Yearbook of Muslims in Europe, Volume 10

The titles published in this series are listed at *brill.com/yme*

Yearbook of Muslims in Europe, Volume 10

Editor-in-Chief

Oliver Scharbrodt

Editors

Samim Akgönül
Ahmet Alibašić
Jørgen S. Nielsen
Egdūnas Račius

BRILL

LEIDEN | BOSTON

Typeface for the Latin, Greek, and Cyrillic scripts: "Brill". See and download: brill.com/brill-typeface.

ISSN 1877-1432
ISBN 978-90-04-38690-7 (hardback)

Copyright 2019 by Koninklijke Brill NV, Leiden, The Netherlands.
Koninklijke Brill NV incorporates the imprints Brill, Brill Hes & De Graaf, Brill Nijhoff, Brill Rodopi, Brill Sense, Hotei Publishing, mentis Verlag, Verlag Ferdinand Schöningh and Wilhelm Fink Verlag.
All rights reserved. No part of this publication may be reproduced, translated, stored in a retrieval system, or transmitted in any form or by any means, electronic, mechanical, photocopying, recording or otherwise, without prior written permission from the publisher.
Authorization to photocopy items for internal or personal use is granted by Koninklijke Brill NV provided that the appropriate fees are paid directly to The Copyright Clearance Center, 222 Rosewood Drive, Suite 910, Danvers, MA 01923, USA. Fees are subject to change.

This book is printed on acid-free paper and produced in a sustainable manner.

Contents

Preface IX
The Editors XIV
List of Technical Terms XVI

Governance of Islam in Europe: An Eastern European Perspective 1
    Egdūnas Račius

Country Surveys

Albania 23
    Olsi Jazexhi

Armenia 41
    Sevak Karamyan and Gevorg Avetikyan

Austria 53
    Dominique Bauer and Astrid Mattes

Azerbaijan 79
    Altay Goyushov

Belarus 95
    Hanna Vasilevich

Belgium 106
    Jean-François Husson

Bosnia and Herzegovina 130
    Nedim Begović

Bulgaria 148
    Aziz Nazmi Shakir

Cyprus 167
    Ali Dayıoğlu and Mete Hatay

Czech Republic   187
    Štěpán Macháček

Denmark   197
    Brian Arly Jacobsen and Niels Valdemar Vinding

Estonia   217
    Ringo Ringvee and Ege Lepa

Finland   230
    Teemu Pauha and Johanna Konttori

France   246
    Anne-Laure Zwilling

Georgia   273
    Thomas Liles and Bayram Balci

Germany   293
    Mathias Rohe

Greece   311
    Konstantinos Tsitselikis and Alexandros Sakellariou

Hungary   327
    Esztella Csiszár

Ireland   342
    James Carr

Italy   360
    Davide Tacchini

Kosovo   379
    Jeton Mehmeti

Latvia   389
    Simona Gurbo

Lithuania 395
    Egdūnas Račius

Luxembourg 409
    Elsa Pirenne

Macedonia 429
    Muhamed Ali

Malta 443
    Ranier Fsadni

Moldova 451
    Aurelia Felea

Montenegro 460
    Sabina Pačariz

The Netherlands 476
    Martijn de Koning

Norway 493
    Sindre Bangstad

Poland 511
    Agata S. Nalborczyk

Portugal 530
    José Mapril, Pedro Soares and Laura Almodovar

Romania 545
    Irina Vainovski-Mihai

Russia 559
    Elmira Akhmetova

Serbia 581
    Ivan Ejub Kostić

Slovakia 594
  Jozef Lenč

Slovenia 608
  Christian Moe

Spain 620
  Jordi Moreras

Sweden 639
  Göran Larsson and Simon Sorgenfrei

Switzerland 655
  Andreas Tunger-Zanetti

Turkey 674
  Ahmet Erdi Öztürk

Ukraine 690
  Mykhaylo Yakubovych

United Kingdom 703
  Stephen H. Jones and Sadek Hamid

Preface

Ten years ago, the first volume of the *Yearbook of Muslims in Europe* was published. Its aim has been to provide comprehensive, accessible and reliable information on the situation of Muslims in every European country. The geographical remit of the *Yearbook* has been extensive, stretching from Portugal to Russia and from Iceland to Azerbaijan. The country reports have provided analysis of public debates on Muslims in a particular country, Church-State relations, and the transnational links of various Muslim organisations, while also including up-to-date demographic information on the Muslim presence in different European countries. It has also sought to answer very practical questions, such as: how many mosques exist in a particular country; how do these countries deal with Muslim burial; and to what extent is halal food available, and what are the legal frameworks around its production?

One of the key questions, addressed both in conceptual and practical terms in the country reports, is the issue of the governance of Islam in different European countries. The governance of Islam is addressed when new pieces of legislation, Church-State relations, and particular policies are discussed in the country reports. It also becomes manifest in very practical questions: to what extent do state institutions provide "chaplaincy" services and pastoral care for Muslims; how do states manage and govern Muslim educational institutions; and what funding structures and arrangements exist between European states and Muslim organisations?

Egdūnas Račius' introductory essay provides a succinct summary of the current state of research on the governance of Islam in Europe, which, as he rightly observes, has focused to a very large extent on Western European countries. Račius tests to what extent models of Church-State relations and Muslim governance that have emerged in Western Europe and have been the subject of significant research, are applicable to Eastern European countries whose historical, political, social and cultural contexts differ in significant areas. For the most part, the Muslim presence in these countries is not the result of immigration in recent decades but is historical, and dates back several centuries. These countries have realigned their policies towards religious communities after the fall of communism. Yet, while these states often recognise the historical presence of Muslims, and classify Islam as one of the "traditional" religions present in the country, the fall of Communism has equally seen the rise of exclusionary ethno-national identities informed by religious allegiance, as the wars after the collapse of Yugoslavia in the early 1990s illustrate. As such, Račius illustrates the limitations of current research on the governance of Islam in Europe, and makes an important contribution to understanding its dynamics in Eastern Europe.

While the different volumes of the *Yearbook* over the last ten years illustrate the rise and intensification of exclusionary discourses directed against European Muslims, they also demonstrate the increasing normalisation of Muslim lives across the continent. This has been through their integration into the cultural life of European societies, their political participation, and the legal recognition of Islamic organisations, institutions, and practices by state authorities. The reports included in this volume of the *Yearbook* attest to these developments, and provide factual (though not necessarily neutral) and topical analysis by expert authors. The particular strength of the *Yearbook* has been the local and regional expertise of its authors, who are usually academic researchers based in the country they report on. As such, they have access to a wealth of material most political and journalistic observers would not have, and are capable of contextualising their data historically, socially, and geographically, based on their research expertise. The editorial team encourages the inclusion of topical and current issues in the reports. At the same time, the editorial team is eager to include information that does not make the headlines, but is equally significant in order to understand developments (long-term in particular) around Muslims in various European countries.

The format of the *Yearbook of Muslims in Europe* ensures a topical focus on the previous calendar year, while not omitting long-term perspectives informed by in-depth research on Islam and Muslims in various European contexts. This tenth volume includes reports on the situation of Muslims in almost every European country, 43 altogether in this volume. The Vatican and the four mini-states of Andorra, Liechtenstein, Monaco, and San Marino have been omitted. Unfortunately, we were not able to secure reports on Croatia and Iceland this year, but hope to include them again in the next volume.

Each report in this volume primarily concentrates on the events, trends, and developments of 2017. By focusing on developments of the previous calendar year, each report offers a fresh annual overview. Over the years, the reports provide cumulative knowledge of ongoing trends and developments around Muslims in different European countries. To facilitate particular attention to events, trends, and developments of the previous calendar year, each report consists of the following sections:

Introduction: The introduction of the report might provide some basic background information in order to contextualise the data presented and discussed in the report. It primarily includes an overview of significant developments and major trends with regards to the Muslim population in each country during 2017, which are then discussed in more detail in the report.

Public Debates: This section presents major issues of public debate around Muslims in each country in 2017. Starting each report with a presentation of topics that dominated public discourse on Muslims in the particular country and of the major actors (whether state or non-governmental, Muslim or non-Muslim) involved in them, sets the scene for the entire report. Thereby, each report highlights what was important in the calendar year.

Transnational Links: Muslim communities and organisations across Europe, in particular those that have an immigrant background, entertain a variety of transnational links to their countries of origin, to other Muslim majority countries, and across Europe. Likewise, the indigenous Muslim populations in Eastern Europe have various links with other Muslim communities that have, for example, the same ethno-national or linguistic background (e.g. Tatars and their links across Eastern Europe), or are connected with governments and non-governmental organisations from Muslim majority countries. This section investigates the significant transnational links of Muslim communities and organisations in each country. Very often, these links have a long history and continued in 2017; in other cases, existing links were reiterated or strengthened by new initiatives, and in some cases, new connections were formed in 2017.

Law and Domestic Politics: In addition to these transnational links, Muslims across Europe are situated in very specific national contexts with their own political and legal cultures, particular Church-State relations, and various types of government interaction with Muslim organisations and institutions. Legal changes and accommodations introduced in 2017, that either directly or indirectly affect Muslims, are discussed in this section, as well as policies and government initiatives that were launched or implemented in that year.

Activities and Initiatives of Main Muslim Organisations: Muslim communities and organisations are involved in and run a variety of activities, some of which are regular and determined by the Islamic religious calendar (*iftar* dinners during the month of Ramadan, celebrations around major Muslim holidays), while others respond to particular events that happened in 2017. Activities and initiatives, presented in this section, can be of a religious, educational, cultural and/or political nature, and can include major public events organised in 2017, the creation of new Muslim organisations, or the opening of new facilities for Muslims, such as mosques, schools, cemeteries etc.

Muslim Population–History and Demographics: This section begins with a brief overview of the history of the Muslim presence in the country, reasons for settlement and/or presence, and significant trajectories of demographic development. Prior to the table providing demographic and statistical information at the end, any issues related to the numbers cited in the table are discussed. Some information on, and discussion of, the sources (e.g. official census, sociological studies etc.) used to arrive at these figures are provided. For example, if there are no clear population or religious affiliation numbers, an explanation is offered to explain the estimates used in the table.

As in previous volumes of the *Yearbook*, the information is presented under the same headings for each country, so that readers who wish to make comparisons across countries can find the information they seek within the same section of each country report. For instance, it is possible to read the section on public debates in different country reports to identify topics that dominated public discourse around Muslims across Europe in 2017.

As reports include less generic information and primarily focus on events, trends, and the developments of 2017, they are of different lengths. In some countries, there is little public discourse around Islam and Muslims, in others, no particular legal changes occurred in 2017. We have therefore not imposed any strict guidelines for the length of individual country reports, except to keep within a guideline maximum, and even that we had to breach in certain, in our view, justified cases. While each report focuses on 2017, particular issues and events often need to be contextualised; certain legal cases might be ongoing for several years, mosque projects initiated might have stalled for a number of years, and particular pieces of new legislation only make sense when placed in the wider context of Church-State relations. Therefore, authors have been asked to provide background information as much as it is needed, or to include references to previous volumes of the *Yearbook* from which this information can be obtained.

More generic information that is unlikely to change every year, is presented in this volume in a table at the end of each country report. The table includes demographic and statistical information and provides a list of the major Muslim organisations in each country. By using a table format, up-to-date information is quickly accessible for each country. Since the 1989 *l'affaire de foulard* in France, and subsequent legislation banning the head scarf in French public schools in 2004, the issue of Muslim dress, in particular in public, has been a constant issue within public debates and legislation in many European countries. Debates and legal initiatives have equally focussed on banning the full face veil (niqab) in some European countries (see, for instance, Denmark and Switzerland in this volume). For this reason, the table includes a new category on Muslim dress, providing a succinct summary of existing legislation, regulations, policies and practices around Muslim dress in every European country.

The following information is contained in the table on demographics, statistics and Muslim organisations:

- Muslim population in numbers and percentage
- Ethnic/national backgrounds
- Inner-Islamic groups
- Geographical spread
- Number and location of mosques
- Number, names and location of Muslim burial sites
- "Chaplaincy" in state institutions
- Halal products
- Muslim dress
- Places of Islamic learning and education
- Muslim media and publications
- Main Muslim organisations

The country reports necessarily use various terms in use by Muslims and others for aspects of Muslim life and worship. Some may be familiar to readers and others not, so we include a list of technical terms which we trust will be useful.

Our thanks are due to the many researchers that have contributed to the volume. We are particularly indebted to Michael Mulryan for the often complicated copy-editing; and colleagues at Brill, Nicolette van den Hoek and Nienke Brienen-Moolenaar, for their continuing enthusiastic support and cooperation.

The editors
Birmingham, Strasbourg, Sarajevo, Copenhagen, Kaunas, June 2018

The Editors

Oliver Scharbrodt
is Professor of Islamic Studies at the University of Birmingham. His research interests include modern and contemporary Islam, Shi'ism, Sufism, and Muslims in Europe. He is the author of *Islam and the Baha'i Faith: a Comparative Study of Muhammad 'Abduh and 'Abdul-Baha 'Abbas* (London: Routledge, 2008) and is co-author of *Muslims in Ireland: Past and Present* (Edinburgh: Edinburgh University Press, 2015).

Samim Akgönül
is Professor at Strasbourg University and researcher at the French National Centre for Scientific Research (CNRS). He also teaches Political Science at Syracuse University, USA, and International Relations at several Turkish universities. Among his recent publications are *The Minority Concept in the Turkish Context: Practices and Perceptions in Turkey, Greece and France* (Leiden: Brill, 2013), *Göçebe Yazılar* (Istanbul: BGST, 2015), and *La Turquie "nouvelle": du rêve d'Europe au cauchemar du Proche Orient* (Paris: Lignes de Repères, 2017).

Ahmet Alibašić
is Associate Professor at the Faculty of Islamic Studies, University of Sarajevo, and Director of the Centre for Advanced Studies in Sarajevo. He writes on Islam in Southeastern Europe, contemporary Islamic political thought, and interreligious relations.

Jørgen S. Nielsen
is Professor of Contemporary European Islam, University of Birmingham, UK, and Honorary Professor of Islamic Studies at the Faculties of Theology and Humanities, University of Copenhagen, Denmark. Since 1978 he has been researching and writing about Islam in Europe. He is the author of *Muslims in Western Europe* (Edinburgh: Edinburgh University Press, 4th edn. with Jonas Otterbeck, 2015), editor of *Islam in Denmark: the Challenge of Diversity* (Lanham: Lexington, 2012), and editor of *Muslim Political Participation in Europe* (Edinburgh: Edinburgh University Press, 2013).

Egdūnas Račius
is Professor of Middle Eastern and Islamic Studies at the Department of Area Studies, Vytautas Magnus University, Kaunas, Lithuania. His field of interest is European Muslim communities in Eastern Europe, particularly European converts to Islam. His most recent publication is *Muslims in Eastern Europe* (Edinburgh: Edinburgh University Press, 2018).

List of Technical Terms

(While many Islamic terms originate in Arabic, many have also acquired local variations. In the following we try to cover the most common variations, and the user will occasionally have to use a bit of imagination to adjust spellings.)

adhan/azan/ezan	call to prayer.
ahl al-bayt/al al-bayt	the family/descendants of the Prophet.
Ahmadi/Ahmadiyya	reform movement founded in India in the 19th century and widely regarded by other Muslims as heretical.
Alevi	movement with roots dating back to the twelfth century, often esoteric in nature and with links to Shi'ism; today especially strong among Turks and Kurds of Eastern Anatolian origin.
Arba'een	Shi'i religious observance, forty days after the day of *'Ashura'*, to commemorate the death of Husayn ibn Ali (third Shi'i Imam).
'Ashura'	festival on the tenth of Muharram (first month of the Islamic calendar) marking the death of Husayn ibn Ali (third Shi'i imam) at the battle of Karbala in 680; a central Shi'i religious observance.
bayram	festival (esp. Turkish for *'Id*, q.v).
Bektashi	a Sufi order with strong Ottoman roots; marginalised during the mid-19th century Ottoman reforms and banned with other Sufi orders by the Turkish Republic in the 1920s.
burqa	specifically the Afghan-style female full body covering, including the face; in common usage in Europe now taken to mean any form of female full body and face covering.
cem	central Alevi communal dance ritual similar to the *sema* ritual of the Mevlevi Sufi order.
cemevi	place in which Alevi *cem* ritual is performed.
da'wa	Islamic term for missionary or proselytising activities.
dershane	"cram school", type of specialised school.
dervish	a common term for Sufi.

LIST OF TECHNICAL TERMS

dhikr	ritual practised by devotees of a Sufi tradition.
fatwa/fetwa	statement of opinion on a point of theology or law issued by an authority in response to an application.
hafiz	person who knows the Qur'an by heart.
hajj	the annual pilgrimage at Mecca at the beginning of the twelfth month of the Islamic calendar; the highpoint is 'Id al-Adha.
halal	permitted.
haram	prohibited.
hijab	head scarf worn by women
hijra	migration of the Prophet and his followers from Mecca to Medina (Yathrib) in 622 CE.
husayniyya	popular centre of learning and devotion in Shi'i Islam.
'id	festival.
'Id al-Adha	Feast of the Sacrifice during the pilgrimage at Mecca.
'Id al-Fitr	festival ending the fast of Ramadan.
iftar	breaking of the fast at the end of the day during Ramadan, increasingly celebrated in invited company by mosques, churches and other organisations.
imam	religious leader, most commonly the one who leads the congregation at the regular prayers; also used about prominent scholars and spiritual leaders. Among Shi'i Muslims, a legitimate leader of the community.
jum'a	Friday noon prayer.
khutba	sermon.
qurban/kurban	sacrifice, as in Turkish *kurban bayramı* (*'Id al-Adha*).
Lailat al-qadr	the "night of power," 27th Ramadan, the celebration of the revelation of the Qur'an.
madhhab	school of law or theology.
madrasa/medrese	school at any level, usually elementary and high Islamic.
majlis	council or body governing Muslim community organisations, in Southeastern Europe in particular (see also *meshihat*).
masjid	mosque.
mawlid/mevlud	birthday of the Prophet Muhammad.

meshihat	council or body governing Muslim community organisations, in Southeastern Europe in particular (see also *majlis*).
mizar/miziar	cemetery
mu'adhdhin/muezzin	the person who calls to prayer.
mufti	person who issues *fatwa*; in some modern states the title of the leading Islamic official.
muftiate	office or institution of mufti.
nafaqa	maintenance and/or alimony payment after divorce.
Nawruz/Nevruz	New Year in the Persian/Kurdish/Turkish tradition.
nikah	marriage formalised in the Islamic tradition.
niqab	female face covering.
qurban/kurban	literally meaning "sacrifice" and often used as a reference to meat of animals during 'Id al-Adha at the end of the annual hajj to Mecca.
ra'is al-'ulama' or just *ra'is* or *reis*	"dean of the scholars", applied in some countries (Eastern European in particular) to the official head of the Muslim community.
Ramadan	the ninth month of the Islamic calendar, the month of fasting.
riba	(unlawful) interest on capital.
rijaset/riyaset	governing council within centralised Muslim community organisations in Southeastern Europe, usually headed by the chief mufti or *ra'is al-'ulama'*.
sabantuj	Tatar and Bashkir cultural festival.
sadaqa	alms given at various occasions, often in connection with a religious festival.
salah/salat	prescribed prayers five times a day.
shari'a	Islamic law and ethics, the principles of good Islamic behaviour.
shaykh/sheikh	leader of a congregation, especially of a Sufi character; honorific for someone learned.
sheikh al-islam	title of leading Muslim scholar or head of official Muslim community organisation in a country; originally, an Ottoman title and therefore used in Muslim communities in regions that were part of the Ottoman Empire.

LIST OF TECHNICAL TERMS

Shi'i/Shi'ism	the branches within Islam which trace their authority through the descendants of 'Ali, the Prophet's nephew and son-in-law. They make up 12–15% of the total number of Muslims worldwide.
Sufi/Sufism	the mystical tradition.
sukuk	commonly used for *shari'a* compliant financial bonds.
Sunni/Sunnism	the majority tradition within Islam, sometimes (mistakenly) called "orthodox".
talaq	divorce by repudiation.
tariqa/tarikat	Sufi order.
tekke/teke	a Sufi meeting place (Turkish).
turba/turbe	tomb of a venerated person ("saint"), often the object of popular devotion.
umma	the global community of believers.
'umra	the lesser pilgrimage at Mecca taking place at times other than hajj.
waqf/vakf	religious foundation (of property) providing income for religious, charitable or educational purposes.
zakah/zakat	obligatory almsgiving.
zawiya	a Sufi meeting place (Arabic).
zikr	see *dhikr*.
ziyara	visiting family graves or tombs of Muslim saints at set times of year.

Governance of Islam in Europe: An Eastern European Perspective

Egdūnas Račius[1]

Introduction

Numerous academic works[2] have been produced dealing from one angle or another with the governance of Islam in Europe. However, on closer inspection, it becomes obvious that their focus rarely ever goes beyond Western Europe, with the overwhelming majority of research focusing on France, Germany and the UK. These three countries are, as a rule, taken to best represent the three ideal types of the governance of religion in Europe. France is portrayed as the representative *par excellence* of what is labelled the "separation system" (also called "secular"), the UK as the representative of the opposite "state church system", and Germany as the archetypical example of the middle path, the "cooperation system" (also called "hybrid").[3] Though this simplified picture of a purportedly tripartite typology of the governance of religion in Western Europe has already been severely criticised,[4] there have hardly been any comparative studies looking at the governance of religion in Europe that also encompasses those systems found in post-communist Eastern Europe.

---

1 Egdūnas Račius is Professor of Middle Eastern and Islamic Studies at Vytautas Magnus University in Kaunas, Lithuania. His most recent book is the monograph *Muslims in Eastern Europe* (Edinburgh: Edinburgh University Press, 2018) that covers 21 post-socialist Eastern European countries.
2 Laurence, Jonathan, *The Emancipation of Europe's Muslims: the State's Role in Minority Integration* (Princeton: Princeton University Press, 2012); Maussen, Marcel, "The governance of Islam in Western Europe. A state of the art report", *IMISCOE Working Paper*, no. 16 (2007), http://www.euro-islam.info/wp-content/uploads/pdfs/governance_of_islam.pdf, accessed 29 April 2018; Sunier, Thijl, "Beyond the domestication of Islam in Europe: a reflection on past and future research on Islam in European societies", *Journal of Muslims in Europe*, vol. 1, no. 1 (2012), pp. 189–208; Elbasani, Arolda, "Governing Islam in plural societies: religious freedom, state neutrality and traditional heritage", *Journal of Balkan and Near Eastern Studies*, vol. 19, no. 1 (2017), pp. 4–18.
3 Leustean, Lucian, "Challenges to church-state relations in contemporary Europe: introduction", *Journal of Religion in Europe*, vol. 1, no. 3, (2008), pp. 247–248.
4 Sandberg, Russell, "Church-state relations in Europe: from legal models to an interdisciplinary approach", *Journal of Religion in Europe*, vol. 1, no. 3, (2008), pp. 329–352 (331); Bowen, John, "A view from France on the internal complexity of national models", *Journal of Ethnic and Migration Studies*, vol. 33, no. 6 (2007), pp. 1003–1016 (1005).

The aim of this article is to contribute to the expansion of both the geographical and theoretical scope of the analysis of the patterns of the governance of religion in Europe. I hope to do this by providing an exposé of the patterns of state-religion relations, and specifically the governance of Islam found in post-communist Eastern European countries, both in member-states of the EU and those that are not. Its secondary aim is to test to what extent the dominant Western European theoretical approaches to the governance of religion (and particularly of Islam) in Europe are applicable (or even relevant) to post-communist Eastern Europe.

The concept of the "governance of religion", which also subsumes the "governance of Islam", in principle is here understood along the lines argued by Maussen, who suggests that "[i]ntroducing the concept of governance in studies on the accommodation of Islam also creates opportunities for a type of analysis that goes beyond the study of (formal) legal arrangements, and also looks at practices of application, implementation and interpretation. It includes the systematic study of customs, conventions and agreements that result in specific forms of regulation, and it widens the scope of actors and institutions that might be involved in one way or the other in the actual accommodation of Islam in Europe".[5] Maussen invites the reader in his analysis to go beyond the static level of formal legal regulations of "State-Church" relations, and instead incorporates into the research more dynamic supra-legal factors, this way significantly expanding the nature of the discussion. Consequently, though the formal legal regulations of "State-Church" relations remain crucial for any debate, they are in themselves not sufficient to disclose a fuller picture of the actual situation of faith communities in a given country, and can at best serve as a starting point from which to start a comprehensive analysis.

However, when arguing for "governance" as an analytical tool, Maussen uses the term "accommodation of Islam" in his work, which he looks to apply to the concept of "governance". Even though, in the Western European context, the term "accommodation" carries a positive resonance, and may be used when talking about the governance of religion, in the Eastern European context, as will be shown further below, such a term may not always be useful. Take, for instance, Slovakia and Kosovo (the latter being a Muslim majority country), where to this day, due to a combination of legal and political impediments, Muslim communities are not able to have legally registered religious organisations, and are forced to operate as NGOs; or Moldova, where, despite the legal registration of a Muslim religious organisation after a long drawn-out process, the Muslim presence faces both a political and social revisionist backlash.

---

5 Maussen, "The governance of Islam in Western Europe", p. 5.

There is also Bosnia and Herzegovina, where the official Muslim community organisation, the Islamic Community of Bosnia and Herzegovina, though possessing representative status for the Muslim majority in the country, still has no comprehensive agreement with the State, even though the representative religious authorities of minority faith communities, such as the Catholic or the Serbian Orthodox Church, do. These and numerous other examples suggest that "accommodation" in many instances, should be prefaced with "lack of …". Therefore, one should not, at least in the Eastern European context, directly tie governance to accommodation; it is better to confine oneself to the use of "governance".

It should also be made clear from the onset that there can be no single, or three-fold model (as suggested by researchers in Western Europe) when discussing the governance of religion (including Islam) in post-communist Eastern Europe. As Sunier aptly notes, though having in mind Western European countries, "… the diverging reactions to Islam in different European nations are best explained by the different discourses of nationhood, the disparate political cultures in those countries, and the different paths emancipation takes".[6] As is shown further below, these factors have heavily influenced the divergent, and at times opposing regimes of governance of religion (*inter alia* Islam) in post-communist Eastern Europe. Basing on his own and others' research, Koening concludes that "[a]s cross-national comparisons show, Church-State relations, national identities, political opportunity structures and deliberate policy initiatives in European countries have led to distinctive patterns of Muslim incorporation, thus giving rise to rather different varieties of European Islam."[7] Though Koening has in mind again primarily Western European countries, this article aims to show that the post-communist countries of Eastern Europe likewise prove this point.

Theoretical Approaches to Patterns of Governance of Religion and of Islam in Particular in Western Europe

As indicated above, the common typology of regimes of governance of religion in Western Europe is based on a three-tier system of State-Church relations,

---

6 Sunier, Thijl, "Religious newcomers and the nation-state: flows and closures", in David Feldman, Leo Lucassen, Jochen Oltmer (eds.), *Paths of Integration Migrants in Western Europe (1880–2004)* (Amsterdam: Amsterdam University Press, 2006), p. 249.

7 Koenig, Matthias, "Europeanising the governance of religious diversity: an institutionalist account of Muslim struggles for public recognition", *Journal of Ethnic and Migration Studies*, vol. 33, no. 6 (2007), pp. 911–932 (912).

comprising "the state church model, the cooperationist (or hybrid) model, and the secular (or separation) model".[8] Sandberg defines these models as follows: "State church systems are those countries characterised by the existence of close links between the state and a particular religious community, which may be styled as a 'state,' 'national,' 'established,' or 'folk' church. (...) By contrast, separation systems include those countries where there is a constitutional barrier forbidding the financial support and establishment of any one religion. (...) Hybrid systems, effectively, are those states whose constitutional provisions concerning religion come in between state church systems and separation systems. Also known as cooperationist systems or sometimes concordatarian systems, these states are characterised by a simple separation of state and church coupled with the recognition of a multitude of common tasks which link state and church activity, which are often recognised in the form of agreements, treaties, and Concordats".[9] Sandberg's examples mainly stem from Western Europe; from among the post-communist Eastern European states, Sandberg assigns Bulgaria to the first model (the "state church"), while Hungary and the Baltic States are assigned to the third (the "hybrid").

Irrespective of the model of religious governance, all states–through their legal systems and particularly, through the legal arrangements of State-Church relations–inevitably regulate a crucial aspect of religious practice and identity. That is to say, the institutionalisation of religion through representative spiritual administrations, as a rule, in the form of religious organisations. However, the legal options for religious communities may differ significantly, ranging from voluntary through to compulsory registration with the State, to rejection or denial of registration (with or without a formal ban of the organisation).

In the case of Islam in Western Europe, the process of the institutionalisation of Muslim religious organisations is often coupled with the corresponding process of the "Europeanisation" of Islam, which is sometimes expected to lead to something labelled "European" Islam, or its national forms, like "German" Islam, "French" Islam and the like. Regulations on the institutionalisation of Islam in general, and the state-guided process of its "Europeanisation", in particular in the Western European context, are often viewed by researchers through the prism of what is called the "domestication of Islam". As Martikainen explains, "'[d]omestication' can have at least two meanings. First, it can refer to processes of adaptation, e.g., with regard to religious institutionalisation. Second,

---

8 Leustean, "Challenges to church-state relations", p. 247.
9 Sandberg, "Church-state relations in Europe", pp. 330–331.

it can refer to the 'taming' of a possible threat to social cohesion or security".[10] Sunier understands the "domestication of Islam" as "the political programmes and modes of governance that emanate from the complex relationship between integration, and political priorities of security and national identity."[11]

However, the domestication of Islam in Western Europe arguably goes beyond institutionalisation, as, according to Sunier, "[d]omestication is a process of containment and pacification based on national identity politics. It is a process that is in the first place and self-evidently about integration of Islam into European societies. But in fact it is more explicitly about the character of nation-states and the challenges they face. Domestication politics revolve around the question of how national states should deal with the presence of Islam in all its perceived facets. Since domestication involves a good deal of monitoring and control of religion, it also implies an intervention in the very content of Islamic practices and convictions."[12] Though it is not stated explicitly in the above quotes, domestication-driven governance of Islam in Western Europe perceives Islam as alien in nature, as an "immigrant religion", or a religion of immigrants. As such, Islam is seen by Western European states as in need of adjustment so as to be integratable; this is what "domestication" in both senses of the word, as explained by Martikainen, means when it is applied to Islam in Western European contexts.

Ultimately, rather than accommodating Muslims in Western Europe, European states, through their governance of Islam, seek to change its institutional structure to fit with the existing organisational and ideological frameworks of State-Church relations. As Laurence argues, European states "are not engaged in the special accommodation of Muslims; they are incorporating Islam into pre-existing State-Church institutions. European governments are trying to create the institutional conditions for the emergence of an Italian or German Islam, e.g., rather than just tolerating Islam 'in' Italy or Germany".[13] Laurence concludes that "religion policy in particular allows European governments to gradually take 'ownership' of their Muslim populations because it grants them unique influence over organizations and leadership within this hard-to-reach minority."[14]

---

10 Martikainen, Tuomas, "The governance of Islam in Finland", *Temenos*, vol. 43, no. 2 (2007), pp. 243–265 (258).
11 Sunier, "Beyond the domestication of Islam in Europe", p. 190.
12 Sunier, "Beyond the domestication of Islam in Europe", p. 190.
13 Laurence, *The Emancipation of Europe's Muslims*, p. 13.
14 Laurence, *The Emancipation of Europe's Muslims*, p. 12.

The governance of religion, in this case of Islam, involves many actors however, of whom the two primary ones are the State and the Muslim community at large, in the person of both common believers and their organisations. The domestication of Islam may have certain unintended consequences for the internal dynamics of the respective country's Muslim population. Martikainen draws attention to several of them, the first of which is that "[c]ertain people are raised to important positions, where they act on behalf of others".[15] This may lead to an unequal distribution of power among different actors and therefore offer opportunities for misuse of held power; it is also unfavourable towards people, who, although of Muslim background, may "hold different views from those who act as their spokespersons".[16] Martikainen sees even larger risks as he argues, "the authorities are actually actively involved in creating 'cultural others'. We may ask whether strong state involvement can lead to the clientisation of immigrants as well as to a pathologisation of cultural and social difference; with time, these processes may create permanent structures that support the status quo, in which many people of immigrant background are in a disadvantaged position".[17] All this points to an integration paradox: while actively involving themselves in the integration of Muslims in their territories through legal measures covering the institutionalisation of Islam, states run the risk of inadvertently "culturally othering" (or, to use the Saidian term, "orientalising"[18]) them.

The Religious Landscape in Eastern Europe

In terms of religious heritage, Eastern Europe is primarily shaped by the heritage of Orthodox Christianity, with Catholicism and Islam sharing second and third places. Unlike Western Europe, in general, in Eastern Europe, Protestantism occupies a negligible part, with Judaism, historically, likely superseding it. Protestantism has only been a dominant force in Estonia, although a large share of Latvia's population has historically been Protestant. Over half a dozen contemporary post-communist Eastern European countries (Lithuania, Poland, Czech Republic, Slovakia, Hungary, Slovenia, and Croatia)

---

15 Martikainen, "The governance of Islam in Finland", p. 258.
16 Martikainen, "The governance of Islam in Finland", p. 258.
17 Martikainen, "The governance of Islam in Finland", p. 258.
18 Said, Edward W., *Orientalism* (New York: Pantheon Books, 1978).

have had Catholic majorities, with almost a dozen, among them the most populous countries (Belarus, Ukraine, Moldova, Russia, Romania, Bulgaria, Macedonia, Serbia, and Montenegro), having Orthodox majorities.

Although it would probably be too far-fetched to compare Orthodox Churches to Protestant Churches, there certainly are similarities between the two, in that they, in the European nation-state context, tend to be national Churches (unlike the Catholic Church), with all the ensuing consequences of that. In this way, the Serbian Orthodox Church, for instance, is similar to, say, the Swedish Lutheran Church. Yet, the Catholic Church in Lithuania, the Catholic Church in Croatia, and the Catholic Church in Poland, are all transnational, in that their rank and file follow and submit to the Vatican, though admittedly they do indeed carry a national flavour. The Orthodox Churches are known to be closely connected to the conceptualisation of nationhood and the very nations in the countries where such Orthodoxy predominates. The close identification of belonging to a nation with belonging to a particular national branch of the Orthodox Church has had repercussions not only to the nation- and state-building processes in Eastern Europe, but also for relations between different religious groups, and ultimately the governance of religion in these countries.

When it comes to the Muslim presence, there is hardly any geographical context in Eastern Europe that, over the course of history, has not had a Muslim presence,[19] though admittedly, some Central European lands (the Czech Republic and Slovakia) have not had any substantial and continuous presence of Muslims on their territories. In two post-communist Eastern European countries (Kosovo and Albania) Muslims constitute clear majorities, while in Bosnia and Herzegovina their share hovers around 50%. As we can see in Table 1, none of the Catholic or Protestant majority countries have a share of population of those with a Muslim background that exceeds 3%. Their share in several Orthodox majority countries is significantly higher: over a third in Macedonia, a fifth in Montenegro, a seventh in Russia, and a twelfth in Bulgaria.

In most Eastern European countries, populations of Muslim background are composed of autochthonous Turkic, Albanian or Slavic speaking ethnic groups. Only within a handful of states–all with a Muslim ratio of less than 1%, and, incidentally, all with nominal Catholic majorities–do Muslims of immigrant Asian and African background constitute the majorities of the national Muslim populations. These countries are Poland, Hungary, the Czech Republic,

---

19 For a brief overview of the history of Islam, see Račius, *Muslims in Eastern Europe*, pp. 23–44.

TABLE 1   Muslim Populations in Eastern Europe[a]

Country	Muslim ratio of population	Muslims in absolute figures	Majority religion
Kosovo	96	1,750,000	Islam
Albania	65	2,300,000	Islam
Bosnia and Herzegovina	51	1,790,000	Islam
Macedonia, FYR of	35	730,000	Orthodoxy
Montenegro	19	119,000	Orthodoxy
Bulgaria	8	600,000	Orthodoxy
Serbia	4	350,000	Orthodoxy
Slovenia	3	60,000	Catholicism
Croatia	1.5	63,000	Catholicism
Ukraine	0.6	250,000	Orthodoxy
Romania	0.3	65,000	Orthodoxy
Hungary	0.3	32,000	Catholicism
Czech Republic	0.3	20,000	Catholicism
Belarus	0.2	20,000	Orthodoxy
Latvia	0.2	6,000	Protestantism
Moldova	0.2	5,000	Orthodoxy
Estonia	0.2	2,000	Protestantism
Lithuania	0.15	4,000	Catholicism
Poland	0.09	35,000	Catholicism
Slovakia	0.09	5,000	Catholicism
TOTAL, up to		8,206,000	
Russia	15	20,000,000	Orthodoxy

a   Based on Račius, *Muslims in Eastern Europe*, p. 155.

and Slovakia, Such countries carry similarities with Western Europe, in that their Muslim populations are also predominantly of immigrant background.

In view of these differences, post-communist Eastern European states may be grouped into several distinct camps: 1) those with primarily indigenous autochthonous Muslim populations (Muslim-majority Albania and Kosovo, and all the successor states of the Socialist Yugoslavia, as well as Bulgaria and Romania); 2) those with mixed autochthonous and immigrant Muslim populations (Poland, Lithuania, Belarus, Ukraine, and Russia); and 3) those with Muslim populations of an overwhelmingly immigrant nature (Central European countries, Moldova, Estonia, and also Latvia where the bulk of

Muslims are immigrants from the Soviet period and their progeny). Besides the autochthonous and immigrant segments of national Muslim populations, there is also an ever increasing segment of local converts to Islam, who, however, rarely identify and socialise with autochthonous Muslims, and instead either group together with those of an immigrant background or create their own social circles.[20]

It may be worth noting that the forms of Islamic religiosity practised by Eastern European Muslims extend from legalist Islam (practised by autochthons and immigrants alike) to Sufi and folk Islam (practised almost exclusively by autochthons), to various strands of revivalist Islam (practised primarily by immigrants and converts, though in some countries also by autochthonous Muslims). Most of the groups espousing these different forms of Islamic religiosity have their communities and organisations, whether registered or unregistered, state recognised or not, led by their respective religious authorities.

State-Church Relations in Post-Communist Eastern Europe

All Eastern European countries in the inter-war period had some sort of legally defined State-Church relationship. They fell into two distinct camps; the first was composed chiefly of the USSR, with its constituent European republics, namely Russia, Ukraine and Belarus. Here, from the Bolshevik takeover in 1917, militant atheism coupled with laicism provided the basis for the legal regulations of State-Church relations. The second distinct camp encompassed all the other sovereign states in this region, that is Yugoslavia, Albania, Bulgaria, Romania, Czechoslovakia, Hungary, Poland and the three Baltic States of Lithuania, Latvia and Estonia. These countries, although applying differing regimes of religious governance, did not share the USSR's ideological aversion towards, and drive to suppress or even eradicate, religion in their respective countries.

These two camps, however, merged into one when, in the aftermath of World War II, USSR-inspired and often heavily-supported local communists took over control of these other countries; the Baltic States were annexed by the USSR, as well as parts of Romania made into the new constituent Soviet Republic of Moldavia. From then until the collapse of the communist system, all of the states East of the Iron Curtain exhibited public belittlement of religion enshrined in their legislation governing State-Church relations.[21] With

---

20   Račius, *Muslims in Eastern Europe*, pp. 157–159.
21   Račius, *Muslims in Eastern Europe*, pp. 45–51, 78–83, 113–114.

the exception of Albania, which in 1967 went completely atheist, all of the communist-ruled Eastern European countries (including the Soviet republics) ultimately settled on a laicist State-Church relations model. However, the communist-era laicism of Eastern European states is not to be confused with the secular model, seen in France. In communist Europe, the state had, through its coercive apparatus, complete control of religion in the public and, to a great extent, the private lives of citizens.

With the fall of the Berlin Wall, and with it the Iron Curtain, the disintegration of the USSR and the collapse of the communist system in Eastern Europe, the newly independent and sovereign states in the region faced a challenge to overhaul their State-Church legislation in general and the governance of religion in particular. Here, once again, the post-communist Eastern European states fell into two distinct camps. There were those that had been independent in the inter-war period, where they could, and often did, fall back to their pre-World War II legal framework regarding State-Church relations. There were also those countries that became sovereign for the first time in their modern history, which had to invent new legislation on this issue, to supplant that of the communist era. These countries included the former Soviet republics of Belarus, Ukraine, Moldova, and the former federal republics of Yugoslavia, such as Slovenia, Croatia, Bosnia and Herzegovina, Macedonia, as well as Kosovo.

Richard Potz, focusing on Orthodox majority post-communist Eastern European countries, claims that for state-religion relations, "… most of the countries emerging from communism opted for the Western European model, considering it more corresponding with their own history and more suitable to their own social structure. This was in principle an understandable choice, but there was of course the question which of the various types of relations available within the Western European system of law on religion was preferred by the post-Communist countries with an Orthodox tradition."[22] However, as will be shown below, such an optimistic view of the regimes of governance of religion and state-religion relations in post-communist Eastern Europe, and particularly in Orthodox majority countries, is superficial. This is because the purportedly Western models chosen by these states either do not function as they should, or function in the same way as they do in Western Europe, or the chosen models are not entirely, or completely, Western European at all. Contrary to what Potz argues, Kalkandjieva maintains that "[a]lthough the Soviet successor-states, Tito's Yugoslavia, and Bulgaria, preserved Lenin's formula of a 'separation of the church from the state,' they did not bring church-state relations closer to the Western model. In fact, post-communist legislation

---

22 Potz, Richard, "State and Church in the European countries with an Orthodox tradition", *Derecho y Religión*, no. 3 (2008), pp. 33–54 (49).

has weakened the principle of separation in the case of the local Orthodox churches by emphasizing their traditional nature or historical roles."[23]

Our own research on state-religion relations in Orthodox majority countries, align with Kalkandijeva's conclusion; this, however, does not imply that non-Orthodox religious communities have not been formally accorded religious rights. Rather, as Elbasani argues, basing her research on the Balkans, "[i]n line with their democratic aspirations, all post-communist states have allocated new religious freedoms, while taking the lead in closely managing the emerging religious groups and activities. Institutionally, post-communist states have continued to 'administer' religious organisations by preserving a multi-tiered system of registrations and institutional controls, subject to unilaterally revocable conditions."[24] Her observations are true for most of the post-communist Eastern European countries. Yet, looking broadly and beyond the Balkans, one can see that some of these states seem not to have followed this pattern, with Estonia and Ukraine, arguably with the most liberal regimes of religious governance, being the obvious examples.

As enacted legislation provides the basis for the governance of religion in post-communist Eastern European states, they can be clustered into several groups. Such groups are, admittedly, largely Weberian ideal types, and, in practice, overlap with each other, and at the same time differ internally. These ideal-type groups are:

1. Though, notably, no state in post-socialist Eastern Europe has an official state religion, there is a significant group of countries that have an unofficial state religion, either regarded by the State as "traditional" *inter alia*, or as the sole "traditional" religion. These countries are: Belarus, Serbia, Bulgaria, Macedonia, Moldova, Romania, and Russia
2. States that have officially recognised "traditional" religions without formally prioritising any one among them: Lithuania, Latvia, Poland, Bosnia, Montenegro, and Albania
3. States that have unofficial "traditional" religions: Ukraine, Slovenia, Croatia, and Kosovo.
4. States that have neither official nor unofficial state or "traditional" religions: Estonia, Czech Republic, Slovakia, and Hungary.

---

23   Kalkandijeva, Daniela, "A comparative analysis on church-state relations in Eastern Orthodoxy: concepts, models, and principles", *Journal of Church and State*, vol. 53, no. 4 (2011), pp. 587–614 (609).
24   Elbasani, Arolda, "State-organised religion and Muslims' commitment to democracy in Albania", *Europe-Asia Studies*, vol. 68, no. 2 (2016), pp. 253–269 (257).

TABLE 2 Status of religions in Eastern Europe

Unofficial state religion	Officially recognised "traditional" religions	Unofficial "traditional" religions	No "traditional" religions
Belarus	Lithuania	Ukraine	Estonia
Serbia	Latvia	Slovenia	Czech Republic
Bulgaria	Poland	Croatia	Slovakia
Macedonia	Bosnia	Kosovo	Hungary
Moldova	Montenegro		
Romania	Albania		
Russia			

Compared to the models of religious governance and state-religion relations in Western Europe, one may argue that the first category is a soft version of the "State-Church" system, although only in those cases where the Orthodox Church is recognised by the constitution or a *lex specialis*, as the representative of the national or traditional confession. Hence, countries falling under this category may be grouped together only very tentatively, as both the formal and actual status of the Orthodox Church in, for instance, Macedonia differs significantly from that in Romania or Belarus, where it is closer to the second category. The second and third categories represent the "cooperative" or "hybrid" system, while the fourth is a chrestomathic example of the "separation" or "secular" system. One may therefore conclude that, even though post-communist Eastern European states can be conditionally placed into these governance models, the reality on the ground is much more complex and fluid than these ideal types would suggest. The main difference between the Western European models of formalised state-religion relations and those formed in Eastern Europe, is that the latter states (with the exception of those falling under the fourth category) recognise multiple "traditional" religions, a feature that is practically non-existent in Western Europe. Moreover, some countries (Serbia, Lithuania, Romania) use a two-tier or even three-tier system of registration for religious organisations,[25] where, as a rule, "traditional" religious groups have much more favourable conditions, compared to those regarded as "non-traditional".

25   Schanda, Balázs, "The recent developments of church–state relations in central Europe", in Silvio Ferrari and Rinaldo Cristofori (eds.), *Law and Religion in the 21st Century: Relations between States and Religious Communities* (London and New York: Routledge, 2010), p. 159.

The countries falling into the final category, with the "separation"/"secular" system, are all of Western Christian heritage, with no historical (autochthonous) Muslim communities, whereas those in the second and third categories include not only Catholic and Orthodox Christian majority countries, but also Muslim majority countries. The first category (those with the "State-Church" system) is comprised of exclusively Orthodox majority countries, and, with the exception of Moldova, all have historical (autochthonous) Muslim communities. Since all these different models (or systems) inevitably produce different practical outcomes from the governance of religion in this part of Europe, at times profoundly, it should not be surprising that there is no uniform regime of governance of Islam in post-communist Eastern Europe, but rather a plethora of systems.

Governance of Islam in Post-Communist Eastern Europe

In addition to the preferential treatment of Orthodox Churches, in many post-communist Eastern European countries, as Elbasani argues, "[r]e-regulating the relationship between the state and Muslim communities proved especially complicated in the context of exclusive national paradigms, long-running ethno-religious animosities, oft-fabricated collective memories, and the inherited majoritarian 'traditions'".[26] In no Eastern European state is Islam recognised as a state religion, as all of the Muslim majority countries in the region (namely, Kosovo, Albania and Bosnia and Herzegovina) one way or another, in their constitutions, declare themselves secular and without a state (official) religion. Furthermore, none of these three national constitutions even refers to Islam, but at the same time affirms constitutional equality among all religions in their respective countries. However, in several post-communist Eastern European countries, Islam, nonetheless, is recognised as a "traditional" religion, either in the constitution or by a *lex specialis*. These countries include Russia, Belarus, Lithuania, Poland, Romania, Macedonia, Montenegro, Serbia, and Bosnia and Herzegovina. In other states, including Muslim majority Albania, Islam (primarily in its legalist form but also in a heterodox form such as Bektashism) is regarded as a "traditional" religion, though there is no specific legislation making this official. So, for instance, in Ukraine, where Muslim Crimean Tatars have been living for more than half a millennium, Islam (in the forms practised by Tatars) is generally accepted as traditional to the country, though there is no explicit official endorsement of this in any legal act. In

---

26   Elbasani, "Governing Islam in plural societies", p. 5.

Bulgaria, the *Law on Religions* "expresses respect" for Islam, next to the other two named religions, namely Christianity and Judaism.

The fact that in a number of post-communist Eastern European states Islam is recognised officially, and in a number, unofficially, as a traditional religion, makes the Eastern European context significantly different from the Western European one when talking about the governance of Islam. Designating Islam as a "traditional religion" may mean that the State recognises Islam, through its followers and their representative organisations, as "indigenous", as opposed to the universal view of Islam in Western Europe as alien, and therefore in need of domestication. For instance, the Lithuanian Constitutional Court has argued that by passing the *Law on Religions*, the Parliament merely acknowledged that Sunni Islam is a traditional religion in Lithuania rather than establishing it as such: "The constitutional establishment of the institute of recognition of churches and religious organisations as traditional means that such recognition by the state is irrevocable. Tradition is neither created nor abolished by an act of the will of the legislature. The naming of churches and religious organisations as traditional is not an act of their establishment as traditional organisations but an act stating both their tradition and the status of their relations with society, which does not depend on the willpower of the legislature."[27] Arguing in this vein, Islam may not be purposefully domesticated by the State, it already is domestic by virtue of having been present in the country for centuries. Though the Lithuanian case may be exceptional and one of the more extreme ones (other similar cases being the Polish and the Belarusian), it nonetheless is symptomatic and representative of the differences in the governance of Islam between Western and Eastern Europe. Furthermore, unlike virtually all of Western Europe, in Eastern Europe, in many cases, the extent of the securitisation of Islam is (still) non-existent, or at least not as discernible.

The recognition of Islam as "traditional" may also mean that the very act of its recognition as a traditional religion is, on the part of the State, an act of domestication, or the completion of the process of domestication. But this is only possible in countries that have a system of traditional religions, and where Islam is not (yet) recognised as such. Latvia could be an example of this, though admittedly this is more a theoretical than practical reality.

The governance of Islam in Eastern Europe, as in Western Europe, is based on, and executed through, the legal regulation of its institutionalisation, which

---

27 The Constitutional Court of the Republic of Lithuania, *Decision on Construing the Provisions of a Constitutional Court Ruling Related with the Status of the Churches and Religious Organisations that are Traditional in Lithuania*, 6 December 2007, http://www.lrkt.lt/en/court-acts/search/170/ta1375/content, accessed 19 April 2018.

itself is an expression of an "accommodation" or "domestication". In connection with this, a rhetorical question may be posed: "How can European states properly comprehend the institutionalization of Islam and channel this process, without too much trauma, towards a system of relations between states and religions that is characteristic of the European tradition?"[28] Ferrari suggests, somewhat idealistically, that the "key to the question may be found in the correct distinction between three fundamental principles underlying the relations between states and religions: freedom, cooperation, and autonomy".[29] However, in those Eastern European countries where there is a national (though not official state) religion or Church (which is locally seen as a foundational part of that State), there might sometimes be inherent obstacles in the way of a full exercise of freedom, cooperation, and autonomy in the relationship between the State and religions. Moldova and Macedonia, with their powerful Orthodox Churches that are openly hostile to Islam and Muslims, are two obvious cases, but other countries (for instance, Serbia and Bulgaria) may also be added.

A top-down institutionalisation of Islam, rather than its accommodation, in post-communist Eastern Europe soon becomes a co-option or even "churchification" of Islam, that is when representative Muslim organisations are expected to model themselves after, and function like, Christian Churches, with their ecclesiastical hierarchical structures. Though this process of churchification of Islam is not universal in Eastern Europe, one may discern its features in half a dozen post-communist Eastern European countries, for instance, Bosnia and Herzegovina, Lithuania, Macedonia, Bulgaria and several others. What is understood here as churchification is the requirement, or at least expectation on the part of the State, that national Muslim communities found representative religious organisations headed by spiritual authorities, who not only serve as interlocutors between the State and the Muslim population, but also as the sole (hierarchically structured) ecclesiastical institution, staffed by religious servants of different ranks in subordination to each other.

In a number of cases in its governance of Islam, a state expects, through its setting of legal requirements, that Muslims form a unitary (umbrella) religious organisation to represent all Muslims of that State, irrespective of their denomination, background or ideology, with the aim to co-opt, but also to enable control over them. Ferrari maintains that "[t]his is the cultural and legal

---

28   Ferrari, Silvio, "The creation of Muslim representative institutions in the 'secular' European states", *The Review of Faith & International Affairs*, vol. 8, no. 2 (2010), pp. 21–27 (24).

29   Ferrari, "The creation of Muslim representative institutions", p. 24.

background that lies behind the request which many states have addressed to the Muslim communities resident in their territories, namely, to provide a representative organization at the national level which is capable of functioning as an interlocutor of the state … This request has sometimes been formulated in an excessively inflexible way, with the state insisting on the need for unitary representation which was not always required from other religious communities (for instance, the Christian ones, which have separate representative institutions)… At other times, the demand to create a single representative institution at the national level has masked delaying tactics by public administrations that were not ready for a productive relationship with Muslims".[30] Hungary, Serbia, Latvia, Macedonia and Slovakia are representatives of this approach by the State, all in their own ways.

So, for instance, in Latvia the law requires religious communities to form representative bodies on the basis of "one body per religion / confession". In order to do that, there have to be at least ten registered congregations of that particular religion. As Muslims can have only one representative religious organisation/association in Latvia, it would require either the unification of disparate registered Muslim religious congregations of different natures (in either denomination or ideology) or the final representative body would be representative of just one particular denomination or ideology, at the expense of all others. There has been no attempt to form such a representative Muslim religious association in the country. In Hungary, two major Muslim religious organisations joined together to form such a representative Muslim umbrella organisation, which has been registered and recognised by the State. In Serbia, there are at least two rival Muslim religious organisations which claim to be representative of the country's Muslim population; however, neither is fully recognised as such by the State. In Macedonia, Bektashis have failed to secure the State's permission to form an independent representative organisation. In Slovakia, in order to register a religious organisation, Muslims have to produce a membership list with 50,000 adult signatories, who need to be citizens of Slovakia permanently residing in the country. In a country where the total estimated number of people with a Muslim background is 5,000, such a requirement is impossible to implement. Thus in Slovakia, institutionalisation (let alone the accommodation) of Islam in the foreseeable future is out of the question.

There is an argument that "[t]he overall proportion of Muslims also plays a decisive role: the greater the number of Muslims, the greater the recognition

---

30   Ferrari, "The creation of Muslim representative institutions", p. 22.

by the state of a representative body".[31] However, this is not necessarily always the case. For instance, in Lithuania, Poland and Belarus, religious organisations of autochthonous Muslim Tatars (having memberships of just a few thousand) are recognised by the State as representative bodies of the respective countries' (entire) Muslim population, though numerically they do not constitute majorities.[32] On the other hand, though Muslims constitute a third of Macedonia's population, for the first decade of its independence, the State there did not recognise Islam as one of the traditional religions in the country. This was only done in the Constitution in the wake of an armed uprising by the Albanian minority, who make up the bulk of the country's Muslim population. In Kosovo, where citizens of a Muslim background constitute an overall majority, Muslim religious organisations to this day have to operate as NGOs because the State has failed to register them as religious organisations.

Ferrari argues that "the need for structured representation at the national level is alien to the Islamic tradition and it thus seems unusual for many Muslims who come from countries where the relationships between state and religion are not organized according to such a model."[33] Though he may be right from an historical point of view in regards to both Muslim majority countries and Western Europe, such an argument is not sustainable in the case of autochthonous Muslim communities in Eastern Europe. Here, in many cases, there has been some sort of structured representation at the national level for decades (and in Russia, for centuries), sometimes since the very founding of certain sovereign nation-states (as with most of the Balkan states, but also Lithuania and Poland) or even earlier (as in Bosnia and Herzegovina). Eastern Europe is different from Western Europe not only in that Islam in many Eastern European countries has been institutionalised for a long time, but also in that these states have recognised representative Muslim religious organisations, couched as spiritual administrations headed by a (chief) mufti.

Rather, the challenge that has emerged is that some Muslim groups reject the authority of the Muslim religious organisations that are recognised by the State as representative of the entire Muslim population in that country. These groups seek to register their own (independent) religious organisations, which then aspire to rival the older established ones in being representative

---

31   Godard, Bernard, "Official recognition of Islam", in Samir Amghar, Amel Boubekeur and Michael Emerson (eds.), *European Islam: Challenges for Public Policy and Society* (Brussels: CEPS Paperbacks, 2007), pp. 183–203 (183).

32   In fact, Tatars are estimated to make up just a tenth of the Muslim population in both Poland and Belarus, while in Lithuania they make up half of the Muslim population in the country.

33   Ferrari, "The creation of Muslim representative institutions", p. 22.

of the country's Muslims, and strive to play the role of interlocutors between the State and Muslims. As Elbasani aptly observes, "[f]rom Bulgaria to Bosnia and Albania, the formalization of religious freedom triggered the fragmentation of the Islamic scene into autonomous groups of faithful, which sometimes complement but at other times compete with the 'official' traditional strand of Islam in terms of the organizational structure, relations to the state and religious doctrine".[34] This is very much true of other, non-Balkan, post-communist Eastern European states. Poland is probably the best example, but Ukraine, Moldova, Serbia, and Romania also fit this pattern. In all of these countries, there are parallel, if not rival, Muslim religious organisations claiming to be representative of, if not the entire Muslim population, then the majority, which then seek recognition by the State as such.

The collapse of both the USSR and socialist Yugoslavia set in motion a process of a nationalisation of Islam in the newly formed states. It was particularly pronounced in the successor states of Yugoslavia, but this is also discernible in such former constituent Soviet republics like Lithuania and Belarus. Though spearheaded by national representative Muslim religious organisations, this process of Islamic nationalisation was very much supported, and at times promoted, by the state authorities themselves. While Bosnia and Herzegovina and Kosovo (Muslim majority countries) are the two most obvious examples of this, Serbia, Macedonia, and Montenegro are other instances of Islamic nationalisation through institutionalisation. Here, formerly pan-Yugoslav Muslim religious organisations became not only national but practically autocephalous, in a process reminiscent of the earlier autocephalization of Orthodox Churches in this part of Europe. Thus, Islam did not merely become "Islam in ... Serbia, Montenegro, Bulgaria etc.", but rather the "Islam of Serbia / Montenegro / Bulgaria etc.", if not "Serbian / Montenegrin / Bulgarian ... Islam". Ultimately, in the Eastern European realm, the institutionalisation of Islam, along with its co-option and bringing under state control, served the purpose of nationalising it: a secondary "domestication". Therefore, the above observation that "religion policy in particular allows European governments to gradually take 'ownership' of their Muslim populations because it grants them unique influence over organizations and leadership within this hard-to-reach minority",[35] is very relevant in the post-communist Eastern European context.

The governance of Islam in countries with autochthonous Muslim communities (with their various forms of Islamic religiosity), significantly differs from

---

34   Elbasani, "Governing Islam in plural societies", p. 15.
35   Laurence, *The Emancipation of Europe's Muslims*, p. 12.

the governance of Islam in Western Europe also in that, in Eastern Europe, "nationalised" Islam is, almost by default, pitted against forms of Islamic religiosity that are deemed alien. In this way, groups espousing revivalist Islam (such as Salafis or Islamists) tend to be doubly marginalised and excluded; first by representative Muslim religious organisations recognised by the State, and then by the states themselves, out of security concerns, but often on the advice from the representative organisations. As such, there is an interplay emerging between the dominant Muslim religious organisations (as a rule run by the autochthonous Muslims) and the State, to control, marginalise and, if need be, eradicate unwelcome forms of Islamic religiosity. With followers of non-indigenous forms of Islamic religiosity still being in a clear minority, such an approach may work. However, if and when Muslims of Salafi and other revivalist leanings grow in numbers (through converts, immigrants and even among autochthonous Muslims), the balance of power may be, if not immediately upset, then at least formidably challenged. Then the states in Eastern Europe may need to reconsider their practised models of state-religion relations and their governance of Islam.

Conclusions

Apart from the main aim of contributing to the expansion of both the geographical and theoretical scope of the analysis on the patterns of the governance of religion in Europe in general, and Islam in particular, the secondary aim of this article was to test to what extent the dominant Western European theoretical approaches to the governance of religion (and of Islam in particular) in Europe are applicable (or even relevant) to post-communist Eastern Europe. The models of state-religion relations and the governance of Islam in Eastern Europe can be placed within the *three-fold* analytical system established in research on state-religion relations in Western Europe, but there are problems with this. By doing so one would have to ignore the multiple aspects peculiar to Eastern Europe, not least of which is the recognition of Islam practised by autochthonous Muslim populations in some Eastern European states as a traditional religion in the respective country. At the same time, the accommodation or domestication of Islam, often talked about in research on Islam in Western Europe, takes a different course in the East of Europe. This is not only because of the different origins and nature of Islam and Muslims in most Eastern European countries. but also because the nation and state building processes there often involved a religious dimension. In a number of Eastern

European countries autocephalous Orthodox Churches are tied in with national identity, with Islam often seen as the antithesis to the very nationhood of the states under question.

Therefore, in many, if not most, post-communist Eastern European states one sees a substantial involvement of the State in seeking to mould Islam (and its representative organisations) into forms acceptable to it. Often, this is being done by co-opting the Islamic leadership through the recognition of their religious organisations as representative of the entire Muslim population of the country. In this way it endorses the chosen form of Islamic religiosity as almost an official Islam in the State, at the expense of other forms of Islamic religiosity. As Elbasani argues, "[t]he way in which institutions, interpretations, and legitimising arguments have developed in post-communist contexts (…) reflects the crucial role of the State in establishing, framing, and maintaining an organised 'religious field'. This organised 'field' implies collaboration between state institutions, intellectual circles, and nationwide religious hierarchies in enforcing 'official' versions of Islam, which develop in tandem with government exigencies and policies".[36]

State-Islam relations and the governance of Islam in Eastern Europe have not been greatly affected by immigration thus far (except within Central European states), when incoming Muslims bring their own forms of Islamic religiosity, which they see as traditional (normative) to their contexts, and which they may want to institutionalise alongside the established forms of Islamic religiosity historically practised in the region. In the current constellation of State-Islam relations, they may find this very difficult if not impossible, as they need to position themselves against both the "representative" Muslim religious organisations and the State. If and when this does happen, Martikainen cautions that "strong state involvement can lead to the clientisation of immigrants as well as to a pathologisation of cultural and social difference".[37] Martikainen's observation, that "with time, these processes may create permanent structures that support the status quo, in which many people of immigrant background are in a disadvantaged position"[38], may also become relevant in Eastern Europe.

---

36   Elbasani, "State-organised religion", p. 254.
37   Martikainen, "The governance of Islam in Finland", p. 258.
38   Martikainen, "The governance of Islam in Finland", p. 258.

Country Surveys

Albania

Olsi Jazexhi[1]

Introduction

The major developments regarding Islam and Muslims in Albania during 2017 were related to the state sponsored efforts to "deradicalise" certain Sunni Muslim groups and to prosecute ISIS sympathisers. There was also the global fight against ISIS, the issue of the presence of the Gülen network in the country, the expanding activities of the Iranian *Mojahedin-e Khalq* organisation, and the debates on the Islamic identity of Albanians in the context of a controversy around Scanderbeg, Albania's national hero. The last debate was provoked by the Qurban Bayram/ 'Id al-Adha prayer, which was held in the main square of Tirana and led certain Christian and secular groups to attack Muslims, to question their "Albanianness", and to defend Scanderbeg's military campaigns against Muslim converts in the 15th century.

Another group of events that drew much media attention was the high-level support that the Iranian *Mojahedin-e Khalq* (MEK) group received from some US senators and a number of Albanian politicians in 2017. The response from the Iranian government to the activities of this group and the protests of some group defectors against the organisation were also widely covered. As in previous years, the arrests of Salafi imams and their followers suspected of supporting terrorism was another issue that drew media attention and condemnation.

Public Debates

The most important debate that concerned Albanian society, media and Muslims of Albania in 2017 was a controversy around Scanderbeg.[2] This debate was provoked by the 'Id Al-Adha prayer that the *Komuniteti Musliman*

---

[1] Olsi Jazexhi holds a PhD in History and Civilisation from the European University Institute, Florence, Italy. He lectures in History at the University of Elbasan Aleksander Xhuvani, and the Aleksander Moisiu University in Durres in Albania.
[2] Scanderbeg is the national hero of Albania. He was made an Albanian hero in the late 19th century when the Austro-Hungarian Empire, and later Italy, sponsored an anti-Turkish version of Albanian nationalism. For more, see Jazexhi, Olsi, *Ottomans into Illyrians: Passages to Nationhood in 20th Century Albania* (PhD dissertation) (Florence: European University Institute, 2011).

i Shqipërisë (Muslim Community of Albania) organised in the central Scanderbeg Square of Tirana. Two large monitors were placed between the statue of Scanderbeg and the congregation, which created the impression that the statute of the national hero of Albania had been purposefully "covered". The covering of the statue was publicised on various websites, and prompted reactions from many politicians and Christian groups. Artan Lame, a close friend of Prime Minister Edi Rama, was the first to accuse the Muslims of covering up the Scanderbeg statue.[3] Eduard Ndocaj, a Catholic politician, published a picture of Scanderbeg with a cross, asking him to guide the Muslims of Albania to Christianity, their original religion, since the Albanians are neither Turks, nor Arabs but genuine Aryans and Christians.[4] Spartak Ngjela, another Christian politician, called for the arrest of the Mufti of Tirana, who, according to him, had called the Albanians Turks. Ngjela declared that Albanians had nothing to do with "Ottoman barbarity" since they were the oldest nation of Europe, descendants of Alexander the Great, Pyrrhus of Epirus, George Kastrioti, Fan Noli and Mother Theresa. They had saved the West from Ottoman barbarity. Ngjela, who described the Mufti of Tirana as "a typical Ottoman", asked for his immediate arrest by the Albanian authorities.[5] Agron Gjekmarkaj, a Catholic lecturer from the University of Tirana, compared the Muslims who prayed on the square with the Taliban. According to him, they had committed a terrorist act by covering Scanderbeg. He asked the leaders of the Muslim Community to make a public apology for destroying the European dream of the Albanians by covering Scanderbeg.[6] Some social media commentators asked the Muslims

---

3 "Artan Lame: Pas 550 vitesh mbi kalë, Skenderbeun e mbuluan me perde!" (Artan Lame: after 550 years on horseback, Skanderbeg covered with hijab!), *Koha Jone*, 1 September 2017, http://www.kohajone.com/2017/09/01/artan-lame-pas-550-vitesh-mbi-kale-skenderbeun-e-mbuluan-me-perde/, accessed 10 March 2018.

4 "Gjesti i rëndë i ish-deputetit shqiptar: Përul myslimanët para kryqit të Skënderbeut!" (A grave provocation by the former Albanian deputy: humble the Muslims before the cross of Skanderbeg!), *Gazeta Express*, 2 September 2017, http://www.gazetaexpress.com/lajme-nga-shqiperia/gjesti-i-rende-i-ish-deputetit-shqiptar-perul-myslimanet-para-kryqit-te-skenderbeut-428288/, accessed 7 February 2018.

5 "Arrestoni myftiun e Tiranës, Ylli Gurra, këtë barbar osman" (Arrest the Tirana Mufti, Ylli Gurra, this Ottoman barbarian), *Gazeta Express*, 6 September 2017, http://www.gazetaexpress.com/lajme-nga-shqiperia/arrestoni-myftiun-e-tiranes-ylli-gurra-kete-barbar-osman-430126/, accessed 7 February 2018.

6 Gjekmarkaj, Agron, "Guxuan të mbulojnë Skënderbeun me perçe" (They dared to cover Scanderbeg with burka), *Gazeta Panorama*, 2 September 2016, http://www.panorama.com.al/guxuan-te-mbulojne-skenderbeun-me-perce/, accessed 7 March 2018.

of Albania to declare if they were Albanians or not,[7] while Kastriot Myftaraj, a well-known Islamophobe and supporter of Anders Breivik, openly declared that "we will squash those who desecrate Scanderbeg like bugs".[8] In one of his Facebook postings, he appealed to his supporters to blow up the "mosque of Erdoğan" in Tirana.[9] These Islamophobic attacks were accompanied by death threats directed against the Mufti of Tirana,[10] Imam Armand Ali,[11] as well as Rudina Xhunga,[12] a TV presenter with Vizion + TV, and other commentators who defended the Muslims and their right to speak against Scanderbeg.

The reactions from Muslims to these Islamophobic attacks, and the role that Scanderbeg has in the national identity of Albanians, were two-fold. On the one hand the Muslim Community of Albania declared that the covering of the statue of Scanderbeg was unintentional, and Scanderbeg was the national hero for Albanian Muslims as well.[13] At the same time though, many

---

7   "Fashizem katolik: Kolec Traboini ve ne dyshim shqiptarine e 90% te shqiptareve" (Catholic fascism: Kolec Traboini questions the Albanianism of 90% of Albanians), *Gazeta Impakt,* 2 September 2016, http://gazetaimpakt.com/fashizem-katolik-kolec-traboini-ve-ne-dyshim-shqiptarine-e-90-te-shqiptareve/, accessed 7 March 2018.

8   Myftaraj, Kastriot, "Mbulimi i Skënderbeut atentat xhihadist / Do t' i shfarosim si insekte ata qe prekin Skenderbeun" (The covering of Scanderbeg was a jihadist attack / we will squash those who desecrate Scanderbeg like bugs), *City News,* 1 September 2017, http://www.citynews.al/2017/09/mbulimi-i-skenderbeut-atentat-xhihadist-do-t-i-shfarosim-si-insekte-ata-qe-prekin-skenderbeun/1, accessed 7 March 2018.

9   "Islamofobi Myftaraj thirrje terroriste për shkatërrimin e xhamisë së madhe të Tiranës" (The Islamophobe Myftaraj makes a terrorist call for the destruction of the great mosque of Tirana), *Gazeta Impakt,* 7 September 2017, http://gazetaimpakt.com/islamofobi-myftaraj-thirrje-terroriste-per-shkaterrimin-e-xhamise-se-madhe-te-tiranes/, accessed 7 March 2018.

10 "Ekrani para Skënderbeut kërcënohet myftiu i Tiranës" (The screen before Scanderbeg, the mufti of Tirana gets threats), *Shqiptarja,* 1 September 2017, https://shqiptarja.com/m/aktualitet/ekrani-para-sk-nderbeut-k-rc-nohet-myftiu-i-tiran-s-438795.html, accessed 7 March 2018.

11 "Kercenohet imam Armand Aliu nga radikalet skenderbegiste" (Scanderbegist radicals make threats against Imam Armand Ali), *Gazeta Impakt,* 2 September 2017, http://gazetaimpakt.com/kercenohet-imam-armand-aliu-nga-radikalet-skenderbegiste/, accessed 7 March 2018.

12 "Emisioni për Skënderbeun, kërcënohet gazetarja Rudina Xhunga. Ja çfarë shkruan" (The Scanderbeg show, journalist Rudina Xhunga is threatened. Here is what she says), *Mapo,* 6 September 2017, http://www.mapo.al/2017/09/emisioni-per-skenderbeun-kercenohet-gazetarja-rudina-xhunga-ja-cfare-shkruan/1, accessed 7 March 2018.

13 "Myftiu Gurra: Skënderbeu, Heroi ynë Kombëtar, më kërcënuan me jetë!" (Mufti Gurra: Scanderbeg is our national hero, I got death threats!), *MAPO,* 2 September 2017, http://www.mapo.al/2017/09/myftiu-gurra-skenderbeu-heroi-yne-kombetar-me-kercenuan-me-jete/1, accessed 7 March 2018.

other commentators, including Imam Armand Ali, rejected Scanderbeg's status as a national hero for all Albanians, stating that he only holds this status for Christians in Albania.[14] The rejection of Scanderbeg by many Muslims led Mustafa Nano, a leading analyst in Albania, to justify Scanderbeg's massacre of Muslims, and to question whether the conversion of Albanians to Islam was a positive historical development.[15] In the debate over Scanderbeg, Prime Minister Edi Rama, in a speech delivered in Parliament, stated that some insignificant groups have suddenly appeared to challenge the role Scanderbeg played in Albanian history.[16]

On 31 December 2017, the Turkish company Ayen Enerji was attacked in Mirdita by a group of Catholic activists. Led by Paulin Zefi, the Director of the Cultural-Historic Office of the city of Lezha, the Mirdita activists vandalised the dam of the company, and destroyed the Turkish flag outside its office, which the company had placed alongside the Albanian flag and the flag with the company's logo. The attack was justified by the Mirditori activists as an attack against Turkey and the Ottoman Empire. They depicted the Turkish company as invading Mirdita with its flag. The Albanian police, who failed to stop the vandalisation of the Turkish flag, later prosecuted 60 activists.[17]

Transnational Links

While the Albanian government continued its policies of targeting Sunni Muslims as possible targets of radicalism, the Iranian *Mojahedin-e Khalq* (MEK) group enjoyed a great deal of support from the Government, many Albanian

---

14   "Imami shqiptar: Kthejini menderen Skënderbeut, ne e kemi për turp që nje mercenar te quhet heroi yne" (The Albanian imam: turn your back on Scanderbeg, we are ashamed to have a mercenary as our hero), *Gazeta TemA*, 2 September 2017, http://www.gazetatema.net/2017/09/02/imami-mysliman-kthejini-menderen-skenderbeut-ne-e-kemi-per-turp-qe-nje-merecenar-te-quhet-heroi-yne-kombetar/, accessed 7 March 2018.

15   "Konvertimi i shqiptarëve në fenë islame ka qenë një proçkë e madhe" (The conversion of Albanians to Islam was a great blunder), *Gazeta Shekulli*, 11 September 2017, http://shekulli.com.al/konvertimi-shqiptareve-ne-fene-islame-ka-qene-nje-procke-e-madhe/, accessed 7 March 2018.

16   "Interesi i gjeneratës tjetër në qendër të politikës dhe të shtetbërjes" (The interest of the next generation at the centre of politics and state-building), *Prime Minister's Official Site*, 11 September 2017, https://kryeministria.al/al/newsroom/fjalime/interesi-i-gjenerates-tjeter-ne-qender-te-politikes-dhe-te-shtetberjes, accessed 7 March 2018.

17   "Ja sesi ekstremistet e Mirdites dhunuan flamurin turk ne HEC-in e Qafe Molles" (This is how the Mirditi extremists violated the Turkish flag at the HEC of Qafe Molla), *Gazeta Impakt*, 31 December 2017, http://gazetaimpakt.com/ja-sesi-ekstremistet-e-mirdites-dhunuan-flamurin-turk-ne-hec-e-qafe-molles/, accessed 10 March 2018.

politicians, and a number of US senators who came to Albania in 2017 to show their support for the MEK. The debate over the presence of the *mojahedins* in Albania started in January 2017, when Albania's Foreign Minister, Ditmir Bushati, was invited to Tehran to discuss the presence of the group, which Tehran views as terrorist.[18] While Ditmir Bushati denied that any discussion about the *mojahedins* took place during his visit to Iran, they continued to expand their activities in Albania. On 22 March 2017, they organised a mass ceremony to celebrate the Day of Nowruz (Iranian New Year). At this event, they were joined by a number of Albanian politicians and ministers, and some US and French officials. Among the foreign officials present were: John Bolton, former US Ambassador to the UN and current National Security Advisor to the US President; Robert Torricelli, former member of the US Senate; David Muniz, deputy US Ambassador in Albania, Jean-Pierre Muller, Mayor of Magny en Vexin and member of Val d'Oise Provincial Council; and Bruno Macé, Mayor of Villiers Adam from France. Elona Gjebrea, Deputy Minister of Interior, Pandeli Majko, former Prime Minister, Fatmir Mediu, former Defence Minister and leader of the Republican Party, the Catholic Archbishop of Tirana George Frendo, and Fatos Klosi, former head of the Albanian Secret Service were some of the Albanian officials present.[19] This event was followed by another event that the *mojahedins* organised in April, when they received US Senator John McCain. In this visit McCain, who supports the calls of Maryam Rajavi, the leader of the MEK, for regime change in Iran, declared that one day her country would be free.[20] In August, the *mojahedins* received another US Senate delegation, led by Roy Blunt, John Cornyn, and Thom Tillis.[21] In these meetings the US Senators urged the Albanian government to give more support to the *mojahedins*, made calls for regime change in Iran, and praised the *mojahedins* for

---

18 "Vizita e Bushatit në Iran shqetëson Perëndimin: Negocioi për muxhahedinët pa pyetur askënd" (Bushati's visit in Iran worries the West: negotiated for the *mojahedins* without asking anyone), *Gazeta Panorama*, 17 January 2017, http://www.panorama.com.al/vizita-e-bushatit-ne-iran-shqeteson-perendimin-negocioi-per-muxhahedinet-pa-pyetur-askend/, accessed 7 March 2018.

19 "Nowruz Celebration in Tirana–2017", *Free Iran Gathering*, 20 March 2017, http://iranfreedom.org/gathering/grand-gathering/grand-gathering-2017/item/276-nowruz-celebration-in-tirana-2017.html, accessed 10 March 2018.

20 "Tiranë, McCain takoi muxhahedinët përgëzoi Shqipërinë për pritjen" (Tirana, McCain met the *mojahedins*, praised Albania for welcoming them), *Shqiptarja*, 16 April 2017, https://shqiptarja.com/m/aktualitet/tiran--mccain-takoi-muxhahedin-t-p-rg-zoi-shqiprin--p-r-pritjen-413766.html, accessed 10 March 2018.

21 "Senior US Senators meet Iran opposition leader In Albania", *The Huffington Post*, 16 August 2017, https://www.huffingtonpost.com/entry/senior-us-senators-meet-iranian-opposition-leader-in_us_598f68fae4b063e2ae058020, accessed 10 March 2018.

their resistance against the Islamic Republic. Fatos Klosi, Albania's ex-head of the Security Service, who in 2016 had declared the *mojahedins* to be a terrorist organisation, now claimed that the US senators had come to Albania to make sure that the Albanian government gave all the necessary protection to the *mojahedins*, who were threatened by Iranian government agents.[22] The "Free Iran" event, that the *mojahedins* organised in Paris on 1 July 2017, was again attended by some Albanian representatives.[23]

However, the MEK organisation had its own problems in 2017. Its activities and meetings with US senators were condemned by the Iranian Embassy in Tirana, which described their meeting with John McCain as a sign of his support for a terrorist organisation.[24] Also, Edward Termado, an Armenian Christian who was member of MEK for twelve years, wrote an open letter to the Catholic Archbishop of Tirana and Durrës, George Anthony Frendo, criticising the MEK.[25] The *mojahedins* were faced with a number of defections from their organisation as well. Some of their members who had defected went to the media and accused the organisation of keeping them in slave-like conditions, monitoring their movements, isolating them from their families, and blackmailing them by cutting their monthly stipends and declaring them to be agents of Iran if they were caught speaking to their families back in the country.[26] Other defectors explained how the *mojahedins* had recruited them to their organisation with promises of smuggling them into Europe, and later brainwashed and radicalised them by separating them from their families

---

22   "Fatos Klosi i cili ne 2016 i shpalli xhihadistet iraniane terroriste, tani thote nuk jane terroriste" (Fatos Klosi who in 2016 declared the Iranians jihadi terrorists, now says they are not terrorists), *Gazeta Impakt,* 16 August 2017, http://gazetaimpakt.com/fatos-klosi-i-cili-ne-2016-i-shpalli-xhihadistet-iraniane-terroriste-tani-thote-nuk-jane-terroriste/, accessed 10 March 2018.

23   "PD dhe PS bëhen bashkë në Paris, ja kush i kryeson" (Democratic Party and Socialist Party come together in Paris, here is who leads them), *Gazeta Infopress,* 2 June 2017, http://gazetainfopress.com/aktualitete/pd-dhe-ps-behen-bashke-ne-paris-ja-kush-kryeson, accessed 10 March 2018.

24   "Ambasada iraniane: McCain përkrahu në Tiranë një qendër terroriste" (The Iranian Embassy: McCain supported a terrorist centre in Tirana), *JavaNews,* 18 April 2017, http://www.javanews.al/ambasada-iraniane-mccain-perkrahu-ne-tirane-nje-qender-terroriste/, accessed 10 March 2018.

25   "Open letter to Archbishop of Tirana-Durrës, George Anthony Frendo", *Sahar Family Foundation,* 28 May 2017, http://www.saharngo.com/en/story/1502, accessed 10 March 2018.

26   "IMPAKT 90–MKO organizate demokratike apo sekt dictatorial" (Impact 90–is MKO a democratic organisation or a dictatorial sect?), *Gazeta Impakt,* 29 August 2017, http://gazetaimpakt.com/impakt-90-mko-organizate-demokratike-apo-sekt-diktatorial/, accessed 10 March 2018.

for many years.[27] Some ex-members also made allegations in the media that the *mojahedins* have cooperated with the Albanian mafia to recruit Albanian youths to join their cause.[28] In November 2017, Anne Khodabandeh, an ex-member, visited Albania, and in her media interviews explained how the *mojahedins* were in Albania not to integrate into Albanian society but to continue their activities in human trafficking and money laundering.[29] Khodabandeh– who gave two interviews, one for TemA TV and another for Ora News–later had her interviews censured and deleted after the *mojahedins* submitted complaints, accusing her of being an Iranian agent and rejecting her allegations.[30] The *mojahedins* declined the requests of Khodabandeh and the TemA TV journalist to participate in a television debate on these issues.

2017 was a difficult year for MEK defectors. Many of them demanded that the Albanian government and the UNHCR support them to live a free life outside the MEK. They complained about their present legal status in Albania, which did not allow them to work or move to other countries and as a result their only form of survival was to maintain their connections to the MEK. In October 2017, an Albanian lawyer and a representative of some defectors, met UNHCR officials in Tirana, repeating allegations of the MEK's pressure on, and isolation of, its members. A defector asked the UNHCR to support him and other defectors financially, but the UNHCR officials declined the request, citing lack of funds.[31]

---

27   "IMPAKT 98: Xhihad 2.0? Cfare duan xhihadistet iraniane ne Shqiperi? (pjesa 2)" (Impact 98: Jihad 2.0? What do the Iranian jihadis want in Albania? (part 2)), *Gazeta Impakt*, 7 November 2017, http://gazetaimpakt.com/impakt-98-xhihad-2-0-cfare-duan-xhihadistet-iraniane-ne-shqiperi-pjesa-2/, accessed 10 March 2018.
28   "SKANDAL! MAFIA SHQIPTARE NDIHMON MUXHEHEDINËT TË REKRUTOJNË FËMIJËT TANË, FRIKËSOHET BE-JA", (Scandal! Albanian Mafia supports the *mojahedins* to recruit our children, the European Union is worried), *Tirana Today*, 20 November 2017, https://tiranatoday.com/skandal-mafia-shqiptare-ndihmon-muxhehedinet-te-rekrutojne-femijet-tane-frikesohet-ja/, accessed 10 March 2018.
29   "Ekskluzive për Ora News, Anne Singelton: Muxhahedinët po rekrutojnë të rinjtë shqiptarë" (Exclusive for Ora News, Anne Singelton: the *mojahedins* are recruiting Albanian youth), *Gazeta Impakt*, 12 November 2017, http://gazetaimpakt.com/ekskluzive-per-ora-news-anne-singelton-muxhahedinet-po-rekrutojne-te-rinjte-shqiptare/, accessed 10 March 2018.
30   "Muxhahedinet iraniane kercenojne lirine e medias, censurojne televizionin Ora News" (Iranian *mojahedins* threaten media freedom, censor Ora News television), *Gazeta Impakt*, 14 November 2017, http://gazetaimpakt.com/muxhahedinet-iraniane-kercenojne-lirine-e-medias-censurojne-televizionin-ora-news/, accessed 10 March 2018.
31   "Legal representative meets with UNHCR in Tirana to clarify the status of MEK defectors", *Sahar Family Foundation*, 16 October 2017, http://www.saharngo.com/en/story/1519, accessed 10 March 2018.

Another Islamic group which drew much media attention in 2017 was the Gülen movement, which runs a number of schools and businesses in Albania. Turkey continued its attacks against the group. Thus, in an interview that the Turkish ambassador, Hidayet Bayraktar, had with the Anadolu Agency in May, he attacked the group's presence in the country, and claimed that Albania was one of the major countries where "FETÖ" (*Fethullahçı Terör Örgütü*–"Gülenist Terror Organisation")–the designation used by the Turkish government for the followers of Gülen since 2016[32]–has its bases, through the network of the schools that they run. He announced that Turkey was working to remove them from Albania, and for this his country had opened the Maarif Foundation, which would open Turkish schools as an alternative in the country.[33] A few days later, Albania's chief prosecutor, Adriatik Llalla, announced that he held a meeting with Turkey's chief prosecutor, Mehmet Akarca, and had received documents pertaining to the alleged coup perpetrators in Turkey who were thought to be hiding in Albania. Llalla confirmed that these cases were investigated.[34] The request to isolate followers of Gülen in Albania also came from the Turkish president Recep Tayyip Erdoğan. In an interview that he gave in June to Top Channel TV, he asked the Albanian public and the Prime Minister to isolate them and cooperate with the Maarif Foundation, which Turkey had brought to Albania.[35] However the Maarif Foundation did not manage to take over any Gülen schools in 2017, nor to open any school of their own. According to media reports, the Maarif Foundation took over the Canadian Institute of Technology, a Qatari funded private university, from its Qatari sponsors.[36]

---

[32] Anadolu Agency, *FETO's Coup Attempt in Turkey: a Timeline* (Ankara: Anadolu Agency, 2016), p. 80.

[33] "Do të jemi në ndjekje deri në pastrimin e anëtarit të fundit të FETO-s nga Shqipëria" (We will pursue them until we remove the last member of FETO from Albania), *Anadoly Agency*, 14 May 2017, http://aa.com.tr/sq/ballkan/do-të-jemi-në-ndjekje-deri-në-pastrim in-e-anëtarit-të-fundit-të-feto-s-nga-shqipëria/818140?amp=1, accessed 10 March 2018.

[34] "Grushti në Turqi, Llalla: Puçistët Dyshohet se fshihen në Shqipëri" (The coup in Turkey, Llalla: it is suspected that the puchists are hiding in Albania), *Shqiptarja*, 23 May 2017, https://shqiptarja.com/m/aktualitet/grushti-n--turqi-llalla-pu-ist-t-dyshohet-se-fshihen-n--shqip-ri-420438.html, accessed 10 March 2018.

[35] "Turkish President Recep Taip Erdogan exclusive interview on Top Story", *Top Channel*, 19 June 2017, http://top-channel.tv/english/turkish-president-recep-taip-erdogan-exclu sive-interview-on-top-story/, accessed 10 March 2018.

[36] "Maarif Foundation will launch its first university in Albania", *World Bulletin*, 12 May 2017, http://www.worldbulletin.net/africa/189391/maarif-foundation-will-launch-its-first-university-in-albania, accessed 10 March 2018.

Extradition requests by the Turkish authorities in Albania did not lead to the deportation of suspected followers of Gülen either. One of these was the case of Muhammed Aydogmus, a teacher from one of the Gülen schools, accused by Turkey to be a terrorist affiliated to "FETÖ". He was arrested in Durres on 8 October 2017 while trying to illegally cross the border to Italy. After being arrested, he was later released on bail, even though the Turkish embassy demanded that Albania extradite him. The Albanian authorities did not follow the Turkish demands, and a few days later he was announced as missing.[37] Turkey did not succeed in convincing the Albanian government that Gülen schools posed a danger to Albania. On 17 May 2017, Lindita Nikolla, the Minister of Education, publicly rejected a speech delivered by a TIKA (Turkish Cooperation and Coordination Agency) representative at the University of Tirana, where he described Gülen schools as terrorist-related.[38]

Law and Domestic Politics

On the domestic front, Albanian Muslims continued to be arrested on charges of terrorism. On 18 January 2017, Emine Alushi, a teacher from the madrasah of Shkodra, was arrested on charges of supporting terrorism. Her arrest came after the programme STOP on Klan TV showed a secret recording of the teacher, where she was describing ISIS as "a Muslim organisation protecting Syria's Muslim population, or that of Palestine, or that of Egypt".[39] While most of the media attacked the teacher, the Mufti of Shkodra, Muhamet Sytari condemned her arrest, calling it illegal and meaningless.[40] The teacher, who, according to

---

37 "Lirimi i terroristit nga gjykata e Durrësit, ambasada turke: Skandal, jemi të zhgënjyer!" (The terrorist was released by Durresi's court, Turkish Embassy: scandal, we are disappointed!), *Gazeta Impakt,* 14 October 2017, http://gazetaimpakt.com/lirimi-terroristit-nga-gjykata-e-durresit-ambasada-turke-skandal-jemi-te-zhgenjyer/, accessed 10 March 2018.

38 "Shkollat e Gylen në Tiranë manipulojnë të rinjtë", ministrja Nikolla përplaset me zyrtarin turk" (Gülen schools are manipulating the youth, Minister Nikolla clashes with Turkish official), *Standard,* 17 May 2017, http://www.standard.al/2017/05/17/shkollat-e-gylen-ne-tirane-manipulojne-te-rinjte-ministrja-nikolla-perplaset-me-zyrtarin-turk-video/, accessed 10 March 2018.

39 "Albanian teacher arrested for pro-IS propaganda", *The Daily Mail,* 19 January 2017, http://www.dailymail.co.uk/wires/ap/article-4135986/Albanian-teacher-arrested-pro-IS-propaganda.html, accessed 10 March 2018.

40 "Xhihadistët dhe "mësuesja" e ISIS, myftiu i Shkodrës: Arrestimet po irritojne myslimanet" (The jihadis and the ISIS "teacher", the mufti of Shkodra: the arrests are angering

her relatives, had her religious rights infringed while in police custody, was later put under house arrest by the Court of Shkodra.[41]

In March 2017, Imam Ahmed Kalaja caused public controversy when, in a Facebook conversation with Andi Lila, a football player in Albania's national team, they both described a Greek priest as "a sex maniac". This scandal was denounced by the Orthodox Church and the media, and Ahmed Kalaja and Andi Lila were forced to make public apologies.[42] In reaction to a complaint by the State Committee on Religions against the imam, the Muslim Community condemned Kalaja's remarks, and threatened to dismiss him from his position.[43]

Some Muslims were attacked in the media for wearing burkinis on public beaches. Mentor Kikia, a journalist, described the practice of women wearing burkinis while Muslim men can wear shorts, as discriminatory.[44] Kikia was supported by Diana Çuli, who attacked the covering of Muslim women, and called their covering as contravening the laws on terrorism.[45] Their remarks provoked a wide debate in Muslim circles. Muslim women countered Diana Çuli, by alleging that she was not in a position to criticise Muslim beliefs and practices since she allegedly collaborated with the security services during the country's communist era.[46]

Muslims), *Balkanweb*, 24 January 2017, http://www.balkanweb.com/site/arrestimet-e-xhihadisteve-myftiu-i-shkodres-irritim-mes-myslimaneve-ndalimi-i-mesueses-i-paligjshem/, accessed 10 March 2018.

41 "Arrest shtëpie për mësuesen që propagandoi për Shtetin Islamik" (House arrest for the teacher who propagated for the Islamic State), *Zeri i Amerikes*, 21 January 2017, https://www.zeriamerikes.com/a/arrest-shtepie-mesuesja-shkoder-isis/3686081.html, accessed 10 March 2018.

42 "VIDEOSKANDALI/ Reagon imami Ahmed Kalaja: Ishte në rafshin e humorit, u keqkuptua" (Video scandal/ Imam Ahmed Kalaja reacts: I was joking, it is a misunderstanding), *Albeu*, 23 March 2017, http://www.albeu.com/opinion/sport/videoskandali-reagon-imami-ahmed-kalaja-ishte-ne-rafshin-e-humorit-/295037/, accessed 10 March 2018.

43 "Videoja tallëse me Andi Lilën, kërkohet shkarkimi i imamit Ahmed Kalaja" (The ridiculing video with Andi Lila, the dismissal of Imam Ahmed Kalaja has been requested), *Tirana Observer*, 28 March 2017, http://www.tiranaobserver.al/videoja-tallese-me-andi-lilen-kerkohet-shkarkimi-i-imamit-ahmed-kalaja/, accessed 10 March 2018.

44 "Fotoja që po ngjall debat: Kafshëri apo nudizëm dhe liri???" (The picture that is provoking a debate: bestiality or nudity and freedom???), *Gazeta Express*, 3 July 2017, http://www.gazetaexpress.com/lajme-nga-shqiperia/fotoja-qe-po-ngjall-debat-kafsheri-apo-nudizem-dhe-liri-398585/, accessed 10 September 2017.

45 Culi, Diana, "Per grate e mbuluar qe kane vape si ne" (For the covered women who feel hot like we do), *Tirana Post*, 6 July 2017, http://www.tiranapost.al/per-grate-e-mbuluara-qe-kane-vape-si-ne/, accessed 10 March 2018.

46 "IMPAKT 85–Racizmi dhe islamofobia e Diana Çulit dhe Mentor Kikise ndaj muslimaneve" (Impact 85–the racism and Islamophobia against Muslims of Diana Culi and Mentor

The courts of Albania continued to prosecute Muslims charged with terrorist offences. In May 2017, the Court of Serious Crimes sentenced Almir Daci to 15 years in prison in absentia, even though Daci was pronounced dead in Syria.[47] In November, the same court was forced to release Xhezair Fishti and Medat Hasani, and later Bekim Protopapa and Ergys Faslia who were arrested one year earlier, on suspicion of planning to attack the Israeli football team during a match in Albania.[48] The court could not find any incriminating evidence for the accused, and since it could no longer extend their detention, was forced to release them while placing them under house arrest.

The Government for its part created a major controversy within the Muslim Community on 16 September 2017, when NATO's highest military authority, the Military Committee and its Chiefs of Defence, held a meeting in Tirana. On that day the police were ordered to close the central mosque of Ethem Beg for two days and halt the *adhan* (call to prayer) while the NATO chiefs were meeting in the Tirana International Hotel in front of the mosque.[49] The news of the closure of the mosque irritated many Muslims and leading imams of Tirana and the leaders of the Muslim Community, who were surprised by this unannounced closure.[50] This incident was publicised in the media and news portals, which denounced this as an unprecedented attack on freedom of religion. The day after the meeting, the police gave instructions to open the mosque again.

As in previous years, in 2017 the Government allocated funds to "traditional" religious communities. The Muslim Community received 31,416,000 Lekë ($286,681), the Bektashi Community 25,840,000 Lekë ($235,877), the

---

Kikia), *Gazeta Impakt,* 19 July 2017, http://gazetaimpakt.com/impakt-85-racizmi-dhe-islamofobia-e-diana-culit-dhe-mentor-kikise-ndaj-muslimaneve/, accessed 10 March 2018.

47 "Rekrutimet në Siri, gjykata shpall fajtor terroristin e vdekur" (Recruitment in Syria, the court declares the dead terrorist guilty), *Top Channel,* 4 May 2017, http://top-channel.tv/2017/05/04/rekrutimet-ne-siri-gjykata-shpall-fajtor-terroristin-e-vdekur/#tab, accessed 10 March 2018.

48 "Lirohen dy të akuzuarit për planifikim sulmi në ndeshjen ndaj Izraelit" (Two of those accused of planning the attack against the match with Israel have been released), *Gazeta Dita,* 7 November 2017, http://www.gazetadita.al/lirohen-dy-te-akuzuarit-per-planifikim-sulmi-ne-ndeshjen-ndaj-izraelit/, accessed 10 March 2018.

49 "Edi Rama mbyll per 2 dite per NATO-n Xhamine e Ethem Beut" (Edi Rama closes the Ethem Beg Mosque for 2 days for NATO), *Gazeta Impakt,* 16 September 2017, http://gazetaimpakt.com/edi-rama-mbyll-per-2-dite-per-nato-n-xhamine-e-ethem-beut/, accessed 10 March 2018.

50 "Mbyllja e xhamisë së Et'hem Beut, reagon KMSH" (The closure of Ethem Beg, MCA reacts), *Nacional Albania,* 17 September 2017, http://www.nacionalalbania.al/2017/09/mbyllja-e-xhamise-se-ethem-beut-reagon-kmsh/, accessed 10 March 2018.

Autocephalous Orthodox Church of Albania 25,872,000 Lekë ($236,242), and the Catholic Church in Albania 25,872,000 Lekë ($236,242).[51]

Activities and Initiatives of Main Muslim Organisations

The Muslim Community of Albania (MCA) organised a number of activities in 2017. On 17 April it organised the annual concert to celebrate the birthday of the Prophet Muhammad in the Palace of Congresses in Tirana. It also organised and participated in a number of symposiums and conferences that dealt with interreligious coexistence,[52] fighting extremism, etc. The chair of the MCA was invited by the German Foreign Minister, Sigmar Gabriel, to attend the conference "Responsibility of Religions for Peace".[53] He was also invited to the United Arab Emirates,[54] and the United States[55] to participate in different conferences.

Muslim Population: History and Demographics

Islam is believed to have entered the regions that constitute modern-day Albania in the ninth century, while steady Islamisation started after the

---

51 "Qeveria i jep 1 mln dollarë komuniteteve fetare shqiptare" (The Government gives 1 million dollars to Albanian religious communities), *Gazeta Monitor*, 19 April 2017, http://www.gazetamonitor.com/qeveria-i-jep-1-mln-dollare-komuniteteve-fetare-shqiptare/, accessed 10 March 2018.

52 "Zhvillohet Simpoziumi i V-të Akademik Ndërfetar, 'Dashuria Hyjnore'" (The Fifth Interreligious Academic Symposium is organised), *Komuniteti Mysliman i Shqiperise*, 15 December 2017, https://www.kmsh.al/al/2017/12/zhvillohet-simpoziumi-i-v-te-akademik-nderfetar-dashuria-hyjnore/, accessed 10 March 2018.

53 "Gjermani, kreu i KMSH-së merr pjesë në konferencën 'Përgjegjësia e feve për paqen'" (Germany, head of MCA participates in the conference "The responsibilities of religions for peace"), *Komuniteti Mysliman i Shqiperise*, 23 May 2017, https://www.kmsh.al/al/2017/05/gjermani-kreu-i-kmsh-se-merr-pjese-ne-konferencen-pergjegjesia-e-feve-per-paqen/, accessed 10 March 2018.

54 "Kreu i KMSH-së merr pjesë në konferencën tre ditore në Abu Dabi" (Chair of MCA takes part in a three day conference in Abu Dhabi), *Komuniteti Mysliman i Shqiperise*, 13 December 2017, https://www.kmsh.al/al/2017/12/kreu-i-kmsh-se-merr-pjese-ne-konferencen-tre-ditore-ne-abu-dabi/, accessed 10 March 2018.

55 "SHBA, kreu i KMSH-së merr pjesë në konferencën e Lidhjes Botërore të Myslimanëve" (USA, chair of MCA takes part in the World Muslim League conference), *Komuniteti Mysliman i Shqiperise*, 18 September 2017, https://www.kmsh.al/al/2017/09/shba-kreu-i-kmsh-se-merr-pjese-ne-konferencen-e-lidhjes-boterore-te-myslimaneve/, accessed 10 March 2018.

17th century, during Ottoman rule.[56] After the collapse of the Ottoman Empire, the number and position of Muslims changed markedly, and Islam lost much of its importance. An important factor was the establishment of a secular Albanian state in 1920, which adopted French style laicism as its official ideology.[57] Islam and other religions of Albania were completely suppressed after World War II, when the communist regime declared the country an atheist state (from 1967 until 1991) and banned all religions. Even though Islam witnessed a revival after the fall of communism, it did not manage to recover the numbers it had before World War II. As a result of Christian missionary activities, past policies of de-Islamisation and negative local and Western depictions of Islam that have accompanied the rebirth of religion after the fall of communism, the majority of the citizens of Albania do not practise or associate themselves publicly with Islam. This is in spite of the fact that in the census of 2011 the majority of Albanian people declared themselves to be Muslims. In recent years many Muslims have converted to Christianity or changed their names and identities in order to receive jobs and residence permits in Western Europe.[58]

The census, which the Albanian government conducted through the National Institute of Statistics in 2011, showed that Albania is still a Muslim majority country. Muslims (Sunnis, Bektashis, and other groups) make up 58.79% of the total population.[59]

Muslim Population   1,646,236 (58.79% of the population) (Census of 2011).

Ethnic/National Backgrounds   While there is no breakdown in the number of Muslims, the Census of 2011 provided the following ethnic breakdown:[60]

Albanian: 82.58%
Greek: 0.87%
Macedonian: 0.20%

---

56   Roka, Dela, and Roberto Moroko, *Kombësija dhe feja në Shqipëri 1920–1944* (*Nation and Religion in Albania 1920–1944*) (Tirana: Eleni Gjika, 1994), p. 20.
57   For more, see Jazexhi, *Ottomans into Illyrians*.
58   An example which shows the reasons behind Albanians converting to Christianity in Italy, can be seen in the film by Gianni Amelio *L'America* (1994): www.youtube.com/watch?v=YR58A4anMR0, accessed 19 December 2014.
59   Instat, *Population and Housing Census 2011* (Shtypshkronja: Adel Print, 2012), p. 71.
60   Instat, *Population and Housing Census 2011*, p. 71.

Montenegrin: 0.01%
Romanian: 0.30%
Roma: 0.30%
Egyptian (Jevgits): 0.12%
Others: 0.09%
Not stated: 1.58%.

Among the above listed minorities, only the Roma and the "Egyptians" (Yevgits) are overwhelmingly Muslim. As a result, we can conclude that most of Albania's Muslims are ethnic Albanians. However, a small number of Bosniaks, Gollobordas, Goranis, and Turks, who do not appear in the census, are also Muslims. In addition, the small number of Syrian, Iranian and other refugees, who have come recently, need to be added.

Inner-Islamic groups State authorities categorise Albanian Muslims into two major groups. The largest group, labelled simply "Muslims," makes up 56.70% of the population. The second group, the Bektashis, according to the census of 2011, make up 2.09% of the population. "Muslims" are usually described as Sunni. However, many Muslims are Salafis, Shi'is, or Ahmadis. Various Sufi orders (Rifa'i, Qadiri, Sa'di, Khalwati, Tijani, etc.) are also present.

Geographical Spread While we do not have any statistics on the distribution of Muslims in Albania, they constitute the majority in almost all the regions of Albania, except in Mirdita and Himara. Since 1991, many Muslims, following a national trend, have migrated towards the capital, Tirana.

Number of Mosques According to Ilir Hoxholli, who served as head of the State Committee on Religions in 2014, the Muslim Community of Albania operates around 650 mosques in the country. However, around a dozen other mosques exist which are not under the jurisdiction of the Muslim Community of Albania.[61] The Bektashis have some 138 Sufi lodges,[62] and the other Sufi orders have altogether an estimated 384 lodges.[63]

Muslim Burial Sites — During communist rule, followers of different religions were buried together. In major cities, like Tirana, Christians, Muslims and people of other beliefs are buried together. Outside Tirana, a number of cemeteries exist where Muslims and Christians are buried separately. In some rural areas the tradition continues where Muslims and Christians have separate graveyards.

"Chaplaincy" in State Institutions — Chaplaincy in state institutions is not organised by the State. There are no chaplains in the Albanian army, hospitals, prisons, or other institutions. However, the Muslim Community and Christian Churches send temporary religious personnel to prisons for pastoral and religious purposes.

Halal Products — In Albania, a number of restaurants and shops exist that provide and serve halal food. Halal slaughter is allowed in private shops, but public institutions do not provide halal food.

Dress Code — There are no laws on Muslim dress in Albania. Muslim women and men wear religious dress only to a limited extent. In general Muslim women wearing the head scarf do not face discrimination. However, women who wear niqabs and sometimes head scarf-wearing girls are not allowed to attend public schools. Head scarf-wearing women can generally find jobs in the private sector, but in public institutions they face difficulties in securing employment.

---

61 "Xhamitë si ndërtimet pa leje, dhjetëra të palegalizuara" (Mosques as illegal constructions, dozens have not been legalised), *Gazeta Dita*, 12 March 2014, www.gazetadita.al/xhamite-si-ndertimet-pa-leje-dhjetera-te-palegalizuara/, accessed 1 April 2017.
62 Information obtained from the Albanian State Committee on Religions, 2 November 2013.
63 Information obtained from the Albanian State Committee on Religions, 2 November 2013.

Places of Islamic Learning and Education

The major places of Islamic learning and education in Albania are the MCA-controlled madrasas and mosques. The MCA operates seven madrasas:

– Madrasa of Tirana H. Mahmud Dashi
– Madrasa of Shkodra H. Sheh Shamia
– Madrasa of Durrës Mustafa Varoshi
– Madrasa of Kavaja Hafiz Ali Korça
– Madrasa of Elbasan Liria
– Madrasa of Berat Vexhi Buharaja
– Madrasa of Korça Abdullah Zemblaku.

The MCA also operates one university called Bedër (Full Moon). Bedër started its activities in 2011, and is presently staffed by the Fethullah Gülen-inspired Turkish Foundation, Sema. Bedër is not a full theological university, but runs one Department of Islamic Sciences which offers a Bachelor's Programme in Islamic Sciences, a Master's Programme in Basic Islamic Sciences and another in Modern Islamic Sciences.[64]

The League of the Imams of Albania, the Ardhmeria Association, and a number of other Muslim NGOs and imams, run Islamic classes as well. Their classes are held in mosques and different centres throughout the country.

Muslim Media and Publications

The main Muslim newspapers, magazines and radio channels in Albania are:

– *Drita Islame* (The Light of Islam), a newspaper of the Muslim Community of Albania.
– *Zani i Naltë*, an academic and cultural journal of the Muslim Community of Albania.
– *Udha Islame* (The Islamic Path), a journal of the Muftiate of Shkodra.

---

64   For more on the programmes of Bedër University, see http://isc.beder.edu.al/en/, accessed 1 April 2017.

- *Drita e Kuranit* (The Light of the Qur'an), a magazine published by the Qur'an Foundation.
- *Lidhja* (The League), a newspaper of the League of the Imams of Albania.
- *Mendimi* (Thought), a newspaper published by the Intellectual Muslim Forum.
- *Radio Kontakt*, a radio channel owned by Ramiz Zeka which broadcasts secular and religious programmes.
- *Albania FM 90.4*, a radio channel owned and operated by the Muftiate of Elbasan. It broadcasts secular and religious programmes.

Main Muslim Organisations

- Muslim Community of Albania (*Komuniteti Musliman i Shqipërisë*–MCA, Rr. George W. Bush, Nr. 50, Tirana, Albania, tel.: ++355 42269123/ 4223701 / 230492, email: info@kmsh.al, www.kmsh.al/). This is the largest Sunni Muslim organisation in Albania, recognised by the State as the national organisation of Islam. It administers most of the mosques, and is viewed as the main representative of Sunni Islam in the country. It was originally founded in 1923, when the Muslims of Albania were officially separated from the Caliphate in Istanbul.[65] After being abolished during the communist era, the Muslim Community was reorganised in 1991.
- World Headquarters of Bektashism (*Kryegjyshata Botërore Bektashiane*, Rruga Dhimiter Kamarda, Tirana, Albania, tel.: ++355 4355227 / 4355090, email: info@komunitetibektashi.org, www.komunitetibektashi.org/). This is the largest Sufi *tariqa* organisation in Albania. *Kryegjyshata Bektashiane* is recognised by the State as a national organisation and a separate religious community. The Bektashis claim their headquarters are the World Headquarters of Bektashism, but this is disputed by Bektashis living outside Albania. *Kryegjyshata Bektashiane* was transferred from Turkey to Albania in 1931, after the prohibition of the order in Turkey in 1925. In 1946, the *tariqa* separated itself officially from the MCA (which represented the Sunnis and other *tariqas*) and became a separate religious community.[66]

---

[65] Jazexhiu, *Ottomans into Illyrians*, pp. 190–194.
[66] Kalicani, Baba Selim, *Bektashizmi si sekt mistik islam* (*Bektashism as a Mystical Sect of Islam*) (Tirana: KOHA, 1999), pp. 228–229.

Apart from the officially recognised organisations, a number of other Muslim bodies are active in the country. One can mention different Sufi *tariqas*, such as the Rifa'is, Qadiris, Sa'dis, Khalwatis, and Tijanis, but also the recent presence of Ahmadiyya Muslims. Important Muslim organisations include a number of NGOs, which run many activities of the MCA:

- Sema Foundation (*Fondacioni Sema*, e-mail: info@sema.edu.al, www.sema.edu.al) runs most of the madrasas and Bedër University.
- "Progress" (*Qendra Kulturore "PROGRESI"*, Vasil Shanto, Rr: Çajupi Shkodër, Albania, tel.: ++355 22254634, www.progresibotime.com). A Sufi Turkish organisation which runs one of the madrasas in Shkodra.
- League of the Imams of Albania (*Lidhja e Hoxhallareve te Shqiperise*, Unaza e Re, Rruga: Teodor Keko mbi Alfa Bank, Tirana, Albania, tel. /fax: ++355 48320160, mobile: ++355 672304520 / 672582271, email: info@lidhjahoxhallareve.com, www.lidhjahoxhallareve.com). A Salafi inspired organisation which represents, supports and defends Salafi imams. It is involved in preaching and publication.
- Albanian Institute of Islamic Thought and Civilisation (*Instituti Shqiptar i Mendimit dhe Qyteterimit Islam*, Rr. Isuf Elezi Nr. 10, VILAT SELIT, P.O. Box. 2905, Tirana, Albania, tel.: ++355 42215087, email: contact@aiitc.net, www.aiitc.net). An NGO directed by Ramiz Zeka which publishes Salafi and nationalist books.
- Future Association (*Ardhmëria Association*, Kutia Postare: P.O. Box 272/1 Tirana, Albania, tel.: ++355 42347728, email: ardhmeriaonline@gmail.com). An NGO which teaches and propagates Islam and runs a number of centres, part-time courses, and publications.
- Alsar Foundation (*Alsar, Fondacion Arsimor Kulturor Humanitar*, Rr. E Bogdanëve, P.Eurocol, Kati 1 Tirana, Albania, tel.: +355 42241852, email: alsar2006al@yahoo.com, http://www.alsar.al). A foundation funded by the Turkish government and Turkish NGOs. It carries out major charitable, political and historical activities on behalf of the Turkish government and institutions in Albania.

Armenia

Sevak Karamyan[1] and Gevorg Avetikyan[2]

Introduction

Armenia has one of the smallest Muslim populations in Europe. It has neither a significant Muslim population nor are there any visible issues of wider social concern about Muslims. There is, however, a growing awareness of Muslim Armenian citizens coming into the country, primarily from neighbouring Turkey. In the years after the collapse of the USSR, the newly independent Armenia conducted two population censuses, in 2001 and 2011. No questions about religion were included in the questionnaire of the 2001 census.[3] Although the questionnaire for the 2011 population census did include a question about religion, and listed "Muslim" among the options, the initial results indicated no specific number of Muslims in Armenia, and grouped them together as "other".[4]

The number of tourists and business people who visit Armenia from Muslim majority countries has grown in recent years. The number of Iranian and Arab restaurants, and other services targeting tourists from these countries and regions, has increased as well. This is also due to the increasing number of Syrian refugees who are actively involved in such services. According to a UNHCR report, there were around 17,000 Syrian and more than 1,000 Iraqi "refugees, asylum-seekers and persons in a refugee-like situation" in Armenia as of December 2015.[5] The number of Syrians reached at least 20,000 persons by the end of 2017.[6] It is worth mentioning, however, that these are predominantly ethnic Armenians fleeing Middle Eastern conflict zones. They are often viewed as repatriates rather than refugees.[7]

---

1 Sevak Karamyan, PhD, is a Senior Fellow at the Centre for Civilisation and Cultural Studies, Yerevan State University.
2 Gevorg Avetikyan, PhD, is an Associate Professor (Iranian Studies) and Co-Director at the Russian and Eurasian Studies (IMARES) Programme, European University at St Petersburg.
3 http://www.armstat.am/file/doc/80.pdf, accessed 23 January 2018.
4 http://armstat.am/file/doc/99486278.pdf, accessed 23 January 2018.
5 http://www.un.am/up/library/UNHCRArmeniaFactSheetDec2015_Eng.pdf, accessed 23 January 2018.
6 https://www.aljazeera.com/indepth/features/2017/12/refugees-improve-armenia-social-fabric-171214061224398.html, accessed 23 January 2018.
7 At least 10,000 Syrian-Armenians were granted Armenian citizenship as early as 2012–2014; only about 800 Syrian-Armenians had refugee status in 2012–13, according to a report by

Public Debates

The local media very rarely covers issues concerning Muslims living in Armenia. However, the coverage of the situation in Turkey and Azerbaijan, as well as the conflicts in Syria, Iraq, Palestine, and Afghanistan is considerable. Public debates with regards to Muslims primarily occur during the celebrations of *Nawruz*, the traditional Iranian New Year, celebrated at the spring equinox. This is when thousands of Iranians come to Armenia to celebrate the holiday, or to attend the concerts held in Yerevan by Iranian artists, who are prohibited from performing in Iran. Three major themes dominate the press coverage during this period. First, the mass visits of Iranian tourists bring economic benefits to Armenia. Second, these visits strengthen Armenian-Iranian relations, and therefore are beneficial for Armenians living in Iran. Third, some media outlets express displeasure with the presence of large numbers of partying Iranians on the streets of Yerevan. In 2017, the State Tourism Committee, an agency affiliated to the Ministry of Economic Development and Investment of Armenia, published brochures in Persian tailored for Iranian tourists.[8] In addition to Iranians, there were also reports about the growing number of Turkish and Saudi tourists in 2017.[9]

On 22 April 2017, a Russian soldier was stabbed to death in the Armenian town of Gyumri.[10] The Russian 102nd Military Base is located there not far from the border with Turkey. The suspect was caught immediately by local inhabitants, and the criminal case investigation lasted until December 2017. Media reports claimed, as early as April, that the perpetrator was an Armenian who had converted to Islam.[11] Local witnesses reported that he was an observant conservative Muslim, had lived in Greece for nearly two decades before returning to Armenia, and "did not look" Armenian.[12] There are very few Muslims living in Armenia. An even smaller number of them are ethnic Armenians. Therefore, it seems, the bystanders were clinging onto details which would explain the otherwise unusual notion of a "Muslim Armenian" for them. Eventually, Arman

---

the Open Society Foundations–Armenia, http://www.osf.am/wp-content/uploads/2017/11/Syrian-Armenians-in-Armenia.-Repatriates-or-Refugees-policy-brief.pdf, accessed 23 January 2018.

8 http://radiomarshall.am/?p=204&l=am/novruz+kam+irancineri+arkacnery+hayastanum, accessed 23 January 2018.

9 https://armeniasputnik.am/tourism/20171229/9993680/arab-turq-hayastan-mexak-apresyan.html, accessed 23 January 2018.

10 https://news.am/eng/news/391251.html, accessed 23 January 2018.

11 http://www.aravot.am/2017/04/25/881146/, accessed 23 January 2018.

12 http://www.aravot.am/2017/04/25/881146/, accessed 23 January 2018.

Janjughazyan, 20, was charged with two violations of the *Armenian Criminal Code*: the illegal carrying of cold steel weapons (*Article 234, Part 4*) and murder out of motives of national, race or religious hatred or fanaticism (*Article 104, Part 2, Point 13*).[13] According to the indictment, he was assisted by unidentified persons presenting themselves as supporters of the so-called Islamic State group.[14]

Another media report claimed that on 28 December 2017 an unidentified citizen of one of the Central Asian republics was refused entry into Armenia at Zvartnots International Airport near Yerevan. Allegedly a member of so-called Islamic State, according to the report he was sent back to Turkey where he had arrived from.[15] There were other mentions of a potential threat emanating from so-called Islamic State earlier in 2017; an armed group was identified and caught on 25 November 2017 in the capital city Yerevan. Media sources claimed that the group may have had ties with so-called Islamic State. According to a representative of the Armenian National Security Service, the group had received financial support worth tens of thousands of US dollars from unidentified sources. He confirmed that Arthur Vardanyan, the alleged leader of the group, had visited Syria in the past and that the investigators would take that fact into consideration.[16] In this sense, there were relatively more references to a potential ISIS threat in Armenia in 2017 compared to previous years. However, there is also a common understanding that Armenia is unlikely to be targeted by ISIS. The country still seems much less vulnerable compared to neighbouring Georgia, Turkey, Iran and Azerbaijan; in other words, there are no public fears of a potential "Islamic threat".

As more and more people in Turkey claim an Armenian ancestry and identity, there is a genuine growing interest in these "crypto" or "hidden" Armenians both in Turkey and in Armenia. Whereas Armenian society is still rather conservative and wary of conversion to Islam, many of them acknowledge that the case of Turkish Armenians is peculiar and more nuanced. Armenian researchers have focused on studying Muslim Armenians in Turkey over the past few years.[17] One of them, Ruben Melkonyan, was elected as Dean of the Oriental Studies Department at Yerevan State University in 2017. This may well lead

---

13   https://168.am/2017/12/28/888395.html, accessed 23 January 2018.
14   https://news.am/eng/news/428788.html, accessed 23 January 2018.
15   http://www.aravot.am/2017/12/28/928836/, accessed 23 January 2018.
16   https://armenpress.am/arm/news/827464/hh-aats-n-pordzum-e-parzel-hancavor-khmbi-finanasavorman.html, accessed 23 January 2018.
17   See, for example, Melkonyan, Ruben, "The problem of Islamized Armenians in Turkey", *21st Century*, vol. 1, no. 3 (2008), available at http://www.noravank.am/upload/pdf/338_en.pdf, accessed 23 January 2018.

to an increase in scholarly work focusing on the topic in the coming years. Turkish Muslim Armenians often travel to Armenia and share their impressions through social media. One such account was published on behalf of a man who travelled to Armenia with his teenage son and daughter.[18] According to him, they were well-received everywhere in the country, while the locals were often surprised to find out that they were Armenian and Muslim at the same time. One passage talks about their visit to a church in downtown Yerevan and a conversation with the local priest. The latter looked shocked but kept repeating "Welcome to Armenia".[19]

Turkish-Armenian writer Vercihan Ziflioğlu also visited Yerevan in 2017 to talk about her work as well as Armenians in Turkey, both Christian and Muslim. In September, 2017, another prominent guest visited Armenia and sparked further interest in the topic. Garo Paylan, a Turkish-Armenian member of the Parliament in Turkey from the Peoples' Democratic Party (HDP), attended the Sixth Armenia-Diaspora Conference. Paylan instantly turned into a celebrity. Officials, journalists and members of the wider public took photos with him to share on social media. Paylan delivered a number of speeches and attended a press conference, where he touched upon several matters, including the question of Muslim Armenians.[20]

Vardan Khachatryan, a professor of theology at Yerevan State University, claimed that it is wrong to categorise Christian and Muslim Armenians as "better or worse", but he also underlined that it was necessary to take measures to help such Muslims integrate into broader Armenian society.[21] At the same time, he warned that one should be careful because "you never know what might be concealed beneath the hidden Armenian label".[22] It is still difficult for many Armenians to reconcile the seemingly contradictory notions of "Armenianness" and "being Muslim". Far right nationalists, for example, still insist that to be Armenian means to speak Armenian and to be Christian. "There are no Muslim Armenians, just as there are no Christian Turks", one of them writes.[23] A Facebook group called "Muslim Armenians", written in Turkish,

---

18   http://armenianhighlands.blogspot.ru/2017/07/inessatashian.html?m=1, accessed 23 January 2018.
19   http://armenianhighlands.blogspot.ru/2017/07/inessatashian.html?m=1, accessed 23 January 2018.
20   http://www.aravot.am/2017/09/19/908366/, accessed 23 January 2018.
21   https://armeniasputnik.am/armenia/20171011/9006679/armenia-hayer-mahmedakan-turqia.html, accessed 23 January 2018.
22   https://armeniasputnik.am/armenia/20171011/9006679/armenia-hayer-mahmedakan-turqia.html, accessed 23 January 2018.
23   http://www.a-rm.de/?p=911, accessed 23 January 2018.

English and Armenian, had more than 13,000 followers as of January 2018.[24] Many of the subscribers reside in Armenia, but it is impossible to determine the number of Muslims among them.

It is generally thought that the war between Armenia and Azerbaijan over the region of Nagorno Karabakh, which broke out immediately after the collapse of the USSR, was not really a religious war. Despite their respective Christian and Muslim backgrounds, the societies in both of these neighbouring post-Soviet countries were fairly secular when the war broke out. However, there have been more recent attempts to instrumentalise religion to promote dialogue and peace but also to mobilise international support against the perceived enemy. Thus, the head of the Armenian Apostolic Church, Catholicos Garegin II met the Azerbaijani religious leader Sheikh al-Islam Allahshukur Pashazade in Moscow on 8 September 2017, upon the Russian Patriarch's initiative.[25] However, the public reception and media coverage of the event were rather sceptical in both Armenia and Azerbaijan. At the same time, Azerbaijani President Ilham Aliyev called upon Muslim majority countries to avoid a close relationship with Armenia several times during 2017, something he has repeated over the past few years.[26]

Transnational Links

The Cultural Centre of the Embassy of the Islamic Republic of Iran in Armenia is a branch of the Iran-based Islamic Culture and Relations Organisation,[27] which has branches all over the world. As mentioned on the organisation's website, the main aim is the "revival and dissemination of Islamic tenets and ideas with a view to spreading the true message of Islam to the people of the world".[28] The activities of the Centre in Yerevan include free Persian language courses, the translation of Persian and Islamic literature into Armenian (in 2006, a translation of the Qur'an was published in Armenian), courses on the Qur'an and calligraphy, as well as exhibitions and conferences both in Armenia and in Iran. In 2017, the Centre organised various events and financed the publication of the Armenian translation of *Shi'a Islam* (*Shi'a dar Islam*)

24 https://www.facebook.com/muslumanermeniler/, accessed 23 January 2018.
25 https://armenianweekly.com/2017/09/08/karekin-ii-blasts-baku/, accessed 23 January 2018.
26 https://www.azatutyun.am/a/28915717.html; http://ru.aravot.am/2017/05/10/241738/, both accessed 23 January 2018.
27 http://www.icro.ir, accessed 23 January 2018.
28 http://en.icro.ir/index.aspx?fkeyid=&siteid=257&pageid=9641, accessed 23 January 2018.

(Yerevan: Edit Print, 2017), a monograph by the prominent Iranian Islamic thinker Mohammad Hossein Tabataba'i.[29] On 5 December 2017, the Centre gave awards to the winners of a contest for *hifz* (learning the Qur'an by heart) and knowledge of Islamic rules at the Blue Mosque in Yerevan. Some of the *hafiz* winners were under 10 years old.[30] The event was organised during the celebration of the birth date of Prophet Muhammad and the sixth Shi'i Imam Ja'far al-Sadiq. As in 2016, the Centre and Yerevan State University also organised a conference entitled "Analysis of the ideas and views of Imam Khomeini" in June 2017.[31] The conference is meant to be a diplomatic gesture towards Iran that is repeated every year.

The Armenian version of the Blue Mosque's website,[32] launched in 2016, shares regular news reports on events in the mosque and the life of the Muslim Iranian community. Built in the 18th century, the Blue Mosque is the only operating mosque in Armenia today. In the Soviet atmosphere of atheism, the building was used for various purposes, and has served as the site of the Museum of the City of Yerevan. The mosque was reopened after the collapse of the Soviet Union with Iranian support and funding. Most of the content available on the website is provided in Persian and Armenian. Summaries of the history of the mosque are also available in Russian and English. An Iranian cleric, Ali Shaja'an, is frequently mentioned as the imam at the Blue Mosque.[33] Besides religious services, the mosque is also the site of a library, and a venue for Persian language classes, has facilities for events and meetings, arts and crafts exhibitions, as well as providing medical services. There are at least two medical doctors and one dentist available, according to the mosque's website.[34] All three of them are Iranian nationals. The mosque also has a Telegram[35] channel, with 145 subscribers as of January 2018.[36]

---

29 http://yerevanmasjed.ir/fa/index.php/2013-11-05-20-23-15/567-2017-03-07-20-27-42, accessed 23 January 2018.
30 http://hy.yerevan.icro.ir/index.aspx?fkeyid=&siteid=250&pageid=38800&newsview=693510, accessed 23 January 2018.
31 http://www.hhpress.am/index.php?sub=hodv&hodv=20170603_5&flag=am, accessed 23 January 2018.
32 http://yerevanmasjed.ir/hy/index.php/2015-11-28-17-52-07/162-2016-02-15-11-15-37, accessed 23 January 2018.
33 http://yerevanmasjed.ir/fa/index.php/2013-11-05-20-23-15/638-2017-12-15-12-04-18, accessed 23 January 2018.
34 http://yerevanmasjed.ir/hy/index.php/2015-11-28-17-36-14/2015-11-28-17-44-47, accessed 23 January 2018.
35 Telegram is a messaging application launched in 2013 by a Russian-led development team. It is widely used in Iran.
36 http://telegram.me/yerevanmasjed, accessed 23 January 2018.

Law and Domestic Politics

Article 95.9 of the *Electoral Code* of the Republic of Armenia, amended as of 29 October 2016 states: "Four mandates of Deputies shall be distributed among national minority representatives by the principle of one mandate to each of the first four national minorities with the largest number of resident population according to the data of the latest census preceding the elections".[37] There is no mention of religious minorities *per se*, but the amended electoral code provided an opportunity for Armenia's non-Christian citizens (including Muslims) to be elected into Parliament.[38] Traditionally, the oldest member of the Armenian parliament is given the honour to chair the inaugural session. The Kurdish representative Knyaz Hasanov, 72, chaired the first session of the newly-elected Parliament on 18 May 2017.

There were no other amendments to existing legislation, and no laws concerning the status of Muslims were introduced in Armenia in 2017.[39]

Activities and Initiatives of Main Muslim Organisations

Muslim festivals are not incorporated into the official calendar of the Republic of Armenia. The Iranian community celebrates Ramadan and commemorates the main Shi'i events, such as 'Ashura'. Muslims were allowed to conduct public mourning rituals in the garden in front of the Blue Mosque for the first time in 2016. 'Ashura' was marked outside the mosque in October 2017 as well. Armenian media did not cover the event this time, but some of the Iranian news agencies wrote about it, and published a video where roughly 200–300 participants could be seen.[40] The official website of the mosque stated that the mourning ceremonies were attended by more than 1,200 people.[41]

The communities of Muslims from the Middle East and South Asia, mainly consisting of students, organise their celebrations in their college dormitories.

---

37   *Electoral Code of the Republic of Armenia*, http://res.elections.am/images/doc/_ecode2016 .pdf, accessed 23 January 2018.
38   https://eurasianet.org/s/armenia-ethnic-minorities-gain-a-voice-in-parliament, accessed 23 January 2018.
39   For more details on Armenian legislature, see Karamyan, Sevak, "Armenia", in Oliver Scharbrodt, Samim Akgönül, Ahmet Alibašić, Jørgen S. Nielsen and Egdūnas Račius (eds.), *Yearbook of Muslims in Europe*, vol. 7 (Leiden: Brill, 2015), pp. 36–37.
40   http://www.irna.ir/fa/News/3527764, accessed 23 January 2018.
41   http://yerevanmasjed.ir/fa/index.php/2013-11-05-20-23-15/619-2017-10-08-17-49-12, accessed 23 January 2018.

The Kurdish community celebrates *Nawruz* on 21 March every year. Numerous performances of music and dance are staged during the celebration, and the events are attended by many guests. Each year, the President of Armenia conveys congratulations to the Kurdish community of Armenia on the occasion of *Nawruz*.[42] In 2017, as in previous years, thousands of Iranians came to Armenia to celebrate it.

Muslim Population: History and Demographics

Islam reached the territory of today's Armenia shortly after its founding. The first Arab invasion of Armenia took place in 640 CE, and thereafter Armenia was under Arab rule for more than 200 years. In the second half of the ninth century, Armenians succeeded in overthrowing Arab rule and restoring their independence, which lasted until the beginning of the eleventh century. From the mid-eleventh century, however, Armenia experienced a number of invasions by Seljuk Turks who, through to the first half of the twelfth century, kept Armenia under their control. As a result of Armenian-Georgian military cooperation, most Armenian territories were liberated from the Seljuk Turks. In 1236, a major military incursion of Mongols took place, after which Armenia remained under Mongol rule for almost two centuries. Throughout the 15th century, Armenia was under the rule of two Turcoman tribes, the *Ak Koyunlu* or *Aq Qoyunlu* (White Sheep) Turcomans, and the *Kara Koyunlu* (Black Sheep) Turcomans.

From the 16th century, Armenia was divided between two Muslim powers, the Ottoman Empire and Safavid Iran. The situation changed after the Russo-Persian wars of the 19th century, when some Armenian territories (including the territory of today's Republic of Armenia) passed to the Russian Empire. In spite of the long presence of Islamic authorities, the majority of Armenians remained strongly attached to their Church and did not change their Christian religion, which the Armenian state had first officially adopted in 301 CE. Some though, for various personal reasons, chose to convert to Islam, especially during the Ottoman period.

During the period of the First Armenian Republic, from 1918 to 1920, as well as in the period following the Soviet Republic, the number of Muslims (Turkic

---

42 http://www.president.am/en/congratulatory/item/2015/03/21/President-Serzh-Sargsyan-congratulation-to-Kurdish-community-in-Armenia/, accessed 23 January 2018.

people later called Azerbaijanis[43] and Kurds) was high, at about 80,000.[44] According to the last Soviet census that took place in 1989, there were 4,151 Kurds and 84,860 Azerbaijanis in Armenia.[45] The majority of these Azerbaijanis left the country during Armenia's conflict with Azerbaijan that began in 1988. Kurds, who used to live in Azerbaijani enclaves in Armenia, by virtue of confessional and cultural relatedness (Kurdish children attending Azerbaijani schools, mixed marriages, etc.) left Armenia along with the Azerbaijanis.

The most recent census that took place in 2011 included an optional question on religious affiliation.[46] According to a report published in 2013, based on the 2011 census, the number of Muslims in Armenia was 812, which is 0.027% of the total population.[47] However, various research publications, as well as information provided by non-governmental organisations, estimate the number of Muslims in Armenia to be around 5,000–6,000. Of these, 80% are resident non-citizens who stay in Armenia for extended periods of time. The majority of Muslims are from Iran, others come from elsewhere in the Middle East and South Asia, and most are business people, students, and diplomats.

There is some contradictory information concerning Kurds in Armenia. The last census showed that there were 2,162 Kurds in Armenia.[48] However, there are more than 35,000[49] Kurdish-speaking people identifying themselves as Yezidis,[50] who detach themselves from Islam in terms of religion and from the

---

43 After 1929, this group began to be called Azerbaijanis in official documents (while formerly called Turks). See Всесоюзная перепись населения 1926г. (*Census of the Population in 1926*), vol. 14 (Moscow: CSU Publishing, 1929), pp. 8, 13.

44 Մկրտումյան Յ, Սարգսյան Հ, Թադևոսյան Ա, *Հայաստանի Հանրապետության ազգային փոքրամասնությունները քաղաքացիական հասարակության կայացման արդի պայմաններում*, Երևան, ՀԳԱԱ, Գիտություն, 2005, էջ 151 (Mkrtumyan, Y., H. Sargsyan and A. Tadevosyan (eds.)), *National Minorities of the Republic of Armenia in the Context of Civil Society Development*, vol. 2 (Yerevan: National Academy of Sciences of the Republic of Armenia, Gitutyun Publishing, 2005) p. 151.

45 Газета Коммунист, № 115 (17002) от 24.05.1990 (*The Communist Newspaper*, no. 115 (17002) of 24 May 1990).

46 www.armstat.am/file/doc/99465273.pdf, accessed 23 January 2018.

47 www.armstat.am/file/article/sv_03_13a_520.pdf, accessed 23 January 2018.

48 http://armstat.am/file/doc/99478353.pdf, accessed 23 January 2018.

49 http://armstat.am/file/doc/99478353.pdf, accessed 23 January 2018.

50 An ethno-confessional group, whose main identity is their religion: Yezidism or Sharfadin. Yezidism is a syncretic doctrine which combines the belief in the one God with the veneration of a Holy Trinity: Malak Tawus (Peacock angel), Shaykh ʿAdi and Sultan Yezid (all being incarnations of God). It also features an extensive popular pantheon, that includes a number of divinities, saints and patron-deities, having parallels with both Iranian and Semitic traditions.

Kurds in terms of ethnicity.[51] Their language is Kurmanji, a Northern Kurdish dialect, although Yezidis call their language Ezdiki in order to underscore their separate identity.[52] It should be mentioned that some Yezidis identify themselves as Kurds or Yezidi-Kurds on the basis of language, traditions and customs.[53] At the same time, the last census showed that only 5% of Kurds (124 individuals) identified themselves as Muslims.

Muslim Population	812 (0.027% of population, Census 2011), but an estimate of about 5,000–6,000 Iranians is provided by the Iranian Cultural Centre.
Ethnic/National Backgrounds	Largest ethnic/national groups: Iranian: 86% (Census 2011) Kurdish: 14% (Census 2011).
Inner-Islamic Groups	No official data available. Estimates are that the ratio of Shi'is to Sunnis is about 4:1.
Geographical Spread	80% of the Muslim population is concentrated in Yerevan.
Number of Mosques	The only operating mosque in Armenia is the Blue Mosque in Yerevan. Besides that, there are at least two non-official prayer rooms in student dormitories in Yerevan.
Muslim Burial Sites	There is no comprehensive data on the exact number and location of Muslim burial sites in Armenia. At least 69 cemeteries were mentioned in an article written in 2007 on the subject.[54] A mausoleum erected in 1413 by Turcoman emirs (Emir Pir-Hussein Mausoleum) is located in Argavand (Ararat marz).

---

51 Asatryan, Garnik, and Victoria Arakelova, *The Ethnic Minorities of Armenia* (Yerevan: Caucasian Centre for Iranian Studies, 2004), p. 10, www.hra.am/file/minorities_en.pdf, accessed 23 January 2018.
52 http://rudaw.net/english/people-places/28052014, accessed 23 January 2018.
53 Սարդար, Ա., *Քրդերը Հայաստանում* (Sardar, A., *Kurds in Armenia*) (Yerevan: Hayastan Press, 1996), p. 59.
54 Bulgadarian, Naira, "Armenia: sad fate of Azeri graves", https://iwpr.net/global-voices/armenia-sad-fate-azeri-graves, accessed 23 January 2018.

"Chaplaincy" in State Institutions	There are no imams in the Armenian armed forces or in any other state institutions, such as hospitals, schools, prisons, etc. However, the *Law Regarding the Relationship between the Republic of Armenia and the Holy Armenian Apostolic Church* allows the Armenian Church to have permanent representatives in hospitals, orphanages, boarding schools, military units, and all places of detention,[55] while the *Law on Freedom of Conscience and Religious Organisations* permits other religious organisations to have representatives in these places on demand only.[56] There is also the *Law on Alternative Military Service* (adopted in 2004, amendments and additions were made to it in 2006).[57] Since 2014, 128 applicants who are followers of the Jehovah's Witnesses have undertaken alternative service in accordance with this Law.[58]
Halal Products	There are at least two halal butchers in Yerevan. One is located in an agricultural market, the other offers halal meat at the Blue Mosque once a week. There is also the so-called Persian market where a wide range of Iranian products are available. In some shops one can find some personal care goods, spices and sweets that are halal. Numerous restaurants in Yerevan offer a wide range of traditional Arab and Iranian dishes, primarily targeting tourists from these countries.

---

55 http://parliament.am/legislation.php?sel=show&ID=2911&lang=arm, accessed 10 December 2016.
56 http://parliament.am/legislation.php?sel=show&ID=2041&lang=arm, accessed 23 January 2018.
57 http://parliament.am/legislation.php?sel=show&ID=1884&lang=arm, accessed 23 January 2018.
58 *Fourth Report Submitted by Armenia Pursuant to Article 25, Paragraph 2 of the Framework Convention For the Protection of National Minorities*, https://rm.coe.int/CoERMPublicCommonSearchServices/DisplayDCTMContent?documentId=09000016800ca9b8#search=Fourth%20Report%20Submitted%20by%20Armenia%20Pursuant%20to%20Article%2025%2C%20Paragraph%202%20of%20the%20Framework%20Convention%20For%20the%20Protection%20of%20National%20Minorities, accessed 23 January 2018.

Dress Code	There are no legal provisions regulating religious dress code in Armenia. Muslim women, predominantly Iranians, often wear head scarves. Veiled women with niqabs are rarely seen.
Places of Islamic Learning and Education	One school that provides optional Islamic education is the educational centre Martyr Fahmideh, sponsored by the Iranian embassy in Armenia. There is no institution for imam training in Armenia.
Muslim Media and Publications	The Blue Mosque of Yerevan (www.yerevanmasjed.ir) publishes the Persian-language monthly journal *Payam-e Masjed* (*Herald of the Mosque*). The journal primarily focuses on religious issues as well as including a news section reporting on the life of Muslims in Armenia. Two other magazines, *Mihr* and *Parsian*, are published by the Iranian Cultural Centre. They are not officially religious, but are rich in Islamic content. Both are published in Persian and Armenian. The website of the Cultural Centre, www.yerevan.icro.ir, is also rich in Islamic content. Two Kurdish tabloids, *Ria Taza* (in Kurdish) and *Zagros* (mainly in Armenian with one or two pages in Kurdish), have no religious content. There is also a 30-minute daily programme in Kurdish on public radio, without any religious content.

Main Muslim Organisations

There are no officially registered Muslim organisations in Armenia. The only institution that carries out regular religious activities in Armenia is the Cultural Centre of the Embassy of the Islamic Republic of Iran.

There are a variety of organisations attached to Muslim ethnic groups, but they do not carry out any religious activities. These include the Association of Iranian Students, the Organisation of Iranian Traders and Entrepreneurs, the National Kurdish Council, the Kurdistan Committee, and the Kurdish Council of Intellectuals.

Austria

Dominique Bauer[1] and Astrid Mattes[2]

Introduction

A previous report referred to 2015 as an *annus horribilis* for Austrian Muslims, and 2017 has brought about further deterioration. In an already hostile climate for Muslims, restrictive policy measures were taken, the most debated among them being the ban of full-face covering. Parliamentary elections brought the radical right-wing[3] Austrian Freedom Party (*Freiheitliche Partei Österreichs–* FPÖ) into a coalition government, a party that for years has placed anti-Islamic sentiments at the centre of its voter mobilisation strategy. The preceding electoral campaign involved heated debates about Islam in Austria. Overall, the centre of the debate shifted somewhat from a focus on security and terrorism to issues of values and belonging, as controversies about illiberal attitudes among Muslims and within Islamic institutions have shown.

The *Islamische Glaubensgemeinschaft in Österreich* (Islamic Religious Community–IGGiÖ) took the lead in a couple of initiatives against extremism and reacted to allegations of lacking support for integration by issuing a series of statements and publications. However, despite significant debate about Islam in Austria, Muslim actors were not particularly visible in these. The legally recognised religious communities were also concerned with the implementation of the 2015 *Islam Law*, which brought up new challenges in the administration of religion and governance in Austria. The Austrian tradition of

---

1 Dominique Bauer is a PhD researcher at the Institute for Islamic Studies at the University of Vienna. She studied International Development Studies and Oriental Studies. Her research areas include gender and religion, European asylum, migration and integration politics, and linguistic diversity in a global perspective.
2 Astrid Mattes is a migration researcher at the Institute for Urban and Regional Research at the Austrian Academy of Sciences. She holds a PhD in Political Science and an MA degree in Comparative Religious Studies. Her main research interests are immigrant integration politics, Islam in Europe, and the governance of (religious) diversity.
3 We use the term "radical right" when we refer to the FPÖ in this article, and thereby stick to the terminology of international political science literature, as used, for example, in Mudde, Cas, *The Populist Radical Right: a Reader* (London-New York: Routledge, 2016). However, other terms are also used to refer to the FPÖ, such as "extreme right" or "right-wing populist party". For an overview of these labels see Carter, Elisabeth L., *The Extreme Right in Western Europe: Success or Failure?* (Manchester-New York: Manchester University Press, 2005).

religion-state cooperation, which has been referred to as tolerant and stable,[4] has changed significantly over the past year or two.

Aside from the deterioration of the legal situation, Muslims in Austria also suffered from violence and defamation. The exact numbers of such cases are not available, but according to a regional anti-discrimination agency, attacks on women wearing the head scarf have increased by 40% in the last five years.[5] As in previous years some cases of religious extremism and foiled terrorist plans were reported.[6] The numbers of Austrian foreign fighters joining the so-called Islamic State in Syria continued to decline according to a now available intelligence report of 2016.[7] Also, transnational political issues, especially with regards to Turkey, continued to be linked to religion in public discourse, as was the case in the previous years. Overall, we consider the religious interests of Muslims in Austria to be largely secured due to the legal privileges of public recognition, but recent legal changes, a strong public anti-Islam discourse, and the presence of the radical right in the Government are matters of concern for Austria's Muslim minority.

Public Debates

The implementation of legal regulations made in the 2015 *Islam Law* had an impact on public debates on Islam and Muslims in 2017. The reform of the original Law from 1912, regarding the legal status of Islam in Austria, forbids any kind of foreign financial inflows. It was only in August 2017 that the grand coalition Government of Social Democrats (*Sozialdemokratische Partei Österreichs*–SPÖ) and the conservative Austrian People's Party (*Österreichische Volkspartei*–ÖVP) decided to enlarge the governmental office in charge of controlling the money given to Islamic associations (*Kultusamt*), after the blame for the late implementation of such a policy was passed back and forth between

---

4 Mattes, Astrid, and Sieglinde Rosenberger, "Islam and Muslims in Austria", in Marian Burchardt and Ines Michalowski (eds.), *After Integration* (Wiesbaden: Springer Fachmedien, 2015), pp. 129–152.
5 Sterkl, Maria, "Frauen mit Schleier 'halten stellvertretend den Kopf hin'", *derstandard.at*, 30 May 2017, https://derstandard.at/2000058422615/Frauen-mit-Schleier-halten-stellvertretend-den-Kopf-hin, accessed 16 February 2018.
6 "Graz: 25-Jähriger wegen Terrorverdachts festgenommen", *diepresse.com*, 17 December 2017, https://diepresse.com/home/panorama/oesterreich/5334751/Graz_25Jaehriger-wegen-Terrorverdachts-festgenommen, accessed 16 February 2018.
7 Bundesamt für Verfassungsschutz und Terrorismusbekämpfung, *Verfassungsschutzbericht 2016* (Vienna: Bundesamt für Verfassungsschutz und Terrorismusbekämpfung, 2017), p. 79.

the two governmental parties.[8] The elections and the consequent change in Government interrupted the processes of implementation, but a more extensive set of tasks for the *Kultusamt* is still being planned. The practical handling of the control over financial flows is not yet clear but the new conservative right-wing Government of the ÖVP and FPÖ is emphasising its interest in a strict implementation.[9]

As 2017 was an election year in Austria, the political debate intensified, and various issues regarding Islam and Muslims had a prominent place in these discussions. As in previous years, the debate about whether or not Islam "belongs to Austria" was brought up by the FPÖ during the election period. Amongst various other expressions against Islam and Muslims in Austria, one election poster contrasted an ÖVP candidate's statement "Islam belongs to Austria" with the FPÖ candidate's statement "Stop Islamisation".[10]

A series of studies covering topics from Muslim refugee's religious attitudes[11] to "Islamic" child care facilities,[12] and the lack of integration efforts in prayer rooms,[13] also caused heated public debates. These occurred due to the alarming results from the survey on religious attitudes, on the one hand, and the severe criticism regarding political interventions[14] and the academic quality of

---

8   Gaul, Bernhard, and Bilal Baltaci, "Auslandsfinanzierung bleibt im Dunkeln", *kurier.at*, 11 July 2017, https://kurier.at/politik/inland/auslandsfinanzierung-bleibt-im-dunkeln/274.603.825, accessed 16 February 2018.
9   Akinyosoye, Clara, "Islam und Blasphemie: Religion im Koalitionsprogramm", *orf.at*, 19 December 2018, http://religion.orf.at/stories/2884656/, accessed 16 February 2018.
10 "FPÖ plakatiert Kurz, Kern und Gusenbauer", *diepresse.com*, 8 September 2017, https://diepresse.com/home/innenpolitik/nationalratswahl/5282218/FPOe-plakatiert-Kurz-Kern-und-Gusenbauer, accessed 16 February 2018.
11 Filzmaier, Peter, and Flooh Perlot, *ÖIF-Forschungsbericht: Muslimische Gruppen in Österreich. Einstellungen von Flüchtlingen, ZuwanderInnen und in Österreich geborenen MuslimInnen im Vergleich* (Vienna: ÖIF, 2017).
12 We use quotation marks because the debated childcare facilities are not explicitly religious. Some are operated by religious, ethnic or language-based associations, others directly address Muslim parents but "Islamic kindergarten" is a label that is commonly used in the public debate rather than an actual category of childcare facilities.
13 Heinisch, Heiko, and Imet Memedi, *Die Rolle der Moschee im Integrationsprozess* (Vienna: ÖIF-Forschungsbericht 2017), https://www.integrationsfonds.at/fileadmin/content/AT/Downloads/Publikationen/Forschungsbericht_Heinisch_Die_Rolle_der_Moschee_web.pdf, accessed 16 February 2018.
14 Kroisleitner, Oona, "Studie zu Islamkindergärten: Einfluss des Ministeriums laut Prüfern 'außer Streit'", *derstandard.at*, 8 November 2017, https://derstandard.at/2000067405072/Kindergartenstudie-Uni-Wien-praesentiert-heute-Pruefergebnis, accessed 16 February 2018.

some works, on the other.[15] These three non-representative studies were (co-) financed and commissioned by the Ministry for Integration or the affiliated Austrian Integration Fund. During the election campaign, the conservative ÖVP in particular used these studies to argue for stricter regulations of Islamic organisations in Austria.[16]

Other parties referred to Islam and Austrian Muslims during their campaigns as well. In September, one month before the parliamentary elections, the party leader of the newly established *Liste Pilz*, a splinter group of the Green Party, published a book focused mainly on the challenges of Islam, among these were "Islamic" child care facilities, the IGGiÖ, and the influence of Salafism and foreign extremists.[17] Around the same time, Austria's liberal party NEOS invited German lawyer Seyran Ateş to an event about liberal Islam.[18]

The SPÖ emphasised their support for Austrian Muslims but also published a video in which the former chancellor chats with a woman in a pub. She says: "I'm not a racist but … it's unacceptable that people wear burqas and I am afraid in my own country," and he replies: "Everyone has to respect our rules."[19] The last statement refers to the most heated debate on issues concerning Islam in Austria over the past year: the ban of face covering. The media around the world reported on the Austrian ban and its unusual violators: a man wearing a shark costume for a PR job,[20] a LEGO ninja,[21] and the mascot of the Austrian

---

15 "Kindergartenstudie: Update zum Prüfbericht", *Medienportal Universität Wien*, 8 November 2017, https://medienportal.univie.ac.at/presse/aktuelle-pressemeldungen/detailansicht/artikel/pruefung-der-kindergartenstudie-kein-wissenschaftliches-fehlverhalten-durch-ednan-aslan-festgeste/, accessed 16 February 2018.

16 "Kurz will islamische Kindergärten schließen lassen", *news.at*, 22 June 2017, https://www.news.at/a/-kurz-islamische-kinderg%C3%A4rten-8201609, accessed 16 February 2018.

17 Pilz, Peter, *Heimat Österreich: Ein Aufruf zur Selbstverteidigung*, (Vienna: Carl Ueberreuter Verlag, 2017).

18 "Stadt, Religion, Befreiung. Ein liberaler Islam in der Stadt–geht das?", *lab.neos.eu*, 20 September 2017, https://lab.neos.eu/neos-events/stadt-religion-befreiung-ein-liberaler-islam-in-der-stadt-geht-das/, accessed 13 March 2018.

19 "Muslims worried as Austria's party leaders put spotlight on Islam", *thelocal.at*, 21 September 2017, https://www.thelocal.at/20170921/muslims-worried-austria-election, accessed 4 March 2018, video available at https://www.youtube.com/watch?v=ItMSxLVQM-U, accessed 4 March 2018.

20 "Shark costume man bitten by Austria's burqa ban", *politico.eu*, 10 September 2017, https://www.politico.eu/article/shark-costume-man-fined-austria-burqa-ban/, accessed 14 February 2018.

21 "Austria 'burqa ban': police raid toy store over a Lego Ninja", *usatoday*, 21 October 2017, https://www.usatoday.com/story/news/world/2017/10/21/austria-burqa-ban-police-raid-toy-store-over-lego-ninja/787167001/, accessed 14 February 2018.

parliament.[22] Many arguments were brought up within the debate about this Law. They ranged from support for the ban from a women's rights perspective,[23] to a cultural supremacist argument, and legal argumentation following the ECtHR ruling on face veiling.[24] There was also criticism of the ban where it was seen as an endorsement of symbolic politics. Negative reactions also came from a women's rights perspective,[25] from an anti-racist stance, and for its legal impracticability[26] and its lack of proportion.[27] The politicisation of Muslim women's appearance was also the topic of a book edited by the Austrian philosopher Amani Abuzahra. The German title *Mehr Kopf als Tuch*,[28] as well as its contributions from eleven Muslim authors, calls for a more holistic perception of Muslim women.

Transnational Links

Following the Turkish constitutional referendum in April 2017, diplomatic relations between Austria and Turkey became increasingly tense, and public suspicion against the Turkish diaspora in Austria, which constitutes the demographically largest Muslim community, continued to grow. According to the state-run Anadolu Agency, 73.23% (38,215) of the eligible Turkish voters in Austria that voted in the referendum did so in favour of a new divisive

---

22   "Bugs ban-ny: Austrian parliament's rabbit mascot is quizzed by police after falling foul of country's burka ban", *dailymail.co.uk*, 20 October 2017, http://www.dailymail.co.uk/news/article-5001474/Austrian-mascot-falls-foul-country-s-burka-ban.html, accessed 14 February 2018.
23   Walterskirchen, Gudula, "Warum das Verhüllungsverbot aus Frauensicht wichtig und richtig ist", *diepresse.com*, 8 October 2017, https://diepresse.com/home/meinung/quergeschrieben/walterskirchen/5299174/Warum-das-Verhuellungsverbot-aus-Frauensicht-wichtig-und-richtig-ist, accessed 14 February 2018.
24   Delcheva, Marina, "Ein Burka-Verbot hat nichts mit Rassismus zu tun", *dasbiber.at*, 15 July 2014, http://www.dasbiber.at/content/ein-burka-verbot-hat-nichts-mit-rassismus-zu-tun, accessed 14 February 2018.
25   "Mein Körper, mein Recht, mein Recht auf Selbstbestimmung", *islamiq.de*, 19 February 2017, http://www.islamiq.de/2017/02/19/mein-koerper-mein-recht-mein-recht-auf-selbstbestimmung/, accessed 14 February 2018.
26   "Scharfe Kritik der Rechtsanwälte am Verhüllungsverbot", *derstandard.at*, 29 September 2017, https://derstandard.at/2000065054517/Scharfe-Kritik-der-Rechtsanwaelte-am-Verhuellungsverbot, accessed 14 February 2018.
27   Klissenbauer, Irene, "Keine Angst vor Pluralität", *derstandard.at*, 28 September 2017, https://derstandard.at/2000064918155/Keine-Angst-vor-Pluralitaet, accessed 14 February 2018.
28   This translates to "more head [meaning brains] than scarf": Abuzahra, Amani (ed.), *Mehr Kopf als Tuch: Muslimische Frauen am Wort* (Innsbruck: Tyrolia Verlag, 2017).

presidential system, which replaced the previous parliamentary model with an executive presidency.[29] Austrian politicians from all parties viewed the election outcome as a clear sign of a failed integration of Turkish immigrants in Austria. However, Peter Pilz, still a member of the Austrian Green Party (*Die Grünen*) at the time, claimed that the outcome was a result of electoral fraud and voter intimidation, while his fellow party member at the time, Efgani Dönmez (now ÖVP), referred to those who voted in favour of the referendum as "blackguards".

Furthermore, electoral roll data of tens of thousands of voters was passed to Austrian authorities and raised questions of illegal dual citizenship. Wolfgang Sobotka from the conservative ÖVP, the Interior Minister at the time, proposed the revocation of Austrian citizenships as well as a financial penalty of up to €5,000 and demanded closer cooperation with the Turkish authorities to identify dual citizenship holders. By the end of 2017, legal action was taken in about 8,000 cases. Subsequently, citizenship was revoked in over 30 cases, however, most of these revocations were still subject to appeal. At this point, the respective rulings of the administrative courts that ensure legal certainty are still pending.[30]

At the EU level, Sebastian Kurz, who at the time was Austria's Foreign Minister and chair of the ÖVP, called upon the European Commission to end membership negotiations with Turkey.[31] After the Austrian legislative election in October 2017, the new government coalition, composed of the ÖVP and the radical right-wing FPÖ, incorporated this demand into their government programme. In reaction to that, Turkish Foreign Ministry officials expressed concerns over the political climate and once again accused Austria of racism and anti-Muslim sentiment, as they had done before in 2016.[32] Thus, Turkey continued to veto any cooperation between NATO and Austria throughout the year,

---

29   The information on the election turnout is inconsistent and differs depending on the sources, ranging from 47.68% to 50.59%. See "Referandum 2017", *ntv.com.tr*, http://referandum.ntv.com.tr/#yurt-disi, accessed 13 February 2018; "Hohe Wahlbeteiligung in Österreich", *derstandard.at*, 10 April 2017, https://derstandard.at/2000055663641/Hohe-Wahlbeteiligung-in-Oesterreich, accessed 14 February 2018.

30   "Doppel-Staatsbürgerschaft: Kaum Verfahren gegen Austro-Türken", *diepresse.com*, 21 January 2018, https://diepresse.com/home/innenpolitik/5357842/DoppelStaatsbuergerschaft_Kaum-Verfahren-gegen-AustroTuerken, accessed 10 February 2018.

31   See Kurz, Sebastian, *twitter.com*, 7 September 2017, https://twitter.com/sebastiankurz/status/905741753982087169, accessed 13 February 2018.

32   "AB Bakanı Çelik'ten Avusturya'da açıklanan yeni hükümet programına tepki", *aa.com.tr*, 17 December 2018, http://aa.com.tr/tr/dunya/ab-bakani-celikten-avusturyada-aciklanan-yeni-hukumet-programina-tepki/1007341, accessed 13 February 2018.

which consequently resulted in a change of procedures that allowed bilateral partnerships to continue.[33]

While the troubled relations between Austria and Turkey are of a political nature, they are predominantly linked to religion in the public discourse. This was fuelled by charges against the *Österreichisch Türkisch-Islamische Union* (Austrian Turkish Islamic Union–ATIB Union), an organisation closely related to the Turkish Presidency of Religious Affairs (*Diyanet İşleri Başkanlığı*), that was allegedly responsible for monitoring Turkish opposition supporters, journalists, Turkish Kurds, and particularly followers of the Islamic preacher Fethullah Gülen.[34] Over 300 organisation officials were interrogated by the State Agency for the Protection of the Constitution and Counterterrorism (*Landesamt für Verfassungsschutz und Terrorismusbekämpfung*–LVT) in the context of these charges. Additionally, investigations were carried out regarding presumptive violations of the prohibition of foreign funding for Islamic organisations.[35]

International jihadi terrorism and its link to Islamic religious groups and the integration of Muslims into Austrian society continued to be the other dominant issues regarding transnational politics. In January 2017, Austrian police arrested 14 suspects in Vienna and Graz as part of a counterterrorism operation that reportedly involved 800 police officers.[36] As of December 2017, seven suspects remained in custody without charge.[37] The Austrian Federal Ministry of the Interior further declared that the murder of an elderly couple in Linz in June 2017 "clearly had a radical Islamist motive",[38] an assessment that has been

---

33 "Türkei blockiert Nato-Kooperation mit Österreich", *diepresse.com*, 23 May 2017, https://diepresse.com/home/ausland/aussenpolitik/5222874/Tuerkei-blockiert-Nato Kooperation-mit-Oesterreich, accessed 10 February 2018.

34 "Schriftliche Anfrage betreffend Auslandsfinanzierungsbericht über die Sonderprüfung des Vereins ATIB", *Austrian Parliament*, https://offenesparlament.at/gesetze/XXV/J_13809/, accessed 9 March 2018.

35 "Stellungnahme der ATIB Union zur parlamentarischen Anfrage", *ots.at*, 13 July 2017, https://www.ots.at/presseaussendung/OTS_20170713_OTS0118/stellungnahme-der-atib-union-zur-parlamentarischen-anfrage, accessed 9 March 2018.

36 "Austria arrests 14 on suspicion of belonging to Islamic State", *reuters.com*, 26 January 2017, https://www.reuters.com/article/us-austria-arrests/austria-arrests-14-on-suspicion-of-belonging-to-islamic-state-idUSKBN15A1IX, accessed 10 February 2018.

37 "Ein Jahr nach Razzia noch 7 von 14 Verdächtigen in U-Haft", *kleinezeitung.at*, 26 January 2018, http://www.kleinezeitung.at/steiermark/chronik/5360590/AntiTerrorEinsatz-in-Graz_Ein-Jahr-nach-Razzia-noch-7-von-14, accessed 10 February 2018.

38 "Doppelmord in Linz: Offensichtlich islamistischer Hintergrund", *bmi.gv.at*, 5 July 2017, http://bmi.gv.at/news.aspx?id=774646774A422F6C6146343D, accessed 10 February 2018.

questioned by Thomas Schmidinger among others, a political scientist and cultural anthropologist who conducts research on jihadism.[39]

Law and Domestic Politics

There is good reason to say that the 2015 *Islam Law* and its implication have opened a new chapter in Austrian state-religion relations, as it marks a breach with the traditional practice of tolerance towards, and cooperation with, legally recognised religious communities. While public resentment against Muslims has been high,[40] and political parties have had significant success in using anti-Islamic and anti-Muslim slogans for voter mobilisation in previous years, the political elites have made no attempts to undermine or limit religious rights, however.[41]

Nevertheless, despite protests from Muslim groups and opposition leaders, the government coalition of the SPÖ and ÖVP passed an *Anti-Face-Covering Act* (*Anti-Gesichtsverhüllungsgesetz*) that came into force in October 2017, two weeks before the Austrian general election. The federal act declared full-face veils illegal, and imposed restrictions on the use of medical face masks and even clown makeup, providing that faces are visible from the hairline to the chin in order to "strengthen social participation and promote peaceful coexistence".[42] Violation of the Law is sanctioned with an administrative penalty of up to €150.[43] In October 2017, administrative penalty proceedings were initiated against a 28-year-old psychologist for wearing a woollen muffler

---

39   "Doppelmord in Linz: Sobotka spricht von 'IS-Hintergrund'", *diepresse.com*, 6 July 2017, https://diepresse.com/home/panorama/oesterreich/5247297/Doppelmord-in-Linz_Sobotka-spricht-von-ISHintergrund, accessed 14 February 2018.

40   Polak, Regina (ed.), *Zukunft-Werte-Europa: die Europäische Wertestudie 1990–2010: Österreich im Vergleich* (Wien: Böhlau, 2011).

41   Gresch, Nora, Leila Hadj-Abdou, Sieglinde Rosenberger, and Birgit Sauer, "Tu felix Austria? The headscarf and the politics of 'non-issues'", *Social Politics: International Studies in Gender, State & Society*, vol. 15, no. 4 (2008), pp. 411–432.

42   *Bundesgesetz über das Verbot der Verhüllung des Gesichts in der Öffentlichkeit (Anti-Gesichtsverhüllungsgesetz–AgesVG)*, 68/2017, BKA, https://www.ris.bka.gv.at/GeltendeFassung.wxe?Abfrage=Bundesnormen&Gesetzesnummer=20009892, accessed 12 March 2018.

43   "Anti-face-covering act", BMEIA, 1 October 2017, https://www.bmeia.gv.at/en/travel-stay/entry-and-residence-in-austria/anti-face-veiling-act/, accessed 12 March 2018.

that partially covered her chin. Her lawyer announced that her case would be presented to the European Court of Human Rights.[44]

With the Austrian general election resulting in a coalition government of the conservative ÖVP and the radical-right FPÖ, the collective discussion of integration, migration, security, and counterterrorism policies, as well as the depiction of Muslims as potentially dangerous, was further accelerated. As an example of this, the new government programme released in December 2017 contains over 20 references to measures targeted directly at Muslims in Austria. While noting that no terrorist attacks have been carried out in the country so far, the programme nevertheless declares "Islamic extremism" to be the greatest danger to internal security. Accordingly, the "fight against political Islam and increasing Islamist radicalisation" was defined as a main objective. Respective measures include unspecified criminal law policies against political Islam, frequent checks on Islamic childcare facilities and educational institutions, with a special focus on the protection of women and girls, and a comprehensive monitoring of the presentation of teachings, including of the Qur'an as the major source of faith. This is carried out in accordance with article 6 of the 2015 *Islam Law*[45] and the amendment of the *Law on Associations* (*Vereinsgesetz 66/2002*) to prevent foreign funding of Islamic religious associations. Such measures were also communicated as part of the prevention of foreign influence, particularly in the educational sector. Authorisation was also given to the security police to instantaneously close religious facilities that aim to support terrorism. Alongside this, cuts were made to the needs-oriented minimum income for those unwilling to integrate, as well as to the housing of Islamist and jihadi-motivated persons inclined to threaten public safety ("*Gefährder*") in separate safety departments. Mandatory security inspections of all external personnel working in prisons, particularly in the field of Islamic spiritual care, were also announced.[46]

Within the framework of this new programme, the Austrian government also explicitly linked political Islam to anti-Semitism, violence, radicalisation, and terrorism. This marks another step towards institutionalising and normalising right-wing arguments aimed at generating causal relations between

---

44   "28-Jährige will Verhüllungsverbot zu Fall bringen", *wien.orf.at*, 17 October 2017, http://wien.orf.at/news/stories/2872778/, accessed 12 March 2018.
45   *Federal Law on the External Legal Relationships of Islamic Religious Societies–Islam Law 2015 (39/2015)*, BMEIA, https://www.bmeia.gv.at/fileadmin/user_upload/Zentrale/Integration/Islamgesetz/Islam_Law.pdf, accessed 14 February 2018.
46   "Zusammen. Für Österreich. Regierungsprogramm 2017–2022", BKA, https://www.bundeskanzleramt.gv.at/regierungsdokumente, accessed 12 February 2018.

Muslim life in Austria and a potential threat to public safety, so as to negotiate the progressive tightening of immigration and security law.[47] Concurrently, the Government expressed that the protection of the majority of Muslims living in accordance with Austrian values from the influences of political Islam was of great concern.[48]

The year 2017 also brought with it the *Integration Act (68/2017)*, according to which immigrants are obliged to sign a mandatory integration declaration and successfully complete German language and value courses by passing statewide unified integration examinations within two years after having obtained a residence permit.[49] Although not mentioned in the legal text, these measures are discursively related to Muslim immigrants.

Finally, as part of fulfilling its legal mandate to implement the *Islam Law*, the University of Vienna introduced a Bachelor's degree programme in Islamic Theological Studies in January 2017 in order to facilitate the education and training of imams and spiritual caretakers in Austria.[50] Likewise, the University of Innsbruck established the independent Institute of Islamic Theology and Education (*Institut für Islamische Theologie und Religionspädagogik*).[51]

Activities and Initiatives of Main Muslim Organisations

Austria has two legally recognised Islamic communities, the Islamic Religious Community in Austria (IGGiÖ), representing the majority of Austria's Sunni and Shi'i Muslim associations, and the *Alevitische Glaubensgemeinschaft in Österreich* (Alevi Religious Community–ALEVI). The much smaller latter community received this status in 2013; the IGGiÖ was established in 1979 on the basis of the 1912 *Islam Law*, and for a long time functioned as the lone point of contact for state actors. While Muslims of Arab origin took a leading role in the IGGiÖ's formative years, Muslims with a Turkish background have become more active over the past few years. Since 2017 the president is Ibrahim Olgun, a former ATIB functionary.

---

47 See Wodak, Ruth, *Politik mit der Angst: Zur Wirkung rechtspopulistischer Diskurse* (Hamburg-Vienna: Edition Konturen, 2016).
48 "Zusammen. Für Österreich. Regierungsprogramm 2017–2022".
49 "Gesamte Rechtsvorschrift für Integrationsgesetz, Fassung vom 14.02.2018", BKA–RIS, https://www.ris.bka.gv.at/GeltendeFassung.wxe?Abfrage=Bundesnormen&Gesetzesnummer=20009891, accessed 14 February 2018.
50 "Bachelorstudium Islamisch-Theologische Studien", https://iits.univie.ac.at/studium-und-lehre/, accessed 12 March 2018.
51 "First Institute of Islamic Theology and Education throughout Austria", https://www.uibk.ac.at/islam-theol/index.html.en, accessed 12 March 2018.

An important part of IGGiÖ's activities were aimed at countering extremism among Muslims. A so-called "imam declaration" was issued, in which over 300 Austrian imams condemned radical interpretations of Islam and any violence committed in the name of the religion.[52] The IGGiÖ also established coaching and mediation training for deradicalisation, which started in January 2018.[53]

Another IGGiÖ initiative was a reaction to the accusations made against local religious communities that they lack support for integration, or even oppose integration altogether.[54] As a consequence, the IGGiÖ developed a series of criteria for local religious communities and their imams to promote integration.[55] Another initiative that has become widely implemented is the "Long Night of Mosques" (*Lange Nacht der Moscheen*). This event, which is conceptualised as a parallel to the "Long Night of Churches" (*Lange Nacht der Kirchen*), opens the doors of many Austrian mosques and prayer sites to the public.[56]

Other Islamic actors are primarily active in civil society and engaged in the election debate. The *Initiative muslimischer ÖsterreicherInnen* (Initiative of Muslim Austrians), a small civic organisation, sent a questionnaire to the leading candidates of all of the political parties running in the parliamentary elections asking what they offer Muslim voters. Although all candidates referred to Islam and Muslims in their campaigns, two of them–Sebastian Kurz from the ÖVP and Peter Pilz from the Green Party splinter group *Liste Pilz*–refrained from answering the questions.[57] Muslim groups were also involved in a series of protests against the ban on head scarves in public offices,[58] which was considered (but only partially implemented) by the ÖVP-SPÖ governmental coalition.[59]

---

52 "Deklaration der Imame in Österreich gegen Extremismus, Gewalt und Terror", *IGGiÖ*, 14 June 2017, http://www.derislam.at/iggo/?f=news&shownews=2088, accessed 14 February 2018.

53 IGGiÖ (ed.), *Lehrgang zum Coach für Prävention und Deradikalisierung mit Schwerpunkt Mediation* (Vienna: IGGiÖ, 2017).

54 Heinisch and Memedi, *Die Rolle der Moschee im Integrationsprozess*, p. 5.

55 Memic, Esad, *Kriterienkatalog für Moscheen und Imame*, (Vienna: IGGiÖ, 2017), http://www.derislam.at/iggo/quellen/News_Medien/Publikationen/IGGOE/Kriterienkatalog.pdf, accessed 16 February 2018.

56 http://www.izwien.at/veranstaltungen/tag-der-offenen-moscheen/, accessed 16 February 2018.

57 Ichner, Bernhard, and Stefanie Rachbauer, "Muslime fordern von Parteien klare Statements zum Islam", *kurier.at*, 14 September 2018, https://kurier.at/chronik/oesterreich/muslime-befragen-spitzenkandidaten-zum-islam/286.239.310, accessed 16 February 2018.

58 "'MuslimBan': Demo von und für muslimische Frauen", *religion.orf.at*, 2 February 2017, http://religion.orf.at/stories/2824112/, accessed 16 February 2018.

59 "NMZ BLOCK–Großdemo gegen Schwarz-Blau", *Netzwerk Muslimische Zivilgesellschaft*, January 2018, http://dieanderen.net/nmz-block-grossdemo-gegen-schwarz-blau/, accessed 16 February 2018.

For the second time now, the *Dokustelle Islamfeindlichkeit und Antimuslimischer Rassismus* (Documentation Centre on Islamophobia and Anti-Muslim Racism), a data collection centre for incidents of defamation and violence against Muslims, published the *Anti-Muslim Racism Report.* This recorded 253 incidents in 2017, that mostly consisted of verbal attacks and hate speech, but also vandalism and hate crimes. In 98% of the reported cases the victims were female.[60]

Muslim Population: History and Demographics

Muslims in Austria were first legally recognised as a religious community in 1874 under the Habsburg Monarchy. Following the occupation of the Ottoman provinces of Bosnia and Herzegovina in 1878, and their subsequent annexation in 1908, the number of Muslims under Austro-Hungarian rule increased considerably. In 1912, the *Islam Law* was passed as an attempt to institutionalise Islam and reduce the institutional influence of the Ottoman Empire.[61] However, the Law only granted Muslims belonging to the majority Sunni-Hanafi tradition legal recognition, an institutional bias that was upheld until a respective amendment was passed in 1988.[62] With the dissolution of the Habsburg Empire after World War I and the separation of the territories that subsequently formed Yugoslavia, the number of Muslims in Austria declined to a few hundred. Starting from the 1960s, the Muslim population increased again significantly with the arrival and settlement of migrant workers from Turkey and Yugoslavia. In 1979, the *Islam Law* was finally renewed after it fell into oblivion following the decay of the Habsburg Empire; subsequently, the Islamic Religious Community (IGGiÖ) was established. Following a legal dispute over the question of whether there could be more than one legally acknowledged Islamic community, the Alevi Religious Community (ALEVI) was recognised in 2013.[63]

---

60 Dokumentations- und Beratungsstelle Islamfeindlichkeit und Antimuslimischer Rassismus, *Antimuslimsicher Rassismus Report 2016* (Vienna: Dokumentations- und Beratungsstelle Islamfeindlichkeit und Antimuslimischer Rassismus, 2017).

61 Kroissenbrunner, Sabine, "Turkish imams in Vienna", in W.A.R. Shahid and P.S. van Koningsveld (eds.), *Intercultural Relations and Religious Authorities: Muslims in the European Union* (Leuven-Paris-Dudley: Peeters, 2002), pp. 184–185.

62 *Gesetz vom 15. Juli 1912, betreffend die Anerkennung der Anhänger des Islams als Religionsgesellschaft*, BKA, https://www.ris.bka.gv.at/Dokument.wxe?Abfrage=Bundesnormen&Dokumentnummer=NOR11009370, accessed 9 March 2018.

63 "Chronologie: Alevitischer Islam in Österreich", ALEVI, http://www.aleviten.at/de/?page_id=136, accessed 9 March 2018.

Over the past few decades, the number of Muslims in Austria has constantly increased, with the Muslim presence becoming more diverse due to global migration flows. Since 2001, religious affiliation was no longer explicitly surveyed by the Austrian census, but as per the 2001 census, approximately 338,988 Austrian residents identified themselves as Muslims; this makes up 4.2% of the total population. A 2016 study conducted by the Vienna Institute of Demography of the Austrian Academy of Sciences, estimates that these numbers have almost doubled in the past 15 years. The list below is based on a statistical projection from 2011 that makes assumptions about four possible scenarios of demographic growth and religious composition. It takes current developments of demographic processes into account, such as migration, fertility, changes in religious affiliation, and religious transmission within families.[64]

Muslim Population	A demographic projection suggests that there are about 700,000 Muslims living in Austria (8% of the total population in 2016).[63]
Ethnic/National Backgrounds	The majority of Muslims are of Turkish and Bosniak heritage and have been living in Austria for decades.[64] Since 2015, there has been a great increase in immigration, particularly from Afghanistan, Syria, Iraq, and Iran as well as from Pakistan, Somalia, the Russian Federation, and Nigeria.[65] There are strong communities from the countries mentioned above, as well as from Kosovo, Macedonia, Montenegro, and to a lesser degree from Egypt, Pakistan, Tunisia, and Bangladesh.[66]

---

64 See Goujon, Anne, Sandra Jurasszovich and Michaela Potancoková, *VID Working Paper 9/2017: Religious Denominations in Vienna & Austria: Baseline Study for 2016–Scenarios until 2046* (Vienna: ÖAW, 2017).
65 Figure based on latest estimate from 2016. See Goujon, Jurasszovich and Potancoková, *VID Working Paper 9/2017*.
66 See Filzmaier and Perlot, *ÖIF-Forschungsbericht*, p. 9.
67 See Goujon, Jurasszovich and Potancoková, *VID Working Paper 9/2017*, p. 13. See also Filzmaier and Perlot, *ÖIF-Forschungsbericht*, p. 9.
68 For the latest figures from 2009, see Marik-Lebeck, Stephan, "Die muslimische Bevölkerung Österreichs: Bestand und Veränderung 2001–2009", in Alexander Janda and Mathias Vogl (eds.), *Islam in Österreich* (Vienna: ÖIF, 2010), p. 7, and Bauer, Werner T., *Islam in Österreich: ein Überblick* (Vienna: OGPP, 2016), p. 30.

Inner-Islamic Groups According to a 2017 survey conducted by the Bertelsmann Foundation, 64% of Muslims in Austria are Sunni (predominantly belonging to the Hanafi school prevalent in Turkey and the Balkans) and 4% are Shi'i, of whom about 18% are Alevi.[69]

Geographical Spread The geographical distribution of the Muslim population is not precisely known, but the distribution in Vienna is very different to that of the rest of the country. As the largest Austrian city (21.3% of the Austrian total population live here) it is home to an estimated 32.5%[70] of Austrian Muslims. There is no particular pattern in the spread of Muslims throughout the country, although some Islamic associations are more active in the Western parts of Austria.[71]

Number of Mosques The IGGiÖ estimates that there are about 400 Muslim prayer sites in Austria.[72] In addition, there are Alevi and other Muslim facilities that are not registered with the IGGiÖ. An exact number is not available. Most of the prayer sites are not very visible and are often located in basements, backyards or on the outskirts of cities.[73] Only four mosques in Austria (Vienna, Telfs, Bad Vöslau, and Saalfelden) have a minaret installed.

---

69 El-Menouar, Yasemin, *Muslims in Europe: Integrated but not Accepted? Results and Country Profiles* (Gütersloh: Bertelsmann Foundation, 2017), p. 12.

70 Based on the projections provided by Goujon, Jurasszovich and Potancoková, *VID Working Paper 9/2017*.

71 Mattes, Astrid, "From Bosnian soldiers to third generation juveniles: 100 years of Islamic identity and the establishment of the youth council of the Islamic religious community in Austria", in Hans Gerald Hödl and Lukas Pokorny (eds.), *Religion in Austria* (Vienna: Praesens Verlag), pp. 81–116.

72 "Muslimische Vereine in Österreich", *Medien-Servicestelle Neue Österreicher/innen*, 23 August 2017, http://medienservicestelle.at/migration_bewegt/2017/08/23/muslim ische-vereine-in-oesterreich/, accessed 2 March 2018.

73 Schuller, Josef P., *Die verborgene Moschee: Zur Sichtbarkeit muslimischer Gebetsräume in Wien* (Vienna: Tectum, 2014).

Muslim Burial Sites

The following is a list of Muslim burial sites in Austria:

- Muslim Cemetery Vienna (*Islamischer Friedhof Wien*, Großmarktstraße 2a, 1230 Vienna, cemetery administration: Ali Ibrahim, tel.: ++43 6764706920, islamischer.friedhof@gmx.at). Operated by the Islamic Religious Community in Austria (IGGiÖ), with 4,000 burial sites.
- Muslim Cemetery Altach (*Islamischer Friedhof Altach*, Schotterried 1, 6844 Altach, cemetery administration: Ali Can, tel.: ++43 6644355927, sila.alican@hotmail.com). Public cemetery, 700 burial sites.
- Interconfessional Cemetery Graz (*Interkonfessioneller Friedhof Graz*, Alte Poststrasse 343, 8020 Graz, ++43 3168872800, bestattung@holding-graz.at). Public cemetery contains a Muslim section with 200 burial sites.
- Central Cemetery Vienna (*Zentralfriedhof Wien*, Simmeringer Hauptstraße 234, 1100 Vienna, ++43 15346928405). The public cemetery contains three sections for Muslims and one specifically for Egyptian Muslims. Since 2011, the Islamic Alevi Religious Community in Austria has a designated section at Vienna's Central Cemetery.
- Municipal Cemetery Pradl, Innsbruck (*Hauptfriedhof Ost*, Pradl, Innsbruck, Kaufmannstraße 1, 6020 Innsbruck). Public cemetery with a Muslim section with 300 burial sites.
- Municipal Cemetery St. Pölten (*Hauptfriedhof St. Pölten*, ++43 27423334600, Goldegger Straße 52, 3100 St. Pölten). Public cemetery with a Muslim section.
- City cemetery Linz / St. Martin (*Stadtfriedhof Linz/St. Martin*, Wiener Bundesstraße 1014050 Traun, ++43 73234006717). Public cemetery with a Muslim section.

- Cemetery Klagenfurt Annabichl, (*Friedhof Klagenfurt Annabichl*, Flughafenstraße 7, 9020 Klagenfurt am Wörthersee, +43 463537487). Public cemetery with a Muslim section.
- Community Cemetery St. Georgen, (*Gemeindefriedhof St. Georgen*, ++43 52626961, Georgenweg 63, 6410 Telfs). Public cemetery with a Muslim section.

"Chaplaincy" in State Institutions

Islamic religious counselling is provided in hospital, prisons, and in the military, though these services are in no way as thorough as those offered by Catholic and Protestant chaplaincies. In recent years the training of counsellors has been professionalised,[74] and public financing has improved. The *Islam Law* of 2015 now provides a legal framework that grants the right to provide pastoral care in state institutions to acknowledged religious communities.[75] In prisons, Islamic-religious counselling is increasingly connected with de-radicalisation work and the countering of religious extremism.[76]

---

[74] "Zertifikatskurs Grundlagen der Islamischen Seelsorge", Universität Wien, https://www.postgraduatecenter.at/weiterbildungsprogramme/internationales-wirtschaft/muslime-in-europa/, accessed 2 March 2018.

[75] Article 11 of the Austrian *Islam Law* states: "(1) The Religious Society has the right to minister to the religious needs of its members, who 1. are members of the armed forces or 2. are in judicial or administrative confinement or 3. are in medical institutions, patient-centred care, nursing homes or similar institutions [...] (3) Material and personnel expenses towards the fulfilment of the matters from para. 1 N 1 are to be born by the Republic." Translation provided by the Ministry of Europe, Integration and Foreign affairs, https://www.bmeia.gv.at/en/integration/the-austrian-islam-law/, accessed 2 March 2018.

[76] Demir, Ramazan, *Unter Extremisten: Ein Gefängnisseelsorger blickt in die Seele radikaler Muslime* (Vienna: edition a, 2017).

Halal Products

Following paragraph 12 of the *Islam Law*, halal slaughtering is permitted and can be performed in Austria. Military facilities, prisons, public hospitals, and public schools have to provide for Muslim dietary needs according to IGGiÖ/ALEVI regulations. Depending on the size of the public institution, the logistics seem to be a challenge, and in the past there have been reports about only vegetarian dishes or meals without pork being offered.[77]

Halal food is widely available, although mostly in specialised supermarkets. There has been a significant outcry from individuals and organisations on the far-right against mainstream supermarket chains listing halal products.

Dress Code

Since 2017, wearing the niqab in public is forbidden in Austria due to the new *Anti-Face-Covering Act*. Wearing the head scarf is restricted. There has been a discussion about banning religious symbols in courts and in the police uniform, but the current regulation has been found sufficient as it already forbids religious symbols for justice and police officers.[78] Following the European Court of Justice ruling on the case of Samira Abichta,[79] some Austrian employers subsequently issued religiously neutral dress codes.[80] Head scarves are common among female Austrian Muslims; face veiling has been, even prior to the Law, a rarely seen practice.

---

77 Reiss, Wolfram, "Der Umgang mit religiösen Minderheiten in der österreichischen Armee", *Interdisciplinary Journal for Religion and Transformation in Contemporary Society*, vol. 2, no. 1, p. 97, https://doi.org/10.14220/jrat.2016.2.1.83, accessed 2 March 2018.
78 "Kopftuchverbot: Nun doch keine Änderung in Österreich", *derstandard.at*, 14 March 2017, https://derstandard.at/2000054168546/Kopftuchverbot-Nun-doch-keine-Aenderung-in-Oesterreich, accessed 15 April 2018.
79 "EU workplace headscarf ban 'can be legal', says ECJ", *bbc.com*, 14 March 2017, http://www.bbc.com/news/world-europe-39264845, accessed 15 April 2018.
80 "Kopftuch: EuGH-Urteil mit Folgen in Österreich", *kurier.at*, 14 March 2017, https://kurier.at/politik/inland/kopftuch-eugh-urteil-mit-ersten-folgen-in-oesterreich/252.053.365, accessed 15 April 2018.

Places of Islamic Learning and Education

– The Institute for Islamic Religion (*Institut Islamische Religion*, Campus Wien-Eitnergasse, Eitnergasse 6, 1230 Vienna) along with the Institute for Alevi Studies (*Institut Alevitische Religion*, Campus Wien-Strebersdorf, Mayerweckstraße 1, 1210 Vienna), both located at the Catholic Teaching Academy (*Kirchliche Pädagogische Hochschule Wien/Krems*–KPH), offer a four-year Bachelor of Education[81] at the primary and secondary level, in cooperation with the IGGiÖ and ALEVI. Students may specialise in Sunni Islamic Studies[82] or Alevi Studies,[83] and upon completion of the primary level teaching degree they can continue with a two-year MA programme to qualify for teaching at the secondary school level. The secondary level BA programme requires a further specialisation in two subjects. As the legal framework for extension studies was announced that it would be amended in 2017, the range of courses available at the secondary level is currently under revision.

– The Institute of Islamic Theology and Religious Education (*Institut für Islamische Theologie und Religionspädagogik*, Karl-Rahner-Platz 1, 6020 Innsbruck)[84] at the University of Innsbruck was established on 1 January 2017, turning the former Department of Islamic Religious Education,

---

81 "Studienangebot–Lehramt Primarstufe", KPH Wien, http://www.kphvie.ac.at/fileadmin/Dateien_KPH/Ausbildung_Allgemein/Studieninteressierte/info-blatt-primarstufe-2018-2-online.pdf, accessed 11 March 2018.

82 "Institut Islamische Religion–Ausbildung", KPH Wien, http://www.kphvie.ac.at/institute/institut-islamische-religion/ausbildung.html, accessed 11 March 2018.

83 "Institut Alevitische Religion", KPH Wien, http://www.kphvie.ac.at/institute/institut-alevitische-religion/ausbildung.html, accessed 11 March 2018.

84 "Bachelor programme Islamic Religious Education", UIBK, https://www.uibk.ac.at/islam-theol/index.html.en, accessed 12 March 2018.

founded in 2013, into an independent institute within the Faculty of Teacher Education. It offers two BA programmes: a three-year BA in Islamic Religious Education, that qualifies graduates for teaching at the elementary and secondary level as well as for spiritual care and counselling; and secondly, a four-year BA in general education for the secondary level with a specialisation in Islamic religion. In January 2017, it was announced that an MA degree in Islamic Religious Education would be introduced by the winter term 2017/18. However, as of December 2017 it had not been implemented.

- The Institute for Islamic-Theological Studies (*Institut für Islamisch-Theologische Studien–* IITS, Schenkenstraße 8–10, 1090 Vienna)[85] at the University of Vienna was also established in 2017 within the Faculty of Philological and Cultural Studies. This replaces the former interdisciplinary and cross-faculty research platform of the Institute for Islamic Studies, founded in 2012 within the Centre for Teacher Education. It offers a three-year BA degree in Islamic-Theological Studies that includes an optional specialisation in Alevi theology as well as a two-year MA degree in Islamic Religious Education. However, a professorial chair for Alevi Theological Studies was not appointed in 2017. The introduction of the BA programme corresponds to the regulations of the *Islam Law*, according to which imams and spiritual caretakers should be trained and educated in Austria.

---

85 "Bachelorstudium Islamisch-Theologische Studien", Universität Wien, https://iits.univie.ac.at/studium-und-lehre/, accessed 12 March 2018.

Confessional Schools

There are four Islamic elementary schools, one comprehensive school for elementary and lower secondary education, six high schools, and one vocational school. Most of them are private with a public status, and as such are in compliance with the Austrian national curriculum. While they enable students to follow religious requirements through access to halal food and prayer rooms, they are also open to non-Muslim students as well as staff.

- Al-Andalus Elementary and New Middle School (*Al-Andalus VS und NMS*, Altmannsdorferstraße 154–156, 1230 Vienna)[86] is a confessional private school with a public status. It is run by the Al-Andalus Association and offers progressive education with an emphasis on nature and health promotion.
- Austrian International Schools Vienna–AISV (Weisselgasse 28/Nordbahnanlage 4, 1210 Vienna)[87] include an elementary school, a new middle school, and a senior high school. They have close relations with the Egyptian Al-Azhar University, and were formerly known as Al-Azhar International Schools. They have a strong focus on Islamic principles and offer Arabic as an elective subject.
- The private Avicenna Elementary School[88] (*Private Volksschule Avicenna*, Pragerstraße 124, 1210 Vienna) was founded in 2013 and is open to Muslim students only.[89] In 2015, it was extended by the Avicenna High School[90] (*Avicenna Privatgymnasium*) located in the same building.

---

86 See www.alandalus.at, accessed 12 March 2018.
87 See www.aisv.at, accessed 12 March 2018.
88 See www.avicenna.schule.wien.at, accessed 12 March 2018.
89 See www.avicenna.schule.wien.at/unsere-schule, accessed 12 March 2018.
90 See www.avicenna-gymnasium.at, accessed 12 March 2018.

- Islamic Grammar School Vienna (*Islamisches Realgymnasium Wien*, Rauchfangkehrergasse 34, 1150 Vienna)[91] with a public status. It was founded and is run by the SOLMIT Association, which promotes intercultural understanding and integration of Muslim youth into Austrian society.
- The Islamic Professional School for Social Education (*Islamische Fachschule für Soziale Bildung*–IFSB, Neustiftgasse 117, 1070 Vienna)[92] is a private vocational school at the intermediate level with a public status. During their three years of education, students receive a general education with a specialisation in the caring professions, and are additionally trained in Islamic teachings and ethics, Qur'an recitation and interpretation, Islamic jurisprudence, Arabic, Turkish (optional), and Arabic calligraphy.
- The confessional Isma Muhammad Asad Private Comprehensive School (*Isma Private Gesamtschule Muhammad Asad*, Reschgasse 20–22, 1120 Vienna)[93] offers comprehensive education for six-to-14-year-old students. It has been run since 2012 by the Isma Association, a self-governing body financed by a religious foundation. It was founded by the International Organisation for Science and Education (IOSE)[94] and has its own curriculum with a comparatively strong focus on Islamic principles.
- Phoenix Elementary School (*Phönix Volksschule*, Gudrunstraße 11, 1100 Vienna) and Phoenix Grammar School (*Phönix Realgymnasium*, Knöllgasse 20–24, 1100 Vienna) are both operated by the Phoenix Association and follow the Austrian national curriculum.

---

91 See www.irgw.at, accessed 12 March 2018.
92 See www.bif-fachschule.at/, accessed 12 March 2018.
93 See www.is-ma.at, accessed 12 March 2018.
94 See www.iose.at, accessed 12 March 2018.

Muslim Media and Publications

- *Eimaan* is a children's magazine in German (first editions were in Bosnian), published by the Bosniak community. All issues are available online, free of charge: https://issuu.com/eimaangraz.
- *Kismet Online* is an independent "Muslim lifestyle" magazine established in 2006. It is intended to promote intercultural dialogue and the protection of human rights. See http://www.kismetonline.at.
- *Qalam* is a magazine for children between the ages of seven and twelve. It was first published in 2016 by the Islamic Centre Vienna (*Islamisches Zentrum Wien*–IZW) and is available for purchase through a subscription. A small section of free issues were made available online, however the website is currently under maintenance: http://www.qalam.at.

Main Muslim Organisations

– Islamic Alevi Religious Community in Austria (*Islamisch Alevitische Glaubensgemeinschaft in Österreich*–ALEVI, Schererstraße 4, 1210 Vienna, tel.: ++43 6764418468, www.aleviten.at/de/). The organisation identifies with the principles of the Turkey-based *CEM Vakfı* (CEM Foundation). They consider Alevism a tradition that stands within Islam. Together with the IGGiÖ it shares the privileges and duties defined in the 2015 *Islam Law*. It is an officially recognised religious community endowed with special privileges and is specified as one of the two main public Muslim bodies in the *Islam Law*.
– Islamic Religious Community in Austria (*Islamische Glaubensgemeinschaft in Österreich*–IGGiÖ, Bernardgasse 5, 1070 Vienna, tel.: ++43 15263122, www.derislam.at/). The IGGiÖ was founded in 1979 and was the only Muslim public institution until the legal recognition of ALEVI in 2013. It functions as an umbrella organisation for a broad spectrum of Islamic associations. The *Islam Law* of 2015 changed the structures of Islamic associations in Austria, as all associations are now forced to become a religious association (*Kultusgemeinde*), and thereby an official branch of the acknowledged

religious communities. This significant, but in a way superficial, legal change resulted in the founding of 27 religious associations thus far, and 20 specialised organisations (*Fachvereine*) that support specific projects. In the course of this restructuring, some existing associations were split into several associations based on their geographical location, while others were merged to constitute a new branch. Notably, those individual communities that merged do not yet have a common public appearance. The following section contains information about these religious associations, and some major specialised organisations, that are all members of the IGGiÖ:

- Albanian Religious Association (*Albanische Kultusgemeinde*, Manzelgasse 15, 1160 Vienna, www.alkig.at, info@alkig.at, ++43 69917374276). The organisation is run by Muslims with roots in Albania and Kosovo, and runs 17 centres in Austria.
- ATIB Religious Association Lower Austria/ Upper Austria/ Salzburg/ Tyrol/ Vorarlberg/ Vienna (*ATIB Kultusgemeinden Niederösterreich/ Oberösterreich/ Salzburg/ Tirol/ Vorarlberg/ Wien*; Viennese address: Sonnleithnergasse 20, 1100 Vienna, tel.: ++43 13346280, www.atib.at/). The ATIB is an organisation closely related to the Turkish Presidency of Religious Affairs (*Diyanet İşleri Başkanlığı*). It is Austria's largest Muslim organisation with 65 mosque communities across the country, organised into six religious associations under the aegis of the IGGiÖ.
- Bosniak Religious Association Central/ North-East/ East/ South-West (*Bosniakische Kultusgemeinde Mitte/ Nord-Ost/ Ost/ Süd-West*; Arndtstrasse 28/2, 1120 Vienna, tel.: ++43 476236664, http://izba.at/). Each of the four regional Bosniak religious associations is related to 40 mosque communities altogether. The relatively new coordinated public appearance of Bosniak Muslims dates back to 2012.
- Islamic Federation Religious Association Arlberg/ Linz/ Lower Austria/ Vienna (*Islamische Föderation Kultusgemeinde Arlberg/ Linz/ Niederösterreich/ Wien*; Viennese address: Rauchfangkehrergasse 36, 1150 Vienna, tel.: ++4319619121, email: info@ifwien.at, www.ifwien.at/). The Islamic Federation is the Austrian branch of the Islamic Community Milli Görüş, a transnational religio-political group originating from Turkey. In Austria, the Islamic Federation is currently organised into five religious associations with around 60 mosque communities.
- Islamic Cultural Centres Union/ Organisation/ Association/ Religious Community (*Islamische Kulturzentren Bündnis/ Organisation / Verband/ Vereinigung/ Kultusgemeinde*; Viennese address: Pelzgasse 9, 1150 Vienna,

tel.: ++43 19831295, www.uikz.org/). The Union is affiliated with the originally Turkish tradition of the followers of Süleyman Hilmi Tunahan, often called Süleymancılar, and runs 42 places of prayer.
- Religious Association Turkish Federation Vienna/ Federal States (*Kultusgemeinde Türkische Föderation Wien/ Bundesländer*, address: Hosnedlygasse 11, 1220 Vienna, tel.: ++43 13349890. https://de-de.facebook.com/ATfederasyon/, email: office@turkfederasyon.at). The Turkish Federation originates from the nationalist Turkish religious movement *Ülkücü* (Idealists), often criticised for its far-right positions. The radical right *Milliyetçi Hareket Partisi* (Nationalist Movement Party) is the political arm of this movement and is active in the Turkish parliament. The Turkish Federation runs about 21 places of prayer and various organisations in Austria.

The following religious associations do not have a coherent public face (i.e. official contact details, website, spokesperson, etc.) but are listed as IGGiÖ members:

- Arab Religious Association (*Arabische Kultusgemeinde*). This religious association loosely unites ten communities of different Arab backgrounds across the country.
- Asian Religious Association (*Asiatische Kultusgemeinde*). This religious association loosely unites ten communities of different Asian backgrounds, among them Afghani and Pakistani, most of them located in Vienna.
- Religious Association of the Islamic-Sufi Community (*Kultusgemeinde der Islamischen-Sufi Gemeinschaft*). This association unites about twelve communities across the country, many of Turkish origin.
- Religious Association of Multicultural Mosque Facilities (*Kultusgemeinde Multikulturelle Moscheeeinrichtungen*). About eleven communities of various origins (Somalia, Morocco, etc.) across Austria are united under this umbrella group.

Here are some of the most prominent specialised organisations (*Fachvereine*) registered with the IGGiÖ:

- Specialised Organisation for the Support of Muslim Youth in Austria (*Verein zur Unterstützung der Muslimischen Jugend in Österreich*–MJÖ, Eitnergasse 6/5, 1230 Vienna, email: office@mjoe.at, www.mjoe.at/). The MJÖ functioned as the official youth branch of the IGGiÖ until 2012, when a new youth organisation of the IGGiÖ (*Jugendrat der Islamischen*

Glaubensgemeinschaft–JIGGiÖ) was established.[95] Since then, there has been a certain estrangement between the MJÖ and the IGGiÖ. The MJÖ, one of the few Austrian Muslim organisations that is not ethnically bound, is highly present in the media and, together with the recently established grassroots Network of Muslim Civil Society (*Netzwerk Muslimische Zivilgesellschaft*–NMZ, http://dieanderen.net/), promotes their self-understanding as Austrian Muslims.
- Specialised Organisation Imam Hatip (*Fachverein Imam Hatip*, Herziggasse 9, 1100 Wien, www.viyanaihl.at/, email: info@viyanaihl.at, + 43 664 235 10 01). This organisation runs educational places for Islamic counsellors and imams. One facility was temporarily closed in 2017, due to violations of the Law on private schools. In early 2018 classes start again but in the form of a religious training course, not as a school, according to Austria's regulations on private schools.[96]
- Specialised Organisation IQRAA University Mosque (*Fachverein IQRAA–Universitätsmoschee*, https://uni-moschee.at/, email: info@uni-moschee.at). This organisation is related to various Muslim associations, and collects donations for the funding of a mosque near the University of Vienna.

Aside from the groups under the aegis of the officially recognised religious communities, there are other relevant Islamic groups that are active in Austria:

- Federation of Alevi Communities in Austria (*Föderation der Aleviten Gemeinden in Österreich*–AABF, Schererstraße 4, 1210 Vienna, http://aleviten.com/index.php/de/). The AABF is a member of the European Alevi Confederation (*Avrupa Alevi Birlikleri Konfederasyonu*), which considers the Alevi tradition not to be Islamic, despite a common heritage. Attempts by the AABF to challenge the status of ALEVI as the only legally acknowledged Alevi religious community, have failed.
- Islamic-Shi'i Religious Community in Austria (*Islamische-Schiitische Glaubensgemeinschaft in Österreich*, Schia, Pezzlgasse 58, 1170 Vienna, tel.: ++43 699111979350, email: office@schia.at). This Shi'i group representing the Iraqi Shi'i *hawza 'ilmiya* tradition was granted the status of an acknowledged faith community in 2013. Their headquarters are within the Islamic Association Ahl-ul-Bayt (*Islamische Vereinigung Ahl-ul-Bayt*, IVAÖ) in Vienna.

---

95 Mattes, "From Bosnian soldiers to third generation juveniles", pp. 81–116.
96 "Neustart für Imam-Lehrgang in Liesing", *kurier.at*, 8 January 2018, https://kurier.at/chronik/wien/neustart-fuer-imam-lehrgang-in-liesing/305.277.103, accessed 14 March 2018.

- Islamic Centre Imam Ali (*Islamisches Zentrum Imam Ali*–IZIA, Mollardgasse 50, 1060 Vienna, tel.: ++43 15977065, email: info@izia.at). IZIA represents Twelver Shi'is in Austria, and is associated with the IGGiÖ. The IZIA operates a mosque and a cultural centre, which is also part of the Islamic Association Ahl-ul-Bayt. This Shi'i umbrella organisation comprises six associations, with members mostly from Iran and Afghanistan.

Azerbaijan

Altay Goyushov[1]

Introduction

2017 was an important year in the religious life of Azerbaijan due to two main developments: first, there was a significant increase in the attendance of 'Ashura' ceremonies in mosques throughout the country and a rising number of pilgrims to the Shi'i shrines of Iraq in Karbala and Najaf during Arba'een (40th day of Imam Husayn's martyrdom). These commemorations proved once more that various types of restrictions implemented by the Government in previous years did little to contain the impressive advance of Shi'i sentiments among the general public. Second, as an attempt to embrace this reality, the ruling elite made significant efforts to demonstrate its loyalty towards so-called "moral national values". For instance, the Foundation for the Promotion of Moral Values (*Mənəvi Dəyərlərin Təbliği Fondu*) was created by a decree of the Azerbaijani President. He also declared 2017 as the Year of Islamic Solidarity in Azerbaijan, and the 4th multinational Islamic Solidarity Games were held in the nation's capital Baku.

There is no doubt that concerns about possible political risks due to rising Shi'i sentiments in the country, and Iran's growing ambitions in the region, were among the priorities which contributed to the active engagement of an Azerbaijani foreign policy with this neighbouring country in 2017. Twice during the year, Azerbaijani President Ilham Aliyev visited Iran and met high-ranking officials, including the country's Supreme Leader Ayatollah Khamenei.[2] Concerns about political risks connected with rising religiosity were also behind the new procedures announced or implemented by Azerbaijani authorities, to further consolidate control over religious life and communities.

---

[1] Altay Goyushov was Professor of Turkic History at Baku State University, Azerbaijan. He received his PhD in the History of Political Islam from the same university in 1993. Currently, his research interests are focused mainly on issues related to political Islam, Islamic education and the secularisation of Azerbaijan during the last two centuries. He has held fellowships and visiting professorships in Italy, France and the United States, including the Bourse "Directeurs d'Études Associés" at the FMSH in Paris, a Fulbright Scholarship at Georgetown University and appointments at Sapienza-Università di Roma, UCLA and the Institut Français d'Études Anatoliennes.

[2] http://www.eurasianet.org/node/86596; http://en.president.az/articles/23008; http://en.president.az/articles/25817, all accessed 25 January 2018.

This year also saw the continuation of special operations taken by the State Security Service against Salafis, which resulted in multiple fatalities of alleged terrorists in various parts of the country. Another notable issue this year were the foreign media reports concerning Azerbaijani nationals' involvement in terrorist activities in neighbouring countries and war zones in the Middle East.

Public Debates

The Government faced rising Shi'i sentiments in 2017, and tried to assure the public of its support for Islamic values in an attempt to mitigate the consequences of its restrictive policies against local Muslims, who have been critical of the authorities in previous years. The crisis around the demolition of an old mosque in the historic Sovetskaya district of the nation's capital, which attracted wide attention and caused major public debates within the local Muslim community, is a vivid example of this.

Located in the centre of Baku, the Sovetskaya neighbourhood was actually built before Soviet rule, during the first oil boom in the late 19th–early 20th century, and was full of mainly art-nouveau style historic buildings. The Government decided to dismantle a huge part of this neighbourhood to clear the space for a massive renovation and beautification project. While the demolition of historic buildings caused surprisingly little criticism from the public and intellectuals, the situation changed drastically when authorities tried to knock down the local, architecturally less significant, Haji Javad mosque in April 2017, which lies in the middle of this area. It seems that resistance of local Shi'is, who defended their place of worship,[3] caught the authorities off guard. This resistance forced the Government to retract its decision, and the President created a special commission to settle the controversy.[4] However, in late June, the Government proceeded with its plans, and demolished the mosque during the night. Several days later the President dismissed the head of the district's executive authority, allegedly for dismantling the mosque. One of the top ranking officials of the President's administration told the media that the dismissed head of the local executive office disregarded the President's order that the mosque should only be demolished after a new community place of worship had been built in another neighbourhood.[5]

---

3 https://www.youtube.com/watch?v=pHWyoLMOf2w, accessed 25 January 2018.
4 http://www.bbc.com/azeri/azerbaijan-39576079, accessed 25 January 2018.
5 https://www.azadliq.org/a/haci-cavad-mescidi-sokulur/28588440.html, accessed 25 January 2018.

Some developments during the yearly 'Ashura' ceremonies of Shi'is, which were commemorated in September, prompted serious criticism from the Azerbaijani public. The first of these were the result of videos showing youths cutting their heads open with knives as part of a self-flagellation ceremony in the outskirts of Baku circulated on Azerbaijani social media; the public was seriously concerned over the revival of this ritual in the metropolitan area of the capital after its decades-long absence. While officials tried to soften public concerns, emphasising the insignificantly small number of Shi'is participating in these ceremonies, the mere reappearance of this long forgotten tradition in the Baku area was regarded as a sign of a failure of the Government's policies to contain the increase in 'Ashura' ceremonies, even in its most extreme expressions.[6] Another issue which drew serious public concern and criticism were small children taking part in various 'Ashura' ceremonies. This concern prompted discussions in Parliament,[7] and information about the preparation of new legislation "that would prohibit children from taking part in 'Ashura' commemorations and similar religious rituals" circulated in the media.[8]

These developments have once again proven that the restrictive measures[9] applied by the Government since 2015 to contain the growing politicisation of Shi'i communities will do little as long as the oppression of secular opposition, independent media, and civil society continues. In fact, shrinking the space for activities by the secular liberal-democratic opposition paves the way for various Muslim groups to replace them with a voice of dissent. The deputy head of the State Committee for Work with Religious Associations, in an interview, acknowledged the existence of a political component of the steadily growing attendance in 'Ashura' ceremonies.[10]

Another type of controversy that stirred public discussion in the pages of local media was the statement by the State Security Service (sss), in which it announced that it had neutralised a group of militants linked to ISIS, who had allegedly planned a terrorist attack on an authorised rally of the secular

---

6 http://www.islaminsesi.info/basi-qeme-ile-yox-elmle-yarmaq-lazimdir-bas-yarma-olayi-ile-bagli-keskin-etiraz--72453.html; https://www.youtube.com/watch?v=cJIYvHqECdA&feature=youtu.be, accessed 2 March 2018.

7 https://apa.az/xeber-az/dini-xeberler/milli-meclis-uzvleri-usaqlarin-dini-merasimlere-celb-edilmesi-yolverilmezdir-9351.html, accessed 25 January 2018.

8 https://eurasianet.org/node/86596, accessed 25 January 2018.

9 Goyushov, Altay, "Azerbaijan", in Oliver Scharbrodt, Samim Akgönül, Ahmet Alibašić, Jørgen S. Nielsen and Egdūnas Račius (eds.), *Yearbook of Muslims in Europe,* vol. 8 (Leiden-Boston: Brill, 2016), pp. 69–81.

10 http://en.apa.az/azerbaijan_religion_news/state-committee-some-forces-in-azerbaijan-seek-to-add-political-elements-into-ashura-commemorations.html, accessed 25 January 2018.

opposition.[11] In autumn 2017, the secular opposition group called the National Council of Democratic Forces (*Demokratik Qüvvələrin Milli Şurası*) held several rallies, protesting against government corruption that had been exposed by international organisations and the media.[12] The State Security Service issued the aforementioned statement about the planned terrorist attack just before one of the October rallies of the National Council. However, the reliability of this statement raised concerns among local independent observers. The secular opposition in question dismissed the sss's statement as baseless and as a politically-motivated manipulation aiming to spread fear among the public in order to reduce the attendance at anti-corruption rallies of opposition groups.[13]

Transnational Links

Fighters from Azerbaijan participating in the wars in Syria and Iraq remained one of the major topics raised by both domestic and foreign media, as well as state agencies in 2017. In September 2017, the head of the State Security Service stated that during previous years, 900 Azerbaijanis joined the ranks of ISIS, and 85 of them were under arrest in Azerbaijan. He added that the citizenship of 195 Azerbaijanis was revoked on the grounds of their participation in the wars in the Middle East as members of terrorist organisations.[14] However, in December, a spokesperson of the General Prosecutor's office reported that the number of those who were stripped of their citizenship for the same reason was 258.[15] The head of the SSS also stated that they were checking the information that suggested 300 Azerbaijanis were killed in the war zones of Iraq.[16]

In July 2017, the Turkish Ministry of the Interior published a report called "Turkey's Fight Against DEASH" (*Türkiye'nin DAEŞ ile Mücadelesi*). According to this report, 252 Azerbaijani nationals have been arrested or deported at Turkish border cities while trying to cross to conflict zones, and 1,677 Azerbaijani

---

11   https://eurasianet.org/node/85726; https://www.azadliq.org/a/drx-mitinq-milli-shura/28815883.html, both accessed 25 January 2018.
12   https://www.theguardian.com/world/2017/sep/04/everything-you-need-to-know-about-the-azerbaijani-laundromat; https://www.rferl.org/a/opposition-activists-hold-anticorruption-rally-baku/28753209.html, all accessed 25 January 2018.
13   http://www.bbc.com/azeri/azerbaijan-41758823, accessed 25 January 2018.
14   http://interfax.az/view/713827, accessed 25 January 2018.
15   https://az.trend.az/azerbaijan/society/2835281.html, accessed 25 January 2018.
16   https://ria.ru/world/20170924/1505438959.html, accessed 25 January 2018.

citizens have been placed on the no-entry list due to their affiliation with terrorism since 2014.[17]

Participation of Azerbaijani women in the conflict zones of Iraq and Syria was another important topic which attracted extensive public attention. In November 2017, Iraqi MP Vian Dakhil reported that about 200 Azerbaijani women had been captured and incarcerated by Iraqi forces for being ISIS members.[18] After ISIS's *de facto* capital Raqqa in Syria had been liberated, the largest Canadian news broadcaster, CBC News, highlighted the story of a young Azerbaijani woman, dubbed the "ISIS bride", who was brought to the war zone by her father and was forced to marry jihadis.[19] In September 2017, local news outlets reported on an ISIS-affiliated Azerbaijani woman who was killed together with her five children in Iraq.[20] Throughout 2017, many other stories discussing the detention and killing of Azerbaijani jihadis in foreign countries surfaced in various news outlets.[21]

However, it should be noted that the media and general public primarily focused their attention on the expanding links between local Shi'i believers and neighbouring Iran. In May 2017, one local newspaper published documents and detailed analysis outlining Iranian financial support for Azerbaijani Shi'i personalities and clerics.[22] In December, one of the most prominent unofficial mouthpieces of the Azerbaijani government published an article about the travelling of local Shi'is to the shrines in Iraq for Arba'een, and connected the

---

17 http://sahipkiran.org/wp-content/uploads/2017/07/Turkiyenin_DAES_ile_Mucadelesi_-_Turkeys-Fight-with-ISIS.pdf, https://www.academia.edu/33832608/T%C3%BCrkiyenin_DAE%C5%9E_ile_M%C3%BCcadelesi_-_Turkeys_Fight_Against_DEASH, accessed 2 March 2018.

18 http://www.thebaghdadpost.com/en/story/19426/Azerbaijan-probes-reports-of-200-ISIS-linked-women-arrested-in-Iraq, accessed 25 January 2018.

19 http://www.cbc.ca/news2/interactives/sh/JBuuQkhhLk/surviving-isis/, accessed 25 January 2018.

20 https://ru.oxu.az/society/212932?fb_comment_id=1646185718786402_1646575675414073#f17f34a12fd7524, accessed 25 January 2018.

21 http://aa.com.tr/en/todays-headlines/turkey-arrests-61-daesh-linked-suspects/950684?amp=1; http://www.milliyet.com.tr/bursa-da-deas-operasyonu-105-gundem-2391173/; http://www.1news.az/news/v-rossii-osuzhden-azerbaydzhanec-verbovavshiy-studentov-v-igil; https://www.dailysabah.com/war-on-terror/2017/05/21/two-daesh-terrorists-killed-during-operation-in-ankara; https://www.ntv.com.tr/turkiye/ankara-valisi-topacadan-oldurulen-daesli-teroristlerle-ilgili-aciklama,jwQFcNWzikyLMK31k2SHTg; http://www.milliyet.com.tr/suriye-sinirinda-yakalanan-deas-li-gundem-2469018/; http://musavat.com/news/telaferde-coxlu-sayda-azerbaycanli-oldurulub-ve-esir-alinib-fotosubutlar_.463420.html; https://m.haqqin.az/news/110175; http://news.lent.az/news/267891, all accessed 25 January 2018.

22 http://muxalifet.az/azrbaycanda-irana-islyn-casus-sbksi-sok-faktlar.html, accessed 25 January 2018.

rising number of pilgrims to a growing Iranian influence.[23] The issue of Iranian influence attracted the attention of independent observers as well.[24]

According to the aforementioned article in the pro-government news website, during Arba'een in 2017, 30,000 Azerbaijanis undertook pilgrimages to the shrines in Iraq, which was 33% more than the previous year.[25] Azerbaijani Shi'i media outlets reported that the authorities of Imam Husayn shrine in Karbala city planned to provide free food and accommodation to 4,000 Azerbaijani pilgrims.[26]

Apart from the concerns over the sharply rising numbers of pilgrims, demonstrations organised by Azerbaijani Shi'is in Karbala, which were critical of the Azerbaijani government and demanded the release of jailed clerics, frustrated Baku's authorities further.[27] Moreover, according to pro-government news outlets, on their way back via Iran, Azerbaijani pilgrims had arranged meetings with prominent Iranian clerics that were very critical of Baku's authorities.[28]

Law and Domestic Politics

In 2017, anti-terrorist operations by the State Security Service (SSS) against alleged terrorists of Salafi background continued in various parts of the country.[29] The law enforcement agencies' raids discovered illegally operating Salafi places of worship in various regions of the country, which were subsequently shut down.[30] As was the case in previous years, some of the operations carried out by the SSS ended with fatalities.[31] In March 2017, an official of the SSS reported that during operations carried out by this agency in the previous six months

---

23 https://haqqin.az/news/117537, accessed 25 January 2018.
24 http://www.eurasianet.org/node/86596, accessed 25 January 2018.
25 https://haqqin.az/news/117537, accessed 25 January 2018.
26 http://ahlibeyt.az/news/a-7481.html, accessed 25 January 2018.
27 http://m.islaminsesi.info/hebsde-olan-ruhaniler-kerbelada-yad-edildi-foto-video--74456.html; http://islamazeri.com/abgul-suleymanov-rbein-zevvarlarina-tesekkur-etdi--20933.html, all accessed 25 January 2018.
28 http://strateq.az/manshet/216284/k%C9%99rb%C9%99la-ziyar%C9%99tind%C9%99n-sui-istifad%C9%99.html, accessed 25 January 2018.
29 http://ru.apa.az/novosti-azerbaydjana/proisshestvie-v-azerbaydjane/sgb-prodolzhaet-antiterroristicheskie-operacii-zaderzhany-eshe-4-uchastnika-boev-v-sirii-i-irake.html, accessed 25 January 2018.
30 http://news.lent.az/news/265139; https://www.azadliq.org/a/berdede-dindarlar-saxlanib/28240824.html, accessed 25 January 2018.
31 http://www.dtx.gov.az/news115.php; http://www.1news.az/news/sgb-azerbaydzhana-lik vidirovala-radikala-voevavshego-v-terroristicheskoy-gruppirovke-za-rubezhom, all accessed 25 January 2018.

in Baku, Sumgait, and the Qusar regions of the country, nine alleged terrorists were killed and four were detained.[32] In December 2017, a spokesperson from the General Prosecutor's office reported that the overall number of those killed in operations against Salafi-affiliated alleged terrorists in the country was 16, and the number of detainees was 21.[33] Those operations with fatalities, carried out by the State Security Service after its restructuring and the appointment of a new head in December 2015, raised public concerns. The legitimacy and professionalism of these operations were questioned by Azerbaijan's independent media, as well as by former security professionals.[34]

In the course of 2017 there were several detentions and arrests of Shi'i clerics and their followers. Mainly Shi'is who were connected with the *Müsəlman Birliyi Hərəkatı* (Union of Muslims Movement) of imprisoned cleric Tale Bagirzade were targeted.[35] The most prominent arrest in 2017 was the imprisonment of Sardar Babayev, a cleric well-known in the Southern regions of the country, and the chief editor of the Shi'i maide.az news website. He was "accused of violating the requirements for conducting religious ceremonies", and was sentenced to three years imprisonment.[36] In three separate trials, the courts delivered lengthy ten to 20 year prison sentences to dozens of Shi'is–members of the aforementioned Union of Muslims Movement[37]–who were arrested in connection with the events in the town of Nardaran in the outskirts of the capital Baku. Here, on 28 November 2015, police arrested the leader of this group, Tale Bagirzade, an operation which ended with the shooting and death of six individuals.[38]

The President of Azerbaijan declared 2017 the Year of Islamic Solidarity,[39] and on 4 May the multinational Islamic Solidarity Games were held in

---

32 https://apa.az/xeber-az/hadise/dtx-nin-sobe-reisi-son-yarim-ilde-azerbaycanda-9-ekstremist-mehv-edilib-4-u-tutulub.html, accessed 25 January 2018.
33 https://az.trend.az/azerbaijan/society/2835281.html, accessed 25 January 2018.
34 https://www.meydan.tv/az/site/politics/26081/, accessed 25 January 2018.
35 http://islamazeri.com/mbh-uzvu-elxan-isgenderov-saxlanilib--8665.html; https://www.meydan.tv/az/site/news/21469; https://www.meydan.tv/az/site/news/25858/; http://www.islamazeri.az/hsen-nuruzadenin-mehkeme-prosesinin-vaxti-melum-oldu--22202.html, all accessed 25 January 2018.
36 http://www.eng.kavkaz-uzel.eu/articles/39967/, accessed 25 January 2018.
37 https://www.amerikaninsesi.org/a/hokm-nardaran-ishi-mehkeme/3691391.html; https://www.amerikaninsesi.org/a/mehkeme/4182411.html; https://www.azadliq.org/a/nardaran-mehkeme/28899896.html, all accessed 25 January 2018.
38 Goyushov, "Azerbaijan", pp. 69–81.
39 http://en.apa.az/azerbaijan-politics/domestic-news/2017-declared-year-of-islamic-solidarity-in-azerbaijan.html, accessed 25 January 2018.

the capital Baku.[40] In October, the President created a new state body, the Foundation for the Promotion of Moral Values (*Mənəvi Dəyərlərin Təbliği Fondu*), which was made subordinate to the State Committee for Work with Religious Associations (SCWRA).[41] In December, the international conference "2017–The Year of Islamic solidarity: interfaith and intercultural dialogue" was held in Baku, aimed at summarising the events dedicated to this occasion.[42]

Activities and Initiatives of Main Muslim Organisations

As usual, the most significant event in the life of Azerbaijani Muslims was the annual 'Ashura' commemoration of Shi'is. After the deadly events in Nardaran village in the outskirts of Baku in 2015, the Azerbaijani government enforced a variety of restrictions to contain 'Ashura' commemorations that had been growing in numbers and size for a number of years. As a result of this policy, the number of attendees of 'Ashura' ceremonies in 2016 was fewer than in 2015. However, 'Ashura' attendance at mosques throughout the country in 2017 became one of, if not the largest, for decades. The effect of this mass event was so impressive that the imprisoned head of the *Azərbaycan İslam Partiyası* (Islamic Party of Azerbaijan), Movsum Samadov, sent his greetings to his followers, congratulating them for the largest 'Ashura' event in recent history.[43] The extensive character of 'Ashura' ceremonies in 2017 in comparison to previous years was commented on by the Supreme Leader of Iran Ayatollah Khamenei, during his meeting with Azerbaijani President Aliyev in Tehran in November 2017, as well. Ayatollah Khamenei described it as proof of the failure of decades-long Soviet atheistic policies in Azerbaijan.[44]

An unexpected dispute arose between various Shi'i groups over the celebrations of the anniversary of the death of the third caliph 'Umar (so-called *Eid-e-Zahra*). Shi'is blame 'Umar for the death of Fatima, the daughter of the Prophet Muhammad and wife of the first Shi'i Imam 'Ali. It should be noted that the majority of Azerbaijani Shi'i clerics, including the popular head of the *Məşədi Dadaş* community, Haji Shahin, publicly criticised this celebration as a danger

---

40   https://www.baku2017.com/, accessed 25 January 2018.
41   https://azertag.az/xeber/Menevi_Deyerlerin_Tebligi_Fondu_yaradilib-1101384, accessed 25 January 2018.
42   https://azertag.az/en/xeber/1123180, accessed 25 January 2018.
43   http://www.islamazeri.az/aip-lideri-movsum-semedov-azerbaycan-xalqina-tesekkur-etdi--18211.html, accessed 25 January 2018.
44   http://m.islaminsesi.info/prezident-ilham-eliyev-iran-islam-respublikasinin-ali-rehberi-ayetulahxamenei-ile-gorusub--74040.html, accessed 25 January 2018.

which can foster internal clashes between Muslims.[45] However, a minority of Shi'is who celebrated the occasion continued to defend their position.

In 2017, problems of religious education were also debated. In July, in an interview with the local media, the head of the SCWRA, Mubariz Gurbanly, stated that there were 2,246 mosques in the country and approximately 900 of them were small neighbourhood ones, and that the appointment of official preachers for these prayer houses had not finished yet. He cited a lack of qualified clerics as one of the major reasons for this shortcoming.[46] In an apparent response to this problem, the SCWRA decided to address this issue by assuming full control over religious educational institutions. In September 2017, the deputy head of the SCWRA criticised the poor education of graduates from Baku Islamic University, which operates under the supervision of the *Qafqaz Müsəlmanları İdarəsi* (Caucasus Muslims Board, CMB).[47] A month earlier, news spread across local media that Baku State University stopped accepting new BA students to its Theology major within the Theology Department.[48] However, the CMB authorities announced that they were planning to construct a new education centre within the *Ilahiyyat* mosque that operates on the campus of Baku State University. The announcement came after the CMB received full authority over this mosque, that was built in the 1990s.[49] Meanwhile, the SCWRA registered ten Islamic Colleges (the word *mədrəsə* has officially been replaced with the word *kollec*) in 2017, which will be under the sole control of the Committee.[50] Moreover, the SCWRA official emphasised that, unlike as before, religious education offered in these colleges will be free of tuition.[51]

In addition, to address the current lack of qualified personnel, amendments to the current legislation–that prohibits the appointment of foreign-educated clerics as official preachers in mosques–were proposed. According to these amendments, some foreign-educated clerics will be allowed to lead prayers and rituals in officially registered mosques.[52] At the same time, the SCWRA

---

45 https://www.youtube.com/watch?v=P1Vcm5GwFs4, accessed 25 January 2018.
46 http://scwra.gov.az/vnews/3609/, accessed 25 January 2018.
47 http://modern.az/az/news/142302#gsc.tab=0, accessed 25 January 2018.
48 http://sherg.az/site/id-34823/%C4%Bolahiyyat_fak%C3%BClt%C9%99si_niy%C9%99_ba%C4%9Fland%C4%B1?#.WpktiOhubIU, accessed 2 March 2018.
49 https://www.azadliq.org/a/ilahiyyat-mescidi-qafqaz-muselmanlarina-verilib/28402265.html, accessed 25 January 2018.
50 http://scwra.gov.az/pages/244/, accessed 25 January 2018.
51 https://report.az/din/gelen-ilden-azerbaycanda-din-xadimlerine-dovlet-terefinden-mevacib-odenilecek/, accessed 25 January 2018.
52 http://az.trend.az/azerbaijan/society/2745723.html, accessed 25 January 2018.

reiterated its opinion that they were against the introduction of religious education in secondary public schools.[53]

The SCWRA also continued its so-called "enlightenment programme" to tackle religious radicalism in state prisons. The well-known head of the *Məşədi Dadaş* mosque, Haji Shahin, also began to participate in these lectures for convicts.[54] This was an important move to improve the efficiency of the programme. In December, the head of the SCWRA announced that, starting in 2018, imams and deputy imams of mosques appointed by the CMB will receive official state salaries via the newly established Foundation for the Promotion of Moral Values.[55] The head of the SCWRA also announced plans to reopen the controversial Salafi Abu Bakr mosque in Baku,[56] which was closed after terrorists threw a bomb inside it in August 2008.

Earlier, in September 2017, the CMB's Council of Qadis decided to replace the word *axund* (*akhund*)–which was used historically in Azerbaijan as an official title for Shi'i clerics appointed to lead Shi'i mosques–with the term imam, which is used as the title for officially appointed clerics in both Sunni and Shi'i mosques.[57] The CMB's head justified this decision with the fact that it is a more commonly used term in the Muslim world, and mentioned Turkey as an example. This decision caused some controversy among some of the independent Shi'i communities, which disapproved, and view it as another move to suppress the distinct Shi'i identity of the country.

Finally, the number of people who travelled to the hajj pilgrimage fell further from 1,040 pilgrims in 2016 to 900 in 2017. This is a trend that started in 2009 (in 2008, the number of pilgrims reached its peak of 6,000[58]) as a result of the formal and informal restrictions applied by the Government to the practice. A fixed price of $3,850 was established by the CMB for a hajj travel package in 2017.[59]

---

53   http://m.apa.az/az/xeber-az/dini-xeberler/dini-komite-azerbaycan-orta-mekteblerinde-dini-tedrisin-tetbiqinin-eleyhinedir-1741, accessed 25 January 2018.
54   http://ahlibeyt.az/news/a-7677.html; http://faktxeber.com/mobil/index.php?H=500215, all accessed 25 January 2018.
55   https://report.az/din/gelen-ilden-azerbaycanda-din-xadimleri-maas-alacaqlar/, accessed 25 January 2018.
56   http://musavat.com/news/mubariz-qurbanli-ziyalilarimiz-islama-qarsi-yox-xurafata-qarsi-mubarize-aparib_455665.html, accessed 25 January 2018.
57   https://report.az/din/qmi-axund-sozunu-legv-edib-yalniz-imam-kelmesi-isledilecek/, accessed 25 January 2018.
58   http://wap.islam.az/news/a-4275.html, accessed 25 January 2018.
59   https://apa.az/xeber-az/dini-xeberler/azerbaycandan-bu-il-hecce-kvotadan-300-nefer-artiq-zevvar-gedir-1119.html, accessed 25 January 2018.

Muslim Population: History and Demographics

The spread of Islam in Azerbaijan started in the middle of the seventh century CE, however, the formation of religious and ethnic identities has gone through numerous changes. In the eleventh century, the formation of the Turkic Seljuk Empire forced a shift in the ethnic composition of the Azerbaijani populace, boosting the proportion of Turkic people and Sunni Islam. In the 16th century, the Sunni version of Islam, patronised by the Seljuk Turks, suffered a severe setback with the rise of the militant Shi'i Safavid dynasty, which was supported by the *Qızılbaş* ("Redhead") Turcoman tribes. Due to this conversion, forcibly imposed by the Safavids, the religious loyalties of the locals were deeply divided. The Sunnis of Azerbaijan were followers of the Hanafi and Shafi'i schools of law, while the Turkic speaking Sunnis of Azerbaijan were mainly Hanafis. The majority of the mountain people, who spoke the native Caucasian languages, followed the Shafi'i branch of Sunni Islam. In turn, the majority of Azerbaijani Shi'is adhered to the Twelver branch of Shi'i Islam.

The Russian conquest of Azerbaijan in the 19th century, and the formation of a local, secular-educated elite under imperial patronage, paved the way for the formation of a new secular nation. Thus, the fall of the tsarist regime was followed by a brief two-year period of independence, when the country was known as the Azerbaijani Democratic Republic. Although the First Republic was swallowed up by the Soviet Union, nation-building in the Soviet Autonomous Republic of Azerbaijan actually made the restoration of independent statehood after the collapse of the communist regime a viable possibility, and on 18 October 1991 the Republic of Azerbaijan declared its independence.

A strong revival of Islam followed the collapse of the Soviet Union. Due to the lack of internal sources of knowledge, which had been wiped out during Soviet rule, foreign actors played a powerful role in the process of revival. Thus, three major groups of practising Muslims now dominate Islamic life in Azerbaijan. These are Twelver Shi'is–who maintain strong spiritual ties with Iran and to some extent with Iraq, via the powerful network of grand ayatollahs (*marja' al-taqlid*) residing there–different Sunni groups connected to organisations and institutions in Turkey, and Salafis connected to various Arab Gulf states.

According to a statement made by the head of the Caucasus Muslim Board, Allahshukur Pashazade, in February 2015, Shi'is made up approximately 65% of the Muslim population, while Sunnis composed roughly 35%.[60]

---

60   http://m.apa.az/?c=show&id=372763&l=az, accessed 31 January 2017.

Muslim Population	According to the State Statistical Committee of the Azerbaijani Republic (SSC), in November 2016 the size of Azerbaijan's population reached nearly 9.8 million people.[61] According to the State Committee on Work with Religious Associations of the Azerbaijani Republic (SCWRA), 96% of the country's population is Muslim.
Ethnic/National Backgrounds	National/ethnic backgrounds: Azerbaijani Turks: 91.6% Lezgi: 2.0% Talish: 1.3% Avar: 0.6% Meskhetian Turks: 0.4% Tatar: 0.3% Tat:[62] 0.3% Others: less than 1%.[63]
Inner-Islamic Groups	Approximately 65% of local Muslims are considered Shi'i and 35% Sunni.[64]
Geographical Spread	In general, the Sunnis and Shi'is of Azerbaijan live in the same areas in different parts of the country. However, Shi'is prevail in the regions of Nakhichevan, Karabakh, Apsheron, Ganja, Mil', Mugan, and Lenkoran. Sunni Islam is strongest in the regions of Sheki-Zaqatala, Quba-Qusar, and Shamakhi-Qabala.[65]

---

61 http://news.lent.az/news/262465, accessed 31 January 2017.
62 Persian speaking minority in Azerbaijan.
63 www.stat.gov.az/source/demoqraphy/ap/indexen.php#, accessed 27 May 2016. It should be noted that the data provided by both the state institutions of the Azerbaijani Republic (i.e. the SCWRA and SSC), cannot be independently verified.
64 http://m.apa.az/?c=show&id=372763&l=az, accessed 31 January 2017.
65 Balci, Bayram, and Altay Goyushov, "Changing Islam in post-Soviet Azerbaijan and its weighting on the Sunnite-Shiite cleavage", in Brigitte Maréchal, and Sami Zemni (eds.), *The Dynamics of Sunni-Shi'i Relationships: Doctrine, Transnationalism, Intellectuals and the Media* (London: Hurst, 2013), pp. 194–195.

Number of Mosques	There are approximately 2,250 mosques in Azerbaijan.[66]
Muslim Burial Sites	Azerbaijan is a Muslim majority country, and Islamic burial rites are followed even by secular families of Muslim origin. Apart from a small number of cemeteries which are designated for deceased followers of other religions (mostly Orthodox Christians and Jews), almost all the cemeteries in large cities, small towns and villages are Muslim burial places.
"Chaplaincy" in State Institutions	There is no chaplaincy provision in state institutions.
Halal Products	Since 1 April 2014, in order to produce and distribute halal food, producers must obtain halal certificates and labels from the State Committee for Standardisation, Metrology, and Patent of the Republic of Azerbaijan (SCSMP).[67]
Dress Code	There are no laws regulating Islamic clothing in public institutions and places. However, wearing the head scarf in photographs for national passports and identity cards is prohibited. In the past some public secondary schools tried to impose restrictions on wearing the head scarf, which caused demonstrations and stirred public debate. Since the fall of the USSR, the Muslim dress code has become more prevalent. Yet, a very small number of Azeri women wear the head scarf.

---

66 https://www.amerikaninsesi.org/a/din/4203699.html, accessed 30 January 2018.
67 www.azstand.gov.az/index.php?id=27&sub_id=42&xid=418&lang=1; http://www.azstand.gov.az/index.php?id=1032&lang=1, both accessed 31 January 2017.

Places of Islamic Learning and Education	– Baku Islamic University. Founded in 1989 under the authority of the Caucasus Muslim Board as Baku Islamic Madrasa. The title of the madrasa was changed a few times, and it was eventually registered by the Ministry of Justice as Baku Islamic University in 1997. The Deputy of the *sheikh al-islam*, the well-known and popular cleric Haji Sabir Hasanli, has served as the rector of this educational institution since its foundation: www.qafqazislam.com/az/biu.php. – Zaqatala city branch of Baku Islamic University. Founded by the Sunni Naqshbandi Aid for Youth Foundation in 1998 in the Northwest of the country, it started operating as an independent educational institution, but was later renamed the Zaqatala city branch of Baku Islamic University: http://zaqatalailahiyyat.edu.az/. – Theology Faculty of Baku State University. Founded with the aid of the official religious institutions of the Republic of Turkey in 1992. The well-known Azerbaijani Arabic language scholar Haji Vasim Mammedaliyev has served as its dean since the foundation of this faculty: http://theology.bsu.edu.az/. – Ten Islamic Colleges, all established in 2017, are officially registered by the State Committee for Work with Religious Associations.[68]
Muslim Media and Publications	– *Dəyərlər* (http://deyerler.org/). Founded and operated by the Shi'i Juma mosque, community led by Haji Ilgar İbrahimoglu. – *Islamın Səsi*: http://www.islaminsesi.info/. News site operated by pro-Shi'i groups. – http://maide.az/. News site operated by pro-Shi'i groups.

---

68 http://scwra.gov.az/pages/244/, accessed 25 January 2018.

- http://ahlibeyt.az/. News site operated by pro-Shi'i groups.
- *Islam.az*: http://islam.az//. Operated by the pro-government Shi'i Islamic Research Centre.
- http://www.islamazeri.com/. News site operated by pro-Shi'i groups.
- *Sələfxəbər*: http://selefxeber.az/. Operated by the Salafi-oriented Abu Bakr mosque community led by Haji Qamat Suleimanov.

Main Muslim Organisations

- State Committee for Work with Religious Associations (*Dini Qurumlarla İş üzrə Dövlət Komitəsi*, Əhməd Cavad Str. N 12, Baku, AZ-1001, tel.: ++994 124926747, info@scwra.gov.az / http://scwra.gov.az/). Established in 2001 by presidential decree as a government agency. In order to operate legally in Azerbaijan, religious communities must go through the official registration process administered by this Committee. The Committee also possesses controlling powers over publication, import and distribution of religious literature. In general, it supervises the life of local religious communities.
- Caucasus Muslim Board (*Qafqaz Müsəlmanları İdarəsi*, QMİ, Mirzə Fətəli Str. № 7, Baku, AZ-1001, tel.: ++994 125945549, qmi@qafqazislam.com, www.qafqaislam.com.az/index/php). This organisation unites Sunni and Shi'i clergy. The head of the organisation is the *sheikh al-islam*, who is Shi'i, while his first deputy is a Sunni mufti.
- Shi'i community of Mashadi Dadash Mosque (*Məşədi Dadaş Məscidi*, Ağadadaş Qurbanov Str. № 37, Baku, tel.: ++994 125968298, http://ahlibeyt.az/). Under the leadership of Haji Shahin, this is the largest Shi'i community in the capital Baku. When the community was created in 2001, as a continuation of the *Ikmal* youth group (dismantled by a court decision in the same year), it was regarded as an independent community frequently critical of the Government's religious policies. However, since late 2012, there has been a rapprochement between the popular leader of this community, Haji Shahin, and the Government. In late 2014, he was appointed the representative of the *sheikh al-islam* in the Nasimi district of Baku.
- Salafi community of the Abu-Bakr Mosque (*Əbu-Bəkr Məscidi*, Ülvi Bünyadzadə Str. № 8, Baku, AZ-1008, tel.: ++994 552017270, www.abubakr-mescidi.com/modules/news/index_topic_id_1_storynum_20_start_20.html, http://selefxeber.az, www.islamevi.az). Under the leadership of Haji Qamet,

once the largest Muslim community in Azerbaijan, it has always been publicly loyal to the Government. The mosque was closed to the public in 2008 after a grenade attack during evening prayer killed three and injured 13, including the mosque's imam, Haji Qamet Suleimanov. In 2017 the head of the SCWRA announced their plans to reopen the mosque in 2018.[69] Haji Qamet still remains the most popular Salafi preacher in the country.

- Shi'i community of the ancient Juma Mosque in the Old City of Baku (*İçəri Şəhər Cümə Məscidi İcması*, http://deyerler.org). Under the leadership of Haji Ilgar, once the largest Shi'i community in Baku, it started declining after the arrest of Haji Ilgar in 2003, and the subsequent takeover of the mosque by the Government in 2004. The well-known leader of the community, Haji Ilgar, has always been critical of government policies. For a long time, he has also maintained strong ties with the secular opposition. However, it should be noted that since the above-discussed rapprochement between Shi'i communities and the Government, Haji Ilgar's critical approach to it has softened.
- Sunni Naqshbandi Community of the Aid for Youth Foundation (*Gəncliyə Yardım Fondu*, Jafarov Qardashlari Str. № 16 Baku, tel.: ++994 124923223, www.gyf.org.az//). This is the Azerbaijani branch of the Turkish Mahmud Hudai Foundation, led by the well-known Naqshbandi leader Osman Nuri Topbash. Until recently, the majority of the religious educational institutions in Azerbaijan belonged to this Foundation.

---

[69] http://musavat.com/news/mubariz-qurbanli-ziyalilarimiz-islama-qarsi-yox-xurafata-qarsi-mubarize-aparib_455665.html, accessed 25 January 2018.

Belarus

Hanna Vasilevich[1]

Introduction

Opened in November 2016, the Minsk Grand Mosque has become a centre of Muslim religious and cultural life in Belarus in 2017. 2017 was also marked by a series of celebrations devoted to the 620th anniversary of the settlement of the Tatar communities on the territory of today's Belarus.

Both Belarusian authorities and religious communities demonstrated their willingness to maintain interfaith dialogue and emphasised the tolerance of Belarusian society. Members of Muslim religious organisations and ethno-cultural communities were actively involved in cultural events both in Belarus and abroad. The anniversary of the Tatar settlement in Belarus and the history of this community throughout these years were substantially covered by Belarusian media outlets in 2017.

Public Debates

In 2017 the Minsk Grand Mosque became a centre of the religious, cultural and educational life for Muslims in Minsk. The year was also marked by the celebration of the 620th anniversary of Tatar settlement on the lands of today's Belarus, which included a series of events which took place in different cities and towns throughout the country. Members of Muslim communities and ethno-cultural organisation representing groups, for whom Islam forms a significant part of their identity and/or cultural heritage, actively participated in dialogue with the authorities. This was done through their participation in consultative bodies under the auspices of the state-appointed Commissioner for Religious and Ethnic Affairs, and other platforms.

There were some events that created public debate within the Muslim communities of Belarus, and demonstrated the determination of their religious leadership to emphasise the long-term embeddedness of the Tatar community in the ethno-religious landscape of Belarus. In early September 2017, a

---

[1] Hanna Vasilevich, PhD, is one of the founders and a board member of the International Centre for Ethnic and Linguistic Diversity Studies (Prague, Czech Republic). Her research interests cover minority issues, inter-ethnic relations and diaspora politics.

conflict erupted at the cemetery in the village of Dukorščyna (Červień district of the Minsk region). Sapar Kanapacki, chair of the Smilavičy Tatar community removed an Orthodox cross at the fresh grave of Maryia Kanapackaja, an Orthodox Christian, whose husband, a Tatar Muslim, wanted her to be buried in the Muslim part of the cemetery. Kanapacki saw the Orthodox cross as a provocation on the eve of the Kurban Bayram ('Id Al-Adha) celebration. The family of the deceased filed a complaint to the local police, which resulted in an administrative investigation. Sapar Kanapacki was told to pay compensation for the removed cross and an administrative fine.[2]

For the past 400 years, the cemetery has been historically seen as a Muslim burial place. However, in the 20th century not only Muslims, but also Christians were buried there. This was largely explained by a high number of mixed marriages in the area. A division of the cemetery into Muslim and non-Muslim parts is not very clear due to its legal status as a public cemetery administered by the local authorities. While the cemetery is divided into Muslim and Christian sections, this division is not always maintained as members of families with mixed religious backgrounds are sometimes buried next to each other regardless of their different religions. Thus, according to the local officials, the family of the deceased did not violate Belarusian legislation and religious traditions by placing a cross on her grave.[3] Both the Mufti of the Muslim Religious Association in Belarus (*муфтый Мусульманскага рэлігійнага аб'яднання ў Рэспубліцы Беларусь*), Abu-Bekir Shabanovich,[4] and the Mufti of the Spiritual Board of Muslims of Belarus (*муфтый Рэспубліканскага рэлігійнага аб'яднання Духоўнае ўпраўленне мусульман у Рэспубліцы Беларусь*), Ali Varanovich,[5] condemned Kanapacki's act, as his actions broke Belarusian laws and provoked incitement of hatred against Muslims in media comments. In addition, the former head of the local community and the imam were removed by the Muftiate and were temporarily replaced with a representative of the Muslim Religious Association. To prevent these conflicts in the future and to settle the situation, meetings with local Muslims were organised with the participation of local authorities.

During the meeting of the Muslim Religious Association in the Minsk Grand Mosque in January 2017, the issue of the participation of members of religious communities in the public life of their organisations was discussed.

---

2 https://www.sb.by/articles/neumestnye-emotsii.html; https://www.kp.by/daily/26768/3801340/, both accessed 31 January 2018.
3 https://krynica.info/ru/2017/11/18/v-smilovichakh-spilili-krest-kotoryjj-muzh-musulmanin-postavil-pravoslavnojj-zhene/, accessed 31 January 2018.
4 https://www.sb.by/articles/neumestnye-emotsii.html, accessed 31 January 2018.
5 http://islam.by/post/kommentarij-po-sobytiyam-v-smilovichakh, accessed 31 January 2018.

The representatives of the Muftiate emphasised that the low participation of the members of the Muslim Tatar community in public religious events might contribute to their gradual assimilation and the loss of their Islamic identity, as it was Islam that has historically allowed Tatars to maintain a distinct religio-cultural identity after the loss of their mother tongue.[6]

Transnational Links

Belarus' Muslim organisations were also actively involved in cooperation with Muslim communities and organisations abroad. For example, the commemoration events celebrating the 620th anniversary of Tatar settlement on the lands of today's Belarus were attended by guests from Muslim, Tatar and ethno-cultural organisations from Poland, Lithuania and Russia.[7] *Inter alia*, they represented the Union of Polish Tatars and the Spiritual Administration of Muslims of Dagestan. In July 2017, a delegation of Poland's Tatar minority visited Belarus. During the joint events, muftis representing both Belarusian and Polish communities emphasised that "Muslim Tatars of Belarus, Lithuania and Poland are one family", and called for closer cooperation.[8]

In April 2018, the Mufti of the Muslim Religious Association in Belarus, Abu-Bekir Shabanovich, attended the Crimean peninsula annexed by Russia to participate in a series of events at the conference "The educational activities of Ismail Gasprinsky and the Muslim world of Russia", in Bakhchysarai. His visit to the Crimea was most likely a violation of Ukrainian legislation on the status of the occupied peninsula, as Shabanovich entered Crimea via Russia. This information was reported by Said Ismagilov, Mufti of the Religious Administration of Muslims of Ukraine "Ummah", and caused outrage in Ukraine.[9] The Ukrainian Ministry of Foreign Affairs announced that it was going to check this information.[10] Belarusian sources, including those related to the Muslim Religious Association in Belarus, provided no information on the participation of Shabanovich at this event.

---

6   http://mechet.by/arch/2.pdf, accessed 31 January 2018.
7   http://mechet.by/arch/7.pdf, accessed 31 January 2018.
8   http://mechet.by/arch/5.pdf, accessed 31 January 2018.
9   http://qha.com.ua/ru/obschestvo/muftii-estonii-i-belarusi-samovolno-sezdili-v-krim/173658/, accessed 31 January 2018.
10 https://ru.krymr.com/a/news/28468198.html, accessed 31 January 2018.

Law and Domestic Politics

In Belarus, religion is separated from the State. This status is ensured by the Constitution, which also guarantees freedom of religion. It is the Constitution that, together with other specific legal instruments, regulates religious issues in Belarus. The main specific Law dealing with religious issues is the *Law on the Freedom of Conscience and Religious Organisations*, adopted in 1992 as amended.[11]

In its preamble, the Law declares Islam's (without specification to any of its denominations) inseparability from the common history of the people of Belarus, which make it one of the so-called "traditional" religions of Belarus. Nevertheless, Belarusian legislation imposes certain obligations onto all religious organisations acting on the territory of the country. First of all, such an organisation should be officially registered, and failure to comply with this norm is subject to criminal prosecution. Secondly, it should reach a minimum threshold of its members and its head must be a Belarusian citizen. Nevertheless, foreigners can serve as clergymen, provided they comply with the requirements (including the knowledge of Belarusian or the Russian language) imposed in the *Enactment on the Approval of the Rules of Residency of Foreign Citizens and Stateless Persons in the Republic of Belarus*,[12] and the *Regulation of the Procedure of Inviting Foreign Citizens and Stateless Persons to the Republic of Belarus with the Aim of Religious Activity*.[13] Foreign clergymen are typically subjects of thorough control by the Belarusian authorities, and their residency may be revoked or not extended at any time by the authorities.

Belarusian legislation also ensures access to services provided by clergymen for people in prisons and hospitals if they want them. However, as the *Belarus 2016 International Religious Freedom Report* demonstrates, access to Muslim

---

11   *Закон Республики Беларусь "О свободе совести и религиозных организациях"* (*Law on the Freedom of Conscience and Religious Organisations*), 17 December 1992, No. 2054-XII, http://etalonline.by/?type=text&regnum=v19202054, accessed 31 January 2018.

12   *Постановление Совета министров Республики Беларусь «Об утверждении правил пребывания иностранных граждан и лиц без гражданства в Республике Беларусь* (*Enactment on the Approval of the Rules of Residency of Foreign Citizens and Stateless Persons in the Republic of Belarus*), 20 January 2006, No. 73, http://pravo.by/document/?guid=3871&po=C20600073, accessed 31 January 2018.

13   *Положение о порядке приглашения иностранных граждан и лиц без гражданства в Республику Беларусь в целях занятия религиозной деятельностью* (*Regulation of the Procedure of Inviting Foreign Citizens and Stateless Persons to the Republic of Belarus with the Aim of Religious Activity*), 30 January 2008, No. 123, https://base.spinform.ru/show_doc.fwx?rgn=21337, accessed 31 January 2018.

clergy for prisoners may often be restricted by the prison authorities.[14] This trend can be seen in some years and places, therefore Muslim clergy are on an unequal footing compared to priests of the Orthodox or Roman Catholic Churches.[15]

Muslim community representatives held meetings within the framework of the Consultative Interfaith Council at the Commissioner for Religious and Ethnic Affairs. During these meetings, the problematic aspects of converting residential and non-residential premises to religious buildings, and the current legislation on the seizure and provision of land for the construction of religious buildings, were discussed.[16]

Activities and Initiatives of Main Muslim Organisations

The year 2017 was marked by the celebration of the 620th anniversary of Tatar settlement on the lands of today's Belarus. The first commemorative events took place in Navahrudak, the first capital of the former Grand Duchy of Lithuania. There, one of the three preserved historical mosques is located; the city is also home to the third-largest Muslim community in Belarus.[17]

The second wave of commemorative events was organised on 4 November 2017 in Iŭje, the town typically referred to as "the capital of Belarusian Tatars". The celebration was attended by the Ambassador of the Republic of Turkey, Kezban Nilvana Darama, and the Ambassador of Palestine, Khaled Arikat.[18] On the same day, the renovated mosque in Iŭje was reopened. The renovation works on the mosque were started by Belarusian Tatars, with financial support from the Turkish Presidency of Religious Affairs (*Diyanet İşleri Başkanlığı*). The final commemorative events took place in December 2017 in Minsk.[19]

Opened in November 2016, the Minsk Grand Mosque has become a centre of cultural, religious and educational life for the Muslim community in the Belarusian capital, hosting various events, meetings and courses. *Inter alia*, the Grand Mosque organises courses for children on the foundations of Islam, master classes on floristry, and events for children connected to Islamic holidays.

---

14   https://www.state.gov/documents/organization/269036.pdf, accessed 31 January 2018.
15   https://www.state.gov/documents/organization/269036.pdf, accessed 31 January 2018.
16   http://mechet.by/arch/7.pdf, accessed 31 January 2018.
17   http://mechet.by/arch/7.pdf, accessed 31 January 2018.
18   http://mechet.by/arch/7.pdf, accessed 31 January 2018.
19   http://mechet.by/arch/7.pdf, accessed 31 January 2018.

The community "Light of Islam" (*Свет Ислама*) in Minsk continued to offer classes on Islam for men and women. These classes include studying the Qur'an, Muslim ceremonies, the history of Islam and the Arabic language.[20]

Muslim Population: History and Demographics

The emergence of the first Muslim communities in Belarus dates back to the 14th–15th centuries. Thousands of Tatar families from the Crimea and the Golden Horde were admitted into the Grand Duchy of Lithuania as soldiers. The region of settlement of the Tatar community in the Grand Duchy of Lithuania primarily encompassed "an area [of today's Belarus and Lithuania] bounded in the north by Troki and Vilna, in the east by Minsk, in the south by Sluck and Slonim and in the west by Hrodna".[21] In the 16th century, there were 60 mosques which served the spiritual needs of around 40,000 Tatars in Belarus.[22] For their services to the State, members of the Tatar community were granted privileges, similar to those of the nobility at that time, and became an integral part of society, which, *inter alia*, included the right to interfaith marriages with Christians. Over the years, this community has linguistically assimilated, switching to Belarusian. Hence, it was only Islam that made this community distinct from other ethnic and religious groups in Belarus. Since the 17th century, and especially after the annexation of Belarus by the Russian Empire, the attitude towards Muslims began to deteriorate. It resulted in an outflow of significant numbers of Tatars to the Crimea and the Ottoman Empire; for instance, in the late 18th century there were approximately 30,000 Muslims in Belarus, while by the beginning of World War I only 14,000 Muslims resided in Belarus.[23]

The communist regime in Belarus in the 20th century was hostile to religious denominations, including Belarusian Muslims. Prior to World War II, there were 19 mosques in Belarus, while only the one in Iŭje remained open in the post-war period.[24] After the collapse of the Soviet Union, the population of Belarus of various backgrounds experienced a growing interest in their

---

20   http://islam.by/post/zanyatiya-po-izucheniyu-islama, accessed 31 January 2018.
21   Akiner, Shirin, *Religious Language of a Belarusian Tatar Kitab: a Cultural Monument of Islam in Europe: with a Latin-script Transliteration of the British Library Tatar Belarusian Kitab* (Wiesbaden: Harrasowitz, 2009), pp. 34–35.
22   Norris, Harry, *Islam in the Baltic: Europe's Early Muslim Community* (London: I.B. Tauris, 2009), p. 135.
23   http://tatarica.narod.ru/archive/09.2003/07_01.09.03.htm, accessed 31 January 2018.
24   Norris, *Islam in the Baltic,* n. 20, p. 135.

ethnic and religious roots. This resulted in the emergence of various religious and ethno-cultural associations, which united ethnic groups for whom Islam formed a significant part of their culture.

The most recent national population census took place in Belarus in 2009. However, religious affiliation has not been included in the set of questions during the censuses in the country. Therefore, the number of Muslims in the State can only be estimated through reference to the ethnicity statistics provided by the 2009 census. Nevertheless, the 2009 National Census results suggest that Belarus accommodates over 30 ethnic groups for whom Islam is an important part of their identity and/or cultural heritage. The number of people who declared their affiliation with these ethnic groups is up to 25,000, of a total population of approximately 9.5 million. As of 2017, the number of Muslims residing in Belarus is estimated to be as high as 35,000.[25]

The available statistics also fail to provide any breakdown of the population according to their citizenship or residency status in Belarus. However, as of 2012, there were 24,500 persons originated from Muslim majority countries residing in Belarus. The ratio between those persons from the former states of the USSR and other countries was 4:1. This situation remains largely unchanged, although the share of Belarus' residents originating from non-Soviet countries with a Muslim majority is growing.

According to the official statistics, there are 24 Sunni and one Shi'i religious organisation in Belarus. All of the Sunni organisations have emerged from the Belarusian Tatar community, which is the oldest in the country. The single Shi'i organisation is affiliated with the Azeri community. There are also ethno-cultural organisations of various ethnic groups whose members are adherents of Islam. Some of these organisations (*inter alia* Afghani, Azeri, Kazakh, Palestinian, Bashkir and Tatar) are represented in the Consultative Inter-Ethnic Council at the Commissioner for Religious and Ethnic Affairs, and in the Consultative Council at the Centre of National Cultures under the auspices of the Ministry of Culture.

---

25   http://www.belintourist.com/rus/welcome_to_belarus/excursions_on_belarus/musulman/, accessed 31 January 2018.

Muslim Population	24,400 (0.26% of total population based on the ethnicity statistics in the 2009 census). Other estimations suggest that the Muslim population of Belarus is as high as 35,000.
Ethnic/National Backgrounds	Largest ethnicities: Tatar: 7,316 Azeri: 5,567 Turkmen: 2,685 Uzbek: 1,593 Kazakh: 1,355 Arab: 1,330.
Inner-Islamic Groups	The majority of Muslims residing in Belarus belong to the Sunni branch of Islam. Being the oldest Muslim community of Belarus, the Tatars have historically been adherents of the Hanafi school. Shi'i Islam is observed by the Azeri and Iranian communities. Members of the Azeri community established the only Shi'i Muslim religious organisation in Belarus.
Geographical Spread	Over 80% is urban. Roughly one third of Muslims (approximately 10,000) reside in Minsk.[26]
Number of Mosques	Eight mosques:[27] Minsk, Iŭje, Navahrudak, Smilavičy, Loŭčycy, Slonim, Maladzie na, and Ašmiany. Five prayer houses: Brest, Homieĺ, Klieck, Mahilioŭ, Vidzy.
Muslim Burial Sites	At least eight: Iŭje, Loŭčycy, Karobčycy, Navahrudak, Slonim (all in Hrodna region), Novaja Myš (Brest region), Dukorščyna (Minsk region), Dokšycy (Viciebsk region).

---

26   https://www.kp.by/daily/26565.5/3581444/, accessed 31 January 2018.
27   https://www.holiday.by/blog/34266, accessed 31 January 2018.

"Chaplaincy" in State Institutions	Belarusian legislation guarantees religious freedom in prisons and hospitals. This includes access to pastoral care provided by religious clergy, literature and other religious services. Specific spaces for religious purposes should also be provided. Belarusian state institutions fail to ensure specific dietary needs of Muslims and other religious denominations.
Halal Products	Halal food is not widely available, although limited access to these products is available through online shops and some food markets (predominantly in Minsk). The Belarusian Centre for Halal Standardisation and Certification–BelHalal (www.halalbel.by) acts under the auspices of the Muslim Religious Association in the Republic of Belarus. It is authorised to provide halal certification for Belarusian products. According to the data available on its website, in 2017 seven certificates were issued to Belarusian food producers.
Dress Code	Belarusian laws do not prohibit the wearing of Muslim dress in public spaces. However, it is not a widespread phenomenon among Muslims in Belarus. At the same time, Belarusian legislation requires that all photos for official documents should be taken without a head scarf, based on the notion that belonging to a religious denomination cannot provide citizens with any advantages over other citizens. Thus, passport photos with a head scarf or any other headgear are not allowed.[28]
Places of Islamic Learning and Education	Muslim organisations offer informal weekend classes in the cities of Minsk, Hrodna and Homieĺ. Imams receive their education abroad, predominantly in Russia, although they must be citizens of Belarus.

---

28 https://krynica.info/ru/2016/10/20/pravozashhitniki-rekomenduyut-mvd-belarusi-razreshit-foto-na-pasport-v-khidzhabe/, accessed 31 January 2018.

Muslim Media and Publications

The magazine Life (*Жизнь*), is available online in a pdf version at the website www.mechet.by in the publications section. The magazine is published by the Muslim Religious Association in the Republic of Belarus. In 2017, seven issues were published.

The website of the Shi'i Muslim community in Belarus http://ahlalbayt.by is an independent educational interactive resource with the focus on Islam related issues.

The website of the Muslim Religious Community "Ahl al-Bayt" (*Мусульманская рэлігійная абшчына «Ахл аль-Бейт»*) is www.ahlibeyt.by.

The website of the Religious Association Spiritual Administration of Muslims in the Republic of Belarus (*Духоўнае ўпраўленне мусульман у Рэспублікы Беларусь*) is www.islam.by. This was the first Muslim portal in Belarus, founded in October 2003.

Main Muslim Organisations

Currently, there are 25 Muslim religious organisations in Belarus. 19 organisations (in Minsk, Smilavičy, Vidzy, Brest, Slonim, Uzda, Ašmiany, Lida, Astryna, Skidzieĺ, Uzda, Mahilioŭ, Orša, Hlybokaje, Dokšycy, and Miadzieĺ) are part of the Muslim Religious Association in the Republic of Belarus. Four Muslim organisations (in Homieĺ, Liachavičy, and Klieck) belong to the Spiritual Administration of Muslims of the Republic of Belarus. Only two organisations do not belong to either of these umbrella associations: the Azeri community of the city of Minsk, and the Muslim community of the city of Hrodna.

– Muslim Religious Association in the Republic of Belarus (*Мусульманскае рэлігійнае аб'яднанне ў Рэспублікы Беларусь*–MRO, vul. Hrybajedava 29, 220035 Minsk, tel.: ++375 173668197, email: mechet@tut.by, http://mechet.by). The head of the association is the Mufti Abu-Bekir Shabanovich. The MRO is registered as a national religious association, and is an umbrella organisation for 19 Muslim religious associations.
– Republican Religious Association Spiritual Administration of Muslims of the Republic of Belarus (*Рэспубліканскае рэлігійнае аб'яднанне Духоўнае*

ўпраўленне мусульман у Рэспублiцы Беларусь–DUM, vul. Šaranhoviča 7-366, 220018 Minsk, tel.: ++375 172006617, email: khuluq@mail.ru, http://www.islam.by/). It is headed by the Mufti Ali Varanovich. The DUM is registered as a national religious association, and is an umbrella organisation for four Muslim religious associations.
- Muslim religious organisation in Hrodna (vul. K. Marksa 9A, 230025 Hrodna, tel.: ++375 296545320).
- International Cultural and Educational Organisation Congress of Azerbaijani Communities (Мiжнароднае грамадскае аб'яднанне Кангрэс азербайджанскiх абшчын, pr. Mašerava 25, Minsk, tel.: ++375 172066900, email: natik-bagirov@rambler.ru).

Belgium

Jean-François Husson[1]

Introduction

Numerous important developments took place in Belgium in 2017. In the aftermath of the 2016 terrorist attacks on the Brussels' metro and airport, most of those regarding Church-State relations, at both the Federal and Regional level,[2] were driven by security concerns. These included issues surrounding financial support, the ending of the special agreement with the *Grande mosquée de Bruxelles* (Great Mosque of Brussels), and the occasion of the King of the Belgians attending an *iftar*. In line with this, specific measures were taken to counter what was considered Saudi and Turkish influence on Belgian Islam. In other public arenas, two out of three Belgian Regions decided to ban slaughter without prior stunning. Alongside this, the demand for Islamic related services (Islamic religious education, cemeteries, halal food) continued to expand in 2017.

Public Debates

The Parliamentary Inquiry Commission set up after the 2016 terrorist attacks in Brussels has now published all its reports,[3] one of which is dedicated to what

---

[1] Jean-François Husson is Coordinator of the *Observatoire des relations administratives entre les cultes, la laïcité organisée et l'Etat* (O.R.A.C.L.E.), an independent monitoring group on Church-State relations. He is a lecturer at the Université Catholique de Louvain, and a Research Associate at the University of Liège. He has been a member of various expert committees, and is the author of numerous reports for public institutions.

[2] In the areas covered by this chapter, the Federal Government is responsible for the recognition of denominations and the regulation of philosophical communities (i.e. Humanists and Buddhists), as well as chaplaincies in the military, in prisons, and in hospitals. The Flemish, Walloon, and Brussels Capital Regions have responsibility for regulating local religious communities, burials, and animal welfare. Flemish, French and German-speaking Communities are responsible for education (including religious education), young offenders, and the media. Provinces (except for the Brussels Capital Region) and municipalities supervise and finance recognised local religious communities, including recognised mosques, and implement regulations coming from the federal and regional authorities.

[3] A summary can be found at www.lachambre.be/kvvcr/pdf_sections/publications/attentats/Brochure_Attentats_Terroristes.pdf, accessed 30 March 2018.

it terms "Islamic radicalism". It mentions the influence of Salafis, the Muslim Brotherhood and foreign states as promoting radical views and/or ideas contrary to Belgian values, such as gender equality. It points to the importance of promoting moderate interpretations of Islam and of countering radical Islam, by providing financial and administrative support to run cultural activities and the screening of, and possible banning, of some organisations.[4] The Commission recommends the introduction of a central registry for all places of worship, and making it more attractive for mosques to be recognised by the *Exécutif des Musulmans de Belgique* (Executive of Muslims in Belgium–EMB), as such a recognition contributes to social cohesion and transparency (most notably concerning foreign funding).

Other recommendations aim at strengthening the Executive of Muslims in Belgium, creating new posts of imams recognised by the Belgian authorities, organising better training for imams, chaplains and teachers of Islamic religion, and looking at the creation of a "House of One", based on the Berlin model; a gathering of the three monotheistic religions in a single place. An important part of the report points to the Great Mosque of Brussels, affiliated to the Muslim World League, and considered an agent of Salafi ideas in Belgium. It occupies a building owned by the Belgian government, based on a 1969 agreement, and was considered in the 1970s as a provisional representative body for Muslims in Belgium, although it never applied for recognition as a mosque to the relevant authorities. The Parliamentary Commission recommended the revocation of the agreement,[5] and the transfer of the management of the mosque to the Executive of Muslims in Belgium.[6]

Other recommendations address radicalism in penitentiary institutions, through various measures including strengthened chaplaincy services in prisons. Other questions raised are the use of new technologies to promote hate messages, and the need to produce a counter discourse; the Commission links a lack of integration and radicalism, and supports the promotion of social and cultural diversity on the one hand, and a stricter screening of migrants, among

---

4 For opposing views, see http://plus.lesoir.be/119681/article/2017-10-17/est-ce-letat-de-dire-quel-est-le-bon-islam, accessed 3 April 2018.

5 The Great Mosque position was further weakened by its poor performance during hearings of the Parliamentary Commission, and some administrative negligence regarding legal regulations. See, for instance: www.lalibre.be/actu/belgique/la-grande-mosquee-ne-dit-pas-tout-58c99473cd705cd98df62dfb and www.lecho.be/dossier/terrorisme/Les-comptes-du-Centre-islamique-et-culturel-de-Belgique-toujours-aussi-flous/9873493, both accessed 3 April 2018.

6 This move is considered to be a sign of growing Islamophobia in the European Report on Islamophobia 2017, see: www.islamophobiaeurope.com/wp-content/uploads/2018/04/Belgium.pdf, accessed 3 April 2018.

them refugees, on the other. Towards the end of the report, the role of culture and employment as integration facilitators, the need to counter radicalism in schools (notably through teacher education) and boroughs (through local police and social workers) are also mentioned.

Regarding counter-terrorism operations, the alert level in Belgium stayed stable at level three, despite isolated terrorist attacks in 2017. The presence of the army in Brussels has been maintained, as well as the so-called "plan canal",[7] which includes screening all associations in some Brussels boroughs, including mosques[8]. Particular attention was also paid to foreign fighters returning from Iraq or Syria.[9]

Tension and hate speech towards minority groups, most notably Shi'is[10] and Jews,[11] continued. Measures were taken against some imams considered radical or a risk to public order. The residence permit of the main imam of the Great Mosque of Brussels was not renewed, his speeches being considered favourable to radicalism.[12] The Muslim Executive suspended an auxiliary imam in Leuven after he had given a sermon in which he gave permission to beating one's wife.[13] The imam of a Somali Verviers-based mosque–who was ordered to leave Belgian territory in July 2015 on the grounds of having delivered hate speeches–appealed against the order to leave Belgian territory while his son was detained in a young offenders institution for hate speech.[14] Imams hoping

---

7   The plan was originally concentrated on Molenbeek and Vilvoorde. It has since been extended to other boroughs of the Brussels Capital Region. See Husson, Jean-François, "Belgium", in Oliver Scharbrodt, Samin Akgönül, Ahmet Alibašić, Jørgen S. Nielsen and Egdūnas Račius (eds.), *Yearbook of Muslims in Europe*, vol. 9 (Leiden: Brill, 2018), pp. 98–120.

8   The scope was quite wide, as, for example, Evangelical churches were among those organisations included.

9   http://plus.lesoir.be/96658/article/2017-05-29/121-returnees-etaient-presents-en-belgique-en-avril-dont-44-en-prison, accessed 30 March 2018.

10 www.dhnet.be/actu/belgique/les-chiites-de-belgique-vivent-dans-la-peur-594d6a61cd70e30bb28053cd, accessed 30 March 2018.

11 www.antisemitisme.be/fr/archives-incidents_fr/2017/ and www.lavenir.net/cnt/dmf20170307_00970564/la-cellule-de-veille-antisemite-relancee, both accessed 3 April 2018.

12 www.rtbf.be/info/belgique/detail_renvoi-de-l-imam-de-la-grande-mosquee-de-bruxelles-il-aurait-du-etre-entendu-clame-son-avocat?id=9745431, accessed 30 March 2017.

13 www.embnet.be/fr/le-president-de-lemb-suspend-limam-auxiliaire-dune-mosquee-de-louvain, accessed 3 April 2018.

14 www.7sur7.be/7s7/fr/1502/Belgique/article/detail/3094746/2017/03/02/Le-fils-de-l-imam-radical-de-Dison-place-en-IPPJ-trois-mois-de-plus.dhtml, accessed 30 March 2018.

to preach in (mainly Turkish) non-recognised mosques, saw their visa applications turned down by the under-minister for immigration.[15]

In previous years, several anti-radicalisation initiatives were taken at different levels of Government. Among these were the *Centre d'aide et de prise en charge des personnes concernées par le radicalisme violent* (Centre for Assistance and Care for People Affected by Violent Radicalism–CAPREV, a hotline for the French-speaking community),[16] the Walloon plan *Prévention de la radicalisation violente* (Prevention of violent radicalisation),[17] and the Flemish plan *Actieplan radicalisering* (Action plan for radicalisation).[18]

As for Islamophobia, references on websites such as *Unia*[19] and the Muslim-organisation *Collectif contre l'islamophobie en Belgique* (Collective against Islamophobia in Belgium–CCIB),[20] appear to have decreased compared to the period immediately after the 2016 attacks. The European Report on Islamophobia 2017 reports fewer Islamophobic verbal or physical attacks, but states there is growing Islamophobia in the media and within some political discourses.[21] Others have argued that criticism of Islam was regularly denounced as Islamophobia, while criticising other religions was seen as legitimate.[22] As a deliberate symbolic gesture, King Philippe of the Belgians celebrated the end of Ramadan with a Muslim family.[23]

---

15   www.7sur7.be/7s7/fr/1502/Belgique/article/detail/3094746/2017/03/02/Le-fils-de-l-imam-radical-de-Dison-place-en-IPPJ-trois-mois-de-plus.dhtml, accessed 30 March 2018.

16   It had received 237 calls in the first months of 2017, see: Parlement de la Communauté française, *Compte rendu intégral*, n° 19, 5 juillet 2017, pp. 9–11, http://archive.pfwb.be/10000000206bodo, accessed 2 April 2018.

17   www.wallonie.be/fr/actualites/2-millions-eu-pour-la-lutte-contre-le-radicalisme, accessed 2 April 2018.

18   https://onderwijs.vlaanderen.be/nl/vlaams-beleid-actieplan-radicalisering, accessed 2 April 2018.

19   *Unia* is the interfederal centre for equal opportunities: www.unia.be/fr/articles/condamnation-de-ladministrateur-de-la-page-facebook-de-la-ligue-de-defense-flamande-vlaamse-verdedigings-liga, accessed 30 March 2018.

20   http://ccib-ctib.be, accessed 28 April 2018.

21   www.islamophobiaeurope.com/wp-content/uploads/2018/04/EIR_2017.pdf, accessed 3 April 2018.

22   See, for instance, www.lecho.be/opinions/analyse/Jeannette-Bougrab-Les-gens-n-osent-pas-critiquer-l-islam-de-peur-d-etre-traites-d-islamophobes/9940692, accessed 3 April 2018.

23   www.rtl.be/info/belgique/famille-royale/le-roi-philippe-rompt-le-jeune-avec-une-famille-musulmane-photos--926343.aspx, accessed 30 March 2018.

In May 2017, the Federal Government adopted a memorandum of understanding aimed at stimulating dialogue between civil authorities, representative bodies of recognised religions, and non-confessional philosophical organisations; all stakeholders signed a declaration on the need for an ongoing dialogue to build a society that guarantees "our core values".[24] In the Flemish Region, the body for a permanent dialogue between life stance associations and regional authorities adopted a charter that was signed, among others, by the Executive of Muslims in Belgium.[25] Representatives of all major religions gathered in Brussels on 22 March to pay tribute to the victims of the terror attacks of 22 March 2016.[26]

From September 2017 to January 2018 the exhibition *L'Islam, c'est aussi notre histoire* (Islam, it's also our history) ran in Brussels,[27] which drew a large audience as well as official visits, including from Muslim chaplains and the Executive of Muslims.

Transnational Links

Despite a large proportion of Muslims in Belgium holding Belgian citizenship, links to countries of origin typically remain strong, especially among Muslims of Moroccan or Turkish descent. As every year, the Moroccan King Hassan II Foundation, sends several dozen imams and other clerics (67 in 2017[28]) to Belgium during Ramadan to support permanent Belgian imams during this busy time. Divisions among the Moroccan community mean they have far less influence than their Turkish counterparts, which are, in contrast, very well-organised through the Turkish Presidency of Religious Affairs (*Diyanet İşleri Başkanlığı*). The main umbrella organisation for Moroccan mosques in Belgium is the *Rassemblement des Musulmans de Belgique* (Union of Muslims in Belgium–RMB), which receives support from Morocco, including symbolic support through the attendance of the Ambassador of Morocco at its main

---

24 http://premier.fgov.be/fr/transcender-la-polarisation-en-rassemblant-les-diff%C3% A9rentes-religions-et-convictions-philosophiques, accessed 2 April 2018.

25 www.kerknet.be/kerknet-redactie/nieuws/permanente-dialoog-tussen-vlaamse-overheid-en-levensbeschouwingen and www.embnet.be/nl/het-emb-ondertekent-charter-voor-interlevensbeschouwelijke-dialoog, both accessed 2 April 2018.

26 www.rtbf.be/info/belgique/detail_attentats-du-22-mars-suivez-en-direct-les-ceremonies-d-hommages-et-les-commemorations?id=9560414, accessed 3 April 2018.

27 http://expo-islam.be/, accessed 3 April 2018.

28 www.bladi.net/maroc-envoi-imam-belgique,48327.html, accessed 30 March 2018.

events, such as its annual *iftar*. Its president, Salah Echallaoui, has been the president of the Muslim Executive since February 2016.

The situation is different in Turkish mosques funded and supported by the Belgian-based branch of the Turkish Presidency of Religious Affairs (*Belçika Diyanet Vakfı*). Turkish officials are present at mosque openings and, when officially recognised, these mosques prefer to employ imams sent by the Diyanet (who usually hold four-year tenures), instead of imams who receive their salaries from the Belgian authorities. Their theological training is not questioned, while their knowledge of Belgian languages and customs is. The Diyanet tries to address this problem by providing imam training in Turkey to young Belgian and French Muslims of Turkish background. It has also been reported that the Diyanet's imams acted as informants for the Turkish authorities after the failed coup attempt in Turkey on 15 July 2016, gathering information on suspected supporters of the Gülen movement in Belgium.[29] There were eruptions of tension and violence between various Turkish groups in Belgium in the aftermath of this coup attempt, and in the context of the presidential referendum of April 2017.[30] These clashes took place between AKP supporters and Kurdish[31] and Gülen organisations.

Law and Domestic Politics

The system of Belgian Church-State relations is based on the recognition of religious denominations and philosophical organisations.[32] Some important legislative changes took place in 2017. The royal decree of 15 February 2016[33] in-

---

29 www.levif.be/actualite/belgique/mosquees-turques-chargees-d-espionner-en-belgique-les-adeptes-de-gulen-cites-dans-le-rapport-belge-de-la-diyanet/article-normal-586709.html, www.demorgen.be/binnenland/turkse-imams-spioneerden-wel-degelijk-in-belgie-b6e8591b/ and http://plus.lesoir.be/archive/recup/1472790/article/actualite/belgique/2017-03-31/turquie-utilise-ses-imams-pour-espionner-partisans-guelen-en-belgique, all accessed 2 April 2018.

30 www.levif.be/actualite/belgique/tension-au-sein-de-la-diaspora-turque-en-belgique/article-normal-639297.html, accessed 2 April 2018.

31 www.rtbf.be/info/belgique/detail_des-kurdes-sont-victimes-d-une-bagarre-a-anvers?id=9748811, accessed 2 April 2018.

32 For a detailed presentation of the system, see Husson, Jean-François, "Belgium", in Oliver Scharbrodt, Samin Akgönül, Ahmet Alibašić, Jørgen S. Nielsen and Egdūnas Račius (eds.), *Yearbook of Muslims in Europe*, vol. 7 (Leiden: Brill, 2016), pp. 95–98.

33 *Arrêté royal du 15 février 2016 portant reconnaissance de l'Exécutif des Musulmans de Belgique*, www.etaamb.be/fr/arrete-royal-du-15-fevrier-2016_n2016009089.html, accessed 20 May 2017.

troduced profound changes to the Muslim Executive.[34] This was challenged in an administrative court, notably by the former president of the Executive, the Diyanet, the *Fédération islamique de Belgique* (Islamic Federation of Belgium) and two mosque unions.[35] As a result, some changes were brought in through another royal decree of 18 April 2017.[36] The latter explicitly enlarges the competences of the Executive to all mosques that are part of it, not only to those recognised by the public authorities.[37] It also details the mission of the Executive, including the training of Muslim clerics.

The Muslim Executive announced its intention to have female preachers; the Minister of Justice declared its support for such a move,[38] an important point in a system where the salaries of religious ministers, including imams, are paid by the State.

As in previous years,[39] the debate over the inclusion of a French-style principle of *laïcité* into the Constitution lingered on. There were a few debates on this,[40] and a proposal to change the Constitution from two MPs who were formerly part of the Flemish nationalist party, the NVA.[41]

If the primary objective of religious leaders' training programmes is to enhance the quality of religious and moral pastoral care to their congregations, such programmes have also been considered useful components of anti-radicalisation policies. This assumes that a properly trained imam is better equipped to counter radical speeches and attitudes.[42] Programmes on Islam

---

34   Husson, "Belgium", *Yearbook of Muslims in Europe*, vol. 9 (2018), p. 104.
35   http://plus.lesoir.be/37873/article/2016-04-28/pourquoi-lislam-turc-conteste-lislam-belge, accessed 10 May 2017.
36   *Arrêté royal du 18 avril 2017 portant modification de l'arrêté royal du 15 février 2016 portant reconnaissance de l'Exécutif des Musulmans de Belgique*, www.etaamb.be/fr/arrete-royal-du-18-avril-2017_n2017040121.html, accessed 2 April 2018.
37   Recognition is a two-level process: a religious community has to be recognised at a federal level and, in a second phase, its representative body may propose local communities for recognition to regional authorities. As a result, non-recognised local communities exist within most of the recognised religious communities, either by choice or because the procedure is pending.
38   www.koengeens.be/fr/news/2017/06/17/l-executif-des-musulmans-veut-creer-une-fonction-de-predicatrice, accessed 3 April 2018.
39   Husson, "Belgium", *Yearbook of Muslims in Europe*, vol. 9 (2018), pp. 104–105.
40   Such as www.entreleslignes.be/agenda/faut-il-inscrire-la-la%C3%AFcit%C3%A9-dans-la-constitution-belge or www.kerknet.be/kerknet-redactie/artikel/waarom-je-het-begrip-la%C3%AFcit%C3%A9-echt-niet-de-grondwet-wil, both accessed 2 April 2018.
41   www.lachambre.be/kvvcr/showpage.cfm?section=/flwb&language=fr&cfm=/site/www cfm/flwb/flwbn.cfm?lang=F&legislat=54&dossierID=2778, accessed 2 April 2018.
42   Husson, Jean-François, and Jérémy Mandin, *Etude de faisabilité en vue de la création d'un institut public d'étude de l'Islam* (Liège: CEDEM-Université de Liège, 2014), https://orbi.uliege.be/handle/2268/184049, accessed 1 April 2018.

within higher education in the Flemish Community[43] have developed with a Master's programme in Islamic Theology and Religious Studies at the KU Leuven.[44] As a result of research carried out in 2014,[45] and a commission's report the following year,[46] the *Institut de promotion des formations sur l'islam* (Institute for the Promotion of Training on Islam, established by the French-speaking Community Decree of 14 December 2016[47]) was formally set up in 2017.[48] The long term goal is to organise a Master's degree in Islamic theology, and in the short term it finances other training organised by various universities. In early 2016, a certificate in Islamic religious education was introduced by the *Université Catholique de Louvain* (Catholic University of Louvain);[49] the first graduates received their diplomas at the end of 2017.[50]

Islamic broadcasting on Flemish public radio and television had been stopped on 31 December 2015; it was decided in 2017 that Muslim programmes would be aired during two Islamic religious holidays on TV per year.[51] A project on the French-speaking side has not yet been implemented; once in place, it should have a wider remit than just broadcasting programmes on specific Islamic holidays.

Despite announcements made in 2014,[52] there was no federal or regional legislation to ban the wearing of religious symbols by public servants providing frontline services.[53] Therefore, in March 2017, in a question referred for a preliminary ruling by the Belgian Court of Cassation (case of *S. Achbita / G4S*

---

43 Husson, "Belgium", *Yearbook of Muslims in Europe*, vol. 7 (2016), pp. 101–102.
44 https://theo.kuleuven.be/islam-studeren, accessed 2 April 2018.
45 Husson and Mandin, *Etude de faisabilité*.
46 Rea, Andrea, Françoise Tulkens, Radouane Attiya, and Brigitte Maréchal, *Rapport de la commission concernant la formation des cadres musulmans et les émissions concédées* (Brussels: Université Catholique de Louvain, 2015), www.uclouvain.be/cps/ucl/doc/cismoc/documents/Rapport_final_commission_Marcourt(1).pdf, accessed 1 March 2016.
47 www.gallilex.cfwb.be/document/pdf/43481_000.pdf, accessed 2 April 2018.
48 www.ares-ac.be/fr/actualites/358-l-institut-de-promotion-des-formations-sur-l-islam-est-lance, accessed 2 April 2018.
49 http://uclouvain.be/fr/etudier/iufc/didactique-du-cours-de-religion-islamique.html, accessed 2 April 2018.
50 https://uclouvain.be/fr/decouvrir/actualites/cder-islam-les-premiers-diplomes.html, accessed 2 April 2018.
51 www.vrt.be/vrtnws/nl/2017/11/30/vrt-gaat-islamitische-erediensten-uitzenden-op-een/, accessed 2 April 2018.
52 Husson, "Belgium", *Yearbook of Muslims in Europe*, vol. 7 (2016), pp. 99–100.
53 www.premier.be/sites/default/files/articles/Accord_de_Gouvernement_-_Regeerakkoord.pdf, accessed 9 July 2015.

Secure Solutions),[54] the Court of Justice of the European Union validated the right for the company to establish a policy of neutrality, requiring staff not to wear religious, philosophical or political signs if certain conditions are met. The Belgian League of Human Rights published an analysis of the head scarf ban, which considered it too excessive, while the leader of the MR parliamentary group (right-wing liberals) restated that civil servants should be "neutral", implying a ban on all religious signs.[55] Conversely, in September 2017, the Public Social Assistance Centre of Leuven allowed the wearing of the head scarf for its employees and civil servants.[56]

After the problems experienced in previous years, the Brussels Capital Region decided not to provide specific venues for animal slaughter for 'Id al-Adha in 2017; it was left to individual families to find a solution; there was little or no controversy made of this in the media. There were similar decisions made in other Regions, sometimes with the support of the Muslim Executive and/or municipalities.[57] New legislation regarding animal slaughter was also introduced in 2017. In Flanders, 'Id al-Adha had led to tensions between political parties.[58] After a report from an ombudsman, the Government decided in March to forbid slaughter without prior stunning by 2019.[59] In May 2017, the Walloon parliament almost unanimously approved a new Law banning slaughter without prior stunning, to be fully implemented for all ritual slaughter by 1 September 2019.[60] These new Laws will be challenged before the Constitutional Court by both Jewish and Muslim[61] organisations,[62] some of which had been

---

54 C-157/15. See: http://curia.europa.eu/juris/document/document.jsf?text=&docid=188852&pageIndex=0&doclang=EN&mode=lst&dir=&occ=first&part=1&cid=253844, accessed 2 April 2018.
55 http://plus.lesoir.be/105883/article/2017-07-23/quand-les-interdictions-du-port-du-voile-sont-illegales, accessed 3 April 2018.
56 www.hln.be/nieuws/binnenland/ocmw-van-leuven-laat-hoofddoek-toe-in-alle-functies~a44828fa/, accessed 3 April 2018.
57 www.embnet.be/fr/communique-mesures-relatives-la-fete-du-sacrifice-dans-les-trois-regions, accessed 3 April 2018.
58 Bombaerts, Jean-Paul, "L'abattage rituel déchaîne les passions en Flandre", *L'Echo*, 9 September 2017, p. 8.
59 www.7sur7.be/7s7/fr/2625/Planete/article/detail/3117095/2017/03/29/L-abattage-sans-etourdissement-interdit-en-Flandre-en-2019.dhtml, accessed 2 April 2018.
60 www.rtbf.be/info/belgique/detail_le-parlement-wallon-adopte-l-interdiction-de-l-abattage-d-animaux-non-etourdis?id=9608502, accessed 2 April 2018.
61 Press release from the Muslim Executive: www.embnet.be/fr/la-communaute-musulmane-poursuit-la-lutte-contre-linterdiction-generale-dabattage-rituel-sans, accessed 2 April 2018.
62 http://plus.lesoir.be/130574/article/2017-12-21/les-decrets-interdisant-labattage-rituel-pourraient-ils-etre-annules, accessed 2 April 2018.

very vocal before the parliamentary votes. Jewish and Muslim communities received support from Christian denominations on this matter, advocating freedom of religion.[63] The Brussels Capital Region still allows slaughter without prior stunning for religious rituals in registered slaughter houses.

Activities and Initiatives of Main Muslim Organisations

All places of worship are free to choose a legal status based on the *Law on Associations*.[64] Alternatively, representative bodies (such as the Muslim Executive) can propose their own recognition of a place of worship to the Region in which they are based (each has its own criteria). In this latter case, the place of worship can benefit from one to three clerics paid by the Federal Government, while part of its running costs and some works to the building are funded by the local government.[65] In the past, mosques in Flanders and the Brussels Capital Region were recognised on a case-by-case basis, with 28 and 14 mosques officially recognised in this way at the beginning of 2017, respectively. Wallonia decided to recognise an initial group of 43 mosques in 2006; since then, four have lost their recognition due to administrative problems, while no further recognition has been granted since then. As the Federal Department of Justice has to give an opinion to the Regions, on security grounds, for any place of worship applying for recognition, a ministerial instruction from September 2017 details the procedure that needs to be followed to gain such recognition.[66]

Contrary to what was thought,[67] such recognition processes have not accelerated in the context of anti-radicalisation plans; in fact, no new mosques have been "recognised", except for three in the Brussels Capital Region in July: Mouhsinin (Saint-Gilles), Al Inaba (Berchem-Sainte-Agathe) and Arrayane (Never-Over-Heembeek).[68] Allegations that Turkish imams spied for the

---

63 www.lalibre.be/actu/belgique/abattage-sans-etourdissement-les-cultes-chretiens-plaident-pour-la-liberte-religieuse-5914b6e5cd70022542c420eb, accessed 3 April 2018.

64 *Loi du 27 juin 1921 sur les associations sans but lucratif, les fondations, les partis politiques européens et les fondations politiques européennes*: www.ejustice.just.fgov.be/cgi_loi/change_lg.pl?language=fr&la=F&table_name=loi&cn=1921062701, accessed 3 April 2018.

65 The system first set up for Catholic, Protestant, and Jewish denominations under Napoléon, has been maintained and extended to include other recognised religions and Humanists. See Husson, "Belgium", *Yearbook of Muslims in Europe*, vol. 7 (2016), pp. 95–98.

66 www.lalibre.be/actu/politique-belge/huit-services-desormais-impliques-dans-le-screening-des-mosquees-59cd396bcd70461d26539fbb, accessed 3 April 2018.

67 Husson, "Belgium", *Yearbook of Muslims in Belgium*, vol. 9 (2018), p. 107.

68 www.islamic-events.be/2017/08/mosquees-reconnues-bruxelles-2017/, accessed 3 April 2018.

Turkish government, led the Flemish Minister to terminate the recognition of the Diyanet Fatih mosque in Beringen, one of the largest in Belgium.[69] She also announced that the recognition criteria would be tightened,[70] as such criteria are supposed to prevent the import of foreign conflicts into Belgium;[71] all pending recognitions were suspended until November 2018.[72] This decision prompted a critical reaction from the Muslim Executive.[73]

The Walloon Region adopted new legislation that listed all the formalities required for the official recognition of places of worship, including their termination, merger etc. Three recognition criteria were established: an adequate building; an adequate legal status; and the absence of activities in contravention with the European Convention on Human Rights or Belgian legislation. A registering phase is a new condition before formal recognition, with the consequence of a delay of all applications already submitted. This general trend[74] to tighten recognition criteria contradicts the announced objective of the process, which was originally meant to have as many mosques as possible officially recognised.

The construction of a new large Fatih mosque in Ghent, with a planned area of 2,500 square metres and two minarets,[75] was opposed by the Flemish nationalist party, the NVA.[76] Another construction is planned in De Leunen (Geel).[77] Works are also to go ahead at another large mosque, the El Houda mosque in Sint-Niklaas.[78] In Norderlaan, Antwerp, the far right party *Vlaams*

---

69 www.rtbf.be/info/belgique/detail_liesbeth-homans-retire-la-reconnaissance-de-la-mosquee-turque-de-beringen?id=9650028 and http://deredactie.be/cm/vrtnieuws/regio/limburg/1.3015275, both accessed 2 April 2018.

70 www.rtbf.be/info/belgique/detail_liesbeth-homans-n-va-veut-durcir-les-criteres-de-reconnaissance-des-mosquees-en-flandre?id=9528274, accessed 2 April 2018.

71 www.n-va.be/nieuws/polarisatie-en-import-buitenlandse-conflicten-in-strijd-met-vlaamse-erkenningscriteria, accessed 2 April 2018.

72 www.knack.be/nieuws/belgie/homans-zal-geen-moskeeen-erkennen-voor-november-2018/article-normal-906621.html, accessed 2 April 2018.

73 www.embnet.be/sites/default/files/communique_de_presse_-_polemique_reconnaissance_mosquees_region_flamande_140217.pdf, accessed 3 April 2018.

74 The Brussels Capital Region also plans new legislation. The (then) Mayor of Brussels proposed new institutions for managing mosques in March 2017, apparently ignoring a regional decree regulating that field: www.lecho.be/opinions/carte-blanche/des-fabriques-de-mosquee-a-bruxelles/9878703.html, accessed 3 April 2018.

75 www.hln.be/nieuws/binnenland/gent-krijgt-grootste-moskee-van-vlaanderen-2-500-m-en-twee-minaretten~a93e6594/, accessed 2 April 2018.

76 www.standaard.be/cnt/dmf20171023_03148247, accessed 2 April 2018.

77 www.gva.be/cnt/dmf20170905_03055421/nieuwe-moskee-op-de-leunen, accessed 2 April 2018.

78 www.tvoost.be/nieuws/exclusieve-inkijk-in-nieuwe-el-houda-moskee-in-sint-niklaas-42968, accessed 2 April 2018.

Belang continued to mobilise against a planned mosque.[79] In the South of the country, a planned mosque in Glain would become the largest in Wallonia; the local Muslim community stressed the solely domestic sources for its funding.[80] A project in Fléron faced some difficulties with local residents and with planning permission.[81] In Liège, the Markaz Attawhid mosque gave up its legal challenge against the municipal decision to shut it down for security reasons.[82]

Public schools (those run by the Flemish, French and German-speaking Communities, or local authorities), organise courses on all recognised religions, as well as courses on non-confessional moral education. In the Flemish and German-speaking Communities, these classes constitute two lessons a week, with exemptions allowed. The possibility of offering such classes in Catholic schools was proposed again in 2017.[83] In the French Community, a one hour lesson on philosophy and citizenship is compulsory, while pupils or their parents have to choose between a second lesson on these topics or a religious or humanist course. Attendance for Islamic religious education classes is also on the rise.

The Brussels Muslim Fair (*Foire Musulmane de Bruxelles*), organised yearly since 2012, was not held in 2017, with the organisers complaining of commercial problems, their Facebook page promoting the Paris Fair instead;[84] it should resume in 2018.[85] Muslim Expo, launched by Emdeo in 2012,[86] was organised for the fourth time in Antwerp on 13–14 May 2017 under a new name: *Medina Expo*. Its counterpart in Charleroi did not see a second edition in 2017.[87]

---

79 https://re-act.be/2017/02/22/300-mensen-met-vlaams-belang-op-straat-tegen-nieuwe-extremistische-moskee-van-850-000-euro-in-antwerpse-wijk-luchtbal/, accessed 2 April 2018.
80 www.lalibre.be/regions/liege/glain-une-mosquee-avec-de-l-argent-clean-59de7574cd70461d268e19d7, accessed 2 April 2018.
81 www.rtbf.be/info/regions/liege/detail_une-etude-sur-la-polemique-generee-par-le-projet-de-mosquee-a-retinne?id=9777958, accessed 2 April 2018.
82 www.rtbf.be/info/regions/liege/detail_la-mosquee-markaz-attawhid-retire-son-recours-contre-l-arrete-de-fermeture?id=9530035, accessed 2 April 2018.
83 www.hln.be/hln/nl/1265/Onderwijs/article/detail/2694974/2016/05/04/Revolutie-in-katholiek-onderwijs-lessen-islam-en-hoofddoeken-welkom.dhtml, accessed 10 May 2017.
84 www.facebook.com/foiremusulmanedebruxelles/, accessed 1 April 2018.
85 www.nsalons.com/foire-musulmane-bruxelles/, accessed 1 April 2018.
86 Website not updated anymore. See Facebook page: www.facebook.com/medinaexpo.be/, accessed 2 April 2018.
87 See Husson, "Belgium", *Yearbook of Muslims in Europe*, vol. 9 (2018) p. 110.

Muslim Population: History and Demographics

As Belgium did not own colonies with a significant Muslim population, the presence of Muslims in Belgium remained marginal, until the signing of labour agreements with some Muslim majority countries in 1964, notably Turkey and Morocco. Estimating religious affiliations is difficult in the absence of a census or the registration of religious or philosophical affiliations; there are only estimates, surveys and "proxies", such as consistent religious education attendance. The issue is also very sensitive when dealing with Islam. On the one hand, there is a general overestimation of numbers, as illustrated by a video from the think tank *Ceci n'est pas une crise*,[88] and by a 2015 Ipsos survey[89] that showed that the number of Muslims in Belgium was estimated to be 29% of the population, 23 points higher than it actually was at the time. On the other hand, some consider that producing such statistics may contribute to a sense of a "Muslim invasion", especially when used in controversial press coverage. Therefore, attempts to put forward some estimates lead to fiery debates among academics, centred on the methodology behind, and the press coverage of, such data.[90]

---

[88] www.cecinestpasunecrise.org/pourcentage-de-musulmans-belgique-stop-aux-prejuges/, accessed 30 March 2018.

[89] www.ipsos-mori.com/researchpublications/researcharchive/3466/Perceptions-are-not-reality-Things-the-world-gets-wrong.aspx, accessed 30 June 2015. The Pew Research Center therefore raised the question about the choice of interviewees, www.pewresearch.org/fact-tank/2015/11/17/5-facts-about-the-muslim-population-in-europe, accessed 5 March 2016.

[90] For a summary, see Husson, "Belgium", *Yearbook of Muslims in Europe*, vol. 7 (2016), p. 106. For more views, see El Battiui, Mohamed, Meryem Kanmaz and Firouzeh Nahavandi (eds.), *Mosquées, imams et professeurs de religion islamique en Belgique: état de la question et enjeux* (Brussels: Fondation Roi Baudouin, 2004), pp. 7–8, www.kbs-frb.be/~/media/Files/Bib/Publications/Older/PUB-1448-Mosquees-imams-prof-islam.pdf, accessed 2 April 2018; Dassetto, Felice, *L'iris et le croissant: Bruxelles et l'islam au défi de la co-inclusion* (Louvain-la-Neuve: Presses universitaires de Louvain, 2011), pp. 21–26, Fadil, Nadia, "Belgium", in Jørgen S. Nielsen, Samim Akönül, Ahmet Alibašić and Egdūnas Račius (eds.), *Yearbook of Muslims in Europe*, vol. 6 (Leiden: Brill, 2014), pp. 84–107 (84–85), Husson, Jean-François, "Le financement des cultes, de la laïcité et des cours philosophiques", *Courrier hebdomadaire du Centre de recherche et d'information socio-politiques*, n° 1703–1704 (2000), pp. 3–90 (84–89); see also http://unia.be/fr/articles/781887-musulmans-en-belgique, www.o-re-la.org/index.php/analyses/item/2183-combien-de-musulmans-en-belgique and www.cecinestpasunecrise.org/pourcentage-de-musulmans-belgique-stop-aux-pre juges/, all accessed 30 March 2018.

Detailed estimates are regularly produced by Jan Hertogen,[91] based on countries of origin.[92] His estimates for 2017 were 859,223 Muslims, or 7.6% of the population; this is up from 6.3% in 2011, 6.5% in 2013 and 7.0% in 2015.[93] This appears in line with data that looks at the attendance of Islamic religious education classes: 62,994 pupils out of 896,273[94] (7.0% vs 6.3% in 2014–15) attended Islamic religious classes in the Flemish Community in 2016–17, as did 9.4% of pupils in the French Community in 2015–16 (up from 5.0% in 1996–97).[95] These are lower estimates as Muslim pupils attending Catholic schools (especially for secondary education) are not considered.[96] All indicators show a regular increase in both the number and percentage of the Muslim

---

91 Mainly, Hertogen, Jan, "Moslims in België van 6.3% naar 6.5% van de Bevolking", 8 October 2014, www.dewereldmorgen.be/blog/janhertogen/2014/10/08/moslims-in-belgie-van-63-naar-65-van-de-bevolking; "In België wonen 628.751 moslims, 6,0% van de bevolking", 11 September 2008, www.npdata.be/BuG/100; "Moslims in België per gewest, provincie en gemeente. Evolutie 2011, 2013 en 2015", 18 September 2015, www.npdata.be/BuG/318-Onderzoekscommissie; www.npdata.be/Data/Vreemdelingen/NIS/Vreemdelingen-gemeenten/2017/Moslims-2017.xls, all accessed 3 April 2018. These estimates will be used in the absence of other more detailed data.

92 Such estimates tend to neglect people from Muslim majority countries who are not Muslims (e.g. Middle Eastern Christians), an aspect considered by Hertogen, as well as converts. See Dassetto, *L'iris et le croissant*, pp. 21–26.

93 www.npdata.be/Data/Vreemdelingen/NIS/Vreemdelingen-gemeenten/2017/Moslims-2017.xls, accessed 3 April 2018.

94 http://data-onderwijs.vlaanderen.be/documenten/bestand.ashx?nr=9788, accessed 2 April 2018.

95 These totals include all educational institutions, including Catholic ones where no Islamic education is provided. If limited to public educational institutions, percentages for 2017–18 are 21.1% in primary education and 19.8% in secondary education (from www.o-re-la.org/index.php/analyses/item/2102-la-frequentation-des-cours-de-religion-et-de-morale-dans-l-enseignement-francophone-en-belgique, accessed 2 April 2018).

96 This does not consider Muslim pupils attending Catholic schools (mainly secondary), which can be estimated to be around 14,000 for Belgium in 2012 (author's own calculations based on Sägesser, Caroline, "Les cours de religion et de morale dans l'enseignement obligatoire", *Courrier hebdomadaire du Centre de recherche et d'information socio-politiques*, no. 2140–2141 (2012), pp. 3–59). The Catholic schools network has produced a note on how to teach the Catholic religion in classes with a majority of Muslim pupils: SeGeC, *Entre enracinement et ouverture: le cours de religion catholique dans les classes du secondaire à forte présence musulmane* (Brussels: 2014), http://enseignement.catholique.be/segec/fileadmin/DocsFede/FESeC/religion/enracinement_ouverture.pdf; for the Flemish-speaking Community, see www.npdata.be/BuG/327-Godsdienstkeuze/, all accessed 3 April 2018.

population in Belgium, with estimates rising to 8.9% by 2030,[97] and even to 11.1% by 2050,[98] this latter estimate being highly contested.[99]

Muslim Population	Estimates for 1 January 2017 are 859,223 Muslims out of a population of 11,322,088 or (7.6% in comparison with 7.2% for 1 January 2016).[100]
Ethnic/National Backgrounds	In 2014, Hertogen estimated that Muslims from a Moroccan background constituted 46.4% of the Muslim population, those from Turkish background 25.8% and others 27.8%.[101]
	More than 91% and 93%, respectively, of Muslim Belgian residents of Moroccan or Turkish background now have Belgian citizenship; a large majority of them have dual citizenship.[102] Higher estimates of converts (who are not counted here) are between 30,000 and 100,000.[103]

---

[97] www.globalreligiousfutures.org/countries/belgium#/?affiliations_religion_id=0&affiliations_year=2030&region_name=All%20Countries&restrictions_year=2014, accessed 26 May 2017. Earlier projections were 10.2%: Pew Research Center, "The future of the global Muslim population. Region: Europe", 27 January 2011, pp. 10–11, 15, www.pewforum.org/2011/01/27/future-of-the-global-muslim-population-regional-europe, accessed 14 June 2015.

[98] www.pewforum.org/2017/11/29/europes-growing-muslim-population/, accessed 3 April 2018.

[99] http://plus.lesoir.be/127158/article/2017-12-01/entre-11-et-18-de-musulmans-en-belgique-dici-2050, accessed 3 April 2018.

[100] www.npdata.be/Data/Vreemdelingen/NIS/Vreemdelingen-gemeenten/2017/Moslims-2017.xls, accessed 1 April 2018.

[101] Hertogen, Jan, "Moslims in België van 6.3% naar 6.5% van de Bevolking", 8 October 2014, www.dewereldmorgen.be/blog/janhertogen/2014/10/08/moslims-in-belgie-van-63-naar-65-van-de-bevolking, accessed 14 June 2015.

[102] Torrekens, Corinne, and Ilke Adam, *Belgo-Marocains, Belgo-Turcs: (auto)portrait de nos concitoyens* (Brussels: Fondation Roi Baudouin, 2015), pp. 33–34, www.kbs-frb.be/uploadedFiles/2012-KBS-FRB/05)_Pictures,_documents_and_external_sites/09)_Publications/3323-POD-BelgoMarocainTurcs_Final.pdf, accessed 3 June 2015.

[103] www.bxlbondyblog.be/se-convertir-a-lislam/, accessed 1 April 2018, and Open Society Foundations, *Restrictions on Muslim Women's Dress in the 28 EU Member States* (New York: Open Society Foundations, 2018), p. 18, www.opensocietyfoundations.org/sites/default/files/restrictions-on-women%27s-dress-in-the-28-eu-member-states-20180425.pdf, accessed 29 April 2018.

Inner-Islamic Groups	There is no official data available on inner-Islamic groups. Shi'is are estimated to be around 30,000 (among which 10,000 are of Moroccan descent and 10,000 of Iranian origin).[104] 20,000 to 40,000 Alevis are also present, and have various organisations.[105]
Geographical Spread	The Muslim population is unevenly spread in the country, concentrating mainly in some parts of Brussels and in (former) industrial and mining areas around Antwerp, Ghent, Liège, Charleroi, and in the province of Limburg.
	In 2017, 34.2% of the Muslim population lived in the Brussels Capital Region, where it represented 24.6% of the entire population.[106]
	43.4% lived in the Flemish Region (5.7% of the population but 8.2% in the Province of Antwerp and 6.9% in the Province of Limburg). The Walloon Region hosts 22.4% of Belgian Muslims and these represent 5.3% of the population (7.7% in the Province of Liège and 5.1% in the Province of Hainaut).[107]
Number of Mosques	There are around 300 mosques; 292 decided to participate in the election of the Executive of Muslims in Belgium (EMB) in 2014, but only 284 sent delegates. Mosques recognised by Belgian Regions are: 17 in the Brussels Capital Region; 39 in Wallonia; and 27 in Flanders.

---

104 Orban, Anne-Claire, "Un quotidien oublié: les chiites bruxellois", *Pax Christi Wallonie Bruxelles Analyse*, May 2016, www.bepax.org/files/files/2016-analyse-un-quotidien-ou blie-les-chiites-bruxellois.pdf, accessed 28 April 2018.
105 http://www.catho-bruxelles.be/wp-content/uploads/2017/01/alevis.pdf, accessed 27 May 2017.
106 Reaching 46.9% in Saint-Josse and 42.5% in Molenbeek, and being between 30–40% in four of the other Brussels Capital Region's 19 municipalities.
107 www.npdata.be/Data/Vreemdelingen/NIS/Vreemdelingen-gemeenten/2017/Moslims-2017.xls, accessed 1 April 2018.

Muslim Burial Sites[108]

Most Muslims of an immigrant background (especially Moroccans) prefer to be buried in their country of origin and sometimes purchase insurance that covers transportation costs. Places of burial in Belgium are segments within local cemeteries, and are in the following places:

Brussels Capital Region:
– Anderlecht, Etterbeek, Forest, Jette, plus interfaith sections in Schaerbeek[109] cemetery (based in the Evere and Zaventem territories), run by an inter-municipal organisation.

Flemish Region:
– Province of Antwerp: Antwerp, Mol, and Turnhout
– Province of West-Flanders: Brugge, Kortrijk, Oostende, and Roeselare
– Province of East-Flanders: Ghent/Zwijnaarde, Ronse, and Sint-Niklaas
– Province of Flemish-Brabant: Leuven, and Tienen
– Province of Limburg: Beringen, Borgloon, Genk, Heuden-Zolder, Houthalen-Helchteren, Leopoldsburg, Lommel, Maaseik, Maasmechelen, Overpelt, Neerpelt, and Sint-Truiden.

Walloon Region:
– Province of Liège: Fleron, Huy, Jupille, Robermont, Visé (Cheratte-Bas), Verviers

---

108 www.embnet.be/fr/annuaire-des-cimetieres and www.embnet.be/nl/lijst-van-de-begraaf plaatsen, both accessed 1 April 2018.
109 www.pouvoirslocaux.irisnet.be/fr/acteurs/les-intercommunales/intercommunale-din humation, accessed 1 April 2018.

- Province of Hainaut: Charleroi (Soleilmont), Farciennes, La Louvière, Manage, Mons, Tournai; planned in Boussu[110] and Morlanwez[111]
- Province of Namur: Andenne, Namur[112], and Sambreville
- Province of Luxembourg: Arlon, Marche-en-Famenne.

"Chaplaincy" in State Institutions	Muslim chaplaincies exist in institutions for young offenders (less than a dozen chaplains), hospitals (although rarely permanently employed by the institution), and penitentiaries[113] (up to 36 in prisons).[114] Recruitment of a Muslim military chaplaincy is thought to be near completion.
Halal Products	Halal food is largely available in small halal shops and in supermarkets, especially in Muslim-populated areas. Slaughtering without stunning is now forbidden in both the Flemish and Walloon Region (from 2019 and 2018 onwards, respectively). Halal meals are available in prisons; some prisons serve no-pork meals to cater for Muslim inmates.[115]

---

110 www.dhnet.be/archive/enfin-une-parcelle-musulmane-51b818d3e4b0de6db99e7ced, accessed 1 April 2018.
111 www.dhnet.be/regions/mons-centre/morlanwelz-une-parcelle-musulmane-dans-le-cimetiere-5a0216d1cd70fa5a061f6ee3, accessed 1 April 2018.
112 www.namur.be/fr/ma-ville/administration/services-communaux/population-etat-civil/reglements/reglement-general-relatif-aux-funerailles-et-sepultures, accessed 1 April 2018.
113 On their mission and recruitment, see: www.embnet.be/fr/conseillers-islamiques, accessed 1 April 2018.
114 www.rtbf.be/info/societe/detail_neuf-nouveaux-conseillers-islamiques-actifs-dans-les-prisons-des-fevrier?id=9475942, accessed 1 April 2018.
115 See the answer in Parliament by the Minister of Justice, Stefaan De Clerck (CD&V), on 23 April 2010: Chambre des Représentants, *Questions et réponses écrites QRVA*, vol. 52, no. 104, pp. 318–319, www.dekamer.be/QRVA/pdf/52/52K0104.pdf, accessed 1 March 2016.

Dress Code

The full-face veil has been banned since 2011 in any place accessible to the public (but permitted in places of worship). As with other religious symbols, wearing the head scarf is forbidden in some public sector institutions; there is no general rule and the situation differs from one institution to another. There is no ban in federal and regional public authorities despite several announcements[116] and each entity of local government establishes its own rule (some local authorities reversed their initial bans). Such a ban may be quite broad or limited to employees providing frontline services. Some restrictions have been challenged in the courts, most of the time successfully.

In primary and secondary education, the ban of head scarfs is quasi-general in public schools, rather extensive in Catholic schools, but permissible in state-funded Muslim schools. A ban has been established in Flemish public educational establishments (legal decisions have therefore brought some limitations), while other regulations are usually determined at school level, with possible variations according to age. There is little restriction in higher education (a ban introduced in 2016 in an institution of higher education in Liège has been overruled in court).

Wearing the head scarf is forbidden for teachers in public education, except for teachers of Islamic religious education, but sometimes limited to their classes.

Recent developments, validated by the European Court of Justice, consider that private companies that include a policy of religious neutrality may

---

116 There was even a recruitment advertisement for the Flemish administration featuring a woman with a head scarf, but it was rapidly withdrawn: www.binnenlandsbestuur.nl/ambtenaar-en-carriere/nieuws/liever-geen-ambtenaar-met-een-hoofddoek.9571147.lynkx (accessed 29 April 2018).

restrict or even forbid all religious, philosophical and political signs; the issue of discrimination is analysed on a case by case basis by the courts.[117]

Places of Islamic Learning and Education

Muslim institutions recognised by the (language-based) Communities:

- Association ECIB (*Enseignement confessionnel islamique de Belgique*) has launched three nursery and primary schools in the Brussels Capital Region: *Al Ghazali* (Etterbeek), *La Plume* (Molenbeek), *La Vertu* (Schaerbeek). A secondary school, *La Vertu*, opened for the 2015–16 school year
- Another primary school, *Institut El Hikma la Sagesse*, opened in 2017, launched by the mosque in Forest (Brussels) of the same name.

These five schools total around 1,200 pupils, with a few hundred on waiting lists.[118] Once recognised, these schools receive the same funding as Catholic, Protestant, or Jewish institutions, and their diplomas/certificates are recognised by all Belgian authorities.

Other Muslim institutions:
These are not recognised by public authorities or the EMB. Despite considering themselves institutions of higher education, their diplomas and certificates are not recognised in Belgium. They do not receive any public funding. Some consider their self-designation as academic institutions as not entirely legal. All are based in the Brussels Capital Region.

---

117 More examples in Open Society Foundations, *Restrictions on Muslim Women's Dress*, pp. 18–27, www.opensocietyfoundations.org/sites/default/files/restrictions-on-women%27s-dress-in-the-28-eu-member-states-20180425.pdf, accessed 29 April 2018.
118 www.lalibre.be/actu/belgique/les-ecoles-islamiques-sont-depassees-par-leur-succes-analyse-59c7cd15cd70129e4188f43c, accessed 1 April 2018.

- European Islamic Institute (*Institut islamique Européen*), linked to the *Centre islamique et culturel de Belgique* and the Muslim World League: http://www.centreislamique.be/node/61.
- *Faculté des sciences islamiques de Bruxelles* (FSIB), www.facebook.com/Facult%C3%A9-des-Sciences-Islamiques-de-Bruxelles-206220459463651/.
- *Académie islamique de Bruxelles* (Brussels Islamic Academy), formerly *Alkhayria Belgica* runs regular conferences and courses in the Islamic sciences, http://aibxl.org/.

Muslim Media and Publications	Two programmes during Islamic holidays are broadcasted yearly on the Flemish public television channel. Plans for such broadcasts on the French-speaking side have not yet been finalised.
	Various private radio stations operate, most notably in Brussels, such as *Arabel FM*.[119] Another enterprise is *Gold FM* (launched in 2005), a commercial and community-based Turkish radio station.[120]

Main Muslim Organisations

– Executive of Muslims in Belgium (*Exécutif des musulmans de Belgique / Executieve van de moslims van België*–EMB, Quai au Bois de Construction 9, 1000 Brussels, tel.: ++32 22100230, www.embnet.be, Facebook page: www.facebook.com/Ex%C3%A9cutif-des-Musulmans-de-BelgiqueExecutief-van-de-Moslims-van-Belgi%C3%AB-476351699186357/). As the representative body to the Belgian authorities, it is recognised and financed by the Federal Government. In 2014, its members were elected in a general assembly, chosen by representatives of the 292 mosques that subscribed to a charter on the renewal procedure for the Executive. There is no such representation for the main organisations listed below; this takes place through their respective mosques.[121]

---

[119] www.arabel.fom, accessed 1 April 2018.
[120] www.goldfeMbe/v2, accessed 3 April 2018.
[121] Husson, "Belgium", *Yearbook of Muslims in Europe*, vol. 7 (2016).

- Council of Theologians (*Conseil des théologiens*, same address as EMB). In connection with the EMB, the Council of Theologians provides answers to questions submitted by the EMB, local mosques, or other national or international religious organisations, and reflects on religious and theological questions relevant to Muslims in Belgium. Any imam hired by a recognised mosque is submitted to the Council for approval. The Council determines the start date of Ramadan and intervenes in public debates.[122]
- Coordination Council of Islamic Institutions (*Conseil de coordination des institutions islamiques de Belgique*–CIB, Quai au Bois de Construction 9, 1000 Brussels, Facebook page: www.facebook.com/Conseil-de-Coordination-des-Institutions-Islamiques-de-Belgique-CIB-1656825377913457/). Set up in the context of the 2014 formation of the EMB, its role is to intervene in public debates on behalf of Muslim communities, whereas the EMB's role is in principle limited to Church-State relations.
- Diyanet (*Belçika Diyanet Vakfi / Diyanet de Belgique / Diyanet van Belgïe*, Chaussée de Haecht 67, 1210 Brussels, tel.: ++32 22185755, www.diyanet.be [in Turkish]). This organisation coordinates all mosques linked to the Turkish government.
- Union of Muslims in Belgium (*Rassemblement des musulmans de Belgique*–RMB, Boulevard Baudouin 18, 1000 Brussels, Facebook page: www.facebook.com/pages/Rassemblement-des-Musulmans-de-Belgique/541296152619233?fref=ts). This organisation is characterised by its links to Morocco, and its commitment to dialogue with other religions.
- Islamic and Cultural Centre of Belgium (*Centre islamique et culturel de Belgique*–CICB, Parc du Cinquantenaire 14, 1000 Brussels, www.centreislamique.be/en/homepage, Facebook page: www.facebook.com/pages/Centre-Islamique-et-Culturel-de-Belgique-Bruxelles/236285763107429?fref=ts). A centre linked to the Saudi-based Muslim World League,[123] it was the first contact organisation for Belgian authorities prior to the formation of the EMB.
- Islamic Federation of Belgium (*Fédération islamique de Belgique / Belçika Islam Federasyonu*–FIB-BIF, Rue Kessels 28–30, Brussels, tel.: ++32 22198079, www.fibif.be, Facebook page: www.facebook.com/belcika.islam.federasyonu [both in Turkish only]). This organisation coordinates the Turkish Milli Görüş mosques.
- Union of Islamic Cultural Centres in Belgium (*Union des centres culturels islamiques de Belgique*–UCCIB, Rue Charles Demeer 1–3, 1020 Brussels,

---

122   www.embnet.be/fr/le-conseil-des-theologiens, accessed 3 April 2018.
123   http://themwl.org/global/content/islamic-center-cultural-belgium, accessed 1 April 2018.

www.selimiye.be – site not working). This organisation coordinates Turkish Sülyemancı mosques.
- There are various local/provincial/regional mosque federations, such as the *Union des mosquées de Liège, Union des mosquées de Bruxelles, Union des mosquées du Hainaut, Union des mosquées de Charleroi*, and the *Unie van Moskeeën en Islamitische Verenigingen in de Provincie Antwerpen* (UMIVPA).
- European Council of Moroccan Oulemas (*Conseil Européen des Oulémas marocains*–CEOM, Avenue Louise 275B, 1000 Brussels, tel.: ++32 26444493, www.ceomeurope.eu [in Arabic only]). The Council considers itself a source of intellectual and religious reference for Moroccans living in Europe, and a contributor to dialogue among cultures and religions in European societies.
- Emdeo (Muslim Expo, Jan van Rijswijcklaan 191, 2020 Antwerp, tel.: ++32 484833181, http://muslimexpo.be, Facebook page: https://www.facebook.com/pages/Moslim-Expo/1824929324399007). Emdeo organises the annual Muslim Expo in Antwerp.
- League of Imams in Belgium (*Ligue des imams de Belgique*, Avenue de Scheut 212, 1070 Brussels, no website. Facebook page: www.facebook.com/ligue.desimams – rarely posts).
- League of Muslims in Belgium (*Ligue des musulmans de Belgique*–LMB, Rue Joseph Claes 69, 1060 Bruxelles, http://lmbonline.be, Facebook page: https://www.facebook.com/lmbelgique/). Established in 2005, it has branches in Brussels, Liège, Verviers, Ghent, and Antwerp, and is the co-organiser of the Brussels Muslim Fair.
- Islamic Relief Belgium (26 Rue Ulens, 1080 Brussels, tel.: ++32 22198184, www.karama-solidarity.be/fr/, Facebook page: www.facebook.com/IRBelgium/). Established around 1990 in Belgium, and part of Islamic Relief Worldwide, it provides humanitarian support to various causes, such as fighting hunger, providing access to clean water in developing countries, and assisting orphans.
- Islamic Assistance League (*Ligue d'entraide islamique*–LEI, 9 Rue Vanderstraeten, 1080 Brussels, tel.: ++ 32 24115679, http://alkhalil.be, Facebook page: www.facebook.com/mosquee.alkhalil/). Established 25 years ago, it is a large network of organisations including the Al Khalil mosque, *Al Khalil* and *La Plume* schools, the Islamic Studies Institute (*Institut des études islamiques*–IEI), and the Wisdom Institute for Languages (*Institut la sagesse pour les langues*–ISL).
- LEAD (formerly *Association belge des professionnels musulmans*–Belgian Association of Muslim Professionals–ABPM, Rue de la Loi 42, 1040 Brussels, www.leadbelgium.be (under construction), Facebook group: www.facebook.com/groups/48136275813/). The association develops contacts among

Muslim professionals, and has started collaborating with the King Baudouin Foundation.
- Muslim Rights Belgium (Rue du Jardinier 82, 1081 Brussels, www.mrb-online.be, Facebook page: www.facebook.com/muslims.rightsbelgium). Established in 2012.
- Collective against Islamophobia in Belgium (*Collectif contre l'islamophobie en Belgique*–CCIB, 40 Rue Emile Wauters, 1020 Brussels, tel.: ++32 484057977, http://ccib-ctib.be, Facebook page: www.facebook.com/islamophobia.ccib.be). Established in September 2014, it publishes a report and collaborates with *Unia* on Islamophobia; it has launched public awareness campaigns around specific themes.
- Federation of Associations of Teachers of the Islamic Religion (*Fédération des associations des enseignants de religion islamique*, www.religion-islamique.be/federation-ri). Created in March 2008 to represent teachers of Islamic religious education.
- Islamic Denominational Education in Belgium (*Enseignement confessionnel islamique de Belgique*–ECIB, 138 Chaussée de Haecht, 1030 Brussels, tel.: ++ 32 27363739). Since 1989, it has established several Muslim schools, and is recognised and financed by public authorities.
- Belgian Secular Muslim Citizen Centre (*Centre citoyen Belge musulman laïque*–CCBML, no known address, Facebook page: https://www.facebook.com/Centre-Citoyen-Belge-Musulman-La%C3%AFque-CCBML-1654789681461563/). An informal organisation very active on Facebook and in the media, promoting a secular view of Islam.

Bosnia and Herzegovina

Nedim Begović[1]

Introduction

In 2017 the progress of Bosnia and Herzegovina (hereafter B&H) in the process of joining the European Union (EU) was slowed down by numerous political disagreements in the country. Only in January 2018 it was published in the media that B&H had finally managed to answer all the questions set out by the European Commission in December 2016. Based on these responses, the European Commission should issue an opinion on B&H's application for membership.

Judgments by the International Criminal Tribunal for the former Yugoslavia (ICTY) in The Hague on Ratko Mladić and the leaders of the self-proclaimed Croatian Community of Herceg-Bosnia, were pronounced in 2017. These represent some compensation for the victims of genocide, and are extremely important because of the historical assessment of the 1990s war in the country.

The *Islamska zajednica u Bosni i Hercegovini* (Islamic Community in Bosnia and Herzegovina–IC in B&H) continued to build on its international links with the aim of improving the status of Bosniak Muslim communities in the diaspora and contributing to the process of institutionalising Islam in EU countries. It also sought to promote a positive image of Islam in European society and fight against radicalism and violent extremism, but also speak out against Islamophobia in Europe. These international endeavours were accompanied by domestic activities, among whose principal aims were the prevention of the radicalisation of young people by the creation of designated spaces for their religious activities, and the promotion of social engagement within the Islamic Community.

Despite the overall sound legal basis for the protection of human rights in the country, Bosnian Muslims still face discrimination at the state level due to

---

1 Nedim Begović, PhD, is Assistant Professor at the Faculty of Islamic Studies of the University of Sarajevo. He holds a BA degree in Islamic Studies, and a MA and PhD in Islamic Law. He is author of the book *Vjerska sloboda i muslimanske manjine u Evropi* (*Religious Freedom and Muslim Minorities in Europe*) (Sarajevo: El-Kalem, 2015), co-author of the book *Sekularnost i religija: BiH i regija* (*Secularity and Religion: B&H and Region*) (Sarajevo: Foundation Public Law Centre, 2015), and is a contributor to the *European Islamophobia Report 2015* (Ankara: SETA–Foundation for Political, Economical and Social Research, 2016). He has also published a number of articles on Islamic law, comparative law, and religion and law.

the lack of political will for an agreement to be signed between the IC and the State of B&H, as well as in parts of the country where Muslims are a minority, as in the Republika Srpska (RS).

Public Debates

On 22 November 2017 the International Criminal Tribunal for the former Yugoslavia (ICTY) in The Hague delivered a judgement that found General Ratko Mladić, the former chief commander of the Army of the RS, guilty of ten out of the eleven counts of the indictments against him. They charged him with genocide in Srebrenica, crimes against humanity and violations of the laws and customs of war, and a life sentence was imposed on him. On 29 November 2017 The Hague Tribunal also convicted the leaders of the self-proclaimed Croatian Community of "Herceg-Bosnia": Jadranko Prlić, Milovoje Petković, Slobodan Praljak, Bruno Stojić, Valentin Ćorić and Borislav Pušić. The existence of a joint criminal enterprise was established in which, in addition to the above people mentioned, the former president of Croatia Franjo Tuđman participated. They aimed to establish a Croatian entity within B&H that would be annexed by the Republic of Croatia in the event of a possible dissolution of B&H.

The verdicts were positively received from the victims of the war, Bosniak politicians and from the international and foreign diplomatic representatives in B&H, but received negative reactions from Bosnian Serb and Croat politicians. In his response to the pronouncement of the verdicts, the leader of the IC in B&H, *ra'is al-'ulama'* Husein Kavazović, said that entire nations should not be identified with the perpetrators of war crimes, but also pointed out the obligation of members of these nations, and their political leaders, to distance themselves from such war criminals.[2]

Transnational Links

In 2017, *ra'is al-'ulama'* Husein Kavazović and other officials of the IC in B&H, as part of their official duties, organised meetings in Sarajevo. They also travelled to many different meetings abroad, with international stakeholders or

---

[2] "Reisu-l-ulema povodom presude zvaničnicima tzv. Herceg-Bosne: Uzmimo pouku iz prošlosti i okrenimo se budućnosti", 29 November 2017, http://islamskazajednica.ba/vijesti/mina-vijesti/25921-reisu-l-ulema-povodom-presude-zvanicnicima-tzv-herceg-bosne-uzmimo-pouku-iz-proslosti-i-okrenimo-se-buducnosti, accessed 24 January 2018.

representatives of different governmental and non-governmental institutions, both from Muslim majority and other countries. Some of these meetings and conferences received wide media coverage, while others did not.

In the context of strengthening the structural unity of the IC and improving cooperation between its organisational units, official visits by delegations of the *riyasat* (presidency) of the IC to Islamic communities in Serbia, Croatia and Slovenia, were undertaken.[3] On 5 and 6 March 2017, *ra'is al-'ulama'* Husein Kavazović visited the *mašihat* (executive council) of the IC in Serbia, in Novi Pazar (Sandžak region), where he met with Mufti Mevlud Dudić, president of the *mašihat*, and his associates. In his speech *ra'is al-'ulama'* stressed the importance of the unity between Bosniaks in Bosnia and Sandžak, and the expectation that the countries in which they live, namely B&H and Serbia, protect their religious and national rights. The delegation of the *riyasat*, headed by deputy of *ra'is al-'ulama'* Husein Smajić, visited the *mašihat* of the IC in Croatia and the *mašihat* of the IC in Slovenia on 14 and 15 November 2017. During these visits they met with the Croatian Mufti Aziz Hasanović and the Slovenian Mufti Nedžad Grabus.[4]

In March 2017 a delegation of the IC, headed by *ra'is al-'ulama'* Husein Kavazović, visited the Islamic Community of North American Bosniaks (ICNAB), where they attended the session of the Assembly of ICNAB and opened two new mosques in Atlanta and Saint Louis.[5] During the visit to the United States *ra'is al-'ulama'* met with high officials of the White House and State Department. The main topics of conversation were: the political and security situation in B&H; the role of religious communities in the promotion of dialogue between their members; the activities of the IC in the fight against violent extremism; and the state of religious freedom in B&H.[6] This was the first official visit to the White House of a high, in this case religious, official from the Balkans since Donald Trump took over the presidency of the United States.

In response to the statements by Kolinda Grabar-Kitarović, the President of Republic of Croatia, on the alleged radicalisation of Bosniaks and "changing

---

3 According to the Constitution of the IC in B&H (art. 1), the *mašihat* of the IC in Serbia, the *mašihat* of the IC in Croatia and the *mašihat* of the IC in Slovenia are integral parts of the IC in B&H. For the Constitution of the Islamic Community, see: www.rijaset.ba/images/stories/Ustavi/Ustav_Iz-e_precisceni_tekst_2014-pdf, accessed 28 July 2015.

4 "Posjeta delegacije Rijaseta mešihatima u Hrvatskoj i Sloveniji", 7 December 2017, https://www.preporod.com/index.php/sve-vijesti/islamska-zajednica/item/8578-posjeta-delegacije-rijaseta-mesihatima-u-hrvatskoj-i-sloveniji, accessed 24 January 2018.

5 "Reisu-l-ulema u posjeti SAD: IZ Bošnjaka Sjeverne Amerike bogatija za dvije nove džamije", *Preporod*, No. 7/1089, 1 April 2017, p. 2.

6 "Reisu-l-ulema razgovarao sa zvaničnicima Bijele Kuće i State Departmenta: Osnažiti prisustvo SAD-a u Bosni i Hercegovini", *Preporod*, No. 7/1089, 1 April 2017, p. 3.

Islam", *ra'is al-'ulama'* Husein Kavazović issued a statement in the media in which he said that the problem of the radicalisation of a small group of extremists in B&H should not be politicised to weaken the political position of Bosniaks, and force them into additional political concessions.[7]

On 3 and 4 May 2017, a delegation of the IC, headed by *ra'is al-'ulama'* Husein Kavazović, visited several EU institutions in Brussels. The members of the delegation met with Mairead McGuinness, Vice President of the European Parliament, Federica Mogherini, High Representative of the EU for Foreign Affairs and Security Policy, Cristian Dan Preda, Special Rapporteur for B&H in the European Parliament, as well as members of the group Friends of Bosnia and Herzegovina in the same Parliament. The topics of conversation were: the historical development of the IC in B&H; its responses to the challenges of extremism; the activities of the IC within the Interreligious Council of B&H (*Međureligijsko vijeće u Bosni i Hercegovini*–MRV BiH); the contribution of religious communities to the path of the European integration of B&H; and the politicisation of the fight against violent extremism and radicalism.[8]

From 19 to 24 May 2017 the *ra'is al-'ulama'* led a delegation of the IC in a visit to Germany where they met with state officials, Bosniak communities, members of the academic community, NGOs and the media. At a meeting with Thomas de Maizière, then German Minister of the Interior, the topics of conversation were the position of Bosniak Muslim communities in Germany and the possibility of obtaining the legal status of public law corporations. The way of how Islamic affairs are administered in a secular state in the experience of Bosniak Muslims and to what extent the elements of their experience could be applied in EU countries with Muslim minorities were also discussed.[9]

At the invitation of a group of European political parties, headed by Cristian Dan Preda, Special Rapporteur of the EU for B&H, *ra'is al-'ulama'* Husein Kavazović participated in the conference "European B&H, Cultural Diversity and Reconciliation", that took place in Brussels on 5 December 2017. The conference was also attended by Bosnian Catholic Cardinal Vinko Puljić.[10]

On 6 November 2017, *ra'is al-'ulama'* Husein Kavazović met with Ali Erbaş, newly appointed president of the Turkish Presidency of Religious Affairs

---

7 "Reisu-l-ulema zatražio pojašnjenje stavova predsjednice Hrvatske: Opasno etiketiranje muslimana u islamofobičnom ambijentu", *Preporod*, No. 7/1089, 1 April 2017, p. 3.
8 "Reisu-l-ulema razgovarao sa visokim zvaničnicima EU u Briselu", *Preporod*, No. 10/1092, 15 May 2018, p. 6.
9 "Reisu-l-ulema u posjeti Njemačkoj: Islamska zajednica je duhovni zavičaj bošnjačkog naroda"\", *Preporod*, No. 11/1093, 1 June 2018, p. 2.
10 http://www.islamskazajednica.ba/vijesti/aktuelno/25939-reisu-l-ulema-u-evropskom-parlamentu, accessed 20 January 2018.

(*Diyanet İşleri Başkanliği*). The conversation was about cooperation between the Diyanet and the IC.[11] On 7 November 2017 *ra'is al-'ulama'* Husein Kavazović attended the opening session of the 27th session of the European Council for Fatwa and Research, which was held in Istanbul.[12]

On 14 December 2017, a memorandum of understanding on the implementation of humanitarian assistance to Rohingya refugees in Bangladesh was signed between the IC in B&H and the Turkish Agency for Cooperation and Coordination (TİKA). According to the document, TİKA was made responsible for delivering 500,000 КМ (€250,000) to Rohignya refugees, through its logistic channels, which was collected from voluntary contributions by mosque communities in B&H and the Bosniak diaspora.[13]

On 16 and 17 December 2017, *ra'is al-'ulama'* attended the second session of the Eurasian Islamic Council for Fatwa that was held in Istanbul, sponsored by the Diyanet. The members of the Council were addressed, among others, by Enes Ljevaković, Mufti of Sarajevo, who also performs the function of deputy secretary of the Eurasian Council.[14]

At the invitation of *shaykh al-islam* Haji Allahshükür Hammat Pashazade, the chief of the Muslim Caucasian Board, *ra'is al-'ulama'* Husein Kavazović went on a two-day visit to Azerbaijan in December 2017. He participated in an international conference in Baku, that was sponsored by the President of the Republic of Azerbaijan Ilham Alijev.[15]

Law and Domestic Politics

The IC in B&H has not yet signed an agreement with the State of B&H, unlike the Catholic Church and the Serbian Orthodox Church, that did so in 2006 and 2008, respectively. The signing of the agreement was delayed by the Serbian

---

11   http://www.islamskazajednica.ba/vijesti/mina-vijesti/25823-reisu-l-ulema-se-sastao-sa-predsjednikom-diyaneta, accessed 20 January 2018.
12   http://www.islamskazajednica.ba/vijesti/mina-vijesti/25820-reisu-l-ulema-na-zasjedanju-evropskog-vijeca-za-fetve-i-istrazivanja, accessed 20 January 2018.
13   https://www.radiosarajevo.ba/vijesti/bosna-i-hercegovina/potpisan-protokol-o-realizaciji-pomoci-narodu-rohinja-prikupljeno-500000-km/284797, accessed 20 January 2018.
14   http://www.islamskazajednica.ba/vijesti/aktuelno/26006-drugi-susret-euroazijskog-islamskog-vijeca-za-fetve-u-istanbulu, accessed 20 January 2018.
15   https://faktor.ba/vijest/reisu-l-ulema-kavazovi-u-azerbejdanu-stanimo-na-put-ideologijama-koje-raspiruju-mrnju-277277, accessed 20 January 2018.

and Croatian members of the Presidency Mladen Ivanić and Dragan Čović.[16] The agreement is expected to improve and strengthen the instruments for protecting the rights of Muslims, especially the rights pertaining to needs unique to Muslims, such as breaks for *jumma* Friday prayer, space for daily prayers etc.

Responding to the appeal of Safet Softić, Deputy President of the House of Peoples of the Parliamentary Assembly of B&H, the Constitutional Court of B&H decided that the prohibition against beards, prescribed by the rulebook on uniforms for the B&H Border Police, is unconstitutional and a violation of the ECHR. According to the Court's decision, the Border Police can prescribe the length of the beard, but cannot "absolutely" prohibit having one, because such a prohibition would infringe on the right to freedom of religion. This decision by the Constitutional Court has wider significance, not only for the employees of the Border Police, but also for all other state agencies, because it will be a precedent for all similar cases.[17]

The Educational and Pedagogical Institute of the Serb-dominated autonomous RS, prepared a proposal of the Code of Ethics, which stipulates, among other things, the dress code for teachers and pupils in elementary schools. In addition to the positive norms envisioned by the code (for instance, clothes should not contain any symbols that offend the feelings of other nations, etc.), it also forbids the wearing of head scarves in schools, thereby preventing some Muslim women from working in schools in the Republic.[18]

Activities and Initiatives of Main Muslim Organisations

In January 2017 the Gazi Husrev-bey madrasa and Gazi Husrev-bey library marked their 480th anniversary. This school, attended today by 490 male and female students, has the status of a secondary school and is funded mostly by the Canton of Sarajevo. The Gazi Husrev-bey library houses more than 100,000 items, some dating back the 12th century. During the 1990s war in B&H and the siege of Sarajevo, the collection was hidden, with 500 of the most valuable

---

16 "Čović i Ivanić blokiraju usvajanje sporazuma Islamske zajednice i države BiH", 7 September 2017, https://www.klix.ba/vijesti/bih/covic-i-ivanic-blokiraju-usvajanje-sporazuma-islamske-zajednice-i-drzave-bih/170905055, accessed 22 January 2018.
17 "Zakonodavci moraju poštovati vjerska prava", 23 December 2017, https://www.preporod.com/index.php/sve-vijesti/drustvo/item/8696-zakonodavci-moraju-postovati-vjerska-prava, accessed 22 January 2018.
18 "Etički kodeks za učenike i nastavnike u RS-u kao mogući paravan za diskriminaciju?: Povreda dva temeljna prava i reduciranje muslimanskog identiteta", *Preporod*, No. 22/1104, 15 November 2017, pp. 14–15.

manuscripts and books locked up in a bank vault. To eliminate the threat that items could be lost, all manuscripts have now been digitised. About 60% of the collection is in Arabic, 30% in Turkish, and the rest is in Persian and Bosnian.[19]

The *waqf* Directorate of the IC established a unique database of *waqf* properties in B&H. In the last 100 years, 90% of *waqf* properties in B&H have been confiscated by various state authorities. Due to a lack of legislation regarding restitution, these properties continue to be under state ownership. The *waqf* Directorate works towards the protection, maintenance and renovation of *waqf* properties in B&H.[20]

The importance of working with young people at all levels of the organisation of the IC, through educational, social, humanitarian, cultural, sporting and recreational activities is an integral part of the activity plan of the Council of Muftis of the IC, adopted at its seventh session held on 11 April 2016 in Sarajevo.[21] Within this context the Office of the Mufti in Sarajevo launched a project in 2017 called "The Youth Network", that is designed to serve as the platform for youth work in the IC at the national level as well as within Bosniak diaspora communities.[22]

On 21 March 2017, the Council of Muftis of the IC adopted the findings of a document prepared by a special commission of the Council, entitled "An Analysis of the Ideology of *takfir* and Violent Extremism". The document discusses the key principles and concepts that radical groups most frequently abuse from ideologies that are derived from established Islamic traditions. These include *takfir* (declaring someone a non-believer), *jihad* (struggle), *hijra* (migration), *taghut* (idols) and "monotheism in government",[23] *dar al-islam*

---

19   "Svečano obilježena 480. godišnjica Gazi Husrev-begove biblioteke", 11 January 2017, http://islamskazajednica.ba/vijesti/aktuelno/24775-svecano-obiljezena-480-godisnjica-gazi-husrev-begove-biblioteke, accessed 21 January 2018; see also "Bosnia opens library housing ancient Islamic manuscripts", 17 January 2014, http://english.islamskazajednica.ba/news/279-bosnia-opens-library-housing-ancient-islamic-manuscripts, accessed 21 January 2018.

20   "Uspostavljena jedinstvena baza podataka vakufske imovine", *Preporod*, No. 3/1061, 1 February 2017, p. 8.

21   A copy of the Activity Plan adopted by the Council of Muftis is in the hands of the author.

22   "Mreža mladih: Konačan odgovor Islamske zajednice kako raditi s mladima?", *Preporod*, No. 6/1088, 15 March 2017, p. 8.

23   The essence of the concept of "monotheism in government" (*tawhid al-hakimiyya*) is that the application of any law that is not based on shari'a law is contrary to the principle of *tawhid*, God's unity and sole authority over the world.

(the abode of Islam), *dar al-harb* (the abode of war), *al-wala' wa-al-bara'* (friendship and hostility), *bid'a* (innovation in religion) etc.[24]

As part of the "Days of *waqf*" which are organised annually by the *waqf* Directorate of the IC, on 22 April 2017 the foundation stone was officially laid as part of the rebuilding of the Arnaudija mosque in Banja Luka (the capital of the RS). The event was attended, among others guests, by Haldun Koç, Turkish ambassador to B&H, and Adnan Ertem, director of the General Directorate of *waqfs* of Turkey. In his speech, Osman Kozlić, the mufti of Banja Luka, said that Aranudija, like the Ferhad Pasha mosque, is part of the spiritual and cultural heritage that belongs not only to Bosniak Muslims, but also to other peoples in B&H, as well as to the Turkish people.[25]

On 23 April 2017 the renovated building of Derviš-hanuma madrasa in Bosanska Gradiška was opened. Several hundred citizens attended the opening ceremony, including many officials of the Municipality of Bosanska Gradiška. The building is intended to be used for educational and cultural programmes. Its construction was funded by the General Directorate of *waqfs* of Turkey.[26] On 12 May 2017, a ceremony was held on the occasion of the reconstruction of the Emperor's mosque in Foča, which was demolished during the 1990s war. The mosque was established by the Ottoman Sultan Bayazid II in 1501. The event was attended by Husein Kavazović, the *ra'is al-'ulama'*, Bakir Izetbegović, a member of the Presidency of B&H, and Veysi Kaynak, the Turkish Deputy Prime Minister. The reconstruction of the Emperor's mosque was partially funded by the Turkish Agency for Cooperation and Coordination (TİKA).[27]

The Faculty of Islamic Studies in Sarajevo marked its 40th anniversary in September 2017. The Faculty, as the leading institution of higher Islamic education in the Balkans, was established on 29 September 1977. The main ceremony took place on 29 September 2017 in Sarajevo in the presence of numerous guests from the country and abroad. One of the other main events for

---

24 "Iz analize ideologije tekfira: Zloupotreba temeljnih koncepata islamskog učenja", *Preporod*, No. 7/1089, 1 April 2017, p. 3; The Islamic Community in Bosnia and Herzegovina–The Council of Muftis, *Ideologija tekfira i nasilni ekstremizam: Analiza* (Sarajevo: The Islamic Community in Bosnia and Herzegovina–The Council of Muftis, 2017).

25 "Svečanost: Aranudija poziva na obnovu međukomšijskih odnosa", *Preporod*, No. 9/1091, 1 May 2017, pp. 2–3.

26 "Svečanost: Derviš-hanumina medresa vraća povjerenje u Bosanskoj Gradišci", *Preporod*, No. 9/1091, 1 May 2017, p. 3.

27 "Svečanosti: Careva džamija kao zalog obnove zajedništva", *Preporod*, No. 10/1092, 15 May 2017, pp. 2–3.

the celebration of the anniversary was the international conference "Islamic Education in Europe", that was held in Sarajevo from 14 to 16 September.[28]

In November and December 2017 *ra'is al-'ulama'* Husein Kavazović visited the *majlises* of the IC in the RS (Foča, Čajniče, Višegrad etc.). In his speech in Višegrad, he emphasised that during his visits to *maktabs* (primary Islamic educational courses in mosques) in the RS, he noticed that, in the majority of cases, they were the only forum for the Islamic education of Bosniak children, and so also the only way to protect their cultural and national identity. He also noted attempts to assimilate Bosniaks through the public educational system of the RS. This was recognised as a new challenge for the IC that should be adequately addressed by the *maktab* curriculum.[29]

Muslim Population: History and Demographics

Bosniaks, or less commonly Bosniacs, are a South Slavic national and ethnic group mainly inhabiting modern Bosnia and Herzegovina. A native minority of this group is also present in other countries of the Balkan Peninsula, especially in the Sandžak region of Serbia and Montenegro (where Bosniaks form a regional majority), as well in Croatia, and in Kosovo. Bosniaks are typically characterised by their historic ties to the historical Bosnian region, their majority adherence to Islam, their common culture, and the Bosnian language. Islam in Bosnia and Herzegovina has a rich and longstanding history, having been introduced to the local population in the 15th and 16th centuries as a result of the Ottoman conquest of the Bosnian Kingdom.[30]

Over the next century, the Bosnians–composed of dualists and Slavic tribes living in the Bosnian Kingdom under the name *bošnjani*[31]–embraced Islam in great numbers under Ottoman rule, which also saw the name *bošnjanin* transform into *bošnjak* ("Bosniak"). By the early 1600s, approximately two thirds of the population of Bosnia were Muslim.[32] Bosnia and Herzegovina remained a

---

28 "40 godina rada Fakulteta islamskih nauka", 13 September 2017, http://www.islamska zajednica.ba/vijesti/aktuelno/25482-40-godina-rada-fakultet-islamskih-nauka, accessed 21 January 2018.
29 "Reisu-l-ulema Kavazović posjetio mekteb u Višegradu", https://www.oslobodjenje.ba/ vijesti/bih/reisu-l-ulema-kavazovic-posjetio-mekteb-u-visegradu, accessed 21 January 2018.
30 See Malcolm, Noel, *Bosnia: a Short History* (New York: New York University Press, 1996).
31 Bašić, Denis, *The Roots of the Religious, Ethnic, and National Identity of the Bosnian-Herzegovinian Muslims* (PhD dissertation) (Seattle: University of Washington, 2009).
32 Malcolm, *Bosnia*.

province of the Ottoman Empire and gained autonomy after the Bosnian uprising in 1831. After the 1878 Congress of Berlin it came under the temporary control of Austria-Hungary. In 1908, Austria-Hungary formally annexed the region.[33]

Since 1971, the term Muslim was used for the national designation of the entire Slav Muslim population in Yugoslavia, and Slav Muslims could officially declare themselves Muslims in the sense of a nation. They became one of the constituent nations of Socialist Yugoslavia.[34] Upon Bosnia and Herzegovina's declaration of independence from Yugoslavia in the early 1990s, the great majority of Bosnian Muslims identified themselves as Bosniaks. In September 1993, at the height of the Bosnian War, the Second Bosniak Congress (*Drugi bošnjački sabor*) formed a basis for the official re-establishment of the historical ethnic name Bosniak, and the rejection of the former designation "Muslim", in use during Socialist Yugoslavia.[35]

During the 1992–95 war, Bosniaks were subjected to ethnic cleansing and genocide. The war caused hundreds of thousands of Bosniaks to flee their homes. The war also caused many drastic demographic changes in Bosnia. Bosniaks were prevalent throughout almost all of Bosnia in 1991, a year before the war broke out. As a result of the war, Bosniaks in Bosnia were concentrated in areas that were held by the Bosnian government during the war for independence. Today Bosniaks make up the majority in Sarajevo and its canton, most of Northwestern Bosnia around Bihać, most of Northeastern Bosnia around Tuzla, as well as in Central Bosnia, the Brčko District, Goražde, and parts of Herzegovina.

According to data from the 2013 census, published by the Agency for Statistics of B&H, Bosniaks constitute 50.11% of the population, Bosnian Serbs 30.78%, Bosnian Croats 15.43%, and others form 2.73%, with the remaining respondents not declaring their ethnicity or not answering this question.[36] The census results are contested by the Republika Srpska (RS) statistical office and

---

33   Imamović, Mustafa, *Historija Bošnjaka* (Sarajevo: Bošnjačka zajednica kulture–Preporod, 1997).
34   Dimitrovova, Bohdana, "Bosniak or Muslim? Dilemma of one nation with two names", *Southeast European Politics*, vol. 2, no. 2 (October 2001), pp. 94–108.
35   Imamović, *Historija Bošnjaka*.
36   *Popis stanovništva, domaćinstava i stanova u Bosni i Hercegovini, 2013.: Rezultati popisa* (*Census of Population, Households and Dwellings in Bosnia and Herzegovina, 2013: Final results*), Agency for Statistics of Bosnia and Herzegovina, Sarajevo, June 2016, http://www.popis2013.ba/doc/Popis2013prvoIzdanje.pdf, accessed 9 December 2016.

by Bosnian Serb politicians,[37] who oppose the inclusion of non-permanent Bosnian residents in the figures.[38] The EU's statistics office, Eurostat, however, concluded that the methodology used by the Bosnian statistical agency was in line with international recommendations.[39] The results of the country's first national census since the 1990s war, showed that Bosnia and Herzegovina had lost nearly a fifth of its pre-war population. The new census counted 824,000 fewer inhabitants that in 1991: a 19% drop.[40]

Muslim Population	Total population 3,531,159 (2013 Census): 1,790,454 individuals declared themselves to be followers of Islam (50.7%), 536,333 as Catholic (15.2%) and 1,085,760 as Orthodox Christian (30.7%). A total of 32,700 declared themselves agnostics (0.9%) and 27,853 atheists (0.8%). 40,655 said that they are of some other faith or belief (1.2%), 32,700 did not declare their religion, and 6,588 did not answer the question of religion (1.1% combined).[41]
Ethnic/National Backgrounds	No official data available. The overwhelming majority of Muslims are Bosnian citizens by birth, with Bosniaks being the largest ethnic group, followed by a small percentage of ethnic Albanians and a negligible number of converts belonging to other ethnicities.

---

37   Toe, Rodolfo, "Census reveals Bosnia's changed demography", *Balkan Insight*, 30 June 2016, http://www.balkaninsight.com/en/article/new-demographic-picture-of-bosnia-finally-revealed-06-30-2016, accessed 22 January 2018.
38   Toe, Rodolfo, "Bosnia to publish census without Serb agreement", *Balkan Insight*, 30 June 2016, http://www.balkaninsight.com/en/article/bosnia-to-release-long-awaited-census-results-on-thursday-06-29-2016, accessed 22 January 2018.
39   "Bosnia-Herzegovina has lost a fifth of its pre-war population, census shows", *The Guardian*, 1 July 2016, https://www.theguardian.com/world/2016/jul/01/bosnia-herzegovina-has-lost-a-fifth-of-its-pre-war-population-census-shows, accessed 22 January 2018.
40   "Bosnia-Herzegovina has lost a fifth of its pre-war population".
41   *Census of Population, Households and Dwellings in Bosnia and Herzegovina, 2013*.

Inner-Islamic Groups   No official data available. The overwhelming majority of Muslims are Sunnis following the Hanafi *madhhab* in Islamic law and the Maturidi school in theology. There are some groups of Salafis, some of whom follow the Hanbali *madhhab* in Islamic law.[42] There are also media reports about some Bosniaks converting to Shi'ism and organising their own communities.[43] No official data is available on the number of Shi'is or Salafis among Bosniaks or sympathisers of Gülen or any other movement.

Geographical Spread   After the changes in the demographic distribution of ethnic groups due to the 1992–95 war, the majority of the Bosnian Muslim population is concentrated in the Northwestern, Central and Northeastern parts of the country around the wider area of the cities of Bihać, Zenica, Sarajevo, and Tuzla, respectively. More than 81% of the RS's inhabitants today are ethnic Serbs (almost all of them declared themselves as Orthodox Christians), while more than 70% of people in the Federation of B&H are Bosniaks (almost all of them declared themselves as Muslims).[44]

The last census in 2013 showed that there are 171,839 (or 14%) Bosniaks/Muslims of the 1,228,423 residents in the RS. This is a decline from 440,746 (or 28%) of 1,569,332 residents, recorded in the census from 1991. This is the result of war atrocities and ethnic cleansing crimes committed against Muslims during the 1992–95 war.

---

42   Some Salafis asked the official Islamic Community to recognise them as followers of the Hanbali *madhhab* in Islamic law. Their letters, sent to the Islamic Community, are available at http://istina.ba/saopcenje-koordinacije-nezavisnih-dzemata-povodom-izvjestaja-rijaseta-iz/, accessed 9 December 2016.
43   See the interview by Sarajevo based magazine *Start* with Bosnian citizen Abdulah Shabar, who spoke about his conversion from Sunnism to Shi'ism, and the Shi'i community in the Bosnian village of Lješevo near Sarajevo: Bečirović, Asaf, "Ne dao Bog sukoba sa sunitima u BiH", *Magazin Start*, 6 December 2016, pp. 16–18.
44   *Census of Population, Households and Dwellings in Bosnia and Herzegovina, 2013*.

Number of Mosques	About 1,700 mosques and *masjids*[45] (most villages and towns with significant Muslim communities have a mosque or *masjid*).
Muslim Burial Sites	There are ca. 4,380 Muslim burial sites in the country, most of which are administrated by the *waqf* Directorate. However, not all of them are active in the sense of Muslims still being buried there. During and after the 1992–95 war, some burial sites where Muslim victims of genocide and war atrocities, as well as soldiers of the Army of the Republic of B&H, were buried became well-known, including: – Memorial Centre Srebrenica Potočari (*Memorijalni centar Srebrenica Potočari*) where victims of the genocide (so far 6,504) are buried. The Centre's web-page is: http://www.potocarimc.org/index.php/memorijalni-centar. – Martyrs Memorial Cemetery Kovači (*Šehidsko spomen mezarje Kovači*) in Sarajevo, where Alija Izetbegović, the first president of the Republic of B&H, and soldiers killed during the siege of Sarajevo, are buried. – Martyrs Memorial Site Bišćani (*Šehidsko spomen obilježje Bišćani*) is situated near to the town of Prijedor, where more than 300 Muslim victims of ethnic cleansing in the area are buried.
"Chaplaincy" in State Institutions	The Agreement on the Establishment of the Military *Mufti* Office, as an integral part of the religious services at the Ministry of Defence and the Armed Forces of B&H, was implemented and signed on 11 September 2007. The Office of the Military Mufti continues to care for Muslims within the defence system of Bosnia and Herzegovina.

---

45 In the Bosnian context, a mosque (*džamija*) is usually expected to have a minaret and a full-time imam. A *masjid* (*mesdžid*) is a smaller place for prayer, usually with occasional services, and in most cases is without a minaret.

The Office of the Military Mufti consists of the following personnel: the military mufti (currently Hadis Pašalić); adviser to the mufti; his secretary; the chief imam and his secretary; one staff imam; six brigadier imams; and five battalion imams. The total number of employees in the structure of the military mufti is 17 persons, who are paid by the Ministry of Defence.

There are imams appointed by the IC to correction facilities and prisons to lead Friday prayers and offer spiritual guidance to inmates. They are not employed by the State or the IC specifically for these services, but some local imams are given these additional duties.[46]

Halal Products

Ritual slaughter is allowed and there are no legal restrictions. No state or military institution, school, prison, hospital, or other organisation, is obliged to make halal food accessible to citizens.

In accordance with its works and mission, the IC in B&H launched a project to form the Agency for Halal Quality Certification, in order to establish in B&H a system that would allow manufacturers to certify their production processes and products and place them on the market labelled as halal.

The Agency has consulted experts from different scientific orientations, from the Faculty of Islamic Studies, Agriculture, Veterinary, Medical, and Technological Faculties in order to develop a project which will comply with Islamic principles of *halal* and *haram* with international requirements in the field of standardisation. The result of the Agency's work is the development of basic regulations, which form a legal basis for carrying out the certification process and control of the quality

---

46 One meeting of imams working in prisons was organised by the Directorate for Religious Affairs of the Islamic Community in Sarajevo, at the end of November 2016, http://www.islamskazajednica.ba/vijesti/aktuelno/24620-sastanak-sa imamima-koji-obavljaju-imamski-poziv-u-kazneno-popravnim-zavodima-u-bih, accessed 11 December 2016.

requirements for halal certification. Certification is undertaken in compliance with other world-recognised standards, such as the International Organization for Standardization (ISO) and Codex Alimentarius HACCAP.

There is a long list of products, companies, hotels, restaurants, and other businesses that comply with halal standards and carry the certified logo, especially with the increase in tourists visiting B&H from the Gulf states.[47]

Dress Code

There are no general laws that prohibit wearing the head scarf and niqab (face veil) in the public, including public schools and universities. Instances are known, however, where Muslim women face discrimination in the employment sector for wearing the head scarf.[48]

On 26 January 2016 the High Judicial and Prosecutorial Council (*Visoko sudsko i tužilačko vijeće Bosne i Hercegovine*–VSTV BiH) upheld a ban on wearing the head scarf and other religious symbols for judges and other employees of the Bosnian judiciary.[49]

Places of Islamic Learning and Education

– The Faculty of Islamic Studies in Sarajevo (Ćemerlina 54, 71000 Sarajevo, tel.: ++387 33251011, fax: ++387 33251044, www.fin.ba).
– Islamic Pedagogical Faculty in Zenica (Prof. Juraja Neidharta 15, 72000 Zenica, tel./fax: ++387 32402919, www.ipf.unze.ba).

---

47 For more on the Agency for Halal Quality, see: www.halal.ba/site/index.php?optino=com_content&view=article&id=489&Itemid=56&lang=en, accessed 8 July 2016.
48 *Riyasat* of the Islamic Community in Bosnia and Herzegovina–Commission for Freedom of Religion, *Izvještaji o registriranim slučajevima kršenja prava na slobodu vjere muslimana u Bosni i Hercegovini za 2016. i 2017. godinu* (*Report on Registered Cases of the Violation of the Right to Freedom of Religion of Muslims in Bosnia and Herzegovina for 2016 and 2017*) (Sarajevo: *Riyasat* of the Islamic Community in Bosnia and Herzegovina–Commission for Freedom of Religion, 2017).
49 "Bosnia judicial authorities uphold hijab ban, despite protests", 11 February 2016, https://www.rferl.org/a/bosnia-judiciary-upholds-ban-on-hijab-despite-protests/27545654.html, accessed 3 April 2018.

- Islamic Pedagogical Faculty in Bihać (Žegarska aleja 14, 77000 Bihać, tel.: ++387 37220 162, fax: ++387 37228160, www.ipf.unbi.ba).
- Gazi Husrev-Bey Madrasa in Sarajevo (Sarači 49, 71000 Sarajevo, phone: ++87 33 534 888, www.medresa.ba).
- Behram-Bey Madrasa in Tuzla (Behram-begova 1, 75000 Tuzla, phone: ++387 35 281 151, fax: ++387 35281154, www.bbm.edu.ba).
- Elči Ibrahim Pasha Madrasa in Travnik (Mostarska bb, 72270 Travnik, phone: ++387 30512023, fax: ++387 30518015, www.medresatravnik.edu.ba).
- Madrasa Osman-ef. Redžović in Visoko (Veliko Čajno 69, 71300 Visoko, phone: ++387 32745771, fax: ++387 32745770 www.medresa.org).
- Madrasa Džemaludin-ef. Čaušević in Cazin (Šepići bb, 77220 Cazin, phone: ++387 37514893, http://medresa-cazin.ba).
- Karađoz Bey Madrasa in Mostar (Maršala Tita 162, 88000 Mostar, phone: ++387 36550920, fax: ++387 36550921, www.medresamostar.com).

Muslim Media and Publications

- *El-Kalem* is the publishing house of the Islamic Community established in 1973, soon after the ruling communist regime eased its restrictions on the activities of religious communities.
- The oldest printed periodical is *Glasnik* (The Herald), a bi-monthly official journal of the Islamic Community (founded in 1933, circulation 2,200).
- The largest and most influential newspaper of the IC is the bi-weekly *Preporod* (The Revival), founded in 1970 (circulation around 25,000, www.preporod.com), which mostly covers current events within the IC, as well as more daily news concerning Islam and Muslims in Bosnia and Herzegovina, and abroad.

- The IC publishes the annual *Takvim*, a hijri calendar with accompanying articles on current issues in religion, culture and society (circulation 50,000).
- The Association of Ulama publishes a quarterly educational magazine *Novi Muallim* (New Teacher, circulation 2,000).
- The Faculty of Islamic Studies publishes *Zbornik Fakulteta islamskih nauka*, an annual collection of scholarly papers, mainly written by its staff (first published in 1989, circulation 300). The Islamic faculties and madrasas also have their own student magazines, the oldest being *Zemzem*, the student magazine of the Gazi Husrev-Bey Madrasa (first published in 1968, circulation around 1,000).
- The Gazi Husrev-Bey Library (founded in 1537, with a collection of 13,000 manuscripts, www.ghb.ba) publishes annuals (*Anali*, first published in 1972, circulation around 500), which include studies and texts in the fields of Islamic Studies, history, and includes a bibliography.

There are also a few Sufi publications: the quarterly magazine *Kelamu'l-Šifa'* (Healing Word, first published in 2004, with a variable circulation), and the older periodical *Šebi Arus* (Wedding Night, first published in 1982).

The Periodical *El-Asr* (Time) publishes analyses of current events concerning Muslims as well as educational articles. Its dominant orientation is Salafi.

In November 2006, the IC established a radio station, BIR, which has been broadcasting 24 hours a day since March 2009. The station produces radio programmes and has a website (www.bir.ba), offering content and information about religious, educational, sporting, and political issues. According to its administration, the radio station is one of the seven most listened to stations in B&H, with their regional frequencies covering an area inhabited by 1.4 million people.

In November 2000, Pazarić based Muslim Television *Igman* began broadcasting its programmes, which have significant religious and educational content. It is owned by the private company *Bandić d.o.o.* Among other religious topics, MTV *Igman* also covers current events in local organisational units (*jamaats*) of the IC in B&H as well as in the Bosniak diaspora.

In 2016 Sarajevo based *TV 5* (http://www.televizija5.ba/) began broadcasting its mostly religiously orientated programmes on local cable networks. Officially, the TV station is owned by the private company *BalkanMedia d.o.o. Adija*, but its editorial concept is pro-Salafi, with several officials and scholars of the IC appearing in some of its programmes.

Main Muslim Organisations

– Islamic Community in Bosnia and Herzegovina (*Islamska zajednica u Bosni i Hercegovini*, Zelenih beretki 17, 71000 Sarajevo, tel.: ++387 33533000, fax: ++387 33 441 800, www.islamskazajednica.ba). The IC is the main Muslim organisation and, according to its constitution, "the sole and united community of Muslims in Bosnia and Herzegovina and Sandžak, Croatia, Slovenia and Serbia, of Bosniaks outside their homelands, and of other Muslims who accepted it as their own".[50] The IC is recognised by the State as the institution that has traditionally represented Islam in Bosnia and Herzegovina. It is independent in terms of regulating its own activities (rituals, Islamic education, management of Islamic endowments, publishing, charity, etc.) and the management of its property. It is financed mainly through *zakat* (alms duty), *sadaqat al-fitr* (a charitable donation given at the end of Ramadan), pious endowments (*waqf*), membership fees, through the revenue of its profit-generating agencies, and through other donations.

---

50   For the Constitution of the Islamic Community, see: www.rijaset.ba/images/stories/Ustavi/Ustav_Iz-e_precisceni_tekst_2014-pdf, accessed 28 July 2015.

Bulgaria

Aziz Nazmi Shakir[1]

Introduction

Bulgaria is home to the largest indigenous Muslim minority within the boundaries of the European Union. Despite the continuing rise of anti-Islamic views with nationalistic and xenophobic overtones, supported even by high-ranking officials, both Bulgaria's historical Muslim population (Turkish and Pomak[2] speakers, as well as Roma), and the recently formed, relatively small, Arab-Muslim community,[3] avoided major conflicts with Bulgaria's non-Muslim majority.

Nevertheless, in 2017, there were several cases in which Muslims, and the symbols of their religious environment, were subjected to various forms of violation. These included vandalised and physically attacked houses of worship, biased representations of religious identity by the media, the refusal of public prosecutors to initiate criminal proceedings for public instigation of religious hatred, as well as discrimination and violence.

After the parliamentary elections held on 26 March 2017, the extreme nationalistic parties in Bulgaria, known for their anti-Muslim positions, united and became coalition partners with the leading centre-right party, the GERB (Citizens for the European Development of Bulgaria–Граждани за европейско развитие на България–ГЕРБ). These extremist parties are the National Front for the Salvation of Bulgaria–NFSB (Национален фронт за спасение на България–НФСБ), the Internal Macedonian Revolutionary Organisation–IMRO (Вътрешна македонска революционна организация–ВМРО), and *Atack* (*Атака*). They were labelled as fascist organisations by the Council of

---

1 Aziz Nazmi Shakir, PhD, is currently working as an Arabic language instructor at the School of Languages at Sabanci University, Istanbul.
2 Pomaks, referred to by most Bulgarian historians as *Българомохамедани* ("Bulgarian Muhammadans"), are concentrated in the central and Western Rhodope Mountains in Southern Bulgaria. On Pomaks, see Todorova, Maria, "Identity (trans)formation among the Pomaks in Bulgaria", in Kürt László and Juliet Langman (eds.), *Beyond Borders: Remaking Cultural Identities in the New East and Central Europe* (Boulder, Colorado: Westview Press, 1997), pp. 63–82; Memişoğlu, Hüseyin, *Balkanlar'da Pomak Türkleri* (*Pomak-Turks in the Balkans*) (İstanbul: Türk Dünyası Araştırmaları Vakfı, 1999).
3 This group consists of immigrants in transit to Western Europe, and former university students who came to the country during the communist period.

Europe's European Commission against Racism and Intolerance.[4] For the first time since the democratic changes in Bulgaria, political parties whose actions contradict the basic principles of democracy and human rights, became part of the Government. They entered politics through the use of hate speech and aggressive stances towards certain vulnerable groups, such as ethnic Roma and Turks belonging to local Muslim communities. Meanwhile the media environment worsened, with the widespread use of slander and manipulation, which tried to discredit civil society organisations dealing with human rights.[5]

For the second time the Supreme Court, which previously has annulled decisions made by the district court in Pazardzhik, returned the eight-year long lawsuit against 13 Muslim clerics, accused of spreading Salafism and imposing shari'a law,[6] to the Court of Appeals in Plovdiv.[7] The Plovdiv court could not reach a final verdict, and in December 2017 it postponed the case until March 2018.[8] Nevertheless, the district court in Pazardzhik freed the defendant Ahmed Musa, who had spent three years behind bars without being convicted.[9]

In March 2017, the results of recent research conducted among Bulgaria's Muslim communities by the *Alpha Research* agency, the New Bulgarian University, and the Konrad Adenauer Foundation, were announced; this showed a tendency towards increasing religiosity. This was reflected both in the performance of important acts of worship, such as Ramadan fasting and

---

4   Emilova, Sonya, "Islamophobia in Bulgaria: national report 2017", in Enes Bayraklı and Farid Hafez, *European Islamophobia Report 2017* (Istanbul: SETA, 2018), p. 132.
5   http://www.bghelsinki.org/en/news/press/single/bulgarian-helsinki-committee-releases-2017-annual-human-rights-report-year-deterioration/, accessed 26 April 2018.
6   For detailed information about the initial stages of the trial, see Shakir, Aziz Nazmi, "Bulgaria", in Jørgen S. Nielsen, Samim Akgönül, Ahmet Alibašić and Egdūnas Racius (eds.), *Yearbook of Muslims in Europe*, vol. 6 (Leiden: Brill, 2014), pp. 141–142.
7   "Делото "Имами: Ахмед Муса отново застана пред съда" (The Imams' case: Ahmed Musa enters court again), https://nova.bg/news/view/2017/12/12/201063/%D0%B4%D0%B5%D0%BB%D0%BE%D1%82%D0%BE-%D0%B8%D0%BC%D0%B0%D0%BC%D0%B8-%D0%B0%D1%85%D0%BC%D0%B5%D0%B4-%D0%BC%D1%83%D1%81%D0%B0-%D0%BE%D1%82%D0%BD%D0%BE%D0%B2%D0%BE-%D0%B7%D0%B0%D1%81%D1%82%D0%B0%D0%BD%D0%B0-%D0%BF%D1%80%D0%B5%D0%B4-%D1%81%D1%8A%D0%B4%D0%B0, accessed 1 March 2018.
8   "Пловдив–Апелативният съд ще гледа делото срещу 13-те имами за радикален Ислям" (Plovdiv: the Court of Appeal will review the lawsuit against the 13 Imams for radical Islam), http://www.focus-news.net/news/2017/11/21/2459202/plovdiv-apelativniyat-sad-shte-gleda-deloto-sreshtu-13-te-imami-za-radikalen-islyam.html, accessed 15 February 2018.
9   "Проповедникът на радикален ислям Ахмед Муса си отива вкъщи" (The radical Islam preacher Ahmed Musa goes home), https://www.blitz.bg/kriminalni/propovednikt-na-radikalen-islyam-akhmed-musa-si-otiva-vkshchi_news562772.html, accessed 20 February 2018.

performing the ritual prayer five times a day, and also in a refraining from eating pork and from drinking alcohol.[10]

Public Debates

Recent public debates on Islam and Muslims in Bulgaria were generated primarily by the far-right political group that formed an alliance for the parliamentary elections in March 2017. Known as United Patriots (*Обединени патриоти*), it used Islamophobia in its campaign to gain public support. It won 9.07% of the votes in the general election, and the alliance became part of the Government on 4 May 2017. This enabled its representatives to move from the periphery of the political landscape in Bulgaria to its centre. Consequently, the leaders of the NFSB and IMRO, Valeri Simeonov and Krasimir Karakachanov, in their capacity as deputy prime ministers, made considerable steps towards institutionalising political hate speech and intolerance towards Muslim citizens. On 24 March 2017, a few days before the parliamentary elections that brought them to power, the two forerunners organised illegal blockades at the Bulgarian-Turkish border. As a result, an unknown number of Bulgarian Muslim voters residing in Turkey were deprived of their right of free movement, and could not execute their constitutional right to vote.[11] Moreover, Simeonov, the deputy prime minister on economic and demographic policy, demonstrably tried to stop an elderly woman from voting, resorted to brute force against her in front of a TV camera covering the incident. Simeonov stated that, thanks to the actions of his followers, the newly founded liberal centrist political party Democrats for Responsibility, Solidarity and Tolerance–DOST (*Демократи за отговорност, свобода и толерантност–ДОСТ*), that mainly represents Muslims in Bulgaria (with only 2.85% of the votes) did not manage to pass the 4% threshold required to be represented in Parliament.[12] The other

---

10   See http://alpharesearch.bg/userfiles/file/Muslim_Graph_%2003_2017_Final.pdf, accessed 1 November 2017.

11   "БХК алармира международни организации за затруднения изборен процес в Турция" (Bulgarian Helsinki Committee alerts international organisations about the difficult electoral process in Turkey), *Bulgarian Helsinki Committee*, 6 April 2017, http://www.bghelsinki.org/bg/novini/press/single/pressobshenie-bhk-alarmira-mezhdunarodni-organizacii-za-zatrudneniya-izboren-proces-v-turciya, accessed 15 February 2018.

12   "Валери Симеонов: Тая баба на границата беше много нагла, знаеше си правата" (Valeri Simeonov: that grandmother on the border was very insolent, she was conscious of her rights), *Faktor*, 30 March 2017, http://www.faktor.bg/bg/articles/novini/balgariya/valeri-simeonov-taya-baba-na-granitsata-beshe-mnogo-nagla-znaeshe-si-pravata, accessed 15 February 2018.

party targeted was the Movement for Rights and Freedoms–MRF (*Движение за права и свободи–ДПС*). This party has counted on incoming voters from Turkey in all previous parliamentary and local elections held since the fall of the iron curtain in the beginning of the 1990s. The extensive blockades set up on all three main roads on the border were also the result of a media campaign that suggested that Turkey used its influence over local religious authorities and Muslim politicians to interfere in Bulgaria's internal affairs. In this period SKAT TV, the television channel owned by Valeri Simeonov, that functions as a media organ of the NFSB, took a very active role in promoting Islamophobia, and race hate and intolerance.[13]

It seems that as part of the actions undertaken by the interim government, headed by Ognian Gerdzhikov, to prevent Turkish interference, the illegal blockades of the United Patriots (on 21 and 24 March) were quietly supported by the Bulgarian Ministry of the Interior. It thus fell short of defending the constitutional rights of Muslims coming from Turkey. On 23 March, the Turkish President Recep Tayyip Erdoğan announced that putting pressure on ethnic Turks in Bulgaria was intolerable. Consequently, the Bulgarian President responded by saying he refused to take "lessons in democracy" from Turkey.[14]

In a special report focusing on the election campaign, the OSCE Office for Democratic Institutions and Human Rights (ODIHR)[15] noted that several international treaties on human rights were gravely violated by the Bulgarian authorities. These included the European Convention on Human Rights, the Framework Convention for the Protection of National Minorities, and several mandatory recommendations by the Parliamentary Assembly of the Council of Europe (PACE) were also ignored. For example, article 32.5 of the 1999 OSCE Istanbul Document, states that people belonging to national minorities (i.e. Muslims and others) have the right "… to disseminate, have access to and

---

13 Tuna, Arda, "Bulgaristan'daki Skat TV, Türklere Karşı Saldırılarına Devam Ediyor" (Skat TV in Bulgaria continues its attacks against Turks), 29 January 2018, http://www.arda-tuna.com/2018/01/29/bulgaristandaki-skat-tv-turklere-karsi-saldirilarina-devam-ediyor/, accessed 27 February 2018.

14 "International election observation mission–Republic of Bulgaria: early parliamentary elections 26 March 2017 osce/odihr limited election observation mission final report", OSCE-ODIHR (not dated), http://www.osce.org/odihr/elections/bulgaria/327171?download=true, p. 9.

15 Based in Warsaw (Poland), the ODIHR is active throughout the 57 participating states of the OSCE. It assists governments in meeting their commitments, as participating states of the OSCE, in the areas of elections, human rights, democracy, rule of law, tolerance and non-discrimination.

exchange information in their mother tongue",[16] yet the use of any language other than Bulgarian during election campaigns in Bulgaria is still banned. An administrative fine of 2,000 BGN (around €1,000) is consistently imposed on political leaders who defy this ban and use their mother tongue, in this case Turkish.

On 27 June 2017, on the third day of Ramadan in Sofia, Deputy Chief Mufti Birali Mümün Birali's wife and two daughters were physically assaulted.[17] Both Muslims and many non-Muslims used different social networks to express their support towards Birali's family, but mainstream media outlets failed to do so. On 12 July 2017, the Supreme Muslim Council (*Висш мюсюлмански съвет*) issued a protest against this incident and other acts of Islamophobia and xenophobia. The National Council of Religious Communities in Bulgaria (NCRCB), the Organisation of Jews in Bulgaria "Shalom", and the Central Israelite Religious Council, also strongly condemned the attack.[18] On 28 July 2017, when the Sofia regional Muftiate started the construction of a residential building for its employees, a group of people tried to stop it, on the pretext that a refuge for radicals would be built. A pig's head was placed on the building's fence and another one dropped into the property.[19]

Although the Minister of Culture Boil Banov made a statement that the mosques in Bulgaria were part of the world's cultural heritage,[20] and that the rights of Muslims ought to be protected throughout 2017 mosques were the most attacked material manifestations of Islam in Bulgaria. The mosque in Silistra was attacked with a 5.5 mm air rifle, the mosque in the village of Krushovitsa, Pleven, was attacked with a self-made bomb, and the mosque in Sofia was damaged by beer bottles and waste bins. The Aziziya mosque

---

16 "ДОСТ пак може да отнесе глоба заради агитация на турски език" (DOST may be fined again for agitation in Turkish language), 18 March 2017, https://clubz.bg/51702-dost_pak_moje_da_otnese_globa_zaradi_agitaciq_na_turski_ezik, accessed 10 December 2017.

17 "Проявена агресия срещу жена със забрадка" (Aggression against a woman with a headscarf), *www.grandmufti.bg* (not dated), http://grandmufti.bg/bg/home/news-room/novini/4299-proyavena-agresiya-sreshtu-zhena-sas-zabradka.html, accessed 1 March 2018.

18 Based on data taken from the unpublished Ahmed, Vedat S., Ahmed Ahmedov and Emin, Hayri (eds.), *Бюлетин 2017/ Bülten 2017/ Annual Report 2017* (Sofia: Chief Mufti's Office, 2018), pp. 179–183: hereafter cited as *Annual Report 2017*.

19 Emilova, "Islamophobia in Bulgaria", p. 139.

20 Chausheva, L., "Minister of Culture Boil Banov: mosques in Bulgaria are world cultural heritage", *www.grandmufti.bg* (not dated), http://www.grandmufti.bg/en/za-nas-3/news/5220-kulturniyat-ministar-boil-banov-dzhamiite-v-balgariya-sa-svetovni-pamet nitzi-na-kulturata-2.html, accessed 7 February 2018.

in Varna was also marked with graffiti containing anti-Muslim and racist expressions.[21] In most of these cases, local Muslim communities were unable to receive sufficient professional support from the Ministry of Interior, whose investigations, despite featuring video evidence and eyewitness statements, proved inconclusive.

In 2017, Muslims were not an active element in public debates concerning issues affecting them. In the few cases where official representatives of the Muslim Denomination (*Мюсюлманско вероизповедание*) were invited to participate in radio and television programmes, they were only invited in order to defend themselves, and to reject certain allegations. For example, between October and November 2017, a number of TV channels (bTV, Bulgaria OnAir etc.)[22] and news websites (offnews, dnes.bg, factor.bg etc.)[23] covered the controversial opinions of journalists, historians, parents, and official representatives of the Muslim Denomination, in reference to a primary school lesson dedicated to the emergence and spread of Islam, as described in a sixth grade History and Civilisation textbook. The text contains quotations from the Qur'an, according to which women are considered inferior to men, giving men the right to beat women (Qur'an 4:3, 34), as well as vague paragraphs about the meaning of jihad in Islam (Qur'an 8:38–40, 9:29). The Deputy Chief Mufti Birali, insisted that the Chief Muftiate should be consulted when this type of text enters school curricula. The authors of the textbook, Alexander Nikolov and Hristo Matanov, stated in their defence that they could not censor the Qur'an. They compared their approach with another lesson from the same textbook, in which information on the Catholic Inquisition could also discomfort Christian students.[24]

21 Emilova, "Islamophobia in Bulgaria", pp. 141–142; *Annual Report 2017*, pp. 169–170.
22 https://www.bgonair.bg/sutreshen-blok/2017-10-19/izuchavaneto-na-dzhihad-v-6-klas-skandalizira-roditeli; https://btvnovinite.bg/videos/tazi-sutrin/kak-e-predstaven-islja mat-v-uchebnika-po-istorija-za-shesti-klas.html, both accessed 25 May 2018.
23 https://www.dnes.bg/obrazovanie/2017/10/19/iz-uchebnici-za-6-klas-ima-li-miasto-dji hadyt-v-uchebnata-programa.356649; https://www.faktor.bg/bg/articles/novini/balgar iya/matyat-nov-skandal-urok-za-dzhihada-i-bieneto-na-zhenite-v-6-klas, both accessed 25 May 2018.
24 "Урок за исляма в учебник за 6 клас: Мъжът може да бие жената" (Lesson about Islam in a 6th-grade history textbook: a man can beat a woman), *Offnews*, 2 November 2017, https://offnews.bg/obshtestvo/urok-za-isliama-v-uchebnik-za-6-klas-mazhat-mozhe-da-bie-zhena-ta-668538.html, accessed 1 March 2018.

Transnational Links

In 2017, the Republic of Turkey (represented by the Turkish Presidency of Religious Affairs (*Diyanet İşleri Başkanlığı*), the Religious Foundation of Turkey (*Türkiye Diyanet Vakfı*–TDV), the Turkish Cooperation and Coordination Agency (*Turk İşbirliği ve Koordinasyon Ajansı*–TİKA)), and other high-ranking officials, municipalities etc., remained the strongest transnational allies of Bulgarian Muslims and their activities. The income of the Muftiate has increased significantly in recent years; for 2017 the expected sum was 6.5 million BGN (around €3,325,000). However, the Muftiate actually spent some 10 million BGN (around €5,115,000) to cover its yearly expenses,[25] and it was the Turkish Diyanet that sponsored most educational events and paid the imams' salaries. This strong bond between the Muslim Denomination and the Diyanet resulted in a number of bilateral official visits, as well as several mutual educational and academic collaborations. In January 2017, Mustafa Tutkun, Secretary General of the TDV, visited the Chief Muftiate in Sofia, and reassured his hosts that as long as the local Muslim community is in need of the Foundation's support they will provide it.[26] On the occasion of the inauguration of Ali Erbaş as the new director of Diyanet (in October 2017), the Bulgarian Chief, Mufti Hadji, travelled to Ankara and met Erbaş, along with other representatives of the Balkan Muslim communities, such as the President of the Islamic Union of Macedonia, Suleyman Efendi Redjeb, and the Chief Mufti of Romania, Murat Yusuf.[27] On 10–11 May 2017, again in Ankara, the Chair of the Supreme Muslim Council, Vedat Ahmed, attended the constituent assembly of the Council on Fetwa, that met to implement a decision taken by the ninth Eurasian Islamic Council, under the initiative of the Supreme Council on Religious Issues of the Diyanet.[28]

On 6 May 2017, supported by the Bursa municipality, the *Kur'an Araştırmaları Merkezi* (Centre for Quranic Research) organised a seminar dedicated to

---

25 "Başmüftü Yardımcısı Murat Pingov İle Başmüftülük Teşkilatının Hukuki, Mali ve Vakıf Hizmetleri Hakkında Mülakat" (An interview with the deputy chief Mufti Murat Pingov about the juridical, financial and waqf services provided by the Chief Muftiate Organisation), *Мюсюлмани-Müslümanlar*, no. 2 (2017), p. 3.

26 "Başmüftülük Türkiye Diyanet İşleri Başkanını Ziyaret Etti" (A delegation from the Chief Muftiate visited the president of the Turkish Presidency of Religious Affairs), *Мюсюлмани-Müslümanlar*, no. 2 (2017), p. 18.

27 "Başmüftülük Heyeti Türkiye Diyanet İşleri Başkanını Ziyaret Etti", p. 18.

28 *Annual Report 2017*, p. 43.

"Islamic Religion and Culture in Bulgaria".[29] Between 17–19 May, the representatives of the Muftiate's Publishing Department participated in the second International Forum for Translators of Religious Literature, that took place in Sapanca, Turkey. More than 150 translators of religious literature from 26 countries took part in the three-day forum. Every year the Education Department of the Muslim Denomination organises summer schools, with cultural and religious training activities. In 2017, five projects, involving about 200 students from Bulgaria, were accomplished together with Turkish host organisations, such as Besader, the Association for Culture, Aziz Mahmud Hüdai, the regional mufti's office in Edirne, and the Diyanet.[30]

Besides the abovementioned events, reflecting the intensive cooperation between Turkish and Bulgarian religious authorities, there were also several other transnational and interreligious forums, bringing together representatives of Bulgaria with their counterparts from different parts of the world. On 22–23 June 2017, the Chief Muftiate participated in the annual conference of the Office for Democratic Institutions and Human Rights (ODIHR) at the Organisation for Security and Cooperation in Europe (OSCE), held in Vienna. The representative of the Muslim Denomination in Bulgaria, Hayri Emin, attended the session entitled "Freedom of Religion or Belief: Issues, Opportunities, and the Specific Challenges of Combatting Anti-Semitism and Intolerance and Discrimination against Christians, Muslims and Members of Other Religions". At it he delivered a special report related to the legislative changes submitted to the Bulgarian parliament by nationalist parties to incriminate "radical Islam".[31]

There are a significant number of activities in which the Muslim Denomination acts as a member of the National Council of Religious Communities in Bulgaria–NCRCB (*Националният съвет на религиозните общности в България*). Between 5–7 April 2017, the NCRCB organised a three-day visit to the Republic of Macedonia, where the representatives of the Bulgarian religious communities (including deputy Chief Mufti Birali and the regional Mufti of Veliko, Tarnovo Syuleyman Masurev) met the Protestant, Catholic and Muslim communities in Skopje and Ohrid.[32]

---

29   "Bulgaristan'da İslam Dini ve Kültürü Paneli Bursa'da Düzenlendi" (A seminar about Islamic religion and culture in Bulgaria was organised in Bursa), *Мюсюлмани-Müslümanlar*, no. 6 (2017), p. 18.
30   *Annual Report 2017*, p. 78.
31   This information was obtained from Hayri Emin, an employee of the Chief Muftiate.
32   *Мюсюлмани-Müslümanlar*, no. 5 (2017), p. 18.

On 11–12 March 2017, the Supreme Council of Islamic Affairs, at the Egyptian Ministry of Waqfs, organised an international conference in Cairo entitled "Terrorism Does Not Have a Religion: the Role of Religious Leaders and Power-Holders in Spreading Peace and Opposing Terrorism and Challenges". The Chair of the Supreme Muslim Council, Vedat Ahmed, took part in the conference that was attended by 40 different state representatives, at the invitation of Minister Muhammad Mukhtar Jumaa.[33]

In recent years, the Chief Muftiate, due to the significant number of Bulgarian Muslims residing in Muslim minority contexts across Europe, organised a series of visits aimed at establishing transnational bonds between these communities and those within the country. This initiative proved to be effective, with funds provided by Bulgarian Muslims living abroad increasing. During Ramadan, Chief Mufti Hadji, accompanied by his secretary-in-chief Dzhelal Faik and the regional Mufti of Sofia, Mustafa Izbishtali, visited Pamplona in Spain and Sweden's capital Stockholm, where he had meetings and conversations with the Bulgarian Muslim diaspora.

Law and Domestic Politics

Shortly after the parliamentary elections of March 2017 the "Turkish interference" theme lost currency, yet during the election campaign the interim government unilaterally cancelled a treaty, signed back in 1998, between the Governments of Bulgaria and Turkey. This treaty aimed at regulating such financial assistance, and the sending of tutors, guest preachers and lecturers from the Diyanet to local religious institutions. The treaty was signed as a result of Bulgaria's inability, or lack of political will, to support its religious institutions in the post-socialist period, and coincided with a moment when relations with Turkey were warmer. At present, the annual subsidy that the Chief Muftiate receives from the State amounts to 360,000 BGN (around €184,000), that is intended for the renovation of old mosques. A separate agreement of cooperation was signed between the Chief Muftiate and the Diyanet in 2002, which does not include a termination clause. These treaties were fully compatible with the *Law of Religions*, according to which, denominations, with the permission of the Diyanet under the supervision of the Council of Ministers of Bulgaria, have the right to invite religious officials from abroad. For example, in 2017, there were 15 imams on secondment from Turkey who preached in

---

33   *Annual Report 2017*, p. 46.

Bulgarian mosques. For more than three months the Bulgarian authorities did not inform the representatives of the Muslim Denomination about the cancellation of the two decades-old treaty, even after being officially asked to do so. At the same time, nearly 630 imams did not receive their salaries for several months, because of annulled money transfers from Turkey.[34] In the last few years, the Chief Muftiate has repeatedly been criticised by the media and certain politicians for receiving financial and staff support from the Diyanet. Besides the funds for imams' salaries, Turkey's financial support also includes the sponsorship of three religious high schools and funding for the Higher Islamic Institute in Sofia.

On 26 May 2017, newly elected members of the 44th Bulgarian parliament from the United Patriots coalition, proposed amendments to the *Penal Code* for the criminalisation of professing "radical Islam", foreseeing imprisonment from one to five years and fines up to 5,000 BGN (around € 2,550).[35] These members stated that terrorism was due to a "radical Islamic ideology" preaching concepts such as jihad and a desire for "establishing an Islamic caliphate". The amendments to the *Penal Code* were passed at first reading on 6 December 2017. In response, on 14 December 2017, the Supreme Muslim Council submitted a petition containing more than 40,016 signatures to the Presidency, the National Assembly, the Council of Ministers and to the Ombudsman of the Republic, condemning the legislative amendments as being discriminatory against citizens professing Islam.[36]

In addition to the aforementioned legislative changes, MPs of the United Patriots coalition in Parliament announced the preparation of bills which stipulated that preaching in places of worship should only be performed in the Bulgarian language, and that the financing of religious institutions from abroad should be banned. As this Bill imposed restrictions on freedom of religion, and offered no alternatives, the Chief Muftiate voiced its opposition to the proposals.[37]

---

34   "Имамите останаха без заплати" (Imams remained without wages), *bTV*, 30 July 2017, http://m.btvnovinite.bg/article/bulgaria/imamite-ostanaha-bez-zaplati.html, accessed 1 March 2018.

35   *Proposed Amendments, National Assembly, May 26, 2017*, http://www.parliament.bg/bills/44/754-01-11.pdf, accessed 1 March 2018.

36   "Muslims submitted petition against the Law on 'Radical Islam'", www.grandmufti.bg (not dated), http://www.grandmufti.bg/en/za-nas-3/news/5093-myusy-ulmanite-vnesoha-podpiska-protiv-zakona-za-radikalniya-islyam-3.html, accessed 25 February 2018. See also, Emilova, "Islamophobia in Bulgaria", p. 135.

37   "Непремерените думи на високопоставените държавни мъже будят негодувание сред мюсюлманите в страната" (Underestimated words of high-ranking politicians

In September 2017, the deputy prime ministers, Valeri Simeonov and Krasimir Karakachanov, submitted an ordinance to the Council of Ministers, according to which imams in Bulgaria have to pass special examinations and loyalty tests.[38] At the same time, the information centre on the National Department of Defence website, declared that there was a danger of radical Islam in Bulgaria, without providing sufficient documentation to support these claims.[39] Karakachanov is also Minister of Defence.

On 22 November 2017, at the Supreme Administrative Court, Rasim Shamatarev, the father of 17-year-old Emine Shamatareva from Valkosel, lost a lawsuit filed, and lost previously by him, at the Administrative Court in Blagoevgrad.[40] A year ago, Emine Shamatareva had been removed from school under the pretext that wearing a head scarf contradicted the school's internal rules. In an interview on 21 December 2017, Rasim said that he would take the case to the European Court of Human Rights in Strasbourg rather than move his daughter to another school. There was a similar case with a former student at a Krumovgrad district high school, who was refused entry to her final exams in May 2016 and May 2017, because she wore a head scarf, and was compelled to wear a wig instead.[41] According to the Civil Association of Turkish and Bulgarian Culture (*Türk ve Bulgar Kültür Derneği–Сдружение за турска и българска култура*), Muslim women wearing head scarves face major problems, not only within education but also in the employment sector.[42]

---

awake resentment among Muslims in the country), *grandmufti.bg* (not dated), http://grand-mufti.bg/bg/home/news-room/pres-saobshteniya/4668-nepremerenite-dumi-na-visokopostavenite-darzhavni-mazhe-budyat-negoduvanie-sred-myusyulmanite-v-stranata, accessed 15 February 2018.

38 Попова, Руманя, "Имамите да минават изпит и тест за лоялност" (Imams have to pass examination and loyalty tests), *bTV*, 27 September 2017, http://btvnovinite.bg/article/bulgaria/predlozhenie-imamite-da-minavat-izpit-i-test-za-lojalnost.html, accessed 13 February 2018.

39 Droznina, Tatyana, "Има ли радикализация сред мюсюлманите в България?" (Is there radicalisation among Muslims in Bulgaria?), *armymedia.bg*, 3 November 2017, http://armymedia.bg/archives/102705, accessed 20 December 2018.

40 Маскръчка, Антоанета, "Забрадената ученичка загуби дело срещу директора на гимназията" (Student with a head scarf lost lawsuit against the high school principal), *24chasa*, 22 November 2017, https://www.24chasa.bg/region/article/6566765, accessed 27 February 2018.

41 Emilova, "Islamophobia in Bulgaria", p. 135.

42 Emilova, "Islamophobia in Bulgaria", p. 111.

Activities and Initiatives of Main Muslim Organisations

In 2017, activities by Bulgarian Muslims were initiated and carried out primarily by the Chief Muftiate and its regional branches. It conducted a broad spectrum of events. These included official meetings, conferences, seminars and courses, both in the country and abroad. It also issued halal certificates and fatwas, published religious literature, and carried out various charity campaigns.

On 19 January 2017, the Chief Mufti, Mustafa Hadji, and the Chair of the Supreme Muslim Council, Vedat Ahmed, paid an official visit to the President of the Republic, Rosen Plevneliev, to commemorate the end of his term in office. On 29 May 2017, the Chief Mufti attended an official *iftar* dinner hosted by the newly elected Bulgarian President Rumen Radev, as a sign of respect to all Bulgarian citizens of Muslim background.[43]

Throughout 2017, Mustafa Hadji had official meetings with several ambassadors to consolidate the existing good relationships between the Muslim Denomination and diplomats in Bulgaria. Hadji hosted Cardinal Leonardo Sandri, the prefect of the Congregation for the Oriental Churches at the Holy See, on 30 June 2017, as well as the Apostolic Nuncio to Bulgaria, Monseigneur Archbishop Anselmo Guido Pecorari, on 6 November 2017.[44]

Representatives of different religious communities came together in Plovdiv to drink the "Coffee of Tolerance", invited by the regional Muftiate. The meeting was held, for the third year in a row, on 14 February, to commemorate the assault against the Dzhumaya mosque on that day in 2014.

On 12 July 2017, in the Grand Hotel Sofia, Mustafa Hadji participated in a conference entitled "Ethics, Values and Religion", which was organised by the Citizens for European Development of Bulgaria, together with the Centre for European Studies Wilfried Martens, and the Konrad Adenauer Foundation. The Deputy Chief Mufti, Birali Birali, at the seminar "Protection of Freedom of Religion and the Struggle against Discrimination and Violence Based on Religion and Belief" (14–17 March 2017), presented the problems which Muslims are facing in Bulgaria. This seminar was organised by the Commission for Protection from Discrimination, in partnership with the US Embassy.

The traditional campaign in support of Islamic education in the month of Ramadan, from 26 May to 25 June 2017, deserves special attention. Funds were raised amounting to €145,000, courses for imams and hafizes took place, in Ustina, Shumen, and Madan, and summer and annual Qur'an courses, totalling

---

43 *Annual Report 2017*, p. 20.
44 *Мюсюлмани-Müslümanlar*, no. 12 (2017), p. 18.

196, were also carried out. A training centre in Rudozem and a dormitory in Velingrad were also opened, among other projects.

The Muslim Denomination in Bulgaria manages and uses *waqf* properties via its special administrative unit at the Chief Muftiate: the *waqfs* Department. Since 2013, 365 projects, mainly aimed at restoring real estate with historical significance, were submitted, most of them were realised, but some 144, worth 25,109,529 BGN (around €12,844,000) are still pending. In the last five years with the support of the Diyanet, TDK, TİKA, NGOs, and with the help of local Muslim communities, more than 170 projects including constructions of new mosques and school buildings for over 10,000,000 BGN (around €5,115,000) were completed.[45]

The Muslim Denomination carries out charitable campaigns in various fields, both related to religious occasions, like Ramadan and ʿId al-Adha, and to ongoing social problems within the community, like providing support to orphans.

In 2017, Bulgarian Muslims celebrated their religious holidays freely and, in accordance with Art. 173, Para. 4 of the *Labour Code*, were officially entitled to a day's holiday for *mawlid*, two days for ʿId al-Fitr, and three days for ʿId al-Adha. Meanwhile the annual hajj, organised by the Muftiate, was performed by 275 pilgrims (42 more than in 2016), who spent 21 days in Mecca and nine in Medina. Prior to their departure, all the regional Muftiates with candidates for pilgrimage carried out training seminars. Such seminars were also held in Turkey for applicants with Bulgarian citizenship. Besides the hajj, in March 2017, for the second year running, the Hajj and Umrah Commission of the Muslim Denomination, organised *ʿumrah* for a group of 30 pilgrims (twelve less than in March 2016).[46]

Muslim Population: History and Demographics

In 1396, the Second Bulgarian Kingdom, founded in 1185, became a core part of the recently conquered Balkan territories of the Ottoman state. Subsequently, Islam spread mainly through a series of resettlement campaigns of Turcoman groups from Asia Minor, aimed at reducing Bulgarian demographic superiority, and by means of the gradual conversion of the local Christian population to Islam. In most of today's Bulgaria, Ottoman rule lasted until 1878, when, as a result of the Russo-Turkish War, and in accordance with the subsequent Treaty

---

45 *Мюсюлмани-Müslümanlar*, no. 2 (2017), p. 4.
46 *Мюсюлмани-Müslümanlar*, no. 4 (2017), p. 18.

of Berlin, the greater part of the Ottoman Danube Vilayet was transformed into a new autonomous region called the Bulgarian Principality.[47] The same treaty gave birth to the semi-autonomous Eastern Rumelian Vilayet, which soon after, in 1885, was incorporated into the Principality. As a result of the First Balkan War in 1912–13, significant areas located in the Rhodope region and Western Thrace, populated overwhelmingly by Muslims,[48] were also incorporated into the Bulgarian state.[49]

The most reliable sources concerning demographic and statistical information on Bulgaria's Muslim population, are the official censuses of the National Statistical Institute. These are carried out every ten years, and include a question on religion. The last three censuses (1992, 2001, 2011) covering the democratic period, show a constant decrease in the number of Bulgarian Muslims; from 1,110,295 in 1991 to 966,978 in 2001, to 577,139 in 2011. This comprises 13.1%, 12.2%, and 7.8% respectively of the total population (8,487,317 in 1991, 7,928,901 in 2001, and 7,364,570 in 2011).[50] The major reason for this decline is emigration. Another explanation for the decrease is the fact that many Muslims declined to declare their religious affiliation. This theory is strongly supported by the following figures: only 444,434 (of an estimated 588,318) Turks, 67,350 (of roughly 160,000 Pomaks) and 42,201 (of 325,343) Roma declared themselves to be Muslim.[51] It is hard to believe, for example, that in ten years the share of Muslims within the Roma community decreased from 40% (148,363 of 370,908 Roma in 2001)[52] to 18%, particularly if we take into account that Roma were not affected by common migration processes; they were the only ethnic group that did not rapidly decrease in number. For the first time in the history of censuses in Bulgaria, the number of Turks (588,318) exceeds the total number of self-declared Muslims (577,139).[53]

---

47   For the history of Islam in Bulgaria in general, see Желязкова, Антонина, Божидар Алексиев и Зорница Назърска (ред.), *Мюсюлманските общности на Балканите и в България* (Zhelyazkova, Antonia, Bozhidar Aleksiev and Zornitsa Nazarska (eds.), *Muslim Communities in the Balkans and in Bulgaria*) (Sofia: IMIR, 1997); Градева, Росица (ред.), *История на мюсюлманската култура по българските земи* (Gradeva, Rositsa (ed.), *History of Muslim Culture in Bulgarian Lands*) (Sofia: IMIR, 2007).

48   Namely the following settlements: Kırcali (Kardjali), Eğridere (Ardino), Koşukavak (Krumovgrad), Darıdere (Zlatograd), Mestanlı (Momchilgrad), Ortaköy (Ivaylovgrad), Dövlen (Devin), Paşmaklı (Smolyan), and Nevrokop.

49   Including South Dobrudja, which was taken from Romania and given to Bulgaria in 1940.

50   *2011 Population Census in Bulgaria (Final Data)*, www.nsi.bg/Census_e/Census_e.htm, accessed 20 January 2017.

51   *2011 Population Census in Bulgaria.*

52   *2011 Population Census in Bulgaria.*

53   *2011 Population Census in Bulgaria.*

Muslim Population	Estimates of around 1 million (ca. 15% of the population). This figure is based on the aforementioned total number of Turks, Pomaks and Roma. The 2011 Census provides a figure of 577,139 (7.8% of population in 2011).[54]
Ethnic/National Backgrounds	Almost all Muslims in Bulgaria are Bulgarian citizens, the only exceptions being the nearly 10,000 refugees (mainly Syrians, Afghans, Iraqis, and Kurds) who entered the country during the crisis in Syria (2013–17).
	Largest ethnic/national groups (number of self-identified Muslims, and total): Turkish: 444,434 (of 588,318) Roma: 42,201 (of 325,343)[55] Pomak: 67,350 (of roughly 160,000)[56] Arab: more than 12,000 Tatar: around 4,500.
Inner-Islamic Groups[57]	Sunni: 546,004 Shi'i: 27,407 (mainly in Razgrad, Ruse, Silistra, Sliven districts) "Muslim": 3,727.
Geographical Spread	The persons who identify themselves as being of Turkish ethnicity are located in several districts: Kardzhali, Razgrad, Targovishte, Shumen, Silistra, Dobrich Ruse, and Burgas, where 63.7% of the population of this ethnic group live. The persons from the Roma ethnic group are distributed in all districts. The areas with the largest share of those

---

54 *2011 Population Census in Bulgaria.*
55 *2011 Population Census in Bulgaria.*
56 Shakir, Aziz Nazmi, "Bulgaria", in Jørgen S. Nielsen, Samim Akgönül, Ahmet Alibašić and Egdūnas Racius (eds.), *Yearbook of Muslims in Europe,* vol. 5 (Leiden: Brill, 2013), p. 146.
57 http://censusresults.nsi.bg/Census/Reports/2/2/R10.aspx, accessed 8 December 2016.

with Roma ethnicity are in the districts of Montana (12.7%) and Sliven (11.8%), followed by Dobrich (8.8%), and Yambol (8.5%), compared to the total for the country (4.9%). Pomaks mainly live in the Rhodope region and the Gotse Delchev district. A very small Tatar community live in Northeastern Bulgaria. The Arab diaspora is mainly based in the capital city, Sofia.

Number of Mosques	1,500 active (400 constructed after 1990); around 30 under construction; 118 not in use.
Muslim Burial Sites	The approximate number of villages and towns with a Muslim population in 13 regions is 2,250. Most of them have separate cemeteries located in their vicinities. Some hamlets and villages share common graveyards. There are also a significant number of abandoned historical cemeteries. The estimated number of burial places is 3,000.
"Chaplaincy" in State Institutions	Imams have access to prisons and may visit patients in hospitals, although no special regulation concerning the issue exists. Imams are not allowed in the armed forces, as military law bans religious activities on the premises of the military and the Ministry of the Armed Forces. This has provoked objections by the Muftiate, in that priests representing the Orthodox Church regularly inaugurate the flags of the Bulgarian Army and perform religious rites at official ceremonies, such as the opening of schools and other institutions.
Halal Products	Muslims have very limited access to halal food. It is available through a number of local shops, which are supplied by a couple of local firms that perform the ritual slaughter. In supermarkets, there are no special signs indicating whether a certain meat product is halal. Nevertheless, private slaughter is not forbidden. Halal food is not available in public institutions.

In 2012, the Supreme Muslim Council accepted "A Regulation Concerning the Basis for the Issuing of Halal Certificates", and formed a commission to deal with matters related to the granting of certificates to companies. The Chief Muftiate's website regularly announces the list of these companies and the halal products they provide. The issued certificates are valid in the Middle East and other countries in the region. In 2017, 53 companies acquired certificates, three of them for the domestic market only, eleven for foreign markets only, and 39 for both.[58]

Dress Code

After the end of the communist era in 1989, there were no formal regulations prohibiting wearing the head scarf in public places. There have been occasional bans in state schools that require school uniform. The niqab (face covering) is not commonly worn by Muslim women in Bulgaria. The burqa was introduced only recently within a few Roma communities, and drew the attention of the Patriotic Front, which, in April 2016, proposed a bill to ban it. This was adopted by the 43rd Bulgarian parliament. The *Law Prohibiting the Wearing of Clothing Concealing One's Face in Public Spaces*, also known as the "Burqa Law", provides fines for violators, as well as for instigators and those who allow it; fines can reach up to 2,000 levs (around €1,000). There is no special regulation prohibiting the wearing of head scarves on ID cards and passport photos. Nevertheless, a person's ears need to be visible in the photographs for these documents.

---

58   *Annual Report 2017*, p. 150.

Places of Islamic Learning and Education	– Higher Islamic Institute in Sofia (*Висш Ислямски Институт*, kv. Vrazhdebna, St. 57, No. 6, tel.: ++359 29456298, fax: ++359 28406366, email: info@islamicinstitute-bg.org, www.islamicinstitute-bg.org) – Religious High School Nuvvab (*СОДУ Нювваб*, гр. Шумен, ул. "Г. С. Раковски" 36, tel.: ++359 54800299, ++359 800301, email: sodu_nuvvab@abv.bg, www.nuvvab.net) – Religious High School–Russe (*СОДУ-Русе*, гр. Русе, ул. Цар Самуил № 3, tel.: ++359 879129188, ++359 879129190, email: sodu.ruse@abv.bg, www.sodu-ruse@com) – Religious High School–Momchilgrad (*СОДУ-гр. Момчилград*, ул. "Вяра" № 6, tel.: ++359 36313213, email: soiu@abv.bg, sodu.momchilgrad@gmail.com, www.sodu-momchilgrad.com) – Scientific Research Centre at the Higher Islamic Institute (*Научноизследователският център (НИЦ)* към Висшия Ислямски Институт, бул. "Мария Луиза" № 27, ет. 3, София, email: research@islamicinstitute-bg.org, http://isrcbg.com/).
Muslim Media and Publications	Since 1990, the Muftiate has published a monthly bilingual journal (in Turkish and Bulgarian) called *Müslümanlar/Мюсюлмани* (Muslims). This includes a children's section called *Hilal* (Crescent), which is available as a pdf file that can be downloaded free of charge from www.grandmufti.bg/bg/home/spisanie-myusyulmani.html. The Higher Islamic Institute publishes the only Muslim scholarly magazine, called *Annual/Годишник*. There are no separate Muslim television or radio channels. National radio broadcasts have a three-hour programme on Islam every Friday. Recently, these programmes have been run by one of the deputy Chief Muftis, Vedat Ahmed.

Main Muslim Organisations

- The Chief Muftiate (*Главно мюфтийство*, Bratia Miladinovi Str. N. 27, Sofia 1301, tel.: ++359 29816001, fax: ++359 29803058, www.grandmufti.bg, www.facebook.com/Grandmufti.bg, email: press@grandmufti.bg, news@grandmufti.bg, fetva@grandmufti.bg, info@grandmufti.bg, hac@grandmufti.bg). The Bulgarian Muslim Denomination (*Мюсюлманско изповедание*) comprises a range of well-developed organisational structures. It is administered by the Supreme Muslim Council (*Висш мюсюлмански съвет*) that consists of 30 members, with its core institution being the Chief Muftiate (Chief Mufti's Office). The Chief Muftiate is staffed by a team of 20 employees, working in departments such as *waqf*, hajj, education, publishing, administration and finances, international protocol and public relations, and *irshad* (spiritual and moral guidance). The managing body of the Muslim Denomination also includes 21 regional muftiates, that are comprised of councils of five to eleven members representing the regional departments of the Denomination. Under their ward there are 1,500 local units, called boards or trusteeships. The current Chief Mufti is Mustafa Alish Hadji, in office since 2005. He has three deputies: Vedat Sabri Ahmed (since 2005), Birali Mümün Birali (since 2008), and Murad Pingov (since 2012). The Supreme Muslim Council is headed by Vedat Sabri Ahmed (since 2014).
- Muslim Sunni-Hanafi Denomination in the Republic of Bulgaria (*Мюсюлманско сунитско ханефитско изповедание в Република България*, Bratia Miladinovi Str. N. 27, Sofia 1301, tel.: ++359 879821051, ++359 884674774, email: nedim_gendjev@abv.bg). This organisation was registered on 9 December 2003 by Nedim Gendzhev, a former chief mufti, who claims that the Chief Muftiate, headed by Mustafa Hadji, illegally represents the Bulgarian Muslim Denomination. This parallel denomination is fighting a legal battle to be acknowledged as the official body representing Bulgarian Muslims, but does not provide sustained religious services and activities.

Cyprus

Ali Dayıoğlu[1] and Mete Hatay[2]

Introduction

The Greek Cypriot administered Republic of Cyprus government (RoC), which controls the Southern part of the island, granted Turkish Cypriots access to religious sites in the area it controls, something it has done the last three years. This included allowing visits by approximately 2,650 Turkish Cypriots and Turkish nationals who are living in the North to the Hala Sultan Tekke Mosque on three occasions. Additionally, seven of the eight functioning mosques in the RoC government-controlled area, with the exception of Hala Sultan Tekke, continued to be open for all five daily prayers, and six mosques had the necessary facilities for ablutions. However, despite long-standing requests, the same Government did not grant permission for Muslim communities to make improvements at these mosques.

One of the most significant developments in North Cyprus (areas not controlled by the RoC) in 2017 was an announcement in favour of religious plurality in schools, delivered by the Turkish Cypriot Ombudsman. It concerned the introduction of compulsory instruction on "religious culture and morality" between the fourth and eighth grades, about which a court case had been brought by the head of the *Kıbrıs Pir Sultan Abdal Kültür Derneği* (Cyprus Pir Sultan Abdal Cultural Society), one of the main Alevi associations on the island. The Ombudsman's report stated that the compulsory course was mainly designed for Sunnis following the Hanafi *madhhab*, and that the failure to present students or their parents with any other choice was discriminatory, and that, therefore, it violated the principles of freedom of religion and conscience, and equality. The report also drew attention to the necessity to make religious

---

1 Ali Dayıoğlu is Associate Professor in the Department of International Relations, European University of Lefke, Northern Cyprus. He researches and writes on the Turkish-Muslim minority in Bulgaria and Greece, the non-Muslim minorities in Turkey, and minorities and Islam in Cyprus.
2 Mete Hatay is Senior Research Consultant at the Peace Research Institute, Oslo (PRIO), and the Cyprus Centre, Nicosia. He primarily researches and writes on the Cyprus conflict, Cypriot cultural history, immigration, Islam, and ethnic and religious minorities in Cyprus.

culture and morality courses elective, or to present the opportunity to be exempt from these courses.[3]

The other important development of 2017 was the ratification on 12 June by the *Vakıflar Örgütü ve Din İşleri Dairesi* (*Waqf* Administration and Religious Affairs Office) of the *Foundation, Duties and Rules of Procedure Amendment Law*. This Law gives authority to the *Din İşleri Dairesi Başkanlığı* (Directorate of Religious Affairs–DRA) to open and run summer religious courses, under the inspection of the Ministry of Education. The DRA was also authorised to arrange the location and teachers for the courses, under the condition that the Ministry would inspect it. In addition to this, the Law enables the DRA to raise the number of its staff from 67 to 346, where necessary.[4]

Public Debates

Religious education in public schools has been a long-standing issue of public debate in North Cyprus. The main controversy surrounds the control over the content and teaching of religion. There is a demand from some families in Cyprus, mostly of non-Cypriot origin, to have religious education made available to their children. The *Adalet ve Kalkınma Partisi* (Justice and Development Party–AKP) government in Turkey has also supported these demands. Teachers' unions in North Cyprus, however, respond that religious practice should not be taught in schools, and that if religion is to be taught, it should be as an academic subject that includes the study of other religions. However, when those families and associations that desire religious education have organised courses in mosques, the teachers' unions have also protested that all religious education should be under the purview of the Ministry of Education. The result has been an impasse that erupts in controversy almost every year; a controversy also fuelled by pressure from the Turkish AKP government, to which many Cypriots object.

In 2009, the centre-right *Ulusal Birlik Partisi* (National Unity Party–UBP) government implemented compulsory instruction in "religious culture and morality" as a one-hour per week class from the fourth through to eighth grades. As in previous years, teachers' trade unions and Alevi organisations protested against the introduction of the course in 2017, as its content was mostly

---

[3] http://ombudsman.gov.ct.tr/anasayfa/haberler.aspx, accessed 8 September 2017; *Kıbrıs*, 9 May 2017, p. 18.
[4] Sonay, Meltem, "Kur'an Kurslarına Yasal Zemin" (Legal basis set for Qur'an courses), *Yenidüzen*, 4 June 2017, pp. 6–7.

devoted to the Hanafi-Sunni doctrine, rather than general knowledge of religion and morality. These organisations claimed that by making this course compulsory, the State was discriminating against people who are not Hanafi-Sunni Muslims.[5]

In 2009, the UBP government implemented summer religious courses, including Qur'an lessons. As in previous years, the most controversial issue regarding these courses in 2017 was that they were solely conducted in mosques, without any authorisation by the Ministry of Education. Talip Atalay, head of the DRA, made a statement in July 2017 declaring that permission to conduct the courses in mosques had been received from the Ministry.[6] He also said that, not only Qur'an lessons, but also basic information on Muslim rituals and prayers, are given in these courses, where attendance is voluntary, and a letter is required from children's parents for enrolment.[7]

Political parties, teachers' trade unions, Alevi associations, and NGOs, objected to the *Foundation, Duties and Rules of Procedure Amendment Law*, mentioned above, on the grounds that it gave powers in education to the DRA, outside the Ministry of Education. Criticism particularly concerned the summer religious courses.[8] In response to protests, the President returned the Law to Parliament for reconsideration, but Parliament approved it on 2 October, after which it came into effect.

In addition to the reaction against these courses, leftist opposition parties, teachers' trade unions, and many NGOs, led by Alevi associations, continued to oppose the opening of the Hala Sultan Divinity College. The College was established through the initiative of a newly established foundation, the *Kıbrıs İlim, Ahlak ve Sosyal Yardımlaşma Vakfı* (Cyprus Science, Ethics and Social Assistance Foundation–KİSAV), which is seen to be close to Turkey's ruling AKP party. Financial assistance came from the *Türkiye Odalar ve Borsalar Birliği* (Union of Chambers and Commodity Exchanges of Turkey–TOBB). In January 2014, the *Kıbrıs Türk Öğretmenler Sendikası* (Cyprus Turkish Teachers Trade Union–KTÖS) and *Kıbrıs Türk Orta Eğitim Öğretmenler Sendikası* (Cyprus Turkish Secondary Education Teachers Union–KTOEÖS) filed a lawsuit against the Ministry of Education over the Hala Sultan Divinity College. They

---

5   *Kıbrıs*, 11 May 2017, p. 26.
6   Güler, Ayşe, and Meltem Sonay, "Manzara Değişmedi" (The view has not changed), *Yenidüzen*, http://www.yeniduzen.com/manzara-degismedi-92067h.htm, accessed 9 October 2017.
7   https://cyprus-mail.com/2017/09/10/power-struggle-sack-mufti-north/, accessed 12 September 2017.
8   For the criticism and protests in question, see *Kıbrıs*, 6 June 2017, p. 18; *Kıbrıs*, 8 June 2017, p. 33; *Kıbrıs*, 9 June 2017, p. 19; *Kıbrıs*, 13 June 2017, p. 13; *Kıbrıs*, 17 June 2017, p. 19; *Kıbrıs*, 5 July 2017, p. 13; *Kıbrıs*, 17 August 2017, p. 32.

demanded that the College be closed, and disapproved of its religion-based education.

The Supreme Administrative Court announced its decision on 17 June 2016, and stated that the decision to open the College had been rescinded as its establishment was unauthorised. Following the Court's decision, the Council of Ministers decided in 28 July 2016 that the Divinity College will continue its educational activities, but under the General Secondary Education Department instead of the Vocational Technical Education Department. As a result of this decision, the issue was once again taken to court by the KTOEÖS, and the school's closure was requested on the grounds that it was against the Constitution. In its decision, delivered on 24 October 2017, the Supreme Administrative Court dismissed the case on the grounds that the teacher union's own charter did not empower it to bring a lawsuit regarding state education policy.[9]

As in previous years, the debate and criticism surrounding the Divinity College continued throughout 2017. Teachers' trade unions and various other groups claimed that the Turkish Republic of Cyprus' (TRNC) Ministry of Education was not allowed to supervise the school, that the school implemented its own curriculum, that the school was not run by the principal appointed by the Ministry, and that the actual person with authority was the vice-principal appointed from Turkey. There were also claims that the vocational teachers who came from Turkey to give courses, such as those on the Qur'an, Islamic law, and Qur'anic interpretation, tried to impose pressure on the other teachers and students to adopt a more conservative lifestyle.[10] Moreover, there were also claims that female students were encouraged to cover their heads, that arts and music classes were not held, that there were not any girls' sports teams in the high school section of the College, and that students who missed any prayers were threatened with expulsion from the dormitory the following academic year.[11] The reactions and criticism regarding the school further intensified when, at the Divinity College graduation ceremony, a female student delivered a speech saying that the College was opened upon Turkish President Recep Tayyip Erdoğan's initiative, as a result of the societal degeneration within the Turkish Cypriot community.[12] Towards the end of 2017

---

9   Uysal, Emine, "İlahiyat Koleji Kapatılmayacak" (Divinity College will not be shut down), *Kıbrıs,* 25 October 2017, p. 9.
10 https://www.havadiskibris.com/hala-sultan-ilahiyat-kolejinde-neler-oluyor-2/, accessed 5 December 2017; https://www.havadiskibris.com/camilerden-ilahiyat-cagrisi/, accessed 1 August 2017.
11 *Kıbrıs,* 9 June 2017, p. 18.
12 https://haberkibris.com/ilahiyat-kolejinde-tepki-ceken-mezuniyet-konusmasi-2017-08-08.html, accessed 5 December 2017.

another incident sparked a new debate at the Divinity College. It was claimed that some of the teachers appointed from Turkey prevented New Year celebrations there, and that students who attended the celebrations were threatened with punishment.[13]

Following the coup attempt in Turkey on 15 July 2016, discussion arose in North Cyprus regarding whether or not the Fethullah Gülen congregation had any ties active in North Cyprus. According to the Turkish Ambassador, Derya Kanbay, the *"Fethullahçı Terör Örgütü / Paralel Devlet Yapılanması"* (Fethullah Terrorist Organization / Parallel State Structure–FETÖ / PDY)–the designation used by the Turkish government–has infiltrated institutions in North Cyprus.[14] In a statement made by the Office of the Attorney General, an investigation was launched within the police organisation.[15] As a result of these investigations, certain civilians, clerics, police officers and soldiers were interrogated or arrested on the grounds that they were members of the Gülen movement.[16] Opposition parties criticised the Government for remaining silent about the investigation and the arrests.[17] The Head of the DRA, Talip Atalay, was also taken into custody in Turkey on suspicion of connections to Gülen,[18] though charges were not brought, and Atalay returned to his position in Cyprus.[19]

One other controversial issue in 2017 was the camp and trip organised by the Turkish Ministry of Youth and Sports, for Turkish Cypriot students to the

---

13   https://www.havadiskibris.com/ilahiyatta-yeni-yil-kutlamalari-yasagi/, accessed 1 January 2018.
14   *Kıbrıs*, 15 July 2017, pp. 14–15.
15   Uysal, Emine, "Soruşturma Var, Zanlılar Artabilir" (Investigations may increase suspects), *Kıbrıs*, 6 September 2017, p. 10.
16   Uysal, Emine, "FETÖ Zanlısı İki Sivil Tutuklandı" (Two FETÖ civilian suspects arrested), *Kıbrıs*, 22 June 2017, p. 10; Vamık, Ahmet, "2 Buçuk Yıl Önce 'Abla' Oldu" (She became a "sister" two years ago), *Kıbrıs*, 28 June 2017, p. 5; Boşnak, Sedef, "Polisten 'FETÖ' Operasyonu" (Police "FETÖ" operation), *Kıbrıs*, 11 August 2017, p. 12; Boşnak, Sedef, "Yeni Tutuklamalar Bekleniyor" (New arrests expected), *Kıbrıs*, 12 August 2017, pp. 10–11; İlktaç, Ahmet, "Şimdi de 2 Astsubay FETÖ Zanlısı" (Now two junior officers are FETÖ suspects), *Kıbrıs*, 15 August 2017, p. 6; *Kıbrıs*, 17 August 2017, p. 12; Uysal, Emine, "FETÖ'den Üç Kişi Daha Tutuklandı" (Three more people from FETÖ were arrested), *Kıbrıs*, 18 August 2017, p. 6; *Kıbrıs*, 25 August 2017, p. 6; *Kıbrıs*, 13 October 2017, p. 8; *Kıbrıs*, 22 October 2017, p. 3; *Kıbrıs*, 27 October 2017, p. 8; Uysal, Emine, "Polisler Başsavcılık'ta Sorgulandı" (Police officers were interrogated at the Office of the Attorney General), *Kıbrıs*, 29 November 2017, p. 8; *Kıbrıs*, 20 December 2017, p. 15.
17   *Kıbrıs*, 6 September 2017, pp. 12–13.
18   http://www.hurriyet.com.tr/gundem/kktc-din-isleri-baskani-talip-atalay-gozaltinda-40515185, accessed 12 December 2017; Özyağcı, Mustafa, "Talip Atalay Sorgulandı" (Talip Atalay questioned), *Kıbrıs*, 11 July 2017, p. 9.
19   http://www.cnnturk.com/turkiye/kktc-din-işşleri-baskani-hakkinda-kara-verildi, accessed 12 December 2017.

Turkish province of Çanakkale. Allegations that the students who were taken to Çanakkale, with the approval of the TRNC Ministry of Education, were then ideologically indoctrinated to support the AKP and Erdoğan, and that students were taken to religious seminars without their teachers' knowledge, were met with a strong reaction from various circles in North Cyprus, led by teachers' trade unions.[20] In response to these reactions, the Ministry of Education and various organisations claimed that the allegations put forward by the trade unions were untrue.[21]

The last significant development in 2017 was the *waqf* Administration's lease of 70 acres of land in Kyrenia to the *Türkiye Maarif Vakfı* (Turkish Maarif Foundation), a charity set up to take over the Fethullah Gülen schools in the world. The lease is for 30 years, in return for a nominal sum of £1,000.[22] While widespread claims were made that the land had been leased to establish an *imam-hatip* school, the General Director of the *waqf* Administration, İbrahim Benter, denied these allegations. According to him, the school would offer the children of underprivileged families the opportunity to receive quality education.[23] Led by teachers' trade unions, various circles protested against this decision, and, as of December 2017, the Council of Ministers had still not approved the agreement to lease the property in question.

Transnational Links

Transnational links in Cyprus are primarily with Turkey, which provides funding to the North Cyprus DRA. While Muslims in the South in the past had links with Arab countries, especially Libya, those links have been cut since the so-called Arab Spring. At the same time, almost half of the clergy in the island's North is from Turkey.

Apart from these links, Cypriot Muslims engage in partnerships with transnational bodies, such as the United Nations Development Programme (UNDP) and the United States Agency for International Development (USAID), as well as with the supranational EU. As in 2016, one of the most successful such

---

20 *Kıbrıs*, 19 July 2017, p. 14; http://www.yeniduzen.com/ktoeos-canakkale-kampinda-neler-oldu-92439h.htm, accessed 31 July 2017; http://www.gazete360.com/egitim-kampindan-skandal-goruntuler/, accessed 1 August 2017; *Kıbrıs*, 1 August 2017, p. 17; *Kıbrıs*, 4 August 2017, p. 14; *Kıbrıs*, 5 August 2017, p. 14; *Kıbrıs*, 19 August 2017, p. 15.
21 *Kıbrıs*, 2 August 2017, p. 10; *Kıbrıs*, 9 September 2017, p. 14.
22 Topal, Bertuğ, "Girne'nin Kalbine İmam Hatip" (Divinity College in the middle of Kyrenia), *Havadis*, 20 December 2017, p. 4.
23 *Kıbrıs*, 22 December 2017, p. 21.

endeavours in 2017, was the bi-communal Technical Committee on Cultural Heritage, which continued its work on the protection and restoration of the cultural heritage in the North and South of Cyprus. Between 2012 and November 2017 approximately €14.7 million have been provided by the EU, through the Aid Programme for the Turkish Cypriot Community, to implement the priorities of the Technical Committee for the preservation of the cultural heritage in Cyprus.[24] In November 2017, the Committee completed a new set of heritage conservation projects. These were: the Ayios Nicolaos/Aynikola mosque in Ayios Nikolaos village; and the Ayios Ioannis/ Ayanni mosque, located in Agios Ioannis village, both situated in the areas controlled by the RoC government.[25]

In addition, the Swedish government, via its embassy and the Office of the Religious Track of the Cyprus Peace Process on the island, has facilitated meetings amongst the island's religious leaders since 2011.[26] These meetings continued throughout 2017. In this context, the head of the DRA, Talip Atalay, Archbishop Chrysostomos II, of the Cyprus Orthodox Church, Archbishop Youssef Souif, of the Maronite Church, Archbishop Varoujan Herkelian, of the Armenian Church, and the representative of Cypriot Roman Catholics (called "Latins" in Cyprus), Bishop George Kraj, attended several meetings throughout 2017. The Office of the Religious Track of the Cyprus Peace Process also convened its third Round Table for Human Rights with the representatives of faith communities, on 28 September 2017.[27]

In addition to the meetings between religious leaders, clergymen from various countries visited North Cyprus. For example, the head of the Islamic Community of Montenegro, Rifat Feyziç, had a meeting with the head of the DRA, Talip Atalay, in January 2017.[28]

Law and Domestic Politics

Apart from the above mentioned *Foundation, Duties and Rules of Procedure Amendment Law*, which gives authority to the DRA to open and run summer

---

[24] http://english.cyprustimes.com/2017/11/24/project-completion-ceremony-conservation-works-technical-committee-cultural-heritage-paphos/, accessed 12 December 2017.

[25] *Kıbrıs*, 25 November 2017, p. 12.

[26] The meetings between the religious leaders are organised by the Office of the Religious Track of the Cyprus Peace Process, under the auspices of the Swedish Embassy. The Office was set up in 2009 by Swedish Religious Social Democrats Chair, Peter Weiderud, with the support of the Swedish Ministry for Foreign Affairs.

[27] See www.religioustrack.com, accessed 7 January 2018.

[28] *Kıbrıs*, 26 January 2017, p. 19.

religious courses, under the inspection of the Ministry of Education there were no other changes in the law or any new legislation adopted regarding Islam in 2017, in either North or South Cyprus. Domestic politics on both sides of the island concentrated mainly on the ongoing negotiations to solve the island's division. However, as the debates in this report indicate, some circles in the Turkish Cypriot community are increasingly worried about Turkey's influence on the island and on domestic politics in the North, suspecting Turkey's ruling AKP party of having an agenda to reshape the religious landscape of the island, and to create a more conservative Muslim environment. Hence, these circles in North Cyprus perceive any kind of economic and cultural activity conducted by the Turkish state as an attempt by Turkey's ruling party to undermine the primarily secular nature of Turkish Cypriot society.[29]

Activities and Initiatives of Main Muslim Organisations

While no Islamic festivals are officially recognised in the South, all Islamic festivals are recognised in the North. As Turkish Cypriot society is for the most part secular, most Turkish Cypriots take part in religious activities primarily during religious festivals, especially the major festivals at the end of Ramadan (*Ramazan Bayramı*) and 'Id al-Adha (*Kurban Bayramı*).

Beginning in the late 1990s, Turkish Cypriots began to celebrate the *Mevlid Kandili*, or the anniversary of the Prophet's birth, as the Week of the Holy Birth (*Kutlu Doğum Haftası*), or *Mevlid-i Nebi*. Although *Mevlid Kandili* had been celebrated previously, under the influence of trends coming from Turkey, this one-day event became a week-long festival (14–20 April 2017), with religious, educational and cultural activities, including conferences, seminars, concerts, and exhibitions. In addition to events sponsored by the DRA, some universities organised special programmes during the Week of the Holy Birth.[30]

As the result of cooperation between the organisation of the North Cyprus Red Crescent and the *waqf* Administration, and the financial support of the Turkish Embassy, *iftar* tents were erected in different districts during Ramadan. Apart from these institutions, the Civil Defence Organisation, several municipalities, political parties, sports associations, private companies, and Muslim

---

29 For example, see "AKP'nin ve Kukla Hükümetlerinin Şecereleri" (The genealogies of the AKP and its puppet governments), *Kıbrıs Türk Orta Eğitim Öğretmenler Sendikası*, 11 July 2013, www.ktoeos.org/akpnin-ve-kukla-hukumetlerin-secereleri/, accessed, 22 April 2017. The discussion about religious influence is also prevalent on social media on the island.

30 *Kıbrıs*, 12 April 2017, p. 34.

civil society organisations also organised *iftar* meals and gave gifts to children. For example, the *Evrensel Sevgi ve Kardeşlik Derneği* (Association of Universal Love and Brotherhood–ESKAD) together with the Cyprus International Student Association, organised an *iftar* meal for foreign students at Cypriot universities coming from 50 different countries.[31] In addition, on the occasion of Ramadan, and with the cooperation of the *waqfs* Administration and the Social Services Department, food aid was given to families in need.

During 'Id al-Adha, and with the help of the Turkish Red Crescent, the North Cyprus Red Crescent distributed sacrificial meat to about 1,000 families in need.[32] The *waqf* Administration also prepared a "Poverty Map", and provided sacrificial meat and food for many poor families.[33]

In 2017, as in previous years, the DRA organised visits to the Hala Sultan Tekke in the island's South. Hala Sultan Tekke allegedly contains the grave of the Prophet Muhammad's aunt. During 'Id al-Fitr (*Ramazan Bayramı*) 818 people from the North visited Hala Sultan Tekke on 27 June 2017.[34] Similar visits to the *tekke* were organised on 5 September and 29 November 2017, on the occasion of 'Id al-Adha (*Kurban Bayramı*) and *Mevlid Kandili* (birth of Prophet Muhammad), respectively.[35]

On 15–22 April 2017, various events were organised to mark the 446th anniversary of the establishment of the *waqf*, as well as the 61st anniversary of the handover of those religious foundations from the British Colonial Administration to the Turkish Cypriot community. In various mosques in North Cyprus, religious memorial services were held in honour of individuals who had made contributions to the *waqf*. As part of the *waqf* week events, on 15 April a programme on "*Waqf* and Woman" and, as in 2016, a day-long "Benevolence Festival", was organised in Nicosia.[36]

Apart from the *waqf* week events, various activities and events were held throughout 2017 in order to spread the theme of "Doing good to others without expecting anything in return". Under this theme, plays[37] and shadow plays[38] were staged for primary school students. As in 2015 and 2016, the *waqf*

---

31   http://ilkha.com/haber/55769/kibrista-50-farkli-ulkeden-kardeslik-iftarda-bulustu, accessed 10 November 2017.
32   http://www.kibrismanset.com/guncel/turk-kizilayi-kktcde-de-kurban-kesecek-h186692.html, accessed 10 December 2017.
33   http://www.evkaf.org/site/sayfa.aspx?pkey=265, accessed 12 November 2017.
34   *Kıbrıs,* 29 June 2017, p. 31.
35   https://www.state.gov/documents/organization/281138.pdf, accessed 18 February 2018.
36   http://www.evkaf.org/site/sayfa.aspx?pkey=291, accessed 19 April 2017.
37   *Kıbrıs,* 11 January 2017, p. 29; *Kıbrıs,* 6 October 2017, p. 28; *Kıbrıs,* 20 November 2017, p. 13; http://www.evkaf.org/site/sayfa.aspx?pkey=265, accessed 26 May 2017.
38   http://www.evkaf.org/site/sayfa.aspx?pkey=362, accessed 12 November 2017.

Administration carried out a project for children and young people to help them understand and promote the spirit of the donation. As part of this project, various foundations (comprising students aged between six and 19) were established under the name "Benevolence Volunteers". On specific dates, students working voluntarily carried out various activities, such as environmental cleaning, visits to old people's homes, providing food-aid for families in need, and feeding animals in animal shelters.[39]

The *waqf* Administration helped many families and their children in need, among whom there were also Syrian refugees.[40] It provided financial support for children receiving special education, and their families.[41] It also carried out various events on important days and weeks, such as on 8 March for International Women's Day, on 18–24 March for Elderly Week, and for *kandils*.[42] Additionally, it sponsored children's festivals.[43] The Administration also supported the restoration and renovation of many museums, schools, sports grounds, and religious and historical sites.[44] It also funded a "Community Kitchen", which was opened for refugees, and sponsored a public service advertisement to raise awareness of the importance of the early diagnosis of cancer.[45] It was announced by the *waqf* Administration that 1,500,000 TL (approximately €275,250) had been allocated for charity, social and cultural aid in 2017.[46]

Apart from the *waqf* Administration and the DRA, which are under the control of the State, Muslim civil society organisations also celebrated special days and organised activities. For example, on 6 May 2017, the ESKAD organised a Mother's Day celebration and a commemoration of Hala Sultan in Famagusta.[47] In November, the same organisation sponsored a "Qur'an Recital Feast" programme in four districts of the island's North.[48] On 7 December, it

---

39 http://www.haberalkibrisli.net/kibris/3-milyon-tllik-hayir-isi-h52849.html, accessed 17 April 2017; Bulut, Ayşe, "Gıda Paketleri Dağıtıldı" (Food packages distributed), *Kıbrıs*, 11 June 2017, p. 13; *Kıbrıs*, 10 July 2017, p. 14; *Kıbrıs*, 10 October 2017, p. 31; *Yenidüzen*, 12 November 2017, p. 3.
40 http://www.evkaf.org/site/sayfa.aspx?pkey=313, accessed 12 November 2017.
41 http://www.evkaf.org/site/sayfa.aspx?pkey=265, accessed 26 May 2017.
42 http://www.evkaf.org/site/sayfa.aspx?pkey=277; http://www.evkaf.org/site/sayfa.aspx?pkey=277, accessed 12 November 2017.
43 http://www.evkaf.org/site/sayfa.aspx?pkey=42, accessed 12 November 2017.
44 *Kıbrıs*, 7 December 2017, p. 5.
45 *Yenidüzen*, 15 October 2017, p. 24.
46 https://www.havadiskibris.com/ibrahim-benterin-sikisan-kalbi-vakiflar/, accessed 15 March 2017.
47 http://www.kibrismanset.com/guncel/eskad-hala-sultan-ve-anneler-gunu-programi-gerceklestirdi-h202954.html, accessed 7 July 2017.
48 http://www.yenisoz.com.tr/kibris-besparmak-ta-dus-gormek-makale-25885, accessed 14 December 2017.

also organised an "Al-Quds Night" in Nicosia.[49] On the night of 31 December 2017, the same organisation held an event in Famagusta to celebrate the conquest of Mecca.[50]

As in previous years, another organisation that carried out numerous events in 2017 was the *Akademi Kıbrıs Gelişim Platformu* (Cyprus Development Platform Academy), a religious educational association that has close links with the AKP and AKP-supported foundations in Turkey. In addition to religious activities throughout the year, the Academy ran various educational events.[51]

Muslim organisations carried out demonstrations and made declarations to protest against the oppression of Muslims in various countries. For example, on 8 December, ESKAD and *Akademi Kıbrıs* protested against the decision of the USA to recognise Jerusalem as the capital city of Israel.[52] On 21 July 2017, after the Friday prayer, ESKAD held a demonstration in Nicosia to protest against attacks by Israeli forces on Palestinian civilians.[53]

Aside from these organisations, several Turkey-based *tariqas* carried out various activities. One of these *tariqas* is known as the *Medeniyet-İrfan-Hayır-Ref Vakfı* (Civilization, Wisdom, Benefaction and Pious Foundation–MİHR), whose leader is İskender Evrenesoğlu. The police received numerous complaints about *tariqa* members carrying out various proselytising events.[54] The distribution of Adnan Oktar's Islamic books, to propagate the *tariqa* without state approval, was another issue that drew reaction. Several MPs brought up the matter in Parliament.[55]

Alevis also freely celebrated their own festivals, such as 'Ashura' and *qurban*. During these celebrations many *dedes* and traditional *ashiks*, or minstrels, are invited from Turkey. In this context, the *KKTC Alevi Kültür Merkezi* (TRNC

---

49 https://web.facebook.com/ESKAD.ORG/videos/1924884780870168/?_rdc=1&_rdr, accessed 4 January 2018.
50 https://www.piccorn.com/tag/eskad, accessed 4 January 2018.
51 For more on Academy Cyprus' activities, see http://www.akademikibris.com/index1.html#, accessed 11 January 2018.
52 İlktaç, Ahmet, "İsrail ve Trump Lânetlendi" (Israel and Trump are cursed), *Kıbrıs*, 9 December 2017, pp. 16–17.
53 http://euturkhaber.com/kibrista-kudus-zulmu-protesto-edilecek/, accessed 28 August 2017.
54 *Yenidüzen*, 5 February 2017, p. 12; http://www.kibrisadahaber.com/tarikatlar-kktcye-desicradi.html, accessed 14 February 2017.
55 Özbil, Ceren, "Kimin Dağıttığı Bilinmiyor" (Nobody knows who distributed them), http://www.kibrisgazetesi.com/haber/kimin-dagittigi-bilinmiyor/16350, accessed 14 April 2017; *Kıbrıs*, 12 April 2017, p. 31.

Alevi Cultural Centre) organised 'Ashura' day on 15 October 2017.[56] The Alevi Cultural Centre also organised a Hacı Bektaşı Veli commemoration event on 17 August.[57]

Additionally, *cem* rituals were performed by the Alevi Cultural Centre in Nicosia and Famagusta on the 8 and 9 February 2017, respectively.[58] Alevi organisations held conferences and events on various topics, including a commemoration of those who died in Turkey's Sivas Massacre in 1993.[59] They carried out demonstrations and protests, as well. For example, on 5 June 2017, the *Kıbrıs Pir Sultan Abdal Kültür Derneği* (Pir Sultan Abdal Cultural Society), together with some other civil society organisations, protested against the new DRA Law.

Muslim Population: History and Demographics

The Muslim presence in Cyprus dates from the seventh century, but Islam took root, grew, and became institutionalised on the island during the period of Ottoman rule (1571–1878). Cyprus was a British colony from 1878 until 1960, when the island gained its independence and the Republic of Cyprus (RoC) was formed. The RoC was based on a consociational system of power-sharing between the Turks and Greeks of the island, each community dealing with its own religious affairs. However, this power-sharing arrangement broke down in 1963, leading to a period of intermittent intercommunal violence over the next decade. During this period, the RoC came under the sole control of Greek Cypriots, while Turkish Cypriots established their own administration in armed enclaves. A Greek-sponsored coup and subsequent Turkish military intervention in 1974 ultimately led to the island's present division. Greek Cypriots residing in the North fled to the South of the island, and Turkish Cypriots in the South moved to the North.

After the division of the island, the RoC, under Greek-Cypriot control, in the South, became the only internationally recognised Government of the island. Turkish Cypriots in 1983 proclaimed a state in the North, the Turkish Republic of Northern Cyprus (TRNC), which remains to this day

---

56 http://www.kibrisgazetesi.com/kultur-sanat/kktc-alevi-kultur-merkezi-pazar-gunu-asure-etkinligi-duzenliyor/28264, accessed 19 October 2017.

57 https://www.gundemkibris.com/kibris/alevi-kultur-merkezi-haci-bektas-veli-yi-anma-etkinligi-duzenliyor-h220518.html, accessed 22 November 2017.

58 http://www.kktcakm.com/kktc-alevi-kultur-merkezi-hizir-cemi-gerceklestirdi-2/, accessed 22 January 2017.

59 *Kıbrıs*, 3 July 2017, p. 11.

unrecognised by any country other than Turkey. Although the RoC is constitutionally a bi-communal state, in 2004 it became a member of the EU without its Turkish Cypriot part. Turkish Cypriots may carry European passports via the RoC, but the Northern part of the island was excluded from the EU's *acquis communautaire*.

According to the 2012 Demographic Report of the RoC Statistical Service Department, the population in the South, in the RoC-controlled area, was 838,897.[60] Of these, 179,547 were foreign residents who do not have Cypriot citizenship. According to information obtained from the Statistical Service Department, the number of Muslim citizens of the RoC, as of May 2014, was 2,492. The number of Muslim citizens from other EU countries living in the South was 611, while the number of Muslims from third countries was 12,152. Information regarding the ethnic origins of these persons was not provided.[61]

According to the 2011 census results, the total *de jure* population in the island's North is 286,257. The census does not include the rotating population of the Turkish military, which is estimated at 30,000–35,000 at any one time. The 2011 census results show that, of the total recorded *de jure* population, 190,494 were citizens of the TRNC, although 31,234 of these gave their birthplace as Turkey.[62] While religion was not listed on the census, and even though the majority of the population is fundamentally secular, Turkish Cypriots are officially considered Muslims.

Muslim Population	South: 15,255 (ca. 2% of entire population) North: 286,257 total population (officially considered to be all Muslims).
Ethnic and National Backgrounds	South: during the civil war in Lebanon, many Lebanese fled and settled in South Cyprus, and Cyprus is today an important receiving country for economic migrants, refugees, and asylum seekers from nearby Muslim majority countries, South East Asia, and Africa. According to the United Nations High Commissioner for Refugees (UNHCR), as of

---

60 www.mof.gov.cy/mof/cystat/statistics.nsf/All/732265957BAC953AC225798300406903?OpenDocument&sub=2&sel=1&e=&print, accessed 8 March 2015.
61 "Rum Tarafında 2 Bin 492 Müslüman Yaşıyor" (2,492 Muslims live in Greek part), *Kıbrıs*, 1 June 2014, p. 8.
62 www.devplan.org/Nufus-2011/nufus%20ikinci_.pdf, accessed 12 January 2014.

the end of 2017, 4,594 asylum seekers were living in Cyprus, the majority of whom were of a Muslim background.[63] Currently 1,250 refugees are living in Cyprus. Asylum applications in 2016 increased by 36% compared to 2015, and this upward trend continued in 2017. Of the total numbers of applications received and processed between 2002 and September 2017, only 15% were accorded protection, the vast majority subsidiary protection (7,718). In 2016–17, the protection rate for Syrians was almost 100%, but only 3% received refugee status compared to the EU average of 60%.[64]

A substantial number of Turkish Cypriots, mostly of Roma origin, moved from the island's North to the South after the 2003 opening of the ceasefire line that divides the island, especially since Cyprus's 2004 EU accession.[65] However, according to a study, the Muslim population of Turkish Cypriot extraction living in the South still does not exceed 1%.[66] According to the 2011 census, there were only 1,405 people who spoke Turkish as their mother tongue and lived in South Cyprus.[67]

North: 80,550 non-TRNC citizen immigrants are nationals of the Republic of Turkey. Amongst them are many Kurdish and Arabic speakers.

---

63   www.unhcr.org.cy/fileadmin/user_upload/CyprusFactSheetMarch2016_003_.pdf; http://www.asylumineurope.org/reports/country/cyprus/statistics, both accessed 18 July 2017.

64   UNHCR Cyprus Web: http://www.unhcr.org/cy/wp-content/uploads/sites/41/2018/05/CyprusFactSheetSeptember2017_updated_latest.pdf, accessed 2 July 2018.

65   It is known, however, that around 300 Roma had already crossed the Green Line, sought asylum, and settled in the RoC controlled areas in the late 1990s. For further information regarding the Roma population movement, see www.domresearchcenter.com/news/cyprus/index.html, accessed 8 March 2014.

66   www.uclouvain.be/cps/ucl/doc/espo/documents/Rapport_parlement_europeen_mai_2007_english.pdf, accessed 3 March 2014.

67   www.mof.gov.cy/mof/cystat/statistics.nsf/census-2011_cystat_en/census-2011_cystat_en?OpenDocument, accessed 5 March 2014.

Inner-Islamic Groups	South: the majority of Muslims are Sunnis. A small number of Iranian residents are Shi'is, while some Arab residents are affiliated with the Salafi movement. Those from South East Asia mainly follow the Hanafi school.
	North: most Kurds are Sunni Muslims, with most following the Shafi'i school. In addition, there is a large Alevi immigrant population, consisting of Turkish nationals from both ethnic Turkish and Kurdish backgrounds. An estimated 10,000 immigrant workers and 8,000 naturalised North Cyprus citizens of Turkish, Kurdish, and Arab origin are Alevis.[68] The majority of Arabic-speaking Turkish nationals are Sunni Muslims of the Hanafi school, but there is also a small population of Alawites or Nusayris (different from Alevis), most of whom are originally from the Hatay area of Southern Turkey.
Geographical Spread	South: most Muslim migrants inhabit the cities, Nicosia in particular, while Muslims of Roma origin are located primarily in Limassol and certain villages in the Paphos district.
	North: Muslims are spread throughout the Northern part of the island, with a concentration of Shi'i students in the Famagusta area, where their university is located.
Number of Mosques	South: eight mosques exist. Prior to the departure of Turkish Cypriots in the 1960s or after 1974, there were 109 mosques in the South as well as four *tekkes*.[69]

---

68 https://www.state.gov/documents/organization/281138.pdf, accessed 18 February 2018.
69 The Republic of Cyprus Department of Antiquities announced that €355,830 had been allocated in 2017 for the restoration and cleaning of Ottoman historical sites, mosques and cemeteries in the South. In another statement, the Department stated that €3.4 million had been spent in the last ten years for the maintenance and restoration of 109 mosques in South Cyprus: *Kıbrıs*, 18 July 2017, p. 20.

	North: as of August 2017, there were 212 mosques and *masjids* in Northern Cyprus.[71]
Muslim Burial Sites	South: only three of the 148 Muslim cemeteries in the South are in good condition.
	North: in the North, there are over 150 Muslim cemeteries. The land is owned by the *waqf* Administration, which also provides for services conducted in these cemeteries. Maintenance is provided by municipalities.
"Chaplaincy" in State Institutions	South: the Central Prison in the South now allows representatives of any religious group to visit prisoners, after complaints by some prisoners that their religious rights were restricted.[72] There are no facilities for Muslim worship in other public institutions.
	North: hospitals, prisons, and military installations have *mescits*, or small chapels for prayer. The military also employs its own imams, while prisons have visiting imams. Facilities for prayer are not available in other state institutions, such as schools or offices.
Halal Products	South: because of demand from Muslim immigrants, there are private companies slaughtering and selling halal meat in the South.
	North: all meat slaughtered in the North is halal, and slaughter is under the control of the municipalities.

---

70 Özyağcı, Mustafa, "Eğitim Yine Sorunlarla Başlayacak" (Education will start the problems again), *Kıbrıs*, 23 August 2017, p. 14; http://www.kibrispostasi.com/c1-KIBRIS_POSTASI_GAZETESI/j97/a31146-Camilerin-ve-okullarin-sayisi, accessed 2 November 2017.
71 www.state.gov/j/dri/rls/irf/2014/eur/238368.htm, accessed 18 June 2016.

Dress Code

South: theoretically, there are no legal restrictions for Muslim dress in the areas controlled by the RoC. However, the *2017 Report on International Religious Freedom: Cyprus*, states that a hotel refused to hire Muslim women as cleaners, because they wore head scarves.[73]

North: beginning in 2017, and apparently under the influence of Turkey, Turkish Cypriots began to change the regulations regarding dress restrictions in official public spaces. The new Law replaced ones that dated to the 1960s, and now allows the head scarf in official public spaces, such as within the police and the military.

Places of Islamic Learning and Education

South: there are no state-supported Islamic schools in South Cyprus, while instruction in the Greek Orthodox religion is compulsory in primary and secondary schools. However, parents of different faiths may submit a written request for their children to be exempted from this subject. Turkish Cypriot pupils who attend schools in the South, if there are reasonable numbers of them, may receive religious instruction in their own language. In 2016, a Turkish Cypriot teacher was giving religious lessons in Turkish in Limassol, where most Turkish Cypriots (mostly of Roma origin) live.

There are no institutions of higher education that offer training for imams or other religious professions in the South.

North: since 2009, compulsory instruction in "religious culture and morality" has been implemented as a one hour per week class from the fourth to eighth grade. There are also summer religion courses, with Qur'an lessons for students who have finished grade three.

---

72 https://www.state.gov/documents/organization/281138.pdf, accessed 3 July 2017.

Institutions of higher religious education are: the Faculty of Theology, Near East University (NEU); Islamic Research Centre, Near East University; The Faculty of Theology, Cyprus Social Sciences University; Hala Sultan Divinity College; and the Open Faculty, Anadolu University.

Muslim Media and Publications

South: the media operate freely in the South, though local media sources do not publish or air informative content about Islam.

North: there are no visual or printed media sources that consistently address religious issues, though some newspapers provide space on Fridays for articles on religion. The NEU Faculty of Theology publishes the *Journal of the NEU Faculty of Theology* and the NEU Islamic Research Centre publishes *Journal of the Near East Islamic Research Centre*. The *Journal of the NEU Faculty of Theology* (whose first two issues were published in 2015 and 2016), focuses on divinity in general. The *Journal of the Near East Islamic Research Centre* (whose first two issues were also published in 2015 and 2016) publishes research into Cyprus' Islamic background and past.

During the main religious festivals, local television and radio stations air religious programmes. All religious publications, including newspapers and magazines that are published in Turkey, are available for sale in the North, and it is possible to view television channels from Turkey with religious content via satellite.

Main Muslim Organisations

- Cyprus *waqf* Administration (*Kıbrıs Vakıflar İdaresi*, PO Box 118, via Mersin 10, Nicosia, Turkey, tel.: ++90 3922283134, www.evkaf.org). Historically, the *waqf* Administration is one of the two primary Muslim organisations in Cyprus. As it represents all Muslims in Cyprus, the *waqf* Administration– currently called *Waqf* Administration and Religious Affairs Office (*Vakıflar*

Örgütü ve Din İşleri Dairesi)–owns all the island's mosques, cemeteries, *tekkes* and *turbes* (shrines), and manages the affairs of land and business holdings that have been donated for religious purposes. Following the 1974 division of the island, the *waqf* lost control of all holdings in the South, both religious and commercial, and now operates solely in the North.
- Mufti, Directorate of Religious Affairs–DRA (*Müftü, KKTC Din İşleri Başkanlığı*, 1A Site Sokak, Din Sitesi, Hamitköy, via Mersin 10, Nicosia, Turkey, tel.: ++90 3922253062, www.kktcdinisleri.com). The *Müftü* (or Mufti) is the official spiritual head of the community in Cyprus. The Mufti is an appointed position, and he is selected by the *waqf* Administration Management Board, which in turn is appointed by the Turkish Cypriot government. Although his remit is technically for the entire island, after 1974 his office moved to the North, and until recently he was effectively without power in the South. While once influential in legal and educational matters, and in areas such as marriage and divorce, the Mufti lost his historical title and privileges in the 1980s, and became simply the Head of the Directorate of Religious Affairs (DRA), although he is still known to Turkish Cypriots as the Mufti.

In addition to these official institutions, there are five important religious associations operating in the North:

- The Association of Universal Love and Brotherhood (*Evrensel Sevgi ve Kardeşlik Derneği*–ESKAD, www.eskad.org). This association was founded in 1996 by a previous Mufti, Ahmet Yönlüer.
- The Turkish Islamic Cultural Association (*Türk İslam Kültür Cemiyeti*, http://turkislamkulturcemiyeti.com). Founded in 1983, this organisation was influenced by the "Turkish-Islamic synthesis", popular in Turkey in the 1980s, which attempted to combine nationalism and Islam.
- Academy Cyprus (*Akademi Kıbrıs Gelişim Platformu*, www.akademikibris.com/index1.html). This association was founded in 2008, and has a close and active relationship with the AKP and various Islamic organisations in Turkey.
- Cyprus Science, Ethics and Social Assistance Foundation (*Kıbrıs İlim, Ahlak ve Sosyal Yardımlaşma Vakfı*–KİSAV, https://tr.facebook.com/pages/K%C4%B1br%C4%B1s-%C4%B0lim-Ahlak-ve-Sosyal-Yard%C4%B1mla%C5%9Fma-Vakf%C4%B1-K%C4%B0SAV/541298235882278). Founded in November 2011. In January 2012, this association leased 200 acres of land belonging to the *waqf* Administration, located in a suburban area of Nicosia. The 30-year lease has a nominal yearly rent of 100 TL (approximately €33), justified by the Foundation's plans to build a *külliye*, a complex of

buildings around a mosque. In 2013, construction of the Hala Sultan Divinity College, the first religious vocational high school in Northern Cyprus, was completed, while construction also began on the Hala Sultan Mosque, both part of this intended religious complex.
- Cyprus Science, Culture and Vocation Foundation (*Kıbrıs İlim, Kültür ve Hizmet Vakfı*, http://www.nurnet.org/tag/kibris-ilim-kultur-ve-hizmet-vakfi/). Founded in 1990 by the followers of Bediüzzaman Said Nursi.
- Cyprus Turkish Islam Association (*Kıbrıs Türk İslam Cemiyeti*, P.O. Box: 099 Lefkoşa, okyaysadikoglu@yahoo.com).
- Certain Sufi *tariqa*s also operate in North Cyprus, the most important being the Naqshbandi *tariqa*, situated in the small town of Lefke (www.saltanat.org).

Along with the Sunni Muslim institutions, there are two Alevi associations:

- TRNC Alevi Cultural Centre (*KKTC Alevi Kültür Merkezi*, www.kktcalevileri.org). In 2006, this organisation acquired land from the Government to build a *cemevi*, or Alevi place of worship. Currently, they use the Association's building for their rituals and gatherings.
- Cyprus Pir Sultan Abdal Cultural Society (*Kıbrıs Pir Sultan Abdal Kültür Derneği*, http://kibrispirsultan.org).

Czech Republic

Štěpán Macháček[1]

Introduction

The small organised part of the Czech Muslims kept a low profile in the public sphere in 2017. This has been the case since 2015 when the immigration wave to Europe inflamed anti-Muslim and anti-Islam voices in Czech society. Some of the short-lived fierce anti-Muslim political platforms gradually disappeared in 2016 and 2017, yet a new far right party Liberty and Direct Democracy (*Svoboda a přímá demokracie*–SPD), established in 2015, with a strong anti-immigrant and anti-Muslim stance, and led by the Czech-Japanese businessman Tomio Okamura–succeeded in gaining a considerable number of seats in the parliamentary elections of October 2017.[2]

In January 2017, the Czech president Miloš Zeman, who uses anti-immigration and anti-Islam rhetoric, said that he was sure that a terrorist attack would one day happen in the Czech Republic.[3] He did not, however, point directly to Czech Muslims as possible perpetrators. At the same time, the Czech Inner Security Service (BIS) clearly stated that it had no evidence pointing to any preparation for a terrorist attack in the Czech Republic, and that there was definitely no such threat stemming from Czech Muslims. According to the BIS, "Muslims comply with Czech law, they do not react to anti-Islamic activities through violence or verbal aggressiveness and remain very restrained in the face of the provocations of Islamophobes".[4] Several minor verbal and

---

[1] Štěpán Macháček is a former research fellow at the Oriental Institute of the Czech Academy of Sciences. Currently he is a Czech Radio correspondent in the Middle East. He graduated in Arabic Philology and Islamic History. His research focuses on contemporary Islam in the Balkans, the Czech Republic and Slovakia.

[2] The quarterly report on extremism for Q1/2018 by the Czech Ministry of the Interior, describes the SPD as a "… non-extremist organisation that has adopted a xenophobic discourse", adding that the SPD put forward a law that would criminalise "… hateful Islamic ideologies": file:///C:/Users/%C5%A0t%C4%9Bp%C3%A1n/Downloads/Extremismus_-_Souhrnna_situacni_zprava_za_1_ctvrtleti_roku_2018.pdf, accessed 17 June 2018.

[3] The video-interview of the Czech president Miloš Zeman by the *Blesk Daily* on 8 January 2017: http://www.blesk.cz/clanek/zpravy-politika/442023/hrozi-cesku-teroristicky-utok-zeman-ano-jsme-na-rade.html, accessed 20 May 2018.

[4] See the Czech on-line daily Aktuálně.cz: https://zpravy.aktualne.cz/domaci/cesti-musli-move-nechteji-vyvolavat-strety-nebo-provokovat-zn/r~8e89bdaed67b11e694810025900fea04/?redirected=1526792581, accessed 20 May 2018.

non-verbal attacks against Muslims in the streets were recorded in the Czech Republic in 2017.[5]

Public Debates

Debates on Islam and Muslims calmed down considerably compared to the rhetoric heard during the migrant and refugee crises of 2015 and early 2016. It appears that the Czech Republic was unaffected by the crisis, and refugees or migrants of a Muslim background did not come into the country in any noticeable numbers.[6] The Czech government ignored the EU relocation plan, and, after accepting twelve refugees taken from Italy and Greece, it stopped the programme altogether in spring 2017. However, the parliamentary elections in October 2017 showed that the fear of Islam could still bring many votes to political parties who decided to profit from this topic. The main anti-immigrant and anti-Muslim party, the SPD, participated in the elections for the first time and won almost 11% of the vote, and gained 22 Members of Parliament. One of its election slogans was "NO to Islam, NO to Terrorism". One of the main manifesto priorities of the party was to "… ban Islam in the Czech Republic".[7] Another priority of the party is to implement a law to facilitate the holding of a referendum on leaving the European Union.[8] No other party with an explicitly anti-Muslim platform made it to Parliament in 2017. Some of the other parties, including the victorious centrist Ano (*Yes*) party of the Prime Minister Andrej Babiš, are very outspoken against the system of EU quotas on distributing asylum seekers among the member states. However, the language of these parties does not target Islam or Muslims specifically.

President Miloš Zeman remains one of the most vocal critics of Islam in the Czech political scene. In one of his regional meetings with local citizens, he

---

[5] https://www.irozhlas.cz/zpravy-domov/potycka-kvuli-hidzabu-zena-v-sarce-napadla-zahalenou-muslimku-pripad-vysetruje_1707221550_rez, accessed 20 May 2018.
[6] The number of asylum seekers in the Czech Republic has decreased slightly since 2015. The total number of applications for asylum in 2017 was 1,450, with a large majority of applications from residents of non-Muslim countries. For Syrians, for example, the Czech authorities recorded less than 80 asylum applications: http://www.ceskenoviny.cz/zpravy/o-azyl-v-cesku-loni-pozadalo-1450-cizincu-mezirocne-o-27-mene/1589711, accessed 20 May 2018.
[7] See the SPD party manifesto: https://www.spd.cz/program, accessed on 17 June 2018.
[8] In the previous Parliament, Tomio Okamura led another party called The Dawn (*Úsvit*), which had a similar anti-Muslim agenda. Okamura left the party after being charged for misappropriating party funds. A few months later, he established the SPD.

reiterated his thesis that Islam had no place in Europe, and that Islamic culture was incompatible with European culture.[9]

The distribution quotas of the EU on asylum seekers were one of the most persistent topics in political debates in 2017. The Czech Republic officially refused to abide by this system, but was out-voted by other member states. According to these quotas, the Czech Republic was supposed to relocate 1,600 refugees, mostly from Greece and Italy. In spring 2017, the Government decided not to continue with any relocations after only twelve refugees were accepted by the Czech Republic.[10] Even though there is a strong anti-Muslim sentiment and a fear of Muslim immigrants in Czech society, related to this EU relocation programme, the Government did not say that most of these refugees would have a Muslim background. Instead, it just mentioned the issue of illegal immigration and the security concerns connected to it. Czech Muslim organisations continued to not take part in public debates on this issue.

The summer of 2017 witnessed controversy over Muslim dress in the Czech Republic. Some public swimming pools refused to allow Muslim women to wear the burkini, while others accepted it. The debate revolved around the hygiene of burkinis rather than religious matters. Those swimming pools that allowed the wearing of burkinis often came under verbal attack from visitors, mostly via social media.[11] These attacks had some anti-Muslim content within them, however most were concerned with the supposed discrimination against those who wear loose shorts rather than proper swimming trunks, who are usually not allowed to swimming pools, in favour of those wearing a burkini.

The first Czech case involving the wearing of a Muslim head scarf in a an educational institution finally came to an end. In 2013, a secondary medical training school prevented two foreign Muslim girls wearing head scarves from taking lessons on the school premises; the students then left the school. In 2015, one of the girls, a Somali asylum seeker, named Ayan Jamaal Ahmadnuur, decided to press charges against the school. She demanded an apology and financial compensation for not being allowed to study; in January 2017, the court refused the demands of the student. According to the court, the student did not show any evidence for discrimination; it said that Ahmadnuur did not meet the admission requirements to study at the school, a fact unconnected to

---

9   https://zpravy.aktualne.cz/domaci/zeman-na-ustecku-za-peroutku-se-neomluvim-islam-k-nam-nepatr/r~ab5a017ea91011e7aacd0025900fea04/, accessed 20 May 2018.
10 https://zpravy.idnes.cz/milan-chovanec-kvoty-uprchlici-ceska-republika-evropska-unie-pud-/domaci.aspx?c=A170605_165247_domaci_fer, accessed 20 May 2018.
11 https://www.expres.cz/burkini-praha-akvacentrum-sutka-muslimky-cesi-fqb-/zpravy.aspx?c=A170807_114331_dx-zpravy_lare, accessed 20 May 2018.

her head scarf.[12] Several anti-Islamic activists, including politicians, were present to hear the verdict, as well as others who supported the Somali student. The verdict, however, gave no clear answers regarding possible future cases involving head scarves in educational institutions in the country.

In recent years, Czech Muslims have made several public appearances to denounce terrorist attacks in Europe. In January 2017, the former head of the *Ústředí muslimských náboženských obcí* (Headquarters of the Muslim Communities in the Czech Republic–UMO), the Czech convert Vladimír Sáňka, together with another Czech convert and well-known academic scholar of Islam, Petr Pelikán, called for a common fight against terrorism. At a conference in Prague, they also publicly denounced the activities of so-called Islamic State.[13]

Transnational Links

Due to their low profile and low level of activity, no particular forms of transnational cooperation or links with Czech Muslim organisations, were observable in 2017. As for security issues, no serious accusations against them, suggesting financial support from transnational or Islamist networks, were raised. Czech Muslim representatives continued to publicly denounce violent attacks. The only security issue connected to Muslims in the country was the case of Jan Silovský, a Czech citizen who tried to join so-called Islamic State. He was caught in 2016 in Istanbul and sent back to the Czech Republic. In 2017 he was sentenced to six years in prison for the spreading and propagation of terrorism.[14] Silovský was not connected with any Czech Muslim organisation. The young man from a small town with a population of less than 3,000 had converted to Islam four years ago after reading the Qur'an on his own and gathering information from websites.[15]

---

12 http://zpravy.e15.cz/domaci/udalosti/muslimska-studentka-neuspela-s-zalobou-kvuli-noseni-satku-ve-skole-1328143, accessed 20 May 2018.
13 http://domaci.eurozpravy.cz/spolecnost/178738-cesti-muslimove-vyzvali-ke-spolecnemu-postupu-proti-terorismu-a-odsoudili-ciny-is/, accessed 20 May 2018.
14 https://plzensky.denik.cz/zlociny-a-soudy/nejvyssi-soud-zamitl-dovolani-jana-silovskeho-ktery-chtel-k-is-20171128.html, accessed 20 May 2018.
15 https://www.irozhlas.cz/zpravy-domov/prvni-cech-ktery-chtel-k-islamskemu-statu-je-obzalovan-hrozi-mu-az-vyjimecny-trest_201612221300_ogolis, accessed 20 May 2018.

Law and Domestic Politics

The UMO is the sole religious representative body for Muslims in the Czech Republic. It has been granted "first level recognition" as a religious community since 2004. "First level recognition" means that the community does not receive public funding, nor is it able to run its own religious schools, or offer religious services in the army. For such rights "second level registration" is needed. According to the UMO leader Hassan Al Rawi, the organisation has postponed an application for this second level status because of the current anti-Muslim atmosphere in Czech society. At the same time though, the UMO has not met the legal conditions required for second level registration either. It admitted gathering 10,000 signatures from Czech Muslims is near to impossible (signatures from at least 0.1% of the Czech population is required for second level registration), and it has also not submitted the required annual reports on its activity to the Czech authorities.[16]

The legal case against a former UMO leader, Czech convert Vladimír Sáňka, ended in February 2018.[17] The court exonerated Sáňka of the charge of spreading hatred towards a group of citizens. According to the initial charge by the police, Sáňka committed this offence by publishing a Czech translation of Bilal Philips' book *The Fundaments of Tawheed*. In September 2016, Sáňka was released and cleared on the grounds that Salafism, as propagated by the book, is not a movement but an ideology, and can therefore not be used as a reason for prosecution. The prosecutor appealed and the process started again in 2017; Sáňka was finally freed in 2018.

Activities and Initiatives of Main Muslim Organisations

The atmosphere in the Czech Republic has become more hostile towards Muslims in the past three years. This is the most likely reason why Czech Muslim organisations have kept a low profile; they did not organise any noticeable activities, and tried to avoid any public confrontations. Activities were limited to a few events, such as public *iftar* dinners during the month of Ramadan etc. In Prague and Brno, Muslim organisations continued to hire congress or sports halls in order to celebrate 'Id al-Adha; for other religious

---

16 https://www.lidovky.cz/islam-v-cesku-zvlastni-prava-neziska-nezverejnuje-vyrocni-zpra vy-109-/zpravy-domov.aspx?c=A150117_142317_ln_domov_mct, accessed 20 May 2018.

17 https://www.irozhlas.cz/zpravy-domov/vladimir-sanka-sireni-radikalni-islamske-knihy-soud_1805111108_jak, accessed 20 May 2018.

feasts, they gathered only in established mosques and prayer rooms. No new mosques were opened in 2017.

A small but active Muslim organisation is the *Muslimský svaz studentů a mládeže* (Muslim Union of Students and Youth–MSSM), also known as *Svaz muslimských studentů v ČR* (Union of Muslim Students in the Czech Republic). It was founded in 1991 by foreign students studying in the Czech Republic. The face of this organisation is the former architecture student Muhammad Abbas al-Mu'tasim, who is of Sudanese origin; the group manages prayer rooms in student dormitories. In the 1990s, al-Mu'tasim and his former *Muslimská unie* (Muslim Union) competed with the *Islámská nadace v Praze* (Islamic Foundation in Prague) to become the leading organisation for Muslims in Prague. Now the MSSM organises summer and winter Islamic congresses and gatherings for Czech Muslims, and also runs a distance-learning course on Islam. Al-Mu'tasim and the MSSM are regarded as a group of more conservative Muslims, who assert shari'a law and a strong Islamic identity for Czech Muslims.

Muslim Population: History and Demographics

The territory of today's Czech Republic has never been under direct Islamic influence or rule, so there are no indigenous ethnic Czech Muslims. After the 1878 Austro-Hungarian occupation of Bosnia-Herzegovina, Czech lands were part of a state with a predominantly Muslim region until 1918. This fact resulted in only a very limited migration of Bosnian Muslims to Czech lands in that period of time.[18] Today, three categories of Muslims in the Czech Republic can be defined: ethnic Czech converts; Czech citizens of foreign origin; and foreigners living in the Czech Republic on the basis of residency permits. There are only a few hundred Czech converts, who are nevertheless very active in Muslim organisations.[19] The second group consists mostly of former students who came from what were socialist-oriented developing countries in order to

---

18   Macháček, Štěpán, "Zákon o islámu z roku 1912: Stát uznal islám na území České republiky před sto lety" (The 1912 Law on Islam: The authorities recognised Islam in what is today the Czech Republic one hundred years ago), *Dějiny a Současnost*, No. 8 (2012), pp. 22–25.

19   Mohamed Alí Šilhavý estimated in the late 1990s the number of Czech converts at around 400. Since then, this number has been often repeated as the closest approximation. However, Vladimír Sáňka, a former representative of the UMO, claimed, in a personal interview on 3 January 2011, that annually, there are tens of conversions of Czechs to Islam. The number of Czech converts is probably growing, but it is impossible to arrive at more exact figures.

study in the former Czechoslovakia, starting from the 1960s. Some stayed after their graduation, married, and obtained citizenship. Most of them came from Arab countries, these being mainly Syria, Libya, South Yemen, Iraq and Sudan. Therefore, a large proportion of the Czech Muslim population consists of educated people and professionals, contrary to some other Western European countries. Muslims from the third category mostly arrived after 1989 as students or entrepreneurs. Their regions of origin were typically Arab countries (especially Egypt, Syria and Iraq) and the Balkans (Bosnia and Herzegovina, Kosovo or Macedonia), followed by Chechnya, Turkey, and Afghanistan. The migrant and refugee crisis of 2015 and 2016 did not significantly increase the number of Muslims in the Czech Republic.

There is no reliable source for the numbers of Muslims in the Czech Republic, as there is no system of identifying citizens according to their religion; in the census, filling in religious affiliation is only optional. Thus, in the 2011 census, only 3,385 people indicated Islam as their religion, which is a much lower figure than the estimates for the number of Muslims, or people of Muslim background, living in the Czech Republic. The gap can be attributed to the fact that many Czech Muslims do not regard Islam as a significant part of their identity, or are simply unwilling to identify themselves as Muslims on the census form.[20] The latest estimates suggest that there are about 22,000 Muslims in the Czech Republic, thus representing 0.2% of the total population.[21] According to the Czech Ministry of the Interior, Muslims are well-integrated into Czech society.[22] There are no specific regions, cities, or neighbourhoods with a noticeable concentration of Muslims. Within the officially recognised major Muslim organisation in the country, the UMO, which is regarded by the Czech authorities as the sole representative of Czech Muslims, only several hundred people are active.

---

20   For the 2011 census results on religious affiliation, see the official site of the Czech Statistical Office: https://www.czso.cz/csu/czso/nabozenska-vira-obyvatel-podle-vysledku-scitani-lidu-2011-61wegp46fl, accessed 20 May 2018.
21   This figure has been widely accepted for several years as the most accurate estimate. It is based on systematic research of the Czech Muslim population by the sociologist Daniel Topinka, who used the statistics from the Ministry of the Interior. The research results were published in Topinka, Daniel (ed.), *Muslimové v Česku: Etablování muslimů a islámu na veřejnosti* (Prague: Barrister and Principal, 2016).
22   For some detail on this, see the audit by the Czech Ministry of the Interior: https://zpravy.aktualne.cz/domaci/muslimove-jsou-v-cesku-dobre-zacleneni-do-spolecnosti-vetsi/r~0d1f1c12b7e711e686630025900fea04/, accessed 20 May 2018.

Muslim Population	Estimated 22,000 (0.2% of total population in 2016).
Ethnic/National Backgrounds	Czech Muslims are of very diverse backgrounds and no ethnic or national group clearly prevails.
Inner-Islamic Groups	No specific Islamic group can be identified as being dominant in the Czech Republic.
Geographical Spread	Most Czech Muslims live dispersed within the two largest cities of Prague and Brno, as well as in some other towns, such as Teplice or Karlovy Vary. No towns, suburbs, or regions have a predominantly Muslim population.
Number of Mosques	Three purpose-built mosques exist: in the capital Prague; the city of Brno; and a private mosque in the village of Kolová, near the spa town of Karlovy Vary. There are about 15 prayer rooms in adapted apartments in different towns within the Czech Republic.
Muslim Burial Sites	Three Muslim sections exist as parts of general burial sites: Olšany burial site in Prague; in the city of Brno; and in the town of Třebíč. Besides these active burial sites, there are cemeteries of Austro-Hungarian Muslim soldiers from World War I and earlier in the cities of Brno and Olomouc, and similar historical graves can be found in several other places.
"Chaplaincy" in State Institutions	In Ruzyně prison, in Prague, a small prayer room has been created by the Islamic Foundation in Prague (IFP). Friday prayers are occasionally led there by an imam provided by the IFP.
Halal Products	Halal slaughter is permitted at official slaughter houses. Usually an Islamic organisation arranges such slaughter with a slaughterhouse, carried out by a Muslim butcher. Halal food is available at

	several grocer shops, and sometimes in supermarkets as well. So far halal food has not been an option in public institutions.
Dress Code	There is has been no legislation on Muslim dress so far. There has been only one incident involving the wearing of the head scarf, as mentioned above. At other schools, girls attend wearing head scarves without any problems. Some swimming pools have banned burkinis, officially for hygienic reasons, others accept them. Muslim women wearing the niqab have not been seen in public.
Places of Islamic Learning and Education	Basic courses on Islam and the Arabic language are provided by the mosques in Prague and Brno for the public. No formal Islamic education is available. An Oriental Studies degree exists at Charles University in Prague, and to a lesser extent at West-Bohemian University in Pilsen and Masaryk University in Brno.
Muslim Media and Publications	Websites only: www.islam.cz (run by the Islamic Foundation in Prague), www.praha.muslim.cz, www.islamweb.cz (both websites run by the Islamic Foundations in Prague and Brno), www.mesita.cz (run by the Islamic Foundation in Brno).

Main Muslim Organisations

- Headquarters of the Muslim Communities in the Czech Republic (*Ústředí muslimských obcí v ČR*–UMO, Blatská 1491, 198 00 Praha 9–Kyje, tel.: ++420 281918876, email: islamcz@islamcz.cz, http://www.umocr.cz/). This is the official Islamic community recognised by the Czech authorities.
- Islamic Foundation in Prague (*Islámská nadace v Praze*–INP, Blatská 1491, 198 00 Praha 9–Kyje, tel.: ++420 281918876, email: praha@muslim.cz, www.praha.muslim.cz). This is the main Islamic organisation that is closely connected to the umbrella organisation UMO.

- Islamic Foundation in Brno (*Islámská nadace v Brně*–INB, Vídeňská 38a, 693 00 Brno, tel.: ++420 543243352, email: brno@muslim.cz, www.brno.muslim.cz). This is the sister organisation of the INP, and is also closely connected to the umbrella UMO.
- Muslim Union of Students and Youth (*Muslimský svaz studentů a mládeže*– MSSM, http://www.svazmuslim.cz/,https://www.facebook.com/V%C5%A1eobecn%C3%BD-Svaz-Muslimsk%C3%BDch-Student%C5%AF-a-Ml%C3%A1de%C5%BEe--114530218565738/). This is an independent Islamic organisation that was founded, and has been managed, by former student Abbas Al Mu'tasim since 1992.
- *Prag Merkez Cami* (*Turecká mešita v Praze*, Pivovarnická 3, Praha 8, tel.: ++420 606141858, ++420 775522174, email: sadeddin44@hotmail.com). Turkish Muslim-run prayer room in Prague.

Denmark

Brian Arly Jacobsen[1] and Niels Valdemar Vinding[2]

Introduction

Just before Christmas 2016, the Danish parliament adopted the last part of an anti-extremism package called *Forkynderloven* (the so-called *Act on Preachers*), which might conflict with the understanding of religious freedom in the Danish Constitution.[3] The Law includes a public sanction list of religious preachers, and Denmark has been accused of singling out Islam, and applying stricter restrictions on Muslims than on other segments of the population. This situation is further elaborated on in two independent reports that look at freedom of religion and discrimination in Denmark. The first is by the UN Special Rapporteur on Freedom of Religion and Belief, which criticises the politically motivated reasons for limiting freedom of religion, with the more or less explicit purpose of limiting Muslim religious practices. The other report, the 2017 report of the European Commission against Racism and Intolerance, lists a number of significant concerns, and highlights that racist and Islamophobic hate speech, in particular directed against Muslims, continues to be a problem, which the Danish government does not address.

---

1 Brian Arly Jacobsen has a PhD in the Sociology of Religion, and is an Associate Professor in the Department of Cross-Cultural and Regional Studies, University of Copenhagen, Denmark. His research is mainly in the area of religion and politics and religious minority groups in Denmark. His publications include "Islam and Muslims in Denmark", in Marian Burchardt and Ines Michalowski (eds.), *After Integration: Islam, Conviviality and Contentious Politics in Europe* (Dordrecht: Springer VS, 2015), pp. 171–186, and "Muslim population trends in Western Europe", in John L. Esposito et al. (eds.), *Oxford Islamic Studies Online*, vol. 2. (Oxford: Oxford University Press, 2014).
2 Niels Valdemar Vinding has a PhD in Islamic Studies and is a post-doctoral researcher at the Department of Cross-Cultural and Regional Studies, University of Copenhagen. He recently co-edited *Exploring the Multitude of Muslims in Europe: Essays in Honour of Jørgen S. Nielsen*, with Egdūnas Račius and Jörn Thielmann (Leiden: Brill, 2018) and also co-edited *Imams in Western Europe: Developments, Transformations, and Institutional Challenges* (Amsterdam: University of Amsterdam Press, 2018) with Mohammed Hashas and Jan Jaap de de Ruiter.
3 *L 18 Proposal for a Law Amending the Criminal Code* (Criminalisation of explicit approval, of certain criminal acts in the context of religious training), adopted 13 December 2016, http://www.ft.dk/samling/20161/lovforslag/l18/index.htm, accessed 18 January 2018.

Public Debates

In May 2017, the Jewish Community in Denmark complained to the police about an anti-Semitic sermon at the Al-Faruq mosque in Nørrebro, Copenhagen[4]. The imam, Mundhir Abdallah, encouraged attacks on Jews during a Friday prayer. On the basis of a video recording of a Friday prayer on 31 March 2017, the Jewish Community in Denmark complained to the police. Imam Mundhir Abdallah quoted a hadith which incites violence against Jews: "Judgement Day will not come until the Muslims fight the Jews and kill them. The Jews will hide behind the rocks and the trees, but the rocks and trees will say: Oh Muslim, oh servant of Allah, there is a Jew behind me, come and kill him". The sermon was posted by the mosque on its YouTube channel, and was brought to the attention of the Jewish Community and Danish media by the Middle East Media Research Institute (MEMRI). The mosque is well-known to be a place for the followers of Hizb ut Tahrir.

Transnational Links

Muslim organisations and groups in Denmark have strong transnational ties based on common nationality, ethnicity or religious conviction. In 2017, this was demonstrated very clearly in a controversial news report, in which the religious advisor at the Turkish Embassy and senior Diyanet official in Denmark, Adnan Bülent Baloğlu, revealed in an interview with the *Christian Daily* newspaper, on 28 April 2017, that the embassy had been collecting sensitive information on Danish Turks and Danish schools.[5] This comes in the wake of similar incidents around Europe after the coup attempt in Turkey on 15 July 2016. What is remarkable in this case is that, while the Embassy in Copenhagen had officially denied documented surveillance of Turks in Denmark, the religious advisor confirmed and defended the intelligence gathering on four men and 14 schools in Denmark, which are considered to be inspired by the Gülen movement. The advisor referred to these activities as the response of a state that has seen a coup attempt, and that the information gathered is

---

4 "Prædiken i dansk moské ses som opfordring til drab på jøder" (Sermon in Danish mosque is seen as an invitation to killing Jews), *Christian Daily,* 10 May 2017.

5 "Leder for tyrkiske imamer i Danmark: Ja, vi samler information om Erdogan-modstandere" (Head of Turkish imams in Denmark: yes, we collect information about Erdogan opponents), *Christian Daily,* 27 April 2017.

"public knowledge" anyway.[6] Danish politicians criticised the practice, and maintained that in Denmark such unauthorised and politicised collection of sensitive political and religious data was not allowed. Following the interview, Adnan Bülent Baloğlu was called home to Turkey by the Diyanet ministerial office in Ankara, which considered the story unfortunate, and sought to end the debates in Denmark and Europe swiftly.[7]

This incident reveals not just that the power and reach of the Diyanet apparatus in Europe is both significant and efficient, but also that the Turkish regime and anti-regime political alignments reach far into the everyday lives of Turkish Muslims in Europe. Following the coup, at least four religious free schools that are considered to be inspired by the Gülen movement have closed down, because Turkish-Danish parents had withdrawn their children due to the fear of repercussions from or in Turkey.[8]

Law and Domestic Politics

In February 2017, a man who filmed himself burning the Qur'an was the first person in 46 years to be charged under Denmark's blasphemy section in the *Danish Criminal Code*.[9] According to the charge, the 42-year-old burned a copy of the Qur'an in his backyard; subsequently, on 27 December 2015, he published a video of the burning on Facebook. It was posted on the public Facebook group: "JA TIL FRIHED—NEJ TIL ISLAM" (YES TO FREEDOM—NO TO ISLAM).[10] The charge led to a discussion in Parliament about the so-called blasphemy article (Art. 140) of the *Danish Criminal Code*. The contentious, 151-year-old law criminalises acts such as burning the Qur'an or the Bible, and states that "… persons carrying out public insults or denigrating, in this country, lawful religious teachings or worships, may be punished with

---

6 "Religiøs rådgiver i Danmark: Kritik af Erdogan er racisme" (Religious adviser in Denmark: critique of Erdogan is racism), *Christian Daily*, 28 April 2017.
7 "Tyrkisk religiøs vejleder sendt hjem" (Turkish religious councillor sent home), *Christian Daily*, 30 April 2017.
8 "Skoleformand på lukket Gülen-skole: 'Dagene op til lukningen var tunge, triste og fyldt med afmagt'" (School chairman at the closed Gülen school: "the days up to the closure were heavy, sad and full of powerlessness"), *Politiken*, 17 December 2016.
9 "Denmark scraps 334-year-old blasphemy law", *The Guardian*, 2 June 2017, https://www.theguardian.com/world/2017/jun/02/denmark-scraps-334-year-old-blasphemy-law, accessed 18 May 2018.
10 Thastum, Mikkel, "Indictment for burning of the Quran", *Anklagemyndigheden*, 22 February 2017, http://anklagemyndigheden.dk/en/indictment-for-burning-of-the-quran, accessed 18 January 2018.

fines or imprisonment up to four months".[11] During the debate, *Venstre*–which is Denmark's Liberal Party and the largest party in the coalition government– changed its stance, and joined a majority agreeing to remove the article from the *Criminal Code*. With this proposal by the Red-Green Alliance to abolish article 140, the prosecutor abandoned the charge against the man who had burned a copy of the Qur'an.[12]

Within the last 20 years, article 140 has been a recurring topic in the debate on value and identity politics. The debate has primarily been about *why* it should be abolished, not *whether* it should be abolished.[13] The Danish People's Party has made such proposals numerous times, but several parties, who otherwise supported the article's abolition, did not agree with the Danish People's Party's critical stance on Islam to justify its removal. In June 2017, the Red–Green Alliance proposed the abolition of the article, which all parties agreed on except the Social Democrats. The Danish People's Party's proposals were all driven by a clear anti-Islam agenda, which meant that the centre-left parties had difficulty voting for the abolition. However, when the Red–Green Alliance took the lead, it also changed the driving force and framework of the debate by adopting a secularist narrative to legitimise its abolition.

A survey in September 2017 showed that a majority of Danes want to ban the burqa and niqab in public.[14] According to the poll, 62% said they supported a full ban on wearing them in public, while 23% said full face veiling should continue to be permitted; 12% were not sure. In a similar survey from 2010, 53% supported a ban on the burqa and niqab, while 38% thought they should be allowed to be worn in public places.[15] The increased opposition against the burqa and niqab among the people is also reflected in Parliament, where several parties support their ban. This means that Denmark is set to become the next European country to ban the burqa and niqab in public spaces. *Venstre*,

---

11   *The Danish Criminal Code, Section 140*, https://www.retsinformation.dk/Forms/R0710.aspx?id=59058 quran, accessed 18 January 2018.

12   L 170 Forslag til lov om ændring af straffeloven (L 170 Proposal for a Law Amending the Criminal Code), 2 June 2017, http://www.ft.dk/samling/20161/lovforslag/l170/index.htm, accessed 18 January 2018.

13   Larsen, Signe E., "Towards the blasphemous self: constructing societal identity in Danish debates on the blasphemy provision in the twentieth and twenty-first centuries", *Journal of Ethnic and Migration Studies*, vol. 40, no. 2 (2014) pp. 194–211.

14   "Et flertal vil forbyde burka og niqab" (A majority will ban burka and niqab), *dr.dk*, 29 September 2017, https://www.dr.dk/ligetil/et-flertal-vil-forbyde-burka-og-niqab, accessed 18 January 2018.

15   "Over halvdelen af danskerne vil have forbud mod burka" (More than half of Danes want a ban on burqas), *dr.dk*, 13 July 2010, https://www.dr.dk/nyheder/indland/over-halvdelen-af-danskerne-vil-have-forbud-mod-burka, accessed 18 January 2018.

the Liberal Party and largest party in the coalition government, decided to back a ban in October. "This is not a ban on religious clothing, this is a ban on masking", Jacob Ellemann-Jensen, spokesman for the Liberal Party, told reporters.[16] This would effectively mean a ban on the niqab and burqa, he added. Around 100–200 women in Denmark wear the niqab (60 of them are converts), and up to three women wear the burqa, according to a study from 2009 by researchers at the University of Copenhagen.[17]

The three-party centre-right minority government, its ally the Danish People's Party, and the main opposition party the Social Democrats, have all expressed their support for a ban, though they are still discussing how it should be designed and enforced. The ban is scheduled to be adopted in 2018. Leaders of Muslim communities, Muslim women's groups, legal rights interest groups, and even voices in the centre-right government, have opposed the ban. They argue that the State should not decide the choice of individuals' clothes in the public space, that it would hamper the integration of the women who wear the burqa and niqab, and also indirectly discriminate against Muslim minorities in their religious practices.[18]

During 2017, nine foreign religious preachers were registered on Denmark's first public list banning them from entering the country, calling them "hate preachers" who posed threats to public order. The first blacklist for hate preachers was published in May and included five Islamic clerics and an American evangelical Christian pastor. "The Government won't accept hate preachers coming to Denmark to preach hate against Danish society and indoctrinate listeners to commit violence against women and children, spread ideas of a caliphate and undermine our founding values", said Inger Støjberg, the Minister for Immigration and Integration: "So I am naturally very pleased that it is now clear to everyone that these people are not welcome in Denmark".[19] Later in 2017, two additional Muslim preachers were banned from entering Denmark

---

16 "Før skændtes de på Facebook: Nu står de bag Venstres burka-kompromis" (Before they argued on Facebook: now they stand behind The Liberal Party's burqa-compromise), *BT*, 6 October 2017.

17 Warburg, Margit et al., *Rapport om brugen af niqab og burka* (*Report on the Use of the Niqab and Burqa*), 2009, http://hum.ku.dk/faknyt/nyheder_fra_2010/2010/brugen-af-niqab-og-burka.pdf, accessed 18 January 2018.

18 "Kirkeminister fastholder kritik af 'tåbeligt burkaforbud'" (Minister of Church Affairs maintains criticism of "foolish burka ban"), *Christian Daily*, 8 November 2017.

19 "Religiøse forkyndere får indrejseforbud" (Religious preachers receive a ban on entry), *Dagbladet Roskilde*, 2 May 2017.

on 15 June, and a Saudi cleric, Abdullah bin Radi Almoaede Alshammar, was put on the list on 12 December 2017.[20]

An upper secondary school, *H.C. Ørsted Gymnasiet*, issued a general ban on all religious ritual during school hours, because a group of Muslim students had been praying in empty classrooms and in the main corridor of the school, which had given rise to conflict. The ban was challenged in the Board of Equal Treatment, which in April 2017 deemed it not to be discriminatory.

This case began in early February 2015, when a group of seven or eight students had gathered to perform prayers, which, on various occasions had delayed teaching and disrupted classes in progress. Individuals from outside the school attended the prayers as well. There were concerns that these students would try to coerce or harass other Muslim students into participating in the prayers. In early March 2015, the school issued new guidelines on "collective and personal conduct". These rules were the result of a longer strategic process and aligning of rules with those of other educational institutions, seeking to make the school a respectful, tolerant and inclusive space, open to all. As such, the rules were not a direct result of the incidents of February. However, because the rules banned political and religious activities, including "… mission and the demanding and controlling of a religious code of conduct", and thus indirectly ban Muslim prayer, the students filed a complaint with the Board of Equal Treatment in May 2015. While the Board of Equal Treatment did not uphold the complaint, there was a minority opinion in the Board of Equal Treatment that held that the school had not justified the rules properly, had not demonstrated the gravity of the interruptions, had not sought alternative solutions, and had not tried to mediate the conflict. Nonetheless, the majority of the Board held that the episodes did cause "disturbance, conflict and insecurity", and that, out of concern for the diversity of the students, and after consulting the student body, the school was justified in issuing the new rules, and found no violation of the principles of equal treatment.

The decision by the Board of Equal Treatment was well received by the Social Democrats and the Danish People's Party. The Social Democrats saw the ruling as support for limiting religious influence in public schools, and a help to those institutions that are struggling with actual problems. The Danish People's Party appreciated in particular that this ban mainly targets Muslim students, and supported a general ban on prayer and prayer rooms that would

---

20 "Religiøse forkyndere med indrejseforbud" (The national sanction list for religious preachers), *The Danish Immigration Service*, https://www.nyidanmark.dk/en-GB/News-Front-Page/2018/03/National-sanktionsliste-udvidet/?anchor=98FA8A72DFA24722AFE2B9D6CE5AE799, accessed 18 January 2018.

apply only to Muslims, because they see Christian prayer as primarily a private exercise.[21]

Addressing the significant challenges faced by Muslims in Denmark, the UN Special Rapporteur on Freedom of Religion and Belief, Heiner Bielefeldt, was openly critical and direct in his report on Denmark for 2016. Overall, the Special Rapporteur criticised the political climate in Denmark, and the politically motivated reasons for limiting freedom of religion and belief, with the more or less explicit purpose of limiting Muslim practices. The Rapporteur's view is that in a number of specific cases, the Danish governance of religion is not in line with international standards. Explicitly, he criticises the unqualified biases that hold all Muslims answerable for the actions of an extreme few. His case in point refers to how the Municipality in Aarhus, where a new mosque building project was authorised in principle, had overturned this decision with explicit reference to a television programme on mosques from 2016.[22]

The Special Rapporteur highlighted the hard-line and overzealous political and legislative responses to religious extremism as the most explicit threat to freedom of religion and belief in Denmark. While extremism warrants a clear political response, the harsh rhetoric targets all Muslims. Furthermore, leading Members of Parliament have even suggested a reinterpretation and significant tightening of the judicial view of the so-called limitation clause in article 67 of the constitution, on the freedom of religion and belief, which states that "… nothing at variance with good morals or public order shall be taught or done". This clause has so far been understood as meaning "against the law", but now there appears to be political will to pass legislation directing the courts to interpret this clause literally. In unequivocal terms, the Special Rapporteur warns that such a legislative move would be out of line with the modern, internationally agreed understanding of freedom of religion and belief, in that it would give legislators free and uncontrolled means of eliminating basic human rights, and is therefore not at all justifiable.[23]

The 2017 report from the European Commission against Racism and Intolerance (ECRI, part of the Council of Europe) lists a number of significant concerns, and highlights that "… racist hate speech, in particular against Muslims, continues to be a problem", and goes on to stress that the

---

21   "Forbud mod bøn på gymnasium er ikke diskrimination–S og DF jubler" (Prohibition of prayer at high school is not discrimination–S and DF cheers), *Jyllands-Posten*, 1 May 2017.
22   "Report of the Special Rapporteur on Freedom of Religion and Belief on his mission to Denmark", *A/HRC/34/50*, p. 9, http://ap.ohchr.org/documents/dpage_e.aspx?si=A/HRC/34/50/Add.1, accessed 18 June 2018.
23   "Report of the Special Rapporteur", p. 10.

"... under-reporting of hate speech is a problem that requires urgent attention".[24] A number of Islamophobic public statements, cases of verbal abuse, insults and public shaming of Muslims especially drew the attention of the ECRI commission.[25] Already in the previous report of 2012, the ECRI recommended that the Danish authorities take initiatives to prevent a climate of hostility towards minority groups like Muslims, and to avoid perpetuating prejudice against Muslims.[26] However, their latest report does not see any such initiatives being taken by the Danish authorities. In fact, the report argues, in line with previous reports, that the number of such hate cases being prosecuted by the police in courts remains too low. The ECRI report also highlights the consequences of the Islamophobic political discourse, and the view of Muslims as unable or unwilling to integrate: "The perception that they will not be accepted as equal members of Danish society merely due to their religion, can easily lead to a vicious circle of marginalisation and radicalisation".[27]

New legislation concerning religious communities was adopted in December 2017.[28] The Danish government proposed legislation concerning all religious communities in Denmark with the exception of the Evangelical-Lutheran Church. Thus, it includes such communities as the Catholic Church, and Buddhist and Islamic organisations. The legislation sets out under which terms religious communities can receive formal recognition from the Danish state, and under what terms such recognition can be withdrawn. In the legislation there is an increased amount of regulation concerning donations and the right to wed couples. Religious communities, including Muslim communities, are generally satisfied with the final result, which largely reflects current unwritten praxis. However, some critics have remarked that the proposals cast suspicion on religious communities, whereas others have raised the point that the Bill might place too large an administrative burden on such communities.

---

24 *ECRI Report on Denmark (Fifth Monitoring Cycle)* (CRI(2017)20), p. 9, https://www.ecoi.net/en/file/local/1399794/1226_1495003288_dnk-cbc-v-2017-020-eng.pdf, accessed 18 June 2018.
25 *ECRI Report on Denmark*, p. 15.
26 *ECRI Report on Denmark*, pp. 26–27.
27 *ECRI Report on Denmark*, p. 26.
28 L19, *Lov om trossamfund uden for folkekirken* (*Act on Religious Communities Outside the Evangelical-Lutheran Church*), http://www.ft.dk/samling/20171/lovforslag/L19/som_vedtaget.htm, accessed 18 January 2018.

Activities and Initiatives of Main Muslim Organisations

CEDAR, the *Center for dansk-muslimske relationer* (Centre for Danish-Muslim Relations), was established in 2016 to formulate a response to the polarising narratives that today permeate the public debate on Islam in Denmark.[29] CEDAR seeks to form bridges between the majority Danes and the diverse Muslim minority. They work for a more inclusive discourse through mappings, analysis and reports, and through campaigns and events, to establish a space for meeting and listening across divides. The organisation seeks to encourage Muslims to participate in the majority community, and to invite the majority to engage with Muslims. CEDAR is focused on the media, politics, Islamophobia, and diversity management. In 2017, CEDAR published a report analysing Islamophobia in Denmark in the fields of politics, integration, the media and hate crimes.[30] According to the report, it appears that almost all new laws and regulations relating to ethnic and religious minorities have been marked by the limitation of their rights.

Muslim Population: History and Demographics

While there have been Muslims in Denmark for centuries, as merchants, scholars, travellers and diplomats, the oldest existing Muslim community in Denmark is the Ahmadiyya community, which was formed in 1956 by missionaries of the Ahmadiyya movement. That early community was largely converts, and were able to build the Nusrat Djahan mosque, which was the first purpose-built mosque in Denmark, in 1957. However, it was only with the significant influx of what was at first labour migrants, then through family reunification, and then refugee movements, that Muslims became a substantial religious group in Denmark.[31]

From the late 1960s, the numbers of Muslims in Denmark became more significant, primarily as a result of immigration. The migration of Muslims to Denmark can be divided into two periods. The first, covering the years from the end of the 1960s to the early 1970s, was the period when people came to

---

29   https://www.cedar.nu/, accessed 18 May 2018.
30   Abasss, Mujahed Sebastian, "Denmark", in Enes Bayrakli and Farid Hafez (eds.), *European Islamophobia Report 2017* (Istanbul: SETA, 2018), http://www.islamophobiaeurope.com/wp-content/uploads/2018/04/EIR_2017.pdf, accessed 18 May 2018.
31   Jacobsen, Brian Arly, Göran Larsson, and Simon Sorgenfrei, "The Ahmadiyya mission to the Nordic countries", in James R. Lewis and Inga Bårdsen Tøllefsen (eds.), *Handbook of Nordic New Religions* (Leiden: Brill, 2015), pp. 359–373.

Denmark as labour migrants from Morocco, Pakistan, Turkey and the former Yugoslavia. The second period, running from the mid-1970s to the present, saw the immigration of refugees and the families of former labour migrants.[32]

The number of Muslims has increased significantly since 1980: from 29,400 (0.6% of the population) in 1980, to an estimated 306,000 (5.3%) on 1 October 2017.[33] The Danish authorities do not register individuals' religious beliefs besides the members of the Church of Denmark. Therefore, it is generally difficult to gather reliable information on individual religious affiliation outside that Church. Statistics Denmark has information on both immigrants and their descendants' national/ethnic background.[34] An estimate of the number of Muslims in Denmark must therefore be based on a number of assumptions about correlations between Statistics Denmark's demographic information on immigrants and their descendants' national/ethnic background and religion. This is based on surveys and other sources of demographic and statistical information on religious adherence among different nationalities. Research conducted regularly between 1999 and 2009, for example, has suggested that only 84% of Iraqi immigrants and their descendants regarded themselves as Muslim in 2008.[35] Statistics Denmark also provides information on the geographical spread of Muslims across the country, and the socio-economic status of the population.

Muslim Population	306,000 (5.3% of population, 1 October 2017).
Ethnic/National Backgrounds	70.4% of Muslims in Denmark are Danish citizens, mostly by naturalisation, and including up to 3,800 converts.

---

[32] Østergaard, Bent, *Indvandrerne i Danmarks Historie: Kultur–og religionsmøder* (*Immigrants in Denmark's History: Meetings of Culture and Religion*) (Odense: Syddansk Universitetsforlag, 2007).

[33] 1980 was the first year in which Statistics Denmark gathered information on both immigrants and their descendants: see www.dst.dk.

[34] www.dst.dk, accessed 18 January 2018.

[35] For background data, see Catinét, *IntegrationsStatus: 10 års fremgang–og hvad nu?* (Copenhagen: Catinét Research, 2009) and Jacobson, Brian Arly, "Muslims in Denmark: a critical evaluation of estimations", in Jørgen S. Nielsen (ed.), *Islam in Denmark: the Challenge of Diversity* (Lanham, Maryland: Lexington, 2012), pp. 165–180.

Largest ethnic/national groups (percentage among immigrants and their descendants):

Turkish: 18.8%
Syrian: 11.8%
Iraqi: 8.9%
Lebanese: 8.3%
Pakistani: 7.8%
Somali: 6.8%
Afghan: 5.9%
Bosniak: 4.2%
Iranian: 4.0%
Moroccan: 3.6%
Others: 20%.

Inner-Islamic Groups A survey from 2008 divides seven ethnic groups (Pakistanis, Iraqis, Iranians, Turks, Somalis, former Yugoslavians and Palestinians) as follows: 57% Sunni, 14% Shi'i, and 29% "Islam, other", which may include Ahmadis (around 0.4%), Alevis (around 2.5%) and Sufis (most Sufis consider themselves to be Sunnis). The rest include non-believers, Christians and other religious categories.[36]

Geographical Spread 42.3% of the Muslim population in Denmark is concentrated in Greater Copenhagen (*Storkøbenhavn*), constituting 9.8% of Greater Copenhagen's population. 8.8% of the Muslim population live in Aarhus, the second largest city of Denmark, constituting 7.9% of the city's population. Odense, the third largest city, has 5.2% of the Muslim population living there, constituting 7.9% of the city's population.

---

36   Catinét, *IntegrationsStatus 10 års fremgang–og hvad nu?*

Number of Mosques

According to a new mapping of mosques in Denmark from Aarhus University, there are 161 mosques in the country, and perhaps up to nine additional mosques, an increase of 115 from 2006.[37] This corresponds to an increase of 40% or 48% in the period 2006–17, if the nine additional mosques are considered. The increase in the number of mosques corresponds roughly with the percentage increase, of approximately 44%, of Muslims in Denmark since 2006. This is estimated to have been between about 206,000 to about 296,000 on 1 January 2017. It also means that there are ca. 1,740 Muslims per mosque in Denmark (1,840 if the number of mosques is 161 in Denmark). The numbers are comparable when looking at the Evangelical Lutheran Church of Denmark, where there are ca. 1,850 members per church building in the country. However, regular attendance is not considered in the numbers.

Muslim Burial Sites

Sections within 21 existing municipal or church cemeteries (all Christian consecrated) have been reserved for Muslim use since 1975 (Vestre cemetery, Copenhagen; Bispebjerg cemetery, Copenhagen; Herstedvester cemetery, Albertslund; Lyngby Park cemetery, Lyngby; Nordre cemetery, Frederiksund Kirkegård, Nykøbing Falster; Risings cemetery, Odense; Korsløkke cemetery, Odense; Fovrfeld burial-ground, Esbjerg; Vestre cemetery, Århus; Østre cemetery, Brande; Østre cemetery, Randers; Østre cemetery, Alborg; Nordre cemetery, Vejle; Nordre cemetery, Holsterbro; Vestre cemetery, Horsens; Gråsten cemetery, Vejen cemetery, Vejen; Sønderborg; Ulkebøl cemetery, Sønderborg; Skive-Resen cemetery, Skive).

---

37 Kühle, Lene, and Malik Larsen, *Moskéer i Danmark II: en ny kortlægning af danske moskéer og muslimske bedesteder* (Aarhus: Center for SamtidsReligion, Institut for Kultur og Samfund, Aarhus Universitet, 2017).

In 2006, a separate Muslim cemetery, owned by the Danish Islamic Burial Fund (*Muslimsk Begravelsesplads*), was established outside Copenhagen (Brøndbyøstervej 180, 2560 Brøndby). The Muslim cemetery in Brøndby has more than 1,100 graves.[38]

"Chaplaincy" in State Institutions

In 2006, the first non-denominational prayer room in the country was established at *Rigshospitalet* (Copenhagen University Hospital), and the first imam began to provide pastoral care for patients. Today eight hospitals, five universities, some colleges and a few high schools have established non-denominational prayer rooms. The local institution's management may decide on whether to establish a prayer room.

According to Danish law, prison inmates have the right to participate in worship with a priest or the equivalent of their own faith. The first "prison imam", financed by the Danish state, was appointed on 1 May 2002.[39] A survey of 2006 shows that ca. 20% of inmates in Danish prisons have a Muslim background.[40] In addition to the one full-time imam at Copenhagen Prison Service, there are two or three part-time imams, and a few others who are brought in on an ad hoc basis. Until recently, there were four state-funded Muslim chaplains, but the future of Muslim prison chaplains has become more uncertain in the current political climate.

---

38   Jacobsen, Brian Arly, "Muslimske gravsteder i Danmark: en multireligiøs begravelsespraksis vinder frem" (Muslim burial sites in Denmark: a multireligious burial practice gaining ground), *Tidsskrift for Islamforskning*, no. 1 (2016), pp. 188–209.
39   "Imam Hansen fra Hatting" (Imam Hansen from Hatting), *Nyt fra Kriminalforsorgen* (*News from the Danish Prison and Probation Service*), no. 3 (2002).
40   Hansen, Helene, "Kirken i fængslet", http://www.kriminalforsorgen.dk/, accessed 30 June 2017.

Halal Products   Halal slaughter is permitted and halal food is widely available in Denmark. Denmark is a major exporter of halal meat to the Arab world.[41] The permit to perform halal slaughter, within certain regulations, has also opened a labour market for halal butchers with halal certifications.[42] Nevertheless, there have been political attempts from right- and left-wing parties to prohibit ritual slaughter since the mid-1990s.[43] Public institutions decide at the local administrative level whether halal food is available, and in many schools, hospitals, prisons, nursing homes and other public institutions, the management has decided to offer halal food in their menus, often after intense public debate.[44]

Dress Code   Muslim dress, especially the head scarf and niqab (face veil) for women, is widely discussed in Danish society. In 2017, the Parliament agreed on a ban on masking, which is primarily aimed at banning the use of the burqa and niqab in public spaces. The head scarf is allowed in public schools and public offices. The Supreme Court, in a verdict from January 2005, upheld the right of retailers and

---

41   Jønsson, Signe, "Mod på eksport til Mellemøsten" (Minding exports to the Middle East), *Eksport Fokus*, no. 1 (14 May 2007).
42   Kühle, Lene, "Mosques and organizations", in Nielsen (ed.), *Islam in Denmark*, p. 90.
43   Jacobsen, Brian A., *Religion som fremmedhed i dansk politik. En sammenligning af italesættelser af jøder i Rigsdagstidende 1903–45 og muslimer i Folketingstidende 1967–2005* (*The Construction of Otherness in the Danish Parliament: a Comparison with the Discussions about Jews and Muslims in the Parliamentary Records from 1903–45 and from 1967–2005 Respectively*) (PhD dissertation) (Copenhagen: University of Copenhagen, 2008), pp. 202–206.
44   Brian Arly Jacobsen, "Byrådspolitikere siger ja til religiøst baserede spiseregler i offentlige institutioner" (City Council's politicians says yes to religiously based dietary rules in public institutions), *religion.dk*, 15 August 2013, https://www.religion.dk/religionsanalysen/byr%C3%A5dspolitikere-siger-ja-til-religi%C3%B8st-baserede-spiseregler-i-offentlige, accessed 30 June 2017; "Hver tredje vil forbyde halalslagtning" (One third of the population will ban halal slaughter), *Christian Daily*, 21 March 2011; The Danish People's Party, "Legislative package for the protection of Danish values", www.danskfolkeparti.dk/Lovpakke_til_værn_for_danske_værdier.asp, accessed 15 October 2015.

others to insist on uniform codes without the female head scarf for employees providing frontline services. In 2009, the former centre-right wing government passed an act that banned judges from wearing religious or political symbols in court. The Law has come to be called the "head scarf act", because its real purpose was to ban Muslim women from wearing head scarves when acting as judges or jurors.

According to a governmental report written by scholars at the University of Copenhagen, the number of women wearing the niqab or burqa in Denmark was, in 2009, respectively 100–200 (60 of them were converts).[45]

Places of Islamic Learning and Education

In Denmark, it is possible for a group of parents to establish "independent schools", which are entitled to state support to cover most of their costs. The first Muslim independent school was established in 1978, and since then over 30 such schools have opened.[46] Many of them offer Arabic and Islamic studies. There are approximately 27 independent Muslim primary schools, with a total of around 5,000 pupils in September 2014, according to the Ministry of Children and Education.[47]

Immigrants with Turkish backgrounds opened the first private Turkish-Danish high school in 2011 (The Copenhagen Private Upper Secondary School).[48] They applied for Turkish language

---

45 Warburg et al., *Rapport om brugen af niqab og burka*.
46 Shakoor, Tallat, "Formål for muslimske friskoler i Danmark: udviklinger i formålserklæringer og vedtægter i danske friskoler for muslimske børn" (Purpose of Islamic schools in Denmark: developments in declarations and regulations in Danish free schools for Muslim children), *Tidsskrift for Islamforskning*, no. 3 (2008), pp. 29–43. Some of these schools have since closed.
47 "Grundtvig med muslimsk fortegn?" (Grundtvig with Muslim sign?), *Jyllands-Posten*, 2 September 2014.
48 *Københavns Private Gymnasium* (*Copenhagen's Private High School*), www.kpgym.dk, accessed 30 June 2017.

teaching in the high school, but were initially turned down by the Ministry of Children and Education in January 2012. After a public discussion on the need for Turkish language teaching in Danish high schools, the former Minister of Education, Christine Antorini, accepted Turkish language teaching in the school.[49]

In 2013, the DIKEV Foundation, an Islamic cultural and educational centre in Denmark, established the first Muslim lower-secondary-level boarding school for 14–17-year-olds (Mina Hindholm School, Fuglebjerg at Zealand). The boarding school opened in 2014.[50]

The University of Copenhagen has offered a "flexible" Masters of Education in Islamic Theology course since January 2016.

Most mosques and Muslim associations provide some form of Islamic instruction outside school hours.

Muslim Media and Publications

There are no Muslim newspapers in Danish, but there are a number of internet sites where Muslims (and non-Muslims) exchange information of various kinds. The largest internet forum is Denmark's United Cyber Muslims (https://www.facebook.com/groups/dfcmuslimer/), formed in 1998. Denmark's United Cyber Muslims is related to one of the oldest websites established to inform Muslims and non-Muslims about Islam in Denmark: www.islam.dk.

---

49 "Elever kan nu lære tyrkisk i gymnasiet" (Students can now learn Turkish in high school), *Ritzaus Bureau,* 21 June 2012, http://www.fyens.dk/indland/Elever-kan-nu-laere-tyrkisk-i-gymnasiet/artikel/2105810, accessed 30 June 2017.

50 "Danmark får sin første muslimske efterskole" (Denmark gets its first Muslim boarding school), *Kristeligt Dagblad,* 3 June 2013, https://www.kristeligt-dagblad.dk/danmark/danmark-f%C3%A5r-sin-f%C3%B8rste-muslimske-efterskole, accessed 30 June 2017.

In 2017, Radio WAIH was established by a group of young Muslims who use the radio medium to address issues relevant to Danish Muslims, and to anyone interested in Islam. Radio WAIH considers itself to be a station that sees the world from the point of view of Danish Muslims, and at the same time deals with topics and news that are particularly relevant to Muslims in Denmark. The radio broadcasts via the web, and the editors and staff produce small video spots for social media on contemporary public and media issues regarding Islam and Muslims (www.waih.dk)

Main Muslim Organisations

- Danish Turkish Islamic Foundation (*Dansk Tyrkisk Islamisk Stiftelse*, Poul Bergsøesvej 14, 2600 Glostrup, http://www.danimarkatdv.org/). The Danish Turkish Islamic Foundation is part of the *Diyanet Isleri Türk Islam Birligi* (Turkish-Islamic Union for Religious Affairs–DITIB). It is indisputably the largest Muslim organisation in Denmark, and almost half of all Turkish migrants, or Danes of Turkish descent, are members of the Diyanet funeral foundation (which has around 28,000 members).[51] It was established in Denmark in 1985, and the foundation's local mosque associations (today 28) were officially recognised by the State as a religious community in 2006.
- Idara Minhaj-ul-Quran International Denmark (Bispevej 25, 2200 Copenhagen NV, tel.: ++45 88429595, www.minhaj.dk). Idara Minhaj-ul-Quran International Denmark was founded in 1987 as a Sunni educational and cultural centre in Copenhagen. It has around 1,500 members, including children. It was officially recognised as a religious community by the State in 1999. Minhaj Denmark and all its sub-associations operate according to the Minhaj-ul-Quran movement's constitution in Pakistan.
- The Islamic Association of Bosniaks in Denmark (*Den Islamiske Forening af Bosniakker i Danmark*, c/o Chairman Abdullah Fejzic, Vesterbrogade 11 C/2, 7100 Vejle). The Association, which has five congregations in Denmark, was officially recognised as a religious community in 2001, and has around 1,900 members.

---

51 *Annual Report of the Funeral Fund* (2011), http://danimarkatdv.org/dansk/sayfa-Årsregnskab-af-begravelse-fonden-135.html, accessed 1 December 2015.

- The Albanian Religious Community (*Det Albanske Trossamfund*, Vodroffsvej 8, 1900 Frederiksberg). The Albanian Religious Community has around 1,000 members and, on an average Friday, 210 people visit the mosque for Friday prayers in Copenhagen. It also has the status of an officially recognised religious community.
- Islamic Cultural Centre in Copenhagen (*Islamisk Kulturcenter*, Horsebakken 2, 2400 Copenhagen, tel.: ++45 38606856). The Islamic Cultural Centre in Copenhagen is one of the largest mosques in the country. It was established in the mid-1970s under the leadership of Imam Sibghatullah Mojaddedi, who was later to become the first president of Afghanistan after the Soviet troops left in the late 1980s.[52] It is an open mosque without membership. Around 80 people visit the mosque on a daily basis for prayers, and 600–1,000 people visit the mosque for Friday prayers.
- Alevi Association in Denmark (*Alevi forbundet i Danmark*, Vibevej 32, 4100 Ringsted, tel.: ++45 25170034, www.alevi.dk). Its present chair is Başkan Feramuz Acar. There are seven local associations, a woman's association, and a national youth association.
- The Islamic Religious Community in Denmark (*Det Islamiske Trossamfund i Danmark*, or *Wakf*, Dortheavej 45–47, 2400 Copenhagen NV, tel.: ++45 38112225, fax ++45 38112226, www.wakf.com). It was founded in 1996, when Palestinians in Copenhagen–headed by the charismatic Imam Ahmed Abu Laban, who died in 2007–collected money to establish their own mosque in the city. Its present chair is Hassan Neffaa, and the association is primarily made up of Sunni immigrant groups from various countries. It has approximately 300–400 paying members, and around 1,000 people attend the *khutba* every Friday, and of these up to 300 are women.[53] *Wakf* is rooted in the Muslim Brotherhood, and has strong ties to Egyptian Muslim organisations. Its perception of Islam is closely identified with Arab culture.
- Young Muslims in Denmark (*Muslimske Unge i Danmark*–MUNIDA, Dortheavej 45–47, 2400 Copenhagen NV, www.munida.dk). Related to *Wakf*.
- Mariam Mosque (*Mariam Moskeen*, Købmagergarde, Copenhagen, https://www.femimam.com/en/home/, Facebook page: https://www.facebook.com/pages/Mariam-Mosque/1580780348897347). The first female-only mosque in Denmark was opened in February 2016. Its imam is Sherin Khankan.

---

[52] See Pedersen, Abdul Wahid, "Towards a European understanding of Islam", in Nielsen, *Islam in Denmark*, pp. 245–254.

[53] Kühle, Lene, *Moskeer i Danmark* (Højbjerg: Forlaget Univers, 2006), p. 118.

- Islamic Centre Jaffariya (Rådmandsgade 56, Copenhagen N). The first Shi'is in Denmark were Twelvers and Ismailis of Pakistani descent. The Ismailis established an association in 1969 (and a *jamaatkhana* in 1970 in Copenhagen), and in 1981 the Islamic Centre Jaffariya became the first mosque of the Twelver branch. It has around 110 members today.
- Association Ahlul Bait in Denmark (*Foreningen Ahlul Bait i Danmark*, Imam Ali mosque, Vibevej 23–29, 2400 Copenhagen NV, http://www.imamalimoske.dk). The substantial migration of refugees with Shi'i backgrounds fleeing from the civil war in Lebanon and the Iran-Iraq war, led to new organisations and mosques being established from the mid-1980s onwards. There are around ten Twelver Shi'i mosques in Denmark, with related associations. Ahlul Bait in Denmark is the largest Shi'i organisation. It opened the first purpose built Shi'i mosque, the Imam Ali mosque, in October 2015. Ahlul Bait was officially recognised as a religious community in 2005.
- Shi'i Islamic Religious Community in Denmark (*Shiamuslimsk Trossamfund i Danmark*, Sturlasgade 14 C. 1, 2300 Copenhagen S).
- *Tariqa Burhaniyya* (Damhus Boulevard 65, 2610 Rødovre, http://www.burhaniya.info/intranet/engl/D_denm_e.htm,).
- *Dialog Forum* (Vesterbrogade 52, 1, 1620 Copenhagen V, tel.: ++45 32175060, http://dialogin.dk/pages/).
- Hizb ut-Tahrir in Denmark (www.hizb-ut-tahrir.dk). The organisation was established in Denmark in 1994. Estimates of its membership numbers are between 100 and 150.[54] Some of their public meetings in Copenhagen have attracted crowds of about 1,000.[55]
- United Council of Muslims (*Muslimernes Fællesråd*, H.J. Holst Vej 28, 2610 Rødovre, www.mfr.nu).
- Union of Islamic Associations (*Forbundet af Islamiske Foreninge*, c/o Forening for Moské og Islamisk Center–FMIC, Postbok 1028, 8200 Aarhus N–tel.: ++45 40762758, http://mosquedenmark.org).
- Danish Muslim Union (*Dansk Muslimsk Union*, Valdemarsgade 17, 1, 1665 Copenhagen V, tel.: ++45 50565908, www.dmu.nu).
- Muslims in Dialogue (*Muslimer i Dialog*, Nørrebrogade 32, 1, 2200 Copenhagen N, http://muslimeridialog.dk).

---

54   SFI–The Danish National Centre for Social Research, *Antidemokratiske og Ekstremistiske miljøer i Danmark: En kortlægning* (*Anti-Democratic and Extremist Milieus in Denmark: a Mapping*) (Copenhagen: The Danish Centre for Social Research, 2014), p. 56.

55   For example, their demonstration against the YouTube amateur movie "Innocence of Muslims", in front of the US embassy in Copenhagen, attracted ca. 1,000 participants on 16 September 2012.

- Danish Islamic Council (*Dansk Islamisk Råd*, Hermodsgade 28, 1, 2200 Copenhagen N, www.disr.com).
- Forum for Critical Muslims (*Forum for kritiske Muslimer*, www.kritiskemuslimer.dk).
- CEDAR, Centre for Danish-Muslim Relations (*Center for dansk-muslimske relationer*, Ryesgade 30B, 2200 Copenhagen, email: info@cedar.nu, www.cedar.nu).

Estonia

Ringo Ringvee[1] and Ege Lepa[2]

Introduction

In 2017, Islam and Muslims were discussed in Estonia in various contexts. Several of the themes that caused discussion in 2017 had their roots in events and developments of the previous years. In 2017, the Muslim population in Estonia continued to grow and diversify, mostly due to growing numbers of foreign students with a Muslim background. Exact numbers are not available because to the lack of statistics. The total population with a Muslim background would probably not exceed 3,000–4,000, that is 0.2% to 0.3% of the total population. For the majority of the Muslim population, Islam is the foremost part of their cultural and/or ethnic identity.

As in previous years the main focus on Islam in the media concentrated on international politics. At the beginning of 2017 discussions on reasons either to build or not build a mosque in Tallinn continued in the media. The criminal investigation on the misuse of the finances of the *Eesti Islami Kogudus* (Estonian Islamic Congregation), that had started in 2016, ended in 2017 with an agreement between the Prosecutors Office and the imam of the Congregation. In 2017, the representatives of Muslim organisations were more present than in previous years on TV programmes in which the refugee and migrant crisis, or Islam in general, was discussed.

Public Debates

In 2017, public debates in Estonia on Islam and Muslims varied from international matters to domestic ones that related mostly to the refugee and migrant

---

1 Ringo Ringvee, PhD, is an adviser at the Religious Affairs Department at the Estonian Ministry of the Interior. His research interests encompass relations between the state and religious institutions in contemporary society. His publications include *Annotated Legal Documents on Islam in Europe: Estonia* (Leiden-Boston: Brill, 2015), "Survival strategies of new religions in a secular consumer society: a case study from Estonia." *Nova Religio. The Journal of Alternative and Emergent Religions*, vol. 20, no. 3 (2017), pp. 57–73.
2 Ege Lepa is a PhD candidate at the University of Tartu, with research interests in the Muslim presence in Estonia.

crisis, European identity, terrorist attacks and issues relating to the Estonian Islamic Congregation, the oldest Islamic organisation in the country.

In January 2017, the daily newspaper *Eesti Päevaleht* asked four members of Parliament representing four different political parties, out of the six represented there, about their opinion on the place of religion in Estonian society and on the prospect of constructing a purpose-built mosque in Estonia. Two of the interviewees rejected the prospect of a new mosque, one mentioned that there is already an Islamic centre known as a mosque, and another did not answer the question.[3] On 9 January 2017 the same paper, *Eesti Päevaleht*, published a report on the Tallinn District Administration Centre's decision to rent a floor in an office building to the Estonian Islamic Congregation in the city centre who had won the bidding in a rental auction. The newspaper speculated about the possibility that a new prayer house would be established there.[4] However, in February the Tallinn District Administration Centre annulled the results of the auction after receiving notification from the Municipality's City Property Department that the renting fee was under the market price, and that the municipality intends to sell the entire building, as the municipal authorities do not have any use for it.[5]

In April 2017, one of two men who were arrested in 2015 and sent to prison on charges of financing terrorism, was released after serving his term. In 2016 their initial five and seven-year sentences were reduced to two and three

---

[3] "Mart Helme: president peaks pühade ajal kirikus käima, sest riik koosneb rituaalidest" (Mart Helme: President should go to church on Christmas as the State is based on rituals), *Eesti Päevaleht*, 5 January 2017, http://epl.delfi.ee/news/arvamus/mart-helme-president-peaks-puhade-ajal-kirikus-kaima-sest-riik-koosneb-rituaalidest?id=76812222, accessed 10 April 2017; "Aivar Sõerd: mingeid mošeesid siia ehitada ei ole vaja" (Aivar Sõerd: there is no need to build a mosque here), *Eesti Päevaleht*, 7 January 2017, http://epl.delfi.ee/news/arvamus/aivar-soerd-mingeid-moseesid-siia-ehitada-ei-ole-vaja?id=76833854, accessed 10 April 2017; "Toomas Jürgenstein: kas te kujutate ette, milline näeks välja kirikuteta Tallinna siluett?" (Toomas Jürgenstein: could you imagine what the silhouette of Tallinn would look like without the churches?), *Eesti Päevaleht*, 9 January 2017, http://epl.delfi.ee/news/arvamus/toomas-jurgenstein-kas-te-kujutate-ette-milline-naeks-valja-kirikuteta-tallinna-siluett?id=76834444, accessed 20 January 2017.

[4] Mallene, Laura, "Peaimaam üüris islami kogudusele Tallinna kesklinnas äriruumid" (Chief Imam rented business space in Tallinn city centre for the Congregation), *Eesti Päevaleht*, 9 January 2017, http://epl.delfi.ee/news/eesti/peaimaam-uuris-islami-kogudusele-tallinna-kesklinnas-ariruumid?id=76841952, accessed 20 January 2017.

[5] Gnadenteich, Uwe, "Linnaosavalitsus ei anna islamikogudusele kesklinnas ruume" (District Administration does not give rooms in city centre to Islamic Congregation), *Postimees* 13 February 2017, https://leht.postimees.ee/4013397/linnaosavalitsus-ei-anna-islamikogudusele-kesklinnas-ruume, accessed 30 April 2017.

years respectively by a Tallinn District Court ruling.[6] This decision was appealed by the defendants in the Supreme Court, but in April 2017 the Supreme Court's decision was not to overrule the previous District Court's decision.[7] In October 2017, Roman Manko, who had served his sentence by April 2017 and was released, announced that his defence lawyer had turned to the European Court of Human Rights.[8] On 13 September 2017 an investigative TV programme *Pealtnägija* focused on the controversies surrounding the imam of the Estonian Islamic Congregation and the possible radicalisation of Muslims. In the programme, the wife of the imam stated that, according to her personal view, both of the convicts were not guilty of anything.[9]

The criminal investigation concerning the management of the assets of the Estonian Islamic Congregation by its head, Imam Ildar Muhhamedšin, that had started in 2016, ended in 2017. Although the Prosecutor's Office found Muhhamedšin guilty of misappropriating the Congregation's assets for his own use, they did not consider criminal punishment proportional. The imam signed a settlement with the Prosecutor's Office and paid a fee of €800.[10]

In September 2017 the University of Tartu Asian Centre organised an international workshop, entitled "Islam in Europe: Challenges of Diversity and

---

6   Mets, Mari, "Ringkonnakohus mõistis terroriprotsessi süüdistatavad osaliselt õigeks" (The District Court partially exculpated the defendants), *Äripäev*, 11 May 2016, www.aripaev.ee/uudised/2016/05/11/ringkonnakohus-moistis-terroriprotsessi-suudistatavad-osaliselt-oigeks, accessed 12 March 2017.

7   "Riigikohus jättis terrorismi toetanud meeste süüdimõistmise jõusse" (Supreme Court did not change conviction of men supporting terrorism), *Supreme Court Website, News*, 10 April 2017, https://www.riigikohus.ee/et/uudiste-arhiiv/riigikohus-jattis-terrorismi-toetanud-meeste-suudimoistmise-jousse, accessed 20 July 2017.

8   "Terrorismi toetamise eest karistatu läheb Eesti vastu inimõiguste kohtusse" (Convicted supporter of terrorism is going to sue Estonia in Human Rights Court), *ERR Uudised* 31 October 2017, https://www.err.ee/639652/terrorismi-toetamise-eest-karistatu-laheb-eesti-vastu-inimoiguste-kohtusse, accessed 10 November 2017.

9   *Pealtnägija*, 13 September 2017, https://etv.err.ee/v/elusaated/pealtnagija/saated/ee97d c3b-058f-46df-be5d-da20ff47d894/pealtnagija, accessed 10 January 2018.

10 "Prokuratuur: peaimaam kasutas koguduse raha isiklikuks tarbeks" (Prosecutor's office: chief imam used congregation money for his own expenses), *ERR Uudised*, 8 September 2017, https://www.err.ee/617336/prokuratuur-peaimaam-kasutas-koguduse-raha-isik likuks-tarbeks, accessed 10 September 2017; Mallene, Laura, "Prokuratuur: peaimaam Muhhamedšin kasutas koguduse raha isiklikuks tarbeks" (Prosecutor's office: Chief Imam Muhhamedšin used congregation's money for his personal expenses), *Eesti Päevaleht*, 8 September 2017, http://epl.delfi.ee/news/eesti/prokuratuur-peaimaam-muhhamedsin-kasutas-koguduse-raha-isiklikuks-tarbeks?id=79438246, accessed 10 September 2017, see also Ringvee, Ringo, "Estonia", in Oliver Scharbrodt, Samim Akgönül, Ahmet Alibašić, Jørgen S. Nielsen and Egdūnas Račius (eds.), *Yearbook of Muslims in Europe*, vol. 9 (Leiden-Boston: Brill), pp. 219–231 (220–221).

Ways to Co-existence", where both academic as well as religious perspectives were presented. The reception of the conference was hosted by the Embassy of the Turkish Republic.[11]

Transnational Links

The transnational links of the Estonian Islamic Congregation in 2017 were maintained, as in previous years, by Imam Ildar Muhhamedšin and his wife. In 2017 he visited several countries, including Turkey and Russia (including Tatarstan).[12] His visit with the Mufti of Belarus to Crimea, annexed by Russia from Ukraine in 2014, received criticism from Ukrainian Muslims, and the Mufti of the Spiritual Administration of the Muslims in Ukraine, Said Ismagilov, also condemned the visit.[13] The main cause of the controversy was that Muhhamedšin entered Crimea via Russia without the permission of the Ukrainian authorities. However, Muhhamedšin said that his visit to Crimea was only of a cultural nature and had no political connotations.[14]

Since 2012 there has been an imam from the Turkish Presidency of Religious Affairs (*Diyanet İşleri Başkanlığı*), appointed for a five-year term, to provide religious services alongside the Estonian Islamic Congregation's imam to Muslims in Estonia. In 2017 the Diyanet replaced the imam sent in 2012 with a new one for a five-year period. In 2017, the Estonian Islamic Congregation, as well as the *Sihtasutus Eesti Islami Keskus* (Estonian Islamic Centre Foundation), continued to have contact with the Turkish Cooperation and Coordination Agency (TİKA). While previously the discussions with TİKA focussed on the possibilities

---

11 University of Tartu Asian Centre Facebook event: www.facebook.com/events/113969472625836/?active_tab=about, accessed 10 January 2018.

12 "Форум ученых стран СНГ по теологии Откровения (вахий) и общественным наукам" (Forum of scientists of CIS countries on theology of Revelation [*wahia*] and social sciences), *Website of the Estonian Islamic Congregation*, http://islami.ee/форум-ученых-стран-снг-по-теологии-отк/, accessed 10 October 2017; "Mufti's travel to Tatarstan," *Website of the Estonian Islamic Congregation*, http://islami.ee/поездка-муфтия-в-татарстан/, accessed 10 October 2017.

13 "Muftis of Estonia and Belarus made unauthorized visit to Crimea", *QHA Crimean News Agency*, 5 May 2017, http://qha.com.ua/en/politics/muftis-of-estonia-and-belarus-made-unauthorized-visit-to-crimea/140643/, accessed 10 May 2017.

14 Koorits, Vahur, "Ukraina moslemeid pahandab Eesti islami koguduse peaimaami Ildar Muhhamedšini visiit Krimmi" (Ukrainian Muslims displeased by the visit of the Estonian Islamic Congregation's chief imam to Crimea), *Delfi*, 5 May 2017, http://www.delfi.ee/news/paevauudised/eesti/ukraina-moslemeid-pahandab-eesti-islami-koguduse-peaimaami-ildar-muhhamedsini-visiit-krimmi?id=78113540, accessed 10 May 2017.

of funding a mosque building in Estonia, the focus in 2017 was on the conservation of historical Muslim cemeteries in Rakvere and Narva.[15]

Law and Domestic Politics

The legal framework concerning Islam did not change in 2017, nor did governmental policies concerning religious associations in general, or Islam in particular.[16] Freedom of religion is protected by the Constitution of the Republic of 1992.[17] *The Churches and Congregations Act* of 2002 provides the legal framework for the implementation of religious freedom, including regulations for founding, managing and liquidating religious association as a legal entity.[18] Religious associations registered according to this Act may have certain exceptions that include taxation, and the possibility to apply for the right of their clergy to conduct marriages with civil validity. There are two Muslim religious associations in Estonia registered in accordance with the *Churches and Congregations Act*. No imams in Estonia have taken the examinations for obtaining the right to conduct marriages which are recognised under civil law, due to their limited access to the Estonian language in which the legal documents need to be written. Religious marriages conducted in the community according to Islamic traditions are, hence, not legally binding and are not recognised by the State.

Activities and Initiatives of Main Muslim Organisations

Since 2009, the centre for Muslim religious life in Estonia has been a building at 9 Keevise Street in Tallinn, maintained since 2015 by the Estonian Islamic Centre Foundation. The building has rooms for lectures, a small library and

---

15 Mallene, Laura, "Türgist tuleb üha rohkem märke Eestisse mošee ehitamisest" (More signs from Turkey to build a mosque in Tallinn), *Eesti Päevaleht*, 14 December 2016, http://epl.delfi.ee/news/eesti/turgist-tuleb-uha-rohkem-marke-eestisse-mosee-ehitamisest?id=76588238, accessed 12 March 2017.

16 On the legal framework in Estonia concerning Islam see Ringvee, Ringo, *Annotated Legal Documents on Islam in Europe: Estonia* (Leiden-Boston: Brill, 2015).

17 *Eesti Vabariigi Põhiseadus* (*Constitution of the Republic of Estonia*), *Riigi Teataja* (*State Gazette*), RT 1992, 26, 349, www.riigiteataja.ee/akt/633949?leiaKehtiv, accessed 12 March 2017.

18 *Kirikute ja koguduste seadus* (*Churches and Congregations Act*), *Riigi Teataja* (*State Gazette*), RT I 2002, 24, 135, https://www.riigiteataja.ee/akt/121062014030?leiaKehtiv, accessed 12 March 2017.

reading room, and a prayer hall that is open daily. There are around ten people with different ethnic backgrounds who are actively involved in the Centre's activities. The main aims of the Estonian Islamic Centre are to provide a space for Friday prayers, to maintain the building of the Centre, and to organise events or provide space for events for the community. On 6 May 2017 the Estonian Islamic Centre organised an open day for the general public.[19] In June 2017 the Centre used the *zakat al-fitr*, collected at the end of Ramadan, for charity purposes.[20]

In the Centre, the imam from the Estonian Islamic Congregation or the imam provided by the Diyanet give the Friday *khutba*s. There are around 100 to 150 male participants at Friday prayers and around 20 female participants. The major religious holidays and *iftars* during Ramadan are held in the Centre. In 2017 the *Ühing EESTÜRK* (Eestürk Association), which has connections to Fethullah Gülen's Hizmet movement, organised a separate *kurban bayramı* celebration outside the Centre as a result of the hostility between followers of Gülen and the Turkish government, after the attempted coup in July 2016.[21] Since 2017 the *khutbas* of the imam of the Estonian Islamic Congregation have been available on the Centre's Facebook page.[22] During the week, the facilities are mostly used by Muslim immigrants and local converts. During the weekends, there are educational activities for children as well as for adults.

In 2017 two Estonian-born students at Medina Islamic University graduated and returned to Estonia. Shortly after their return they established an association called *Tallinna Islamkeskus* (Tallinn Islamic Centre). The main objective was seemingly to manage the building at 9 Keevise Street, where the Estonian Islamic Centre resides. The intent behind establishing the association has remained unclear, and the organisation seems to be already defunct. One of the graduates who returned leads Friday prayers in Maardu, a satellite-town of Tallinn, which has a small Tatar community. The other graduate has become involved in the activities of the Estonian Islamic Congregation.

---

19 Estonian Islamic Centre Facebook event: https://www.facebook.com/events/1804851856509202/, accessed 10 September 2017.
20 Estonian Islamic Centre Facebook page: https://www.facebook.com/media/set/?set=a.715585958621831.1073741842.449884078525355&type=3, accessed 12 August 2017.
21 Eesti Foorum/Eestürk Facebook event: https://www.facebook.com/events/338390166603768/, accessed 10 January 2018.
22 Estonian Islamic Centre Facebook page: www.facebook.com/IslamiKeskus/, accessed 29 April 2018.

On 11 March 2017, the Estonian Islamic Congregation held its annual general meeting at the Ülemiste hotel in Tallinn, with about 70 participants.[23] As in previous years the Congregation did not organise hajj for Muslims from Estonia.

Muslim Population: History and Demographics

Tatars have a history in Estonia that goes back more than 200 years, and they have remained the largest ethnic group among Estonian Muslims.[24] In 1928, Estonian Tatars registered their first Muslim religious association, *Narva Muhameedlaste Usuühing* (Muslim Religious Society in Narva). During the Soviet period, the Tatar community became more diverse due to immigration from Tatarstan, as well from other parts of the Soviet Union. During that period, Muslims of other ethnicities also arrived to Estonia from the Muslim majority regions of the Soviet Union.

In 1989, the Tatar Cultural Society registered the first Muslim religious association since the beginning of Soviet rule, *Tallinna Islami Kogudus* (Tallinn Islamic Congregation). In 1994, ethnic group-based cultural societies with a Muslim identity in Estonia restructured the Congregation as the *Eesti Islami Kogudus* (Estonian Islamic Congregation), that unites both Sunni and Shi'i Muslims. While Tatars, the largest ethnic group, are Sunni Muslims, the majority of Shi'i Muslims are Azerbaijanis, who settled in Estonia during the Soviet period. The relations between Sunni and Shi'i Muslims have been traditionally good in Estonia.

In the 2010s, the Muslim population both grew in number as well as diversified, due to immigration and ethnic Estonian and Russian converts. According to the 2011 Population and Housing Census, one third of Muslims over 15-years of age were born in Estonia, while Tatars are the largest ethnic group of Muslims in Estonia, with 40% of the total Muslim population. However, one of the demographic trends of the Muslim population, according to the 2000 and 2011 population censuses, is the declining number of Tatars who identify themselves as Muslims, as well as the decreasing number of Tatars in general.[25]

---

23   http://islami.ee/общее-собрание-исламского-прихода-эс-2/, accessed 10 January 2018.
24   Abiline, Toomas and Ringo Ringvee, "Estonia", in Ingvar Svanberg and David Westerlund (eds.), *Muslim Tatars in the Baltic Sea Region*, (Leiden: Brill, 2016), pp. 105–127.
25   *Estonian Statistics, Statistical Database: Population and Housing Census Database 2000*, Religious Affiliation, http://pub.stat.ee/px-web.2001/I_Databas/Population_census/PHC 2000/16Religious_affiliation/16Religious_affiliation.asp; *Estonian Statistics, Statistical Database: Population and Housing Census Database 2011*, Religious Affiliation, http://pub.stat.ee/px-web.2001/I_Databas/Population_census/PHC2011/01Demographic_and_

The overwhelming majority of Estonia's Muslims are located in and around the capital city Tallinn, and in the industrial area in the Northeast of the country. According to the 2011 census, Muslims are the most urban religious group in Estonia, with 90% of Muslims living in cities.[26] There have been different estimations concerning the number of Muslims in Estonia over the years, ranging from 1,500 to 80,000.[27] The only reliable number is from the 2011 Housing and Population Census, that counted 1,508 Muslims who were 15-years of age or older, but the number has increased since then, and could be estimated to be around 3,000 to 4,000 now. However, the number of practising Muslims does not exceed a couple of hundred, based on regular participation at Friday midday prayers.

The population censuses from 2000 and 2011 also show that one cannot count all the representatives whose ethnicities have their roots in Muslim majority countries as Muslims, as their religious affiliation is often diverse, or they may have no religious affiliation at all. For example, only 37% of Tatars, the largest ethnic group among the Muslim population of Estonia, identified themselves as Muslims in the 2011 population census. Similarly, of Azerbaijanis, only 37% consider themselves to be Muslims; a similar picture emerges with other ethnic groups with a background in the Muslim majority regions of the former Soviet Union. Likewise, not all Pakistanis living in Estonia identified themselves as Muslims.

The number of participants in 'Id Al-Fitr and 'Id al-Adha events continued to be around 400. The Friday prayers at the Islamic Centre usually had around 100–150 male participants, most of them with a recent immigrant or convert background; there were around 20 female participants, most of them older generation Tatar women.

---

ethno_cultural_characteristics/08Religious_affiliation/08Religious_affiliation.asp, all accessed 12 March 2017.

26 *Estonian Statistics, Statistical Database: Population and Housing Census*, http://pub.stat.ee/pxweb.2001/I_Databas/Population_Census/databasetree.asp, accessed 12 March 2017.

27 Ringvee, Ringo, "Estonia", in Jørgen S. Nielsen, Samim Akgönül, Ahmet Alibašić and Egdūnas Račius (eds.) *Yearbook of Muslims in Europe*, vol. 5 (Leiden: Brill, 2013), pp. 229–236 (230); "Erdoğan, Minsk'te cami açılışına katılacak", *Aksam*, 4 November 2016, http://www.aksam.com.tr/guncel/erdogan-minskte-cami-acilisina-katilacak/haber-563532, accessed 12 March 2017.

Muslim Population	According to the 2011 census data there were 1,508 Muslims over 15-years of age living in Estonia (0.1% of the entire population. Over the years there have been different estimates of the number of Muslims in Estonia.[28] In the early 1990s the Muslims estimated their number in Estonia to be 10,000. After the 2000 and 2011 population censuses these estimates have decreased. The current number of people who consider themselves Muslims could be estimated to be between 3,000 and 4,000, including children (0.2–0.3% of the entire population).

The majority of Muslims in Estonia are from the ethnic groups who migrated to the country during the Soviet era, from the 1940s to the late 1980s. Although there are no exact numbers concerning conversion to Islam or Muslim immigration in the 21st century, it could be argued that these processes have slightly increased the Muslim population in Estonia. According to the 2011 Census, 33% of the Muslim population older than 15-years of age was born in Estonia. |
| **Ethnic/National Backgrounds** | According to the 2011 Census (that only includes respondents older than 15 years of age), the largest ethnic/national groups were:

Tatar: 604 (40% of Muslim population)
Azerbaijani: 299 (19.8%)
Estonian: 148 (9.8%)
Russian: 107 (7.1%)
Bedouin/Arab: 50 (3.3%)
Lezgin: 34 (2.25%)
Turkish: 33 (2.18%)
Others: 233 (16.05%). |

---

28 "Erdoğan, Minsk'te cami açılışına katılacak", *Aksam*, 4 November 2016, http://www.aksam.com.tr/guncel/erdogan-minskte-cami-acilisina-katilacak/haber-563532, accessed 12 March 2017.

Inner-Islamic Groups	No official data available. The Estonian Islamic Congregation operates as a religious association for both Sunni and Shi'i Muslims. The other Muslim religious association *Eesti Muhameedlaste Sunniitide Kogudus* (Estonian Muslim Sunni Congregation) represents Sunni Muslims exclusively. According to the available data, the vast majority of Muslims in Estonia are Sunnis. Although there exists a NGO for Ahmadis, the Ahmadiyya Muslim Jamaat in Estonia, their activities have not been visible.
Geographical Spread	According to the 2011 Census, 54.2% of the Muslim population is concentrated in Estonia's capital Tallinn. 90.7% of Muslims live in urban areas.
Number of Mosques	One prayer room in Tallinn, that operates within the Estonian Islamic Centre (*Eesti Islami Keskus*). The prayer room on 9 Keevise Street has also been known as Tallinn mosque. Outside of Tallinn, Muslims rent facilities for Friday prayers and religious festivals.
Muslim Burial Sites	During the Tsarist period, Estonian Muslims (Tatar settlers from inner Russia) maintained separate cemeteries in Narva, Rakvere and Tallinn. In the first years of the Soviet occupation (1940–41), they were closed and later destroyed. Estonian Muslims have since been using general cemeteries for burial, where they have a separate section. No request for a separate Muslim cemetery has been filed.
"Chaplaincy" in State Institutions	A "chaplaincy" service is provided in the following state institutions: defence forces, prisons, police, and border guard. The chaplains in these institutions are required to organise the religious or spiritual services for people of different religious affiliations. For this the chaplains pass the requests to the clergy required. While there is no Muslim chaplain in these institutions, the clergy of registered religious associations have the right to visit prisons and detention houses if required.

Halal Products	According to the *Animal Protection Act*[29] the slaughtering of animals that have not been stunned on religious grounds for consumption by members of a religious community is allowed. However, it must take place in slaughterhouses, and the slaughtering should not have commercial purposes. There is no special halal menu in public institutions, instead a vegetarian option is provided. In March 2017 the first halal-shop, NUR-Market, was opened (https://nur.ee). Additional information on the availability of halal products is available from the website: www.islamikeskus.eu/et/halal-shops-in-estonia.
Dress Code	There are no restrictions on Muslim dress (including head scarf and niqab (face veil)) in Estonia. Mostly new immigrants from Muslim majority countries and local female converts wear the head scarf. There are a couple of women in Estonia who wear the niqab.
Places of Islamic Learning and Education	There are no institutions for Islamic learning and education in Estonia.
Muslim Media and Publications	In 2017 there were no publications published by Muslims in Estonia.

Main Muslim Organisations

– Estonian Islamic Centre Foundation (*Sihtasutus Eesti Islami Keskus*, 9 Keevise Street, 11415 Tallinn, Estonia, ++372 51938795, ++372 6015220; email: info@islamikeskus.eu; www.islamikeskus.eu). The Estonian Islamic Centre was registered as a foundation in 2015. The Estonian Islamic Centre governs the building at 9 Keevise Street that has been used as a prayer house

---

29 *Loomakaitseseadus* (*Animal Protection Act*), *Riigi Teataja* (*State Gazette*), RT I 2001, 3, 4; RT I, 16.06.2016, 13, English translation available at: https://www.riigiteataja.ee/en/eli/514072016003/consolide, accessed 15 April 2017.

and centre for Muslim activities since 2009. The religious services in the Centre (including Friday prayers) are provided by the Estonian Islamic Congregation.
- Estonian Islamic Congregation (*Eesti Islami Kogudus*, 21a-7 Tina Street, 10216 Tallinn, Estonia, tel.: ++372 55947689, email: ildar.muhhamedsin@yahoo.com, www.islami.ee). The Estonian Islamic Congregation is the oldest Muslim religious association in Estonia, with its roots dating back to the Narva Muslim Religious Society established by Tatars in 1928. In 1989 the congregation was re-established as the Tallinn Islamic Congregation (*Tallinna Islami Kogudus*). The association has had its present name since 1994; it unites both Sunni and Shi'i Muslims, although Sunnis form the majority. The association mostly represents the "traditional" ethnic Muslim communities in Estonia. The prayers are conducted at the 9 Keevise Street building, managed since 2015 by the Estonian Islamic Centre. Since 2002, the imam of the congregation has been Ildar Muhhamedšin.
- Estonian Muslim Sunni Congregation (*Eesti Muhameedlaste Sunniitide Kogudus*, 12–13 Retke tee, 13415 Tallinn, Estonia, tel.: ++372 56666341, email: harrasov@gmail.com). The religious association was established in 1995 after a split in the Estonian Islamic Congregation. The congregation is relatively small and consists mostly of older generation Tatars. The Friday prayers are conducted in rented facilities and are led by Imam Ali Harrasov.
- Estonian Muslims (*Mittetulundusühing Eesti Moslemid*, 9 Keevise Street, 11415 Tallinn, Estonia, email: juhatus@eestimoslemid.eu). The Association was formed in 2015 to represent the Estonian converts and foreign-citizens not included in the Estonian Islamic Congregation. The association is registered as a regular non-profit association.
- Turath-Pärand Cultural Centre (*Kultuurikeskus Turath-Pärand*, 9 Keevise Street, 11415 Tallinn, Estonia, tel.: ++372 55947689, email: ildar.muhhamedsin@yahoo.com). The Turath-Pärand Cultural Centre was established in 2012 by the Imam of the Estonian Islamic Congregation, Muhhamedšin, and his wife Makhmutova. The Centre mostly organises educational activities.
- Association of Muslim Women in the Baltics (*Baltimaade Mosleminaiste Ühendus*, 9 Keevise Street, 11415 Tallinn, Estonia; tel.: ++372 55582953, email: mahmutova@yahoo.com). The association was established in 2012 by the imam of the Estonian Islamic Congregation and his wife.
- Iqra Cultural Centre (*Kultuurikeskus Iqra*, 1 Eha Street, 93811 Kuressaare, Estonia, email: keskus@islam.pri.ee, www.islam.pri.ee). The Iqra Cultural Centre was founded in 2012 by ethnic Estonian converts to Sunni Islam. The Centre has been active in previous years through translating, producing and publishing religious materials in the Estonian language.

- Ahmadiyya Muslim Jamaat in Estonia (*Mittetulundusühing Ahmadiyya Muslim Jamaat in Estonia*, 7-4 Paide, 11312 Tallinn, Estonia, tel.: ++372 5295720, www.alislam.org). The organisation of Ahmadiyya Muslims was registered in 2009. However, there are no signs of any activity and the number of Ahmadiyya Muslims in Estonia is unknown.
- Estonia–Turkey International Business, Culture and Education Association Eestürk, (*Ühing EESTÜRK*, 20 Pirita tee, 10127 Tallinn, Estonia, tel./fax.: ++372 6012070, email: estonya@eesturk.ee, www.eesturk.ee). The Association was established in 2010 by Turkish business persons in Estonia to encourage cultural, educational and business exchange between Turkey and Estonia. Although the association is not religious, the founders have identified themselves through the Hizmet movement of Fethullah Gülen.
- Tallinn Islamic Centre (*Tallinna Islamikeskus*, 9 Keevise, 11415 Tallinn, Estonia, email: islamikeskus@gmail.com). A non-profit association that was registered in November 2017 by two graduates from Medina University. The association had not become active by the end of 2017.

Finland

Teemu Pauha[1] and Johanna Konttori[2]

Introduction

In 2017, the Finnish public discussion of Islam was centred on similar issues as previous years, such as the debate on the plan to construct a "grand mosque" in Helsinki, terrorist attacks, especially in Europe, and the issue of the funding of terrorism. There was one new topic, however, that received substantial media coverage: the presumed terrorist attack in the city of Turku. The police have so far declined to comment on the motives of the attacker, but have announced that the attacks are being investigated as "murders with terrorist intent".[3]

The debate on the Helsinki mosque came to an end, at least for now, when the Urban Environment Committee of the City of Helsinki decided to reject the application to reserve a plot for the mosque. The mosque project had received much media attention for several years. It now remains to be seen whether there will be a new mosque project in the coming years.

Public Debates

The year 2017 saw what may have been the first Islamist terrorist attack on Finnish soil. On 18 August, Moroccan-born Abderrahman Bouanane carried out a knife attack in central Turku, killing two and injuring eight, before being shot in the leg by the police. Bouanane had entered Finland as an asylum

---

1 Teemu Pauha is a psychologist of religion. In his doctoral thesis (PhD 2018, University of Helsinki, Study of Religions), Pauha studies the social psychology of identity construction among young Finnish Muslims. Besides the psychology of religion and Islam, Pauha's main academic interests include nationalism, globalisation, and apostasy.
2 Johanna Konttori is a sociologist of religion. In her doctoral work (PhD 2015, University of Helsinki, Study of Religions) she examines the political debates on head scarves and full face veils in 21st century France. Her main areas of expertise include head scarf and full veil debates, state-religion relations, religions in the public sphere, and Islam, all in the European context.
3 Mäkelä, Kalle, and Yrjö Hjelt, "Turun puukotuksista epäilty on siirretty Turun vankilaan–koostimme juttuun tutkinnan vaiheet ja sen, mitä seuraavaksi tapahtuu" (The suspect of the Turku stabbings has been moved to the Turku Prison–we gathered here the stages of the investigation and what happens next), *Yle Uutiset*, 17 October 2017, https://yle.fi/uutiset/3-9821241, accessed 24 January 2018.

seeker in 2016, initially using the name Abderrahman Mechkah. His asylum application was later refused. Already half a year before the attack, the police had received warnings of Bouanane possibly being radicalised, but the warnings did not lead to action. After the attack, the police reportedly obtained a manifesto and video made by Bouanane, but their contents have so far not been made public. No terrorist organisation has taken responsibility for the attack, and the police have not found anything that would connect Bouanane to any organised group. Immediately after the attacks, the police arrested three other men suspected of being complicit in it. However, all three were soon released without charge.[4] The ambiguity surrounding the motives has led to debates whether the Turku incident constitutes an act of Islamist terrorism. Soon after the attack, terrorism researcher Leena Malkki assessed that the information available on Bouanane's religious views suggests a terrorist motivation.[5]

The Helsinki mosque project received much public attention also in 2017. One of the main questions was its funding, as the construction of the mosque was planned to be financed with foreign funding. There was also one written question by a parliamentarian and three municipal citizens' initiatives launched in 2017 that were linked to the Helsinki mosque project.

Transnational Links

The number of Muslims who left Finland and travelled to Syria and Iraq as foreign fighters still remained relatively low in 2017, even though it was increasing. The Finnish Security Intelligence Service estimated the number to be approximately 80, whereas in 2016 it was estimated to be 70.[6]

In November 2017, three men were charged with preparation of a crime with terrorist intent. According to the subpoena the men had travelled to Syria in order to join the group *Jaysh al-Muhajirin wal-Ansar* (The Army of the Emigrants and Supporters). In addition, one of the men was charged with

---

4 Mäkelä and Hjelt, "Turun puukotuksista epäilty on siirretty Turun vankilaan".
5 Malkki, Leena, "Oliko Turun puukotus terrori-isku?" (Was the Turku stabbing a terrorist attack?), *Politiikasta*, 28 August 2017, http://politiikasta.fi/oliko-turun-puukotus-terrori-isku/, accessed 24 January 2018.
6 Pauha, Teemu, "Finland", in Oliver Scharbrodt, Samim Akgönül, Ahmet Alibašić, Jørgen S. Nielsen and Egdūnas Račius (eds.), *Yearbook of Muslims in Europe,* vol. 9 (Leiden: Brill, 2017), pp. 232–247 (234); Finnish Security Intelligence Service, "Kansainvälinen radikaali-islamist inen terrorismi ja siihen liittyvät ilmiöt" (International radical Islamist terrorism and phenomena related to it), *SUPO News*, 11 September 2017, https://www.supo.fi/tiedotteet/1/0/kansainvalinen_radikaali-islamistinen_terrorismi_ja_siihen_liittyvat_ilmiot_64055, accessed 21 January 2018.

giving training in committing a terrorist crime, and another man with recruitment of people to commit terrorist crimes.[7]

The foreign sources of funding were a key point of contention with regard to the plans for the Helsinki mosque. The cost of the mosque's construction was estimated to be in the range of €110 to 140 million, and the annual maintenance costs in the range of €6 to 7 million. The Kingdom of Bahrain had offered the initial funding, as well as help in coordinating the fundraising activities. The involvement of Bahrain raised public concerns over foreign influence in the planned mosque.[8] This, together with the lack of other confirmed funding sources, led the Urban Environment Committee of the City of Helsinki to reject the application to reserve a plot for the mosque.[9]

Law and Domestic Politics

In 2017, the European Union Agency for Fundamental Rights (FRA) published its Second European Union Minorities and Discrimination Survey (EU-MIDIS II). The Finnish Muslim sample, the respondents of which were mostly of Somali descent, had the highest average level of attachment to the country of residence (4.6–5%) and the lowest percentage of respondents not at all attached (1%) in the entire survey. Almost half of the respondents (45%) had experienced harassment due to ethnic or immigrant background in the twelve months before the survey, a percentage significantly higher than the EU average of 27%. Experiences of overall discrimination were also more prevalent than in the EU generally. However, the percentage of Muslims who perceived discrimination to be widespread due to religion, ethnicity, or skin colour, was lower in Finland than in the EU on average.[10] Furthermore, Finnish respondents were more active than average in reporting experiences of discrimination to authorities, and they had the highest level of trust in the

---

7   Nuuttila, Sakari, "Kolmelle syyte terrorismin valmistelusta–matkustivat Suomesta Syyriaan liittyäkseen terrorijärjestöön" (Three charged with preparation of terrorism–travelled from Finland to Syria to join a terrorist organisation), *Iltalehti*, 7 November 2017, http://www.iltalehti.fi/kotimaa/201711072200515992_uo.shtml, accessed 28 January 2018.

8   Pauha, Teemu, and Tuomas Martikainen, *Lausunto Oasis-hankkeesta* (*Report on the Oasis Project*) (Turku: Siirtolaisuusinstituutti, 2017), pp. 3, 23.

9   City of Helsinki, Urban Environment committee, "Päätöstiedote nro 17" (Decision notice #17), https://www.hel.fi/static/public/hela/Kaupunkiymparistolautakunta/Suomi/Paatostiedote/2017/Kymp_2017-12-12_Kylk_17_Pt/index.html, accessed 13 December 2017.

10 38% of the Finnish respondents perceived widespread discrimination with regard to religion, 45% with regard to ethnicity, and 43% with regard to skin colour. The respective percentages in the EU as a whole were 58%, 54%, and 48%.

police.[11] The reasons for the apparent discrepancy between personal experiences and general perceptions are not known. However, some clue may be inferred from a study in which young Muslims wrote letters about life in Finland. In the letters, Finland was portrayed positively as a free and safe country with a high standard of living. The Finnish people, in contrast, were described in more ambiguous terms as sometimes racist and in any case different from Muslims.[12]

In order to gain background information on a certain topic, a member of the Finnish parliament may present a written question to the responsible minister, who then has 21 days to answer the question. In 2017, there were two written questions that dealt with Islam. In March 2017, MP Päivi Räsänen (Christian Democrats) issued a question on the Helsinki mosque project: its purposes, finances, and possible security issues.[13] In her answer, the Minister of the Interior, Paula Risikko, pointed out that her ministry was actively monitoring the project and collaborating with the City of Helsinki, among others.[14]

In May 2017, Juho Eerola, an MP of the Finns Party, issued a question on the monitoring and prevention of "multicultural hate speech" (*monikulttuurinen vihapuhe*). In his question Eerola pointed out that hate speech in Finland occurred not only in the national languages but in Somali and Arabic as well. Eerola referred such "multicultural hate speech" to radical Islam, and asked whether the police had enough personnel with knowledge of the Somali and Arabic languages.[15] In her response, the Minister of the Interior, Paula Risikko, pointed out that the police, the Finnish Security Intelligence Service as well as the National Bureau of Investigation had already received additional resources to fight against hate speech and extremist movements. In addition, she noted

---

11 European Union Agency for Fundamental Rights, *Second European Union Minorities and Discrimination Survey: Muslims–Selected findings* (Luxembourg: Publications Office of the European Union, 2017), pp. 19–20, 21, 35, 40, 43, 56.

12 Pauha, Teemu, and Inga Jasinskaja-Lahti, "'Don't ever convert to a Finn': Young Muslims writing about Finnishness", *Diaconia*, vol. 4, no. 2 (2013), pp. 172–193.

13 Räsänen, Päivi, "Kirjallinen kysymys Helsingin suurmoskeijahankkeen taustoista ja rahoituksesta" (Written question on the background and funding of the Helsinki grand mosque project), 17 March 2017, https://www.eduskunta.fi/FI/vaski/Kysymys/Documents/KK_105+2017.pdf, accessed 24 January 2018.

14 Risikko, Paula, "Vastaus kirjalliseen kysymykseen Helsingin suurmoskeijahankkeen taustoista ja rahoituksesta" (Reply to the written question on the background and funding of the Helsinki grand mosque project), 11 April 2017, https://www.eduskunta.fi/FI/vaski/Kysymys/Documents/KKV_105+2017.pdf, accessed 24 January 2018.

15 Eerola, Juho, "Kirjallinen kysymys monikulttuurisen vihapuheen seurannasta ja torjunnasta" (Written question on the monitoring and prevention of multicultural hate speech), 12 May 2017, https://www.eduskunta.fi/FI/vaski/Kysymys/Documents/KK_200+2017.pdf, accessed 28 January 2018.

that the police could also use interpreters and technical solutions in identifying hate speech, when needed.[16]

It is possible to make citizens' initiatives both at national and local levels in Finland. In 2017, three municipal citizens' initiatives dealing with Islam were launched in Helsinki. One of the initiatives was against the building of a "grand mosque", one against the building of minarets, and one demanded a municipal referendum on the mosque project. At the time of writing, two of these initiatives are still open, and one has been sent to the municipality.[17]

Activities and Initiatives of Main Muslim Organisations

In 2015, the City of Helsinki received an application for land for constructing "a grand mosque" and a cultural centre in Helsinki. The application was prepared by a conglomeration of three organisations: *Suomen Muslimiliitto ry* (Finnish Muslim Union), *Suomen Musliminaiset ry* (Finnish Muslim Women), and *Kulttuuri–ja uskontofoorumi FOKUS ry* (Forum for Culture and Religion FOKUS).[18] In practice, the core group behind the project consisted of Pia Jardi, her husband Abdessalam Jardi, and retired ambassador Ilari Rantakari. The applicants wanted the project to remain independent of existing mosque associations, and therefore created a separate foundation named Oasis to manage the affairs of the planned mosque complex.[19]

Despite the applicant organisations representing a relatively small share of Finnish Muslims, the outspoken goal of the core group was to establish a mosque that would welcome everybody. The mosque project received public support from the broader Muslim community, with the Shi'i *Resalat* being an

---

16   Risikko, Paula, "Vastaus kirjalliseen kysymykseen monikulttuurisen vihapuheen seurannasta ja torjunnasta" (Reply to the written question on the monitoring and prevention of multicultural hate speech), 2 June 2017, https://www.eduskunta.fi/FI/vaski/Kysymys/Documents/KKV_200+2017.pdf, accessed 28 January 2018.

17   "Ei suurmoskeijaa" (No grand mosque), https://www.kuntalaisaloite.fi/fi/aloite/4714 "Minareettien kielto Helsinkiin" (Minaret ban to Helsinki), https://www.kuntalaisaloite.fi/fi/aloite/3949; "Kunnallinen kansanäänestys suurmoskeijahankkeesta Helsingissä" (Municipal referendum on the grand mosque project in Helsinki), https://www.kuntalaisaloite.fi/fi/aloite/4643, all accessed 29 January 2018.

18   The two former are Muslim advocacy organisations. The latter, in turn, is a non-denominational and ecumenical association that is actively engaged in interfaith and intercultural dialogue.

19   Pauha and Martikainen, *Lausunto Oasis-hankkeesta*, pp. 3, 14–16.

exception. Despite the general support, some in the community criticised, for example, the central role of a Christian (Rantakari) in the project.[20]

In December 2017, after receiving assessments from several ministries and the Finnish Institute of Migration, the Urban Environment Division of the City of Helsinki proposed the acceptance of the application and the reservation of a plot for the mosque complex, albeit with several conditions.[21] However, the very next week, the Urban Environment Committee held a meeting and unanimously rejected the application. The Committee considered the application to be untenable because "the scope of the project and the still open questions and uncertainty factors, above all the origin of the funding and the possible effects of the funding sources do not provide a sustainable foundation for this solution to be realised".[22] The matter was scheduled to be further considered by the Helsinki City Board, but after the decision of the Urban Environment Committee, the applicants decided to withdraw their application.[23]

After the terrorist attack of 9/11, President Tarja Halonen convened meetings of Finnish religious leaders. Ten years later, the National Forum for Cooperation of Religions in Finland (*Uskontojen yhteistyö Suomessa–USKOT-foorumi ry / Religionernas samarbete i Finland–RESA-forumet rf.*) was founded to continue the work started in the meetings and "to foster peace in Finnish society".[24] Since its foundation, the Forum has consisted of five member organisations: the *Suomen Juutalaisten Seurakuntien Keskusneuvosto ry* (Central Council of Jewish Communities in Finland), the *Suomen evankelis-luterilainen kirkko* (Evangelical Lutheran Church of Finland), the *Suomen Ekumeeninen Neuvosto* (Finnish Ecumenical Council), the *Suomen Islam-seurakunta* (Finnish Islamic Congregation), and *Suomen Islamilainen Neuvosto ry* (Islamic Council

---

20   Pauha and Martikainen, *Lausunto Oasis-hankkeesta*, pp. 14, 20.
21   City of Helsinki, "Moskeijalle ja monitoimikeskukselle esitetään suunnitteluvarausta Sörnäisiin" (A planning reservation in Sörnäinen is proposed for the mosque and community centre), https://www.hel.fi/uutiset/fi/kaupunkiymparisto/moskeija-ja-monitoimikeskushankkeesta-paatoksia-tana-talvena, accessed 13 December 2017.
22   City of Helsinki, Urban Environment committee, "Päätöstiedote nro 17."
23   Malmberg, Lari, "Helsinkiin suunniteltu suurmoskeija kaatui lopullisesti–Hankkeen vetäjät peruivat tonttivaraushakemuksensa" (The Grand Mosque planned in Helsinki has collapsed for good–the project leaders withdrew their application for a plot), *Helsingin Sanomat*, 14 December 2017, https://www.hs.fi/kaupunki/art-2000005490463.html, accessed 3 January 2018.
24   Juusela, Pauli, "Suomalainen uskontojen vuoropuhelu kiinnostaa Yhdysvaltain kongressia" (The United States Congress is interested in Finnish religious dialogue), *Kirkko ja kaupunki*, 1 December 2017, https://www.kirkkojakaupunki.fi/-/suomalainen-uskontojen-vuoropuhelu-kiinnostaa-yhdysvaltain-kongressia, accessed 29 January 2018.

of Finland).[25] The Forum has been active in promoting religious dialogue and denouncing religious violence. After the Turku attack in August 2017, the Forum and the *Suomen Muslimiverkosto* (Finnish Muslim Network) organised a vigil to commemorate the victims and to pray for peace. The Finnish Muslim Network also published a Facebook statement condemning the attack.[26]

Muslim Population: History and Demographics

The Finnish Muslim population dates back to the time when Finland was a Grand Duchy under the rule of the Russian emperor (1809–1917). The Russian military that was stationed in the country is known to have had Muslim soldiers, including Kazakhs and Tatars, serving in it, at least from the 1830s onward. In the 1870s, a permanent Muslim community was formed when Tatar Muslims from the Russian Nizhni Novgorod region settled in the country. When Finland became independent in 1917, these Muslims were granted citizenship and a right to organise themselves into a religious community. Until the 1990s, the growth of the Muslim population remained slow, and increased mostly due to marriage, tourism, and work-related migration. At the turn of the 1990s, a change occurred and the number of Muslims began to rise rapidly as Finland increased its intake of UNHCR quota refugees and asylum seekers from Muslim majority countries.[27]

Due to the lack of census data, there are no official or precise statistics regarding the number of self-identified Muslims in Finland.[28] Instead, the only exact figures available relate to the number and membership of registered religious communities. In early 2018, there were 46 religious communities and 87 other registered associations with a name containing the word "Islam",

---

25 National Forum for Cooperation of Religions in Finland (CORE), "Rules in English", http://www.uskot-resa.fi/en/rules_in_english/, accessed 29 January 2018.

26 Juusela, Pauli, "Narinkkatorilla vietettiin uskontojen hiljainen hetki Turun iskun takia" (A vigil of religions was held at Narinkkatori because of the Turku attack), *Kirkko ja kaupunki*, 21 August 2017, https://www.kirkkojakaupunki.fi/-/narinkkatorilla-vietettiin-uskontojen-hiljainen-hetki-turun-iskun-takia, accessed 29 January 2018. The Finnish Muslim Network (*Suomen Muslimiverkosto*) is a nation-wide organisation that was founded in January 2017 to represent Muslims within society (see Suomen Muslimiverkosto, "About", https://www.facebook.com/pg/muslimiverkosto/about/?ref=page_internal, accessed 29 January 2018).

27 Pauha, Teemu, and Tuomas Martikainen, "Finland", in Jørgen S. Nielsen, Samim Akgönül, Ahmet Alibašić and Egdūnas Račius (eds.), *Yearbook of Muslims in Europe*, vol. 6 (Leiden: Brill, 2014), pp. 218–228 (218).

28 Pauha and Martikainen, "Finland", p. 219.

"Muslim", or their derivatives. Four religious communities and one other association were newly registered in 2017.[29] At the end of the year 2016, Islamic religious communities had 14,141 members in total.[30] These figures do not represent a complete picture, however, because, as is often emphasised, the majority of Finnish Muslims do not belong to a registered religious community.[31] Accordingly, the estimates below are, for the most part, provided by Finnish Muslim leaders, or calculated by experts on the basis of figures pertaining to nationality, native language, or country of origin, for example.

Muslim Population	The total number of Muslims is unknown, but estimated to be at least 70,000[32] (1.3% of the total population in 2017).
Ethnic/National Backgrounds	Official figures are available only with regard to the Tatars. During recent years, the total number of members from the two Tatar communities has

---

29 http://yhdistysrekisteri.prh.fi/ryhaku.htx, accessed 3 January 2018. Associations and religious communities are governed by different legislation, which grants them a different legal status. For example, an association must be democratically administered and have a board of several members, whereas a religious community does not. Furthermore, a religious community may be granted the right to conduct marriages, and members of a religious community may be entitled to receive religious education in their own religion at public schools. See, for example, *HE 170/2002. Hallituksen esitys Eduskunnalle uskonnonvapauslaiksi ja eräiksi siihen liittyviksi laeiksi* (*Government's Proposal to the Parliament with Regard to the Freedom of Religion Act and Some Raws Related to it*), http://www.finlex.fi/fi/esitykset/he/2002/20020170#idp5318496, accessed 29 January 2018.
30 Statistics Finland, *Statistical Yearbook of Finland 2017* (Helsinki: Statistics Finland, 2017), p. 466.
31 See, for example, Martikainen, Tuomas, "Muslimit suomalaisessa yhteiskunnassa" (Muslims in Finnish society), in Tuomas Martikainen, Tuula Sakaranaho and Marko Juntunen (eds.), *Islam Suomessa: Muslimit arjessa, mediassa ja yhteiskunnassa* (*Islam in Finland: Muslims in Everyday Life, Media and Society*) (Helsinki: Suomalaisen Kirjallisuuden Seura, 2008), pp. 62–84 (71). The low rate of organisation does not only apply to Muslims, but to predominantly migrant religious groups more generally. Statistics Finland has reported that at the end of 2013, only 16% of foreign language speakers in Finland belonged to a registered religious community. See *Quality Description: Population Structure 2013* (Helsinki: Statistics Finland, 2014), http://www.stat.fi/til/vaerak/2013/01/vaerak_2013_01_2014-09-26_laa_001_en.html, accessed 29 January 2018.
32 Sohlberg, Jussi, and Kimmo Ketola, "Uskonnolliset yhteisöt Suomessa" (The religious communities in Finland), in Kimmo Ketola, Maarit Hytönen, Veli-Matti Salminen, Jussi Sohlberg and Leena Sorsa (eds.), *Osallistuva luterilaisuus: Suomen evankelis-luterilainen kirkko vuosina 2012–2015: Tutkimus kirkosta ja suomalaisista* (*Participating Lutheranism: The Evangelical Lutheran Church of Finland in the Years 2012–2015: A Study on the Church and Finns*), (Tampere: Kirkon tutkimuskeskus, 2016), pp. 15–46 (24).

remained at around 600, with a trend of slow decline.[33] The vast majority of Finnish Muslims are first-generation immigrants who have come to the country as refugees or asylum seekers or through family reunion. The largest national and ethnic groups are Somalis, Arabs, Kurds, Turks, Bosniaks, Afghans, Iranians and Kosovo Albanians.[34] In 2012, the number of ethnic Finnish converts to Islam was estimated to lie around 1,500.[35]

Inner-Islamic Groups   It is estimated that ca. 10% of Finnish Muslims are Shi'is.[36] However, there is no official data available to confirm this.

Geographical Spread   The Muslim population is concentrated in the capital region of Helsinki and a few large cities, especially Turku and Tampere.[37] However, no official figures are available about distribution.

---

33 The Religions in Finland Project, "Suomen Islam-seurakunta", http://www.uskonnot.fi/yhteisot/view.php?orgId=85, accessed 8 January 2018; The Religions in Finland Project, "Tampereen islamilainen seurakunta", http://www.uskonnot.fi/yhteisot/view.php?orgId=441, accessed 8 January 2018. One of the communities, *Tampereen islamilainen seurakunta*, resides in Tampere, while the other, *Suomen Islam-seurakunta*, is active in other parts of Southern Finland.

34 Martikainen, Tuomas, and Marja Tiilikainen, "Johdanto: islamin hallinta" (Introduction: the governance of Islam), in Tuomas Martikainen and Marja Tiilikainen (eds.), *Islam, hallinta ja turvallisuus (Islam, Governance and Security)*, (Turku: Eetos, 2013), pp. 9–23 (12); Pauha and Martikainen, "Finland", pp. 218–219.

35 The figure is an estimate by the Muslim activist Isra Lehtinen (see Pauha and Martikainen, "Finland", pp. 218–219), but it is supported by figures regarding the Finnish-speaking membership of Muslim organisations. In 2011, the official number of Finnish-speaking members was 1,575. See *Haastettu kirkko: Suomen evankelis-luterilainen kirkko vuosina 2008–2011 (The Challenged Church: The Evangelical-Lutheran Church of Finland in the Years 2008–2011)* (Tampere: Kirkon tutkimuskeskus, 2012), p. 33.

36 Pauha and Martikainen, "Finland", p. 218.

37 Martikainen and Tiilikainen, "Johdanto: islamin hallinta", p. 12; Pauha and Martikainen, "Finland", pp. 218–219.

Number of Mosques	It is estimated that there are approximately 80 mosques in Finland, of which ca. 30 are in the capital region.[38] Of these, only two are purpose-built: the Tatars built a wooden mosque in Järvenpää in 1942, as well as "an Islam house" in central Helsinki, one floor of which is used for worship.[39] There are plans for the construction of mosques in the cities of Turku and Oulu. In both cities, there have been also previous mosque construction initiatives, but so far they have not come to fruition because of funding difficulties.[40]
Muslim Burial Sites	The Finnish Tatar community has its own cemeteries in the cities of Helsinki and Turku. Furthermore, a local Muslim community maintains a cemetery in the town of Jyväskylä in central Finland. In large towns, parts of cemeteries that are maintained by the Lutheran Church may be reserved for the burial of Muslims.[41]
"Chaplaincy" in State Institutions	Finnish state institutions are increasingly recognising Islam as a religion that is to be included in chaplaincy services. However, Muslim chaplaincy is so far not provided systematically. Several state institutions have guidelines for dealing with

---

[38] The estimates are given by Anas Hajjar, the Chairperson of the Islamic Council of Finland. See Salminen, Reeta, "Vaikuttajaimaami: 'Pääkaupunkiseudulle tarvitaan jopa viisi suurmoskeijaa'" (Influential imam: "At least five grand mosques needed in the capital region"), *Yle Uutiset*, 28 October 2015, https://yle.fi/uutiset/3-8412539, accessed 29 January 2018.

[39] Pauha and Martikainen, "Finland", p. 221.

[40] Pauha and Martikainen, *Lausunto Oasis-hankkeesta*, pp. 9–10.

[41] Grönholm, Pauliina, "Puhtaus on muslimeille olennaista" (Purity is essential for Muslims), *Helsingin Sanomat*, 1 November 2014, http://www.hs.fi/kotimaa/a1414738147609, accessed 29 January 2018; Latva-Teikari, Kati, "Buddhalaiselle tuhkaus, muslimille oikea ilmansuunta–pikkukunnissa hautaus aiheuttaa päänvaivaa" (Cremation for the Buddhist, the right direction for the Muslim–burial causes puzzlement in small municipalities), *Yle Uutiset*, 6 October 2016, http://yle.fi/uutiset/3-9211207, accessed 6 February 2017; Pauha and Martikainen, "Finland", p. 223.

Muslims, but it is not known how these guidelines are implemented.[42]

Halal Products

The *Animal Welfare Act* of 1996 permits halal slaughter with the provision that the animal is stunned at the same time as the bleeding out has begun. The Act is currently under revision, and the new act is scheduled to take effect in 2020. In its proposed form, the new act will demand the stunning to precede the bleeding out.[43] Four abattoirs are producing halal meat, but domestic produce is nevertheless small.[44] Halal stores are, by and large, concentrated in the major cities. The halal selection in common grocery shops is rather limited.

Dress Code

In Finland there are no laws that prohibit the use of the head scarf or niqab in the public sphere or in the workplace. People are allowed to express their religiosity in public. There are two exceptions, namely the police and the army, where the dress code does not allow religious symbols. Otherwise, the only two reasons for restricting the use of religious symbols are hygiene and safety. Thus, for instance, pupils and teachers are allowed to wear head scarves and even niqabs, and many large

---

42 The general regulations of the Finnish Defence Forces, for example, contain information on fasting, praying, and other Islamic religious practices that should be taken into account with regard to Muslim soldiers. See, Defence Command, "Yleinen palvelusohjesääntö", http://puolustusvoimat.fi/documents/1948673/2258487/PEVIESTOS_YLPALVO+2017/3684dac2-c7ac-4d93-b792-34649f6e2f5d, accessed 29 January 2018.

43 Ministry of Agriculture and Forestry, *Hallituksen esitys eduskunnalle laiksi eläinten hyvinvoinnista ja laeiksi eräiden siihen liittyvien lakien muuttamisesta* (*Government's Proposal to the Parliament with Regard to the Animal Welfare Act and Some Laws Related to it*), 21 December 2017, http://mmm.fi/documents/1410837/6017006/Luonnos_Hallituksen+esitys+laiksi+el%C3%A4inten+hyvinvoinnista_+21.12.2017.pdf/b8bca450-95a8-463e-bfe0-78135f0dc679, accessed 17 January 2018, pp. 3, 140.

44 Finnish Food Safety Authority Evira, "Usein kysyttyä teurastuksesta" (Frequently asked questions about slaughter), https://www.evira.fi/elaimet/elainsuojelu-ja-elainten-pito/elainsuojelu-teurastuksessa-ja-lopetuksessa/usein-kysyttya-teurastuksesta/, accessed 17 January 2018.

companies have added head scarves to their uniforms.[45]

No research data exists on the number of girls and women who wear a head scarf or a niqab in Finland. However, it is safe to say that the number of women wearing a face veil is considerably smaller than the number of women wearing a head scarf.

Places of Islamic Learning and Education

The *Religious Freedom Act* of 2003 obliges the municipalities to organise Religious Education (RE) in Islamic and other minority faiths if there are at least three pupils requesting it. In public schools, RE is provided in a non-confessional manner. In other words, RE concentrates on providing the pupil with information about her or his own religion, and religious practice is not permitted. In 2016, 2.1% of pupils in grades 1–6 of comprehensive school, and 1.9% of pupils in grades 7–9 of comprehensive school participated in Islamic RE.[46] In general upper secondary education (*lukio*), the share of pupils in the Islamic RE course is lower, firstly because the share of Muslims among pupils is lower in general, and secondly, because a matriculation exam cannot yet be taken in the Islamic religion. Compared to the total number of pupils participating in Islamic RE in Finland, the number of qualified teachers is low: in 2015, there were only 14 teachers with a formal qualification to teach Islam in a public school. The Finnish National Agency

---

45   Sorsa, Leena, *Uskonnolliset tavat ja julkinen tila Suomessa (Religious Customs and the Public Sphere in Finland)* (Tampere, Kirkon tutkimuskeskus, 2018), pp. 52, 54–58, http://sakasti.evl.fi/julkaisut.nsf/43A7EEF29E2743E6C225822100301852/$FILE/Uskonnolliset%20tavat%20ja%20julkinen%20tila%20Suomessa_55.pdf, accessed 19 February 2018.

46   Vipunen–Education Statistics Finland, *Pupils' Subject Choices*, https://vipunen.fi/en-gb/basic/Pages/Kieli--ja-muut-ainevalinnat.aspx, accessed 17 January 2018.

for Education has published textbooks for teaching Islam up until the seventh grade.[47]

Currently, there are no Islamic schools in Finland. However, the capital region has at least one private Muslim kindergarten (*Islamilainen päiväkoti*), and many mosques organise Qur'an classes for children. In addition, there is a post-secondary level school called the European Institute Islamic of Human Sciences in Helsinki, where teaching is done in Arabic.[48] As for university education, the Faculty of Theology at the University of Helsinki opened a new, permanent position of University Lecturer in Islamic Theology in late 2017. The Lecturer will begin her work in Autumn 2018.[49]

Muslim Media and Publications

Currently, the youth magazine *Ana* is the only regularly published Finnish-language Muslim periodical. Tatars and other ethnic communities have their own publications that do not necessarily concentrate on religion, but nevertheless contain religious material.[50] Besides print media, the internet provides an important communication platform, especially for the younger generation of Finnish

---

47 Pauha, Teemu, Suaad Onniselkä and Abbas Bahmanpour, "Kaksi vuosisataa suomalaista islamia" (Two centuries of Finnish Islam), in Ruth Illman, Kimmo Ketola, Riitta Latvio and Sohlberg Jussi (eds.), *Monien uskontojen ja katsomusten Suomi (Finland of Many Religions and World Views)* (Tampere: Kirkon tutkimuskeskus, 2017), pp. 104–115 (111).

48 Haikala, Topias. "Suomalaisen islamkoulun perustaja: 'Tärkeää ei ole, millä nimellä kutsut itseäsi, vaan mitä teet'" (The founder of Finnish school of Islam: "The important thing is not what you call yourself, but what you do"), *Kirkko & kaupunki*, 16 October 2017, https://www.kirkkojakaupunki.fi/-/suomalaisen-islamkoulun-perustaja-tarkeaa-ei-ole-milla-nimella-kutsut-itseasi-vaan-mita-teet-, accessed 29 January 2018.

49 Toivanen, Olli-Pekka, "Islamilaista teologiaa moniulotteisesti ja elävästi" (Islamic theology in a multidimensional and lively manner), *Teologia.fi*, 13 January 2018, https://www.teologia.fi/ajankohtaista/1519-islamilaista-teologiaa-moniulotteisesti-ja-elaevaesti, accessed 15 January 2018.

50 Pauha and Martikainen, "Finland", p. 225.

Muslims. Besides message boards and information portals, such as *Tulevaisuus.org*, there are also several Facebook groups and blogs maintained by young Muslims. Of particular prominence is the Facebook group *Suomen Nuorten Muslimit* that has over 6,900 subscribers.[51]

Main Muslim Organisations

- Helsinki Islamic Centre (*Helsinki Islam Keskus*, Veturitori 4, 00520 Helsinki, tel.: ++35 8451282818, http://www.hic.fi/fin/). With over 2,600 members, *Helsinki Islam Keskus* is officially the largest Muslim organisation in Finland. The majority of its members are of Somali origin. Besides maintaining a mosque in central Helsinki, *Helsinki Islam Keskus* also provides Qur'an classes and family counselling.[52]
- Islamic Multicultural Da'wah Centre (Munkkiniemen puistotie 4 A, 00331 Helsinki, tel.: ++35 895882579, http://www.masjidiman.com/). The Islamic Multicultural Da'wah Centre is a Sunni Muslim organisation that maintains a mosque in Western Helsinki. The number of members is approximately 250, of whom the majority are immigrants of African or Arab origin.[53]
- Islamic Society of Northern Finland (*Pohjois-Suomen Islamilainen Yhdyskunta*, Kajaaninkatu 36, 90100 Oulu). With close to 900 members, *Pohjois-Suomen Islamilainen Yhdyskunta* is the largest Muslim organisation in the North of Finland. It has its own mosque in the city of Oulu.[54]
- Resalat Islamic Society (*Resalat Islamilainen Yhdyskunta*, Kaunispääntie 5, 00970 Helsinki, http://resalat.fi). With approximately 750 members, *Resalat Islamilainen Yhdyskunta* is the largest Shi'i organisation in Finland. It maintains a community centre in Northern Helsinki, and actively participates in public discussions on Islam.[55]

---

51 https://www.facebook.com/MuslimiNuoretSuomessa, accessed 15 January 2018.
52 The Religions in Finland Project, "Helsinki Islam Keskus", http://www.uskonnot.fi/yhteisot/view.php?orgId=132, accessed 29 January 2018.
53 The Religions in Finland Project, "Islamic Multicultural Da'wah Center", http://www.uskonnot.fi/yhteisot/view.php?orgId=746, accessed 29 January 2018.
54 The Religions in Finland Project, "Pohjois-Suomen Islamilainen Yhdyskunta", http://www.uskonnot.fi/yhteisot/view.php?orgId=450, accessed 29 January 2018.
55 The Religions in Finland Project, "Resalat Islamilainen Yhdyskunta", http://www.uskonnot.fi/yhteisot/view.php?orgId=133, accessed 29 January 2018.

- Islamic Council of Finland (*Suomen Islamilainen Neuvosto ry*–SINE, Kastelholmantie 3, 00900 Helsinki, tel.: ++35 8465964103, http://sine.fi/). *Suomen Islamilainen Neuvosto ry* (SINE) is an umbrella organisation that brings together ca. 20 Finnish Muslim groups. Besides providing a discussion forum for its member organisations, SINE is an important discussion partner for the Finnish state, as well as other non-Muslim actors.[56] Since 2013, SINE has been in serious financial difficulties that have forced it to restrict its activities and move its offices.[57]
- Finnish Islamic Society (*Suomen Islamilainen Yhdyskunta*, Lönnrotinkatu 22 A 5, 00120 Helsinki, tel.: ++35 8465964103, http://www.rabita.fi/). With over 1,600 members, *Suomen Islamilainen Yhdyskunta* is the second largest Muslim organisation in Finland. It runs its own mosque in central Helsinki and an Islamic day care centre in the Eastern suburb of Herttoniemi. *Suomen Islamilainen Yhdyskunta* is a member organisation of the Federation of Islamic Organisations in Europe (FIOE), and is also linked to the Muslim World League.[58]
- Helsinki Muslims (*Helsingin Muslimit*, Viljatie 4 C 20, 00700 Helsinki, tel.: ++35 8458825681, http://helsinginmuslimit.fi/). Although being relatively small with regard to membership figures, *Helsingin Muslimit* has been markedly visible in the public sphere and media. The group has actively engaged in missionary work, and also became involved in several public controversies.[59] Anthropologist Marko Juntunen has characterised the group as Salafi-oriented. The membership largely consists of young adults and ethnic Finnish converts to Islam.[60]
- Finnish Islamic Congregation (*Suomen Islam-Seurakunta*, Fredrikinkatu 33 A, 00120 Helsinki, tel.: ++35 89643579, http://tatar.fi). As the oldest Muslim organisation in Finland, *Suomen Islam-Seurakunta* accepts only Mishar

---

56 The Religions in Finland Project, "Suomen Islamilainen Neuvosto ry", http://www.uskonnot.fi/yhteisot/view.php?orgId=733, accessed 29 January 2018.
57 Haikala, Topias, "Suomen islamilainen neuvosto vaikeuksissa: kymmenien tuhansien valtiontuet poikki taloudellisten epäselvyyksien vuoksi" (Islamic Council of Finland in trouble: state subsidies of tens of thousands of euros stopped because of financial obscurities), *Kirkko ja kaupunki*, 6 March 2017, https://www.kirkkojakaupunki.fi/-/suomen-islamilainen-neuvosto-vaikeuksissa-kymmenien-tuhansien-valtiontuet-poikki-rahankayton-epaselvyyksien-vuoksi, accessed 8 January 2018.
58 The Religions in Finland Project, "Suomen Islamilainen Yhdyskunta", http://www.uskonnot.fi/yhteisot/view.php?orgId=442, accessed 29 January 2018.
59 See Pauha, "Finland", p. 246.
60 Juntunen, Marko, "Islamin monimuotoisuus on lisääntynyt Länsi-Euroopassa" (The diversity of Islam has increased in Western Europe), *Helsingin Sanomat*, 16 May 2014, https://www.hs.fi/paakirjoitukset/art-2000002731544.html, accessed 17 January 2018.

Tatars as members. The organisation has prayer rooms in four towns in Southern Finland: Helsinki, Järvenpää, Kotka, and Turku. The organisation's size has been in decline, and is now down to approximately 500 members.[61]
- Tampere Islam Society (*Tampereen Islamin Yhdyskunta*, Yliopistonkatu 60 A, 33100 Tampere, tel.: ++35 8503235594, http://www.islamtampere.com/). With over 1,400 members, *Tampereen Islamin Yhdyskunta* is one of the largest Muslim organisations in Finland, and the largest outside Helsinki. It maintains a prayer room in central Tampere.[62]
- Islamic Society of Turku (*Turun Islamilainen Yhdyskunta*, Yliopistonkatu 7, 20100 Turku, http://www.tisy.fi/). With its approximately 650 members, *Turun Islamilainen Yhdyskunta* is the largest Muslim organisation in Southwest Finland. It maintains a mosque in central Turku.[63]

---

61   The Religions in Finland Project, "Suomen Islam-seurakunta", http://www.uskonnot.fi/yhteisot/view.php?orgId=85, accessed 29 January 2018.
62   *Haastettu kirkko*, p. 30; The Religions in Finland Project, "Tampereen Islamin Yhdyskunta", http://www.uskonnot.fi/yhteisot/view.php?orgId=131, accessed 29 January 2018.
63   The Religions in Finland Project, "Turun Islamilainen Yhdyskunta", http://www.uskonnot.fi/yhteisot/view.php?orgId=1058, accessed 29 January 2018.

France

Anne-Laure Zwilling[1]

Introduction

2017 was a year of presidential elections in France. Matters concerning religion took only a limited place in the political debate. As usual, secularism (*laïcité*) remained the main topic of these discreet public debates in France, often to implicitly target French Muslims. Nevertheless, although many issues in 2017 were quite similar to those in previous years, it seems that in general the situation for Muslims in France is not worsening. As an illustration, one can mention that for the second year in a row, the number of registered acts of aggression against Muslims decreased in France: from 185 in 2016 to 121 in 2017 (-34.5%). Threats against Muslims also decreased (-58.5%): from 118 in 2016 to 49 in 2017.[2] For the Government, the setting up of the *Délégation interministérielle à la lutte contre le racisme, l'antisémitisme et la haine anti-*LGBT (Interministerial Delegation to Combat Racism, Antisemitism and Anti-LGBT Hate–DILCRAH) in 2012 is one of the reasons for this decrease.

Public Debates

A disturbing statement was issued by the ombudsperson responsible for the protection of civil liberties (*Contrôleur général des lieux de privation de liberté*), Adeline Hazan, on the matter of respecting fundamental rights in France.[3] Among the different issues raised (overpopulation, non-compliance with rights), the matter of dealing with detainees suspected of religious

---

[1] Anne-Laure Zwilling is a research fellow at the joint research unit *Droit, religion, entreprise, société* of the University of Strasbourg and the French National Scientific Research Centre (CNRS). She holds a MA degree in Philosophy, a MA in Religious Studies, a PhD and a *Habilitation à diriger les recherches* in Religious Studies. She is the director of several research projects, among them the *Eurel* project (www.eurel.info). Her fields of interest are religious diversity, and religious minorities in France and Europe.

[2] *Bilan 2017 des actes racistes, antisémites, antimusulmans et antichrétiens recensés par le Service central du renseignement territorial (SCRT) de la Direction centrale de la sécurité publique (DCSP)*, https://www.interieur.gouv.fr/Le-ministre/Communiques/Bilan-2017-des-actes-racistes-antisemites-antimusulmans-et-antichretiens, accessed 25 February 2018.

[3] Contrôleur général des lieux de privation de liberté, *Rapport d'activité 2016*, http://www.cglpl.fr/2017/publication-du-rapport-dactivite-2016/, accessed 25 February 2018.

radicalisation was raised in the light of the respect of human rights; this mainly concerns Muslims.

The question of religious slaughter was also one of the debates of 2017. Religious prescriptions of Jews and Muslims often lead them to forbid the stunning of animals prior to slaughtering, which has been grounds for a heated debate. The legal text for the slaughtering of animals, *Article R. 214-70* of the *Rural Code* on animal slaughter, currently stipulates "… that stunning is compulsory, unless it is not compatible with the practices of ritual slaughter".[4] At the beginning of the year, the association whose job it is to raise awareness of, provide information on, and defend Muslim consumers (*Association de sensibilisation, d'information et de défense de consommateurs musulmans*) tried to obtain from the Council of State an abrogation of any requirements for prior stunning for any kind of slaughter, whether ritual or not. Their request was rejected.[5] Later in the year, an official report was issued on the conditions of the killing of animals for slaughter in French slaughterhouses; this report also deals with ritual slaughter.[6] After referring back to the legal framework granting exemption to the rules of slaughter for religious reasons, it proposes to amend the current Law, namely article *R. 214-74* of the *Rural Code*. The new Law would impose reversible stunning and post-jugulation stunning of sheep and cattle, even in the case of ritual slaughter. This recommendation has not yet encouraged a proposal for a new law or for a modification of the existing Law.

According to an IPSOS survey,[7] a majority of the French (60%) think that living alongside different religions is not working well in France. Only 39% of French people believe that "… the way in which the Muslim religion is practised today in France is compatible with the values of French society" (compared to 47% in 2014; see also the figure of 83% for the Jewish religion and 94% for the Catholic religion). As a result, many people approve the proposals limiting Islam to the private sphere: 79% are in favour of banning the head scarf in universities, and 77% are in favour of banning the burkini in the public

---

4 *Code rural et de la pêche maritime* (articles R. 214-70 to 214-75), www.legifrance.gouv.fr/affich Code.do?idSectionTA=LEGISCTA000006193366&cidTexte=LEGITEXT000006071367&dateTe xte=20160325, accessed 25 February 2018.
5 *Conseil d'État N° 391499, 13 March 2017*, https://www.legifrance.gouv.fr/affichJuriAdmin.do?o ldAction=rechJuriAdmin&idTexte=CETATEXT000034267058&fastReqId=1750887432&fastP os=3, accessed 25 February 2018.
6 Caullet, Jean-Yves, *Rapport n° 4038 fait au nom de la Commission d'enquête sur les conditions d'abattage des animaux de boucherie dans les abattoirs français*, September 2016, http://www .assemblee-nationale.fr/14/pdf/rap-enq/r4038-ti.pdf, accessed 25 February 2018.
7 "La place de la religion et de la laïcité dans l'élection présidentielle", *Ipsos / Sopra Steria*, 22 March 2017, http://www.ipsos.fr/decrypter-societe/2017-03-22-presidentielle-2017-place-religion-et-laicite-dans-l-election-presidentielle, accessed 25 February 2018.

sphere. In addition, 60% of the French are opposed to the public funding of mosques. However, according to a report by the Bertelsmann Foundation, the percentage of non-Muslim respondents who would not want to have Muslim neighbours is lowest in France compared to the rest of Europe, at 14%. In the United Kingdom it is 21%, Germany 19%, and Switzerland 17%.[8]

In September 2017, the results of a wide-ranging survey of Muslims living in Europe were made public by the European Agency for Fundamental Rights.[9] According to this survey, France holds the equal largest number of Muslims, with around 4.7 million in the country. Together with Germany, which has the same number, this makes up for 46% of all Muslims in the EU. Muslim respondents from North Africa feel discriminated against in France (31%).[10] The level of attachment to the country of residence, on a scale of 1 to 5, is highest among Muslims surveyed in Finland (4.6), Sweden (4.4), the United Kingdom (4.3), and France (4.3). It is somewhat higher among Muslim respondents who hold citizenship of the survey country. However, in France, the children of Muslim immigrants feel slightly less strongly attached than first-generation immigrants.[11] First-generation immigrants also show higher levels of trust in the legal system, and their children a slightly lower level of trust than the general population. The opinion difference between first- and second-generation Muslims is largest in France. These patterns are even more pronounced when it comes to trust in the police.[12]

A conference on Islamophobia had to be cancelled in October 2017 at the University of Lyon, under pressure from local associations.[13] The conference organisers had invited not only academics, but also members of associations such as the *Collectif contre l'islamophobie en France* (Collective against

---

8   Bertelsmann Foundation, *Intégration islam en Europe*, https://www.bertelsmann-stif tung.de/fileadmin/files/BSt/Publikationen/GrauePublikationen/Study_LW_Religion-Monitor-2017_Muslims-in-Europe_Results-and-Country-Profiles.pdf, accessed 25 February 2018.
9   *Second European Union Minorities and Discrimination Survey (EU-MIDIS II) Muslims–Main results*, 21 September 2017, http://fra.europa.eu/en/publication/2017/eumidis-ii-main-results, accessed 25 February 2018; Gauquelin, Blaise, "Les musulmans sont bien intégrés en Europe", *Le Monde*, 21 September 2017, http://www.lemonde.fr/interna tional/article/2017/09/21/les-musulmans-sont-bien-integres-en-europe_5188855_3210 .html#fQ85lb3cwORO8AcR.99, accessed 25 February 2018.
10 *EU-MIDIS II Muslims–Main results*, p. 31.
11 *EU-MIDIS II Muslims–Main results*, p. 20.
12 *EU-MIDIS II Muslims–Main results*, p. 23.
13 Tosseri, Bénévent, "Un colloque sur l'islamophobie annulé sous la pression d'associations", *La Croix*, 4 October 2017, https://www.la-croix.com/Religion/Laicite/colloque-lislam-ophobie-annule-pression-dassociations-anti-racistes-2017-10-04-1200881931, accessed 25 February 2018.

Islamophobia in France–CCIF), and the association *Participation et spiritualité musulmane* (Muslim Participation and Spirituality–PSM). Opponents of the event claimed that it was organised to allow political Islam to gain a foothold on the university campus.

Transnational Links

At the end of 2017, a complaint was filed against the Swiss theologian Tariq Ramadan for rape and sexual assault. Tariq Ramadan is the grandson of the founder of the Muslim Brotherhood in Egypt, Hasan al-Banna. He is Professor of Contemporary Islamic Studies at Oxford University (UK). The plaintiff, Henda Ayari, was a Salafi who became a feminist and secular activist.[14] Two other women later also pressed charges. The news of these charges against Tariq Ramadan triggered a surge of violent and sometimes anti-Semitic reactions from his supporters, particularly against his alleged victims.[15]

Law and Domestic Politics

In France, for historical reasons, a distinct legal system applies to the region of Alsace-Moselle.[16] The legal differences are especially apparent in the field of religion; in particular, blasphemy was prohibited within its distinct legislation. In January 2015, representatives of the Catholic, Protestant, Jewish, and Islamic denominations in Alsace-Moselle proposed to abrogate this prohibition and align the region, on the question of blasphemy, with *Article 32* of the *Law*

---

14 "Plainte déposée à Rouen contre Tariq Ramadan pour viol", *Paris-Normandie*, 20 October 2017, http://www.paris-normandie.fr/actualites/faits-divers/plainte-deposee-a-rouen-contre-tariq-ramadan-pour-viol-NC11209051, accessed 25 February 2018.

15 Lefebvre, Barbara, "L'affaire Ramadan, révélatrice du 'nouvel' antisémitisme", *Le Figaro*, 31 October 2017, http://www.lefigaro.fr/vox/societe/2017/10/31/31003-20171031ARTFIG00217-l-affaire-ramadan-revelatrice-du-nouvel-antisemitisme.php; Chambraud, Cécile, "Plainte contre Tariq Ramadan: l'antisémitisme se déchaîne envers Henda Ayari", *Le Monde*, 28 October 2017, http://www.lemonde.fr/societe/article/2017/10/28/plainte-contre-tariq-ramadan-l-antisemitisme-se-dechaine-envers-henda-ayari_5207247_3224.html, both accessed 25 February 2018.

16 See Curtit, Françoise, "Organising the faiths: local systems", *Eurel-France*, July 2017, http://www.eurel.info/spip.php?rubrique345, accessed 25 February 2018.

of 1905.[17] The corresponding Amendment (no. 833) was adopted in June 2016, and the Law was promulgated in January 2017.[18]

The *Fondation de l'islam de France* (Foundation of Islam of France[19]) elected its council, which counts eleven women among its 30 members.[20] Created in 2016, the Foundation was set up to help promote secularism, support interreligious and intercultural dialogue with Islam, train imams according to Republican values, and enhance the teaching of Islam at universities. Jean-Pierre Chevènement, its president, affirms that training imams is the best defence against Salafism.[21]

The *Terra Nova* think tank published a report in February entitled *The Emancipation of Islam in France*. While the document proposed a decentralised organisation of Islam in France, the ensuing public debate was limited to the proposal to introduce a Jewish and a Muslim holiday in place of the Easter and Pentecost Mondays. The authors of this study argue that the way public authorities have been trying, since the late 1990s, to organise the representation of Islam on French territory, has never fully grasped the reality of Islam in France, the different denominations that exist and the different nationalities that make it up. Public authorities have been proposing a very centralised institutional framework that is unsuitable. *Terra Nova* advocates an organisational structure that is less centralised and better adapted to the local needs of Muslim communities.[22]

---

17 *Loi de séparation des Eglises et de l'Etat* (*Law of Separation of the Churches and the State*), 1905, https://fr.wikisource.org/wiki/Loi_du_9_d%C3%A9cembre_1905_concernant_la_s%C3%A9paration_des_%C3%89glises_et_de_l%E2%80%99%C3%89tat, accessed 25 February 2018.

18 *Loi n° 2017-86 du 27 janvier 2017 relative à l'égalité et à la citoyenneté* (*Law of 27 January 2017 on Equality and Citizenship*), https://www.legifrance.gouv.fr/affichTexte.do;jsessionid=97D4CBA088FDFB8A0663313C310E35F1.tpdila11v_2?cidTexte=JORFTEXT000033934948&categorieLien=id, accessed 25 February 2018.

19 http://fondationdelislamdefrance.fr/, accessed 25 February 2018.

20 Hoffner, Anne-Bénédicte, "La fondation de l'islam de France s'ouvre aux femmes", *La Croix*, 16 March 2017, http://www.la-croix.com/Religion/Islam/La-Fondation-lislam-France-souvre-femmes-2017-03-16-1200832426, accessed 25 February 2018.

21 Sauvaget, Bernadette, "Jean-Pierre Chevènement: il faut mener une lutte culturelle contre le salafisme", *Libération*, 2 February 2017, http://www.liberation.fr/france/2017/02/02/jean-pierre-chevenement-il-faut-mener-une-lutte-culturelle-contre-le-salafisme_1545861, accessed 25 February 2018.

22 Christnacht, Alain, and Marc-Olivier Padis, "L'émancipation de l'islam de France", *Terra Nova*, February 2017, http://tnova.fr/etudes/l-emancipation-de-l-islam-de-france, accessed 25 February 2018.

A circular on the application of the principles of secularism to civil servants was issued on 15 March 2017.[23] This circular draws upon the conclusions of the 2016 Zucarelli report on secularism and public service.[24] It essentially argues for the necessity of training civil servants to a better understanding of secularism.

The UN Human Rights Committee expressed its views under Article 5, Paragraph 4, of the Optional Protocol to the International Covenant on Civil and Political Rights (108th session). The committee concluded that the regulation of the State Party (France) requiring persons to appear bareheaded in their passport photographs is a disproportionate limitation that infringes on freedom of religion and constitutes a violation of Article 18 of the Covenant.[25]

Several Islamic institutions were closed due to decisions made by the public authorities in 2017. In September 2017, the deputies at the French National Assembly adopted an amendment which widens the grounds for administrative closure of a place of worship.[26] This closure could henceforth be justified by the "ideas and theories" that are disseminated therein for the purpose of supporting terrorism, and not merely by evidence explicitly provided through written or spoken words. 16 mosques have already been closed since the 2015 terrorist attacks in Paris and Marseille. Only one political party, *La France insoumise* (left-wing), judged this article "against the basic freedom of religion". Under the State of Emergency Act, the Department Prefect has the power to close places of any kind in which statements are made that constitute a provocation to hatred or violence or a provocation to commit acts of terrorism or call for such acts. Since September 2017, several mosques have been closed on such grounds. In the Bouches-du-Rhône department, the Dar-es-Salam mosque was under surveillance by the Ministry of the Interior because of its imam, Charef

---

23 *Circulaire du 15 mars 2017 relative au respect du principe de laïcité dans la fonction publique* (*Circular of 15 March 2017 on Respecting the Principle of Secularism in Public Services*), http://circulaires.legifrance.gouv.fr/pdf/2017/03/cir_41960.pdf, accessed 25 February 2018.
24 Zucarelli, Emile, *Rapport de la commission "Laïcité et fonction publique"*, December 2016, http://www.fonction-publique.gouv.fr/files/files/publications/rapports-missionnes/Rapport-Laicite-et-Fonction-publique.pdf, accessed 25 February 2018.
25 Jacquin, Jean-Baptiste, "Europe: les entreprises peuvent interdire le voile sous conditions", *Le Monde*, 14 March 2017, http://www.lemonde.fr/emploi/article/2017/03/14/la-justice-europeenne-se-penche-sur-le-port-du-voile-islamique-au-travail_5093936_1698637.html, accessed 25 February 2018.
26 "Antiterrorisme: les députés étendent les motifs de fermeture administrative de lieux de culte", *Le Monde*, 13 September 2017, http://www.lemonde.fr/societe/article/2017/09/13/antiterrorisme-les-deputes-etendent-les-motifs-de-fermeture-administrative-de-lieux-de-culte_5185192_3224.html#W1bdIb7EuEumRR39.99, accessed 25 February 2018.

M'Rabet. It was closed in February.[27] In March, the Prefect of Hérault closed the Es-Sunna mosque in Sète until further notice, after leaflets containing hate messages had been found during a police raid.[28] The Ministry of the Interior allowed the reopening of the mosque of Stains which had been closed in 2016 for threatening public order.[29]

An Islamic school was legally closed in Toulouse in 2016. However, the director continued to run the school and admitted pupils, leading to another forced closure in March 2017.[30] Finally, the Administrative Court of Toulon judged that the building permit of the mosque of Fréjus, issued in April 2011 to the El Fath association, expired when the construction began, which renders an amending permit issued in 2013 illegal. Despite this verdict, the Court of Appeal of Aix-en-Provence did not order the demolition of this religious building.[31]

A report on the training of imams[32] underlines the importance of the courses offered at universities to help prevent religious radicalisation.[33] The 2016–17 report of the Observatory on Secularism (*Observatoire de la laïcité*)[34] lists that

27 Leroux, Luc, "Une mosquée fermée pour 'menace contre la sécurité' à Aix-en-Provence", *Le Monde*, 2 February 2017, http://www.lemonde.fr/societe/article/2017/02/02/une-mosquee-fermee-pour-menace-contre-la-securite-a-aix-en-provence_5073435_3224.html, accessed 25 February 2018.

28 "Le prefet de l'Hérault ferme une mosquée après une perquisition", *Le Monde*, 6 April 2017, http://www.lemonde.fr/societe/article/2017/04/06/le-prefet-de-l-herault-ferme-une-mosquee-apres-une-perquisition_5106615_3224.html, accessed 25 February 2018.

29 Vincent, Elise, "Le ministère de l'intérieur autorise la réouverture de la mosquée de Stains", *Le Monde*, 11 May 2017, http://www.lemonde.fr/societe/article/2017/05/11/le-ministere-de-l-interieur-autorise-la-reouverture-de-la-mosquee-de-stains_5125784_3224.html, accessed 25 February 2018.

30 Battaglia, Mattea, and Philippe Gagnebet, "A Toulouse, l'école Al-Badr refuse de fermer", *Le Monde*, 4 February 2017.

31 "La mosquée de Fréjust échappe de nouveau à la démolition", *Le Monde*, 21 March 2017, http://www.lemonde.fr/societe/article/2017/03/21/la-mosquee-de-frejus-echappe-de-nouveau-a-la-demolition_5098409_3224.html, accessed 25 February 2018.

32 Mayeur-Jaouen, Catherine, Mathilde Philip-Gay and Rachid Benzine, *Mission de réflexion sur la formation des imams et des cadres religieux musulmans*, http://www.letudiant.fr/static/uploads/mediatheque/EDU_EDU/6/3/1455063-rapport-sur-la-formation-des-imams-4-original.pdf, accessed 25 February 2018.

33 "La piste des universités pour mieux former les imams", *Le Monde*, 17 March 2017, http://www.lemonde.fr/campus/article/2017/03/17/la-piste-des-universites-pour-mieux-former-les-imams_5096389_4401467.html#rR54QdHMTDPP7VMg.99. See also https://mobile.interieur.gouv.fr/Archives/Archives-des-communiques-de-presse/2017-Communiques/Formation-des-imams-et-des-cadres-religieux-musulmans, both accessed 25 February 2018.

34 Observatoire de la laïcité, *Rapport annuel 2016–2017*, http://www.gouvernement.fr/rapport-annuel-de-l-observatoire-de-la-laicite-2016-2017, accessed 25 February 2018.

several training programmes supported by the State exist at French universities: 14 existed in 2017, and five more will start soon. These university training courses are largely funded by the Ministry of the Interior and are organised around three main themes: the social sciences of religions; secularism and republican institutions; law of religions; and the organisation of religion.

Religious matters were not important issues in the presidential election campaign, although, according to a survey, 77% of the French think that it took up too much space in the election campaign.[35] A survey of votes, after the legislative elections of June 2017, provided information on the distribution of votes according to religious adherence.[36] Catholics and Jews in France mostly voted for parties on the right, and Muslims mostly for those on the left. In the first round of the presidential election, Jean-Luc Mélenchon (extreme-left) came out on top amongst the Muslim electorate and scored twice his national score. Several specifically Muslim political parties have put forward candidates for the legislative election; for example, the Equality and Justice Party, that claims to originate from the Turkish AKP, presented 52 candidates.[37] This party, as well as others supported by Muslims associations, obtained marginal votes.

In June 2017, the newly elected President of France Emmanuel Macron met representatives of Islam from the *Conseil français du culte musulman* (French Council of the Muslim Faith–CFCM). He called on Muslims to fight against "fanaticism".[38] He also claimed that he wanted Islam to be "compatible with the Republic".[39] At the end of the year, when presenting his good wishes to the religious authorities, Emmanuel Macron affirmed that he would speak "dispassionately" of secularism, and that a "structuring of Islam in France" was necessary. The main challenge will be to set up a representative and legitimate body: the CFCM, created in 2003 by Nicolas Sarkozy, seems to have failed in this

---

35 "La place de la religion et de la laïcité dans l'élection présidentielle", *Ipsos / Sopra Steria*, 22 March 2017, http://www.ipsos.fr/decrypter-societe/2017-03-22-presidentielle-2017-place-religion-et-laicite-dans-l-election-presidentielle, accessed 25 February 2018.

36 "Un vote confessionnel lors des législatives ?", *IFOP focus*, no. 163, June 2017, http://www.ifop.fr/?option=com_publication&type=publication&id=984, accessed 25 February 2018.

37 Fourquet, Jérôme, and Sylvain Manternach, "Législatives: y a-t-il eu des votes catholique, juif et musulman?", *Le Figaro*, 27 June 2017, http://www.lefigaro.fr/elections/legislatives/2017/06/27/38001-20170627ARTFIG00234-legislatives-y-a-t-il-eu-des-votes-catholique-juif-et-musulman.php, accessed 25 February 2018.

38 Chambraud, Cécile, "Macron appelle les musulmans au 'combat' contre le 'fanatisme'", *Le Monde*, 21 June 2017.

39 Guénois, Jean-Marie, "Macron veut un islam compatible avec la République", *Le Figaro*, 21 June 2017, http://www.lefigaro.fr/actualite-france/2017/06/21/01016-20170621ARTFIG00001-macron-veut-un-islam-compatible-avec-la-republique.php, accessed 25 February 2018.

mission. However, setting up a new body must be done while not offending the spirit of secularism.[40]

An expert committee looking at questions of secularism at school (*Conseil des sages sur la laïcité à l'école*) was established in 2017. The Committee has 13 members. This new body was set up by the Minister of Education, Jean-Michel Blanquer, to "clarify the position of the school institution with regard to secularism and religion". The Minister's intention is to bring together supporters of both "open" and "closed" secularism, two distinct ways of understanding *laïcité*; the former takes into account the existence of religious groups, the latter relegates religion to the private sphere.[41] The president of this Council is the sociologist Dominique Schnapper, and the group is comprised of academics from different disciplines.

The mayor of Chalon-sur-Saône, Gilles Platret, banned meals without pork from school canteens in 2015. The administrative court of Dijon cancelled this decision in the name of the "superior interest of the children", arguing that there is no proof, contrary to what the mayor claimed, that providing such meals would force the children to group together according to their religious background.[42]

An industrial norm has been set up for halal food in France in 2017, as part of a trial.[43] It was welcomed by the industry sector who had long been asking for such a norm. The industrial norm mainly lists "haram" products which should not be included in halal food. The CFCM has criticised this norm, recalling that they withdrew from the working group in 2015.[44] The CFCM claims

---

[40] "Emmanuel macron juge indispensable une structuration de l'islam en France", *Le Monde*, 4 January 2018, http://www.lemonde.fr/emmanuel-macron/article/2018/01/04/emmanuel-macron-juge-indispensable-une-structuration-de-l-islam-en-france_5237661_5008430.html, accessed 25 February 2018.

[41] Chambraud, Cécile, and Mattea Battaglia, "Laïcité à l'école: pas encore nommé, le Conseil des sages fait déjà débat", *Le Monde*, 8 January 2018, http://www.lemonde.fr/education/article/2018/01/08/laicite-a-l-ecole-pas-encore-nomme-le-conseil-des-sages-fait-deja-debat_5238735_1473685.html, accessed 25 February 2018.

[42] Moullot, Pauline, "Repas sans porc dans les cantines: l'argument fallacieux du maire de Chalon-sur-Saône", *Libération*, 31 August 2017, http://www.liberation.fr/desintox/2017/08/31/repas-sans-porc-dans-les-cantines-l-argument-fallacieux-du-maire-de-chalon-sur-saone_1593301, accessed 25 February 2018.

[43] "Création de la première norme française pour les aliments halal", *Le Monde*, 15 September 2017, http://www.lemonde.fr/religions/article/2017/09/15/creation-de-la-premiere-norme-francaise-pour-les-aliments-halal_5185949_1653130.html, accessed 25 February 2018.

[44] "La nouvelle norme pour le halal critiquée par les autorités religieuses", *Le Monde*, 18 September 2017, http://www.lemonde.fr/religions/article/2017/09/18/la-nouvelle-norme-pour-le-halal-critiquee-par-les-instances-representatives-du-culte-musulman_5187373_1653130.html, accessed 25 February 2018.

that defining halal is the sole responsibility of religious authorities, and not the task of the French Association for Industry Standards and Norms (*Association française de normalisation*–AFNOR).

For several years now in France, street prayers have regularly taken place in protest against the inadequacy of existing premises used as Muslim places of worship. In November 2017, in Clichy-la-Garenne (a Parisian suburb), the Member of Parliament, municipal, departmental, and regional councillors from several right-wing parties, marched behind a banner proclaiming "Stop illegal street prayers". 200 local Muslims had been protesting against the closure of their place of worship in the city centre in March, accusing the mayor of not offering them "suitable land with an option to buy" so that they could build a new one.[45] The *Association des associations musulmanes de Clichy* (Association of Muslim Associations in Clichy) finally cancelled the protest, which was to take place in front of the town hall.[46]

Several legal decisions in 2017 concerned the wearing of religious attire at the work place. On 22 November, the Court of Cassation granted a company the right to prohibit the wearing of religious signs by an employee providing frontline services, if its internal regulations provided for it.[47] In December 2017, the case of a medical intern was rejected by the Versailles Administrative Court of Appeal. The plaintiff had been dismissed in February 2014 due to the wearing of a beard deemed religiously ostentatious. The Court held that the wearing of the beard "cannot by itself constitute a sign of religious affiliation", but that the context justified the decision.[48]

The Randstad Group issued their annual report on religion at the workplace in October 2017,[49] observing that the number of issues in relation to religion

---

45   Jocard, Alain, "Une centaine d'élus tentent d'empêcher une prière de rue", *La République des Pyréenées*, 10 November 2017, http://www.larepubliquedespyrenees.fr/2017/11/10/clichy-une-centaine-d-elus-tentent-d-empecher-une-priere-de-rue,2216836.php, accessed 25 February 2018.

46   "Clichy: négociations en cours à propos des 'prières de rue'", *Cnews* n° 2162, 24 November 2017, p. 12.

47   "Une entreprise peut interdire le port de signes religieux selon la Cour de cassation", *La Croix*, 23 November 2017, https://www.la-croix.com/Religion/Laicite/entreprise-peut-interdire-port-signes-religieux-selon-Cour-cassation-2017-11-23-1200894252, accessed 25 February 2018.

48   "Laïcité: un médecin, écarté d'un hôpital en raison de sa barbe, débouté en justice", *Le Monde*, 30 December 2017, http://www.lemonde.fr/societe/article/2017/12/30/laicite-un-medecin-ecarte-d-un-hopital-en-raison-de-sa-barbe-deboute-en-justice_5235928_3224.html, accessed 25 February 2018.

49   Groupe Randstad, *L'entreprise, le travail et la religion*, October 2017, http://grouperandstad.fr/desormais-banalise-le-fait-religieux-cesse-en-2017-de-progresser-dans-les-entreprises-2/, accessed 25 February 2018.

has remained stable. The main difficulties arising because of religion at the workplace are the wearing of obvious religious symbols (22%), the requesting of leave for religious holidays (18%), and prayer during breaks (10%). Only 28% of interviewees (both employers and employees) think that companies should adapt to religious demands (compared to 40% in 2016).[50]

Activities and Initiatives of Main Muslim Organisations

In 2016, Tariq Ramadan opened the Islamic Institute for Ethics Training (*Institut islamique de formation à l'ethique*–IIFE).[51] Aiming both at theoretical and practical education, the institute claims to be "transdisciplinary". It offers courses in Islamic law and jurisprudence, philosophy, and theology, and one-day monthly seminars, or on-line courses.

The *Union des organisations islamiques de France* (Union of Islamic Organisations of France–UIOF) decided in February to change its name.[52] By removing the word "*islamique*", which in French evokes radical Islam, the organisation intended to dissociate itself from the Muslim Brotherhood, from which it originated in 1983. *Musulmans de France* (Muslims of France) is the new name of the organisation.[53] Although one of its members, Tareq Obrou, affirmed that "the new name does not claim to represent all French Muslims", leaders of other Islamic organisations expressed their irritation over the name change. Abdallah Zekri, the general secretary of the French Council of the Muslim Faith (CFCM), the representative body of Islam to public authorities, declared that the "… UOIF does not have the monopoly of Muslims of France".[54] Lydia Guirous, from *Les républicains* (centre-right political party), and Marine

---

50   Maillard, Denis, *Quand la religion s'invite dans l'entreprise* (Paris: Fayard, 2017).
51   https://iife.tariqramadan.com/, accessed 25 February 2018.
52   The website of the association still contains its old name, www.uoif-online.com/, accessed 25 February 2018.
53   Besmond de Senneville, Loup, "L'UOIF devient musulmans de France", *La Croix*, 28 February 2017, http://www.la-croix.com/Religion/Islam/LUOIF-devient-Musulmans-France-2017-02-28-1200828273; "Changement de nom pour l'UOIF, désormais appelée 'Musulmans de France'", *BFMTV*, 15 April 2017, http://www.bfmtv.com/societe/changement-de-nom-pour-l-uoif-desormais-appelee-musulmans-de-france-1143540.html; "L'UOIF s'appelle désormais 'Musulmans de France'", *Yabiladi*, 16 April 2017, https://www.yabiladi.com/articles/details/52877/l-uoif-s-appelle-desormais-musulmans-france.html, all accessed 25 February 2018.
54   http://www.20minutes.fr/france/2050683-20170415-uoifchange-nom-appelle-desormais-musulmans-france, accessed 25 February 2018.

Le Pen, from the *Front national* (extreme-right political party), called for the dissolution of the organisation,[55] claiming that it conveys political Islam in France.

The annual meeting of French Muslims, *Rassemblement annuel des musulmans de France*[56], which has been organised annually in April by the UOIF for over 35 years, remains the most important gathering of Muslims in the country, with some 50,000 attendants. However, it seems that the number of people attending is diminishing, and regional gatherings are becoming more important.

Multiple crises have regularly shaken the French Council of the Muslim Faith (CFCM), the representative body of Islam in France. In April, the CFCM published a charter for imams. Five federations–among them *La grande mosquée de Paris* (The Grand Mosque of Paris) and the UOIF–accused the president of the CFCM, Anouar Kbibech, the day after the publication, of having produced working papers prematurely, while they were still in preparation.[57] In 2017, for the first time since its creation in 2003, the CFCM elected as president a representative of Turkish Islam in France; previous presidents had been exclusively North Africans.[58] Ahmet Ogras, former vice-president of the CFCM, is 46 years old; he is better known in France as a promoter of Franco-Turkish relations than for his religious commitment. He has been criticised for his lack of theological training. He was also co-founder of the Union of European Turkish Democrats, a youth movement sponsored by President Erdoğan.

Several controversies erupted around the celebration of Islamic holidays. In September 2017, disagreements emerged on determining a common date for 'Id al-Adha among different Muslim organisations. Brigitte Bardot, a famous actress and someone engaged in the protection of animals, denounced the "barbarian traditions" associated with the festival in a letter posted on Twitter. The extensive consumption of livestock in such a short time leads to sanitary, logistical and financial problems. Mobile slaughterhouses are not always sufficient, while Muslim organisations are required to use only legally approved

---

55 Guirous, Lydia, "Tribune", *Valeurs Actuelles*, 15 April 2017, https://www.valeursactuelles.com/societe/tribune-uoif-ou-musulmans-de-france-la-reponse-est-la-meme-dissolution-80480, accessed 25 February 2018.

56 https://www.ramf-uoif.fr/, accessed 25 February 2018.

57 Guénois, Jean-Marie, "La 'Charte de l'imam' provoque une crise au sein de l'islam de France", *Le Figaro*, 30 March 2017, http://www.lefigaro.fr/actualite-france/2017/03/30/01016-20170330ARTFIG00242-la-charte-de-l-imam-provoque-une-crise-au-sein-de-l-islam-de-france.php, accessed 25 February 2018.

58 "Qui est Ahmet Ogras, nouveau président du CFCM", *RFI*, 1 July 2017, http://www.rfi.fr/france/20170701-est-ahmet-ogras-nouveau-president-cfcm, accessed 25 February 2018.

slaughterhouses.[59] New difficulties arose in December, when Shi'i Muslims wanted to celebrate *mawlid*, the birth of the Prophet Muhammad. The CFCM demanded tolerance towards Muslims celebrating it, while Salafis have vigorously fought against its celebration.[60]

Muslim Population: History and Demographics

The Muslim presence in metropolitan France is mainly the result of immigration,[61] which started to be noticeable at the end of World War I, when men from Northern African countries served in the French army. These immigrants were mostly from Algeria, which was at the time a French colony, and from Tunisia and Morocco, which were then French protectorates. Immigration continued after that, with a marked increase after World War II,[62] mostly men responding to a French demand for cheap labour. In 1962, at the end of the Algerian war of independence, 160,000 Algerians who had been soldiers in the French army, found themselves in a difficult situation, and many sought refuge in France. These ex-soldiers, called *Harkis*, and their families arrived in France between 1962 and 1968; their number is generally estimated to be around 91,000. They were not very well-received, and were often badly housed in what should have been temporary, poorly equipped housing, but which turned out to be long-term structures.

In 1964, France and the Turkish government signed a labour agreement, which caused many Turks to migrate to France (18,000 in 1970, 200,000 in the early 1990s and 450,000 by 2005). A number of immigrants also came from former French colonies and other countries with a Muslim population, such as Senegal and India. In 1974, the Government passed a law allowing the families of immigrants to join them, which caused many immigrants' children and wives to move to France. Because of all these factors, the Muslim population

---

59   "Aïd el-Kébir 2017: la fête gâchée par les polémiques en France?", *L'internaute*, 1 September 2017, http://www.linternaute.com/actualite/societe/1242541-aid-el-kebir-2017-la-fete-gachee-par-les-polemiques/, accessed 25 February 2018.
60   Hoffner, Anne-Bénédicte, "Fêter le mawlid, ou comment résister à l'interdit salafiste", *La Croix*, 30 November 2017, https://www.la-croix.com/Religion/Islam/Feter-mawlid-comment-resister-linterdit-salafiste-2017-11-30-1200896038, accessed 25 February 2018.
61   Godard, Bernard, and Sylvie Taussig, *Les musulmans en France–courants, institutions, communautés: un état des lieux* (Paris: Robert Laffont, 2007).
62   Blanchard, Pascal, Éric Deroo, Driss El Yazami, Pierre Fourni and Gilles Manceron, "L'immigration: l'installation en métropole des populations du Maghreb", in Pascal Blanchard and Sandrine Lemaire (eds.), *Culture impériale 1931–1961* (Paris: Éditions Autrement, 2004), pp. 213–222.

in France is currently made up of people predominantly from North Africa (Algeria, Morocco, and Tunisia), Turkey, and Sub-Saharan Africa, and their children, and now grandchildren, born in France. There are also South Asians (Tamils, and Gujaratis, for example)[63] and migrants from the Middle East. Bosniaks and Albanians arrived after the Yugoslav wars (1991–2001), and, in recent years, an increase in migrants from Africa and the Middle East can be observed.

Because many immigrants came to France for work, the number of Muslims is high in former industrial and mining areas such as the North or Haut-Rhin, as well as along the Mediterranean coast, geographically close to North Africa. Turkish people living in France are mostly concentrated in Paris, Alsace and Lorraine,[64] and the region of Nord-Pas-de-Calais, where they live mainly in the cities of Calais, Lille, and Roubaix.[65] Very few Muslims live in rural areas. The concentration of the Muslim population is high in socially deprived areas, major urban centres, and suburbs. Many are in the region around Paris, especially Seine-Saint-Denis and Val-de-Marne.

Questions on religious affiliation are not included in the census in France, although a recent report underlined that having access to such information would be helpful.[66] The only available way to gather demographic and statistical information on the Muslim population of France is through surveys carried out by private institutions and governmental estimates.[67] A regularly updated list of surveys dealing with religious groups in France can be found at the Eurel website.[68] Since there are no official statistics in France regarding the number of Muslims, all numbers given below are estimates. On this basis, it is nearly

---

63 Moliner, Christine, "L'immigration sud-asiatique en France: discrète et exemplaire?", *Infos migrations*, 12 November 2009, www.immigration.interieur.gouv.fr/Info-ressources/Statistiques/Etudes-et-publications/Publications/Numeros-parus-en-2009/L-immigration-sud-asiatique-en-France-discrete-et-exemplaire, accessed 25 February 2018.

64 Akgönül, Samim, Murielle Maffessoli, Muharrem Koç and Stéphane De Tapia, *40 ans de présence turque en Alsace: constats et évolutions* (Strasbourg: Neotheque, 2009).

65 "Analyse: 1989–2011, enquête sur l'implantation et l'évolution de l'Islam de France", *IFOP*, July 2011, www.ifop.com/media/pressdocument/343-1-document_file.pdf, accessed 25 February 2018.

66 Goulet, Nathalie, and André Reichard, *De l'islam en France à un islam de France, établir la transparence et lever les ambiguïtés*, www.senat.fr/notice-rapport/2015/r15-757-notice.html, accessed 25 February 2018.

67 An article in the newspaper *Le Monde* summarises the available information concerning the numbers of the Muslim population, www.lemonde.fr/les-decodeurs/article/2015/01/21/que-pese-l-islam-en-france_4559859_4355770.html, accessed 25 February 2018.

68 The *Eurel* website for France is: www.eurel.info/spip.php?rubrique351, accessed 25 February 2018.

impossible to have a proper understanding of developments or trends with regards to the Muslim population.[69] The estimates of the Muslim population in France range from 2.1 million to between 4 and 5 million (estimates by the Ministry of the Interior based on country of origin).[70] More precisely, according to the extensive survey *Trajectoires et origines* (Trajectories and Origins), there are 2.4 million Muslims among the 18 to 60-year old population. For the entire population, estimates are between 3.9 and 4.2 million Muslims.[71] According to a recent survey by the European Union,[72] the largest numbers of Muslims in Europe live in France and Germany, with around 4.7 million in each country.

Muslim Population	The National Institute of Statistics (INSEE) estimates the Muslim population to be between 2.1 and 4 million, which is up to 7% of the total population (66,990,826 in January 2017).[73] Recent EU estimates suggest a figure of around 4.7 million.[74]
Ethnic/National Backgrounds	Most French Muslims come from the Maghreb area (Morocco, Algeria, and Tunisia). There are also many Turks, and people originating from sub-Saharan African countries (e.g. Senegal, Cameroon). Recently, the number of Muslims coming from Eastern Europe (Albania, Bulgaria) has increased as well. The survey by the *Institut Montaigne*,[75] conducted in 2016, provides the following numbers as percentages of the overall Muslim population:

---

69   Dargent, Claude, "La population musulmane de France: de l'ombre à la lumière?", *Revue française de sociologie*, vol. 51, no. 2 (2010), pp. 219–246.
70   On this subject, see Godard, Bernard, *La question musulmane en France* (Paris: Fayard, 2015).
71   Simon, Patrick, and Vincent Tiberj, "Sécularisation ou regain religieux: la religiosité des immigrants et de leurs descendants", *Documents de travail de l'INED*, vol. 196 (2013), https://www.ined.fr/fr/publications/document-travail/secularisation-regain-religieux/, accessed 25 February 2018.
72   *EU-MIDIS II Muslims–Main results*.
73   Numbers are from the National Institute of Statistics (INSEE), https://www.insee.fr/fr/statistiques/2381474, accessed 25 February 2018.
74   *EU-MIDIS II Muslims–Main results*.
75   Institut Montaigne, *Un islam français est possible*, p. 26, available at: http://www.institutmontaigne.org/publications/un-islam-francais-est-possible, accessed 25 February 2018.

Algerian: 31%
Moroccan: 20%
Tunisian: 8%
Other African: 15%
Turkish: 5%.

Inner-Islamic Groups	No official data is available. The majority of Muslims in France are Sunnis following the Maliki school (as practised in North Africa).[76] Other Sunnis are predominantly Hanafi from Turkey or Pakistan. There are also Alevi (about one third of the Muslims from Turkey), and some Sufi brotherhoods, mainly among Senegalese Muslims.[77]
Geographical Spread	The highest concentration of Muslims can be found in the region around Paris (Muslims are more than 10% of the population in the departments of Val d'Oise, Seine-Saint-Denis, and Val de Marne); they are also found in the region of Lyon and Bouches-du-Rhône, and in the Eastern part of France.[78]
Number of Mosques	The Ministry of the Interior counts 2,502 places of worship (2,131 for metropolitan France) in 2015; there were 1,300 in the year 2000.[79] Only 90 are purpose-built mosques; others are either places of worship inside a multi-purpose building, such as a

---

[76] It is interesting to note that young French Muslims were unable to state whether they were Sunni or Shi'i, and the corresponding question had to be withdrawn from a study on "Youth, law, school and the family". See UPYC–IPSOS, *Les adolescents, la loi, la famille et l'école, enquête*, February 2016, p. 91, https://drive.google.com/file/d/0B0Fh_ENuJ_tYcWd la1VmQU13SlU/view, accessed 25 February 2018.

[77] Havard, Jean-François, "Les stratégies de visibilisation des étudiants mourides en Alsace", in Anne-Laure Zwilling (ed.), *Minorités religieuses, religions minoritaires dans l'espace public: visibilité et reconnaissance* (Strasbourg: Presses Universitaires de Strasbourg, 2014), pp. 217–228.

[78] "Enquête sur l'implantation et l'évolution de l'islam de France", *IFOP Focus* n° 40, 1989–2011, http://www.ifop.fr/?option=com_publication&type=publication&id=343, accessed 25 February 2018.

[79] www.senat.fr/compte-rendu-commissions/20160125/mi_islam.html, accessed 25 February 2018.

cultural centre or a suburban house, or a repurposed building like a former factory, for example. Most of them are located around Paris (Île-de-France) or in the Southern part of France (Rhône-Alpes and Provence-Alpes-Côte-d'Azur). 70 mosques can be considered very large ("cathedral mosques"), 6% of mosques can accommodate 500 to 1,000 believers; 1,500 can accommodate 150 persons at the most. Most mosque construction projects are funded by local communities. There are many plans to build more mosques: 315 projects are pending,[80] of which 3% are major projects.[81]

Muslim Burial Sites

Given the French principle of *laïcité*, there is theoretically no legal possibility of religious burial places in public cemeteries in France.[82] According to the Ministry of the Interior, around 75% of Muslims, after their death, are repatriated to be buried in their countries of origin. The only Muslim cemetery in France is the historical *Cimetière musulman de Bobigny*, originally a private burial place, opened in 1943. However, several decrees (1975, 1991, recalled in a circular in 2008)[83] have made it possible for mayors to group Muslim burial spaces together in communal cemeteries, creating what is called a *carré musulman* (Muslim section). Their number is growing, from only around ten such spaces in communal cemeteries in France in the 1980s (mostly military burial places for soldiers

---

80   Godard, *La question musulmane*, p. 316.
81   "Compte rendu de la mission organisation, place et financement de l'islam en France", 27 January 2016, http://www.senat.fr/compte-rendu-commissions/20160704/mi_islam.html, accessed 25 February 2018; "Mosquées en France: combien en existe-t-il et qui les finance?", BFMTV, 7 April 2015, www.bfmtv.com/societe/mosquees-en-france-combien-en-existe-t-il-et-qui-les-finance-875069.html, accessed 25 February 2018.
82   *Law of 14 November 1881*, www.legirel.cnrs.fr/spip.php?article283, accessed 20 May 2015. See also Goulet and Reichard, *De l'islam en France*.
83   *Circulaire NOR/INT/A/08/00038/C du 19 février 2008 relative à la police des lieux de sépulture, aux aménagements des cimetières et aux groupements confessionnels des sépultures*, www.legirel.cnrs.fr/IMG/pdf/080219.pdf, accessed 25 February 2018.

from the World Wars), to around 200 currently.[84] In 2006, a report recommended the establishment of Muslim sections.[85] In the Alsace-Moselle region regional law allows for religious cemeteries; one Muslim cemetery opened in Strasbourg in 2012.[86]

"Chaplaincy" in State Institutions

There are 198 Muslim prison chaplains[87] among a total of 1,518 prison chaplains,[88] as of 1 August 2015 (175 receive a stipend from the State).[89] However, prison chaplains are neither civil servants nor government employees.[90]

In state hospitals, the management of chaplaincy is the responsibility of the board of directors; chaplains are paid from the hospital budget. There are around 50 Muslim hospital chaplains on a part-time salary paid by the hospitals.[91]

---

84   Benbassa, Esther, and Jean-René Lecerf, *La lutte contre les discriminations: de l'incantation à l'action, Rapport d'information no. 94 (2014–2015)*, 12 November 2014, www.senat.fr/rap/r14-094/r14-094.html, accessed 25 February 2018.

85   Sueur, Jean-Pierre, and Jean-René Lecerf, *Rapport d'information no. 372 (2005–2006), Bilan et perspectives de la législation funéraire–Sérénité des vivants et respect des défunts*, May 2006, www.senat.fr/rap/r05-372/r05-3721.pdf, accessed 25 February 2018.

86   Legrand, Thierry, and Anne-Laure Zwilling, "Lire le religieux dans le paysage des cimetières: fondements juifs, chrétiens et musulmans", in Matthieu Gaultier, Anne Dietrich and Alexis Corrochano (eds.), *Rencontre autour des paysages du cimetière médiéval et moderne: actes des 5es rencontres du groupe d'anthropologie et d'archéologie funéraire* (Tours: FERACF, 2015), pp. 255–267.

87   Galembert, Claire de, "De l'utilitarisme religieux de la république laïque en monde pénitentiaire", *Mouvements*, vol. 4, no. 88 (2016), pp. 75–84.

88   Most information concerning chaplaincy can be found in Goulet and Reichard, *De l'islam en France*.

89   Portelli, Hugues, "Projet de loi de finances pour 2016: administration pénitentiaire", *Avis n° 170 (2015–2016), déposé le 19 novembre 2015*, www.senat.fr/rap/a15-170-8/a15-170-83.html, accessed 25 February 2018.

90   *Circulaire NOR/JUSK1240021C du 20 septembre 2012 relative à l'agrément des aumôniers (On the Accreditation of Chaplains)*, www.legirel.cnrs.fr/IMG/pdf/120920.pdf, accessed 25 February 2018.

91   www.france24.com/fr/20100803-france-imam-hopital-francais-sante-paris-aumoniers-religion-islam-musulmans-malades, accessed 25 February 2018.

Muslim chaplaincy services were officially opened in 2006; the National Council of Muslim Hospital Chaplaincy (*Conseil national de l'aumônerie musulmane hospitalière*–CNAMH) was created as an association under the *Law of 1901* in 2013.

Military chaplaincy services were established in 2005;[92] since 2012 there have been Muslim chaplains in the army.[93] There are currently a total of 51 Muslim military chaplains.[94]

Halal Products

French law rules that stunning prior to slaughter is compulsory.[95] However, an exception to this principle is provided for ritual slaughter, when stunning is not compatible with religious prescriptions.[96]

The Administrative Court stated in September 2015 that it is not compulsory to offer vegetarian or alternative meals in school canteens when pork was on the menu.[97] It had also stated in 2014 that it is not compulsory to serve halal meals in prisons.

The halal industry is a quickly growing business.[98] There are several bodies of halal certification in France: AVS (*À votre service*, At Your Service),

---

92 http://aumonerie-musulmane.over-blog.com/, accessed 25 February 2018.
93 www.legifrance.gouv.fr/affichTexte.do?cidTexte=JORFTEXT000026052467, accessed 25 February 2018.
94 Merchet, Jean-Dominique, "Les armées comptent une quarantaine d'aumôniers musulmans", *L'opinion*, 16 March 2015, www.lopinion.fr/blog/secret-defense/armees-comptent-quarantaine-d-aumoniers-musulmans-22321, accessed 25 February 2018.
95 *Decree of 12 December 1997*, www.legifrance.gouv.fr/affichTexte.do?cidTexte=JORFTE XT000000204001, accessed 25 February 2018.
96 *Code rural et de la pêche maritime* (articles R. 214–70 to 214–75. See also Zwilling, Anne-Laure, and Anne Fornerod, "Ritual slaughter", *Eurel-France*, www.eurel.info/spip .php?article23, accessed 25 February 2018.
97 Zimmerlin, Catherine, "Septembre 2015: menus de substitution vs menus végétariens dans les cantines scolaires", *Eurel-France*, www.eurel.info/spip.php?rubrique362, accessed 25 February 2018.
98 Bergeaud-Blackler, Florence, *Les sens du halal: une norme dans un marché mondial* (Paris: CNRS alpha éditions, 2015); Bergeaud-Blackler, Florence, Johan Fischer and John Lever (eds.), *Halal Matters: Islam, Politics and Markets in Global Perspective* (London: Routledge, 2015).

which works with the UOIF and now certifies only meat, and the SFCVH (*Société française de contrôle de la viande halal*, French Society of Control of Halal Meat). The SFCVH was linked to the *Grande mosquée de Paris*, but the ties were severed in 2016.[99] In 2015, the SFCVH registered a net profit of €500,000 from a revenue of €1.5 million.[100] The halal business, although thriving, is reserved for traditional shops; for instance, the 2,500 Muslim butcher shops in France make the majority of that revenue. Overall, the halal business in France is estimated to be worth between €5 and 7 billion.[101]

An industrial norm was set up for halal food in France in 2017.[102] It has been welcomed by the industry sector, but the CFCM criticised it for not sufficiently complying with Islamic definitions of halal food.

Dress Code

In 2004, the Law on wearing ostentatious religious signs at school (*Loi sur le port de signes religieux ostensibles à l'école*[103]) banned the wearing of all "conspicuous" religious signs in public schools. This applies to staff and pupils, but not to parents accompanying a school outing.

---

99 "Halal: lettre de la mosquée de Paris aux industriels (contre la SFCVH)", *Al-Kanz*, 18 March 2016, https://www.al-kanz.org/2016/03/18/halal-mosquee-de-paris-sfcvh/, accessed 25 February 2018.
100 Sauvaget, Bernadette, "Ramadan, les paniers de l'islam", *Libération*, 5 June 2016, www.liberation.fr/france/2016/06/05/ramadan-les-paniers-de-l-islam_1457474, accessed 25 February 2018.
101 Sauvaget, "Ramadan, les paniers de l'islam".
102 "Création de la première norme française pour les aliments halal", *Le Monde*, 15 September 2017, http://www.lemonde.fr/religions/article/2017/09/15/creation-de-la-premiere-norme-francaise-pour-les-aliments-halal_5185949_1653130.html, accessed 25 February 2018.
103 *Loi n°2004-228 du 15 mars 2004 encadrant, en application du principe de laïcité, le port de signes ou de tenues manifestant une appartenance religieuse dans les écoles, collèges et lycées publics*, http://www.legirel.cnrs.fr/spip.php?article138, accessed 5 May 2018.

Since 2010, the Law[104] prohibits the concealment of the face in public spaces, which, de facto, bans the wearing of the niqab.

In 2017, the Court of Cassation[105] stated that it is only legal to ban religious clothing or signs at the work place inasmuch as the internal regulations of the enterprise contains a "neutrality clause", which can only apply to employees who provide frontline services.

Places of Islamic Learning and Education

Primary education:
There are around 40 Muslim primary schools in France, most of which are private schools (without state support).[106] They have around 2,000 pupils.[107] 80% of the pupils in Muslim schools belong to four educational regions: Versailles (1,443 pupils), Lyon (802), Lille (727), and Créteil (near Paris, 611). Two schools (Villeneuve-Saint-Georges and Strasbourg) are run by the Fethullah Gülen movement, and educate about 300 pupils.[108]

Secondary education:
Five establishments have signed a contract with the State (Averroès College in Lille, Al-Kindi School and Secondary School in the suburbs of Lyon, Ibn Khaldun Secondary School in Marseille, and *Education et savoir* secondary school and college in Vitry-sur-Seine).[109]

---

104 *Loi n° 2010-1192 du 11 octobre 2010 interdisant la dissimulation du visage dans l'espace public*, http://www.legirel.cnrs.fr/spip.php?article93, accessed 5 May 2018.
105 *Cass. Soc. 22 November 2017, n° 2484 / 13-19.855*.
106 www.al-kanz.org/2014/10/11/enseignement-prive-musulman/, accessed 25 February 2018.
107 Graveleau, Séverin, "La loi sur le voile à l'école n'a pas résolu la question des 'signes religieux ostensibles'", *Le Monde*, 11 October 2015, www.lemonde.fr/religions/article/2015/10/10/la-loi-sur-le-voile-a-l-ecole-n-a-pas-resolu-la-question-des-signes-religieux-ostensibles_4786958_1653130.html, accessed 25 February 2018.
108 Godard, *La question musulmane*, p. 309.
109 Graveleau, "La loi sur le voile".

Other secondary schools have not obtained such a contract: *La réussite* (Success), in Aubervilliers, opened in 2001; Montigny-le-Bretonneux, opened in 2009, and failed to obtain this contract in 2014.[110] The Fethullah Gülen movement opened a secondary school, *Collège privé educ'active*, in 2010, near Paris (Villeneuve-la-Garenne). A secondary school opened in March 2016 in Toulouse, called *Collège Alif*. Altogether, some 4,000 to 5,000 children and young people are educated in Muslim institutions.

Higher education:
Muslim higher education and the religious training of imams in France are only provided in private institutions with ties to Muslim associations.[111] This includes the *Institut européen des sciences humaines* (European Institute for Human Sciences–IESH), which is located on two sites: IESH Centre de Bouteloin (Château Chinon, 58120 Saint-Léger-en-Fougeret, tel.: ++33 386794062, www.iesh.org) and IESH de Paris (13 Boulevard de la libération, 93200 Saint-Denis, tel.: ++33 148201515, www.ieshdeparis.fr). There is also the *Institut Ghazali* (*Grande mosquée de Paris*, 5 Place du Puits de l'Ermite, 75005 Paris, tel.: +33 145357460, www.institut-al-ghazali.fr/), and the *Institut français des études et sciences islamiques* (French Institute for Islamic Studies and Sciences, 11B, Avenue Charles de Gaulle, 94470 Boissy-Saint-Léger, tel.: ++33 145991583, www.ifesi.com, www.facebook.com/institutifesi).

---

110   Le Bars, Stéphanie, "Un collège musulman 'sous le choc' après le refus de l'État de le prendre sous contrat", *Le Monde*, 13 June 2014, www.lemonde.fr/education/article/2014/06/13/un-college-musulman-sous-le-choc-apres-le-refus-de-l-etat-de-le-prendre-sous-contrat_4437748_1473685.html, accessed 25 February 2018.

111   See Messner, Francis, *Rapport sur la formation des cadres religieux musulmans*, http://dres.misha.cnrs.fr/IMG/pdf/rapp_messner_version_diffusion.pdf, accessed 25 February 2018.

The State provides funding for some one-year programmes on civic education (*Diplôme d'université*), open to all, but mainly aimed at imams. These are now offered at several universities:[112] Aix-en-Provence–Institute of Political Studies, Bordeaux, Lille 2, Université Lyon 3 and *Université Catholique de Lyon, Université du Maine* and *Université de Nantes*, Montpellier–Faculty of Law and Political Sciences, *Institut catholique* of Paris, Paris 1 Sorbonne, *Paris Sud*, Strasbourg–Faculty of Law, Strasbourg–Faculty of Catholic Theology, Toulouse I Capitole.

Muslim Media and Publications

- A 30-minute weekly programme called *Islam*, on the public broadcaster *France 2*, is managed by an association called *Vivre l'islam* (To Live Islam).[113]
- French Muslim television programme, *La chaîne musulmane francophone*.[114]
- Muslim information websites: *Saphir news* (www.saphirnews.com/); *Mejliss* (mejliss.com/); *Oumma* (Oumma.com); *Zaman France*, (www.zamanfrance.fr/); *Le journal du musulman* (The Muslim Newspaper, journaldumusulman.fr/); *Islam en France* (Islam in France, www.islamenfrance.fr/); *Ajib* (www.ajib.fr/); and *Al-Kanz* (www.al-kanz.org/), a website with information and news on Islamic finance and the economy worldwide.
- There is a scholarly review, *Les cahiers de l'islam* (www.lescahiersdelislam.fr/); there is also *Al Moukhtarat*,[115] the pedagogical journal of the *Institut du monde arabe* (Institute of the Arab World, Paris).

---

112 Zwilling, Anne-Laure, "Training in secularism", *Eurel-France*, www.eurel.info/spip.php?article2587, accessed 25 February 2018.
113 https://www.france.tv/france-2/islam/, accessed 25 February 2018.
114 islamfrench-tv.fr/, accessed 25 February 2018.
115 www.imarabe.org/librairie/librairie-boutique/revue-al-moukhtarat, accessed 25 February 2018.

- In 2016, a new publishing house *Les éditions du grand remplacement* was launched by Mehdi Meklat, Badroudine Saïd Abdallah, and Mouloud Achour. It has published a journal, *Téléramadan* (this title was an intended pun on one of the most popular French television magazines, *Télérama*), and it also intends to publish books.[116] The journal does not seem to exist anymore.

Main Muslim Organisations

Religious groups in France can either have the specific status of *association cultuelle* (denominational association), or have the common association status, according to the *Law of 1901*.[117] Most Muslim groups and associations are organised according to the *Law of Associations*, and registered as such. There are a very large number of Muslim associations, most of them only of local importance. Some associations, however, are of national significance.

- French Council of the Muslim Faith (*Conseil français du culte musulman*– CFCM, 270 rue Lecourbe, 75015 Paris, tel.: ++33 145580573). The president is Ahmet Ogras. This organisation is the official body representing Muslims to the State. It was founded in 2003 at the request of the French authorities. Its general assembly is composed of 194 members who are either elected by the leaders of the main mosques, or represent the main mosques and federations. It deals with issues such as the construction of mosques, sections for Muslim burial in cemeteries, halal slaughter, the nomination of chaplains, and the training of imams, but it has no real prerogatives nor any executive power. Its purpose, to represent all French Muslims, has sometimes been questioned by Muslims themselves.[118]

---

116   www.lemonde.fr/actualite-medias/article/2016/06/06/teleramadan-la-revue-qui-veut-contrer-les-idees-nauseabondes_4938197_3236.html, access 25 February 2018.
117   For further information concerning the French legal framework for religious groups, see *Associations religieuses*, www.interieur.gouv.fr/A-votre-service/Mes-demarches/Associations#F21925, accessed 25 February 2018 and *Le support institutionnel de l'exercice du culte*, NOR/IOC/D/10/16585/C, www.legirel.cnrs.fr/IMG/pdf/100623-1.pdf, accessed 25 February 2018.
118   www.interieur.gouv.fr/fr/Archives/Archives-presse/Communiques-de-presse/Election-d-un-nouveau-bureau-pour-le-CFCM, accessed 15 February 2017.

- Muslim Institute of the Grand Mosque of Paris (*Institut musulman de la Grande mosquée de Paris*, Place du Puits de l'Ermite, 75005 Paris, tel.: ++33 145359733, www.mosquee-de-paris.org). This is the official organisation representing Algerian Islam (Sunni), promoting a "Republican" Islam, that is, fully in accordance with French laws and way of life.
- Muslims of France (*Musulmans de France*, 20 rue de la Prevôté, 93120 La Courneuve, tel.: ++33 143111060, https://www.facebook.com/MusulmansdeFranceMF/, www.uoif-online.com). The president is Amar Lasfar. The association changed its name in 2017; it was previously known as the Union of Islamic Organisations of France (*Union des organisations islamiques de France*–UOIF). The former UOIF follows the ideals of the Muslim Brotherhood. It aims at promoting a conservative Islam adapted to Western ideas and societies. This federation brings together more than 200 local or specific Muslim associations (such as cultural associations, women's groups, and student organisations).
- National Federation of French Muslims (*Fédération nationale des musulmans de France*–FNMF), created in 1985 with the support of the World Islamic League. At first a gathering of several different Islamic orientations, it finally became mainly a representation of Moroccan Islam. Selected in 2000 by the public authorities (during the consultation launched by Jean-Pierre Chevènement) to represent Moroccan mosques in France, it thus obtained, the support of the Moroccan consular network. In 2005, a split led to the creation of a new Moroccan body within Islam in France: the Union of French Muslims.
- Union of French Muslims (*Rassemblement des musulmans de France*–RMF, www.lermf.com). It is considered one of the major organisations of Islam in France. Created from a split within the *Fédération nationale des musulmans de France*, the RMF is an organisation of Moroccan Muslims, established in 2007. It promotes a traditionalist, devotional form of Islam.
- Coordinating Committee of Turkish Muslims in France (*Comité de coordination des musulmans Turcs de France*, 2 Boulevard Saint Martin, 75010 Paris, tel.: ++33 142001936, www.facebook.com/Comit%C3%A9-de-Coordination-des-Musulmans-Turcs-de-France-CCMTF-333690070165341/). Created in 2005 from the DITIB network, it officially represents Turkish Muslims in France, and is close to the Turkish Presidency of Religious Affairs (*Diyanet İşleri Başkanlığı*) and its French branch (*Fransa Diyanet İşleri Türk Islam Birliği*).
- Union of French Mosques (*Union des mosquées de France*, 65 rue d'Amsterdam, 75008 Paris, tel.: ++33 153161897, www.umfrance.fr/). The president is Mohammed Moussaoui. Created from a split within the *Fédération*

nationale des musulmans de France, the RMF is an organisation of Moroccan Muslims formed in 2013. It has close ties with the Moroccan Ministry of Habous and Religious Affairs.
- Faith and Practice (*Foi et pratique*, 83 rue Faubourg St Denis, 75010 Paris, tel.: ++33 143574513). Created in 1972, *Foi et pratique* is one of the French associations of the Tablighi Jama'at.
- French Federation of Islamic Associations of Africa, Comoros, and the Antilles (*Fédération française des associations islamiques d'Afrique, des Comores et des Antilles*–FFAIACA, 37 rue de Chabrol, 75010 Paris, tel.: ++33 142460507). Created in 1989, this association brings together Muslims from Sub-Saharan Africa and the Antilles.
- Millî Görüş Islamic Community of France (*Communauté islamique Millî Görüş de France*, 64 rue du Faubourg, Saint-Denis, 75010 Paris, tel.: ++33 145234150, www.cimgfrance.com). An orthodox and nationalist Turkish association, which brings together a third of French-Turkish mosques.
- Other Turkish brotherhoods have networks in France, such as Süleymanci (*Fédération centres culturels Turcs de Paris*) or Fethullahci (fr.fgulen.com/).[119]
- Tabligh Al Dawa Il Allah Federation (*Fédération tabligh Al Dawa Il Allah*), was created after a split from *Foi et pratique*, to form the other branch of the French Tablighi Jama'at.
- The Sufi house (*La maison soufie*, 8 Rue Raspail, 93400 Saint-Ouen, tel.: +33 764145726, www.lamaisonsoufie.fr/) represents Naqshbandi Sufism in France.
- The Council of French Imams (*Conseil des imams de France*, 3 impasse Charles Cousin, 93300 Aubervilliers, tel.: ++33 664674561, www.leconseildesimamsdefrance.org/). The council brings together several hundred imams (out of the 2,500 or more imams in France). The general secretary is Meskine Dhaou.
- National Federation of Muslim Private Education (*Fédération nationale de l'enseignement privé musulman*–FNEM, http://www.fnem.fr/). Created on 24 March 2014, this is the first representative body for private Muslim education in France; the director is Makhlouf Mameche.
- French Muslim Theological Council (*Conseil théologique musulman de France*–CTMF, www.facebook.com/ConseilTheologique/). Created on 25 May 2015, this council aims at helping French Muslims to "live fully both their religion and their French citizenship".

---

119 Balci, Bayram, "Le hizmet de Fethullah Gülen. Quelle place dans l'islam en France et en Europe?", *Études*, vol. 6 (June 2015), pp. 19–31.

- Foundation of Islam of France (*Fondation de l'islam de France*, 7 rue Saint-Dominique, 75007 Paris, tel.: ++33 145028213, email: contact@fondationdelislamdefrance.fr). Created by the French government, the foundation aims at promoting secularism, supporting interreligious and intercultural dialogue with Islam, training imams according to Republican values, and enhancing the teaching of Islam at universities. The president is former politician Jean-Pierre Chevènement, a non-Muslim.

Georgia

Thomas Liles[1] and Bayram Balci[2]

Introduction

In 2017, Muslim sacred spaces and discrimination against Muslims continued to take centre stage in public debates around Islam. The ongoing involvement of Georgian nationals with ISIS dominated narratives around transnational links, although all Muslim communities and organisations maintained or strengthened peaceful links with transnational actors. In the area of law and politics, 2017 witnessed an uptick in controversial counterterrorism operations within Georgia. Additionally, state-associated entities continued to pursue a top-down approach to managing Muslim affairs, particularly with regards to financing, property issues, and mediating domestic communities' transnational links. Finally, Adjara's Muslim population continued to advocate for the construction of a second mosque in Batumi, while the Shi'i community in Marneuli filed lawsuits against state bodies regarding mosque restitution issues. As in previous years, most Muslim communities pursued primarily spiritual and educational initiatives.

Public Debates

In the village of Mokhe (Adigeni Municipality, Samtskhe-Javakheti region), tensions continued to simmer between local Muslims and Orthodox Christians over the religious origins of a derelict building. Public debate first erupted in October 2014 when local police arrested members of Mokhe's Muslim community–who claim that the building is an historic mosque–during a peaceful demonstration against the municipality's planned conversion of the structure

[1] Thomas Liles holds an MA in Russia, Eastern Europe, and Central Asia Studies from Harvard University. He has researched Muslim issues in Georgia and the wider Caucasus in affiliation with the European Centre for Minority Issues Caucasus, the US Embassy in Tbilisi, and as a Fulbright Research Fellow in Baku, Azerbaijan.
[2] Bayram Balci is director of l'Institut français d'études anatoliennes in Istanbul, Turkey, where his research focuses on Turkey and Turkish foreign policy in Central Asia and the Caucasus. He is also a non-resident scholar with the Carnegie Endowment's Russia and Eurasia Programme, and is affiliated with CERI Sciences Po in Paris, France.

into a cultural centre.³ The Georgian Orthodox Church quickly countered that the structure was an historic Orthodox church, after which the State Agency for Religious Issues (რელიგიის საკითხთა სახელმწიფო სააგენტოს, hereafter the State Agency) created a commission to study the building's origins. The commission remained largely dormant, and only in late 2016 issued a recommendation to keep the building under state ownership as a "disputed property", rather than addressing the contradictory historic ownership claims.⁴ In May 2017, the State acted on the commission's recommendation and transferred the disputed site to the Agency of State Property (National Agency for Cultural Heritage Preservation of Georgia), while the Ministry of Culture and Monument Protection was charged with preserving the structure. Simultaneously, the State allocated a separate plot of land for the construction of a new mosque.⁵

On 14 September 2017, local officials sealed off the property with a fence to prepare the disputed building for preservation, thus preventing Mokhe's Muslims from conducting Friday prayers in front of the ruins, as many had regularly done since late 2016. According to eyewitnesses, Nikoloz Getsadze, who serves as archimandrite of the nearby Zarzma Monastery, and has actively touted the Georgian Orthodox Church's ownership claims to the building, appeared at the site and threatened to break anyone's legs who attempted to enter the sealed area. When local Muslims gathered the following day to conduct Friday prayers, Getsadze blocked their entrance to the property.⁶

On a broader level, the ownership dispute has further aggravated interreligious tensions, as neighbourly relations between Muslim and Orthodox villagers in Mokhe continued to deteriorate throughout 2017. The controversy

---

3   http://www.kavkaz-uzel.eu/articles/251172/, accessed 1 November 2014.
4   In December 2016, the Muslim community published archival administrative documents from late Imperial Russia, which indicate the presence of a mosque in Mokhe as of 1870 (see Liles, Thomas, and Bayram Balci, "Georgia", in Oliver Scharbrodt, Samim Akgönül, Ahmet Alibašić, Jørgen S. Nielsen and Egdūnas Račius (eds.), *Yearbook of Muslims in Europe*, vol. 9 (Leiden: Brill, 2018), p. 274). Independent art historian Kristine Mujiri corroborated this evidence, noting that many 19th century mosques in Georgia were initially built from wood and later reconstructed from stone. She suggests that the 1870 archival record likely corresponds to the disputed building in Mokhe, which was probably reconstructed with stone in the 1930s or 1940s. See http://www.forum18.org/archive.php?article_id=2260, accessed 28 February 2017.
5   Mokhe's Muslims had traditionally prayed in a private home, and began praying among the disputed building's ruins from October 2016: http://tdi.ge/en/statement/brief-issues-batumi-and-mokhe-mosques, accessed 16 May 2017.
6   Getsadze did not appear the following Friday: http://oc-media.org/georgias-mokhe-muslims-threatened-by-christian-leader/, accessed 8 October 2017.

also underscored distrust among local Muslims toward the Administration of Muslims of All Georgia (სრულიად საქართველოს მუსლიმთა სამმართველო, hereafter AMAG), officially an independent body, but which many perceive as representing the interests of the State above those of the Muslim population. Indeed in early October, officials from AMAG's Western Muftiate[7] visited Mokhe and held prayers in the new mosque then being constructed on state-allocated land.[8] Nevertheless, some Muslim villagers refused to participate in AMAG's initiative and continued to pray outside the fence of the disputed site.[9] Moreover, the non-governmental Tolerance and Diversity Institute (ტოლერანტობის და მრავალფეროვნების ინსტიტუტი, hereafter TDI), which routinely represents Muslim interests in legal disputes, revealed that Mokhe's new mosque was in fact being built without a construction permit. Without proper construction permits, the TDI notes that the mosque remains in a tenuous legal status and could easily be dismantled by municipal authorities in the future.[10]

Advocacy and human rights organisations highlighted multiple cases of discrimination against Muslims in 2017. In March, the TDI published an assessment of an internal audit by the Ministry of Education and Science in relation to a discrimination case in Mokhe. The case alleged that a local Orthodox resident with openly hostile attitudes towards Muslims became acting director of Mokhe's high school in September 2016, and threatened to prevent the enrolment of a female student due to the student's preference to wear a head scarf.[11] Although the Ministry found no proof of discrimination, the TDI's assessment noted that the audit was not supported by factual information and, moreover, discussed the permissibility of prohibiting head scarves in public schools.[12] In September, the TDI met with ethnic Georgian Muslim representatives in the

---

7   Based in Adjara's capital Batumi, AMAG's Western Muftiate nominally represents ethnic Georgian Sunnis in Western Georgia.
8   https://www.facebook.com/SruliadSakartvelosMuslimtaSammartvelo/posts/1622230024467092, accessed 8 October 2017.
9   http://oc-media.org/voice-from-meskheti-whether-in-rain-or-thunderstorms-we-pray-outside/, accessed 25 January 2018.
10 http://tdi.ge/en/news/509-new-mosque-being-built-without-permission-mokhe, accessed 15 February 2018.
11 http://tdi.ge/en/statement/tdi-studies-alleged-facts-discrimination-mokhe-public-school, accessed 30 December 2016.
12 http://tdi.ge/en/statement/assessment-internal-audit-report-mokhe-public-school, accessed 3 August 2017.

Republic of Adjara, where they addressed problems surrounding discriminatory treatment and obstacles to building new mosques.[13]

In May 2017, the TDI and the non-governmental Human Rights Education and Monitoring Centre (ადამიანის უფლებების სწავლებისა და მონიტორინგის ცენტრი, hereafter EMC) notified the governmental Public Defender of Georgia (საქართველოს სახალხო დამცველი, hereafter the Public Defender) of alleged violations of Georgian Muslims' religious freedom at the Sarpi border crossing to Turkey. The Public Defender subsequently confirmed at least three cases of discriminatory treatment, which included strip searches, confiscation of copies of the Qur'an and other religious literature, and hours-long interrogations regarding Muslim travellers' connections to Turkey.[14] In its annual report released in September 2017, the Public Defender noted a total of seven instances of confiscation of religious literature. The Public Defender also issued a general proposal urging the Minister of Education and Science to "assess the fitness" of the acting director of Mokhe's high school, as well as to "establish a uniform approach for all public schools" to ensure female Muslim students' right to wear head scarves. Moreover, the report noted increasingly aggressive attitudes towards Muslim students in the village of Nigvziani (Lanchkhuti Municipality, Guria region), and urged the Minister to organise training on the importance of tolerance and multicultural instruction, particularly in regions populated by religious and ethnic minorities.[15]

Debate over Muslim religious attire emerged again in late September 2017, when a 14-year-old girl in the Azeri-populated village of Karajala (Telavi Municipality, Kakheti region) was told to remove her head scarf whilst at school. The girl's family contended that the school violated the girl's religious freedom and claimed that the school's director, Elza Ashurova, sent the girl home on several occasions. Ashurova claimed never to have prevented the girl from attending classes and countered that the school's policy prohibited head coverings of all types, a position that the Ministry of Education and Science later echoed.[16] In contrast to Mokhe–where the head scarf debate underscored

---

13   http://tdi.ge/en/news/469-tdis-visit-adjara-meetings-religious-organizations-and-state-representatives, accessed 21 November 2017.
14   http://www.kavkaz-uzel.eu/articles/302250/, accessed 5 June 2017. These instances affected ethnic Georgian Muslims and indicate an uptick in scrutiny among border guards vis-à-vis Georgia's domestic Muslim communities. Similar scrutiny has not been reported for Turkish nationals or Georgian Christians who use the Sarpi crossing. See http://oc-media.org/islamic-literature-confiscated-at-georgian-turkish-border/, accessed 24 October 2017.
15   http://www.ombudsman.ge/uploads/other/4/4826.pdf, accessed 24 October 2017.
16   http://oc-media.org/girl-prohibited-from-wearing-hijab-in-east-georgia-school/, http://oc-media.org/georgian-education-ministry-unfortunate-school-hijab-dispute-seen-as-restriction-of-religious-freedom/, both accessed 28 September 2017.

confessional cleavages between Orthodox and Muslim ethnic Georgians and essentially revolved around mutually exclusive conceptions of Georgian national identity–the incident in Karajala arose among ethnic Azeris, all of whom are Muslim, and essentially pitted "traditional" conceptions of Islam against the uptick in conservative Sunnism that has been noted in Karajala over the past decade.[17] Accordingly, Ashurova argued that the Muslim head scarf is alien to Karajala's local customs, and that there would be no such internal school regulation had the head scarf been a more prominent aspect of local religious observance. She also claimed that the parents in this case are forcing fundamentalist practices on the student.[18] The girl's parents argued that the family is simply religious, and wants to resolve the conflict to ensure both access to education and religious observance. Other parents in the village have indicated plans to keep their daughters at home after the age of 14 unless the school revises its policy.[19]

In early October 2017, the opposition political party Development Movement (შენების მოძრაობა) filed a complaint with the Inter-Agency Commission for Free and Fair Elections against local activists from the ruling Georgian Dream Party (ქართული ოცნება-დემოკრატიული საქართველო). The activists allegedly forced ethnic Azeri Muslims in Irganchai village (Dmanisi Municipality, Kvemo-Kartli region) to swear on the Qur'an to vote for Georgian Dream candidates in the 21 October local elections, threatening to cut off the villagers' social welfare if they failed to follow directions. Georgian Dream denied the complaint as a pre-election smear campaign, although TV Pirveli confirmed the claims, and indicated similar cases in other villages. Minister of Justice Tea Tsulukiani subsequently condemned the incident.[20]

---

17 See Liles, Thomas, and Bayram Balci, "Georgia", in Oliver Scharbrodt, Samim Akgönül, Ahmet Alibašić, Jørgen S. Nielsen and Egdūnas Račius (eds.), *Yearbook of Muslims in Europe*, vol. 8 (Leiden: Brill, 2017), p. 291.

18 http://oc-media.org/girl-prohibited-from-wearing-hijab-in-east-georgia-school/, accessed 28 September 2017; in a 2015 interview, Ashurova indicated that students from religious families regularly missed school during the Ramadan fast, an issue for which she attempted to negotiate a solution with the local *akhund* to no avail: https://jam-news.net/?p=4967&lang=ru, accessed 18 February 2018.

19 http://dfwatch.net/either-school-hijab-daughters-will-not-go-school-without-hijab-49310, accessed 18 October 2017.

20 http://oc-media.org/muslims-forced-to-swear-on-quran-to-vote-for-georgian-dream/, accessed 6 October 2017.

Transnational Links

Since approximately 2013, the involvement of Georgian nationals in the ranks of the so-called Islamic State (ISIS) and other extremist Sunni groups in Syria has taken centre stage in questions surrounding transnational links, particularly in relation to Pankisi's Kist community. In June 2017, 25-year-old Duisi native Mukhmad Baghakashvili was reported killed while fighting for ISIS in Syria.[21] In August, 31-year-old Omalo native Levan Tokhosashvili and his family were reported killed as a result of aerial bombing in Syria,[22] although these claims were retracted after Tokhosashvili contacted relatives in Pankisi several days later.[23] In December, a high-profile Kist field commander by the name of Giorgi Margoshvili (a.k.a. Salahuddin al-Shishani)[24] was reported killed after a Russian air raid in Northern Syria. Margoshvili headed the *Jaish al-Muhajirin wal Ansar* (Army of Emigrants and Supporters) unit, until disagreements arose with the group's Saudi faction. Thereafter, he formed a smaller group consisting primarily of Kists and North Caucasians.[25] As of March 2016, Georgia's State Security Service (SSS) indicated there were up to 50 Georgian citizens fighting for extremist groups in Iraq and Syria.[26] According to one Georgian expert, 25 Pankisi natives, ten ethnic Georgian Muslims and ten ethnic Azeris had been killed in action as of November 2017, with a total of approximately 50 Pankisi and Adjara natives currently fighting in the region.[27]

Notwithstanding the predominance of international terrorism in the news cycle, all of Georgia's Muslim communities and organisations maintained or strengthened peaceful religious and financial links with transnational actors to some extent. This was especially true for Georgia's ethnic Azeri Shi'i community, which hosted prominent Iranian Shi'i figures on several occasions. In mid-March, *Əhli-Beyt* (Ahli-Beyt), a Shi'i spiritual and educational organisation with traditionally close ties to Iran, received Ayatollah Kazem Sedighi at its office in Marneuli (Kvemo-Kartli region). Sedighi, a high-ranking Shi'i scholar who currently serves as Tehran's Friday Prayer Imam, discussed the organisation's activities with Ahli-Beyt Director Rasim Mammadov, and offered advice

---

21 http://civil.ge/eng/article.php?id=30162, accessed 6 June 2017.
22 http://civil.ge/eng/article.php?id=30392, accessed 28 August 2017.
23 http://www.apsny.ge/2017/conf/1506996067.php, accessed 2 October 2017.
24 Margoshvili is alternatively known by the forename and surname Feyzulla and Kushtanashvili, respectively: http://www.chechensinsyria.com/?p=23682, accessed 28 December 2017.
25 http://dfwatch.net/al-qaeda-commander-pankisi-reported-dead-syria-49623, accessed 27 December 2017.
26 http://civil.ge/eng/article.php?id=30392, accessed 28 August 2017.
27 http://www.kavkaz-uzel.eu/articles/313111/, accessed 30 November 2017.

on future initiatives.[28] Sedighi likewise met with AMAG's Sheikh Ramin Igidov, and participated in a conference on Islam and family values.[29] In a move that underscored the high-level nature of the visit, Sedighi subsequently met with Georgian Orthodox Church Patriarch Ilya II.[30] In May, AMAG and the Tbilisi-based Shi'i educational organisation Alul-Bayt,[31] jointly organised a conference on the concept of the saviour (i.e. Imam Mahdi) in Islam, which featured remarks by Ali Akbar Odjaq Nejad.[32] Nejad, a prominent Iranian cleric who serves as the representative of Iran's Supreme Leader Ayatollah Ali Khamenei in Azerbaijan, subsequently took part in an AMAG-organised conference in Gardabani on the occasion of Imam Mahdi's birthday.[33]

September saw further high-level transnational Shi'i contacts with the visit of Ayatollah Mujtahid Shabistari to Georgia. Shabistari, who formerly served as imam in Tabriz, appeared as the main speaker at a conference entitled "Lessons from the 'Ashura' Movement" organised by Ahli-Beyt.[34] Shabistari also made several site visits in Gardabani Municipality (Kvemo-Kartli), including Marağa mosque and Əl-Hikmə madrasa, where he discussed their activities with local clergy. He also participated in the opening of a new mosque in Qara Təhlə village.[35] Finally, in November, several Azeri Shi'i leaders associated with Ahli-Beyt attended a conference in Tehran devoted to countering "takfirism" (i.e. radical movements within Salafism that declare other Muslims such as Shi'is as apostates).[36]

---

28 http://www.ahlibeyt.ge/georgia/16017-gurcustan-ehli-beyt-e-cemiyyetinde-ayetullah-kazim-siddiqi-ile-gorus-foto.html, accessed 27 December 2017.

29 http://www.ahlibeyt.ge/georgia/16035-gurcustan-muselmanlar-daresnn-dn-rehberler-ayetullah-kazm-sddq-le-gorusub-foto.html, http://www.ahlibeyt.ge/georgia/16034-tblsde-saglam-ale-ve-saglam-cemyyet-movzusunda-elm-konfrans-kecrlb-vdeo.html, both accessed 27 December 2017.

30 http://www.ahlibeyt.ge/georgia/16044-ayetullah-kazm-sddq-gurcustan-patrarx-lya-le-gorusdu-foto.html, accessed 27 December 2017.

31 Although similar in name and mission, Ahli-Beyt and Alul-Bayt are separate organisations.

32 http://amag.ge/index.php/news/item/407-2017-05-07-19-23-31, accessed 23 December 2017.

33 http://www.ahlibeyt.ge/georgia/17076-rustav-sehernde-hz-mam-mehdnn-e-movludu-le-bagl-merasm-kecrld-foto.html, accessed 27 December 2017.

34 http://www.ahlibeyt.ge/georgia/18627-gurcustan-ehli-beyt-e-cemiyyetinde-asura-her ekatindan-dersler-movzusunda-elmi-konfrans-kecirildi-foto.html, accessed 27 December 2017.

35 http://www.ahlibeyt.ge/georgia/18639-ayetullah-sebisteri-qardabani-rayonunu-ziyaret-etdi-foto.html, accessed 27 December 2017.

36 A select few ethnic Georgian Sunni figures also attended, including Aslan Sharashidze, who was appointed as Mufti of Adjara's Shuakhevi Municipality in 2016: http://www.ahlibeyt.ge/georgia/19361-gurcustanli-din-xadimleri-tekfirciliyin-sebeblerinin-arasdiril masi-movzusunda-konfransda-foto.html, accessed 27 December 2017.

Georgia's Sunnis also strengthened transnational ties. In April, AMAG representatives Beglar Kamashidze and Iasin Aliyev[37] visited Saudi Arabia, where they met with the Saudi Minister of Hajj and Umra Mohammad Saleh bin Taher Benten, and discussed the participation of Georgia's Muslims in the hajj.[38] In December, Iasin Aliyev met with several Muslim officials from Russia's Republic of Dagestan, including Deputy Mufti Muhammad Manguyev, and officials involved in Islamic education. In a reference to Georgia's ethnic Avar population in the Kvareli Municipality, Aliyev noted that Georgia was home to Muslims of Dagestani origin, thus suggesting a greater initiative towards strengthening AMAG's relationship with ethnic Avars and their transnational links in the North Caucasus.[39] Meanwhile, the Batumi-based World Alliance of Georgian Muslims (მსოფლიო ქართველ მუსლიმთა კავშირი, hereafter the World Alliance) bolstered its connections with Turkey, which has traditionally been a key source of spiritual and material support for Adjara's Muslims. In December, the World Alliance hosted Turkish theologian Süleyman Uludağ, who gave lectures on religion to Muslim students in Batumi and Khulo.[40] Similarly, World Alliance Director Zurab Kemal Tsetskhladze strengthened ties with ethnic Georgian diaspora communities in Turkey during visits to the cities of İnegöl and Bursa in March[41] and İznik in January, where Mayor Osman Sargın underlined İznik's sister city status with Khulo, and promised further mutual visits and cooperation.[42]

Law and Domestic Politics

In contrast to previous years, 2017 was particularly notable for the scale and intensity of counterterrorism operations conducted within Georgia. On the night of 21 November, the State Security Service (SSS) Counterterrorism Department began an operation to arrest an unspecified number of foreign nationals who had been under surveillance for several weeks at an apartment block in

---

37   Kamashidze is an ethnic Georgian Sunni from Adjara, who serves as Mufti of Western Georgia. Aliyev is an ethnic Azeri Sunni who serves as Mufti of Eastern Georgia, and nominally represents Sunnis of all ethnic backgrounds in Kvemo-Kartli, Kakheti, and Shida-Kartli.
38   http://amag.ge/index.php/news/item/408-2017-05-16-10-19-26, accessed 23 December 2017.
39   http://amag.ge/index.php/news/item/435-2017-12-18-07-21-00, accessed 23 December 2017.
40   Khulo is a mountainous district in Adjara, where Muslims comprise a higher proportion of the population compared to lowland districts.
41   goo.gl/rQUm7G, accessed 18 December 2017.
42   https://m.sondakika.com/haber/haber-baskan-sargin-dunya-gurcu-muslumanlari-birligini-9132917/, accessed 18 December 2017.

Tbilisi's Isani district. According to the SSS, the suspects opened fire at law enforcement personnel, setting off a firefight that stretched into the next afternoon, and led to the evacuation and blockade of the apartment building. Three suspects were killed and one arrested, while one SSS officer was killed and four wounded.[43] On 3 December, SSS confirmed one of the casualties as ISIS operative Akhmed Chatayev, a Russian citizen and Chechnya native suspected of organising the July 2016 terrorist attack on Istanbul's Atatürk Airport.[44] In late December, the remaining two casualties were identified as North Caucasus natives Ibrahim Adashev and Aslanbeg Soltakhmadov. Simultaneously, SSS identified Georgian citizen Gocha (a.k.a. Ali) Saginadze to Turkish authorities as Chatayev's accomplice.[45]

On 26 December 2017, SSS carried out another special operation in the villages of Omalo and Duisi in Pankisi Gorge. Security personnel detained five villagers who had allegedly helped Chatayev's group cross the border into Georgia from Turkey and establish a safe haven in Tbilisi. Investigators also found a secret weapons cache, which they claimed the suspects were planning to use for terrorist attacks in Georgia and Turkey.[46] According to official statements, one detainee–18-year-old Temirlan Machalikashvili–was shot in the head by security forces and hospitalised after attempting to put up resistance with a grenade, although Machalikashvili's family disputed the official version and claimed that security personnel planted the grenade.[47] On 27 December, Pankisi's Council of Elders convened a public meeting and called on authorities to carry out an objective investigation of the operation and Machalikashvili's injuries. Several hundred locals subsequently held a rally in Duisi, where speakers indicated that the aggressive nature of the operation had "caused great outrage" in the gorge and rolled back years of positive developments between locals and Georgian law enforcement.[48] On 28 December, the Tbilisi City Court placed the four remaining detainees in pre-trial detention on charges of aiding terrorists, while Machalikashvili remained in a critical condition.[49] Pankisi's

---

43 http://civil.ge/eng/article.php?id=30658, accessed 22 November 2017.
44 http://dfwatch.net/authorities-confirm-akhmed-chatayev-died-siege-49539, accessed 29 December 2017.
45 Turkish Police arrested Saginadze in Trabzon on 29 December: http://www.interpressnews.ge/ru/2010-05-25-09-34-34/100601-2017-12-29-05-22-23.html?ar=A, accessed 29 December 2017.
46 http://www.kavkaz-uzel.eu/articles/314342/, accessed 26 December 2017.
47 http://www.kavkaz-uzel.eu/articles/314361/, accessed 27 December 2017.
48 http://civil.ge/eng/article.php?id=30764, accessed 28 December 2017.
49 http://www.kavkaz-uzel.eu/articles/314448/, accessed 28 December 2017.

Council of Elders publicly expressed serious doubts regarding the involvement of Machalikashvili and detainee Ramaz Margoshvili in terrorist activities.[50]

In addition to an uptick in counterterrorism operations, government bodies maintained an active role in the management of domestic Muslim affairs.[51] In particular, the State Agency continued to play an implicit mediating role between domestic Shi'i communities and their various transnational counterparts. State Agency Director Zaza Vashakmadze met with essentially every Iranian Shi'i figure that visited Georgia in 2017, including Kazem Sedighi,[52] Ayatollah Shabistari,[53] and Islamic Culture and Relations Organisation (ICRO) Director Abuzar Ebrahimi.[54] The State Agency also deepened its involvement in the realm of religious education during an October meeting with an Iranian delegation, in which the two sides discussed opening an Iranian-sponsored Shi'i school in Georgia.[55] Additionally, Vashakmadze conducted meetings with *sheikh al-islam* Allahshukhur Pashazade–Azerbaijan's leading Shi'i official who heads the Baku-based Caucasus Muslim Board[56]–and Selahattin Özgündüz, the head of Turkey's Jafari Shi'i community.[57]

Similarly, the State Agency worked in conjunction with AMAG on Muslim financial and property issues. In March 2017, Vashakmadze and Sheikh Ramin Igidov convened a meeting with AMAG's Supreme Religious Council[58]

---

50   http://www.kavkaz-uzel.eu/articles/314542/, accessed 31 December 2017.
51   This trend has been evident since the Saakashvili government's unilateral creation of AMAG in 2011, as well as the Georgian Dream government's creation of the State Agency for Religious Issues in 2014. The two bodies have often worked in tandem to coordinate Muslim affairs from above, particularly with regards to overseeing transnational links, registering Muslim religious property and clergy, and distributing financial support to Muslim constituencies.
52   AMAG Sheikh Ramin Igidov and Iran's recently-appointed ambassador to Georgia, Javad Ghavam Shahidi, also attended the meeting: http://religion.geo.gov.ge/eng/news/zaza-vashakmadze-hosted-clerical-delegation-from, accessed 23 December 2017.
53   http://religion.geo.gov.ge/eng/news/meeting-with-ayatollah-shabistan, accessed 23 December 2017.
54   http://religion.geo.gov.ge/eng/news/meeting-with-the-head-of-the-islamic-culture-and, accessed 23 December 2017.
55   http://religion.geo.gov.ge/eng/news/visit-of-the-iranian-delegation-to-the-religion, accessed 23 December 2017.
56   Until the creation of AMAG in 2011, Pashazade nominally represented Georgia's entire Muslim population: http://religion.geo.gov.ge/eng/news/the-pm-of-georgia-met-azerbaijani-delegation-of, accessed 23 December 2017.
57   http://religion.geo.gov.ge/eng/news/meeting-with-selahattin-ozgunduz, accessed 23 December 2017.
58   The Council was formed in 2014, and consists of prominent Azeri Shi'i clerics from Kvemo-Kartli and Tbilisi, including Ahli-Beyt Director Rasim Mammadov: see Liles, Thomas, and Bayram Balci, "Georgia", in Oliver Scharbrodt, Samim Akgönül, Ahmet Alibašić,

to discuss the legal status of mosques in Eastern Georgia, and state financial assistance to ethnic Azeri Muslim communities.[59] Similar initiatives were taken in Adjara, where the State Agency contributed funds for the renovation of a mosque in the Khelvachauri Municipality[60] and formally transferred ten mosques in the mountainous Shuakhevi Municipality to AMAG ownership.[61]

Activities and Initiatives of Main Muslim Organisations

AMAG continued to play its own coordinating role vis-à-vis Georgia's various Muslim communities, as the body receives significant state funds and is essentially the only Muslim entity to which mosques have formally been transferred. In August, AMAG Sheikh Igidov stated that over 40 mosques were currently under renovation and another ten under construction in various parts of Georgia.[62] While Sheikh Igidov and other AMAG officials attended almost all events involving domestic Shi'i communities and transnational actors, the Mufti of Eastern Georgia, Iasin Aliyev, likewise coordinated with Eastern Georgian Sunni communities, reviewing 2016 activities with the region's Sunni clergy in January, as well as the "action plan" for 2017.[63] In July 2017, Igidov and Aliyev convened the first meeting of AMAG's Halal Commission near Tbilisi's main mosque, which was attended by a group of ethnic Azeri clergy members, and covered issues such as certification for halal distributors and halal best practices.[64] AMAG also hosted several events in the calendar year, including a conference dedicated to Georgia's Shi'i sayyids[65] and a celebration of AMAG's

---

Jørgen S. Nielsen and Egdūnas Račius (eds.), *Yearbook of Muslims in Europe*, vol. 7 (Leiden: Brill, 2015), p. 260.

59 http://religion.geo.gov.ge/eng/news/meeting-with-muslim-community-of-georgia, accessed 3 April 2017.
60 The current Mufti of Western Georgia, Beglar Kamashidze, previously served as Khelvachauri's district mufti; http://religion.geo.gov.ge/eng/news/zaza-vashakmadze-visited-the-central-mosque-in, accessed 3 April 2017.
61 http://ajaratv.ge/news/en/21061/10-mosques-operating-in-shuakh.html.html, accessed 8 October 2017.
62 http://salamnews.ru/ru/news/read/282589, accessed 8 October 2017.
63 http://amag.ge/index.php/news/item/371-2017-01-21-14-02-46, accessed 16 January 2017.
64 http://amag.ge/index.php/news/item/394-halal, accessed 4 July 2017.
65 http://www.ahlibeyt.ge/georgia/19144-seydlk-meqam-ve-gurcustan-seydler-movzusunda-konfrans-kecrld-foto.html, accessed 27 December 2017.

establishment, where officials presented the administration's 2017 annual report.⁶⁶

In Adjara's capital city of Batumi, local Muslims continued to lobby for permission to construct a second place of worship due to frequent overcrowding in the city's main Orta Jame mosque. In April, Tariel Nakaidze, head of the Georgian Muslims Union (ქართველ მუსლიმთა კავშირი, hereafter GMU), indicated that the initiative group New Mosque Building Foundation in Batumi (ბათუმში ახალი მეჩეთის მშენებლობის ფონდი, hereafter the New Mosque Foundation) had submitted a request to Batumi City Hall for permission to construct a second mosque on a plot of land purchased by the group in 2016.⁶⁷ Nakaidze also stated that the Government of Adjara, which previously touted controversial plans simply to expand Orta Jame,⁶⁸ had expressed verbal support for a new mosque during a meeting with the Chairman of the Government of the Autonomous Republic of Adjara, Zurab Pataradze.⁶⁹ The Muftiate of Western Georgia, which had always echoed government positions on the issue, likewise changed its view. In April, Deputy Mufti of Western Georgia Adam Shantadze also complained of overcrowding in Orta Jame and acknowledged the need for a new structure.⁷⁰

Nevertheless, on 5 May Batumi City Hall turned down the New Mosque Foundation's requests, citing issues with building religious structures in residential zones.⁷¹ On 26 May, one day before the beginning of Ramadan, Adjaran Muslims protested City Hall's decision by holding a symbolic "mosque opening ceremony" at the proposed construction site, which included speeches by prominent local Muslim leaders and open-air prayers. Nakaidze also noted the discriminatory nature of City Hall's decision, given that the residential zone in question contains seven churches.⁷² Supporters of a new mosque continued to conduct prayers at the site throughout the month of Ramadan.⁷³ In June, the

---

66   http://amag.ge/index.php/report/item/434-2017-12-05-10-38-40, accessed 23 December 2017.
67   The initiative group had previously collected over 12,000 signatures in support of a new mosque, http://www.apsny.ge/2017/pol/1492112070.php, accessed 13 April 2017.
68   See Liles and Balci, "Georgia", *Yearbook of Muslims in Europe*, vol. 7 (2015) and vol. 8 (2016).
69   http://www.apsny.ge/2017/pol/1492112070.php, accessed 13 April 2017.
70   http://tv25.ge/news.php?id=1538&lang=ge, accessed 13 April 2017.
71   https://emc.org.ge/2017/05/11/emc-278/, accessed 11 May 2017.
72   http://oc-media.org/batumi-muslims-convene-open-air-mosque/, accessed 8 October 2017.
73   goo.gl/MTL322, accessed 8 October 2017.

TDI and EMC jointly filed a lawsuit against Batumi City Hall on behalf of the New Mosque Foundation, citing state discrimination on religious grounds.[74]

Meanwhile, in Marneuli, independent Shi'i actors associated with *Ümum Gürcüstan Müsəlmanları Ali Dini İdarəsi* (Supreme Religious Administration of All Georgia's Moslems, hereafter ÜGMADİ)[75] and the Imam Ali mosque continued to mobilise against state policy on Muslim property. In September, the EMC filed a restitution lawsuit on behalf of the Imam Ali mosque council against the State Agency, the National Agency of State Property, and the Ministry of Economy and Sustainable Development. The mosque council and the EMC contended that the State Agency's unilateral transfer of the Imam Ali mosque to AMAG's control in 2014 violated the ownership rights of local religious organisations, as Marneuli's Shi'i community financed the restoration of the mosque in the 1990s, and the mosque council had served as its governing body since 2004.[76] The plaintiffs also argued that the State Agency's approach to minority religious property restitution since 2014 has been selective, non-systematic, and politically motivated.[77] In early October, immediately after 'Ashura' celebrations in Marneuli, members of the mosque council repeated demands for the legal transfer of Muslim religious property from AMAG's control to local religious communities.[78] On 5 December, the Tbilisi City Court held its first hearing on the case, with additional proceedings scheduled for 2018.[79]

In November, ÜGMADİ filed another lawsuit against the State Agency pertaining to transparency of expenditures. ÜGMADİ Sheikh Mirtagi Asadov had previously sent a written request to the State Agency regarding the amount of budgetary allocations to Muslim organisations registered as Legal Entities of

---

74 http://tdi.ge/ge/news/433-batumshi-mechetis-msheneblobis-nebartvaze-tdi-m-da-emc-m-sasamartlos-mimartes, accessed 1 October 2017.

75 ÜGMADİ was established in 2013 in opposition to AMAG, and claims to represent Shi'is in Kvemo-Kartli through a parallel independent sheikh.

76 The mosque council still serves as the mosque's *de facto* governing body, although the issue of formal ownership continues to be a major point of contention for many Muslims in the community: http://georgiatoday.ge/news/7937/The-Marneuli-Mosque-Dispute, accessed 25 October 2017.

77 https://emc.org.ge/2017/09/26/emc-359/, accessed 1 October 2017.

78 https://www.facebook.com/328999030888577/videos/359310754524071/, accessed 28 December 2017.

79 https://www.facebook.com/permalink.php?story_fbid=385643375224142&id=328999030888577, accessed 28 December 2017.

Public Law (LEPL),[80] although the Agency refused to release the information.[81] ÜGMADİ countered that the Agency was obliged to answer such requests given its status as a public entity. The Tbilisi City Court held the first hearing in December with further hearings scheduled for January 2018.[82] In addition to legal action against state bodies, ÜGMADİ Sheikh Mirtagi Asadov demonstrated solidarity with Adjara's Muslims on the Batumi mosque issue, and visited the open-air mosque in July.[83]

Despite the political overtones of the Batumi and Marneuli mosque issues, and widespread scepticism toward the State's approach to Islam, most Muslim organisations primarily pursued religious and educational initiatives. In particular, Shi'i organisations were very active in holding conferences on religious themes, and publicising weekly sermons by popular clerics through Facebook and portals such as *"Əhli-beyt" internet qəzeti* (Ahli-Beyt Online Newspaper). Shi'i organisations likewise staged frequent public celebrations on major holidays (e.g., 'Ashura', Tasua, Arba'een)[84] and arranged trips to holy cities in Iraq and Iran, including to Najaf and Karbala during Arba'een,[85] as well as Qom and Mashhad.[86]

Among ethnic Georgian Sunnis, the World Alliance continued its educational initiatives in Adjara, organising a summer school for religious studies in Khulo,[87] as well as seminars with Muslim high school and college students in advance of the 2017–18 academic year.[88] In addition to its coordination

---

80 A 2011 amendment to Georgia's *Civil Code* made organisations with "close religious ties to Georgia" eligible for LEPL status and, by extension, state funding. AMAG immediately gained LEPL status, with Ahli-Beyt, the Salafi-leaning Association of Muslims of Georgia, and ÜGMADİ gaining LEPL status in 2014. See Liles and Balci, "Georgia", *Yearbook of Muslims in Europe*, vol. 9 (2018), pp. 281–282.
81 goo.gl/Wg5Nam, accessed 28 December 2017.
82 https://www.facebook.com/permalink.php?story_fbid=392096157912197&id=328999030 888577, accessed 28 December 2017.
83 https://www.facebook.com/permalink.php?story_fbid=329675244154289&id=328999030 888577, accessed 28 December 2017.
84 http://ahlibeyt.ge/georgia/, accessed 28 December 2017.
85 Trip organisers included Ahli-Beyt and ÜGMADİ, with approximately 300 Shi'i participants from Georgia: http://www.ahlibeyt.ge/georgia/19274-gurcustandan-erbein-ziyaret ine-geden-zevvarlar-vetene-donubler-foto.html, accessed 27 December 2017.
86 Approximately 30 Ahli-Beyt members participated in the latter visit in May 2017: http://www.ahlibeyt.ge/georgia/16970-muqeddes-seherlere-ziyaret-turu-bas-tutudu.html, accessed 27 December 2017.
87 https://www.facebook.com/permalink.php?story_fbid=1993878940846884&id=17015713 63410978, accessed 28 December 2017.
88 https://www.facebook.com/permalink.php?story_fbid=2027112824190162&id=1701571 363410978, https://www.facebook.com/permalink.php?story_fbid=2023521951215916&id= 1701571363410978, both accessed 28 December 2017.

activities with the State Agency, AMAG was active in organising celebrations on religious holidays, including *iftar* dinners with government officials in Rustavi,[89] Lagodekhi,[90] and Marneuli[91] in June 2017.

Muslim Population: History and Demographics

Muslims account for approximately 11% of Georgia's population of 3.7 million, and consist of a diverse array of ethno-confessional groups, including ethnic Georgian Sunnis, ethnic Azeris of predominantly Shi'i orientation, and smaller groups of Sunni Kists and Avars. Islam has had a permanent presence in Georgia since the Arab conquests of the eighth century and Tbilisi's subsequent transformation into the capital of an Islamic emirate. Initially confined to urban centres, Islam spread to rural areas with the settlement of Turkic-speaking Muslim tribes in Southern and Eastern Georgia in the eleventh, 16th, and 17th centuries. Branded as "Tatars" under Russian imperial rule, and eventually Azeris/Azerbaijanis in the 20th century, these Turkic populations mainly adhered to Shi'ism due to Safavid control over Georgian territory in the 16th and 17th centuries. Meanwhile, Ottoman suzerainty led to Islamisation in Adjara and parts of Samtskhe-Javakheti in the 18th and 19th centuries, while Sufi Kists–ethnic cousins of Chechens and Ingush–migrated to Pankisi from the North Caucasus in the early 1800s. Ethnic Avars from Dagestan migrated to Kakheti's Kvareli district in the 1800s and 1950s.[92]

Statistical information on Muslim populations was taken from the 2014 population census (released 2016), which includes detailed data on ethnicity and religion by region.[93] For Muslim population by ethnic/national group, best estimates were made for Azeri and Kist shares by splitting each group's respective number against the country's total Muslim population. The same method was used to estimate ethnic Georgians' share of the Muslim population,

---

89 http://amag.ge/index.php/news/item/421-2017-06-22-21-33-09, accessed 23 December 2017.

90 http://amag.ge/index.php/news/item/422-2017-06-22-21-38-54, accessed 23 December 2017.

91 http://amag.ge/index.php/news/item/420-2017-06-22-20-46-19, accessed 23 December 2017.

92 See Sanikidze, George, and Edward W. Walker, "Islam and Islamic practices in Georgia", *Berkeley Program in Soviet and Post-Soviet Studies Working Paper Series* (Fall 2004), http://georgica.tsu.edu.ge/files/03-Society/Religion/Sanikidze&Walken-2004.pdf, accessed 24 November 2015.

93 See "Population by regions and religion" and "Total population by regions and ethnicity", http://census.ge/en/results/census, accessed 4 May 2016.

specifically by combining the total number of Muslims living in Adjara, Guria, Imereti, and Samtskhe-Javakheti.

Muslim Population	398,677 (10.74% of population, 2014).
Ethnic/National Backgrounds	Largest ethnic groups as share of Muslim population: Azeri: 58.45% (233,024) Georgian: 38.33% (ca. 152,794) Chechen-Kist: 1.43% (5,697) Other: <2%.
Inner-Islamic Groups	Georgia's Azeri population is predominantly Shi'i, with the exception of Karajala and Ponichala. Ethnic Georgian Muslims in Adjara subscribe to Hanafi Sunni Islam, as do Adjaran ecological migrants in other regions.[94] Young ethnic Kists in Pankisi adhere almost entirely to Salafism, whereas older believers largely follow the Qadiriyya Sufi order.[95] Avars in Kvareli are Sunnis of the Shafi'i *madhhab*,[96] while a small number of Sunni Meskhetian Turks reside in Southern and Western Georgia.[97]

---

94   In this context, the term ecological migrants (or "eco-migrants") refers to families from Adjara's highland districts who have been resettled in other regions of Georgia since the 1980s as a result of flooding, landslides, and avalanches in Adjara. Many eco-migrant families have retained their Muslim identity. See Lyle, Justin, "Resettlement of ecological migrants in Georgia: recent developments and trends in policy, implementation, and perceptions", *European Centre for Minority Issues Working Paper*, no. 53 (January 2012).
95   Gould, Rebecca, "Secularism and belief in Georgia's Pankisi Gorge", *Journal of Islamic Studies*, vol. 22, no. 3 (2011), p. 364.
96   Sanikidze and Walker, "Islam and Islamic practices in Georgia", p. 25.
97   Meskhetians are a Turkic Muslim subgroup that resided primarily in Georgia's Samtskhe-Javakheti region until their deportation by the Soviet government to Central Asia in 1944. A small number have been repatriated to Georgia since the end of the Soviet Union. See Menagarishvili, Irakli, Giorgi Lobjanidze, Netal Sakhokia, and Giorgi Gvimradze, "Political aspects of Islam in Georgia", *Strategic Research Institute* (2013), pp. 71–73.

Geographical Spread	Kvemo-Kartli: 45.71% (Muslims as percentage of each region's total population) Adjara: 33.32% Kakheti: 9.7% Tbilisi: 4.08% Guria: 3.25% Samtskhe-Javakheti: 1.52% Shida-Kartli: 1.42% Mtskheta-Mtianeti: 0.58% Imereti: 0.23% Samegrelo-Zemo Svaneti: 0.19%.
Number of Mosques	Previous estimates put the number of operational mosques at 200 in Adjara and 79 in Kvemo-Kartli, Shida-Kartli, and Kakheti,[98] although the total number in Eastern Georgia appears to exceed 90 as of early 2018.[99] Smaller numbers are located in Samtskhe-Javakheti and Guria. According to AMAG, there were 312 functioning mosques in Georgia as of September 2016,[100] with 40 under renovation and an additional ten under construction as of August 2017.[101]
Muslim Burial Sites	There are two Muslim cemeteries in Tbilisi, as well as numerous Muslim burial sites and shrines in Adjaran, Azeri, Kist, and Avar villages.[102] Some villages with Orthodox majorities and Muslim ecological migrant minorities lack separate burial sites for Muslims, and the prospect of allocating land for a separate cemetery arose as a point of contention in the village of

98 Liles and Balci, "Georgia", *Yearbook of Muslims in Europe*, vol. 7 (2015), p. 268.
99 http://www.ahlibeyt.ge/mescidler/, accessed 12 January 2018.
100 http://www.salamnews.org/ru/news/read/234248, accessed 2 September 2016.
101 http://salamnews.ru/ru/news/read/282589, accessed 8 October 2017.
102 Mkrtchyan, Satenik, and Ketevan Khutsishvili, "Georgia", in Jørgen S. Nielsen, Samim Akgönül, Ahmet Alibašić and Egdūnas Račius (eds.), *Yearbook of Muslims in Europe*, vol. 6 (Leiden: Brill, 2014), p. 255.

	Adigeni in 2016. Eventually the two communities agreed to share the existing cemetery.[103]
"Chaplaincy" in State Institutions	Muslim prayer rooms have operated in prisons since 2014, with prison-based religious education introduced in 2015.[104] In 2016, the Ministry of Defence opened Muslim prayer rooms at army bases in Kutaisi and Samtredia,[105] as well as the Marneuli Air Base.[106]
Halal Products	Halal food is accessible in the Muslim-populated areas of Kvemo-Kartli, Kakheti, and Tbilisi, with no apparent restrictions on halal slaughter.[107] In Adjara, Muslim charitable organisations provide halal food on Muslim holidays. Penitentiary facilities have increased access to halal products in recent years,[108] as did the army in 2016.[109] In 2017, AMAG announced the creation of a special halal commission for the purposes of halal certification and improvement in halal slaughter.[110]
Dress Code	Although there are no explicit regulations against Muslim dress, many Muslim women in Adjara have reported problems gaining or keeping employment on account of their decision to wear head scarves. Visibly Muslim women are often referred to pejoratively as "Turks" or

---

103 http://dfwatch.net/christians-and-muslims-in-adigeni-agree-to-share-cemetery-40622, accessed 2 March 2016.
104 http://m.apa.az/az/dini-xeberler/gurcustan-muselmanlari-idaresinin-illik-hesabat-konfransi-kecirilib, accessed 5 May 2018.
105 http://www.rferl.org/a/georgia-first-mosque-armed-forces/27593944.html, accessed 7 March 2016; http://amag.ge/index.php/news/item/245-2016-03-15-12-43-56, accessed 15 March 2016.
106 goo.gl/fMJQzQ, accessed 10 January 2018.
107 Fieldwork trip to Marneuli, Karajala, and Pankisi, January 2016.
108 Telephone interview with Ruslan Baramidze, February 2016.
109 http://www.eurasianet.org/node/77621, accessed 1 March 2016.
110 http://amag.ge/index.php/news/item/394-halal, accessed 4 July 2017.

	"Tatars" in everyday public settings.[111] The head scarf issue has become especially divisive in public schools in recent years, as underlined by incidents in Adigeni and Karajala.
Places of Islamic Learning and Education	Two prominent Shi'i madrasas operate in Marneuli, while Alul-Bayt operates a madrasa in Tbilisi's Ortachala neighbourhood. A number of smaller madrasas also operate in Gardabani District (Kvemo-Kartli). There are approximately 80 madrasas of varying size and activeness in Adjara.[112] In Pankisi, a Salafi madrasa operates with transnational funding.[113] Tbilisi's Juma Mosque has a madrasa attached,[114] while the official Muftiate in Batumi began weekly seminars on Islam for students in 2016.[115]
Muslim Media and Publications	– Amag.ge (Official site of Administration of All Georgia, AMAG) – *Əhli-beyt" internet qəzeti*, http://www.ahlibeyt.ge/ (Ahli-Beyt online newspaper) – Muslims of Georgia *Gündəlik İnternet Qəzet*, www.mgeo.com (news portal with links to Imam Ali Charitable Foundation and ÜGMADİ)

Main Muslim Organisations

– Administration of Muslims of All Georgia (სრულიად საქართველოს მუსლიმთა სამმართველო, *Bütün Gürcüstan Musəlmanları İdarəsi*– AMAG, 23 Esma Oniani Street, Tbilisi, tel.: +995 32531630, www.amag.ge/

---

111 See Popovaite, Inga, "Religious and national aspects of Georgian Muslim women's identity in the autonomous Republic of Adjara", *CEU Nationalism Studies Program* (2014), pp. 63–64.
112 Liles and Balci, "Georgia", *Yearbook of Muslims in Europe*, vol. 7 (2015), p. 269.
113 http://dfwatch.net/pankisi-youth-choose-radical-islam-over-grim-reality-94931-32304, accessed 21 November 2014.
114 Mkrtchyan and Khutsishvili, "Georgia", p. 255.
115 http://amag.ge/index.php/news/item/242-2016-03-12-10-49-02, accessed 3 January 2017.

www.bgmi.ge). AMAG was established in 2011 and is the main recipient of state funding for Islam. It is subdivided along ethno-sectarian lines, with three branches representing, respectively, Sunni Adjarans; Shi'i Azeris; and Sunni Azeris, Kists, and Avars in Eastern Georgia.

- Ahli-Beyt (*Əhli-Beyt*, Marneuli, email: ahlibeyt.ge@mail.ru, www.ahlibeyt.ge). Ahli-Beyt is an independent, Marneuli based Shi'i organisation, which runs a madrasa and arranges other educational initiatives. It organises religious celebrations and reports on religious and global events through an associated media arm.
- Alul-Bayt (10 Bezhan Kalandadze Street, Tbilisi). Established in 2005 with funding from Grand Ayatollah Ali Al-Sistani, Alul-Bayt provides religious and secular education for Azeri students. The organisation runs a small madrasa in Tbilisi, and often hosts religious events in an attached conference hall.
- Georgian Muslims Union (არტველ მუსლიმთა კავშირი–GMU, Batumi, email: info@islam.ge, www.islam.ge). Batumi-based GMU advocates for Muslim rights and better interfaith relations, and often criticises state policies on religion.
- Supreme Religious Administration of All Muslims of Georgia (*Ümum Gürcüstan Müsəlmanları Ali Dini İdarəsi*, სრულიად საქართველოს მუსლიმთა უმაღლესი სასულიერო სამმართველო–ÜGMADİ, www.mgeo.ge). Established in 2013 in opposition to AMAG, ÜGMADİ is critical of state initiatives and appointed a parallel, independent sheikh.
- World Alliance of Georgian Muslims (მსოფლიო ქართველ მუსლიმთა კავშირი, Batumi, https://goo.gl/oJCnTS). The Batumi-based World Alliance was established in 2015 and focuses mainly on spiritual and educational initiatives, as well as strengthening relations with Turkey's Georgian diaspora.

Germany

Mathias Rohe[1]

Introduction

In 2017, two major developments and trends regarding the Muslim population and public debates on Islam can be discerned. First, the ongoing conflict between the Turkish and German governments affected Muslims of a Turkish background living in Germany. This was due to illegal interventions by the Turkish secret service, with its abuse of religious organisations for political propaganda and for espionage. Second, the outspoken Islamophobic and anti-refugee party Alternative for Germany (*Alternative für Deutschland*–AfD) achieved remarkable success in the federal election in September, obtaining 94 out of 709 seats in Parliament, winning 12.6% of the votes (compared to 4.7% in 2013). Indeed, in the state of Saxonia, where there is a strong anti-Muslim movement,[2] the AfD became the largest party. After years of continuous successes in previous state elections, the ultimate rise of this party at the federal level had a strong impact on political debates about Muslims. Among centre-right political parties and actors, several tendencies became visible; they aimed to gain voters back by criticising "political Islam" and targeting the small number of women wearing a niqab (face veil) in public.

In general, the immigration of a large number of Muslim refugees and migrants since 2015 (approximately 1 million) has triggered widespread fear and led to broad and emotional debates on home and identity. As a result, according to representative polls from December 2017, while Church affiliation among Christians continues to decrease, the desire to stress the "Christian culture" of the country through public symbols is increasing.[3]

---

1 Mathias Rohe studied Law and Islamic Studies. He holds the Chair for Civil Law, Private International Law and Comparative Law at the University of Erlangen-Nuremberg, and is the founding director of the Erlangen Centre for Islam and Law in Europe. He has been a judge at the Court of Appeals of Nuremberg and participated in the *Deutsche Islamkonferenz* (German Islam Conference) from 2006 to 2017.
2 On PEGIDA in Dresden, see Rohe, Mathias, "Germany", in Oliver Scharbrodt, Samim Akgönül, Ahmet Alibašić, Jørgen S. Nielsen and Egdūnas Račius (eds.), *Yearbook of Muslims in Europe*, vol. 8 (Leiden: Brill, 2016), p. 306; Rohe, Mathias, "Germany", in Oliver Scharbrodt, Samim Akgönül, Ahmet Alibašić, Jørgen S. Nielsen and Egdūnas Račius (eds.), *Yearbook of Muslims in Europe*, vol. 9, (Leiden: Brill, 2017), p. 294.
3 See the results of representative polls in December 2017, published in *Frankfurter Allgemeine Zeitung* 20 December 2017, p. 10.

Public Debates

In 2017, the debate on Islam, and news relating to Muslims, still took place, to a large extent, under the shadow of the terrorist attacks that occurred in several parts of Europe and beyond. New legal instruments for security authorities were discussed, and were to a large extent based on the intention to efficiently combat Muslim violent extremism.

The number of attacks on Muslims has also continued at a high level. The first statistics on anti-Muslim crimes in 2017 show that at least 950 incidents (assaults on Muslims, attacks on mosques, insults, etc.) occurred in 2017; 33 persons were injured.[4] Detailed information about anti-Muslim hate crimes during the first three months of 2017 is provided by the Federal Government.[5]

Debates on Islam were still focused on, and mixed with, the debate on the huge number of refugees and migrants entering the country, since September 2015 in particular. Yet, there is a continuing broad acceptance of refugees both by the German authorities and within politics and society as a whole; scores of volunteers are engaged in all kinds of support. At the same time, anti-Muslim forces also continued their activities, particularly in Eastern Germany, such as PEGIDA in Dresden, and the "Identitarians" (*Identitäre*) and right-wing think tanks, like the Institute for Statemanship (*Institut für Staatspolitik*) in Rittergut Schnellroda in Saxony-Anhalt.[6]

Nevertheless, these tensions in the public debate seemingly had little impact on one important aspect of Muslim daily life: the labour market. According to representative data (not including those refugees and migrants that have recently arrived), the employment status of Muslims does not significantly differ from the rest of the population. Both groups are at 60% in full-time employment, 21% and 20% respectively in part-time employment, 14% in no employment (by choice), and both are at 5% unemployed.[7]

---

4 "Innenministerium zählt 2017 mindestens 950 islamfeindliche Straftaten", *Tagesspiegel*, 3 March 2018, https://www.tagesspiegel.de/politik/islamophobie-in-deutschland-innenministerium-zaehlt-2017-mindestens-950-islamfeindliche-straftaten/21028412.html, accessed 20 May 2018.

5 See the answer of the Federal Ministry of the Interior to a parliamentary request dated 26 May 2017, available at https://www.ulla-jelpke.de/wp-content/uploads/2017/06/KA-18_12319-Antimusmlimische-Straftaten-Q-I-2017.pdf, accessed 20 May 2018.

6 Rohe, "Germany", *Yearbook of Muslims in Europe*, vol. 8, pp. 306–308; "Rechtes vom Rittergut", *Die Zeit*, 28 February 2017, https://www.zeit.de/gesellschaft/2017-02/schnellroda-sachsen-anhalt-afd-goetz-kubitschek, accessed 6 June 2018.

7 Halm, Dirk, and Martina Sauer, *Muslime in Europa – Integriert aber nicht akzeptiert. Bertelsmann Stiftung Religionsmonitor, 2017* (Gütersloh: Bertelsmann Stiftung, 2017, p. 30, https://www

Transnational Links

A considerable number of the German Muslim population has a "migration background", mainly due to labour immigration in the 1960s and early 1970s from Turkey and the Balkans, and the immigration of their family members. There have also been a large number of asylum seekers from Muslim majority countries since then. Thus, many Muslim organisations still have a mixed character, being religious as well as ethnically oriented. Over the course of time though, and with a new generation in charge of their leadership, the religious element is increasingly prevailing over the ethnic one. Still, most of the ca. 2,600 mosques in Germany are called Turkish, Albanian, Arab, etc., and only the increasing Salafi movement seems to easily reach out to a German speaking youth beyond ethnic categories.

During the period of mass immigration of predominantly Arab Muslim refugees since 2015, Arab mosques and organisations have gained more influence in public space and within Muslim communities. Turkish dominated organisations like the DITIB reacted by offering their services to an Arabic speaking public, and by engaging in support projects for refugees and migrants, funded by German authorities.[8]

The strongest political and ethnic links still exist between Muslims of Turkish origin and the Turkish Republic. There are close personal and financial links between the Turkish religious authority via the Presidency of Religious Affairs (*Diyanet İşleri Başkanlığı*) and its German branch the DITIB (*Diyanet Işleri Türk İslam Birliği, Türkisch-Islamische Union der Anstalt für Religion*– Turkish-Islamic Union of the Institution for Religious Affairs), which is by far the largest organisation, running around 900 mosques all over the country. Other organisations maintain links to the countries of their ethnic background, or to organisations sharing their ideological preferences.

For a long time, the DITIB and the Turkish religious administration–the Diyanet, which has a strong influence on the former[9]–were perceived by many German politicians and governments to be a reliable "moderate" cooperative partner in various fields. This view has fundamentally changed in the aftermath of the coup attempt in Turkey on 15 July 2016. The Turkish government

---

.bertelsmann-stiftung.de/fileadmin/files/BSt/Publikationen/GrauePublikationen/Studie_LW_Religionsmonitor-2017_Muslime-in-Europa.pdf, accessed 18 February 2018.
8 Information given to the author by several representatives of such organisations.
9 The Diyanet pays the salaries for the imams sent to German DITIB mosques. In addition, the statutes of the DITIB grant Diyanet representatives a remarkably strong position. For details see, for example, Yaşar, Aysun, *Die DITIB zwischen der Türkei und Deutschland* (Würzburg: Ergon, 2012).

blamed the Gülen movement for the coup, and now considers it to be a terrorist group, using the designation "FETÖ" to refer to it.[10] It persecutes all actual and alleged members of the movement as severely as possible, even though no reliable evidence has been presented so far to prove the Turkish government's allegations towards the movement, according to German security services.[11]

The Diyanet has also asked imams working in DITIB mosques abroad to collect information about the members and institutions of the Gülen movement. The request was distributed by three Turkish consulates in Düsseldorf, Cologne and Munich, and 19 imams allegedly responded. In December 2017, inquiries by the Federal Attorney General, that started in February in 2017, were terminated without filing charges. In seven of these cases, this was due to the fact that the imams had already left the country, in five cases it was because the allegations turned out to be only minor violations of the Law, and in another seven cases it was because no indications of criminal offences were provided.[12] Similar activities by the Turkish secret security forces were reported and continue to take place. The Federal Attorney General started eleven inquiries against members of the Turkish secret service in 2017; thus 19 inquiries are now pending altogether, which is an increase of 300% compared to the last five years.[13] The polarisation within the Turkish community is still strong, and aggressive nationalism is strongly supported by the Turkish authorities and the media under their control.

The tension and distrust between the Turkish government and many German politicians, and much of society towards the DITIB, increased in 2017, due to the potential influence of a more authoritarian Turkish government, and its very strong links to the Diyanet. Several (although not all) cooperation projects with the DITIB were stopped or suspended. The many volunteers working within the organisation are deeply disappointed about these developments, and debates focused on a fundamental restructuring of the organisation have emerged, although with little success up till now. Also, the board of the youth organisation of the DITIB collectively stepped down in early 2017, after the very liberal and active board of a central mosque in Berlin was replaced by a much

---

10   This stands for *Fethullahçı Terör Örgütü* ("Gülenist terror organisation").
11   "Türkische Spionage ist ein Fall für die Justiz", *Tagesspiegel*, 28 March 2017, https://www.tagesspiegel.de/politik/bespitzelung-von-guelen-anhaengern-tuerkische-spionage-ist-ein-fall-fuer-die-justiz/19579348.html, accessed 6 June 2018.
12   "Spionageermittlungen eingestellt", *Frankfurter Allgemeine Zeitung*, 7 December 2017, p. 4.
13   "Zahl der Verfahren gegen türkische Spione verdreifacht", *Stuttgarter Nachrichten*, 26 October 2017, https://www.stuttgarter-nachrichten.de/inhalt.tuerkischer-geheimdienst-in-deutschland-zahl-der-verfahren-gegen-tuerkische-spione-verdreifacht.b77d8754-a439-421b-8fee-de2c82c00d3b.html, accessed 20 May 2018.

more conservative one, seemingly following pressure from the Turkish General Consulate. The election of a new board at the federal level of the DITIB, was also disappointing for those who hoped for significantly more influence from domestic representatives, since the dominance of Turkish state officials continued, to the detriment of Germany-based volunteers.[14]

Law and Domestic Politics

Legal debates on banning religious dress in state institutions intensified in 2017 in several states, such as in Lower Saxony, where the new Law of 16 August 2017 bans the wearing of the niqab in public schools.[15] In Bavaria, according to the Law of 6 August 2017,[16] wearing a niqab is, or can be, forbidden in several public spaces, such as for state officers and employees, in public schools, nurseries and universities. At the federal level, a law dating from 8 July 2017[17] forbids the wearing of the niqab by federal state officers and soldiers during service, and demands its removal in situations where the identity of a person has to be proven.

A number of court decisions dealt with the scope and limits of religious freedom claimed by Muslim parties.[18] The Federal Constitutional Court upheld the ban on head scarves for postgraduates in legal training in courts, in an interlocutory decision due to the particular necessities of granting neutrality in courtrooms.[19] Yet, a judge sitting in family cases was held to be prejudiced because he prevented a wife from taking part in divorce procedures because

---

14 "DITIB Jugendverband schmeißt hin", *dtj*, 12 May 2017, https://dtj-online.de/ditib-jugend-bdmj-ruecktritt-83748, accessed 20 May 2018.
15 Para. 58 sect. 2 of the *Gesetz zur Verankerung der Pflichten von Schülerinnen und Schülern im Niedersächsischen Schulgesetz*, http://aktuell.schure.de/index.php/nieders-schulgesetz/45-kopftuchgesetz, accessed 20 May 2018.
16 *Gesetz über Verbote der Gesichtsverhüllung*, Bayerischer Landtag Drucksache 17/17603.
17 *Gesetz zu bereichsspezifischen Regelungen der Gesichtsverhüllung und zur Änderung weiterer dienstrechtlicher Vorschriften*, Bundesgesetzblatt 2017 I, no. 36, p. 1570.
18 For the general legal framework in Germany, see Rohe, Mathias, "Germany", in Jørgen S. Nielsen, Samim Akgönül, Ahmet Alibašić and Egdūnas Račius (eds.), *Yearbook of Muslims in Europe*, vol. 6 (Leiden: Brill, 2016), pp. 263–266; for details see Rohe, Mathias, *Der Islam in Deutschland–eine Bestandsaufnahme* (Munich: C.H. Beck, 2016), pp. 175–202.
19 Federal Constitutional Court decision of 27 June 2017, NJW 2017, pp. 2333–2337.

she wore her head scarf.[20] Also, at Würzburg University, a (female) professor had to apologise to a Muslim student whom she had previously instructed to remove her head scarf in her lectures.[21]

In November 2017, the Administrative Court of Appeals of North Rhine-Westphalia[22] rejected the claim of two Muslim organisations–*Zentralrat der Muslime in Deutschland* (Central Council of Muslims in Germany) and *Islamrat für die Bundesrepublik Deutschland* (Islam Council of the Federal Republic of Germany)–to implement Islamic religious education in state public schools, as part of the cooperation model provided by Art. 7 sect. 3 of the German constitution; procedures had been pending for years on this topic. The court rejected the claim for two reasons mainly. First, the court held that the two umbrella organisations did not hold the necessary extent of the religious authority within the various associations they are comprised of. Second, the two umbrella organisations lacked the ability to engage in identity-creating religious activities, which would have been necessary for recognising them as religious associations in the constitutional sense. The Court's judgment was criticised by some organisations,[23] but others remarked that the preparation for the proceedings by the claimants was not sufficiently professional. Since then, the state of North Rhine-Westphalia has been seeking solutions for continuing the current model of Islamic religious education in schools, in cooperation with several Muslim organisations that have been brought together to form an advisory council. The current model will legally come to an end in 2019.

German jurisprudence on the scope and limits of wearing religious dress in public spaces and within state institutions, differs considerably from the much more restrictive approach of the current jurisprudence of the European Court

---

20 "Richter nach Kopftuch-Verbot wegen Befangenheit abgelehnt", *Süddeutsche Zeitung*, 23 August 2017, http://www.sueddeutsche.de/news/panorama/prozesse---luckenwalde-richter-nach-kopftuch-verbot-wegen-befangenheit-abgelehnt-dpa.urn-newsml-dpa-com-20090101-170823-99-751344, accessed 20 May 2018.

21 "Kopftuch-Streit: Professorin entschuldigt sich bei Muslima", *Süddeutsche Zeitung*, 1 November 2017, http://www.sueddeutsche.de/bayern/wuerzburg-kopftuch-streit-professorin-entschuldigt-sich-bei-muslima-1.3730961, accessed 20 May 2018. Wearing head scarves cannot be forbidden in German schools and universities.

22 Judgment dated 9 November 2017 (19 A 997/02), http://www.justiz.nrw.de/nrwe/ovgs/ovg_nrw/j2017/19_A_997_02_Urteil_20171109.html, accessed 19 May 2018.

23 See the statement of the Coordination Council of Muslims dated 13 November 2017, http://islam.de/files/pdf/u/KRM_PM_OVGUrteil13112017.pdf, accessed 19 May 2018.

of Human Rights (ECtHR)[24] and the European Court of Justice (ECJ).[25] Yet, Muslim dress is rejected by large parts of the population.[26]

The issue of marriages with minors and their recognition in Germany, led to federal legislation banning such recognition across the country. The issue arose in the context of the mass immigration of mostly Muslim refugees since 2015. According to governmental research, some 1,475 married minors (mostly female) lived in Germany in 2016, 361 of them under the age of 14.[27] In reaction to this, the legal exception for marriage in Germany under the age of 18 was abolished and marriages concluded abroad are taken to be void if one of the spouses was under 16. There is no exception given even if the spouses continued living together without knowledge of the German legal system, something that was heavily criticised by nearly all experts involved in the legislative procedure.[28] For minors between the ages of 16 and 18, the marriage is void and has to be brought into a respective legal procedure by the German authorities, except in cases of undue hardship. The debate in Parliament and in the media was extremely polarised; thus, experts who supported the protection of minors, by looking at particular cases, had little opportunity to make their voices heard. The resulting new legislation appears to have been enacted due to public pressure, and does not promise the protection of those in need of it.

Within private legal cases, the German courts and authorities have to apply Islamic norms (as formulated in the laws of Muslim majority countries) according to the rules of private international law (PIL), within the limits set by "public order" (*ordre public international*).[29] The Court of Appeals of Frankfurt am Main, in an Iranian case, held that stipulations in marriage contracts on the payment of dower to the wife do not generally violate German public order. In the case, it was decided that the husband had to pay 600 gold coins *bahare*

---

24 See the decision in Ebrahimian vs. France, ECtHR 26 November 2015 (*64846/11*), http://hudoc.echr.coe.int/eng#{%22itemid%22:[%22001-158878%22]}, accessed 4 May 2018.

25 Decisions of Achbita and Bougnaoui of 14 March 2017 (*C 157/15* and *C 188/15*), http://eur-lex.europa.eu/legal-content/EN/TXT/?uri=CELEX:62015CJ0157; http://curia.europa.eu/juris/document/document.jsf?text=&docid=188853&pageIndex=0&doclang=EN&mode=lst&dir=&occ=first&part=1&cid=1350298, both accessed 4 May 2018.

26 See, for example, the result of representative polls in 2016: 51% supported the ban of head scarves in schools; see "Kopftuch-Verbot", *Focus online*, 2 May 2016, https://www.focus.de/politik/videos/kopftuch-verbot-umfrage-zeigt-jeder-zweite-deutsche-ist-gegen-kopftuecher-an-schulen_id_5490206.html, accessed 7 June 2018.

27 Data provided in *Bundestags-Drucksache* (*Proceedings of the Federal Parliament*), 18/12086, p. 14.

28 Including the author. For the debate see Rohe, Mathias, "Die rechtliche Behandlung von Minderjährigenehen in Deutschland", *Das Standesamt, StAZ* (2018), pp. 73–79.

29 Rohe, Mathias, *Islamic Law in Past and Present* (Leiden-Boston: Brill, 2015), pp. 468–469.

azadi.[30] While Iranian family law is not gender-neutral, the court held that the examination of violations of public order has to be evaluated on a case-by-case basis, not by simply assessing it on the basis of the applicable foreign law.[31] As a consequence, while a foreign norm might be incompatible with the principle of a domestic law, the outcome of its application in a particular case might still be acceptable.[32] This kind of approach is still prevalent in German courts.[33]

Regarding domestic labour law, the Labour Court of Mannheim held that the contract of a Muslim nurse (a Lithuanian convert to Islam) could be terminated after she had refused to partake in bodily care for male patients.[34]

Some other administrative and court procedures and decisions were aimed at preventing and punishing extremist Muslim and anti-Muslim activities. The ban of the association *Die wahre Religion* (The true religion) and its *Lies*-campaign ("Read")[35] became final after its former chair, Abou-Nagie, withdrew his claim in the Federal Constitutional Court.[36] An 18 year old supporter of ISIS was sentenced to eight years imprisonment for attempted murder in seven cases, after throwing Molotov-cocktails into a shopping centre. His 15 year old sister had already been sentenced for stabbing a policeman in a railway station.[37]

A nurse was sentenced to a payment of 70 daily rates,[38] inter alia, for the violation of para. 166 sect. 2 of the *German Criminal Code*; this regards the defamation of religions, and religious and ideological associations. This norm is rarely applied due to a broad understanding of freedom of speech in Germany, but in

---

30 The standard gold coin struck in the Islamic Republic of Iran.
31 Court of Appeals Frankfurt am Main, decision of 5 August 2016, NJW 2017, 896–898.
32 For further details see Rohe, *Islamic Law*, pp. 470–475.
33 See Rohe, Mathias, "Marriage in Islam and its treatment under European Laws", in University of Braga, *Código Civil des 1966* (Braga: Universidade do Minho, 2017), pp. 249–276.
34 "Pflegerin wollte keine Männer waschen: Kündigung rechtens", *Südwestpresse*, 20 March 2017, https://www.swp.de/suedwesten/landespolitik/pflegerin-wollte-keine-maenner-waschen_-kuendigung-rechtens-23397759.html, accessed 20 May 2018.
35 See Rohe, "Germany", *Yearbook of Muslims in Europe*, vol. 9, p. 302.
36 "Salafismus: Verbot der 'Koran-Verteiler' ist endgültig–Abou-Nagie zieht Klage zurück", *Kölner Stadtanzeiger*, 19 December 2017, https://www.ksta.de/nrw/salafismus-verbot-der--koran-verteiler--ist-endgueltig---abou-nagie-zieht-klage-zurueck-29322482, accessed 20 May 2018.
37 "IS-sympathisant muss für Mordversuch ins Gefängnis", *Nürnberger Nachrichten*, 9 June 2017, p. 4.
38 The daily rate amount is dependent on income (i.e. 30 rates is the entire income, excluding the minimum amount for living expenses).

this case the court determined that an offence took place, since the culprit had published a picture of a dog defecating on the Kaaba.[39]

The establishment of Islamic religious education in public schools and the introduction of Islamic confessional theology in universities, continued. In Lower Saxony, training for teachers of Islamic religious education in secondary schools, was implemented; this has already been introduced in North Rhine-Westphalia and Baden-Württemberg.[40] A new academic organisation, bringing together the representatives of Islamic theology in German universities (*Akademie für Islam in Wissenschaft und Gesellschaft*–AIWG: Academy for Islam in Scholarship and Society) was founded. This was set up to enable Muslim scholars to develop academic standards for Islamic theology and to start research in this field, which could be relevant for Muslim practitioners and society as a whole. It is funded by the federal government and the Mercator Foundation.[41]

Cooperation between German states (*Bundesländer*) and municipalities and Muslim organisations continued in 2017, but suffered a serious setback with the controversy surrounding the largest organisation, the DITIB, as a result of the repercussions of the failed coup attempt in Turkey. In the state of Hesse, the DITIB is recognised as a partner for Islamic religious education in public schools. Due to intense public pressure, the Ministry of Education commissioned three experts to evaluate whether this cooperation should continue. Aside from technical matters, the core question was whether the Hessian state branch of the DITIB was independent from the political influence of the Turkish government, this being a prerequisite for its recognition as a *religious* organisation.[42] The evaluation of the performance of Islamic religious education in Hesse was very positive, nevertheless, this was in part due to the fact that the Government was ready to fill some organisational gaps during the period of its implementation. The studies revealed several difficulties typical of Muslim organisations, regarding the registration of members–which is legally necessary, but a novel concept for many Muslims–and weaknesses

---

39 Local Court Munich, judgment of 19 April 2017 (841 Cs 113 Js 172972/16) (unpublished).
40 "Islam-Unterricht an Gymnasien", *NWZ*, 10 July 2017, https://www.nwzonline.de/schule/islam-unterricht-an-gymnasien_a_31,3,1943684977.html, accessed 20 May 2018.
41 https://aiwg.de/, accessed 6 June 2018.
42 The three expert opinions were given by Günther Seufert (regarding the role of the Diyanet and its relations to the DITIB), by the author (regarding the organisational side of the DITIB in Germany and their activities in Hesse), and by Josef Isensee (on the basis of these two opinions for a legal evaluation under German administrative and constitutional law). Their evaluations are available at https://kultusministerium.hessen.de/presse/pressemitteilung/ditib-hessen-als-kooperationspartner-fuer-bekenntnisorientierten-islamischen-religionsunterricht-0, accessed 20 May 2018.

due to very limited personnel and financial resources. No evidence was found with respect to political influence by Turkey, or undue political activities by the organisation itself. Nevertheless, relevant statutory regulations secure the organisation's strong ties with the Turkish authorities via the federal umbrella organisation; thus Turkish authorities could intervene at any time. In addition, imams working at the local and regional level, are still directly affiliated to the Diyanet, and are thus governed not by the DİTİB, but by Turkish diplomatic agencies in Germany. Thus, pursuant to the recommendations given by the experts, the state government required that the state branch of the DİTİB fill its organisational gaps, and negotiate more institutional independence from the Turkish authorities to ensure a purely religious character for the organisation by the end of 2018. A number of municipalities stopped their long lasting cooperation with local DİTİB branches, due to a general suspicion of their activity, in spite of trusting relationships at the local level in the past.

Activities and Initiatives of Main Muslim Organisations

Shi'i communities are increasingly participating in German public life, and cooperating in projects with the State, such as with the establishment of Islamic theological studies courses in the state of Berlin.[43] The Alevi community also established a programme to educate Alevi ministers and volunteers in spiritual care activities in hospitals and prisons. It will begin in the state of North Rhine-Westphalia, and includes modules on Alevi spiritual care in Germany, intercultural communication, professional cooperation and supervision, and conflict management in clinics, hospices and prisons.[44]

The *Junge Islam Konferenz* (Young Islam Conference) continued and broadened its activities in 2017.[45] Besides organising public lectures and conferences,

---

43 "Das Islam-Institut gehört zu Berlin", *Tagesspiegel*, 16 May 2018, https://www.tagesspiegel.de/politik/islamische-theologie-an-der-humboldt-universitaet-das-islam-institut-gehoert-zu-berlin/21894906.html, accessed 7 June 2018. For developments see Langer, Robert, and Benjamin Weineck, "Shiite 'communities of practice' in Germany", *Journal of Muslims in Europe*, vol. 6 (2017), pp. 216–240 with further references.

44 "Die Alevitische Gemeinde Deutschland bildet Geistliche in der Seelsorge aus", *Alevilerin Sesi*, December 2017, p. 30.

45 "Junge Islamkonferenz in Bonn will Zusammenleben verbessern", *Generalanzeiger Bonn*, 20 November 2017, http://www.general-anzeiger-bonn.de/bonn/stadt-bonn/Junge-Islamkonferenz-in-Bonn-will-Zusammenleben-verbessern-article3705336.html, accessed 20 May 2018; cf. https://www.junge-islam-konferenz.de/, accessed 7 June 2018.

it provides a platform for exchange of information and ideas, and supports and coordinates local and regional activities.[46]

Many public activities and declarations by Muslim organisations were aimed at combating extremism, and expressing solidarity with society as a whole.[47] Many Muslim organisations continued their *iftar* invitations, with an overwhelming reaction, particularly among the large numbers of refugees and migrants, who were also provided with copies of the Qur'an, prayer carpets and goods for their daily needs. Some organisations send out *iftar* invitations to foreign embassies or institutions.[48]

Major Muslim organisations continued to support refugees and migrants. According to some reports, mosques were even overburdened by the number of tasks they had to undertake, and by the needs of refugees and migrants.[49] Many mosques use the national holiday of 3 October (Unification Day) as a "day of the open mosque" (*Tag der offenen Moschee*), inviting the public to visit mosques and to gain information about Islam.

An already broad range of dialogue initiatives continued and widened; for instance, the Federal Minister of the Interior agreed to continue meetings with representatives of Muslim and migrant organisations, due to the current wave of prejudice, fear and assaults. As a result of these meetings, police statistics have included "anti-Muslim hate crimes" (*islamfeindliche Straftaten*) as a particular sub-category of political offenses since 2017.[50]

Muslim Population: History and Demographics

The presence of considerable numbers of Muslims in Germany is still a relatively new phenomenon, compared to the UK or France.[51] Since the 1960s, thousands of so-called *Gastarbeiter* ("guest workers") were attracted to Germany

---

46   See the information on the website https://www.junge-islam-konferenz.de/, accessed 7 June 2018.
47   See the declaration of Muslim theologians at Frankfurt University (ZEFIS) on 12 January 2015: www. http://www.uni-frankfurt.de/53652821, accessed 4 May 2018.
48   See, for example, "Aus Premiere wurde Tradition", *islam.de*, 14 June 2017, http://islam.de/28919, accessed 4 May 2018, on the *iftar* jointly organised by the Central Council of Muslims in Germany (ZMD) and the embassy of the United Arab Emirates in Berlin.
49   "Überforderte Moscheen", *qantara.de*, 8 August 2016, https://de.qantara.de/inhalt/fluechtlinge-in-deutschland-ueberforderte-moscheen, accessed 4 May 2018.
50   "Gemeinsam gegen Islamfeindlichkeit", *IslamiQ*, 15 October 2016, http://www.islamiq.de/2016/10/25/gemeinsam-fuer-einen-gesellschaftlichen-zusammenhalt/, accessed 4 May 2018.
51   For details see Rohe, *Der Islam in Deutschland*, pp. 59–74.

for work; most were Turkish nationals, followed by people from the Balkan region (mainly Yugoslavia and Albania). There was also continuous immigration of often well-educated people from the Middle East and beyond (mainly from Syria, Lebanon, Iran and Afghanistan), but these were limited in number. A third motivation for Muslim immigration was the search for asylum. Their countries of origin are mainly to be found in the Middle East, followed by South and Central Asia. Since 2015, approximately 1 million Muslim asylum seekers have arrived in Germany, but no precise statistical data is available on this group so far. As well as this, there are also Muslim business people, students and academics living in Germany for a short or long period. At first, the "guest workers" themselves, and the German authorities, did not expect their presence in the country to be long-lasting, but it has become clear since the 1970s that large numbers of Muslims have become part of German society, and increasingly have become German citizens as well.

Up to now, the best source for demographic and statistical information on Germany's Muslim population is the study *Muslim Life in Germany: a Study Conducted on Behalf of the German Conference on Islam*, by the Federal Office for Migration and Refugees (*Bundesamt für Migration und Flüchtlinge*–BAMF), produced in June 2009,[52] and its amended version based on the census of 2011. There is also more recent data published by the same institution in 2016.[53] The 2016 study only covers the number of Muslims and their regional backgrounds. The data given below regarding these two issues are taken from this latest study, while other data is based on the earlier studies. Due to the very large numbers of refugees and migrants that came into the country in 2015 and 2016, the ratio of Muslims of Turkish origin has dropped, from approximately two thirds to half of the overall Muslim population in Germany, while the number of Muslims from the Middle East has doubled (now close to 20%). The number of German converts to Islam is unknown. According to a special study concerning refugees, published in 2016 by the BAMF, only 50% of native Iranians living in Germany identify themselves as Muslims; among Iranian refugees it was less than 20%, compared to more than 20% who identified themselves as non-religious and more than 50% who identified themselves as Christians.[54]

---

52 https://www.bamf.de/SharedDocs/Anlagen/EN/Publikationen/Forschungsberichte/fb06-muslimisches-leben.pdf;jsessionid=0973F04A752E9254DE91DFD5FB3CE7E8.1_cid359?__blob=publicationFile, accessed 4 May 2018.

53 https://www.bamf.de/SharedDocs/Anlagen/DE/Publikationen/WorkingPapers/wp71-zahl-muslime-deutschland.pdf?__blob=publicationFile, accessed 4 May 2018.

54 https://www.bamf.de/SharedDocs/Anlagen/DE/Publikationen/Forschungsberichte/fb28-fluechtlingsstudie-2014.pdf?__blob=publicationFile, pp. 206–208, accessed 4 May 2018.

Thus, figures derived from a person's nationality alone are not very reliable for determining the actual number of Muslims.

Muslim Population	4.4–4.7 million (5.4–5.7% of the total population in 2015).
Ethnic/National Backgrounds	45% of Muslims in Germany are German citizens (mostly by naturalisation and including an unknown number of converts).
	Largest ethnic/national groups: Turkish: 50.6% Southeast European: 11.5% Middle Eastern: 17.1% North African: 5.8% South/Southeast Asian: 8.2% Iranian: 1.9% Sub-Sahara African: 2.5% Central Asian/CIS: 2.4%.
Inner-Islamic Groups	Sunnis: 74.1% Alevis: 12.7% Shi'is: 7.1% Ahmadis: 1.7% Ibadis: 0.3% Sufis: 0.1% Others: 4.0%.
Geographical Spread	Baden-Württemberg: 16.6% Bavaria: 13.2% Berlin: 6.9% Brandenburg: 0.1% Bremen: 1.6% Hamburg: 3.5% Hesse: 10.3% Lower Saxony: 6.2% Mecklenburg-Western Pomerania: 0.1% North Rhine-Westphalia: 33.1% Rhineland-Palatinate: 4.0% Saarland: 0.8%

	Saxony: 0.7% Saxony-Anhalt: 0.4% Schleswig-Holstein: 2.1% Thuringia: 0.2%.
Number of Mosques	About 2,350 (including Alevi *cem* houses), 2,179 of them have an imam (or *dede* for Alevis).
Muslim Burial Sites	In an increasing numbers of cities and villages, Muslim burial sites–in nearly all cases parts of municipal cemeteries–are to be found across Germany. In 2008, their number was ca. 200, according to the *Museum für Sepulkralkultur* in Kassel. The oldest is the Turkish Cemetery at the Columbiadamm in Berlin-Neukölln, founded in 1866.
"Chaplaincy" in State Institutions	Chaplaincy in state institutions is run in cooperation between the State and recognised religious communities, which fulfil the necessary organisational conditions. No Muslim organisation has achieved this status so far. Until now, there are mostly provisional solutions on a local level, particularly in hospitals and prisons. The state of Lower Saxony signed an agreement with three major organisations in December 2012[55] to create a stable framework of cooperation regarding chaplaincy in prisons.
Halal Products	Halal food can be imported to Germany, which regularly occurs. According to a verdict of the Federal Constitutional Court in 2002,[56] Muslims are entitled to apply for an exemption from the general prohibition of slaughtering without pre-stunning, according to the *Animal Protection Act* (art. 4a sect. 2).

---

55 https://www.mj.niedersachsen.de/download/73665/zum_Download.pdf, accessed 4 May 2018.
56 *Entscheidungen des Bundesverfassungsgerichts*, vol. 104 (Tübingen: Mohr, 2002), p. 337.

Since then, some Muslim butchers have applied for such exceptions, which were often refused by administrations or only granted under very restrictive conditions. The Federal Administrative Court has repeatedly decided in favour of Muslim applicants,[57] but administrative and lower court resistance has not yet ceased. In September 2009, the Federal Constitutional Court,[58] in an unusually clear judgement, quashed decisions made by the Administrative Court of Giessen[59] and the Administrative Court of Appeals of Hesse,[60] which were unfavourable to the Muslim applicant. Nevertheless, in a questionable decision of November 2009, the Bavarian Administrative Court of Appeals[61] stated that the claim of a Muslim applicant to slaughter animals for 'Id al-Adha was taken to be merely culturally based, thus not coming under freedom of religion. Repeated reports confirm that local administrations are handling exemption applications in a very restrictive manner.[62]

Access to halal food is widespread, since more and more shops, restaurants, and supermarkets offer it, mainly in areas with large Muslim populations. Regarding Islamic banking and finance, a number of banks and financial services offer *sukuk* and other forms of Islamic investments, or interest-free accounts.

---

57 "Federal Administrative Court judgement of 23 November 2006", *Neue Zeitschrift für Verwaltungsrecht,* vol. 4 (2007), p. 461.
58 "Decision of 28 September 2009", *Neue Zeitschrift für Verwaltungsrecht,* vol. 15 (2009), p. 945.
59 "Decision of 25 February 2009 (*10 L 80/09.GI*)", www.kostenlose-urteile.de/Verwaltungsgericht-erlaubt-Schaechten-unter-Auflagen.news7501.htm, accessed 4 May 2018.
60 Decision of 26 May 2009 (unpublished).
61 Decision of 26 November 2009 (*9 CE 09.2917*), https://openjur.de/u/480173.html, accessed 4 May 2018.
62 See Rohe, *Der Islam in Deutschland,* pp. 190–191. for further references.

Dress Code	The head scarf and niqab (face veil) are both permitted in public spaces in general. With respect to the niqab, according to federal legislation, and its equivalents in some states, it is forbidden for people such as judges, teachers or state officers to wear one at work; the ban also applies to students in schools in some states. The legal situation regarding university students is still unclear. In addition, there is an explicit ban on head scarves for judges in some states; up to now no Muslim judge wears a head scarf. In other contexts (regarding school teachers in particular), wearing head scarves is generally allowed, according to the jurisprudence of the Federal Constitutional Court.
Places of Islamic Learning and Education	Since 2011, four centres of Islamic Theology at six universities have been set up: Erlangen-Nuremberg (www.dirs.phil.fau.de/), Frankfurt (www.uni-frankfurt.de/42913326) with Giessen (www.uni-giessen.de/fbz/fb04/institute/islamtheo), Münster/Osnabrück (www.uni-muenster.de/ZIT/, www.islamische-theologie.uni-osnabrueck.de), which were later split into two independent institutions, and Tübingen (www.uni-tuebingen.de/fakultaeten/zentrum-fuer-islamische-theologie/zentrum.html). They have been established with the support of the Federal Ministry of Education and Research. Moreover Islamic Theology can be studied in Paderborn (www.kw.uni-paderborn.de/sit/), Ludwigsburg (www.ph-ludwigsburg.de/6029+M52087573abo.html), and Karlsruhe (www.ph-karlsruhe.de/institute/ph/institut-fuer-islamische-theologiereligionspaedagogik/). At the *Pädagogische Hochschule Weingarten*, Alevi religious studies have been offered since 2011 (www.ph-weingarten.de/alevitische_religion/). Since 1995, there has been a private state-recognised Islamic primary school in Berlin (www.islamische-grundschule.de/index.html).

Muslim Media and Publications

- *Islamische Zeitung*, founded in 1995 by the lawyer Andreas Abu Bakr Rieger; a monthly publication (www.islamische-zeitung.de/).
- *Al-Fadschr–Die Morgenröte*, a quarterly with a special section for children (*Salam*) in German, edited by the Islamic Centre Hamburg, a Shi'i institution (www.al-fadschr.com/).

On the internet, a large number of various publications are to be found (websites, blogs, chats, TV programmes and videos, etc.).

Numerous publishing houses exist, publishing in various languages on a broad variety of subjects.

Main Muslim Organisations

- Ahmadiyya Muslim Jamaat Germany (*Ahmadiyya Muslim Jamaat Deutschland K.d.ö.R.*, Genfer Straße 11, D-60437 Frankfurt am Main, email: kontakt@ahmadiyya.de, www.ahmadiyya.de). Founded in 1957 in Hesse; since 2013 it is a corporation by Public Law (*Körperschaft des öffentlichen Rechts*).
- DITIB (*Diyanet İşleri Türk-İslam Birliği, Türkisch-Islamische Union der Anstalt für Religion e.V.*, Venloer Str. 160, D-50823 Cologne, email: info@ditib.de, www.ditib.de). Founded in 1985.
- Islamic Community Jama'at un-Nur (*Islamische Gemeinschaft Köln e.V. Dachverband Deutschland (Nurculuk-Bewegung)*, Neustraße 11, D-51063 Cologne, email: info@igjn.de, www.jamaatunnur.com). Founded in 1967.
- Islamic Community Millî Görüş (*Islamische Gemeinschaft Millî Görüş e.V.–IGMG*, Boschstraße 61–65, D-50171 Kerpen, email: info@igmg.org, www.igmg.de). Founded in 1976.
- Islamic Community of Shi'i Congregations of Germany (*Islamische Gemeinschaft der schiitischen Gemeinden Deutschlands–IGS, e.V.*, Harzer Str. 51–52, D-12059 Berlin, email: info@igs-deutschland.org, www.igs-deutschland.org). Founded in 2009, it is the umbrella organisation for Shi'i mosques and associations.
- Islamic Council of the Federal Republic of Germany (*Islamrat für die Bundesrepublik Deutschland*, Mehrheimer Str. 229, D-50733 Cologne, email:

info@islamrat.de, www.islamrat.de). Founded in 1986, originally as a federal umbrella organisation, it has now established branches in various states (*Bundesländer*).
- Alevi Community Germany (*Alevitische Gemeinde Deutschland e.V. / Almanya Alevi Birlikleri Federasyonu*–AABF, Stolberger Str. 317, D-50933 Cologne, email: info@alevi.com, www.alevi.com/). Founded in 1990, in several states it is recognised as a religious community according to art. 7 sec. 3 of the Constitution (this article of the German constitution regulates religious instruction in public schools). The relationship between Alevism and Islam is debated, but the organisation is a member of the German Islam Conference (*Deutsche Islamkonferenz*).
- Central Council of Muslims in Germany (*Zentralrat der Muslime in Deutschland e.V.*–ZMD, Sachsenring 20, D-50677 Cologne, email: sekretariat@zentralrat.de, www.islam.de). Founded in 1989 originally as a federal umbrella organisation, but has now established branches in various states.

Greece

Konstantinos Tsitselikis[1] and Alexandros Sakellariou[2]

Introduction

Although the situation with regard to migrants and refugees stabilised to some extent in 2017, it was still one of the main issues in public discussions. It is estimated that approximately 55,000 persons have been detained in Greece waiting to be transferred to other European countries, while according to the available data around 32,000 individuals arrived on the Aegean islands crossing the borders with Turkey.[3] One crucial aspect of this development was the treatment of these migrants and refugees. During the last months of 2017 many problems were reported especially in the Eastern islands of the Aegean Sea (Samos, Chios, Lesvos), which are islands greatly affected by the arrival of migrants and refugees. The second feature of this issue was the incorporation of refugee children into Greek schools–a programme initiated in 2016 and continued in 2017, and which was in general accepted, although some reactions from local communities took place sparked by extreme-right wing groups.

A second development in 2017 was the continuation of the construction work of the first purpose-built mosque of Athens, with new amendments legislated and voted on by the Greek parliament in June 2017, including the decision on the establishment of the mosque's administrative board in August. However, and despite these developments, the mosque is still under construction and a clear timetable has not been made available by the Government, causing frustration among Muslims in Greece.

---

1 Konstantinos Tsitselikis is Professor of Human Rights and International Organisations at the University of Macedonia, Thessaloniki. He has published articles and monographs on minorities and migrants. His latest academic interests focus on Muslim communities in Christian majority countries and Christian minorities in Muslim majority countries. He was chair of the Hellenic League for Human Rights until March 2017.
2 Alexandros Sakellariou holds a PhD in the Sociology of Religion from Panteion University of Social and Political Sciences of Athens. He teaches Sociology at the Hellenic Open University and he is a post-doctoral researcher at Panteion University working in EU-funded research projects. His scientific interests include among others politics and religion, Church-state relations, religious communities in Greek society, religious freedom, religion and globalisation, youth activism and civic participation, and right-wing extremism. He is a member of the Hellenic League for Human Rights.
3 http://migration.iom.int/europe/, accessed 19 December 2017.

A third development of the year was related to the Muslims of Thrace, triggered by case law from the European Court of Human Rights. In November 2017, the Greek Prime Minister announced that a new piece of legislation will be presented in Parliament that will make the implementation of shari'a law in Thrace optional, meaning that Greece will cease to be the only European country officially recognising and implementing shari'a law for its historical Muslim minority. In December, the Ministry of Education and Religious Affairs initiated the discussion about the possible change of the current legislation with regard to the Muftis in Thrace, arguing that they should probably be elected by local Muslim communities and not appointed by the Greek state, as has been the case until now. Also, an amendment to the Law would allow such minority associations to use the appellation "Turkish" in their titles when officially registering, in order to comply with three relevant judgments of the European Court of Human Rights in Strasbourg.

A final issue that should be reported is the continued presence of Islamophobic discourse in Greek society similar to previous years. The main agents were again specific political parties, mainly of the extreme right, but not exclusively; some media, social media, blogs and websites, as well as certain religious figures from the Orthodox Church of Greece were also involved in this. As expected, all the above developments, together with those on the international stage, e.g. the terrorist attacks in Manchester and Barcelona, have been instrumentalised by Islamophobic actors in order to express and propagate their hostility towards Islam and Muslims.

Public Debates

Public debates during 2017 were mainly focused on the migrant and refugee issue, the construction of the mosque in Athens and the Muslim minority of Thrace. Contrary to trends in other European countries around Islamophobia, serious attacks on Muslims and their interests based exclusively on a religious motivation have not been recorded in Greece. Reports in Greece usually count xenophobic and racist attacks with no particular focus on any religious motivation, perhaps because in most of the cases such a distinction is not always possible. Attacks against immigrants, for example, which during the second half of 2017 were on the rise in Aspropyrgos, a region near Athens, mainly targeted Muslims from Pakistan. However, it is not easy to classify them as Islamophobic. The most appropriate way is, probably, to count them both as xenophobic and Islamophobic. These attacks reached 70 or 80 in number in 2017, and it has been suggested that the perpetrators in Aspropyrgos returned to the local offices of the Golden Dawn (GD) party in the region after the attacks there.[4]

In October 2017, a new extremist group emerged in Athens, under the name *Crypteia*, inspired by an ancient Spartan group.[5] They claimed to be behind an attack against the house of a small Afghan boy;[6] he was chosen to hold the Greek flag in the national commemoration day celebrations of 28 October, although his school administrators later changed their minds. *Crypteia* also claimed to be behind an assault against two Muslim immigrants, one of them being an imam, in November 2017.[7]

Discussions with Muslims[8] suggest that Islamophobia in Greece is not as severe as in other European countries, and probably declined compared to previous years, especially with regard to physical assaults. In their view, such assaults are racially and not religiously motivated, meaning that most of them are xenophobic and not Islamophobic, and that they do not speak for Greek society on the whole. The findings of a study of the European Union Agency for Fundamental Rights (FRA) seem to verify the view that Muslims in Greece do not consider such assaults as Islamophobic. Muslims themselves consider these assaults as primarily based on their ethnic or immigrant background, then on their skin colour and finally on their religion, although it should also be added that in most of the cases they hesitate, or are afraid, of reporting such assaults.[9] They also mentioned that a key-issue is that state authorities, and more particularly the police and the secret service, seem to hold Islamophobic attitudes and views, as well as stereotypical opinions of Muslims.[10]

It is important to mention that a variety of opinion polls show that negative views about Islam and Muslims in Greece are still strong. In a PEW study

---

4   http://www.tanea.gr/news/greece/article/5476327/exoyn-ginei-70-80-ratsistikes-epitheseis-mono-ston-aspropyrgo-to-2017/, accessed 6 December 2017.

5   The *crypteia* in ancient Sparta was a secret police organised by the Spartan elites in order to terrorise the slave/peasant population, especially their leaders, and those who were brave enough to start uprisings. For this purpose young Spartans with knives were sent out during the night to assassinate these people in order to create fear among them.

6   This was the first time that the group appeared. They broke the windows of the family's house by throwing stones; they then called the offices of a newspaper and claimed to be behind the attack.

7   http://www.thetoc.gr/koinwnia/article/omada-krupteia-i-fasistiki-organwsi-pou-xtupaei-metanastes, accessed 6 December 2017.

8   These discussions and interviews took place during ethnographic research conducted by one of the authors of this report (A. Sakellariou).

9   *Second European Union Minorities and Discrimination Survey–Muslims, Selected Findings* (Luxembourg: European Union Agency for Fundamental Rights, 2017), pp. 27, 35, 40.

10 Information collected from interviews and informal discussions with Muslims.

published in 2017 on attitudes towards Muslims, 62% of Greeks stated that they would not accept a Muslim being a member of their family, 28% would not accept a Muslim as their neighbour, and 21% would not accept Muslims as full citizens of the country.[11] In another study, when participants were asked to mention what comes to their mind when they hear the word "Muslim", 46.4% said something "bad" and 36.3% something "good", while 32.4% argued that in their view most Muslims around the world supported the terrorist attacks committed by the so-called Islamic State. Finally, with regard to the mosque of Athens, 31% responded that they would certainly be disturbed by the construction of a mosque in Greece, and 10.3% responded that they would probably be disturbed. The majority of respondents, however, said they would not be disturbed.[12]

In the field of politics, Golden Dawn (GD) is the most significant actor with regard to the reproduction of Islamophobia and anti-Muslim hatred. In 2017, GD continued voicing such views, quite often via the party's official website, arguing that "through the arrival of immigrants and refugees the Islamisation of Greece has already started".[13] GD's Islamophobic discourse was also evident in parliamentary debates about the construction of the mosque of Athens, or in discussions about immigration in which the GD's MPs, especially after the terrorist attacks in Europe, argued that "jihadists are killing people and children throughout Europe",[14] implying that a mosque in Athens and all immigrants and refugees constitute a direct threat.[15]

Apart from GD, politicians from the right, liberal or even the centre-left have expressed views which could be considered as Islamophobic in relation to immigration, in particular after the terrorist attacks in European cities. The former Prime Minister, Antonis Samaras, for example, argued in his talk in a meeting of a European People's Party think tank, that Europe was threatened

---

11 *Religious Belief and National Belonging in Central and Eastern Europe*, Pew Research Center (10 May, 2017), p. 161 and a study of the National Centre for Social Research, https://www.efsyn.gr/arthro/zoyme-ton-mytho-mas-gia-toys-metanastes, accessed 19 December 2017.

12 https://www.dianeosis.org/wp-content/uploads/2017/03/ti_pistevoun_oi_ellines_final_version.pdf, accessed 3 January 2018.

13 http://www.xryshaygh.com/enimerosi/view/h-islamopoihsh-ths-eurwphs-me-arithmous-sthn-ellada-eichame-ejaplasiasmo-to, accessed 6 December 2017.

14 Parliamentary Proceedings, session PKE, 25 May 2017 and session PAZ, 21 June 2017, http://www.hellenicparliament.gr/UserFiles/a08fc2dd-61a9-4a83-b09a-09f4c564609d/es20170525.pdf and http://www.hellenicparliament.gr/UserFiles/a08fc2dd-61a9-4a83-b09a-09f4c564609d/es20170621.pdf, both accessed 3 February 2018.

15 Sakellariou, Alexandros, "Fear of Islam in Greece: migration, terrorism and 'ghosts' from the past", *Nationalities Papers*, vol. 45, no. 4 (July 2017), pp. 511–523.

by a "tsunami of immigrants" that arrive in Europe, and in Greece were practising "all kinds of smuggling, trafficking or even Jihad".[16] In the same vein, Andreas Loverdos, an MP of the centre-left socialist party (PASOK) made the following statement after the attack in Barcelona: "the problem of Islamic [sic] terrorism is related to immigration and this is where the main focus of Europe should be".[17] Thanos Tzimeros, the president of a small neo-liberal party, also argued after the Barcelona attack that "Europe should forbid halal food for Muslims because that way they will have nothing to eat, and they will leave".[18] Similarly, the mayor of Argos, in the Peloponnese, stated that Europe and, of course Greece, was in a process of Islamisation through the rise of immigrants and refugees and that "there is a plan to destroy national identities and eliminate the national consciousness of the next generation".[19]

The second agent in Greece with regard to Islamophobia are some members of the Orthodox Church in the country, especially some Metropolitans of the Holy Synod. It is important to note that the Church on the whole is not Islamophobic and does not express hatred against Muslims; however there are some cases that need to be taken seriously. The Metropolitan of Piraeus, Serafeim, is a central figure in such discourses since he continuously argues that Islam is a false religion and Muhammad a false prophet, adding that Islam is violent and very dangerous.[20] Similarly the Office for Heresies and Para-religions of the Metropolis of Piraeus released an announcement arguing that it was impossible to see Islam in another way because nowadays "Islam is conquering the West", and because Islam was "theocratic, fascist and imperialist and of course violent using jihad to expand".[21] Another Metropolitan who also commonly speaks out against Islam is the Metropolitan of Kalavryta, Ambrosios, who has repeatedly expressed views against immigrants, especially Muslims, who, he argues, "invade Greece and Europe and have already conquered it and started their criminal activity with attacks, thefts, injuries and murders of innocent Greek people!"[22]

16 http://www.protothema.gr/politics/article/717600/samaras-sto-elk-i-europi-kinduneuei-apo-to-tsounami-tis-anexelegtis-metanasteusis-/, accessed 8 December 2017.
17 https://www.thepressproject.gr/article/115516/Strofi-Loberdou-sto-akrodeksio-koino, accessed 8 December 2017.
18 https://twitter.com/thanostzimeros/status/898268459590713346, accessed 8 December 2017.
19 http://koinosparanomastis.blogspot.gr/2017/02/blog-post_14.html, accessed 8 December 2017.
20 http://goo.gl/mqStGV, accessed 7 December 2017.
21 https://www.ekklisiaonline.gr/mitropoleis/boroume-na-doume-islam-allo-tropo/, accessed 8 December 2017.
22 http://mkka.blogspot.gr/2017/01/blog-post_23.html, accessed 8 December 2017.

Lastly, an organisation named the "Group of High Policing" (Ομάδα υψηλής αστυνόμευσης / *Omada ypsilis astynomefsis*), in October 2017, called for the extreme right-wing group "Guardians of Thrace" (Φρουροί της Θράκης / *Frouroi tis Thrakis*) to take action against members of the board of the Turkish Union of Xanthi (*Tourkiki Enosi Xanthis / İskeçe Türk Birliği*).[23] This open intimidation has to be seen in relation to the discussion to allow minority associations to include in their names the appellation "Turkish".

Transnational Links

Muslims from Thrace have regular relations with Turkey in terms of Islamic or folklore festivals, and they also collaborate with the Turkish Presidency of Religious Affairs (*Diyanet İşleri Başkanlığı*) and certain Turkish NGOs of national-religious profile in joint activities (*kurban, mevlut,* folk festivals, *zekat,* visits to religious or cultural sites etc.). These transnational activities are conducted by local minority organisations in Thrace sympathetic to Turkey.

Migrant Muslims' interactions with Muslims abroad are sporadic and not focused on specific kinds of activities. Other migrant national communities also have sporadic contacts with organisations in their countries of origin (for example, Pakistan or Bangladesh). There are no interstate joint functions, agreements, visits or bilateral cooperation on Islamic issues between the Greek government and other states, except for a series of scholarships offered by Arab states to students coming from Greece, which may also include Muslim students pursuing Islamic Studies abroad. In some cases there is collaboration between Muslim groups in Athens and institutes or associations abroad, for example, the Conveying Islamic Message Society (CIMC) in Egypt translates, produces and distributes brochures, booklets, and leaflets about Islam in the Greek language.[24]

The political crisis that has embroiled Turkey after the failed coup in July 2016, had repercussions in Thrace where, as in Turkey, there was increasing pressure to clarify allegiances (even for those who previously supported the Gülen movement and who "switched sides" after the failed coup attempt).

---

23 http://paratiritis-news.gr/article/195431/Apo-ton-pato-tou-pio-bromerou-bothrou, accessed 24 December 2017.

24 The Conveying Islamic Message Society (CIMC) was established in 1974, and licensed by the Ministry of Social Affairs in Egypt. Its aim is to acquaint the world with Islam's principles through books and pamphlets in different languages, and answer Islamic questions and inquires with the help of the scholars of Al-Azhar. For more details see http://www.islamic-message.net/cims/default.aspx, accessed 3 February 2018.

There were ensuing social divisions and the exclusion of those branded as supporters of Fethullah Gülen by the dominant segment of the Turkish community of Thrace. Hundreds of Turks, who cannot live under the increasingly authoritarian regime in Turkey, and others who were accused of being supporters of the "terrorist organisation FETÖ", have sought refuge in Greece and even asylum under the terms of the Convention of Geneva (1951). Supporters of the Gülen movement are no longer tolerated in Thrace, and as such bilateral Greek-Turkish relations have faced new tensions as a consequence.

The visit of President Erdoğan to Greece (Athens and Thrace) on 8–10 December 2017 triggered again the discussion over the status of this minority, as he requested modifications to the Treaty of Lausanne[25] and a change to the mode of selection of the Mufti. President Erdoğan named the minority as "being of a common Turkish descent (*soydaş*)", and he mentioned three groups "Turks, Pomaks and Roma" that all are seen under the "common denominator of Islam".[26]

Law and Domestic Politics

In May 2017, the Government passed a new Law (*Law 4473/ 2017, FEK A 78, article 5*)[27] that determined the composition of the administrative board that will manage the new mosque of Athens. In August, the Ministry of Education and Religious Affairs appointed the seven members of the board with only two of them being Muslim. However, while it was announced that the construction of the mosque should be completed during the late summer or early autumn of 2017, construction was still not completed by the end of the year. In our discussions with some Muslims on the mosque project, it became clear they were quite pessimistic about its opening, suggesting it would not happen under the current Government–despite being left-wing and supportive of the project–because of its collaboration with a populist right-wing party (Independent Greeks/ Ανεξάρτητοι Έλληνες).

The issue of establishing an Islamic cemetery in Athens is still pending. For this reason, 34 Members of Parliament of the SYRIZA ruling party asked the Minister of Education and Religious Affairs about the Government's plan to

---

25   According to Articles 37–45 of the Treaty of Lausanne (1923) the Muslims of Greece and the non-Muslims of Turkey enjoy a series of minority rights.
26   http://www.tovima.gr/politics/article/?aid=923246, accessed 18 December 2017.
27   Μέτρα για την επιτάχυνση του κυβερνητικού έργου σε θέματα εκπαίδευσης (Measures to Accelerate Government Work on Education) http://www.et.gr/index.php/anazitisi-fek, accessed 3 February 2018.

open one, with the Minister replying that the Government sees this positively and will act accordingly,[28] but without providing a concrete schedule for its establishment.

An amendment to the *Civil Procedure Law* (*Law 4491/2017*, FEK A 152, *articles 29 and 30*) now allows for the rehearing of cases which the European Court of Human Rights found that current legislation violated the right to association. In January 2017, the European Court of Human Rights concluded that a case that had already been adjudicated could be examined again as the Greek government had to find the means to redress the violation, namely, to allow the registration of an association belonging to the minority of Thrace under the name "Turkish".[29]

A case related to the legal position of shari'a law in the Greek legal system, pending before the First Section of the European Court of Human Rights since 2013, was referred to the Grand Chamber.[30] A Muslim man drafted a public will according to which his wife would inherit all of his property. As they do not have children, after he passed away, his widow acquired the properties. The public will was challenged by the sisters of the deceased on the grounds that shari'a law has to be implemented, according to which they are heirs of three-quarters of the bequeathed properties. While the first instance court and the Court of Appeal of Thrace upheld that the public will is valid and shari'a law cannot be implemented without consent, the Court of Cassation upheld the reverse, i.e. that shari'a law is the exclusive law applicable to all Muslims of Thrace in the framework of the minority protection law. The Grand Chamber of the Court of Strasbourg heard the case on 6 December 2017 and initiated a series of changes in law and policies around the position of the Mufti and Islamic law, as long as the judgment of the Court was made public by mid-2018. In November 2017, the Prime Minister announced from Komotini in Thrace that shari'a law will cease to be obligatory and will become voluntary to those who wish to follow it, receiving positive comments from human rights organisations.[31] In December, the Minister of Education and Religious

---

28   http://www.kathimerini.gr/910332/article/epikairothta/ellada/erwthsh-34-voyleytwn-toy-syriza-gia-dhmioyrgia-moysoylmanikoy-nekrotafeioy, and http://www.liberal.gr/arthro/140116/politiki/2017/tin-idrusi-mousoulmanikou-nekrotafeiou-sto-schisto-schedi azei-kai-ulopoiei-i-kubernisi.html, all accessed 19 December 2017.

29   ECtHR, *Bekir-Ousta and Others v Greece*, 7050/14, judgment 12–1-2017.

30   ECtHR, *Molla Sali v Greece*, 20452/14.

31   http://www.avgi.gr/article/10811/8568942/saria-telos-mia-istorike-stigme, and http://www.hlhr.gr/%CE%BA%CE%B1%CF%84%CE%AC%CF%81%CE%B3%CE%B7%CF%83%CE%B7-%CF%84%CE%B7%CF%82-%CF%85%CF%80%CE%BF%CF%87%CF%81%CE%B5%CF%89%CF%84%CE%B9%CE%BA%CE%AE%CF%82-%CE%B5%CF%86%CE%B1%CF%81%CE%BC%CE%BF%CE%B3%CE%AE/, both accessed 19 December 2017.

Affairs submitted the relevant Bill of Law for discussion in Parliament.[32] In December, it was also announced that the Government considered changing the current status of the three Muftis in Thrace, who are currently appointed by the Greek government, introducing elections instead of appointing them, as happens until now. Such an initiative caused reactions from some right and extreme-right-wing elements, with some media referring to such a decision as "treason".[33] It should be noted that, as mentioned in the media in January 2017, the Government had already taken the decision to dismiss the current Mufti of Xanthi, despite his tenure not meant to officially end until 2021.[34]

In the area of education, the new curriculum and religious textbooks introduced in 2016 as a pilot in selected schools, was expanded to cover every school nationwide in 2017. This new religious educational material, or "educational files" as they are now called, that replaced the existing textbooks, build upon a more balanced and objective presentation of all the major religions, including Islam, contrary to the previous curriculum. This change caused reactions from parents who, with the support of extreme-right groups–such as GD[35] among others, and some Church and theological groups[36]–strongly protested against this new educational material. Some parents filled in a document arguing that they "do not accept their children being taught about other religions, which are presented in a biased way concealing their true teachings", which, in their view, include "fanaticism, racism and hatred", mainly referring to Islam. They returned this new educational material to the Ministry of Education, describing it as "unacceptable".

The programme of the Ministry of Education for refugee children continued to be implemented in 2017 in different regions throughout Greece despite some local complaints and obstacles.[37] There have been some angry reactions reported in various regions of Greece (e.g. in Oraiokastro and Filippiada), but

---

32 http://www.parliament.gr/Nomothetiko-Ergo/Anazitisi-Nomothetikou-Ergou?law_id=fdd50036-9d9d-48d0-a326-a83f0135c69d, accessed 19 December 2017.

33 https://www.efsyn.gr/arthro/eklogi-moyfti-me-pliri-sevasmo-sti-meionotita, and http://www.stoxos.gr/2017/12/gavroglou.html, both accessed 19 December 2017.

34 http://tvxs.gr/news/ellada/i-kybernisi-teleionei-moyfti-ksanthi, accessed 19 December 2017.

35 http://www.xryshaygh.com/koinovoulio/view/erwthsh-gia-tis-aparadektes-leptomerhs-anafores-sto-islam-apo-to-biblio-ths, accessed 6 December 2017.

36 http://www.petheol.gr/nea/ellenaxypnaertheeoraantistasetoratoupanagiotetsankare-gengrammateatespanelleniasenosestheologon, accessed 6 December 2017.

37 For the legal background of these two cases, see Tsitselikis, Konstantinos, and Alexandros Sakellariou, "Greece", in Oliver Scharbrodt, Samim Akgönül, Ahmet Alibašić, Jørgen S. Nielsen and Egdūnas Račius (eds.), *Yearbook of Muslims in Europe*, vol. 9 (Leiden-Boston: Brill, 2017), p. 320.

not to the same extent as in 2016,[38] against the decision to include refugee children in the school programme in order to incorporate them and avoid their social exclusion. Another case that was extensively discussed was the reaction to the decision that an eleven-year-old student from Afghanistan would hold the Greek flag during the national commemoration day of 28 October. He was chosen randomly, according to the new educational legislation, to hold it in the students' parade. However, the school administration and the school's parents association reversed the decision, and only gave him the sign with the school's name to hold, not the flag itself.[39]

Activities and Initiatives of Main Muslim Organisations

There are a number of Muslim organisations in Greece, but their activities are quite limited and mainly focused on organising religious festivals and celebrations, like Ramadan. This festival in 2017 was celebrated once again in a public space, at the open area of the Olympic Stadium of Athens and at the Stadium of Peace and Friendship in Piraeus, after permission was given by the Ministries of Education and Religious Affairs, of Culture and of Public Order.[40] The festival was also celebrated in existing prayer houses and in some of the camps for migrants and refugees.[41] Shi'is, as in 2016, organised the commemoration of 'Ashura' in Piraeus in the autumn.[42] In March, Syed Aijaz Haider, one of the first Shi'i Muslims in Greece, passed away in Athens; the local community organised a memorial service in the cultural centre of the Municipality of Aghios Ioannis Rentis.[43]

The Muslim Association of Greece (Μουσουλμανική Ένωση Ελλάδας) along with the Pakistani, Afghan and Bangladeshi communities gathered to protest against the killing of Rohingya in Myanmar, and delivered a letter of

---

38 http://www.nooz.gr/greece/neo-skiniko-ekfovismoi-paidion-sto-oraiokastro, and http://www.athina984.gr/2017/03/24/ektos-scholiou-70-prosfygopoula-logo-ton-ratsistikon-antidraseon-sti-filippiada/, both accessed 8 December 2017.
39 http://tvxs.gr/news/ellada/piran-ti-simaia-tis-parelasis-apo-11xrono-amir, accessed 6 December 2017.
40 https://left.gr/news/oaka-kai-sef-sti-diathesi-ton-moysoylmanon-gia-ramazani, accessed 20 December 2017.
41 https://www.altsantiri.gr/ellada/eid-al-fitr-h-giorti-ton-mousoulmanon-pou-simatodoti-telos-tou-ramazaniou-ikones/ and https://www.thepressproject.gr/article/111915/Ramazani#.WSvfoQmXfCs.facebook, both accessed 20 December 2017.
42 http://www.lifo.gr/now/greece/162281, accessed 20 December 2017.
43 http://www.huffingtonpost.gr/2017/04/09/koinonia-ekdilosi-mnimis-gia-ton-idryth-ton-siiton-mousoulmanv-sthn-ellada_n_15896020.html, accessed 20 December 2017.

condemnation to the consulate of Myanmar in Athens. The Muslim Association of Greece also expressed its solidarity with Qatar over the summer after the Saudi-led embargo of Arab Gulf countries, and also gave its support to the Palestinians after the decision by US President Donald J. Trump to transfer the US embassy and recognise Jerusalem as Israel's capital. The Association also participated in initiatives to help migrants and refugees arriving in Greece.

The Arab Hellenic Centre for Culture and Civilisation (Ελληνο-Αραβικό Πολιτιστικό Κέντρο), apart from organising religious festivals, continued to run courses in the Arabic and Greek languages for Arabs and Greeks who are interested in learning either language; they also ran a Qur'anic competition for Muslim children. Islam for Greeks,[44] a website run by Salah us Salih (former Al Rahman) through the cultural association Ptolemy (Πτολεμαίος), has been active through the posting of videos, classes, publications and online articles in order to engage in *da'wa*, explaining what Islam is, its theology and practices. The director of the organisation and manager of the website, a Greek Muslim of Egyptian origin, born and raised in Greece, emphasises the peaceful face of Islam, arguing against those who commit terrorist attacks.

Muslim Population: History and Demographics

At the establishment of Greece as an independent state (1830), Muslims constituted a very small group within the then borders of the country, with almost no institutional special protection. By 1881 and with the annexation of Thessalia, Muslim communities (numbering about 40,000 at that time) were protected as a minority by the Treaty of Constantinople. In effect, the Ottoman *millet* system (ethno-religious communal institutional autonomy) was preserved. By the end of the Balkan Wars (1912–13) and with the annexation of the New Territories by Greece, the same status was extended to more than 500,000 Muslims who opted to become Greek citizens. After the Greek-Turkish war of 1919–22, a population exchange took place under the Lausanne Convention (1923) and 450,000 Muslims left Greece for Turkey. 92,000 Muslims with Greek citizenship remained in Thrace (Turkish-speakers and Bulgarian-speakers or Pomaks) and 26,000 Albanian-speakers stayed in Epirus. The latter were forced to flee to Albania in 1945 at the end of the German occupation. In 1947, when the Dodecanese Islands were annexed by Greece, a population of about 12,000 Muslims (Greek and Turkish speaking) became Greek citizens. For political and economic reasons, in the context of Greek-Turkish confrontations in

---

44   https://islamforgreeks.org/, accessed 20 December 2017.

the 1960s and 1970s, a wave of Muslims emigrated from Thrace to Turkey and Germany (more than 120,000 are estimated to live abroad). Muslims of Greek citizenship are mostly Turkish-speakers and express Turkish national feelings. About 20,000 of them have Pomak (a Bulgarian dialect) as their mother tongue, partly expressing an ethnic Pomak identity, often along with a Turkish (national) identity, and about 5,000 speak Roma (partly expressing an ethnic Roma identity), although most of the Muslim Roma are monolingual Turkish speakers. As religion and mother tongue ceased to be a question in the national census after 1951, all the above figures are rough estimates.

Migrant Muslims have been an important presence in Greece since 1990 as part of the general flow of migration. Muslim immigrants come from African and Asian countries (after 2001) and from Albania (after 1990). The 2011 census registered 911,929 non-Greek citizens (199,101 European Union citizens, 708,003 citizens of third countries, and 4,825 of non-identified citizenship; 52.7% were Albanians and 3.7% Pakistanis). Of this number, some 250,000 were estimated to be Muslims (this figure does not include Albanians who, although of a Muslim background, do not identify with Islam). There are no official figures on the number of Muslims in Greece. The numbers provided below are estimates based on nationalities from the national census[45] and on figures provided by leaders of Muslim organisations. The numbers refer to permanent residents and not those who pass through, transit or stay for a few weeks.

Muslim Population	Approx. 380,000 (unofficial estimate, about 2% of entire population). Muslim migrants and refugees in transit or of a minimum stay are not taken into account.
Ethnic/National Backgrounds	Approx. 25% of Muslims in Greece are Greek citizens (mostly comprising the Turkish-Muslim minority of Thrace, the communities of Rhodes and Kos; also small number of naturalised immigrants or Greek converts).
	Largest ethnic/national groups (estimates): Turkish: 90,000 (Greek nationals) Pomak: 15,000 (Greek nationals) Roma: 10,000 (Greek nationals)

45   http://www.statistics.gr/2011-census-pop-hous, accessed 3 February 2018.

	Non-Greek nationals (estimates and 2011 census figures in parenthesis): Pakistani: 70,000 (34,178) Bangladeshi: 35,000 (11,076) Syrian: 40,000 (7,628) Iraqi: 10,000 (3,692) Palestinian: 5,000 (976) Afghan: 25,000 (6,911) Egyptian: 15,000 (10,455) Other: 50,000.
Inner-Islamic Groups	No official data available. Sunni Islam is the most widespread form of Islam and is practised by immigrants from North and Sub-Saharan Africa, Bangladesh, Pakistan, Arab countries and by the Muslim minority in Thrace. Shi'ism is far less widespread, existing mainly among Kurdish, Pakistani and Iranian communities, while Alevism is found mostly among Turks and Kurds.
Geographical Spread	Muslims of Greek citizenship residing in Greece (in total about 115,000) are mainly concentrated in Thrace (about 85,000), in Athens and Thessaloniki, and on Rhodes and Kos (Dodecanese Islands), with about 2,000 on each island. Around 15,000 have emigrated from Thrace to Athens or other Greek cities for economic reasons. It is estimated that more than 65% of the overall Muslim population (mostly immigrants) is concentrated in the greater Athens metropolitan area.
Number of Mosques	Ca. 300 mosques in Thrace, two in Kos and one in Rhodes are officially registered as mosques, and around 50 unofficial prayer houses function in greater Athens (also in Thessaloniki and other cities) run by migrant Muslims. Five officially registered prayer houses are operational in Athens, Piraeus and Thiva.

Muslim Burial Sites	– Muslim cemetery of Xanthi, Anat. Romylias, 67100, Xanthi – Muslim cemetery of Komotini, Yenice, terma Adrianoupoleos, 69100 Komotini – Muslim cemetery Komotini, Kahveci, terma Adrianoupoleos, 69100, Komotini – Muslim cemetery of Rodhes, G. Papanikolaou st., 85100, Rodhes – Muslim cemetery of Kos, Platani, 85300, Kos.
"Chaplaincy" in State Institutions	A prayer room is available in two public hospitals in Komotini and Xanthi (Thrace).
Halal Products	Halal products are mainly available in Thrace where the Muslim minority lives, but shops and restaurants offering halal products can be found in Athens as well.
Dress Code	According to Greek law there are no restrictions on how someone can dress in public. The head scarf is widely worn among religious parts of the minority of Thrace and Muslim immigrants and refugees. The niqab is very rarely worn by immigrant Muslim women.
Places of Islamic Learning and Education	In Thrace (related to the Muslim minority) – in all minority schools (elementary and secondary) – Medrese (secondary school) of Komotini – Medrese (secondary school) of Ehinos – Qur'anic course (*Kuran kursu*) offered privately (under the auspices of the "parallel Muftis"[46]) in a number of villages and city neighbourhoods.

---

46   Two parallel muftis were elected in 1991 by a limited electorate of Muslim male voters as a counterweight to the three muftis appointed by the Greek government. They are based in Xanthi and Komotini and are affiliated to Turkey, and not recognised by the Greek authorities. For the Greek-Turkish antagonism over the Muftiates of Thrace, see Tsitselikis, Konstantinos, *Old and New Islam: From Historical Minorities to Immigrant Newcomers* (Leiden-Boston: Martinus Nijhoff, 2012), pp. 421–427.

In Athens (related to immigrant Muslims) courses of Islamic education are offered by

- the Arab-Hellenic Centre for Culture and Civilisation
- the Muslim Association (Union) of Greece
- certain prayer halls (in urban centres) according to the initiative and availability of imams.

Muslim Media and Publications

Awaz, a weekly newspaper in Urdu that has been in print since August 2000 and has a high circulation; other newspapers in Urdu also circulate in Greece, such as *Dais Perdais, Khabarnama* or *Dunya News* imported from Pakistan or having a special edition for Greece. Often, they are backed by a network of websites in Urdu and English (such as www.daisperdais.gr or www.ujaalanews.com) which deal with Pakistani immigrants in Greece.

El Dhafatain (since 2004); *Al Mouhajir*, a bi-monthly newspaper; and *Athens Weekly Report*, a weekly newspaper that offers announcements of social and economic interest.

A number of websites have been online since 2009 enhancing dialogue among members of the Muslim communities and in some cases with Greeks: www.islam.gr, www.elladapalestini.blogspot.com (by the Hellenic-Palestinian Friendship Association) and islamforgreeks.gr.

Main Muslim Organisations

There is no central national Muslim organisation, but there are many associations of Muslims of Greek citizenship as well as of immigrant Muslims. Very limited contacts are observed between minority and migrant associations, and these occur only in Athens. In Thrace, there are a number of cultural, educational and sports associations that are Turkish in character, a few regarded as Muslim Roma and one Pomak. There are also a few that may be identified as Bektashi or Alevi.

- Association of University Graduates of the Minority of Thrace (*Batı Trakya Azınlığı Yüksek Tahsilliler Derneği*, Egnatias 75, 69100 Komotini, tel.: ++30 25310 29705). The Association was founded in 1982 bringing together all university graduates from the Muslim minority of Thrace.
- Turkish Union of Xanthi (*İskeçe Türk Birliği*, not yet registered, P. Ydras 2, 67100, Xanthi, tel.: ++30 25410 23614, www.iskeceturkbirligi.org). The Union, established in 1936, has a modernist Turkish profile, and is the most prestigious and contested among the minority associations. Its legal status was recalled in 1984 as a counter measure to the proclamation of the Turkish Republic of Northern Cyprus. For the European Court of Human Rights this constituted a violation of Article 10 of the ECHR in its verdict.[47]
- Arab-Hellenic Centre for Culture and Civilisation (*Ελληνο-Αραβικό Πολιτιστικό κέντρο*, Kyprou 2 & Pireos str., Moshato 18346, Athens, tel.: ++30 2106910492). The Centre was founded in 2001, and since 2007 has been based in Moshato (Athens) after a Saudi businessman purchased and offered a building to the Centre.
- Muslim Association of Greece (*Μουσουλμανική Ένωση Ελλάδας*, 9 Galaxia str, N. Kosmos, Athens, tel.: ++30 2106916055). The Association was established in 2003 and is based in Athens. It has played an active role in lobbying for the construction of a mosque and a cemetery in Athens as well as in organising public prayers.
- Shia Muslim Community of Greece (*Κοινότητα Σιιτών Μουσουλμάνων Ελλάδας*, Dimitras Str. 5, Piraeus, Postal code 18540, tel.: ++30 6936952264, shiacommunitygreece@gmail.com).

---

47 ECtHR, *Tourkiki Enosi Xanthis v Greece*, 26698/05, judgment of March 2008.

Hungary

Esztella Csiszár[1]

Introduction

In 2017 the Muslims of Hungary were mostly influenced by the impact from the anti-refugee nature of public discourse, as a result of the 2015 migrant and refugee crisis that hit Europe from the early spring to late November that year. From the spring of 2015, Hungary had become one of the major entry points into the European Union for migrants, many of them war refugees from Syria and elsewhere in the Middle East. The crisis provoked a remarkably strong wave of xenophobia and Islamophobia in Hungary in 2015, which has not ceased after two years, despite the significant decrease in the numbers of migrants and refugees who reached the country.

In 2017, 3,397 asylum seekers were newly registered, 2,049 claims were suspended and 2,880 rejected; only a small proportion of claims were accepted (1,291), that includes applications from 2016. These asylum seekers mainly came from Afghanistan (1,432), Iraq (812), Syria (577), Pakistan (163) and Iran (109).[2]

The construction of the 175 kilometre-long fence along the two Southern borders with Serbia and Croatia in September 2015 significantly decreased the number of border crossings. To secure Hungary against another wave of mass migration from the Balkan route, in April 2017 a second fence, this time a 155 kilometre-long double fence system, was completed along the Hungarian-Serbian border.[3]

---

[1] Esztella Csiszár is a PhD candidate in International Relations at Corvinus University of Budapest, Hungary. Her research interests include contemporary social and political discourses on Islam. Her dissertation focuses on the political identity of Muslims in Bosnia and Herzegovina. This report was funded by a scholarship from the Bosnian Centre of Advanced Studies (CNS).

[2] In comparison, in 2016, 29,432 migrants and refugees applied for political asylum, following the record number of 177,135 in 2015: http://www.iom.hu/migration-issues-hungary; http://bmbah.hu/images/statisztikak/180131%20IAO%20Statistics%202017.xls, both accessed 17 February 2018.

[3] http://www.kormany.hu/en/ministry-of-interior/news/second-fence-completed-along-the-hungarian-serbian-border, accessed 17 February 2017.

Public Debates

Despite the low numbers of asylum seekers, xenophobic and Islamophobic tendencies have been steadily increasing in Hungary since the introduction of the Hungarian government's strong anti-immigration rhetoric and policies, which began in 2015. The topic of the migrant and refugee crisis has been framed and presented to the public as a series of criminal, economic and cultural threats that mass migration allegedly brings. The trope of the Islamist migrant who is conspiring against Hungarian and European Christian culture, has pervaded public opinion at large. The mainstream media usually link migration to criminality and terrorism, and promote cultural fears by contrasting Christian Europe with Muslim migrants. On 30 March 2017, Prime Minister Viktor Orbán delivered a speech at the European People's Party Congress in Valletta, Malta, where he stated: "Migration turned out to be the Trojan horse of terrorism. Migration turned out to be a false solution to labour shortages. Migration turned out to be more and more an NGO-business. Migration revealed that we have taken in significant anti-Semitic potential to Europe. Migration revealed that the newcomers rather living in parallel societies instead of being integrated to the mainstream society."[4]

In 2017, two national consultations were initiated by the Government, both raising the issue of immigration into Hungary. In March 2017, the Hungarian government launched a national consultation entitled "Let's stop Brussels" focusing on six specific issues. The questionnaires reached every household in Hungary. The survey came with a letter from Prime Minister Viktor Orbán in which he "calls on the people of Hungary to stand up for national independence and fill out the questionnaire to support the Government's efforts to combat mistaken proposals on the part of Brussels".[5]

Among the six issues, one refers to immigration directly. Though Europe suffers from terror attacks, Brussels want to resettle "illegal immigrants" in Hungary:. "What do you think Hungary should do? (a) For the sake of the safety of Hungarians these people should be placed under supervision (...) while the authorities decide their fate. (b) Allow the illegal immigrants to move freely in Hungary".[6] The Government declared that the consultation had been record-

---

4 http://abouthungary.hu/speeches-and-remarks/speech-of-viktor-orban-at-the-european-peoples-party-congress/, accessed 18 February 2018.

5 http://www.kormany.hu/en/cabinet-office-of-the-prime-minister/news/the-national-consultation-packages-are-already-being-delivered-including-a-letter-from-the-prime-minister, accessed 18 February 2018.

6 http://hungarianspectrum.org/2017/04/02/national-consultation-2017-lets-stop-brussels/, accessed 20 February 2018.

breaking as they received 1.68 million responses to the national consultation questionnaire. The European Commission responded to the questions in the national consultation, emphasising that several of the claims made in the consultation "are factually incorrect or highly misleading", and set the record straight on its website.[7] Prime Minister Orbán insisted that the high participation in the Government's latest nationwide public survey means that "a whole nation is looking for ways to support its position of denying entry to people of a different culture or civilization".[8]

In September 2017, the Government announced that it would organise a new national consultation on the so-called Soros Plan. The seventh national consultation addresses the "Soros Plan", which is, according to government statements, to bring 1 million illegal immigrants to Europe. The Government's interpretation is that EU institutions wish to accelerate the approval of a mandatory, permanent quota system based on the redistribution of asylum-seekers.[9] According to Prime Minister Orbán the essence of the mandatory quota system is the plan of George Soros, who devised it and published it under his own name.[10] Previously, in July 2017, Prime Minister Orbán referred to the menace of the so-called Soros Plan to an audience at Balvanyos Summer Open University: "… the red line was however when this Soros Empire ventured into the territory of national security: that was unforgiveable. George Soros began using his money, people and institutions to transport migrants into Europe …".[11] Orbán, in his speech for the opening of the parliamentary year, addressed the issue of migration, the so-called Soros Plan, and the civilisational aspect of these political positions. According to him, "… the old world economic and political order is over and a new world order rises and cannot be prevented". The establishment of this "new world order" is responsible for the current large population movements, which go hand in hand with "the new global offensive of one of the main religions, Islam".[12]

---

7   https://ec.europa.eu/commission/publications/stop-brussels-european-commission-responds-hungarian-national-consultation_en, accessed 20 February 2018.
8   http://abouthungary.hu/news-in-brief/hungarians-have-decided-that-they-do-not-want-illegal-immigrants-in-their-country/, accessed 20 February 2018.
9   Questions on the "Stop Soros" plan: http://abouthungary.hu/news-in-brief/national-consultation-on-the-soros-plan/, accessed 20 February 2018.
10 http://www.miniszterelnok.hu/hungary-will-never-be-an-immigrant-country/, accessed 20 February 2018.
11 http://www.kormany.hu/en/the-prime-minister/the-prime-minister-s-speeches/viktor-orban-s-answers-to-questions-from-audience-members-after-his-speech-at-the-balvanyos-summer-open-university-and-student-camp, accessed 18 February 2018.
12 http://www.kormany.hu/hu/a-miniszterelnok/hirek/sikerult-a-munkaalapu-gazdasag-felepitese, accessed 18 February 2018.

Against this background, Hungarian citizens perceived immigration as one of the most important problems facing the country in 2017. In the Standard Eurobarometer survey, based on data gathered in May 2017, 27% of Hungarian respondents believed that immigration was one of the two most pressing problems in the country. Hungarians only considered health and social security to be more important (41%).[13] According to research conducted by the Pew Research Center, only in Hungary, among the European countries, was the influx of refugees and migrants coming from places like Iraq and Syria named as the greatest threat, where 66% consider the movement of refugees a major danger. This figure is even higher than those concerned about ISIS; 64% of Hungarian respondents named ISIS as the greatest threat, with only 37% responding that the condition of the global economy was a major problem.[14]

According to the leadership of the *Magyar Iszlám Közösség* (Hungarian Islamic Community–HIC), in 2017 the fear-mongering public discourse concerning migrants and refugees resulted in Islamophobia remaining at the same level as they experienced in 2016. Muslims and their communities were subject to verbal and physical attacks. The other main Muslim organisation had similar experiences. Szultan Sulok, president of the *Magyarországi Muszlimok Egyháza* (Organisation of Muslims in Hungary–OMH) acknowledged that Muslims felt threatened in Hungary owing to the shift in the official discourse on Islam. He said that Hungarian Muslims had been turned into migrants in their own country, and was afraid that this situation could deteriorate further. Even pogroms against the Muslim population in Hungary were not unthinkable, according to him.[15]

On 5 November 2017, the leader of the FIDESZ parliamentary group, Gergely Gulyás, declared on the pro-government television channel Echo TV, that there will be no mosques in Hungary, and argued that such places have a negative security impact.[16] The *Magyar Iszlám Jogvédő Egyesület* (Hungarian Islamic League for the Defence of Human Rights–HILDHR) reacted to this in a statement, indicating that Gergely Gulyás "… has alluded to restrictions of numerous

---

13 "Public opinion–European Commission (What do you think are the two most important issues facing [your country] at the moment?)", http://ec.europa.eu/commfrontoffice/publicopinion/index.cfm/Chart/getChart/chartType/gridChart//themeKy/42/groupKy/208/savFile/54, accessed 25 January 2017.
14 http://www.pewglobal.org/2017/08/01/globally-people-point-to-isis-and-climate-change-as-leading-security-threats/, accessed 08. February 2018.
15 https://mno.hu/belfold/migransok-a-hazajukban-muszlimellenes-pogromoktol-tartanak-2454603, accessed 20 March 2018.
16 https://index.hu/belfold/2017/11/05/magyarorszagon_nem_lesznek_mecsetek_tiltakoznak_az_iszlam_jogvedok/, accessed 20 March 2018.

international treaties and European laws, and to freedoms guaranteed in Article VII of the Fundamental Law".[17] The Hungarian Islamic Community (HIC) also reacted in a communiqué, emphasising that "Gulyas's statement is unacceptable as it goes against the Fundamental Law, human rights and international norms. For several years, Muslims have been experiencing Islamophobia but none of the Hungarian politicians nor any representatives of the Churches stand by Muslims against the discriminatory declarations ... We are not 'migrants', this is our homeland!".[18]

The HILDHR published an annual report for 2017 on the situation of Muslims in Hungary on its Facebook page. The report emphasised that Islamophobia and xenophobia reached a new level in Hungary in 2017 in four areas they examined: political communication, the media, general public opinion, and the assaults the HILDHR directly suffered. The intention to spread mistrust towards Hungarian Muslims has become an official part of political communication. The media also follow suit, even those more open-minded media outlets provide a platform for individuals with anti-Muslim attitudes. General public opinion echoes these discourses. The HILDHR regularly receives death threats on Facebook, typically from fake profiles. Despite these negative attitudes, the HILDHR's report emphasises that there are still people "... who uphold the principle of peaceful co-existence, and who are open to experience the real, peaceful face of Hungarian Muslim communities, who make all efforts to overcome the virtual reality created by the media and politics".[19]

Transnational Links

The two most influential Muslim organisations, the HIC and the OMH, are part of different European Muslim umbrella organisations. The OMH is a member of the Federation of Islamic Organisations in Europe (FIOE), and has ties to Western European Muslim community organisations.

Building on their common historical heritage, the HIC has been seeking a partnership with the Islamic Community of Bosnia and Herzegovina. As in 2016 the cooperation between the two communities halted, with the HIC shifting more towards Turkish Muslim communities in Germany (Hasane Foundation)

---

[17] https://budapestbeacon.com/gergely-gulyas-will-no-mosques-hungary/, accessed 19 March 2018.
[18] http://mandiner.hu/cikk/20171106_magyar_iszlam_kozosseg_valasz_gulyas_gergely_nyilatkozatara, accessed 20 February 2018.
[19] https://www.facebook.com/iszlamjogvedoliga/posts/1634029266663866, accessed 24 February 2018.

and Austria. It also strengthened its cooperation with the Islamic Community in Subotica (Szabadka), a Serbian town close to the Hungarian-Serbian border.

Law and Domestic Politics

There were no legal changes nor specific new laws directly affecting the Muslim population in 2017. Islam has had the status of a recognised religion in Hungary since 1916. The activities and benefits given to religious communities in Hungary were regulated up until 2012 by the 1990 *Act on the Freedom of Conscience*. The new Law, the *Law on Religion* (Act CCVI/2011[20], Act VII/2012[21]), was adopted to strictly regulate religious institutions, thus the number of Churches and religious organisations decreased from 300 to 35. The new regulation acknowledges the Hungarian Islamic Council as an umbrella organisation formed by the two largest communities, the Hungarian Islamic Community and the Organisation of Muslims in Hungary. The two communities are registered as separate legal entities, whereas the Council is not a legal entity, and its activities are based on the member organisations. All other Islamic organisations operate as foundations. However, ongoing legal changes in immigration policy have had a considerable impact on Muslims in Hungary, as 80–90% of Muslims are of immigrant origin and many of them asylum-seekers.

On 24 November 2016, Laszlo Toroczkai, the mayor of the southern Hungarian village of Ásotthalom, near the border with Serbia (and also vice president of the far-right Jobbik Party), banned public displays of both Islam and homosexuality. Mosque construction, the use of a muezzin at prayer times, and the wearing of clothes such as the niqab and burkini, were forbidden by his ordinance. Toroczkai says the ordinance was adopted to defend the village's "community and traditions" from any EU scheme to resettle asylum-seekers. In April 2017, Hungary's Constitutional Court repealed the ban and deemed it unconstitutional as it "aims to limit directly the freedom of conscience and religion, as well as freedom of speech".[22] Toroczkai banned the burqa again in 2017, avoiding any direct reference to Islam and presenting it as a generic ban on any kind of face veiling.[23]

20   http://net.jogtar.hu/jr/gen/hjegy_doc.cgi?docid=A1100206.TV, accessed 2 January 2017.
21   http://mkogy.jogtar.hu/?page=show&docid=a1200007.TV, accessed 2 January 2017.
22   https://mno.hu/belfold/megsemmisitette-toroczkai-rendeletet-az-alkotmanybirosag-2394424, accessed 22 February 2018.
23   https://hirtv.hu/ahirtvhirei/asotthalmon-ismet-betiltottak-a-burkat-2429929, accessed 22 February 2018.

Activities and Initiatives of Main Muslim Organisations

In December 2016, the HIC purchased a house in the XIV district in Budapest to create a new Islamic centre for the community (*Germanus Gyula Iszlám Kulturális Központ*–Gyula Germanus Islamic Cultural Centre). Deputy Chief of Mission of the US Embassy in Hungary, David Kostelancik, attended the opening ceremony that took place in March 2017.[24]

The two main Muslim organisations in Hungary, the OMH and the HIC regularly organise lectures on religious themes and summer camps for adults and children. As part of interreligious charitable cooperation, Muslim organisations distribute food to the poor with other Churches. The OMH offers a variety of educational programmes for Muslims; they organise lectures every Saturday, as well as study groups for new converts, monthly women's meetings, and also run the Noor School on Saturdays for elementary and high school children, teaching them the Arabic language, the Qur'an, and Islam. The OMH also provides the Friday sermon (*khutba*) in the Budapest mosque and in the Al-Huda mosque, in Budapest, as well as in the Yakovali Hassan mosque in Pécs. In Pécs, they also organise programmes for female converts. The OMH took its share in helping migrants and refugees at the borders and in Budapest, providing food, tents, clothes and also interpreters to migrants and refugees. As the OMH leadership tries to avoid any active political participation, their help largely remained unnoticed by the public.

The *Muszlim Fiatalok Társasága* (Muslim Youth Association) and the Hungarian Islamic League for the Defence of Human Rights (HILDHR), attached to the OMH, are also involved in initiatives to raise the community's profile in Hungary. The HILDHR was registered as an NGO at the beginning of 2016 by its founder Abdul-Fattah Munif. Its mission is to prevent acts of hate against Muslims in Hungary by registering these attacks, and by informing the public about all kinds of verbal or physical Islamophobic incidents. They invite Muslims to share their accounts if they experience any anti-Muslim hatred, such as hate speech, verbal insults, or physical assault.

The HIC ran several projects in 2017, and was active in aiding Muslims and non-Muslims as in previous years. The organisation distributed durable food for needy non-Muslim families in several villages, and second hand clothes for needy Muslim families during 2017; it also paid utility bill arrears for Muslim families living in extreme poverty, as well as distributing monthly food vouchers. The old prayer house in the XIII district was donated to the Charity

---

24 https://hu.usembassy.gov/remarks-opening-ceremony-gyula-germanus-islamic-cultural-center/, accessed 21 February 2018.

Foundation of the HIC after the establishment of the new Islamic centre. The organisation financed *iftar* dinners not only in Budapest but also for the communities in Debrecen, Győr, and Siklós. For the 'Id al-Adha celebration, they distributed the meat of sacrificial animals to more than 200 families.

The HIC regularly organises weekly lectures on Islamic themes in Budapest and in the countryside. The HIC restored and continuously maintains the Muslim parcel of land in the New Public Cemetery of Budapest. As they are running out of graveyard space, they are also negotiating with local authorities for permission to purchase a new burial ground in a village near Budapest.

An initiative that started in 2014 attracted many visitors interested in Islam to Hungary in 2017; the Budapest-based tour operator *Sétaműhely* (Budapest Walkshop) runs 30 different walks taking visitors around the city's architectural and cultural sites, including those related to the Jewish and Muslim communities. The tours visit mosques, schools and halal shops, while guests can meet local and immigrant Muslims as well as community leaders to learn about the basics of Islam. In 2017, the "Muslims who live among us" walking tour became very popular among the citizens of Budapest, as it gives an insight into the life of Muslims in the country.[25]

Muslim Population: History and Demographics

Before the Ottoman conquest of Hungary, a tiny mercantile minority of Muslims called *böszörmény* existed in medieval Hungary between 1100 and 1300. In the 16th and 17th centuries, the 150 years of Ottoman rule over a part of Hungary was the country's main contact with the world of Islam. After the withdrawal of the Ottoman Empire in 1699, Islam very soon disappeared from Hungary. The question of Islam only emerged almost two centuries later with the occupation of Bosnia and Herzegovina after the Congress of Berlin (1878). With the annexation of Bosnia and Herzegovina in 1908, the Austro-Hungarian Monarchy gained a large Muslim population that led to discussions about the place of Islam in Austria-Hungary in a new context of a multi-religious empire. During World War I, the Turkish alliance contributed to the adoption of *Act XVII* of 1916, which legally acknowledged Islam as a "recognised religion" and has never been withdrawn.

With the arrival of communism after World War II, religious practice was strictly limited: the communist leaders intended to eliminate all Churches within four or five years, and wipe out religious thinking in two generations.

---

25   https://setamuhely.hu/seta/koztunk-elo-muszlimok/, accessed 17 March 2018.

In the final years of the socialist era, in 1988, when the Hungarian Islamic Community was founded, only 14 Muslim converts to Islam could be found. Another group of six non-Muslims would have to be added to the list of founding members of the Hungarian Islamic Community for the organisation to be officially recognised. The Organisation of Muslims in Hungary (OMH) was established in September 2000, but it dates its origins back to 1987 when the very first Islamic organisation, the Muslim Students' Association, was founded. In the beginning, the OMH shared space with another Islamic foundation, the Dar As-Salam mosque, but then moved to another building which provided a space for approximately 100 individuals. As their number grew, the OMH needed a larger building. From donations from Gulf countries, the three-storey building of the Budapest Mecset (Budapest mosque) first opened its door during Ramadan in 2011.

Muslims in Hungary account for a very small portion of the population (about 0.3%), but an exact figure is very difficult to establish. The figures presented here are based on available data. The Pew Research Center reports that the number of Muslims in Hungary is around 25,000 (0.3%) which is significantly lower than the estimate of the Organisation of Muslims in Hungary, with 32,600 (including Muslim students) in 2010. Among them, around 5,000–10,000 are regularly involved in the activities of Muslim community organisations. Demographic and statistical information on converts, together with Hungarian citizens of foreign origin, can be found in the latest official Hungarian Census, which was carried out in 2011. It includes a question on religion and provides information on the national backgrounds, occupational and socio-economic status, and educational level of the Muslim population. According to the Census, 5,579 people identified themselves as Muslim (0.056% of the total population).[26] Of these, 4,097 (73.4%) declared themselves as Hungarian, while 2,369 (42.5%) as Arab by ethnicity. As the people of Hungary can declare more than one ethnicity (the sum is greater than the whole), some people identified themselves as both Hungarian and Arab.[27] Therefore, there are 3,210 ethnic Hungarian Muslims, according to the Census.

The majority (90%) of Muslims in Hungary are immigrants coming from a wide variety of backgrounds. They consist mainly of Arab, Turkish, African,

---

26 The Census enumerated Hungarian citizens living in the country or staying temporarily abroad for a period of less than twelve months, and all foreign citizens and stateless persons living in Hungary for a period of more than three months. The reason for a significantly lower number of 5,579 can be explained by the fact that half of the population (4.5 million) did not declare any religious affiliation: 2.7 million refused to reply the question of religion, while 1.8 million chose the answer of not following any religion.

27 www.ksh.hu/nepszamlalas/tablak_teruleti_00, accessed 2 February 2017.

Afghan and Iranian immigrants, many of them naturalised, alongside a small number of Hungarian converts. Their presence is not yet regarded as a significant phenomenon by the State owing primarily to their relatively small numbers, but a growing concern can be detected as a result of the securitisation discourse in the aftermath of the migrant and refugee crisis. The Muslim population lives predominantly in Budapest, but also in some of the larger cities (Debrecen, Pécs, Szeged). Communities in the countryside generally have affiliations with the two major Muslim organisations in the capital: the Organisation of Muslims in Hungary (OMH) and the Hungarian Islamic Community (HIC). Muslims are not concentrated in certain districts within the cities, which effectively prevents their segregation. Nevertheless, living far from each other raises difficulties in organising an active community life and Muslim educational or day-care centres for children.

Muslim Population	25,000–32,000 est. with 2,000–3,000 Hungarian converts (0.3% of total population of Hungary). Some estimations report a much higher number of 45,000–50,000.[28] According to the official census conducted by the National Statistical Office in 2011, 5,579 declared themselves as Muslim.
Ethnic/National Backgrounds	Approximately 60% of Muslims have Arab origins, 30% are from different African and Asian backgrounds (mainly Turkish, but also Sub-Saharan African and Iranian Muslims), and less than 10% are native Hungarians.[29]
Inner-Islamic Groups	No official data available. The Muslims of Hungary are predominantly Sunni with a small Shi'i community in Budapest (200–300 people), who are mainly Iranians. There are also small Sufi groups.

28 Estimate given by Zoltan Sulok, president of the OMH.
29 Figures provided by the OMH and the HIC.

Geographical Spread	The Muslim population is concentrated in Budapest and other major cities (Debrecen, Pécs, Szeged).
Number of Mosques	There are ca. 14 mosques and prayer houses (mostly in Budapest):

- Gyula Germanus Islamic Centre, 60 Paskál Street, Budapest
- Budapest Mosque, 41 Fehérvári Street, Budapest
- Dar as-Salam Mosque, 29 Bartók Béla Street, Budapest
- Al Huda Mosque, 21 Dobozi Street, Budapest
- *Magyarországi Iszlám Kulturális Egyesület*, 6/A Makk Street, Budapest
- Egyptian mosque, 6 Dózsa György Road, Budapest
- Afghan mosque, Ganz telep, Budapest
- Mosque in Győr, 6 Hunyadi út Győr
- Mosque in Debrecen, 56 Egyetem Sugárút, Debrecen
- Aluakf Mosque, 30 Huba Street, Miskolc
- Mekka Mosque, 23 Gogol Street, Szeged
- The Jami of Malkocs bej, 15 Kossuth Square, Siklós
- The Jami of Pasha Jakovali Hassan, 2 Rákóczi Street, Pécs
- Oratory: Turkish lorry parking place in Lajosmizse.

Muslim Burial Sites	A Muslim parcel of land is available in the New Public Cemetery at Kozma Street, Budapest, next to the cemetery for Turkish soldiers who died in World War 1. Due to the limited capacity of the Kozma Street cemetery, the HIC has been negotiating with the authorities to open a new burial place for Muslims. Muslim burial places can also be found in the countryside at Sopron, Siklós (old cemeteries for Muslim soldiers). Separate Muslim areas are also available in other public cemeteries in larger cities, e.g. Pécs, Debrecen, Szeged.

"Chaplaincy" in State Institutions	The HIC carries out prison chaplaincy services in line with the cooperation contract between the HIC and the Hungarian Prison Service (BVOP). In Budapest, a weekly chaplaincy service is provided; in the prisons of Szeged, Tiszalök, Márianosztra, Debrecen, and Vác such a service is provided on a monthly basis.
Halal Products	There are halal food products offered in special restaurants and shops. Halal slaughtering is done mostly in the slaughterhouses of companies with a halal certificate, predominantly for export. The Islamic Information and Documentation Centre in Hungary (IIDZ) is affiliated with the Austrian IIDZ, which observes the strict requirements for halal certification that are recognised internationally. The IIDZ cooperates with the World Halal Food Council and is a member of the International Halal Integrity Alliance. In 2014, the Hungarian Islamic Community also gained official accreditation from the United Arab Emirates to approve the certificate for halal foods exported to that country. Halal food is available in several restaurants and in some hotels, but is not available in public institutions. Halal slaughtering for Islamic festivals is performed by Muslims in their own houses.
Dress Code	At the national level there is no legal ban, or any proposal of such a ban, on Islamic clothing. At municipal level, Laszlo Toroczkai, the Mayor of Asotthalom, issued a decree that bans the wearing of all forms of face covering (including the niqab, burqa and burkini) in 2016 and in 2017. However, the Constitutional Court of Hungary annulled the ban as unconstitutional. Although there is no legal ban on Muslim dress, many Muslim women do not wear the head scarf in public in order to avoid harassment, in particular in the aftermath of the migrant and refugee crisis.

Places of Islamic Learning and Education	There are no Islamic schools in Hungary; religious instruction is available in mosques. – Orchidea, Turkish kindergarten, primary and secondary school at Cserkesz Street, x district, and Hajdú Street, xiii district, Budapest, founded by the Turkish government. The multicultural institution offers Hungarian and English bilingual education and follows the Hungarian national curriculum. – the OMH organises a weekend school for Muslim children. – the HIC runs a nursery and a primary school in Eastern Hungary as part of the Roma Integration Programme, and is active in delivering Islamic religious lectures in public schools and in its Cultural Centre.
Muslim Media and Publications	Muslim organisations are active in running websites and in using Facebook rather than publishing printed media. – OMH: www.iszlam.com, www.mohamed.hu, www.iszlam.net. – HIC: www.magyariszlam, http://napiiszlam.blog.hu, http://www.nurtoday.com/.

Main Muslim Organisations

– Organisation of Muslims in Hungary (*Magyarországi Muszlimok Egyháza*– OMH, 41 Fehérvári út, Budapest 1119, tel.: ++36 202045852, http://www.iszlamweb.hu). It is a member of the Hungarian Islamic Council with the Hungarian Islamic Community, but the two communities are registered as separate legal entities under the *Law on Religion*. The members of the OMH mainly consist of Arabs, South Asians and Hungarians. The aims of the OMH are to promote an Islamic lifestyle, to encourage interfaith dialogue, the education of non-Muslim Hungarians about Islam and Muslims, and the organisation of pilgrimages (hajj and '*umra*) to Mecca. The organisation

does not see itself interfering in domestic politics. Due to its mission of integrating Muslims into European societies, the OMH does not follow one particular school of Islamic jurisprudence (*madhhab*).
- Hungarian Islamic Community (*Magyar Iszlám Közösség*–HIC, 60 Paskál utca, Budapest 1141, tel.: ++36 302729865, http://www.magyariszlam.hu). The HIC follows the Hanafi school of Islamic jurisprudence. Its members are mainly Turks, Sub-Saharan Africans and Hungarians. Among the Hungarian organisations, the HIC is the most active in politics, trying to build connections with the governing parties. Previous ties with the Hungarian far-right movement (Jobbik) have broken due to the party's openly Islamophobic stance during the migrant and refugee crisis. Its main projects and activities within the community include running the mosques in Budapest, Győr, Miskolc, and Debrecen, and providing regular *sadaqa* (aid) for Muslims and non-Muslims in need (especially clothing and food) in Hungary, but also abroad. For example, between 2004 and 2007 it gave aid to Sudan, in 2007 and 2013 to Syria, in 2005 to Indonesia after the Tsunami, in 2009 to Gaza, in 2011 to Libya, in 2014 to Bosnia and Herzegovina after floods, and in 2015 to refugees travelling through Hungary. The HIC is also responsible for the regular maintenance of the Muslim cemetery in Budapest (a separate parcel of land in the New Public Cemetery of Budapest), as well as conducting research on Islamic historical places in Hungary, organising the hajj and '*umra* to Mecca, providing lectures for Muslims and non-Muslims, and providing legal and social services in refugee camps and prisons, with the permission of the Government.
- Islamic Organisation–Charitable Peace Foundation (*Iszlám Egyház–Jótékonysági Béke Alapítvány*–IO, 29 Bartók Béla út, Budapest 1115, tel.: ++36 13651502, http://www.iszlam.hu). This organisation operates as a charitable foundation. Muslims from different ethnic groups attend the prayers in the mosque of the IO, which has the most diverse community. The IO does not participate in politics.
- Platform of Dialogue (*Dialógus platform*, 16 Andrássy út, Budapest 1062, tel.: ++36 13320635, http://dialogusplatform.hu). The Fethullah Gülen movement-inspired organisation was established by Turkish and Hungarian members in 2005, with the aim of advancing and promoting intercultural and interfaith dialogue.
- Islamic Cultural Trust of Hungary (*Magyar Iszlám Kulturális Egyesület*, 6/a Makk utca, Budapest). This organisation includes the Hungarian followers of the Sufi Süleyman Hilmi Tunahan, and started its activities by running a Qur'an school in 2006.

- Hungarian Islamic League for the Defence of Human Rights (*Magyar Iszlám Jogvédő Egyesület*–HILDHR, 41 Fehérvári út, Budapest 1119, email: iszlamjogvedoliga@gmail.com, https://www.facebook.com/iszlamjogvedoliga/,). The Hungarian Islamic League for the Defence of Human Rights was registered as an NGO in 2016 by its founder Abdul-Fattah Munif. Its mission is to prevent acts of hate against Muslims in Hungary by registering these attacks, and by informing the public about all kind of verbal or physical Islamophobic acts and legal procedures. The organisation provides legal advice for Muslims regarding their religious rights under Hungarian legislation. The League also promotes interfaith dialogue among the religious groups of Hungary, and conducts research on Islam and its culture.
- Hungarian Youth Society (*Muszlim Ifjúsági Társaság*, 41 Fehérvári út, Budapest 1119, tel.: ++36 705825102, ++36 308598081, email: info@mmemit.com). A group of young Muslim activists attached to the OMH established the Hungarian Youth Society in September 2015, with the aim of supporting young Muslims living in Hungary by organising programmes and making their voices heard in society at large.

Ireland

James Carr[1]

Introduction

Ireland's Muslim presence continues to grow, as indeed does the range of initiatives involving men and women affiliated to various Islamic organisations in the country. 2017 witnessed various debates play out among Muslim communities in Ireland in the spheres of radicalisation, extremism and state regulation of Islam. Catalysed by local and international events, leading representatives of different Islamic organisations in Ireland debated their role vis-à-vis challenging the issues of radicalisation and extremism within and outside Ireland's Muslim communities. Calls that more needs to be done were levelled against some of the key Islamic organisations in the Irish context, who countered that they were already active in this regard.[2] Outside of the Islamic organisations themselves, a leading Islamic figure in Ireland, Sheikh Umar Al-Qadri, called for Irish authorities to restrict international funding for Muslim organisations/structures; and, in addition to these financial restrictions, that a prohibition be placed on international Islamic "hate preachers" from visiting the country.[3] These latter points formed part of Sheikh Al-Qadri's broader stance, which advocates for state regulation of Islam in Ireland.

Outside of these debates, reports of local anti-Muslim hostility and discrimination continue to come to the fore. At a political level, actors from both

---

[1] James Carr, PhD, lectures in the Department of Sociology at the University of Limerick, Ireland. Building on previous scholarly and policy oriented publications, in 2016 he published his book *Experiences of Islamophobia: Living with Racism in the Neoliberal Era* (London-New York: Routledge) which focused on anti-Muslim racism in Ireland set in an international context. He has also undertaken and published research with the Immigrant Council of Ireland, supported by the Open Society Foundations, entitled "Islamophobia in Dublin: experiences and how to respond". He is a co-editor on the recently published collection of essays *Public and Political Discourses of Migration* (London: Rowman and Littlefield) and was a contributor to the *Yearbook of Muslims in Europe* for Ireland for 2015 and 2016.

[2] Sheehan, Maeve, "Death of Dublin jihadi confirms worst fears of the enemy within; Khalid Kelly was suspected of radicalising Muslim converts before he blew himself up in Mosul earlier this month, writes Maeve Sheehan", *Sunday Independent,* 20 November 2016.

[3] Limerick Civic Trust, *Autumn Lecture Series 2017,* "Sheikh Dr Umar Al-Qadri discusses Immigration and Integration", https://www.youtube.com/watch?v=IxdvWdcv2bE, accessed 30 March 2018; Riegel, Ralph, "As Muslims, it is our duty to speak up against extremists", *Irish Independent*, 25 May 2017.

mainstream political parties in Ireland, and newcomers with European pedigree, such as Generation Identity UK and Éire, have been vocal in disseminating anti-Muslim sentiments.[4] This report highlights the international connectedness of Muslim communities in Ireland as well as some of the domestic activities undertaken by Islamic organisations in the State. Muslim communities in Ireland continue to demonstrate strong links with Islamic scholars and institutions internationally. At a domestic level, Islamic bodies in Ireland continue to encourage greater political engagement within Muslim communities. In addition to political work, a range of Muslim organisations continue to participate in charitable activities, particularly with Ireland's homeless. The final part of this report brings to light some insights of Muslims in Ireland derived from data presented from the most recent Census.

Public Debates

2017 witnessed ongoing public debates on the subject of Muslims in Ireland. Yet again, reports of anti-Muslim hostility and discrimination in Ireland were made evident in the publication of the *European Islamophobia Report*, and the submission for Ireland therein, as well as in national print media.[5] These reports referred to lived experiences of anti-Muslim hostility and discrimination, as well as problematic media reporting practices on issues relating to Muslim communities. These included: the co-location of the words "Muslim" and "Islam(ic)" with terms such as "terrorism" and "extremism"; themes of an alleged "clash of civilisations", and Muslims described as an "enemy within" were also evident.[6] The question of Muslims in Ireland and their role in combatting, or allegedly promoting terrorism, was visible in debates within Muslim communities throughout 2017, as were discussions on their integration and the broader role of the State in facilitating this.

The most visible debates around Muslims and Islam in Ireland were those relating to an alleged terrorist threat coming from certain Irish Muslims; the issues of regulation of religious activities and integration were the most evident though. These issues can be set within a context of other events that amplified

---

4   Carr, James, "Ireland", in Enes Bayrakli and Farid Hafez (eds.), *European Islamophobia Report 2017*, (Ankara: SETA 2018), pp. 326–341, http://www.islamophobiaeurope.com/, accessed 30 March 2018.
5   Carr, "Ireland", *European Islamophobia Report 2017*; Phelan, Andrew, "Woman (58) pulled veil off 17-year-old's face and roared abuse at her in attack on city street", *Irish Independent*, 2 October 2017.
6   Carr, "Ireland", *European Islamophobia Report 2017*.

the debate. These included, in particular, the case of the Irish female convert to Islam who claimed to have been radicalised; and relatedly, albeit to a lesser extent, the public pronouncements on social media of another, this time male, Irish convert to Islam.

In the aftermath of the terrorist attacks on London Bridge in June 2017 a press conference was held in the Al Mustafa Islamic Centre in Dublin, organised by Sheikh Umar Al-Qadri.[7] Sheikh Al-Qadri has been a key figure in Ireland for raising awareness of the potential for extremism and radicalisation within and without Ireland.[8] The focus of this press conference was a Muslim woman with the alias "Aaliya." The woman, whose face was concealed behind a niqab, stated that she was born and brought up in Ireland and converted to Islam when she was 18, inspired, she claimed, by the attacks in New York and Washington on 11 September 2001.[9] She moved to London aged 23 where she was, according to her own account, "radicalised". Over a period of time she met with Anjem Choudary in Ireland and the UK, and also met two of the men who carried out the London Bridge attack. During her press conference, "Aalyia" claimed that there are 150 "Muslim extremists" residing in Ireland. "Aaliya" also claimed that these "extremists" saw Ireland as lenient when it comes to policing their activities.[10]

Shortly before this press conference took place, reports in the media emerged in relation to another Irish Muslim who allegedly posted "inflammatory messages under the name 'Abu Yusuf Al Irlandi'", and was also critical towards "Muslims who condemn jihadi terror attacks".[11] According to reports, "Al Irlandi" was very active on at least two social media sites–including one known as Islam4Ireland–both are no longer active–and attended mosques in Dublin.[12] Responding to the reports of "Al Irlandi's" activities, Sheikh Umar

---

7 Anderson, Nicola, "'There are at least 150 extremists here who see Ireland as a soft touch: Nicola Anderson talks to a young Muslim woman about how she became deradicalised after being a jihadi wife", *Irish Independent*, 10 June, 2017.

8 Carr, James, "Ireland", in Oliver Scharbrodt, Samim Akgönül, Ahmet Alibašić, Jørgen S. Nielsen and Egdūnas Račius (eds.), *Yearbook of Muslims in Europe*, vol. 8 (Leiden: Brill, 2017), pp. 362–379; Irish Muslim Peace and Integration Council, "Not in our name protest against ISIS", http://impic.ie/not-in-our-name-protest-against-isis.html, accessed 29 March 2018.

9 Anderson, "There are at least 150 extremists here who see Ireland as a soft touch".

10 Anderson, "'There are at least 150 extremists here who see Ireland as a soft touch".

11 O'Neill, Katie, and Ali Bracken, "The Irish voice of Islamist fanatics; hard line Muslim convert spouts hate speech online and is 'engaging' with mosque youths. London terror aftermath: the Irish fanatic defending jihad", *Irish Daily Mail*, 7 June, 2017.

12 O'Neill and Bracken, "The Irish voice of Islamist fanatics".

Al-Qadri spoke out to denounce the individual and his actions, and called on other imams in Ireland to distance themselves from him.[13]

His comments point to an important aspect of the public debates in question. These are the claims by individuals such as Sheikh Umar Al-Qadri and others, that "radicalism" and "extremism" are issues that need to be addressed but are being ignored by other leaders of Islamic organisations in Ireland, with him and others calling for more to be done.[14] In addition to singling out the mosque on the South Circular Road in Dublin, where the Islamic Foundation of Ireland is located, Sheikh Al-Qadri was also critical of Sheikh Hussein Halawa, imam at the Islamic Cultural Centre of Ireland (ICCI) in Clonskeagh, also in Dublin, the largest mosque in the country, for being "friends" with "Al-Irlandi" on Facebook.

The points raised by Sheikh Al-Qadri resulted in the imam of the Dublin Mosque distancing himself and his community from "Al Irlandi".[15] However, Sheikh Halawa, responding in an article published a few days later, stated that, in relation to Facebook and "Al Irlandi": "I have hundreds or maybe thousands of followers. I don't access their pages, I don't know what they support and what they do not support ...".[16] In this wide ranging article, Sheikh Halawa responded to many of the other criticisms that have been directed at him in the recent past. These included the condemnation of terrorist activity and the need for it to be addressed through the appropriate authorities.[17] Addressing the allegations that he is a member of the Muslim Brotherhood, he stated that: "... I have never been a member of that group ...". Speaking to another Irish newspaper, Halawa addressed the issue of radicalisation in Ireland, using unequivocal language: "A very positive thing is the Muslim community in Ireland just doesn't accept any radicalism or terrorism–they despise it and they vocally put effort into despising it ... The majority [of Muslims] would disown anyone that has those opinions".[18]

Sheikh Halawa also distanced his son, Ibrahim, from membership of the Muslim Brotherhood.[19] Ibrahim was, at that point, still imprisoned in Egypt after participating in protests against the military coup, led by the current

---

13   O'Neill and Bracken, "The Irish voice of Islamist fanatics".
14   Sheehan, "Death of Dublin jihadi confirms worst fears of the enemy within".
15   O'Neill and Bracken, "The Irish voice of Islamist fanatics".
16   "'Islam does not accept any form of terrorism', says Sheikh Halawa", *Sunday Independent*, 11 June 2017.
17   "'Islam does not accept any form of terrorism', says Sheikh Halawa", *Sunday Independent*.
18   O'Neill, Katie, "Muslims in Ireland have no tolerance for radicals", *Irish Daily Mail*, 8 June 2017.
19   "'Islam does not accept any form of terrorism', says Sheikh Halawa", *Sunday Independent*.

Egyptian president Abdel-Fattah Sisi in 2013. Ibrahim was held in prison for four years, a period in which his trial adjourned a total of 28 times, before he was eventually released in October 2017.[20] The alleged links between Sheikh Halawa and his son with the Muslim Brotherhood repeatedly emerged in discussions about Ibrahim's detention, upon and after his release.[21] Sheikh Umar Al-Qadri raised the issue on social media stating that he did not "understand why most reports of Ibrahim Halawa in the media fail to mention the strong Muslim Brotherhood link of his household".[22] Speaking at an event in Limerick as part of a public lecture series, Sheikh Al-Qadri stated that Ibrahim Halawa travelled to Egypt with the intention of participating in political events, a point denied by Ibrahim himself.[23] Sheikh Al-Qadri continued that Ibrahim's father, as an imam, should be encouraging Muslim youth to stay in Ireland and participate and contribute to Irish society, while also discouraging participation in international conflicts.[24] Sheikh-Al Qadri also noted the racist statements that were made about Ibrahim Halawa in Ireland during his detention, and hoped for his speedy release.[25]

Other issues raised publicly by Sheikh Umar Al-Qadri in his Limerick address related to broader aspects of Islam in Ireland.[26] Reiterating calls made in late 2016, in the aftermath of an attack on a Berlin Christmas market, Sheikh Al-Qadri called again for the establishment of a regulatory body for Muslim affairs in Ireland, facilitated by the State.[27] Previous calls for the establishment

---

20 Fegan, Catherine, "An innocent abroad? As campaigners await his release after four years of detention, is it time to start asking questions about why Ibrahim Halawa and his sisters went to Egypt, why they joined Muslim Brotherhood protests … and why they refused a safe passage home negotiated by the Irish Government?", *Irish Daily Mail,* 7 October, 2017.

21 See e.g. RTÉ, "Ibrahim Halawa says he was never a member of the Muslim Brotherhood", https://www.rte.ie/news/2017/1103/917389-halawa/, accessed 25 January 2018; Farrell, Craig, "'Not members'. Jailed Ibrahim Halawa's dad insists none of his family are members of an Islamic terrorist organisation", *The Irish Sun,* 8 October 2017; Creighton, Lucinda, "People who raise legitimate and necessary questions about Ibrahim Halawa are not racist–they are concerned", *The Irish Sun,* 8 November 2017.

22 Mitchell, Susan, "Ireland's leading imam on fatwas, feminism and his son Ibrahim Halawa", *Sunday Business Post*, 7 October 2017.

23 Limerick Civic Trust, *Autumn Lecture Series 2017*; RTÉ, "Ibrhaim Halawa says he was never a member of the Muslim Brotherhood", https://www.rte.ie/news/2017/1103/917389-halawa/, accessed 30 March 2018.

24 Limerick Civic Trust, *Autumn Lecture Series 2017.*

25 Limerick Civic Trust, *Autumn Lecture Series 2017.*

26 Limerick Civic Trust, *Autumn Lecture Series 2017.*

27 Limerick Civic Trust, *Autumn Lecture Series 2017.*

of such a body were rejected by the former Taoiseach (prime minister) Enda Kenny (in office from 2011 to 2017).[28]

Sheikh Al-Qadri raised this issue in Limerick, when making reference to the proposed construction of a new mosque in Blanchardstown, a suburb of Dublin, for which a submission for planning permission was made in September 2017.[29] The new mosque project, driven by Taufiq Al Sattar and the Shuhada Foundation, will include halal food store(s), sports facilities and a private primary level school. Al Sattar made a pledge to construct the mosque following the tragic deaths of his wife, daughter, and two sons in an arson attack in the UK city of Leicester in 2013.[30] According to reports, Al Sattar will fund the construction of the new mosque from his own private resources, from donations from the people of Leicester, as well as through fund raising initiatives with medical students in Pakistan and Saudi Arabia.[31] Sheikh Al-Qadri questioned the funding of the mosque project, and raised queries as to the backgrounds of those behind it, alleging links with Wahhabi Islam. He claimed that those behind the project were "secretive about it".[32] Sheikh Al-Qadri called on the Irish government to ban international funding for the construction of mosques.

In a similar vein, earlier in 2017, Sheikh Al-Qadri stated that he supports "legislation that bans hate preachers from entering the EU and also deports their sympathisers".[33] Sheikh Al-Qadri called for the State instead to support the needs of the Muslim communities in Ireland by supporting Islamic centres whose values align with that of the State; that through such centres, the State can establish a set of common standards to be met across Islamic organisations, standards that must be met if support is to be provided. Sheikh Al-Qadri noted that such state initiatives would eliminate foreign influence on Islam in Ireland.[34]

In terms of the constitution of the proposed regulatory body, Sheikh Al-Qadri noted that such a body would be inclusive of all aspects of Islam in Ireland. This body would agree on issues such as educational programmes to

---

28 Hutton, Brian, "Berlin-style terror attack in Ireland 'cannot be ruled out', Enda Kenny warns", *Irish Independent,* 24 December 2016.
29 Power, Jack, "Plans submitted for large mosque centre in Blanchardstown", *The Irish Times*, 2 September 2017.
30 Power, "Plans submitted for large mosque centre in Blanchardstown".
31 Limerick Civic Trust, *Autumn Lecture Series 2017*.
32 Limerick Civic Trust, *Autumn Lecture Series 2017*.
33 Riegel, Ralph, "As Muslims, it is our duty to speak up against extremists", *Irish Independent*, 25 May 2017.
34 Limerick Civic Trust, *Autumn Lecture Series 2017*.

be delivered in religious schools, and also ensure a sort of uniformity of message in sermons, for example, a common position discouraging young Muslims from travelling to international conflict zones but encouraging them to participate in civic life in Ireland instead.[35] In terms of governmental actions, Sheikh Al-Qadri called for the State itself to play a greater role in facilitating the integration of Muslim communities in Ireland, that, "[W]hen people feel part of a community and valued, the risk of radicalisation disappears".[36] Al-Qadri was also critical of the Irish government for failing to design and implement a programme to counter radicalisation in Ireland.[37] It is worth noting that the Irish Muslim Board, when meeting in January 2017, also addressed the need for greater inclusion, but their position on "extremism" in Ireland is at odds with Sheikh Al-Qadri's.[38]

As for anti-Muslim hostility and discrimination, reports emerged in the media of attacks on mosques in Limerick and Galway. These included the breaking of a window in one incident, while others included the receipt in the post of a Qur'an wrapped in pork.[39] Reports also emerged in September 2017 of a local Councillor for the Dún Laoghaire-Rathdown County Council, Brian Murphy–a member of the main party in the Irish government, Fine Gael–and the dissemination of anti-Muslim messages on social media.[40] Reports stated that Murphy posted comments on social media including: "Sharia law is operating in Ireland and most of the political class either do not know or do not care. It is a subversion of our legal system".[41] The Fine Gael party whip was removed from Cllr Murphy for twelve months by the Party Executive, meaning that he cannot claim to represent nor affiliate himself with the party.[42]

---

35 Limerick Civic Trust, *Autumn Lecture Series 2017*.
36 Meagher, John, "Muslims in Ireland: a growing community that's keen for more integration", *Irish Independent*, 22 April 2017.
37 "Assessing jihadist levels: optimism will not stop terror attack", *Irish Examiner*, 30 August 2017.
38 Pollak, Sorcha, "Greater effort needed to ensure inclusion of Irish Muslims, group hears", *The Irish Times*, 19 January 2017.
39 Dunne, Séan, "Muslims 'terrified' after Galway mosque attacked during prayers", *The Irish Times*, 6 June 2017; Sheridan, Anne, "Verse of the Quran wrapped in bacon are sent to Muslim leader", *Limerick Leader*, 10 June 2017.
40 McQuinn, Cormac, and Kathy Armstrong, "'We will take any necessary action'– Taoiseach distances himself from FG councillors comments on Islam and refugees", *Irish Independent*, 7 September 2017.
41 McQuinn and Armstrong, "We will take any necessary action".
42 McMahon, Aíne, "FG councillor loses party whip after 'Sharia law" comment", *The Irish Times*, 3 November 2017.

The establishment in Ireland of an Identitarian affiliated group is important to note: Generation Identity UK and Ireland (GI) are an anti-Islamic, anti-immigration group.[43] GI launched in the summer of 2017, and their activities have included meetings. They have promoted themselves through videos, media activities and the distribution of literature.[44]

Transnational Links

Questions regarding the connection between Irish Islamic organisations and those at an international level have been noted in the past and are discussed in the above section.[45] These aside, 2017 provided further examples of the connectivity between Muslim communities in Ireland and those abroad. As in previous years, internationally based Islamic scholars and speakers visited Ireland to participate in seminars and lectures. For example, in January, Sheikh Majidi Aqil delivered a lecture on the topic of Muslim women living in the West. Sheikh Aqil is based in Manchester Mosque and is a graduate from Al-Azhar and Manchester Universities and a lecturer at the University of Gaza, in the Palestinian Territories.[46]

In addition to these activities, interactions between Muslim organisations in Ireland and international political delegations also took place in 2017. The Islamic Cultural Centre of Ireland welcomed a ten-member parliamentary delegation from Indonesia in March. The delegation were hosted by Nooh Al-Kaddo, Chief Executive of the Islamic Cultural Centre of Ireland, and Imam Sheikh Halawa, among others.[47] Towards the end of 2017, Sheikh Umar Al-Qadri met with the Pakistani Minister for Religious Affairs, Sardar Muhammad

---

43   Identitarian Movement, "Home", https://identitarian-movement.org/, accessed 10 January 2018.
44   Generation Identity Ireland/Northern Ireland Facebook page: https://www.facebook.com/giEIRE/, accessed 10 January 2018.
45   Scharbrodt, Oliver, Tuula Sakaranaho, Adil Hussain Khan, Yafa Shanneik and Vivian Ibrahim, *Muslims in Ireland: Past and Present* (Edinburgh: Edinburgh University Press, 2015), pp. 91–112.
46   Islamic Foundation of Ireland, "Muslim girls in the West", http://www.islaminireland.com/news/muslim-girls-in-the-west/, accessed 2 February 2018.
47   Islamic Cultural Centre of Ireland, "Indonesian delegation visits ICCI", http://www.islamireland.ie/news/indonesian-delegation-visits-icci/, accessed 2 February 2018; McGarry, Patsy, "Who is Dr Noh al-Kaddo, Chief Executive of Islamic Centre?", *The Irish Times,* 12 March 2018.

Yousuf, in Abu Dhabi.[48] The international aspect of Ireland's Muslim communities is not limited to hosting or visiting events such as those discussed here. Islamic organisations based in Ireland have also been vocal in condemning international terrorism; the atrocities visited upon the Rohingya people in Myanmar; and also the decision of US President Donald J. Trump to move the US Embassy in Israel to Jerusalem.[49]

Law and Domestic Politics

Broader developments impacted on Muslim communities in Ireland in 2017. The year started with a conference in Dublin, organised by the Irish Muslim Board. The IMB event included a range of speakers from academia and politics, including Davide Stanton, Minister of State for Equality, Immigration and Integration, who addressed the audience at the beginning of the event. Issues debated by participants included: current legislation around the rights of children from minority religions to access the school of their choice; societal inclusion; the need for hate crime legislation; and broader social issues facing Muslims and non-Muslims in Ireland.[50] It is interesting to note that in the weeks after the IMB event, Minister Stanton's own Department published its Migrant Integration Strategy document.[51] The cover of the document includes an image of Muslim women wearing a head scarf, yet, the document only refers to Muslim communities once: "Radicalisation has been a particular issue for other European societies where ideologies that seek to undermine the state

---

48   Irish Muslim Peace and Integration Council, "Shaykh Al-Qadri meets Pakistani Minister for Religious Affairs", http://impic.ie/h-e-shaykh-al-qadri-meets-pakistani-minister-of-religious-affairs-h-e-sardar-muhammad-yousuf.html, accessed 2 February 2018.

49   Islamic Foundation of Ireland, "Press release", http://www.islaminireland.com/news/urgent-appeal-for-protection-of-rohingya-press-release/; Islamic Cultural Centre of Ireland, "Press release", http://www.islamireland.ie/news/press-release-urgent-appeal-for-protecton-and-safety-of-rohingya-in-rakhine-state/; Irish Muslim Peace and Integration Council, "Press release", http://impic.ie/press-release-impic-condemns-persecution-of-rohingya-will-protest-on-friday-8th-september-at-5pm.html; Islamic Foundation of Ireland, "Press release", http://www.islaminireland.com/news/press-release-jerusalem/; Islamic Cultural Centre of Ireland, "Press release", http://www.islamireland.ie/news/jerusalem-press-release/, all accessed 2 February 2018.

50   Pollak, "Greater effort needed to ensure inclusion of Irish Muslims, group hears".

51   Pollak, Sorcha, and Elaine Edwards, "Hate crime legislation needed 'as matter of urgency'", *The Irish Times*, 23 March 2017; Department of Justice and Equality, *The Migrant Integration Strategy: a Blueprint for the Future*, http://www.integration.ie/website/omi/omiwebv6.nsf/page/JWKY-AJEE6A1021139-en/$File/Migrant_Integration_Strategy_English.pdf, accessed 10 January 2018.

have prompted some young people, particularly second-generation Muslim immigrants, to undertake terrorist actions".[52]

In June 2017, the Minister for Education, Richard Bruton, proposed that schools–the patronage of which in Ireland largely resides with the Catholic Church–will no longer be able to discriminate in admissions on the basis of religious identity.[53] Heretofore, schools could offer preferential treatment to potential students on the basis that their faith identity aligned with that of the school.[54] Exceptions exist for minority faith schools, which will still be allowed to consider the religious identity of the person seeking admission in their decision. If not, the Minister argued, minority faith schools may not be able to maintain their religious ethos.[55]

Activities and Initiatives of Main Muslim Organisations

2017 commenced with the Irish Muslim Board (IMB) hosting an event that addressed political issues and engaged actors from the Government, inter alia, in a debate on a range of issues affecting Muslim communities in Ireland. The IMB is a relatively new organisation that focuses on Muslim communities' engagement with the main political parties in the country.[56] The IMB developed out of the South Dublin Muslim Board, which was formed to engage with political groups in Ireland and encourage Muslim participation in the lead up to the last general election.[57] This was just one of a range of activities organised by the main Muslim organisations in Ireland.[58]

Muslim community groups were active when it comes to challenging anti-Muslim sentiment and policies. The group known as the Muslim Sisters of Eire (MSOE) organised a number of events. The first was held in March 2017 in the context of the ruling by the European Court of Justice vis-à-vis "political, philosophical or religious symbols" in the workplace; MSOE held a protest

---

52   Department of Justice and Equality, *The Migrant Integration Strategy*.
53   Doyle, Kevin, "'Baptism barrier' to end as Bruton plans to stop Catholic schools admitting on basis of religion", *Irish Independent,* 28 June 2017.
54   For more information on the Irish legal position vis-à-vis hate crime, please refer to Carr, "Ireland", *European Islamophobia Report 2017*.
55   Doyle, Kevin, "'Baptism barrier'".
56   Irish Muslim Board, Facebook page: https://www.facebook.com/irishmuslimboard/?ref=page_interna, accessed 30 March 2018.
57   McGarry, Patsy, "New Muslim group in Dublin to encourage engagement with politics", *The Irish Times,* 28 December 2015.
58   For example, see: Islamic Cultural Centre of Ireland, "News", http://www.islamireland.ie/news/, accessed 30 March 2018.

outside the European Commission office in Dublin.[59] In April, the group organised a conference entitled "Being Me: Muslim Women Defying Stereotypes", with speakers from different sectors providing insights on the experiences of Muslim women in Ireland and abroad.[60] The MSOE and partners also made the news in December in relation to their ongoing voluntary work providing food and clothing to homeless people in Dublin, a service they provide every Friday evening in the city centre.[61] During Ramadan Muslim youth groups organised an open *iftar*. Branded as "Under One Tent", the three-day event was held on the grounds of St Patrick's Cathedral, Dublin on the green area outside the main building.[62]

Among the many diverse events organised throughout 2017 by the main Muslim organisations in Ireland, lectures relating to "Muslim Girls in the West",[63] and two conferences on the issue of mental health awareness took place.[64] Muslim organisations also participated in interfaith events,[65] and a public fund raising campaign took place to raise monies to purchase the premises currently utilised as Al Furqan mosque in Limerick City.[66]

Events that attracted national media attention included the charitable activities of the Islamic Cultural Centre of Ireland (ICCI) linked to the impact of Ex-Hurricane Ophelia. In advance of the storm's arrival, an invitation was issued to members of the local community and homeless people to take shelter in the Centre. The doors of the Centre remained open for a 24-hour period

---

59 MacDonald, Sarah, "'Backlash' against ruling allowing hijab ban in workplace", *Irish Independent,* 20 March 2017; Pollack, Sorcha, "Protestors warn ECJ ruling to further alienate Muslim women", *The Irish Times,* 21 March 2017.

60 Dublin City Interfaith Forum, "Events", https://www.dublincityinterfaithforum.org/event/109/being-me-ndash-muslim-women-defying-stereotypes, accessed 12 January 2018.

61 Brophy, Darragh, "'We're just trying to do as much as we can': the volunteers handing out food and giving haircuts at the GPO every Friday", *The Journal,* 9 December 2018, http://www.thejournal.ie/gpo-homeless-services-3740663-Dec2017/, accessed 26 January 2017.

62 Dublin City Interfaith Forum, "Events", https://www.dublincityinterfaithforum.org/event/113/under-one-tent accessed 26 January 2018.

63 Islamic Foundation of Ireland, "Muslim girls in the West".

64 Islamic Foundation of Ireland, "Mental health awareness", http://www.islaminireland.com/news/mental-health-awareness-2017/, accessed 2 February 2018; Islamic Cultural Centre of Ireland, "Mental health conference", http://www.islamireland.ie/news/mental-health-conference-november-4th/, accessed 2 February 2018.

65 Islamic Cultural Centre of Ireland, "ICCI hosts interfaith meeting", http://www.islamireland.ie/news/icci-hosts-an-interfaith-meeting/, accessed 1 February 2018.

66 Rabbits, Nick, "Limerick mosque crowdfunds €50,000 in a single month to prevent closure", *Limerick Leader,* 8 November 2017.

during this time.[67] The ICCI opened its doors again to members of Dublin's homeless community during a particularly severe cold spell in late November 2017, offering shelter from the elements as well as food and refreshments.[68] Earlier in 2017, the ICCI also opened its doors to the Irish Taoiseach (prime minister) to celebrate 'Id al-Fitr.[69]

Towards the end of 2017, the National Ahlul Bayt Islamic Centre in Milltown, Dublin hosted the Eleventh Annual Imam Hussain Condolence Conference in November. This public event again comprised speakers from a range of backgrounds, including those from academia, local communities, and representatives of other faiths. Continuing the international dimension of Ireland's Muslim communities, the event was attended by the Shi'i cleric Shamshad Rezavi, who is based in Oslo.

Muslim Population: History and Demographics

Albeit with minor exceptions, that included particular individuals or within certain industries, up until the mid-20th century it was difficult to discern the presence of Muslim communities in Ireland. This was to change from the late 1950s onwards. Starting from modest numbers in the low hundreds, Muslim immigrants, predominantly from a middle-class background, started to migrate to Ireland for the purpose of third-level education. This pattern of educational migration, in relatively low numbers, was maintained until the early 1990s. However, motivated by the need to seek refuge or economic opportunities, the 1990s witnessed not only a growth in the number of Muslims coming to Ireland but also an increase in the ethno-national, religious (in broad terms: Sunni, Shi'a, Sufi, Ahmadiyya) and class diversity within the Muslim communities of Ireland.[70]

With the publication of data taken from the Census of 2016, new statistical insights on the demographic constitution of the Muslim population in Ireland became available in 2017. According to this data, there are now 63,443 Muslims

---

67   Islamic Cultural Centre of Ireland, "Press-release: Ex-Hurricane Ophelia", http://www.islamireland.ie/news/press-release-ex-hurricane-ophelia/, accessed 1 February 2018.
68   Islamic Cultural Centre of Ireland, "Doors open to homeless during 'polar low'", http://www.islamireland.ie/news/doors-open-to-homeless-during-polar-low/, accessed 1 February 2018.
69   Islamic Cultural Centre of Ireland, "Press Release", http://www.islamireland.ie/news/an-taoiseach-leo-varadkars-eid-visit-to-the-icci/, accessed 2 February 2018.
70   Carr, *Experiences of Islamophobia*, pp. 154–155.

living in Ireland.[71] This may seem a small number (1.3% of the population) but to put this in context, in data from the 1991 Census in Ireland the figure was just 3,875 Muslims living in the country.[72] Thus, the pace at which the Muslim population has grown in Ireland is tremendous. To put it another way, the number of Muslims in Ireland has increased by almost 100% from the 2006 figure of 32,539 Muslim men, women and children.[73] In terms of diversity, the Muslim presence in Ireland is diverse, as can be seen in the data below. Interestingly, the majority of Muslims in Ireland are Irish citizens (56%) (predominantly naturalised citizens). Moreover, just over a quarter (26%) of all Muslims in Ireland were born in the State.[74]

Muslim Population	63,443 (1.3% of total population in 2016).
Ethnic/National Backgrounds	National backgrounds:[190]
	Irish: 33,971 (55%)
	Pakistani: 6,823 (11.4%)
	British: 2,069 (3.4%)
	Saudi: 1,775 (2.9%)
	Bangladeshi: 1,209 (2%)
	Afghan: 1,160 (1.9%)
	Other European: 1,473 (2.3%)
	Various African countries: 5,293 (8.5%).
Inner-Islamic Groups	Official statistics with regards to religious diversity among Muslims in Ireland are not available. The majority of Muslims in Ireland align with Sunni

---

71　Central Statistics Office, "Census of population 2016–profile 8 Irish travellers, ethnicity and religion", http://www.cso.ie/en/releasesandpublications/ep/p-cp8iter/p8iter/p8rnc/, accessed 29 March 2018.
72　Central Statistics Office, "Census of population 2016".
73　Central Statistics Office, "Census of population 2016".
74　Central Statistics Office, "Census of population 2016".
75　Percentage figure is based on the number of responses to the question on nationality in the Census, which are 62,032, of a total figure of those who identified as Muslim of 63,443. For more see: Central Statistics Office Reports: http://www.cso.ie/px/pxeirestat/Statire/SelectVarVal/Define.asp?maintable=E7016&PLanguage=0, accessed 29 March 2018, and also Central Statistics Office, "Census of population 2016".

traditions. However, there is an estimated aggregate figure of 6,000 Shi'i Muslims in Ireland; the number of the Ahmadiyya community is estimated to have grown to be greater than 500.[76]

Geographical Spread Almost half (47%) of Ireland's Muslim population lives in Dublin. Outside of Dublin, approximately 6% live in Limerick City and County; the next most populated areas are Cork County (4.5%) and Cork City (3.6%), while the smallest percentage population of Muslims residing in any county in Ireland is in Leitrim (0.4%).

Number of Mosques Such is the character of prayer rooms and mosques in Ireland that detailed research is required to map the number of mosques across the country. A conservative estimate would place the figure at greater than 50.

Muslim Burial Sites Ireland has one dedicated Muslim cemetery, whilst other cemeteries facilitate Muslim burial. These include:

- Muslim Cemetery (dedicated), Ballyhaunis, Co. Mayo
- Muslim section in St. Patrick's Cemetery, Dowdallshill, Co. Louth
- Muslim section in Newtown Cemetery, South Dublin
- Muslim section in Passage West Cemetery, County Cork
- Muslim sections in Galway City cemeteries
- Muslim section in Chetwynd Cemetery, Togher, County Cork.

---

76 Email communication from Ahmadiyya community leader, 18 January 2016.

"Chaplaincy" in State Institutions	The Health Service Executive provides guidance on its website as to how medical staff can contact a local imam should the patient request it; only Sunni and Shi'i imams are referred to. The Prison Service also facilitates visits from local imams if requested. The Irish Defence Forces do not refer to the option of chaplaincy for Muslim staff.[77]
Halal Products	Halal slaughter is permitted and practised in specialist firms such as Nour Foods in Ballyhaunis, Co. Mayo, which has a long tradition of halal meat production and distribution.[78] Interestingly, discussions with Irish Muslims indicate that a considerable number of mainstream meat producers also engage in halal production but do not publicise it for political reasons. Information on halal food is readily available via Islamic centres, as is access to it, particularly in larger urban locations. Access to halal food is available in public institutions.
Dress Code	There are no state level prohibitions on any form of Muslim dress in Ireland for both men and women. However, research has demonstrated that Muslim women and girls have experienced discriminatory practices in/accessing work and at secondary school level vis-à-vis the wearing of the head scarf. In terms of numbers wearing the head scarf, it is common place among Muslim women in Ireland; the niqab is far less common, with the estimated numbers of wearers in the low tens.[79]

---

77   Health Service Executive, "Care of the ill", www.hse.ie/eng/services/Publications/SocialInclusion/InterculturalGuide/Islam/contact.html, accessed 30 January 2018; Irish Prison Service, "Chaplaincy", https://www.irishprisons.ie/prisoner-services/chaplaincy-service/, accessed 30 January 2018; Defence Forces Ireland, "Chaplaincy Service", http://militarychaplaincy.ie/, accessed 30 January 2018.
78   Nour Foods, "Home", http://www.nourfoods.com/, accessed 30 January 2018.
79   Carr, *Experiences of Islamophobia*.

Places of Islamic Learning and Education	In terms of formal education, there are three Muslim primary schools in Ireland, all based in Dublin. Two of these schools are public and the most recent, established in 2014, is private.[80] Muslim organisations and mosques around the country also organise and run Arabic and Qur'an classes locally.
Muslim Media and Publications	n/a.

Main Muslim Organisations

- Ahlul Bayt Islamic Centre (Shia Islamic Centre, Milltown Bridge, Dundrum, Dublin 14, tel.: ++353 12604491, http://homepage.tinet.ie/~ahlulbyteassociation/). Located in the suburbs of South Dublin, the Ahlul Bayt Shi'i Muslim centre is frequented predominantly by Shi'is of Iranian and Iraqi background. The Ahlul Bayt Islamic Centre itself is one of the few purpose-built mosques in Ireland.
- Ahmadiyya Muslim Association Ireland (67 Well Park Grove, Galway, tel.: ++353 191768832, http://galway-mosque.ie/index.html). The Irish branch of the global Ahmadiyya Muslim community is situated in the West of Ireland in Galway. The community is comprised predominantly of Pakistani men and women as well as Irish converts. As with the previous organisation, the relatively new Ahmadiyya mosque in Galway, Masjid Maryam, is one of the few purpose-built facilities in Ireland.
- Al-Mustafa Islamic Centre (31 Coolmine Industrial Estate, Blanchardstown, Dublin 15, tel.: ++353 15156206, www.islamiccentre.ie). Al-Mustafa is a Sunni Sufi organisation. The imam has Pakistani roots while the broader congregation itself is a mix of African, Arab and Asian. Al-Mustafa Islamic Centre is led by Sheikh Umar Al-Qadri, who is heavily involved in socio-political issues relating to Muslim communities in Ireland. As a result of this activity, the Al-Mustafa Centre, although small, has hosted high profile media and political events.

---

80   Islamic Foundation of Ireland, "Education", www.islaminireland.com/education/, accessed 23 January 2017; Shaheeda Zainab Muslim Independent Primary School, "Home", www.szainabschool.com/, accessed 2 February 2018.

- Cork Dawah Centre (73 Shandon Street, Cork, tel.: ++353 214217003, www.corkdawahcentre.ie/). Located in inner city Cork, the Cork Dawah centre congregation is Sunni, and consists of mainly Asian and Arab Muslims. The Dawah Centre provides classes on the Qur'an, lectures on Islam related topics, as well as facilities for women and new Muslims.
- Cork Islamic Cultural Centre (60 Tramore Road, Turners Cross, Cork, tel.: ++353 214320301, www.corkmosque.org/index.html). This centre serves members of the Sunni community in Cork and has an ethnically very mixed congregation. One of the most established Muslim centres in Cork, work is continuing on the construction of a purpose-built mosque, the first in the city.
- Galway Mosque and Islamic Society (13 Sandyview Drive, Riverside, Galway, tel.: ++353 91751621, www.gicc.ie/index.php/contactus). The Galway Mosque and Islamic Society, or Galway Islamic Cultural Centre, caters for Galway's and the surrounding regions' Sunni communities. The Centre is predominantly frequented by Arab and Asian Muslims. Although having gone through a number of iterations in terms of name, the Galway Islamic Cultural Centre is the longest established official Muslim presence in the Galway area, with its roots dating back to the 1970s.
- Irish Muslim Board (Online presence only, https://www.facebook.com/irishmuslimboard/). The IMB is a relatively new organisation that focuses on Muslim communities' engagement with the main political parties in Ireland. The IMB developed out of the South Dublin Muslim Board, which was formed to engage with political groups in Ireland and to encourage Muslim participation in elections.
- Irish Sufi Foundation, Anwar-E-Madina (8–9 Talbott Street, Dublin; email: manan@madina.ie).
- Islamic Cultural Centre of Ireland (19 Roebuck Road, Clonskeagh, Dublin 14, tel.: ++353 12080000, www.islamireland.ie). The Islamic Cultural Centre of Ireland (ICCI) has, in many ways, come to be perceived as the "face of Islam in Ireland". Catering to Dublin's Sunni communities, the congregation is mainly Arab in terms of ethnic background. The ICCI is home to one of the aforementioned Muslim primary schools.
- Islamic Foundation of Ireland (163 South Circular Road, Dublin 8, tel.: ++353 14533242, www.islaminireland.com). This is the oldest Muslim organisation in Ireland, initially established by Muslim students as the Dublin Islamic Society in 1959.
- Kerry Islamic Cultural Centre (Fort Field, Tralee, Co. Kerry; no landline telephone available). The Kerry Islamic Cultural Centre and Tralee Mosque host a diverse Muslim congregation which, although mainly Bangladeshi, also

includes Pakistani, Kosovan, Sudanese, and Afghan people, among others. Although a small town when compared to, for example, Dublin, Tralee is host to a vibrant Muslim community, as discussed above.
- Kilkenny Islamic Centre (Desert Villa, Freshford Road, Kilkenny) is a Sunni organisation in the Southeast of Ireland. Led by Sheikh Ebrahim Ndure, the KIC provides a range of services to the local Muslim communities of Kilkenny and surrounding areas.
- Limerick Islamic Centre (LIC, Old Dooradoyle Road, Limerick, tel.: ++353 61635151). Although a number of mosques and prayer rooms are dotted across the city of Limerick (including the relatively large Al-Furquan mosque in the city centre), the LIC is the location that is most well-known locally. The LIC is Sunni in orientation, and the congregation is mainly Asian.
- Muslim Association of Ireland (Tallaght Mosque, Unit 2, Greenhills Business Centre, Greenhills Road, Tallaght, Dublin 24, tel.: ++353 14523416). The Muslim Association of Ireland, located in South County Dublin serves the local Sunni and mainly Arab communities in the area. As with others mentioned above, the Muslim Association of Ireland engages in community outreach, working with NGOs on the topic of integration and communication. It also provides Islamic services to the local communities.

Italy

Davide Tacchini[1]

Introduction

2017 was a year during which, at least in the last five months, the attention of the media and of political parties, shifted from ISIS and terrorism[2] to migrants and refugees, and the major issue of the conditions for acquiring Italian citizenship. The education and training of imams and, in connection with this, the question of Muslims in prisons were among the new issues that appeared in 2017. For the first time both the media and, less effectively, the State, realised that the role played by prisons in the process of radicalisation of (young) Muslims cannot be ignored any more. For the first time the issue of de-radicalisation was addressed, as part of training programmes for penitentiary officers.

Lega (the League, formerly The Northern League), in particular, has made the struggle against Islam an important and highly visible part of its political platform. The electoral campaign in the lead-up to the 2018 general elections started in 2017. Some of the most frequent themes on which the ballot result has been decided, concerned immigration and Islam and Muslims in Italy.

Public Debates

As mentioned above, in 2017, Italy has witnessed strong debates on a number of topics. They included: ISIS, terror attacks, and the issue of so called "foreign fighters"; immigration, the issue of asylum seekers, in particular; and pathways to Italian citizenship and debates around *ius soli* and *ius culturae*.

---

[1] Davide Tacchini, PhD, is currently Research Fellow and Project Coordinator at the Friedrich-Schiller-Universität (Jena Centre for Reconciliation Studies) in Jena, Germany, and is Visiting Professor of Arabic Language and Literature at the University of Parma, Italy. He is author of *Radicalismo islamico: Con il diario del soggiorno di Sayyid Qutb, negli Stati Uniti dal 1948 al 1950* (*Radical Islamism: With the Diary of Sayyid Qutb's Trip to the US from 1948 to 1950*) (Milan: Obarrao Editore, 2015), and *Islam e integrazione in Italia* (*Islam and Integration in Italy*) (Milan-Venice: Marsilio Editore, 2014), edited with A. Angelucci and Maria Bombardieri. He has also authored a number of articles on radical Islam, Christian-Muslim relations, Islam in Europe and the West, and Islamic reform, and lectures widely on both sides of the Atlantic and in the Arab world.

[2] http://www.ednh.news/it/cronologia-degli-attacchi-terroristici-in-europa-dal-2004-al-2017/, accessed 16 April 2018.

Public discourse was not dominated by the ISIS phenomenon as much as in 2016, but, at least until September, the terrorist attacks for which ISIS claimed responsibility, represented one of the main issues concerning Islam and Muslims in Italy. Almost after every attack, especially after those in London (22 March and 3 June) and Barcelona–Cambrils (17–18 August), public debates occurred. On 18 and 19 August, all major Italian newspapers dedicated their headlines to the attacks in Spain,[3] which reported three Italian casualties. The same thing happened on 23 March and 4 June in the aftermath of the Westminster and London Bridge attacks. Articles in newspapers focused, among other issues, on the relationship between terrorism and the policies of welcoming refugees and asylum seekers.[4]

After every attack, Muslim community leaders condemned ISIS, and criticised not only its criminal acts, but also their Muslim identity, frequently quoting verses from the Qur'an and / or passages from other sources from the Islamic tradition. Emblematic in this regard is the Fatwa of European Muslims against Terrorism,[5] a 2013 document that was republished by the *Unione delle comunità islamiche d'Italia* (Union of the Islamic Communities of Italy–U. Co.I.I.) on its official website on 26 July 2017.[6]

What spurred more in depth public debates, though, has been the political analysis of the attacks, and views developed on Islam by the different parties. A polarisation of positions between the right and left is clearly visible in newspapers. Some of the headlines of the right-wing press focused on the Muslim background of the perpetrators and their allegiance to so-called Islamic State,[7] and used the terrorist incidents as an argument against immigration.[8] The

---

3   *Il Corriere della Sera, Repubblica, La Stampa, Il messaggero, Il Fatto Quotidiano.* The websites www.velvetnews.it and www.dire.it provide the first page of all major Italian newspapers on a daily basis.
4   http://sicurezzainternazionale.luiss.it/2017/12/05/minniti-integrazione-cruciale-evitare-fusione-migranti-terrorismo/, accessed 1 July 2018.
5   http://www.U.Co.I.I..org/documento/la-fatwa-dei-musulmani-deuropa-terrorismo/, accessed 17 April 2018.
6   Another example of the public condemnation of the terror attacks is this U.Co.I.I. press release, on their official website: https://www.U.Co.I.I..org/3464/comunicati-stampa/attacchi-terroristici-spagna/, accessed 22 May 2018.
7   "Rambla, bastardo in fuga. Il gesto: cosa ha fatto dopo aver ucciso 15 persone" (Rambla, the bastard is running away. The deed: what he did after killing 15 people), *Libero*, 20 August 2017. *Libero* removed the adjective "bastard", which it had used on 14 September 2015, after the Paris attacks.
8   "I soldati del Califfato: l'ISIS esulta si Internet e rivendica la mattanza. Il capo di Wikileaks, lo dice anche Assange: è colpa dell'accoglienza" (The caliphate's soldiers: ISIS celebrates on the web and claims the carnage. Wikileaks' leader: welcoming refugees is the cause of these attacks), *Libero*, 19 August 2017.

(perceived) connection between the high number of asylum seekers that have reached the Italian coasts in the last few years and ISIS-related attacks in Europe was a permanent feature throughout the year.

Debates on TV, in which politicians also participated, highlighted that most of the attackers in Belgium, Britain and France, were citizens of the country in which they carried out these attacks. This observation was then used to argue against easier access to Italian citizenship.

The *ius soli* pathway to Italian citizenship is included in the citizenship reform proposal, issued in 2016, which, in 2017, was only passed in one chamber of Parliament. The main reform, compared to the current Law, consists of a new way of obtaining Italian citizenship at birth (*ius soli*), and through schooling or attending formative courses (*ius culturae*). According to the wording approved in the lower chamber of Parliament, anyone may immediately become a citizen of the Republic of Italy who was born in the country to foreign parents. At least one of them must be on permanent leave to remain (*ius soli*). One of the parents is entitled to apply for the citizenship of his/her son/daughter born in Italy.

A foreign minor, who was either born in Italy, or immigrated at the age of twelve or younger, and who has attended a school recognised by the Italian Ministry of Education for at least five years, may become a citizen of the Republic of Italy. If the five years of school attended by the young foreigner are those of primary school, it is required that he/she completes the courses successfully. One of the parents is then entitled to apply for the citizenship of his/her son/daughter born in Italy.[9]

Both of the above mentioned scenarios may involve the children of Muslim immigrants. Therefore, debates on easier access to Italian citizenship also focused on the prospect of an increasing number of Muslim immigrants and their children obtaining it. Most of the political debates in the last months of 2017, in preparation for the 2018 general elections, had the *ius soli* Law as their main topic. *Lega*'s leader, Matteo Salvini, widely used on social networks the two hashtags #*noiussoli* and #*stopinvasione*, sometimes together.[10] As such, the three issues dominating public debates about Muslims in Italy

---

9   http://www.camera.it/leg17/465?tema=integrazione_cittadinanza, accessed 26 April 2018.
10 http://www.repubblica.it/politica/2017/09/12/news/senato_ius_soli_non_in_calendario_per_settembre-175289715/?ref=search, accessed 26 April 2017, is just an example of the wide use of these hashtags.

in 2017–terrorism, the arrival of asylum seekers, and citizenship reform–were connected to one another by right-wing politicians and media outlets.[11]

Transnational Links

All the main Italian Muslim organisations have links with other Islamic associations or governments of either European or Muslim majority countries. The U.Co.I.I.[12] has close relationships with the Qatar Charity Foundation, which supports some of its purpose-built mosques (for example in Bergamo and Ravenna), as well as existing Islamic centres (in Rome, Piacenza and elsewhere).

The Qatar Charity Foundation has provided €25 million to build several U.Co.I.I. affiliated mosques and Islamic centres over the last three years. The Foundation has funded 43 mosques, including those in Ravenna, Catania, Piacenza, Colle Val d'Elsa, Vicenza, Saronno, and Mirandola.[13] This financial support has been endorsed by the Ministry of the Interior as part of article 10 of the *Patto nazionale per un islam Italiano*[14] (National Pact for an Italian Islam).

The *Associazione degli imam e delle guide religiose in Italia* (Italian Islamic Association of Imams and Religious Guides) reiterated its existing links with Tariq Ramadan.[15] As for European connections, the *Associazione degli imam* is linked to the European Council for Fatwa and Research, and also with the Federation of Islamic Organisations in Europe; both organisations are close to European and global networks of the Muslim Brotherhood.[16]

---

11   "La cittadinanza si conquista e non si regala ..." (Citizenship must be deserved and must not be given as a gift) and "La cittadinanza non è un regalo elettorale ..." (Citizenship is not a gift to be given before elections) are two public statements made by Matteo Salvini several times, the last of which on 10 December 2017. See: https://www.youtube.com/watch?v=7UI4i_DJJsQ, accessed 26 April 2018.

12   Some U.Co.I.I. leaders have links with the Muslim Brotherhood in the Middle East and Europe.

13   https://www.huffingtonpost.it/2017/02/02/accordo-islam-italia_n_14572256.html, accessed 16 April 2018.

14   The English version of the full text is available at: http://www.interno.gov.it/sites/default/files/patto_nazionale_per_un_islam_italiano_en_1.2.2017.pdf, accessed 16 April 2018.

15   http://www.ildialogo.org/cEv.php?f=http://www.ildialogo.org/islam/rassegna_1510645573.htm, accessed 20 May 2018.

16   www.facebook.com/Associazione.ImamItalia/posts/1715995841953948, accessed 12 May 2018.

The *Associazione donne musulmane d'Italia* (Association of Muslim Women of Italy–ADMI),[17] the female branch of the U.Co.I.I., restated its relationship with the European Network of Women by participating in its events, mostly focused on Islamophobia, women's rights, and European Muslim identity. In 2016 in reference to the discrimination that affects Muslim women, the European Network against Racism[18] presented the Italian report[19] of a two-year project called: "Forgotten Women: The Impact of Islamophobia on Muslim Women".[20] Italian Muslim women have experienced the same inequalities as other women regarding employment, and verbal and physical violence, but they are compounded by additional factors of (perceived) religion and/or ethnicity.

The *Alleanza islamica d'Italia* (Islamic Alliance of Italy) through the *Volontari alleanza islamica* group (Volunteers of Islamic Alliance) is one of the most active Italian Muslim associations for political causes; it has campaigned on Palestine, Egypt (pro-Morsi, Muslim Brotherhood), and on Syria.[21] It frequently organises demonstrations and raises money for overseas charitable causes in those countries.

Giovani musulmani d'Italia (Muslim Youth of Italy–GMI), the youth branch of the U.Co.I.I., continues to organise volunteer and charity events with Islamic Relief Italia.[22] The GMI still maintains its membership with the Forum of European Muslim Youth and Student Organisations.

The *Comunità religiosa islamica italiana* (Italian Islamic Religious Community–COREIS) has links with international cultural, interfaith and

---

17   Souheir Katkhouda, former president of the *Associazione donne musulmane d'Italia* (ADMI), and Marisa Iannucci, the president of the *Lega islamica femminile Europa* and Life Onlus, have represented Italy at international conferences.
18   www.enar-eu.org/, accessed 23 May 2018.
19   The aim of the Italian report is to document the disproportionate effect of Islamophobia on Muslim women in the fields of employment and racist violence and speech. The report presents an overview of national legislative provisions, practices, academic literature, debates, case law, surveys and opinion polls, press reviews, and consultations with stakeholders. Muslim women of different backgrounds, staff members of anti-racist and feminist associations, MPs, public anti-discrimination centre employees, public officials, lawyers and experts in anti-discrimination law (a total of about 45 people) were interviewed by Giulia Dessi, the researcher who carried out the Italian study: www.enar-eu. org/IMG/pdf/forgotten_women_report_italy_-_final.pdf; www.enar-eu.org/IMG/pdf/ factsheet-italy_web.pdf, both accessed 10 January 2017.
20   www.youtube.com/watch?v=E2K_SwDjCG0; www.enar-eu.org/IMG/pdf/20095_forgotten womenpublication_v5_1_.pdf, both accessed 10 January 2017.
21   www.facebook.com/Foiegi/photos/a.1063330640376634.1073741828.1063303767045988/114 3924405650590/?type=3&theater, accessed 20 May 2018.
22   https://www.islamic-relief.it/chi-siamo/cosa-facciamo/emergenze-umanitarie, accessed 20 May 2018.

economic networks. Its president, Imam Yahya Pallavicini, is one of the Islamic Educational, Scientific and Cultural Organisation (ISESCO) ambassadors, and is also a member of the European Council of Religious Leaders (ECRL).[23] He takes part in symposia and conferences debating the role of religious communities in integrating migrants. Moreover COREIS, through its president, has links with Malaysia, in order to promote training programmes on interreligious dialogue, and sustainable development in both Italy and Malaysia. In Malaysia and the Gulf region, COREIS is involved in halal market networks through its halal agency, Halal Italia.[24]

Three of the main Moroccan organisations in Italy maintain links to their home country. The *Istituto culturale islamico d'Italia* (Islamic Cultural Institute of Italy), the only Islamic organisation that has been legally recognised by the Italian state,[25] is led by Abdallah Redouane,[26] who was directly nominated by Morocco. The *Confederazione islamica italiana* (Italian Islamic Confederation–CII), a network of Moroccan mosques, is funded by Morocco. Moroccan Qur'an reciters, imams and even singers, were invited to several Italian mosques, both under the patronage of the U.Co.I.I. and of other associations. The majority Moroccan *Confederazione islamica Italiana* (Italian Islamic Federation–C.I.I.) has relationships with other European Muslim confederations of Moroccans. Members of the *Partecipazione e spiritualità musulmana* (Muslim Participation and Spirituality–PSM) share the same religious opinions as the group Al-Adl wal-Ihsan.

Zahoor Ahmad Zargar, of the U.Co.I.I., has been cooperating for the last years with the South Korean, UN recognised NGO, Heavenly Culture, World Peace, Restoration of Light (HWPL).[27] On 17–19 September 2017 he took part in the World Alliance of Religions for Peace (WARP) annual meeting,[28] together with 1,200 political and religious leaders, youth groups, and members of women's associations. He was the only Muslim from Italy attending, as he had been invited to represent the U.Co.I.I..

---

23 This is a multi-religious coalition accredited to the United Nations, advancing common action among the world's religious communities for peace. See: http://rfp-europe.eu/, accessed 20 May 2018.
24 http://www.halalitalia.org, accessed 23 May 2018.
25 This recognition means that the *Istituto culturale islamico d'Italia* is the only religious entity which is legally able to represent Islam in Italy.
26 Redouane is also the director of the Great Mosque of Rome.
27 Founded in 2012, it is a non-profit, non-governmental organisation, the purpose of which is achieving world peace and the cessation of war. HWPL has 70 branches in Korea and another 100 branches around the world. It works in conjunction with the International Women's Peace Group (IWPG) and the International Youth Peace Group (IPYG).
28 http://warpsummit.org, accessed 1 July 2018.

Law and Domestic Politics

In Italy, a country in which there are no non-confessional divinity schools or schools of religious studies, there is a desperate need for trained Muslim community leaders. In the last five to six years, different governments have formed, from time to time, special commissions, committees, and other workshops to address the issue of training for imams.[29] In most mosques imams are still self-trained, or they are hired from abroad, and may have earned diplomas or doctorates from recognised Islamic Institutions. Up to 2017, only a few local Muslim communities have organised short programmes for the training of imams.[30] In 2013, the Tunisian Ministry for Religious Affairs signed an agreement with the U.Co.I.I. to send imams and religious leaders to Italy.

The U.Co.I.I., on 1 February 2017, signed an agreement, the *Patto nazionale per un islam italiano* (National Pact for Italian Islam) with the *Consiglio per l'islam italiano* (Council for Italian Islam).[31] It is not a direct agreement with the Ministry of the Interior, but rather with the official consultation group, convened by it.[32]

The National Pact, signed by the U.Co.I.I. and COREIS and some other minor associations,[33] is a significant step forward for religions without official recognition by the State (referred to as *intesa*).[34] Other than the Catholic Church–which

---

29 *Consulta per l'Islam Italiano, 2005,* http://www1.interno.gov.it/mininterno/export/sites/default/it/sezioni/sala_stampa/notizie/immigrazione/app_notizia_22030.html; *Comitato dell'Islam Italiano, 2010,* http://www.padovaislam.it/files/nuovocomitato20101.pdf., both accessed 16 April 2018.

30 An example here is the imam training programme held in Padua between 14–17 May 2013, organised by the Al Qods Acharif association, together with ISESCO. Morocco has also financially supported the building of the mosque in Turin.

31 Members of the committee (est. 19 January 2016) chaired by Paolo Naso (La Sapienza, University of Rome) are: Stefano Allievi, Enzo Pace, Annalisa Frisina (University of Padua), Pasquale Annicchino (European Institute of Fiesole), Massimo Campanini (University of Trento), Alessandro Ferrari (University of Insubria), Shahrazad Housmand (Gregorian University of Rome), Younis Tawfik (University of Genova), Francesco Zannini (University PISAI), Ida Zilio Grandi (Ca' Foscari University of Venice), and Khalil Altoubat (member of the *Associazione comunità del mondo arabo*–COMAI, and the *Associazione medici stranieri in Italia*–AMSI).

32 The full text of the document is available at: http://www.U.Co.I.I..org/wp-content/uploads/2017/02/patto_nazionale_per_un_islam_italiano.pdf, accessed 21 May 2018.

33 The CII, CICI, UAMI., Ahmadou Bamba association, *Associazione Madri e Bimbi Somali* (Association of Somali Mothers and Children), *A. I. Imam e guide religiose* (Italian Imam and Religious Leaders Association), and the *A.I. Pakistana Muhammadiah.*

34 The Law related to religious traditions that do not have an *intesa* with the State, as far as preachers and ministries are concerned, is still the one promulgated in 1929, the *Legge 24*

has a special agreement with the State,[35] signed in 1929 and updated in 1984–most of the Reformed Churches[36] currently possess official recognition by the State, together with the *Unione delle comunità ebraiche italiane* (Union of the Italian Jewish Communities), the *Unione buddhista italiana* (Italian Buddhist Union), the *Istituto buddista* (sic) *italiano Soka Gakkai* (Soka Gakkai Italian Buddhist Institute), and the *Unione induista italiana* (Italian Hindu Union).

As far as counter radicalisation policies are concerned, the *Scuole nazionali di polizia penitenziaria* (National Schools for Penitentiary Officers) implemented training courses on Muslim culture and traditions. Both Muslim and non-Muslim professors, scholars, practitioners, religious leaders, and intercultural facilitators, have taught classes to penitentiary officers, social workers, prison directors, and other personnel throughout the year.[37]

Activities and Initiatives of Main Muslim Organisations

Up to August 2017 all the main Muslim organisations condemned ISIS-related attacks, either through press conferences and releases, or posts on social media, etc.[38] Compared to their 2015 and 2016 official press releases, Italian Muslim organisations have developed much more detailed communications. In 2017, they did not limit themselves to just condemning the attacks and separating themselves from the atrocities and their perpetrators.[39] Press releases in 2017 included references to Muslim sources that openly show that both the

---

giugno 1929, n.1159: http://presidenza.governo.it/USRI/ufficio_studi/normativa/Legge%20 24%20giugno%201929,%20n.1159.pdf, accessed 16 April 2018.

35 http://www.vatican.va/roman_curia/secretariat_state/archivio/documents/rc_seg-st_198 50603_santa-sede-italia_it.html, accessed 16 April 2018.

36 *Assemblee di Dio in Italia* (Assemblies of God in Italy), *Unione delle chiese cristiane avventiste del 7° giorno* (Union of the Seventh-Day Adventist Churches), *Tavola Valdese* (Waldesian Evangelical Church), *Chiesa evangelica luterana in Italia* (Lutheran Evangelical Church in Italy), *Sacra arcidiocesi ortodossa d'Italia e Malta ed esarcato per l'Europa meridionale* (Greek Orthodox Archdiocese of Italy and Malta and Exarchate of Southern Europe), and the *Chiesa apostolica in Italia* (Apostolic Church of Italy).

37 http://www.ansa.it/sito/notizie/cronaca/2017/01/02/primo-prof-islam-scuole-penitenzi aria_bc86a719-f8ef-4a43-ba9d-c9f068f10f9f.html, accessed 16 April 2018.

38 As an example, see above, about the fatwa of European Muslims against terrorism: http:// www.U.Co.I.I..org/documento/la-fatwa-dei-musulmani-deuropa-terrorismo/, accessed 17 April 2018.

39 One year after the attack in Nice, France, U.Co.I.I. shared a Facebook post by a political science student to commemorate the victims: http://www.U.Co.I.I..org/2829/news-even ti/uniti-la-paura/, accessed 18 April 2018.

attackers and the whole idea of a caliphate, as promulgated by ISIS, have no basis in the Islamic tradition.

The oldest and better organised national Muslim associations, as well as some of the most structured local mosques, have been very active in 2017. This has been in educational activities (Sunday schools, conferences on Islamic topics), interfaith initiatives and events, and programmes to promote a better knowledge of Islam, addressed to Italian public schools, Churches, and the wider public. Several leaders of Muslim organisations gave seminars for the Masters programme "Judaism, Christianity and Islam: Religions of Abraham" at the Catholic University of Milan.[40]

The U.Co.I.I. was very active, with a number of initiatives and events on different topics, such as interfaith dialogue, imam training, and public conferences.[41] It has been very active in the last few years, as well as in 2017, in starting initiatives towards promoting the integration of Muslims into Italian and European societies,[42] examining the condition of women,[43] and encouraging initiatives against Islamophobia, for example. The participation of its president at the presentation of *Fondazione Oasis*' e-book *Cittadinanza e Libertà Religiosa: Il Ruolo delle Città* (Citizenship and Religious Freedom: The Role of Cities) and the speech he delivered there, is another example of this trend.[44]

As far as the training of imams and Muslim religious leaders is concerned, on 20 January 2017, the U.Co.I.I., together with other Muslim associations, met the then Minister of the Interior, Marco Minniti at the *Tavolo di confronto con i rappresentanti delle associazioni e delle comunità islamiche presenti in Italia* (Round Table with Representatives of Islamic Associations and Communities Present in Italy). During this formal meeting, among other topics, the training of imams, the official recognition of Muslim places of worship and Muslim worship associations, were addressed.[45] U.Co.I.I. representatives also attended the training course for religious leaders, the *Corso di formazione degli esponenti delle comunità religiose presenti in Italia che non hanno stipulato intese con*

40 https://milano.unicatt.it/master/master-Guide_Master_monoteismi_123X165_on_line3 .pdf, accessed 17 April 2018. The Masters programme ended in December 2017.
41 https://www.U.Co.I.I..org/blog-izzeddin/festival-delle-religioni-2017-incontro-dalai-la ma/, accessed 17 April 2018.
42 http://www.U.Co.I.I..org/2288/news-eventi/integrarsi/, accessed 22 May 2018.
43 http://www.U.Co.I.I..org/2295/news-eventi/islamofobia-tra-realta-e-illusioni/, accessed 22 May 2018.
44 http://www.U.Co.I.I..org/2321/uncategorized/cittadinanza-liberta-religiosa/, accessed 20 May 2018.
45 http://www.U.Co.I.I..org/2066/news-eventi/U.Co.I.I.-al-tavolo-del-ministro-minniti/, accessed 23 May 2018.

lo Stato (Training Course for the Representatives of Religious Communities Which do not Have a Formal Agreement [*Intesa*] with the Italian State). This is promoted by the Ministry of the Interior, through Ravenna's *Fondazione familia*. The course ended on 28 November 2017, with a public event organised by the Ministry of the Interior.[46]

The U.Co.I.I. also published a paper entitled *Moschee e imam in Italia, le linee guida* (Guidelines for Imams and Mosques in Italy), the main aim of which is to provide guidelines to the imams at the mosques affiliated to the organisation. Leaders of the U.Co.I.I. also frequently took part in meetings, gatherings, and conferences on interfaith dialogue, Christian-Muslim relations,[47] as well as appearing on radio and TV broadcasts.[48]

During Ramadan in 2017, many initiatives, activities and events took place throughout the country. The *Interculturalità parte dalla luna* (Interculturality Starts from the Moon) event took place on 26 May 2017. During it, 18 imams from North-Eastern Italy gathered at the National Astronomical Observatory in Padua to observe the first crescent moon, and to officially begin the month of fasting.[49]

The *Giovani musulmani d'Italia* (Young Muslims of Italy–GMI) communicates most effectively through their Facebook page, and Twitter and Instagram accounts.[50] Its president, Nadia Bouzekri, made the headlines on 27 September, when she accused the airport personnel at *Orio al Serio* (Bergamo, one of the airports of Milan) of racially profiling her during a security check.[51] They asked her to remove her head scarf. The association is very active and organises summer camps, and meetings with young Catholics and young people of other religions, both at the local and national levels.[52] They have joined with both Muslim and non-Muslim associations for single activities as well as for

---

46 http://www.U.Co.I.I..org/3582/news-eventi/formazione-degli-esponenti-delle-comunita-religiose-non-stipulato-intese-lo/, accessed 23 May 2018.
47 http://www.U.Co.I.I..org/2444/news-eventi/religioni-monoteiste-serve-conoscenza/, and http://www.confronti.net/confronti/?wysija-page=1&controller=email&action=view&email_id=286&wysijap=subscriptions, both accessed 23 May 2018.
48 http://www.U.Co.I.I..org/2459/news-eventi/incontro-papa-francesco-grande-imam-della-mosche-al-azhar/, accessed 10 May 2018.
49 http://www.media.inaf.it/2017/05/27/ramadan-astronomia/, accessed 10 May 2018.
50 https://www.facebook.com/GiovaniMusulmanidItaliaGMI/, accessed 4 April 2018.
51 http://milano.repubblica.it/cronaca/2017/09/28/news/velo_aeroporto_orio_al_serio-176769065/, accessed July 10, 2018.
52 Regional and local branches have very active Facebook pages, as well as Twitter accounts and Instagram profiles.

longer collaborations, such as with AVIS, ACLI Emergency, ARCI, Islamic Relief, *Comunità di Sant'Egidio*, and others.[53]

The *Comunità Religiosa Islamica* (Islamic Religious Community–COREIS), is also very active in interfaith dialogue, and issuing public information about Islam, mainly through its president, Yahya Pallavicini.[54] On 12 November 2017, the COREIS founder and honorary president, 'Abd al-Wahid Pallavicini, father of Yahya, passed away at the age of 91.[55] He converted to Islam in 1951, and has been one of the few Italians to embrace Islam in the 20th century. President Pallavicini took part in a number of conferences and public events, at the national and international level.[56]

Locally, almost every mosque organised initiatives and/or public events. These included a collaboration with *Caritas-banco alimentare*, which provides meals to people in need (80% of which are Italians), mosque open-days, as well as *iftar* dinners with the local authorities and/or people in need.

The *Centro islamico culturale d'Italia*[57] (Islamic Cultural Centre of Italy–CICI or CCII) hosted conferences, public events, and meetings, usually sponsored by the kingdoms of Morocco or Saudi Arabia.[58]

On 17 October 2017, Khalid Chaouki, deputy chair of the *Partito democratico*, was elected president of the *Centro culturale islamico d'Italia* (Islamic Cultural Centre of Italy). This election was also very important symbolically;[59] Chaouki, 34, is a child of Moroccan immigrants, and has been one of the strongest supporters of the *ius soli* Law.[60]

The group *Partcipazione e spiritualità musulmana* (Participation and Muslim Spirituality–PSM) was also very active, especially in the field of education, both with children and teachers, organising the 18th workshop for Arabic language teachers of children on 16 November 2017, in co-operation

---

53   https://www.forumnazionalegiovani.it/associazioni/10-associazioni/51-giovani-musulmani-d-italia.html, accessed 23 May 2018.
54   https://www.strasbourgconsortium.org/content/blurb/files/Pallavicini%20Yahya%20Bio.pdf, accessed 23 May 2018.
55   http://www.coreis.it/wp/in-memoriam-shaykh-abd-al-wahid/, accessed 23 May 2018.
56   http://www.coreis.it/wp/una-nuova-alleanza-per-il-mediterraneo/, accessed 23 May 2018.
57   https://it-it.facebook.com/centroislamicoculturale/, accessed 17 April 2018.
58   http://www.archidiap.com/opera/moschea-e-centro-culturale-islamico/, accessed 10 July 2018.
59   http://formiche.net/2017/10/khalid-chaouki-moschea/, accessed April 4, 2018.
60   http://milano.repubblica.it/cronaca/2017/09/28/news/velo_aeroporto_orio_al_serio-176769065/http://milano.repubblica.it/cronaca/2017/09/28/news/velo_aeroporto_orio_al_serio-176769065/, accessed 4 April 2018.

with the *Unione musulmana italiana per l'infanzia* (Italian Muslim Union for Childhood–UMII).[61] The PSM annual meeting is usually a major event; there were 1,700 participants in 2017.[62] The title of the 2017 edition was *Islam e rinnovamento* (Islam and Renewal) and involved the municipal authorities of the city of Turin as well as Muslim scholars.[63] The young advisory board member Brahim Baya, is one of the most active representatives of the PSM on social media.

Muslim Population: History and Demographics

In the second half of the 1970s, Italy experienced its first major inflow of Muslim migration. These migrants, made up of young and educated individuals from urban areas, had fled territories with few job opportunities. They came mostly from Middle Eastern countries like Syria, Lebanon, and Palestine. The first wave of Muslims looked for a better education and, therefore, most of them enrolled at the *Università per stranieri* (University for Foreigners) in Perugia. From their countries of origin, they brought with them a strong Islamic identity and made their presence felt, visibly organising themselves into associations in the 1980s and 1990s.[64] Some had a background in Islamist movements such as the Muslim Brotherhood. In the 1990s, there was a second major wave of Muslim migration into Italy, with an increasingly illegal presence in the country. They had mainly North African origins, coming from Morocco, Tunisia, Egypt, and Algeria. The second wave of Muslims came in search of steady employment but, in comparison with the first wave of Muslims, they had lower levels of education. These later flows of Muslims constitute the majority of Muslims attending mosques, while those of the earlier migration wave have developed leadership roles in Islamic associations and mosques.

Family reunification policies in the 1990s and 2000s led to an increase in arrivals of women and children. Gender imbalances were most evident in immigration from Mali (10% women) and Senegal (26%), while the most gender-balanced community is the Moroccan one with 231,000 women (44.1% of all Moroccan immigrants), followed by the Tunisian (45,000 women, 36.5%

---

61 http://www.psm-italia.it/seminario-insegnanti-arabo-per-bambini/, accessed 4 April 2018.
62 http://www.psm-italia.it/conferenzastampa/, accessed 4 April 2018.
63 http://www.psm-italia.it/category/aattivita/convegno/, accessed 4 April 2018.
64 Allievi, Stefano, and Felice Dassetto, *Il ritorno dell'Islam: i musulmani in Italia* (Rome: Edizioni Lavoro, 1992).

of Tunisians), and Egyptian (40,000 women, 29.5% of Egyptians) groups.[65] Subsequent to the Syrian civil war and the Arab uprisings from 2011, Italy experienced its third major wave of Muslim immigration, with migrants escaping war, violence, poverty and unemployment.

Religion is not part of the official census in Italy. Hence, sources for demographic information on Muslims in Italy are based on sociological research and empirical studies.[66] At present, in Italy, there are an estimated 1,645,331 Muslims,[67] 32.6% of the 5,047,028 foreign residents. Converts are estimated to be more than 100,000.[68] Compared with the 2016 figures of Muslims by national background, the number of Albanians and Egyptians increased, whereas those from the Maghreb (Morocco, Tunisia, Algeria) decreased.[69]

Muslim Population	No official data is available, estimates vary significantly: 2,870,000 (4.78% of the total population) from Pew Research,[70] and 1,645,331 (2.74%) from the *Dossier statistico immigrazione*.[71]
Ethnic/National Backgrounds	Albanian: 449,000 Moroccan: 418,000 Bangladeshi: 121,000 Egyptian: 111,000 Tunisian: 93,000 Senegalese: 87,000[72]

---

65   Centro studi e ricerche IDOS, *Dossier statistico immigrazione 2014: Rapporto UNAR "dalle discriminazioni ai diritti"* (Rome: UNAR, 2014).

66   Allievi, Stefano, and Gianpiero Dalla Zuanna, *Tutto quello che non vi hanno mai detto sull'immigrazione* (Rome-Bari: Editori Laterza, 2016), pp. 118–135.

67   According to Pew Research (http://www.pewforum.org/2017/11/29/europes-growing-muslim-population/, accessed 1 July 2018) the number of Muslims is 2,870,000. This number is much higher than the ones provided by *Dossier immigrazione* and all other statistical sources.

68   Allievi, Stefano, *I nuovi musulmani: I convertiti all'Islam* (Rome, Edizioni Lavoro, 1999).

69   http://www.dossierimmigrazione.it/docnews/file/2017_scheda%20dossier.pdf, accessed 9 July 2018.

70   http://www.pewforum.org/2017/11/29/europes-growing-muslim-population/, accessed 20 May 2018.

71   http://www.dossierimmigrazione.it/docnews/file/2017_scheda%20dossier.pdf, p. 3, accessed 20 May 2018.

72   http://www.dossierimmigrazione.it/docnews/file/2017_scheda%20dossier.pdf, p. 4, accessed 20 May 2018.

Inner-Islamic Groups	No official data available. The majority of Muslim organisations are Sunni. However, there are at least four Shi'i organisations: three in the North of Italy and one in the South.
Geographical Spread	Muslims are more numerous in the North than the South, and are mostly concentrated in the urban areas of Northern Italy (Lombardy, Emilia Romagna, Veneto and Piedmont). They also live in the South, mainly in Lazio, Campania, and Sicily. Their different levels of concentration depend on employment opportunities in the Italian regions.
Number of Mosques	Muslim prayer halls are more numerous in the North than the South, because of the larger immigrant presence in these regions and their higher level of organisation. This is one of the important factors that explains the low visibility of Italian Islam, in a significantly hostile cultural climate. According to the latest academic survey, 769 Islamic places of worship existed in 2010.[73] The estimated numbers in 2016 were 848 Islamic places of worship and four mosques, based on the Ministry of the Interior census in 2016.[74] The U.Co.I.I. provides a figure of 1,219 Islamic centres.[75] The website www.arab.it provides a list of Islamic centres and places of worship that is constantly updated.[76]
Muslim Burial Sites	There is no official data available. Spaces within municipal cemeteries for Muslim or Islamic burial sites are available in the main Italian cities. In 2011, Maria Bombardieri gave an estimate of 63 Muslim burial sites located in all regions, except Molise,

---

73 Bombardieri, Maria, *Moschee d'Italia* (Bologna, EMI, 2011).
74 http://ucs.interno.gov.it/ucs/contenuti/Le_statistiche_ufficiali_del_ministero_dell_interno_ed._2016-5010589.htm, accessed 10 July 2018.
75 http://www.U.Co.I.I..org/3523/news-eventi/geopolitica-religioni-trieste/, accessed 10 July 2018.
76 http://www.arab.it/almarkaz.html, accessed 23 May 2018.

Basilicata, and Sardinia.[77] The oldest Islamic cemetery is a Turkish one in Trieste.

"Chaplaincy" in State Institutions

According to the data provided by the Ministry of the Interior, 14 Muslim chaplains are allowed to enter Italian prisons for counselling, spiritual assistance, and Friday prayer.[78] 148 imams are chosen among Muslim inmates to lead congregational prayers within prisons. In 2016, there were 11,029 Muslims among the 54,881 foreign inmates in Italy. Muslim inmates who attend congregational prayer are 7,600.[79] Moreover, 69 out of 190 Italian prisons have a mosque inside; the others do not have specific spaces for Muslims and use the courtyard or inmates' rooms as mosques on Friday.

No official data is available on Muslim religious counselling and/or ritual services for Muslims in health care centres, universities, and the armed forces.

Halal Products

Muslims quite often have access to halal products in the major Italian stores, such as Coop supermarkets. Halal slaughter is permitted, but halal food is not yet available in most public institutions.

The most important halal certification agencies are: Halal Italy Authority (the Italian branch of Halal International Authority); *Halal Italia*; Halal Global; and Whad World Halal Development (*Halal Roma*).

---

77 Bombardieri, *Moschee d'Italia*.
78 Rhazzali, Khalid, *L'Islam in carcere: L'esperienza religiosa dei giovani musulmani nelle prigioni italiane* (Milan: Francoangeli, 1st edn. 2010), p. 12. He claims that there are 29 authorised religious leaders.
79 Rhazzali, *L'Islam in carcere*, p. 13.
80 http://www.normattiva.it/uri-res/N2Ls?urn:nir:stato:legge:1977;533, accessed 1 July 2018.

Dress Code	There are no specific laws on Muslim dress such as the head scarf or full face veil (niqab). *Law 152* (1975), modified in 1978 (*Law 533*)[80] does not allow the use of full face helmets or any other item that might mask the recognition of people in public, without any "justified reason". Some of the interpretations of this Law, frequently coming from right-wing parties, call for a *de-facto* ban of face veils.[81]
Places of Islamic Learning and Education	Several of the better organised mosques and Islamic centres offer both Qur'an and Islamic schooling for children, as well as courses on the Arabic language, for young native speakers and for the general public. The main private Islamic learning and education institutes are: the Interreligious Studies Academy (*Accademia ISA*) and the Italian Institute of Islamic Studies (*Istituto italiano degli studi islamici*). Both have organised several Islamic training courses for Muslims and non-Muslims. The latest project, started in 2016, is the Islamic University of Italy (*Università islamica d'Italia*). The first and only Islamic university in the country offered, in 2016 and 2017, a postgraduate course on Qur'anic Theology and Western Society (*Laurea triennale in teologia coranica e società occidentale*). There is also the IISI (*Istituto Italiano di Studi Islamici*), the mission of which is to provide Italian and European Muslims with knowledge of Islam. It claims to have a scholarly approach. Their programmes are especially aimed at Italian Muslims, to train them to be active in Italian and European society. Its reference institution is the European Council for Fatwa and Research.

---

81 https://pagellapolitica.it/dichiarazioni/6897/indossare-il-burqa-in-italia-e-vietato, accessed 1 July 2018.

Muslim Media and Publications	The publishing house *Edizioni del calamo* edits the online journal *Il messaggero dell'Islam* (The Messenger of Islam). The *Yalla Italia* blog is edited by young Italian Muslims and non-Muslims from Arab countries.

Main Muslim Organisations[82]

– Union of Islamic Communities of Italy (*Unione delle comunità islamiche d'Italia*–U.Co.I.I., via Tor de' Schiavi 17–19, 00172 Rome, tel.: ++39 0692929864, email: info@ucoii.org, info@ucoii.org). Established in 1990 and promoted by the Muslim Students' Union in Italy (*Unione degli studenti musulmani d'Italia*–USMI), the U.Co.I.I. represents Muslim Sunni groups in the country. It is one of the best-known Muslim organisations, and is associated with about 200 Islamic centres.
– Islamic Association of Italy (*Associazione islamica d'Italia*, viale Monza 50, 21100 Milan, tel.: ++39 0236553368, email: info@alleanza-islamica.it, www.alleanza-islamica.it). Established formally in 2010, but operating since 2000, it is part of the Federation of Islamic Organisations in Europe (FIOE) and is linked to the Muslim Brotherhood.
– Islamic Association of Imams and Religious Guides in Italy (*Associazione islamica italiana degli imam e delle guide religiose*, via Federico Garofoli 244, San Giovanni Lupatoto, 37057 Verona, www.imamitalia.it; www.facebook.com/Associazione.ImamItalia). Established in 2012, in order to offer a better understanding of the shari'a to Muslims, and to provide training to imams.
– Islamic Cultural Centre of Italy (*Centro islamico culturale d'Italia*, viale della Moschea 85, 00197 Rome, www.facebook.com/centroislamicoculturale/timeline). The Centre promoted the construction of the Rome mosque in the 1970s, and is the only Muslim body officially recognised by the State. It is connected with the embassies of Muslim majority states (ambassadors are members of its administrative board), and with the Muslim World League–Italy.
– Islamic Religious Community (*Comunità religiosa islamica italiana*–COREIS., via Giuseppe Meda 9, 20136 Milan, tel.: ++39 028393340, email:

---

82 For a quick video overview of the pluralistic Italian Muslim population and its associations, see: https://www.youtube.com/watch?v=LllslbB3EeA, accessed 16 April 2018.

coreis@coreis.it, www.coreis.it). An independent organisation but part of the Sufi order Ahmadiyya Idrisiyya Shadiliyya in Europe, and is mostly made up of Italian converts. It particularly promotes interfaith dialogue and cultural initiatives.
- Muslim Participation and Spirituality (*Partecipazione e spiritualità musulmana*–PSM, email: info@psm-italia.it, www.psm-italia.it). An umbrella-association, set up by local mosques whose purpose is to promote spiritual and cultural activities; is linked to the Moroccan Al-Adl wal-Ihsan movement.
- Italian Islamic Confederation (*Confederazione islamica italiana*, via Ferrarese 156/57, 40128 Bologna, tel.: ++39 0519240127, www.conf-islamica.it/confederazione-islamica-italiana/; email: c.islamica.italiana@gmail.com). This organisation was promoted by the *Centro islamico culturale d'Italia* and the Moroccan ambassador in Italy in 2012. It includes around 250 mosques and Muslim associations, mainly catering to Moroccan Muslims.
- Young Muslims of Italy (*Giovani musulmani d'Italia*–GMI, viale Monza 50, 20127 Milan, email: info@giovanimusulmani.it, www.giovanimusulmani.it). Linked to the U.Co.I.I., the GMI is one of the most active organisations of young Muslims.
- Association of Italian Muslim Women (*Associazione donne musulmane d'Italia*–ADMI, viale Monza 50, 20127 Milan, www.admitalia.org). Organisation of Muslim women, connected to the U.Co.I.I.. Yamina Saleh is the current president.
- Association of Moroccan Women in Italy (*Associazione donne marocchine in Italia*–ACMID-DONNA, tel.: ++39 0648913386, email: info@acmid-donna.it, www.acmid-donna.it). It organises cultural initiatives aimed at promoting dialogue between Italian and Moroccan women, and runs projects to defend the rights of immigrant women.
- Islamic Association Imam Mahdi a.j. (*Associazione islamica Imam Mahdi a.j.*, via Gualdo Tadino 17, 00181 Rome, tel.: ++39 3394968095, email: imam_mahdi59@yahoo.it, www.islamshia.org). This is the main organisation set up by Shi'i Muslims in Italy, in 2004. It includes Shi'i Muslims from Iran, Afghanistan, Pakistan, Iraq, Lebanon, and Italy. The Association translates religious Shi'i books into Italian, and organises public events.
- Italian Islamic Branch Association (*Associazione sezione islamica italiana*, 15033 Casale Monferrato, www.sezioneislamicaitaliana.it, email: sezioneislamicaitaliana@hotmail.it). Established by a small group of Salafi Italian converts, the organisation offers translations of religious books into Italian and undertakes *da'wa*. Some of its members have attended courses at the Islamic University of Medina in Saudi Arabia.

- Community of the Arab World in Italy (*Comunità del mondo arabo in Italia*–Co.Mai, c/o F.K.T. Salvetti Sito in Piazza degli Ontani 11, 00172 Rome, tel.: ++39 3387177238, ++39 0686214184, email: foadaodi@hotmail.com, segreteriaorganizzativa12@gmail.com, http://co-mai.org/). Established by secular Muslims with the aim of promoting Arab culture and social and cultural integration in Italy. Its president is Foad Aodi.

Kosovo

Jeton Mehmeti[1]

Introduction

The legal status of religious communities became one of the topics of parliamentary debate in late 2017, when the newly formed Government of Kosovo introduced a new Draft Law on Freedom of Religion. The new legislature approved in principle the Draft Law, something that previous legislature had failed to do. The new Draft Law foresees the mechanisms for religious communities to register in Kosovo, and to acquire the status of a legal person. *Bashkësia Islame e Kosovës* (Islamic Community of Kosovo), as the official body representing Kosovo Muslims, did not manage to include most of its recommendations in the final draft. Among the main requests of the Islamic Community was the allocation of public funds from the state budget for paying the employees of religious organisations, and such funds to be allocated according to the number of adherents of a particular religion. On the contrary, the Draft Law foresaw that the Government should not finance any religious community. Moreover, the Islamic Community failed to prevent the Government's recognition of the *Bashkësia e Tarikateve të Kosovës* (Union of Kosovo Tarikats) as an independent religious community, which, as an umbrella organisation for different Sufi orders, has so far operated under the Islamic Community. In addition to the legal framework, the commitment of state institutions to fight violent extremism and radicalisation continued throughout 2017. New trials and appeals of Kosovans charged with terrorism offences received significant media attention.

Public Debates

According to the US Department of State's *Report on Terrorism*, released in 2017, Kosovo has demonstrated political will to address the threats related to terrorism. According to the report, during 2016, Kosovan authorities arrested 32 individuals on terrorism-related charges. Seven citizens were sentenced to a cumulative 42 years of imprisonment on terrorism charges, and five others

---

[1] Jeton Mehmeti is a PhD candidate at the University of Graz.

received 49 years of imprisonment for their involvement with ISIS.[2] During 2017, most of them continued their trials and appeals. In some cases that were appealed the defendants received reduced sentences due to errors made by the prosecutors.

In one such case, the prosecutor accused a Kosovan citizen of fighting for a non-existing organisation. Arben Livoreka was initially sentenced to three years and six months imprisonment for allegedly joining an organisation called "Harausham". When his case was appealed, the new prosecutor corrected the name of the organisation to "Ahrar al-Sham", and the defendant's sentence was reduced to a two and a half years conditional sentence.[3] In some cases, lower sentences, like house arrests, were given for a Facebook post, that was interpreted by the prosecutor as a call to join foreign military groups.[4] Another person was sentenced to 18 months imprisonment for airing a YouTube song which was considered by the prosecutor as a call to attack state institutions and foreign embassies in Kosovo.[5]

One of the cases that received wide media coverage concerned the former imam of the grand mosque Mehmet Fatih in Prishtina, Shefqet Krasniqi. In December 2017 he appeared in a Prishtina court to face charges for intentionally spreading messages through his public talks and social media, which, according to the prosecutor, have encouraged others to join militant groups in Syria and Iraq. He was also charged for characterising certain religious groups in Kosovo as enemies of Sunni-Muslims, hence spreading hatred against other religious groups that live in Kosovo.[6] In a separate trial, four other imams, Mazllam Mazllami, Enes Gogaj, Bedri Robaj, Idriz Bilibani and a religious political figure Fuad Ramiqi, appeared in court to face charges related to terrorism.[7]

---

[2] US Department of State, Country Reports on Terrorism 2016, https://www.state.gov/documents/organization/272488.pdf, accessed 25 April 2018.
[3] http://kallxo.com/denim-per-terrorizem-ne-rastin-harausham/, accessed 25 April 2018.
[4] http://kallxo.com/arrest-shtepiak-te-dyshuarit-per-terrorizem/, accessed 27 April 2018.
[5] http://kallxo.com/gjnk/historia-e-planit-terrorist-per-ti-sulmuar-lideret-e-shtetit/, accessed 27 April 2018.
[6] http://kallxo.com/shefqet-krasniqi-ne-gjykate-per-shtytje-ne-terrorizem/, accessed 28 April 2018.
[7] http://kallxo.com/debatet-per-gjakderdhjen-dhe-shpaten-ne-gjykimin-e-imameve/, accessed 28 April 2018.

Transnational Links

The Islamic Community of Kosovo maintains a strong relationship with the Muslim Community of Albania, the Islamic Community of Macedonia and the Turkish Presidency of Religious Affairs (*Diyanet İşleri Başkanlığı*). Various religious and educational activities are often organised among the three institutions.

Throughout 2017, representatives of the Islamic Community participated in various international events, such as: the Eurasian Fatwa Council, held in Istanbul;[8] the International Forum on Peace Promotion in Islamic Societies, in the United Arab Emirates;[9] as well as a visit to the head office of the Diyanet in Ankara,[10] among others. It is worth mentioning that the Islamic Community has a special relationship with the Diyanet as well as with the governmental Turkish Cooperation and Coordination Agency (TİKA). The latter is involved in the restoration of religious and cultural monuments in Kosovo, in particular historical Ottoman mosques.

Law and Domestic Politics

The new Government of Kosovo that was formed in the autumn of 2017, proposed a new Law on religious communities to Parliament. In November, the Kosovo parliament approved in principle the *Draft-Law on the Amendment and Supplementation of Law No.02/L-31 on Freedom of Religion in Kosovo*.[11] Although the final approval of the Law is not completed yet, its principal acceptance was considered a success, as previous legislative attempts had never reached this stage. The new Law aims to regulate issues such as the registration of religious communities, their legal status, the position within the Prime Minister's Office that will be responsible for registering religious communities, the number of followers needed in order to register as a separate religious community, the issues of cemeteries and funeral rites, as well as the transparency and financial accountability of religious communities.[12]

---

8   http://bislame.net/keshillit-te-fetvave-i-organizates-islame-te-shteteve-te-evroazise/, accessed 4 May 2018.
9   http://bislame.net/forumi-abu-dhabi/, accessed 4 May 2018.
10 http://bislame.net/myftiu-viziton-dijanetin/, accessed 4 May 2018.
11 http://www.kuvendikosoves.org/common/docs/proc/trans_s_2017_11_23_10_7106_al.pdf, accessed 5 June 2018.
12 http://www.kuvendikosoves.org/common/docs/proc/trans_s_2017_11_23_10_7106_al.pdf, accessed 5 June 2018.

This Draft Law aims to regulate, first and foremost, the legal status of religious communities. A religious community without the status of a legal entity may not possess or exercise certain rights, such as the right of property ownership or lease of property, the maintaining of bank accounts, the employment of workers, and the provision of legal protection for the community, its members and its assets.

In addition to the five religious communities that are recognised by the current Law (the Islamic Community of Kosovo, the Serbian Orthodox Church, the Catholic Church, the Jewish Community of Faith, and the Kosovo Protestant Evangelical Church), a sixth religious community, i.e. the Union of Kosovo Tarikats, was added to these recognised communities in the Draft Law. According to the explanatory memorandum of the Draft Law, the Union of Tarikats, which is primarily Bektashis, has about 60,000 members with a long existence in Kosovo of 350 years.[13]

The Draft Law also foresees the creation of an agency that will issue a certificate of registration as a legal entity of the above mentioned religious communities. The new Law also guarantees the freedom to manifest the religion or belief of all individuals, alone or communally, even if they are not registered and not provided with the status of legal entity. The condition is that religious communities on the occasion of their foundation have at least 50 members who are adult citizens of the Republic of Kosovo.

The Draft Law also regulates on the issue of cemeteries and rites of burial. Cemetery places shall be assigned on a neutral and non-discriminatory basis by public authorities without the intervention of other religious communities, and religious rites are to be performed in accordance with the requests of the deceased, or if there are none they are to be made in accordance with the requests of the families and relatives of the deceased, unless it is contrary to public order. Burials and burial rites in cemeteries are to be organised in a neutral way, and persons belonging to a religious or philosophical minority should not be dependent on persons belonging to a majority religious group for aspects of their burial. On this matter the Government plans secondary legislation.

With regard to funding, the Draft Law states that the Government shall not finance any religious communities.[14] However, various tax exemptions for religious communities are also regulated by other laws: the Law on immovable property tax contains an exemption from tax on the immovable property of

---

13 http://ligjet.kuvendikosoves.org/Uploads/Data/Documents/06-L-001Memorandumish pjegues_meSxXgzWyG.pdf, accessed 4 May 2018.

14 http://ligjet.kuvendikosoves.org/Uploads/Data/Documents/06-L-001_pCErUBna5B.pdf, accessed 4 May 2018.

religious institutions, whose property is maintained and used for religious purposes. Moreover, the Draft Law states that the Government may invite religious communities to receive funds for the maintenance of cultural monuments that are owned by them. The Draft Law also demands that the revenues of religious communities, including foreign donations, must comply with existing legislation to ensure transparency.

The Islamic Community, which represents the largest religious community, objected to some of the new provisions of the Draft Law, however. To begin with, it was against the new provision which recognises the *Bashkësia e Tarikateve të Kosovës* (Union of Kosovo Tarikats) as a separate religious community.[15] Traditionally all Sufi orders in Kosovo have operated under the authority of the Islamic Community. The new change will affect the Islamic Community also in terms of demographics, since Muslims belonging to Sufi orders will register in the future as a separate religious community. The Islamic Community also suggested that the number of required members to register as a new religious organisation should be 500 instead of 50, and that the Draft Law should prohibit the activities of non-governmental religious organisations without the prior permission of the relevant recognised religious community. However, none of these objections and suggestions were taken into account when the new Law was drafted.

With regard to funds and financial reporting, the Islamic Community suggested the Government should allocate funds from the state budget to provide the monthly income of their employees, and finances should be allocated to fund religious communities based on the number of their adherents.[16] This request was not taken into account either. The Islamic Community also requested that secondary education should include religious education, to be represented in elective courses.[17] This was also rejected by the Government.

The Government's rejections of the requests of the Islamic Community are often justified with reference to the secular nature of the State. The Constitution of Kosovo defines the country as a secular state, with a neutral attitude towards religious affairs. This neutrality is further emphasised by the fact that the Constitution does not mention by name any of the existing religions in Kosovo. However, freedom of belief is explicitly regulated in Article 38

---

15   http://www.evropaelire.org/a/28026050.html, accessed 1 April 2017.
16   http://ligjet.kuvendikosoves.org/Uploads/Data/Documents/06-L-001Memorandumish pjegues_meSxXgzWyG.pdf, accessed 5 May 2018.
17   http://ligjet.kuvendikosoves.org/Uploads/Data/Documents/06-L-001Memorandumish pjegues_meSxXgzWyG.pdf, accessed 5 May 2018.

and 39 of the Constitution. Freedom of expression and freedom of association are also guaranteed by specific laws.

Activities and Initiatives of Main Muslim Organisations

Among the most important educational activities of the Islamic Community in 2017 was the organisation of an academic conference entitled "60 Years of Islamic Literature in the Albanian Language in Kosovo".[18] This conference brought together researchers and the academic community who analysed the Islamic Community's publications since 1957. The Islamic Community of Kosovo has three regular publications: *Dituria Islame* (Islamic Knowledge), *Edukata Islame* (Islamic Education), and *Takvimi*. In May 2017, the Islamic Community organised another international conference to commemorate the 65th anniversary of Medreseja Alauddin. The event was attended by political leaders, religious figures and renowned academics.[19] Another academic conference organised by the Islamic Community investigated "Albanian Muslims in the Balkans".[20]

In addition to organising the hajj every year, the Islamic Community has started organising a regular *'umrah* visit for Kosovan Muslims. The first such trip occurred in December 2017, whereby 59 pilgrims set off to visit Mecca and Medina.[21]

Almost each year new mosques are built and some old ones are renovated. The laying of the foundation stone for a new mosque in the municipality of Shtimje was celebrated by the Islamic Community. The mosque will be co-financed by the Al-Maktoum Foundation from the United Arab Emirates.[22] The laying of a foundation stone for a new mosque was also celebrated in the municipality of Drenas.[23] At least six new mosques opened during 2017, in: Shtimje;[24] Lipjan;[25] Peja;[26] Prizren;[27] Suhareka;[28] and Rahovec.[29]

---

18 http://bislame.net/6ovjetori/, accessed 27 April 2018.
19 http://bislame.net/medreseja65/, accessed 4 May 2018.
20 http://bislame.net/konferenca-myslimanet-shqiptare-ne-ballkan/, accessed 4 May 2018.
21 http://bislame.net/umreja-e-pare/, accessed 27 April 2018.
22 http://bislame.net/xhamia-shtime/, accessed 25 April 2018.
23 http://bislame.net/xhamia-terdevc-te-drenasit/, accessed 25 April 2018.
24 http://bislame.net/mollopolc-2/, accessed 25 April 2018.
25 http://bislame.net/xhamia-bujan/, accessed 26 April 2018.
26 http://bislame.net/xhamianure/, accessed 26 April 2018.
27 http://bislame.net/xhamia-ne-fshatin-caparc/, accessed 26 April 2018.
28 http://bislame.net/dubrave-e-suharekes/, accessed 26 April 2018.
29 http://bislame.net/xhamia-re-rahovec/, accessed 26 April 2018.

The Islamic Community is building a new madrasa and training centre in Gjakova.[30] This will be an addition to the current secondary schools that provide religious education to both male and female students and operate in three different cities: Prishtina, Prizren and Gjilan. Many of its graduates pursue their studies at the Faculty of Islamic Studies, which provides studies at the Bachelor's and Master's level. Both the madrasas and the faculty operate under the authority of the Islamic Community. The Islamic Community has its own charity organisation too, called *Bereqeti* (from Arabic *baraka*, meaning blessing), which works mostly on delivering free food and clothes to those in need.

Muslim Population: History and Demographics

The Muslim presence in Kosovo goes back to the Ottoman period when Islam spread extensively among Albanians. Since then, Kosovo has had a predominantly Muslim population. Although the majority of Kosovo Muslims are Albanian, other ethnic groups like Turks and Bosniaks also constitute a large number of Muslims. In addition to the overwhelming Sunni majority, there are small Sufi orders active in Kosovo, such as the Bektashi, the Saadi, the Kaderi, the Rufai, and the Malami. The *Bashkësia Islame e Kosovës* (Islamic Community of Kosovo) is the official institution that represents the Muslim population in Kosovo. Before 1993 the Islamic Community was part of the Islamic Religious Community of Yugoslavia, a centralised body with its headquarters in Sarajevo.

According to the latest national population census, organised in Kosovo in 2011, the overwhelming majority of the population declared themselves Muslim. Out of a population of nearly 1.8 million people, over 95% declared themselves to be Muslim (1,663,412), 2.2% to be Catholic (38,438), and 1.5% to be Christian Orthodox (25,837). Since the 2011 census was boycotted by most Kosovan Serbs, who predominantly belong to the Orthodox Church, the exact number of the Christian Orthodox population is unknown. There are other communities too, like Protestants, Jews, and those who did not declare their religious affiliation.

---

30   http://bislame.net/myftiu-ternava-inspektoi-punimet-ne-kompleksin-e-medresese-se-vogel-ne-gjakove/, accessed 27 April 2018.

Muslim Population	Total population 1,820,631 (95% of them declared themselves Muslim in the 2011 census).
Ethnic/National Backgrounds	93% of Muslims in Kosovo are Albanians. Other ethnic groups: Bosniak: 1.6% Turkish: 1.1% Roma, Ashkali and Egyptian:[31] 1.3% Gorani: 0.9%.
Inner-Islamic Groups	In addition to the overwhelming Sunni majority, there are small Sufi orders active in Kosovo. The Bektashi order mainly resides in Gjakova, where their Grand Tekke is also located. Other Sufi orders active in Kosovo are the Saadi, Kaderi, Rufai, and Malami.
Geographical Spread	The Sunni population is spread throughout Kosovo. The Sufi orders are mainly based around Prizren, Gjakova, Rahovec and the Mitrovica region.
Number of Mosques	There are over 800 mosques in use around Kosovo.
Muslim Burial Sites	Each municipality in Kosovo provides sites for burial. There are no specific places for Muslim cemeteries. Typically, cemeteries are mixed in terms of religious background.
"Chaplaincy" in State Institutions	The secular nature of the State prohibits organised religious activities in state institutions, including public hospitals, universities, police, and army premises.

---

31   The members of the Egyptian community are not Egyptian Arabs.

Halal Products	Halal food is widely available in the country, as halal slaughter is common.
Dress Code	Muslim dress, especially for women, in the form of the head scarf is common and allowed in public, and there is no legal restriction on wearing the niqab (face veil). However, both, head scarf and niqab, are prohibited for girls attending public schools.
Places of Islamic Learning and Education	– High school Medreseja (madrasa) Aluddin with its main campus in Prishtina and two branches in Prizren and Gjilan. Established in 1952: http://medreseja.com/ – *Fakulteti i Studimeve Islame* (Faculty of Islamic Studies), based in Prishtina. It offers Bachelor's and Master's degrees in Islamic Education, and was established in 1992: http://www.fsi92.net/ – *Instituti i Hifzit* (Hifz Institute) in Gjakova. Established in 2005 as a private school. – Gymnasium Hasan Hani in Prishtina: private high school established in 2013. The school is run by the Gülen movement.
Muslim Media and Publications	– The Islamic Community of Kosovo has three regular publications: *Dituria Islame* (Islamic Knowledge), a monthly magazine since 1986; *Edukata Islame* (Islamic Education), a quarterly journal since 1971; and *Takvimi*, an annual journal since 1970. – Peace TV–the Albanian version is made in Kosovo. *Online media*: – www.bislame.net: the website of the Islamic Community of Kosovo – www.islamgjakova.net: online news resource run by the Islamic Community, from their Gjakova office

- www.mesazhi.com: online newspaper with local news, and news from other Muslim majority countries
- www.kohaislame.net: private online newspaper with Islamic news and content.

Main Muslim Organisations

- Islamic Community of the Republic of Kosovo (*Bashkesia Islame e Republikes se Kosoves*, Str. Bajram Kelmendi, No. 84, 10000 Prishtina, tel.: ++381 38224024, www.bislame.net). This is the formal institution that represents the Muslims of Kosovo in religious affairs.
- Union of Kosovo Tarikats (*Bashkesia e Tarikateve te Kosoves*, Str. Kaqaniku nr. 3, 20000 Prizren, e-mail: contact@btkonline.net, www.btkonline.net). This is an independent religious community representing various Sufi orders in Kosovo.

Latvia

Simona Gurbo[1]

Introduction

Muslim community organisations in Latvia kept a low profile in 2017 with hardly any activities and attention being drawn. A strong anti-refugee sentiment continues to prevail in Latvia, however, but it has more to do with a wider anti-immigration stance rather than specific anti-Islamic attitudes. The leadership of Muslim community organisations reported continued instances of hate speech on the internet on pages that focus on local Muslims or the refugees that have settled in Latvia from Muslim majority countries. As in 2016, despite efforts on the part of various political groups, the Ministry of Justice and law enforcement agencies since 2015, no laws were passed on the issue of banning the covering of the face in public. The local media continued to cover terrorist attacks perpetrated by various groups across the globe. By and large, however, few activities by Muslim community organisations in Latvia took place.

Public Debates

In 2017, the majority of articles and debates in the media on Islam and Muslims focused on reports either on the refugee and migrant crisis in Europe, or more commonly on terrorism cases across the world. In May 2017, the Security Police published its annual report, in which it made the same observations as in previous years. These being that former director of the *Latvijas Islāma kultūras centrs* (Islamic Cultural Centre in Latvia–ICCL) who joined ISIS in 2015, Oļegs Imrans Petrovs, continues to remain an authority among a small group of local converts. However, the majority of Muslims do not sympathise with him, terrorism levels in Latvia are low, and since ISIS activities in the Middle East are now on the decline, few Muslims have shown any interest in travelling to Syria.[2]

---

[1] Simona Gurbo is a visiting lecturer at the Department of Political Science at Rīga Stradiņš University, and teaches Religion and Politics. Her research interests include Church-State relations, the political behaviour of clergy of various Christian denominations, as well as political behaviour in general.

[2] *Publiskais pārskats par Drošības policijas darbu 2016. gadā* (Annual Report of the Security Police), 18 April 2017, http://dp.gov.lv/lv/noderigi/publikacijas/drosibas-policija-publice-par-skatu-par-dienesta-darbibu-2016.-gada.art70, accessed 14 February 2018.

Līga Fatima Legzdiņa, a local convert and one of the three Muslim women in Latvia that wear a niqab, continued to draw people's attention to Muslim affairs in Latvia. Because of her post on Facebook that "Western civilization is evil", she caused uproar on social media, garnering some interest from other media as well.[3]

Hamza Jānis Luciņš, the leader of the Islamic Cultural Centre, reiterated that anti-Muslim hate speech mostly in the form of posts on social media and comments on news articles continued to present a problem; however no reports were made either to the police or to the Ombudsman of the Republic of Latvia. The anti-Muslim rhetoric is hardly surprising, since in the latest survey from 2014 by the Marketing and Public Opinion Research Centre (SKDS), 53% of Latvians held negative attitudes towards Muslims.[4]

Transnational Links

Global events had little impact on Muslims in Latvia. After the departure of Oļegs Imrans Petrovs in 2016–who had studied in Saudi Arabia and was well-connected with other Muslim organisations in Europe, such as the German branch of the Tablighi Jama'at–the Islamic Cultural Centre in Latvia lost many of its ties with Muslim organisations in other countries. Tablighi Jama'at representatives have not visited Latvia since 2014.

Law and Domestic Politics

In 2017, no legal changes were made that affected the Muslim population in Latvia. In November 2015, the Cabinet of Ministers had tasked the Ministry of Justice with the drafting of a law regarding face covering. The Law was eventually drafted in late spring 2016 in anticipation of the incoming refugees as part of the European wide asylum seeker relocation programme. It took more than a year for the Ministry of Justice to include a reference on the European Court of Human Rights (ECtHR) conclusions on similar bans in Belgium and France.

---

3 "Islāmticīgās latvietes Līgas Fātimas ieraksts 'Facebook' izraisa traci sociālajos tīklos" (Latvian Muslim's Liga Fatima's post on "Facebook" stirs an uproar on social media), 24 August 2017, http://jauns.lv/raksts/zinas/251598-islamticigas-latvietes-ligas-fatimas-ieraksts-facebook-izraisa-traci-socialajos-tiklos, accessed 19 February 2018.

4 Department of State, *Starptautiskais ziņojums par reliģijas brīvību pasaulē: Latvija* (*International Religious Freedom Report. Latvia*), 2016, https://lv.usembassy.gov/wp-content/uploads/sites/58/IRRF2016_LV.pdf, accessed 19 February 2018.

On 22 August 2017, the proposal finally went before the Cabinet of Ministers, which approved the preliminary draft despite objections from the Ministry of Foreign Affairs, which pointed out that some cases could reach the ECtHR.[5] The Law has yet to be approved by Parliament. Whereas previously progress on the Law stirred much interest and public discussion, it received very little coverage in 2017.

Activities and Initiatives of Main Muslim Organisations

The number of Muslim organisations, according to the records of the Central Statistical Bureau of Latvia, remained at 16 (the data for 2017 is still unavailable).[6] According to Hamza Jānis Luciņš, less than 100 Muslims meet for Friday prayers on a weekly basis in Riga, and a few do so in other locations across Latvia. The activities of the Islamic Cultural Centre continued to decline (presumably still due to the leadership change in 2015), however another organisation, *Kultūras un izglītības centrs Miras* (Cultural and Education Centre *Miras*) became more active; it was involved in various social activities and refugee integration discussions. The Islamic Cultural Centre to date has not opened the prayer centre building that it acquired in 2013, as they still have not met the necessary fire and safety requirements as set out by the Riga City Construction Board.

In July 2017, the Cultural and Educational Centre *Miras* engaged with representatives of non-governmental organisations to discuss how they can support refugees and provide them with integration opportunities in Latvian society. No public events were organised in 2017. Muslim organisations continued to operate with little public visibility and did not participate in any public discussions.

---

5 "Valdība atbalsta Sejas aizsegšanas ierobežojumu" (The Government approves limitations on face covering), *TVNET/LETA*, 22 August 2017, http://www.tvnet.lv/zinas/latvija/674084-valdiba_atbalsta_sejas_aizsegsanas_ierobezojumu, accessed 22 August 2017.

6 Centrālā Statistikas pārvalde, "Valstī reģistrēto reliģisko draudžu skaits sadalījumā pa konfesijām gada beigās" (Number of registered religious congregations by denomination at the end of the year), http://data.csb.gov.lv/pxweb/lv/visp/visp__ikgad__politika/PR0130.px/table/tableViewLayout2/?rxid=a79839fe-11ba-4ecd-8cc3-4035692c5fc8, accessed 19 February 2018.

Muslim Population: History and Demographics

Though Muslims (mainly Volga Tatar immigrants and other Muslims decommissioned from the Russian Tsarist army) started arriving and settling in the then Russian-ruled Latvia in the second part of the 19th century, the first Muslim congregation in Riga was established only in 1902. By World War I, it had grown to around 1,000 members, but by 1920 the Muslim presence in the now independent Latvia had shrunk to a mere 150, and further declined to about 60 by 1935. Today, most Latvian Muslims are settlers, and descendants of settlers, from the Soviet period, when scores of people from the then Soviet Central Asian and Caucasus republics, as well as the Volga region, moved to the Baltics. The last Soviet census of 1989 reported more than 12,000 people of Muslim background (Tatars, Azerbaijanis, Kazakhs, Uzbeks, etc.) living in Soviet Latvia, although most of them did not practise Islam. Quite a few of them chose to leave after Latvia had regained independence in the early 1990s.[7]

No official data on the number of Muslims is available, as official censuses in Latvia do not include a question on religious identity. However, the best source, in order to gain some demographic and statistical information, on Latvia's Muslim population, is still the official census, which was last carried out in 2011 by the Central Statistical Bureau of Latvia, and provides information on the ethnic and national backgrounds of the population.

Muslim Population	Estimates based on data about ethnic/national background, suggest that there are approximately 5,000 to 6,000 Muslims in the country (ca. 0.25% of the population). Population estimates by Muslim organisations, as expressed on their website www.islammuslim.lv, report approximately 1,000 practising Muslims in Latvia (0.05% of the population in 2017). However, the *Annual Report of Religious Organisations and Their Activities* lists only 295 members, a decrease from 315 in 2016.[8]

---

7 Ščerbinskis, Valters, *Ienācēji no tālienes: Austrumu un Dienvidu tautu pārstāvji Latvijā no 19. gadsimta beigām līdz mūsdienām.* (*Newcomers from Remoteness: Representatives of the Eastern and Southern Nations in Latvia from the End of the 19th Century to the Present Day*) (Rīga: Nordik, 1998).

8 Tieslietu ministrija, *Ziņojums par Tieslietu ministrijā iesniegtajiem reliģisko organizāciju pārskatiem par darbību 2016. gadā* (*Annual Report of Religious Organisations and their Activities in 2016 to the Ministry of Justice*), 30 June 2017, https://www.tm.gov.lv/lv/ministrija/gada-parskati/2016-gada-publiskie-parskati, accessed 15 February 2018.

Ethnic/National Backgrounds	Largest ethnic/national groups (2011):[9] Tatar: 2,164 Azerbaijani: 1,657 Uzbek: 339 Kazakh: 241 Other: 828.
Inner-Islamic Groups	No official data available. Estimates provided by www.islammuslim.lv suggest that the majority of Azerbaijani Muslims in Latvia are Shi'is.
Geographical Spread	The majority of the Muslim population is concentrated in Riga, with a much smaller community in Daugavpils.
Number of Mosques	1 prayer hall in Riga, usually referred to as a mosque by local Muslims and the general public.
Muslim Burial Sites	– Musulmaņu sektors Miķeļa kapos, Gaujas iela 4, Rīga, Latvija – Musulmaņu sektors Jaunciema kapos, Jaunciema 8. šķērslīnija 10, Rīga, Latvija.
"Chaplaincy" in State Institutions	None.
Halal Products	There are a few stores and a few restaurants that offer halal food, however halal food is not widely available in public institutions. Halal slaughter has been permitted in Latvia since 2009.

---

9 LR Centrālā statistikas pārvalde, "Latvijas Pastāvīgie iedzīvotāji pēc tautības, dzimuma un pa vecuma grupām 2011. gada 1. martā" (Permanent residents of Latvia by nationality, sex and age group on 1 March 2011), http://data.csb.gov.lv/pxweb/lv/tautassk_11/tautassk_11__tsk2011/TSG11-06.px/table/tableViewLayout1/?rxid=cdcb978c-22b0-416a-aacc-aa650d3e2ce0, accessed 17 January 2015.

Dress Code	There are no limitations on Muslim dress. Several women wear head scarves (primarily international students), three women wear a niqab in Latvia.
Places of Islamic Education and Learning	*Brīvdienas skola bērniem* (Holiday School for Children), Brīvības 104, Rīga, Latvija.
Muslim Publications and Media	No data available.

Main Muslim Organisations

- Islamic Cultural Centre in Latvia (*Latvijas Islāma kultūras centrs*–ICCL, Brīvības iela 104–22, Rīga, Latvija, tel.: ++371 28625625, www.likc.lv). The ICCL represents the following Muslim congregations: Iman, Koran, Islam, Mardžani (mostly Tatar Muslims), Alshabab Almuslim, Makka, Amina, Halal in Riga, and Ideļ (mostly Kazan Tatars) in Daugavpils.
- Culture and Education Centre Miras (*Kultūras un izglītības centrs Miras*, Lāčplēša iela 35–2, Rīga, Latvija, tel.: ++371 26210643). The Centre ncludes Azerbaijanis, Bashkirs, Georgians, Kazakhs, Latvians, Pakistanis, and Russians.

Lithuania

Egdūnas Račius[1]

Introduction

By the expiry of the European Commission refugee relocation and resettlement programme towards the end of 2017, Lithuania had admitted less than half of the set quota of 1,105 displaced persons, chiefly from Syria and Iraq, the overwhelming majority of them being of a Muslim background. However, more than two-thirds chose to move on to Western Europe. For this reason, during the two-year period of the programme, the country's Muslim population increased by little more than 100 persons.

Compared to 2015–with its migrant and refugee crisis and resulting public anxiety in anticipation of impending relocation/resettlement–and compared to 2016–when issues surrounding incoming refugee integration and their *en masse* flight out of Lithuania were widely discussed–the year 2017 was relatively quiet. There were no heated debates on either political side; neither among those who had vehemently opposed the EU resettlement programme, nor among those who expressed solidarity with displaced persons.

The new Government, formed just before 2017, did not in any way change the State's course regarding Lithuania's stance on the migrant and refugee crisis. Internally its rhetoric did not betray any tilt toward anti-immigrant or anti-Muslim populism. In general, 2017 was not in any way an exceptional year in regards to Islam and the Muslim presence in Lithuania. Muslim communities kept, as usual, a low profile, and no major events took place in the country to draw any sustained public attention.

Public Debates

As in previous years, in 2017, the national media continued to devote time and space to reflect on the aftermath of the migrant and refugee crisis. However, this was done in an incoherent manner; mainly through *ad hoc* and one-off reports on refugee integration related to wider issues in Europe or in Lithuania.

---

[1] Egdūnas Račius is Professor of Middle Eastern and Islamic Studies at Vytautas Magnus University in Kaunas, Lithuania. His most recent book is *Muslims in Eastern Europe* (Edinburgh: Edinburgh University Press, 2018).

There were also some articles in the printed media and reports on TV and radio about aspects of the religion of Islam, individuals of Muslim background in Lithuania, and Lithuanian Tatar Muslims. None of these stories caused any public reaction, let alone public debate, however.

The exception to this was the publication of the annual national security threat assessment of 2016,[2] that was released in early 2017. Among the threats described, two relate to Lithuanian residents of Muslim background. One of them explicitly addresses the perceived vulnerability of Lithuanian Tatars to Russian influence: to make them more favourable toward Russia and its policies, including those related to the annexed Crimea. The other point draws attention to the potential radicalisation of Lithuania's Muslims. In its annual report for 2016 (released in April 2017),[3] the State Security Department provided some details on its monitoring activities of some 70 Lithuanian citizens and expatriates of Muslim background on suspicion that they had been radicalised. Though the report does not indicate to which particular groups or organisations the monitored individuals may have belonged, it suggests that several of them were sympathetic to the so-called Islamic State. Both these reports caused a swift reaction from the Lithuanian Tatar Muslim leadership,[4] who rejected outright the insinuations of the intelligence community as absurd, and repeatedly reaffirmed Tatar (and by extension, the country's Muslims') loyalty to the country.

Apart from this rare public appearance, the Lithuanian Muslim leadership as always kept a low profile, with the Mufti Romas Jakubauskas, and several other prominent indigenous Muslim Tatars, agreeing on only a few interviews, in which they shunned any controversies and squarely placed themselves within the framework of a tolerant and peaceful Islam. In this way they gave no ground to any concerned side who wished to drag them into possible wider, prolonged, public discussion.

Transnational Links

In the years preceding 2017, Lithuanian Muslims, particularly converts, showed high levels of cooperation with their coreligionists in Latvia and Estonia through

---

2 https://www.vsd.lt/wp-content/uploads/2017/03/AKATSKT_DRAFT-3-31-EN-HQ.pdf, accessed 26 January 2018.
3 https://www.vsd.lt/wp-content/uploads/2016/10/2016_veiklos-ataskaitaVIESA_0330.pdf, accessed 26 January 2018.
4 https://www.balctictimes.com/head_of_tatar_community__we_are_patriots_of_lithuania/, accessed 26 January 2018.

the organisation of joint seminars, lectures and the like. However, in 2017 there were hardly any joint functions. This, in part, may have been the result of internal tensions within the Latvian and Estonian Muslim communities,[5] with which Lithuanian Muslims have had close personal and institutional relations.

In 2017, the Mufti, as the official head and representative of the country's Muslim population, took part in a number of activities organised by Muslim religious organisations and bodies abroad, from the UK to Turkey, Azerbaijan, Ukraine, Russia, and Finland. It should be noted that, though invited by the Russian-controlled Crimean Muslim authorities to visit the occupied Crimea, unlike his Estonian[6] and Belarusian colleagues, the Lithuanian Mufti did not accept the invitation and did not travel to Crimea. Rather, he took part in commemoration functions at the Ukrainian parliament, thereby reaffirming the general Lithuanian stance on Russia's policies regarding Crimea and its Muslim population.

Lithuanian Tatars maintain quite close relations not only with their ethnic kin in neighbouring Poland and Belarus, but also with those in Tatarstan in the Russian Federation. Here though their interaction has less of a religious colour and is more about cultural and academic exchange, and, recently, political issues, like the situation of Crimean Tatars under Russian occupation. With the annexation of Crimea by the Russian Federation, anti-Russian Crimean Tatars became quite frequent guests in Lithuania, welcomed not only by the local Tatar leadership–the head of the *Lietuvos totorių bendruomenių sąjunga* (Union of Lithuanian Tatar Communities), Adas Jakubauskas, is a Lithuanian representative in the Crimean Tatar Majlis–but also by Lithuania's political establishment.

A UK-based Muslim religious organisation iERA, that is engaged in global proselytisation activities, reported of a New Muslim Retreat taking place in the Lithuanian town of Elektrėnai in October of 2017, which is claimed by the organisation to have been the first of its sort outside the UK.[7] Though it hosted just half a dozen converts (all males), besides Lithuanians there were three

---

5 Ringvee, Ringo, "Estonia", in Oliver Scharbrodt, Samim Akgönül, Ahmet Alibašić, Jørgen S. Nielsen and Egdūnas Račius (eds.), *Yearbook of Muslims in Europe*, vol. 9 (Leiden: Brill, 2017), pp. 219–231; Gurbo, Simona, "Latvia", in Oliver Scharbrodt, Samim Akgönül, Ahmet Alibašić, Jørgen S. Nielsen and Egdūnas Račius (eds.), *Yearbook of Muslims in Europe*, vol. 9 (Leiden: Brill, 2017), pp. 404–410.
6 http://rus.delfi.ee/daily/estonia/musulmane-ukrainy-nedovolny-vizitom-estonskogo-imama-ildara-muhamedshina-v-krym?id=78116696, accessed 25 January 2018.
7 https://iera.org/ieras-new-muslim-retreat-goes-international-lithuania/, accessed 25 January 2018.

participants from Latvia. However, this event is not known to have been coordinated with any of Lithuania's Muslim organisations.

Law and Domestic Politics

The only legal action taken in 2017 that has had an effect on the Muslim population in the country was an explanation by the Constitutional Court that the clergy of traditional faith communities (among them Sunni Muslims) may be drafted into the country's armed forces only in cases of war; otherwise they are exempt from this obligation.

In January 2018, the High Administrative Court dealt with a case of a Latvian citizen, who, because of his belonging to and activity in Tablighi Jamaat, was banned in 2016 by the Department of Migration from entering Lithuania for five years.[8] The Department based its decision on information supplied by the State Security Department, which had argued that Tablighi Jamaat and its individual members pose a serious security threat to Lithuania because it is engaged in activities leading to the potential radicalisation of Muslims under its influence. The High Administrative Court ruled that there were no grounds for banning the person from entering Lithuania, as there was no evidence that his activities (both in the past and in the foreseeable future) had been in breach of any laws, or showed signs of leading to such a breach. The Court's decision is final and may not be appealed. It should also be mentioned that the Court included in its argument that Tablighi Jamaat is not banned in Lithuania.

On the municipal level, the Muftiate has pursued the objective of building a mosque in Vilnius on a plot to be allocated by the municipality as compensation for the nationalised (during the Soviet period) land on which the Vilnius mosque once stood. Though the City Council had proposed a number of plots, the Muftiate was not satisfied with the offers and has rejected them. The current mayor of Vilnius, Remigijus Šimašius (of the Liberal Movement), made public comments in 2015 in which he assured the public that the City Council would not consider the mosque issue for the time being.[9] As of the end of 2017, the negotiations for the land plot had not moved any further.[10]

---

8   http://eteismai.lt/byla/262212711484074/A-1048-624/2017, accessed 26 January 2018.
9   "Simasius–no plans for mosque in Vilnius", *The Baltic Times*, 25 September 2015, http://www.baltictimes.com/simasius_-_no_plans_for_mosque_in_vilnius/, accessed 26 January 2018.
10 Interview with Mufti Romas Jakubauskas, 23 January 2018.

In 2017, as in previous years, the Lithuanian government allocated an annual subsidy for the officially recognised nine "traditional" religious communities, among them Sunni Muslims, who received a modest sum of €3,600. Although there is no law requiring the Government to allocate any money to religious communities, it has been doing so for some 20 years. The amounts paid vary, but their share depends on the estimated number of adherents of the "traditional" religions.

In July 2017, the Speaker of the Parliament received a delegation of Lithuanian Tatars, with the Mufti among them,[11] and in September himself paid a courtesy visit to Kaunas mosque, where he met with the Mufti and the acting Turkish imam.[12]

Activities and Initiatives of Main Muslim Organisations

The Muftiate, which is officially recognised by the State as the sole representative religious organisation of Muslims in Lithuania, kept its usual low public profile in 2017, and organised hardly any events or functions in its own name. Rather, it was a joint venture between Halal Control Lithuania (founded in 2016, in which the Mufti plays a prominent role) and the Muslim community of the once Tatar-dominated Keturiasdešimt totorių village, that co-organised several activities for the community, such as the celebrations of 'Id Al-Adha (August) and *mawlid* (December). In September 2017, the Muslim community of Keturiasdešimt totorių village also organised a public celebration of 'Ashura', perceived in a specific Lithuanian Tatar not a Shi'i way, where the story of the death of Husayn is devoid of any Sunni-Shi'a conflict and with an emphasis on special meals.

Representatives (including the Mufti) of Halal Control Lithuania met with officials of the Ministry of Agriculture in September to discuss co-operation in the promotion and export of Lithuania-produced halal meat products. In November 2017, the Mufti was part of an official Lithuanian delegation that visited Algeria, where the export of halal products from Lithuania was discussed with the Algerians (Ministry of Agriculture, Ministry of Foreign Affairs).

---

11 http://www.lrs.lt/sip/portal.show?p_r=15259&p_k=1&p_a=media_object_viewer&guid=83BAC04C-85FE-4627-9F97-BA2775B93919, accessed 25 January 2018.
12 http://islamasvisiems.lt/oficialus-vizitas-kauno-meceteje/, accessed 25 January 2018.

The Kaunas mosque-based NGO *Švietimas ir paveldas* (Education and Heritage)–established in 2014 by a group of young Muslims (mainly converts but also some young Lithuanian Tatars)–has been a much more active organisation since its foundation than the Muftiate. It has been mainly devoted to both spiritual counselling for new converts and the promotion of Islam among the Lithuanian-speaking population. In 2017, as in previous years, the organisation was active in maintaining Qur'an and Arabic language weekend classes in the Kaunas mosque and on the premises of the Islamic Cultural and Educational Centre. It also organised occasional public lectures, workshops and other meetings, primarily aimed at local Muslims but open to the general public. It hosted representatives of the Third Generation University in the Kaunas mosque in November 2017. It was also instrumental in organising the celebrations of the two major Islamic holidays, 'Id al-Fitr and 'Id al-Adha around the country, particularly in Kaunas where the meat of slaughtered animals during 'Id al-Adha was distributed among Muslims in the city. This organisation's website (islamasvisiems.lt) remained the only one that regularly updated information (mainly in Lithuanian but also occasionally in English) on upcoming events in 2017. The website also contains a growing list of online books on Islamic doctrine and practices that is translated into Lithuanian by community members.

The Kaunas Muslim community engages in humanitarian aid; in January 2017 it took clothes and toys to refugees housed in the Refugee Reception Centre in Rukla, and met with some of them. The *Islamo kultūros ir švietimo centras* (Centre of Islamic Culture and Education) founded by the Muftiate as a platform for its public relations activities, that first appeared in 2016, did not report any activities in 2017.

The recently established Ahmadiyya association made its first public appearance by organising a clean-up of the country's main square (the Cathedral Square in the capital city Vilnius) in the early hours of 1 January 2017.[13] In March, members of the association gave blood to the National Blood Centre.[14]

---

13   http://www.bernardinai.lt/straipsnis/2017-01-02-sausio-1-aja-musulmonu-bendruomene-tvarke-katedros-aikste-vilniuje/153577, accessed 24 January 2018.

14   https://v2.kraujodonoryste.lt/naujienos/ahmadija-nariai-savo-asociacijos-sukurimo-metines-iprasmino-lietuvos-ligoniams-dovanodami-kraujo.html, accessed 24 January 2018.

Muslim Population: History and Demographics

The history of Islam in Lithuania dates back to the 14th century when the first migrants–political refugees from the Golden Horde and later the Crimean Khanate–came to the then Grand Duchy of Lithuania. Soon they were joined by new arrivals, consisting chiefly of mercenaries hired by Lithuanian grand dukes, and more refugees and prisoners of war who, once freed, chose to stay. The immigrants, the majority of whom were recently Islamised Turkic speakers (eventually to be called "Lipka" (Lithuanian) Tatars), settled in the Northwestern parts of the Duchy, mainly in village communities around the capital Vilnius. Upon settlement, the Tatar elite were granted the rank of nobility and given tracts of land to be used as fiefs, that later went into their personal possession.

Despite, or because, Muslims were only a tiny minority of the citizenry of the Duchy,[15] they enjoyed most of the rights and freedoms that their Christian fellow citizens did. Throughout the centuries, with a few brief exceptions, Lithuanian Tatars were allowed to publicly observe all Islamic duties and rituals. It is believed that mosques on the then territory of the Grand Duchy were being built as early as the late 14th or beginning of the 15th century.

After the final partition of the Republic of Two Nations (formed with Poland in 1569) in 1795, most Tatars of the former Grand Duchy of Lithuania found themselves subjects of the Russian Empire, and the local Tatar community was entrusted to the care of the Simferopol-based (Crimea) Mohammedan Spiritual Governing Board. Available archival material suggests, however, that the Muslims of the lands of the former Grand Duchy insisted on retaining their religious independence from the Mohammadan Spiritual Governing Board. Eventually, in 1851, the Russian government ascended to the Tatars' requests and officially allowed them to elect *mullas* from among themselves. An attempt by some local Muslims in the middle of the 19th century to convince the Russian government to establish a separate spiritual governing body (muftiate) for the Muslims of the Western provinces failed however.

In interwar independent Lithuania, the Muslim population was still comprised mainly of Tatars, though its numbers had been drastically reduced (the number hovered around 1,100) because Muslims living in Vilnius and surrounding areas became citizens of Poland, which controlled the Vilnius region until the end of 1939. However, it was during the interwar period when the

---

15   Though precise data is not available, it can be safely assumed that at no time in history did the Muslim population of the Grand Duchy of Lithuania exceed 100,000 individuals.

first brick mosque in Lithuania (in the interim capital Kaunas) was built; it opened its doors in the early 1930s. During the Soviet period, Muslim communal life, due to anti-religious state policies, came to a virtual standstill despite a significant influx (counted in the tens of thousands) of people of Muslim background from the Soviet Caucasus and Central Asia. With the regaining of independence in the early 1990s, the Lithuanian Muslim Tatar community regained its mosques and revived its communal activities.

The sole source of demographic and statistical, though not necessarily very reliable, information on Lithuania's Muslim population, is the official Lithuanian Census carried out every ten years, which includes a question on religion. The data from the last Lithuanian Census of 2011 provides information on the age, gender, national background, and geographical spread of Muslims across the country.

Muslim Population	Officially less than 3,000 Sunni Muslims (2,727 or 0.1% of population, according to 2011 census).[16] With little immigration and emigration of Muslim citizens, the number of Muslims for 2017 should have not changed significantly from 2011. Mosque attendance on Fridays and involvement in community activities suggest a much lower number of practising Muslims (around 500).
	No official data on Shi'is or other groups exist.
Ethnic/National Backgrounds	The overwhelming majority of Muslims in Lithuania are Lithuanian citizens.
	Largest ethnic/national groups (according to 2011 census):
	Tatar: 1,441 (52.8% of all Sunni Muslims)
	Lithuanian: 374 (13.7%)
	Russian: 73 (2.7%)

---

16   Department of Statistics, *Gyventojai pagal tautybę, gimtąją kalbą ir tikybą* (*Population by Ethnicity, Native Language, and Faith*) (Vilnius: Statistikos departamentas, 2013), p. 14, https://osp.stat.gov.lt/documents/10180/217110/Gyv_kalba_tikyba.pdf/1d9dac9a-3d 45-4798-93f5-941fed00503f, accessed 26 January 2018.

Others: 794 (29.1%, from among 157 Uzbeks, 144 Kazakhs, 93 Arabs, 88 Turks, 84 Bashkirs, 76 Chechens, 43 Tajiks, 30 Turkmen, 29 Egyptians, 19 Pakistanis, 18 Kyrgyz and 10 Afghans).

Between 100 and 150 Syrian and Iraqi refugees of Muslim background resettled or relocated to Lithuania between 2015 and 2017.

Inner-Islamic Groups No public official data is available on other Muslim groups as the published census results only include Sunni Muslims (as a "traditional" faith-community).

There is, however, a more than 600-strong Azerbaijani community, and some among them could be at least nominal Twelver Shi'is. There are also several dozen Shi'i immigrants from Lebanon and Iran, but there is no specific Shi'i congregation, and some individual Shi'is pray at Sunni mosques.

The Hizmet (Gülen movement) has a presence in the country and runs a private school (Vilnius International Meridian School, VIMS), however, the number of its adherents (chiefly Turkish citizens) is not known. Until the split between the Turkish government and Gülen, members of the movement were an integral part of the Sunni community in Lithuania. However, since then, and particularly since the attempted *coup d'état* in Turkey in July 2016, they, under pressure from both the Diyanet and the Turkish embassy, have been marginalised within the broader Muslim institutional field and premises in Vilnius.

The Ahmadiyya movement, although making an appearance in the country in the beginning of the 1990s, failed to gain followers, and is currently represented by just a few families of immigrants and converts united by the Ahmadiyya association (https://www.facebook.com/AhmadijaLT/).

Geographical Spread	Almost half of Lithuania's Muslims live in the capital city Vilnius and its district, followed by the centrally located second largest city Kaunas, and Southern Alytus (both with around 13%), and then Western Klaipėda (10%).
Number of Mosques	Four purpose-built historical mosques (three wooden, built in the 19th and early 20th centuries,[17] and one brick, built in the early 1930s) owned by local Lithuanian Tatar congregations, of which only the mosque in Kaunas (Totorių Street 6) is regularly used for Friday prayers and is served by a Turkish imam paid by the Diyanet. The other mosques, in the villages of Raižiai, Nemėžis and Keturiasdešimt totorių (Forty Tatars), are open mainly during religious festivals, although during warm seasons occasional Friday prayers also take place, with local Tatar imams leading the prayers.

In addition, in the capital Vilnius, there is a spacious prayer hall (and a separate one for women) at the premises of the Muftiate/Centre of Islamic Culture and Education, which is open throughout the day. It has a Turkish imam whose salary is paid by the Diyanet.

In the Western seaport city of Klaipėda, Muslims make use of rented premises.

Vilnius City Municipality over the course of over 20 years has offered various plots of land for the purpose of building a mosque as a compensation for the land, on which the original Vilnius mosque stood, that was nationalised by the communist authorities in the Soviet era. However, since the current mayor assumed office in 2014, the negotiations between the Mufti and the city authorities have been stalled.

---

17 The interior of these mosques can be viewed at http://www.panoramas.lt/index.php?page_id=133&pan_type=242&show=yes&search_katalog=mosque, accessed 26 January 2018.

Muslim Burial Sites

The main burial place for Lithuanian Muslims is a vast cemetery in Raižiai village (Alytus district) in the South of the country. Raižiai is the location of one of the historical Tatar mosques, and this particular mosque was the only one which functioned during the Soviet period. The Forty Tatars village, besides a historical (unused) Muslim cemetery around the mosque, has a new spacious community cemetery, to which it accepts all deceased Muslims, including expatriates. Nemėžis (yet another village with a mosque) also has a cemetery which, though still in use, has limited capacity. Muslims of the Western seaport city of Klaipėda have recently secured a section in the city's public cemetery. Likewise, there is a separate section allocated to Muslims in one of Vilnius' cemeteries. According to the Mufti, as only around 30 funerals take place annually, there are currently no concerns over space.[18]

However, many Tatars, particularly the more secularised ones, bury their deceased in cemeteries used by people of different faiths.

"Chaplaincy" in State Institutions

Though by law Sunni Muslims in state institutions may seek spiritual guidance, there has so far been no demand for Muslim chaplains in the armed forces or hospitals. The few Muslim inmates serving terms in the Lithuanian penitentiary system who sought an imam's counselling have been occasionally visited by the Mufti.

---

18   Interview with Mufti Romas Jakubauskas, 23 January 2018.
19   Interview with Mufti Romas Jakubauskas, 23 January 2018.

Halal Products	A dozen or so Lithuanian meat processing plants have halal certificates issued by the Lithuanian Mufti through Halal Control Lithuania (http://halalcontrol.lt/apie-mus). Halal Control Lithuania employs several local Muslims as butchers, but the bulk are expatriates, among them several resettled/relocated displaced persons from Iraq and Syria. Though most of the produce made by these companies is exported, the Mufti asserted[19] that all chicken products sold in Lithuanian shops are halal, though they are not officially certified as such. An increasing number of kabab stalls serve purportedly halal meat, though they do not carry any papers confirming that claim.
Dress Code	By law, Sunni Muslims (like believers of other traditional faiths) may wear clothes they deem required by religion, just short of covering the face. There is a general law, not aimed at any religious group, prohibiting face covering for security reasons; hence, the niqab is by default proscribed. Consequently, Muslims may pose for official photos in such non-face covering attire as a head scarf (*hijab*), *jilbab, abaya, chador*, turban, cap and the like, provided they have a document signed by the Mufti stating that the holder is a Muslim and it is required of her/him to wear such particular clothes and/or headgear. However, practically no Muslim women wear the head scarf, except for Turkish expatriates (mainly Hizmet followers) and a few converts.
Places of Islamic Learning and Education	Lithuanian Muslims still have no institutions of formal education and only run weekend schools in Kaunas and Vilnius where the basics of religion and Arabic and Turkish languages are taught. Even though in 2016 the organisation of these schools was stepped up–the one in Kaunas was given a name (*Iqra*) and a formal curriculum created and

announced publicly–in 2017, due to low attendance levels, the weekend schools did not expand. Plans to found a kindergarten in Vilnius were not realised in 2017. Lithuanian converts to Islam prefer informal study groups that regularly meet at someone's home.

Muslim Media and Publications

The sole printed publication (also available online) produced by local Muslims is the Tatar-run *Lietuvos totoriai* (Lithuanian Tatars) which has sections in Lithuanian, Russian and Polish and is aimed at an exclusively Tatar readership. Strictly religious topics tend to be irregular and scarce, with the bulk of articles focused on the history and heritage of the Tatars of the once Grand Duchy of Lithuania. Though previously a regular monthly publication, for the past few years *Lietuvos totoriai* has only been released irregularly, to the extent of being just published annually. During the more than 20 years of its existence, *Lietuvos totoriai* has released 163 issues.[20]

Islamasvisiems.lt is an informational, educational, missionary website maintained by the NGO Education and Heritage. In 2017 it was practically the only public channel of communication for local Muslim communities.

Main Muslim Organisations

– Spiritual Centre of the Lithuanian Sunni Muslims–Muftiate (*Lietuvos Musulmonų Sunitų Dvasinis Centras–Muftiatas*, Smolensko 19, Vilnius, tel.: ++370 67417710, email: ramadan@inbox.lt, https://www.facebook.com/Sunni-Muslim-Religious-centre-in-Lithuania-Muftiate-936258176516705/). Headed by Mufti Romas Jakubauskas, this is an umbrella organisation for the mainly Tatar-established and controlled Muslim communities around the country. As of 2017 these are officially ten, but only six are functioning.

---

20   http://www.tbn.lt/files/File/Tiurkai/Laikra160-1.pdf, accessed 25 January 2018.

They submit to the authority of the Muftiate and their representatives serve as members of the Muftiate's board. No alternative or rival religious organisations to the Muftiate have yet been established.

- Centre of Islamic Culture and Education (*Islamo kultūros ir švietimo centras*, Smolensko 19, Vilnius, tel.: ++370 67903415, email: beganskas@islamocentras.lt). In 2013, the Muftiate, jointly with the Diyanet, established a separate organisation which formally runs the premises where the Muftiate's and Vilnius Tatar community's offices are located. The current director is Aleksandras Beganskas.
- Halal Control Lithuania (Ševčenkos 7, tel.: ++370 63657777, email: info@halalcontrol.lt, http://halalcontrol.lt). Though technically a business, because of the heavy involvement of the Mufti in its activities, it significantly contributes to the religious life of the country's Muslims by sponsoring religious festivals.
- Education and Heritage (*Švietimas ir paveldas*, Lygybės 21–86, Kaunas, tel.: ++370 61230735, email: info@islamasvisiems.lt, www.islamasvisiems.lt). Founded by converts and young Tatars in 2014, it has its base in the Kaunas mosque and has become the most active Muslim organisation in the fields of Islamic religious education, publication and outreach in both Kaunas and Vilnius. The current chairperson is Nelli Mažitova.

Luxembourg

Elsa Pirenne[1]

Introduction

Following the debates that occurred in 2016 in Luxembourg, the year 2017 was still dominated by the discussion about the legislation of concealing the face in certain public spaces. The Government approved a draft law on concealing the face in specific public spaces in July 2017.[2] At the end of November 2017, however, the Council of State rejected the bill.[3] The debates will probably continue in 2018.

The other significant concern in the country is linked to the terrorist attacks that took place in Europe in recent years and the question of radicalisation. Until now, Luxembourg has not been targeted by such attacks, but the country is not shielded from the potential radicalisation processes that could take place among segments of the Muslim communities. For this reason, the non-profit association "SOS Radicalisation" was set up in May 2017,[4] and is attempting to tackle this phenomenon. The association plays an advocacy, prevention, training and mentoring role both at the familial and societal level. The members of this organisation also intend to set up a research group to understand, hear about and be able to intervene in any radicalisation process (political or religious).

After the agreement signed in January 2015 between the State and the *Shoura*, the body representing Muslims in the country and unique interlocutor with the State,[5] and after a Law of July 2016, that concerns relations between churches and the State, came into effect, Muslim communities have been

---

[1] Elsa Pirenne is a PhD candidate at the University of Luxembourg and the Catholic University of Louvain in Belgium (UCL). She is working on the sociography of Muslim communities and the institutionalisation of Islam in Luxembourg (2014–18). She studied Islamic Studies and Arabic language at UCL.
[2] https://www.wort.lu/fr/politique/projet-de-loi-approuve-le-port-du-voile-integral-interdit-dans-l-espace-public-5978bbdca5e74263e13c4c0a#, accessed 23 November 2017.
[3] http://www.rtl.lu/letzebuerg/archiv/1099512.html, http://www.rtl.lu/letzebuerg/1097408.html, both accessed 2 January 2018.
[4] http://respect.lu/index-fr.php, accessed 23 November 2017.
[5] See Pirenne, Elsa, and Waltzer, Lucie, "Luxembourg", in Oliver Scharbrodt, Samim Akgönül, Ahmet Alibašić, Jørgen S. Nielsen and Egdūnas Račius (eds.), *Yearbook of Muslims in Europe*, vol. 8 (Leiden: Brill, 2017), pp. 422–440 (422).

reorganising themselves. The *Shoura* hired a secretary general in March 2017[6] in order to streamline its organisation, and to be more professional with regard to its relations with the State and society at large.

In September 2017, the new school subject "Life and Society" (*Vie et Société*), which started in 2016 for secondary schools,[7] began in primary schools. This subject replaces Catholic religious education and provides an introduction to the different religions of the world, in particular those that are established in Luxembourg.[8]

Public Debates

The press reported on a conference that looked at gender equality and freedom of religion held in April 2017.[9] The Imam of the *Centre Culturel Islamique du Grand-Duché du Luxembourg* (Cultural and Islamic Centre of the Grand-Duchy of Luxembourg), Halil Ahmetspahic, intervened during a session of questions and answers at the end of the conference;[10] the event was organised by the National Council of Women of Luxembourg (*Conseil National des Femmes du Luxembourg*).[11] In that context, the imam said, in a personal intervention, that the Qur'an condemns homosexuality. Reacting to it, the Members of Parliament Laurent Mosar, Diane Adehm and Gilles Roth (CSV Party)[12] asked a parliamentary question[13] in order to know if these statements

---

[6] http://www.identitet.lu/offre-demploi-secretaire-general-de-la-shoura/, accessed 23 November 2017.

[7] Pirenne, Elsa, "Luxembourg", in Oliver Scharbrodt, Samim Akgönül, Ahmet Alibašić, Jørgen S. Nielsen and Egdūnas Račius (eds.), *Yearbook of Muslims in Europe*, vol. 9 (Leiden: Brill, 2018), pp. 423–441 (423, 430).

[8] http://www.men.public.lu/fr/actualites/articles/communiques-conference-presse/2017/07/11-vote-vieso/index.html, http://portal.education.lu/vieso/, accessed 4 January 2018.

[9] https://www.neimenster.lu/Culture/Offre-diversifiee-Calendrier-shop-visites/Programmation/Conferences/Egalite-des-sexes-et-liberte-de-religion-Monday-27-March-2017-4-00-00-pm, accessed 23 November 2017.

[10] https://www.lequotidien.lu/a-la-une/limam-de-mamer-inquiete-certains-politiques-du-pays/, accessed 23 November 2017.

[11] http://www.cnfl.lu/site/, accessed 23 November 2017.

[12] The CSV Party is a Catholic political party in Luxembourg.

[13] http://chd.lu/wps/portal/public/Accueil/TravailALaChambre/Recherche/RoleDesAffaires?action=doQuestpaDetails&id=15305, accessed 23 November 2017.

are compatible with the convention[14] signed between the State and the *Shoura* in 2015. The MPs were particularly concerned about the promotion of human rights, equality of treatment and gender equality guaranteed in the latest convention. On 18 April 2017, the response of the Ministry in charge of religions, Xavier Bettel, was that a theological divergence does not affect the convention previously signed by the *Shoura*.

A controversy took place at the Superior Court of Justice of Luxembourg on 21 September 2017. It happened at the official ceremony of the Bar Association, when newly trained jurists need to take an oath, at which a Muslim woman, wearing the head scarf, also participated. The President of the Bar Association let her know that, while wearing her head scarf, her oath would be refused by the Superior Court of Justice. According to her, neither during her studies nor during the graduation ceremony, did anyone inform her that there is an obligation to take the oath without wearing any kind of religious or confessional symbols. There is no precedent for such a case in Luxembourg and this caused a wider debate in the country. Almost all the local media reported the incident.[15] In a press release, the *Shoura* expressed its regret about this situation and the way it occurred.[16] According to the President of the Luxembourg Bar, François Prum, "The lawyer's robe is a tradition for them, and should be worn without any religious, philosophical or political symbol."[17] The woman involved decided not to participate at the ceremony in order to avoid any further embarrassment. She eventually participated, without the head scarf, in December 2017.[18]

During the campaign for the municipal elections of October 2017, a Luxembourgish candidate on the ADR list,[19] Christiane Kies, posted Islamophobic statements on Facebook in September 2017. She wrote that "Muslims are and stay terrorists". She erased the messages and apologised for

---

14   http://shoura.lu/wp-content/uploads/2017/05/MEMORIAL-CONVENTION.pdf, accessed 23 November 2017.
15   http://paperjam.lu/news/le-foulard-islamique-incompatible-avec-la-robe-davocat, http://5minutes.rtl.lu/grande-region/laune/1080751.html, http://paperjam.lu/news/le-foulard-de-laspirante-avocate-intrigue, all accessed 23 November 2017.
16   http://shoura.lu/?p=162, both accessed 23 November 2017.
17   http://paperjam.lu/news/le-foulard-islamique-incompatible-avec-la-robe-davocat, accessed 23 November 2017.
18   http://jeudi.lu/revirement-de-laspirante-avocate-laffaire-foulard/, accessed 8 January 2018.
19   https://adr.lu/, accessed 8 January 2018. The ADR is the Alternative and Democratic Reform Party in Luxembourg. It is a right-wing, conservative and populist party.

her statements. Nevertheless, she had to withdraw her candidacy for the elections, as well as her position in the ADR party.[20]

A documentary discussing different confessional cemeteries in the country, shown on the occasion of All Saints' Day by the Luxemburgish channel RTL, provoked a lot of reactions on the internet. The section concerning Muslim graves provoked hundreds of comments, most of them negative, some even Islamophobic. After the first version aired, the documentary was removed from the channel's website and was replaced by a shorter, less controversial, version, including less references to Muslim burial sites.[21]

Transnational Links

Luxembourg is a very small country, with common borders with France, Germany and Belgium.[22] Transnational, as well as the trans-regional links, are very important. As the Muslim communities in Luxembourg mainly come from the Balkans, the transnational links with this European region are very strong in terms of religious, cultural, economic and political support or connections. Most Bosniak events take place in mosques and in Islamic centres, where Bosniak speakers are invited for lectures. Usually, the same person is invited and travels to the different associations. For instance, for the *mawlid* celebration, the *Centre Islamique de Luxembourg* (Islamic Centre of Luxembourg) and the *Centre Culturel Islamique du Nord* (Islamic Cultural Centre of the North) held their events using the same speaker, Safvet Halilovic, in their centres on 2 and 3 December 2017.

In the case of *Le Juste Milieu* (The Middle Ground) association, the links with border countries are also important. The members of this association

---

20 https://www.lequotidien.lu/politique-et-societe/propos-islamophobes-christiane-kies-demissionne-de-ladr/, https://www.wort.lu/de/politik/adr-kandidatin-kies-sorgt-fuer-aufregung-muslime-sinn-a-bleiwen-terroristen-59b7d23c56202b51b13c31d5?variant=B&utm_expid=83959466-12.SpI6vqyGSSyCfbAQ6TzOyQ.2&utm_referrer=https%3A%2F%2Fwww.google.lu%2F, http://www.rtl.lu/letzebuerg/1074841.html,http://5minutes.rtl.lu/grande-region/luxembourg/1074897.html?_x_preview=1, http://paperjam.lu/news/une-candidate-adr-demissionne, all accessed 29 November 2017.

21 http://5minutes.rtl.lu/grande-region/luxembourg/1092262.html, accessed 23 November 2017.

22 Luxembourg's population numbers about 590,667 residents (as of 1 January 2017). Among them, 308,919 are Luxembourgers and 281,748 have a foreign nationality, representing 47.7% of the entire population. See more on http://www.luxembourg.public.lu/en/, accessed 4 January 2018.

organised events, lectures, and weekly lessons given by Islamic scholars from Belgium and France. These scholars mainly come from a Muslim Brotherhood background in Europe. Ties with the European Institute of Human Sciences in Paris and in Château-Chinon are also pertinent.[23]

The Sufi order of the Mouride Brotherhood, composed of people of Senegalese origin, possess extremely strong transnational links. The order, organised as an informal group in Luxembourg, is set up hierarchically. At the bottom, different groups (local *dahira*), from Luxembourg, Nancy, Metz (France, region of Lorraine), form a regional structure. At the next level up, there is a "federation" in Strasbourg, gathering together all these small local groups; together with other local *dahira* (like Dijon, Mulhouse, Belfort, Besançon), they form the "Great East" group of the Mouride Brotherhood. They also have a "dual organisation": the first applies to each local group related to internal organisation (activities, conferences, etc.); the second concerns the federation in general. The local group have to participate, organise, and give funds for larger activities (events, feasts, etc.) for the federation. Currently, they are collecting funds in order to buy a house in Strasbourg. At the top of this Brotherhood there is the Sufi order in Touba, Senegal, the holy city and spiritual and administrative centre of the order. The sheikhs travel around European countries to meet their followers, stopping from time to time in Luxembourg. An example of the links between the diverse Mouride groups is the famous event known as the Grand Magal of Touba.[24] For this commemoration, the Luxembourgish order joined other groups in Dijon (France) in 2017 to celebrate it together.

Among other Sufi orders, the Burhaniya Order[25] maintains relations with Luxembourg through the presence of some of its members (Luxembourgish or living in the country). The members of the Order travel to Germany for festivals and prayer, in particular to its European mother order in Salzhausen (in the countryside, 45 km from Hamburg).[26] The Burhaniya Order also participated in the exhibition "Pray".[27] For this, members of the Order were in contact with another Sufi group, not directly present in Luxembourg either, the

---

23   For example, http://www.ljm.lu/3/69/rencontre-mensuelle-09-2017, accessed 29 November 2017, http://www.iesh.org, accessed 4 January 2018.
24   The Magal of Touba is the celebration of an annual religious pilgrimage by the Senegalese Mouridiyya Order. The Mourids celebrate the life and teachings of the founder of the order, Sheikh Amadou Bamba.
25   The Burhaniya is a Sufi order coming from Sudan, and was founded by Abu Al-Hasan Al-Shadhili and Ibrahim Dasuqi in the 13th century.
26   http://burhaniya.info, accessed 29 November 2017.
27   https://www.lsrs.lu/organisation-organisation/formation-des-adultes/pray-fotoausstellung-und-buch-uber-religiose-gemeinschaften-in-luxemburg/pray-fotoausstellung-uber-religiose-gemeinschaften-in-luxemburg.html, accessed 29 November 2017.

Alawiya Order (AISA Saarland–Lorraine–Luxembourg), based in Saarbrucken in Germany. The inter-regional section of this group is part of the global Alawiya Sufi Order.[28] These two Sufi orders are not established as organised associations in Luxembourg, but both have links to followers in the country.

The *Association des soufis tijanis du Luxembourg* (Tijani Sufi Association of Luxembourg) is a member of *Le cercle des souffles* (The Circle of Breaths),[29] based in Morocco. The Luxembourgish association, linked to the Sufi order of the Tijaniya,[30] maintains links with neighbouring countries, and sheikhs are invited to Luxembourg or to the border region.

Law and Domestic Politics

In January 2017, the MPs Diane Adehm and Gilles Roth (CSV Party) asked a parliamentary question about the participation of young women in swimming lessons at school.[31] Referring to a Swiss case heard by the European Court of Human Rights on 10 January 2017 about the "non-violation of the freedom of religion by the Swiss authorities in the case of a rejection of participation at the swimming class by two Muslims pupils", the MPs anticipated a similar situation occurring in Luxembourg. They submitted a parliamentary question to the Minister of National Education, Childhood and Youth, Claude Meisch.[32] His answer, on 17 February 2017, was a reminder of Luxembourgish school legislation, which is in accordance with the decision of the European Court of Human Rights. At primary schools (*Art. 4 Law 6/Feb. 2009*) as well as at secondary schools, no exemption for religious conviction would be warranted. A ministerial letter of 26 June 2014 contains guidelines on the principles of the neutrality of public schools, tolerance and non-discrimination at these institutions.[33]

---

28 http://aisa-ong.org, accessed 29 November 2017.
29 https://fr-fr.facebook.com/MouvementCS/, accessed 10 January 2018.
30 http://www.tidjaniya.com/en/tariqa-tidjaniya.php, accessed 29 November 2017.
31 http://chd.lu/wps/portal/public/Accueil/TravailALaChambre/Recherche/RoleDesAffair es?action=doQuestpaDetails&id=15064, accessed 29 November 2017.
32 http://chd.lu/wps/portal/public/Accueil/TravailALaChambre/Recherche/RoleDesAffair es?action=doQuestpaDetails&id=15064, accessed 20 March 2018.
33 http://www.men.public.lu/fr/actualites/articles/communiques-conference-presse/2014/ 07/01-neutralite-religieuse/circulaire.pdf, accessed 29 November 2017.

A draft law concerning a ban on concealing the face in some public places was approved in July 2017 by the Government.[34] This question, as well as the legal question, has to be understood in the context of a general debate on freedom of expression in Luxembourg, initiated in 2016.[35] This law, project number 7179, was presented and tabled on 5 September 2017 by the Minister of Justice Félix Braz (*déi Gréng*) as a draft law amending *Article 563* of the *Penal Code*. The draft law includes a ban on concealing the face in certain public spaces.[36] The proposition was made by the Government under pressure from ministers in the coalition from the ADR and CSV parties; primarily it argues for a ban based on security reasons. This draft law also includes a fine of between €25 to €250 in case of violation. The ban targets any action that conceals the face–such as "a motorcycle helmet, a hood or a full-veiling"[37]–that renders the recognition and identification of the face and the person impossible. The law provides for some exceptions, similar to those existing in the Belgian and French law on this matter. The Government identified the public spaces where the law should apply,[38] providing a balance between the right of citizens to wear and to appear in public as they wish, and the minimal requirements of society concerning communication between each other and co-existence. The proposal includes restrictions on the wearing of the niqab as well as the burqa,[39] and follows the debates that took place in 2016 in Luxembourg.[40]

---

34 https://www.wort.lu/en/luxembourg/article-563-luxembourg-law-foresees-partial-ban-of-face-veils-in-public-spaces-59888ea2a5e74263e13c5632, http://www.lequotidien.lu/a-la-une/une-loi-pour-interdire-le-voile-integral-au-luxembourg-va-voir-le-jour/, both accessed 29 November 2017.

35 http://paperjam.lu/news/sale-quart-dheure-a-la-chambre, accessed 23 January 2017.

36 *Projet de loi portant modification de l'article 563 du Code pénal en créant une infraction de dissimulation du visage dans certains lieux publics*, http://chd.lu/wps/portal/public/Accueil/TravailALaChambre/Recherche/RoleDesAffaires?action=doDocpaDetails&backto=/wps/portal/public/Accueil/Actualite&id=7179, accessed 28 March 2018.

37 See p. 8 in section "Comments on single-article" in *Document 7179/00*, tabled 5 September 2017: http://chd.lu/wps/portal/public/Accueil/TravailALaChambre/Recherche/RoleDesAffaires?action=doDocpaDetails&backto=/wps/portal/public/Accueil/Actualite&id=7179, accessed 28 March 2018.

38 https://www.wort.lu/fr/politique/projet-de-loi-le-voile-integral-interdit-oui-mais-pas-partout-5989b033a5e74263e13c56ff, accessed 29 November 2017.

39 http://chd.lu/wps/portal/public/Accueil/TravailALaChambre/Recherche/RoleDesAffaires?action=doDocpaDetails&backto=/wps/portal/public/Accueil/Actualite&id=7179, accessed 2 January 2018.

40 See Pirenne, "Luxembourg", pp. 429–430.

This debate on concealing the face in public spaces in Luxembourg is clearly influenced by the same debates taking place in neighbouring countries, even though wearing a niqab or burqa is not a common practice among Muslim women in Luxembourg. According to Nicolas Schmit, Minister of Labour, the full-face veil has no place in Luxembourgish society, and is a question of women's rights.[41] The Minister could not accept that each municipality had to take its own decision on this sensitive subject, as had been the case until the passing of this new law. The *Shoura* reacted to this new draft law,[42] estimating that the debate about the burqa is of foremost interest to the media, and had been used as a popular subject by some political parties in order to gain votes for the municipal elections of October 2017. As part of the preparation of the draft law, the legal opinions of various institutions (Chamber of Deputies, Prosecutors) were consulted. The Council of State rejected the law at the end of November 2017; it wants more details concerning the places covered by the law, in particular on public transport, in schools (primary and secondary) and in public offices.[43] The debate is still on-going as of January 2018.[44]

The Luxembourg police registered 17 cases of allegedly radicalised individuals in 2017;[45] all of them were linked to Islam. Even though this figure was very low, the Governing Council[46] decided to set up a listening and support service for people confronted with extremism and radicalisation on 29 July 2016. As a consequence, the association "SOS Radicalisation "was founded in May 2017 and the centre linked to it, Respect.lu, started working on 3 July 2017.[47] According to the statutes of this Association, it has been created due to the terrorist threat and the professionalisation of propaganda and methods of

---

41 https://www.wort.lu/fr/luxembourg/port-du-voile-integral-au-luxembourg-nicolas-schmit-confirme-le-gouvernement-veut-legiferer-5890b267a5e74263e13a9dd2, accessed 28 March 2018.

42 http://shoura.lu/?p=155, accessed 23 November 2017.

43 http://www.rtl.lu/letzebuerg/archiv/1099512.html, http://5minutes.rtl.lu/grande-region/luxembourg/1098674.html, http://www.rtl.lu/letzebuerg/1097408.html, all accessed 2 January 2018.

44 http://www.rtl.lu/letzebuerg/1121151.html#, accessed 23 January 2018.

45 According to SOS Radicalisation, nine radicalised cases have been identified in 2017, including two women.

46 http://www.gouvernement.lu/7111678/05--respect-lu, accessed 23 November 2017.

47 http://www.gouvernement.lu/7111699/Dossier-de-presse_Centre-contre-la-radicalisation_respect_lu-.pdf, accessed 29 November 2017.

recruitment by terrorist groups in the world. The Association is working to prevent the spread of such groups and their ideas in Luxembourg.

Activities and Initiatives of Main Muslim Organisations

Islamic groups in Luxembourg were again active in 2017, in particular since the signature of the convention in January 2015. Three new associations emerged: the *Association Fraternelle Musulmane* (Muslim Fraternal Association) at the very end of December 2016, located in Mersch; the *Centre culturel islamique du Foutah* (Islamic Cultural Centre of the Foutah) in February 2017, based in Rumelange; and the *Association Islamique et Culturelle–al Rahma* (Islamic and Cultural Association al Rahma), founded in Differdange in April 2017. Even though this number of new groups seems small, it is a significant number for a small country like Luxembourg.

The *Shoura: Assemblée de la Communauté Musulmane du Grand-Duché de Luxembourg* (Assembly of the Muslim Community of the Grand Duchy of Luxembourg), changed its statutes in July 2017, following the rules adopted by the *Law of 23 July 2016*, that turned it into a legal personality under public law. This organisation is no longer a non-profit organisation (*association sans but lucratif*–asbl), having been removed from the register of associations. Due to this change in the legal status of the *Shoura*, its internal rules are under modification and are to be adjusted to fit its new standing.

The *Shoura* moved to new premises at the end of November 2017, to the Rue du Potager, L-2347 Luxembourg–Kirchberg.[48] At the same time, new Islamic associations have become members (Islamic and Cultural Association of Afnane, in July 2017) or are in the process of becoming members of the *Shoura*. These include: the *Association Islamique de Wiltz Luxembourg* (Islamic Association of Wiltz Luxembourg) and the *Centre Islamique et Culturel Bosniaque de Luxembourg* (Islamic and Cultural Bosniak Centre of Luxembourg). New rules for incorporating Islamic associations since the institutionalisation of 2015 were adopted. These are to prevent smaller congregations without significant members, activities or places of worship from being included in the annual budget the *Shoura* receives from the State: €450,000 in 2017.[49]

48　http://www.identitet.lu/novi-uspjeh-muslimana-luksemburga-otvoreno-sjediste-sure-kirchbergu/, http://shoura.lu/?page_id=18, both accessed 2 January 2018.

49　See Pirenne and Waltzer, "Luxembourg", p. 430, and Pirenne, "Luxembourg", vol. 9, p. 430.

The *Shoura* hired a general secretary, Eric Risch, who started working on 1 April 2017. He is the first member of the *Shoura* who is a full-time, permanent employee, his salary being financed by the budget resulting from the new convention signed with the Luxemburgish state in January 2015. He is a young Luxembourgish convert, fluent in French, German, Luxembourgish, as well as in English and Arabic. He also knows the Luxembourgish context, as well as the Muslim associations in the country. His role is to manage the administrative tasks and internal communications, and to assist the *Shoura* in its meetings. He is also in charge of maintaining the organisation's accounts and the public relations of the *Shoura* in Luxembourg.

In April 2017, a series of radio programmes on Islam was made by a young Muslim, Mohammed Hamdi, for the radio channel 100.7.[50] The main aim of the series was to facilitate a better understanding of Islam in general, and in particular of Muslims in Luxembourg, among the wider public.

A new initiative for a private Muslim school called *Madrassaty* was launched at the end of December 2016.[51] This project is, in a way, a continuation of the previous school project *Wëssenbuerg*,[52] which had caused considerable debate in 2016, and which closed in the summer of 2017 without having ever opened its doors to students.[53] The members of the Association intended to open *Madrassaty* at the beginning of September 2017 if they found a suitable venue. The initial goal was to combat low achievement at school, a particular problem for pupils with a migrant background. At the end of 2017, no news about this specific initiative had been given, and the project seems to have been suspended.

It is important to mention that, like every year for the *Te Deum*,[54] a representative from a Muslim organisation was invited to represent Islam during this official ceremony. This event takes place on the National Day of Luxembourg, on 23 June, at the Cathedral in Luxembourg city. In 2017, the imam who accepted this role for the event was the imam of the association The Middle Ground, Sheikh Mustapha Turki. He lives in Belgium, is the imam of the mosque El Itissam in Liège, and is close to the ideology of the Muslim Brotherhood in

---

50   100.7 is Luxembourg's public service radio. Its programmes focus on information, cultural events and music, both classical and contemporary. See more on https://www.100komma7.lu/program/episode/143956/201704261040-201704261050, accessed 29 November 2017.
51   http://madrassaty.lu, accessed on 29 November 2017.
52   See Pirenne, "Luxembourg", pp. 423, 425–426.
53   http://5minutes.rtl.lu/grande-region/luxembourg/1066576.html, accessed on 22 December 2017.
54   The *Te Deum* is a Christian celebration occurring on the National Day of the Grand-Duchy (23 June 2016), at the Notre-Dame de Luxembourg Cathedral.

Europe. He recited a verse of the Qur'an in Arabic and gave a short speech about the need to establish harmony among the people of Luxembourg.[55]

As for the Turkish association *Turkuaz*, its links with the Gülen movement still exist, even though the association is weak since the coup attempt in Turkey in 2016.[56] For the second time in Luxembourg, *Turkuaz* organised "The colours of Luxembourg" (*Les Couleurs du Luxembourg*) on 24 March 2017. The project gathered young talented people in Luxembourg to sing in their mother tongues, dance, and play instruments.[57] The association also organised several "dinners of friendship",[58] and created a stand at the Festival of Migrations and Cultures (*Festival des Migrations et des Cultures*). In spring 2017, *Turkuaz* also organised an evening with the Belgian president of the Hizmet Forum, Hüseyin Cakmak.[59] At this event the documentary "Love is a verb" about Fethullah Gülen and the Hizment movement was shown, directed by Terry Spencer Hesser.

The Muslim association The Middle Ground organised an annual brotherhood weekend on 29 April 2017 in Lultzhausen.[60] The centre frequently organises conferences and events, and invites lecturers, mainly from Muslim Brotherhood networks in Belgium and France, throughout the year.[61]

The largest event of 2017 was probably the conference held by Elvedin Pezic[62] on 11 February 2017 in Luxembourg city, in Tramschapp.[63] It was organised by four Islamic associations of the country with a Bosniak majority: the Cultural and Islamic Centre of Luxembourg; the Islamic and Cultural Association of the South; the Islamic and Cultural Association Afnane; and the Islamic Association of Luxembourg; all under the patronage of the *Shoura*. During his time in Luxembourg, Pezic gave *khutbas* in the mosques which ran the event. The evening itself gathered around 500 people from Luxembourg, but also from neighbouring countries, such as Switzerland and the Netherlands. Stands offered Islamic literature and multimedia material for the participants. Sandžak TV made a report on the event.

---

55 https://www.youtube.com/watch?v=KoXgtN8_hA0, accessed 22 December 2017.
56 See Pirenne, "Luxembourg", p. 427.
57 http://lescouleursduluxembourg.lu/, accessed 2 January 2018.
58 http://turkuaz.lu, accessed 23 November 2017.
59 http://hizmetforum.be/, accessed 4 January 2018.
60 http://www.ljm.lu/3/59/week-end-fraternel---29-avril-01-mai-2017, accessed 2 January 2018.
61 http://www.ljm.lu/2/evenements, accessed 2 January 2018.
62 http://www.identitet.lu/mr-elvedin-pezic-semin-rizvic-luksemburgu-video-foto-reportaza/, and http://www.identitet.lu/velika-tribina-11-februara-luksemburgu-gost-mr-elvedin-pezic/, accessed 23 November 2017.
63 https://youtu.be/SW-6oDl5PDs, and https://youtu.be/iBMBtSyo80M, accessed 2 January 2018.

The commemoration of the massacre of Srebrenica was held on 24 June 2017 and was organised by several Bosniak associations.[64] A Viber group called "Us Srebrenica" (*Mi smo Srebrenica*) was formed. For the event, the committee of this group invited the President of the Association of Women Victims of War, Bakira Hasečić, the wartime commander in Srebrenica, Velid Sabic, and the writer Mustafa Širbic.

Muslim Population: History and Demographics

The Muslim presence in Luxembourg was established mainly through immigration and refugees. Historically, the first waves of immigrants came during the 1960s as a workforce, following a labour agreement between Luxembourg and the former Republic of Yugoslavia. However, the first Muslims were Turkish families, who established the first mosque in Luxembourg. Most Muslim immigrants from the former Yugoslavia came as asylum seekers during the 1990s, after the economic and political breakdown of their country during the civil war. Islam in Luxembourg is thus still predominantly "Balkan". This, though, should not conceal the fact that the Muslim presence in Luxembourg spans a wide range of countries of birth and languages, and includes a growing number of converts. The Friday sermons in mosques reflect this multicultural background, and are held in Arabic, Bosnian, French and English.

Islam has, step by step, become a constitutive element of the Luxembourgish religious landscape. According to the Pew Research Centre on Religion and Life (2017), 3.2% of the national population is Muslim in Luxembourg, so around 18,000 persons.[65] A growth in the size of the Muslim population in Luxembourg over the last 30 years has been noticed, especially with the arrival of refugees since 2015. Nevertheless, in absolute terms, the Muslim population is still very small in the country.

Since 1979,[66] the date of the last census in Luxembourg which included a question on religious affiliation, it is legally prohibited to assess such affiliation through the census. This absence of information creates an important restriction, as it means citizenship is the only criterion for identifying religious

---

64   http://sandzakpress.net/bosnjaci-u-luksemburgu-spremaju-komemoraciju-povodom-genocida-u-srebrenici, accessed 23 November 2017.
65   http://www.pewforum.org/2017/11/29/europes-growing-muslim-population/, accessed 4 January 2018.
66   Article 15 in the *Law of 31 March 1979* on the use of data in a databank forbids the collection and registration of data concerning individuals' activities and opinions in the following fields: politics, trade union activities, and philosophical and religious affiliation.

minorities, and thus excludes all individuals having adopted or possessing Luxembourgish citizenship, including Luxembourgish converts. Citizenship is also not a good indicator for religious affiliation because there is not always an overlap between ethnic, national and religious identification, especially after the population movements during the civil war in Yugoslavia. Moreover, citizenship can only inform us about the religious background of the country of origin of a person, but does not say anything about their real religious preferences. Further, numbers are usually underestimated, because a great number of Serbs come from the Muslim region of Sandžak in Serbia but as Serbian citizens are not usually counted as Muslims. A similar problem arises regarding the Syrian refugee population, making it impossible to have an accurate knowledge regarding their actual religious affiliation. As such, it is difficult to estimate the changes occurring within the Muslim population over time. Due to the restrictions mentioned above, it is not possible to give an accurate estimate as to Muslim numbers in Luxembourg.

Muslim Population	Estimated at around 18,000 (3.2%[67] of the population, which was 590,667 on 1 January 2017). The *Shoura* estimates a Muslim population of 20,000, a figure to which recently arrived Muslim refugees need to be added.
Ethnic/National Backgrounds	As of 1 January 2017, on the basis of nationality and by collecting the percentage of Muslims from each country of origin, the largest groups with Muslim backgrounds were as follows:[68]
	Maghreb (Moroccan, Algerian, Tunisian): around 1,800 Kosovar: around 1,500 Syrian: around 1,098

---

[67] http://www.pewforum.org/2017/11/29/europes-growing-muslim-population/pf_11-29-17_muslims-update-20/, accessed 1 December 2017.

[68] Statec, www.statistiques.public.lu/fr/acteurs/statec/index.html, accessed 4 January 2018. The author compared the data of the Pew Research Centre (http://www.pewforum.org/2011/01/27/table-muslim-population-by-country/) with the data collected on http://www.liberte-religieuse.org/ to provide the ethnic and national backgrounds of Muslims in Luxembourg. Nevertheless, these figures do not give any clue as to the religious practices of these individuals, and does not reflect the lived religious realities, in particular among Muslims from the Maghreb countries.

	Bosniak: around 1,000 Sub-Africa: around 650 Iraqi: around 848 Montenegrin: around 800 Albanian: around 450 Turkish: around 645 Former Yugoslav Republic of Macedonia: around 200 Iranian: around 420 Afghan: around 333 Serb:[69] around 80 Converts: no official data available.
Inner-Islamic Groups	The majority of Muslims are Sunnis. There is a small community of Shi'is. The presence of the Ahmadiyya can also be mentioned. The Gülen movement is also present in the country. No further data is available.
Geographical Spread	No official data is available, but based on location of places of worship one can surmise that the Muslim population is mainly concentrated in the larger cities (Luxembourg, Esch-sur-Alzette, Wiltz, Differdange).
Number of Mosques	13 places of worship are spread throughout the country: Mamer (1), Esch-sur-Alzette (3), Diekirch (1), Mersch (1), Luxembourg (3), Differdange (2), Wiltz (2).
Muslim Burial Sites	– Cemetery of Merl, Coin Rue des Aubépines, Val Sainte-Croix, L-1371 Luxembourg, cimetieres@vdl.lu

---

69 Furthermore, we can assume that during the wars in the former Yugoslavia in the 1990s, the majority of the people who left the area were Muslims, although not exclusively. Bosniaks are dominant in the Sandžak region, located in Serbia and Montenegro. In Luxembourg, a certain number of Serbs come from Sandžak and constitute one of the largest Muslim groups in the country.

- Cemetery of Lallange, rue de Mondercange, L-4247 Esch-sur-Alzette
- Cemetery of Betzdorf, Commune administration, 11 rue du Château, L-6922 Berg, ++352 770049-1, fax: ++352 77 00 82, info@betzdorf.lu, www.betzdorf.lu

"Chaplaincy" in State Institutions

In Schrassig prison and in the detention centre of Givenich, Islamic prayers are organised weekly. Since March 2016, an imam is part of the chaplaincy team in Schrassig (Detention centre of Luxembourg in Schrassig, Um Kuelebierg, L-5299 Schrassig, B.P. 35 L-5201 Sandweiler, tel.: ++ 352 3596211, fax: ++352 350217).

Imams of the different mosques also visit Muslims patients in hospitals upon request. No data is available on Muslim chaplaincy in the armed forces.

Halal Products

Ritual slaughter has been legally forbidden in Luxembourg since 1995. Therefore, halal butchers must import meat from neighbouring countries. For halal products in general, most Muslims travel to the neighbouring countries, shop online or at some small markets (Luxembourg, Esch). Moreover, they visit the weekly markets at the border region.

There are at least four halal butchers in the country, two in Luxembourg city: "Lux Halal" and "Ma boucherie", and one in Strassen: "A la belle viande", which opened a branch in Ettelbruck at the beginning of 2017, also called "A la belle viande". There are also halal products available in some supermarkets (Cora, Delhaize), as well as at the wholesaler *La Provençale*.

Dress Code

According to the ministerial circular of Claude Meisch, Minister of National Education, Childhood and Youth, young girls can wear a head scarf at school.[70] Nevertheless, it is forbidden for their teachers. No more legislation on Muslim dress code exists in the country.

Places of Islamic Learning and Education	Centre Avicenne Luxembourg (CAL), 32 Dernier Sol, L-2543 Luxembourg, ++352 26481153, ++352 621179581, http://avicenne.lu, email: avicenne@gmail.com. The majority of the Muslims associations offer Islamic education, language lessons and organise conferences on religious topics.
Muslim Media and Publications	– Online Muslim Bookshop "Eslamshop", http://www.librairie-boutique-musulmane.com/,[71] ++352 621359657, Skype name: e-slamshop.com (Mon–Fri 7PM–9.30PM, Sat–Sun 9AM–5.30PM). – *Institut de Recherche, d'Education et de Dialogue Interculturel* (IREDI), asbl, 73, route de Volmerange, L-3593 Dudelange, tel.: ++352 661420855, email: info@iredi.lu, contact@iredi.lu, www.iredi.lu (under construction). Established in February 2016, it publishes books on Islamic topics, intends to edit an annual review called *Sukun* and is building up a monitoring centre for Islamophobia. The website www.identitet.lu is dedicated to Bosniak-Muslim identity. Under the term "identity", the goal of this portal is to give insights on discoveries, knowledge, and experiences for readers from the Bosnian-speaking area, gathering together intellectuals and activists from Bosnia, Sandžak and the diaspora.

---

70 http://www.men.public.lu/fr/actualites/articles/communiques-conference-presse/2014/07/01-neutralite-religieuse/circulaire.pdf, http://www.lessentiel.lu/fr/luxembourg/story/Le-voile-a-bien-sa-place-dans-la-sphere-publique-13531241, both accessed 30 March 2018.
71 The website was inaccessible on 4 January 2018. The Facebook page is still online.

Main Muslim Organisations

- *Shoura*, Assembly of the Muslim Community of the Grand-Duchy of Luxembourg (*Shoura: Assemblée de la Communauté Musulmane du Grand-Duché de Luxembourg*, rue du Potager 1, 2347 Luxembourg, tel.: ++352 621354318, email: contact@shoura.lu, www.shoura.lu.) Composed of seven Islamic associations (CCIL, LJM, AICSUD, CCINS, AIL, CIL, CICD-A), the structure is a legal personality and is the only interlocutor with the State in matters of Islam. The *Shoura* was established in 2003.
- Cultural and Islamic Centre of the Grand-Duchy of Luxembourg (*Centre Culturel Islamique du Grand-Duché de Luxembourg*–CCIL, asbl, route d'Arlon 2, 8210 Mamer, tel.: ++352 310060, email: info@islam.lu, www.islam.lu). It organises Friday prayers in Arabic, French, English and Bosnian, as well as daily prayers, Islamic education, Bosnian and Arabic language teaching and public conferences. The CCIL was the first Muslim centre in the country, founded in February 1984. Bosniaks represent the majority of its members.
- Islamic Association of Luxembourg (*Association Islamique de Luxembourg*–AIL, asbl, rue Nicolas Martha 17–19, 2133 Luxembourg, email: subulusselam@hotmail.com, http://assalam.lu).[72] The Association offers daily prayers and is mainly composed of Bosniaks, Kosovars and Montenegrins, coming mostly from the Sandžak region. The centre was established in August 1999.
- Islamic Cultural Centre of the North (*Centre Culturel Islamique du Nord*–CCIN, asbl, route de Noertange 26, 9543 Wiltz, tel.: ++352 26950680, ++352 691734408, fax: ++352 26950681). The Centre was established in September 2000 and is mostly composed of Muslims from the Serbian Sandžak region. It offers religious classes for children (*mekteb*).
- Mutual of CCIL (*Mutuelle du CCIL*, route d'Arlon 2, 8210 Mamer, tel.: ++352 310060, fax: ++ 352 31260431, email: mutuelle.ccil@gmail.com, https://sites.google.com/site/mutuelleduccilluxembourg/home). This mutual insurance group is a non-profit solidarity project created in 2001 to provide spiritual and material support at the time of the death of a parent. Their services include (if needed) assistance with administrative formalities with the consulate, and the organisation of ritual funeral rites and the transportation of the body to the cemetery up to a maximum distance of 2,000 km. Its members have to pay an annual fee in order to benefit from its services.
- Islamic and Religious Association of the South (*Association Islamique et Cultuelle du Sud*–AIC-SUD, asbl, rue de Luxembourg 44, 4220 Esch-sur-Alzette, tel.: ++352 26540788, email: aicsud@gmail.com, www.aicsudlive

---

[72] The website was inaccessible on 20 December 2017.

.com). This Association was established in March 2002, and most of its members are from the Sandžak region in Montenegro and Serbia. The centre organises Friday and daily prayers in Bosnian as well as Islamic education.
- Islamique Association of Wiltz, Luxembourg (*Association Islamique de Wiltz, Luxembourg*–AIWL, asbl, rue X Septembre 39, 9560 Wiltz, tel.: ++352 691153008, email: aiwl@hotmail.de, www.aiwl.lu). The Association is mostly composed of Bosniak people from Sandžak; it was established in February 2007.
- The Middle Ground (*Le Juste Milieu*–LJM, asbl, Dernier Sol 32, 2543 Luxembourg, tel.: ++352 26481153, email: ljmaccueil@gmail.com, www.ljm.lu). The association organises Islamic education for children, Arabic language teaching for children and adults and public conferences around Islamic and interreligious matters, as well as Friday prayers (two services) in Arabic and in French, and daily prayers. It was established in February 2008. Its founding members are mostly people of Arab descent.
- Islamic Cultural Centre NordStad (*Centre Culturel Islamique NordStad*–CCINS, asbl, avenue de la Gare 29, 9233 Diekirch, email: ccie@live.fr). The location of the new centre will be rue Bamertal 22, 9209 Diekirch, and the members use it as an address for correspondence. Friday prayers are men only, and there is a school on Sunday mornings. Members are from Bosnia and Herzegovina and Sandžak. The Centre was founded in October 2008.
- Islamic Centre of Luxembourg (*Centre Islamique Luxembourg*–CIL, asbl, bd. d'Avranches 6, email: cil1430@yahoo.com). Daily prayers, Islamic education and Bosnian language teaching are organised. The Centre was established in December 2008 and is mainly composed of Bosniaks.
- Multicultural Association of the West (*Association Multiculturelle de l'Ouest*–AMCO, asbl, rue du Brill 10–12, 4041 Esch-sur-Alzette). Registered office at 132 Bd J.F. Kennedy L-4171 on the corner with 94 Rue Dicks L-4082 Esch-sur-Alzette. Created in May 2011. Friday and daily prayers take place.
- Muslim Association Ahmadiyya Luxembourg (*Association Musulmane Ahmadiyya Luxembourg*–AMAL, asbl, rue de Strasbourg 62, 2560 Luxembourg, email: info@ahmadiyya.lu, www.islam-ahmadiyya.org). The Association was established in October 2012, even though it was already registered in 1989.
- Islamic Finance Professionals Association (IFPA, asbl, avenue de la Gare 13, 1611 Luxembourg). It was created in May 2012. The main objectives are to promote the interests of professionals active in the field of Islamic finance in Luxembourg.
- Association of Tijani Sufis of Luxembourg (*Association des soufis tijanis du Luxembourg*–ASTL, asbl, rue Jean-François Gangler 59, 1613 Luxembourg).

Member of The Circle of Breaths (*Le Cercle des Souffles*), constituted in 2012 and composed mainly of Muslims of Senegalese origin.
- Association of Muslim Professionals of Luxembourg (*Association des Professionnels Musulmans du Luxembourg*–APML, asbl, email: apml.luxembourg@gmail.com, www.apml.lu,[73] rue des champs 11, L-1323 Luxembourg). Monthly meetings on religious subjects are chosen at the beginning of the academic year by its members. The Association was created in 2013.
- Islamic Fellowship and Charity Association of Luxembourg (IFCAL, asbl, place Léon XIII 2, 1929 Luxembourg). Formerly known as Dawah Luxembourg (until April 2014), it was established in October 2013. Its goals are to promote the spiritual life of its members through worship, prayer and fasting, and to provide assistance and educational facilities to persons in need and to contribute to the development of the local community through community services. The members of the community are mostly from Nigeria.
- Islamic and Cultural Centre Afnane (*Centre Islamique et Culturelle de Differdange–Afnane*–CICD-A, asbl, 41, Rue J-F Kennedy, L-4599 Differdange). The Association was established in April 2014 and organises cultural activities, and teaching, spiritual and material assistance for sick and vulnerable people.
- Aid and Support Association for those Expelled by Islamic State Hostilities (ASAEISH, asbl, boulevard Kaltreis 58, 1882 Luxembourg). Established in November 2014, this humanitarian association provides information about the victims of ISIS, living in refugee camps in Iraq, and collects donations to help them.
- Islamic and Cultural Bosniak Centre of Luxembourg (*Centre islamique et culturel bosniaque de Luxembourg*–CICBL, asbl, rue d'Ehlerange 13, 4108 Esch-sur-Alzette, cicbl@outlook.com). Friday prayers take place, and religious education for children and adults is organised on Saturdays and Sundays. The Centre was created in May 2015. Members mostly come from the Sandžak region in Montenegro and Serbia.
- Islamic Finance Initiative (asbl, rue du Fort Wallis 2, 2714 Luxembourg). Formed for the promotion finance according to shari'a law. It created an Islamic financial centre, and constituted a shari'a council in Luxembourg in May 2015.
- Institute of Research, Education and Intercultural Dialogue (*Institut de Recherche, d'Education et de Dialogue Interculturel*–IREDI, asbl, route de Volmerange 73, 3593 Dudelange, tel.: ++352 661420855, email: info@iredi

---

73 The website was inaccessible on 4 January 2018.

.lu, contact@iredi.lu, www.iredi.lu).[74] Created in February 2016, the Institute undertakes research and education in different languages on Islam and Muslims in Luxembourg in particular, and in Europe in general. The main goals of the institute are to publish books, an annual review called *Sukun*, and to establish an observatory on Islamophobia (starting January 2018).
- Muslim Fraternal Association (*Association Fraternelle Musulmane*, asbl, rue Grand-Duc Jean 14, 7545 Berschbach, tel.: ++352 621658498 email: fraternelle.musulmane@gmail.com). The members meet at 5, rue Wenzel L-7393 Beringen in a room rented by the Association. The Association was founded in December 2016 and organises Friday prayers.
- Islamic Cultural Centre of Foutah (*Centre culturel islamique du Foutah*– CCIF, asbl, Rue du cimetière 133, 3715 Rumelange, tel.: ++352 661422022, email: ccif2017@gmail.com). The Centre was created in February 2017 and is composed of Muslims from Guinea and the Fula people. The Centre does not have a place of worship.
- Islamic and Cultural Association al-Rahma (*Association Islamique et Culturelle al-Rahma*–AIC Al Rahma, asbl, Avenue de la Liberté 96, 4601 Niederkorn). The Association was founded in April 2017 and organises Friday and daily prayers.

---

74   The website is still under construction, as of 28 March 2018.

Macedonia

Muhamed Ali[1]

Introduction

In 2017, the educational and schooling institutions in Macedonia that function under the Islamic Religious Community–IRC (*Исламска Верска Заедница–Bashkësia Fetare Islame*), played a major role in preparing new professional places in order to support local religious activities. Furthermore, 2017 witnessed a rise in Muslim media activities and NGOs defending the religious values of Muslims in Macedonia. This year also saw a continuation of interreligious dialogue between the representatives of various religions and a relative respect given by the political elite towards representatives of Islamic organisations. In this context, Macedonian Muslims, through the IRC, requested the same political and financial treatment by the State as the Christian population. The IRC and other Muslim NGOs, through their relations with foreign actors–especially Turkey, Kuwait, Saudi Arabia, Qatar and the United Arab Emirates–supported local Muslim religious activities.

Public Debates

In an interview for Radio Free Europe, the Head of the Islamic Religious Community in Macedonia, Sulejman Rexhepi, highlighted that while Western Europe experienced a number of terrorist attacks, Albanian imams, that are appointed by the IRC to work within Albanian communities in the Western European diaspora, should assume a more prominent public role to represent Islam in those countries. According to him, interreligious relations in Macedonia are good, however these good relations are often attacked by politicians.[2] One of the most discussed cases related to the IRC in 2017 was an award Rexhepi received from the US President Donald J. Trump for his life achievements. During the award ceremony held in Skopje, Rexhepi thanked

---

[1] Muhamed Ali is Assistant Professor at the International University of Sarajevo, where he teaches courses in the areas of international law and political sciences. Previously, he served as an Assistant Professor at the Faculty of Islamic Studies in Skopje, where he taught courses on Islamic law.

[2] https://www.evropaelire.org/a/bfi-xhamia-maqedoni-sulejman-rexhepi/28577677.html/, accessed 09 April 2018.

Otto von Feigenblatt, who handed over the award.[3] According to Rexhepi, he received this award for his stance against extremism, Islamophobia, radicalism, and his support for humanitarian aid activities.[4] This award caused various reactions among the public in Macedonia. While some congratulated Rexhepi, others were suspicious about the validity of this award, as the US Ambassador to Macedonia, Jess L. Baily, did not attend the award ceremony.[5]

One of the most discussed debates in 2017 was related to the Bleta kindergarten in Skopje. On social networks, photos circulated that showed children performing Islamic rituals. There were different reactions, as some claimed that the kindergarten did not possess a licence to operate, that it was spreading religious extremism, and violated the children's rights etc. There were also some Islamophobic reactions on social media. In response, Bekir Halimi, an imam from Skopje and a representative of the Bleta kindergarten, declared that Bleta did not operate as a licensed kindergarten, but is the name of an NGO which provides educational services for children and women. The Ombudsman of the Republic of Macedonia, Ixhet Memeti, stated that he would collect all relevant data on the organisation and produce a special report to decide whether the children's rights were violated in the institution. The IRC Head Rexhepi explicitly distanced himself from the Bleta kindergarten, as an initiative not endorsed by the IRC.[6]

In 2017, the house of IRC Head Rexhepi was a target of an attack. However, his security team managed to apprehend the attacker and handed him over to the police.[7] According to the official statement from the Macedonian authorities, the attack was caused by two people who were under the influence of alcohol.[8] This incident caused numerous debates on local social networks and media.

---

3 https://www.medial.mk/2017/12/28/kreu-bfi-se-dekorohet-nga-presidenti-tramp-cmimin-presidencial-per-arritje-jetesore/, accessed 3 April 2018.
4 https://telegrafi.com/sulejman-efendi-rexhepi-te-nderohet-nga-presidenti-donald-trump/, accessed 22 May 2018.
5 https://shigjeta.net/skandal-bfi-po-genjen-e-mashtruan-keq-mulla-sulen/, accessed 22 May 2018.
6 http://portalb.mk/430309-cfare-fshihet-pas-kopshtit-bleta-qe-beri-buje-ne-opinion-me-ligjeratat-fetare/, accessed 2 April 2018.
7 http://gazetainfopress.com/aktualitete/rexhepi-tregon-ekskluzivisht-per-sulmin-ne-shtepine-e-tij-video/, accessed 3 May 2018.
8 https://www.tetova1.mk/2017/03/19/ja-cka-ka-nodhur-ne-shtepine-e-sulejman-rexhepit/, accessed 23 May 2018.

Transnational Links

Sulejman Rexhepi, together with an IRC delegation, carried out the first official visit to the leadership of the Islamic Community of Serbia, in Belgrade, on 21 February 2017; they met its head Sead Nasufovic, his associates, as well as a significant number of imams of the Islamic Community there. The most discussed topic of this meeting was the phenomena of extremism, radicalism, and the poor representation of Islam in the region. Nasufovic reciprocated the visit on 4 December 2017, giving lectures to students at the Isa Beu Madrasa in Skopje.[9]

During 2017, the good relations between the IRC and the Turkish Presidency of Religious Affairs (*Diyanet İşleri Başkanlığı*) continued. Among other foreign visits carried out by Rexhepi, was his official visit to the Diyanet, where he was welcomed by his counterpart, Ali Erbaş, who had just been appointed as its new director.[10] Rexhepi also met with the Mufti of Istanbul, Hasan Kamil Yilmaz. They discussed the situation, the achievements and the obstacles of the IRC in Macedonia.[11] Rexhepi, through a letter he sent to the President of the Republic of Turkey, Recep Tayyip Erdoğan, expressed his support for constitutional changes that were decided at the 16 April 2017 referendum. Rexhepi wished that the referendum would be a beacon of hope, and guidance for Turkey, the Islamic world, the Balkans and everyone in the world who is oppressed.[12] On the occasion of the first anniversary of the coup attempt in Turkey, the IRC gave instructions to 700 mosques in Macedonia to hold a Friday sermon, on 14 July 2017, and dedicate it to those who lost their lives during the coup attempt.[13]

Sulejman Rexhepi gave a declaration on the decision of US President Trump to relocate the US embassy to Jerusalem: he stated that this issue is "… very complicated, but it is more of an issue of a political character, it is very problematic for the Islamic Religious Community to issue an opinion for that matter, so while it is a political matter, in my opinion, there is no need for a religious opinion in that direction".[14]

---

9   https://www.tetovasot.com/2017/12/reisi-i-serbise-bfi-ne-rm-model-funksionimi-per-tegjithe-bashkesite-islame-ne-ballkan-e-ne-evrope/, accessed 22 April 2018.
10 https://bfi.mk/al/reisul-ulema-per-vizite-zyrtare-ne-turqi/, accessed 6 May 2018.
11 http://bfi.mk/al/reisul-ulema-bfi-h-sulejman-ef-rexhepi-vizite-muftinise-se-stambollit/, accessed 5 May 2018.
12 http://kohaislame.com/kreu-i-bfi-se-mbeshtetje-presidentit-erdogan-per-referendumin/, accessed 8 May 2018.
13 http://kohaislame.com/ne-maqedoni-dhe-kosove-do-te-lexohet-hutbe-dedikuar-deshmoreve-te-15-korrikut/, accessed 5 April 2018.
14 https://www.almakos.com/rexhepi-ceshtja-e-jerusalemit-karakter-politik-por-jo-edhe-fetar/, accessed 6 May 2018.

Law and Domestic Politics

The Head of the Islamic Religious Community of Macedonia, in an interview for Radio Free Europe, declared that the institution he was leading has been continuously discriminated by official state institutions in the last ten years. He addressed the Government of the Republic of Macedonia in a letter, in which he asked that the Islamic Religious Community of Macedonia be treated the same as the Orthodox Church of Macedonia. According to Rexhepi, the discriminating policies of the State towards the Islamic Religious Community of Macedonia are related to public funding.[15]

In 2017, the Ministry of Labour and Social Policy of the Republic of Macedonia initiated a new draft law, entitled the *Law on Prevention and Protection against Discrimination*, which also includes discrimination on the basis of religion. According to this draft law, the members of the Commission for Protection against Discrimination should be appointed based on professional merit in a non-partisan manner.[16] This draft law stipulates fines between €500–5000 for legal entities, and fines between €100–500 for individuals, for those who perform discriminatory actions, including discrimination based on religion.[17]

The Venice Commission criticised some pieces of the abovementioned draft law. Some of the criticism was related to the lack of transparency in appointing and dismissing the members of the Commission for Protection against Discrimination. Some of its other criticisms related to the preparation mechanism of the draft law, which, with the exception of the international community and NGOs, did not include any input from marginalised groups nor public opinion.[18]

Activities and Initiatives of Main Muslim Organisations

In September 2017, a cornerstone of the new mosque in the Topansko Pole neighbourhood in Skopje was laid, which is financed by Turkey's Diyanet Foundation (*Türkiye Diyanet Vakfı*). Representatives of the Turkish embassy and Cair municipality, where this mosque is located, took part in the laying

---

15 https://www.evropaelire.org/a/bfi-xhamia-maqedoni-sulejman-rexhepi/28577677.html/, accessed 9 April 2018.
16 https://www.akademik.mk/javna-debata-za-noviot-zakon-za-sprechuvane-i-zashtita-od-diskriminatsija/, accessed 27 May 2018.
17 https://www.akademik.mk/javna-debata-za-noviot-zakon-za-sprechuvane-i-zashtita-od-diskriminatsija/, accessed 19 May 2018.
18 https://republika.mk/896505/, accessed 27 May 2018.

ceremony, as well as a delegation of the IRC, led by Rexhepi. This large complex, which will serve as a mosque for regular prayers, will also be a cultural and academic centre, and will host lectures, conferences and other academic activities.[19]

In July 2017, a group of Muslims from the Skopje Sever neighbourhood, in the Butel municipality, started an initiative to build a new mosque in their neighbourhood. They gathered 910 signatures from the residents of the neighbourhood, and handed them over to the Butel Municipality as a project proposal to build a mosque on a designated piece of land. The Islamic Religious Community provided strong support for the initiative.[20]

In June 2017, during the month of Ramadan, the Dean of the Faculty for Islamic Studies (FIS), Faredin Ebibi, organised an *iftar*. The staff of the Faculty, and many representatives of the IRC took part, as well as the Macedonian Ministry of Education, led by the Deputy Minister for Education and Science, Visar Ganiu.[21] During Ramadan, the President of Macedonia, Gjorgji Ivanov, organised an *iftar* for representatives of the IRC, which members of the diplomatic core also attended.[22]

In September 2017, on the occasion of the Islamic (hijri) New Year, the Islamic Religious Community organised its traditional event, with an artistic and religious programme, in the hall of the Macedonian Opera and Ballet. During the event, the Myfti Vebi Dibra[23] certificate of gratitude was presented, as well as diplomas of *hifz* for the new students who had memorised the Qur'an during 2017.[24] In September 2017, on the premises of the Isa Beu Madrasa, Gostivar branch, the Head of the IRC awarded the Speaker of the Parliament of Macedonia, Talat Xhaferi, the Myfti Vebi Dibra Award. This award is given by the IRC leadership for achievements by distinguished Macedonian Muslim personalities.[25]

---

19 http://kohaislame.com/xhami-e-re-ne-lagjen-fushe-topane-ne-shkup-kthim-i vlerave-autoktone/, accessed 15 April 2018.
20 https://www.almakos.com/bfi-mbeshtet-deri-ne-fund-ndertimin-e-xhamise-ne-shkup-veri/, accessed 12 April 2018.
21 http://www.fshi.edu.mk/content/?id=348/, accessed 2 April 2018.
22 www.zhurnal.mk/content/?id=17621215/, accessed 22 April 2018.
23 Vehbi Dibra (1867–1937) was an Albanian politician and prominent Muslim scholar born in Dibër (a city recently divided between Albania and Macedonia). He was the first Grand Mufti of Albania between 1920–1929 and the first chair of the Albanian senate.
24 https://www.aktuale.mk/manifestimi-tradicional-kushtuar-hixhretit-1439-2017-foto/, accessed 12 April 2018.
25 http://www.aktuale.mk/reisi-dekoroi-kryeparlamentarin-xhaferi-me-titullin-myfti-vehbi-dibra/, accessed 8 April 2018.

The *Forumi Rinor Islam* (Islamic Youth Forum), for the 17th time in a row, organised the traditional celebration of the Islamic (hijri) New Year in the National Macedonian Theatre in Skopje. The best students from numerous colleges and various towns in Macedonia were awarded prizes; the best university students from various institutions were also given awards.[26]

In 2017, different NGOs–such as *Kalliri i Mirësisë, Merhamet, Vizioni M, Throni, Ensar*–organised many activities and events related to humanitarian aid, culture and education. In April 2017, the humanitarian aid organisation *Kalliri i Mirësisë* organised an event named "Orphan's Week". Among the most important activities at this event were; debates, collecting of donations, organising of humanitarian concerts and various excursions.[27] In 2017, *Kalliri i Mirësisë* also played a role in distributing *qurban* meat to 4,500 poor families in need.[28] In September 2017, the Foundation for Science, Culture and Humanitarian Activities, *Throni*, located in Tetovo, was visited by former Prime Minister of the Republic of Turkey Ahmed Davutoğlu. During this visit he was informed about *Throni*'s main activities and future strategies.[29] In 2017, the Education and Thought Association *Fettah Efendi* played active role in organising different seminars, debates, and public lectures, attended by academics as well as students. On the occasion of 'Id Al-Adha, the Cultural Association *Vision M*, in cooperation with the City of Skopje, organised the traditional display of *kandilat e bajramit* ("'Id Candles").[30]

The Islamic High School Isa Beu Madrasa held a ceremony on 10 July 2017 to award diplomas to the graduates of that academic year. More than 178 students were awarded with a high-school diploma. The Head of the IRC, Rexhepi, and his associates, were present at this ceremony. This included all the IRC's muftis, the Assembly Chair of the IRC, the Dean of the FIS, as well as various professors and guests from Macedonia and abroad.[31] On 27 September 2017, the Isa Beu Madrasa established a branch in Gostivar, opening a new building there. At this opening ceremony, the Head of the IRC, and the Speaker of the Parliament, Talat Xhaferi, took part, as well as the mayors of Gostivar and Vrapciste, and

---

26 http://portalb.mk/463705-forumi-rinor-islam-dekoroi-me-te-miret/, accessed 2 May 2018.
27 http://portalb.mk/395028-kalliri-i-miresise-nis-fushaten-java-e-jetimeve/, accessed 29 May 2018.
28 https://www.tetova1.mk/2017/09/03/kalliri-miresise-shperdnan-kurbane-per-4-500-familje/, accessed 29 May 2018.
29 http://throni.org/archives/2818/, accessed 29 May 2018.
30 https://www.almakos.com/vizioni-m-edhe-sivjet-organizon-kandilat-e-bajramit/, accessed 29 May 2018.
31 http://medreseja-isabeu.com/178-kandila-te-dijes-diplomuan-ne-medresene-isa-beu-2/, accessed 1 May 2018.

the Macedonian Minister of Health. Participants from the local political scene and guests from the mufti institutions of Albania and Turkey also attended.[32] During 2017, the second cycle of studies in the field of Islamic Pedagogy at the Faculty of Islamic Studies (under the auspices of the IRC) started.[33]

The IRC organised the travel for the hajj and decided to set the price for a pilgrimage package at €3,900 from 27 January 2016.[34] In 2017, the IRC also carried out the *qurbani* sacrifice; the value of a single *qurbani* in Macedonia was €120.

Muslim Population: History and Demographics

Although the territories of the Balkan Peninsula, including Macedonia, were introduced to Islam before their contact with the Ottomans, the widespread conversion of Albanian Christians to Islam took place when it became a part of the Ottoman Empire (early 14th century). The 20th century marked a new period for Muslims in Macedonia. During this time, besides World Wars and economic and social crises, Muslims also faced the challenges of various political systems, like a monarchy (Kingdom of Yugoslavia) and communism (Socialist Yugoslavia). The end of the Cold War brought changes to the organisation of religious life in the country. Up to the 1990s, religious life in Macedonia was organised in a limited way by the *riyasa/muftinia*, the only institution for this purpose that existed in this period.

Population registration in Balkan countries is considered to be a very complicated and sensitive process, because ethnic and religious demographics play an important role in policy making within various social groups in the region, given their diverse demographic structure. Macedonian society is equally multicultural, multi-ethnic and multi-religious, while Macedonian public institutions often lack stability and experience in dealing with this diversity.

According to the last census in Macedonia, carried out in 2002, the majority of the population in the country is made up of ethnic Macedonians, followed by Albanians. 64.8% of the population are Christian Orthodox, and the vast majority of them are members of the Macedonian Orthodox Church. Muslims constitute 33.3% of the population. Macedonia possesses the fifth highest proportion of Muslims in a European country; the majority of Muslims

---

32   http://medreseja-isabeu.com/medreseja-isa-beu-paralelja-e-vajzave-gostivar-me-objekt-te-saj-te-ri/, accessed 22 April 2018.
33   http://portalb.mk/474453-filluan-ligjeratat-e-para-te-studimeve-te-magjistratures-ne-fakultetin-e-shkencave-islame-ne-shkup/, accessed 24 April 2018.
34   www.bfi.mk/, accessed 4 May 2018.

are Albanians, Turks, Romas, Bosniaks, with a very small percentage that are Torbeshis and Macedonian converts. In recent years, there has been a decrease in the birth rate of Macedonian families with a Christian background, while there has been a visible increase in the birth rate of Albanian families with a Muslim background. According to the 2002 census, 47% of children up the age of four are from families with a Muslim background.[35]

Muslim Population	702,492 (33.3% of total population).[37]
Ethnic/National Backgrounds	The majority of Muslims in Macedonia are Albanians, Turks, Romas, Bosniaks, with a very small percentage that are Torbeshis and Macedonian converts. Albanian Muslims in Macedonia represent the majority of Muslims in the country, and number approximately 72% (509,083) out of 702,492 Muslims in the country. Turkish Muslims represent 11% (77,959), and Romas 8% (53,879). Torbeshis, together with converted Macedonian Muslims, are 5%, (35,000) with Bosniaks 4% (25,000).[38]
Inner-Islamic Groups	Most of the Muslim population belongs to the Hanafi school of jurisprudence and the Maturidi school in theology, but there are some small Salafi groups. Some groups are part of various Sufi orders, like the Rifaʿis, Bektashis, Malamatis etc.
Geographical Spread	The vast majority of Muslims live in the Northwestern and Western parts of the country. Muslims in general are concentrated in the towns around Skopje, Kumanovo, Tetovo, Gostivar, Kicevo, and Struga. A small percentage lives in the towns of Bitola, Ohrid, Shtip, Prilep, and Radovish.

---

35 http://worldpopulationreview.com/countries/macedonia-population/, accessed 5 April 2018.

36 https://www.cia.gov/library/publications/the-world-factbook/geos/mk.html/, accessed 5 April 2018; http://studies.aljazeera.net/en/reports/2013/10/20131088412517496.html/, accessed 22 May 2018.

37 http://studies.aljazeera.net/en/reports/2013/10/20131088412517496.html/, accessed 22 May 2018.

Number of Mosques	There are approximately 641 registered mosques within the territory of the Republic of Macedonia.[39] Mufti office of Skopje: 115; Mufti office of Shtip: 45; Mufti office of Resen: 11; Mufti office of Gostivar: 73; Mufti office of Debar: 50; Mufti office of Tetovo: 159; Mufti office of Kumanovo: 36; Mufti office of Kicevo: 44; Mufti office of Struga: 36; Mufti office of Ohrid: 11; Mufti office of Bitola: 26; Mufti office of Veles: 11; Mufti office of Prilep: 24.[40]
Muslim Burial Sites	Every town and village in Macedonia has special cemeteries for the burial of Muslims. Within the IRC, a burial service called Er-Rahatu has been established which provides services in all Macedonian cities, and also in the diaspora (address: Cairska 52, Skopje, 1000, Macedonia, tel.: ++389 75374402).
"Chaplaincy" in State Institutions	Although there is not any legal obstacle regarding this issue, so far there is not such practice in public institutions.
Halal Products	The Agency for Halal Standards that, functions within the IRC, is in close coordination with the local Ministry of Economy for implementing halal standards for products in Macedonia.[41] Until December 2017, 49 companies in Macedonia have implemented the halal system. Also, nine companies have discontinued halal standards for various reasons.[42]

---

38   http://www.kovz.gov.mk/WBStorage/Files/karta%20i%20tekst%20spoeno.pdf/, accessed 18 April 2018.
39   http://www.kovz.gov.mk/WBStorage/Files/karta%20i%20tekst%20spoeno.pdf/, accessed 18 April 2018.
40   http://bfi.mk/en/halal-standard/, accessed 12 April 2018.
41   https://www.alsat-m.tv/trajnohen-kuadro-te-reja-te-kompanive-qe-zbatojne-standardin-hallall/, accessed 4 May 2018.

Dress Code	There are no laws restricting the wearing of Muslim dress in Macedonia. So far, any evidence of discrimination against Muslim women due to their Muslim dress in their everyday life does not exist.
Places of Islamic Learning and Education	– Islamic High School, Isa Beu Madrasa in Skopje. Although located in Skopje, it has branches in a few other towns in Macedonia. Besides the central madrasa for male students in Skopje, this school has branches for female students in Skopje, Tetovo and Gostivar, as well as one more branch for male students in Shtip. Address: Skopje, 80–1060 Gj. Petrov, Republic of Macedonia, tel.: ++389 22058540, tel./fax: ++389 22058541; email: medreseja.isabeu@gmail.com, www.medreseja-isabeu.com.[43] – Faculty of Islamic Studies, Skopje: this Faculty offers Bachelor's degrees in Islamic Studies and Master's degrees in the field of Islamic Pedagogy. It is the only educational institution for Islamic higher education in Macedonia and is located in Kondovo, near Skopje. Address: 1000 Skopje, Macedonia, tel.: ++389 22057270, email: dekanati@fshi.edu.mk, www.fshi.edu.mk.[44]
Muslim Media and Publications	– *Ikre*: religious and cultural magazine in Albanian, Turkish and Macedonian languages, published by the students of the Isa Beu Madrasa[45] – *Hikmet*: an academic international magazine, published by *Qendra për Arsim, Kulturë dhe Art* ADEKSAM (Centre for Education, Culture and Arts ADEKSAM)[46]

---

42   www.medreseja-isabeu.com/, accessed 13 April 2018.
43   www.fshi.edu.mk/, accessed 11 April 2018.
44   http://medreseja-isabeu.com/revista/, accessed 10 April 2018.
45   http://hikmetdergisi.org/wp-content/uploads/hikmet25.pdf/, accessed 16 April 2018.

- *Hëna e Re*: Islamic monthly cultural magazine in the Albanian language, published by the IRC.[47]
- *Köprü*: cultural, artistic and academic magazine, published by the cultural organisation Kopru, with its headquarters in Skopje. The articles of this magazine are published in Turkish.
- *Hilal*: cultural Islamic magazine in the Macedonian and Turkish language, published by the IRC.
- *Kardelen*: children's magazine in the Turkish language for Muslim children of a Turkish background. Published by the Kopru cultural organisation, with its headquarters in Skopje.[48]
- *Centrum*: academic international magazine; it has been published by the Centre for Understanding and Institutional Cooperation since 2013: http://centrum.mk. Address: Bul. Krste Misirkov 57a, Lok. 3 1000 Skopje, tel./fax: ++389 02/3232186, email: centrum.qmbi@gmail.com.
- *Revista Shkencore Përmbledhje Punimesh*: academic magazine that is published by the Faculty of Islamic Studies in Skopje.[49]

Main Muslim Organisations

- Islamic Religious Community of Macedonia (*Исламска Верска Заедница на Македонија–Bashkësia Fetare Islame e Maqedonisë*, Cairska 52, Skopje, 1000, Macedonia, email: rijaseti.bfi@gmail.com, www.bfi.mk). The Islamic Religious Community of Macedonia is the only official organisation that organises the religious life of Muslims in the country and Macedonian Muslims abroad. This institution follows the Hanafi school of jurisprudence. The IRC headquarters are located in Skopje. The IRC's organs are: the Mufti Office, the Leadership of the IRC, the Head of the IRC, and the Assembly of the IRC.

---

46 http://bfi.mk/en/hena-e-re-291/, accessed 12 April 2018.
47 http://www.dunyabulteni.net/haberler/384731/makedonyada-turk-cocuklari-icin-bir-dergi-kardelen/, accessed 11 April 2018.
48 http://www.fshi.edu.mk/revistashkencore/, accessed 1 April 2018.

Some of the IRC's most important institutions are: the Department of *waqf*, High Schools–Madrasas, the Faculty of Islamic Studies, the Isa Beu Library and archives, Sufi shrines (Rufai, Bektashi, Halveti etc.), *hans* (Turkish inns) and *hamams* (Turkish baths), a publishing and information centre, the El Hilal charity organisation, and Er-Rahatu burial services etc.[49]

- Foundation Centre of Islamic Civilisation, FOCIC (*Фондација Центар за Исламска Цивилизација*, Samoilova 10, 1000 Skopje, email: info@focic.org.mk, tel.: ++389 22600036/ ++389 23211256/fax: ++389 22611508, www.focic.org.mk). A non-governmental organisation, focused on educational activities, referring to Islamic values.[50] This foundation was founded in 2006 by Bajram Benjamin Idriz, Adnan Ismaili, and Tadjudin Shabani.[51]
- Association for the Affirmation of Women (*Asociacioni për Afirmimin e Gruas*–AAG, email: aagsecretariat@gmail.com, http://www.aag-m.org). A non-governmental organisation for women, that aims at the realisation of personal and/or collective freedoms and rights.
- Islamic Youth Forum (*Forumi Rinor Islam*–FRI, Rr. Krste Misirkov nr. 57 a lok. 3, 1000, Shkup, tel./fax: ++389 23233659, www.fri.org.mk, email: shkupi@fri.org.mk). The FRI is a non-governmental youth organisation, founded in 2000. It is a legal organisation, registered with the juridical organs of the Republic of Macedonia on 25 August 2000.[52]
- Merhamet Cultural Humanitarian Organisation (*Organizata Kulturore Humanitare Merhamet*, rr. 11-ра Македонска бригада, numër.10/7–qendra tregtare "Treska", Skopje). Cultural and humanitarian organisation with headquarters in Skopje. The main objectives of this organisation are the advancement of culture, humanitarian activities, and efforts to promote interreligious tolerance. It was registered in 1999.[53]
- Fettah Efendi Education and Thought Association (*Fettah Efendi Eğitim ve Düşünce Derneği*, email: info@fettahefendi.com, http://www.fettahefendi.com). Educational organisation, founded in Skopje in 2016. Its main objective is the promotion of education among young Muslims.
- Vizioni M Cultural Association (*Shoqata Kulturore Vizioni M*, Samoilova no. 6, Samoilova, Skopje, Macedonia (FYROM), tel.: ++389 23125119). This organisation was founded in 1998 under the name *Vizioni Multikulturor* (Multicultural Vision), a name that, for administrative purposes, had to be

---

49 Bfi.mk/, accessed 11 March 2018.
50 http://www.focic.org.mk/programme-principle.html/, accessed 2 April 2018.
51 http://www.focic.org.mk/foundations-history.html/, accessed 2 April 2018.
52 Fri.org.mk/, accessed 1 April 2018.
53 http://www.slvesnik.com.mk/Issues/4F5E166A79054527ADA50804B19A1239.pdf/, accessed 3 April 2018.

changed into the Vizioni M Cultural Organisation. Generally its projects are youth-related, like theatre performances, courses, lectures, seminars and youth meetings.[54]
- Nun Civil Association (*Shoqata NUN*, tel.: ++389 71441412, ++389 71334359, ++389 7033598). Humanitarian and cultural organisation based in Skopje.
- Centre for Education, Culture and Arts ADEKSAM (*Qendra për Arsim, Kulturë dhe Art ADEKSAM*, JNA bb, Gostivar, tel.: ++389 42214319). An organisation that was established in 1997 with headquarters in Gostivar. It organises cultural, educational and artistic activities, with a special focus on Islamic values.[55]
- Ensar Cultural Humanitarian Organisation (*Shoqata Humanitare dhe Kulturore Ensar*, Bezisten, Çarshia e vjetër, Skopje, tel.: ++389 23231398). An organisation registered in Skopje. It is active in the field of humanitarian, cultural and educational work. The director of the organisation is Sulejman Baki.
- Dituria Foundation (*Fondacioni Dituria*, Brakja Gjinoski 156, Gostivar 1230, tel.: ++389 42221431). Established in 2013 in Gostivar, Macedonia. Most of its activities involve giving scholarships to Bachelor's, Master's and PhD degree students. The director of this organisation is Musa Musai.
- Centre for Understanding and Institutional Cooperation (*Qendra për Mirëkuptim dhe Bashkëpunim Institucional*–QMBI, Bul. Krste Misirkov 57a, Lok. 3, 1000, Skopje, tel./fax: ++389 02/3232186, email: infoqmbi@gmail.com, www.qmbi.org.mk). The objectives of this Centre include the preservation of the cultural, national and religious identity and heritage of Macedonian Muslims. They also include child and youth welfare, the promotion and provision of education, and cultural dialogue between different ethnic and religious communities, with the aim of providing social stability. The director of this organisation is Muhamed Murtezi.[56]
- Kalliri i mirësisë Humanitarian Aid Organisation (*Organizata Humanitare Kalliri i Mirësisë*, Joakim Krcovski b.b. Skopje, tel.: ++389 23112629, email: kallirimiresise@gmail.com, http://kalliri.org/). A humanitarian and charitable organisation focusing on the care of orphans; its headquarters are in Skopje. The director of this organisation is Rufat Sherifi.[57]
- El Hilal Humanitarian Aid Organisation (*El Hilal Organizatë Humanitare*, Samoilova 106 no.64/2–Old Bazaar, Skopje, tel.: ++389 23121927).

---

54 http://vizioni-m.mk/, accessed 3 April 2018.
55 http://adeksam.mk/, accessed 3 April 2018.
56 http://qmbi.org.mk/, accessed 2 May 2018.
57 http://kalliri.org/, accessed 3 May 2018.

Non-governmental organisation with its headquarters in Skopje. The activities of this organisation are generally focused on humanitarian and cultural activities. Its director is Behixhudin Shehapi.
- Throni Foundation for Science, Culture and Humanitarian Activities (*Fondacioni Throni për Shkencë, Kulturë dhe Aktivitete Humanitare*, Kumanovska nr. 16, 1200, Tetovë, tel.: ++389 71275989, email: info@throni.org, www.throni.org). Non-governmental organisation that is active in the sphere of culture and education, with headquarters in Tetovo. Its general director is Metin Izeti.[58]
- Mustafa Pasha Foundation (*Fondacioni Mustafa Pasha*, Drvarska Br.28, Stara Carsija, Skopje, 1000, tel.: +389 23232124). An organisation that promotes education and culture, and provides humanitarian aid.

---

58 http://throni.org/rreth-nesh/, accessed 2 May 2018.

Malta

Ranier Fsadni[1]

Introduction

There are two background features that are salient to understanding recent developments among Malta's Muslims: sustained, strong economic growth, and rapid population growth, due to net migration from within the EU and Third Countries to service the needs of the labour market. At the same time, irregular migration from Africa virtually stopped, with Italy giving safe harbour to almost all refugee and migrant boats arriving from Libya in 2017. At the beginning of 2017, non-Maltese people made up 11.8% of the population, a striking rise that made the headlines and provoked public debate.[2] One consequence of this growth in the number of all foreigners is that it has tended to reframe public discussion about the growth of the specifically Muslim population, which is now increasingly seen as one group among several contributing to economic prosperity, rather than being constituted of dependents on welfare services.

The current estimate of the size of the Muslim population, as given by the Islamic Centre, is in the order of 35,000. In 2015, the same Centre had given an estimate of around 10,000–15,000. The dramatic difference could be partly the result of an upward revision of the 2015 figure. It should be kept in mind that these figures are both informed and self-interested; Muslim representatives are using these figures to argue for official permits for new places of worship, for which, however, there is a real urgent need.

In the news, the petitions for and against official permits for new places of worship intermittently occupied media attention in 2017, even if the related public incidents were fewer than in 2016. In that year, for several successive

---

[1] Ranier Fsadni is Assistant Lecturer in the Department of Anthropological Sciences of the University of Malta. He has conducted fieldwork in Libya among the Warfalla, and his teaching responsibilities include the anthropology of Islam and the contemporary Arab world. He has previously served as Director Operations in the European Commission-League of Arab States Liaison Office, and as an Advisor on Mediterranean Affairs to the Prime Minister of Malta.

[2] The total population of Malta is now officially given as 460,297 by the National Statistics Office, in revising its number upwards. In 2006, the total stood at 405,616. See: "Malta's population rises to 460,000 in 2016", *The Malta Independent Online*, 12 February 2018, http://www.independent.com.mt/articles/2018-02-12/local-news/Malta-s-population-rose-to-460-000-in-2016-6736184720, accessed 5 March 2018.

Fridays, around 200 Muslims gathered to pray in public after they were evicted from their informal place of worship. In general, there continues to be a growth in the demand of the resources of the Islamic Centre in Paola. This institution suffered from a massive loss of Libyan funding after 2011, and its problems began to reach a head in 2017, when the secondary school-section of the Mariam Albatool Muslim School had to be shut down.

The June 2017 general election campaign saw a new small Islamophobic party, *Moviment Patrijotti Maltin* (Movement of Maltese Patriots) contest the general election for the first time. It performed miserably in terms of votes but has been very active in social media, warning against an "invasion" and rejecting "integration", its memes touching a chord and highlighting the current lack of cultural policy addressing the growing number of minorities in Malta.

Public Debates

In January 2016, around 200 Muslims gathered to pray at the Msida seafront, a highly visible space, for three successive Fridays, after they were evicted from their previous place of worship. It prompted a social media furore, and the *Patrijotti Maltin* organised protests, including the distribution of ham sandwiches. A temporary agreement with the authorities was reached that permitted prayer at the Ospizio complex in Floriana,[3] until a permanent solution was found. The growing size of the Muslim population, its fragmentation as it grows more diverse, as well as significant traffic congestion, make attendance at the Friday prayer at the Paola mosque during the lunch break impracticable. However, by the end of 2017, a permanent solution had not yet been found, with planning applications for identified venues in the centre of Malta always turned down. Currently, Friday prayers are organised in at least nine places, including the Paola mosque and the main general hospital.[4]

In February 2017, the Mariam Albatool Muslim School (est. 1977) announced it was closing down its secondary school due to lack of funds. It had greatly depended on a subsidy from the Libyan government but these funds were lost

---

[3] The Ospizio forms part of a set of buildings occupied by the civil services' Education Department. See "Muslim community's Friday prayers move to Ospizio in Floriana", *The Times of Malta Online*, 22 January 2016, https://www.timesofmalta.com/articles/view/20160122/local/muslim-communitys-friday-prayers-move-to-ospizio-in-floriana.599701, accessed 9 July 2018.

[4] "Muslims still praying for a place to pray", *The Times of Malta Online*, 17 January 2018, https://www.timesofmalta.com/articles/view/20180117/local/muslims-still-praying-for-a-place-to-pray.668016, accessed 5 March 2018.

after 2011. The subsidy given by the Maltese government, as well as interest-free loans given in 2011 and 2012, were not enough to make up for the shortfall.[5] As a result of the crisis of the Mariam Albatool School, talks also began with the Ministry of Education to have Islam taught to Muslim students at state schools. It was a controversial proposal in terms of public opinion.[6] The Archbishop of Malta quickly made public his own support, saying he was open to a similar measure in Church schools if feasible.[7] However, the president of the Ahmadiyya Muslim Jamaat, Laiq Ahmed Atif, said that state schools ought to be secular and not teach religious doctrine.[8] Information given by the Islamic Centre suggests that the proposal has stalled because of a lack of teachers.

The June general election saw the *Patrijotti Maltin* given a platform, literally, at the widely covered University of Malta debates. Although the party's votes were negligible, it has given an organised voice to Islamophobia online and in press reports. Although there are several initiatives to counter Islamophobia and harassment of Muslims, there is no organised Muslim initiative which speaks on behalf of Muslims on this matter, and a survey has found that fewer than 10% of Muslims are aware of organisations that could offer advice to victims of discrimination.[9]

Transnational Links

There is no information about any formal transnational links set up in Malta, in 2017, between any Muslim community organisation and its country of origin. Many of the affluent members of the Libyan community maintain business links with Libya; but despite a felt need (at least in private conversations) for a

---

[5] "Muslim secondary school to shut down after 20 years", *The Times of Malta Online*, 17 February 2017, https://www.timesofmalta.com/articles/view/20170211/local/muslim-secondary-school-to-shut-down-after-20-years.639202, accessed 5 March 2018.

[6] "Maltese split on teaching of Islam in state schools", *MaltaToday Online*, 17 April 2017, https://www.maltatoday.com.mt/news/data_and_surveys/76301/survey__maltese_split_on_teaching_of_islam_in_state_schools#.Wy3uE7snYgE, accessed 5 March 2018.

[7] "Imam 'stunned' by Archbishop Scicluna's openness", *MaltaToday Online*, 5 April 2017, https://www.maltatoday.com.mt/news/national/75932/imam_stunned_by_sciclunas_openness#.WoYN1rsnYgE, accessed 9 July 2018.

[8] "State schools should not teach religious doctrine, says Muslim community leader", *The Times of Malta Online*, 28 March 2017, https://www.timesofmalta.com/articles/view/20170328/local/state-schools-should-not-teach-religious-doctrine-says-muslim-leader.643805, accessed 9 July 2018.

[9] Ezabe Malliue, Sara, *Islamophobia in Malta: National Report 2017*, in Eynes Bayraklı and Farid Hafez, *European Islamophobia Report 2017* (Istanbul: SETA, 2018) pp. 410–420.

formal Malta-Libyan charitable foundation to help the less fortunate Libyans in Malta, nothing seems to have come of it.

Law and Domestic Politics

In 2015, a handful of politicians, from both the major political parties represented in Parliament, attracted media attention when they suggested banning the burqa (which is hardly seen in Malta) on their social media pages. Yet, no legislative proposal resulted from this, and the matter was a non-issue in 2017.

Other issues–like public Friday prayers, and the teaching of Islam to Muslim students at state schools–also largely faded from public view; discussions between the authorities and Muslim representatives are ongoing. At the heart of all these outstanding issues is the shift from toleration of informal, laissez-faire practices, to official, rights-based recognition and legitimisation. Politicians and legislators are likely to approach the latter cautiously because of their own uncertainty concerning the social and electoral consequences.

Activities and Initiatives of Main Muslim Organisations

The Islamic Centre is the main officially recognised organisation, conducting pastoral charity work and liaising with other institutions to help recently arrived Muslims find jobs or accommodation. Imam Mohammed al-Sadi is periodically in the news either meeting a government minister, being quoted in the press on issues of the day, or participating in TV debates. In 2017, the state broadcaster reported his proposal that, if parliamentary quotas for women are introduced, it would be worth considering quotas for Muslims.[10]

While the Ahmadiyya Muslim Jamaat is responsible for many activities and publications, it reaches the wider public mainly by periodic opinion articles in the mainstream newspapers and interviews, which argue for interfaith understanding and peace.[11] Its activities in 2017 included a peace symposium on

---

10   "Imam wants Muslim representation in Parliament", *TVM*, 21 July 2017, https://www.tvm.com.mt/en/news/imam-wants-muslim-representation-in-parliament/, accessed 5 March 2018.
11   For example, Ahmed Atif, Laiq, "Humanitarian calamity", *The Times of Malta Online*, 15 April 2017, https://www.timesofmalta.com/articles/view/20170415/opinion/Humanitarian-calamity.645245, accessed 6 July 2018.

jihad and terrorism,[12] an *iftar* dinner,[13] and participation in a televised annual national charity event: *L-Istrina*.[14]

The Malta Muslim Council Foundation's main work currently is in formulating petitions to the authorities for official permits for new places of worship, and being a contact point for journalists. It is conducting a census of the Muslim population.

Muslim Population: History and Demographics

The Muslim presence in Malta dates back to the so-called Arab Period (870–1091). It is a matter of dispute among historians whether the Maltese inhabitants in their majority converted from Christianity to Islam at this time. Muslims continued to worship freely until the 13th century. The most significant cultural inheritance from this period is the Maltese language, originally an Arabic dialect. Whether myth or history, the idea that Christianity was continually practised by the Maltese majority from the time of St Paul is an important feature of popular national identity, and this, together with the annual commemoration of the Ottoman siege of 1565, shapes not just Maltese national identity, but also the popular perception of Muslims today among a segment of the population.

In the 20th century, the socially significant presence of Muslims began in the 1970s, with growing official, commercial, and informal ties with Libya, which led to the establishment of the Mariam Albatool mosque, among other institutions. From 2002, much publicity was given to growing irregular immigration from Africa, including Muslim majority countries like Somalia and Sudan, with popular anxiety over Malta's capacity to absorb large, unexpected numbers of migrants often overlapping with Islamophobia. The Syrian conflict has seen many refugees arriving from that country. The Libyan conflict and its aftermath saw many Libyans come to Malta for health care, for work in the informal

---

12   "Maltese Muslims call for peace at annual symposium", *Rabwah Times*, 5 April 2017, https://www.rabwah.net/maltese-muslims-call-peace-annual-symposium/, accessed 6 July 2018.

13   "Ahmadiyya Malta celebrates Ramadan iftar at peace lab", *Ahmadiyya Muslim Jamaat Malta*, 22 June 2017, https://ahmadiyyamalta.org/2017/06/22/ramadan-iftar-at-peace-lab/, accessed 6 July 2018.

14   "Ahmadiyya participated in L-Istrina 2017", *Ahmadiyya Muslim Jamaat Malta*, 29 December 2017, https://ahmadiyyamalta.org/2017/12/29/ahmadiyya-participated-in-l-istrina-2017/, accessed 6 July 2018.

economy, or, in the case of the more affluent, a safe place in which to raise a family. The impact on fashionable districts, especially their shopping centres and coffee-shop life, has been highly visible, and rents in areas like Sliema and St Julians have risen exponentially.

The Muslim population has continued to grow. There are no official figures categorised in terms of religion, and the last national household survey (which would give national backgrounds) was conducted in 2011. It is a growth not just of number but of diversity, which has therefore meant fragmentation in terms of collective representation. In 2017, the Islamic Centre's estimate for Maltese converts to Islam is 1,000 (up from 500 in 2015), with the main reason for conversion being attributed to Maltese women marrying non-Maltese Muslim men. In terms of geographical spread, up until a few years ago the main residential clusters were to be found in central and North Malta. However, rapidly rising rents have seen all foreign residents spread across Malta. The growing Muslim population has led to increasing demands for new places of worship, not only but not least because of the logistical difficulty of attending Friday prayers during the work lunch break.

Muslim Population	Estimate provided by the Islamic Centre: ca. 35,000 (7.6% of total population of 460,300, as of 31 December 2016).
Ethnic/National Backgrounds	The largest national backgrounds represented are Somali and Libyan, although public figures of various prominence include people of Syrian, Palestinian, Moroccan and Pakistani background or nationality. No recent official figures are available. The number of Maltese converts is estimated at 1,000.
Inner-Islamic Groups	The vast majority of Muslims in Malta are Sunni. The Ahmadi community, mainly of Pakistani origin, is made up of a few dozen members. The number of Shi'is is small. Although there is a growing Turkish community, what percentage are Alevi is unknown.
Geographical Spread	There are no official figures.

Number of Mosques	There is one central mosque in Paola, the Mariam Albatool mosque, and several unofficial places of worship. The Ahmadi community has a prayer room.
Muslim Burial Sites	There is one cemetery in use, which is part of the precincts of the Islamic Centre (Corradino Hill, Paola PLA 9037, tel.: ++356 21697203). A 19th century historic Turkish cemetery in Marsa is no longer in use.
"Chaplaincy" in State Institutions	There is no provision of Muslim religious counselling and/or ritual services for Muslims in public institutions.
Halal Products	Halal slaughter is permitted. Halal food is widely available commercially, but is not available in public institutions.
Dress Code	There is no legal restriction on specifically Muslim dress codes. The 2015 debate on social media about the legality of the niqab did not lead to new legislation by 2017. On the contrary, in 2015 the police declared it was not illegal to wear the "burqa" while driving.[15] Article 338 (n) of the *Criminal Code* has a general prohibition on the wearing of masks and disguises, except at the time and in the manner allowed by Law, but this has not been invoked to prohibit Muslim dress codes. Commercial establishments have the right to impose a special dress code, but there have been no reported incidents involving Muslim dress.

---

15 "In Malta, wearing a burqa while driving is 'not illegal'–police", *The Malta Independent Online*, 11 July 2015, http://www.independent.com.mt/articles/2015-07-11/local-news/In-Malta-wearing-a-burqa-while-driving-is-not-illegal-police-6736138692, accessed 5 July 2018.

Places of Islamic Learning and Education	– Mariam Albatool School, kindergarten and primary school (Dom Mintoff Road, Paola PLA 9037, tel.: ++356 21664791). The secondary school section had to close down in 2017 due to lack of funds. – 24 December Libyan School, offering a Libyan educational curriculum (Lapsi Street, Ta' Giorni, St. Julians).
Muslim Media and Publications	There are no influential, specifically Muslim media outlets. The Malta Muslim Council Foundation has a Facebook page: https://facebook.com/mmcfMalta. The Ahmadiyya Muslim Jamaat has several publications and a website: http://ahmadiyya.mt.

Main Muslim Organisations

– Islamic Centre (Corradino Hill, Paola PLA 9037, tel.: ++356 21697203, email: islamicsociety@melita.com; no active website). It is officially recognised and its congregation comes from various national backgrounds, although it is associated especially with the Libyan community.
– Malta Muslim Council Foundation (no premises, tel.: ++356 99001007, https://facebook.com/mmcfMalta). An independent, voluntary, non-profit foundation, which, among other things, represents Muslims seeking official permits for new places of worship.
– Ahmadiyya Muslim Jamaat (30 Turu Rizzo Street, Gzira GZR 1645, tel.: ++356 79320139, email: amjmalta@gmail.com, http://ahmadiyya.mt/). A non-governmental organisation, established in 2005, with a predominantly Pakistani membership.

Moldova

Aurelia Felea[1]

Introduction

The *Liga Islamică din Republica Moldova* (Islamic League of the Republic of Moldova) is the only Muslim religious organisation officially recognised by the State. Various aspects of the life of this community organisation are reflected in public discourses, as the organisation's leadership is regularly involved in debates on topics of general interest. The activities of other Islamic groups are not as visible. Although there are no accurate estimates of the number of members the League has, based on several years of observation it is probably the largest Muslim community organisation in the country. In 2017, the focus of Islamic activities lied in organising communal events (Friday prayers, festivals and charity events), the study of the Qur'an and Islamic literature, and charitable support for those in need. In the case of the Islamic League, interreligious dialogue between Muslims and representatives of other religions in Moldova should be added to the set of important activities that were carried out.

Public Debates

In response to the arrest of a Moldovan citizen who published messages on online platforms and social media supporting terrorist groups, an official press statement was released in January 2017 by the Information and Security Service of the Republic of Moldova, together with the Prosecutor's Office of the Chișinău Municipality. It stated that his conversion to Islam was the first step in the process of his radicalisation.[2] The particular wording suggested that embracing Islam was inevitably followed by the adoption of an extremist

---

[1] Aurelia Felea, PhD, is Associate Professor at the State University of Tiraspol in Chișinău. Her areas of academic interest include the history of Central and Eastern Europe, totalitarian and post-totalitarian societies, testimonies about the communist era, higher education and the formation of elites in Soviet Moldova.

[2] http://www.sis.md/en/comunicare/noutati/moldovean-retinut-propaganda-favoarea-orga nizatiilor-teroriste-internationale, accessed 13 May 2018.

position.[3] The press release did not arouse notable reactions in Moldovan society, even among the Islamic League and other Muslim organisations in the country.

The Russian television channel Alif TV aired a programme on "How the Muslims of Russia and CIS see the world" (*Взгляд мусульман России и СНГ на мир вокруг*). This included a documentary on a young Moldavian Jew, born in Tighina, who converted to Islam, and emigrated to Turkey, and now works in an editorial business.[4]

The newspaper *Moldova Suverană*, formerly a government publication, published an article which, in line with the far-right discourse across Europe, suggested a decline in European civilisation, which is abandoning its identity in the face of "intruders", as Muslims are presented. The newspaper included articles from various media sources that cast doubt on the will and capacity for social integration among Muslims in European countries and, while refraining from explicitly anti-Muslim statements, published the articles under Islamophobic titles, such as: "Europe besieged and terrorised by Muslim refugees".[5] The newspaper *Moldova Suverană* supports the current President Igor Dodon. In the 2016 presidential election campaign, Igor Dodon's supporters circulated the idea that any proximity between the Republic of Moldova and the European Union would involve the danger of the latter "placing" a large number of refugees in Moldova. The President, in contrast, has pleaded for closer ties with Russia and Turkey, which he regards as Moldova's "strategic partners".[6]

---

3 "Un moldovean reținut pentru propaganda organizațiilor teroriste internaționale" (A Moldovan arrested for promoting international terrorist organisations), https://www.timpul.md/articol/un-moldovean-retinut-pentru-propaganda-organizatiilor-teroriste-internationale-102808.html, accessed 21 April 2018.

4 "Сердце со шрамом. Эмигрант" (A scarred heart. The emigrant), https://alif.tv/islam-i-stambul-dlya-moldavskogo-romantika-serdtse-so-shramom/, accessed 23 April 2018.

5 "Suedia, țara în care femeile au dispărut de pe străzi, de frica imigranților. Ziarista britanică Katie Hopkins a realizat pentru Daily Mail un reportaj terifiant pe străzile din Suedia, țara considerată cea mai liberală din lume" (Sweden, the country where fear of immigrants keeps women off the streets. British journalist Katie Hopkins did a terrifying piece for the Daily Mail on the streets of Sweden, the country considered the most liberal in the world), http://moldova-suverana.md/article/europa-asediata-si-terorizata-de-catre-refugiatii-musulmani_17311, accessed 21 April 2018; Buducă, Ioan, "Islamul, da, creștinismul, nu" (Islam, yes, Christianity, no), http://moldova-suverana.md/article/islamul-da-crestinismul-nu_20332, accessed 21 April 2018; "Strania moarte a Europei: imigrare, identitate, islam" (The curious death of Europe: immigration, identity, Islam), http://moldova-suverana.md/article/strania-moarte-a-europei-imigrare-identitate-islam_19328, accessed 21 April 2018.

6 "Turcia a decis să finanțeze integral lucrările de reparație a clădirii Președinției, preconizate a fi finalizate pînă în luna mai 2018" (Turkey has decided to fully finance the repairs of

Transnational Links

The Islamic League communicates with its counterparts and relevant organisations from Ukraine (*Духовне управління мусульман України "Умма"*–the Spiritual Administration of Ukrainian Muslims "Ummah"–SAUM "Ummah"), Romania (*Liga Islamică și Culturală din România*–Islamic and Cultural League in Romania; *Fundația Centrul Cultural Islamic "Islamul azi"*–The Islamic Cultural Centre Foundation "Islam Today"; *Asociația Musulmanilor din România*–Association of Muslims of Romania), Turkey, Saudi Arabia, Syria, Qatar and others. The Islamic League refers to decisions by the European Council for Fatwa and Research when determining the beginning and end of Ramadan, for example.[7]

Law and Domestic Politics

The *International Religious Freedom Report*, an annual report for the US Department of State, points to the Moldavian government's preferential treatment of the Orthodox Church and its strong influence on government policies. According to the report, government authorities react passively to incidents where minority religious groups are subjected to abuse (threats, insults, physical violence, and vandalism of places of worship). In addition, the report points at the influence of the Orthodox Church in pre-university education, which is manifest in the presence of Christian symbols in classrooms, in the participation of Orthodox priests in school events, especially at the beginning and at the end of the school year, and in providing religious education in schools. Studying religion in pre-university education is optional, but students who do not attend religious classes are not provided with an educational alternative. The school programme offers two types of courses: one for Orthodox and Catholic Christians, and another for Evangelicals and Seventh-day Adventists. The first course, taught by Orthodox teachers or priests, focuses primarily on the Orthodox Christian religion. The State Department also points out that the separatist regime in the Transnistria region continued to discriminate, restrict and monitor the activities of minority religious groups. Out of fear of

---

the presidential building, scheduled to be completed by May 2018), http://www.presedinte .md/rom/comunicate-de-presa/turtsiya-prinyala-reshenie-o-polnom-finansirovanii-rabot- po-remontu-zdaniya-prezidentury-pri-etom-remontnye-raboty-dolzhny-zakonchitisya-do- maya-2018-goda, accessed 23 April 2018.

7 Facebook: Мусульмане Молдовы–Liga Islamica RM.

the persecution they were subjected to in the past, Muslim communities in the Transnistria region refrain from running religious activities.[8]

In July 2016, Parliament adopted amendments to the Law which allow individuals, but not companies or other legal entities, to redirect 2% of their income tax to NGOs or religious organisations. Religious groups wanting to benefit from these new provisions must register with the Ministry of Justice, and use the amounts received for social, moral, cultural and/or charitable activities only. The Law exempts religious organisations from paying tax on the income received, as a donation under the 2% law, and from registration fees.[9]

Activities and Initiatives of Main Muslim Organisations

The Islamic League leadership has repeatedly condemned the use of violence in the name of Islam. The sermons given at the League's prayer congregations plead for mercy and mutual understanding, not only towards co-religionists, but towards all human beings.[10]

Muslim Population: History and Demographics

The first encounters with Islam in Moldova probably occurred as early as the 13th–14th centuries. While encounters took place for a number of centuries, with variable intensity and in various forms, there are no historic Muslim communities and continuous Islamic traditions within the territory of the modern Republic of Moldova.[11]

The last population census in the country was conducted between 12–25 May 2014. The total population in Moldova was given as 2,804,801; 2,611,759 respondents declared their religion, while 193,042 did not. Of those who declared their religion, 2,528,152 (96.8%) consider themselves Orthodox Christians. The exponents of other religions were Baptists (Evangelical Christian Baptists): 1.0%, Jehovah's Witnesses: 0.7%, Pentecostal Christians: 0.4%, the Seventh-day

---

8   *International Religious Freedom Report for 2016. Moldova*, http://www.state.gov/j/drl/rls/irf/religiousfreedom/index.htm?year=2016&dlid=268844, accessed 21 April 2018.
9   *International Religious Freedom Report for 2016. Moldova.*
10 Facebook: Мусульмане Молдовы–Liga Islamica RM.
11 For the history of such contacts, see Felea, Aurelia, "Moldova", in Oliver Scharbrodt, Samim Akgönül, Ahmet Alibašić, Jørgen S. Nielsen and Egdūnas Račius (eds.), *Yearbook of Muslims in Europe*, vol. 8 (Leiden: Brill, 2016), pp. 463–478 (471–472).

Adventists: 0.3%, while Catholics represent 1%. The share of persons who identified themselves as atheists and non-religious (agnostics) was 0.2%.[12]

Muslim Population	The 2014 census recorded 2,009 Muslims (0.072% of the total population); of these 1,235 were men and 774 were women.
Ethnic/National Backgrounds	The Muslim population in the Republic of Moldova is an ethnically heterogeneous religious minority composed of Arabs, Turks, Tatars, Azeris, Moldovan converts and others.
Inner-Islamic Groups	No data available. Most Muslims identify themselves as Sunnis.
Geographical Spread	According to the 2014 Census data, the largest concentration of Muslims is in Chișinău, the capital of the country (985). A significant number of Muslims were registered in places like Comrat, the capital of the Gagauz administrative-territorial unit (176), Bălți (71), Anenii Noi (68) and Cahul (54).
Number of Mosques	Three locations fulfil the role of mosques in Chișinău. One belongs to the Islamic League of the Republic of Moldova,[13] and the other serves as a place of prayer, but is also used for educational activities for members of the NGO *Grădinile liniștii* (The Gardens of Peace). A group of Turkish citizens have created their own community centre in Chișinău. This group meets at the headquarters of the *Fundația de susținere a Culturii și Tradițiilor Islamice în Republica Moldova* (Foundation for the

---

12   "The population of the Republic of Moldova at the time of the census was 2,998,235, 31.03.2017", http://www.statistica.md/newsview.php?l=en&id=5582&idc=30; see also: http://www.statistica.md/public/files/Recensamint/Recensamint_pop_2014/Nota_informativa_Preliminare_Recensamint_2014.pdf, both accessed 19 April 2018.
13   The online page *Beautiful Mosque Gallery* shows photographs of this building, which, before being transformed into a mosque, was part of an industrial unit: https://www.beautifulmosque.com/Chisinau-Mosque-Moldova, accessed 19 April 2018.

Support of Islamic Culture and Traditions in Moldova), an imposing building constructed with financial support from the Turkish government, and opened in 2015.

Muslim Burial Sites — There are no Muslim cemeteries in the Republic of Moldova. There is a sector in Saint Lazarus Cemetery, located in the capital, where Muslims are buried (Doina street 189, Chișinău, tel.: ++373 22460880, Funeral services, http://serviciifunerare.md/824-2/cimitirului-sf-lazar/).

"Chaplaincy" in State Institutions — The relevant Law allows all religious groups to hold services at state facilities, including prisons, orphanages, hospitals, schools, and military and police institutions, at the request of individuals in such institutions, provided they obtain the approval of the institution's administration.[14] The main Church in Moldova, the Moldovan Orthodox Church (MOC), has signed agreements with state institutions to facilitate the access of its clergy to public institutions.[15] Some data points to the presence in the country's penitentiaries of people who have a Muslim background or originate from countries with a Muslim majority population, including persons convicted of advocating terrorism.[16] For Muslim convicts in general to get in touch with their co-religionists is rare. According to Islamic organisation leaders, interaction is hard to establish, especially because of complicated bureaucratic procedures.[17]

---

14   *International Religious Freedom Report for 2016. Moldova.*
15   *International Religious Freedom Report for 2016. Moldova.*
16   "Cetățean al Republicii Arabe Siriene reținut de către ofițerii BMA" (Citizen of the Syrian Arab Republic detained by BMA officers), http://bma.gov.md/ro/content/cet%C4%83%C8%9Bean-al-republicii-arabe-siriene-re%C8%9Binut-de-c%C4%83tre-ofi%C8%9Berii-bma, accessed 19 April 2018. The BMA is the Migration and Asylum Bureau of the Ministry of the Interior of the Republic of Moldova.
17   Personal interview conducted by author.

Halal Products	There are no special legal provisions concerning procedures for slaughtering animals according to certain religious norms. Halal food is not available in public institutions. In its information and advertising materials, Franzeluţa SA, the largest Moldovan company specialising in bakery products, pastry, and pasta–with 56% of the statutory capital belonging to the State–notes that the company has kosher and halal certificates.[18] There is a Halal Restaurant in Chişinău (its Facebook page is Halal Market). Several Muslim families buy livestock from local producers, livestock that is later slaughtered according to Islamic norms. This is the common practice, not only in cases of daily consumption of halal meat, but also during Muslim holidays. Islamic communities distribute food and halal meat to their members on Islamic holidays.
Dress Code	There are no legal provisions regarding the head scarf or any other types of Muslim head or face covering. Muslim women wearing head scarves can often be seen in public spaces. Wearing a full face-veil (niqab) has not been observed
Places of Islamic Learning and Education	There are no institutions of Islamic education in the Republic of Moldova. The Islamic League works with Muslims in Romania to develop interactive online courses to study Islam and the Arabic language. An Islamic Studies Course organised by the *Centrul de Studii Islamice. Asociaţia Musulmanilor din România* (Centre for Islamic Studies of the Association of Muslims of Romania), began on 16 October 2017, and was to be held for nine months. An Arabic language course, organised by the same Centre, started on 22 November 2017, and contained three modules of 16 weeks each.[19]

---

18 "Top 100 de branduri 2016. Franzeluţa" (Top 100 brands in 2016), http://vipmagazin.md/wp-content/uploads/2017/03/Top-100-Branduri-2016.pdf, accessed 19 April 2018.

19 See http://www.asociatiamusulmanilor.ro/, accessed 19 April 2018.

Muslim Media and Publications

Islamic organisations in the country do not own radio and television stations and do not publish any regular print media. Muslims in the Republic of Moldova consult a number of online resources from abroad. By analysing the Islamic League's social network activity, it can be seen that, in 2017, members of the League have consulted a number of sources that provide information about Islamic dogma, practices and rituals.[20] Other media sources serve to inform about events that took place in countries with a Muslim majority population, and the situation of Muslims in Western Europe.[21]

Main Muslim Organisations

– The Islamic League of the Republic of Moldova (*Liga Islamică din Republica Moldova*, Mesager street 9, Chişinău MD 2029, tel.: ++373 22922755, 079420046, Facebook: Мусульмане Молдовы–Liga Islamica RM). Mufti Sergiu Sochirca leads the Islamic League, which was officially registered on 14 March 2011. The Islamic League includes two entities that have been officially registered as non-governmental organisations: The League of Muslim Women in the Republic of Moldova (*Liga Femeilor Musulmane din Moldova*, chair: Natalia Tkacenko, Nicolae Sulac street 4/18, Chişinău MD 2075, officially registered on 29 November 2010), and the Islamic Association "Assalam" in Moldova (*Asociaţia Islamică "Assalam" în Republica Moldova*, https://assalammd.com/). The organisation interacts closely with state authorities

---

20 *Ислам для всех!* (*Islam for All!*), http://islam.com.ua; *Моя Религия Ислам* (*Islam is my Religion*), https://www.instagram.com/abu.atika/; *Umma.ru–Достоверно!* (*Umma.ru–Reliable!*), https://umma.ru/; *Alif TV*, http://arifov.com.ua/2016/12/3742/, all accessed 19 April 2018.

21 *Голос Ислама* (*Voice of Islam*), https://golosislama.com/; *Al Jazeera*, https://www.aljazeera.com/; *TRT World*, https://www.trtworld.com/; *The Independent*, https://www.independent.co.uk/; *Русская служба Би-би-си–BBC Russian Service*, http://www.bbcrussian.com/; *OnePath Network*, https://www.onepathnetwork.com/; IHH Humanitarian Relief Foundation, https://www.ihh.org.tr/en; Peace House, http://www.peacehouse.us/; *АрабМир–Окно в арабский мир* (*ArabMir–Window into the Arabian World*), http://arabmir.net/; ATTN, https://www.attn.com/; *Солидарность* (*Solidarity*), http://solidarnost.su/; *AJ+*, http://www.ajplus.net/english/; *Channel 4 News*, https://www.channel4.com/news/, all accessed 19 April 2018.

and international organisations (United Nations, Organisation for Security and Cooperation in Europe, and others).
- The Gardens of Peace (*Grădinile liniștii*, Rezeni 1, Ialoveni MD 7727, tel.: ++373 79156707). The chair of the organisation is Talgat Mashaev; it has public organisation status and was officially registered on 26 December 2006.[22] A number of requests for it to be recognised as a religious organisation by the State, submitted by this group from 2000, have failed. Nevertheless, its registration as a public organisation means it performs Islamic religious activities, including prayers, lessons for children, etc. The organisation appears to follow a more conservative brand of Islam.
- The Foundation for the Support of Islamic Culture and Traditions in Moldova (*Fundația de susținere a Culturii și Tradițiilor Islamice în Republica Moldova*, Albișoara street 80/8, Chișinău). This Foundation has public organisation status, and was officially registered on 25 June 2001.

---

22 *State Register of Non-Profit Organisations*, http://rson.justice.md/organization/view/4244, accessed 19 April 2018.

Montenegro

Sabina Pačariz[1]

Introduction

The Muslims of Montenegro are organised religiously around the *Islamska Zajednica u Crnoj Gori* (Islamic Community of Montenegro–ICM), an independent organisation formally recognised by the State. Its members are predominantly Sunnis of the Hanafi *madhhab*. As autochthonous people, constituting almost 20% of the overall population, Montenegrin Muslims are actively included in the political, social and cultural life of the country. They were a major contributing force during key moments in the country`s recent past, such as the independence vote in 2006, and support for the alliance with the North Atlantic Treaty Organisation (NATO) in 2017. As such, the Islamic Community has supported the policies of the ruling Democratic Party of Socialists (*Demokratska partija socijalista*) in Montenegro and its president Milo Djukanović, who has interchangeably served as the State's Prime Minister and President ever since 1991. The political leverage of the Muslims of Montenegro is often publicly recognised (not only by the ruling regime), and therefore explored in various ways by themselves, but also by non-Muslim actors.

However, some events of 2017 questioned the hitherto accepted notion of the multi-confessional nature of Montenegrin society. A donation, which started with the intention of preserving the common cultural heritage of the Montenegrin capital, in the form of the Clock Tower of Podgorica, was followed by serious disagreements among different religious institutions, and ended up disturbing the sense of belonging of many Montenegrin Muslims. Although now fully renovated, the Clock Tower aroused a great deal of bitterness between different communities.

Certain gaps in the legal regulations within religious education became more obvious in 2017, once the Islamic Community of Montenegro (ICM) raised the issue of legality of religious schools sponsored by the Islamic Community of a neighbouring country. The official state institutions struggled over defining

---

[1] Sabina Pačariz is a PhD candidate at the School of Politics and International Relations, Queen Mary University of London. Her doctoral thesis explores Turkish influence in the Balkans. She completed her Master's Degree in International Relations at Marmara University in Istanbul, and graduated from the University of Ss. Cyril and Methodius in Skopje, Macedonia, in the Department of Interpreting of English and German Languages. She also researches identity and migrations in the Balkans.

exact responsibilities, while the ICM and the Islamic Community in Serbia[2] exchanged inflammatory accusations.

In 2017, the ICM completed several building projects and implemented a few, but also initiated new ones. 2017 was another year that saw the continuation of traditionally good relations with neighbouring Islamic communities. Additionally, close cooperation with some more distant regions allowed several capital projects to come to fruition.

Public Debates

In 2017 the prevalent public debate centred on religious symbols, a debate that for Montenegrin Muslims disturbed the notion of being part of multi-confessional state. The cultural identity of the Montenegrin capital was fiercely debated, as one of its hallmarks underwent restoration. The Clock Tower, located in the centre of Podgorica, was built in the 17th century (during Ottoman rule), as part of the *waqf* of Mehmet Paša Osmanagić. In 1890 (during the Kingdom of Montenegro) a metal cross was added atop the Clock Tower. In 2017 the Turkish Agency for Cooperation and Coordination (TİKA), provided €400,000 to finance the restoration of the Clock Tower and the surrounding Bećir Beg Osmanagić Square, as part of its projects for the preservation of Ottoman cultural heritage.

During the course of the restoration, the cross was removed for practical reasons, initiating numerous discussions about whether and when it would be returned. From the beginning, the Islamic Community of Montenegro (ICM) clearly stated its disagreement with returning the cross, as none of the other Islamic architectural landmarks of the country included a cross. According to the ICM's press release, the "Christening" of the Clock Tower was a more recent addition, and only one of numerous usurpations of the property of the ICM.[3] The head of the ICM, *reis* Rifat Fejzić, as the signer of the press release, stated: "We could not believe learning from the media that the top municipal authorities of Podgorica had arranged the design of the Clock Tower with the Serbian Orthodox Church leadership, while completely circumventing the

---

2 There are two Islamic Communities functioning in the Republic of Serbia. One of them is the Islamic Community of Serbia (*Islamska zajednica Srbije*–IZS), organised in an independent *rijaset*, whose head is a *ra'is al-'ulama*. The other is the Islamic Community in Serbia (*Mešihat islamske zajednice u Srbiji*–IZuS), as a component *meshihat* within the *rijaset* of the Islamic Community of Bosnia and Herzegovina. The second organisation is active in Montenegro.

3 http://balkans.aljazeera.net/vijesti/crnogorska-iz-protiv-krsta-na-sahat-kuli-u-podgorici, accessed 13 March 2018.

Islamic Community, a party directly involved".[4] The Podgorica imam, Džemo Redžematović, participating in a television debate addressing this issue, expressing hopes that by the next elections the Muslims of Podgorica would evaluate the attitude of the capital toward their cultural heritage.[5] In his opinion, the Clock Tower is not a symbol of victories or defeats, but is supposed to measure time, and therefore requests for religious demarcations are groundless.

The representatives of the Montenegrin branch of the Serbian Orthodox Church (*Mitropolija Crnogorsko-Primorska*) considered the rhetoric of the ICM as overly harsh and irresponsible, especially since no Muslim had raised that issue before. In addition, both the Tower and the cross are part of cultural heritage, so when someone claims that "it is now time to remove the cross", then of course the people will respond that if it was there for hundred years, it should stay from now on.[6]

The Directorate for Cultural Heritage explained that the Clock Tower was officially registered as cultural heritage in 1957, and therefore the metal element on top of it was registered as an integral part of it. Once the restoration works are completed, it has to be returned, in order to match the officially registered appearance.[7] The mayor of Podgorica, Slavoljub Stijepović, also confirmed that the metal element was only temporarily removed for restoration purposes, and was going to be returned to comply with the previous structure.[8]

The media also consulted historians, academics and intellectuals regarding "the return of the cross". Novak Kilibarda, writer, professor and former politician, considered this act to be against the national harmony of the country, especially since "if it was not for the Muslim votes in 2006, Montenegro would not have been an independent State today".[9] The historian Živko Andrijasević expressed similar views, stating that the Clock Tower served the urban life of Podgorica, and as such could not have any religious symbols. Dragana Kujović, an expert in Oriental Studies at the Montenegrin History Institute confirmed that the cross did not originally belong to the tower.[10]

---

4   http://balkans.aljazeera.net/vijesti/crnogorska-iz-protiv-krsta-na-sahat-kuli-u-podgorici, accessed 13 March 2018.
5   https://www.youtube.com/watch?time_continue=13&v=CwDK223g5_w, accessed 15 March 2018.
6   https://www.youtube.com/watch?v=46fJ7t_oHcI, accessed 15 March 2018.
7   https://www.youtube.com/watch?v=46fJ7t_oHcI, accessed 15 March 2018.
8   http://balkans.aljazeera.net/vijesti/crnogorska-iz-protiv-krsta-na-sahat-kuli-u-podgorici, accessed 15 March 2018.
9   https://fosmedia.me/infos/drustvo/kilibarda-zahtjev-da-se-vrati-krst-na-sahat-kuli-nepotreban-i-nekulturan, accessed March 2018, accessed 15 March 2018.
10 https://fosmedia.me/infos/drustvo/kilibarda-zahtjev-da-se-vrati-krst-na-sahat-kuli-nepotreban-i-nekulturan, accessed 15 March 2018.

The metal cross was returned to the top of the Clock Tower on 27 October 2017, by which time the restoration works were concluded.[11] The Serbian Orthodox Church saluted the return of the cross, expressing hopes for the simultaneous return of peace amongst the citizens of Podgorica. The ICM condemned this as an attack on multi-confessional Montenegro.[12]

The ICM and the Serbian Orthodox Church had major disagreements on other issues as well. *Reis* Fejzić reacted to the statements of the Amfilohije Metropolitan, whereby Podgorica mosques are built on the foundations of Serbian churches and monasteries. According to the *reis*, cadastres and archival evidence can prove the history of the mosques. For him, such claims are just another example of the tendencies of the Serbian Orthodox Church to appropriate Islamic heritage sites in the country.[13]

Another public debate focused on the introduction of a new national holiday to celebrate the Montenegrin statesmen and poet Petar Petrović Njegoš. His most famous work *Gorski Vjenac* (The Mountain Wreath) is considered a lyrical masterpiece in Montenegrin literature. However, the main event in the poem is the "extermination of the Turkicised," in the 17th century, in which Metropolitan Danilo allegedly executed all converts to Islam. As a result, the ICM expressed discomfort with such a national holiday. According to *reis* Fejzić, Muslims in Montenegro do not impugn the personality, the political leadership capabilities or even the poetry of Njegoš, but verses that speak of Islam as a fake religion are offensive to them. Many parts of this widely quoted poem are extremely problematic for Muslims, and therefore "first and foremost, the Ministry of Culture, but also all other authorities should show more responsibility against creating artificial problems".[14]

The year 2017 witnessed a publicised case of violence due to Islamophobia, in which three Libyan students from the Airways Aviation Academy, based in Nikšić, were attacked. The police statements indicated that it was motivated by religious hatred, with several references made to connections between Muslims and terrorism. Ted Kabut, the director of the Airways Aviation Academy, expressed fear for the future, since the incident happened within the first seven days of the students' stay in Montenegro. He called upon the Montenegrin authorities to be diligent in dealing with racially motivated violence, as the

---

11   http://www.vijesti.me/vijesti/metalni-krst-vracen-na-sahat-kulu-960426, accessed 15 March 2018.
12   https://www.blic.rs/vesti/svet/podgorica-mitropolija-pozdravila-vracanje-krsta-na-sahat-kulu/8jphtvt, accessed 15 March 2018.
13   http://www.vijesti.me/vijesti/fejzic-amfilohije-tendencioznim-izjavama-ugrozava-meduvjerski-sklad-955360, accessed 15 March 2018.
14   http://www.infomediabalkan.com/vijest.php?pro_id=11397, accessed 15 March 2018.

efforts of the Academy to brand Montenegro as a stable and safe country will prove fruitless if such attacks are repeated.[15]

Transnational Links

The majority of Montenegrin Muslims are of either Bosniak or Albanian ethnic background, which is reflected in their institutional collaboration with organisations in these neighbouring countries. The year 2017 witnessed several examples of cooperation between the ICM and various governmental and non-governmental institutions throughout the region.

As part of his official visit to Montenegro, the chairman of the Council of Ministers of Bosnia and Herzegovina, Denis Zvizdić, visited the ICM and the Mehmed Fatih Madrasah in February, where participants discussed the position of Bosniaks in the Montenegrin context. Zvizdić expressed his satisfaction with the formal recognition of the role of Bosniaks in Montenegro; they hold many high positions in the Government, and were among the strongest promotors of Montenegro's independence and membership of NATO.[16]

The mayor of Sarajevo, Abdullah Skaka, also visited the ICM. After exchanging words of hospitality and friendship with *reis* Fejzić, they held a joint meeting with influential Bosniaks from the political and public sphere of Montenegro.[17] The Council of the Congress of Bosniak Intellectuals, led by Nedžad Mulabegović, paid a visit to the ICM leadership as well. The national, cultural and political situation of Bosniaks in the region was discussed at the meeting.[18]

The ICM also marked its continuing good relations with the Islamic Community of Albania. In that regard, a pilgrimage was again jointly organised in 2017. A total of 83 pilgrims travelled to Tirana, from where they continued their journey to Mecca.[19]

---

15   http://mondo.rs/a1034272/Info/Ex-Yu/Niksic-napadnuti-libijski-studenti-jer-su-muslimani.html, accessed 12 May 2018.

16   http://ba.n1info.com/a137880/Vijesti/Vijesti/Zvizdic-se-sastao-sa-reisom-Fejzicem-i-Bugarijem.html, accessed 5 April 2018.

17   http://www.monteislam.com/aktuelnosti/gradonacelnik-sarajeva-posjetio-reisa-fejzica, accessed 5 April 2018.

18   http://www.monteislam.com/aktuelnosti/delegacija-vijeca-kongresa-bosnjaka-sastala-se-sa-reisom, accessed 5 April 2018.

19   https://m.cdm.me/drustvo/iz-cg-na-hadz-otputovala-83-vjernika-sve-duse-su-srecne-sto-posjecuju-meku-medinu/, accessed 5 April 2018.

The Bektashi community of Albania is another example of well nurtured mutual relations. Every year the Bektashis organise *iftar* dinners, where representatives of all neighbouring Islamic Communities are invited, along with the state leadership and diplomatic corps. *Reis* Fejzić, together with deputy *reis* Omer Kajoshaj, took part in the 2017 traditional ceremony.[20]

A training programme, entitled "Contemporary Methods and Types of Work in Religious Schools", was held in Sarajevo for the teachers of the Mehmed Fatih Madrasah. The seminar was co-organised by the Centre for Advanced Studies in Sarajevo, providing the teachers the opportunity to discuss the theoretical and practical aspects of religious education.[21]

Many transnational activities were implemented through the non-governmental organisation (NGO) *Horizonti*, whose president, Omer Kajoshaj, is also the acting director of the Foreign Relations Office of the ICM. In cooperation with the Centre for Advanced Studies from Sarajevo, the Vesatija Centre for Dialogue, and the Centre for Personal and Professional Development Sarajevo, the seventh summer school "Islam in the Contemporary World" was completed in 2017. 34 undergraduate and postgraduate students from the region and abroad participated in the programme, which focused on contemporary Islamic thought, Muslim communities and culture, and communication skills.[22] In a collaboration project with the European Muslim Network and the NGO *Ardhmeria* from Albania, *Horizonti* co-organised a conference entitled "Populism and beyond Islamophobia", where related topics were explored in the Albanian, regional Balkan, and wider European context.[23]

The ICM traditionally nurtures very close relations with Turkey, which was clearly demonstrated in 2017 through several visits by *reis* Fejzić to Turkey, where he met with state and religious officials. During his May visit, Fejzić held meetings with the President of the Grand National Assembly of Turkey, Ismail Kahraman,[24] and later participated in a programme in Konya, organised by the then director of the Turkish Presidency of Religious Affairs (*Diyanet İşleri Başkanlığı*), Mehmet Görmez.[25] Upon the initiative of the Montenegrin *reis*,

---

20 http://shqiptarja.com/lajm/kryegjyshi-i-bektashinjve-iftar-per-br-besimtaret-ben-thirrje-per-harmoni?r=pop5s, accessed 5 April 2018.
21 http://cns.ba/vijesti/odrzan-seminar-za-profesore-medrese-u-podgorici/, accessed 10 April 2018.
22 http://cns.ba/vijesti/zavrsena-sedma-cns-ljetna-skola/, accessed 10 April 2018.
23 http://ardhmeria.org.al/2017/06/12/seminari-populizmi-dhe-pertej-islamofobise-tarik-ramadan/, accessed 10 April 2018.
24 http://www.monteislam.com/novosti/prijem-kod-predsjednika-skupstine-republike-turske-i-druge-vazne-posjete, accessed 10 April 2018.
25 http://www.monteislam.com/novosti/velicanstven-program-u-turskoj-konya-gradi-islamski-centar-u-bijelom-polju, accessed 10 April 2018.

the Muftiate and the Municipality of Konya established formal "brotherhood" with the Bijelo Polje *mesihat* of the Montenegrin IC. As a result of this cooperation, the Muftiate, together with the Municipality of Konya, committed to support the building of an Islamic centre in Bijelo Polje.[26] In late September, a delegation from the Municipality of Konya repaid a visit to the ICM, during which they inspected the intended location for the centre in Bijelo Polje, and discussed the prospects of the project.[27]

In September 2017, *reis* Rifat Fejzić visited the newly appointed head of the Turkish Diyanet, Ali Erbas, to extend his congratulations on his new post.[28] The two religious leaders met again in November, when Fejzić paid another official visit to Turkey.[29] On this occasion, Fejzić also met with the Deputy Prime Minister, Bekir Bozdağ, and expressed hope that Turkey would continue its support for the ICM in the future.[30]

The Turkish Deputy Minister of Education, Orhan Erdem, met with the leadership of the ICM in Podgorica, and visited the Madrasah in Tuzi.[31] The two sides discussed potential cooperation projects between the Madrasah and Turkish religious high schools (Imam Hatip Schools). Another Turkish education official also met with the leadership of the ICM. On this occasion, *reis* Fejzić thanked Mehmet Köse, head of the Presidency for Turks Abroad and Related Communities, for the support of numerous Montenegrin students who are studying in Turkey on state-funded scholarships.[32]

Relations between the two countries were also explored by non-state actors. For example, the NGO ISKED, from Istanbul, organised a ceremonial *iftar*

---

26 The ICM proposed this as a priority project for assistance for several reasons. First of all, demographically, town's Muslims constitute 44% of its overall population, but only have access to one small mosque. Also, during the recent wars, the property of the ICM was severely damaged in the town. This project would include the construction of a central mosque, with several adjacent buildings.

27 http://www.monteislam.com/aktuelnosti/delegacija-turske-opstine-konya-posjetila-medzlis-iz-bijelo-polje, accessed 4 May 2018.

28 http://www.monteislam.com/aktuelnosti/reis-fejzic-posjetio-je-reisa-turake-prof-dr-ali-erbasa, accessed 4 May 2018.

29 http://www.monteislam.com/aktuelnosti/reis-fejzic-posjetio-reisa-republike-turske, accessed 6 May 2018.

30 http://www.monteislam.com/aktuelnosti/reis-fejzic-u-posjeti-bekiru-bozdagu-potpredsjedniku-vlade-republike-turske, accessed 6 May 2018.

31 http://www.monteislam.com/aktuelnosti/pomocnik-ministra-prosvjete-republike-turske-posjetio-islamsku-zajednicu, accessed 6 May 2018.

32 http://www.monteislam.com/aktuelnosti/direktor-direkcije-za-tursku-dijasporu-srodne-zajednice-i-strane-studente-posjetio-islamsku-zajednicu, accessed 6 May 2018.

dinner in Ulcinj, and financially supported the construction of a dormitory for the female Madrasah in Ulcinj.[33]

The ICM closely cooperates with certain Gulf countries, which is seen in the extent of support the ICM receives for various construction projects. Kuwait financed the completion of the female madrasah in Tuzi, the building of a mosque near Ulcinj, and the completion of the Han Islamic Centre in Bijelo Polje. The financing of these projects was arranged in September 2017, during the official visit to Kuwait by the director of the Foreign Relations Office of the ICM, Omer Kajoshaj. The visit included meetings with the Directorate of Vakfs, the Ministry of Vakfs, and the Bejtu Zekat and Rahme Alemiye organisations.[34]

Qatar also provided support for a capital project of the ICM. During Kajoshaj's visit to the Qatari Ministry of *waqf*, Qatar committed €1.5 million for the construction of a Youth Centre in Podgorica.[35] Improvement in cooperation in the fields of education, da'wa, and charity work, were also among the topics of discussion at these meetings.

Law and Domestic Politics

During 2017 there were many discussions over the legality of certain Islamic religious schools in Montenegro. There is a female madrasah in Rožaje, a branch of the Islamic Community in Serbia (IZuS). In Rožaje and Petnica there are several other kindergartens and Qur'an schools aligned with the IZuS. The *reis* Rifat Fejzić raised the issue of their legality and called upon Montenegrin authorities to check the status of these schools. He argued that it should be impossible for "another state" to open religious schools in Montenegro, without any control of its programme and curriculum, or treatment of students.[36]

Within the formal legal context of Montenegro, article 17 of the Agreement signed in 2012 between the Montenegrin government and the ICM, provides the ICM with the right to form religious schools and educational institutions to educate personnel working for it. However, there are no formulations regulating the existence of alternative educational institutions, such as the ones in Rožaje and Petnica. Article 20 of the same Agreement states that, in compliance with

---

33 http://www.monteislam.com/aktuelnosti/veliki-iftar-u-ulcinju, accessed 6 May 2018.
34 http://www.monteislam.com/novosti/omer-kajoshaj-direktor-uprave-za-saradnju-sa-inostranstvom-u-sluzbenoj-posjeti-kuvajtu, accessed 8 May 2018.
35 http://www.monteislam.com/novosti/omer-kajoshaj-direktor-uprave-za-saradnju-sa-inostranstvom-u-sluzbenoj-posjeti-kataru, accessed 8 May 2018.
36 https://www.slobodnaevropa.org/amp/nelegalne-islamske-vjerske-skole-crna-gora/28302443.html, accessed 10 May 2018.

the principles of religious freedom, parents have the right to religiously educate their children; but this provision does not grant this responsibility exclusively to the ICM.[37]

In February 2017, the Ministry of Education explained that religious schools were not licensed according to standard procedures. The ICM-run Mehmet Fatih Madrasa is listed among the schools with publicly recognised educational programmes, that is, their diplomas are recognised within the formal state educational system, that enables its students to continue with higher education after graduating from the madrasa. The municipal authorities in Rožaje, where the religious schools run by the Islamic Community in Serbia (IZuS) are based, did not provide any answers about the legal status of these institutions.[38]

The ICM also brought up this issue with the Ministry of Human and Minority Rights, where, within the eighth session of the Mixed Committee for Tracking the Implementation of the Agreement for Regulation of Relations of Common Interests between the Government of Montenegro and the Islamic Community in Montenegro, the problematic aspects were analysed in more detail. According to the official information circulated by the Ministry, all necessary information related to opening religious schools by other countries or communities will be collected in the near future. That official statement concluded that "… all members of the Mixed Committee agree that more robust solutions should be provided for dealing with illegal schools, especially considering that the Mehmed Fatih Madrasah is the only religious school conducting a publicly recognised educational programme".[39]

The authorities from the Islamic Community in Serbia (IZuS) did not remain silent on these developments, expressing surprise with Fejzić's reaction, since he personally taught in one of their schools for the past few years. Fejzić explained that this was in the period when Serbia and Montenegro formed a state union and other schools did not exist. In independent Montenegro, however, the ICM possesses the sole jurisdiction over matters pertaining to Islam, and opened its own madrasah in accordance with its Agreement with the State.

---

[37] http://www.rtcg.me/vijesti/drustvo/186228/rozajske-vjerske-skole-nelegalne.html, accessed 10 May 2018.

[38] https://www.slobodnaevropa.org/amp/nelegalne-islamske-vjerske-skole-crna-gora/28302443.html, accessed 10 May 2018.

[39] https://m.cdm.me/drustvo/da-li-je-neka-druga-drzava-otvorila-vjersku-skolu-u-crnojgori/, accessed 10 May 2018.

Activities and Initiatives of Main Muslim Organisations

The opening of a newly built mosque in Bukovica was an important event for the ICM, as Muslims in this region remember the forced expulsion of the Muslim population during the 1990s.[40] The former mosque was set on fire in 1943, and the remaining minaret was destroyed by explosives in 1993.[41] The vice-president of the Montenegrin government, Rafet Husović, was present at the opening ceremony, emphasising that the Government had provided substantial funding for the infrastructure and building of 110 houses for the Muslim returnees. Promising that the Government would support the reconstruction of other destroyed or derelict mosques, Husović added: "I am sure that independent, civil, multi-confessional and NATO member Montenegro will never allow crimes in this region".[42] *Reis* Fejzić expressed hope that the return process of dispersed persons would continue.[43] With its opening, the Bukovica mosque became the 138th in Montenegro.

Cornerstones for the construction of a new mosque were placed in the village of Trubina, near Bijelo Polje. The owners of the land turned their property into a *waqf* for the future mosque.[44] The population of the village of Dobrodole, the majority of whom have migrated to Western Europe for economic reasons, collected funds for the construction of a new mosque on a site gifted to them.[45]

In December 2017, foundations for a female dormitory were laid within the campus of the Mehmed Fatih Madrasa in Podgorica. The project is being implemented through the Office for International Relations of the Islamic Community, with the support of charity organisations from Kuwait.[46]

---

40   Technically, there was no war in Montenegro during the 1990s, but in the context of the extreme nationalism present in the region at that time, this politics of fear often spilt over into Montenegro, and led to the expulsion of Muslims and the destruction of Islamic places of worship in Montenegrin territory.
41   http://www.rtcg.me/vijesti/drustvo/174932/bukovica-otvorena-rekonstruisana-dzamija.html, accessed 12 May 2018.
42   http://www.monteislam.com/aktuelnosti/svecano-otvorena-dzamija-u-rascicima-bukvi capljevlja, accessed 12 May 2018.
43   http://pvportal.me/2017/08/otvorena-dzamija-u-rascicima/, accessed 12 May 2018.
44   http://www.monteislam.com/aktuelnosti/postavljen-kamen-temeljac-za-dzamiju-u-se lu-trubina, accessed 14 May 2018.
45   http://www.monteislam.com/aktuelnosti/postavljen-kamen-temeljac-za-izgradnju-dza mije-u-selu-dobrodole, accessed 14 May 2018.
46   http://www.monteislam.com/aktuelnosti/postavljen-kamen-temeljac-internata-za-uce nice-medrese, accessed 14 May 2018.

Muslim Population: History and Demographics

The majority of Montenegrin Muslims accepted Islam during Ottoman rule, starting from the 15th century, though several earlier contacts with Arab sailors are noted in coastal areas. With the establishment of a new state after the Berlin Congress of 1878, the processes of cultural and demographic "de-Ottomanisation" took place in Montenegro as well. Historians note several cases of forced assimilation, exodus and even persecution of local Muslims during the outbreak of nationalistic movements in this period. After the Second World War, Montenegro became one of the six Federative Socialist Yugoslav republics, where the communist regime did not favour any religion in particular. However, due to economic, but also hidden political pressures, Muslims emigrated in much higher numbers than the non-Muslim population of Montenegro. The early 1990s brought the collapse of Federal Yugoslavia, followed by a damaged economy and severed relations between the different religious and ethnic groups of the region. The nationalistic political movements during these years were marked by several bitter events in the collective memory of Muslims. Montenegrin independence in 2006 symbolised a shift in the treatment of Montenegrin Muslims, but also in their self-perception, as they mostly supported independence, and thus significantly contributed to it.

Ethnically, Montenegrin Muslims self-identify themselves into several groups: Bosniaks; Albanians; ethnic "Muslims";[47] Bosnian; Bosniak-Muslims; Montenegrin-Muslims; Goran etc. The differences among some of these groups are barely visible, but a lot of confusion was created due to certain practices dominant during the communist era. Namely, the former Yugoslavia did not recognise the existence of Bosniaks as a separate ethnic group, while the notion of Muslim (with a capital "M") could also be used to refer to ethnic belonging, but only within the larger national pool of Serbs, Croats or Bosnians.

---

47   Here national identity differs from religion. In Montenegrin practice, "Muslim" (with a capital M) stands for nationality and "muslim" for religion, a relic of the Yugoslav past. The concept of "Muslim" by nationality was created in the time of Socialist Yugoslavia to refer to all Muslims, by religion, living in the federal Yugoslav republics, and at the time recognised the Serbo-Croatian language as their mother tongue.

Muslim Population	118,477 (19.11% according to the 2011 Census).
Ethnic/National Backgrounds	In terms of ethnicity,[48] Muslims self-identify as: Bosniak: 8.65% Albanian: 4.9% Muslim: 3.31% Bosnian: 0.068% Bosniak-Muslim: 0.029% Montenegrin-Muslim: 0.028% Goran:[49] 0.031% Muslim-Bosniak: 0.029% Muslim-Montenegrin: 0.041% Turkish: 0.016%.
Inner-Islamic Groups	Most Muslims of Montenegro are Sunnis who adhere to the Hanafi *madhhab*. There is no reliable data available on the existence of other groups.
Geographical Spread	The Bosniak population is mostly concentrated in the North of the country (Sandžak region), although lately Bosniaks have been migrating to the capital. The Albanians of Montenegro mostly live in the Southeastern part adjacent to Albania, and around the capital, Podgorica. Those who identify as "Muslims" by nationality are present in the Central and Southeastern parts of the country. Based on the Census of 2011, the percentage of the Muslim population in municipalities where they are the majority are: Rožaje: 94.95 % Plav: 76.64 % Ulcinj: 71.82 %.

---

[48] www.monstat.org/cg/page.php?id=534&pageid=322, accessed 23 December 2017.
[49] Gorans originate from the region of Gora, in Kosovo. They accepted Islam during Ottoman times, but preserved their mother tongue, which is very close to certain Macedonian dialects.

The municipalities where Muslims form a significant part of the population are:

Bijelo Pole: 42.64 %
Bar: 30.14 %
Berane: 27.96 %
Pljevlja: 16.37 %.

Although the headquarters of the Islamic Community in Montenegro is in the capital city, Podgorica, this municipality only has a Muslim population of 11.23%.

Number of Mosques

There are 138 mosques and four *masjids* (prayer houses) on the territory of Montenegro. The first mosque built on Montenegrin territory was the Sailors' Mosque in Ulcinj, constructed by African and Arab sailors in the 14th century. It was entirely destroyed in 1931, but its reconstruction was completed in 2012. Most of the mosques were built during Ottoman rule. In the 1980s, mosques began to be rebuilt, and 71 mosques had been renovated or newly built by 2017.

Muslim Burial Sites

Almost every municipality that is populated by Muslims has a Muslim cemetery. Exceptions are the municipalities of Budva, Herceg Novi, Kotor, and Tivat, where local Muslims are still waiting for an official permit from the municipal authorities. It is difficult to ascertain the specific number of Muslim burial places, since some municipalities have several and the place of burial is determined by membership of a particular family. The single graveyard which is officially registered as Muslim is the Cijevna Muslim cemetery in Podgorica, but it should be noted that Muslims are buried within the Podgorica City Cemetery as well.

"Chaplaincy" in State Institutions

Since 2011, an imam nominated by the *meshihat* leads the 'Id (*Bayram*) prayers in the Institution for

Execution of Criminal Sanctions (*Zavod za izvršenje krivičnih sankcija*–ZIKS), the state prison of Montenegro. After intensive negotiations between the *meshihat* of the Islamic Community and the Ministry of Justice of Montenegro, that started in November 2013, the *jum'a* prayer (Friday midday prayer) is regularly performed in the state prison.

Halal Products

There are two food companies in Montenegro that have officially acquired a halal food certificate: *Mesopromet Bijelo Polje* and Gradina Company from Rožaje. Both companies are involved in the meat production industry. The concept of halal food was for the first time officially addressed in 2012, due to the signing of the Memorandum of Understanding between the Government and the Islamic Community in Montenegro.[50] Generally, Montenegrin Muslims are quite familiar with the concept of halal food, and usually buy food from Muslims. Meat can easily be provided through individual slaughter as well.

Dress Code

The signing of the *Agreement for Regulation of Relations of Common Interests between the Government of Montenegro and the Islamic Community in Montenegro*, from 2012, enabled women to wear a head scarf in photos for personal identification documents (exposing the face is a legal requirement). The Agreement also gave women unlimited access to all levels of education, as well as employment in the private and public sector. The implementation of such rights is followed by the Mixed Committee for Tracking the Implementation of the Agreement for Regulation of Relations of Common Interests between the

---

50   Pačariz, Sabina, "Montenegro", in Jørgen S. Nielsen, Samim Akgönül, Ahmet Alibašić and Egdūnas Račius (eds.), *Yearbook of Muslims in Europe*, vol. 5 (Leiden: Brill, 2013), p. 417.

Government of Montenegro and the Islamic Community in Montenegro. Even though there are women who wear the niqab, there are no rights that guarantee their equal access to education and employment.

Places of Islamic Learning and Education

The Mehmed Fatih Madrasah in Podgorica is the main institution of Islamic education in Montenegro. The male madrasah was established in 2008, while the female branch of the madrasah was established in 2014. There are also units of this female branch in Rožaje and Ulcinj. A female branch of the Novi Pazar Madrasah of the Islamic Community in Serbia also functions in Rožaje, though its work is highly disputed by the Islamic Community in Montenegro.

Classes on Islam (known as *mekteb*) are held within some mosques and prayer houses all over the country, but they are organised on a voluntary basis and have no official status.

Muslim Media and Publications

Printed media:

– *Elif*–review of the Islamic Community in Montenegro, issued every other month
– *Ikre*–review by the students of the Mehmed Fatih Madrasah, issued twice a year
– *Forum*–review of the Forum of Bosnian Muslims, issued every month
– *Bošnjačke novine*–newspaper of the Bosniak Informative Centre, issued every month
– *Almanah*–periodical focused on preserving the cultural and historical heritage of Bosniaks/Muslims of Montenegro, issued once a year.

Radio and Television:

– *Radio Fatih*–radio station of the Islamic Community in Montenegro.

Internet media:

- Web pages of the Islamic Community in Montenegro: www.monteislam.com and www.islam.org.me
- Web page of the NGO *Horizonti*: www.horizonti.me.

Main Muslim Organisations

- Islamic Community in Montenegro (*Islamska zajednica u Crnoj Gori*, Ul. Gojka Radonjica br 54, pf 42, 81 000 Podgorica, tel.: ++382 20622408, fax: ++382 20623812, www.islam.org.me and www.monteislam.com). The Islamic Community functions through its 14 regional branches. Its main administrative body is the *meshihat* (*Mešihat Islamske zajednice*). The head of the Islamic Community is the chief mufti (*ra'is or reis*), elected every six years. The current chief mufti is Rifat Fejzić, elected for the first time in 2003 and re-elected in 2009 and 2015.
- NGO Horizonti–Centre for Cross-Cultural Understanding (*NVO Horizonti*, 81206 Tuzi bb., tel./fax: ++382 20870508, www.horizonti.me). Founded in 2007, this NGO is independent, but acts in close collaboration with the Islamic Community in Montenegro. The director of the NGO is Omer Kajoshaj, who is also the director of the Foreign Relations Office of the Islamic Community in Montenegro.

The Netherlands

Martijn de Koning[1]

Introduction

In the Netherlands, 2017 was dominated by the general elections which took place in March. With slogans such as "Islam is a threat to Dutch identity",[2] and "The Netherlands should close its borders to Islamic migrants",[3] Islam and migration were the predominant themes during debates in the run-up to the general elections.

Public Debates

After the Brexit vote in the UK and Trump's victory in the US presidential elections in 2016, there was great concern amongst candidates and electorate alike about the Dutch elections being effected by right-wing populism, something evident in the elections in France and Germany in 2017 as well. However, unexpectedly, the Freedom Party (*Partij voor de Vrijheid*–PVV), headed by Geert Wilders, did not win the election, but only came second, with the conservative liberal VVD taking first place. However, Wilders' Freedom Party did gain seats. Furthermore, a new far-right populist party entered the Dutch parliament, the Forum for Democracy (*Forum voor Democratie*), whose leader Thierry Baudet was very vocal about his fear that more migrants would lead to a "homeopathic dilution" of the Dutch population. This refers both to a dilution of Dutch identity, and a racial dilution of the majority white Dutch population.[4] After long coalition talks a new Government was formed made up of four parties: the conservative liberals (VVD), with incumbent Prime Minister Mark Rutte; the

---

1 Martijn de Koning is an anthropologist at the University of Amsterdam and at Radboud University, Nijmegen. He has been working on an on NWO funded project that examines interventions made by Muslims in public debates since 1989, and is also currently involved in a project about Muslim marriage. He maintains his own blog at: http://religionresearch.org/closer.
2 "Rode Hoed Debat", *RTL Nieuws*, 26 February 2017, https://www.rtlnieuws.nl/nieuws/laatste-videos-nieuws/hoogtepunten-rode-hoed-debat, accessed 10 May 2018.
3 https://tweedekamer2017.stemwijzer.nl, accessed 10 May 2018.
4 "Dit is de Dag", *NPO Radio 1*, 17 March 2017, https://www.nporadio1.nl/dit-is-de-dag/onderwerpen/400417-baudet-snapt-ophef-om-homeopatische-verdunning-niet, accessed 10 May 2018.

Christian-Democrats (CDA); the progressive liberals (D66); and the conservative Christians (CU).

At an election rally held in March 2014, the populist anti-Islam and anti-EU politician, Geert Wilders, spoke in a market square in The Hague and called for "fewer Moroccans" in the Netherlands. He repeated this message on the night after the local elections and, in December 2014, the Public Prosecutor announced that it would take Wilders to court for discrimination and inciting hatred.[5] In December 2016, the court found Geert Wilders not guilty of inciting hatred, stating that the language he used did not amount to a call for violence. He was, however, found guilty of inciting discrimination, as the court concluded that one of his comments had contributed to a further polarisation of Dutch society. Mutual respect was imperative in a "pluralistic" Netherlands, the judges said. "This statement [by Wilders] can be regarded as affecting the dignity of this group as a whole. It is insulting for the entire group."[6] According to the court, "freedom of speech is one of the foundations of our democratic society. But freedom of speech can be limited, for example, to protect the rights and freedoms of others, and that is what this case is about."[7] However, the court did not impose a fine (as was demanded by the Public Prosecutor), ruling that a criminal conviction was sufficient punishment for a politician in Wilders' position. Wilders' lawyer and the Public Prosecutor subsequently announced their intention to appeal the verdict, the preparations for which began in October 2017; the actual appeal is scheduled to take place in May 2018.[8]

Transnational Links

Throughout 2017, Turkish-Dutch relations have been severely strained. In the context of the debates about Dutch integration and Islam, the Turkish influence exerted on Turkish-Dutch citizens has always been a contested issue. Some political parties and opinion makers regard the influence of the Turkish

---

5 "Wilders & 'fewer Moroccans'–exposing and challenging racism in the Netherlands", *CLOSER*, 26 March 2016, https://religionresearch.org/closer/2014/03/26/wilders-less-moroccans-exposing-challenging-racism-netherlands/, accessed 18 May 2018.
6 "Discrimination & hatred?–the verdict in the second Wilders trial", *CLOSER*, 9 December 2016, https://religionresearch.org/closer/2016/12/09/discrimination-hatred-the-verdict-in-the-second-wilders-trial, accessed 10 May 2018.
7 "Discrimination & hatred?".
8 "Beslissingen Haagse hof op verzoeken regiezittingen in zaak Wilders", *Rechtspraak. nl*, 9 November 2017, https://www.rechtspraak.nl/Organisatie-en-contact/Organisatie/Gerechtshoven/Gerechtshof-Den-Haag/Nieuws/Paginas/Beslissingen-Haagse-hof-op-verzoeken-regiezittingen-in-zaak-Wilders.aspx, accessed 20 May 2018.

state and Turkish-Islamic organisations as detrimental to the integration of Turkish Muslims, while others perceive it as a buffer against radicalisation.[9] In recent years, even before the 2016 coup, the Turkish Presidency of Religious Affairs (*Diyanet İşleri Başkanlığı*, in short Diyanet) has been heavily criticised in the Netherlands for being an agent of the Turkish state, for mixing religion and politics, and for hindering the integrative process by its practice of having only Turkish-speaking imams, and by emphasising that Turkish-Dutch citizens should remain loyal to Turkey.[10]

Relations were already tense when, in July 2016, a failed coup took place in Turkey which raised this tension to new heights during the Dutch election campaign, which coincided with the Turkish referendum campaign. When the Turkish Minister of Foreign Affairs, Mevlüt Cavasoğlu, expressed a desire to visit the Netherlands (the city of Rotterdam), he was prevented from doing so by the Dutch police. The Turkish state then sent its Deputy Minister, Fatma Betül Sayan Kaya, from Germany to the Netherlands, arriving by car at the Turkish consulate in Rotterdam. There she was met by armed police and escorted back to Germany which led to violent riots across Rotterdam.[11]

Concerns have been raised about Dutch foreign fighters and their families returning to the Netherlands after the military collapse of so-called Islamic State. According to the intelligence and security service, about 50 people have already returned and pose a severe security risk.[12] One Dutch woman who travelled to Syria and Iraq while her husband allegedly fought with the so-called Islamic State group, was convicted in November 2017 of supporting terrorist acts, and was sentenced to two years' imprisonment (with a 13 month suspension).[13]

---

9   Sunier, Thijl, Heleen van der Linden and Ellen van de Bovenkamp, "The long arm of the State? Transnationalism, Islam, and nation-building: the case of Turkey and Morocco", *Contemporary Islam*, vol. 10, no. 3 (2016), pp. 401–420.

10 Sunier et al., "The long arm of the State?".

11 "Hoe de rel met Turkije in Rotterdam volledig uit de hand liep", RTL, 12 March 2017, https://www.rtlnieuws.nl/nederland/hoe-de-rel-met-turkije-in-rotterdam-volledig-uit-de-hand-liep, accessed 10 May 2018.

12 "Dreigingsbeeld Terrorisme Nederland 46", AIVD, 20 November 2017, https://www.aivd.nl/publicaties/kamerstukken/2017/11/20/dreigingsbeeld-terrorisme-nederland-46, accessed 20 May 2018.

13 Isitman, Elif, "Rechtbank: Laura Hansen ging willens en wetens naar IS", *Elsevier*, 13 November 2017, https://www.elsevierweekblad.nl/nederland/achtergrond/2017/11/twee-jaar-cel-voor-jihadbruid-laura-hansen-559093/, accessed 10 May 2018.

Law and Domestic Politics

In May 2015, the Dutch government announced a partial ban on face covering, aimed in particular at banning the wearing of the niqab (full face veil) in public areas. Violating the ban could incur a fine of up to €405. Despite legal advice to reject the ban, the Government announced that it would pursue it and, in 2016, the proposal was discussed in the *Tweede Kamer* and was accepted.[14] In 2017 the *Eerste Kamer* started its deliberations, which had been delayed by the elections and the long coalition negotiations; it is expected that the vote on the proposal will take place at some time during 2018.[15]

After the Party for Animals' (*Partij voor de Dieren*–PvdD) first proposal for a ban on the ritual slaughter of animals without prior stunning was turned down in 2012, and then the working agreement between religious organisations, the meat industry and the Government was seen by them to have failed, it announced in 2017 its intention to work on a new proposal. This proposal has not yet been presented.[16]

In July 2017 a court ruling in favour of the *Stichting Islamitisch Onderwijs* (Foundation of Islamic Education–SIO) allowed the Foundation to establish a publicly-funded Islamic secondary school in Amsterdam, the second one in the Netherlands. The Amsterdam municipality and the Ministry of Education rejected the ruling however, because one former board member of the Foundation had expressed his support for so-called Islamic State. This was a remark on Facebook which was misinterpreted, according to the board member in question.[17] Relations between the SIO and the municipality had already been strained because of problems with an Islamic secondary school in Amsterdam that had to close in 2010. The new school, Cornelis Haga Lyceum, opened its doors in September 2017. A few hours before the opening, activists from the far-right Identity Resistance group (*Identitair Verzet*) climbed onto the rooftop and displayed a banner that stated "Whoever sows Islam, reaps sharia".[18]

---

14 The Dutch parliament consists of two chambers, the *Tweede Kamer* and *Eerste Kamer*: a house of representatives and a senate.
15 "Wet gedeeltelijk verbod gezichtsbedekkende kleding", https://www.eerstekamer.nl/wetsvoorstel/34349_wet_gedeeltelijk_verbod, accessed 20 May 2018.
16 "Onverdoofd ritueel slachten", *Partij voor de Dieren*, https://www.partijvoordedieren.nl/items/onverdoofd-ritueel-slachten, accessed 20 May 2018.
17 Couzy, Michiel, and Lorianne van Gelder, "Wat weten we over het islamitische Cornelis Haga Lyceum?", *Het Parool*, 9 September 2017, https://www.parool.nl/amsterdam/wat-weten-we-over-het-islamitische-cornelis-haga-lyceum~a4515759/, accessed 10 May 2018.
18 Couzy and Gelder, "Wat weten we over het islamitische Cornelis Haga Lyceum?".

Activities and Initiatives of Main Muslim Organisations

In April 2017, Milli Görüş organisations held demonstrations in several cities, during which they distributed white roses under the slogan #hallowijzijnmoslims ("Hello We are Muslims") in order to reach out to people and improve the public image of Islam.[19]

Two anti-Islamophobia organisations *Meld Islamofobie* (Call Islamophobia) and the *Platform Islamitische Organisaties Rijnmond* (Platform for Islamic Organisations Rijnmond–SPIOR) have called for attention to be paid to rising Islamophobia and, after an attack was made on a mosque in Canada, Christian organisations in the Netherlands organised solidarity meetings with Muslim organisations and mosques.[20]

Muslim networks and organisations have been active in encouraging Muslims to vote. Small but vocal campaigns have been launched, claiming that voting is not just allowed in Islam, but imperative.[21]

In September 2017, the women's organisation *Al Nisa* celebrated its 35th anniversary, making it one of the oldest Muslim organisations in the Netherlands. The key note speaker at their gala event was Daisy Khan, director of the Women's Islamic Initiative in Spirituality and Equality (WISE) in the United States.[22]

In September 2017 police officer Sara Izat launched a campaign to have the head scarf approved as an optional part of the police uniform. Although the Dutch human rights and equal opportunities commission supported the campaign, in December the police announced that it would disregard the committee's ruling. According to the police, a neutral appearance is crucial to good

---

19 "#Hallowijzijnmoslims–Publieksactie van moslims in Europa", *CLOSER*, https://religionresearch.org/closer/2017/04/29/hallowijzijnmoslims-publieksactie-van-moslims-in-europa/, accessed 20 May 2018.

20 "Jaarrapport: Meld Islamofobie" (Annual report: Call Islamophobia), *CLOSER*, http://religionresearch.org/act/2016/04/14/jaarrapport-meld-islamofobie-toename-islamofoob-geweld-na-aanslagen-parijs-in-2015/, accessed 28 March 2018; "Onderzoeksrapport Islamofobie SPIOR" (Research report Islamophobia SPIOR), http://religionresearch.org/act/2016/05/25/spior-onderzoeksrapport-islamofobie-in-zicht/, accessed 28 March 2018.

21 "Een impressie van twee gesprekken over Nederland–Solidair met moslims en #Ikbenmoslimenikstem", *CLOSER*, 15 March 2018, http://religionresearch.org/closer/2017/03/15/een-impressie-van-twee-gesprekken-over-nederland-solidair-met-moslims-en-ikbenmoslimenikstem/, accessed 10 May 2018.

22 "Persbericht Daisy Khan op het jubileum van Al Nisa", *Al Nisa*, 18 September 2017, http://www.alnisa.nl/daisy-khan/, accessed 10 May 2018.

policing, and a head scarf is not compatible with such an appearance.[23] Sarah Izat continues to work for the police providing frontline services.

In 2017, the European Court announced that an organisation's internal rules prohibiting the visible wearing of any political, philosophical or religious sign did not constitute direct discrimination. After this, several Islamic (women's) organisations and human rights organisations asked to meet the Dutch government for a consultation about the consequences of the ruling for the Netherlands. To date this has not taken place.[24]

The as-Salaamah wal-'Adaalah (*Veiligheid en Rechtvaardigheid* / Security and Justice) Foundation has stepped up its campaign to support the Rohingya minority in Myanmar in the wake of an increasingly intense campaign waged by the Myanmar army against so-called militants. According to Zeid Ra'ad Al Hussein, United Nations High Commissioner for Human Rights, this campaign is, in fact, targeting the entire Rohingya population.[25]

Muslim Population: History and Demographics

From the 17th century onwards, small groups of Muslims have settled in the Netherlands in a number of ways.[26] Surinam (known as Dutch Guyana from 1667 to 1954) and Indonesia (known as the Dutch East-Indies from 1816 to 1949)

---

23 "Nationale Politie blijft erbij: Rotterdamse medewerker mag geen uniform dragen in combinatie met hoofddoek", *De Volkskrant*, 20 December 2017, https://www.volkskrant.nl/nieuws-achtergrond/nationale-politie-blijft-erbij-rotterdamse-medewerker-mag-geen-uniform-dragen-in-combinatie-met-hoofddoek~bocd1079/, accessed 10 May 2018.

24 "European Court on political, philosophical or religious signs and direct discrimination", *CLOSER*, 14 March 2017, https://religionresearch.org/closer/2017/03/14/european-court-on-political-philosophical-or-religious-signs-and-direct-discrimination/, accessed 10 May 2018.

25 United Nations, "Darker and more dangerous: High Commissioner updates the Human Rights Council on human rights issues in 40 countries", *Human Rights Council 36th Session. Opening Statement by Zeid Ra'ad Al Hussein, United Nations High Commissioner for Human Rights*, 11 September 2017, http://www.ohchr.org/EN/NewsEvents/Pages/DisplayNews.aspx?NewsID=22041&LangID=E, accessed 10 May 2018.

26 Wiegers, Gerard, and Mercedes Garcia-Arenal, *Samuel Pallache: Koopman, kaper en diplomaat tussen Marrakesh en Amsterdam* (*Samuel Pallache: Merchant, Pirate and Diplomat between Marrakesh and Amsterdam*) (Amsterdam: Amsterdam University Press, 2014); van Gelder, Maartje, "Tussen Noord-Afrika en de Republiek. Nederlandse bekeerlingen tot de islam in de zeventiende eeuw" (Between North-Africa and the Republic: Dutch converts to Islam in the seventeenth century), *Tijdschrift voor Geschiedenis*, vol. 126, no. 1 (2013), pp. 17–33; Kaplan, Benjamin J., *Muslims in the Dutch Golden Age: Representations and Realities of Religious Toleration* (Amsterdam: Amsterdam University Press 2007).

were Dutch colonies, and as such part of the Kingdom of the Netherlands. These colonies were populated with large numbers of Muslims, in particular in Indonesia. Muslims from Surinam, and their descendants, were often slaves, but most Muslim immigrants came to the Netherlands as contract labourers from India and Indonesia (Java). During the interwar period in the 20th century, converts and Indonesian students in the Netherlands played a significant role in establishing national and transnational networks of Muslims.[27] With the arrival of guest workers from Morocco and Turkey in the 1960s and 1970s, the hitherto small Muslim communities within the country of the Netherlands (as part of the Kingdom) grew significantly, at about the same time as Dutch society was becoming increasingly secular.

The Netherlands does not have a state religion, nor does it have a policy of officially recognising religious denominations. Muslims have the same rights as other religious groups and, if they comply with the principles applied to those groups, such as Christian Churches, they can achieve recognition of their denominational claims (although often with great difficulty).

The Netherlands does not hold a census of its population, but the Government and various academic institutions have a long tradition of accumulating statistics. Early assessments made by Statistics Netherlands have provided estimates of Muslim numbers based on ethnic origins,[28] but in 2005 and 2006 a new methodology was introduced, based upon self-identification surveys,[29] which has led to a new assessment of the numbers.

Muslim Population   The overall percentage of people in the Netherlands categorising themselves as Muslim in the surveys of Statistics Netherlands has been relatively stable in recent years: 4.5% in 2010 and 4.9% in 2014 (825,000 Muslims). Among 18–25 years old, the percentage of Muslims has risen from 6.8% in 2010 to 8.2% in 2014, and among 35–45 years old it has risen from 6.5% to 8.0%. Within the category of "non-Western"

---

[27] Ryad, Umar. "Among the believers in the land of the colonizer: Mohammed Ali van Beetem's role among the Indonesian community in the Netherlands in the interwar period", *Journal of Religion in Europe*, vol. 5, no. 2 (2012), pp. 273–310.

[28] Phalet, Karen, and Jessica Ter Wal, *Moslim in Nederland* (*Muslim in the Netherlands*) (The Hague: Sociaal en Cultureel Planbureau, 2004).

[29] Maliepaard, Mieke, and Merove Gijsberts, *Moslim in Nederland* (*Muslim in the Netherlands*) (The Hague: Sociaal en Cultureel Planbureau, 2012).

persons (meaning a person from a non-Western country, or with one parent from a non-Western country), 40% identify themselves as Muslim.[30]

Ethnic/National Backgrounds

Percentages of ethnic/national groups self-identifying as Muslim:

Turkish Dutch: 94%
Moroccan-Dutch: 97%
Afghan-Dutch: 85%
Iraqi-Dutch: 61%
Iranian-Dutch: 34%
Somali-Dutch: 93%.[31]

Inner-Islamic Groups

The Muslim population includes Sunnis, Shi'is, Alevis, and Ahmadis.

Self-identification as Sunni:
Turkish-Dutch/Moroccan-Dutch: 89%
Somali-Dutch: 81%
Afghan-Dutch: 66%
Iraqi-Dutch: 56%.

This does not mean that the other ethnic groups identify themselves as Shi'i, Alevi, or Ahmadi, since all of these groups, in particular the Turkish-Dutch, Moroccan-Dutch and Somali-Dutch, contain individuals who identify themselves only as Muslim, without mentioning a specific branch. In the Turkish-Dutch group, 7% identify themselves as Alevis. Shi'i Muslims in the Netherlands are mainly part of the Iranian diaspora (81% of the

---

30   Statistics Netherlands 2015, *Religieuze betrokkenheid van bevolkingsgroepen 2010–2014 (Religious Involvement of Groups in the Population 2010–2014)* (Den Haag: Statistics Netherlands, 2015), pp. 8–9.
31   Unless otherwise indicated, the numbers in this section are taken from Maliepaard and Gijsberts, *Moslim in Nederland*, pp. 71 and 87.

Iranian-Dutch).[32] Among Surinamese Muslims, the Ahmadi-Lahore community is well-represented (although no reliable statistics exist), and is very active with its own mosques and a national organisation. Turkish migrants are divided along other lines: the Milli Görüş movement, the Nurcus, Hizmet (Gülen), and the Sülyemanlıs, all have strong networks in Dutch society. The differences between the branches of Islam matter, but Muslims are divided predominantly along ethnic lines when it comes to representation and (mosque) organisations.

Geographical Spread — Most Muslims live in the Western part of the Netherlands, in particular in the provinces Noord-Holland, Zuid-Holland, Utrecht, and Flevoland.[33]

Number of Mosques — About 453 mosques exist in the Netherlands (ca. 100 purpose built).[34]
Turkish-Dutch:

- Diyanet: 140 mosques
- Milli Görüş: 35 mosques
- Sülyemanlıs: 38 mosques

Moroccan-Dutch mosques: 150
Surinamese-Dutch: 77

- World Islamic Mission: 25 mosques
- Ahmadiyya: 5 mosques

---

32   Hessels, Thomas, *Iraniërs in Nederland: een profiel* (*Iranians in the Netherlands: a Profile*) (The Hague: Ministerie van Binnenlandse Zaken en Koninkrijksrelaties, 2002), www.justitie.nl/images/Iraniers_in_Nederland_tcm74-38879_tcm34-18120.pdf, accessed 10 March 2009; Ghorashi, Halleh, *Ways to Survive, Battles to Win: Iranian Women Exiles in the Netherlands and the US* (Nijmegen: Katholieke Universiteit Nijmegen, 2001).
33   Statistics Netherlands 2015, *Religieuze betrokkenheid*, p. 5.
34   Allievi, Stefano, *Conflicts over Mosques in Europe: Policy Issues and Trends* (London: Alliance Publishing Trust-Network of European Foundations, 2009), p. 30.

Others (including Somali-Dutch): 62 mosques.[35]

In 1998, 9% of Moroccan-Dutch Muslims visited a mosque at least once a week; by 2011 this had increased to 33% (and among Turkish-Dutch the percentage increased from 23% to 35%).[36]

Muslim Burial Sites   In 2007, the National Organisation of Cemeteries (*Landelijke Organisatie van Begraafplaatsen*) published a handbook for Muslim burials.[37] There are more than 80 Muslim burial sites (out of a total of 3,500 in the Netherlands), all of them situated within municipal cemeteries. The first one was established in The Hague in 1932. In 2007, the city of Almere founded the first dedicated Islamic cemetery, Raza Ul Mawa. This cemetery is managed by the Foundation of Almere Muslims (*Stichting Almeerse Moslims*, Edvard Munchweg 2, 1328 MA Almere, www.alraza.nl). In 2012, a second one was established in Nuenen (Beekstraat 48a te 5673 NA, Nuenen) and, although part of a municipal burial site, it is managed by an Islamic institution: the Islamic Burial Society (*Islamitisch Begrafeniswezen Ibw*, www.stichtingibw.nl). Negotiations with local authorities for establishing more dedicated Islamic cemeteries are still ongoing.[38] Almere and Nuenen wish to maintain "eternal peace" for buried Muslims, meaning the graves will not be removed.

---

35   Douwes, Dick, Martijn de Koning and Welmoet Boender, *Nederlandse moslims: van migrant tot burger* (*Dutch Muslims: from Migrant to Citizen*) (Amsterdam: Salomé/ Amsterdam University Press, 2005).
36   Maliepaard and Gijsberts, *Moslim in Nederland*.
37   *Handboek Islamitisch Begraven* (*Handbook of Islamic Burials*), 2007, www.begraafplaats .nl/publicaties, accessed 1 May 2010.
38   Wojtkowiak, Joanna, and Gerard Wiegers, "Moslims doen het helemaal zelf: veranderende islamitische uitvaartrituelen in Nederland" (Muslims do it all themselves: changing Islamic burial rituals in the Netherlands), in Eric Venbrux, Meike Heessels and Sophie Bolt (eds.), *Rituele Creativiteit* (*Ritual Creativity*) (Zoetermeer: Meinema, 2008), pp. 31–44.

The municipal cemeteries in Utrecht and Zwolle also maintain an "eternal peace" approach for their Islamic sections.

"Chaplaincy" in State Institutions

There are Muslim chaplains (*geestelijk verzorgers*) in several hospitals, prisons, and homes for the elderly. Several universities have prayer rooms for Muslims, paid for by the universities. In 2009, the Dutch army recruited two Muslim clerics (one Moroccan-Dutch and one Turkish-Dutch) to give spiritual support to both Muslims and non-Muslims in the armed forces. They are civilian employees, but are required to wear a uniform.

Halal Products

Halal food is important for many Muslims in the Netherlands, with many eating halal food every day. This is especially true for the Moroccan-Dutch (94%), Somali-Dutch (83%) and the Turkish-Dutch (80%). The numbers are significantly lower among Iraqi-Dutch (69%), Afghani-Dutch (66%) and in particular among the Iranian-Dutch (34%).[39] Under Dutch law, animals must be rendered unconscious before slaughter, but exceptions are made for Jewish and Islamic ritual slaughter. This is opposed by some political parties and animal rights groups.

There have been attempts to produce a unified certification for halal food, but so far these have not been successful and are resulting in a lack of trust among consumers.

Almost every city with a Muslim minority has at least one or two halal butcher shops. Several of the larger supermarket chains have special shelves with halal products.

Dress Code

The Netherlands has no national or local restrictions for Muslim women's dress yet. A proposal

---

[39] Maliepaard and Gijsberts, *Moslim in Nederland*, p. 14.

for a partial ban on the face veil is still to be implemented.[40] There have been several cases of women with head scarves being discriminated against at work or when applying for a job.[41]

Places of Islamic Learning and Education

- Islamic University of Rotterdam (*Islamitische Universiteit Rotterdam*, IUR, Bergsingel 135 Rotterdam 3037, GC, www.islamicuniversity.nl). A Sunni-oriented and Süleymanlı dominated institute of higher learning. Its Islamic theology and its Islamic chaplaincy education are recognised by the Dutch Ministry of Education as higher vocational studies, and are therefore publicly funded.
- Islamic University Europe (*Islamitische Universiteit Europa*, Statenweg 200, 3033 JA Rotterdam, www.iue-edu.nl). Theological and Islamic training through private funding.
- Dar al Ilm (Paul Krugerlaan 177, 2571 HE Den Haag, info@islamstudies.nl). A privately funded Sunni institute.
- Dar al-Fahm Centre for Islamic Learning (*Dar al-Fahm Centrum voor Islamitisch Onderwijs*, Almere, www.daralfahm.nl) cooperates with Sabeel (Sabeel.org.uk) in the UK, and Muslim Youth Almere (*Moslimjongeren Almere*, MJA), among others, and is a privately funded Salafi educational initiative.
- Fahm Institute (*Fahm Instituut*, Utrecht, www.fahminstituut). Sunni oriented institute presenting itself as engaging with Islam in a critical, progressive way. It is privately funded.

---

40 "Voorstel deelverbod gezichtsbedekkende kleding", https://www.eerstekamer.nl/wetsvoorstel/34349_wet_gedeeltelijk_verbod, 10 May 2018.
41 Jung, Mariska, "Forgotten women: the impact of Islamophobia on Muslim women in the Netherlands", *ENAR*, (2016), http://www.enar-eu.org/IMG/pdf/forgotten_women_report_netherlands_-_final.pdf, accessed 10 May 2018.

- Teacher of Islam (*HBO Lerarenopleiding Islamgodsdienst*, Hogeschool Inholland, Boelelaan 1109, 1081 HV Amsterdam, tel.: ++31 204951111). Higher vocational education with public funding
- Centre for Islamic Theology (*Vrije Universiteit Amsterdam, Faculteit Godgeleerdheid*, Boelelaan 1109, 1081 HV Amsterdam, www.godgeleerdheid.vu.nl/nl/onderzoek/onderzoek-en-secties/islamitische-theologie/index.aspx). Offers Bachelor's and Master's degrees in Theology courses at the Free University of Amsterdam, with public funding
- Avicenna College (Postbus 53290, 3008 HG Rotterdam, www.avicenna-college.com). Publically funded Islamic secondary school
- Cornelius Haga Lyceum (Naritaweg 30, Bedrijventerrein Sloterdijk Amsterdam). Publically funded Islamic secondary school.
- Institute for Training and Education (*Instituut voor Opvoeding en Educatie*, IVOE, Pahud de Mortangesdreef 41 3562 AB Utrecht, www.ivoe.nl). Salafi oriented and privately funded.
- Al-Islah Institute for Training and Learning (*Al-Islah Instituut voor Opvoeding en Onderwijs*, Ampsenseweg 8, 7241 NB Lochem, www.alislah.nl). One of the oldest privately funded boarding schools for Islamic learning in the Netherlands; Sunni oriented.
- Institute Tarbiya (*Instituut Tarbiya*, Geraardsbergenstraat 14, 4821 CS, Breda, www.tarbiya.nl). Privately funded courses; Sunni oriented.
- Madrasah Darul-Erkam (www.madrasah-darulerkam.nl). Online courses and training for children and adults. Privately funded and Sunni oriented.
- Madrasah Raayatun Nabiy (Foundation Islamic Organisations The Netherlands, *Stichting Islamitische Organisatie Nederland*–StION, Postbus 63588, 2502 JN Den Haag). Privately funded, Sunni oriented, following the Hanafi *madhhab*.

THE NETHERLANDS 489

– Dar el Huda (Piet Mondriaanstraat 147, 1061 TS Amsterdam). Offers courses in the Arabic language and memorising the Qur'an.

Muslim Media and Publications

In 2016, a licence to broadcast was given to the Muslim Broadcasting Company (*MoslimOmroep–MO*) under the umbrella of the NTR. The NTR is the public broadcasting company responsible by Law for information, education, culture, youth, and diversity on radio and television. As a consequence of the licence having expired, there is no special channel for Muslims anymore (and the same goes for Jews, Buddhists, Hindus and Humanists).

There are several small-circulation magazines, such as *Al Nisa Maandblad* (Al Nisa Monthly, www.alnisa.nl), produced by the *Al Nisa* women's organisation, which also publishes *Anti Wa Anta*, a quarterly magazine for children, and *As Siraata* (for young women over 16).

Time Media Group (related to the Fethullah Gülen movement) publishes *Zaman Nederland* (www.zamanhollanda.nl), a free monthly newspaper distributed among researchers, universities, Islamic institutions, policy makers etc.

The Ahmadiyya branch has its own monthly magazine, *Al-Islaam* (www.ahmadiyya-islam.nl), and Hizb ut-Tahrir publishes *Expliciet* (www.expliciet.nl) four times a year. *The Muslim Voice International* describes itself as an independent press agency of the Muslim world, located in the Netherlands. Their main publication is *Stem van de Ummah* (Voice of the Ummah)

There are several mailing lists, discussion sites and mosque sites on the internet. One of the best known Dutch weblogs is *Wij Blijven Hier* ("We stay here", www.wijblijvenhier.nl). Since 2010, *Nieuwemoskee* (New Mosque, wwwwww.nieuwemoskee.nl) has presented itself as an Islamic platform for contemporary critical thinkers. The website focuses on encouraging debate about Islam (in the West) and engaging in dialogue with other religious and secular groups about Islam and Muslims in the Netherlands. The Muslim Newspaper (*De Moslimkrant*, www.demoslimkrant.nl) gives a voice to a variety of Muslim writers, journalists, politicians, and activists.

Main Muslim Organisations

– Muslim Contact Agency (*Contact Moslims Overheid*–CMO, Koninginnegracht 63, 2514 AG Den Haag, Postbus 85518, 2508 CE Den Haag, www.cmoweb.nl). The CMO is the national representative for mosque organisations in the Netherlands, and consists mainly of organisations representing Sunni mosques. The Muslim Contact Agency was established in 2001, but the Turkish and Moroccan Sunni groups excluded any Ahmadi organisations. CMO unites five Turkish organisations: Islamic Foundation Netherlands (*Islamitische Stichting Nederland*–ISN); the Turkish Islamic Cultural Foundation (*Turks Islamitische Culturele Federatie*–TICF); both sections of the Milli Görüş movement; and the Foundation Islamic Centre The Netherlands (*Stichting Islamitisch Centrum Nederland*–SICN). CMO also includes the Union of Moroccan Mosque Organisations The Netherlands (*Unie van Marokkaanse Moskee Organisaties Nederland*–UMMON), the Surinamese-Hindustani World Islamic Mission (WIM), and the Shi'i Association (*Overkoepelende Sjiitische Vereniging*–OSV), which is mainly Iraqi Shi'i. These organisations claim to represent 369 mainly Sunni mosques.
– Islamic Foundation The Netherlands (*Islamitische Stichting Nederland*–ISN, Javastraat 2, 2585 AM Den Haag, www.diyanet.nl). The ISN is a national organisation of Turkish-Dutch Sunni mosque groups, controlled by the Turkish state through the Diyanet. The tasks of the ISN are restricted to religious affairs only, unlike the TICF (below).
– Turkish Islamic Cultural Foundation (*Turks Islamitische Culturele Federatie*–TICF, Afrikaanderplein 40, 3072 EC Rotterdam, www.ticf.nl). The TICF is a national organisation of Turkish-Dutch Sunni groups, controlled by the Turkish state through the Diyanet, and established in opposition to the SICN (below).
– Foundation Islamic Centre The Netherlands (*Stichting Islamitisch Centrum Nederland*–SICN Süleymanlı, Van Lieflandlaan 3, 3571 AA Utrecht, jwww.sicn.nl). The SICN is the national organisation of Turkish-Dutch Süleymanlı mosques.

- Union of Moroccan Mosque Organisations The Netherlands (*Unie van Marokkaanse Moskee Organisaties Nederland*–UMMON, Weesperzijde 74, 1091 EH Amsterdam, Postbus 94384). The UMMON is the national organisation for Moroccan-Dutch mosques.
- World Islamic Mission (WIM, Iqra Moskee, Hoogoord 257, 1102 CN Amsterdam, www.wimnet.org, www.worldislamicmission.nl). The WIM is the main national organisation for Surinamese-Dutch mosques.
- Shi'i Association (*Overkoepelende Sjiitische Vereniging*–OSV, Postbus 1113, 3260 AC Oud-Beijerland, www.shiaparlement.com). The OSV is the main Shi'i organisation in the Netherlands, consisting of mostly Iraqi and Lebanese member organisations.
- Lahore Ahmadiyya Movement for the Propagation of Islam The Netherlands, (*Ahmadiyya Anjuman Isha'at-e-Islam* (*Lahore*) *Nederland*–AAII(L)N, Paul Krugerlaan 16, 2571 HK Den Haag, www.aaiiln.nl). The AAII(L)N is one of the national Ahmadiyya organisations.
- Council of Moroccan Mosques in the Netherlands, (*Raad voor Marokkaanse Moskeeën in Nederland*–RMMN, Finlandpad 2, 3402 TV IJsselstein, www.rmmn.nl). The RMMN is a national organisation for Moroccan-Dutch mosques in opposition to the UMMON, which is deemed to be close to the Moroccan government.
- Association of Imams in the Netherlands (*Vereniging voor Imams in Nederland*–VIN, Burgemeester Schneiderlaan 5, 4706 CK, Roosendaal, www.imamonline.nl). This is the national Sunni organisation for Dutch imams.
- National Platform New Muslims (*Landelijk Platform Nieuwe Moslims*–LPNM, www.facebook.com/LPNMnl). National organisation for Muslim converts.
- Al Nisa Foundation (*Stichting Al Nisa*, Postbus 9, 3500 AA Utrecht, www.alnisa.nl). The national organisation for Muslim women; consists mainly of converts and is Sunni oriented.
- Platform INS (Rochussenstraat 221, 3021 NT Rotterdam, www.platformins.nl). One of the Dutch branches of the Gülen movement.
- Platform for Islamic Organisations in Rijnmond (*Stichting Platform Islamitische Organisaties Rijnmond*, Teilingerstraat 122, 3032 AW Rotterdam, www.spior.nl).
- Islamic School Boards Association (*Islamitische Schoolbesturen Organisatie*–ISBO, Zielhorsterweg 83 3813 ZX Amersfoort, www.isbo.nl). ISBO is the national organisation for publicly funded Islamic schools.
- Halal Nutrition and Food Inspection Authority (*Halal Voeding en Voedsel*–HVV/HFFIA, Postbus 16786, 2500 BT Den Haag, www.halal.nl). One of the three main halal food certifiers, working according the rules of all four Sunni Islamic schools of law.

- Halal Correct Certification (HCC, P.B. 179, 2300 AD Leiden, www.halalcorrect.com). Halal food certifier also working according to the rules of the four Sunni schools of Islamic law, and supervised by the Islamic Board for Fatwa and Research in the Netherlands, which is part of the Islamic University of Rotterdam.
- Control Office of Halal Slaughtering/Halal Quality Control (COHS/HQC, Laan van Meerdevoort 53d, 2517 AE Den Haag, tel.: ++31 703469795, fax: ++31 703450033, www.halaloffice.com). Halal food certifier working according to the rules of the four Sunni schools of Islamic law.
- Islamic Burial Society (*Islamitisch Begrafeniswezen*–IBW, www.stichtingibw.nl). The national foundation for Islamic burial arrangements; Sunni oriented and set up by converts.
- Collective against Islamophobia and Discrimination (*Collectief tegen Islamofobie en Discriminatie*–CTID, Eerste Weteringplantsoen 2c Amsterdam, tel.: ++31 204288825, www.meldpunt-islamofobie.nl).
- Report Islamophobia (*Meld Islamofobie*, www.meldislamofobie.org, tel.: ++31 638657499).

Norway

Sindre Bangstad[1]

Introduction

2017 proved an exceptionally difficult year for established Muslim umbrella organisations in Norway. After the use of state funding to employ a niqab-wearing Norwegian-Bosnian Muslim female as a secretary, five of the largest mosque congregations in Norway finally left the *Islamsk Råd Norge* (Islamic Council of Norway–IRN) and established their own and rival umbrella organisation, *Muslimsk dialognettverk* (Muslim Dialogue Network). Expressing political dissatisfaction with the ways in which state funding, to be used for the specific purpose of furthering the IRN's work on "bridge-building and dialogue", had been allocated by the IRN's board, the Conservative Party-controlled Ministry of Culture, under Culture Minister Linda Hofstad Helleland, suspended, and later terminated, state funding for the IRN. Norway's largest meat producer NORTURA reacted by terminating its long-standing co-operation with the IRN on halal certification, thus depriving the IRN of another important source of revenue. Citing a lack of co-operation from the IRN Board and the IRN's secretary-general, the national ecumenical organisation *Samarbeidsrådet for tros- og livssynssamfunn* (The Council for Religious and Life-Stance Communities–STL) by mutual agreement suspended the IRN from its long-standing and central membership role for a period of six months.[2] After years of unresolved tensions between the leadership of the STL and the IRN, this was in effect, a *fait accompli* which neither party publicly opposes.

In other developments, anti-Muslim rhetoric continued unabated, with a national representative survey finding that no less than 34.9% of the Norwegian population in 2017 held strongly negative views of Muslims.[3] In September's parliamentary elections, the right-wing coalition Government of the Conservative Party (*Høyre*) and the populist right-wing Progress Party

---

[1] Sindre Bangstad is a social anthropologist and a research associate based at KIFO (Institute for Church, Religion and Worldview Research) in Oslo, Norway.
[2] STL was established in 1996, and since then has been a central national actor in the field of interreligious dialogue in Norway; the IRN is a central member. See: http://www.trooglivssyn.no/index.cfm?id=136722, accessed 5 February 2018.
[3] For the HL-Centre Report, see: http://www.hlsenteret.no/forskning/jodisk-historie-og-anti-semittisme/befolkningsundersokelse:-holdninger-til-joder-og-a/hl-rapport_13des-web.pdf, accessed March 8 2018.

(*Fremskrittspartiet*) was re-elected on a ticket of, *inter alia*, introducing further restrictions in Norwegian immigration policies, and increasing state surveillance of mosques and mosque congregations in Norway.[4] Reported anti-Muslim hate crimes in the Norwegian capital of Oslo continued to rise, and increasingly targeted Muslim women in the public sphere. With the support of a group of Norwegian corporate billionaires from Oslo West, far-right and anti-Muslim online media continued to expand and gain increasing traction in the Norwegian mainstream media and the public sphere.

Norwegian Salafi groupings appeared to experience not only dwindling media attention but also dwindling levels of support from Muslim youth in Norway. Though Salafi-jihadi terrorist attacks in Stockholm in neighbouring Sweden in April 2017 generated new concerns, and was predictably enough played up by both Norwegian mainstream media and prominent Norwegian terrorism researchers, the Norwegian Police Security Services (PST) continued to declare the threat from "Islamist extremists" represents the pre-eminent terror threat in Norway.[5] Yet, 2017 saw hardly any new recruitment of Norwegian "foreign fighters" to the battlefields of Syria, Iraq or Somalia.

A proposed new law on faith and life-stance communities was tabled for discussion by the Government in September 2017, and included provisions which would severely curtail the number of congregations eligible for state support in Norway.[6]

Public Debates

2017 was in all respects a challenging year for the established Muslim umbrella organisation IRN in Norway. It was in late March 2017 that Norwegian media were able to disclose that the IRN had used an additional 484,000 Norwegian kroner, provided by the Ministry of Culture (led by Linda Hofstad Helleland of the Conservative Party) in order to strengthen the IRN's work on "bridge-building and dialogue" to employ the then 32-year old Leila Hasic, from the

---

[4] https://tif.ssrc.org/2017/05/19/a-state-of-suspicion-counter-radicalization-in-norway/, accessed November 6 2017.

[5] For the PST's Annual Open Threat Assessment for 2017, see: https://www.pst.no/alle-artikler/trusselvurderinger/trusselvurdering-2017/, accessed 4 December 2017. For a critique, see: https://www.opendemocracy.net/sindre-bangstad/lessons-from-norway-s-terror-attack-that-world-failed-to-heed, accessed 15 December 2017.

[6] https://www.regjeringen.no/contentassets/3e1f412509d348f28dc19343779026b5/no/pdfs/horingsnotat-forslag-til-ny-lov-om-tros--og-livssy.pdf, accessed 15 February 2018.

Eastern Norwegian town of Sarpsborg, as a communication advisor.[7] Though the IRN's secretary-general, Mehtab Afsar, was quick to point out that Hasic would not be used as a spokesperson for the IRN, the IRN board's decision to employ the niqab-wearing Hasic, originally a refugee from Bosnia and Herzegovina, against the advice and wishes of a significant faction in the IRN board, quickly resulted in another heated Norwegian media debate. The IRN board and the IRN secretary-general found themselves facing widespread condemnation not only from Norwegian politicians and media commentators from all parts of the political spectrum, but also from within the ranks of the IRN's own board. When Norwegian media started exploring Hasic's activities in social media prior to her appointment, it quickly came to light that she had long-standing Salafi sympathies, and had engaged in and promoted anti-Semitic conspiracy theories about al-Qaida's attacks on the USA on 11 September 2001.[8] Hasic had in the past been a central member of the female-headed sub-grouping of the Norwegian Salafi organisation IslamNet,[9] known as "Sister's Corner", and had, as a student at Østfold University College, played an active role in pro-niqab activism on and off campus. She had published op-ed letters in Norwegian mainstream media arguing that the opposition to her wearing the niqab in public involved denying her the right to religious freedom, and accusing named Norwegian politicians and public intellectuals of Muslim background of "making her daily life torture."[10] It is certainly the case that Hasic, who in a prior life had even been a fashion model and was the mother of small children, had experienced racist harassment on account of her wearing the niqab. This is attested by a Norwegian court verdict from 2012 when a non-Muslim Norwegian man was sentenced for racially abusing her in a public street in her hometown of Sarpsborg.

In the course of the heated media debate over Hasic's appointment by the IRN, there were also unconfirmed allegations to the effect that Hasic had been centrally involved in organising support for a small group of Norwegian Salafi-jihadi sympathisers known as *Profetens Ummah* (The Prophet's Ummah), which in the period 2012–14 has been alleged to have been involved in the recruitment

---

[7] https://www.aftenposten.no/kultur/i/xoBdQ/Islamsk-Rad-fikk-statlig-stotte-til-bro bygging-og-dialog-Ansatte-medarbeider-med-niqab, accessed 12 September 2017.

[8] https://www.dagbladet.no/nyheter/beskrevet-som-en-sentral-person-i-det-kvinnelige-islamistmiljoet-og-spredte-konspirasjonsteorier-om-119---hun-angrer/67439339, accessed 20 September 2017.

[9] A standard reference on IslamNet in Norway is Bangstad, Sindre, and Marius Linge, "'*Da'wa* is our identity'–Salafism and Islamnet's rationales for action in a Norwegian context", *Journal of Muslims in Europe* vol. 4, no. 2 (2015), pp. 174–196.

[10] https://www.aftenposten.no/meninger/kronikk/i/onypB/Hvor-er-min-rett-til-a-prak tisere-islam, accessed 25 September 2017.

of Norwegian Muslim "foreign fighters" for ISIS and *Jabhat al-Nusra* in Syria and Iraq. As the best-selling Norwegian popular author Åsne Seierstad's 2017 book *To Søstre* (Two Sisters) documents, in the case of two young Norwegian-Somali teenage sisters who ended up as ISIS' "jihadi brides" in Raqqa, Syria, it is certainly the case that some of Hasic's fellow members in IslamNet's "Sister's Corner" turned into Salafi-jihadi sympathizers.[11] The heated media debate around Hasic's appointment led to a temporary shut-down of communication from the IRN, and in the absence of any direct comments to the media from Hasic herself, IRN's secretary-general Afsar tried to defend Hasic by arguing that she now took exception to her previous statements. However, the damage was already done, and after some initial hesitation, large congregations of Norwegian-Bosnian, Norwegian-Albanian, Norwegian-Arab and Norwegian-Pakistani Muslims in the cities of Oslo and Drammen announced their intention to withdraw from the IRN on a permanent basis. They were led by Senaid Kobilica (b. 1974), chief imam of the *Islamska Zajednica Bošnjaka u Norveškoj* (Islamic Community of Bosniaks in Norway–IZBIH), and a former secretary-general of the IRN from 2007 to 2013. Kobilica's disapproval of the leadership of the IRN under Mehtab Afsar had by then long been a matter of public record.

Among the mosque congregations which left the IRN and established the rival umbrella organisation *Muslimsk Dialognettverk* (Muslim Dialogue Network–MD) in October 2017,[12] one finds historically and numerically important and influential urban congregations in Oslo and Drammen. However, Afsar and the IRN board counted on relatively strong support from smaller, and historically less influential, mosque congregations outside of Oslo, and in the cities of Stavanger and Bergen in particular. Afsar and the IRN board's decision to appoint Hasic could also be read as a means of cementing power by reaching out to the Norwegian Salafi groupings from which Hasic originated, given IslamNet's prior history of public and vicious antagonism towards the IRN. This had, in the period 2008 to 2013, been centred on the figure of Senaid Kobilica, in his capacity as the then secretary-general of the IRN. The first chairperson of the interim board of the MD appointed in October 2017 was Kobilica.

As a direct result of the termination of state funding of the IRN, which was announced by the then Minister of Culture Linda Hofstad Helleland in the summer of 2017, the IRN lost state funding of 1.3 million Norwegian

---

11 Seierstad, Åsne, *Two Sisters: a Father, His Daughters, and Their Journey into the Syrian Jihad* (translated from the Norwegian by Sean Kinsella) (New York: Farrar, Strauss and Giroux, 2018).

12 See https://www.nrk.no/norge/oppretter-nytt-muslim-nettverk-1.13757094, accessed 10 October 2017.

kroner (NOK) (€140,000) in less than a year.[13] The Norwegian meat producer NORTURA, which controls close to 80% of the meat and poultry market in Norway, in early October announced that it would not renew its halal certification contract with the IRN when this expired at the end of 2017. NORTURA had by then co-operated as a privileged partner with the IRN since 2006. IRN's halal certification of NORTURA's products, the result of extensive co-operation between the IRN and NORTURA dating back to 2006, was formalised in 2012, and is estimated to have provided the IRN with an extra revenue of 1.4 million Norwegian kroner (NOK) (€150,000) in 2017.[14] Having contracted lawyers to represent them vis-à-vis the Ministry of Culture, the IRN submitted a formal complaint to the Ministry over the termination of state funding for its activities. The Government's termination of state funding for the IRN was upheld by the Norwegian parliament's sub-committee on Families and Culture in October 2017.[15] In December 2017, the state funding originally intended for the IRN was reallocated by the Ministry of Culture to four different religious bodies in Norway, including the newly-established Muslim Dialogue Network.[16]

As a result of all of these developments, a Norwegian Islamic landscape which has long been fractured and polarised has arguably become even more so. In the face of the shortfall of funds to run the organisation, the IRN was throughout 2017 barely able to exercise any functions as spokesperson for the wider and more general interests of practising Muslims in Norway. At the end of 2017, it also seemed clear that the rival organisation MD, with state funding of only 190,000 Norwegian kroner (NOK) (€20,000) at its disposal, and operating out of a private flat in a suburb of Oslo, had little in the way of capacity or resources to act in this role either. In a comparative perspective, the fact that Norway has since the mid-1990s a single dominant and reasonably unified Muslim umbrella organisation has made the Norwegian case somewhat exceptional. One could argue that given the long-standing fractures in the Muslim body politic in Norway, that exceptionality was bound to fall sooner or later, and that the current situation represents a realignment which brings the Norwegian case closer to the situation in other European countries, as far as their organisational landscape and infrastructure are concerned.

---

13   See: https://www.dagbladet.no/nyheter/muslimske-ledere-stotter-statens-stans-av-stotte-til-islamsk-rad/68281177, accessed 12 February 2018.
14   See: https://www.vg.no/nyheter/innenriks/i/95dmq/nortura-fornyer-ikke-kjoettavtale-med-islamsk-raad, accessed 14 February 2018.
15   See: https://www.dagbladet.no/nyheter/ga-islamsk-rad-dodsdommen---det-er-sjelden-man-blir-sa-skuffet-og-trist-over-a-ha-fatt-rett/68769175, accessed 8 December 2017.
16   See: https://www.aftenposten.no/norge/i/qnAqvm/Fire-aktorer-deler-pa-stotten-Islamsk-Rad-ble-fratatt, accessed 15 January 2018.

2017 also saw the publication of two important new books tailored to a general audience but written by young Norwegian feminists of Muslim background, both of which received much media attention. In *Skamløs (Shameless)*,[17] the feminist authors Nancy Herz, Amina Bile and Sofia N. Srour tackle the social control experienced by Muslim girls and young women growing up in Norway through a recounting of personal experiences. This book became a significant publishing success following the national and international popularity of the NRK state broadcaster's TV series *Skam (Shame)*, which provided a sympathetic and nuanced portrait of a fictional young Norwegian Muslim teenager. The Norwegian-Pakistani medical doctor and public intellectual Bushra Ishaq's *Hvem snakker for oss? Muslimer i dagens Norge–hvem er de og hva tenker de? (Who speaks for us? Muslims in Today's Norway–Who Are They and What Do They Think?)*,[18] on the other hand, adopts a much less stridently feminist tone. Ishaq's book, modelled on John L. Esposito and Dalia Moghahed's 2008 *Who Speaks for Islam?: What a Billion Muslims Really Think*,[19] outlines the findings of the largest survey ever conducted on the views and opinions of Norwegian Muslims. The book documents that Norwegian Muslims generally hold rather moderate and mainstream views on gender equality, democracy, freedom of expression and terror. The media, public and political reception of these two books in Norway in 2017, however, provided yet another vivid illustration of the extent to which Norwegian media and politics is dominated by long-standing secular feminist ideas and tropes, which revolve around the tacit exclusion of the views of a certain class of practising Muslim women.[20] Herz, Bile and Srour's book, speaking as it was to Norwegian secular feminist ideas about the struggle for women's rights and gender equality in Norway, being now primarily about "emancipating Muslim women", was widely hailed by media commentators, academics and politicians of all political stripes in Norway. This was to the extent that its authors, still in their 20s, became a regular fixture in meetings and consultations at Norwegian Conservative Prime Minister Erna Solberg's office throughout 2017, and received an honorary award from the

---

17 Herz, Nancy, Amina Bile, and Sofia N. Srour, *Skamløs* (Oslo: Gyldendal, 2017).
18 Ishaq, Bushra, *Hvem snakker for oss? Muslimer i dagens Norge–hvem er de og hva tenker de?* (Oslo: Cappelen Damm, 2017).
19 Esposito, John L. and Dalia Moghahed, *Who Speaks For Islam? What a Billion Muslims Really Think* (New York: Gallup, 2008).
20 The most detailed exploration of the exclusion of immigrant and minority, as well as working-class, women in the history of Norwegian state feminism in the past, is provided by Holst, Catherine, *Feminism, Epistemology and Morality* (Münster: VDM Verlag, 2010). For this tendency on a broader and international level, see Scott, Joan W. *Sex and Secularism* (Princeton-London: Princeton University Press, 2017).

freedom of expression foundation *Fritt Ord* in March 2017. Being highly conscientious about the perils of allowing their feminism to be appropriated for the purpose of instrumentalisation, even by Norwegian far-right and Islamophobic activists, who more often than not support the current Norwegian right-wing government, Herz, Bile and Srour spent much time and energy on distancing themselves and their project from the most overt forms of politicisation in the public sphere. Ishaq's book, which though critical of both Salafism and the notion that Saudi Arabia or Iran "represent" anything worthy of emulation for Norwegian Muslims, was widely attacked and ridiculed by groups of self-identified secular and liberal Muslims, who have long enjoyed privileged platforms in Norwegian mainstream media and privileged personal relationships with Norwegian media editors as media commentators and book reviewers. Book reviewers contrasted the two books, making their preference for Herz, Bile and Srour's book perfectly clear. The coverage and reception of these two books in Norwegian mainstream media and their instrumentalisation by Norwegian politicians, testifies to the importance of what Sara R. Farris has characterised as "femo-nationalism" in the Norwegian public and political sphere.[21]

2017 also saw the emergence of a 20-year old Norwegian poet and public intellectual of Norwegian-Somali background, namely Sumaya Jirde Ali.[22] Originally a refugee from war-torn Somalia, the multi-talented and head scarf-wearing Jirde Ali grew up in the Northern Norwegian town of Bodø. Jirde Ali occupies something of an intermediate position of articulation between Herz, Bile, Srour and Ishaq, and in her celebrated writings draws much more clearly on a specifically black American feminist tradition, combined with a clear anchoring in Islamic feminism. Jirde Ali published her first poetry collection in 2017 and became something of a fixture in Norwegian media, and received a number of awards for her writings in 2017, including the Norwegian Zola Prize for 2017. Vocal and strident in her opposition to the expanding Norwegian far-right and its Islamophobia, she opposed Norway's far-right Minister of Immigration, Sylvi Listhaug of the Progress Party in a televised debate on NRK Television.

---

21 Farris, Sara R., *In the Name of Women's Rights: the Rise of Femonationalism* (Durham-London: Duke University Press, 2017).
22 Ali, Sumaya J., *Kvinner som hater menn* (Oslo: Minotenk, 2017).

Transnational Links

Muslim organisations in Norway have for a long time been embedded in transnational networks of various kinds, indicating the presence of what John R. Bowen has referred to as a "transnational Islamic public space".[23] The importance of this has, if anything, increased in recent years, due to the ease of online communication. Islamic scholars from the Middle East, South Asia, Europe and the USA are regularly invited to Norway to present lectures and pre-prayer *khutbas*. In the case of Norwegian Salafi organisations (IslamNet), an important organisational point of reference is the Mumbai-based Islamic Research Foundation (IRF) in India, run by the Islamic televangelist Zakir Naik, and the Islamic legal reference point Islamic Scholars Online, both of whom are Saudi-based. The Sufi Minhaj-ul-Qur'an, which for a number of years has attracted a significant number of Muslim youth in Norway, regularly hosts Minhaj delegates from Pakistan. For certain sections of well-educated Muslim youth of conservative leanings, Hamza Yusuf and his Zaytuna College in the USA has in recent years become an important point of reference. In late 2014 and early 2015, the Atlanta-based Madina Institute also established a presence in Norway.

According to the most recent figures from the Norwegian Secret Police, some 90 Norwegian Muslims have travelled to Syria and/or Iraq since 2011 in order to join armed groups such as *Jabhat al-Nusra* and the so-called Islamic State of Iraq and Syria (ISIS). As ISIS lost control over much of its territory in Iraq and Syria over the course of 2017, there were no new reports of Norwegian Muslims travelling to Iraq or Syria as "foreign fighters". 40 Norwegian Muslims, who in the period 2011–15 travelled to Iraq and Syria as "foreign fighters" for ISIS or *Jabhat al-Nusra*, remain unaccounted for according to the Norwegian Secret Police, the PST.[24]

Law and Domestic Politics

The right-wing governing coalition, comprised of the Conservative Party *Høyre* and the populist right-wing Progress Party (*Fremskrittspartiet*), which first came to power in Norway in October 2013, was re-elected in the Norwegian

---

[23] Bowen, John R., "Beyond migration: Islam as a transnational public space", *Journal of Ethnic and Migration Studies*, vol. 30, no. 5 (2004), pp. 879–894.

[24] See: https://www.aftenposten.no/norge/i/owxQo/PST-frykter-fremmedkrigere-kan-komme-hjem-til-Norge, accessed 20 January 2018.

parliamentary elections of October 2017. By the end of the year 2017, a new Government had yet to be formed, since it depends on the parliamentary support of the Christian Democratic Party (KrF) and the social-liberal party *Venstre*. The Conservative Prime Minister Erna Solberg had wanted to expand her platform by drawing these parties into negotiations about forming part of the new Government. Since 2013, the Government has issued new restrictions on immigration to Norway, but these restrictions do not target Muslim immigrants in particular. It is nevertheless the case that many refugees and asylum seekers of Muslim background have been greatly affected by the Government's emphasis on meeting new and stringent deportation quotas.

For Norwegian Muslims, the most significant new legal and political initiative came in the form of a Government draft for a new law regulating state support[25] for what in Norway is known as "faith and life-stance communities".[26] As a result of long-standing Norwegian laws and legal practice dating back to the early 1980s, any faith or life-stance community in Norway is entitled to state funding in support of their activities, subject to certain legal conditions, and in proportion to their number of registered members. State support can, under Norwegian law dating from 1969, even be given to faith and life-stance communities with a single member. The newly proposed law, which was tabled for public and political interpellation and discussion by the Ministry of Culture in October 2017, indicated that the Government sees an urgent need to make oversight and control over this system of state support easier and more transparent. This support had been administered by the State's provincial bureaucrats, the *fylkesmannen*, in each of Norway's 19 provinces.

This comes as a direct result of the rapidly increasing number of faith congregations in Norway in the past few years. The number of faith congregations has risen particularly fast among Muslims in Norway, a fact which very much suggests that the, by now widespread, Norwegian notion of a "unified" Norwegian Muslim "interest", is a myth. The new proposal suggests meeting a threshold of 500 registered members of a particular faith congregation as a central criterion for state support. This threshold will have consequences for a great number of smaller Muslim faith congregations in Norway. However, this high threshold is unlikely to garner the required parliamentary support

---

25 For the Government's proposal, see: https://www.regjeringen.no/contentassets/3e1f412 509d348f28dc19343779026b5/no/pdfs/horingsnotat-forslag-til-ny-lov-om-tros--og-livssy .pdf, accessed 1 March 2018.

26 In the Norwegian context, this also includes the Norwegian Humanist Association (*Human-Etisk Forbund*–HEF) and various believers in Norse-inspired and/or New Age life-stances.

in Norway. A new threshold of 100 registered members is, however, an increasingly likely prospect.

Activities and Initiatives of Main Muslim Organisations

On an organisational level, Muslims in Norway have seen an increased internal pluralisation and polarisation in the course of the year 2017. These developments are not new, but were exacerbated by the profound and continuous crises that the main Muslim umbrella organisation, the IRN found itself in as a result of its decision to employ a niqab-wearing and Salafi-oriented administrative consultant in March 2017. As a result of these multiple crises of internal and external confidence–the cessation of state funding, the loss of revenue from halal certification, and the suspension of its long-standing membership in the ecumenical organisation STL–the Sunni-dominated IRN for all practical purposes ceased functioning as a public representative for wider Muslim interests and concerns, vis-à-vis the Norwegian public and political spheres. In the vacuum that has emerged, Norwegian Shi'i Muslims have emerged as increasingly vocal and public.[27]

Muslim Population: History and Demographics

The very first Muslims to settle in Norway were probably Pakistani Ahmadi proselytisers, who arrived in the 1940s. From the late 1960s until the introduction of legislation aimed at curbing labour migration, laid out by the Norwegian parliament in 1975, predominantly male labour migrants started arriving from Pakistan, Morocco and Turkey. They were later supplemented by family members from their countries of origin through family reunification, and refugees from countries such as Iran, Somalia, Bosnia and Herzegovina, Kosovo, Iraq and Afghanistan, from the 1980s onwards.[28]

There are no official records relating to the number of Muslims in Norway. Norwegian state bodies collect a wide array of information about the population of Norway, pertaining to education, employment, contact with health

---

27   For an excellent survey of Shi'i Muslims in Norway, see Bøe, Marianne, and Ingvild Flaskerud, "A minority in the making: the Shia Muslim community in Norway", *Journal of Muslims in Europe*, vol. 6, no. 2 (2017), pp. 179–197.

28   For further background on the history of Muslim migration to, and settlement in, Norway, see Bangstad, Sindre, *The Politics of Mediated Presence: Exploring the Voices of Muslims in Norway's Mediated Spheres* (Oslo: Scandinavian Academic Press, 2014), pp. 41–81.

services, marital status etc. Much of this information is aggregated and made available on the website of Statistics Norway (www.ssb.no). Unless indicated otherwise, all numbers and statistics here are retrieved from that site, using the latest available data. However, information about citizen's religious beliefs is not collected by the State. In order to provide an estimate of the number of Muslims in Norway, one therefore has to go via two indirect routes. The first is to base one's estimate on the number of persons of immigrant background from Muslim majority countries. Using this method, the Muslim population in Norway in 2017 amounted to ca. 263,667, making up some 5.0 % of the total population of 5.3 million. This indicator, however, excludes Norwegian converts to Islam. It will also include persons who do not necessarily self-identify as "Muslims," including immigrants from Muslim majority countries who may not be practising Muslims at all. Using this method, one probably arrives at a too high a number of persons who self-identify as Muslims. Alternatively, one may make an estimate based on membership in mosques in Norway. The State of Norway gives economic support to religious communities in proportion to the number of registered members, and there is therefore a strong impetus for mosques to enrol people as members. By 1 January 2017, there were 148,189 registered members of Norwegian mosques. This method, however, might provide a number of self-identifying Muslims that is too low. The number of persons in Norway who self-identify as Muslim may therefore fall somewhere between 148,189 and 263,667, or between 2.8% and 5% of the total population.

Muslim Population	148,189–263, 667 (2.8–5% of population in 2017).
Ethnic/National Backgrounds	The overwhelming majority of Muslims in Norway are persons of immigrant background or descent. In addition, there are an estimated 3,000 Norwegian converts to Islam.
	The largest ethnic/national groups of Muslim background (in absolute numbers–figures from 2016) are:[29] Somali: 40,100 Pakistani: 36,026 Iraqi: 31,490

---

[29] http://www.ssb.no/befolkning/artikler-og-publikasjoner/4-prosent-muslimer-i-norge, accessed 5 March 2018.

	Iranian: 20,461 Turkish: 17,870 Bosniak: 17,402 Afghan: 17,519 Kosovar: 14,959 Moroccan: 9,995 Norwegian converts to Islam (estimate): 3,000.
Inter-Islamic Groups	Figures are uncertain, but it is generally assumed that ca. 20% of Muslims in Norway are Shi'i and 80% are Sunni Muslims. There is a small Ahmadiyya community as well, estimated at 1,500 in 2010. Among Sunni Muslims, most of the mosques cater for specific ethnicities. Though there is still no academic research on the topic, there is also some evidence to suggest that the Deobandi Tablighi Jamaat (TJ) has been gaining ground in some mosques in the Oslo area in recent years.
Geographical Spread	Norway's Muslim population is largely an urban one, with the greatest concentration of Muslims found in and around the capital of Oslo, and in larger urban centres mainly in Eastern Norway, but also in Stavanger in Western Norway and Kristiansand in Southern Norway.
Number of Mosques	Up to 150.
Muslim Burial Sites	In terms of current Norwegian law and legal practice, Norwegian Muslims do not have separate burial grounds. Instead Muslims, under the *Funeral Law* (*Gravferdslova*) of 1996, last amended by the Norwegian parliament in 2010, are allocated separate plots in municipal burial grounds administered by Joint Parish Councils (*Kirkelige Fellesråd*) affiliated with the Lutheran State Church in Norway. This is a consequence of the fact that under Norwegian law only municipal burial grounds receive public funding, and that the *Funeral Law* privileges the

Lutheran State Church. There were in 2013 a total of over 2,000 burial grounds in Norway, but less than 15 of these were non-church burial grounds. To date, no separate Islamic burial grounds exist, but an estimated 50 municipal burial grounds across Norway have sections for Muslims. In May 2013, the newspaper *Aftenposten* reported an acute future lack of burial grounds for Muslims in Oslo. Muslim and inter-denominational concerns over this issue led to the establishment of a Burial Council (*Gravferdsråd*) in Oslo in November 2013, in which the Muslim umbrella organisation the Islamic Council of Norway, also takes part.[30]

"Chaplaincy" in State Institutions

Norway has not institutionalised Muslim chaplaincy in state institutions. Norway obtained its first ever salaried Muslim military chaplain in 2016, when *Hæren*, the Norwegian Armed Forces, hired both a Muslim and a Humanist chaplain. Late in 2016, the position as Muslim chaplain was given to Najeeb Naz. Naz had formerly been employed as an imam in the Sufi- and Barelwi-oriented mosque World Islamic Mission (WIM) in Oslo. Apart from this, there are no salaried Muslim chaplains employed in hospitals, prisons or other parts of the military in Norway. However, in Oslo Prison, occasional visits by volunteer imams are organised for the purpose of Friday congregational prayers and pastoral care.

Halal Products

Provision of halal-slaughtered meat has historically been quite erratic in Norway, with ethnographic research on processes of halal provision and certification, undertaken by Sindre Bangstad and

---

30 This section draws on Van den Breemer, Rosemarie, "Graveyards and secularism in Norway: in search of a fitting category", in Rosemarie van den Breemer, José Casanova and Trygve Wyller (eds.), *Secular or Sacred? The Scandinavian Case of Human Rights, Law and Public Space* (Göttingen-Bristol, Connecticut: Vandenhoeck & Ruprecht, 2013), pp. 170–96.

Ragna Lillevik.[31] This suggests that Norwegian Muslims have been forced to resort to private slaughter by tacit agreement with select Norwegian farmers; or private import from neighbouring countries such as Sweden; or to a wide range of small-scale Muslim and non-Muslim private enterprises offering "halal certification" with dubious guarantees. Securing state support for the establishment of a Muslim-controlled halal certification regime acceptable to most, if not all, Norwegian Muslims, has therefore been a crucially important priority for the Islamic Council of Norway (IRN) since the 1990s. The IRN established its own halal certification in 2012, and has a standing halal certification committee responsible for assessing halal certification applications from producers, distributors and restaurants. The establishment of the IRN's halal certification also meant that the IRN accepted submitting the slaughter of halal meat to Norwegian animal welfare regulations, which requires the animal not to be fully conscious when being slaughtered. This has caused some Muslim congregations under the IRN's own umbrella, most notably the Turkish Suleimanci-oriented *Diksin*, to opt out of the IRN's halal certification, since they consider these methods of slaughter to fail to meet standards of "proper" halal slaughter. They rely instead on the limited state import quota for halal meat, which allows for the import of a limited amount of halal products from producers in Germany and Turkey.

Upon certification from the IRN, the applicants are provided with a right to use the Islamic Council of Norway's halal certification brand in marketing. As of 1 January 2017, the IRN has certified

---

31 The research was conducted under the auspices of a Norwegian Research Council (NRC)-funded project: *Muslim Politics and the Governance of Islam* (2015–2019), co-ordinated by Olav Elgvin.

21 producers and distributors and eleven restaurants and public institutions, mostly in urban centres of Norway, as offering halal products. Among public institutions, only one hospital, namely Akershus University Hospital at Lørenskog outside Oslo, is certified by the IRN. Non-pork options are however available to prison inmates in Norwegian prisons in Oslo and the larger cities, as well as at Ullevål Sykehus in Oslo. In the provision of halal certified meat in Norway, the largest meat industry business overall in Norway, NORTURA, which has halal certified meat-producing plants in five different locations across the country, and its own halal meat brand, Alfathi, is by far the largest producer. Until the end of 2017 by virtue of its agreement with the IRN, NORTURA also paid 1% of the revenue from its sales of halal certified meat to the IRN. NORTURA's decision not to renew its halal certification contract with the IRN beyond 2017, which followed in the wake of the Ministry of Culture's termination of state funding of the IRN, has not only deprived the IRN of its most important source of revenue, but also raised the question as to which Muslim civil society actor will in the future certify products from NORTURA and other smaller meat and poultry producers' halal production lines.

Dress Code

Restrictions on forms of dress of public employees entail that female Norwegian police officers may not wear the head scarf or the niqab as part of their police uniform. Female soldiers and officers in the various branches of the Norwegian Armed Forces may however use the head scarf as part of their military uniform. In spite of various political efforts by the populist right-wing Progress Party (*Fremskrittspartiet, FrP*)–in Government since 2013–to introduce restrictions on the wearing of the head scarf for underage girls in Norwegian schools in the past decade, there are still no such restrictions on the public wearing of the head scarf in Norway. Various university colleges and high schools in the country have, however, introduced a variety of local restrictions on the wearing of the niqab. In October 2017, the then Conservative Minister of Education Torbjørn Røe Isaksen, stated in Parliament that the Government was in the process of preparing national legislation against the wearing of the niqab in Norwegian schools, university colleges and universities.[32]

There are no reliable statistics on the number of women wearing the niqab in Norway, but estimates suggest between 50–100 nationally.

Places of Islamic Learning and Education	There are at present no Islamic primary or secondary schools in Norway.
Muslim Media and Publications	Norwegian Muslims have generally not established specifically Muslim media outlets, preferring instead to express their interests and views through Norwegian mainstream media. Muslim civil society organisations do however have their own websites. The Muslim Student Society (MSS) at the University of Oslo (UiO) ran a quarterly print magazine entitled *Salam* for a number of years, but no edition of this title has appeared since the Spring of 2014. 2014 also saw the establishment of an online magazine by Muslims, entitled minareten.no.

Main Muslim Organisations

– Islamic Council of Norway (*Islamsk Råd Norge*–IRN, Storgaten 39, 5. etg. N-0184 Oslo, http://www.irn.no). An umbrella organisation for most of the Sunni mosque congregations in Norway, excluding Tablighi Jamaat (TJ) and with a very limited number of Shi'i mosque congregations as members, the Islamic Council of Norway was established in 1993. The IRN has since then been the preferred dialogue partner for various Norwegian state bodies in

---

32   See: https://www.tv2.no/nyheter/8638161/, accessed 20 November 2017.

Islamic matters. The internal structure is more or less democratic, with the members (the mosques) choosing a board and a secretary general. The secretary general is the only salaried employee at the organisation. The IRN frequently finds itself under criticism, both from media pundits and politicians (Muslim and non-Muslim alike) who perceive them as too conservative, and from conservative Muslims who perceive them as too lenient towards Norwegian mainstream society and values. The IRN experienced its most fundamental crisis of legitimacy and funding since its establishment in 1993, in 2017.

- Muslim Dialogue Network (*Muslimsk Dialognettverk*, Fougners vei 2A, 0571 Oslo). A break-away faction of the Islamic Council of Norway (IRN), established in October 2017, and led by the Norwegian-Bosniak imam of Norway, Senaid Kobilica, this group organises five large mosque congregations, including the Norwegian-Pakistani Islamic Cultural Centre (ICC) in Oslo, the Norwegian-Albanian Muslim congregation in Oslo, the Norwegian-Arab-dominated and moderate Islamist Rabita Congregation in Oslo, and the Norwegian-Bosnian IZBIH in Oslo and Drammen.
- Muslim Student Society (*Muslimsk Studentsamfunn*–MSS, Postboks 22, Blindern, 0313 Oslo, http://www.mss.no). While it has a limited membership base, the MSS has, since its establishment in 1995, nevertheless played an important role in the Islamic scene in Norway. The MSS is based at the University of Oslo, where it frequently hosts meetings and invited lectures, and has published the irregular magazine *Salam*. MSS has, by virtue of tradition and its close links with the Islamic Council of Norway, held a place on the board of the Council, and has been involved in dialogue with both government bodies and Christian and Jewish faith communities. Several of the leaders of MSS have also participated actively in public debates in Norway. MSS has thus served a role as a platform for Muslim voices engaging with the Norwegian mediated public sphere.
- Islamic Network (*IslamNet*, Postboks 38, 1469 Rasta, http://www.islamnet.no). IslamNet is the largest Muslim student and youth group in Norway, and was established by a group of engineering students at the then Oslo University College (*Høgskolen i Oslo*–HiO) in 2008. From the outset, it has had a clear Salafi orientation. IslamNet has focused on organising large conferences where they invite high-profile (and often controversial) Muslim preachers, and see their goal as reaching out to non-practising Muslims as well as to non-Muslims. They have often taken a confrontational stance towards non-Muslim and Muslim critics alike.
- *Minotenk* (*Torggata 1, 0181 Oslo*, http://www.minotenk.no). A civil society organisation and think tank, founded in 2010 by Abid Raja, a Norwegian

social-liberal politician, parliamentarian and former mosque spokesperson for the World Islamic Mission (WIM) mosque in Oslo. Norwegian converts to Islam currently play an important role in the organisation. *Minotenk* has in recent years emerged as an important interlocutor for the Government in its "counter-radicalisation" work. While not having any members in the proper sense, it is nevertheless regarded as a central Muslim voice in Norwegian media. *Minotenk* has increasingly taken a critical stand towards the Islamic Council of Norway and the institutionalised Islamic scene in Norway.

- Equality, Integration and Diversity (*Likestilling, Integrering og Mangfold*– LIM, Fredshuset Møllergata 12, 0179 Oslo, www.lim.no). LIM is a Muslim civil society organisation in Norway which was founded by persons of Muslim background in 2010. It is strongly secular in orientation, and is currently led by a Norwegian-Iranian Conservative Party politician and local councillor by the name of Mahmoud Farahmand. Often vocally opposed to, and critical of, any practising Muslim in Norway, LIM has, under the current right-wing Government, been a favoured interlocutor for government ministries.
- The Islamic Community of Bosnia and Herzegovina (*Det Islamske Felleskap Bosnia og Herzegovina*, IZBIH, Frogners vei 2A, 0571 Oslo). The most important mosque congregation for Bosnian Muslims in Norway.
- The Islamic Federation of Norway (*Det Islamske Forbundet Norge*, Rabita, Calmeyers gate 8, 0183 Oslo, http://www.rabita.no). A main mosque congregation for Arabic-speaking Sunni Muslims in Oslo, with historical links to the FIOE (Federation of Islamic Organisations in Europe).
- Islamic Cultural Centre in Norway (Det Islamske kultursenter i Norge– DIKSIN, Tordenskjoldsgate 40, 3044 Drammen). Turkish Sunni mosque congregation.
- Ahmadiyya Muslim Community Norway (Ahmadiyya Muslim Jama'at Norge, Postboks 200, Furuset, 1001 Oslo, http://www.ahmadiyya.no/).
- Islamic Cultural Centre (ICC, Tøyenbekken 24, 0188 Oslo, http://www.islamic.no/). Norway's first mosque congregation, established 1974, with the highest number of mosque congregants; dominated by Norwegian-Pakistani Sunni Muslims.

Poland

Agata S. Nalborczyk[1]

Introduction

Islam and Muslims in Poland usually do not attract much media attention. Their number is estimated at about 25,000–35,000, which represents only 0.07–0.09% of the total population of Poland. It was mostly due to the terrorist attacks carried out in Western Europe that some specific issues were discussed in the media. Similar to 2016, a growing number of anti-Muslim websites, Facebook profiles, and organisations (albeit only popular among a small number of supporters) were more active than before, and continued to attract mainstream media attention, mostly media outlets supporting the ruling party Law and Justice (*Prawo i Sprawiedliwość*). Polish Muslim Tatars, Poland's indigenous Muslim population, are not targeted in the media or experience assaults in public.

There were a few important developments with regards to the Muslim population in the country in 2017:

- Celebrations were held to commemorate 620 years of Muslim Tatar settlement in Lithuania and Poland.
- A growing number of manifestations of enmity towards Islam and Muslims were again noticeable. This included attacks on kebab shops or banners carried during the Independence March on 11 November 2017.
- To counteract these expressions of enmity, various events were organised, very often spontaneously, by Polish citizens and organisations as a way of showing support for the victims of these attacks.

---

1   Agata S. Nalborczyk, PhD, is Assistant Professor in the Department for European Islam Studies, Faculty of Oriental Studies, University of Warsaw. She has an MA in Iranian studies, Arabic and Islamic Studies, a PhD in Arabic and Islamic Studies, and a habilitation doctorate in Religious Studies–Islamic Studies. She is a member of the editorial board of the series *Annotated Legal Documents on Islam in Europe* (Leiden: Brill; first volume published in 2014) and is a member of the editorial board of the journal *Sociology of Religion*. Her research focuses on Islam in Europe (especially Poland, Central and Eastern Europe), the legal status and history of European Muslim minorities, Polish-Lithuanian Tatars, gender issues in Islam, Christian-Muslim relations, and the image of Islam and Muslims in Europe.

- Celebrations were held for the 20th anniversary of the establishment of the Common Council of Catholics and Muslims.
- A 16th century Polish translation of the Qur'an was discovered.

Public Debates

Although the refugee and migrant crisis in Europe was less felt and discussed in Poland in 2017, the number of physical assaults on people of foreign ethnic and national background rose to 947 in the first half of the year. As a comparison, in the corresponding period in 2016 such a number was 863, and in 2015 it was 848. The most frequently assaulted persons were individuals of a Muslim background; about 20% of the assaults, with 192 prosecution proceedings.[2] The first week of 2017 was already difficult in this respect; six racist attacks took place in the first four days. On New Year's Eve, one incident further escalated. In the city of Ełk, a young Pole threw a firecracker inside a kebab shop run by Arab immigrants, that caused them to run after him; one of the owners then killed him with a knife. As a result of this incident the shop was destroyed, the police arriving too late to prevent it.[3] During the following days further attacks on kebab shops run by immigrants took place in Lubin (the shop is run by a Hindu), in Wrocław (run by a Yezidi Kurd), and again on the same shop in Ełk (the police arrested 28 persons).[4] The attacks took place throughout the year and were perpetrated mainly on take away shops operated by immigrants, as well as on individuals who appeared to have a Muslim background.

It is estimated that about 60,000 people took part in the "Independence March" on 11 November 2017, organised by Polish nationalist and right-wing groups on the occasion of Independence Day. Some participants marched under the official slogan of the march "We Want God!", words from an old Polish religious song. Other demonstrators with faces covered chanted "Pure Poland, white Poland!" and "Refugees get out!" The participants also highlighted their Islamophobic leanings by carrying a banner depicting a refugee as a suicide bomber on board a Trojan horse. State broadcaster TVP, which reflects the conservative government's line, called it a "great march of patriots," and the Minister of the Interior, Mariusz Błaszczak, said "It was a beautiful sight".

---

2 http://wyborcza.pl/7,75398,22861475,coraz-wiecej-przestepstw-z-nienawisci-prokuratura-krajowa-opublikowala.html, accessed 6 May 2018.
3 http://poznan.wyborcza.pl/poznan/1,36037,21208820,demonstracja-przeciwko-rasizmowi-w-sobote-na-placu-wolnosci.html, accessed 6 May 2018.
4 http://wyborcza.pl/7,75398,21210226,w-polsce-bija-z-nienawisci-szesc-rasistowskich-atakow-w-cztery.html, accessed 6 May 2018.

Around 5,000 people attended a counter-protest organised by the anti-fascist movement, holding banners with the words "For your freedom and ours", "Women against fascism," and "Nationalism is a disease".[5]

On 27 November 2017, at night, the mosque of the *Liga Muzułmańska w Rzeczpospolitej Polskiej* (Muslim League in the Republic of Poland–LM) in Warsaw was attacked with pieces of concrete and stones; several glass panes were broken. The perpetrators were recorded by the CCTV cameras installed on the premises. The next day, a Polish flag was put behind one of the broken windows and candles were arranged in the shape of the letters OKM (*Ośrodek Kultury Muzułmańskiej*–Centre of Islamic Culture). A letter of support for the attacked mosque community was sent by the Government Plenipotentiary for Equal Treatment, Adam Lipiński, and the Minister of the Interior and Administration, Mariusz Błaszczak, expressed the hope that the perpetrators would be quickly captured. On 15 December, the police arrested the identified perpetrator, and in his flat found leaflets inciting hatred based on race and religion.[6]

As in 2016, against that backdrop, numerous meetings, seminars, and public debates were organised, with the intention of broadening public knowledge of the issues related to immigrants, their religion, and the modes of receiving and accepting those who would arrive. Some of these events were again organised spontaneously after xenophobic incidents or after attacks on people of different ethnic backgrounds. On 29 November 2017, in response to the attack on the mosque in Warsaw, a rally under the motto: "Stop racist attacks–no to Islamophobia" was organised in the square next to the Centrum metro station. It was supported, among others, by the Together Party (*Partia Razem*), the Green Party (*Zieloni*), the LGBT community, the Ocalenie Foundation (*Fundacja Ocalenie*) and other organisations working on the integration of immigrants into Polish society.[7]

At the end of June 2017, a recording of a lecture, which was given at the *Muzułmańskie Centrum Kulturalno-Oświatowe* (Muslim Cultural and Educational Centre) in Poznań, appeared on the internet. The person who made the recording suggested that it showed the Poznan imam of the LM, Youssef Chadid, calling for aggression against Poles. The film was manipulated to discredit the imam. After right-wing portals had published the manipulated

---

5 http://wyborcza.pl/7,75398,22634227,11-listopada-jeden-z-najwiekszych-marszow-niepodleglosci-w.html, accessed 17 January 2018.
6 https://warszawa.onet.pl/warszawa-policja-zatrzymala-mezczyzne-ktory-zdewastowal-osrodek-muzulmanski/b3nnb18, accessed 17 January 2018.
7 https://www.facebook.com/events/2027629694189068/, accessed 17 January 2018.

recording, the imam and his family started to receive death threats. The imam declared that he would leave Poland, where he had been living for 21 years. On 6 July 2017 hundreds of residents of Poznan gathered to show their support for him. They held a banner that read "First you must kill me!".[8]

On 5 March 5 2017, a letter on the occasion of Lent by Cardinal Kazimierz Nycz, the Archbishop of Warsaw, was read in the churches of Warsaw. It talked about humanitarian corridors.[9] According to the Cardinal, the programme is safe and Church charities and dioceses are prepared for it. Most importantly, he said, there is also a readiness to take on the subject of humanitarian corridors by local governments: "Of course, we need the openness of state authorities and we wait for it", he stressed. The Cardinal also called for an abstaining from words that incited hatred.[10]

In June 2017, the representatives of different Muslim organisations appealed to Parliament to take action in order to protect Muslims in Poland. In a letter addressed to the Speaker of the Parliament and to the Parliamentary Commission for National and Ethnic Minorities, they wrote: "Disseminated on the media, public statements that say that the Muslim community is a threat to Poland, is a manifestation of prejudices and stereotypes". The letter was signed by the heads of the Muslim League, the *Muzułmański Związek Religijny w Rzeczpospolitej Polskiej* (Muslim Religious Union in the Republic of Poland), the *Muzułmańskie Stowarzyszenie Kształtowania Kulturalnego* (Muslim Association for Cultural Formation), and the *Stowarzyszenie Studentów Muzułmańskich w Polsce* (Association of Muslim Students in Poland).[11] As a response to the letter, representatives of Muslim organisations were invited to two meetings of the Parliamentary Commission for National and Ethnic Minorities, on 14 September 2017 and 7 December 2017. The Ministry of the

---

8   https://poznan.onet.pl/poznaniacy-staneli-w-obronie-imama-ktory-dostaje-grozby-smierci-najpierw-musicie/wsqt3g5/, accessed 17 May 2018.

9   "Humanitarian corridors" refer to small groups of Syrian refugees who need the most help, i.e. victims of persecution, torture and violence, as well as families with children, elderly people, sick people, and persons with disabilities. Their stay and support in Poland was supposed to be financed by the Roman Catholic Church, mostly through Caritas Poland. A humanitarian corridor was supposed to guarantee them legal entry into Polish territory with humanitarian visas. However, the Government refused to participate in this initiative, and failed to issue humanitarian visas for the refugees selected; Nalborczyk, Agata S., "Poland", in Oliver Scharbrodt, Samim Akgönül, Ahmet Alibašić, Jørgen S. Nielsen, and Egdūnas Račius (eds.), *Yearbook of Muslims in Europe*, vol. 9 (Leiden: Brill, 2017), p. 523.

10 http://wiez.com.pl/2017/02/26/kard-nycz-jestesmy-gotowi-na-przyjecie-uchodzcow-czekamy-na-otwartosc-wladz/, accessed 7 May 2018.

11 http://bialystok.wyborcza.pl/bialystok/7,35241,22384133,polscy-muzulmanie-czuja-sie-zagrozeni-apeluja-do-polskiego.htm, accessed 7 May 2018.

Interior and Administration in response to the Commission's inquiry, stated that there were no problems in Poland with hatred based on race or religion.[12]

In 2017, the political grouping that rules Poland (mainly the party Law and Justice) denied the existence of dislike or hatred on the basis of religion, race or skin colour. The Minister of the Interior and Administration, Mariusz Błaszczak, after the series of incidents at the beginning of 2017, expressed the opinion that Poland had no hate crime problems.[13] Yet at the same time, some members of the ruling government coalition expressed Islamophobic or xenophobic opinions themselves. For example, the Minister for Refugees, Beata Kempa, stated in public, when talking about humanitarian corridors, that "Anyone who knows the rules of Islamic culture is aware that, even if we took those few children here for treatment, they would no longer have the right to return to their families, because after they were among the so-called infidels, they would no longer be accepted at home".[14] In 2017, state television and other media supporting the current Government reported false information and allegations against Muslims,[15] and persons invited to public discussions were selected because of their anti-Muslim views.[16]

Muslim organisations continued to issue statements condemning the terrorist acts in Europe. For instance, on 23 March 2017, the LM published a statement condemning the terrorist act of 22 March in London. It also expressed sympathy for the victims' families, and expressed the belief that all religions care for human life and peaceful coexistence with people of different faiths.[17] On 18 August the LM published a statement condemning the terrorist acts of 17 August in Barcelona and Cambrils, and acts of terrorism in general, as inconsistent with the teachings of Islam. It again expressed sympathy for the victims' families.[18]

---

12   http://www.sejm.gov.pl/sejm8.nsf/biuletyn.xsp?documentId=DA4DA8EE75763591C12582 09004F90B2, accessed 7 May 2018.

13   http://wyborcza.pl/7,75398,21210226,w-polsce-bija-z-nienawisci-szesc-rasistowskich-atakow-w-cztery.html/, accessed 17 May 2018.

14   https://wiadomosci.onet.pl/kraj/beata-kempa-uchodzcom-trzeba-pomagac-madrze/zrzxd3q/, accessed 17 May 2018.

15   See for example: http://wiadomosci.gazeta.pl/wiadomosci/7,114883,21314214,krzysztof-ziemiec-o-szerzeniu-nieprawdy-w-wiadomosciach-wiecej.html, accessed 6 May 2018.

16   For more details see: Piela, Anna, and Anna Łukjanowicz, "Islamophobia in Poland: national report 2017", in Enes Bayrakli and Farid Hafez (eds.), *European Islamophobia Report 2017* (Istanbul–Washington DC–Cairo: Seta, 2018), pp. 471–473.

17   http://isni.pl/oswiadczenie-ligi-muzulmanskiej-w-rp-dot-zamachu-w-londynie/, accessed 9 February 2018.

18   http://islam.info.pl/oswiadczenie-lm-w-rp-w-sprawie-zamachu-terrorystycznego-w-barcelonie/, accessed 9 February 2018.

In October 2017, the identification of a Polish translation of the Qur'an from the second half of the 16th century by a group of researchers from the Nicolaus Copernicus University in Toruń, was officially announced. However, this translation exists only in handwritten copies from the 17th–20th centuries, and is written in Polish in a specially adapted Arabic alphabet. These manuscripts were called *tefsirs* by Polish-Lithuanian Muslim Tatars, because they did not consider such translations to be the Qur'an itself; according to Islam, a *tafsir* is a commentary on the Qur'an. They are of variable quality in terms of their readability, so their transliteration into the Latin alphabet alone is an enormous task. Nevertheless, the Arabic alphabet was always a barrier that made these texts inaccessible for direct research by philologists. For this reason, specialists were unaware that the first translation of the Qur'an into a Slavonic language was made as early as the 16th century. This makes Polish the third European language that the Qur'an was translated into, after Latin and Italian. The researchers are planning to publish this translation.[19]

Transnational Links

In 2017, the Polish-Lithuanian Tatar community celebrated 620 years of Tatar settlement in Lithuania. Among several smaller events there was a large international conference on the 27 and 28 June 2017 at Vilnius University (Lithuania). On 29 and 30 June, the conference moved to the headquarters of the local Muslim religious community (MZR) in Bohoniki (Poland); the conference was organised by to the Centre for Kitab Studies at Nicolaus Copernicus University, and the University in Białystok. The title of the conference was "Tatars-Muslims in the Grand Duchy of Lithuania: Past, Present and Future", where about 30 papers were presented by academics from Poland, Lithuania, Belarus, Tatarstan, Turkey, Bulgaria, and Russia.[20]

The Polish Tatar-Muslim community maintains links with other Tatar communities across Europe, mostly with other Polish-Lithuanian Tatars in Belarus and Lithuania. The Muslim Religious Union, and its Mufti Tomasz Miskiewicz, organised, as in previous years, a trip to Belarus on 22–24 July 2017, and to Lithuania on 26 and 27 August 2017. The aim of the trip was to visit Belarus' traditional Tatar mosques in Nowogródek, Iwie, Łowczyce, and its cemeteries

---

19   http://forsal.pl/lifestyle/nauka/artykuly/1078445,badacze-z-torunia-przeklad-koranu-polskich-tatarow-byl-trzecim-na-swiecie-po-lacinskim-i-wloskim.html/, accessed 17 May 2018.

20   http://www.atsi.fsf.vu.lt/dokumentai/PROGRAMME.pdf/, accessed 17 May 2018.

in Wasiliszki, Niekraszuńce, Uzda, Ogrodniczki, Skidel, Mir, and Osmołów. In Lithuania, MZR representatives visited mosques in Niemież, Rejże, Sorok Tatary, and Kaunas.[21] On 1 December 2017, in Minsk, Tomasz Miśkiewicz, with a delegation of representatives of the MZR, participated in the celebrations for the 620th anniversary of Tatar settlement in the lands of the Grand Duchy of Lithuania; it was organised by the Mufti of Belarus, Abu Bekir Szabanowicz.[22]

An exhibition "Tradition and Contemporaneity of Tatars, Polish Muslims" was jointly organised by the Muslim Religious Union and the Polish Ministry of Foreign Affairs. The exhibition was shown from 29 November to 15 December at Bilkent University in Ankara,[23] between 9 and 14 November in Astana (Kazakhstan),[24] and between 20 and 24 November at the Hamad Bin Khalifa University in Doha (Qatar).[25]

Contacts between the MZR and Turkey were also strengthened in 2017. Over the last three years, TİKA (Turkish Cooperation and Coordination Agency) funding was used to renovate the surroundings of the mosque in Bohoniki, the funeral home, and the Tatar cemetery in Warsaw, and to rebuild the prayer house in Suchowola. Further projects are at various stages of implementation, such as the construction of a fence around the historic Tatar cemetery in Zastawek, and the renovation of the minaret in Gdańsk. Diyanet has also financed the translation and publication of six Turkish religious instruction textbooks for children; the original graphical layout has been preserved, but the translation was from Russian. Also, on the occasion of the exhibition on Tatar Muslims mentioned above, the Mufti of the MZR, Tomasz Miśkiewicz, visited the Diyanet offices in Turkey and several other institutions; on October 16 he also had a meeting with the leadership of TİKA in Bialystok in Poland.[26]

The issue of the annexation of the Crimean peninsula by Russia in March 2014, is still present in the Tatar media. Articles on Crimea and Crimean Tatars appear regularly in Tatar-Muslim journals, for example in *Przegląd Tatarski* (Tatar Review). Tatar refugees and their children have become an important element of the Polish Tatar-Muslim community, and are noticeable during religious and cultural events.

---

21   http://bibliotekatatarska.pl/?publications=przeglad-tatarski-36, accessed 6 May 2018.
22   http://mzr.pl/620-lat-osadnictwa-tatarow-uroczystosci-w-minsku/, accessed 6 May 2018.
23   http://mzr.pl/wystawa-o-tatarach-w-turcji/, accessed 6 May 2018.
24   https://www.msz.gov.pl/pl/p/astana_kz_a_pl/aktualnosci/wystawa_i_seminarium_nt__tradycji_i_wspolczesnosci_tatarow___polskich_muzulmanow/, accessed 6 May 2018.
25   http://mzr.pl/tradycja-i-wspolczesnosc-polskich-tatarow-w-katarze/, accessed 6 May 2018.
26   http://mzr.pl/spotkanie-z-kierownictwem-tika/, accessed 6 May 2018.

Law and Domestic Politics

Representatives of the Polish Muslim population met with the Ombudsman and politicians (representing the opposition) on 28 February 2017. As promised during a previous meeting with him on 21 June 2016, the Ombudsman presented a special report on hate speech towards Muslims in the Polish press.[27] During this meeting the report was discussed and Muslims complained again about intolerance and growing xenophobia, including Islamophobia. They again emphasised the major role of the media and politicians in creating a negative image of Muslims.[28]

In 2017 one of the Tatar journals, *Życie Tatarskie* (The Tatar Life), published by the *Związek Tatarów Rzeczpospolitej Polskiej* (Association of Tatars in the Republic of Poland), stopped receiving any financial support from the Government. This support had been via the Ministry of the Interior and Administration, Department of Religious Denominations and Ethnic Minorities in previous years. As a journal for an ethnic minority, however, it should continue to be financially supported, according to the *Act on Ethnic Minorities*.[29] Instead, issue number 45 (2017) was published together with the Common Council of Catholics and Muslims–on the occasion of the 20th anniversary of the Council–and was financed by the Council.

During the 18th All-Polish Congress of the MZR on 17–18 November 2012, its participants voted in favour of separating the office of the mufti from that of the chair of the Highest Muslim Board. They also decided to hold elections for a new mufti in 2013. However, this resolution taken during the Congress was at variance with the *Act of Parliament of 1936* (still in force), that states that the mufti must be simultaneously the chair of the Highest Muslim Board. As a result of action subsequently taken by the Department of Religious Affairs and Religious Minorities, the Ministry of the Interior and Administration confirmed Tomasz Miśkiewicz as the Mufti of the MZR, and also the chair of the Board. He was elected to both positions in 2004. In 2017, however, there was

---

27 "The negative portrayal of Muslims in the Polish press. an analysis of selected examples published between 2015–2016", *A Report by the Kultura Liberalna's Public Debate Observatory*, https://www.rpo.gov.pl/sites/default/files/Raport%20Negatywny%20obraz%20muzu%C5%82man%C3%B3w%20w%20polskiej%20prasie.%20Analiza%20wybranych%20przyk%C5%82ad%C3%B3w%20z%20lat%202015-2016.pdf, accessed 6 May 2018.

28 https://www.rpo.gov.pl/pl/content/mowa-nienawi%C5%9Bci-spotkanie-polityk%C3%B3w-i-przedstawicieli-%C5%9Brodowiska-muzu%C5%82ma%C5%84skiego-w-biurze-rpo, accessed 6 May 2018.

29 Information from the editor-in-chief of the journal.

another attempt to remove him from his post. Representatives of the local community in Kruszyniany, in Warsaw, and several other MZR members, organised a congress on 15 October 2016, during which they voted for the annulment of the 2004 election of Miśkiewicz, and elected a new mufti, Imam Janusz Aleksandrowicz from Kruszyniany. Information about the congress only became public in March 2017, when its participants sent letters informing the Prime Minister, the President, and the Minister of the Interior and Administration, about the election of Aleksandrowicz. On 20 July 2017, though, the Ministry of the Interior and Administration again confirmed Miśkiewicz as the Mufti of the MZR, as, according to the *Act of Parliament of 1936* (art. 4.2) the post of the mufti is for life.[30]

Activities and Initiatives of Main Muslim Organisations

Polish Islamic religious organisations, as well as cultural associations, were again very active in 2017. On 15 January 2017 members of the Muslim League (LM) in Gdańsk took part in the "Great Orchestra for Christmas Charity", an annual event to raise funds for hospital medical equipment, with the help of thousands of volunteers.[31] LM members prepared and served Syrian tea as a way of raising funds for the orchestra.[32]

From January 2017 the LM organised a series of meetings in Warsaw entitled "Others but the Same"; the first meeting discussed charity. Beside such meetings there was also blood donations for civilians in Aleppo.[33] On the occasion of the 700th anniversary of the establishment of the city of Lublin in 2017, the Lublin branch of the LM organised a series of lectures and debates on Islam entitled "700 Questions about Islam".[34]

On 26 January 2017, Mufti Tomasz Miśkiewicz and delegates of the *Muzułmańska Gmina Wyznaniowa* (Muslim Religious Community–MZR) in Białystok, were among the representatives of religious communities met by the Polish president during the traditional New Year reception at the presidential

---

30 http://mzr.pl/oswiadczenie-w-sprawie-janusza-aleksandrowicza/, accessed 6 May 2018.
31 In 2017 the orchestra collected almost 105.6 million PLN, which amounts to €25 million.
32 https://www.facebook.com/pg/Liga-Muzu%C5%82ma%C5%84ska-w-RP-Oddzia%C5% 82-Pomorski-681502515303524/photos/?tab=album&album_id=1220060574781046, accessed 6 May 2018.
33 http://islam.info.pl/zapraszamy-na-pierwsze-spotkanie-z-cyklu-inni-ale-tacy-sami/, accessed 6 May 2018.
34 http://islam.info.pl/700-pytan-o-islam-cykl-debat-o-islamie/, accessed 6 May 2018.

palace. The Mufti was among the religious leaders asked to deliver a speech on that occasion.[35]

After three years of reconstruction, the local MZR prayer house, the Tatar Cultural Centre of Islam in Suchowola, was opened on 13 May 2017. The reconstruction was financed by TİKA. The building was also reconstructed on the outside; a small tower with a dome was added. The opening ceremony was attended by the MZR authorities, local MZR communities, the Mufti of Lithuania, representatives of the State and of local government authorities, the embassies of Turkey and Saudi Arabia, as well as the delegate of TİKA.[36]

The Associations of Tatars in the Republic of Poland organised the Fifth Festival of Tatar Culture in the Białystok Rural Museum on 29–30 July 2017. The programme of the festival included performances by the Tatar dance group *Buńczuk* and the Chechen *Lovzar* group, as well as tastings of Tatar food.[37]

On 20 August 2017, the eleventh *sabantuj* in Kruszyniany was held. *Sabantuj* is a rural Tatar festival; the name itself means the feast of the plough, and the holiday is a combination of rural celebrations, dancing, and singing. The event was organised by the Tatar Yurt restaurant–owned by Dżenneta Bogdanowicz, a prominent person involved in promoting Tatar culture–and the *Muzułmańska Gmina Wyznaniowa* (Muslim Religious Community) in Kruszyniany. There was a tasting of Tatar dishes, cooking contests, archery, Turkish wrestling, falconry and historical weapon shows. A reconstruction of the Battle of Parkany of 1683–during which a Tatar, Samuel Krzeczowski, was supposed to have saved the life of the Polish king, John III Sobieski, the victor from Vienna–took place at the end of the event. Tatar dance groups performed on stage, including the Polish *Buńczuk*, as well as dance groups from Tatarstan, Belarus, Lithuania, and Ukraine.[38]

The 19th Summer Academy of Polish Tatar Lore (*XIX Letnia Akademia Wiedzy o Tatarach Polskich*) organised by the Association of Tatars in the Republic of Poland (ZTRP) took place on 19 August 2017 in the Białystok Rural Museum. The title of this year's academy was: "Identity and Religion of the Tatars of the

---

35 http://www.prezydent.pl/aktualnosci/wypowiedzi-prezydenta-rp/wystapienia/art,150,noworoczne-spotkanie-miedzyreligijne-w-palacu-prezydenckim.html/, accessed 6 May 2018.
36 http://mzr.pl/uroczyste-otwarcie-tatarskiego-centrum-kultury-islamu-w-suchowoli-2/, accessed 6 May 2018.
37 http://ztrp.pl/v-festiwal-kultury-tatarskiej-program/, accessed 17 April 2018.
38 https://isokolka.eu/krynki/21563-sabantuj-2017-tatarskie-swieto-w-kruszynianach-wideo-foto, accessed 5 March 2017.

Grand Duchy of Lithuania: The 620th Anniversary of Tatar Settlement in the Grand Duchy of Lithuania".[39]

On 11 November 2017, the local Muslim Religious Community in Białystok (MZR) organised a prayer for the welfare of the home country in the MZR prayer hall, as part of the celebrations for Independence Day.[40] This is a continuation of the pre-war tradition, when such prayers were required by the *Act of Parliament of 1936*. In connection with the Independence Day celebrations, a singing of patriotic songs and a lecture were organised as part of the Muslim religion class at the MZR in Białystok, in the primary school where Muslim religion education is provided. On the same day, the MZR Mufti, Tomasz Miśkiewicz, participated in the main state celebrations of Independence Day in Warsaw.[41]

Dances, organised during Muslim holidays, are a traditional part of Polish Tatar cultural life, and are called "Tartar balls". On 25 June 2017, a ball was held on the first day of Ramadan Bayram ('Id al-Fitr). Representatives of the Tatar community gathered at a local restaurant and danced to music typically played at Polish functions, i.e. world evergreen songs, traditional Polish melodies, as well as Tatar music. They were also served traditional Tatar dishes. As usual, the event was financed by the Ministry of the Interior and Administration.[42]

Interreligious encounters, both those organised by Muslims and those to which Muslims were invited, were held in various locations in Poland. On 26 January 2017, the 17th Day of Islam, organised by the Roman Catholic Church in Poland, was celebrated in several Polish cities. The introduction of the Day of Islam, which is celebrated every year on 26 January, is one of the main achievements of the Common Council of Catholics and Muslims (*Rada Wspólna Katolików i Muzułmanów*, est. 1997).[43] The Day of Islam is incorporated into the Roman Catholic Church's calendar of events, and every year its subject is taken from the "Message for the End of Ramadan", issued by the Pontifical Council for Interreligious Dialogue. The subject in 2017 was: "Christians and

---

39   http://ztrp.pl/tozsamosc-a-religia-tatarow-wielkiego-ksiestwa-litewskiego/, accessed 15 April 2018. The local action group *Szlak Tatarski* (Tatar Trail), that was a co-organiser of previous academies, in 2017 organised its own 19th Summer Academy of Polish Tatar Lore on 1 July 2017 in Bohoniki. This was not an academic event, however. It was organised without Artur Konopacki, who organised the academic event mentioned above.

40   http://ztrp.pl/tozsamosc-a-religia-tatarow-wielkiego-ksiestwa-litewskiego/, accessed 24 June 2018; https://bialystok.onet.pl/swieto-niepodleglosci-muzulmanie-modlili-sie-za-ojczyzne/bzzpwzj, accessed 10 May 2018.

41   https://bialystok.onet.pl/swieto-niepodleglosci-muzulmanie-modlili-sie-za-ojczyzne/bzzpwzj, accessed 10 May 2018.

42   http://mzr.pl/bal-tatarski-2017/, accessed 5 May 2018.

43   http://www.radawspolna.pl/, accessed 7 April 2018.

Muslims: Beneficiaries and Instruments of Divine Mercy". In 2017, the main celebration was held for the first time in Białystok, the seat of Bishop Henryk Ciereszko, the new delegate for dialogue between Catholics and Muslims of the Polish Bishops' Conference, and the president of the Committee for Dialogue with Non-Christian Religions. Local celebrations were also held in Kraków, Katowice, and, for the first time, in Płock. Muslims were invited as guests and as participants, delivering speeches, reciting the Qur'an, and praying.[44]

The fifth Day of Christianity among Polish Muslims was held on 25 May 2017 at the *Centrum Kultury i Dialogu Doha* (Centre for Culture and Dialogue Doha) in Katowice, and was organised by the local branch of the Muslim League. The main theme focused on Mary and her role in the Bible. Representatives of the city authorities, Christian clergy, the local Jewish community, and the Common Council of Catholic and Muslims took part in the meeting. The Day of Christianity is organised as a response to the Day of Islam, organised by the Roman Catholic Church in Poland, but the event is much smaller, announced only locally, and it is not open to the public. Its aim is to acquaint Polish Muslims from the LM with Christianity.[45]

On 30 June 2017, the MZR organised the "Prayer for Peace and Justice in the World" event, held in Bohoniki. Such prayers had been organised previously, but there was a one year gap last year, and in 2017 the event was much smaller. Representatives from the local government and administration, clergy of various Churches, members of the Common Council of Catholics and Muslims, and representatives of the diplomatic corps of Muslim majority countries, were invited.[46]

Christians and Muslims also took part in a "world peace meditation". The six-day meditation took place between 17 and 23 July 2017 in Karczówka, in Kielce. It was organised by the Institute for Meeting and Dialogue (which is affiliated with the Jan Karski Association) and by the School of Sufi Teaching.[47] The meditation and prayers were led by the Catholic priest Jacek Prusak SJ and Sheikh Hazrat Hamid Hasan.[48]

---

44 http://www.radawspolna.pl/index_XVII_DzIsl.html, accessed 7 April 2018.
45 http://islam.info.pl/v-dzien-chrzescijanstwa-wsrod-muzulmanow/, accessed 7 April 2018. On 4 May 2017 there was also a Day of Judaism among Polish Muslims, organised in the same Islamic centre; the title of the event was "People of the Book, Messengers of God": http://islam.info.pl/i-dzien-judaizmu-wsrod-muzulmanow/, accessed 7 April 2018.
46 http://mzr.pl/modlitwa-o-pokoj-i-sprawiedliwosc-na-swiecie/, accessed 5 May 2018.
47 The School of Sufi Teaching in Poland was established in 1996 by Andrzej Ahmed Saramowicz, a student of the Sheikh Hazrat Azad Rasool. The School is the first Islamic Sufi *tariqa* in Poland, and offers the teaching and practices of the Nakshbandiyya-Mujaddidiyya. It is connected to the Polish Sufi Jalaleddin Rumi Foundation.
48 Information from one of the organisers.

Muslim Population: History and Demographics

The presence of Muslims in Poland goes back to the turn of the 14th/15th centuries when some Tatars (prisoners of war and refugees from the Golden Horde[49]) were settled in the Grand Duchy of Lithuania.[50] By the 16th century, they had lost their mother tongue but retained their religion and customs.[51] In the second part of the 17th century, a wave of Tatar settlers was given land in Podlachia (Polish Podlasie, present day Northeast Poland).[52] When the Polish state regained independence after World War I, only 19 Muslim religious communities, with their mosques and cemeteries, remained within its new borders. After World War II and the movement of the Polish border westwards, only a tiny part (about 10%) of the territories settled by Tatars remained within the new Polish state. Post-war migrations dispersed Tatars, resulting in small communities living in Gdańsk, Gorzów Wielkopolski, Szczecin, and Wrocław, places far from their original settlements in the Białystok district (in the Northeast of the country) and Warsaw.

Muslim foreign students began arriving in Poland in the 1970s. Some of them married locally and settled. After the democratic reforms of the late 1980s, they were joined by Muslim refugees, traders, and professionals from the Arab Middle East and Turkey. These people have primarily come from Arab countries (Iraq, Palestine, Syria, and Yemen) and the Balkans, and live mainly in university cities (Warsaw, Gdańsk, Lublin, Wrocław, Bydgoszcz, Kraków, Poznań, Opole, Łódź, and Rzeszów). The refugee population is mainly from Chechnya,[53] Afghanistan, and Iraq.[54]

---

49   Borawski, Piotr, and Aleksander Dubiński, *Tatarzy polscy: dzieje, obrzędy, legendy, tradycje* (*Polish Tatars: History, Rituals, Legends, Traditions*) (Warsaw: Iskry, 1986), p. 15.
50   At that time a shared monarchy with Poland, later forming the Kingdom of Two Nations. See Tyszkiewicz, Jan, *Z historii Tatarów polskich, 1794–1944* (*A History of the Polish Tatars, 1794–1944*) (Pułtusk: Wyższa Szkoła Humanistyczna, 2002), p. 15.
51   Borawski, Piotr, *Tatarzy w dawnej Rzeczpospolitej* (*Tatars in the Erstwhile Commonwealth* [of Poland and Lithuania]) (Warsaw: LSW, 1986), pp. 199–202.
52   Sobczak, Jacek, *Położenie prawne ludności tatarskiej w Wielkim Księstwie Litewskim* (*The Legal Position of the Tatar Population in the Grand Dutchy of Lithuania*) (Warsaw-Poznań: PWN, 1984), pp. 34–38.
53   For more details see Łukasiewicz, Karolina, "Strategies of reconstructing Islam in exile: a case of Chechens in Poland", in Katarzyna Górak-Sosnowska (ed.), *Muslims in Eastern Europe: Widening the European Discourse on Islam* (Warsaw: University of Warsaw, 2011), pp. 88–107.
54   Settlers, contractors, and refugees are categorised according to their former/present citizenship, not their religious affiliation.

There is no official data on the total number of Muslims in the country, since the Constitution (section 7, article 53) rules out asking a question about religious affiliation in the census. Therefore, the Polish national population census does not include a question about religion, and it is necessary to rely on estimates, which differ depending on the source.[55]

Muslim Population	The number of Muslims in Poland is estimated at 25,000–35,000, which represents 0.07–0.09% of the total population of Poland.
Ethnic/National Backgrounds	The overwhelming majority of Muslims in Poland are Polish citizens, excluding refugees (who are mostly from Chechnya), or Turkish business persons.
	Largest ethnic/national groups: Tatar: approx. 5,000 Others: Arabs, Turks, Bosniaks, Chechens, and Polish converts.
Inner-Islamic Groups	No data on Muslim groups is available. Polish Tatars are traditionally Sunni, and so are most of the Muslims from immigrant backgrounds. However, there are also several dozen Shi'i Polish converts and refugees from Iran.
	Some adherents of Fethullah Gülen's Hizmet movement are also present in the country, however their numbers (mostly consisting of Turkish citizens) are not known, but the community has grown in 2017 due to the political situation in Turkey. They have established a local religious community in Warsaw as part of the MZR organisation. There is also a small group of adherents of the Ahmadiyya Muslim community.

---

55   The sources are: numbers of members given by Islamic religious organisations; numbers of Polish citizens with immigrant backgrounds from Muslim majority countries; numbers of foreign citizens coming from Muslim majority countries; and data from the Central Statistical Office of Poland. Islamic religious organisations usually give the highest estimates.

Geographical Spread	It is estimated that 11,000 Polish Muslims live in Warsaw, the capital city. Traditional Muslim Tatar settlements are in the Northeastern part of Poland, in Białystok and its surroundings. Other concentrations of Muslims, mostly of immigrant origin, are in larger cities like Kraków, Katowice, Gdańsk, Poznań, Lublin, etc.
Number of Mosques	There are four purpose-built mosques. Three belong to the MZR, and are in Bohoniki and Kruszyniany in Northeastern Poland, and date from the 18th–19th centuries. The other MZR mosque is in Gdańsk, and opened in 1990. The LM opened a new mosque in Warsaw in 2015.
	There are Islamic centres in Białystok, Warsaw, Gdańsk, Lublin, Wrocław, Poznań, Katowice, and Cracow.[56] There are prayer houses in Warsaw, Raszyn, Białystok, and Suchowola,[57] but the total number of them is not known.
Muslim Burial Sites	Three Muslim cemeteries are currently in use: in Bohoniki, established in the second half of the 18th century; in Kruszyniany, established in the 17th/18th century; and in Tatarska Street, Warsaw, opened in 1868. Separate sections are reserved for Muslims in communal cemeteries in Gdańsk, Wroclaw, and Poznań.
"Chaplaincy" in State Institutions	Particular laws, regulating the organisation of public institutions, make it possible to establish an organised ministry, including a Muslim ministry. The *Act of 1936 on Relations Between the State and the Muslim Religious Union*, Art. 22, makes it possible to establish a Muslim ministry in the Polish Army "as needed". Its structure would be regulated by special laws issued by the Minister of National Defence.

---

56 islam-bialystok.dzs.pl/indeks/liga-muzulmanska-w-rp/, accessed 17 April 2018.
57 mzr.pl/gminy-mzr-w-rp/, accessed 17 April 2018.

Currently, however, there are no Muslim chaplains permanently employed in Polish public institutions. This is due to the fact that the numbers of Muslims are small, and so their needs can be met informally through the community.

Halal Products   Before the legal disputes concerning Islamic slaughter,[58] halal meat was mainly imported. Only a few shops and some restaurants with Middle Eastern cuisine offered, and still offer it, in the country. None of the Muslim religious organisations give the addresses of shops or restaurants which offer halal food. Some, however, can be found on internet fora, where Muslims exchange opinions and give advice. Apparently in some cities where Muslims live, frozen halal chicken meat and beef from farms in the city environs can be occasionally obtained at the local Muslim centre.

Dress Code   There are no formal limitations in the Polish legal system regarding Muslim dress. Wearing religious clothing is treated as a way of manifesting one's faith, and as such the freedom to do it is guaranteed by Article 53, Section 2 of the Constitution of the Republic of Poland. Muslim dress is not prohibited directly even in the case of state employees, e.g. teachers or civil servants.

---

58   For more details see Nalborczyk, Agata S., and Stanisław Grodź, "Poland", in Jørgen S. Nielsen, Samim Akgönül, Ahmet Alibašić and Egdūnas Račius (eds.), *Yearbook of Muslims in Europe*, vol. 6 (Leiden: Brill, 2014), p. 481, and Nalborczyk, Agata S., "Poland", in Oliver Scharbrodt, Samim Akgönül, Ahmet Alibašić, Jørgen S. Nielsen, and Egdūnas Račius (eds.), *Yearbook of Muslims in Europe*, vol. 7 (Leiden: Brill, 2015), p. 455.

Places of Islamic Learning and Education

The MZR, as a religious organisation operating under an act of Parliament, has the right to teach religion in public schools, and its teachers are paid by the State (in Białystok there is an inter-school class). In Warsaw, the LM also runs an inter-school group (in a public school) for Muslim religious instruction, at the primary school level, for pupils from the Mazowsze district in Warsaw.

In other parts of the country, religious education for Muslim children is provided by local Muslim communities independently of the school system, via weekend classes.

Muslim Media and Publications

Muslim periodicals cover various aspects of Muslim culture and religious matters. The MZR started a new webpage dedicated to the periodicals and books they have published: *Biblioteka Tatarska*, www.bibliotekatatarska.pl/. Many issues can be downloaded as PDFs.

The most important journals include:
- The quarterly *Przegląd Tatarski* (Tatar Review), published by the MZR. Four issues were published in 2017 (accessible on the webpage *Biblioteka Tatarska* (Tatar Library), www.bibliotekatatarska.pl/przeglad-tatarski/).
- *As-Salam* (www.as-salam.pl), published by the LM, with no issues in 2017.
- *Życie Tatarskie* (Tatar Life), an academic journal published by the Association of Tatars in the Republic of Poland, with one issue in 2017 (www.zycietatarskie.pl).
- *Rocznik Tatarów Polskich* (Yearbook of Polish Tatars), published by the MZR, one issue (series 2, issue 4) published in 2017, and accessible on the webpage *Biblioteka Tatarska*, bibliotekatatarska.pl/rocznik-tatarow-polskich/).

Main Muslim Organisations[59]

1. Denominational Organisations (*związki wyznaniowe*):[60]

- Muslim Religious Union in the Republic of Poland (*Muzułmański Związek Religijny w Rzeczypospolitej Polskiej*–MZR, 15–052 Białystok, ul. Piastowska 13F, 42; tel.: ++48 857324023, www.mzr.pl). This is a Sunni organisation, established in 1925, functioning on the basis of the *Act of Parliament of 1936*. The Mufti of the Republic of Poland and chair of the Highest Muslim Board of the Muslim Religious Union in Poland, is Tomasz Miśkiewicz. Some local MZR communities run their own websites or Facebook profiles (e.g. Kruszyniany: www.kruszyniany.com.pl; Gdańsk: www.meczetgdansk.com; Białystok: Facebook profile–*Muzułmańska Gmina Wyznaniowa w Białymstoku*).
- Muslim League in the Republic of Poland (*Liga Muzułmańska w Rzeczypospolitej Polskiej*–LM, 01–046 Warszawa, ul. Niska 25/43, www.islam.info.pl). A Sunni organisation established in 2001 and registered in 2004. The chairman of the General Council is Youssef Chadid (elected 2016), and the Mufti of the LM is Nidal Abu Tabaq. Some local LM communities run their own websites or Facebook profiles (e.g. Białystok: www.islam-bialystok.dzs.pl; Katowice: www.islam-katowice.pl; Poznań: www.islam.poznan.pl, www.facebook.com/MCKO.Poznan/; Gdańsk: www.facebook.com/Liga-Muzułmańska-w-RP-Oddział-Pomorski-681502515303524/; Warsaw: www.okmwarszawa.pl, www.facebook.com/okmwarszawa/).
- Muslim Unity Society (*Stowarzyszenie Jedności Muzulmańskiej*, 02–679 Warsaw, ul. Pieńkowskiego 4/91, www.shiapoland.com, www.al-islam.org.pl, www.facebook.com/shiapoland/). Shi'i organisation, registered in 1990.

---

59 Depending on the type of registration, these organisations can be divided into: denominational organisations; associations; and foundations. For more details see Nalborczyk, Agata S., and Monika Ryszewska, "Islamic organizations in Poland: from monopoly to pluralism", in Matthias Kortmann and Kerstin Rosenow-Williams (eds.), *Islamic Organizations in Europe and the USA: a Multidisciplinary Perspective* (Basingstoke–New York: Palgrave Macmillan, 2013), pp. 16–21.

60 Denominational organisations function within the legal framework of Church–State relations in Poland. There are two categories of denominational organisation in Poland: 1) organisations operating on the basis of separate acts and agreements with the Government; and 2) organisations entered into the register of Churches and other religious communities functioning under the *Act of 17 May 1989 on the Guarantees of Freedom of Conscience and Religion*.

- Ahl-ul-Bayt Islamic Assembly (*Islamskie Zgromadzenie Ahl-ul-Bayt*, 05–840 Brwinów, Moszna 4a, skr.poczt.108, 05–800 Pruszków, www.abia.pl). Shi'i organisation established in 1979 and registered in 1990.
- Ahmadiyya Muslim Association (*Stowarzyszenie Muzulmańskie Ahmadiyya*, ul. Dymna 17, 02–411 Warszawa, www.alislam.pl). Registered in 1990.

2. Muslim Associations:[61]

- Association of Muslim Students in Poland (*Stowarzyszenie Studentów Muzulmańskich w Polsce*, ul. Hetmańska 63, 15–727 Białystok, www.facebook.com/ssm.poland/).
- Muslim Association for Cultural Formation (*Muzułmańskie Stowarzyszenie Ksztaltowania Kulturalnego*, ul. Kolejowa 15, skr.poczt.109, Białystok).
- Association of Tatars in the Republic of Poland (*Związek Tatarów Rzeczpospolitej Polskiej*, Bohoniki 23, 16–100 Sokólka, ztrp.pl, www.facebook.com/ZwiazekTatarowRP/).
- Institute for the Study of Islam (*Instytut Studiów nad Islamem*, al. Kasprowicza 24; 51–137 Wrocław; isni.pl, www.facebook.com/InstytutStudiaIslam/).

3. Islamic Foundations:[62]

- Danube Dialogue Institute (Dunaj Instytut Dialogu–DID, ul. Wiejska 18/7a, 00–490 Warsaw, www.dialoginstytut.pl/). Affiliated to Fethullah Gülen's Hizmet movement.
- Polish Sufi Jalaleddin Rumi Foundation (*Polska Fundacja Sufich im. Dżelaladdina Rumiego*, ul. Pogodna 5, 05–502 Wólka Kozodawska/Piaseczno, www.facebook.com/FundacjaSufich/).
- Tatar Cultural Society Foundation (*Fundacja Tatarskie Towarzystwo Kulturalne*, ul. Stoczni Gdańskiej 76, 15–571 Białystok, www.fttk.org, www.facebook.com/fttk.org/).

---

61 Polish citizens and people with a residence permit are free to establish their associations in line with the general regulations of the *8 March 1989 Act on Associations*. To become a legal entity, an association must be entered into the National Court Register. An association does not function within the legal framework of Church-State relations in Poland.

62 Foundations in Poland may be established on the basis of the provisions of the *Act of 6 April 1984 on Foundations*. To become a legal entity, a foundation must be entered into the National Court Register. A foundation does not function within the legal framework of Church-State relations in Poland.

Portugal

José Mapril[1], Pedro Soares[2] and Laura Almodovar[3]

Introduction

In 2017, public debates that discussed Portuguese Muslims were related to Islamophobia in the country, international political events, interfaith activities, and the creation of a purpose-built mosque in Lisbon. The social, religious, and demographic complexities of Portuguese Muslims were also looked at, as well as questions of citizenship and belonging. Throughout 2017, several activities were organised by Islamic institutions, some associated with the Islamic calendar and others for charitable purposes.

---

1 José Mapril is Assistant Professor at the Department of Anthropology of the New University of Lisbon and a researcher at CRIA (Centre for Research in Anthropology). He finished his PhD in Anthropology at the Institute of Social Sciences, University of Lisbon, in 2008, with a thesis on transnationalism and Islam among Bangladeshis in Lisbon. In recent years, he has worked on Islamic education in Portugal and is currently beginning a new research project on remigration and expectations about the future among Portuguese-Bangladeshis. He is the author of *Transnacionalismo e Islão: uma etnografia entre Portugal e o Bangladesh* (Lisbon: ICS, 2012); "The patron and the madman: migration, success and the (in)visibility of failure among Bangladeshis in Portugal", *Social Anthropology*, vol. 19, no. 3 (2011), pp. 288–296; and "'Aren't you looking for citizenship in the wrong place?'. Islamic education, secularities, and the Portuguese Muslim", *Religion and Society: Advances in Research*, vol. 5, no. 1 (2014), pp. 65–82.
2 Pedro Pestana Soares is a doctoral student in Anthropology at the New University of Lisbon, where he researches Sufi-inspired Islamic movements in the outskirts of Lisbon. In 2016, he completed his Masters in Anthropology at ISCTE-IUL, with an ethnography of Angolan Catholic missions that host children accused of witchcraft. Previously, as a member of Númena–Research Centre in Social Sciences and Humanities, he worked on minority religions and religious discrimination in Portugal, and participated in the multidisciplinary *The Pilgrimage Project: a Study of Motivations and Experiences in Sacred Spaces*, undertaking fieldwork in several Christian and neopagan pilgrimage sites around Europe.
3 Laura Almodovar graduated in 2015 in Anthropology at the New University of Lisbon (FCSH-UNL). During 2016, she was a research fellow with the project *Fora do Padrão–Lembranças da Exposição de 1940*, at the Centre for Research in Anthropology–CRIA. She has just finished her Master's thesis at the New University of Lisbon. It looks at civic participation, religion, social class and citizenship through an ethnographic study of an Islamic association in a working-class context in the urban periphery of Lisbon.

Public Debates

Public debates on Portuguese Islam and Muslims, in 2017, addressed several topics and themes, namely Islamophobia, interfaith activities, the impact of terrorism on Portuguese Muslim communities, and citizenship and belonging.

In 2017, the *Mesquita Central de Lisboa* (Central Mosque of Lisbon–CML) was again vandalised,[4] and the topic was addressed in the media on several occasions. It sparked further debates about the growing presence of Islamophobia in contemporary Portuguese society, in spite of dominant discourses that emphasised the absence of such forms of racism.[5]

In November 2017, the imam of Lisbon Central Mosque publicly condemned in the media the terrorist attack on a Sufi mosque in the Sinai Peninsula, Egypt,[6] arguing that such acts have tremendous negative consequences for all Muslims worldwide, and thus should be vehemently condemned by all, Muslims and non-Muslims alike.

The construction of a new square in Lisbon, the *Praça da Mouraria* ("Moorish Square"), will, over the next few years, also include a new mosque and cultural centre in the Mouraria neighbourhood of central Lisbon.[7] Such a project continues to raise questions as to the role of the State in religious affairs, security issues, expropriations, vigilance and control, and processes of gentrification, among other topics. Several critics argued that the project could contribute to the "ghettoisation" of Muslims in the city and, simultaneously, could pose a serious security threat due to radicalisation processes resulting from this. In contrast, the city hall, the members of the executive committee of the *Comunidade Islâmica do Bangladesh* (Islamic Community of Bangladesh–CIB) and the main interlocutors in the project, continue to emphasise that this

---

4 Mapril, José, "Portugal", in Oliver Scharbrodt, Samim Akgönül, Ahmet Alibašić, Jørgen S. Nielsen and Egdūnas Račius (eds.), *Yearbook of Muslims in Europe*, vol. 8 (Leiden: Brill, 2016), pp. 549–560.

5 https://www.publico.pt/2017/12/01/mundo/opiniao/vamos-falar-sobre-islamofobia-1794482; https://www.rtp.pt/play/p50/e334581/a-fe-dos-homens, both accessed 8 June 2018.

6 http://rr.sapo.pt/noticia/99300/sheik-munir-muculmanos-sao-as-maiores-vitimas-dos-atentados, accessed 8 June 2018.

7 This is the Moorish quarter, whose name evokes the historical presence of Muslims in this area of Lisbon in the late medieval period. This historical reference has become increasingly patrimonialised, and now the quarter is an area that is under increasing pressure from gentrification.

mosque would be part and parcel of the construction of a plural and inclusive society.[8]

Another set of topics addressed in the media during 2017, as in previous years, are the complex issues surrounding Portuguese and European Muslims. Several topics were addressed, but some of the most prominent focused on ideas of European citizenship and belonging.[9]

Ten tears after laying the foundation stone, the *Associação da Comunidade Islâmica da Tapada das Mercês* (Islamic Community Association of Tapada das Mercês) pushed forward the project to construct a new purpose-built mosque and community centre on a plot of land given by the Sintra municipality. The leaders of the Association, argue that this will be the second purpose-built mosque in the country, and recognition of their work in the municipality. Until now, there have been no public objections to the mosque, due perhaps to the role played by this Islamic organisation in social solidarity initiatives. These include a foodbank and literacy classes for all the inhabitants in the area, Muslims and non-Muslims alike. Equally, this Association is also well supported by the Sintra municipality and Aga Khan Foundation, through its *Kapacidades* programme, a project developed to support poor urban communities.[10]

Transnational Links

In the Bangladeshi Baitul Mukarram mosque, transnational links are mainly fostered by the historical and political connections of its members to Bangladesh. Several members of the executive committee are engaged transnationally with Bangladesh, through "long distance nationalism".[11] In spite of this, the mosque uses two or three languages, depending on the congregation:

---

8   https://www.publico.pt/2017/03/28/local/noticia/mesquita-da-mouraria-para-a-camara-so-falta-a-publicacao-em-diario-da-republica-1766805; http://sicnoticias.sapo.pt/pais/2017-06-06-A-polemica-da-construcao-de-uma-nova-mesquita-em-Lisboa; https://www.tsf.pt/sociedade/interior/casos-de-radicalizacao-preocupam-ima-da-mesquita-central-de-lisboa-8536211.html, both accessed 8 June 2018.

9   https://www.dn.pt/mundo/interior/nao-ha-um-so-islao-e-o-islao-na-europa-tem-de-ser-europeu-8858104.html; https://www.dn.pt/lusa/interior/maioria-de-muculmanos-na-europa-sente-se-ligada-ao-pais-em-que-vive---estudo-8788069.html; http://visao.sapo.pt/actualidade/sociedade/2017-03-01-Nosmuculmanos, all accessed 8 June 2018.

10 Almodovar, Laura, *Islão periférico na Tapada das Mercês: entre pertenças de religião e de classe* (MA dissertation) (Lisbon: New University of Lisbon, 2017).

11 Anderson, Benedict, *The Spectre of Comparisons: Nationalism, Southeast Asia and the World* (London: Verso, 1998).

Bengali, Urdu, and Portuguese. It thus appeals not only to Bangladeshis but also to the wider Muslim community in Lisbon.

In the Al-Qadriyah mosque, transnational connections are mostly maintained with Mozambique, where most of the mosque's founders were born. Besides the regular flow of members of the congregation between the two countries, mainly motivated by business and family issues, the Al-Qadriyah mosque maintains an informal but close connection with the *Comunidade Islâmica de Moçambique* (Islamic Community of Mozambique–CIMO), a Muslim organisation that represents the Barelvi-inspired version of modern South Asian Islam that is predominant among Muslims from the North of Mozambique. In 2017, representatives of this mosque and close associates of the CIMO, collaborated in drawing up the statutes for a new association that will represent Muslims linked with the Al-Qadriyah mosque, thus reinforcing its alignment with the doctrinal tenets of its Mozambican sister organisation.

Law and Domestic Politics

No laws, policies or regulations, that directly or indirectly affected the Muslim population in Portugal, were issued or debated in 2017.

Activities and Initiatives of Main Muslim Organisations

In 2017, Portuguese Muslim organisations carried out many activities, the most important of which were related to the main celebrations of the Islamic calendar. They also included several public debate events, and solidarity initiatives.

During 2017, the two main festivals of the Islamic calendar, 'Id al-Fitr and 'Id al-Adha, were celebrated in the main mosques in the country.[12] In the Martim Moniz area, the Islamic Community of Bangladesh (ICB), with the Baitul Mukarram mosque and Martim Moniz mosque, organised two prayer events in the main square. The permissions for these open-air prayers, that have taken place in this same location over the past four years, were negotiated with Lisbon City Council within the larger context of the planned creation of a purpose-built mosque in central Lisbon, and, in 2017, gathered, according to its organisers, more than 3,000 worshippers.

During Ramadan, as has been the case for several decades, the ICB/Baitul Mukarram mosque organised a monthly *iftar* for the entire congregation. These

---

12   Based on fieldwork and research undertaken by José Mapril.

are usually sponsored either by the mosque executive committee, based on donations, or, as in 2017, an important entrepreneur sponsored all the meals. As part of a larger claim to visibility in Lisbon (related to the construction of a new mosque), on two occasions the ICB executive committee invited several local politicians, members of political parties, local association representatives, academics, diplomats, journalists, and others, in order to introduce them to the community and the Association. During 2017, the ICB created a Facebook page where major religious and ritual events of the year are announced, together with sermons and other statements made by religious scholars located in other parts of the world.[13]

In the Central Mosque of Lisbon, the "Dinner Debates of the Al-Mutamid Philosophy Club" continued throughout 2017. This is a monthly initiative in close collaboration with the Religious Studies Unit of the Universidade Lusófona. Members of several Islamic organisations in Portugal, politicians, and academics attended these meetings, whose themes included an homage to Mário Soares (1924–2017) on 7 February, who passed away in January 2017. He was an important political figure in contemporary Portuguese society, as founder and a former leader of the Socialist Party. Other seminars discussed gender violence, religion, and citizenship, to mention just a few.

The campaign "Soup for everyone" (*sopa para todos*) continued throughout the year in the Central Mosque; it served 8,000 hot meals in its canteen. Resuming the work done in previous years, the programme was organised in close cooperation with several civil society institutions, local parishes, the Lisbon municipality and NGOs. In 2017, in recognition of this programme, the President of the Portuguese Republic, Marcelo Rebelo de Sousa, visited the premises of the Central Mosque.

The Central Mosque also organised several student visits to its premises throughout the year, the objective of which was to continue an open-door policy that, according to its organisers, favours the sharing of knowledge, tolerance and the deconstruction of feelings of mistrust in relation to Muslims in Portuguese society. Also, at the end of Ramadan, the Central Mosque organised an intercultural lunch gathering refugees and migrants, from diverse backgrounds (Syria, Bangladesh, Pakistan, among others). This was organised in close collaboration with Lisbon city council and the High Commissioner for Migration. The objective was to bring together different groups of Muslims and non-Muslims.[14]

13   https://www.facebook.com/cib.mbm/, accessed 22 June 2018.
14   See http://comunidadeislamica.pt/pt/, accessed 22 June 2018.

In the outskirts of Lisbon, the municipalities of Odivelas (North of the capital), and Almada (on the south bank of the Tejo/Tagus river) have included significant Muslim populations since the 1980s, which have, since then, established regular ties with local institutions and civil society. In 2017, the largest places of Muslim worship in these municipalities reinforced their connection with other social actors by cooperating with government organisations, the Catholic Church, and NGOs, through various events and initiatives, mainly related to welfare. In Almada, the *Associação Islâmica Sul do Tejo* (Islamic Association of the South Bank of the Tagus), together with the Al-Madinah mosque, promoted several social care initiatives, in collaboration with other non-Muslim partner institutions. These included the annual solidarity meal for vulnerable groups (mostly homeless people), organised jointly with Catholic associations and NGOs; the local mayor, representatives of the *Comunidade Islâmica de Lisboa* (Islamic Community of Lisbon–CIL), and Catholic clergy, were in attendance. The Islamic Association of the South Bank of the Tagus has a regular presence in the public space, that is strengthened by very visible events, such as the collective prayers in the Peace Park (*Parque da Paz*), the largest green leisure area in the municipality of Almada.

In Odivelas, a municipality at the Northern edge of Lisbon, the Aisha Siddika mosque cooperates with local authorities on a regular basis. In 2017, these joint efforts resulted in several events of great public visibility, such as the Prayer for Peace/Peace Day and the World Week of Interfaith Harmony. For the municipality of Odivelas, the Aisha Siddika mosque and its representatives are those who stand out most clearly among the other minority religions participating in these interfaith celebrations, due to the high profile and proactive stance of its leaders. As such, contacts between the mosque and civil society have led to several instances of cooperation with the local authorities in 2017. This also materialised in many educational initiatives, such as regular visits by local students to the mosque, under the joint guidance of Aisha Siddika's communications officer and representatives of the culture department of the Odivelas municipality.

In Odivelas, the *Associação cultural Colinas do Cruzeiro* (Cruzeiro Hills Cultural Association) was legally constituted in September 2017. This is a new organisation led by a former imam of the Aisha Siddika mosque, and is currently responsible for the education of converts to Islam in Lisbon's Central Mosque. This Association aims to promote educational, cultural, and training activities for non-Muslims and other groups and institutions, from civil society. These activities can be considered a continuation of similar activities in the Central Mosque in terms of interfaith dialogue; these are organised in direct collaboration with the Islamic Community of Lisbon, and take place in facilities already acquired by the Association. The new premises of the Association will officially open in 2018. Reflecting this wish for visibility, the headquarters of the association will include art galleries, training and meeting rooms, and an auditorium.

In June 2017, after the tragic forest fires that resulted in several dozen fatalities in central Portugal, a campaign was coordinated by the *Fundação Islâmica de Palmela* (Palmela Islamic Foundation), which manages the International School of Palmela. The Foundation mobilised several mosques and Islamic associations, mainly in the Greater Lisbon area, to gather food and non-food relief items for the firefighters battling the wild fire. The Odivelas and Almada mosques were some of the main contributors to this campaign.

Both Odivelas and Almada also have Islamic places of worship that follow a Barelvi doctrinal orientation. The Gausiyah mosque in Odivelas, proceeded with restructuring its premises, with the construction of a refectory and the completion of works in the prayer hall. The Al-Qadriyah mosque in Almada took its first steps towards greater cooperation with civil society by collaborating with a Catholic institution and the Portuguese Red Cross in a joint initiative to distribute blankets and other relief items to homeless people in the city. In order to formalise this new openness towards other social actors, the leaders of the Al-Qadriyah mosque started working on the constitution of an association, the *Associação Islâmica e Cultural da Margem Sul* (Islamic and Cultural Association of the South Bank). They formulated its by-laws and initiated the formalisation process, which is expected to be concluded in the first months of 2018.[15]

During 2017, the *Associação da Comunidade Islâmica da Tapada das Mercês* (Islamic Community Association of Tapada das Mercês–ACITM) developed its social services and religious activities. In terms of social intervention, the ACITM resumed its foodbank, every Friday, for people from low socio-economic backgrounds. IT classes were also made available to children and adults.[16]

Muslim Population: History and Demographics

For around 30 years, Muslims have represented the largest non-Christian religious minority in Portugal. Muslims in Portugal constitute a diverse presence, in terms of ethnicity, socio-economic integration, and their religious affiliation

---

15 Based on fieldwork research undertaken by Pedro Soares.
16 Based on fieldwork research undertaken by José Mapril.

within Islam.[17] The contemporary Muslim presence has no demographic linkage to the historical Islamic presence in the region, rather it is largely the result of post-colonial movements of middle-class Ismaili and Sunni families of Indian/South Asian background who came from Mozambique in the early/mid 1970s. It also includes Fulas and Mandingas (at first, mainly male workers) from Guinea-Bissau, who arrived slightly later.[18] Like other cases of former European empires, the first Muslims who settled in the cities came for educational purposes *before* decolonisation, in this case from Mozambique, made up of single male students from Sunni families of Indian origin. From the late 1950s, as these students joined Lisbon's faculties of law, economics and medicine, up until today, and with the arrival of Bangladeshis, the Muslim population in Portugal has steadily increased.

Shortly after the revolution of 25 April 1974, namely in May of the very same year, around 500 Muslims arrived in Lisbon. In 1982, the Islamic Community of Lisbon (CIL, founded in 1968) counted 15,000 people who had left Mozambique. The second wave of immigration which shaped the Muslim presence in Portugal had its point of departure in Guinea-Bissau. The profile of this second type of Muslims arriving from the late 1980s is different, with only a very small number of students, something also due to their different age profile. This wave rarely featured families, but was generally young men looking for work in civil construction, and finding it in and around Lisbon and the Algarve. In

---

17 For different Islamic groups and organisations see Vakil, Abdool Karim, "Comunidade Islâmica em Portugal", in Fernando Alves Cristovão, Maria Adelina Amorim, Maria Lúcia Garcia Marques and Susana Brites Moita (eds.), *Dicionário Temático da Lusofonia* (Lisboa: Associação de Cultura Lusófona-Instituto Camões, 2005), pp. 219–222. A general introduction on Muslims in contemporary Portugal is provided by Tiesler, Nina Clara, "Muçulmanos na margem: a nova presença Islâmica em Portugal", *Sociologia, Problemas e Práticas*, vol. 34 (December 2000), pp. 117–144. See also Loja, Fernando Soares, "Islam in Portugal", in Shireen T. Hunter (ed.), *Islam, Europe's Second Religion: the New Social, Cultural, and Political Landscape* (Westport, Connecticut: Prager, 2002), pp. 191–203.

18 An extensive study on migrants from Guinea-Bissau and their communities is provided by Machado, Fernando Luís, *Contrastes e Continuidades. Migração, Etnicidade e Integração dos Guineenses em Portugal* (Oeiras: Celta, 2002). As for Guinean Muslims, see Abranches, Maria, *Pertenças Fechadas em Espaços Abertos. Estratégias de (re)Construcção Identitária de Mulheres Muçulmanas em Portugal* (Lisbon: Alto-Comissariado para a imigração e diálogo intercultural, 2004). For people of Indian descent and their communities, see Malheiros, Jorge M., *Imigrantes na Região de Lisboa: os Anos da Mudança, Imigração e Processo de Integração das Comunidades de Origem Indiana* (Lisboa: Colibri, 1996). An account of the Ismaili community, with a special focus on women, is provided by Keshavjee, Faranaz, *A Mulher Muçulmana em Portugal: processos psicosociológicos de diferenciação entre os sexo, tese de mestrado em psicologia social e das organizações* (Lisboa: ISCTE, 1996).

the 1980s, the number of Muslims of Indian descent was overtaken by Muslims hailing from Guinea-Bissau. With immigration from Guinea-Bissau, the number of Muslims doubled to approximately 30,000 at the beginning of the 1990s.[19]

Immigration patterns in Portugal changed in the early 1990s, and respective policies and academic research now contrast the ongoing immigration from the ex-colonies with strongly increasing immigration from Eastern Europe and countries which are not part of the Schengen Treaty area. Portugal, a small country at the margins of Western Europe (population ca. 10 Million) became a "promising destination" for migrants until the early 21st century. This meant that migrants without any colonial connections to Portugal began to arrive in the country. While immigration from Portuguese-speaking African countries and Brazil continued, most of the "new" migrants hailed from Eastern Europe, and, to a lesser extent, from Morocco, Senegal, Bangladesh, and Pakistan.[20] Most of the latter have joined the existing infrastructures of the still overwhelmingly Portuguese-speaking Muslim communities, which are mainly concentrated in and around Lisbon.

Thus, Portugal has a Muslim population which has grown mostly since its empire ended in 1974. Estimates produced by these communities themselves, and by researchers, suggest that there are between 48,000 and 55,000 Muslims in the country, among them ca. 8,000 Ismailis. The Muslim population is mainly Sunni, of South Asian origin from Mozambique, and, in greater numbers, from Guinea-Bissau. Though some 60% of them are Portuguese citizens, the percentage is lower for those of Guinean origin. Other Muslim groupings from Pakistan and Bangladesh arrived more recently, noticeably since the early 1990s. Small numbers of Muslims stem from Morocco, Algeria, Senegal, and India. The recent increase in the Muslim population derives from family reunifications, namely among Bangladeshis, and, less so, among Pakistanis.

---

19   Vakil, "Comunidade Islâmica", pp. 219–22.
20   The particular case of Muslims from Bangladesh is approached by Mapril, José, "The new South Asians: the political economy of migrations between Bangladesh and Portugal", *Revista Oriente*, vol. 17 (2007), pp. 81–99; Mapril, José "'Bangla masdjid': Islão e bengalidade entre os bangladeshianos em Lisboa", *Análise Social*, vol. 39 (2005), pp. 851–873; and Mapril, José, "'Maulana says the Prophet is human, not God': Milads and hierarchies among Bengali Muslims in Lisbon", *Lusotopie*, vol. 14, no. 1 (2007), pp. 255–270. For Moroccan immigrants, see Faria, Rita Gomes, "Imigrantes marroquinos em Portugal: o papel da religião na formação de comunidade e na incorporação na sociedade portuguesa", *Lusotopie*, vol. 14, no. 1 (2007), pp. 205–221.

While there are small Muslim communities established in the North (mainly in Porto and Coimbra), in the South (in the Algarve), and on the island of Madeira, the overwhelming majority of Muslims live in and around the capital city Lisbon. The majority of Moroccan Muslims live in and around Porto and the Algarve. Within and near Lisbon, there are some, although not significant, geographical concentrations of Muslims in single neighbourhoods. These are in the areas of Laranjeiro, Odivelas, Damaia, and Sintra, all of which have well established, representative mosques.

The best sources for demographic and statistical information on the Portuguese Muslim population are (i) from the main institutional representative for Islam in Portugal, namely the Islamic Community in Portugal (CIL), (ii) through the statistical data provided by the border police (*Serviço de Estrangeiros e Fronteiras*), and (iii) from the last Portuguese census, in 2011.

Muslim Population	The estimated numbers (source CIL) vary between 48,000 and 55,000 (ca. 0.5% of total population). According to the census, the number is just 9,134.[21]
Ethnic/National Backgrounds	60% of Muslims in Portugal are Portuguese citizens.[22]
	Largest ethnic/national groups:[23] Bissau-Guinean: 16,604 Guinea Conakry: 1,561 Indian: 8,268 Pakistani: 3,643 Bangladeshi: 3,236 Moroccan: 1,668 Senegalese: 1,469.
	In the case of India and Guinea-Bissau, the ratio of Muslims is uncertain.

---

21 The main reason for this discrepancy is due to the fact that, in the census, the questions related to religious belonging are optional and not mandatory. The numbers provided by the CIL, however, are based on data gathered among the main Islamic institutions in the country.

22 Tiesler, Nina Clara, and David Cairns, "Representing Islam and Lisbon youth: Portuguese Muslims of Indian Mozambican origin", *Lusotopie*, vol. 14, no. 1 (2007), pp. 222–238.

23 These numbers were taken from the 2016 report by the Border Police (*Serviço de Estrangeiros e Fronteiras*).

Inner-Islamic Groups	The majority are Sunnis but there are also 8,000 members of the Nizari Ismaili Community.
Geographical Spread	Most Muslims in Portugal live in the main urban centres, such as Lisbon, Porto, Coimbra, and Faro.
Number of Mosques	57 cultural centres, mosques, and prayer halls exist across the country, the majority of which are located in the Lisbon metropolitan area.
Muslim Burial Sites	In Portugal it is possible to find general cemeteries with specific plots for Muslims, namely in Lumiar, Feijó, and Odivelas. Other Muslim burial sites: – Cemitério do Lumiar, Azinhaga das Lajes, 1600–484, Lisbon – Cemitério de Vale Flores, Rua de Vale Flores, 2810, Feijó – Cemitério Municipal de Odivelas, Rua Antero de Quental, 2675–482, Odivelas.
"Chaplaincy" in State Institutions	In Portuguese institutions (hospitals, prisons, etc.), patients need to request religious assistance from that institution, that in turn contacts the corresponding religious communities. In practice, it is usually a Catholic priest, close to the institution, that mediates the contacts with other religious groups.
Halal Products	In the main cities of Portugal, especially in urban areas with a significant concentration of Muslims (Mouraria, Odivelas, Almada, among many others), it is possible to find several halal butchers, kebab shops, and restaurants. In Lisbon's central area alone, there are four halal butchers and many other kebab shops and restaurants that sell halal products and meals. In 2015, the Halal Institute of Portugal (*Instituto Halal de Portugal*) was created in order to analyse, monitor, inspect, and certify halal products.

Dress Code

In Portugal, no legal restrictions on wearing Muslim dress, such as the head scarf or niqab, exist. Although there is an absence of a systematic study on the subject, random case studies[24] and media reports,[25] reveal the use of different types of veils, in distinct segments of Muslim populations.

In March 2017, the Court of Justice of the European Union (CJEU) ruled that employers can ban women from wearing head scarves and religious symbols in the workplace, which led to some public debate about the importance of this issue in Portugal. Spokespersons from the Portuguese Council for Refugees (*Concelho Português para os Refugiados*), from the Catholic Church, the Jewish Community, and the Imam of the Central Mosque of Lisbon, expressed their disagreement with the decision.[26]

Places of Islamic Learning and Education

The majority of mosques and prayer halls have Qur'anic classes for the younger generation. Besides these, it is important to mention the existence of two faith-based schools. There is the International School of Palmela, which offers a secular (the Cambridge plan of studies) and an Islamic curriculum. This institution also has a building in Amadora, in the Lisbon metropolitan area. There is also the Darul-Uloom Kadria-Ashrafia school in Odivelas.

Muslim Media and Publications

Muslims take part, alongside other religious groups, in two television and radio programmes on the public TV channel RTP 2 and on the public broadcasting radio station Antena 1, namely *A Fé dos Homens* (The Faith of Men) and *Caminhos* (Routes). The time given to them is dependent on

---

24 Coelho, Alexandra, and Daniel Rocha, *Muçulmanos em Portugal: onde fica Meca quando se olha de Lisboa* (Lisboa: Público, 2005).
25 http://revista.delas.pt/familia/muculmanas-em-portugal/, accessed 27 June 2018.
26 http://www.jornaleconomico.sapo.pt/noticias/proibicao-do-veu-islamico-o-mais-certo-e-que-haja-mulheres-que-deixem-de-trabalhar-133500, accessed 27 June 2018.

the numbers in those communities. In practice, this means that most airtime is occupied by the Catholic Church, and then the Protestant and Pentecostal Churches.

There are some chatrooms,[27] where one can also submit questions to be answered by an imam, and there are several blogs used by young Muslims in Portuguese.[28] There is currently only one Muslim printed journal, *Al-Furqan*, which is also available online.[29]

Main Muslim Organisations

- Central Mosque of Lisbon (*Mesquita Central de Lisboa*,[30] Rua da Mesquita in Bairro Azul (à Praça de Espanha), 1070–283 Lisbon, tel.: ++351 213874142 / 213879184; fax: ++351 213872230; email: info@comunidadeislamica.pt, www.comunidadeislamica.pt). Founded in 1985, its imam is Sheikh David Munir. This is the home of the Islamic Community of Lisbon (*Comunidade Islâmica de Lisboa*, CIL) and provides space for meetings and projects for other Muslim associations.
- Islamic Community of Palmela (*Comunidade Islâmica de Palmela*, Av. Vila Amélia, lote 171, 172, Cabanas, 2950–805 Palmela, tel.: ++351 212110530, fax: ++351 212110539, email: cipalmela@hotmail.com).
- Ismaili Cultural Centre and Aga Khan Foundation (*Centro Cultural Ismaili e Fundação Aga Khan*, Rua Abranches Ferrao, 1600–001 Lisbon, tel.: ++351 217229000, fax: ++351 217229045, email: nationalcouncil@netcabo.pt). The Aga Khan Foundation Portugal is currently running a capacity development project, called *K'Cidade*.[31] Its objective is to improve individual (education, integration into the labour market, citizenship training programmes) and community (child care, children's education) capacities in urban contexts.

---

27 www.aliasoft.com/forumislam, accessed 27 July 2016.
28 muculmana.blog.com; islamicchat.blogspot.com; Portugal-islamico.blogspot.com, all accessed 27 July 2016.
29 www.alfurqan.pt, accessed 27 July 2016.
30 For details see Tiesler, Nina Clara, "No bad news from the European margin: the new Islamic presence in Portugal", *Islam and Christian-Muslim Relations*, vol. 12, no. 1 (2001), pp. 71–91.
31 In Portuguese this term is pronounced "capa-cidade", so including the term "city" with the term "capacity".

- Shi'i Community of Portugal (*Comunidade Shi'ita de Portugal* (Ithna Ashari), Avenida das Forças Armadas, 11 D, Almada; tel.: ++351 218106030; email: Bremtula_pnegra@netcabo.pt). The main Twelver Shi'i organisation in Portugal.
- Baitul Mukarram mosque or *Mesquita do Martim Moniz* (Rua do Benformoso, 119–1°/2°/3°, 1100–083 Lisbon, tel.: ++351 917385367). In 2004, Muslims from Bangladesh founded the Baitul Mukarram mosque (named after Dhaka central mosque), also known informally as *Mesquita do Martim Moniz* or *Mesquita do Benformoso*.[32] It is managed by the Islamic Community of Bangladesh (*Comunidade Islâmica do Bangladesh*–CIB), an association formally recognised by the Portuguese state.
- Association for Islamic Education in Portugal (*Associação para a Educação Islâmica em Portugal*, Rua 3 de Abril de 1964, 12-A–14-A, 2675–300 Odivelas). This association is based at the Gausiyah mosque (former Darul-Uloom Kadria-Ashrafia), in Odivelas, and has close ties with the Al-Qadriyah mosque, in Laranjeiro. Stated goals include the promotion of religious activities and education programmes inspired by "Sufi traditional values", namely of the Barelvi orientation. This place of worship was founded by Mozambicans who arrived in Portugal after the 1974 Revolution, and was the result of a split in the mid-1990s, with about 150 Muslims leaving the Aisha Siddika mosque, associated with the Tablighi Jamaat missionary movement, to found the Darul-ulum Kadria-Ashrafia (nowadays the Gausiyah mosque), of Barelvi inspiration, just a few metres away. This group was formalised in 1997 as the *Associação para a Educação Islâmica em Portugal* (Association for Islamic Education in Portugal), cementing its status and sustainability through a set of partnerships with Sufi transnational organisations, such as the Islamic Educational and Cultural Research Center (based in Sacramento, California) and the Indian-British Spiritual Foundation (based in Leicester, UK, and in Kichhauchha, India), of which it is presently the Portuguese branch.
- Association of the Disciples of Serigne Touba of Portugal (*Association des Disciples de Serigne Touba au Portugal*, Rua Passos Manuel, no 20 R/C, 1150–260, Lisbon, tel.: ++351 932407559). It is an association linked to the Mouride brotherhood or the Sufi order; they opened a prayer hall in the central Lisbon district of Anjos in 2010.

---

32   For a more comprehensive account of the historical process behind the creation of this mosque, see Mapril, "Bangla masdjid".

- Multicultural and Islamic Association (*Associação Multicultural e Islâmica*, Rua luis gomes nº 11, 2700–529, Mina, Amadora).[33] Founded by Luso-Guineans from Conakry and Bissau, its objective is to organise not only religious services and classes, but also to teach Portuguese.
- Halal Institute of Portugal (Instituto Halal de Portugal, Avenida Vila Amélia, lote 171/172, 2950–805, Quinta do Anjo, Palmela). It was created to inform the general Portuguese population, and Muslims in particular, about halal products in the country.
- Islamic Community Association of Tapada das Mercês (and Mem-Martins) (*Associação Islâmica da Tapada das Mercês (e Mem-Martins)*–ACITM/ ACITMMM, Av. Miguel Torga nº48-B Tapada das Mercês 2725–540 Mem-Martins; tel.: ++351 920278204, email: geral@acitmmm.org, www.acitmmm.org). The ACITM was created in 2007, and is an organisation that first appeared as an informal group for a segregated Muslim population in one of Lisbon's suburbs. In 2007, this Association moved to a garage to use as a mosque and a common space, and in 2008, it received support from the *K'Cidade* programme of the Aga Kahn Foundation (AKF). The next step was its institutionalisation and formalisation, with the active support of the AKF and the municipality, that led to the opening of a community centre, separated from the mosque. Soon after 2012, there was decrease in the activities of the ACITM. The local repercussions of the global economic crisis brought instability to its fragile structure, mainly its economic sustainability, due to cuts in public funding, and management issues. As a reaction, the ACITM's activities were reduced, with it giving priority to social needs, namely food redistribution. In parallel, religious activities were maintained. This situation changed in 2016, largely because of the collective aspiration to build a new purpose-built mosque and community centre in a plot of land given by the Sintra municipality. The ACITM has improved the community centre and re-established some of its courses and activities, with the help of their partners.

---

33 Mapril, "Aren't you looking for citizenship in the wrong place?".

Romania

Irina Vainovski-Mihai[1]

Introduction

In 2017, international public opinion and the media continued to focus on the flow of Middle Eastern migrants and refugees into Europe, and, implicitly, into Romania. They even questioned if Romania was ready to deal with its rising number of migrants. Yet, Romania remains a rather limited transit region for migrants and refugees, most of whom were trying to reach Western Europe.[2] The *coup d'état* attempt in Turkey, which took place on 15 July 2016, continued to reverberate in Romania during 2017. The main incident in this respect concerned the Turkish basketball star Enes Kanter, an NBA player for Oklahoma City Thunder, who could not enter Romania because the Turkish authorities had cancelled his passport.

Public Debates

An issue that re-emerged in public debates in 2017 was the project to build a grand mosque in Bucharest, with the financial aid of the Turkish state. On 27 May 2015, the Government decided to allot the Muftiate a plot of about 11,000 m², free of charge, for a period of 49 years, for the purpose of constructing "a compound of buildings".[3] The Government's decision was followed

---

[1] Irina Vainovski-Mihai is Professor of Arab Studies at the Dimitrie Cantemir Christian University, Bucharest. She holds a degree in Arabic language and literature, and a PhD in Philology. She has published on Arabic literature, comparative literature and intercultural stereotyping.

[2] Gherasim, Cristian, "Is Romania ready to deal with its rising migrant numbers?", *Euronews*, 16 September 2017, http://www.euronews.com/2017/09/16/is-romania-ready-to-deal-with-its-rising-migrant-numbers?utm_term=Autofeed&utm_campaign=Echobox&utm_medium=Social&utm_source=Facebook#link_time=1505577103, accessed 17 September 2017.

[3] "Hotărârea nr. 372/2015" (Decision No 372/2015), *Lege*[5], http://lege5.ro/Gratuit/gy4dcnrxhe/hotararea-nr-372-2015-privind-trecerea-unui-imobil-teren-din-domeniul-privat-al-statului-si-administrarea-regiei-autonome-administrarea-patrimoniului-protocolului-de-stat-in-domeniul-public-al-statulu, accessed 17 April 2017.

immediately by several declarations and a series of protests.[4] In the first months of 2017, several Romanian media sources referred to the dimension, structure and shape of the project,[5] as presented by the Turkish Presidency of Religious Affairs (*Diyanet İşleri Başkanlığı*).[6]

The *coup d'état* attempt in Turkey which took place on 15 July 2016 continued to reverberate in Romania in 2017. In February, the Romanian press announced that the Turkish Ministry of Justice had requested the extradition from Romania of two members of the "Gülen Organisation".[7] No specific names were made public. On 20 May 2017, the Turkish basketball star Enes Kanter, an NBA player for Oklahoma City Thunder, could not enter Romania because the Turkish authorities had cancelled his passport.[8] The incident caused a major public stir in Romania, and also made headlines in the media abroad.[9] Enes Kanter, a Turkish national, and professional basketball player in the USA, is an outspoken opponent of the Erdoğan government, and is a supporter of the Hizmet movement of Fethullah Gülen. He was expected to be in Romania as part of a tour of several countries organised by the Enes Kanter Light

---

4 Odobescu, Vlad, "Romania's Turkey-funded mosque sparks anti-Muslim backlash, terror fears", *The Washington Times*, 12 August 2015, http://www.washingtontimes.com/news/2015/aug/12/bucharest-romanias-turkey-funded-mosque-sparks-ant/, accessed 17 April 2017.

5 "Galerie foto. Autoritatea religioasa din Turcia a dezvaluit proiectul Marii Moschei ce se va construi in Bucuresti" (Photo gallery. The religious authority of Turkey unveiled the project of the Grand Mosque which would be built in Bucharest), HotNews.ro, Friday, 19 May 2017, http://www.hotnews.ro/stiri-esential-21775341-foto-autoritatea-religioasa-din-turcia-dez valuie-proiectul-marii-moschei-construi-bucuresti.htm, accessed 15 January 2018.

6 "Romanya Bükreş Camii" (The Grand Mosque of Bucharest Romania), in *Camilerimiz, Türkiye Diyanet Vakfi*, n.d., pp. 76–77, available on the site of the Diyanet at: https://www.tdv.org/Media/files/Tan%C4%B1t%C4%B1m%20Kataloklar%C4%B1/Camilerimiz_TR.pdf, accessed 27 April 2018.

7 Cristea, Irina, and Angela Sârbu, "Turcia: Ministerul Justiţiei a cerut extrădarea unor membri ai organizaţiei lui Gulen din 16 state, inclusiv România" (Turkey: the Ministry of Justice requested the extradition of members of the Gülen organisation from 16 states, including Romania), *Romanian National New Agency AGERPRES*, 10 February 2017, https://www.agerpres.ro/externe/2017/02/10/turcia-ministerul-justitiei-a-cerut-extradarea-unor-membri-ai-organizatiei-lui-gulen-din-16-state-inclusiv-romania-20-09-21, accessed 15 January 2018.

8 "NBA star Enes Kanter–blocked on Otopeni Airport by the Romanian authorities. Melescanu: Romania respected the decision taken by Turkey, who cancelled the passport of the basketball player Kanter", *NINE O'CLOCK.ro*, 22 May, http://www.nineoclock.ro/nba-star-enes-kanter-blocked-on-otopeni-airport-by-the-romanian-authorities-melescanu-romania-respected-the-decision-taken-by-turkey-who-canceled-the-passport-of-the-basketball-player-kan/, accessed 15 January 2018.

9 "Enes Kanter, NBA star and Gulen supporter, briefly detained in Romania after 'Turkey cancels passport'", *HAARETZ*, 21 May 2017, https://www.haaretz.com/middle-east-news/turkey/nba-s-enes-kanter-briefly-detained-after-turkey-cancels-passport-1.5474720, accessed 15 January 2018.

Foundation.[10] A few days before the incident the Romanian press announced that Kanter would come to Bucharest to take part in several basketball events, and would celebrate his birthday as part of the city's Multicultural Festival.[11] Kanter was invited to Romania by *Lumina Wolves*, a sporting club launched in February 2017,[12] upon the initiative of *Lumina Instituții de Învățământ* (Lumina Educational Institutions[13]), a network of Gülen-inspired schools in Romania.

In July 2017, a Romanian national who had converted to Islam prior to her marriage to a Palestinian, went on hunger strike for five days in the city centre of Bucharest requesting support from the public and state authorities for the repatriation of her three daughters from the Gaza Strip. The mother declared that she was afraid that their lives were in danger because their father, whom she divorced many years ago, was keeping them in Gaza against their will. According to the mother, the daughters were Romanian nationals, but had no documents to prove that. Eventually, with the mediation of the Romanian Ministry of Foreign Affairs, and mobile consular teams sent to the Erez border point in Israel and to Jordan, the three girls were reunited with their mother in Bucharest.[14]

The flow of Middle Eastern migrants and refugees into Romania and the debates around this topic, were still present in 2017, although less than they were in 2016. There were a few incidents when the Romanian coast guard intervened to rescue migrants and refugees from ships in distress on the Black Sea.[15] Romania is mostly a transit country for migrants trying to reach Western

---

10 http://www.eneskanter11.com/partnerships-projects/the-light-foundation/, accessed 15 January 2018.
11 Nueleanu, Iulia, "Comunicat de presă–Un star din NBA își sărbătorește ziua de naștere la București" (Press release: an NBA star celebrates his birthday in Bucharest), *Romanian National New Agency AGERPRES*, 17 May 2017, https://www.agerpres.ro/comunicate/2017/05/17/comunicat-de-presa-un-star-din-nba-isi-sarbatoreste-ziua-de-nastere-la-bucuresti-10-03-47, accessed 25 May 2017.
12 Miu, Alin, "VIDEO. Lumina Wolves, un nou concept pe piața baschetului românesc. Proiect susținut de un star din NBA!" (VIDEO: Lumina Wolves, a new concept in Romanian basketball. Project supported by an NBA star), *FANATIK.RO*, 24 February 2017, http://www.fanatik.ro/video-lumina-wolves-un-nou-concept-pe-piata-baschetului-romanesc-proiect-sustinut-de-un-star-din-nba-903185, accessed 25 May 2017.
13 http://fundatia.lumina.org/; http://www.lumina.ro/, accessed 25 May 2017.
14 Lazar, Valeriu, "Update: MAE brings the three girls from Gaza strip back to Romania, mother stops hunger strike. 'It was now or never'...", *The Romanian Journal*, 26 July 2017, https://www.romaniajournal.ro/update-mae-brings-the-three-girls-from-gaza-strip-back-to-romania-mother-stops-hunger-strike-it-was-now-or-never/, accessed 19 November 2017.
15 Gheorghiu, Olimpiu, "Romanian coast guards rescues 157 migrants from Black Sea", *USNEWS*, 13 September 2017, https://www.usnews.com/news/world/articles/2017-09-13/romania-coast-guards-rescues-157-migrants-from-black-sea, accessed 19 November 2017.

Europe. In July 2017, the Timisoara police disbanded a camp set up illegally by migrants and refugees (including children) from Iraq, Syria and Iran. All of them had left the migrant centres where they were hosted, and settled on the outskirts of the town in makeshift shelters waiting for a guide to take them across the border to either Serbia or Hungary.[16]

In the media, a diverse range of stories about the month of Ramadan appeared. They ranged from general information,[17] specific information given by Mufti Murat Iusuf,[18] as well comments on the charity activities carried out by the Turkish Cooperation and Coordination Agency (*Türk İşbirliği ve Koordinasyon İdaresi Başkanlığı*–TİKA),[19] and advice to the tens of thousands of Romanian non-Muslim tourists visiting Dubai during Ramadan.[20]

Transnational Links

In 2017, the Mufti of Romania, Murat Iusuf, further promoted the Muftiate's international relationships. On 13 March, he participated, together with the president of the Turkish Democratic Union of Romania (in Romanian: *Uniunea Democrată Turcă din România*–UDTR; in Turkish: *Romanya Demokrat Türk Birliği*), Osman Fedbi, and other officials, in a series of events that took place in the town of Braila. They were organised by the Consulate General of the Republic of Turkey in Constantza, on the occasion of the "Day of Turkish

---

16 "Tabără ilegală în care locuiau refugiați din Siria, Iran și Irak, desființată la Timișoara" (Illegal camp of refugees from Syria, Iran and Iraq, disbanded in Timisoara), *Știrile TVR*, 31 July 2017, http://stiri.tvr.ro/tabara-ilegala-in-care-locuiau-refugia-i-din-siria-iran-i-irak-desfiin-ata-la-timi-oara_820566.html#view, accessed 1 August 2017.

17 "1 miliard și jumătate de musulmani intră astăzi în postul Ramadanului" (One billion and a half Muslims enter the fast of Ramadan today), *Radio România Actualități*, 27 May 2017, http://www.romania-actualitati.ro/1_miliard_si_jumatate_de_musulmani_intra_astazi_in_postul_ramadanului-103123, accessed 5 November 2017.

18 "Musulmanii intră de sâmbătă în postul Ramadanului" (Starting with Saturday, Muslims enter the fast of Ramadan), *Telegraf*, 26 May 2017, https://www.telegrafonline.ro/musulmanii-intra-de-sambata-in-postul-ramadanului, accessed 5 November 2017.

19 "Turkish aid agency sends Ramadan aid to Romania", *Daily Sabah. Turkey*, 19 June 2017, https://www.dailysabah.com/turkey/2017/06/19/turkish-aid-agency-sends-ramadan-aid-to-romania, accessed 5 November 2017.

20 "Ce trebuie să știți despre perioada Ramadanului în Dubai" (What you should know about the period of Ramadan in Dubai), *DC NEWS*, 23 May 2017, https://www.dcnews.ro/ce-trebuie-sa-stiti-despre-perioada-ramadanului-in-dubai_543631.html, accessed 5 November 2017.

Heroes".[21] Similar commemorations for the battle of Çanakkale took place in Bucharest, attended by the Turkish Ambassador to Romania, Osman Koray Ertaş.[22]

The Muftiate, with the aid of the Turkish Cooperation and Coordination Agency (TİKA), started the renovation of the historical Hunchiar mosque in Constantza.[23] The mosque dates back to 1867.

In the Turkish constitutional referendum designed to give the President more executive power, Turkish nationals in Romania casted their votes on 13–15 April at the Consulates in Bucharest and Constantza. According to Romanian media, citing the Embassy of Turkey, more than 30% of the 6,351 registered voters participated, and 44.6% voted in favour of the constitutional changes.[24]

Law and Domestic Politics

Romania is a secular republic with no state religion, though Orthodox Christians constitute the majority of the population (according to the 2011 census).[25] The Islamic faith community, as one of the 18 religious denominations recognised by law (*Law 489/2006*), is considered a public-utility legal entity.[26] Costs are covered primarily from the Muslim communities' own income. Through their officially recognised national leadership and representative

---

21 This is the day, each year around 18 March, when Turkey commemorates the Turkish soldiers fallen in the Galliopoli campaign during World War I. Ceremonies are organised in Romania in cities such as Bucharest and Braila.
22 İbraim, Nurcan, "Çanakkale Deniz Savaşları Zaferi" (Çanakkale naval war victory), *Haksez: Romanya Türk Demokrat Birliği yayın organıdır*, p. 4 and Asan, Sorina, "Ziua eroilor turci, marcată la Brăila şi Bucureşti" (The day of Turkish heroes, marked in Braila and Bucharest), *Haksez: Romanya Türk Demokrat Birliği yayın organıdır*, p. 5.
23 Baciu, Nicoleta, "Geamia 'Hunchiar', reabilitată cu ajutorul Agenţiei de Cooperare şi Coordonare Turcă. Va urma Moscheea 'Carol I'" (The "Hunchiar" Mosque renovated with the aid of the Turkish Cooperation and Coordination Agency: the "Carol I" Mosque will follow), *Ziua de Constanţa*, 29 April 2017, https://www.ziuaconstanta.ro/stiri/imobiliare/geamia-hunchiar-reabilitata-cu-sustinerea-agentiei-de-cooperare-si-coordonare-turca-va-urma-moscheea-carol-i-629720.html, accessed 3 October 2017.
24 "Referendum. Cum au votat turcii din România" (Referendum: how did the Turks from Romania vote), *DIGI24 HD*, 16 April 2017, https://www.digi24.ro/stiri/externe/mapamond/referendum-cum-au-votat-turcii-din-romania-707718, accessed 1 August 2017.
25 *Ce ne spune recensământul din anul 2011 despre religie?* (*What Does the 2011 Census Tell Us about Religion?*) (Bucharest: Institutul Naţional de Statistică România, October 2013), p. 6.
26 "Hotărâre de guvern privind statutul cultului musulman" (Government decision regarding the recognition of the Muslim denomination), www.muftiyat.ro/muftiatul/statutul-mcm/, accessed 17 April 2017.

body (the Muftiate), Muslims can receive material support from the State for the maintenance of mosques, monuments, and other communal buildings. As these funds are rather scarce, the Diyanet, and Turkish citizens with businesses in Romania, make substantial contributions.

Activities and Initiatives of Main Muslim Organisations

As every year, 'Id al-Fitr (in Turkish: *Ramazan Bayram*) and 'Id al-Adha (in Turkish: *Qurban Bayram*) were celebrated as the main Islamic religious events. On 25 May, two days before the beginning of the month of Ramadan, the Muftiate, in collaboration with the Hasene Organisation from Germany,[27] sent packages with food to Muslim families in need.[28] At the end of Ramadan, on the first day of 'Id al-Fitr (25 June 2017),[29] and on the morning of 'Id al-Adha (1 September 2017), Mufti Murat Iusuf headed the special prayers (in Turkish: *bayram namazı*) at the Hunchiar mosque in Constantza. After the communal prayer occasioned by the beginning of 'Id al-Adha, the Mufti participated in ritual sacrifices and the distribution of *qurban* meat and other food to families in need from the Southeastern counties of Constantza, Tulcea and Călăraşi. These offerings were provided by the Muftiate of Romania, the Diyanet, and charities from Europe.[30]

As in the past, Gülen-inspired schools in Romania and the *Fundaţia Tuna* (Tuna Foundation) were involved in charity activities throughout 2017, as well as cultural festivals, like the annual Multicultural Festival[31] and the Turkish

---

[27] https://www.hasene.de/hasene-organization-comes-together-with-all-its-observers/?lang=en, accessed 2 June 2018.

[28] "Pachete pentru familiile nevoiaşe din multe localităţi, în pragul Lunii Ramazan" (Packages for needy families from many towns), *Curier local*, 24 May 2017, https://curierlocal.ro/7354/pachete-pentru-familiile-nevoiase-din-mai-multe-localitati-pragul-lunii-ramazan/, accessed 2 June 2018.

[29] "Începe sărbătorirea Ramazan Bairam" (The feast of Ramazan Bayram begins), *Telegraf*, 23 June, 2017, https://www.telegrafonline.ro/incepe-sarbatorirea-ramazan-bairam, accessed 2 June 2018. For a video report on feasting during *Ramazan Bayram* in the Dobrudjan town of Medgidia, see: RAMAZAN BAYRAM, TREI ZILE DE SĂRBĂTOARE PENTRU MUSULMANI [VIDEO] (Ramazan Bayram, three days of feast for Muslims [video]), *alpha media*, 26 June 2017, http://tvalphamedia.ro/2017/06/26/ramazan-bayram-trei-zile-de-sarbatoare-pentru-musulmani-video/, accessed 2 June 2018.

[30] "Zi de sărbătoare pentru musulmani. Începe Kurban Bayram" (Day of feast for Mulisms. Qurban Bayram begins), *CONSTANTA 100%*, 1 September 2017, http://www.ct100.ro/zi-de-sarbatoare-pentru-musulmani-incepe-kurban-bayram/, accessed 2 June 2018.

[31] https://issuu.com/isb.romania/docs/multicultural_festival_presentation, accessed 15 October 2017.

Festival; the latter included the dances of whirling dervishes and music performances. However, most of the public festivities, festivals, and contests, and awards granted, have mainly ethnic rather than religious dimensions. Examples include traditional Tatar and Turkish music concerts, and the competition for children "The Traditional Turkish House",[32] organised by the Turkish Democratic Union of Romania. There are also transnational Turkic spring celebrations, such as *hâdârlez*[33] or *tepreş*,[34] organised by the Democratic Union of Turkish-Muslim Tatars in Romania.

Muslim Population: History and Demographics

The first Muslims in Romania settled mainly in Northern Dobrudja and along the lower Danube in the 14th century, when Ottoman rule was established in the region. Dobrudja remained part of the Ottoman Empire for five centuries. After the Russo-Ottoman War of 1877–78, Romania gained its independence, and the Treaty of Berlin (1878) acknowledged Dobrudja as part of Romanian territory. As a result of economic and political conditions in the early 20th century, most Turks and Tatars emigrated from Dobrudja to Turkey. While the census of 1879 recorded Muslims as representing 56% of the population in the Dobrudjan county of Constantza, by the census of 1909 the percentage had dropped to 10.8%.[35]

---

32 "Concurs între elevii din COBADIN: 'Casa Tradiţională Turcească'" (Contest among the pupils of Cobadin: "The Traditional Turkish House"), *Radio România Constanţa*, 12 April 2017, http://radioconstanta.ro/2017/04/12/concurs-intre-elevii-din-cobadin-casa-traditionala-turceasca/, accessed 10 August 2017.

33 Ghiulşen, Ismail-Iusuf, "Musulmanii sărbătoresc astăzi Kidirlez (Hidirlez)" (Muslims are celebrating Kidirlez [Hidirlez] today), *Radio România Constanţa*, 6 May 2017, http://radioconstanta.ro/2017/05/06/musulmanii-sarbatoresc-astazi-kidirlez-hidirlez/, accessed 10 August 2017.

34 "TEPREŞ. Lupte tătăreşti şi mâncare tradiţională, la Murfatlar" (TEPREŞ: Tatar wrestling and traditional cuisine at Murfatlar), *Replica*, 8 July 2017, https://www.replicaonline.ro/tepres-lupte-tataresti-si-mancare-traditionala-la-murfatlar-324060/, accessed 10 August 2017.

35 Schmidt-Rösler, Andrea, "Dobrudscha", in Michael Weithmann (ed.), *Der ruhelose Balkan: die Konfliktregionen Südosteuropas* (Munich: Deutscher Taschenbuch Verlag, 1993), pp. 94–106 (101), quoted in Bara, Maria, "Relaţii interetnice dintre creştinii ortodocşi şi musulmani în Dobrogea. Studiu de caz: Medgidia şi Cobadin" (Muslim-Orthodox Christian interethnic relations in Dobrudja. A case study: Medgidia and Cobadin), *Philologica Jassyensia*, vol. 2, no. 1 (2006), pp. 93–104 (95).

Today, the majority of Muslims in Romania live in Dobrudja, and are mainly made up of ethnic groups with a well-established historical presence. After the fall of the communist regime in 1989, new Muslim groups appeared in major cities, such as Bucharest, Iasi, Cluj, and Timisoara. These groups were made up of Middle Eastern businesspersons, former students who studied in Romania before the fall of the communist regime, as well as refugees and converts. These new groups have not joined with the old Muslim communities of Romania, and the two groups live largely parallel lives.[36] Discussion does not focus on the question of *who* is a Muslim, but rather what kind of Muslim someone is, and to which extent they adhere to the religion.[37] Many disputes at international level also reverberate within Romania, and influence the way in which Muslims define themselves and practise Islam in the country.[38] The size of the Muslim population, by ethnic/national background, given below, is based on the 2011 Census; it is the only detailed data available.

Muslim Population	64,337 (0.3% of total population in 2011).[40] According to estimates by the Muftiate, the Muslim population now numbers 70,000.[41]
Ethnic/National Backgrounds	The vast majority of Muslims in Romania are Romanian citizens, with a Turkish and Tatar ethnic background.
	Ethnic/national groups: Turkish: 26,903 Tatar: 20,060 Romanian: 6,281 Hungarian: 86

---

36 Grigore, George, "Muslims in Romania", *ISIM Newsletter*, 3 July 1999, p. 34.
37 Kozák, Gyula, "Romániai muzulmán intézmények diskurzusa az identitásról és integrációról" (The discourse on identity and integration of Muslim institutions from Romania), *Korunk*, no. 5 (May 2009), pp. 54–61 (54).
38 Isac Alak, Alina, "Types of religious identities within Romanian Muslim communities", *Journal for the Study of Religions and Ideologies*, vol. 14, no. 41 (Summer 2015), pp. 148–173 (148).
39 The results of the 2011 Census, by religion, are available on the site of the National Institute of Statistics, www.recensamantromania.ro/wp-content/uploads/2015/05/vol2_t11.xls, accessed 17 April 2017.
40 Data available on the site of the Muftiate at: http://www.muftiyat.ro/comunitatea-musulmana-din-romania/, accessed 17 April 2017.

Roma: 3,356
Ukrainian: 10
German: 25
Lipovan Russian: 21
Serbian: 24
Bulgarian: 6
Greek: 10
Jewish: 58[42]
Chinese: 10
Csango: 141[43]
Macedonian: 16
Other: 6,906
Undeclared: 417.[44]

Inner-Islamic Groups   The majority of Romania's Muslims follow the Sunni Hanafi *madhhab*.

Geographical Spread   Dobrudja has a sizeable Muslim population (90% of the ethnic Turks and 96% of the ethnic Tatars live in the Dubrudjan county of Constanza).[45] According to the Romanian Muftiate, 85% of Muslims live in the county of Constantza, 12% live in the county of Tulcea, and the others live in different Southern urban centres, such as Bucharest, Brăila, Galaţi, Călăraşi, Giurgiu, Olteniţa, and Turnu Severin.[46]

---

41   It is not clear what this self-identification as ethnically "Jewish", and religiously "Muslim", signifies.

42   The Csangos are a Catholic ethnic minority, speaking an old dialect of the Hungarian language. The individuals who identified themselves as Muslims are most likely converts.

43   The results of the 2011 Census, by religion and ethnicity, are available on the site of the National Institute of Statistics, www.recensamantromania.ro/wp-content/uploads/2015/05/vol2_t14.xls, accessed 17 April 2017.

44   The results of the 2011 Census, with the demographic characteristics of the population, are available on the site of the National Institute of Statistics, www.recensamantromania.ro/wp-content/uploads/2013/07/REZULTATE-DEFINITIVE-RPL_2011.pdf, accessed 17 April 2017.

45   Data available on the site of the Muftiate at: http://www.muftiyat.ro/comunitatea-musulmana-din-romania/, accessed 17 April 2017.

Number of Mosques	There are 77 officially recognised mosques.[47] Legally, only the Muftiate can endorse the founding and the functioning of a mosque, be it the property of either a legal or individual entity.
Muslim Burial Sites	The Muftiate (as the only legal representative of the Islamic faith community in Romania) owns 108 cemeteries.[48] They are all located in the region of Dobrudja. In some cities (e.g. Bucharest), there is an acute need for cemetery space, while in others (e.g. Constantza), there is some need for additional provision. The creation of a Muslim cemetery in Bucharest was placed on the municipality's agenda some ten years ago.
"Chaplaincy" in State Institutions	There are no imams in the armed forces. The Muftiate can assign an imam to visit a prison inmate at the inmate's request and at the Muftiate's expense. The same applies to patients in hospitals. Most prisons and state hospitals have only Orthodox Christian chapels.
Halal Products	In the main cities, there are several halal food shops with both Muslim and non-Muslim customers, as well as numerous ethnic restaurants, which offer Arab and Turkish halal food and do not serve alcohol. The meat for these shops and restaurants is supplied by halal slaughter houses operating in Romania and certified by the Muftiate. Moreover, Romania exports meat to several Muslim majority

---

46 Information available on the site of the State Secretariat for Religious Denominations (*Secretariatul de Stat pentru Culte*), http://culte.gov.ro/?page_id=770, accessed 6 October 2018.

47 Data available on the site of the State Secretariat for Religious Denominations at: http://culte.gov.ro/?page_id=770, accessed 6 October 2018.

countries, such as Jordan.[49] Generally, halal food is not available in Romania either in public institutions or in supermarkets.

Dress Code

There are no laws or regulations limiting Muslim dress in public or for pupils in schools. In the last few years, many convert women have started wearing the head scarf. Muslim women can ask permission from the authorities to have their ID or passport photo with them wearing a head scarf. Muslim women wearing the niqab have not been observed.

Places of Islamic Learning and Education

According to the *Law of Education* (*Law of National Education 2011/* ch. I, art. 18), religion is taught in public schools and pupils, or their parents, can express the wish to take courses in a particular religion (including Islam). Only persons authorised by the Ministry of Education and the heads of the legally recognised denominations, can teach religion in public schools.

The Turkish high school in the Dobrudjan town of Medgidia (in Romanian: *Colegiul Național Kemal Atatürk*, in Turkish: *Kemal Atatürk Ulusal Koleji*, Medgidia, str. Română, nr. 2, tel.: ++40 241818105, www.isjcta.ro/ofertaeduc/licee/ColegiulNationalKemalAtaturk/index.html; https://ro-ro.facebook.com/kolejimiz) teaches a course on Islamic Theology. The school operates under the joint support of the Romanian and Turkish governments.

Islam is also taught in mosques and by religious and cultural associations on an extra-curricular and private basis. Such private schools are: the Jerusalem School of Bucharest (*Madrasat*

---

48 "Surplus of local, imported meat available during Ramadan", *The Jordan Times*, 8 June 2017, http://www.jordantimes.com/news/local/surplus-local-imported-meat-available-during-ramadan%E2%80%99, accessed 5 August 2017.

al-Quds fi Bukharist, Bucharest, Şos. Fabrica de gheaţă, tel.: ++40 726474674, https://www.facebook.com/pages/Jerusalem-School-of-Bucharest-JSB-/104230119701663), under the patronage of the Islamic and Cultural League; the Crescent School and Kindergarten (*Şcoala şi Grădiniţa Semiluna*, Bucharest, str. Munţii Gurghiului, nr. 50–52, tel.: ++40 720952143, www.gradiscoalasemiluna.ro/, https://en-gb.facebook.com/people/Scoala-Si-Gradinita-Semiluna/100006749146914), under the auspices of the Crescent Islamic Cultural Centre.

The *Asociaţia Musulmanilor din România* (Association of Muslims of Romania) also offers online courses on Islam.[50]

Muslim Media and Publications

The main printed media presenting general information and news regarding the life of Muslim communities, are the monthly *Hakses* (The Authentic Voice), published by UDTR (Constantza, str Crişanei, nr. 44, tel.: ++40 241550903; online issues: http://hakses.turc.ro/#gsc.tab=0) and *Zaman Romania* (http://zamanromania.ro/). This was formerly the Romanian edition of the Turkish *Zaman* newspaper, and maintains an editorial policy critical of the Turkish authorities, and whose representative has publicly denied any financial link with Fethullah Gülen.[51] Launched in 1993, it has been published in Romanian and Turkish (both on paper and online), with a special section for news from Dobrudja. An entirely separate Romanian edition was launched in February 2013.

---

49   http://www.asociatiamusulmanilor.ro/index.php?option=com_content&view=category&layout=blog&id=69&Itemid=74, accessed 4 June 2018.

50   Siclitaru, Lavinia, "'Imperiul' lui Gulen din Constanţa–Şcoala Spectrum şi Liceul Internaţional, Fundaţia Tuna şi ziarul bilingv Zaman" (The "empire" of Gülen–Spectrum School and the International High School, Tuna Foundation and the bilingual journal Zaman), *Ziua de Constanţa*, 18 July 2016, http://www.ziuaconstanta.ro/stiri/deschidere-editie/imperiul-lui-gulen-din-constanta-scoala-spectrum-si-liceul-international-fundatia-tuna-si-ziarul-bilingv-zaman-document-600521.html, accessed 17 April 2017.

Radio T (Constantza, str. Bogdan Vodă nr. 75, tel.: ++40 341820073, http://radio-t.ro/), is a broadcasting station opened in 2009 by the UDTR, UDTTMR and the Muftiate. It airs programmes on various topics in Romanian, Turkish and Tatar.

The web portal *Islam Romania* (http://islam-romania.ro/) is administered by the Islamic and Cultural League. It continues to increase its activities, and presents information from diverse sources in the Romanian language, and offers downloadable books and journals.

Meant to be the first online Islamic TV channel in Romania, *RouaTV* (www.rouatv.ro) mainly broadcasts sermons, delivered in Arabic, by Abu al Ola Nagi Al Ghithy, the president of the Cultural Centre Islam Today.

Main Muslim Organisations

– Great Mufti's Office of the Muslim Community of Romania (*Muftiatul cultului musulman*, Str. Bogdan Voda nr. 75, Constantza, tel./fax: ++40 241611390, email: muftiyat.muftiyat@yahoo.com,www.muftiyat.ro,https://www.facebook.com/Muftiatul). This is the only religious institution that legally represents the followers of Islam in Romania.
– The Turkish and Tatar minorities are represented by the Muftiate's Synodal Council (Romanian: *Consiliu Sinodal*, Turkish: *Şura-i Islam*). In the Parliament of Romania the Turkish minority is represented by the Turkish Democratic Union of Romania (*Uniunea Democrată Turcă din România*– UDTR, Str. Crişana nr. 44, Constantza, tel./fax: ++40 241550903, email: udtr@turc.ro, www.rdtb.ro/, https://www.facebook.com/UniuneaTurca). Until 2016, the Tatar minority was represented in Parliament by the Democratic Union of Turkish-Muslim Tatars in Romania (*Uniunea Democrată a Tătarilor Turco-Musulmani din România*–UDTTMR, Str. B.P. Haşdeu, nr. 53, Constantza, tel./fax: ++40 241616643; ++40 241520186, email: udttmr@yahoo.com, http://uniuneatatara.ro; https://www.facebook.com/udttmroficial).

Newly established associations, and foundations dominated by immigrants from various ethnic backgrounds and converts, are also actively engaged in public activities, charities, and the translation and publishing of religious literature, as well as the teaching of Arabic. The main organisations are:

- Crescent Islamic Cultural Centre Foundation (*Fundaţia Centrul Cultural Islamic Semiluna*, Bucharest, sector 6, Str. Munţii Gurghiului, nr. 50–52, tel.: ++40 212238258, www.musulman.ro/;https://www.facebook.com/CentrulCulturalIslamicSemiluna).
- Islamic Cultural Centre Islam Today Foundation (*Fundaţia Centrul Cultural Islamic Islamul Azi*, Bucharest, sector 2, Şos. Colentina, nr. 373, tel.: ++40 212410280; Constantza, Str. Maior Şofran, nr. 11, tel.: ++40 726170204, www.islamulazi.ro/, https://ro-ro.facebook.com/CCI.IslamulAzi). Formerly the Taiba Foundation.
- Muslim Sisters Association (*Asociaţia Surori Musulmane*, at the same addresses as the Cultural Centre Islam Today Foundation in Bucharest and Constantza, tel.: ++40 766805530, email: surorimusulmane@yahoo.com; https://ro-ro.facebook.com/asociatiasurorimusulmane).
- Tuna Foundation (*Fundaţia Tuna*, Bucharest, Bd. Regina Maria, nr. 34, tel.: ++40 213355858, email: elena@halt.ro, http://www.tuna.ro/, https://www.facebook.com/FundatiaTuna/). Linked to the Gülen Movement.
- Islamic and Cultural League in Romania (*Liga Islamică şi Culturală din România*), has its main branch in Bucharest (Bucharest, sector 2, Str. Fabrica de Gheaţă, nr.14, www.islamromania.ro; https://ro-ro.facebook.com/LigaIslamicaSiCulturala) and others in Cluj-Napoca (Cluj-Napoca, str. Pastorului, nr. 17), Constantza (at the same address as the Cultural Centre Islam Today Foundation), Timisoara (str. Dr. Ioan Mureşan, nr. 15), Iasi (str. Morilor nr. 20), and Craiova (str. Grigore Pleşoianu, nr. 11).
- Association of Muslims of Romania (*Asociaţia Musulmanilor din România*, Constantza, Str. Egalităţii, nr. 9b, tel.: ++40 72317710, email: office@asociatiamusulmanilor.ro; www.asociatiamusulmanilor.ro/).

Russia

Elmira Akhmetova[1]

Introduction

Following developments in 2016, Muslims in Russia continued to focus on both their internal affairs and international diplomacy in 2017. At the beginning of the year, the activities of the *Soviet Muftiyev Rossii* (Russian Council of Muftis–RCM), the most influential Islamic establishment in Russia, were centred on the issues related to the restrictions on the Muslim head scarf. Following a supplementary chapter to the *Law on Education No. 273 FZ* from 29 December 2012–which stipulates a secular dress code, excluding any religious or cultural characteristics for all pupils in primary and secondary schools nationwide–many schools announced a rule banning school girls from wearing the head scarf. Since then, the cases of head scarf-wearing Muslim school-girls being prevented from entering schools and universities, and various types of discrimination against, and harassment of, Muslim girls by school authorities were recorded as escalating sharply between the end of 2016 and the beginning of 2017. Dozens of school teachers wearing the head scarf were expelled from schools in the Republic of Mordovia, in the city of Ulyanovsk, and in other regions of the country.

Olga Vasilyeva, Minister of Education and Science of the Russian Federation, pointed out during a press conference on 21 January 2017 that there is no place for the head scarf in Russian public schools. On 25 January 2017, Ramzan Kadirov, the President of the Republic of Chechnya, opposed the suggestion of Vasilyeva to ban head scarves in Russian public schools and, by referring to freedom of conscience and religion embedded in the Russian Constitution, declared that his daughters would not take their head scarves off in schools.[2] Leaders of Muslim organisations and intellectuals condemned discrimination on the basis of religious attributes, and called upon the Government to allow Muslim women to dress according to their religious rulings. As a result, the

---

1 Elmira Akhmetova holds a PhD in History and Civilisation from the International Islamic University of Malaysia (IIUM) and is currently Assistant Professor in History and Civilisation at the same university. She is the author of *Islam in Russia: Historical Facts and Current Developments* (Kuala Lumpur: IAIS Malaysia, 2013) and of various papers about Islam in Russia, Middle Eastern history and political issues.
2 "Chechnya's Kadyrov: my daughters won't take their hijabs off in schools", *Jam News*, 16 January 2017, https://jam-news.net/?p=14140, accessed 18 February 2018.

court in Mordovia ruled to allow the wearing of head scarves in public schools within the Republic, both for teachers and pupils, in February 2017.[3]

Another source of tension between Muslims of a Tatar ethnic origin and the authorities was caused by the issue of teaching the Tatar language at public schools in the Republics of Tatarstan and Bashkortostan. In Russia, Tatar is considered the language of Islamic education and the symbol of Muslim identity. In Russian colonial history, the Russian language has been utilised to assimilate and Russify Muslim subjects within the majority of ethnic Russians. In the 1990s, Tatarstan recognised Tatar as an official language of the Republic along with Russian, and learning Tatar became mandatory for all inhabitants, although, in reality, this policy has not been effectively implemented. In 2017, the teaching hours for the Tatar language at schools were reduced down to two hours weekly. In addition, such teaching could now only be implemented on a voluntary basis with the written request of parents. Many Tatar parents, especially in cities, have started to remove their children from Tatar language classes as it is considered unpractical, as all examinations and higher education is solely in Russian throughout the country. Tatar national activists saw this move by the Russian government as a new blow to their religious and ethnic identities, and a form of discrimination against their rights as a minority to learn their native language and culture. In addition, school principals who refused to reduce the hours given to the Tatar language in their schools were prosecuted.[4]

Close to the end of 2017, many Russian Muslims were excited and motivated as Aina Gamzatova submitted the required documents to Russia's Central Election Commission for her self-nomination for the Russian presidency. She is the wife of the Mufti of the Republic of Dagestan, and the head of Russia's largest Muslim media holding, Islam.ru, which comprises television, radio and print outlets. Russia held its seventh presidential election on 18 March 2018.[5] Although Russia's Central Election Commission (CEC) refused to register Aina Gamzatova, referring to a lack of documents, this move by a Muslim woman in

---

3 "Advokatlar: Azyurkada Yaulikny Yakladik–Emma By Waqitlicha Jingu" (Lawyers: we defended scarf in Azyurka although it is a short-term victory), *Radio Liberty*, https://www.azatliq.org/a/28403536.html, accessed 18 February 2018.

4 "Kazan school director faces suspension for refusal to abolish mandatory Tatar classes", *Radio Liberty*, 8 December 2017, https://www.rferl.org/a/russia-tatarstan-teacher-refuses-abolish-mandatory-tatar-language-classes/28905231.html, accessed 20 February 2018.

5 "Dagestani Mufti's wife submits documents for Russia's 2018 presidential run," *Russian News Agency*, 1 January 2018, http://tass.com/politics/983888, Mirovalev, Mansur, "Aina Gamzatova: the Muslim woman challenging Putin", *Al-Jazeera*, 31 December 2017, http://www.aljazeera.com/news/2017/12/aina-gamzatova-muslim-woman-challenging-putin-171230123254169.html, both accessed 20 February 2018.

a head scarf became a symbol for the existence of religious freedom in Russia, especially for the media.

At the official level, high-ranking Russian officials continued to appreciate the contributions by Muslims to the betterment of Russian society. The tenth report by the Organisation of Islamic Cooperation (OIC) on Islamophobia, states that Putin is among one of the world leaders, who showed "friendly" gestures towards Muslims and Islam. On various occasions, he highlighted that there is no link between Islam and terrorism.[6] On the occasion of the 'Id al-Fitr 2017, for instance, Vladimir Putin acknowledged the enormous impact that Muslims, as a united *umma* (community), had on the development of international and interreligious dialogue.[7]

At the same time, domestic anti-Muslim policies by the Government continued in 2017, including the cases of arrests of Muslims on allegations of being involved in terrorist activities. Respect for the rights to freedom of expression, and peaceful assembly and association have largely declined in Russia since the Russian intervention in Crimea in March 2014. The authorities dominate the print and broadcast media, and further extended their control over the internet. NGOs faced further harassment and reprisals under the "foreign agents" law, while their access to foreign funding was further restricted by a new law banning "undesirable" organisations. Published by the Ukrainian Institute for the Future, a new but well-connected think tank based in Kiev, the report entitled "Crimea: Three Years of Occupation" noted that, under Moscow's administration, Crimea has seen the imposition of a raft of draconian new laws, governing everything from military conscription to alcohol consumption. According to the report, there has also been a surge in human rights abuses, and the "systemic persecution" of the region's indigenous Tatar population, whose governing body, the *mejlis*, has been formally banned as a "terrorist organisation". The goal of this effort is twofold: to subjugate the region's native population and to tether it more closely to Moscow.[8] As Al-Jazeera observes, Muslims in the Russian occupied Crimea remain under pressure, marginalised and persecuted by the Government. The religious freedom of Crimean

---

6 *Tenth OIC Observatory Report on Islamophobia, Presented to the 44th Council of Foreign Ministers*, Abidjan, Republic of Côte d'Ivoire, 10–11 July 2017, p. 67, http://rusisworld.com/sites/default/files/images/files/10th_islamophobia_rep_en.pdf, accessed 20 February 2018.

7 "Putin Pozdravil Musulman v Rossii s Prazdnikom Kurban Bayram (Putin congratulated Muslims in Russia on Kurban Bayram), *RIA News*, 25 September 2017, https://ria.ru/religion/20170901/1501529152.html, accessed 15 February 2018.

8 Berman, Ilan "How Russian rule has changed Crimea," *Foreign Affairs*, 13 July 2017, https://www.foreignaffairs.com/articles/eastern-europe-caucasus/2017-07-13/how-russian-rule-has-changed-crimea?cid=nlc-fa_fatoday-20170713, accessed 20 February 2018.

Muslims is under threat as many mosques across the peninsula have had CCTV cameras installed and are monitored by Russian security services.[9]

In 2017, cases of discriminations against Muslims and violation of Muslims' rights under the pretext of "fighting against religious extremism" and "Islamic terrorism" continued in Russia. A number of Islamic books were ruled "extremist" and several practising Muslims were detained for reading banned literature. Cases of racism, Islamophobia and xenophobia continued to be visible to the Russian public. Sociological research conducted by Levada Analytical Centre on 14–17 July 2017 detected a decline in xenophobia and racism in Russia in 2017.[10] The SOVA Centre for Information and Analysis, a Moscow-based Russian non-governmental organisation and think-tank, conducting sociological research primarily on nationalism and racism in post-Soviet Russia, also noted a slow decline in violent attacks on individuals with a non-Slavic appearance. Central Asian Muslims, however, continue to be the main targets of racist violence, with eleven people injured in 2017, along with three persons injured from the Caucasus, and five individuals, simply identified as "non-Slavic in appearance", injured.[11]

Public Debates

The phenomenon of Islamophobia and the politics of hatred towards everything Islamic continues in Russia. Consequently, several negative developments took place in 2017, such as cases of public and official objections by the Orthodox Church, regional administrations, and non-Muslim populations, to the construction of new mosques or to the celebration of Islamic festivals. Alongside this we also saw the refusal to employ head scarf-wearing women and bearded men, the dismissal of head scarf-wearing women from their jobs, and cases where head scarf-wearing girls were not allowed to enter educational institutions.

The shortage of mosques and places of worship continued to be a major issue for Russia's Muslims. The non-Muslim population and local governments in many Russian regions strongly objected to new mosques, claiming that

---

9   Coffey, Luke, "Russia continues to oppress Crimea's Tatars", *Al-Jazeera*, 19 March, 2016, http://www.aljazeera.com/indepth/opinion/2016/03/russia-continues-oppress-crimea-tatars-160308054208716.html, accessed 19 February 2018.

10 http://www.sova-center.ru/racism-xenophobia/discussions/2017/08/d37739, accessed 20 February 2018.

11 http://www.sova-center.ru/racism-xenophobia/publications/2018/01/d38732, accessed 20 February 2018.

they would spread "Islamic radicalism" and "Islamic extremism." The Mufti of Russia, Ravil Gainutdin, in his speech at the pre-election tour of Vladimir Putin to Ufa on 25 January 2018, mentioned the cases of public and official reaction against new mosques in the country in 2017.[12] More mosques and prayer houses are needed for practising Muslims in many Russian cities especially in Moscow, which is home to about 2 million Muslims (14% of the total population of the city).[13] There are only five mosques in Moscow, the largest of which, the Moscow Cathedral Mosque, can accommodate around 10,000 worshipers at one time. However, the number of worshippers who came to pray during 'Id al-Fitr on 25 June 2017 at the Moscow Cathedral Mosque was over 250,000, according to a police report.[14] Sergey Sobyanin, the then-mayor of Moscow, warned Muslims in 2013 that no permission would be granted to build new mosques in Moscow, and this decision did not change in 2017. Yekaterinburg, the fourth-largest city in the Russian Federation, and the administrative centre of the Sverdlovsk region, has a large Muslim population (700,000 in the Sverdlovsk region), but the community suffers from a lack of mosques in the city. On 24 November 2007, the foundation stone was laid for the construction of a large Cathedral Mosque with four minarets. The construction, however, was stopped in 2010, after about 26 million Russian Rubles (€350,000) had been spent, and the land, where there was a temporary prayer hall, was transferred to the city administration. In 2017, the city administration ordered the destruction of the temporary prayer hall, with a deadline of 1 September. Another mosque in Yekaterinburg, the Rahmat mosque, was designated for demolition in 2017, as it interferes with the administration's plan to build a new railway.[15] There is also no mosque in the city of Voronezh, which is home to about 30,000–50,000 Muslim residents (about 1% of the total population). The persistent appeals from the local Muslim organisation to obtain land for

---

12 Kharrasova, Landysh, "Muftiler Putinga telaganen Aitkanme?" (Did muftis tell Putin what they wanted?), *Radio Liberty*, https://www.azatliq.org/a/28997960.html, accessed 20 February 2018.
13 Hanrahan, Mark, "Moscow is largest Muslim city in Europe", *International Business Times*, 23 July 2015, http://www.ibtimes.com/moscow-largest-muslim-city-europe-faithful-face-discrimination-public-authorities-2020858, accessed 20 February 2017; and "Moscow population 2018," *World Population Review*, http://worldpopulationreview.com/world-cities/moscow-population, accessed 22 February 2018.
14 "250,000 Muslims flock to Moscow's cathedral mosque for Eid prayer", *RT*, 25 June 2017, https://www.rt.com/news/394009-russia-celebrates-eid-festival, accessed 22 February 2018.
15 http://www.info-islam.ru/publ/stati/aktualno/musulmane_ekaterinburga_ostalis_bez_sobornoj_mecheti/49-1-0-44823; https://www.azatliq.org/a/28677746.html, both accessed 22 February 2018.

a mosque were rejected by the regional administration and local inhabitants. The Muslim community in Kolomna, a city in the central European part of Russia, has for 15 years appealed to the city administration for them to grant land for a mosque, but the city administration has not approved their requests.

The construction of a mosque in Kaliningrad, a seaport city on the Baltic Sea, formerly called Königsberg, is also blocked by the city administration. The Muslim population of the city is believed to be more than 100,000 and does not have a proper place to perform their religious rituals. They have appealed repeatedly to the city administration to obtain permission to build a mosque for more than 20 years. Official permission was granted in 2009, and the construction was almost complete, when in 2013 the Kaliningrad Court made a decision claiming that the mosque land was located in a recreational area and of regional and cultural importance, and so annulled the decision of land allocation. The Russian Supreme Court rejected an appeal against this court decision on 28 November 2014, after which the local government authorities demanded that the mosque, of which 80% had been built, be demolished. As a consequence, the Muslims of Kaliningrad appealed to the European Court of Human Rights on 29 November 2014 and the case was accepted in December 2014.[16] The city administration then granted land for a new mosque in another part of the city, but still demands the destruction of the built mosque.[17] Such cases of the closure of functioning mosques, or of those which are still under construction, by local governments under the pretext of "unsuitable" location or public objection, happen repeatedly in many Russian cities.[18]

Such negative developments have had an overwhelming impact on the security, rights and well-being of Russia's Muslims. The most integrated traditional Russian Muslims such as Tatars and Bashkirs, whose religious adherence is not noticeable, do not face serious adverse public opinion from non-Muslims. Muslims from the North Caucasus region and Central Asian immigrants, however, are often unwelcome in Russian cities. Central Asians and other Muslims are called "darkies" by Russians due to their skin colour. Millions of Central

---

16 Sukharkin, Sergey, "Is Kaliningrad on the brink of inter-ethnic conflict?", *Eurasia Daily Monitor*, vol. 14, issue 132 (2017), https://jamestown.org/program/is-kaliningrad-on-the-brink-of-inter-ethnic-conflict; "ECHR accepts application for mosque from Russian Muslims", *World Bulletin*, 31 December 2014, www.worldbulletin.net/news/151983/echm-accepts-application-for-mosque-from-russian-muslims; Arnold, Victoria, "Russia: Kaliningrad and Moscow struggles for places of worship", *Forum 18*, 16 December 2014, www.forum18.org/archive.php?article_id=2024, all accessed 25 February 2018; http://en.news-4-u.ru/in-the-op-and-the-hrc-urged-local-authorities-to-pay-more-attention-to-the-rights-of-the-muslims.html, all accessed 9 February 2017.

17 http://www.islamnews.ru/news-486858.html, accessed 25 February 2018.

18 https://www.azatliq.org/a/28997960.html, accessed 25 February 2018.

Asians, mostly from Uzbekistan, Tajikistan and Kyrgyzstan, work in Russia, usually in low-paid jobs, thus their label of a blue-collar workforce. According to a survey conducted by the independent Levada polling agency in July 2017, 27% of Russians feel "irritation, dislike or fear" towards Central Asians, and almost one in five Russians think that their presence in Russia has to be "limited". In February 2017, 38% of respondents had negative feelings about migrants from Central Asia, and 41% felt the same about migrants from the North Caucasus, while the respondents who shared this feeling towards migrants from Belarus and Ukraine were only 13% and 19% respectively.[19] Within the last ten years, hundreds of Central Asians have been killed and thousands wounded in hate attacks by ultra-nationalists and skinheads, and corrupt police officers routinely prey on them to extort money, by threatening detention or deportation.[20] An opinion poll conducted by the Echo of Moscow (*Ekho Moskvy*) on 28 October 2017, revealed that 83% of respondents expressed their unwillingness to see migrants in their cities.[21] Another poll conducted by the same public opinion agency on 3 June 2017, revealed that 65% of respondents do not want to have neighbours of non-Slavic origin, while only 27% did not mind.[22]

Such Islamophobic sentiments persisted among the Russian public in 2017, as various other opinion polls reveal. To the question asked by the Echo of Moscow on 31 March 2017: "Is there a need for menu varieties at public schools to accommodate the religious dietary requirements of minority groups?", 83% of respondents answered no, while only 13% believed in the necessity of providing a special menu to accommodate religious minority dietary requirements.[23] On the same day, the Echo of Moscow conducted another poll, asking "Can we allow pupils at public schools to wear clothes according to their religious requirements?"; 85% of respondents answered no, and only 12% responded yes.[24]

The attitude of the Russian public remained unchanged on the Muslim head scarf issue; it is considered a religious symbol among the Russian public. The Echo of Moscow's poll, conducted in 29 January 2017, reveals that 87% of respondents support the prohibition of the head scarf or any other religious and

---

19 "Attitudes towards migrants", *Levada*, 29 May 2017, https://www.levada.ru/en/2017/05/29/attitudes-toward-migrants, accessed 25 February 2018.
20 Mirovalev, Mansur, "Muslim migrants succeed in Russia despite xenophobia", *Al-Jazeera*, 24 December 2017, http://www.aljazeera.com/news/2017/12/muslims-succeed-russia-xenophobia-171224055010711.html, accessed 10 February 2018.
21 https://echo.msk.ru/polls/2082150-echo.html, accessed 26 February 2018.
22 https://echo.msk.ru/polls/1993544-echo.html, accessed 26 February 2018.
23 https://echo.msk.ru/polls/1954482-echo.html, accessed 26 February 2018.
24 https://echo.msk.ru/polls/1954594-echo.html, accessed 26 February 2018.

ideological symbols in schools, while only 10% are against banning religious symbols.[25] Yet, public opinion commonly depends on stereotypes, created by the media and entertainment industry. On 24 August, the Echo of Moscow conducted two public opinion polls online, asking the same question with slightly different phrasings. To the question "Are girls in scarves beautiful?",[26] 26% responded positively, while 66% responded negatively.[27] In another question, the agency used the word "hijab", which means Muslim head scarf; only 9% of respondents answered yes to the question "Are girls in hijabs beautiful", while 86% responded negatively.[28]

Yet, such extreme public dislike of religious attributes in Russia cannot simply be the result of widespread Islamophobia alone. In general, sentiments of religiosity are barely noticeable among the Russian public, and there is a strong public antagonism towards everything associated with any type of religion or religious symbol. On 15 July 2017, the Echo of Moscow asked "Do you need a prayer room at the workplace?", without specifying the type of prayer room. Only 3% of respondents indicated their need for a prayer room at work, while 96% responded negatively.[29] As the results of another public poll conducted on the same day indicate, 91% of respondents are against having prayer halls at workplaces, while only 8% of the respondents are fine with it.[30] The poll carried out on 14 May shows that 57% of the respondents do not believe in God at all, and only 35% answered that they do.[31] The high level of Islamophobic sentiments prevailing in Russia can thus be explained by a general anti-religious attitude, that is deeply rooted from the time of the Soviet Union.

Another public opinion survey conducted by the independent Levada Centre in December 2017 throughout the whole of Russia, asked the question "Who would you say are Russia's enemies?" The USA goes is in first place with 68%, and Ukraine is second with 29%. Surprisingly, radical Islamists, supporters of Islamic extremism and ISIS are number nine in the list with 5%.[32] Another poll conducted by the leading Russian Public Opinion Research Centre, WCIOM, in September 2017, reveals that the Russian public still considers ISIS to be the largest threat to the well-being and security of the country (23%), while Islam

---

25 https://echo.msk.ru/polls/1918448-echo.html, accessed 26 February 2018.
26 The original term used in this question was *platok*, the Russian word for any type of scarf.
27 https://echo.msk.ru/polls/2042776-echo.html, accessed 26 February 2018.
28 https://echo.msk.ru/polls/2042756-echo.html, accessed 26 February 2018.
29 https://echo.msk.ru/polls/2019166-echo.html, accessed 27 February 2018.
30 https://echo.msk.ru/polls/2019170-echo.html, accessed 27 February 2018.
31 https://echo.msk.ru/polls/1980830-echo.html, accessed 27 February 2018.
32 https://www.levada.ru/en/2018/02/02/enemies, accessed 3 March 2018.

and Muslims are considered to be the second greatest threat with 11%. The USA is number three in the threat list with 10%.[33]

Ethnic Russian nationalism remained present in the public sphere in 2017. Reported skinhead attacks were mainly directed against immigrants from Central Asia and are largely confined to a few cities such as Moscow, St Petersburg and Nizhniy Novgorod. Yet, experts suggest there has been a decline in the level of xenophobia and ultra-nationalism among the Russian public.[34]

Transnational Links

In 2017, the RCM represented the voice of Russia's Muslims at various significant international conferences and gatherings related to Islam and Muslim affairs. These include: the International Conference "2017–Year of Islamic Solidarity: Interreligious and Intercultural Dialogue" in Baku, Azerbaijan, in December 2017; the 13th International Muslim Forum on "Qur'anic Humanism and Global Problems of Modernity" on 11 December 2017 in Helsinki, Finland; the International Conference on "The Role of Fatwas in Social Stability" in 17–19 October in Cairo, Egypt; the International Islamic Conference "Muslims and Resistance against Terrorism and Extremism" on 31 July in Brazil; the International Conference on "Islam and Contemporary Challenges" in April in Jordan; and the International Conference "City Hebron: Reality and Challenges" on 23–25th April in the Palestinian Territories. On 27 December 2017, the RCM also took part in an international conference in Jiddah, Saudi Arabia, to discuss the present and future situation of Mecca and its surrounding areas.[35]

Damir Mukhetdinov, First Deputy to the Head of the RCM, while addressing the International Conference on "2017–Year of Islamic Solidarity: Interreligious and Intercultural Dialogue" on 22 December in Baku, stressed that 2017 was a productive year for Russia's Muslims in terms of spreading worldwide solidarity. *Blagotvoritel'niy Fond Zakat* (the Zakat Aid Foundation, affiliated to the RCM) organised the collection of humanitarian aid for Syrian refugees in Lebanon, and Rohingya Muslim refugees in Bangladesh.[36] Mufti Ravil Gainutdin strongly condemned the statement of Donald Trump on Jerusalem, saying that the

---

33   https://wciom.ru/index.php?id=236&uid=116378, accessed 3 March 2018.
34   http://www.sova-center.ru/racism-xenophobia/discussions/2017/08/d37739, accessed 20 February 2018.
35   https://muslim.ru/articles/279/19829, accessed 3 March 2018.
36   https://muslim.ru/articles/287/19803, accessed 3 March 2018.

recognition of Jerusalem as the capital of Israel lessens the city's importance as the spiritual centre of three religions, Islam, Christianity and Judaism.[37] On behalf of Russia's Muslims, the RCM made an official declaration on 7 December, stating that the recognition of Jerusalem as the capital of Israel will escalate the conflict in the region. This declaration points out that Russia's Muslims fully support the official position of the Russian government on the Israeli-Palestinian conflict, that is the formation of an independent Palestinian state with East Jerusalem as its capital.[38]

The RCM has maintained its function as a bridge between the Muslim world and the Russian government. In 2017, the RCM received the official delegations from a number of Muslim majority countries and the representatives of those from Muslim minority communities including the Palestinian leader Mahmud Abbas on 13 May, to discuss cooperation between the two countries in terms of religion, education, culture and fighting extremism. It also hosted Khaidar Hadi, the ambassador of Iraq to Russia on 12 May, as well as Dato' Mohd Johari, Deputy Defence Minister of Malaysia, and Shaikh Saad al-Shasri, advisor to the Government of the Kingdom of Saudi Arabia on 30 May. A delegation of members of the Turkish parliament was also received on 5 December to discuss the prospects of cooperation between Russia and Turkey in establishing peace and stability in the region, and combating extremism and terrorism. Further delegations included Mohammad Yasmin bin Hj Umar, Minister of Energy and Industry of Brunei Darussalam, to discuss the further joint strategies between two countries; a delegation from Ministry of Tourism of Indonesia on 16 November to form a joint strategy in developing halal tourism and industry; and a delegation from Iran on 31 October to strengthen ties between Islamic universities in Russia and Iran. The RCM also met with a delegation of members of the Indonesian parliament on 13 July to exchange the experiences of both parliaments in bringing peace and integration into multi-national societies; it also met with Malik Ruiz, the President of the Muslim Community of Granada, Spain, on 7 June 2017. When Ravil Gainutdin was re-elected as a Head of the RCM in December 2017, the embassies of Bahrain, Jordan, Iran, Iraq and Algeria sent official congratulations to him.[39] The RCM organised meetings with the ambassadors to Russia of France, Spain and Switzerland on 31 May 2017.

37   https://muslim.ru/articles/278/19683, accessed 3 March 2018.
38   https://muslim.ru/articles/280/19649, accessed 3 March 2018.
39   https://muslim.ru/articles/287/19840, accessed 3 March 2018.

Law and Domestic Politics

The 1997 *Law on Freedom of Conscience*, a supplemental *Law on Religion*, does not recognise a state religion. However, its preamble identifies Russian Orthodoxy, Judaism, Islam and Buddhism as traditional religions and recognises the special contribution of Orthodoxy to the history of Russia and the establishment and development of Russian spirituality and culture. Islam is repeatedly affirmed to be part of Russian society by the Russian authorities and political leaders. Yet, in the wake of the Russian *Law on Extremism* of 2002, cases of discrimination against Muslims and violation of Muslims' rights under the pretext of "fighting against religious extremism" or "Islamic terrorism" have significantly increased in Russia. Dozens of mainstream Islamic books such as the *Riyadh al-Salihin* (The Gardens of the Righteous), *Sorok Khadisov* (Forty Hadiths) of Al-Nawawi, *Mizan al-Amal* (Balanced Criterion of Action) of Imam Ghazali, *Jizn' Proroka Muhammada* (The Life of the Prophet Muhammad) of Ibn Hisham and *al-Mubarakfuri*, and parts from the *Risale-i Nur* of Said Nursi, have been indiscriminately banned in various district courts in Russia for allegedly inciting interreligious and interracial hatred, and promoting exclusivity and superiority on the basis of religion.

In 2017, Islamic literature continued to be ruled "extremist" and placed on the Justice Ministry's Federal List of Extremist Materials, although most of it does not contain any violent or racist content. On 3 March 2017, Svetly City Court in Kaliningrad region banned a book entitled *Muslim Aqidah*, written by Ahmed Saim Kilavuz. The Ministry of Justice added it to the Federal List on 7 June 2017, noting explicitly that the Qur'anic quotations it contains are not banned, in accordance with the 2015 amendment to the *Extremism Law*. On 1 February 2017, Kirov District Court in Ufa banned *Selected Hadith*, a Russian translation of several hundred selected sayings of the Prophet Muhammad. The collection was compiled by Muhammad Yusuf Kandahlawi (1917–1965), a major figure in the Jama'at al-Tabligh movement, which is outlawed as "extremist" in Russia.[40] The Federal Service for Supervision of Communications, Information Technology, and Mass Media (*Roskomnadzor*) also has the authority to block sites, apps, and webpages without recourse to the courts. Libraries, educational institutions, and even internet cafes are also frequently

---

40 Arnold, Victoria, "Russia: Jehovah's Witness Bible, Jewish, Christian, Muslim books banned", *Forum 18 News Service*, 29 September 2017, http://www.forum18.org/archive.php?article_id=2319, accessed 5 March 2018.

reprimanded for failing to put in place adequate content filters to prevent users of their networks from accessing "extremist" material online.[41]

In addition, a number of Muslim organisations, movements and societies such as Hizb ut-Tahrir, Jama'at al-Tabligh, Nurcular (followers of Said Nursi and Fethullah Gülen), the so-called Ahl al-Sunna, Islamic Jamaat, Salafism, Wahhabism and others have been banned in Russia as being "extremist" and "contradictory to the traditional Hanafi *madhhab*," according to the 2002 *Law on Extremism*. These bans have inevitably led to the arrests of dozens if not hundreds of Muslims in Russia on allegations of belonging to "extremist groups." In 2017, several Muslims were detained for running an organisation which, according to human rights activists and lawyers, does not exist. The Oslo-based Forum 18 News Service said that, after a relative lull in law enforcement activity against readers of Said Nursi's books in 2012 and into 2013, raids and investigations have been carried out in different regions across Russia in Krasnoyarsk, Chelyabinsk, Novosibirsk, and Makhachkala, and about 40 people have been charged since the beginning of 2013. These individuals face charges under *Article 282.2, Parts 1 and 2* ("Organisation of …" or "participation in …" "… the activity of a social or religious association or other organisation in relation to which a court has adopted a decision legally in force on the liquidation or ban of the activity in connection with the carrying out of extremist activity").[42] The FSB security service is responsible for all these investigations. Two of the detainees awaiting trial in 2017 were charged for the second (Komil Odilov in Novosibirsk) or third time (Andrei Dedkov in Krasnoyarsk) for identical "crimes", that is organising a "cell" of the banned "extremist" organisation Nurcular. The appeal by Komil Odilov against his first conviction is still under consideration at the European Court of Human Rights (ECtHR). Law enforcement agents arrested an Azerbaijani-born Russian citizen Ilgar Aliyev in an armed raid on the night of 19–20 April 2017. He faces up to ten years imprisonment if convicted of charges of being connected to the Nurcular movement.[43]

In 2017, four Muslims were given criminal convictions and imprisoned for meeting with others to read Said Nursi's works in Dagestan. On 7 November 2017 at Lenin District Court in Makhachkala, Ziyavdin Dapayev was sentenced to four years in prison; in the same trial Sukhrab Kaltuyev and Artur Kaltuyev were sentenced to three years each. In a separate trial on 19 June 2017, Yevgeny

---

41 Arnold, Victoria, "Russia: 'extremism' religious freedom survey", *Forum 18 News Service*, 13 September 2016, http://forum18.org/archive.php?article_id=2215, accessed 5 March 2018.
42 Arnold, "Russia: 'extremism'".
43 http://www.forum18.org/archive.php?article_id=2358, accessed 5 March 2018.

Lvovich Kim was sentenced to three years and nine months in prison by Blagoveshchensk City Court.[44]

Forum 18 also observed that the prosecutions of Muslims who read Nursi's works usually begin with (often armed) raids on the homes of people whom law enforcement agencies suspect of "continuing the activities of a banned extremist organisation (*Nurdzhular*)".[45] Such raids involve the seizure of computers, phones, and religious literature, and the arrest and interrogation of individuals. Suspects are sometimes then kept in pre-trial detention, or are put under house arrest or travel restrictions as the investigation continues, which may take several months. Under Article 109 of *the Criminal Procedural Code*, individuals can initially be held in custody for up to two months, and investigators must seek any necessary extensions to this period by application to a district court. Pre-trial detention in extremism-related prosecutions can generally be extended to a maximum of six months, with a maximum of one year in serious cases.[46]

Based on material collected while monitoring alleged "Islamic extremism" criminal cases, Forum 18 asserts that since Vladimir Putin's re-election as President in May 2012, the Russian federal government has increasingly restricted the possibility of exercising freedom of religion and belief. Law enforcement agencies have displayed rising hostility towards independent public activity of all kinds. Since 2012, the authorities have labelled many Russian civil society and human rights groups "foreign agents". State hostility to independent civil societies, and government assertions of alleged external threats, have increased since Russia's March 2014 annexation of Crimea and the September 2015 intervention in Syria.[47] Most cases of abuse of the fundamental rights of Muslims are the consequence of the 2002 *Law on Extremism*. In fact, the Russian government does not have a policy of restricting freedom of religion or belief, but a too broad definition of "extremism" in the *Law on Extremism* has opened a space for corrupt officials to gain financial benefits under the pretext of fighting against such "extremism."

On 14 March 2017, 15 Muslims were detained in the Republic of Tatarstan for allegedly reading banned Hizb ut-Tahrir literature, and for the "establishment of a terrorist organisation". On 8 December, eight of them were given

---

44   Arnold, Victoria, "Ten years' jail for religious study meetings?", *Forum 18 News Service*, 1 March 2018, http://www.forum18.org/archive.php?article_id=2358, accessed 5 March 2018.
45   Arnold, "Ten years' jail".
46   Arnold, "Ten years' jail".
47   Arnold, Victoria, "Russia: religious freedom survey, January 2017", *Forum 18 News Service*, 13 January 2017, http://www.forum18.org/archive.php?article_id=2246, accessed 5 March 2018.

criminal convictions by the Kazan Military Court, from 16 to 19 years of imprisonment.[48] Human Rights Centre Memorial acknowledged all detainees as political prisoners.[49]

As Forum 18 observes, the State's "counter-extremism" strategy in the North Caucasus is far cruder. In the republics of Chechnya and Dagestan in particular, those dubbed "Wahhabis"–which can sometimes be men merely with a devout Muslim appearance–may be detained as "extremists" by law enforcement agencies. Local residents reported that they were frequently tortured, and in some cases they disappeared, allegations occasionally confirmed by state officials.[50]

Activities and Initiatives of Main Muslim Organisations

Throughout 2017, the leaders of Muslim organisations and intellectuals endeavoured to enhance the well-being and security of the Muslim population, and were involved in public debates on various social issues, such as the question of immigrant workers, crime, and religious and racial tolerance. Russia's Muslims and their umbrella organisations were also engaged in various local and international interfaith activities, as well as organising round tables, seminars, conferences and public lectures on interreligious dialogue, and greeting followers of other faiths at their religious festivals. Inviting such groups to *iftars* and other Islamic festivals has become a tradition in modern Russia. Joint sports, cultural and religious events between followers of different faiths also occasionally took place. In Moscow, the RCM annually organises the so-called *Shater Ramadana* (Ramadan Tent), a cultural charity project, where diplomats from Muslim majority countries, as well as local Muslim and non-Muslim political leaders, activists, scholars, public figures, the media, representatives of other religions and soldiers, as well as ordinary citizens, are invited to attend cultural programmes and share *iftar* with Muslim religious leaders. The 2017 tent programme, for instance, included discussions on various topics highlighted in the Qur'an, parties for orphans, Qur'an memorisation contests, lectures, as well as other cultural and sports activities, and was attended by more than 15,000 participants. Similar Ramadan tents were organised in Kazan in

---

48   https://memohrc.org/ru/news_old/sud-v-kazani-prigovoril-k-bolshim-srokam-vos meryh-musulman-po-ocherednomu-delu-hizb-ut, accessed 5 March 2018.

49   https://memohrc.org/ru/news_old/sud-v-kazani-prigovoril-k-bolshim-srokam-vos meryh-musulman-po-ocherednomu-delu-hizb-ut, accessed 5 March 2018.

50   Arnold, "Russia: 'extremism'".

Tatarstan, Yekaterinburg in the Sverdlovsk region, Makhachkala in Dagestan, and in other cities.

Several significant developments took place in 2017 in terms of the halal industry as well. The Eighth International Halal Exhibition in Moscow (Moscow Halal Expo 2017) was organised by the RCM with the support of the Russian ministries of Agriculture, Trade and Foreign Affairs and the Moscow City Administration, on 16–18 November 2017. More than 200 Russian and foreign companies from different countries including Turkey, the United Arab Emirates, Bahrain, Palestine, Tunisia, Iran, Uzbekistan, the Philippines, Poland, Thailand, Spain, Malaysia, Brunei, and Indonesia took part in the exhibition displaying food and beverages, cosmetic products, medicine, Islamic books and clothes. Seminars on Islamic finance, banking and insurance as well as Islamic business meetings and a Muslim Fashion Forum were held during the exhibition.[51]

International and domestic conferences and seminars were organised in different cities around the country discussing the principles of Islamic banking and the prospect of establishing Islamic banks in Russia. The most noteworthy among them was the Kazan Summit–International Islamic and Finance Summit, which has taken place annually in Kazan since 2009. This has the aim of strengthening trade and economic, scientific-technical, social, and cultural ties between Russia and the Organisation of Islamic Cooperation member countries. The Kazan Summit 2017 brought together 2,641 participants from international organisations, federal and local authorities, financial institutions, embassies of 15 states, Members of Parliament, investors and businesspeople, representing 50 countries, and 250 journalists.[52]

The diverse ethnic and cultural backgrounds of Russia's Muslim population gave rise to numerous cultural events throughout 2017. They ranged across various sporting, arts and religious events, and attracted local as well as international participants. Qur'an recitation competitions for men, women and children are organised by Muslim communities every year in various parts of Russia. The main event is the Moscow International Qur'an Reciting Competition, which attracts participants from Muslim majority countries and from Muslim minority communities. More than 40 participants from Arab countries, Turkey, Iran, the UK, Brunei Darussalam, Malaysia, Indonesia, Finland, South Africa, the USA, Central Asia, and Russia took part in the 2017 competition.

---

51 "Results of Moscow halal expo", https://www.muslim.ru/en/articles/138/19581, accessed 10 April 2018.
52 https://kazansummit.com, accessed 5 March 2018.

Muslim Population: History and Demographics

Islam first entered the territory of the modern Russian Federation through Dagestan from the mid-seventh century when, in 641, a Muslim army under the leadership of 'Abd Rahman ibn Rabi'a al-Bakhili reached the Southern Caucasus. In 685–86, Arabs took the city of Derbend, which subsequently became the focus for the Islamisation of the Northeastern Caucasus, referred to as *bab al-jihad* (the gateway of jihad).[53] In another part of modern Russia, the upper Volga basin, Islam gradually took root through trade and other economic relations with the Muslim world. The first Muslim state in the region was the Bulghar Kingdom,[54] which voluntarily accepted Islam as an official state religion in 922 in the presence of a delegation sent by the Abbasid Caliph Ja'far al-Muqtadir Billah.[55] From there, Islam spread to other parts of modern Russia, culminating during the period of the Golden Horde (*Altyn Orda*), which was established in 1242 as a result of the Mongol invasion of the Bulghar Kingdom and other neighbouring territories. Under the rule of Uzbek Khan (1312–42), Islam became the official religion of the State and, from the mid-14th century until the demise of the Golden Horde in 1437, the Volga Bulghar elite dominated the cultural and Islamic discourse of the empire.

At the beginning of the 15th century a number of independent Islamic khanates (or states), including the Kazan, Crimean, Siberian, Noghay, and Astrakhan khanates, emerged from the Golden Horde. From the 16th century, these Muslim states were conquered one after another and incorporated into a newly centralised Muscovite state of proto-Russians. Today the majority of Muslims live in their historical territories of the Volga-Urals basin, Western Siberia and the Northern Caucasus.

Russia has the largest Muslim minority population in Europe. There is no official record of the number of Muslims in the Russian Federation as the 2010 census did not include a question on religious beliefs. However, according to that same census, the total number of members of Muslim ethnic groups indigenous to Russia is about 15 million, and there are significant numbers of labour migrants from Central Asian states, such as Kyrgyzstan, Uzbekistan

---

53   Yemelianova, Galina, "Islam in Russia: an historical perspective", in Hilary Pilkington and Galina Yemelianova (eds.), *Islam in Post-Soviet Russia: Public and Private Faces* (New York: Routledge Curzon, 2003), p. 28.

54   The Bulghar Kingdom existed in the Middle Volga region (a territory within the modern republic of Tatarstan) from the eighth century until the Mongol invasion in 1236.

55   Wimbush, Enders, "Islam in Central Asia and the Caucasus", in John Esposito (ed.), *The Oxford Encyclopedia of the Modern Islamic World* (New York: Oxford University Press, 2001), vol. 2, pp. 271–272; Yemelianova, Galina, *Russia and Islam: a Historical Survey* (New York: Palgrave, 2002), p. 7.

and Tajikistan, whose expatriates form a significant portion of the approximately 10 million officially registered.[56] Ethnic Russian converts are believed to number around 100,000.[57] The Religious Diversity Index (RDI) of the Pew Research Center shows that Muslims in Russia constitute at least 10% of total population.[58]

Muslim Population	14–20 million (10%-15% of population in 2017).
Ethnic/National Backgrounds	Muslims of Russia, excluding labour migrants, are Russian citizens who have lived in their native lands for centuries. They belong to more than 40 different ethnic groups.
	Largest ethnic/national groups: Tatar: 20.3% Bashkir: 6.0% Chechen: 5.5% Avar: 3.5% Kazakh: 2.5% Azerbaijani: 2.3% Dargin: 2.3% Others: 57.6 %.
Inner-Islamic Groups	The majority of Russia's Muslims follow two Sunni schools of Islamic jurisprudence: the Hanafi and Shafi'i *madhhabs*. Muslims of the Volga-Urals region and the Nogais, Karachays and Balkars in the Northern Caucasus follow the Hanafi *madhhab*, while Muslims of Dagestan, Chechnya and Ingushetia are Shafi'is. Shi'is are a small minority to be found almost exclusively in the Caucasus, among Azerbaijanis and their diaspora, and among Dagestan's small Muslim ethnic group, the Lezgins.

---

56 "Kolichesvto Migrantov V Rossii na 2016 God" (Number of migrants in Russia in 2016), http://topmigrant.ru/migraciya/obshhaya-informaciya/migranty-v-rossii.html, accessed 5 March 2018.
57 http://voprosik.net/russkie-musulmane-segodnya, accessed 3 March 2018.
58 www.pewforum.org/2014/04/04/religious-diversity-index-scores-by-country/, accessed 3 March 2018.

Geographical Spread	Ethnic Muslims are predominant in seven out of 21 republics of the Russian Federation: Bashkortostan and Tatarstan in the Volga-Urals region, and Chechnya, Ingushetia, Dagestan, Kabardino-Balkaria and Karachay-Cherkessia in the Northern Caucasus. Other parts of Russia, including large cities such as Moscow, Nizhniy Novgorod and St Petersburg also have significant Muslim populations.
Number of Mosques	ca. 7,200 (the majority of them in the Volga-Urals and North Caucasus regions).
Main Muslim Burial Sites	Muslim cemeteries exist in all parts of the predominantly Muslim republics and also in Muslim populated villages in other regions, such as Orenburg, Saratov, Yekaterinburg, Penza and Chelyabinsk. Special sections are reserved for Muslims in communal cemeteries in most Russian cities:

- In Moscow, special Muslim sections exist in Kuzminskoe, Perepechenskoe, Domodedovskoe, Butovskoe and other cemeteries.
- In St. Petersburg, special sections for Muslims exist in Kovalevskoe, Yuzhnoe and Poroshkinskoe cemeteries.

"Chaplaincy" in State Institutions	There are officially appointed Muslim chaplains in some units of the Russian army in the Northern Caucasus. In some places imams pay occasional visits to the armed forces; Muslim religious representatives are often invited to new soldiers' swearing-in ceremonies. Some private hospitals in Moscow, Kazan, Ufa, and in cities of the Northern Caucasus have prayer rooms for Muslim patients and staff. There are no officially appointed Muslim chaplains in prisons, although some prisons in Tatarstan, Bashkortostan, Nizhny Novgorod, Chelyabinsk, Mordovia, Penza, Sverdlovsk and other regions have mosques and prayer houses

with regular imams, usually appointed from among the detainees.

Halal Products

There are no restrictions in Russia on the slaughtering of animals according to Islamic regulations. Halal certification is carried out by Muslim religious authorities, who issue halal certificates to food manufacturers and suppliers. In 2002, the RCM established the Centre for Halal Standardisation and Certification. Halal standards have been recognised by the governments of Tatarstan and Bashkortostan. Most regional Muslim religious boards have established halal committees for the development and promotion of halal standards. They have issued the halal logo, control its usage, and notify the authorities of the illegal use of the halal sign on manufactured products. Halal restaurants and shops are widespread in predominantly Muslim republics. A number of confectionary and bakery companies in Tatarstan produce halal cakes, sweets, chocolate products and pastries.

Dress Code

There were no legal restrictions on the wearing of Muslim dress in public until 2013. In 2002, Muslim women won a court case that allowed them to be photographed with the head scarf for official identification documents. In 2012, the Stavropol regional court ruled to ban head scarves in schools. On 10 July 2013, the Supreme Court of the Russian Federation confirmed the validity of this ruling issued by the Stavropol regional court. From 1 September 2013, a new *Law on Education* came into force, which established the requirements for a school uniform chosen by the school administration. According to this Law, every school has the right to decide what its students may or may not wear.

There are no legal restrictions on wearing the niqab in the Russian Federation, although it is a rare occurrence that is mainly seen in the Republic of Dagestan.

Places of Islamic Learning and Education	– Moscow Islamic University (*Moskovskiy Islamskiy Universitet*, 12 proyezd Kirova, Moscow, tel.: ++7 4953513067, www.miu.su) – Russian Islamic University, Kazan (*Rossiyskiy Islamskiy Universitet*, riu, 19 Gazovaya str., Kazan, Tatarstan, tel.: ++7 8432775536, kazanriu.ru) – Russian Islamic University, Ufa (*Rossiyskiy Islamskiy Universitet*, 5 Chernyshevskogo str., 450077, Ufa, Bashkortostan; tel.: ++7 3472519787, http://rio.bspu.ru) – Moscow Spiritual Islamic College (7 Vipolzov by-street, 129090, Moscow, tel.: ++7 4952844704) – Muhammadiya Madrasa in Kazan (34 Gabdulla Tukay st., 420021, Kazan, tel.: ++7 8432931706, http://mohammadiya.tatar) – Mahinur Madrasa in Nizhniy Novgorod (6, Kazanskaya Naberezhnaya str., Nizhniy Novgorod) – Imeni M. Sultanovoi Madrasa in Ufa (3 Mustay Karim str., Ufa, tel.: ++7 3472723858) – Nur al-Iman Madrasa in Sterlitamak (73 Bogdan Hmelnitskiy str., 453100, Sterlitamak; tel.: ++7 3473252223) – Bolghar Islamic Academy (1A, Kul Gali str., Bolghar, 422840, Tatarstan, tel.: ++7 8435902379, email: info.biacademy@gmail.com, bia.tatar).
Muslim Media and Publications	– *Al-RTV*: the first Russian-language Islamic TV channel under the patronage of the RCM, which seeks to promote dialogue among the different Muslim ethnic groups in Russia and advocates "moderate" Islam – *Islam TV*: Islamic Russian language internet channel established in 2007 under the supervision of RCM and private individuals. Its programmes include Islamic lectures, documentaries, news, children's programme, sermons, etc.

- The Medina Publishing House in Nizhniy Novgorod (www.idmedina.ru), which produces four academic journals and a newspaper; it also aims to produce a 12-volume encyclopaedia, *Islam v Rossiyskoi Federatsii* (Islam in the Russian Federation).
- *Safinat*, Islamic FM radio channel in Russian (http://radiotut.ru)
- The most popular Islamic websites are www.islam.ru, http://islam-today.ru; http://islamnews.ru, http://ansar.ru, http://umma.ru and http://islamrf.ru.

Main Muslim Organisations

- Russian Council of Muftis (*Soviet Muftiyev Rossii*–RCM, 7, Vypolzov by-street, 129090, Moscow, tel./fax: ++7 4956814904, www.muslim.ru.). RCM is an umbrella organisation founded in July 1996 that unites Sunni religious Muslim organisations in the Russian Federation on a voluntary basis. Among its main tasks are: the consolidation of Muslim religious organisations of the Russian Federation, with the aim of finding solutions to problems affecting all Muslims in Russia; coordination and mutual assistance with respect to activities organised by individual religious boards; clarification of the Council's official position with regard to various issues in relations with public authorities on the federal and local level, organisations representing other confessions, international, and foreign organisations; organisation of hajj, conferences, public relations campaigns concerning the Muslim population, the Government, and the non-Muslim population.
- Central Spiritual Board of Muslims of Russia and European Countries of the Commonwealth of Independent States (*Tsentral'noe Duxovnoe Upravlenie Musul'man Rossii i Evropeiskix Stran*, SNG–CSBM, 50, Tukaeva str., 450057, Ufa, Republic of Bashkortostan, RF, tel.: ++7 3472508086/ 2508079, http://cdum.ru.). The origins of the CSBM go back to 1788, when the Empress Catherine II ordered the establishment of the "Ufa Spiritual Gathering for Mohametan Law". Regional Muslim religious boards in the Russian Federation, except the North Caucasus region, are registered with either the RCM or the CSBM, and every local Muslim community must be affiliated to a

regional Muslim religious board in order to be officially recognised as a legal organisation. These two organisations enjoy equal rights and status in the government structure and are recognised by the State as umbrella Muslim organisations of Russia.
- Coordinating Centre of the Muslims of the Northern Caucasus (*Koordinatsionniy Center Musul'man Severnogo Kavkaza*–CCMNC, 49, Ostojenka str., 119034, Moscow, RF, tel.: ++7 4992552147, email: coorcenter@mail.ru.). The CCMNC was established in 1998 and unites almost all regional Muslim religious boards of the North Caucasus region.

Serbia

Ivan Ejub Kostić[1]

Introduction

In Serbia, a deterioration in political and press freedom marked 2017, which also had certain consequences for the Muslim minority in the country. Right-wing parties, which were quite successful in the parliamentary elections of 2016, used this momentum to reaffirm nationalistic discourses in the public sphere. Those narratives were very similar to those used in the 1990s, when Serbia did not prevent the genocide and ethnic cleansing against the Muslim population of Bosnia and Herzegovina and Kosovo, and did not punish those responsible. The main representatives of such discourse in Serbia are the Serbian Radical Party (*Srpska radikalna stranka*), with Vojislav Šešelj as its leader, and the nationalistic Serbian Movement known as DVERI. Both of these parties are now represented in the Serbian parliament. Beside the role of political parties, hate speech is very much present in the mass media as well, particularly in pro-government media outlets, like the *Informer* newspaper. Therefore, if we consider previous experiences of Muslims especially Bosniaks and Albanians, in the 1990s in particular, the current political and social climate in Serbia has made this minority feel unsafe and uncertain about their future.[2]

The dispute between the two organisations, *Islamska Zajednica Srbije* (Islamic Community of Serbia–IZS) and *Islamska zajednica u Srbiji* (Islamic Community in Serbia–IZuS) remains unresolved. Both claim to be the legitimate representative of the legally recognised *Islamska zajednica* (Islamic Community–IZ). Their registration in the register of official religious

---

1 Ivan Ejub Kostic is a PhD candidate at the Faculty of Political Sciences, University of Belgrade. He holds a degree in Islamic Studies and a Bachelor's degree in Arabic Studies from the Faculty of Philology, University of Belgrade. He is the director of the Balkan Centre for the Middle East in Belgrade, author of *Persecuted Islam* (Belgrade: Utopia, 2013), and has written numerous articles on issues related to the position of Muslims in Serbia and the Balkans.
2 The "Final Report on Serbia" by the European Commission against Racism and Intolerance (ECRI), which was published in 2017, highlighted the position of the media in Serbia since 2012 compared to the previous period. The report emphasises that the independence of the media is in great danger, and the rise of hate speech is especially highlighted. The year 2012, when the ECRI began the five-year monitoring of Serbia, coincides precisely with the arrival of the Serbian Progressive Party, which has been in power since that year.

communities, as well as the restitution of property claimed by both of these institutions, also remain pending.[3]

Public Debates

The question of Kosovo was the most dominant topic among the public, and affects many other questions that are of central concern for Serbian citizens, like the process of European integration, amendments to the Constitution, and economic development. The question of Kosovo also significantly shapes the relationship between the Serbian government and the Albanian Muslim minority, that has suffered for a long time now from many types of discrimination in Serbia. In debates over Kosovo, right-wing political circles implicitly accept the independence of Kosovo on the provision that the Bosnian autonomous *Republika Srpska* becomes part of Serbia. For example, in an interview with *Deutsche Welle*, the President of the *Republika Srpska*, Milorad Dodik, accepted Kosovo's independence, but likewise expressed the aim to achieve a similar status for the *Republika Srpska*.[4] This interview was held one week after an interview with Bakir Izetbegovic, also with *Deutsche Welle*, in which he, as the Bosniak representative in the Presidency of Bosnia and Herzegovina, referred to potential military action to preserve the territorial integrity of Bosnia and Herzegovina.[5] Serbian media responded furiously to Izetbegovic's statement, which also triggered a lot of hate speech toward Bosniaks.

Beside Kosovo, the trial and verdict of Ratko Mladić, former commander of the *Republika Srpska* army, by the International Criminal Tribunal for the former Yugoslavia, has drawn a lot of attention in Serbia. Ratko Mladić has been sentenced to life imprisonment after being convicted of being responsible for the Srebrenica genocide in 1995, as well as war crimes and crimes against humanity committed against the Bosnian Muslim population during the Bosnian war.[6] Nataša Kandić, founder of the Humanitarian Law Centre, was among

---

3   For more on the split in the Serbian Islamic Community, see Kostić, Ivan Ejub, "Serbia", in Oliver Scharbrodt, Samim Akgönül, Ahmet Alibašić, Jørgen S. Nielsen and Egdūnas Račius (eds.), *Yearbook of Muslims in Europe*, vol. 7 (Leiden: Brill, 2015), pp. 502–503.
4   http://rs.n1info.com/a343300/Svet/Region/Dodik-za-DW-crtao-mapu-Balkana-kako-ga-vidii .html, accessed 20 November 2017.
5   http://www.dw.com/bs/izetbegović-onaj-ko-voli-ovu-zemlju-mora-biti-spreman-ići-do-kraja/a-41333199, accessed 13 November 2017.
6   https://edition.cnn.com/2017/11/22/europe/ratko-mladic-verdict/index.html, accessed 22 November 2017.

many Serbian NGO representatives who gave a positive reaction to this verdict.[7] Other Serbian NGOs, like the Youth Initiative for Human Rights, the Helsinki Committee for Human Rights, and Women in Black, also gave positive statements regarding Mladic's verdict. Yet, Patriarch Irinej of the Serbian Orthodox Church said that the verdict was "something we expected", and nothing but the "devil's work".[8]

Two comprehensive surveys were carried out in 2017. These surveys about the wars in the 1990s, which were published in August and December respectively, clearly showed the extent of unawareness and lack of information among the Serbian Orthodox majority population about crimes committed during the wars in the 1990s. Upon the request of the daily newspaper *Danas*, the Demostat Research and Publishing Centre conducted the first survey in August 2017, which was entitled "Awareness of Serbian Citizens about the Wars in the 1990s, War Crimes and Trials of Those Indicted for War Crimes". In December, the Humanitarian Law Centre published its research entitled "Initial Report on the Implementation of the National Strategy for War Crimes Prosecution".[9] One of the events that caused a lot of debate in the public sphere was the demolition of a mosque in a suburb of Belgrade known as Zemun polje. The mosque was demolished during the night between 25 and 26 May 2017, at the very beginning of the month of Ramadan; it was done by Belgrade authorities in the presence of special force units.[10] The majority of this suburb of Belgrade is inhabited by Roma, and the mosque was financed by them, despite the fact that they are the most socially disadvantaged group in Serbian society. The reason given for the demolition was that the mosque was built without permission by the local authorities, notwithstanding that the majority of buildings in this suburb, including a Serbian Orthodox church close to the mosque, do not have planning permissions either.[11] Because of the reason given for the demolition of the mosque in Zemun polje, representatives of the IZS accused the Belgrade municipal authorities of double-standards

---

7   http://rs.n1info.com/a343884/Vesti/Vesti/Reakcije-na-presudu-Mladicu.html, accessed 22 November 2017.

8   http://rs.n1info.com/a344349/Vesti/Vesti/Patrijarh-o-presudi-Mladicu.html, accessed 24 November 2017.

9   See http://www.hlc-rdc.org/wp-content/uploads/2018/01/Istrazivanje_javnog_mnjenja_Sudjenja_za_ratne_zlocine_Demostat_logo_EU_i_Svajcarska_ambasada.pdf i http://www.hlc-rdc.org/wp-content/ uploads/2017/12/Izvestaj_Strategija_I.pdf, accessed 24 November 2017.

10 http://rs.n1info.com/a251443/Vesti/Vesti/Srusena-dzamija-u-Zemun-Polju.html, accessed 26 May 2017.

11 http://rs.n1info.com/a251493/Vesti/Vesti/Jusufspahic-o-rusenju-u-Zemnu-Polju.html, accessed 26 May 2017.

when enforcing planning permissions. The demolition of this mosque brought together Muslims from both the IZS and the IZuS, as well as different political parties and ethnic groups. The demolition was condemned by the Party of Democratic Action (*Stranka demokratske akcije*), which is led by a Bosniak from Sandžak, Sulejman Ugljanin, and the Bosniak Democratic Community (*Bošnjačka demokratska zajednica*), led by another Bosniak from Sandžak and former mufti, Muamer Zukorlić. Both the IZS and the IZuS in Serbia, but also parties and organisations from the Albanian and Roma communities also protested about the fate of the mosque.[12]

However, these debates after the demolition also exposed the existing political cleavages among Muslims in Serbia. For example, Enis Imamović, representative of the Party for Democratic Action of Sandžak in the National Assembly of Serbia, said that "the demolition of a mosque is a concrete step towards a definition of those who are Vučić's Muslims and those who are not". The phrase "Vučić's Muslims" is a reference to representatives of the Bosniak Democratic Community (*Bošnjačka demokratska zajednica*) and their leader Muamer Zukorlić, former mufti of the IZuS; Zukorlić is currently in a coalition government with the Serbian Progressive Party, whose president is Aleksandar Vučić. Muamer Zukorlić himself has been accused of constructing a building without planning permission; he built an extension to the Islamic Faculty building that encroached over the entire main square in the city of Novi Pazar, without facing any legal consequences. The IZuS was also accused of embezzlement when, at the beginning of 2017, Novi Pazar Regional Television released an audio recording of an alleged conversation in which two high ranking employees of the IZuS are trying to convince an imam to take personal responsibility for the misappropriation of funds, in order to protect the reputation of the IZuS.[13] The conference "Fourth Attack Wave on the Islamic Community in Serbia" was immediately organised by the IZuS as a response to this accusation. During the conference, current member of the Serbian parliament and former mufti Muamer Zukorlić and other representatives of the IZuS rejected the allegations.[14]

The "Final Report on Serbia" by the European Commission against Racism and Intolerance (ECRI, part of the Council of Europe), was published in 2017, covering a period of five years from 2012 to 2016. Despite the report's recommendations, it did not receive any public attention. With regards to the Muslim

---

12   http://balkans.aljazeera.net/vijesti/vlasti-tokom-noci-srusile-dzamiju-u-beogradu, accessed 26 May 2017.
13   https://www.danas.rs/drustvo/zukorlicevi-prisluskivani-razgovori-u-dnevniku/, accessed 1 January 2017.
14   See *Glas islama*, vol. 280 (February 2017), pp. 3–9.

minority in the country, this report criticises the lack of effort made to address past war crimes, and the rise of hate speech in the media. The report also contains statistics on the Roma population in Serbia. Although the 2011 Census provides a figure of 147,604 Roma living in Serbia, the ECRI report provides an estimate of up to 600,000. The statistical invisibility of the Roma population is explained by the fact that most of their settlements are informal. The ECRI also advised the Serbian authorities to take more serious steps towards the integration of Roma into society, and to show more respect to existing anti-discriminatory laws that are already in place, but that are currently rarely implemented and enforced. For instance, the police do not respond to charges pressed by Roma.[15]

Transnational Links

In organisational terms, the IZuS is part of the Islamic Community of Bosnia and Herzegovina (IZBiH), which is why it has close relationships with other Islamic communities in the region, as well as other international Islamic organisations and institutions that the IZBiH has signed agreements of cooperation with. Apart from those international relationships that the IZuS has established due to being part of the IZBiH, the IZuS has also, independently, held several important meetings with representatives from various Muslim majority countries. In 2017, IZuS officials undertook a series of monthly visits to its diaspora communities across Europe. The IZuS carried out visits to Bosniak communities in Germany, Switzerland, Austria, Sweden, and France. The IZuS also visited several neighbouring Islamic communities and Bosniak organisations in the region. In 2017, the IZuS also signed several memoranda of understanding with the Hifz Foundation in Sarajevo, the Ministry of Awqaf and Islamic Affairs in Kuwait,[16] and with representatives from the Turkish General Directorate of Waqfs about the restoration of an old Turkish bath in Novi Pazar.[17] In addition, representatives of the IZuS also hosted representatives from the Ministry of Education of Saudi Arabia,[18] from a delegation of

---

15 European Commission against Racism and Intolerance (ECRI), "Final Report on Serbia", English version available at: https://www.coe.int/t/dghl/monitoring/ecri/Country-by-country/Serbia/SRB-CbC-V-2017-021-ENG.pdf, accessed 24 November 2017.
16 "Potpisan sporazum između Mešihata I Ministarstva vaukufa iz Kuvajta", *Glas islama*, vol. 284 (August 2017), p. 40.
17 "Rekonstrukcija Isa-Begovog Hamama", *Glasi slama*, vol. 287 (December 2017), p. 40.
18 "Manifestacija 'Deset godina od agresije na Islamsku zajednicu'", *Glas slama*, vol. 286 (November 2017), p. 30.

the European Union in Serbia,[19] from an OSCE delegation in Serbia, and also hosted the political advisor of the US ambassador in Serbia.[20]

Representatives of the IZuS have also participated in a few important conferences. Mufti Dudić participated in the conference "Civil Dialogue Between the Muslim world and the United States of America", organised by the Islamic World League–Rabita, in New York on 16 and 17 September 2017.[21] The principal of the Gazi Isa Bey Madrasa, Rešad Plojović as a representative of the IzuS, participated in the conference "The Role of Fatwa in Achieving and Maintaining Stability in the Community", organised by the General Secreteriat for Fatwa Authorities Worldwide, and by the office of the Grand Mufti of Egypt (*Dar al-ifta*).[22] In November 2017, Mufti Dudić presented his paper at the international conference "Charter by Islamic Ulema on Fundamental Principles in Islam", organised by the International Union of Muslim Scholars, and the Presidency of Religious Affairs (*Diyanet İşleri Başkanlığı*) in Turkey.[23]

As for transnational links with Serbia's other Islamic organisation, the IZS, it was, as in previous years, less active. But the IZS continued to maintain relationships with the representatives of various embassies from Muslim majority countries in Serbia in 2017.

Law and Domestic Politics

There were no significant legal changes in Serbia in 2017 with regards to its Muslim population. The main issue, in addition to the unresolved status of the Islamic Community (IZ), was still property restitution. State authorities continued to refuse to engage in restitution on the grounds that there are two organisations that claim to be the legitimate representatives of the IZ, as defined by the *Law on Churches and Religious Communities*. As a consequence, the IZ has not received any property legally owed to them by the State.

---

19   "Predsjednik Mešihata primio šefa delegacije Evropske unije u Srbiji", *Glas islama*, vol. 280 (February 2017), p. 71.
20   "Muftija Dudić sa američkim diplomatom: još uvijek traje pritisak na vjeronauku, *Glas islama*, vol. 286 (November 2017), p. 33.
21   "Muftija Dudić u Nju Jorku", *Glas islama*, vol. 285 (September 2017), p. 57.
22   "U Kairu održana konferencija 'Uloga fetve u satbilnosti zajednice'", *Glas islama*, vol. 286 (November 2017), p. 35.
23   "Muftija Dudić na konferenciji u Istanbulu", *Glas islama*, vol. 287 (December 2017), p. 41.

The process of rehabilitating leading figures from the Chetniks movement,[24] and a number of other individuals who were at the head of the Serbian collaborationist government during World War II, continued in 2017. This process goes hand in hand with the aforementioned process of reaffirming a Serbian nationalist ideology. In 2017, the Higher Court in Valjevo rehabilitated Nikola Kalabić, Commander of the Oplenac Corps of the Yugoslav Army in the Fatherland. It is believed that Kalabić was responsible for many assassinations and killings of both civilians and members of the partisan movement, as well as Roma. This case of legal rehabilitation was only the latest in a series of similar court decisions, such as the rehabilitation of Dragoljub Draža Mihajlović, leader of the Chetniks' movement, back in 2015.[25] The consequences of such court decisions were highlighted by a report by the European Commission against Racism and Intolerance (ECRI). According to the report, the rehabilitation of those who were responsible for mass killings and the deportations of Bosniaks, Albanians and Roma during World War II, cannot possibly contribute to a sense of security among these ethnic minorities and general stability in the region.[26] The ECRI report also highlighted that the processes of putting on trial and sentencing those indicted for war crimes and genocide committed in the 1990s had been progressing very slowly, and that persons who are high-ranking officials are not tried at all for war crimes.[27]

Activities and Initiatives of Main Muslim Organisations

For a second year in a row, the Faculty of Islamic Studies in Novi Pazar, affiliated with the IZuS, organised the conference "Methods of Teaching and Learning of the Qur'an". The conference was organised in cooperation with the Islamic Organisation for Education, Science and Culture of Morocco, and the World Organisation for Hifz in Jeddah.[28] The IZuS also organised a visit of popular scholar Yusuf Estes to Novi Pazar.[29] The IZuS also opened two new mosques

---

24 The Chetnik Detachments of the Yugoslav Army, also known as the Yugoslav Army in the Fatherland (commonly known as the Chetniks), was a World War II partisan force in Yugoslavia led by Draža Mihailović.
25 See Kostić, Ivan Ejub, "Serbia", in Oliver Scharbrodt, Samim Akgönül, Ahmet Alibašić, Jørgen S. Nielsen and Egdūnas Račius (eds.), *Yearbook of Muslims in Europe*, vol. 8 (Leiden: Brill, 2017), pp. 603–604.
26 ECRI, "Final Report on Serbia".
27 ECRI, "Final Report on Serbia".
28 "Četvorodnevna naučna konferencijana FIS-u", *Glas islama*, vol. 282 (April 2017), p. 34.
29 "Muftija Duduić primio Jusuf Estetesa", *Glas islama*, vol. 283 (June 2017), p. 35.

in 2017. In May, the Ana Vatan mosque was opened in the village of Crnoča, and another was opened in the suburb Novi Pazar-Lug III.[30] In November, the IZuS opened a new educational-cultural centre called "Academia" in Malmö, Sweden.[31] It has also become a tradition to organise a Night of Prayer in Novi Pazar during the month of Ramadan. In 2017, the Night of Prayer was led by a reciter from Saudi Arabia. Furthermore, the IZuS organised events that were of an exclusively ethno-national character, concerning questions of Bosniak identity, as well as commemorative meetings dedicated to victims of the wars during the dissolution of Yugoslavia in the 1990s.

The NGO *Svetionik* (Lighthouse), located in Novi Pazar, organised numerous religious lectures throughout the year, through its head Muhamed Demirović, who is very popular with the Muslim youth in the Sandžak region. Moreover, the same NGO managed to gather charitable contributions for those in need, and collected enough capital to provide scholarships for young students who are unable to pay for their own education. *Svetionik* also ran a humanitarian campaign called "Donate Kurban", and organised very well-attended cultural activities in advance of Ramadan, as well as the project "The Prophet in My Heart". The Salafi organisation *Put sredine* (The Middle Path) has been very active locally, and is involved in charitable and humanitarian aid, as well as running a well-attended lecture series.

Muslim Population: History and Demographics

The history of Muslims in Serbia is directly connected to the expansion of the Ottoman Empire into the Balkan Peninsula. Following the Battle of Maritsa in 1371, and the Battle of Kosovo in 1389, Serbia became a de facto part of the Ottoman Empire, remaining so until the Congress of Berlin in 1878, when it was recognised as an independent state. Over the course of nearly five centuries spent under Ottoman rule, a vast number of Southern Slavs in Serbia gradually converted to Islam.

Due to the fact that Islam came to Serbia with the Ottoman Empire, Muslims in Serbia have predominantly been followers of the Hanafi school of religious jurisprudence and the Maturidi school in theology. There have also been a significant number of Sufi brotherhoods. During Ottoman rule, the Muslim

---

30   "Nastavak radova I otvaranje novih džamija–proučena dova za nastavak radova na džamiji na Gazilaru", *Glas islama*, vol. 282 (May 2017), p. 33.

31   "U Malmeu svečano otvorena bošnjačka palata, kulturno-edukativnicentar 'Akademia'", *Glas islama*, vol. 286 (November 2017), p. 26.

population was particularly concentrated in the Western and central parts of the country, as well as in the Southeastern region. Upon Serbian liberation from Ottoman rule–which was achieved gradually, starting in the 18th century–a great number of Muslims were forced into exile. Likewise, many mosques and places of worship were destroyed or torn down during that period. For instance, in Užice, Smederevo and Belgrade, dozens of mosques were destroyed.[32]

The agreement adopted at the Congress of Berlin in 1878, aimed at ending the persecution of the Muslim population, whereby Serbia was obliged to ensure the safety of Muslims that wished to stay in the newly established Serbian state. However, this obligation was only theoretically observed most of the time. Following the Balkan Wars of 1912 to 1914, Serbia took over Ottoman territories in the Sandžak region of Novi Pazar and Kosovo, where Muslims represented the majority of the population. Consequently, this resulted in another proportional increase in the Muslim population of Serbia. However, after World War I and World War II, and during the communist era, there was once again a rapid decline in the Muslim population.

Once the former Yugoslavia began to fall apart, and Slobodan Milošević started to implement his nationalist and populist politics, war broke out, which led to many Muslims being killed in Bosnia and Herzegovina, and Kosovo. Although there were no military operations by Serbian armed forces in Sandžak, local Muslims suffered systematic repression, which was carried out through different means. Once Slobodan Milošević was overthrown in 2000, and the first democratically elected government in 50 years came to power, the situation of Muslims in Serbia improved significantly. Nowadays, Bosniaks make up the largest percentage of the Muslim population, but there is also a considerable number of Albanians and Roma, which makes the composition of the Muslim population in Serbia very heterogeneous. This had led to many disagreements regarding the organisation of the Islamic Community in Serbia.[33]

The data from the 2011 Census does not fully represent the actual figure of Muslims living in Serbia. Albanians from the Southeastern Preševo Valley, bordering Kosovo and Macedonia, boycotted the census altogether, while the representatives of the IZuS, who are known to have great influence over Sandžak's Bosniaks, organised a campaign to also boycott the census, because

---

32 In those three cities, only one mosque remains from the Ottoman period: the Bajrakli mosque in Belgrade.
33 This ethnic factor is very important among Muslims in Serbia. Ethnic differences are quite often exploited for political purposes, by both the Government and ethnic minority parties.

of what representatives of the Bosniak population called "discriminations and state sponsored terror perpetrated by the Government", and "census ballots not being printed in the Bosnian language or the Latin alphabet".[34] The census data for Serbia's Roma population does not reflect their real numbers either, since many of them are without official documents, and their records are not kept due to their immense poverty and exclusion from Serbian society.

Muslim Population[35]	222,828 (3.1% of population in 2011).
Ethnic/National Backgrounds	65% of Muslims in Serbia are Bosniaks. The other 35% are Roma, Muslims by nationality[36], and Serbian Muslims.[37]
Inner-Islamic Groups	No official data is available. Estimates provided by Twelver Shi'i communities in Serbia, suggest that there are 100–200 Shi'is in the country.
Geographical Spread	Around 80% of the Muslim population live in the Sandžak region, which is located in Southwest Serbia. Around 15% of the Muslim population is based in Belgrade.
Number of Mosques	About 195, 130 of which are in Sandžak, 60 are in the Preševo Valley, and the rest are in Belgrade, Subotica, Šabac, Niš, and Mali Zvornik.

---

34 www.b92.net/info/vesti/index.php?yyyy=2011&mm=09&dd=29&nav_id=545626, accessed 7 January 2015.

35 The 222,828 Muslims, recorded by the 2011 Census, did not include Albanians from the Preševo Valley. The 2002 Census, which was not boycotted by Albanians, registered 67,647 Albanians in Serbia, which means that the actual number of Muslims, including Albanians, would be 290,475. One must also not forget to add the significant number of Sandžak's Bosniaks to this total, since they were asked to boycott the 2011 Census by the IZuS. Finally, there are a number of non-registered people from the Roma population.

36 "Muslim" as a national identity is an artefact of the communist period. At the time of the SFRY (Socialist Federal Republic of Yugoslavia), Muslims from Bosnia and Herzegovina and the Sandžak region were not recognised as Bosniaks, but they were allowed to define themselves as Muslims in a national sense. A number of citizens are still identified in this way. In the last census, 22,301 citizens gave "Muslim" as their national identity.

37 This percentage does not include the Preševo Valley Albanians, who boycotted the Census in 2011.

Muslim Burial Sites	The exact number of Muslim cemeteries in Serbia is unknown. While they exist in almost every major town, the largest are located in the larger Sandžak communities. Two cemeteries are located in Novi Pazar: Gazilar, an old-town cemetery; and the New Cemetery. The Baruthana Cemetery is located in Sjenica, and the Kosovac Cemetery is in Prijepolje. While there are no special Muslim cemeteries in Belgrade, every larger cemetery has a designated section for Muslims.
"Chaplaincy" in State Institutions	In Serbia, legal regulations provide for the possibility of imams to be permanently employed at public institutions, such as prisons, hospitals, and the military. However, due to their lack of resources, the IZS and the IZuS have not made use of that legal right. Presently, there is one chief military imam, whose office is at the Serbian Army General Staff in Belgrade.
Halal Products	In Serbia, there is a halal agency under the aegis of the IZuS which is very active, and has awarded halal certificates to many Serbian manufacturers. It is possible to buy certified halal food at most of the larger supermarkets, as well as in some private butcher shops, which sell only certified halal meat and meat products. However, there is no halal food available at kindergartens, schools, halls of residence, or canteens in public institutions.
Dress Code	In Serbia, there is no law regulating the wearing of the head scarf. There are no legal restrictions on wearing it in schools or when taking photographs for official documents. A restriction exists for wearing the niqab in photographs for official documents, but there is no such ban for wearing it in schools. Data on discrimination or hate crimes due to wearing the head scarf or niqab does not exist.

Wearing the head scarf is quite common in the regions inhabited by predominantly Muslim populations, such as Sandžak and the Preševo Valley. Some women wear the niqab in predominantly Muslim regions, but it is extremely rare.

Places of Islamic Learning and Education	The IZuS and IZS have parallel school systems. The IZS runs the Nahla preschool, the Sinan Bey Madrasa in Novi Pazar, and the women's Bakija Hanume Madrasa in Prijepoje, as well as the Faculty of Islamic Studies in Belgrade. The IZuS runs the preschool and *mekteb* Reuda and Wildan, the Gazi Isa Bey Madrasa in Novi Pazar, and the Faculty of Islamic Studies in Novi Pazar.
Muslim Media and Publications	In 2017, the only regularly published Muslim media outlet was *Glas Islama* (Voice of Islam) of the IZuS.[38] There are official websites for the IZuS and IZS, and some other Islamic online portals.

Main Muslim Organisations

– Islamic Community in Serbia (*Mešihat islamske zajednice u Srbiji*–IZuS, Gradska 1, 36 300, Novi Pazar, tel.: ++381 20315452, www.mesihat.org). The IZuS is under the jurisdiction of the larger Islamic Community of Bosnia and Herzegovina (IZBiH). There are three muftiates within the IZuS: the Sandžak; the Presevo; and the Novi Sad-Belgrade Muftiate. Since 2014, the president of the Council of the IZuS has been Mevlud Dudić. He replaced Muamer Zukorlić, who had been president of the Council of the IZuS since its foundation in 1993. Zukorlić remained the Mufti of Sandžak until 2016, when he was replaced by Mevlud Dudić. The IZuS, and its activities, are primarily concentrated in the Sandžak region, despite having muftiates across Serbia.
– Islamic Community of Serbia (*Islamska zajednica Srbije*–IZS, Gospodar Jevremova 11, 11 000, Beograd, tel.: ++381 112622428, www.izs.rs). The IZS was founded in 2007. It is not recognised by the IZBiH and IZuS, that claim that it was founded illegitimately. The founders of the IZS were dissatisfied

---

38 In 2017, *Glas islama* celebrated its 20th anniversary.

imams of the IZuS, who accused Mufti Muamer Zukorlić of nepotism. These imams had the support of the Belgrade Mufti Hamdija Jusufspahić, the Party of Democratic Action, and the Serbian government at that time.[39] In the organisational body of the IZS, there are three muftiates: the Serbian; the Sandžak; and the Preševo Muftiate. Since its establishment in 2007 up to 2016, the IZS was headed by the former Tutin Imam of the IZuS, Adem Zilkić. Currently, the head of the IZS is *ra'is* Sead Nasufović.

– In addition to the IZuS and IZS, there are several other Muslim non-governmental organisations. Worthy of mention are two competing NGOs among the youth of Sandžak: the pro-Sufi Lighthouse (*Svetionik*, Šabana Koče 11, Novi Pazar, tel.: ++381 66317317, http://www.svetionik.rs/); and the Salafi organisation Middle Path (*Put sredine*, https://putsredine.com).

---

39 Hamdija Jusufspahić became the Mufti of Belgrade in 1968. Even prior to the breakup of Yugoslavia and the Islamic Community of Yugoslavia in 1991, Hamdija Jusufspahić was removed from the position of Mufti of Belgrade. However, he refused to acknowledge this decision, and with the help of the Serbian government, declared the independence of the Belgrade Muftiate from the rest of the Islamic Community. Since then, the Bajrakli mosque has been under the control of the Jusufspahić family. Hamdija Jusufspahić was succeeded in the position of Mufti of Belgrade by his son, Muhamed Jusufspahić.

Slovakia

Jozef Lenč[1]

Introduction

The Muslim presence in Slovakia is one of the smallest in the European Union. The Muslim population is not recognised by the State as a religious community, and Muslim organisations only have the status of NGOs. Muslims have neither an official representative organisation nor a purpose-built mosque. Despite its public invisibility, the Muslim presence has been, for several years, the focus of Slovak politicians (populists and nationalists), the media (especially tabloids) and various extremist groups. In the years 2012 to 2015, this interest was marginal, but the turning point came before the parliamentary elections in 2016, which was also reflected in the life of Muslims in 2017.

A significant change in the life of Slovak Muslims in 2017 was that public expressions of Islamophobia were transferred from social media to the Slovak parliament. These debates became part of Slovak politics and Slovak political debates. At the end of 2016, the National Council of the Slovak Republic (*Národná rada Slovenskej republiky*, NR SR), the Parliament of Slovakia, after ten years, submitted again a law, which prevented the official registration of Islam in Slovakia.[2] Politicians who disseminate Islamophobic views have received more attention from media outlets, not just before the elections in 2016,

---

1 Jozef Lenč is an Assistant Professor at the Department of Philosophy and Applied Philosophy at the University of Ss. Cyril and Methodius in Trnava. He earned his PhD at the Institute of Political Science of the Slovak Academy of Sciences in Bratislava. In his work he addresses the issue of the relationship between religion and politics with a focus on Islam and Islamic philosophy. He is a commentator on Slovak and international politics (especially the Middle East). He is co-author of the book Stefančík, Radoslav, and Jozef Lenč, *Mladí migranti v slovenskej spoločnosti: medzinárodná migrácia, muslimovia, štát a verejná mienka* (*Young Migrants in Slovak Society*) (Brno: Tribun EU 2012) and author of the book *Náboženstvo v politike a pozícia náboženských politických strán* (*Religion in Politics and the Position of Religious Political Parties*) (Trnava: Univerzita sv. Cyrila a Metoda v Trnave 2015). He actively publishes on IslamOnline.sk as well. He is part of a research project on Islamophobia in the East of the European Union (2018–22), funded by the Social Sciences and Humanities Research Council of Canada.
2 "Začína sa to kebabom, vyhlásil Danko. Šéf SNS chystá bič na moslimov" (It begins with kebab, said Danko. The head of the SNS is preparing a whip on Muslims), *Aktuality*, 4 October 2017, https://www.aktuality.sk/clanok/378223/zacina-to-kebabom-vyhlasil-danko-sef-sns-chysta-bic-na-moslimov/, accessed 18 December 2017.

but have been the focus of attention during any political debate that concentrates on topics where the "threat of Islam" is mentioned.[3]

This is the result of several factors that are reflected in the reactions of some Slovak politicians. The first factor is a sense of acute danger that has spread due to repeated terrorist attacks in Europe. Despite the absence of any experience of terrorism, these events have resonated markedly in Slovakia. The second factor is that right-wing extremists managed to gain seats in the Slovak parliament for the first time since 1989 (Kotleba–People's Party Our Slovakia; *Kotleba–Ľudová strana Naše Slovensko* K-LSNS). The third factor is that the vocabulary of extremists is increasingly used by representatives of mainstream democratic parties, as well as by the Prime Minister Robert Fico and the Speaker of the Parliament Andrej Danko. Political statements against Muslims were part of most of the parliamentary debates concerning laws that tightened the registration of Churches and tried to ban the construction of mosques in Slovakia, or those that addressed issues of migration or the future of the European Union.

In 2017, Muslims were the subject of a number of political debates in which politicians (from both the government coalition and many of the opposition parties) used the fear of Muslims when communicating to the media or to their voters on social networks, and also used this tactic during the campaign before the regional elections. A significant number of politicians ignored the fact that Muslims are also citizens of the Slovak Republic and that they have the same rights and obligations as other citizens of the country. Their presence is overlooked or often irresponsibly associated with terrorism and illegal migration. These ideas were spread by some non-governmental organisations that try to influence public opinion and the decisions of Slovak politicians (such as the *Centrum pre štúdium politického islámu*; Centre for the Study of Political Islam).[4] Marginal Christian associations (*Inštitút Leva XIII*; Institute of Leo XIII,[5] Magnificat,[6] etc.) repeatedly spread misinformation about Islam, and called for a ban on constructing mosques or the "burqa" (which in most cases is understood as any Muslim head dress).[7]

---

3 "Jeden a pol roka islamofóbie na Slovensku" (One and half years of Islamophobia in Slovakia), *IslamOnline*, 29 September 2017, http://www.islamonline.sk/2017/09/jeden-a-pol-roka-islamofobie-na-slovensku/, accessed 18 December 2017.
4 https://www.cspii.org/sk, accessed 22. December 2017.
5 http://www.instituteofleoxiii.org/, accessed 22. December 2017.
6 http://www.magnificat.sk/, accessed 22. December 2017.
7 "Farnosti po celom Slovensku zaplavili knihy vykresľujúce proroka Muhammada ako predchodcu antikrista" (Parishes throughout Slovakia flooded books depicting the Prophet Muhammad as the forerunner of the Antichrist), *IslamOnline*, 8 August 2017, http://www.islamonline.sk/2017/08/farnosti-po-celom-slovensku-zaplavili-knihy-vykreslujuce-proroka-muhammada-ako-predchodcu-antikrista/, accessed 22 December 2017.

A positive sign was the public defence of Muslims by the President of the Slovak Republic, Andrej Kiska, who received representatives of the *Islamská nadácia na Slovensku* (Islamic Foundation in Slovakia), and in his New Year's speech condemned hate speech against Muslims and migrants.[8] In 2017, NGOs, the smaller Christian Churches and the Jewish community were also engaged in mitigating tensions between the majority of society and Muslim communities.[9]

The perception of Muslims has not changed significantly compared to 2016. At the end of 2017, the Slovak Academy of Sciences published the results of research which showed that up to 54% of Slovak citizens would not want to have a Muslim neighbour. It should be noted that in 2008 only about 20% of the population had this attitude. A number of negative reports about Muslims have also affected the attitudes of the Slovak public towards Muslims.[10]

Public Debates

Parliamentary debates were to some extent directed against Slovak Muslims. In February 2017, opposition MP Milan Krajniak (We Are Family–Boris Kollar, *Sme rodina–Boris Kollár*, SR-BK) proposed a change to two laws to ban the construction of mosques. He described the mosques as "terrorist recruitment centres", and presented the theory that terrorist attacks do not occur in countries that have no mosques. His proposals were not approved by parliamentarians, but a parliamentary platform was used to spread misinformation about Islam and Muslims.[11]

---

8   "Prezident v novoročnom prejave hovoril o nenávisti na internete. Zastal sa muslimov aj Rómov" (The President, in a New Year's speech, talked about internet hatred. He defended Muslims and Roma), *IslamOnline*, 1 January 2017, http://www.islamonline.sk/2017/01/prezident-v-novorocnom-prejave-hovoril-o-nenavisti-na-internete-zastal-sa-muslimov-i-romov/, accessed 22 December 2017.

9   "Zišli sa na diskusiách žid, moslim a kresťan: slovenská realita, nie vtip" (Jews, Muslims and Christians met for a discussion: Slovak reality, not a joke), *Dennik N*, 23 January 2018, https://dennikn.sk/1006584/zisli-sa-na-diskusiach-zid-moslim-a-krestan-slovenska-realita-nie-vtip/, accessed 25 January 2018.

10 Tížik, Miroslav (eds.), *Naše hodnoty 2017. Prezentácia výskumu európskych hodnôt* (Bratislava: Sociologický ústav SAV, 2017); "Čoraz viac Slovákov nechce susediť s muslimom či homosexuálom" (More and more Slovaks do not want to be neighbours with a Muslim or a homosexual), *Aktuality*, 18 December 2017, https://www.aktuality.sk/clanok/548957/coraz-viac-slovakov-nechce-susedit-s-moslimom-ci-homosexualom/, accessed 10 January 2018.

11 "Poslanec, ktorý si hovorí posledný križiak, navrhol zakázať na Slovensku mešity" (MP, who calls himself the last crusader, has proposed banning mosques in Slovakia),

The second half of 2017 was linked to an election campaign for regional governments in which political parties and some independent candidates used anti-Islamic and anti-migrant rhetoric. In the campaign, misconceptions about the Islamisation of Slovakia through migrants from Muslim majority countries were repeated. At the end of 2017, Prime Minister Robert Fico (SMER-SD) returned to similar rhetoric, and reiterated after the EU summit in December 2017, that he will not allow "a comprehensive Muslim community to be established in Slovakia".[12]

The Slovak media has been using the same line for several years, which indirectly supports deeply-rooted stereotypes about Islam and Muslims. Certain news and commentaries in mainstream media could not be distinguished from tabloid news reports and also engaged in conspiracy theories around Muslims. The media that talked about Muslims mostly used inappropriate images that supported stereotypes about Islam. In most cases, reports used the image of a woman in a niqab or burqa, or depicted violent events in the Middle East. Such illustrative images support stereotypes about the inequality of women in Islam and the religion's violent nature.

Another factor that exacerbates the perception of Muslims in Slovak society is the tabloid character of reports about Islam and its adherents. Most information about Muslims is related to terrorist attacks, regardless of the fact that the victims of terrorism are mainly Muslims. In 2017, there were many unverified reports and hoaxes about religiously motivated attacks in Muslim majority countries or Western European cities.

The latest phenomenon that has helped support the growing trend of Islamophobia in Slovakia is the misuse of Islamic terminology, in particular: Islam and Islamism, jihad and jihadism. In the first case, the terms are often used interchangeably and or employed to suggest that certain actions are religiously sanctioned in Islam. Reports suggested that rape is part of Islamic behaviour, that abuse of social benefits is a religious practice of Islam etc.[13] In

---

IslamOnline, 9 February 2017, http://www.islamonline.sk/2017/02/poslanec-ktory-si-hovori-posledny-kriziak-navrhol-zakazat-na-slovensku-mesity/, accessed 30 December 2017.

12 "EÚ chce lepšie utesniť Stredozemné more. Dá viac peňazí Taliansku" (The EU wants to better seal the Mediterranean Sea. Gives more money to Italy), *Euractiv*, 22 October 2017, https://euractiv.sk/section/buducnost-eu/news/eu-chce-lepsie-utesnit-stredomorsku-cestu-da-viac-penazi-taliansku/, accessed 30 December 2017; "Fico: Sme bezpečná krajina, nevidím dôvod, aby sme sem navozili tisícky moslimov" (Fico: we are a safe country, I don't see a reason to bring thousands of Muslims here), *Pravda*, 26 January 2018, https://spravy.pravda.sk/domace/clanok/456245-fico-sme-bezpecna-krajina-nevidim-dovod-na-to-aby-sme-sem-navozili-tisicky-moslimov/, accessed 27 January 2018.

13 "Traja migranti brutálne znásilnili pätnásťročné dievča" (Three immigrants brutally raped a 15-year-old girl), *Parlamentne listy*, 18 May 2017, http://www.parlamentnelisty.sk/arena/

addition, public discourses associate the word "Islamist" with "terrorist", and thereby use the label "terrorist" for those who have nothing to do with terrorism. These simplifications occur mainly in the Slovakian tabloids (*Nový Čas, Plus 1 Deň*, etc.) and media outlets disseminating conspiracy theories. In the latter case, the problem is that the Slovak public discourse links jihad with violence and so-called holy war. All Slovak media (SME, *Dennik N,.týždeň, Pravda, Nový Čas*, RTVS, TV JoJ, TV *Markíza*, radio stations or various online media) contribute to this, as they present "jihad" as a synonym for terrorism, and "jihadi" is synonymous with terrorist.[14] This creates the misconception that Muslims who practice jihad are terrorists.[15] The open dissemination of Islamophobia and xenophobia are most prevalent in the media outlets engaging in conspiracy theories, such as *Hlavné správy*,[16] *Parlamentné listy*,[17] *Medzičas*[18] and, until March 2017, the website of the MP Milan Krajniak, known as *Konzervatívny výber*.[19] The active dissemination of Islamophobia also includes the internet portal[20] of Tibor E. Rostas, *Zem a Vek*.[21]

The verbal attacks against Muslims in Slovakia in 2017 were mainly aimed at the leaders of Muslim organisations who appeared in the media. Most attacks

---

monitor/Traja-imigranti-brutalne-znasilnili-patnastrocne-dievca-Policajti-nabehli-do-uteceneckeho-centra-a-preverili-uplne-vsetkych-288196, accessed 5 January 2018.

14 "Jozef Lenč: Islamista neznamená terorista" (Jozef Lenc: Islamist is not a terrorist), *Teraz.sk*, 21 April 2017, http://www.teraz.sk/publicistika/j-lenc-islamista-neznamena-terorista/255620-clanok.html, accessed 5 January 2018.

15 "Fico označuje dva denníky za džihád" (Fico denounces two newspapers for their jihad), *O médiách*, 3 August 2017, https://www.omediach.com/blog/item/11509-fico-oznacuje-dva-denniky-za-dzihad, accessed 5 January 2018; "Bugár otvorene v HN TV: Vedie sa proti mne džihád. Je jedno, čo urobíte, aj tak dostanete" (Bugar says openly on HN TV: the Jihad is against me. No matter what you do, you can get it), *Hospodárske noviny*, 2 June 2017, https://slovensko.hnonline.sk/970439-bugar-otvorene-v-hntelevizii-vedie-sa-proti-mne-dzihad-je-jedno-co-urobite-aj-tak-dostanete, accessed 5 January 2018.

16 https://www.hlavnespravy.sk/category/svetonazor, accessed 1 April 2018.

17 http://www.parlamentnelisty.sk/zahranicie, accessed 1 April 2018.

18 http://medzicas.sk/category/imigracia/, accessed 1 April 2018.

19 "MP Milan Krajniak announces the end of his web site *Konzervatívny výber*", *poslednykriziak.sk*, 13 March 2017, http://www.poslednykriziak.sk/koniec-konzervativneho-vyberu-podakovanie-citatelom/1664/, accessed 1 April 2018.

20 Link to articles about Islam published on the web site *Zem a Vek*: http://zemavek.sk/?s=islam&aTHczbAnwNJyBDU=AJO2yR5IYzN%40pov&NMOVrRZloQm=Qok*pNOq8S9&SrkiqPaNZFWQY=*%5DFGOaPgWisxj&yILGDjtFzYMOkP=njXVxRO25ye7Yc, accessed 1 April 2018.

21 "Príručka pre stredné školy: Klamstvá a konšpirácie" (Secondary school guide: lies and conspiracy), *Denník N*, 2 April 2017, https://dennikn.sk/718059/prirucka-pre-stredne-skoly-klamstva-a-konspiracie/, accessed 5 January 2018.

targeted the Islamic Foundation.[22] Alongside these verbal attacks against Slovak Muslim community leaders, verbal attacks on some diplomats were also reported, especially women wearing the head scarf. Some Muslim women reported that they had been the victims of "stalking" as a result of a media campaign against the so-called burkini, especially during the summer in public swimming pools and in spa towns (Piestany, etc.).[23]

Transnational Links

The Slovak Muslim presence is very small, but very diverse. Several ethnic groups of Muslims, Muslims of different generations and with different socio-economic backgrounds live in Slovakia. They also differ in terms of their legal status, the reasons for their stay in Slovakia and the level of their religiosity. All these factors affect their connections to the Slovak Republic and their ties to their countries of origin. Some Slovak Muslims are closely linked to Muslim communities in Austria (in particular Muslims from the Balkans and Turkey), the United Kingdom, Scandinavia, Middle Eastern countries and the Gulf states (Muslims with Middle Eastern roots, Somalis, Afghans, etc.).[24]

What is interesting is the close cooperation between the Slovak and Czech Muslim communities. The Czech Muslim presence is–unlike the Slovak–recognised by the State, but is largely passive in terms of activities for Muslims. The Islamic Foundation in Slovakia currently runs *IslamOnline.sk*, which covers news and topics for the Czech Republic, as does *al-Islam* magazine (since 2011), which is published in the Slovak and Czech languages.

Law and Domestic Politics

In 2017, the political and social situation stabilised in Slovakia, as a result of a surprise after the parliamentary elections in March 2016. This was the entry of

---

22   "Fanúšikovia Kotlebu zdieľajú príhovor predsedu Islamskej nadácie M. S. Hasnu. Vyhrážajú sa mu smrťou" (Kotleba's fans share a speech by the president of the Islamic Foundation M. S. Hasna. They threatened him with death), *IslamOnline*, 14 July 2017, http://www.islamonline.sk/2017/07/fanusikovia-kotlebu-zdielali-prihovor-predsedu-islamskej-nadacie-m-s-hasnu-vyhrazaju-sa-mu-smrtou/, accessed 6 January 2018.

23   "A long-tolerant spa town feels the chill of Slovak populism", *New York Times*, 12 September 2017, https://www.nytimes.com/2017/09/12/world/europe/piestany-arabs-slovak-nationalism.html, accessed 6 January 2018.

24   Štefančík and Lenč, *Mladí migranti v slovenskej spoločnosti*, pp. 157–160.

right-wing parties into Parliament, with the establishment of a ruling coalition that included: the Direction–Social Democracy (*Smer–Sociálna demokracia*, SMER-SD), the Slovak National Party (*Slovenská národná strana*, SNS), and The Bridge–Civic Party (*Most-Híd Občianska strana*, Most-Híd).

Law 308/1991, adopted after the Velvet Revolution to strengthen the religious freedom of Czechoslovakia, has become the cornerstone of the "wall", that prevents Slovak Muslims from becoming a state-recognised religious community. The Law stipulated that, in addition to the Churches and religious societies listed in the Law's appendix, other communities that want to operate in the territory of the Slovak Republic, and benefit from state recognition status,[25] must pass through the registration process. In the appendix to *Law 308/1991*, only Christian Churches and the Jewish community were registered. The process of selecting registered Churches and communities was not clearly explained in the Law, and the state authorities had not officially recognised Islam in the territory of Czechoslovakia in the past.[26]

The Law's original wording stated that the application for registration could be "filed if it is proven that at least 20,000 members are registered with the Church or religious community", and determined that the signature of the community members is only valid from those who "have a permanent residence in the territory of the Slovak Republic and are citizens of the Slovak Republic".[27] At the turn of 2016 and 2017, there was a passionate parliamentary debate on the draft amendments to *Law 308/1991*[28], which was intended to further tighten the legislation around the registration of Churches and religious communities in Slovakia. The approved amendments meant that now 50,000

---

25   Churches and religious communities registered under *Law 308/1991* have the right to: financial support, the issuance of internal regulations that do not contravene the legal norms of the State, provide spiritual and material services, teach religion, educate clergy at their own schools, organise without permission their meetings, and operate dedicated facilities, participate in the provision of social and spiritual services in state facilities etc. The Law, in addition to the right to freedom of religion, has strengthened the status of registered Churches and religious societies to the detriment of those that have not been recognised by the State or failed to meet the required membership requirements. See: *Law 308/1991*, Letavajová, Silvia, "Zmiešané slovensko-afgánske manželstvá ako príklad etnokultúrnych aspektov migrácie cudzincov na Slovensku", *Etnologické rozhľady*, vol. XIV, no. 2 (2007), pp. 25–43.

26   Štefančík and Lenč, *Mladí migranti v slovenskej spoločnosti*, pp. 124–126.

27   Zákon č. 201/2007, Z. z. zmena zákona o slobode náboženskej viery a postavení cirkví (*The Amendment to the Law on Freedom of Religious Belief and the Status of Churches*) [online], https://www.noveaspi.sk/products/lawText/1/65138/1/2, accessed 29 December 2017.

28   Zákon č. 308/1991 Zb., Zákon o slobode náboženskej viery a postavení cirkví a náboženských obcí (*The Law of Freedom of Religion and the Status of Churches and Religious Communities*) [online], http://www.zakonypreludi.sk/zz/1991-308, accessed 29 December 2017.

signatures were required from members of a religious community in order to be registered. This amendment to *Law 308/1991* was approved in November 2016, but President Kiska refused to sign it.[29] However he was overruled, which deepened the unequal position of Muslims in Slovak society.[30]

The process of registering Islam in Slovakia has been complicated by the signing of the *Vatican Treaty*[31] and *Law 395/2004*,[32] both of which strengthened the privileged position of the Catholic Church in Slovakia. Slovak Muslims are in the position of a religious community that is discriminated against. With the adoption of *Law 201/2007*,[33] that supplemented and amended *Law 308/1991*, the chance of registering any new religious community–in particular Muslim–thus became even slimmer.

During the debate in Parliament, many offensive statements about Islam and Muslims were voiced.[34] Some of these statements were scrutinised by the parliamentary Mandate and Immunity Committee, which, in December 2017, ruled that the MPs Milan Mazurek and Stanislav Mizík (both from the K-ĽSNS party) must publicly apologise for what they said. Mizík said that Islam was the "Satanic paedophile work of the devil", and Mazurek stated that Islam

---

29 "Andrej Kiska: taký vysoký počet osôb na registráciu cirkvi "mieri proti ľudskej dôstojnosti"" (Andrej Kiska: such a high number of people for the registration of the Church "stands against human dignity"), *IslamOnline*, 21 December 2016, http://www.islamonline.sk/2016/12/andrej-kiska-tak-vysoky-pocet-osob-na-registraciu-cirkvi-mieri-proti-ludskej-dostojnosti/, accessed 29 December 2017; "Prezident Kiska vetoval ďalší zákon SNS" (President Kiska vetoed another law), *Aktuality*, 20 December 2016, https://www.aktuality.sk/clanok/400926/prezident-kiska-vetoval-dalsi-zakon-sns/, accessed 29 December 2017.

30 "Poslanci prelomili veto prezidenta, sprísnia sa podmienky registrácie cirkví" (MPs break the veto of the President, the conditions for registering Churches will be tightened), *Pravda*, 31 January 2017, https://spravy.pravda.sk/domace/clanok/418488-poslanci-prelomili-veto-prezidenta-schvalili-zakon-o-cirkvach/, accessed 29 December 2017.

31 Zmluva č. 326/2001 Z. z., *Základná zmluva medzi Slovenskou republikou a Svätou stolicou* (*The Basic Treaty between the Slovak Republic and the Holy See*) [online], http://www.culture.gov.sk/vdoc/251/zakladna-zmluva-medzi-sr-a-svatou-stolicou-5b.html, accessed 29 December 2017.

32 Zákon č. 395/2004 Z. z., *Dohoda medzi Slovenskou republikou registrovanými cirkvami a náboženskými spoločnosťami o náboženskej výchove a vzdelávaní* (*Agreement between the Slovak Republic and Registered Churches and Religious Communities on Religious Education and Training*) [online], https://www.minedu.sk/data/att/705.pdf, accessed 29 December 2017.

33 Zákon č. 201/2007 Z. z., *zmena zákona o slobode náboženskej viery a postavení cirkví* (*The Amendment to the Law on Freedom of Religious Belief and the Status of Churches*) [online], https://www.noveaspi.sk/products/lawText/1/65138/1/2, accessed 29 December 2017.

34 "Nevychovateľní hulváti z poslaneckých lavíc" (Undisciplined bores from Parliament), *IslamOnline*, 1 February 2017, http://www.islamonline.sk/2017/02/nevychovatelni-hulvati-z-poslaneckych-lavic/, accessed 7 January 2018.

was a "cruel, disgusting and inhumane system". The speech was supplemented by words about the alleged enslavement and murder of Slovaks by Muslims.[35] The remarks by these K-ĽSNS MP's were noted by the Attorney General Jaromír Čižnár, who said that the only way to prevent the spread of extremism in Parliament is the revocation of immunity for its members.[36]

In February 2017, MP Krajniak made a proposal to ban the construction of mosques in Slovakia. Krajniakov's proposed a "law on the prohibition of mosques", that was to be an amendment to two laws: *Law 50/1976*[37] and *Law 308/1991*. For the construction law, *Law 50/1976*, he proposed adding a condition that would allow the construction of a religious building (mosque) only if the applicant submits proof that his faith is registered under *Law 308/1991*. In *Law 308/1991*, he proposed to change the registration procedure so that religious communities must first obtain confirmation from the Slovak Secret Service that they do not pose a security risk. MP Krajniak said that Slovakia was a safe country because there were no mosques in it.[38] Other MPs of the extreme right supported his views. In Parliament, the proposal was supported by only eleven MPs; 48 members voted against it and there were 77 abstentions.[39]

To sum up: in 2017, Slovakia tightened legislation which a) increased the number of signatures necessary for the registration of Churches and religious communities in Slovakia from 20,000 to 50,000 signatures; b) confirmed the condition that the signatures of a religious community must be citizens of the Slovak Republic; (c) signatures must be confirmed by the transmission of personal data. Such registration conditions are discriminatory because at

---

35   "Kotlebovci sa za svoje výroky v parlamente neospravedlnili" (Kotleba MPs didn't apologise for his statements in Parliament), *Pravda*, 1 February 2017, https://spravy.pravda.sk/domace/clanok/418536-kotlebovci-sa-za-vyroky-v-parlamente-neospravedlnili/, accessed 7 January 2018.

36   "Čižnár: Extrémistickým prejavom v NRSR zabráni zrušenie imunity" (Čižnár: Extremist expression in the NR SR will prevent immunity being lifted), *Aktuality*, 1 February 2017, https://www.aktuality.sk/clanok/411743/ciznar-extremistickym-prejavom-v-nrsr-zabrani-zrusenie-imunity/, accessed 7 January 2018.

37   Zákon č. 50/1976 Zb., *O územnom plánovaní a stavebnom poriadku /stavebný zákon/* (*Law on Town Planning and Building Regulations /Building Law/*) [online], http://www.zakonypreludi.sk/zz/1976-50, accessed 9 January 2018.

38   "Strana Borisa Kollára predloží návrh na zákaz stavby mešít" (Boris Kollar's party will submit a proposal to ban the construction of mosques), *IslamOnline*, 28 February 2017, http://www.islamonline.sk/2017/02/strana-borila-kollara-predlozi-navrh-na-zakaz-stavby-mesit-oznamil-to-dnes-ich-posledny-kriziak/, accessed 10 January 2018.

39   "Krajniak neuspel, zákaz mešít sa zavádzať nebude" (Krajniak failed, no ban against mosques will be introduced), *Aktuality*, 5 April 2017, https://www.aktuality.sk/clanok/460920/krajniak-neuspel-zakaz-mesit-sa-zavadzat-nebude/, accessed 10 January 2018.

this current time only four of the 18 already registered Churches fulfil these criteria.[40]

Activities and Initiatives of Main Muslim Organisations

Muslims in Slovakia are involved in a number of activities which can be divided into the following categories: a) religious community activities, including the organisation of Friday prayers, programmes during the month of Ramadan, and pastoral care and educational services (funerals, private Islamic classes, etc.); (b) activities for the non-Muslim majority, in particular participation in public debates or lectures at schools; c) contacts with the media, in particular interviews on topical issues and the stating of opinions on current events concerning Muslims; d) contacts with State and public institutions at a local and national level.

In February 2017, the Islamic Foundation published a statement expressing concerns about activities leading to greater discrimination against Muslims in Slovakia.[41] In April 2017, a meeting of representatives of the Islamic Foundation, along with representatives of the Jewish and Muslim communities of Vienna, took place at the Córdoba Centre in Bratislava.[42] At the beginning of June, the Islamic Foundation organised a public *iftar* for Muslims and non-Muslims. The invitation was accepted by the representatives of embassies and religious communities, experts in the field of democracy and human rights, journalists and academics, as well as representatives of the state administration and the non-profit sector and those from Slovak Muslim organisations.[43] Representatives

---

40 "Počet veriacich podľa sčítania obyvateľov" (Number of believers according to census), *Ministerstvo kultúry Slovenskej republiky*, 15 March 2017, http://www.mksr.sk/posobnost-ministerstva/cirkvi-a-nabozenske-spolocnosti-/registrovane-cirkvi-a-nabozenske-spolocnosti-f9.html, accessed 26 January 2018.

41 "Stanovisko Islámskej nadácie k opozičnému návrhu obmedziť práva skupiny občanov Slovenskej republiky" (The opinion of the Islamic Foundation on the opposition proposal to limit the right of citizens of the Slovak Republic), *IslamOnline*, 28 February 2017, http://www.islamonline.sk/2017/02/stanovisko-islamskej-nadacie-k-opozicnemu-navrhu-obmedzit-prava-skupiny-obcanov-slovenskej-republiky/, accessed 30 December 2017.

42 "Muslimsko-židovská delegácia z Viedne v Bratislave" (Muslim-Jewish delegation from Vienna to Bratislava), *IslamOnline*, 2 April 2017, http://www.islamonline.sk/2017/04/muslimsko-zidovska-delegacia-z-viedne-v-bratislave/, accessed 30 December 2017.

43 "Ramadán v Bratislave: Spoločná večera s rabínom, farárkou, diplomatmi, novinármi a aktivistami" (Ramadan in Bratislava: joint dinner with rabbi, clergywoman, diplomats, journalists and activists), *IslamOnline*, 12 June 2017, http://www.islamonline.sk/2017/06/ramadan-v-bratislave-spolocna-vecera-s-rabinom-fararkou-diplomatmi-novinarmi-a-aktivistami/, accessed 30 December 2017.

of the Islamic Foundation also participated in several debates that focused on solving problems around migration[44] and interreligious dialogue.[45] In December 2017, a representative of the Islamic Foundation, along with a rabbi and Evangelical minister, took part in interreligious discussions at secondary schools.[46]

Muslim Population: History and Demographics

Muslims lived in parts of Slovakia between 1554 and 1687 during Ottoman rule. At this time, in these areas, systematic efforts to proselytise were not undertaken. As a consequence, the Muslim presence diminished markedly after the Ottoman withdrawal from Slovakia.[47]

Information about Muslims living in Slovakia during the Czechoslovak Republic (1918–38) is minimal. A Slovak Muslim presence began to be formed shortly after World War II; it was, however, not an organised community. It was mainly made up of migrants from Yugoslavia and other Balkan states who searched for work or moved to be with relatives who had lived in Slovakia before the War. Their descendants today form the third to fourth generation of Muslims in Slovakia. In the 1950s and early 1960s, Muslims from Arab countries, especially students, came to Slovakia.

The first prayer room was opened in Bratislava in the early 1990s. In 1993, Czechoslovakia collapsed and the Muslim presence divided as a consequence. In both countries, Muslims had to face the same problems of registering their organisation at the municipality so as to be able to build a mosque. The *Všeobecný zväz muslimských študentov* (General Union of Muslim Students),

---

44 "O utečencoch v Bratislave diskutovali katolícky biskup, predseda Islamskej nadácie, farár a aktivista" (Refugees in Bratislava discussed by Catholic bishop, president of the Islamic Foundation, vicar and activist), *IslamOnline*, 29 September 2017, http://www.islamonline.sk/2017/09/o-utecencoch-v-bratislave-diskutovali-katolicky-biskup-predseda-islamskej-nadacie-farar-a-aktivistka/, accessed 3 January 2018.

45 "V srdci Bratislavy sa stretli predstavitelia troch ambrahámskych náboženstiev" (In the heart of Bratislava, representatives of three Abrahamic religions met), *IslamOnline*, 24 October 2017, http://www.islamonline.sk/2017/10/predstavitelia-troch-abrahamskych-nabozenstiev-pod-zastitou-primatora-diskutovali-o-ulohe-viery/, accessed 3 January 2018.

46 "Rabín, kňaz a imám cestujú po slovenských školách a hovoria so žiakmi o tolerancii" (Rabbi, priest and imam travel to Slovak schools and talk to students about tolerance), *IslamOnline*, 3 January 2018, http://www.islamonline.sk/2018/01/rabin-knaz-a-imam-cestuju-po-slovenskych-skolach-a-hovoria-so-ziakmi-o-tolerancii/, accessed 19 January 2018.

47 Stefančík and Lenč, *Mladí migranti v slovenskej spoločnosti*, pp. 124–126.

established in 1993, represented the interests of foreign students with a Muslim background. Some of its members later founded the Islamic Foundation in Slovakia in 1999. The Foundation opened the Córdoba Cultural Centre in 2009, which is located in the centre of Bratislava.[48]

Muslim Population	4,800–5,000 (0.09% of the total population, 2017).[49]
Ethnic/National Backgrounds	Arabs (Syria, Algeria, Saudi Arabia, Egypt and Sudan), Albanians (from Macedonia and Kosovo), Afghans, Bosniaks, Muslims from the former Soviet Union, Turks, Muslims from Sub-Saharan Africa (Somalia in particular), Muslims from other part of the South and South-East Asia (Pakistan, Indonesia, India), Slovak converts (primarily women).
Inner-Islamic Groups	No data available.
Geographical Spread	Most Muslims live in Bratislava and in university towns (Martin, Košice or Nitra). Others live scattered across the whole of Slovakia.
Number of Mosques	There is no official mosque in Slovakia. Muslims use only prayer rooms that are part of foundations or located in private homes.
Muslim Burial Sites	The only known place for burial is in Bratislava in the cemetery in Slávičie údolie, which Muslims can use. It is not designated as a Muslim burial site.
"Chaplaincy" in State Institutions	Islam is not officially registered in Slovakia, and thus Muslims cannot provide pastoral services in state institutions.
Halal Products	Halal food is available in restaurants run by Muslims. There are several shops in Slovakia that offer halal products.

---

48   Štefančík and Lenč, *Mladí migranti v slovenskej spoločnosti*, pp. 154–160.
49   "Europe's growing Muslim population", 29 November 2017, http://www.pewforum.org/2017/11/29/europes-growing-muslim-population/, accessed 1 April 2018.

Dress Code	There are no laws proscribing wearing the head scarf or niqab.
Places of Islamic Learning and Education	No data available.
Muslim Media and Publications	– IslamOnline.sk. This is the website of the Islamic Foundation in Slovakia that gives daily information about the life of Muslims in Slovakia and the Czech Republic, and monitors the various manifestations of Islamophobia in both countries. – *al-Islam*. A quarterly publication, issued by the Islamic Foundation; published in the Slovak and Czech languages. It provides information related to local issues and the wider world.

Main Muslim Organisations

- Islamic Foundation in Slovakia (*Islamská nadácia na Slovensku*, PO Box 247, Bratislava 81499, www.islamonline.sk) Generally regarded as the official institution representing Muslims. This organisation also runs the Cordoba Cultural Centre (*Kultúrne centrum Córdoba*, Obchodná 31, 81106 Bratislava, tel: ++421 944 560 161) The Foundation publishes a bulletin (*al-Islam*), manages a web page (www.islamonline.sk) and runs a Facebook group (*IslamOnline.sk*) with 8,262 followers.
- Association of Friends of Islamic Literature (*Združenie priateľov islámskej literatúry*, Žabotova 2, 811 04, Bratislava) and the Muslim Community in Slovakia (*Komunita muslimov na Slovensku*, Žabotova 2, 81104, Bratislava) were founded by Abdulwahab Al Sbenaty, but both organisations are not active except for the running of the web site koran.sk.
- Muslim Foundation in Slovakia (*Nadácia moslimov na Slovensku*, Peterská 2, 83101 Bratislava). Established in 2009 by Ammar Qari and Chiboub Hibdani; the Foundation is currently in the process of being dissolved, however.[50]

---

50   https://finstat.sk/42172098, accessed 20 January 2018.

- Turkish-Slovak Alliance for Education and Development (TSAFED, Obchodná 66, 81106 Bratislava, tel: ++421 254690600, www.tsafed.org). Established in 2011, it is formally a non-profit organisation dedicated to the development of trade and educational links; it is affiliated with the Hizmet movement.
- Foundation al-Huda (*Nadácia al-Huda*, Hemerkova 33, 04023 Košice, Masjid Alhuda, Rožňavská 10, 04011 Košice, email: mohamadfarah42@gmail.com).
- Association of Muslims in Central Slovakia–al-Bakara (*Združenie moslimov na strednom Slovensku–al-Bakara*, Mešita al-Bakara, Jesenského 27, 03601 Martin, email: albakaramt@gmail.com).

Slovenia

Christian Moe[1]

Introduction

In 2017, the main Islamic organisation in Slovenia, *Islamska skupnost* (Islamic Community–IC), celebrated several major anniversaries. It was able to look back on considerable successes in institutionalising Islamic activities in the country, though its major project–completing the Islamic Cultural Centre in Ljubljana–remained on hold for lack of funding. The IC also remained concerned about Islamophobic outbursts from the political right, and the "fragmentation" of the Islamic scene by Muslim organisations outside its control. Talks between religious communities and the Government in the Council for Dialogue on Religious Freedom, continued to slowly and cautiously address some obstacles to Muslim religious practice in public institutions.

Public Debates

In the early 2000s, public debates on Islam were focused on the mosque-building project in Ljubljana. After a favourably disposed mayor and city council gave the necessary approvals, however, the project became a financial rather than a political problem for the Islamic Community. In recent years though, and particularly since the 2015 refugee and migrant crisis, right-wing media and politicians have increasingly adopted Islamophobic and anti-migrant discourses, similar to those in many other parts of Europe. In 2017, with the mosque construction at a hiatus due to a lack of funding, the building was again made a political issue on at least two occasions. In Ljubljana, city councillors for the *Slovenska demokratska stranka* (Slovene Democratic Party–SDS) and *Nova Slovenia* (New Slovenia–NSi) parties[2] unsuccessfully opposed the proposal to

---

[1] Christian Moe is a freelance writer in Slovenia. His research focuses on Balkan Muslims, human rights, and religious reform. He is co-editor of *Gender Equality in Muslim Family Law* (London: I.B. Tauris, 2013), and has been a contributor to *Yearbook of Muslims in Europe* since its inception.

[2] The SDS and NSi are right-wing parties affiliated with the European People's Party. The SDS, headed by Janez Janša, is a nationalist populist party that has, in recent years, adopted a hard-line anti-migrant rhetoric, aligning itself with Hungary's Prime Minister, Victor Orbán. The NSi is a pro-business Christian democratic party that has not focused on migration

name an access road to the mosque *Džamijska ulica*, "Mosque Street", arguing that the city did not have a "Church Street", and that the proposal was "divisive" and a "provocation".[3] At the national level, a prominent parliamentarian for the SDS party used the blockade of Qatar as an occasion for raising fears about the Ljubljana mosque. Branko Grims, who headed the parliamentary oversight committee for the security and intelligence services, noted accusations that Qatar supported terrorism, and stated that this had security implications for Slovenia, since Qatar was the main sponsor of the mosque. While speaking of "infiltration" of people from "that environment" into "various positions" in the EU, he asked the Government why foreign funding of religious communities from abroad was not forbidden. The IC took these remarks as preparing the ground for "demolishing the mosque and lynching Muslims in Slovenia", and asked politicians in positions of power to stop creating negative images of the mosque and Muslims.[4]

Yet, the IC was also concerned about foreign Islamic influences, specifically about small groups of Muslims in Slovenia who did not work within the IC's framework, and did not adhere to the same Islamic tradition. In November 2017, it published a brief report on "Alternative Muslim organisations in Slovenia." As described in the report, the *Slovenska muslimanska skupnost* (Slovenian Muslim Community), an officially registered breakaway group from the IC, had initially been "ideological"–a claim the report left unclear–but was not currently in tension with the IC. The report also briefly mentioned the Ahmadiyya mission in Maribor; an informal congregation of IC members on the coast, named *Teblig*; and several dervish groups said to be operating informally in Maribor. More problematic were the *El-Iman* and *Resnica-Haq* cultural societies, which were described as "exclusivist", as having had contacts with persons accused of terrorism, and as being in conflict with congregations of the IC. Similarly, the *Srednja Pot* cultural society carried out its religious programme and its own mosque-building project in isolation from the IC.

---

issues. In 2017, the parties were in opposition both in the Ljubljana city council and at the national level.

3 Jesenšek, Maša, "Žabja, Džamijska in Plečnikova ulica ter Kocbekov park" (Frog, Mosque and Plečnik Street and Kocbek Park), *Delo*, 27 June 2017, p. 11. The word for mosque in Slovene has traditionally been *mošeja*, but the Bosnian *džamija*, consistently used by Slovenian Muslims themselves, has gained wide currency.

4 "Blokada Katarja ima po besedah Grimsa posledice tudi za Slovenijo" (In Grims' words, the blockade of Qatar has consequences for Slovenia too), STA, 8 June 2017, https://www.sta .si/2396509/blokada-katarja-ima-po-besedah-grimsa-posledice-tudi-za-slovenijo; IC, "Načrti za rušenje džamije" (Plans for demolishing the mosque), *Press Release*, 8 June 2017, http:// www.islamska-skupnost.si?p=10368, all accessed 24 January 2018.

The report avoided terms like "Salafi", and instead described the groups in broad terms. They were said to be "ideological", and dealt with "marginal" issues of "formal religiosity", to attract young people with insecure identities, and exacerbated the "isolation and ghettoisation" of Muslims from society. The IC found itself having to answer the public's questions about these groups, for which it had no responsibility. The report dealt with this "fragmentation" of Islamic activities as a negative phenomenon that also led to the polarisation of Muslims and their stigmatisation in Slovenian society. At the same time, the report recognised such groups as part of the "plurality" of religions in democratic societies, which had to be respected, but not to the point of allowing "wrong" interpretations to cause conflicts among Muslims. It concluded that the IC should pass a resolution condemning all Islamic actors it had not authorised as "ill-intentioned" and harmful.[5]

The IC, then, reiterated its dissatisfaction with the legal situation in Slovenia, which allows anyone with the requisite minimum number of founding members to establish Muslim cultural organisations, or even register an Islamic religious community without the IC's approval. The IC effectively argues that it could help society combat radicalisation if the State let it control what organisations could brand themselves "Islamic" or "Muslim". These arguments have not convinced the Slovenian government to change its approach. Still, the IC raised the issue on several occasions in 2017. In his *Bayram* sermon, which coincided with Slovenia's Statehood Day, the Mufti argued that Slovenia was the only country with Austro-Hungarian legal heritage to introduce "pluralism" in the Islamic field, and that this had been an error.[6]

---

[5] Mešihat Islamske skupnosti v RS, "Alternativne muslimanske organizacije v Sloveniji" (Alternative Muslim organisations in Slovenia) (adopted 8 November 2017), *Islamska skupnost*, 16 November 2017, www.islamska-skupnost.si?p=10862, accessed 24 January 2018.

[6] "Bajramska hutba–nagovor muftija prof. dr. Nedžada Grabusa" (Bayram khutba–address by Mufti Prof Dr Nedžad Grabus), *Islamska skupnost*, 25 June 2017, www.islamska-skupnost.s?p=10459; "Delovni sestanek imamov v Ljubljani" (Working meeting of imams in Ljubljana), *Islamska skupnost*, 24 August 2017, http://www.islamska-skupnost.si?p=10612, both accessed 24 January 2018. This is not the place to assess the Mufti's claim about Slovenia's uniqueness, but various other legal models in the region do give one Islamic organisation a special position, and grant it control over Islamic nomenclature, from the Austrian *Islamgesetz* (Law on Islam), *Official Gazette of Austria* no. 39/2015, art. 9, to the Bosnian *Zakon o slobodi vjere i pravnom položaju crkava i vjerskih zajednica* (Law on Religious Freedom and the Legal Position of Churches and Religious Communities), *Official Gazette of BiH* no. 5/2004, art. 5 (e).

Transnational Links

Slovenian Muslims are primarily linked to their communities of origin in other parts of the former Yugoslavia (Bosnia and Herzegovina, the Sandžak region in Serbia and Montenegro, Kosovo, etc.). The IC in Slovenia is affiliated with the Islamic Community of Bosnia and Herzegovina, and nurtures ties with Islamic institutions in that country, with other affiliates in the region (especially in neighbouring Croatia), and in the Bosnian diaspora. These ties were maintained also in 2017, *inter alia* through an official delegation from the Bosnian *riyasat* (leadership) to its Slovenian affiliate in mid-November.[7] The IC also seeks to maintain good relations with relevant institutions in a range of Muslim majority countries, including Turkey, with which Slovenian Muslims share an Ottoman heritage, and Qatar, the main sponsor of the Islamic Cultural Centre in Ljubljana. Representatives of the IC also take part in various international Muslim, inter-religious, and official dialogues. In 2017, these included a meeting of the European Council of Religious Leaders in Finland (of which Mufti Grabus is a member), and two OSCE/ODIHR events in Olzstyn (Poland) and Vienna on hate speech. The IC also took part in a Muslim–Jewish conference in Sarajevo, and the 13th Muslim International Forum in Helsinki, hosted by the Grand Mufti of Russia.[8]

Law and Domestic Politics

In 2017, talks between religious communities and the Government made cautious progress on several issues of concern to the IC, while the courts turned down a Muslim citizen's private complaint over holidays.

In 2014, Almir Talić brought a constitutional complaint against the *Law on Holidays and Work-Free Days*, which he claimed was discriminatory, since a number of Christian holidays (but no Muslim ones) were officially recognised as work-free days.[9] In this way, he argued, it disadvantaged him personally as a Muslim, non-Christian employee, since, unlike Christians, he had to take time off out of his regular vacation time for festivals, and was at a disadvantage in

---

[7] "Namestnik Reisu-l-uleme in člani Rijaseta obiskali Mešihat" (The deputy *ra'is al-'ulama'* and members of the *riyasat* visited the *mashihat*), *Islamska skupnost*, 21 November 2017, www.islamska-skupnost.si?p=10875, accessed 24 January 2018.
[8] Various reports on www.islamska-skupnost.si, accessed 24 January 2018.
[9] Moe, Christian, "Slovenia", in Oliver Scharbrodt, Samim Akgönül, Ahmet Alibašić, Jørgen S. Nielsen and Egdūnas Račius (eds.), *Yearbook of Muslims in Europe*, vol. 7 (Leiden: Brill, 2016), pp. 523–533 (528–529).

negotiating time off with his employer. This, he argued, was in conflict with the religious freedom provisions of Article 41 of the Slovenian Constitution; it was also discriminatory against non-Christian religious communities in general, in conflict with Articles 7 and 14 of the Constitution.[10] The Constitutional Court accepted the latter claims for review as well, considering that individual believers had a legal interest in the equal rights of their communities, but rejected the complaint as manifestly unfounded. Namely, the Law distinguished between state holidays (*prazniki*) and other work-free days; the latter were not celebrated by the State, and the legislature had not chosen them for their religious content, but for their historical or traditional association with Slovene heritage, the Court held. The strict proportionality test previously laid down by the Court, for differential treatment that impaired the exercise of a religion-based human right, did not apply here, as religious communities and individuals remained free to manifest their beliefs, regardless of the holidays law. The work-free days were for individuals to do with as they liked, and the legislature was free to determine those days as it liked, including "… as an expression of the identity of the people who have historically lived in the area of the present State and who are connected with a European heritage".[11]

The Islamic Community had not been party to the complaint, and had distanced itself from it from the beginning. In response to the ruling, the IC reiterated its views in a press release: first, the IC did not seek rights at others' expense, and would not be so unreasonable as to oppose the rights of Catholics and other Christians to their holidays. Second, this matter did not need to be resolved in court, but should be pursued through an open dialogue between Slovenian institutions, experts and all the religious communities affected, an option that was far from exhausted. Third, since the problem affected some 15% of the population, a solution needed to be found, and the Croatian Law on holidays, which provided for extra work-free days for those observing various religious holidays, might serve as a model.[12]

The IC continued, instead, to advance its interests through participation in the Slovenian government's Council for Dialogue on Religious Freedom (*Svet za dialog o verski svobodi*), which has, since 2016, brought together religious communities, Churches, government offices, and experts, under the auspices of the

---

10   Zakon o praznikih in dela prostih dnevih (Law on Holidays and Work-Free Days), *Official Gazette* no. 112/05, 52/10, 19/15 and 83/16. Complaint: *Initiative U-I-67/14 for Assessment of Constitutionality*, 19 March 2014.
11   *Constitutional Court Decision U-I-67/14*, 19 January 2017.
12   "Sporočilo za javnost Islamske skupnosti v zvezi z odločbo Ustavnega sodišča" (Press release in connection with the Constitutional Court decision), *Islamska skupnost*, 2 March 2017, http://www.islamska-skupnost.si?p=10029, accessed 24 January 2018.

Ministry of Culture. The Council held two meetings in January and October 2017, and deliberated on three issues raised by the IC: spiritual care in hospitals; spiritual care in the army; and male circumcision.

Not all hospitals and other health-care institutions set aside a space for religious purposes, and those that do have a Catholic chapel, with the exception of the hospital in Celje, which has a room for ritual use by all religious communities. The IC wanted a small room where a visiting imam could meet and pray with patients without disturbing their room-mates. It also wished to be informed by hospitals about patients seeking Islamic spiritual care, but was told that for privacy reasons, hospitals could not give out such lists. Officials pointed out that hospitals reported little demand for such care, and suggested that there was scope for working out local solutions case by case. The IC and the Catholic Church supported each other in arguing that sharing Catholic chapels was not an appropriate solution, and that a separate space should be found for Islamic care.[13] By the next meeting, officials were pleased to report that the hospitals in Ljubljana and Maribor had promised to set aside a space for other religious communities, while that in Jesenice (with a large Muslim population) had no space available, but had intensified its efforts to inform patients about the availability of spiritual care.[14]

The Chaplaincy of the Slovenian Armed Forces (*Vojaški vikariat Slovenske vojske*) is responsible for the spiritual care of all soldiers, but has, since 2000, employed only Catholic and Protestant chaplains, based on special agreements between the State and these Churches. In the Council meeting, a defence official suggested that a military imam was not currently needed, because no-one had made use of opportunities offered to Muslim soldiers in the past. The IC objected that the need was unknown, as the number of Muslims serving in the armed forces was unknown, and some might not wish to call attention to their identity but might want to use the services of an imam if provided. However, their numbers were almost certainly higher than those of Protestants, who had their own chaplain; in any case, the IC and the armed forces could cooperate on provision of spiritual care even without the army's chaplaincy employing its own imam. The Catholic Church representative supported the inclusion of both Muslim and Serbian Orthodox chaplains. Various possible arrangements

---

13 "Zapisnik 2. seje Sveta vlade Republike Slovenije za dialog o verski svobodi" (Minutes of the 2nd meeting of the Council), *no. 013–2/2017/21*, 23 February 2017. This and other Council documents are available at: http://www.mk.gov.si/si/delovna_podrocja/urad_za_verske_skupnosti/svet_vlade_rs_za_dialog_o_verski_svobodi/, accessed 5 May 2018.

14 "Zapisnik 3. seje Sveta vlade Republike Slovenije za dialog o verski svobodi" (Minutes of the 3rd meeting of the Council), *no. 013–12/2017/56*, 22 January 2018.

were discussed, and it was pointed out that interested parties should engage with the on-going parliamentary procedure over a new defence bill.[15]

Concerning circumcision, the IC complained that access to surgery had been jeopardised by the Human Rights Ombudsman's 2012 statement that intervening in the bodily integrity of children for no medical reason, but based only on the parents' religious wishes, was unacceptable and could incur criminal liability.[16] Some health-care providers had stopped offering circumcision; some still offered it, but the IC considered the price prohibitively high. The IC requested the Government to clarify that circumcision was legal, and to regulate an affordable price. A physician and Ministry of Health representative noted that the Ljubljana university clinic had stopped offering the procedure due to growing waiting lists for medically necessary child surgery. However, they did frequently have to treat complications in children who had been inexpertly circumcised elsewhere, and it would be best to provide the procedure in a safe environment, but this was not possible with the current capacity of the health services. A representative of the Ombudsman's office rejected calls for the Ombudsman to reconsider the opinion, stating that even thousand-year old traditions did not justify violations of children's rights, and that any legalisation of circumcision would have to come not from them but through legislation, in which the legislature would decide the appropriate balance between religious freedom and children's right to bodily integrity. A government official, however, pointed out that circumcision was not treated as a criminal act in Slovenian judicial practice; relevant cases had not been prosecuted for the procedure itself, but only when malpractice was involved. The discussion ended without a conclusion in 2017.[17]

Activities and Initiatives of Main Muslim Organisations

The *Islamska skupnost* (Islamic Community–IC) hosted several events to celebrate various anniversaries, chiefly "100 years of institutional activity in Slovenia". They took as their starting point the 1917 visit by the Bosnian *ra'is al-'ulama'* and the military mufti to a mosque built for Bosnian Muslim soldiers

---

15   "Zapisnik 3. seje".
16   Office of the Human Rights Ombudsman (Varuh človekovih pravic), "Obrezovanje fantkov iz nemedicinskih razlogov je kršitev otrokovih pravic" (Circumcision of little boys on non-medical grounds is a violation of children's rights), 3 February 2012, http://www.varuh-rs.si/medijsko-sredisce/aktualni-primeri/novice/detajl/obrezovanje-fantkov-iz-nemedicinskih-razlogov-je-krsitev-otrokovih-pravic/, accessed 5 May 2018.
17   "Zapisnik 3. seje".

serving in the Austro-Hungarian army on the Soča (Isonzo) front.[18] It should be noted that there has not in fact been institutional continuity since then, but only since the local congregation in Ljubljana started (or "renewed") its work in 1967, a 50-year anniversary that was also celebrated.[19] The anniversary was marked in September 2017 with a commemoration in Log pod Mangartom, site of the former mosque and graveyard of some 100 Muslim soldiers, which was attended by representatives of the military chaplaincies of both Slovenia and Bosnia and Herzegovina. The anniversary was further marked in October with an academic conference in Ljubljana organised by the Averroes Institute, attended by academics from Bosnia and Herzegovina and Slovenia. Between these two formal events, on 2–7 October, the local imam in Celje, Nazif Topuz, went on a 140-kilometre "run for peace" from Log pod Mangartom to Ljubljana, during which he also met with Slovenia's president Borut Pahor.

For many years, the project of constructing an Islamic Cultural Centre and mosque in Ljubljana has consumed most of the IC's energy. The centre has now been built, but is not yet functional. In late 2018, Mufti Grabus estimated that another €13 million would be needed to complete construction work and to furnish and equip the centre, on top of the unexpectedly high €22 million the project has already cost. The Mufti remained hopeful that Qatar, which had already contributed €15 million, would come to the IC's aid again.[20] Meanwhile, the IC continues to rent sports halls for its holiday prayers. Still, the new urban landmark with its 40-metre minaret is a historical milestone. It serves as the symbolic backdrop for various events. In May 2017, leaders of the Catholic, Evangelical and Orthodox Churches in Slovenia joined the Mufti in planting a tree of peace and friendship on the mosque grounds.[21]

As every year, the IC organised the hajj, *Bayram* prayers, and other events in the ritual calendar, including a *mawlid* celebration on 22 April 2017. Noteworthy additions to Slovenia's home-grown Islamic literature included a book of sermons by Ljubljana imam Špendi Fidani, as well as IC secretary Nevzet Porić's MA thesis, completed at the Faculty of Islamic Sciences in Sarajevo, on four Slovene translations of the Qur'an.[22]

18   As announced in *Slovenec*, vol. 45, no. 244 (24 October 1917), p. 5.
19   "Džemat Ljubljana zaznamoval pomemben jubilej" (Ljubljana congregation marked important anniversary), *Islamska skupnost*, 5 December 2017, http://www.islamska-skupnost.si?p=10910, accessed 24 January 2018.
20   Pozničr Cvetko, Sonja, "Burke so danes bolj politično kot versko vprašanje", STA, 9 December 2017, www.sta.si/2459390 (excerpt), full text available at www.islamska-skupnost.si?p=10949, accessed 24 January 2018.
21   Lešničar, Tina, "Generacijski projekt še čaka na zeleno vejo", *Delo*, 24 May 2017.
22   Fidani, Špendi, *Dogovor je pobjeda* (*Agreement is Victory*) (Ljubljana: Averroes, 2017), in Bosnian, see www.islamska-skupnost.si?p=10321; Porić, Nevzet, *Prevodi Kur'ana v slovenski jezik in njihova percepcija* (*Translations of the Qur'an into Slovene and their Perception*)

Muslim Population: History and Demographics

Muslims in Slovenia mostly come from other parts of the former Yugoslavia, as labour migrants from the 1960s onwards, and as refugees in the 1990s. They have almost exclusively settled in urban, industrial areas; the majority are Bosniaks. They look like Slovenes, have a closely related mother tongue, and share some of the same historical and cultural heritage, including extensive experience with secularisation, yet remain "othered" by ethnicity, cultural differences, religion, and social position. Slovenia has a Catholic majority, and a small but historically important Protestant minority. Though Muslims may make up less than 3% of Slovenia's population of 2 million, they likely form the second largest religious community, followed by the Serbian Orthodox.

The 2002 census was the last to ask about religious or national identity, and thus gives the last official count of the Muslim population (excluding short-term guest workers). These figures are likely an underestimate, as some Muslims would be among the 23% of the population that did not officially declare a religion, but it tallies reasonably well with nationality data and with the loose membership figures (in terms of families) quoted by the IC. From 2002 to 2011, the population as a whole grew by 4.4%.

Muslim Population	47,488 (2.4% of total population, according to the 2002 census, the last to ask about religion); ca. 7,500 families (according to various IC membership estimates).
Ethnic/National Backgrounds	As a percentage of the Muslim population in the 2002 census:[23]
	Bosniak or related categories (Bosnian, *Muslimani*): 19,923 (74%)
	Albanian: 5,237 (11%)
	Slovene: 2,804 (6%)
	Unknown (several categories): 1,125 (2%)
	Roma: 868 (2%)

(MA dissertation) (Sarajevo: Faculty of Islamic Studies, 2017): see www.islamska-skupnost.si?p=10668, both accessed 24 January 2018.

23   Komac, Miran (ed.), *Priseljenci: Študije o priseljevanju in vključevanju v slovensko družbo* (*Immigrants: Studies on Immigration and Inclusion into Slovenian Society*) (Ljubljana: Inštitut za narodnostna vprašanja, 2007), table 10, p. 536.

	Montenegrin: 634 (2%) Macedonian: 507 (1%) Other: 445 (1%).
Inner-Islamic Groups	The vast majority of Muslims, and both the two officially registered Islamic organisations, belong to Sunni Islam of the Hanafi rite.
Geographical Spread	Muslims are concentrated in industrial towns and ports. In 2002, they made up 4.1% of the urban and 0.6% of the rural population. Over 50% lived in four towns: Ljubljana (the capital), Jesenice, Velenje and Koper. The town with the highest proportion of Muslims was Jesenice (28%), followed by Velenje, Hrastnik, Trbovlje and Izola (each over 10%).
Number of Mosques	The first purpose-built mosque and Islamic cultural Centre, in Ljubljana, remains to be furnished and put to use. The IC has some 18 venues used for regular prayers.
Muslim Burial Sites	Cemeteries are publicly owned. Some towns have allotted separate sections for Muslims (Jesenice, Maribor, Celje, Kranj, Krško). Repatriation of remains to countries of origin also takes place. The IC has restored a burial site in Log pod Mangartom, where Muslim soldiers fell in World War I.
"Chaplaincy" in State Institutions	Imams have the right to provide spiritual care in public institutions. The provision of these services is limited in practice by capacity and various obstacles, which were addressed in talks between the different religious communities and the Government in 2017. Regular prison visits are carried out. The armed forces have Catholic and Protestant chaplains, but no Muslim ones.
Halal Products	Halal products are not generally available. A few butcher shops exist, and shopping trips to Austria are a viable alternative for some. Ritual slaughter is

no longer exempt from the legal requirement that the animal be rendered unconscious first.[24] The IC has raised the problem of access to halal food in schools.

Dress Code	Muslim women in Slovenia only began wearing head scarves in the 1990s, and many still do not, except at religious occasions. The IC disapproves of full face veils (niqab). There is no law restricting Muslim dress. A 2015 proposal to ban burqas in public spaces failed to receive parliamentary support. There is discussion of a policy for schools, but this has not been a prominent issue.
Places of Islamic Learning and Education	The IC conducts Islamic education for children on its various premises, as well as some evening classes for adults. There are no Islamic schools; the closest option is the secondary school (madrasa) in Zagreb, Croatia. The IC is reportedly exploring the possibility of starting a private secondary school and boarding home.[25]
Muslim Media and Publications	– www.islamska-skupnost.si (IC website) – *Amber* (IC internal newsletter) – *Preporod* (Bosnian IC newspaper) – *Ibn Rušd* (journal of the Averroes institute) – Various websites and Facebook pages of small Islamic cultural societies outside the IC, more or less Salafi-inspired – Other media targeting a Bosniak and generally Muslim audience include *Bošnjak* magazine and the web portal bosnjak.si.

---

24   Amendment to *Zakon o zaščiti živali* (*ZZZiv, Animal Protection Act*), art. 25, *Official Gazette* no. 32/2013.
25   Cvetko, "Burke so danes bolj politično kot versko vprašanje".

Main Muslim Organisations

- Islamic Community (*Islamska skupnost–IS RS* (referred to as IC above), Grablovičeva 14, PO Box 2725, 1001 Ljubljana, tel.: ++386 12313625, fax: ++386 12313626, email: mesihat@islamska-skupnost.si, www.islamska-skupnost.si). Headed by Mufti Nedžad Grabus and affiliated with the Islamic Community of Bosnia and Herzagovina, this is the main organisation in charge of Islamic life in Slovenia, with 17 local branches across the country.
- Slovenian Muslim Community (*Slovenska muslimanska skupnost*–SMO, Ledina centre, Prostor št. 33, Kotnikova ul. 5, 1000 Ljubljana, tel.: ++386 14304866, fax: ++386 14304866, email: odbor@smskupnost.si, www.smskupnost.si). Started by Osman Đogić after he was replaced as Mufti in 2006, the SMO claims to have only a few hundred members. It is the only officially registered Islamic religious community beside the IC.
- Averroes Institute (*Kulturno-izobraževalni zavod Averroes*, same address/phone as the IC, info@averroes.si, www.averroes.si). It was established by the IC to carry out cultural and educational projects, including publishing, organising public lectures, and running a library.
- Zemzem Women's Association (*Žensko združenje Zemzem*, Cesta Andreja Bitenca 70, 1000 Ljubljana, email: zemzem@islamska-skupnost.si). It organises a wide range of activities, including the annual Bosnian Food Festival.
- Humanitarian Society Merhamet (*Humanitarno društvo Merhamet*, same address as the IC, tel.: ++386 41255692, email: info@merhamet.si, www.merhamet.si). Muslim charity organisation.
- Outside the IC's orbit there are small, independent Islamic groups, promoting a more Salafi-oriented Islam, organised as cultural societies. The Middle Road Society (*Kulturno Društvo Srednja pot*, Tbilisijska 83a, Ljubljana, www.srednjapot.si), established in 2014, is establishing a new centre, while the Resnica-Haq Society (*Društvo za promocijo islamske kulture v Sloveniji Resnica-Hak*, Cesta Maršala Tita 68, Jesenice) and the El-Iman Society (*Društvo za promocijo islamske kulture v Sloveniji El-Iman*, Dunajska cesta 190, Ljubljana) share a website at www.resnica-haq.com, and struggle with accusations of links to extremists.
- The Ahmadiyya Community (*Društvo za informiranje o islamu: Muslimanska skupnost Ahmadija*, Zrkovska c. 144, 200 Maribor, tel.: ++386 40718105, fax: ++386 83888342, email: info@alislam.si, www.alislam.si). It operates a mission based in Slovenia's second largest town Maribor.

Spain

Jordi Moreras[1]

Introduction

The impact of the terrorist attacks in Barcelona and Cambrils in August 2017 has marked the future of Muslim communities in Spain. 13 years after the attacks on commuter trains in Madrid in 2004, Spain witnessed once again a terrorist attack. In 2017, the political tension between the Spanish state and Catalan nationalist parties that argue for Catalonian independence became an issue in the aftermath of the attack during the discussion over what occurred. The different groups fighting against Islamophobia warned of an increase in aggression against Muslims and mosques as a result of the attacks. Likewise, the concern among the Spanish public in relation to international terrorism increased considerably.

For the first time since 2013, the numbers of foreign people in Spain grew again slightly, breaking the downward trend of previous years. The number of foreign residents from Muslim majority countries equally rose. The estimate, based on foreign residents with documentation in Spain, indicates that an increase occurred, from 1,034,116 in 2016 to 1,063,302 in 2017. The largest Muslim group in Spain are still Moroccans (773,478 residents in 2017, compared to 756,796 in 2016). Other national groups from Pakistan and Senegal, increased their numbers to 78,350 and 61,644, respectively. In 2016, a total of 30,506 people from Muslim majority countries obtained Spanish citizenship. No data is available for 2017, but there has been a decline in the number of such naturalisations, given the modification of the procedure for granting citizenship through continuing residence. This includes assumptions such as "good civic conduct" and "sufficient degree of integration", which are very difficult to determine.

Alongside such official data, information that is provided by the Andalusi Observatory (*Observatorio Andalusi*), a body set up by the *Unión de Comunidades Islámicas de España* (Union of Islamic Communities in Spain)

---

[1] Jordi Moreras is Professor of Social Anthropology at the Faculty of Humanities, University Rovira i Virgili (Tarragona, Spain). His latest works include *Identidades a la intemperie: Una mirada antropológica a los procesos de radicalización en Europa* (Unprotected Identities: an Anthropological Look at Radicalisation Processes in Europe) (Barcelona: Bellaterra, 2018); Moreras, Jordi, (ed.), *Diàspores i rituals. El cicle festiu dels musulmans a Catalunya* (Diasporas and Rituals: The Festive Cycle of Muslims in Catalonia) (Barcelona: Departament de Cultura-Generalitat de Catalunya, 2017).

in 2003, must also be included.[2] Its annual report provides a much more generous estimate of the number of Muslims in Spain, that includes: naturalisations (309,708);[3] the residents of Ceuta and Melilla (72,355); those born to Muslim families in Spain (564,766);[4] and converts, called *naturales* (24,440). According to this report, 43% of Muslims in Spain are Spanish citizens, part of a total figure of 1,946,300 Muslims in Spain, which is 4.2% of the Spanish population.

2017 marked the 25th anniversary of the signing of the Cooperation Agreement between the Spanish state and the *Comisión Islámica de España* (Islamic Commission of Spain). Different commemorations took place, such as a celebration in the Congress of Deputies on 13 November 2017, which the Minister of Justice, Rafael Catalá, and the Speaker of the Spanish parliament, Ana Pastor, attended. The main representatives of the Protestant, Jewish and Muslim communities were also at the event. Riay Tatary Bakri acted as the representative of the Islamic Commission of Spain, the entity created from the union of the two main Islamic federations, the *Unión de Comunidades Islámicas de España* (Union of Islamic Communities of Spain–UCIDE), and the *Federación Española de Entidades Religiosas Islámicas* (Spanish Federation of Islamic Religious Entities–FEERI). The dispute between these two federations still generates an anomalous leadership split that hinders and obstructs a proper representation of Muslim groups in Spain. The public budget given by the Spanish state to Muslim community organisations, takes this internal division for granted.[5] However, in 2017, it was decided that Muslims, Jews and Protestants, as well as the Catholic Church, will be audited by the State for the first time regarding the public subsidies they receive.

---

2 Observatorio Andalusi, *Estudio demográfico de la población musulmana. Explotación estadística del censo de ciudadanos musulmanes en España referido a a fecha 31 de diciembre de 2017* (*Demographic Study of the the Census of Muslim Citizens in Spain Conducted 31 December 2017*) (Madrid: Unión de Comunidades Islámicas de España, 2018). See http://observatorio.hispanomuslim.es, accessed 23 February 2018.

3 This figure represents the sum of the naturalisations between 1968 and 2016.

4 This data should be questioned, since Spanish citizenship is not obtained automatically by being born in Spain, if both parents are foreigners. Despite the doubts regarding the methodology of this report, its estimates are beginning to be accepted: for example, in the *Informe Anual sobre la situación de la libertad religiosa en España de 2016* (*Annual Report on Religious Freedom in Spain 2016*) (Ministry of Justice, 2017), data from the *Observatorio Andalusi* is cited to establish the number of Muslims in Spain.

5 In 2017, the Islamic Commission of Spain received an annual subsidy of €255,000 from the Ministry of Justice's Foundation for Pluralism and Coexistence. This budget is distributed as follows: €150,000 for UCIDE, €85,000 for FEERI, and €20,000 is reserved for the management of the Islamic Commission of Spain, as a representative organisation. See the *Annual Report of the Foundation for Pluralism and Coexistence*: www.pluralismoyconvivencia.es, accessed 5 October 2017.

Due to the economic recovery after the global economic and financial crisis, Muslim communities relaunched initiatives and projects that had to be temporarily suspended due to a lack of economic resources. Initiatives aimed at religious socialisation are again being developed, as well as projects to improve or expand spaces of worship and charitable programmes for Muslim families in need. The latter involves the organisation of activities, and the collecting of food and basic products, especially during the month of Ramadan.

Public Debates

On the afternoon of 17 August, a truck drove onto the central pavement of the Ramblas in Barcelona, running over numerous people, resulting in 14 dead and 140 injured people. The perpetrator of this attack took flight, and while escaping the police hunt for him, murdered a young man to steal his car. Nine hours later there was another attack at the seafront of Cambrils (Tarragona), when a car with five young men tried to run over passers-by. The young men left the car and stabbed and killed a woman and hurt others. The Catalan police (*Mossos d'Esquadra*) shot the perpetrators, who were wearing fake explosive vests. The initial investigations indicated that it was a group of young people of Moroccan origin who lived in Ripoll (Girona), a town in the interior of Catalonia, about 107 km from Barcelona. Immediately a direct relationship was established with an explosion the previous day in a house in the coastal town of Alcanar (Tarragona), in which two people died and another was injured. One of the deceased was identified as Abdelbaki Es-Satty, who was the imam of one of the mosques of Ripoll, and who was considered the leader of the group. Four days after the attacks, the last member of the cell, the ringleader of the massive attack in Barcelona, was also killed by the Catalan police in the town of Subirats, some 50 km from Barcelona. The police investigations concluded weeks later that this group intended to commit a series of attacks on emblematic buildings in Barcelona (the Church of La Sagrada Familia, among others), and had prepared the necessary explosives.[6]

The impact of these two improvised attacks created a great deal of tension, with a mixture of condemnation of the terrorists and solidarity with the victims, and denunciations of Islamophobia, as well as racist discourses, especially on social networks. In the days following the attacks, several mosques in

---

6 For more details, see Reinares, Fernando, and Carola García Calvo, "'Spaniards, you are going to suffer': the inside story of the August 2017 attacks in Barcelona and Cambrils", *CTC Sentinel*, vol. 11(1) (Jan 2018), pp. 1–10.

Spain and Catalonia were damaged, and some Muslims (particularly women) were verbally and physically assaulted; such incidents were denounced by the civic platforms that combat intolerance. A viral campaign appeared, promoted by the City Council of Barcelona, which later became the motto of the demonstration of August 26 through the hashtag #notincpor (I'm not afraid). This was aimed at showing an image of unity between citizens and political institutions in light of the attacks.[7]

However, these atrocities were viewed within the unique context of Catalonian politics, the result of the struggle between the Spanish government and Catalan nationalist parties that are committed to the region's independence. It had seemed as if the attacks had interrupted or distracted public attention away from the sovereignty issue, even though a date of 1 October was already set for a referendum on the unilateral independence of Catalonia. Just ten days later though,[8] the Catalan media once again placed the issue of sovereignty on their front covers, with the terrorist attacks only spoken of as another argument within this political struggle, with questions asked as to the role of the security forces. No public enquiry was immediately proposed to investigate the course of events in Barcelona and Cambrils, and it was only six months later when the first public reports on the attacks appeared.[9]

In previous years, public debates on the Muslim presence in Spain centred on terrorist attacks in Europe and the migrant and refugee crisis, provoked by the armed conflict in Syria and Iraq. In 2017, the attacks in Barcelona and Cambrils provoked an increase in concern about international terrorism among the Spanish public. Those who saw this issue as a major concern rose to 15.6%, as it became the fifth most serious problem for Spaniards, behind unemployment, political corruption, and the progress of the economy in a survey conducted in September 2017.[10] However, this fell to 3.7% in the following month.

The terrorist acts also overshadowed the issue of the migrant and refugee crisis among the Spanish public. There was continued public support in favour of receiving refugees, although the Spanish government failed to comply with

---

7   See the official website created by Barcelona City Council: https://notincpor.barcelona.cat/ca/, accessed 27 August 2017.
8   Moreras, Jordi, "Ten days in August", in Moussa Bourekba (ed.), *Revisiting the Barcelona Attacks: Reactions, Explanations and Pending Discussions*, (CIDOB Report n° 2 February 2018), pp. 31–40.
9   Bourekba, *Revisiting the Barcelona Attacks*.
10 According to the barometer of opinion released each month by the *Centro de Investigaciones Sociológicas*, Barómetro CIS september 2017: http://datos.cis.es/pdf/Es3187mar_A.pdf, accessed 13 February 2018.

its commitments as set out by the European Union. According to them, Spain should have accepted a total of 17,337 refugees; by the end of 2017 it had only allowed in 2,782 refugees (16% of the assigned quota).[11] So far, no Spanish political force has yet capitalised on these anti-Muslim sentiments. Xenophobic parties remain very marginal in Spanish political life, but often take advantage of the controversies surrounding Muslims to continue spreading their message against Islam.

Transnational Links

Islam in Spain shows a strong internal heterogeneity, displaying a varied representation of the main doctrinal currents and transnational movements within Islam. There are various national groups that maintain relations with their countries of origin through cultural associations. In the case of Moroccans, the collaborative network created in the 1970s and 80s around the *Amicales de Trabajadores Marroquíes* (Moroccan Workers' Associations), linked to the various consular delegations, gave way in the 1990s to another kind of association with a social and cultural focus. At the same time, an associative network was formed around local prayer houses, that have a greater degree of independence from Morocco's official political sphere. A significant part of this Moroccan associative network claims a Berber identity, since a very significant part of the Moroccan community comes from the Rif region. In Catalonia, albeit without official statistics, it is estimated that between 60–70% of Moroccans come from the Rif.

Organisations that are part of transnational Islamic movements also favour connections with Muslims across Europe. The Muslim Brotherhood has had a presence in Spain since the 1970s, and played an important role at the beginning of the institutionalisation of Islam in the country.[12] At present, the different centres connected to this movement carry out various initiatives and programmes that are especially aimed at young Muslims. The other transnational Islamic pietist movement, the Tablighi Jamaat, has also been working

---

11 See "España ha acogido a 2.782 refugiados dentro del programa puesto en marcha por la UE", ABC, 22 March 2018, http://www.abc.es/espana/abci-espana-acogido-2782-refugiados-dentro-programa-puesto-marcha-201803220238_noticia.html, accessed 23 March 2018.
12 See Arigita, Elena, and Rafael Ortega "The Muslim Brotherhood in Spain", in Frank Peter and Rafael Ortega (eds.), *Islamic Movements of Europe* (London: I.B. Tauris, 2014), pp. 139–144.

in Spain since the 1970s.[13] This movement has played a very prominent role in the history of the Muslim population in Catalonia, and one of its main emirs continues to head the *Consejo Islámico y Cultural de Cataluña* (Islamic and Cultural Council of Catalonia).

Among Pakistanis, the activities of the Minhaj ul-Quran movement and Dawat-e Islami must be highlighted, both of which have been active in Spain since the 1990s. Among Pakistanis there are also some Shi'i communities, which have recently acquired some notoriety due to the public celebration of the 'Ashura' ceremony in Barcelona.[14] Among African groups (from Senegal and Gambia), the Sufi brotherhoods of Muridiyya and Tijaniyya play a very important organisational role, and their growth in Spain's Levante region has been consolidated since the 1980s.

Currently the most active bodies at the transnational level are those connected to Salafism;[15] they organise numerous meetings and training activities, and invite different sheikhs to the country from across Europe, the Middle East and the Maghreb. This movement is considered by the police to be the main group promoting radical interpretations of Islam. It is estimated that in Catalonia 100 mosques are influenced by Salafi doctrine, which accounts for a third of the total in this region. Although there is no federation representing these Salafi communities, they control two of the five large mosques built in Catalonia in recent years.[16]

Law and Domestic Politics

One of the singularities of Islam in Spain was the early recognition of the religion as a confession with an historical rootedness in Spanish society. The signing of the Cooperation Agreement in 1992 between the Spanish state and

---

13   See Tarrés, Sol, "The Tablighi Jama'at in Spain", in Frank Peter and Rafael Ortega (eds.), *Islamic Movements of Europe* (London: I.B. Tauris, 2014), pp. 257–262.

14   After the controversies generated in previous years (see Alonso-Kabré, Marta, Khalid Ghali, Alberto López Bargados, Jordi Moreras and Ariadna Solé Arrarás, "Invisible rituals: Islamic religious acts in Catalan public space", in Ana I. Planet (ed.), *Observing Islam in Spain: Contemporary Politics and Social Dynamics* (Leiden: Brill, 2018), pp. 85–112.), the city council of Barcelona has explicitly included 'Ashura' in a government measure adopted to guarantee the equality of religious activities in public space (approved in December 2017).

15   See Moreras, Jordi, and Sol Tarrés, "The development of Salafi doctrine in Spain", in Frank Peter and Rafael Ortega (eds.), *Islamic Movements of Europe* (London: I.B. Tauris, 2014), pp. 219–224.

16   See Moreras, *Identidades a la intemperie*.

the Islamic Commission of Spain, established a legal framework that aimed to guarantee the exercise of the Islamic religion and to promote its social recognition. At the time it was one of the most advanced legal frameworks of this sort in Western Europe, but it has yet to be fully developed even after 25 years. Apart from the official celebration mentioned above, the anniversary of this Agreement has gone virtually unnoticed, and only a few local communities have held events and conferences to highlight its continued lack of implementation.

The first issue that is still pending is the official representation of Muslim community organisations. This is because the differences between the two federations that make up the Islamic Commission of Spain, and the emergence of new federal entities, calls into question the model of representation established in the Cooperation Agreement. This has been the main argument used to explain its failure. However, there are other reasons as well. It may be due to developments within the Muslim communities themselves, which have brought up new issues that were not contemplated when the Cooperation Agreement was set up. These include the religious socialisation of young people, the social role of mosques, and the radicalisation processes among young Muslims.

In addition, the Agreement covers issues that pertain to competencies of the State which have now been transferred to the regional administrations. This has meant that new public Muslim actors have emerged at regional level, each with their respective agendas, having new demands and initiating negotiations without the existence of a minimum level of coordination in the decisions taken at regional level. Finally, the spread of a widely-accepted discourse regarding the supposedly problematic character of the Muslim presence in Spain, and all the issues that relate to that, has hindered the attempts by political actors to fully implement this Agreement.

The result is that relevant issues still need to be addressed, for example the implementation of Islamic religious education. The main demands of Muslim communities still focus on education, since not all Spanish regions offer Islamic religious education. In November 2014, a teaching curriculum for Islam in primary education was agreed. Islamic religious education is taught only in Andalusia, Aragon, the Canary Islands, the Basque Country, Castilla y León, Ceuta, Melilla, and Madrid (only at secondary level). For the 2017/18 school year, only 61 teachers have been employed for such courses, while the number of Muslim pupils stands at 308,767. According to the *Observatorio Andalusí*, 95% of Muslim students do not receive lessons in Islamic religious education.

Catalonia, which has the highest number of Muslim students (84,018), has not developed Islamic religious education at all.[17]

A collaborative agreement between the Spanish state and the Islamic Commission of Spain was signed in July 2007, to finance chaplaincy services in prisons. This agreement was implemented in 2011, but the financial contribution from the State has been considerably reduced in the last few years.[18] In 2017 the budget remained the same as the previous year (€9,000), which contrasts with the budget granted to the Catholic Church (€600,000). This agreement determines that Muslim chaplains would be paid by the Spanish state, provided they cater for a group of ten or more prisoners. In Spanish prisons, there are around 7,400 Muslim prisoners. The 20 imams in charge of this service must be accredited by the Islamic Commission of Spain. The fear of the influence of radical imams who may visit prisoners has led to efforts to control pastoral care. Prison authorities consider the reports given by the Spanish National Intelligence Centre, which determine the adequacy of these imams. The Ministry of the Interior closely follows 271 prisoners, considered jihadi or who are susceptible to adhere to radical and militant forms of Islam, and have developed a plan to detect the processes of radicalisation between these inmates. These detainees are distributed over a total of 53 prisons, and respond to a varying typology: group A (149 inmates) are pre-trial prisoners or those convicted of acts related to terrorism; group B (35 inmates) are inmates not convicted of terrorism offences, but who are considered recruiters of future jihadis; and in group C (87 inmates) are prisoners who, although not involved in terrorist activities, present signs of radicalisation, and are considered particularly vulnerable.[19] The Ministry of the Interior is also developing (from 2017) a specific programme to assess the risk of radicalisation in prisons.[20]

Spanish police estimate that some 222 people left the country to fight in Syria and Iraq for ISIS and other groups (199 men and 23 women). Of these, it is estimated that 47 died in combat and that 35 have returned to Spain. According to the reformed *Penal Code* of 2015, those who have participated in

---

17   See http://observatorio.hispanomuslim.es, accessed 23 February 2018.
18   From €41,000 in the budget for 2007, to €9,000 for 2011, down to €3,930 for 2015.
19   "271 presos yihadistas tienen un seguimiento especial", *El País*, 1 September 2017, https://politica.elpais.com/politica/2017/09/01/actualidad/1504288960_939227.html, accessed 12 September 2017.
20   "La radicalización de 79 reclusos comunes obliga a Interior a reforzar su plan yihadistas", *El País*, 16 April 2018, https://politica.elpais.com/politica/2018/04/16/actualidad/1523904096_658658.html, accessed 24 April 2018.

terrorist actions face a prison term, while the rest are subject to special monitoring by the Spanish police.[21]

The National Strategic Plan on Combating Violent Radicalisation was approved in February 2015,[22] and an agreement was also reached between the main Spanish political parties to modify the *Penal Code* to better combat jihadi terrorism. As a result, the Spanish police strategy is shifting more towards prevention. In December 2015, the Spanish police announced the creation of a web page and a telephone line where people could report issues related to radicalism. Under the title "*Stop Radicalismos*", citizens could now help the police, in line with similar programmes elsewhere in Europe.[23] Between December 2015 and September 2017, a total of 4,761 reports were received. 805 of them were considered relevant, but only one or two were of particular interest to the police. A detailed study of these reports by the public indicated that 34% contained information considered to be of police interest.[24]

In November 2015, the Catalan police force (*Mossos d'Esquadra*) announced the implementation of a programme for detecting Islamist radicalisation in primary and high schools in Catalonia. It has been variously criticised by Muslim representatives and teachers,[25] but the *Proderai* strategy (Procedure for Detection of Islamist Radicalisation), has been implemented, with the collaboration of the Department of Education in the Catalan government. To date, no evidence has been shown that indicates that this strategy has intervened in any concrete case. The Catalan ombudsman (*Síndic de Greuges*) produced a report in November 2017 where he reviewed the initiatives set up for the prevention of radicalisation developed in Catalonia, especially the *Proderai* protocol in the field of education.[26]

---

21 Reinares, Fernando, and Carola García Calvo, "Marroquíes y segundas generaciones entre los yihadistas en España" (Moroccans and second generations among the jihadists in Spain), *ARI-Real Instituto Elcano*, no. 61 (2018).

22 http://www.interior.gob.es/web/servicios-al-ciudadano/plan-estrategico-nacional-de-lucha-contra-la-radicalizacion-violenta/plan-estrategico-nacional, accessed 12 March 2015.

23 https://stop-radicalismos.ses.mir.es/?language=en, accessed 13 March 2016.

24 "La web de Interior 'Stop Radicalismos' ha recibido 4.761 comunicaciones desde su puesta en marcha en 2015", *La Vanguardia*, 16 September 2017, http://www.lavanguardia.com/vida/20170916/431328311582/la-web-de-interior-stop-radicalismos-ha-recibido-4761-comunicaciones-desde-su-puesta-en-marcha-en-2015.html, accessed 25 September 2017.

25 Moreras, Jordi, "Minority report? El Proderai como artefacto de prevención del precrimen", in SOS Racismo-SOS Arrazakeria, *Islamofobia y género. Mujeres feminismos, instituciones y discursos frente al sexismo y el racismo* (San Sebastián: SOS Racismo, 2017), pp. 64–75.

26 http://www.sindic.cat/site/unitFiles/4871/Informe%20prevencio%20radicalitzacio%20i%20terrorisme%20a%20Catalunya.pdf, accessed 12 February 2018.

After announcing it in 2015, the Basque government presented a plan to prevent radicalisation in November 2017, under the title "Plan of Action against International Terrorism of Religious Pretext".[27] Likewise, the Málaga City Council presented a transversal "Plan for Coexistence and Prevention against Violent Radicalisation",[28] which is the first plan developed specifically by a Spanish municipality on this subject.

In January 2017, the City Council of Barcelona approved a plan to combat Islamophobia,[29] which includes 28 measures and a budget that exceeds €100,000. It aims to support the most vulnerable victims, Muslim women, and its main foci are prevention, awareness, and commitment to interculturality and social cohesion.

Activities and Initiatives of Main Muslim Organisations

In the last five years, new groups have been formed by young Muslims that maintain a certain distance with respect to mosques and Muslim federations. However, they have created intense activity around the promotion of Muslim identity among young people, and have maintained contacts with other similar European movements. Two examples of such groups are the *Asociación de Chicas Musulmanas de España* (Association of Muslim Girls of Spain– ACHIME), created in Madrid in 2012, and *Juventud Multicultural Musulmana* (Muslim Multicultural Youth), created in Barcelona in 2014.[30] They have both acquired significant public relevance in recent years.

Although they had played a very important role in previous years, communities formed by Muslims converts have lost some relevance in the configuration of Spanish Islam. Although they continue to be present on the boards of the two main Islamic federations, they no longer appear among the main public figures that represent Muslim communities to the wider public. Amparo Sanchez, who had been vice president of the Islamic Community of Spain, left his post at the end of 2017, while the members of the *Junta Islámica* (Islamic Council)–an entity that played an important role in the founding of

---

27 https://www.irekia.euskadi.eus/uploads/attachments/10561/PLAN_frente_al_Terrorismo_Internacional_2017.pdf?1511173607, accessed 21 December 2017.

28 https://riuma.uma.es/xmlui/bitstream/handle/10630/13800/I%20Plan%20Transversal%20por%20la%20Convivencia.pdf?sequence=1, accessed 12 February 2018.

29 http://ajuntament.barcelona.cat/bcnacciointercultural/es/noticia/contra-la-islamofobia-y-a-favor-de-fortalecer-la-cohesion-social, accessed 10 February 2017.

30 https://joventutmulticulturalmusulmana.com/ and www.asociacionachime.com, both accessed 15 May 2017.

the *Federación Española de Entidades Religiosas Islámicas* (Spanish Federation of Islamic Entities–FEERI)–are now focused on the implementation of halal standards in food products and other services. Other activists, like Abdennur Prado,[31] Laure Rodriguez,[32] and Natalia Andujar,[33] are engaged in intellectual activism within the contexts of Islamic feminism and postcolonial thought.

Three elements have contributed to the consolidation of the Muslim presence in the public sphere in Spain. Firstly, there is the intensive use of social media by different Islamic organisations, especially among those with an umbrella structure. The presence of these organisations on Facebook has become useful not only for following their activities or learning of their views or positions, but it has also allowed more people to hear their opinion on controversial issues. An example of this is the international charity organisation, Islamic Relief, that has been present in Spain since 2011. It has organised various events to promote humanitarian action programmes and cooperation through social media, especially related to the crisis in Syria. In recent years, it is also taking action to promote action aimed especially at young Spanish Muslims, by organising collective *iftars* during Ramadan, and collaborating in activities with other Islamic organisations. In this way, they have acquired an important visibility. Some media outlets reported in the winter of 2017 that Islamic Relief had begun to develop volunteer initiatives distributing food to homeless people, in collaboration with other NGOs.[34]

In view of the increase in Islamophobic incidents since 2015, and especially after the attacks in Barcelona and Cambrils, Muslim community organisations have developed different initiatives to denounce these events. These platforms include Muslim communities but also other civil society groups engaged in defending civil liberties and fighting intolerance. The *Plataforma Ciudadana*

---

31 Abdennur Prado (born Barcelona 1967) is a prolific author who explores the Islamic tradition in an innovative way. His last book is *Genealogía del monoteísmo: La religión como dispositivo colonial* (*Genealogy of Monotheism: Religion as a Colonial Device*) (Madrid: Editorial Akal, 2018).

32 Laure Rodriguez (born Paris 1975) is the author of *Falsos mitos de la mujer en el islam* (*False Myths of Women in Islam*) (Cordoba: Editorial Almuzara 2017), and is one of the most critical voices from the feminist perspective.

33 Natalia Andújar (born Barcelona 1972) is an online activist, especially involved in educational projects. She was the promoter of the Educaislam initiative in 2013, that is linked to the *Junta Islámica*. See https://nataliaandujar.wordpress.com/, accessed 8 March 2017.

34 See "La ONG islámica que alimenta a los mendigos españoles y sus planes para expandirse", *El Confidencial*, 12 January 2017, https://www.elconfidencial.com/espana/2017-01-12/ong-islamic-relief-espana-mendigos-planes-expansion_1315294/, accessed 12 February 2018.

contra la Islamofobia (Civic Platform against Islamophobia)[35] was created in 2011 by a number of different organisations. Its report that covers 2017 gathered 546 cases of Islamophobia: 50% were expressions of hate towards Muslims and Islam in general; 21% were against women for the use of the head scarf; and 7% were related to acts of vandalism or opposition related to the opening of mosques. The report points at the low number of complaints that reach the Spanish courts, and warns of the increase of xenophobia in social networks, taking advantage of the anonymity they offer.

In 2017, the *Observatorio de la Islamofobia en los Medios* (Observatory of Islamophobia in the Media)[36] was created by a joint initiative between the *Fundación Al-Fanar* (Al-Fanar Foundation), the *Instituto Europeo del Mediterráneo* (European Institute of the Mediterranean), *Casa Árabe* (Arab House), and the *Fundación Tres Culturas* (Three Cultures Foundation), to which different entities, platforms and universities have been incorporated. Its objective is to analyse and respond to Islamophobic discourses present in the Spanish press.

Muslim Population: History and Demographics

The establishment of a Muslim space in Spain is closely related to the development of relations between the State and religious confessions. During the Franco period (1939–75), the regime's Catholic confessional character prevented the recognition of other religions. It was not until 1967 that the first Post-Civil War law on religious freedom recognised the possibility of the monitored practice of religions other than Catholicism. In 1968 the first Muslim association was created in Melilla, given the large Muslim population in this North African city, and in 1971, the *Asociación Musulmana de España* (Muslim Association of Spain) was formed in Madrid. The political transition opened up the possibility of new freedoms in Spanish society, among them that of religion. This favoured the development of Muslim associations, particularly among groups of Spanish converts in Andalusia.[37] In the 1980s the first prayer halls set up

---

35   http://www.observatorioislamofobia.org/wp-content/uploads/2018/03/Informe-Islamofobia-en-Espa%C3%B1a.-PCCI-Informe-Anual-2018.pdf, accessed 8 March 2018.
36   See http://www.observatorioislamofobia.org/, accessed 13 May 2017.
37   López Barrios, Francisco, and Miguel José Haguerty, *Murieron para vivir. El resurgimiento del islam y del sufismo en España* (Barcelona: Argos-Vergara, 1983) and Cabrera, Hashim, *Memoria de la Junta Islámica: 25 años de espiritualidad, pensamiento y acción* (Córdoba: Junta Islámica, 2014).

by immigrant groups–mainly Moroccans but also Sub-Saharan Africans and Pakistanis–began to appear as a result of incoming migratory flows of people settling-in. The year 1992 is crucial in the recent history of Islam in Spain. In the April of that year the Cooperation Agreement, between the Spanish state and the Islamic Commission of Spain, was signed. This Agreement marks a milestone in the recognition of the Muslim presence in Spain, as it allowed for the creation of a specific legislative body to regulate the basic principles of Muslim religious practices.

Counting religious affiliation is prohibited by the 1978 Spanish constitution (article 16.2). As such, the number of Muslims in Spain is the subject of estimates that are not always based on reliable criteria. Moreover, the Spanish case presents the peculiarity of also including the North African cities of Ceuta and Melilla, where a significant Muslim population has resided for centuries. Due to the increase in the number of people who have obtained Spanish citizenship, it is no longer appropriate to use statistics of foreign residents from Muslim majority countries. For this reason, we refer below to the data produced by the *Observatorio Andalusí*, with some modifications.

Muslim Population	1,946,300 (4.2% of population) (in 2017).[38]
Ethnic/National Backgrounds	43% of Muslims in Spain are Spanish citizens (a total figure of 834,058; 24,440 of whom are converts).
	Largest ethnic/national groups: Moroccan: 38.4% Pakistani: 4.1% Senegalese: 3.2% Algerian: 3% Malien: 1.2% Gambian: 0.9% Bangladeshi: 0.7%.
Inner-Islamic Groups	No official data available, but the majority of Muslims in Spain are Sunnis.

---

38 Observatorio Andalusi, *Estudio demográfico de la población musulmana*.

Geographical Spread	The Muslim presence extends throughout Spanish territory. The four regions with the largest presence are Catalonia, Andalusia, Madrid and Valencia.
Number of Mosques	The report published by the Observatory of Religious Pluralism in Spain (*Observatorio del Pluralismo Religioso en España*),[39] in December 2017, estimates that there are 1,569 Muslim places of worship in Spain (14 of them major Muslim centres), and 1,643 Muslim religious entities in the official register of the Ministry of Justice. These religious institutions are divided among the 47 Islamic federations. The three regions with most mosques are Catalonia (299), Andalucia (225) and the Valencian Community (209).
Muslim Burial Sites	In Spain there are two private Muslim cemeteries (Benalmádena and Fuengirola) and another 28 parcels of land reserved in municipal cemeteries for Islamic burials. Nevertheless, the main tendency (around 90%) of some ethnic groups (Moroccans or Senegalese) remains the repatriation of the corpse to their region of origin.[40]
	Ceuta (18th century)
	Granada (created during the civil war (1936–39), and reopened in 2003)
	Seville (created during the civil war (1936–39), and reopened in 1987)

---

[39] The Observatory of Religious Pluralism in Spain is an institution that depends on the Foundation for Pluralism and Coexistence (*Fundación Pluralismo y Convivencia*). Its main aim is "to provide public authorities with guidelines for managing religious freedom, that are in line with constitutional principles and the legal framework regulating the exercise of the right to religious freedom in Spain." See: http://observatorioreligion.es, accessed 24 February 2017.

[40] See Moreras, Jordi, and Ariadna Solé, "Genealogies of death. A comparison between the Moroccan and Senegalese funerary rituals in diaspora", in Eerika Koskinen-Korvisto, Hanna Snellman and Samira Saramo (eds.), *Transnational Death* (Helsinki: Helsinki Studia Fennica Ethnologia Series, 2018), pp. 184–200.

Griñón-Madrid (created during the civil war (1936–39), reopened in 1978 and 2015)
Córdoba (created during the civil war (1936–39), and reopened in 1992)
Zaragoza (created during the civil war (1936–39), and reopened in 2002)
Burgos (created during the civil war (1936–39), and reopened in 2009)
León (created during the civil war (1936–39), and reopened in 2010)
Melilla (1992)
Fuengirola (Málaga) (1996)
Barcelona (1996)
Murcia (1997)
Almódovar del Río (Córdoba) (1998)
Benalmádena (Málaga) (1999)
Valencia (2000)
Jerez de la Frontera (Cádiz) (2001)
La Puebla de Don Fadrique (Granada) (2002)
Manresa (Barcelona) (2002)
Lucena (Córdoba) (2004)
Riba-roja de Turia (Valencia) (2007)
Las Palmas de Gran Canaria (2007)
Santa Cruz de Tenerife (2007)
Bilbao (2008)
Palma de Mallorca (2008)
Alcobendas (Madrid) (2008)
Órgiva (Granada) (2009)
Lucena (Córdoba)(2009)
Logroño (2010)
Sant Feliu de Guíxols (Girona) (2012)
Sant Antoni de Calonge (Girona) (2012).

"Chaplaincy" in State Institutions	According to the *Observatorio Andalusi*, 20 imams offer chaplaincy services in prisons, and another seven do so in Spanish hospitals. There are no imams providing chaplaincy services in the armed forces.

Halal Products	According the Cooperation Agreement of 1992, the State must ensure that a halal menu is provided in public institutions, such as hospitals, prisons or in the army. In reality, it does not follow the provisions of the Law. Muslim representatives have requested to have halal menus in schools and in hospitals, and found different responses from those responsible for these institutions.
Dress Code	After the controversies over the prohibition of the full face veil in 2011, there has been no further controversy over the use of the head scarf. There is still no regulation that prohibits its use in public spaces or in the workplace. However, that does not prevent numerous cases existing where Muslim women are not hired for employment because they wear the head scarf, something repeatedly reported by Muslim organisations.
Places of Islamic Learning and Education	Umm al-Qura school. The only Islamic school in Spain, which forms part of the Madrid Islamic Cultural Centre complex. It provides pre-school, primary and secondary education. The school was recognised by the Spanish state in April 1998, and has around 400 students and 30 teachers. In September 2016, the project to create the first Islamic University of Spain, which would be located in San Sebastián (Basque Country), was announced. The initiative, which is linked with the Islamic University of Minnesota (USA), should have started its virtual classes in the 2016–17 academic year, but they have yet to begin. Its head, Rachid Boutarbouch, is associated with the Moroccan movement Justice and Charity.[41]

---

41 https://politica.elpais.com/politica/2016/09/09/actualidad/1473432256_159464.html, accessed 25 March 2017.

| Muslim Media and Publications | – *Islam Hoy* (Islam Today): http://islamhoy.com. Promoted by the Islamic Community in Spain (an entity created in the 1980s, and linked with the international Morabitun movement). Bimonthly magazine (paper and digital)
– *Webislam*: www.webislam.com. Created in 1997 by *Junta Islámica*, the main internet portal in the Spanish Muslim blogosphere (digital)
– *Nurain* Magazine: http://www.nurainmagazine.info. Promoted by the Canary Islamic Cultural Centre (Las Palmas de Gran Canaria) (digital). |

Main Muslim Organisations

- Union of Islamic Communities of Spain (*Unión de Comunidades Islámicas de España*–UCIDE, Anastasio Herrero, 5 28020 Madrid, www.ucide.org). The main Muslim umbrella organisation in Spain. Created in 1991 by Riay Tatary Bakri, of Syrian origin, who, in 1971, created the Muslim Association of Spain, which manages the Abu Bakr mosque in Madrid. Since then, Riay Tatary has continued to chair the Federation that brings together the majority of Muslim communities in Spain.
- Spanish Federation of Islamic Religious Entities (*Federación Española de Entidades Religiosas Islámicas*–FEERI, General Ricardo Ortega, 1, 3A, 07006 Palma de Mallorca, www.feeri.es). The FEERI was the first Muslim umbrella organisation, created in 1989 through the initiative of Muslim converts. The president of FEERI is Mounir Benjelloun, one of the main leaders of the Moroccan 'Adl wa al-Ihsan (Justice and Charity) movement in Spain. In October 2009, he replaced the previous board, made up of members of the Union of Muslims of Ceuta, who supported the Moroccan government's policies.
- Islamic Council Federation of Catalonia (*Federación Consell Islàmic de Catalunya*, Nou de Sadurní, 9, local 3B 08001, Barcelona www.consellislamic.org). Created in 2000 by Mohamed Chaib, the first deputy of the Catalan parliament of Moroccan origin. The Council includes a group of Muslim communities in Catalonia that are mainly Moroccan. In 2002 Chaib signed a collaboration agreement with the Catalan government, thus becoming the unofficial representative of Islam in Catalonia.

Other Muslim umbrella organisations:

- Supreme Islamic Council of the Valencian Community (*Consejo Islámico Superior de la Comunidad Valenciana*, CISCOVA), Arquitecto Rodriguez, 21 Bajo 46019 Valencia, www.ciscova.org/es.
- Muslim Federation of the Valencian Communiy (*Federación Musulmana de la Comunidad Valenciana*, FEMCOVA), Avenida de Castellón, 49 P 8 Villarreal 12540 Castellón, www.femcova.org/index.php.
- Islamic Federation of the Region of Murcia (*Federación Islámica de la Región de Murcia*–FIRM), General Martín de la Carrera, 13 30011 Murcia, http://islamenmurcia.blogspot.com.es.
- Union of Islamic Communities of Catalonia (*Unión de Comunidades Islámicas de Cataluña*, Jaén, 34 bajos izquierda Terrassa 08226 Barcelona, www.ucidecatalunya.blogspot.com.es.
- Islamic Federation of Cataloniya (*Federación Islámica de Cataluña*–FICAT), Merlet, 12 Igualada 08700 Barcelona, www.ficonlin.blogspot.com.es.
- Federation of African Muslim Communities of Spain (*Federación de Comunidades Musulmanas Africanas de España*–FCMAE), Bernardina García, 15 local 28047 Madrid.
- Muslim Federation of Spain (*Federación Musulmana de España*–FEME), Pío XII, 4 bajo Collado Villalba 28400 Madrid.
- Federation of Islamic Groups for Coexistence in Spain (*Federación de Agrupaciones Islámicas por la Convivencia en España*–FAICE), Granada, 23 bajo derecha 46006 Valencia, www.facebook.com/FederacionFAICE.
- Islamic Federation of Andalucia (*Federación Islámica de Andalucía*–FIDA), México s/n Bollullos del Condado 21710 Huelva, www.facebook.com/pages/Federacion-islamica-de-andalucia/1422868437945247.
- Islamic Federation of the Autonomous Communty of the Balearan Islands (*Federación Islámica para la Comunidad Autónoma de las Islas Baleares*–FICAIB), Regalo, 71 bajos 07008 Palma de Mallorca, www.federacionislamica.wordpress.com.
- Islamic Federation of Aragon, Navarro and Rioja (*Federación Islámica de Aragón, Navarra y Rioja*–FIARNARI), Nuestra Señora de Salz, 15 B, 3º A 50017 Zaragoza, www.fiarnari.com.
- Islamic Federation of the Basque Country (*Federación Islámica del País Vasco / Euskal Herriko Islamiar Federakundea*–FIVASCO), Paseo Herrera, 20 San Sebastián 20017 Guipúzcoa, www.fivasco.blogspot.com.es.
- Islamic Council of the Basque Country (*Consejo Islámico de Euskadi / Euskadiko Kontseilu Islamiarra*), Fuente de la Salud, 10 Vitoria-Gasteiz 01003

Álava, www.facebook.com/pages/Consejo-Islámico-del-Pa%C3%ADs-Vasco/316539715112000.
- Board of Mosques of Castilla-La Mancha and Madrid (*Coordinadora de Mezquitas de Castilla-La Mancha y Madrid*–COMECAM), San Adrián, 47 Albarreal de Tajo 45522 Toledo, www.islamancha.blogspot.com.es.
- Federation of Islamic Communities of Castilla-La Mancha (*Federación de Comunidades Islámicas de Castilla-La Mancha*–FECOM), Benjamín Domínguez, 4 Tarancón 16400 Cuenca, www.fecomclm.blogspot.com.es.
- Islamic Federation of the Canaries (*Federación Islámica de Canarias*–FIDC), Juan Carlos I, 30 bajo. Los Cristianos-Arona 38686 Santa Cruz de Tenerife, www.fidc.es.

Sweden

Göran Larsson[1] and Simon Sorgenfrei[2]

Introduction

As in previous years, debates over Islam and Muslims were much informed by questions regarding issues such as immigration, integration and terrorism. This has especially been the case since the terror attack on Drottninggatan on 7 April 2017, when an Uzbek citizen and asylum-seeker, Rakhmat Akilov, killed five people and injured 15 with a lorry. Akilov claimed he acted on behalf of the so-called Islamic State (ISIS). ISIS has not in any way acknowledged Akilov or the attack, however.

The Swedish Secret Police have estimated the number of individuals in Sweden sympathising with ISIS and similar organisations at approximately 2,000 individuals, a great increase over earlier approximations.[3] More research is needed to verify the number and to analyse the characteristics of such support. For instance, do such individuals support ISIS theologically, or as an anti-Western phenomenon? Does such support suggest a greater willingness to commit terrorist acts themselves, or could it rather be understood as a counter-cultural expression?

Although Swedish policy on migration changed dramatically in 2015, there were no major changes in 2017. The new policy is strict, and the public debate in printed media, on radio and in social media, is highly shaped by vigorous debates over migration and integration,[4] two issues that have a bearing on Islam and Muslims in Sweden.

---

1 Göran Larsson is Professor of Religious Studies at the University of Gothenburg, Sweden. His research focuses on Islam and Muslims in Europe. His latest book is *Annotated Legal Documents on Islam in Europe: Sweden* (Leiden and Boston: Brill, 2017), written together with Mosa Sayed of Uppsala University.

2 Simon Sorgenfrei is Associate Professor of the Study of Religion at Södertörn University, Sweden. His research focuses on Islam and Muslims in the West, as well as on medieval Sufi literature. His latest book is *Islam i Sverige–de första 1300 åren* (*Islam in Sweden–The First 1300 Years*) (Stockholm: Myndigheten för stöd till trossamfund, 2018).

3 SÄPO, "2000 våldsbejakande islamistiska extremister", http://www.sakerhetspolisen.se/ovrigt/pressrum/aktuellt/aktuellt/2017-07-03-sa-mycket-har-extremistmiljoerna-vuxit.html, accessed 4 February 2018.

4 Eriksson, Mats, "Brott och integration dominerar nyheterna och sociala medier", *Sveriges Radio*, 23 November 2017, http://sverigesradio.se/sida/artikel.aspx?programid=83&artikel=6827129, accessed 2 February 2018.

Public Debates

The question of how to combat violent extremism was a recurring theme in public debates on Islam and Muslims in Sweden in 2017, especially after the terror attack committed by Rakhmat Akilov on 7 April. Major Muslim organisations in Sweden condemned the terror attack committed by Akilov, and a joint statement was issued by the Swedish Inter-religious Council (*Sveriges Inter religiösa råd*).[5] As in the previous year, the Swedish Ahmadiyya community has been very active with regard to these questions, and has continued its work with the campaign against violent extremism, known as *Stoppa krisen* ("Stop the Crisis"). This resulted in a large number of lectures, articles, panel discussions and web TV broadcasts in 2017.[6]

The report *Swedish Foreign Fighters in Iraq and Syria: an Analysis of Open-Source Intelligence and Statistical Data* by Linus Gustafsson and Magnus Ranstorp–both of whom are connected to the Swedish Defence University (*Försvarshögskolan*)[7]–for the first time provided a systematic overview of the biographical backgrounds of those who had travelled to Syria. The report also contained estimates of how many Swedish foreign fighters have died or returned to Sweden. The report indicates that the average age of the foreign fighters who have travelled to Iraq and Syria is 26, that one quarter are women and that most come from so-called particularly vulnerable areas (Swedish "*särskilt utsatta områden*"). These are areas that the police have defined as neighbourhoods suffering from high levels of criminality, drug abuse and a general sense of lawlessness.[8] Of the three hundred travellers who have been identified, 106 were reported to have returned to Sweden in 2017. The returnees have caused heated public and political debates concerning what to do with them; should they be helped to be reintegrated into society, or should they lose

---

5 http://www.sverigesmuslimskarad.org/nyheter/120-uttalande-fran-sveriges-interreligiosa-rad-med-anledning-av-dadet-i-stockholm, accessed 2 February 2018.

6 https://www.google.se/search?site=&source=hp&q=stoppa+krisen&oq=stoppa+krisen&gs_l=hp.3..0.642.2458.0.2708.14.13.0.1.1.0.244.898.11j0j1.12.0....0...1c.1.64.hp..1.12.656.0..35i39k1j0i131k1j0i67k1j0i22i30k1.2v2xiVpvhsw, accessed 18 January 2017.

7 Gustafsson, Linus, and Magnus Ranstorp, *Swedish Foreign Fighters in Iraq and Syria: an Analysis of Open-Source Intelligence and Statistical Data* (Stockholm: Försvarshögskolan, 2017), http://fhs.diva-portal.org/smash/get/diva2:1110355/FULLTEXT01.pdf, accessed 1 February 2018.

8 In 2017 Sweden had 23 "particularly vulnerable areas" according to the police. See *Utsatta områden–social ordning, kriminella strukturer och utmaningar för polisen*. (Stockholm: Nationella operativa avdelningen, 2017), https://polisen.se/PageFiles/683149/Utsatta%20områden%20-%20social%20ordning,%20kriminell%20struktur%20och%20utmaningar%20för%20polisen.pdf, accessed 2 February 2018.

their citizenship? In 2017, the Swedish government gave the National Board of Health and Welfare (*Socialstyrelsen*) an assignment to develop national guidelines for social workers who come into contact with foreign fighters who have returned to Sweden. The guidelines should be presented to the Government no later than 19 February 2018.[9]

As in most European countries, there are competing opinions about how to explain why so many Europeans, and in particular Swedes, have joined groups like ISIS or the al-Nusra Front. While some argue that the main explanation is to be found in the ideology of these groups, others point to social reasons, arguing that it is discrimination, racism and segregation that drives and motivates young Muslims to identify with the ideologies of such organisations. It is also argued that it is the adventure of going to a war zone, the attraction of a so-called "jihadi cool" lifestyle and the ability to live a criminal and violent existence that motivates these young individuals. Some point to the use of social media to recruit youngsters who seek an identity and lifestyle that resembles how life is portrayed in action movies and video games. Although it is difficult to isolate any singular explanatory factor, the preferred or chosen explanation will have an impact on how society and its actors prevent young individuals from becoming violent extremists. How to explain and prevent individuals picking up arms and turning to violence remained a contested issue in public debates in Sweden, and the lack of common ground regarding good practice created room for political mobilisation, as well as causing a fundamental split within society.[10]

A central component in the fight against violent extremism, encouraged by the national coordinator against violent extremism in Sweden, is the development of so-called action plans to be used in specific cities or by municipalities. Cities and municipalities that have not developed such plans have often been criticised by politicians and in public debates.[11] However, a critical study conducted by the Swedish Association of Local Authorities and Regions (*Sveriges*

---

9 *Uppdrag till Socialstyrelsen att ta fram en nationell vägledning för socialtjänstens arbete med återvändare m.fl.*, http://www.regeringen.se/49df87/contentassets/6f7ae41f458b4398af3866d2f710c454/uppdrag-till-socialstyrelsen-att-ta-fram-en-nationell-vagledning-for-socialtjanstens-arbete-med-atervandare-m.fl, accessed 2 February 2018.

10 An overview of the current research on violent extremism can be found in *Våldbejakande extremism–en forskningsantologi* (Stockholm: Fritze, SOU 2017:67). See also Kaati, Lisa (ed.), *Det digitala kalifatet: En studie av Islamiska statens propaganda* (Stockholm: FOI, 2017).

11 See, for example, Esping, Ylva, Helena Petersen Schön and Olle Palm, "Fiasko för Malmös arbete mot våldsbejakande extremism", *Svt*, 1 February 2017, https://www.svt.se/nyheter/lokalt/skane/fiasko-for-malmos-arbete-mot-valdsbejakande-extremism, accessed 2 February 2017.

kommuner och landsting) in cooperation with the Segerstedt Institute at the University of Gothenburg, came to the conclusion that several of these action plans were not based on a thorough investigation of the problems that have emerged from the local context, and that most of them were written to target violent interpretations of Islam, even though some cities and municipalities hardly had any Muslims. At the same time, for example, white supremacist groups, who have been more visible and active over the last couple of years, were left out of the plans. Some of the plans could even be construed as advocating breaking existing laws relating to, for example, the freedom to hold meetings and gatherings, and they were also criticised for encouraging schoolteachers and social workers to report "suspicious" activities. The Segerstedt Institute report indicates that the public and political perception is that Islam and Muslims are a more serious threat than neo-Nazi groups.[12] A similar criticism, directed towards the Swedish Secret Police and other security and law enforcement agencies, was made by Mattias Gardell, Professor of the Study of Religions at Uppsala University, in an examination of the so-called lone-wolf phenomenon. In the study, Gardell shows that the Secret Police and other security forces in Sweden tend to downplay or neglect the threat from far-right extremists, while giving a great deal of attention to so-called Islamic extremism. This is in spite of the fact that far-right extremists have conducted far more attacks and killings in Sweden in recent decades than extremists of Islamic backgrounds or convictions.[13]

In a jointly written article published in *Dagens Nyheter*, Imam Salahuddin Barakat, Archbishop Antje Jackelén of Sweden, Anna Carlstedt (the national coordinator against violent extremism) and Aron Verständig (from the Swedish Jewish congregation–*Judiska centralrådet*) argued that religion can also help and support the struggle against violence and intolerance. This initiative attempted to show that interpretations of religion can also lead to peace, harmony and conflict resolution.[14] While the article was applauded by

---

12   Andersson Malmros, Robin, and Christer Mattsson, *Från ord till handlingsplan: En rapport om kommunala handlingsplaner mot våldsbejakande extremism* (Stockholm: Sveriges Kommuner och Landsting, 2017), https://webbutik.skl.se/bilder/artiklar/pdf/7585-580-6.pdf?issuusl=ignore, accessed 2 February 2017.
13   Gardell, Mattias, "Lone wolves–hotet från ensamagerande politiska våldsbrottslingar", in Heléne Lööw, Mattias Gardell and Michael Dahlberg-Grundberg (eds.), *Den ensamme terroristen?: om lone wolves, näthat och brinnande flyktingförläggningar* (Stockholm: Ordfront, 2017), pp. 87–202.
14   Barakat, Salahuddin, Antje Jackelén, Anna Carlstedt and Aron Verständig, "Religion kan leda människor ut ur våldsbejakande extremism", *Dagens Nyheter*, 1 July 2017, https://www.dn.se/debatt/religion-kan-leda-manniskor-ut-ur-valdsbejakande-extremism/, accessed 2 February 2018.

some segments of society, it was heavily criticised by others. Both Barakat and Jackelén received support for their interpretations of Islam and Christianity, but they were also criticised by fellow Muslims and Christians respectively for being naïve and for selling out their faith. This criticism has not prevented Barakat and Jackelén from attending further engagements, and they both participated in joint discussions and seminars in 2017.[15]

Tensions and conflicts in society can also be related to the fact that Sweden has received large numbers of migrants and asylum seekers due to the wars in Syria and Iraq. According to EXPO, a Swedish NGO that documents far-right activities, 92 homes for asylum-seekers and migrants were, for example, attacked by firebombs and other means in 2017.[16] However, a report produced by the Swedish Civil Contingencies Agency (MSB) shows that many of the fires seem to have started within the homes or to have been due to accidents.[17] Whatever the case, an increase in attacks against asylum homes can certainly be observed, and it is not unlikely that this development is related to public discussions about migration, integration, religion and Islam.

Transnational Links

Like their European counterparts, Muslim organisations in Sweden have extensive contacts with international and global Muslim groups and networks. Many of them are also rooted in and associated with international organisations such as the Turkish Presidency of Religious Affairs (*Diyanet İşleri Başkanlığı*), the Islamic Community of Bosnia and Herzegovina (*Islamska zajednica Bosne i Hercegovine*), the Muslim Brotherhood, a number of Sufi organisations, Shi'i organisations, and others such as the Ahmadiyya community, the Pakistani Tablighi Jamaat and the Turkish Millî Görüş.[18]

When it comes to international and transnational links, much attention was given to a report on the Muslim Brotherhood's alleged presence in Sweden,

---

15 See, for example, http://muslimerforfred.org/sv/blog/2015/06/29/salahuddin-barakat-pa-almedalen/ and https://www.svenskakyrkan.se/almedalsveckan/arkebiskopen, both accessed 2 February 2018.
16 http://expo.se/2017/92-anlagda-brander-pa-asylboenden-forra-aret_7245.html, accessed 1 February 2018.
17 https://www.msb.se/Upload/Kunskapsbank/Olycksundersokningar_ovrigt/Lages beskrivning_kring_brander_i_flyktingboenden_2012-2016.pdf, accessed 2 February 2018.
18 For more information about transnational links, see Larsson, Göran, *Islam och muslimer i Sverige* (Stockholm: SST, 2014); Sorgenfrei, Simon, *Sufism i Sverige* (Stockholm: SST, 2016); Sorgenfrei, Simon, *Islam i Sverige–de första 1300 åren* (Stockholm: SST, 2018).

published by the Swedish Civil Contingencies Agency (MSB). It was written by Magnus Norell, former researcher at the Swedish Defence University, Aje Carlbom, social anthropologist at Malmö University, and Pierre Durrani. In the report, the writers claim that a number of Muslim organisations, primarily the *Islamiska förbundet i Sverige* (Islamic Association of Sweden–IFiS), *Sveriges unga muslimer* (Sweden's Young Muslims–SUM) and the Adult Education Institute Ibn Rushd, represent the Muslim Brotherhood in Sweden, despite their denials. Further the authors of the report argued that the Brotherhood aims at creating a parallel society with the help of "political elites" (including journalists and academics) who are fostering a culture of silence that makes it impossible to criticise Islam or study and analyse politically-oriented Islam critically in Sweden. Norell *et al.* claim further that the Brotherhood is working to increase the number of Muslims in Sweden, which will supposedly pose a long-term challenge to Sweden's social cohesion, and is thus a threat to democracy and the Swedish state.[19]

However, the report was heavily criticised by more than 20 Swedish Religious and Islamic studies scholars, who stated that it ignored existing research on Islam and Muslims in Sweden. They pointed to the fact that the serious claims made in the report were not substantiated by any references or sources.[20] After the debate, the MSB announced further research funding to analyse what it calls the impact of Islamist information in Sweden.[21]

The conflicts in Syria and Iraq highlighted yet again the extent to which international militant organisations exploit transnational links, and that these international terrorist organisations do not observe geographical boundaries. International terrorism has large sums of money at its disposal, and consequently the Swedish state should pay more attention to financial fraud, illegal economical transactions and the misuse of social benefits that could be used for funding terrorism both within and outside Sweden. In a report issued by the Swedish Defence Academy, the need to raise awareness among Swedish businesses and banks was stressed in 2017.[22]

---

19 https://www.msb.se/Upload/Kunskapsbank/Studier/Muslimska_Brodraskapet_i_Sverige_DNR_2107-1287.pdf, accessed 3 February 2018.
20 http://religionsvetenskapligakommentarer.blogspot.se/2017/03/debatt-undermalig-forskning-i-svensk.html, accessed 3 February 2018.
21 https://www.msb.se/sv/Om-MSB/Nyheter-och-press/Nyheter/Nyheter-fran-MSB/Tematisk-utlysning-for-forskning-inom-informationspaverkan/, accessed 3 February 2018.
22 Normark, Magnus, Magnus Ranstorp and Filip Ahlin, *Finansiella aktiviteter kopplade till personer från Sverige och Danmark som anslutit sig till terrorgrupper i Syrien och Irak mellan 2013–2016: Rapport på uppdrag av Finansinspektiionen* (Stockholm: CATS, 2017).

Muslim organisations that have been associated with the Muslim Brotherhood, Millî Görüş or Salafi movements attracted some negative media attention. The question of who is and who is not linked to these organisations or ideas entered into public debates about transnational links, as well as the influence, if any, of global Muslim organisations over Muslims who live in Sweden.[23] However, it is also clear that international conflicts in the Middle East and elsewhere are spilling over into Sweden. For example, in several news articles, investigative journalist Niklas Orrenius describes how the tensions between Sunni and Shi'i Muslim groups in Sweden have become more common.[24] Some individuals or groups have even turned to violence. For example, on 11 October 2016 a Shi'i Muslim mosque in Malmö was set on fire and a Sunni man who had shown sympathies for so-called Islamic State was arrested and suspected of carrying out the attack. This action was also supported by so-called Islamic State, which publicly stated in its journal *an-Naba* that it was responsible for the attack.[25] The suspect, who was arrested by the police, was accused of arson, but he was later released and all the charges against him dropped. Although the police could demonstrate that he had shown sympathies for so-called Islamic State, they did not have enough evidence to link him to the crime.[26]

However, the attack in Malmö was not unique, and in May 2017 the large Shi'i mosque in Järfälla just north of Stockholm (Imam Ali mosque) was also set on fire, causing extensive destruction.[27] Again a person of Sunni background was suspected, and Shi'i Muslims in Sweden stated that they were worried about the growing threats from Sunni extremists operating in Sweden.[28]

---

23 See, for example, www.aftonbladet.se/nyheter/article16628650.ab, accessed 11 May 2015. The newspaper *Gefle Dagbladet* also produced a series of articles in September 2015 on Salafi tendencies in the town of Gävle. For more information see, for example, www.gd.se/gastrikland/gavle/gavles-moske-vill-sprida-extrem-tolkning-av-islam, accessed 21 February 2016; http://religionsvetenskapligakommentarer.blogspot.se/2016/07/dunkelt-skrivet-dunkelt-tankt-norell.html, accessed 18 January 2017.

24 Some of Orrenius' reports from *Dagens Nyheter* have been collected in the following link https://fokus.dn.se/radikala-islamismen-i-sverige/, accessed 1 February 2018.

25 Kudo, Per, "IS tar på sig ansvar för attentat i Malmö", *Svenska Dagbladet* 20 October, 2016, https://www.svd.se/is-pastar-sig-ligga-bakom-dad-i-malmo/om/det-skarpta-sakerhetslaget, accessed 1 February 2018.

26 Bauler, Carl-Johan, "IS-anhängare vill ha 150 000 Kronor", *Skånda Dagbladet* 31 May 2017, http://www.skd.se/2017/05/31/is-anhangare-vill-ha-150-000-kronor/, accessed 4 February 2018.

27 Lagercrantz, Maja, "Moskébranden misstänks vara anlagd", *Sveriges Radio*, http://sverigesradio.se/sida/artikel.aspx?programid=83&artikel=6686994, accessed 1 February 2018.

28 https://www.svt.se/nyheter/inrikes/utbredd-oro-bland-svenska-shiamuslimer, accessed 4 February 2018.

On September 26, the large Sunni mosque in Örebro was also set on fire, and parts of the building were destroyed. The mosque had earlier been attacked in 2014, but on that occasion the fire did not spread. The police arrested a man who confessed that he had left Islam after a divorce and that it was he who had set the mosque on fire.[29]

Other examples point to the fact that political developments in Turkey have influenced Turkish diaspora communities in Sweden. The political control of the Erdoğan government and its religious affairs office, the Diyanet, have also had an impact on Sweden. For example, the above-mentioned journalist Niklas Orrenius reported that the Diyanet has tried to exert control over specific mosques, and that several mosques have tried to control and register members' political opinions. Those who express anti-Erdoğan sentiments have received threats according to Orrenius, who has investigated reports published in the Swedish daily paper, *Dagens Nyheter*.[30]

Another example of how Sweden is affected by international affairs is the protests following Donald Trump's administration announcing that the American embassy in Israel would be moved from Tel Aviv to Jerusalem. This decision provoked demonstrations and protests in both the Middle East and other parts of the world. Following a public demonstration against the Trump administration in Gothenburg on 9 December 2017, the Jewish community in Gothenburg was targeted, and more than 20 perpetrators tried to set the large synagogue and its congregational house on fire.[31] Demonstrations against the American government that were organised in Malmö also featured openly anti-Semitic statements.[32] For all its complexity, this seems to illustrate that anti-Semitic sentiments are on the rise in Sweden, not least among many mi-

---

29   Malmgren, Kim, Magnus Hellberg and Johanna Karlsson, "20-åringen lämnade islam–misstänkt för moskébrand", *Expressen*, 29 September, 2017, https://www.expressen.se/nyheter/brottscentralen/20-aring-misstanks-for-moskebranden/, accessed 2 February 2018. See also, http://www.sverigesmuslimskarad.org/nyheter/121-pressmeddelande-misstankt-mordbrand-mot-orebro-moske, accessed 2 February 2018.

30   See, for example, Orrenius, Niklas, "Erdogans kampanj sprider rädsla bland turksvenskar", *Dagens Nyheter*, 4 April 2017, https://www.dn.se/nyheter/sverige/erdogans-kampanj-sprider-radsla-bland-turksvenskar/, and Orrenius, Niklas, "Erdogans auktoritära arm når svenska bostadsområden", *Dagens Nyheter*, 24 November 2017, https://www.dn.se/nyheter/sverige/niklas-orrenius-erdogans-auktoritara-arm-nar-svenska-bostadsomraden/, both accessed 1 February 2018.

31   "Attacken fångad på film–tre personer kunde gripas", *Expressen*, 9 December 2017, https://www.expressen.se/gt/brinnande-foremal-har-kastats-mot-synagoga-polisen-pa-plats-med-flera-patruller/, accessed 1 February 2018.

32   Monikander, Katarina, "Hot mot judar under demonstration i Malmö", *Sydsvenskan*, 9 December 2017, https://www.sydsvenskan.se/2017-12-09/hot-mot-judar-under-demonstration-i-malmo, accessed 4 February 2017.

grants with a Middle Eastern background, a problem that has been highlighted in political discussions.[33]

In direct connection with the demonstrations mentioned above, we can also see a number of Muslim organisations and representatives joining forces with local Jewish communities to speak out against anti-Semitism and call for greater co-operation between Jews and Muslims in Sweden.[34] One further example of such co-operation is the *Amanah* project focused on interreligious dialogue and founded by Imam Salahuddin Barakat and Rabbi Moshe-David HaCohen in Malmö.[35]

Law and Domestic Politics

Most debates on law and domestic politics in 2017 focused on international terrorism and how to deal with the fact that a relatively large number of Swedes left Sweden to join ISIS and similar movements in the wars in Syria and Iraq, and that at least 106 individuals have returned to Sweden from these war zones. Following the terror attack on Drottninggatan on 7 April 2017, the police were applauded for their work against terrorism and for how they handled the attack by Akilov in Stockholm.[36]

In December 2017, the national coordinator against violent extremism (*Nationella samordnaren mot våldsbejakande extremism*) presented the final report in the form of a public enquiry.[37] In the report, the coordinator describes its work as proceeding in three phases. The first phase, the report stated, is focused on putting the problem of extremism on the agenda, creating awareness and starting mobilisation among the country's municipalities. The

---

33 See for example, Bachner, Henrik, "Forskning: Antisemitism är mer utbredd bland svenska muslimer", *Aftonbladet*, 12 December 2017, https://www.aftonbladet.se/nyheter/samhalle/a/oEnPLo/forskning-antisemitism-mer-utbredd-bland-svenska-muslimer, and Karlsson, Pär, "Löfven oroad över antisemitism bland invandrare från Mellanöstern", *Aftonbladet*, 11 December 2017, both accessed 4 February 2017.
34 https://www.thelocal.se/20171210/muslim-and-christian-leaders-express-support-for-swedens-jewish-community, accessed 2 April 2018.
35 https://www.dn.se/nyheter/sverige/har-gar-judar-och-muslimer-samman-mot-hatet/ accessed 2 April 2018.
36 Schori, Martin, "Så hyllas polisen–efter lastbildsdådet", *Aftonbladet*, 8 April 2017, https://www.aftonbladet.se/nyheter/a/5aPPE/sa-hyllas-polisen--efter-lastbilsdadet, accessed 4 February 2018.
37 *Värna demokratin mot våldsbejakande extremism: Hinder och möjligheter* (SOU 2017:110), https://data.riksdagen.se/fil/oE5BA25E-665E-4F41-A5A1-A41A2248BCF5, accessed 6 April 2018.

second phase is described as centred on building a structure for local preventive efforts, most importantly appointing a staff member in every municipality responsible for coordinating these efforts. Thirdly, all municipalities are to produce action plans based on situational reports.[38]

With these preparations in place, the report concludes that municipalities would be considered well-equipped to conduct preventive efforts. However, the need to support local efforts to prevent violent extremism in the future is also mentioned. Moreover, the report emphasises the need for central government support in developing, describing and evaluating methods for local efforts to prevent violent extremism.[39]

Although there seems to be a consensus in society that individuals who have gone to Syria to fight for ISIS and who have committed offences should be punished when they return, there is no consensus regarding how to treat or help those who return from international war zones or who are willing to leave violent groups like ISIS. For example, Magnus Norell, former researcher at the Swedish Defence University, suggested that all Swedes who return from ISIS-controlled areas should be arrested and placed in custody as soon as they return to Sweden.[40] The question is whether they should be given treatment and help to (re)integrate into society (many of them suffer from psycho-social problems and war trauma), or simply be punished.[41] These questions caused intense public debate in Sweden, and the cities and municipalities that have to handle these questions tend to be heavily criticised, no matter what action they take.[42]

Activities and Initiatives of Main Muslim Organisations

There are few national activities among Muslim groups that could be included in this report because most such activities take place at the local level. In

---

38 http://www.regeringen.se/48e153/contentassets/d9eb44c5d8054f63baa71f199390341b/varna-demokratin-mot-valdsbejakande-extremism---hinder-och-mojligheter-sou-2017110, accessed 4 February 2018.

39 http://www.regeringen.se/48e153/contentassets/d9eb44c5d8054f63baa71f199390341b/varna-demokratin-mot-valdsbejakande-extremism---hinder-och-mojligheter-sou-2017110, accessed 4 February 2018.

40 https://www.svd.se/terrorexpert-hakta-alla-som-kommer-hem-fran-is-omrade, accessed 12 January 2017.

41 http://www.expressen.se/nyheter/sa-ska-is-avhoppare-tas-emot-i-sverige/, accessed 20 January 2017.

42 https://www.svd.se/kritik-mot-stockholms-satsning-mot-extremister, accessed 27 February 2017.

Stockholm, Gothenburg, Malmö and other cities, it is possible to find examples of local initiatives organised by Muslim groups and congregations related to religious festivities and visits by international Muslim scholars and representatives. Nationally, the most important event is still the annual Muslim Family Day, organised by the *Islamiska Förbundet i Sverige* (Islamic Association of Sweden–IFiS) in Stockholm. This initiative includes lectures, seminars, concerts and family activities for both children and adults, and it attracts a large number of mainly Sunni Muslims, many of whom were young adults.[43]

As in earlier years, some of Sweden's Sufi organisations have arranged assemblies, retreats and national meetings. The most visible and best known is probably the annual "Where the Land Meets the Sea" retreat in Åsa, outside Gothenburg. In 2017, the retreat was visited by the international Sufi Sheikh Fadlallah Haeri, now based in South America.[44]

Muslim Population: History and Demographics

The Muslim population of Sweden is diverse and heterogeneous when it comes to its ethnic, cultural, linguistic and religious backgrounds. Most Muslims in Sweden arrived as guest workers, migrants or refugees, but a growing number of Swedish Muslims today were born and raised in Sweden. While the first guest workers arrived in the late 1960s and early 1970s, Sweden's contacts with the wider Muslim world date back much earlier. As early as the Viking period (ca. 900 CE) there are indications of contacts via trade, business and most likely also wars, especially during the so-called Viking raids into Eastern Europe and Russia and on the Iberian Peninsula. From the 16th century onwards, Sweden had regular diplomatic contacts with Muslim dynasties, such as the Khanates in Kazan or the Crimea, as well as with the Ottoman Empire and Iran. In these centuries, we also know of Swedes converting to Islam and Muslims coming to Sweden.

The first known Muslim man to move to Sweden and stay in the country of his own volition was the Russian Tatar furrier Ebrahim Umerkajeff (d. 1954). He was later followed by a number of other Turk and Tatar immigrants who arrived in the first half of the 20th century, especially in the last years of World War II.[45] Other sources indicate that a small number of individuals were identified as Muslims in the 1930 census, the last to include information about

---

43   See, for example, http://muslimskafamiljedagarna.se/2017/, accessed 2 February 2018.
44   https://vimeo.com/channels/1291249, accessed 2 February 2018.
45   Sorgenfrei, *Islam i Sverige*.

religious affiliation.[46] However, starting from the mid-1970s, and especially during the 1980s and 1990s, Muslims became much more visible in Sweden, when major Islamic institutions and the first mosques were set up, some of them purpose-built.

Islam has become the second largest religion in Sweden. In contemporary Sweden, collecting census data on religious affiliation is not allowed. One of the few sources that one can draw on for information about religious groups in Sweden is the Swedish Agency for Support for Faith Communities (SST).[47] However, this source of information only contains statistical data based on information submitted by the religious communities themselves, and only includes Islamic congregations receiving state support. According to statistics provided by the SST, 154,140 Muslims were active members of congregations in receipt of state grants in 2017.[48] However, other estimates are available, for example, based on ethnicity or migration patterns (i.e. the homeland of migrants), or on self-identification, such as the work of the American PEW think-tank, which estimates that there are 800,000 Muslims in Sweden.[49] These studies are generally very problematic and do not provide reliable information on religious backgrounds, attitudes or behaviour. As with other religious communities, individuals of Muslim background tend to make use of religious services in connection with life-cycle rituals (e.g. birth, marriage, sickness and death) and during religious festivals and holidays. If we compare the data provided by the SST to the statistics provided by PEW, they suggest that just one in five individuals with a Muslim background identify as members of a Muslim organisation in Sweden. Although this figure indicates that many individuals are not that interested in religion, it is also likely that the low figure is due to the simple fact that it is unusual to be a member of a religious organisation in many parts of the world, and that one can take part in what congregations offer without being a fee paying member. Reliable data on Muslims in Sweden is generally very difficult to obtain and verify. Even though, in comparison to many other European countries, Sweden has a relatively large population with a Muslim cultural background, few Muslims are organised into Muslim organisations or congregations, and the existing organisations are also fragmented into a number of different ideological, theological or ethnic branches. Hence,

---

46   *Folkräkningen den 31 December 1930* (Stockholm: Statiska Centralbyrå, 1937).
47   For more information, see www.sst.a.se, accessed 4 June 2018.
48   Data given in email correspondence with Åsa Hole (SST), 5 February 2018.
49   http://www.pewforum.org/2017/11/29/europes-growing-muslim-population/, accessed 3 February 2018.

there is no one organisation that talks for all, or even a majority, of Muslims in Sweden.

Muslim Population	No data available, but the PEW estimates mentioned above give a figure of approximately 800,000 with a Muslim background (8.1% of the entire population).[50]
Ethnic/National Backgrounds	No data available, but it is clear that the Muslim population of Sweden includes individuals and groups from all the Muslim majority regions and countries around the world. The majority of asylum-seekers in recent years have come from Syria, Afghanistan and Iraq.[51]
Inner-Islamic Groups	The Muslim population is dominated by Sunni Muslims. However, a large number of Shi'i Muslims also live in the country. Besides these two groups, there are also Muslims who are Ahmadis. No exact figure exists for inner-Islamic groups.
Geographical Spread	The vast majority of Muslims live in Stockholm, Gothenburg and Malmö.
Number of Mosques	There are eight purpose-built mosques in Sweden (five Sunni mosques, in Malmö, Uppsala and Gothenburg, and two in Stockholm; one Shi'i mosque in Trollhättan; and two Ahmadiyya mosques in Gothenburg and Malmö). In Stockholm, Gävle, Västerås and Sundsvall, Muslims have bought old churches and converted them into mosques. There are no reliable figures for mosques located in basements, flats or warehouses.

50   http://www.pewforum.org/2017/11/29/europes-growing-muslim-population/pf_11-29-17_muslims-update-20/, accessed 4 February 2018.
51   http://www.migrationpolicy.org/article/overwhelmed-refugee-flows-scandinavia-tempers-its-warm-welcome, accessed 4 February 2018.

Muslim Burial Sites	There is no systematic mapping of Muslim burial sites, but the larger cities in Sweden (e.g. Stockholm, Gothenburg and Malmö) have burial sites for Muslims. Some of them are located close to or within predominantly Christian cemeteries.
"Chaplaincy" in State Institutions	The *Sveriges muslimska råd* (Swedish Muslim Council, or SMR) has an agreement with the Swedish Prison and Probation Service to provide counselling and ritual services in prisons (www.sverigesmuslimskarad.org/andlig-vard/start). Other Muslim organisations are allowed to provide similar services, but the formal agreement is limited to the SMR. The Swedish Agency for Support for Faith Communities (SST) has also helped Muslim organisations set up a network of Muslim spiritual care-workers in hospitals. This service receives financial support from the SST, but it is run by Muslim organisations (www.muslimsksjukhuskoordinator.se). There is no Muslim chaplaincy service for the armed forces.
Halal Products	Since halal slaughter is forbidden in Sweden, Muslims have to import halal meat and other halal products. However, most grocery stores provide halal alternatives, and halal food (vegetarian food or fish) is generally available in public institutions, such as hospitals, prisons and schools.
Dress Code	In 2017, the Christian Democrat Party's youth organisation (*Kristdemokratiska ungdomsförbundet*, KDU) argued for a ban on the niqab and burqa in the public sphere.[52] The suggestion was criticised[53] and did not lead to any significant debate. However,

---

52 https://www.expressen.se/debatt/forbjud-burka-och-niqab-i-offentlig-verksamhet/, accessed 8 March 2018.
53 https://www.expressen.se/kronikorer/hanne-kjoller/forbud-mot-burka-ar-rent-vansinne/, accessed 8 March 2018.

when a woman was denied a job for the Scandinavian Airlines Company (SAS) because she wore the head scarf,[54] this generated a debate on when and where religious symbols, such as the head scarf, were to be allowed or banned.

Places of Islamic Learning and Education	The last estimate of confessional independent schools from 2010 was 68, of which nine had an Islamic profile. There are no institutions of higher Islamic learning or madrasas in Sweden, but some minor Muslim organisations have tried to set up online courses to provide Islamic religious education (for example, *Islam Akademin* (www.islamakademin.se), and *Al-Ghazali-institutet* (www.ghazali.se)).
Muslim Media and Publications	Most Islamic media activities are online or on social media, such as Facebook, Twitter and Instagram. There has been no systematic research on how Swedish Muslims make use of social media.

Main Muslim Organisations

– Union of Islamic Congregations (*Förenade Islamiska Församlingar i Sverige*–FIFS, Kapellgränd 10, SE-116 25 Stockholm, www.fifs.se). This is the oldest national Muslim organisation in Sweden. It was launched in 1974, and it has both Sunni and Shi'i Muslim congregations.
– Swedish Muslim Union (*Sveriges Muslimska Förbund*–SMF, Kyrkbacken 14, bv. SE-169 62 Solna). This organisation was launched in 1982 because of an internal split in the Union of Islamic Congregations.
– Swedish Muslim Council (*Sveriges Muslimska Råd*–SMR, Sundbybergsvägen 1C, 171 73 Solna, www.sverigesmuslimskarad.se). Despite the tensions between the Union of Islamic Congregations and the Swedish Muslim Union, they have managed to cooperate under the umbrella organisation of the Swedish Muslim Council. This organisation is often associated with the ideologies of the Muslim Brotherhood. In 2017, it seems that SMR was dormant.

---

54   https://www.svt.se/nyheter/lokalt/stockholm/sas-vagrar-anstalla-aye-for-att-hon-bar-sloja, accessed 8 March 2018.

- Union of Islamic Cultural Centres (*Islamiska Kulturcenterunionen*–IKUS, Box 61, SE-191 21 Sollentuna). This organisation was launched in 1984 after a split in the Swedish Muslim Union, and most of its members are of Turkish ethnic background. The organisation is close to the Süleymaci movement and its counterpart in Germany.
- Swedish Islamic Assemblies (*Svenska Islamiska Församlingar*–SIF, Moränvägen 13, SE-136 51 Haninge). This organisation was launched in 2002 following a split within IKUS.
- Islamic Shi'i Communities in Sweden (*Islamisk Shiasamfund*–ISS, Box 690, SE-175 27 Järfälla, www.shiasamfund.se/sida1.html). As the name indicates, this is an umbrella organisation for Shi'i communities. Members are of Iraqi, Iranian and Lebanese backgrounds. However, most South Asian Shi'i congregations are members of the Union of Islamic Congregations, an organisation that includes both Sunni and Shi'i congregations.
- Swedish Ahmadiyya Community (*Ahmadiyya Muslimska Samfundet*, Nasir Moské, Tolvskillingsgatan 1, SE-414 82 Gothenburg, www.ahmadiyya.se). This is the national body for Ahmadi Muslims in Sweden.
- Islamic Association (*Islamiska förbundet*, Västanforsgatan 21B, 214 50 Malmö, www.islamiskaforbundet.se/sv/). This organisation is particularly influenced by the ideologies of the Muslim Brotherhood.
- Islamic Fatwa Bureau in Sweden (*Islamiska Fatwabyrån i Sverige*, http://www.ifbs.se/). This organisation is connected to the Al-Ahbash movement.

Switzerland

Andreas Tunger-Zanetti[1]

Introduction

"Swiss feel threatened by Islam" was the headline of the Sunday tabloid newspaper *Sonntagsblick* on 27 August 2017.[2] The claim was supported by a survey and can be seen as expressing in a nutshell a widespread perception in Switzerland. A much more nuanced picture was shown a few days earlier by the *Religionsmonitor*, a much more comprehensive survey by the German Bertelsmann Foundation, aptly condensed into the title "Integrated, but not accepted?"[3] While the article under the first headline explicitly makes reference to unacceptable speeches in some mosques and to the radicalisation of young Muslims, the second expresses a broader range of issues. For Muslims and Islam in Switzerland, the year 2017 was marked by a constant oscillation between these two poles of a gloomy picture prevalent in media reporting, on the one hand, and an inconspicuous normality, on the other.

The debate on "radicalisation", supposed hate speech and Islamist activities, was stoked by a few new cases, such as that of a Libyan imam in Biel-Bienne. Regularly, proposals in the political debate asking, for example, for a stricter control of imams and the financing of mosques, are quick to follow, and with this the "burqa ban initiative" was successfully launched. The combination of a representative democracy alongside the high participation of citizens through direct-democratic processes in Switzerland, offers citizens the chance to overturn government policy and parliamentary decisions, or to pressurise it towards a desired course indirectly by initiating a referendum. At the same time, in the absence of a constitutional court, there is no judicial institution in the country with the competence to cancel articles of law which are contrary to European and international human rights conventions.

At the same time, the political system offers local testing grounds for policy, that is attentively watched by the larger confederation. For example, the small

---

1 Andreas Tunger-Zanetti is the coordinator of the Centre for Research on Religion at the University of Lucerne.
2 Faki, Sermîn, and Florian Blumer, "Schweizer fühlen sich vom Islam bedroht", *Sonntagsblick*, 27 August 2017, pp. 2–3.
3 Halm, Dirk, and Martina Sauer, *Muslime in Europa: integriert, aber nicht akzeptiert?* (Gütersloh: Bertelsmann Stiftung, 2017), https://www.bertelsmann-stiftung.de/de/publikationen/publikation/did/muslime-in-europa/, accessed 22 April 2018.

canton of Glarus in 2017 refused to introduce a "burqa ban" on its territory, after the canton of Ticino had opted for a ban in 2013. Public authorities and judicial courts continue to pursue policies less unsettled than public opinion as, for example, in the case of the controversial question of how to treat groups of young men distributing copies of the Qur'an for free in the street.

Public Debates

Extremism, real or supposed, has been the major topic of political and media debates in Switzerland in 2017. Voices in the debate rarely distinguish between criminal or other illegal action, and opinions or behaviour that may seem unacceptable but are still within the law.

As in previous years the an-Nur mosque in the outskirts of the industrial city of Winterthur (canton of Zurich) continued to produce newspaper headlines as a hotspot of jihadi sympathisers, with at least seven young people having left to join armed groups, mainly in Syria and Iraq. The young imam, an asylum seeker of Ethiopian nationality, had been arrested with others on 2 November 2016 and stood trial on 23 November 2017. He was found guilty of incitement to use violence against Muslims who do not pray in the mosque community.[4] He was sentenced conditionally to 18 months in prison, but put in custody for deportation since the authorities had rejected his request for asylum. The police raid on the mosque on 2 November 2016 was followed by a second raid on 21 February 2017, when the police arrested nine adults and one minor. They are charged of having assaulted, injured, bullied and threatened two mosque-attendees whom they suspected of having provided a journalist with recordings of the imam's hate speech.[5] By August 2017, all of them were released and awaiting trial. The mosque itself was shut down by the an-Nur association itself, which had been unable to find a new premise after the owner of the prayer hall had terminated the rental contract.[6]

A new case of an imam delivering a possibly radical speech was published in August by Kurt Pelda, the investigative journalist who had set in motion the Winterthur case, jointly with Swiss TV. The reports dealt with Abu Ramadan, a Libyan who came to Switzerland in 1998 and occasionally officiates in the

---

4 Baumgartner, Fabian, "120 Sekunden Hass", *Neue Zürcher Zeitung*, 24 November 2017, p. 17.
5 A detailed reconstruction of the events is offered by Knellwolf, Thomas, "Todesangst in der Moschee", *Tages-Anzeiger*, 19 August 2017, p. 35.
6 Müller, André, and Florian Schoop, "Anklage gegen neun Mitglieder der ehemaligen An-Nur-Moschee", *Neue Zürcher Zeitung*, 2 February 2018, p. 18.

ar-Rahman mosque in Biel-Bienne. He is quoted by the media as asking God in a prayer to "destroy the enemies of our religion, the Jews, the Christians and the Hindus and the Russians and the Shia".[7] A dispute arose about the appropriate translation and interpretation of his speech, given in Arabic.[8] That Abu Ramadan had lived completely on social security benefits for 13 years and had received nearly 600,000 Swiss Francs, created a much more significant public stir. Subsequently, more instigative speeches of Abu Ramadan came to light.[9] The prosecutor is examining the case.

On 22 February 2017, police in the canton of Ticino arrested a 32-year old Turkish and Swiss citizen on suspicion of recruiting fighters for *Jabhat al-Nusra*. The accused agreed to an abridged legal procedure, admitting guilt for receiving a reduced sentence.[10] On 7 November 2017 Swiss police in the Romandy, and French police, arrested ten members of a suspected terror group. One of them, a 27-year old Swiss convert of Croatian origin, is thought to be the head of the group, which formulated several terror plots for an attack in Switzerland.[11]

The dilemma of a liberal society with Islamist activists in it has been most tangible in the debate about the "Lies!" campaign ("Read!", referring to Qur'an 96:1). Typically small groups of young bearded men would set up a stand on a street in a Swiss or other European city and offer a free copy of a German or French translation of the Qur'an to passers-by. Their Salafi sympathies are obvious. A number of Swiss jihadis had contact with the "Lies!" campaign before their departure for the Middle East.[12] Some voices in the Swiss debate called for a ban on the campaign. The most prominent voice among them has been Mario Fehr, a socialist member of the Government of the Canton of Zurich, and head of its Security Department. On 5 May 2017, Fehr, referring to

---

7   Pelda, Kurt, "Hassprediger hetzt gegen Christen und Juden", *Tages-Anzeiger*, 23 August 2017, p. 5; "Sozialhilfe für Hassprediger: Radikaler Imam lebt vom Staat", SRF, "Rundschau", 23 August 2017; https://www.srf.ch/play/tv/rundschau/video/sozialhilfe-fuer-hasspredi ger-radikaler-imam-lebt-vom-staat?id=315c1839-494f-40c7-a429-f359bdc5c8d9, accessed 22 April 2018.
8   Baumann, Michael, and Philipp Gut, "In den Mund gelegt", *Die Weltwoche*, 7 September 2017, p. 22–23; Islamischer Zentralrat Schweiz, "Ausführliche Stellungnahme zur Polemik gegen Shaykh Abu Ramadan", n.d.; http://www.izrs.ch/ausfuehrliche-stellungnahme-zur -polemik-gegen-shaykh-abu-ramadan.html, accessed 8 October 2018.
9   Pelda, Kurt, "Uralte antisemitische Klischees", *Tages-Anzeiger*, 6 October 2017, p. 5.
10 "Radikaler Islamist bald wieder frei", *Berner Zeitung*, 19 August 2017, p. 11.
11 Botti, Dominique, "Verhafteter Westschweizer soll Kopf einer Terrorzelle sein", *Sonntags-Zeitung*, 12 November 2017, p. 9.
12 Pelda, Kurt, and Thomas Knellwolf, "Koranverteiler im Radikalisierungslabor", *Tages-Anzeiger*, 5 May 2017, p. 19.

commissioned legal advice by Markus Rüssli,[13] recommended to the local authorities not to approve requests for setting up stands of the "Lies!" campaign.[14] In October the Police Department of the canton of Berne issued a similar recommendation. In the Federal Parliament, MP Walter Wobmann demanded an outright ban of the "Lies!" campaign "and similar organisations".[15] However, the Federal Government rejected the demand on the grounds that there is no sufficient legal basis for this. Moreover, the Federal Intelligence Service stated only in May 2017 that "there is no substantiated evidence that the street campaigns observed in this country promote violent extremist or terrorist activities and thereby threaten internal security. A ban on activities is out of the question, as there is no established structure present in Switzerland and the target of such a ban would be unclear".[16] While the political and legal debates have not yet ended, the street activists have begun to change method: instead of setting up stands they now walk around in teams of two, for which no permission is required, distributing German and French copies of a biography on the Prophet Muhammad instead of the Qur'an.[17]

From 2016 to 2017 the number of individuals leaving Switzerland to join armed groups in Syria or Iraq rose from 81 to 93, of which 24 are unconfirmed cases. The figure includes all cases since 2001.[18] The authorities have registered no departures since 2016. At the same time they estimate around a hundred individuals in Switzerland are radicalised, and have been in contact with so-called Islamic State.[19] Also, on 4 December 2017, the Security Network

---

13   Rüssli, Markus, *Rechtsgutachten zur Verteilung des Korans auf öffentlichem Grund im Rahmen der Aktion «Lies!»*, erstattet zuhanden der Sicherheitsdirektion des Kantons Zürich, Zürich, 26 April 2017, https://ds.zh.ch/dam/sicherheitsdirektion/direktion/veroeffentlichungen_gs/Rechtsgutachten_%C2%ABLies!%C2%BB.pdf, accessed 22 April 2018.

14   Pelda, Kurt, "Koranverteiler unerwünscht", *Tages-Anzeiger*, 6 May 2017, p. 23.

15   *Motion 17.3583*, brought to the Federal Parliament on 16 June 2017.

16   Federal Intelligence Service, *Switzerland's Security. Situation Report 2017*, Berne, 2 May 2017, p. 42, www.newsd.admin.ch/newsd/message/attachments/48136.pdf, accessed 22 April 2018.

17   Bamarni, Jotiar, *Muhammad: die faszinierende Lebensgeschichte des letzten Propheten* (Mannheim: We Love Muhammad, 2nd edn., 2017).

18   For the most recent figures and earlier communiques, see Federal Department of Defence, *Civil Protection and Sport DDPS* (Eidgenössisches Departement für Verteidigung, Bevölkerungsschutz und Sport VBS), www.vbs.admin.ch/de/themen/nachrichtenbeschaffung/dschihadreisende.html, accessed 22 April 2018.

19   Federal Department of Defence, *Civil Protection and Sport DDPS* (Eidgenössisches Departement für Verteidigung, Bevölkerungsschutz und Sport VBS), "Entwicklung bei der Anzahl Risikopersonen und den im Dschihad-Monitoring des NDB verzeichneten Fälle", 30 November 2017, www.vbs.admin.ch/content/vbs-internet/de/ueber-das-vbs/organisation-des-vbs/die-verwaltungseinheiten-des-vbs/-der-nachrichtendienst-des-bundes.

Switzerland (*Sicherheitsverbund Schweiz / Réseau national de sécurité*) published a "National Action Plan to Prevent and Counter Radicalisation and Violent Extremism". The document does not propose a major strategic shift, rather it systematises and argues for the coordination of existing measures and projects.[20]

At the end of August 2017 households in some communes in the cantons of St. Gallen, Schwyz, and Zurich, saw a flyer in their private letter boxes. It showed a view of the respective commune with a minaret added. The text, signed by a fictitious "Islamic Central Council" of the respective commune, announced "that we will soon be the majority", and asked women to wear the head scarf.[21] The flyer had not been sent by the *Islamischer Zentralrat Schweiz* (Islamic Central Council Switzerland). The authorities soon identified the author of the flyer. He may have to face punishment for race discrimination, violating the freedom of worship, and other charges.[22]

In mid-October 2017, 15 of the 22 graves in the Muslim section of Bois-de-Vaux cemetery in Lausanne were vandalised, with flowers pulled out and anti-Muslim slogans sprayed on them.[23] The section had been opened in 2016 after long debates. The tombs of people with Arabic names in the same cemetery had already been vandalised before in 2015. Hostilities against Muslims of less drastic and more common types, were the topic of a conference organised on

---

detail.nsb.html/69026.html, accessed 22 April 2018. A remarkable MA thesis has analysed the individual motivations of Swiss jihadi fighters: Bielmann, Florent, *Combattants terroristes étrangers: Analyse des motivations individuelles des djihadistes de Suisse* (Geneva: Université de Genève, 2017), www.unige.ch/gsi/files/4214/9682/0523/Memoire_Master_F_BIELMANN.pdf, accessed 22 April 2018.

20 www.newsd.admin.ch/newsd/message/attachments/50703.pdf, accessed 22 April 2018. An academic article comments on what initiatives of a similar nature Muslim organisations in Switzerland have created themselves: Merz, Fabien, and Darius Farman, "Das Engagement Muslimischer Organisationen in der Schweiz gegen gewaltbereiten Extremismus", *Bulletin 2017 zur schweizerischen Sicherheitspolitik*, 2017, pp. 33–57; www.css.ethz.ch/content/dam/ethz/special-interest/gess/cis/center-for-securities-studies/pdfs/Bulletin_2017_04_FM.pdf, accessed 22 April 2018.

21 Tjon-A-Meeuw, Olivia, "Fragwürdige Postkarte verkündet Islamisierung", *St.Galler Tagblatt*, 30 August 2017, p. 33.

22 Schibschid, Christine, "Islam-Flyer: Ermittler haben Verdächtigen im Visier", *Südostschweiz*, 18 October 2017, www.suedostschweiz.ch/ereignisse/2017-10-18/islam-flyer-ermittler-haben-verdaechtigen-im-visier, accessed 22 April 2018.

23 "Le carré musulman de Lausanne a été vandalisé", *Le Temps*, 14 October 2017, www.letemps.ch/suisse/carre-musulman-lausanne-vandalise, accessed 22 April 2018.

11 September 2017 at the University of Fribourg by the National Commission against Racism.[24]

On 28 September 2017 Saïda Keller-Messahli published her book *Switzerland as an Islamist Hub*.[25] The subtitle promises "a glimpse behind the scenes of the mosques". However, on 150 pages it essentially offers a mixture of speculations, based on media reports and internet sources, designed to support her hypothesis that half of the mosques in Switzerland follow an Islamist tendency, and should be closed. Keller-Messahli is a 60-year old Tunisian-born freelance author who has spent most of her life in Switzerland. She is the founder and president of the *Forum für einen fortschrittlichen Islam* (Forum for Progressive Islam), and probably the single most cited voice in the press in relation to Islam.[26] She is increasingly criticised and is accused of not substantiating her claims.[27]

A less confrontational stance is taken by Kerem Adıgüzel. On 22 October 2017, Adıgüzel, a 30-year old IT engineer,[28] together with other like-minded people, founded the association *Al-Rahman–mit Vernunft und Hingabe* (Al-Rahman–With Reason and Devotion).[29] Its main goal is to promote a modern reading of the Qur'an that is compatible with liberal democracy.

In the field of academic studies related to Islam, the University of Fribourg welcomed 34-year old Amir Dziri as the new Professor of Islamic Studies in September 2017. Tunisian-born Dziri has spent most of his life in Germany. His main research interests are hermeneutics, epistemology and political philosophy. In the same month, Jordanian-born Rana Alsoufi, a specialist in the history of Islamic law, began work on a part-time basis at the University of Lucerne as the first Assistant Professor of Islamic Theology. The visiting professorship at the University of Zurich for the autumn semester of 2017 was held by Armina Omerika, a specialist in the history of ideas. Since 2017, the University

---

24 The conference and the state of the debate in Switzerland are documented in the Commission's Review: National Commission against Racism, "Muslimfeindlichkeit: Gesellschaft, Medien und Politik. Tagungsbericht der EKR", *Tangram*, vol. 40, December 2017. www.ekr.admin.ch/pdf/Tangram_40_Web.pdf, accessed 22 April 2017.

25 Keller-Messahli, Saïda, *Islamistische Drehscheibe Schweiz: ein Blick hinter die Kulissen der Moscheen* (Zurich: NZZ libro, 2017).

26 For a portrait see Schoop, Florian, "Die Getriebene", *Neue Zürcher Zeitung*, 1 September 2017, p. 15.

27 Eberhard, Fabian, "Islam-Kritikerin von Hassprediger angezeigt", *Blick*, 1 October 2017, p. 8.

28 Vögeli, Dorothee, "Mit dem Koran gegen religiösen Fanatismus", *Neue Zürcher Zeitung*, 10 August 2017, p. 20.

29 See the statutes online: www.alrahman.de/statuten-al-rahman-mit-vernunft-und-hingabe/, accessed 22 April 2018.

of Geneva offers a training course for imams and Islamic religious teachers in French and socio-cultural comprehension.[30]

On 4 November 2017, the *Tribune de Genève* added a Swiss dimension to the accusations directed against the Muslim intellectual Tariq Ramadan by women in France. Ramadan, a Swiss national born in Geneva in 1962, and grandson of Hasan al-Banna, is said to have abused his position as a teacher of French and philosophy in two grammar schools in Geneva in the 1980s and 1990s. According to five women, then aged between 14 and 18, their teacher had unduly approached them, forcing three of them to have sexual intercourse with him repeatedly.[31] While cases from later dates in France motivated the women in Geneva to speak to the newspaper anonymously, none of them reported the incidents to the police.[32]

Throughout 2017, the largest mosque in Geneva, a Saudi-run foundation, was a topic in the media. The departure of two youths among the mosque-attendees to Syria, the employment of controversial imams and persons suspected by French authorities to represent security risks, as well as financial non-transparency, were the main points of criticism, to which the mosque's general director Ahmed Beyari initially answered in a newspaper interview in January.[33] The cantonal state authority in charge of supervising the foundation, discovered a large number of financial irregularities, and commissioned a detailed audit of the accounting.[34] In November 2017, two imams and two other employees of the mosque were dismissed, which Mohammed bin Abdulkarim al-Issa, Secretary General of the Islamic World League, announced a few days earlier in a newspaper interview.[35]

---

30   www.unige.ch/formcont/cas-langue-decodage, accessed 22 April 2018.
31   Roselli, Sophie, "A Genève, le professeur Tariq Ramadan séduisait ses élèves mineures", *Tribune de Genève*, 4 November 2017, p. 4; Roselli, Sophie, "Un nouveau cas d'abus au Collège dénoncé", *Tribune de Genève*, 9 December 2017, p. 2.
32   Another case, dating from 2008, led another woman to report to the police, that was reported by the *Tribune de Genève* on 14 April 2018.
33   Roselli, Sophie, "Les maux de la mosquée", *Tribune de Genève*, 31 January 2017, p. 18. Online version with helpful links: www.tdg.ch/geneve/actu-genevoise/mosquee-face-critiques/story/21523115, accessed 22 April 2018.
34   Sophie Roselli, "Grosse pagaille dénoncée dans la gestion de la plus grande mosquée de Suisse", *Tribune de Genève*, 15 August 2017, p. 13.
35   Sophie Roselli, "'Je vais remettre de l'ordre à la mosquée'", *Tribune de Genève*, 17 November 2017, p. 4; "Quatre employés fichés S [rated "security risk" by French intelligence] sont renvoyés de la mosque", *Tribune de Genève*, 24 November 2017, p. 13.

Transnational Links

The Turkish community in Switzerland has repeatedly been a subject in the media in 2017. One aspect was the climate of intimidation against opponents of President Erdoğan, nurtured by agencies related to the Turkish state. These activities have led to dwindling demand for schools related to the Gülen movement; the institution in Basel closed in summer 2017. In April the police of the canton of Basel-Stadt suspended a Turkish citizen from office who was employed in tasks unrelated to security. He was suspected of having spied on Turks in Basel. He received a minor sentence for abuse of office for various unauthorised requests in the police's database, but charges of espionage were not substantiated.[36] The constitutional referendum in Turkey on 16 April 2017 brought 53% of Turks living in Switzerland to the polling stations; 62% of them voted against the proposed Bill providing the President with more executive power.[37]

Law and Domestic Politics

The most widely noted political developments in 2017 were related to the issue of face covering. On 7 May 2017, the *Landsgemeinde* of the small canton of Glarus, the annual open-air gathering of the electorates, had to vote on a citizen's request to introduce a ban on disguising one's face in public, irrespective of the motives and the details of the attire. After public discussion, a majority of two to one rejected the request.[38] The content of the request in Glarus was nearly identical to the ban accepted by the electorate of the canton of Ticino in 2013, brought into effect in 2016, as well as the national initiative launched by the Egerkingen committee, named after the village in which the initiators of the minaret ban had first assembled in 2006. On 15 September 2017, the committee delivered 105,553 valid signatures of Swiss citizens entitled to vote,

---

36   Albrecht, Serkan, "Strafbefehl gegen Türkei-Spitzel", *Basler Zeitung*, 19 July 2017, p. 15. See also the critical analysis of the media reporting on this case: Bangerter, Annika, and Christian Mensch, "Spion oder nicht? Wie sich Basel einen Spion schuf", *Basellandschaftliche Zeitung*, 29 September 2017, www.bzbasel.ch/basel/basel-stadt/spion-oder-nicht-wie-sich-basel-einen-spitzel-schuf-131737871, accessed 22 April 2018.

37   Chassot, Sylviane, and Simon Gemperli, "Schweizer Türken sagen Nein", *Neue Zürcher Zeitung*, 19 April 2017, p. 13.

38   Canton of Glarus (Kanton Glarus), *Protokoll der Landsgemeinde vom 7. Mai 2017*, pp. 3–7. https://www.gl.ch/route/cmiglarus-dokument-getSitzungDokument/dok_guid/cd9f1cbd648947d18cbdafb486640379, accessed 8 October 2018; Krummenacher, Jörg, "Glarus will kein Verhüllungsverbot", *Neue Zürcher Zeitung*, 8 May 2017, p. 9.

asking for a nationwide ban of the full face veil. On 20 December, the Federal Government dismissed the initiative, arguing that each canton should remain free to act; as a symbolic concession it announced minor legal adjustments.[39] In any case, both chambers of Parliament will also pronounce their opinion on the subject, before a national referendum, not before 2019, will decide on the matter.

As in the run-up to the minaret referendum held in 2009, promotors of the ban tried to lay the groundwork for success by keeping the topic on the national agenda. They did so in the canton of St. Gallen, where on 28 November 2017 a small majority of the Parliament opted for a ban. Yet soon after, the youth wings of most of the political parties opposed it, and decided to collect the necessary 4,000 signatures to bring about a cantonal referendum on the *Law no 22.17.02*, in order to prevent the ban's implementation.

The Federal Parliament has been the arena of numerous debates related to Islam. For example, a majority of 94 to 89 MPs wanted the Federal Government to propose a law regulating mosques. According to *Law no 16.3330*, mosques should not be allowed to accept funds from abroad, they should be obliged to give full account of their finances and how they are used, and imams must preach in the local language. The Council of States, the Senate, has yet to announce an opinion on the matter. In a separate move, MP Walter Wobman, a member of the Swiss People's Party (*Schweizerische Volkspartei / Union Démocratique du Centre*–SVP/UDC) and the driving force behind the bans on minarets and face covering, went one step further by asking the Federal Government to constantly observe all mosques in the country (*motion 17.3681*, pending).

Returning to regional politics, the Parliament of the canton of Valais on 15 December 2017, declared unconstitutional, and therefore invalid, a legal proposal by the Swiss People's Party to ban head scarves from public schools. The initiative of the Swiss People's Party had been backed by the signatures of 4,329 citizens entitled to vote.[40]

In the canton of Vaud, the Swiss People's Party tried to launch an initiative "against religious fundamentalism". The party wanted the cantonal constitution to specify as inadmissible any religiously motivated claims concerning topics such as religious instruction, the wearing of head scarves, or halal meals

---

39   Federal Council (Bundesrat), "Kein Verhüllungsverbot in der Verfassung, aber gesetzliche Regeln", *Communiqué*, 20 December 2017, www.admin.ch/gov/de/start/dokumentation/medienmitteilungen/bundesrat.msg-id-69303.html, accessed 22 April 2018.

40   Carrupt, Romain, "Les Valaisans ne voteront pas sur le voile à l'école", *24 heures*, 16 December 2017, p. 7.

in public schools. However, it failed to collect more than 3,000 of the 12,000 signatures necessary to enforce a referendum.[41]

Matters concerning the public position of religious communities are slowly moving against what the Swiss People's Party would prefer, especially in the French-speaking part of Switzerland (Romandy).[42] In Geneva, as in Neuchâtel–the two cantons with a strict separation between religious communities and the State–legal proposals to allow a minimal type of partnership between the two are under discussion, but have been sent back for revision. In the canton of Vaud, the umbrella organisation *Union Vaudoise des Associations Musulmanes* (Vaudois Union of Muslim Associations–UVAM) has been attentively following recognition requests by three small Christian denominations, but is itself still at the stage of intensive internal debate on the matter.[43]

In the judicial arena, on 23 May 2017 a district court in the canton of Valais found Jean-Luc Addor, national MP of the Swiss People's Party since November 2015, guilty of race discrimination, committed in a tweet in 2014.[44]

On 21 September 2017, the Office of the Attorney General of Switzerland brought charges of spreading terrorist propaganda against three board members of the *Islamischer Zentralrat Schweiz* (Islamic Central Councils Switzerland). The object of dispute is a 38-minute video interview, led in 2015 by one of the three, along with Abdallah al-Muhaysini, a leading al-Qaida member in Syria. The video interview is seen as uncritical, and hence suspected of promoting terrorism.[45] The case is scheduled to be heard in 2018.

---

41   "L'UDC a prêché dans le désert avec son initiative religieuse", *24 heures*, 10 May 2017, p. 17.
42   Schneuwly Purdie, Mallory, and Andreas Tunger-Zanetti, "Switzerland", in Oliver Scharbrodt, Samim Akgönül, Ahmet Alibašić, Jørgen S. Nielsen, and Egdūnas Račius (eds.), *Yearbook of Muslims in Europe*, vol. 8 (Leiden: Brill, 2016), pp. 660–670.
43   Collet, Cécile, "Les musulmans réunis pour leurs assises ont questionné l'"islam vaudois", *24 heures*, 8 May 2017, p. 17. See also https://www.uvam.ch/uvam/reconnaissance/, accessed 22 April 2018.
44   Commenting on the killing of an ethnic Albanian by another in a mosque in St. Gallen in 2014, Addor had tweeted "On en redemande!" (More of this!); "SVP-Nationalrat Addor verurteilt", *Neue Zürcher Zeitung*, 18 August 2017, p. 14.
45   Office of the Attorney General, "Office of the Attorney General of Switzerland has filed an indictment against three committee members of the Islamic Central Council of Switzerland (ICCS)", www.bundesanwaltschaft.ch/mpc/en/home/medien/archiv-medienmitteilungen/news-seite.msg-id-68176.html, accessed 22 April 2018; Pelda, Kurt, and Thomas Knellwolf, "IZRS-Spitze muss vor Gericht", *Tages-Anzeiger*, 22 September 2017, p. 6.

On 10 January 2017, the European Court of Human Rights ruled that the Swiss courts had been right to refuse exemption from swimming lessons in a public school on religious grounds.[46]

Activities and Initiatives of Main Muslim Organisations

Largely unnoticed by the public, during the summer 2017 the Vaudois Union of Muslim Associations applied for the status of a "body of public interest", a minor form of legal recognition in the canton of Vaud. It is the first time in Switzerland that a Sunni umbrella organisation has applied for this status.[47] The request, communicated by the association's president Pascal Gemperli,[48] triggered a lengthy process of comprehensive screening, and an adjustment of the member associations to the standards of the canton.

On 20 March 2017, the two Albanian Islamic national umbrella organisations signed a charter[49] confirming their commitment to democracy and the rule of Swiss law, their will to promote integration, and to cooperate with each other. This last point is noteworthy since the *Union der albanischen Imame in der Schweiz* (Union of Albanian Imams in Switzerland) and the *Albanisch-Islamischer Verband Schweiz* (Albanian Islamic Association Switzerland) have never cooperated before. It was Naim Malaj, the previous Ambassador of Kosovo to Switzerland, who had brought about the charter which was signed in the House of Religions in Berne.[50]

---

46   European Court of Human Rights, *Information Note 203, January 2017*, pp. 19–21, https://www.echr.coe.int/Documents/CLIN_2017_01_203_ENG.pdf, accessed 22 April 2018.

47   Two Alevi associations obtained a similar status in the canton of Basel-Stadt in 2012. So far, no Muslim association has applied for the more comprehensive status of a body governed under public law, which is the status of the Roman Catholic Church and the Protestant Church in most cantons. Contrary to its minor status, a "body of public interest" entails the right to levy a Church tax from its members.

48   "L'invité de la redaction–Pascal Gemperli", RTS, 14 July 2017, https://www.rts.ch/play/radio/linvite-de-la-redaction/audio/linvite-de-la-redaction-pascal-gemperli-president-de-lunion-vaudoise-des-associations-musulmanes?id=8760215&station=a9e7621504c6959e35c3ecbe7f6bed0446cdf8da, accessed 12 May 2018.

49   For the German text, see http://www.uais.ch/2017/03/21/die-charta/, accessed 22 April 2018.

50   "Führer der albanisch-isalmischen Gemeinde unterzeichnen Sekularismus-Deklaration [sic] mit dem Schweizer Staat", *albinfo*, 19 March 2017, www.albinfo.ch/de/fuehrer-der-albanisch-islamischen-gemeinde-unterzeichnen-sekularismus-deklaration-mit-dem-schweizer-staat/, accessed 22 April 2018.

The month of May saw three Albanian mosques inaugurated: a purpose-built one in Wil (canton of St. Gallen),[51] and two others in converted buildings in Gebenstorf (canton of Aargau) and Plan-les-Ouates (canton of Geneva). On 10 December 2017, an important assembly took place in the new Albanian mosque in Wil; dozens of imams and other representatives of Albanian congregations gathered to transform the Union of Albanian Imams, founded in 2012, into the *Bashkësive Islame Shqiptare në Zvicër* (Umbrella Organisation of Albanian Islamic Communities in Switzerland). The body represents more than 40 Islamic congregations of Albanian origin across Switzerland.[52]

Biel-Bienne was the birthplace of another charter. The industrial city situated on the border of the French and the German-speaking parts of the canton of Berne, has some 55,000 inhabitants, 10% of whom are Muslims. Mohamed Hamdaoui, local deputy of the Socialist Party to the cantonal parliament, together with the association *Tasamouh* (Tolerance), launched the idea of a charter of self-commitment to Muslim citizens' rights and obligations.[53] The charter, which is of a purely symbolical nature, is meant to serve as a separation line against radical ideas of any origin.

On 12 November 2017 in Geneva, the Muslim youth groups of the French-speaking part of Switzerland held their second assembly. As in the previous year, it offered a broad variety of workshops and presentations. In Geneva, the *Fondation DIAC* (*De l'individuel au collectif*) founded in 2016, launched activities in the fields of integration (work, leisure time) and the fight against discrimination. It is run by Muslim youths, but is aiming at disadvantaged young people of any background.[54] The Muslim youth organisation of Fribourg, *FRislam*, also explored new avenues by giving its third public *iftar* event a humorous approach, something that was widely appreciated.[55]

---

51 See the website of the mosque: http://moschee-wil.ch, accessed 22 April 2018.

52 "Gründungsversammlung des Dachverbandes der Albanisch-Islamischen Gemeinschaften in der Schweiz, Wahl der Führungsorgane", www.uais.ch/2017/12/13/grundungsversammlung-des-dachverbandes-der-albanisch-islamischen-gemeinschaften-in-der-schweiz-wahl-der-fuhrungsorgane/, accessed 22 April 2018. Homepage of the new organisation: https://daigs.ch.

53 Enssle, Doreen, "Une 'Landsgemeinde' musulmane à Bienne", *Le Temps*, 23 November 2017, www.letemps.ch/suisse/une-landsgemeinde-musulmane-bienne, accessed 22 April 2018; "Schweizer Muslime verabschieden eine Charta gegen Extremismus an der 'Landsgemeinde'", *Neue Zürcher Zeitung*, https://www.nzz.ch/schweiz/aktuelle-themen/schweizer-muslime-verabschieden-charta-an-landsgemeinde-ld.1332545, accessed 22 April 2018.

54 Homepage: http://diac-reseau.ch, accessed 22 April 2018.

55 "Humorvolles Fastenbrechen in Freiburg zieht 900 Leute an", www.kath.ch/newsd/humorvolles-fastenbrechen-in-freiburg-zieht-900-leute-an/, accessed 22 April 2018.

Muslim Population: History and Demographics

The first traces of a Muslim population in Switzerland date back to the tenth century when the Saracens crossed the Alps. They were Arabs, but their exact origin remains a mystery. Scattered chronicles and sparse archaeological evidence show that they were present in some valleys of today's canton of Valais, as well as in some places in the Grisons. Their presence lasted a few decades involving "only irregular troops–mercenaries, pirates, adventurers".[56]

In contemporary Switzerland, the Muslim presence is dated to the second half of the 20th century. Since the 1960s, people with a Muslim background have migrated to Switzerland for three main reasons:

1. Economic immigration: since 1960, Switzerland has recruited Turkish and Balkan (farm and factory) workers to respond to the demands of its growing economy. They were essentially male workers, migrating without their wives and families. In those early years, they mostly lived in Switzerland as temporary residents.
2. Familial reunification: since the 1970s, Switzerland changed its regulations concerning migration and authorised family reunion. This modified the composition of the Muslim population in terms of age and gender.
3. Humanitarian and political immigration: from 1960 onwards, asylum seekers from various countries (North Africa, the Middle East, Central Asia, the horn of Africa) have migrated to Switzerland.

Since 2010, the Federal Statistical Office (FSO) modified its method of analysing the Swiss population. It now conducts a yearly survey of a sample of 200,000 respondents. In January 2017, the FOS published its latest results based on the pooling of five consecutive years (2010–15). Thus, the following results are based on a sample of 1 million respondents. Some of the data presented in this paper was taken from the 2014 annual survey, whereas other data has been drawn from the 2010–15 pooling. Potential respondents must be permanent residents, above 15 years of age and living in private households. As such, it excludes asylum seekers, refugees, diplomats, and a considerable number of expatriate workers, as well as prison inmates and people living in social and

---

[56] Versteegh, Kees, "The Arab presence in France and Switzerland in the 10th century", *Arabica*, vol. 37, no. 3 (1990), pp. 359–388 (360–361).

medical institutions. Based on this, the Muslim population in Switzerland can be presented as follows:[57]

Muslim Population	Approx. 500,000 (5.5% of the total population, including those under the age of 15 and Alevis); the official number, limited to persons 15 years and older, is 362,973 as of 2016 (191,576 men, 171,398 women).
Ethnic/National Backgrounds	35.4% of Muslims over 15 in Switzerland are Swiss citizens (including around 8,000 converts); Alevis are estimated to number between 30,000 to 50,000.
	Largest ethnic/national groups (as a percentage of overall Muslim population): Balkans: 38% Turkish (Alevis included): 12% North African: 4% Middle Eastern: 4% EU member states: 4% Sub-Saharan African: 2% Central Asian: 1% East Asian: 1%.
Inner-Islamic Groups	Muslims in Switzerland are mostly Sunni. Since this data is not collected, we can only estimate as follows: 80% are Sunni, 7% Shi'is and up to 11% Alevis. The residual percentage includes minority community members, such as the Ahmadiyya movement and Sufi orders.
Geographical Spread	The Muslim population is present in every region of Switzerland:
	– German speaking region: 77% – French speaking region: 21% – Italian speaking region: 2%.

---

57 The data and percentages presented in this appendix were collected by the Federal Office of Statistics between 2010 and 2017. This is the most recent data describing the Swiss population at present.

Number of Mosques	Switzerland has some 260 mosques and prayer halls. Four of them have a minaret.[58] Recently built mosques show modest features of Islamic architecture, e.g. the Albanian mosque completed in December 2016 in Netstal (canton of Glarus) or the one in Wil (canton of St. Gallen), inaugurated in May 2017. Construction of further mosques is under way in Grenchen (canton of Solothurn), and Frauenfeld (canton of Thurgau).
Muslim Burial Sites	Geneva (opened in 1978)
	Basel (2000)
	Bern (2000)
	Lugano (2002)
	Olten (2003)
	Zurich (2004)
	Sissach (2006)
	Liestal (2008)
	Birsfelden (2008)
	Pratteln (2008)
	Bottmingen (2008)
	Münchenstein (2008)
	Allschwil (2008)
	Oberwil (2008)
	Luzern (2008)
	Thun (2009)
	La Chaux-de-Fonds (2011)
	Le Locle (2011)
	Neuchâtel (2011)
	Biel (2011)
	Köniz (2012)
	Winterthur (2012)
	St. Gallen (2013)
	Lausanne (2016).

---

58 On 29 November 2009, Swiss citizens in a national referendum decided to prohibit the construction of minarets in Switzerland. The existing mosques with minarets are in Zurich (inaugurated in 1963, run by the Ahmadiyya movement), and Geneva (1978, financed by Saudi Arabia). Those with a more symbolic shape are in Winterthur (2005, run by Muslims of Albanian background) and Wangen (2009, run by Muslims of Turkish background).

"Chaplaincy" in State Institutions	Traditionally, state institutions only hosted Christian chaplains. Nonetheless, the pluralisation of religion in the country has meant the implementation of local Muslim chaplaincy initiatives, in prison as well as in hospitals. The Muslim Emergency Chaplaincy (*Muslimische Notfallseelsorge*) in the Zurich canton is being transformed into a broader institution in cooperation with the Swiss Centre on Islam and Society of the University in Fribourg, and with support of the cantonal government. The University of Berne offers a Certificate of Advanced Studies (CAS) in Religious Care in Migration Contexts (www.religiouscare.unibe.ch).
Halal Products	Halal slaughter without prior stunning is not permitted in Switzerland. The quantity of imported halal meat is limited to 350 tonnes of beef and 175 tonnes of mutton per year.[59] Some butchers sell meat as halal which has been slaughtered by a Muslim after the animal was stunned. Halal food is usually not available in public institutions.
Dress Code	Switzerland has no legal restrictions on dress except for the canton of Ticino, where the wearing of the niqab has been banned since 2016. Private enterprises are free to enact dress codes for their employees, and very few allow the head scarf. In 1996 the strictly laicist canton of Geneva prohibited a woman teacher from wearing the head scarf at school, a decision backed by all courts up to the European Courts of Human Rights. The huge majority of Muslim women in Switzerland do not cover their hair. Those wearing a head scarf face difficulties in finding employment and accommodation. Resident women wearing a niqab are no more than a handful.

---

59 Federal Council (Bundesrat), *Decree on the Importation of Agricultural Products, 916.01*, 26 October 2011, www.admin.ch/opc/de/classified-compilation/20110403/index.html, accessed 22 April 2018.

Places of Islamic Learning and Education

Islamic education for children in Switzerland is taught in Qur'an classes organised by mosque associations or, less frequently, on an entirely private basis. Islamic education in public schools is found in very few municipalities (Kriens and Ebikon, canton of Lucerne, since 2003, Kreuzlingen, canton of Thurgau, since 2010, see www.viuk.ch). Alevi classes in public schools exist in Basel. People seeking more religious knowledge of a Sunni tradition may attend courses given by Mag. Amir Zaidan from Vienna. Recently he has changed from local courses to a webinar system (www.islam-wissen.com/).

The Swiss Centre on Islam and Society (CSIS), founded in 2015, offers courses aiming at self-reflective Muslim learning and dialogue, for Muslims and non-Muslims alike. In 2015, the University of Zurich established a visiting professorship for Islamic Theology and Education, which in 2017 was held by Armina Omerika.[60]

Muslim Media and Publications

Among the regularly updated Muslim websites with extensive textual content are:

- *Föderation islamischer Dachorganisationen der Schweiz / Fédération des organisations islamiques de Suisse* (www.fids.ch)
- *Vereinigung der Islamischen Organisationen in Zürich* (www.vioz.ch)
- *l'Union vaudoise des associations musulmanes* (www.uvam.ch)
- Diyanet (www.diyanet.ch) with its Swiss edition of *Post gazetesi* (http://www.postgazetesi.ch)
- *Schweizerische Islamische Glaubensgemeindschaft* (www.sig-net.ch)
- *Centre Islamique de Genève* (www.cige.org/cige).
- *Islamischer Zentralrat Schweiz* (IZRS, www.izrs.ch).

---

60 http://www.aoi.uzh.ch/de/islamwissenschaft/personen/gastprofessur.html, accessed 22 April 2018.

Main Muslim Organisations

- Federation of Islamic Organisations of Switzerland (*Föderation islamischer Dachorganisationen der Schweiz*–FIDS / *Fédération des organisations islamiques de Suisse*–FOIS, Bahnstrasse 80, 8105 Regensdorf, www.fids.ch). Headed by Montassar BenMrad, it brings together 14 cantonal or ethnic organisations, which makes it by far the most representative Muslim umbrella organisation.
- Islamic Central Council Switzerland (*Islamischer Zentralrat Schweiz*–IZRS / *Conseil central islamique Suisse*–CCIS, Postfach 695, 3000 Bern 9, www.izrs.ch). The IZRS is headed by converts Nicolas Blancho (president) and Abdel Aziz Qassim Illi (spokesperson). It has between 3,000 and 4,000 individual members, and has Salafi tendencies.
- Turkish Islamic Foundation of Switzerland (*Türkisch Islamische Stiftung / İsviçre Türk Diyanet Vakfı*–İTDV, Schwamendingenstrasse 102, 8050 Zürich, www.diyanet.ch). Since its foundation in 1987, it is the official agency of the Turkish Republic for religious affairs in Switzerland, assisting some 40 local mosque associations all over the country. The İTDV became a member of the FIDS in 2017.
- Swiss Islamic Community (*Schweizerische Islamische Gemeinschaft / İsviçre İslam Toplumu*–SIG, Bahnstrasse 80, 8105 Regensdorf, www.sig-net.ch). Founded in 1999, it represents 18 local mosques of the Millî Görüş movement in Switzerland, and one in the Principality of Liechtenstein. The SIG is a member of the FIDS.
- Albanian Islamic Association Switzerland (*Albanisch Islamischer Verband Schweiz*–AIVS, Widistrasse 15, 4528 Zuchwil). Founded in 2005, it is headed by, and centred around, the widely-known imam Mustafa Memeti in Bern. The AIVS brings together some 20–30 mosque associations from all the linguistic regions of Switzerland.
- Umbrella Organisation of Albanian Islamic Communities in Switzerland (*Bashkësive Islame Shqiptare në Zvicër / Dachverband der albanisch-islamischen Gemeinschaften in der Schweiz*, Rautistrasse 58, 8048 Zürich, www.daigs.ch). Founded in 2017 as a successor to the Union of Albanian Imams in Switzerland (*Unioni imamëve shqiptarë në Zvicër*, www.uais.ch), the new organisation aims at bringing together most Albanian-speaking communities. With Islamic teaching being the main field of activity of the new union, imams are still as predominant as they were in the precursory body.
- Union of Islamic Organisations in Zurich (*Vereinigung der islamischen Organisationen in Zürich*–VIOZ, Badenerstrasse 808, 8048 Zürich, www.vioz.ch). Founded in 1995, it represents some 35 associations running over 40

mosques throughout the canton. It is the most active among the cantonal umbrella organisations.
- Federation of Alevi Congregations in Switzerland (*Föderation der Alevitischen Gemeinden in der Schweiz*–FAGS / *İsviçre Alevi Birlikerli Federasyonu*–İABF, Grabenstrasse 1, 8952 Schlieren, www.iabf.ch). The Federation was founded in 1998, and represents 13 Alevi associations in the German and French-speaking parts of the country.
- Forum for Progressive Islam (*Forum für einen fortschrittlichen Islam*–FFI / *Forum pour un Islam progressiste*–FIP, Postfach 191, 4005 Basel, www.forum-islam.ch). The organisation is not a congregation of practising Muslims. Its president since its foundation in 2004, Saïda Keller-Messahli, frequently expresses in the media fundamental opposition to mainstream Islam as practised in traditional mosque associations.

Turkey

Ahmet Erdi Öztürk[1]

Introduction

2017 passed under the influence of the aftershock of one of the greatest political earthquakes of contemporary history for the Republic of Turkey: the 15 July 2016 *coup d'état* attempt. The main aim of the coup attempt was to overthrow President Recep Tayyip Erdoğan and the ruling Justice and Development Party (*Adalet ve Kalkınma Partisi*–AKP). All the investigations, detentions and trials revolved around one Sunni Islamic group: the Gülen movement, and its leader Fethullah Gülen.[2] Immediately after the coup attempt, Erdoğan, followed by almost all political actors, public intellectuals, veteran journalists and the vast majority of Turkish society, come to the agreement that Gülen was the mastermind behind the coup attempt. Yet, beyond that, Erdoğan and the AKP have instrumentalised this issue to expedite an authoritarian drift in Turkey and to browbeat various opposition groups. Therefore, religion was one of the focal points of Turkey's socio-political transformation in 2017.

Initially, after the coup attempt, Erdoğan declared a state of emergency for three months. Such an emergency allows the President and cabinet to bypass Parliament when drafting new laws and to restrict or suspend rights and freedoms. Under these circumstances, more than 41,000 people have been imprisoned pending trial in connection with the attempted coup, out of 100,000 who

---

[1] Ahmet Erdi Öztürk is a research assistant at the Faculty of Law, Social Science, and History at the University of Strasbourg. He is also a Swedish Institute Scholarship holder at the Institute for Research on Migration, Ethnicity and Society. He is the co-editor of *Authoritarian Politics in Turkey: Elections, Resistance and the AKP* (London: I.B. Tauris, 2017) and is a guest editor of the *Journal of Religion, Politics and Ideology* for 2018. He has published articles in peer reviewed journals including the: *Journal of Religion and Politics, European Political Science, Journal of Southeast European and Black Sea Studies, Journal of Critical Studies on Terrorism*, and the *Journal of Balkan and Near East Studies*.

[2] Fethullah Gülen (b. 1941) is a Turkish preacher, former imam, writer, and a political figure. He is also the founder of the Gülen movement which is known as the *Hizmet* (service) movement among his followers. Yet, in this paper, in the interest of academic objectivity and critical distance, I prefer to use the term "Gülen movement". Notwithstanding the movement's claims that they are a non-political organisation, it is known that it was the largest unofficial coalition partner of the AKP between 2002–2013. Even though the movement and the AKP did have a mutually beneficial relationship, since 2013 there has been a conflict of interest in regard to the control of socio-political power in Turkey, the coup attempt being the last stage in this conflict.

faced prosecution. Some 120,000 people, including soldiers, police officers, scholars, teachers, judges and journalists, have been suspended or dismissed since the coup, although thousands of them have since been restored to their posts.[3] After this, under the state of emergency conditions, Turkey performed one of its most important and contradictive political turning points: the 16 April 2017 constitutional referendum. The referendum approved 18 proposed amendments to the Turkish constitution that were brought forward by the AKP and the National Action Party (*Milliyetçi Hareket Partisi*–MHP). The main purpose of the referendum was to change the governmental system from a parliamentary democracy to a unique form of a presidential system.[4]

Turkey's foreign policy was also in a constant state of crisis in 2017. Beyond the populist and election-based crises with the Netherlands,[5] and Germany,[6] one could argue that Turkey experienced a change in orientation in its state identity and foreign policy during 2017. Traditionally, Turkish foreign policy was Western-oriented and realist, but currently the AKP has changed this to a more adventurist and ethno-religious (Sunni Islamic and Turkish) approach. This shift has created tensions in Turkey's relations with Western powers such as the USA,[7] and European Union.[8]

At this point it should be noted that, since roughly 2011, the Turkish state and the AKP have been experiencing a process of mutual transformation. Initially advancing a pro-democratic agenda, the AKP has taken a clear authoritarian turn where religion is one of the actors in this process. Even though the AKP is not the first pro-Sunni Islamic political party in the history of contemporary Turkey, one might claim that it is the first religious-oriented party which has managed to control all the state mechanisms, courtesy of its long-lasting ruling period. During this long ruling period, the AKP's leading cadre and their indisputable leader Erdoğan have used Sunni Islam as a dual weapon. That is, religion is both the instrument to keep themselves in power but also a

---

[3] http://www.dw.com/en/turkey-extends-state-of-emergency-by-three-months/a-39720340, accessed 29 November 2017.

[4] For a comprehensive analysis on the conditions in Turkey before and after the referendum see https://theconversation.com/erdogan-la-guerre-tous-azimuts-64916, accessed 10 December 2017.

[5] https://www.haaretz.com/world-news/europe/1.776716, accessed 30 November 2017.

[6] https://www.express.co.uk/news/world/830716/turkey-germany-arrests-merkel-erdogan-eu-suspensions, accessed 30 November 2017.

[7] For a comprehensive analysis of the problems between the USA and Turkey, see: https://www.al-monitor.com/pulse/originals/2017/10/turkey-us-crisis-visa-worst-yet-to-come.html, accessed 30 November 2017.

[8] https://www.reuters.com/article/us-turkey-eu/turkeys-eu-dream-is-over-for-now-top-official-says-idUSKBN17Y0U0, accessed 30 November 2017.

determinant during the transformation of the State's identity to a more ethno-religious one. In other words, for the AKP, Sunni-Islamic discourse, and some of its pro-Sunni Islamic policies, have been employed to consolidate conservative and pious supporters under the same umbrella. On the other hand, the AKP started to transform state apparatuses into a more religious structure under the control of Erdoğan and his party.[9] From this point of view, one could say that the AKP's long-term project for Turkey is a kind of "Sunnification" under the repressive implementations of its authoritarian turn.

Public Debates

The central role of the Diyanet in the Turkish understanding of *laiklik* (a type of secularism) and in the AKP's hegemonic Sunnification project for Turkish society, produced various public debates. Primarily these included the issue of education, the *Civil Law Code* and the role of imams in issuing marriage contracts, the new president of the Diyanet, and his statements on secularism.

Before moving onto the most significant public debates, we need to explain one of the most unexpected events of 2017 in Turkey: the decision by Mehmet Görmez, former president of the Diyanet, to retire from his post. After his retirement, Yalova University Rector Ali Erbaş was appointed as the new president of the Diyanet. The appointment of Erbaş was published in the official newspaper on 18 August 2018.[10] According to the mainstream media in Turkey, the Government will appoint Görmez as the rector of the Turkey International Islam, Science and Technology University, whose foundation was ratified in the Parliament in 2015.[11]

During Görmez's term, due to the AKP's pro-Islamic policies, the Diyanet reached its peak of influence in terms of its national and international activities. The Diyanet was also transformed into a pliable state apparatus, geared towards implementing the political ideology of the ruling party. Moreover, during the failed coup attempt of 2016, the Diyanet played a far more significant role in organising the resistance against it compared to other state institutions. In the first couple of hours of the coup attempt, Görmez issued an order

---

9   Irak, Dağhan, and Ahmet Erdi Öztürk, "Redefinition of state apparatuses: AKP's formal–informal networks in the online realm", *Journal of Balkan and Near Eastern Studies*, vol. 20, no. 5 (2017), pp. 439–458.
10 http://en.ilkha.com/haber/2676/appointment-to-presidency-of-diyanet, accessed 2 February 2018.
11 http://www.hurriyetdailynews.com/former-head-of-turkeys-top-religious-body-to-become-university-rector-116291, accessed 5 December 2017.

to all imams of the Turkish Republic to go to their mosques and called upon the people to do the same. This resulted in the first *sala* prayer being read at mosques around the country almost simultaneously all throughout the night of the attempted coup. Furthermore, after the coup attempt, Görmez's Diyanet announced that coup suspects would not receive an Islamic burial, and stated that Fethullah Gülen was not a Muslim scholar but rather the head of a terrorist organisation.[12] Taking into account all of these activities and statements, it is clear that Görmez's tenure as head of the Diyanet saw the implementation of the policies of the AKP government and President Erdoğan. However, unexpectedly he retired from his post on 31 July 2017, although his term was not supposed to end until 2020. According to some political commentators, Erdoğan dismissed Görmez since his views on Islam were found to be too reformist and modernist, compared to the more rigid and conservative voices that are becoming increasingly assertive in Turkey.[13]

Erbaş gave an indication of his approach and priorities in his first message as the new head of the Diyanet. During his inauguration he declared that "we have to work more than ever to deliver the eternal call of God and the Prophet to humanity, which is endangered by secularism and nihilism".[14] This statement was sufficiently controversial to discomfort the opposition and secular groups who have been disconcerted by the Sunnification project of the AKP.

With the appointment of Erbaş as the president of the Diyanet, one significant change occurred in the history of the institution; Huriye Martı was appointed as its vice-president. It is the first time a woman has been appointed to this post.[15] Even though the Diyanet has employed female preachers (*vaizeler*) in the past, who have performed many activities outside of mosques, both in Turkey and abroad,[16] the gender issue and some of the recent fatwas on gender topics, have been some of the most disputable elements of the Diyanet's activities. The increasing relative prominence of women in the Diyanet could

12 Öztürk, Ahmet Erdi, "Turkey", in Oliver Scharbrodt, Samim Akgönül, Ahmet Alibašić, Jørgen S. Nielsen and Egdūnas Račius (eds.), *Yearbook of Muslims in Europe*, vol. 9 (Leiden: Brill, 2017), p. 687.
13 One of the most comprehensive op-eds was written by Mustafa Akyol, see https://www.al-monitor.com/pulse/originals/2017/08/turkey-why-erdogan-dismiss-top-cleric.html, accessed 3 December 2017.
14 http://www.hurriyetdailynews.com/turkeys-new-top-cleric-enters-office-vows-to-continue-struggle-against-feto-118113, accessed 3 December 2017.
15 http://bianet.org/english/women/191702-prof-dr-marti-becomes-first-woman-religious-affairs-vice-president?bia_source=rss, accessed 3 December 2017.
16 Maritato, Chiara, "Performing *irşad*: female preachers' (*vaizeler's*) religious assistance within the framework of the Turkish state", *Turkish Studies*, vol. 16, no. 3 (2015), pp. 433–447.

be read as a result of the conflict between the AKP and the Gülen movement. It is known that the Gülen movement has a strong organisational structure, namely *ablalar* (elder sisters) who have worked as female imams within the movement, and have established communication with other pious women both in Turkey and in Turkish diaspora communities abroad.[17]

Another of the focal points of the AKP's Sunnification project is education. Further new education policies were implemented in 2017 as well. Turkey's national school curriculum was revised, leaving out evolution but adding the concept of jihad. In the new national school curriculum, children have started to be taught about renowned Turkish and Muslim scientists alongside Einstein and Newton, the number of lessons on applied science have been reduced, and the number of lessons on culture and religion, and knowledge of ethics, increased.[18] The new curriculum concentrates on values, for instance, the notions of national unity and solidarity, as well as national, moral and universal values. The new curriculum refers to such a value-based education as having a cultural impact, claiming that it will be significant in turning these values into new norms and daily behaviours in society in the future. Positivism and secularism are taught in the section on "problems of faith", in which students have started to learn about deism, agnosticism, atheism, nihilism, reincarnation and false prophets.[19] Right after the declaration of the new curriculum many opposition groups raised concerns about it. For instance, *Egitim-Sen*, a teachers' union often critical of government policies, opposed the curriculum as encouraging a narrow-minded religious and nationalist mindset, with its emphasis on Turkishness and Sunni Islam.[20]

A major public debate in the field of the relationship between religion and the State occurred on the topic of Islamic marriages and the permission of muftis to perform civil marriage ceremonies. After some discussion, the AKP government has passed a new law that allows muftis to conduct civil marriage ceremonies; opposition was voiced by secular and liberal groups. The legislation was signed by Erdoğan in the first half of November 2017, and has given clerics the same powers to perform marriages as civil authorities, like judges. Before the law was passed, couples would have needed to be married by a

---

17   Ebaugh, Helen Rose, *The Gülen Movement: a Sociological Analysis of a Civic Movement Rooted in Moderate Islam* (Heidelberg: Springer Dordrech, 2009), pp. 50–52.
18   http://www.hurriyetdailynews.com/turkish-education-ministry-reveals-new-curriculum-evolution-out-jihad-in-115673, accessed 3 December 2017.
19   http://politicalcritique.org/world/2017/turkey-curriculum-schools/, accessed 2 February 2018.
20   For a comprehensive discussion, see https://www.politico.eu/article/erdogan-turkey-education-news-coup-analysis-curriculum-history-istanbul/, accessed 3 December 2017.

state authority and could also have had an Islamic ceremony performed by an imam in addition to this. Now, couples can bypass the state authority altogether, and conduct a single marriage ceremony under the auspices of a mufti, which is sufficient to gain civil recognition of the marriage. Among the many different reactions to this new regulation, that of the independent member of the Parliament, Aylin Nazlı Aka's was particularly striking. According to her, this new regulation is an effort to prepare the legal groundwork for the sexual abuse of children by legalising underage marriages. Some secular groups claimed that this was yet another move away from the Turkish model of secularism (*laiklik*).[21] After the new law came into force, the first "imam marriage" was performed in Diyarbakır's Bismil district. 30 couples were married by a mufti, Ahmet Durmuş, in a mass wedding ceremony held in Bismil. During the marriage ceremony Durmuş urged couples to have at least five children, a campaign long encouraged by Erdoğan.[22]

At this point, it should be noted that despite the political discussions around this new law, in principle, giving an official licence to imams and muftis to conduct civil marriage ceremonies does not directly contravene Turkey's classical model of state-secularism. Since the State, as the main regulator and controller of religion, officially categorises imams and muftis as civil servants, it can entitle them to perform civil duties. However, in light of the other Islamist policies of the AKP, the concerns of secular and liberal opposition groups around an implicit Sunnification agenda of the AKP appear legitimate.

In 2017, another debate concerned the Syriac community[23] in Turkey and their religious properties. The issue first appeared on a website called *Demokrat Haber*. According to the site, Turkey's Mardin Governorate decided to hand over a number of properties, including monasteries, churches and cemeteries, which have belonged to Turkey's Syriac community in Mardin province. Tens of churches, monasteries and cemeteries were reportedly given by the commission to the Diyanet, and some cemeteries were given to the Mardin Municipality.[24] The Syriac community applied to the court to stop and annul

---

21 http://www.telegraph.co.uk/news/2017/11/03/new-turkish-marriage-law-prompts-fears-child-weddings/, accessed 10 December 2017.

22 http://www.hurriyetdailynews.com/first-mufti-marriage-performed-in-turkeys-southeast-122511, accessed 10 December 2017.

23 Syriacs are an indigenous Semitic ethnic group and a minority in Turkey (and also in Northern Iraq and Northeast Syria) with a presence in the region dating to as far back as the 25th century BCE, making them the oldest ethnic group in the nation. Some regions of what is now Southeastern Turkey were an integral part of Assyria from the 25th century BC to the seventh century CE, including its final capital, Harran.

24 http://www.demokrathaber.org/siyaset/suryani-cemaatine-ait-cok-sayida-kilise-manastir-ve-mezarlik-diyanet-e-h85782.html, accessed 10 December 2017.

the systematic and official confiscation of its property. The court made a judgement in November, and the Syriac community welcomed the imminent return of its legal ownership of their properties. Right after the court decision Deputy Prime Minister Hakan Cavuşoğlu declared that the properties were mistakenly transferred to the state treasury.[25]

Some of the Diyanet's fatwas also sparked debates in 2017. For instance, on 1 December 2017, it issued a fatwa on dyeing hair, stating that dyeing men's hair black is inappropriate, according to Islam. The Diyanet also addressed Islamic rules regarding people who work in places that sell alcoholic beverages.[26] It also declared that the digital currency Bitcoin was not appropriate according to Islamic law. In its response to a question on purchasing digital currencies such as Bitcoin and Ethereum for investment purposes, the Diyanet noted that digital currencies are not under a central authority or under the guarantee of any state or financial institution, and therefore beyond the Islamic understanding of legitimate financial transactions.[27]

Transnational Links

Throughout 2017, outside the borders of Turkey, the most important issue was also the conflict between the AKP and the Gülen movement. In this regard, the Diyanet gathered intelligence and prepared reports on Gülen supporters in countries such as Albania, Austria Azerbaijan, Bosnia and Herzegovina, Bulgaria, Montenegro, Kazakhstan, Kyrgyzstan, Kosovo, Macedonia, Romania, Tajikistan, and Turkmenistan.[28]

Among the various cases, the Bulgarian one seems to be the most pertinent. The Bulgarian press reported on 21 February 2017 that Uğur Emiroğlu, the Diyanet's official in Bulgaria, was declared *persona non grata* for engaging in activities in the religious sphere. Emiroğlu's activities in Bulgaria were deemed "incompatible with his diplomatic status", although the nature of these activities was not specified. There were two claims about Emiroğlu: the first was about his spying on Gülen supporters in Bulgaria, the second one concerned the division between two Turkish parties in the country: the DOST (The

---

25   http://www.hurriyetdailynews.com/turkeys-syriac-community-welcomes-mor-gabriel-monasterys-return-122914, accessed 3 February 2018.
26   http://www.hurriyetdailynews.com/turkeys-top-religious-body-issues-fatwa-on-hair-dye-123368, accessed 3 December 2017.
27   http://www.yenisafak.com/bitcoin-caiz-mi-h-2843237, accessed 6 December 2017.
28   https://www.gatestoneinstitute.org/9640/turkey-long-arm-in-europe, accessed 2 February 2018.

Movements for Rights and Freedoms/ *Демократи за отговорност, свобода и толерантност*/ *Sorumluluk, Özgürlük ve Hoşgörü için Demokratlar*) and the DPS (Democrats for Responsibility, Solidarity and Tolerance Party/ *Движение за права и свободи*/ *Hak ve Özgürlükler Hareketi Parti*). The historical pro-Turkish DPS split, and some of its leading political figures established DOST.[29] At this point, according to the Bulgarian press, Emiroğlu pressured Bulgarian Muslims to support DOST following orders from Ankara.[30]

Turkey continued to support Muslim organisations and the governments of Muslim-majority countries across the world. In this regard, the Diyanet and TİKA (Turkish Cooperation and Coordination Agency Directorate–*Türk İşbirliği ve Koordinasyon Ajansı Başkanlığı*) opened and renovated mosques and religious structures in the Balkans and Central Asia throughout 2017. In addition, the Diyanet gave financial, and contributions in kind to various countries. For instance, Turkey sent a total of 2,000 copies of the Qur'an to Samoa after translating them into Samoan for the 130 Muslims living in the remote South Pacific country.[31]

Law and Domestic Politics

The issue of Syrian "visitors"[32] was one of the important issues in Turkey's domestic politics in 2017. There were 235,000 refugees in temporary refugee centres in Turkey, including around 228,000 Syrians and around 7,000 Iraqis, in the Southern and Southeastern provinces of Hatay, Gaziantep, Şanlıurfa, Kilis, and Mardin. In order to provide religious services to them, the Diyanet decided to employ at least 100 Syrian imams. Furthermore, the Diyanet also announced trips to be organised for around 500 Syrian refugee children for them to visit religious, historical and cultural sites across Turkey.[33]

---

29 In 2015, a group headed by Lütfi Mestan split off from the DPS and formed DOST after he was ousted from the HÖH leadership after openly backing Turkey in the conflict with Russia, after a Russian fighter jet was shot down in November 2015.

30 For a comprehensive discussion, see http://bnr.bg/en/post/100662409/on-turkish-persona-non-grata-and-more, accessed 5 December 2017.

31 http://www.hurriyetdailynews.com/turkey-sends-samoan-quran-to-samoa-for-130-muslims-112604, accessed 3 December 2017.

32 The status of Syrian refugees in Turkey is disputed. According to Turkish authorities, they are "visitors" in the country, but on legal documents they are individuals who have obtained temporary protection status. For a detailed explanation see https://140journos.com/legal-status-of-syrian-citizens-in-turkey-1e6b5cfaff97, accessed 2 February 2018.

33 http://www.hurriyetdailynews.com/100-syrian-imams-to-be-employed-across-turkey-122042, accessed 5 December 2017.

Historically, Turkey has a poor record on the protection of freedom of religion and minority rights, including the rights of Alevis, but in 2017 this latter long-lasting issue was finally resolved. The European Court of Human Rights (ECtHR) in Strasbourg reached an important decision on the relationship between the Turkish state and Alevis. In its ruling on 20 June 2017, the ECtHR decided that the Turkish state must pay compensation amounting to €54,000 to an Alevi foundation on the grounds of religious discrimination. The case arose after the failed request by the cultural centre of the *Cumhuriyetçi Eğitim Ve Kültür Merkezi Vakfı* (Foundation for Republican Education and Culture), which runs a number of *cemevis* in Turkey, for exemption from electricity bills in 2006, in line with Turkish law that exempts places of worships from paying them.[34]

As well as this ruling of the ECtHR, in 2017, Turkey's Council of State ruled in another landmark decision that the State should cover the electric expenses of *cemevis*, Alevi houses of worships that are not officially recognised by the State. The 13th Chamber of the Council noted that "everyone, without discriminating based on language, race, gender, political view, philosophy, belief, religion, sect and similar reasons, stands equal in front of law. State organs and administrative authorities should act in accordance with the principle of equality before the law."[35]

Activities and Initiatives of Main Muslim Organisations

Notwithstanding the AKP's pro-Islamic ideological orientation, legally the establishment of political parties based on religious affiliation is forbidden in Turkey, which is one of the main characteristics of the Turkish understanding of *laiklik*. Thus, in legal terms, there is no official religious political party in Turkey, and all the parties officially declare that they are respectful to the *laik* norms of the country, even though the AKP's policies and orientation contradict this legal framework. There are also some other pro-Islamic parties which cannot officially declare their orientation in Turkey. The first one is *Saadet Partisi* (Felicity Party), which was founded in 2001 and whose roots are Islamic; it is largely supported by conservative Muslims in Turkey. Similarly, *Hür Dava*

---

34 http://www.hurriyetdailynews.com/euro-court-fines-turkey-54000-euros-for-discrimination-against-alevi-foundation-114533, accessed 5 December 2017.
35 http://www.hurriyetdailynews.com/turkish-council-of-state-hands-down-historic-decision-on-electricity-expenses-of-cemevis-115961, accessed 3 December 2017.

Partisi (Independent Dawah Party) is a far-right Sunni Islamist political party that is only active in the Kurdish region.

Based on the same *laiklik* principles, there has also been a ban on the establishment of Sufi brotherhoods (*tariqas*), since the early republican period in the 1920s. Though this ban remains *de jure, de facto*, it does not exist. Perhaps the most visible example of this is the Gülen movement. Yet, beyond it the Mevlevi and Bektashi orders continue to hold official endorsement, and the Naqshabandi and Qadiri Sufi groupings, as well as neo-Sufi religious groupings (namely Nurcus and Sülyemancıs), have a social representation in various civil society organisations.

Alevis are also another and very important part of Turkey's Muslim structure.[36] Turkish Alevis can be divided into traditionalists and reformists. While traditionalists use more Islamic-rooted idioms and language, the reformists are more secular and utilise a more political language. Traditionalist Alevi organisations consist of individual associations or foundations, gathered around *cemevis*, such as *Şahkulu Sultan Vakfı* (Şahkulu Sultan Foundation),[37] *Karacaahmet Sultan Derneği* (Karacaahmet Sultan Association),[38] and *Garip Dede Kültür ve Cemevi Derneği* (Garip Dede Culture and Cemevi Association).[39] Reformist Alevi organisations are composed of associations with multiple branches, like *Hacı Bektaş Veli Kültür Derneği* (Hacı Bektaş Veli Cultural Association),[40] and *Pir Sultan Abdal Kültür Derneği* (Pir Sultan Abdal Cultural Association).[41] Another form of foundation includes *Hacı Bektaş Veli Anadolu Kültür Vakfı* (Hacı Bektaş Veli Anatolian Cultural Association),[42] and *CEM Vakfı* (*Cumhuriyetçi Eğitim ve Kültür Merkezi Vakfı*–Republication Educational and Cultural Centre Association).[43]

---

36 Even though Alevis are considered to be Muslims, some Sunnis consider them "heretics". Beyond that, some Alevi organisations in Turkey do not place themselves within the Islamic tradition. Therefore, the issue is disputed in the religious field in Turkey.
37 http://sahkulu.org, accessed 5 December 2017.
38 http://www.karacaahmet.org.tr, 5 December 2017.
39 http://www.garipdede.org, accessed 5 December 2017.
40 http://www.hacibektasdernegi.com, accessed 5 December 2017.
41 http://pirsultan.net, accessed 5 December 2017.
42 http://www.hacibektasvakfi.web.tr, accessed 5 December 2017.
43 http://www.cemvakfi.org, accessed 5 December 2017.

Muslim Population: History and Demographics

Since 1937, Turkey has been officially defined as a *laik* state (a term that has been used instead of *laic* and/or secular), albeit with a Sunni Muslim majority population. *Laik* is the term used for the State's control of religion in the public sphere, as opposed to secularism, which implies the separation of state and religion; *laiklik* is the concept that is preferred by Turkey's republican founding fathers.[44] Despite this definition of *laiklik*, the concept has been altered in Turkey. One of the most common meanings for the term seems to be that the State should not be totally blind to religious issues, but also that it is better not to define religion openly as one particular faith, which is Sunni Islam. Before the official declaration of *laiklik*, the Diyanet was established in 1924, with its primary purpose being to ensure the tight management and control of religion by the state authorities within the state structure. The Diyanet is thus an administrative unit that has been charged with the management of religion–particularly the regulation of the Sunni Islamic faith, its practice and education, and the maintenance of places of prayer–from the early republican period.

The Diyanet is a guardianship mechanism for the Turkish state, and has the ability to act both ideologically and repressively at the same time. In this regard, one may argue that it is a hybrid state apparatus. Historically speaking, the reasons behind the nature of the Diyanet as a hybrid state apparatus are closely linked to the evolution of *laiklik*. In the context of Turkey, Zürcher argues that "secularism meant not so much the separation of church and state as the subjugation and integration of religion into the state bureaucracy".[45] To highlight the role of the Diyanet in *laiklik*, Gözaydın claims that the ruling elite both took religion under their control and managed to break the Diyanet's potentially sacred significance.[46] These provisions reveal that on the one hand, the founding fathers recognised the inevitable importance of religion in Turkish society. On the other hand, they were determined to control its social influence and to introduce a framework for the State that excluded religious interference.

During the early republican period all the dervish and Sufi lodges (*tekke* and *zaviye*) were closed and the activities of their leaders outlawed. Yet, in the late 1940s, in the context of the first multi-party system, political parties realised that religious rhetoric could be transformed into votes, and therefore started

---

44   Öztürk, Ahmet Erdi, "Turkey", in Oliver Scharbrodt, Samim Akgönül, Ahmet Alibašić, Jørgen S. Nielsen and Egdūnas Račius (eds.), *Yearbook of Muslims in Europe*, vol. 9 (Leiden: Brill, 2017), p. 684.
45   Zürcher, Eric J, *Turkey: a Modern History* (London: I.B.Tauris, 2004), p. 233.
46   Gözaydın, İştar, "Diyanet and politics", *The Muslim World*, vol. 98, nos. 2–3 (2008), p. 217.

to instrumentalise both the Diyanet and other Islamic groups for their sociopolitical agendas. Indeed, this relationship has been mutual; while political figures have collected support via religion, religious groups and the Diyanet have become more visible and powerful.[47]

One of the most significant turning points for state-religion relations in Turkey was the 1980 *coup d'état* and its subsequent new constitution. This made the Diyanet constitutionally responsible for the protection of the Turkish national identity, which also includes Sunni Islam. Yet, one could argue that the largest alteration in regard to the activities of the Diyanet and the role of religion occurred during AKP rule. The Diyanet's budget, administrative capacity (due to legal reforms at 2010) and activities have gradually expanded, and its policies have been synchronised with those of the AKP.[48] Furthermore, there have been a growing number of mosques, Qur'an classes and religious schools all around the country during the AKP's rule.[49]

Turkey's legally *laik* structure does not allow for any official survey on an individual's religious beliefs. Yet, it is well-known that the established presence of Islam in the region that now constitutes modern Turkey, dates back to the latter half of the eleventh century. According to Turkey's Statistics Administration's latest report of December 2016, the population of Turkey was 79,814,871.[50] Surveys claim that, in terms of religion, 99.8% are Muslim (mostly Sunni), and the remaining 0.2% are mostly Christians and Jews.[51] It should be noted that even though most of the population consider themselves to be Muslims, many do not follow the rules of Islam very strictly. This means that there are gaps among believing-belonging and behaving categories of religion in Turkey.

---

47 Akgönül, Samim, "Türkiye'de Sunni Olmayan Azınlıklar ve Laiklik", in Samim Akgönül (ed.), *Tartışılan Laiklik: Fransa ve Türkiye'de ilkeler ve Algılamalar* (İstanbul: İstanbul Bilgi Üniversitesi Yayınları, 2011), p. 183.
48 Öztürk, Ahmet Erdi, "Turkey's Diyanet under AKP rule: from protector to imposer of state ideology?", *Southeast and European and Black Sea Studies*, vol. 16, no. 4 (2016), pp. 633–635.
49 https://www.reuters.com/investigates/special-report/turkey-erdogan-education/, accessed 3 February 2018.
50 file:///Users/Erdi8620/Downloads/Adrese_Dayal%C4%B1_N%C3%BCfus_Kay%C4%B1t_Sist_31.01.2017.pdf, accessed 11 December 2017.
51 TÜİK figures are available at http://www.tuik.gov.tr/PreTablo.do?alt_id=1059, accessed 9 December 2017.

Muslim Population	According to estimates by state officials and the general public, almost 97–98% of Turkey's citizens are Muslims.
Ethnic/National Backgrounds	The majority are of Turkish, and Kurdish background.[52] The remainder are: Albanian: 500,000–6,000,000 Arab: 420,000 Azeri: 800,000 Bosniak: 4 million Bulgarian/Pomak: 600,000 Circassian: 2.5 million Dagestani; Crimean Tatar; Iranian: 500,000 Kabarday; Kabarday; Karachay; Kazakh: 30,000 Kyrgyz: 5,000.
Inner-Islamic Groups	Sunni-Hanafi and Shafi'i: 70% to 85% Alevi: 15% to 25% Twelver Shi'i: 4% Nusayri: 1%.
Geographical Spread	n/a.
Number of Mosques	86,762.[53]
Muslim Burial Sites	There is no official data on the number of Muslim cemeteries in Turkey. Local authorities are in charge of conducting funerals in accordance with Islamic practice and relevant legislation, and maintaining cemeteries.
"Chaplaincy" in State Institutions	Providing Muslim religious counselling and ritual services for Muslims in public institutions (such as health services, elderly care homes, prisons, juvenile

---

52 http://www.milliyet.com.tr/---milyon-kisi--etnik-olarak--turk/guncel/haberdetayar siv/22.03.2007/250844/default.htm, accessed 9 December 2017.

53 http://www.risalehaber.com/turkiyede-kac-cami-var-iste-il-il-cami-sayisi-277112h.htm, accessed 9 December 2017.

	detention centres, and the like) are among the responsibilities of the Diyanet.[54]
Halal Products	Halal slaughter is widely provided, and halal food is available in public institutions.
Dress Code	Right after the 1980 military coup, in the 1982 Constitution, the head scarf was outlawed for civil servants and at universities, but in 2013, in the second AKP term, the ban was lifted as part of its democratisation legislative initiative.
Places of Islamic Learning and Education	There are 75 Faculties of Theology and 132,725 religious schools (*imam hatip*) in Turkey.[55]
Muslim Media and Publications	The conflict between the AKP and the Gülen movement had a strong impact in the past few years in creating a polarisation of the media outlets, between those that are supportive of the AKP and those that are not. In 2016 and 2017, the AKP government seized all the media branches of the Gülen movement, but some Gülen supporters have established new online media outlets abroad. Among various new pro-Gülen web based outlets, the website of the Stockholm Centre for Freedom[56] is one of the most impactful and visible. Apart from pro-Gülen online newspapers, most of Turkey's newspapers have started to shift towards a more religious bent. Furthermore, other papers, such as *Yeni Şafak, Türkiye, Milli Gazete, Vakit* and *Yeni Asya*, are known to be affiliated to religious groups. After the failed coup, the Turkish government closed all TV channels run by the Gülen movement, but some pro-Gülen journalists have started to open YouTube channels to make themselves heard

---

54 http://www.mevzuat.gov.tr/Metin.Aspx?MevzuatKod=1.5.633&MevzuatIliski=0&source XmlSearch=, accessed 3 December 2017.
55 http://www.egitimajansi.com/kose-yazisi-yazdir/850, accessed 11 December 2017.
56 https://stockholmcf.org, accessed 11 December 2017.

and to unite Gülen sympathisers. The YouTube channel of Ekrem Dumanlı, former editor in chief of daily *Zaman*, is the most popular one.[312] Other important TV channels, such as *Kanal 7*, *TGRT Haber*, *Ülke TV*, and *Kanal A* continue to broadcast and have become more popular under AKP government rule.

Main Muslim Organisations

As mentioned above, there has been a *de jure* ban on the establishment of Sufi brotherhoods (*tariqas*) since 1925; however, this is not the case in practice. Four different Naqshbandi groups (*İsmail Ağa, İskender Paşa, Erenköy* and *Menzil*) have dominated the Naqshbandi orders in Turkey since the Ottoman period. Some Sufi groupings, including the Mevlevi and Bektashi orders, as well as neo-Sufi religious groups (namely Nurcus and Suleymancis), are represented by various civil society organisations in Turkey and abroad. Among these, the Gülen movement's future remains ambiguous in light of the failed coup and the government clampdown on it in Turkey and abroad. It should be noted that these organisations do not have any official and approved addresses and explanatory websites.

Apart from these historical and traditional Islamic groups and their organisations, there are several other notable Islamic organisations that can be categorised as Sunni and Alevi:

Main Sunni organisations:

- Presidency of Religious Affairs (*Diyanet İşleri Başkanlığı*, Eskişehir Yolu 9. km. Çankaya-Ankara, tel.: ++90 3122957000). This is the most important official organisation overseeing a vast array of Islamic institutions in Turkey and abroad.[58]
- Turkish Foundation of Religious Affairs (*Türkiye Diyanet Vakfı*, Dr. Mediha Eldem Sokak, No. 72/B, 06640 Kocatepe, Ankara, tel.: ++90 3124171235, fax: ++90 3124181900, email: tdv@diyanetvakfi.org.tr). Established on 13 March 1975, it is a tax exempt foundation, has the right to collect donations

---

57 https://www.youtube.com/channel/UC05bvpZ3mS6G5e2nimHADWQ/videos, accessed 10 December 2017.
58 http://www.diyanet.gov.tr, accessed 5 December 2017.

without prior permission, and is the largest foundation in Turkey in terms of its financial resources.[59]
– Foundation for Turkish Volunteer Associations (*Türkiye Gönüllü Teşekküller Vakfı*, TGTV, Otakçılar Mh. Savaklar Cd. No: 1, 134050, Edirnekapı/ Eyüp/ Istanbul, tel.: ++90 212534040708, fax: ++90 2123104679, email: tgtv@tgtv .org). Established on 22 January 1994 and based in Istanbul, it is an umbrella organisation made up of 700 foundations, associations and unions that have Islamic and Turkish nationalist leanings.[60]

Main Alevi organisations:

– Karacaahmet Sultan Association (*Karacaahmet Sultan Derneği*, http://karacaahmet.org.tr/). One of the oldest Alevi organisations which is based in the Üsküdar district of Istanbul.
– Erikli Baba Cultural and Cemevi Association (*Erikli Baba Kültür ve Cemevi Derneği*, www.eriklibaba.org.tr/). The historical background of the Erikli Baba Cultural and Cemevi Association goes back to the early Ottoman period. Even though its centre is located in İstanbul's Zeytiburnu district, it has many members in the different cities of Anatolia.
– Hacı Bektaş Veli Anatolian Cultural Association (*Hacı Bektaş Veli Anadolu Kültür Vakfı*, www.hacibektasvakfi.web.tr/). The Association claims to follow the path of Hacı Bektaş Veli. Tuncer Baş is the official director of the Association, which is known as one of the largest Alevi organisations in Turkey. It was founded in 1994 and has 44 branches all over the country.
– Republication Educational and Cultural Centre Association (*Cumhuriyetçi Eğitim ve Kültür Merkezi Vakfı, CEM Vakfı*, www.cemvakfi.org.tr/). It was founded in 1995 and the current head of the Association is Erdoğan Döner. Its main area of activity is education and it has provided scholarships for students in need. It has 50 branches which are mostly located in Anatolia.
– Federation of Alevi-Bektashi Unions of Turkey (*Alevi Bektaşi Birlikleri Federasyonu*, http://alevifederasyonu.org.tr/index.php?option=com_content&view=article&id=222&Itemid=258) It was founded in 2002 as an umbrella organisation for Alevi groups. Muhittin Yıldız is the current head of the Federation, which has women and youth branches as well.

---

59   http://www.diyanetvakfi.org.tr, accessed 5 December 2017.
60   http://www.tgtv.org, accessed 5 December 2017.

Ukraine

Mykhaylo Yakubovych[1]

Introduction

In 2017, further major reconfigurations occurred within Ukrainian Muslim communities, as part of a long-term reaction to the changes imposed by the Russian annexation of Crimea and the military conflict in the Donbass region of Eastern Ukraine. In general, Islam-related activities in Ukraine were affected by a few major developments, the first of these being the most problematic: Crimean and Russian policies towards Muslims on the peninsula, as well as Ukrainian policies towards Crimean Tatars in the "continental" part of the country. Most of the outputs in the Ukrainian media related to Islam were concerned with Crimea, in particular police raids and arrests of Muslims.

As for religious institutions, the newly established Spiritual Administration of Muslims of the Autonomous Republic of Crimea (*Духовне управління мусульман Автономної республіки Крим*, ДУМАРК / SAMARC) has been officially registered as a "religious administration" (*релігійне управління*) in the State Department for Religions and Nationalities of the Ministry of Culture of Ukraine. Some joint initiatives by Muslim organisations also occurred in 2017, such as the signing of *The Social Doctrine of Ukrainian Muslims*, a 20-page document (jointly prepared by SAUM "Ummah" and SAMARK) that outlines Muslim attitudes towards the State, politics, society, economy and other areas. More broadly, most Islamic organisations continued to pursue their own activities, ranging from religious events to participating in different meetings with state officials.

2017 was also the final year in which state-prescribed changes to the statutes of all religious organisations (including Muslim ones) had to be implemented.

---

1 Mykhaylo Yakubovych, PhD, is Director of the Centre for Islamic Studies, The National University of Ostroh Academy, Ostroh, Ukraine. He is the author of the first complete translation of the Qur'an into Ukrainian (four editions since 2013). He has held numerous academic fellowships in Poland (University of Warsaw), Saudi Arabia (Academic Department, King Fahd Qur'an Printing Complex, Medina), the USA (Institute for Advanced Study, Princeton) and recently Germany (IOS Regensburg and Freie Universität Berlin). Currently, he works on the history of Islamic intellectual traditions in Eastern Europe. His recent publications include monographs on the history of Islam in Ukraine, and the participation of Muslims in the military conflict in the Donbass region.

However, in December, the Ukrainian parliament announced an extension of the deadline for such implementations until 2018. Another well-discussed issue was the migration of Muslims into Ukraine. The nature of the debate was similar to that taking place in other European countries, despite the fact that the number of migrants of a Muslim background coming to Ukraine was far less than in most EU countries. A more specific issue was the presence of Muslim refugees from Russia, who are mostly representatives of organisations that are not loyal to the "official" Islamic institutions in Russia (Salafis, members of Hizb ut-Tahrir etc.). Some of these individuals established the Union of Displaced Muslims "Azan" (*Союз мусульман-переселенців «Азан»*). All these developments clearly indicate how the Muslims of Ukraine adapted to confront the new challenges imposed by the military conflict that started in 2014.

Public Debates

One of the first topics to cause some attention in the media in 2017 was the issue of Crimean Tatar autonomy. This notion of "autonomy" was discussed after the end of the Russian annexation of Crimea, as a means to defend the rights of the peninsula's indigenous people., This idea was raised for the first time in 2014 by the representatives of the Mejlis of the Crimean Tatar People (*Меджліс кримськотатарського народу*), and already by 2015 and 2016 the concept had begun to be discussed at the highest level. In May 2017, President Petro Poroshenko supported the idea of some "cultural autonomy" for Crimean Tatars, but said that it required the support of the Ukrainian parliament in order to change the Constitution.[2] Finally, a law related to this was proposed (*No. 6315*, dated 7 April 2017, Status of the Crimean Tatar People in Ukraine, *Закон про статус кримськотатарського народу в Україні*).[3] This move caused a great deal of debate among Ukrainian observers, with active supporters–mostly Crimean Tatars and some liberal politicians–and opponents of this idea–represented by some pro-Russian forces and right-wing Ukrainian nationalists–taking part.[4]

Another Crimean matter appearing in the media was the series of repressive measures taking place against Tatars in Crimea. While the Russian media

---

[2] http://www.pravda.com.ua/news/2017/05/14/7143874/, accessed 22 December 2017.
[3] http://w1.c1.rada.gov.ua/pls/zweb2/webproc4_1?pf3511=61537, accessed 22 December 2017.
[4] https://ru.tsn.ua/blogi/themes/politics/krymskotatarskaya-avtonomiya-pro-et-contra-868140.html, accessed 22 December 2017.

(and the Russian-controlled media in Crimea) keep almost completely silent about these events, various reports from elsewhere provided information about police raids, arrests and prosecutions.[5] Not only the Ukrainian media, but also international human rights organisations, supported claims that a major clampdown on Muslim organisations and activists in Crimea was occurring. Amnesty International reported that the Russian authorities used allegations of possession of "extremist literature" and membership of the Islamist organisation Hizb ut-Tahrir, as a pretext for house raids of ethnic Crimean Tatars (predominantly Muslims), and arrests. At least 19 men were arrested as alleged members of Hizb ut-Tahrir, while by 18 December 2017 the total number of "politically-motivated" investigations reached 72, most of them against Crimean Tatars.[6] Four men from Sevastopol were put on trial in a military court in Russia, in violation of international humanitarian law governing occupied territories; they were sentenced to between five and seven years in prison. During the trial, nearly all prosecution witnesses tried to retract their earlier statements, claiming that these had been forcibly extracted under threat of criminal prosecution by members of the Russian Security Service.[7] The release of Mejlis member Ilmi Umerov and Crimean Tatar activist Ahtem Chiygoz (arrested in Crimea by the Russian authorities in 2015) was made possible by the negotiations between Turkish President Recep Erdoğan and Vladimir Putin.

Nevertheless, when it comes to wider Islamic issues in Ukrainian society, there appears to be some shift in social attitudes. The Razumkov Centre (Ukrainian Centre for Economic and Political Studies, named after Olexander Razumkov), one of the most advanced Ukrainian centres for research on public opinion, published the study *Religion and Church in Ukrainian Society*.[8] Based on research conducted in March 2017, the results include demographic information on the followers of the larger religious "denominations" in Ukraine, as well as the attitude towards them. Muslims constitute only 0.2% of the population (excluding Crimea and part of the Donbass region; yet in 2016, the figure was given as 1.1%, also excluding Crimea and the Donbass). Most Muslims live in Southern and Central Ukraine. In terms of attitudes, in 2017 only 12.6% of Ukrainians expressed a "positive opinion" about Islam (in 2016 it was 16.1%), while 20.1% expressed a negative opinion (19.9% in 2016).

---

5   http://qha.com.ua/en/society/another-wave-of-repression-against-crimean-tatars-in-crimea/141822/, accessed 22 December 2017.
6   https://www.unian.ua/politics/2303884-za-den-u-krimu-provedut-72-sudovih-zasidannya-u-spravah-krimskih-tatar.html, accessed 22 December 2017.
7   https://www.amnesty.org/en/countries/europe-and-central-asia/ukraine/report-ukraine/, accessed 22 December 2017.
8   http://razumkov.org.ua/uploads/article/2017_Religiya.pdf, accessed 22 December 2017.

Most respondents held an indifferent attitude towards Islam (37.6% in 2017 and 41.6% in 2016). From this, it could be concluded that Islam is one of the most negatively perceived religions (for instance, 15.4% held a "negative" opinion about Judaism in 2017, with 19.6% for Charismatic Christian Movements). In the South of Ukraine, almost a third of people (32.3%) expressed a negative attitude towards Islam (for Judaism and Charismatic Movements it was a quarter of people, 25% and 25.6% respectively).[9]

The Mufti of SAUM "Ummah", Said Ismagilov, was ranked among the top-100 most influential Ukrainian people by the tabloid magazine *Correspondent*; he was the only Muslim on the list.[10] Leaders of the largest Islamic organisations (such as SAUM "Ummah", Духовне управління мусульман України «Умма») also highlighted the fact that the Muslim cemetery in Kiev had run out of burial spaces. As of December 2017, the Kiev city authorities had made no efforts towards allocating land for a new Muslim cemetery.[11]

Transnational Links

In 2017, the main Muslim organisation in the annexed Crimea (the Spiritual Administration of Muslims of the Republic of Crimean and the City of Sevastopol (SAMRCCS), Духовне управління мусульман Республіки Крим та міста Севастопіль) continued to develop contacts with other Islamic organisations from Russia. Delegations from SAMRCCS participated in various events in Dagestan,[12] Moscow,[13] Ufa,[14] and other parts of Russia. Many new agreements were signed, including one with the Holy Qur'an Memorisation International Organisation, in Saudi Arabia.[15] In terms of educational

---

9   http://razumkov.org.ua/uploads/article/2017_Religiya.pdf, accessed 22 December 2017.
10 https://korrespondent.net/ukraine/3921084-top-100-vlyiatelnykh-ukrayntsev-v-2017-hodu, accessed 22 December 2017.
11 http://project.weekend.today/funeral, accessed22 December 2017.
12 http://qmdi.org/v-dagestane-proshla-konferentsiya-na-temu-vozrozhdeniya-traditsiy-rossiyskih-musulman/, accessed 22 December 2017.
13 http://qmdi.org/v-moskve-prohodit-x-mezhdunarodnaya-teologicheskaya-nauchno-obrazovatelnaya-konferentsiya-chteniya-imeni-galimdzhana-barudi/, accessed 22 December 2017.
14 http://qmdi.org/v-ufe-sostoyalas-x-mezhdunarodnaya-konferentsiya-posvyashhennaya-voprosam-islamskogo-obrazovaniya/, accessed 22 December 2017.
15 http://qmdi.org/muftiyat-kryima-podpisal-dogovor-o-sotrudnichestve-so-vsemirnoy-organizatsiey-po-izucheniyu-korana/, accessed 22 December 2017.

programmes, some ties with Russian institutions, like the newly established Bolgar Islamic Academy, were also established.[16]

Since the Crimea became internationally isolated (due to the sanctions imposed on Russia after its annexation), visits by foreign Muslim guests are rare. The only exceptions for this year were the Muftis from Belarus, Abu-Bekir Shabanovich, and Estonia, Ildar Muhametshin, who attended some events in Crimea. It is not known whether they entered Crimea with official permission from Ukraine or via Russia without Ukrainian consent.[17]

SAUM "Ummah" was internationally active in 2017 as well. Mufti Said Ismagilov undertook official visits to Istanbul, first to a conference of the Federation of Muslim Organisations in Europe, and the second for a meeting with the Mufti of Istanbul, Hasan Kamil Yılmaz.[18] The Association "Alraid" (Асоціація «Альраїд»), closely related to SAUM "Ummah", also hosted many foreign guests in its headquarters in Kiev, ranging from Islamic scholars from the Middle East[19] to the representatives of various NGOs from EU countries.[20] In December 2017, "Alraid" co-organised an international conference called "Muslim Presence in the South of Ukraine: History, Culture, Religion". This was attended by academics and religious authorities from Moldova, Azerbaijan, Belarus and Turkey; one of the notable speakers was the well-known Turkish expert on Ottoman history Mehmet Maksutoğlu.

The newly established Spiritual Administration of Muslims of the Autonomous Republic of Crimea (Духовне управління мусульман Автономної республіки Крим, ДУМАРК / SAMARC) also forged some new links with Turkish religious bodies, by visiting the Turkish Presidency of Religious Affairs (Diyanet İşleri Başkanlığı) as well as the Mufti of Istanbul.[21] The Spiritual Administration of Muslims of Ukraine (Духовне управління мусульман України, SACM) was internationally active as well; its leader, Mufti Ahmad Tamim, attended a few conferences abroad, for example in Azerbaijan,[22] and also hosted some Islamic

---

16   http://qmdi.org/bolgarskaya-islamskaya-akademiya-priglashaet-na-uchebu-kryimskih-musulman-foto/, accessed 22 December 2017.

17   http://qha.com.ua/ru/obschestvo/muftii-estonii-i-belarusi-samovolno-sezdili-v-krim/173658/, accessed 22 December 2017.

18   http://islam.in.ua/ua/novyny-u-sviti/muftiyi-dumu-umma-i-stambula-obgovoryly-spiv robitnyctvo-mizh-musulmanamy-ukrayiny-i/, accessed 22 December 2017.

19   http://www.arraid.org/ru/node/5533, http://www.arraid.org/ru/node/5797, accessed 22 December 2017.

20   http://www.arraid.org/ru/node/5813, accessed 22 December 2017.

21   http://qha.com.ua/ru/obschestvo/muftii-dumk-i-glava-soveta-ulemov-posetili-turtsiyu/172837//, accessed 22 December 2017.

22   http://qha.com.ua/ru/obschestvo/muftii-dumk-i-glava-soveta-ulemov-posetili-turtsiyu/172837//, accessed 22 December 2017.

scholars from Lebanon.[23] These various transnational links in 2017 clearly illustrate that Turkey has become an important partner for Muslims in Ukraine. This is primarily due to Turkey's position of supporting Crimean Tatars, and the growth of an "Islamic dimension" to Erdoğan's foreign politics. Turkey is also active in sponsoring projects in the region, most obviously in its support for the construction of a new mosque in Kiev.[24]

Law and Domestic Politics

2017 was the last year for religious organisations to implement changes to their statutes. According to *Law no. 5050 (Про внесення змін до Податкового кодексу України /On the Changes to the Tax Code of Ukraine*), registered religious communities (*релігійні організації*/religious organisations) are exempted from paying taxes when the funds are used for the aims prescribed in their statutes. The Law clearly states that the income of registered religious communities may be freely used for humanitarian aims, like the distribution of goods and so on. In order to benefit from these tax exemptions every non-profit organisation (including registered religious communities) was initially required to make changes to their statutes by 1 January 2018, but in December 2017, this deadline was extended due to numerous requests for this from religious leaders. Registered religious communities also enjoy subsidised utility bills; gas prices, for example, have a 50% reduction.

Another issue discussed was the wearing of the head scarf in photographs for official documents. On 5 December 2017, the representatives of some Muslim organisations (the NGO "Vetan" and others) organised a panel discussion on this topic, hosted by Crimean House (*Кримський Дім*) in Kiev. Some officials from the Ministry of the Interior and the Ministry of Culture also attended the event.[25] The matter is still not solved, since in most cases Muslims women are required to take off their head scarves when taking their photographs for official documents.

Some controversy surrounded two local branches of the Islamic organisation SAUM "Ummah", one in Sumy, the other in Zhytomyr. Officials from the Security Service of Ukraine (SBU, *Служба безпеки України*) and National

---

23 http://islam.ua/novosti/ediny-v-lyubvi-k-proroku//, accessed 22 December 2017.

24 http://qha.com.ua/ru/obschestvo/djemilev-turtsiya-postroit-v-kieve-mechet-i-jile-dlya-pereselentsev/180929//, accessed 22 December 2017.

25 http://qha.com.ua/ru/obschestvo/razresheno-li-v-ukraine-fotografirovatsya-v-hidjabe-na-dokumenti/183225//, accessed 22 December 2017.

Police (*Національна поліція*) undertook raids on their offices, confiscating Islamic literature.[26] However, as of December 2017, no court decision had been made following these events, and the branches continue to operate. Mufti Said Ismagilov, in recent interviews, claimed that some of the confiscated books were brought to the mosques by unidentified people, so the communities cannot be responsible for their content.[27] The reasons for the series of police raids are unknown, but they are probably the result of internal conflicts between various Islamic religious organisations in Ukraine, with the leaders of some organisations claiming that rival groups are "extremists".

Activities and Initiatives of Main Muslim Organisations

In 2017, SAMARC (Spiritual Administration of Muslims of the Autonomous Republic of Crimea, *Духовне управління мусульман Автономної республіки Крим*) was mostly active in the organisation of various social events, engaging primarily in distributing Islamic knowledge among Crimean Tatars (book publications etc.).[28] Construction work for a new mosque (*Джума Джамі*, meaning "Cathedral mosque") started in Sympheropoil, which is designed to become the main, and largest, mosque in Crimea.[29] According to the plan, the mosque will open in 2019. In February 2017, the Mufti of SAMRCCS, Emirali Ablaev, heading Crimean Tatars loyal to Russia, complained that the Crimea was still a place for many "deviant Islamic groups", primarily Hizb ut-Tahrir.[30] In many ways, this corresponds to the official line taken by the Russian authorities, that want to stop the activities not only of Hizb ut-Tahrir in Crimea (the organisation is banned in Russia but can freely operate in Ukraine), but also the Tablighi Jamaat.[31]

SAUM "Ummah" was active both in religious and social events. Together with "Alraid", it organised the 19th competition of Qur'an recitation.[32] Members of SAUM "Ummah" also participated in demonstrations in support of Rohingya

---

26 http://tyzhden.ua/Society/199096/PrintView/, accessed 22 December 2017.
27 http://zik.ua/news/2017/12/12/muftiy_ismagilov_musulmanam_u_zhytomyri_ekstremistsku_literaturu_pidkynuly_1224785/, accessed 22 December 2017.
28 http://news.allcrimea.net/news/2017/11/6/muftiyat-v-krymu-predstavil-posobie-po-izucheniju-islama-v-doshkolnom-vozraste-91576//, accessed 22 December 2017.
29 https://ria.ru/society/20170422/1492853724.html/, accessed 22 December 2017.
30 http://tass.ru/proisshestviya/3995952/, accessed 22 December 2017.
31 https://ria.ru/incidents/20171002/1505973709.html/, accessed 22 December 2017.
32 https://15minut.org/articles/174753-ctartuye-vzhe-xix-vseukrayinskij-konkurs-chitciv-svyaschennogo-koranu/, accessed 22 December 2017.

Muslims; other Muslim leaders like the head of the Association of Ukrainian Muslims (*Асоціація мусульман України*) Sulayman Khayrullev, also took part.[33] Mufti Said Ismagilov also made a statement saying that at least one of the Muslim religious holidays of ʿId al-Fitr or ʿId al-Adha, should be an official holiday in Ukraine, like Christmas.[34]

SAUM "Ummah" and "Alraid" were the first to sign the document *The Social Doctrine of Ukrainian Muslims* (*Соціальна концепція мусульман України*), followed by the representatives of more than 30 Islamic organisations, including "Alraid", SAUM "Ummah", SAMARC, AMU, and others.[35] The document is made up of eleven sections, starting with a general outline of Islamic principles, and finishing with the relationships between Islam and ecology, Islam and peace, Islam and medicine, and Islam and inter religious dialogue.

SAUM "Ummah" was involved in military chaplaincy, visiting military units in the conflict zone in the East of Ukraine. SACM, with its header Mufti Ahmad Tamim, was mostly active in the events organised by the All-Ukrainian Council of Churches and Religious Organisations (*Всеукраїнська Рада Церков і релігійних організацій*, ACCRO). Ahmed Tamim was the head of this Council during the latter half of 2017.[36] In May, members of ACCRO visited the European parliament.[37] Other Islamic events were generally purely religious or related to school teaching, the celebration of religious festivals, *iftar* dinners etc.

As for other communities, SAMARC started being active in 2017. Mufti Ayder Rustemov was present in the media; he represented the Crimean Tatar community at the celebrations of the 100th anniversary of the *qurultay* (All-Crimean Tatar Council), held at the Ukrainian parliament on 5 December 2017. Other Islamic leaders from Ukraine were also present, as well as international guests like the muftis from Romania, Lithuania and Poland.[38]

---

33   https://www.radiosvoboda.org/a/28716512.html/, accessed 22 December 2017.
34   http://qha.com.ua/ru/obschestvo/muftii-said-ismagilov-prizval-sdelat-kurbanbairam-vihodnim-dnem/182519//, accessed 22 December 2017.
35   https://risu.org.ua/en/index/exclusive/reportage/69342//, accessed 22 December 2017.
36   http://islam.ua/novosti/muftij-ukrainy-stal-glavoj-vstsiro//, accessed 22 December 2017.
37   http://islam.ua/novosti/muftij-ukrainy-posetil-evropejskij-parlament//, accessed 22 December 2017.
38   https://112.ua/politika/mid-ukrainy-proveryaet-informaciyu-o-priezde-v-krym-muftiev-iz-belarusi-i-estonii-388108.html, accessed 22 December 2017.

Muslim Population: History and Demographics

Historically, the first contacts between Ukraine and Muslims can be traced back to the tenth and eleventh centuries, with merchants arriving from Arab lands, Iran, and Volga Bulgaria. A well-known Crimean legend states that the first Muslims on the Crimean peninsula were the followers of the Prophet Muhammad's companions Malik Ashtar and Ghazi Mansur, although the historical accuracy of this legend has been doubted. Since the 14th century, Crimea and Southern Ukraine became more widely Islamised, being ruled by the Golden Horde. A few centuries later, the Crimean Khanate (15th–18th centuries) and the Ottoman cities (Caffa–now Feodosia, Akkerman–now Belgorod) represented one of the most prosperous Muslim areas in this part of Eurasia. In Western Ukraine, the first Muslim settlements appeared in the 16th century, being associated with the so-called Lipka Tatars, who lived mostly in the land of present-day Belarus, Lithuania, and Poland. These communities lived in the various regions of Volyn until the middle of the 20th century; a small Muslim population of Tatar origin also existed in Galicia (Lviv). After 1944, when the majority of the Crimean Tatars were deported from Crimea, Muslim communities ceased to exist, although some of them had already disappeared by the end of the 1920s. It was only after 1989, when thousands of Crimean Tatars returned to their homeland, that Islam experienced a period of revival.

By 2013, just a year before the Crimean and Donbass crisis, the number of Muslims in Ukraine was around 600,000; more than half of them lived in Crimea and Donbass. In the years 2014–17, the majority of Ukrainian Muslims lived in Russian-controlled Crimea and the self-proclaimed "Donetsk People's Republic" and "Luhansk People's Republic". Emigration from these parts of Ukraine resulted in a rise in the Muslim population in the Central and Western parts of the country, more than 20,000 Crimean Tatars relocated there. Other Muslims originate from Arab, Azerbaijani, Volga Tatar, Uzbek, Chechen, Turkish, and other ethnic groups, including a few thousand converts of Ukrainian and Russian origin.

The only official source to determine the exact number of Muslims, on the basis of ethnicity, is the All-Ukrainian National Census of 2001 (the next one is planned for 2019); however, all the figures provided need to be updated. Another resource is the data provided by the Ministry of Culture of Ukraine every year. It provides a statistical report with the exact number of registered religious communities (excluding Crimea). Some estimates have also been made by Islamic organisations, however their figures usually overestimate the actual number of Muslims. Taking all this into consideration, the numbers given in the table below are based on the author's own research and personal conversations with the representatives of the main Islamic organisations in the country.

Muslim Population	Ca. 520,000 in 2017 (1.2% of total population).
Ethnic/National Backgrounds	The largest ethnic groups are: Crimean Tatars: around 300,000 Volga Tatars: 70,000 Azerbaijanis: 100,000 Chechens, Daghestanis, Turks, Iranians, Arabs, Uzbeks as well as Ukrainian, Belarusian and Russian converts: approx. 50,000.
Inner-Islamic Groups	Sunnis (mostly Hanafi, significant number of Shafi'i), including Neo-Sufis and Salafis (various schools), constitute the majority. Twelver Shi'is are relatively small in number, not exceeding 20,000.
Geographical Spread	Around 50% of Ukrainian Muslims live in Crimea; more than 30% live in Kiev and Eastern Ukraine (Kharkiv, Donetsk, Luhansk), around 20% in other regions.
Number of Mosques	Around 400 (approx. 300 in Crimea).
Muslim Burial Sites	– Muslim cemetery on Lukyanivska str., Kiev – Abdal Muslim cemetery, Symferopol, Crimea – Ghazi-Mansur cemetery, Bakhcisaray, Crimea – Muslim cemetery in Zhytomyr – Muslim cemetery in Luck – Historical Muslim cemetery in Yuwkiwci (Khme'nyc'ka obl.), the largest one in Western Ukraine.
"Chaplaincy" in State Institutions	Provided by SAUM "Ummah" for the Ukrainian Armed Forces; SAUM "Ummah" also provides some chaplaincy services in prisons.

Halal Products	The main Muslim organisations, like "Alraid", certify halal products of Ukrainian origin; "Alraid" owns a special centre of certification, the same centre is operated by SAUM. Some products, like halal chicken meat, milk and sweets are available in all Ukrainian markets and stores, while special halal shops can be found mostly in larger cities. The exception to this is the Crimea, where halal meat is also produced and sold in small villages with Crimean Tatar communities. There are no legal restrictions on halal slaughter.
Muslim Dress Code	The head scarf and niqab are rarely worn in Ukraine. Wearing them in public is not prohibited, but taking photographs wearing the head scarf for official documents (for example, passports and ID cards) is not allowed.
Places of Islamic Learning and Education	– Al-Irshad Islamic School and University (Lukyanivska str, 46, Kiev, 04071, tel.: ++380 44651877/78, fax: ++380 44651876). – Al-Nur Islamic School (Dehtiarivska Str., 25-a, Kiev, 04119, tel.: ++380 44909900, fax: ++380 44909922). – Azov Medrese of Islamic Sciences (Majskoje, Dzankoj region, Crimea, Gasprinskogo str., 1, tel.: ++380 656450691, fax: ++380 656454535).
Muslim Media and Publications	– *Alraid*, Islamic magazine (in Russian, published monthly by the Association "Alraid"), www.arraid.org/ru/taxonomy/term/103. – *Ummah*, Islamic magazine (in Ukrainian, published monthly by SAUM "Ummah"), http://umma.in.ua/?cat=54. – *Istochnik Mudrosti* ("Source of Wisdom", in Russian and Crimean Tatar, published monthly by SAMRCCS). – *Minaret*, Islamic magazine (in Russian, published monthly by SAUM), www.islamyat.org/gazeta-minaret.

Main Muslim Organisations

- Spiritual Administration of Ukrainian Muslims "Ummah" (*Духовне управління мусульман України "Умма"*, SAUM "Ummah", Dehtiarivska str., 25, Kiev, 04119, tel.: ++380 44909900, fax: ++380 44909922, email: dumu.umma@gmail.com, http://umma.in.ua). Founded in 2008, the Spiritual Administration represents more than 30 communities from all around Ukraine. Its leader, Sheikh Said Ismagilov, often appears in Ukrainian media. SAUM "Ummah" follows a mainstream Sunni creed with a strong admiration for the concept of "moderation" (*wasatiya*) in Islam. It has very close relations with the "Alraid" association (their headquarters are located in the same building).
- All-Ukrainian Association of the Organisation "Alraid" (*Всеукраїнська асоціація громадських організацій "Альраїд"*, Main office, Dehtiarivska Str., 25-a, Kiev, 04119, tel.: ++380 44909900, fax: ++380 44909922, email: offfijice@arraid.org, www.arraid.org). This organisation, founded in 1997 by the Arab diaspora in Ukraine, is officially registered as an NGO. It has around 15 divisions in the regions of Ukraine, including Crimea. "Alraid" is very active in publishing and media, propagating cultural relationships between Ukraine and Middle Eastern states.
- Spiritual Administration of Ukrainian Muslims (*Духовне управління мусульман України*, SAUM, Lukyanivska str, 46, Kiev, 04071, tel.: ++380 44651877/78, fax: ++380 44651876, email: info@islam.ua, www.islam.ua). This organisation is among the oldest (founded in 1992) and is headed by Mufti Ahmad Tamim. From a theological viewpoint, it follows Sunni Sufi Islam, primarily the order of 'Abd Allah al-Harrari (1910–2008) from Lebanon (known as the "Al-Ahbash group").
- Spiritual Administration of Muslim of the Autonomous Republic of Crimea (*Духовне управління мусульман Автономної республіки Крим*, Sedovtsiv 22/14, Kiev, 01014). Established in 2017. The main office is located in the building of the Mejlis of the Crimean Tatars. SAMARC currently consists of six officially registered, and eight unregistered, communities, and has its headquarters in Kiev.
- Muftiate of Kiev (*Київський муфтіят*, Nevska str., 10-A, Kiev, 03062, tel.: ++380 44496546, email: tugantel@gmail.com). This Muftiate (founded in 2007) represents the Volga Tatar communities of Ukraine, and propagates their cultural heritage. It has established good relations with the Muslims of Tatarstan, and is mostly concerned with the preservation of their cultural heritage in Ukraine.
- Spiritual Administration of the Muslims of the Republic of Crimea and the City of Sevastopol (*Духовне управління мусульман Республіки Крим*

і міста Севастопіль, SAMRCCS, Kurchatova str., 4, Symferopil, 95000, tel.: ++380 652274353, email: muftiyat@qirimmuftiyat.org.ua, www.qmdi.org). Before the Russian annexation of the peninsula it operated as the Spiritual Administration of Crimean Muslims. The organisation unifies most Crimean communities. It was founded in 1992 to preserve the religious identity of Crimean Tatars; it represents the Hanafi-Maturidi school of law and theology.

- Central Spiritual Administration of Crimean Muslims "Tavrian Muftiyate" (*Центральное духовное управление мусульман–"Таврический Муфтият"*, email: info@cdumk.ru, www.cdumk.ru/). Established in 2014 with the help of the Central Spiritual Administration of Russian Muslims, this organisation has just started its activities. It seems to support a Sufi notion of Sunni Islam.
- Spiritual Centre of Ukrainian Muslims (*Духовний центр мусульман України*, Donetsk, Marshal Zhukov str., 1, 83071). This centre was established in 1995 to unify the Muslim communities of Donbass. By the end of the 1990s, it included more than 20 local communities in the Donetsk and Luhansk areas. It has reduced its activities, mostly because of the military conflict in Eastern Ukraine.
- Association of Ukrainian Muslims (*Асоціація мусульман України*, AUM, Kiev, Borschahivska str., 128, email: lifeislam.org@gmail.com, http://lifeislam.org). Established in 2012, AUM represents Sunni Muslims, a group which has increased after the influx of internally displaced people from Crimea. Recently, AUM started to operate beyond Kiev (Lviv, Vinnytsia, Chernihiv), registering new communities.

United Kingdom

Stephen H. Jones[1] and Sadek Hamid[2]

Introduction

While the political landscape in 2017 was dominated by the process of the UK exiting the European Union and responses to the first year of the presidency of Donald Trump, the country experienced three of the most deadly attacks on British soil since July 2005.[3] The first was an attack on the Palace of Westminster in March, which led to four deaths; the second was a suicide bombing that took place at a pop concert at the Manchester Arena in May in which 23 people were killed; and the third was an attack on London Bridge and Borough Market in June in which ten were killed. All of these attacks led to a spike in anti-Muslim hate crime; the most significant instance of such happened on 19 June when a van was driven into Muslims leaving the nightly Ramadan *tarawih* prayers in Finsbury Park in North London, killing one person and leaving eight injured. In September, 58 year-old surgeon Nasser Kurdy, who treated victims of the Manchester Arena attack, was also stabbed in the back of his neck as he walked into his local mosque in Altrincham, Manchester.[4]

Anti-Muslim narratives were promoted to new audiences by the new US President, who, on 29 November, shared a series of tweets composed by the far-right ultra-nationalist organisation Britain First, a group that has organised several "mosque invasions", and refuses to recognise the legitimacy of politicians

---

1 Stephen H. Jones is a lecturer in the Department of Theology and Religion, University of Birmingham. He is a sociologist specialising in Islam in the UK, with research interests in religion and social change, faith-based political participation, religion and education and the impact of public policy on religious organisations. He has been General Secretary of the Muslims in Britain Research Network (MBRN) since 2017.
2 Sadek Hamid is Research Associate at the University of Oxford Centre for Islamic Studies. He has written widely on Islam in Britain, and is co-author with Philip Lewis of *British Muslims: New Directions in Islamic Thought, Creativity and Activism* (Edinburgh: Edinburgh University Press, 2018), is the author of *Sufis, Salafis and Islamists: the Contested Ground of British Islamic Activism* (London: I.B. Tauris, 2017) and is editor of *Young British Muslims: Between Rhetoric and Realities* (London: Routledge, 2016).
3 These events amounted to three of the four most deadly mass killings since 2005. The fourth was a mass killing and suicide in Cumbria in 2010, the motivation for which has never been determined.
4 The man who carried out the attack was found not guilty of attempted murder in March 2018, with the jury accepting the defence's case that Kurdy was not attacked because of his religious background.

who are Muslim, notably the Mayor of London Sadiq Khan. Alongside these events, several public controversies, all discussed below, impacted upon British Muslims. The placing of a reportedly Christian child with Muslim foster carers prompted media outcry, while an Islamic school in Birmingham, Al-Hijrah, was judged to be discriminating unlawfully and failing to act in accordance with "fundamental British values" by keeping boys and girls largely separate. British counter-terror policies, and their intertwining with other domains of governance, remained a significant source of concern among British Muslims, scholars and human rights activists.

At the same time, 2017 witnessed the publication of potentially influential reports on British Muslims' social mobility and Islamophobia. The year also saw advances in Muslim representation: the actor Riz Ahmed became the first Muslim man to win an Emmy award; Mohamed "Mo" Farah, the most successful British track athlete in modern Olympic Games history, was knighted; and Mohamed Salah, an Egyptian player for Liverpool Football Club, received the BBC African Footballer of the Year Award 2017. Following a general election in June the number of Muslim MPs in the House of Commons also grew.

Public Debates

A number of themes continued to dominate media debates about British Muslims, including fears about religious radicalisation, terrorism, child sexual exploitation gangs and rising Islamophobia and anti-Muslim hate crime. Britain experienced five UK terrorist attacks in 2017, which left 35 dead and many other casualties. According to the security services, nine attacks were intercepted, including one said to have targeted Downing Street and the Prime Minister.[5] As ISIS appeared to be imploding overseas, the Government signalled its concern over British citizens returning from Syria, and in particular over the risk that some would return undetected and would commit acts of terror in the UK. About 850 British citizens were estimated to have travelled to Syria to fight, according to a detailed database of British foreign fighters compiled by the BBC. This database listed the names of 100 people who had been convicted of offences relating to the conflict, along with around 150 people who had either died or who were still in the region as of October 2017.[6]

---

5 http://www.middleeasteye.net/columns/islamophobia-and-radicalisation-age-disinformation-1495373932, accessed 23 March 2018.
6 http://www.bbc.co.uk/news/uk-32026985, accessed 18 March 2018.

These challenges for the British government were compounded by problems implementing its Prevent counter-terrorism policy, which received repeated criticism from Muslim community groups, teachers and other agencies, who considered it to be counter-productive and ineffectual. Prevent has been accused of dividing communities and having resulted in the over-referral of Muslim young people, the silencing of dissent, the stigmatising of religious practice and the creation of a climate of fear.[7] Former cabinet Minister Baroness Sayeeda Warsi published a high-profile book, *The Enemy Within: a Tale of Muslim Britain*, in which she argued that the Prevent policy was too focused on jihadi ideology as the sole cause of radicalisation when other factors, such as upbringing and drug and gang culture, played more significant roles.[8] The Government insisted that its policy was working and, after the Manchester Arena bombings in May, announced plans for a "Commission for Countering Extremism". This will be established as a statutory body advising the Government on how to fight all forms of extremism, develop new policies and consider the need for any new powers.[9]

The over-representation of South Asian Muslim men in gangs that groom and sexually exploit predominately young white girls continued to be a highly charged political debate, in which claims often focused on the race and religion of the perpetrators. Grooming gangs in Rotherham, Rochdale, Oxford, Bradford and Newcastle abused and trafficked large numbers of young women, leading to allegations that Pakistani Muslim men had failed to integrate into British society and held racist, misogynistic views towards non-Muslim women. Rotherham Labour MP Sarah Champion was sacked from the role of Shadow Minister for Women and Equalities over a newspaper article published in *The Sun* in which she claimed "Britain has a problem with British Pakistani men raping and exploiting white girls".[10] Media coverage of the issue spiked again due to the controversial "counter-extremism" think-tank Quilliam's report *Group Based Child Exploitation: Dissecting Grooming Gangs*, which claimed

---

[7] http://www.middleeasteye.net/columns/what-prevent-referral-figures-don-t-saythe-impact-muslim-young-people-1836550075, accessed 20 March 2018.

[8] http://www.theguardian.com/politics/2017/may/29/sayeeda-warsi-uk-policy-on-radicalisation-has-been-flawed-for-years, accessed 19 March 2018. See also Warsi, Sayeeda, *The Enemy Within: a Tale of Muslim Britain* (London: Allen Lane, 2017).

[9] For details see https://www.gov.uk/government/publications/charter-for-the-commission-for-countering-extremism/charter-for-the-commission-for-countering-extremism, accessed 18 March 2018.

[10] http://www.independent.co.uk/news/uk/politics/sarah-champion-mp-britsh-pakistani-men-raping-white-girls-exploit-rotherham-labour-equalities-a7896626.html, accessed 18 March 2018.

that Asian Muslims made up 80% of child groomers.[11] The credibility of the report was vigorously challenged and the figures disputed, however, with Nazir Afzal, the former chief prosecutor of sexual abuse rings in Telford and Rochdale, counter-claiming that Quilliam's figure focused only on offences carried out by groups, and that across all cases of child sexual abuse more than 80% of offenders are white British men.[12]

Prejudice against Muslims tends to peak after terrorist incidents and public scandals, and this partly explained the increased rates of anti-Muslim prejudice and discrimination towards Muslims that occurred against the backdrop of the Westminster attacks and the controversies over child grooming. One notable case was the intervention of US President Donald Trump when he retweeted three anti-Muslim videos from the far-right group Britain First in late November. The British Prime Minister Theresa May criticised Trump, albeit indirectly, for posting the inflammatory videos on his Twitter page,[13] to which Trump responded in a remarkably undiplomatic manner.[14] This prompted a number of politicians to call for the cancellation of the planned presidential state visit, including the London Mayor Sadiq Khan.[15]

Other cases of prejudice and discrimination against Muslims were less obvious. A report commissioned by the Government concluded that British Muslim men and women were less likely to succeed in the labour market compared with people from other faith groups. The Social Mobility Commission research, conducted by academics at Sheffield Hallam University, warned that young Muslims living in Britain "face an enormous social mobility challenge and are being held back from reaching their full potential at every stage of their lives".[16] Nearly half of the Muslim population live in the 10% most deprived local authority districts, and this was found to impact upon Muslims' educational success, access to higher education, employment prospects and progression routes at postgraduate and managerial levels. The report identified

---

11 Quilliam, *Group Based Child Sexual Exploitation: Dissecting Grooming Gangs* (London: Quilliam International, 2017).
12 https://www.newstatesman.com/politics/uk/2018/03/child-sexual-abuse-grooming-rings-are-biggest-recruiter-far-right-rochdale-and-telford-prosecutor, accessed 19 March 2018.
13 https://www.theguardian.com/us-news/2017/nov/29/trump-account-retweets-anti-muslim-videos-of-british-far-right-leader, accessed 22 March 2018.
14 https://twitter.com/realdonaldtrump/status/936037588372283392?lang=en, accessed 22 March 2018.
15 https://twitter.com/sadiqkhan/status/936172776637026304?lang=en, accessed 22 March 2018.
16 https://www.gov.uk/government/news/young-muslims-in-the-uk-face-enormous-social-mobility-barriers, accessed 22 March 2018.

significant barriers to improved social mobility from school to university and the workplace: many young people experience Islamophobia, discrimination and racism, and this, the authors concluded, was part of the reason why "young Muslims are more likely to be unemployed, under-employed, in insecure employment and/or in receipt of low pay".[17] More troubling cases of discrimination were visible in the rise in anti-Muslim hate crime across the country. In London a five-fold increase in hate crime was witnessed after the London Bridge attacks, according to the Mayor's office.[18] Similarly, Greater Manchester Police recorded a 500% rise in anti-Muslim hate crime following the concert bombing at the Manchester Arena.[19] Some of this violence is also associated with the continued fallout after the Brexit vote and the growth of xenophobic and anti-refugee sentiment.[20]

This increased anti-Muslim sentiment in society led, however, to greater co-operation between inter-faith organisations and other forms of solidarity.[21] The Runnymede Trust published a follow-up to its highly influential report *Islamophobia: a Challenge for us All*, which was published in 1997. *Islamophobia: Still A Challenge for us All* included contributions from academics, activists and policymakers, and made the case for recognition of Islamophobia as a form of racism, urging the Government to recognise this and tackle Islamophobia in line with other policies that address racial discrimination more generally.[22] In some cases, alliances occurred largely by chance, as in the case of a widely circulated photo of the artist and activist Saffiyah Khan standing up to a member of the far-right English Defence League who was abusing a head scarf wearing woman, Saira Zafar.[23]

Muslim religious practices continued to be a subject of significant media interest, with a number of programmes exploring the role of faith in everyday life. Channel 4 offered a number of such programmes throughout the year. In

---

17   Stevenson, Jacqueline, Sean Demack, Bernie Stiell, Muna Abdi, Lisa Clarkson, Farhana Ghaffar, and Shaima Hassan, *The Social Mobility Challenges Faced by Young Muslims* (London: Social Mobility Commission, 2017), p. 4.
18   http://www.theguardian.com/uk-news/2017/jun/07/anti-muslim-hate-crimes-increase-fivefold-since-london-bridge-attacks, accessed 20 March 2018.
19   https://www.theguardian.com/uk-news/2017/jun/22/islamophobic-attacks-manchester-increase-arena-attack, accessed 20 March 2018.
20   https://www.independent.co.uk/news/science/brexit-prejudice-scientists-link-foreigners-immigrants-racism-xenophobia-leave-eu-a8078586.html, accessed 20 March 2018.
21   http://aa.com.tr/en/europe/uk-vigil-held-to-protest-islamophobic-attacks/855253, accessed 23 March 2018.
22   Elahi, Farah, and Omar Khan (eds.), *Islamophobia: Still a Challenge for Us All* (London: Runnymede, 2017).
23   http://www.bbc.co.uk/news/uk-england-birmingham-39545256, accessed 22 March 2018.

Extremely British Muslims, audiences were introduced to a number of different Muslim residents of Birmingham to illustrate the day-to-day challenges that they encountered.[24] *My Week as a Muslim* attempted to challenge common misconceptions as it followed Katie Freeman over seven days while she spent time with a Muslim family in Manchester and began to question her hostile views of Islam. The programme came under fierce criticism for its voyeurism and because Freeman wore a prosthetic nose and darkened her skin colour in order to feign "Muslimness".[25]

The Truth about Muslim Marriage highlighted how many British Muslims were married in religious ceremonies that were not registered in law.[26] A study linked to this programme interviewed 923 women married in Britain in 14 British cities and found that 60% (and 80% of those under 25) were not in legally recognised marriages because they did not have a civil ceremony after their religious wedding.[27] This situation has occurred partly due to the fact that only 10% of mosques in Britain are licensed for the solemnisation of marriages, and just 31% of Muslim women married in the UK had been married in a mosque. The programme also explored attitudes to polygamy, finding that 89% of the women did not wish to be in a polygamous relationship, and that 37% of the 11% who were in such a relationship had not agreed to it.

Within the sphere of advertising, attempts at more positive representation were made when British Muslims appeared in a television marketing campaign for the supermarket chain Tesco. The company featured a Muslim family in its Christmas advert, the apparent aim being to show a variety of families preparing to celebrate the festive season.[28] This mainstreaming of Muslims continued in another Christmas advert produced by the Penny Appeal charity, as it attempted to challenge the misconception that Muslims were against Christmas, and implied that Muslims in the UK are "as British as a cup of tea".[29] This helped to normalise Muslims' presence, and also demonstrated the increased financial power of the "Muslim Pound," which has grown as Muslim

---

24 http://www.theguardian.com/tv-and-radio/2017/mar/17/extremely-british-muslims-review-the-only-extreme-thing-round-here-is-the-size-of-the-rats, accessed 22 March 2018.

25 http://www.theguardian.com/tv-and-radio/2017/oct/23/my-week-as-a-muslim-review-a-cynical-concept-and-spectacularly-odd, accessed 22 March 2018.

26 http://www.channel4.com/programmes/the-truth-about-muslim-marriage, accessed 19 March 2018.

27 https://assemble.me/uploads/websites/39/files/5a140876945ed.pdf, accessed 19 March 2018.

28 The advert can be viewed at https://www.youtube.com/watch?v=sWCeMGMtkG8.

29 The advert can be viewed at https://www.youtube.com/watch?v=5JydnCgyGxY.

consumers stimulate the market for, among other things, shari'a compliant finance and halal goods and services in British high street retail outlets.

Transnational Links

British Muslim organisations have extensive connections overseas, and many Islamic institutions host and draw direct inspiration from institutions and religious leaders in South Asia and the Middle East.[30] Such networks tend, however, to remain below the public radar, attracting little immediate attention. In 2017, the most high-profile example of transnational relationship building came from a different source: London's Muslim mayor Sadiq Khan, who took the highly unusual step of making an official visit to Pakistan and India as part of the same trip, even going so far as to cross the disputed border between the two on foot.[31] On the same trip, Khan became the first high-ranking British official to call for an apology for the Jallianwala Bagh massacre in Amritsar in 1919, although his statement on the subject was overshadowed somewhat by a BBC reporter who attracted widespread criticism after he asked Khan whether his visit to Pakistan felt "like coming home".[32]

Elsewhere, the three most significant transnational issues connecting British Muslims with other Muslims globally were the humanitarian crises in Yemen, Myanmar and on-going concern for the victims of the Syrian civil war. These tragedies inspired various charitable efforts by British Muslims to fundraise for those affected on the ground, including an emergency Yemen appeal by Islamic Relief,[33] and appeals for aid in Syria by Islamic Relief, Muslim Aid and Muslim Hands. British Muslims, such as the politician and activist Salma Yaqoob, also placed pressure on the UK Government to speak more forcefully against the ethnic cleansing of Rohingya Muslims in Myanmar, with many comparing the conflict to the genocide of Bosnian Muslims in the mid-1990s.[34]

---

30 For examples see Geaves, Ron, "The symbolic construction of the walls of Deoband", *Islam and Christian–Muslim Relations*, vol. 23, no. 3 (2012), pp. 315–328; Inge, Anabel, *The Making of a Salafi Muslim Woman: Paths to Conversion* (Oxford: Oxford University Press, 2016).

31 https://www.standard.co.uk/news/world/sadiq-khan-makes-historic-border-crossing-on-foot-from-india-to-pakistan-a3712026.html, accessed 1 May 2018.

32 http://www.bbc.co.uk/news/world-asia-india-42262338, accessed 1 May 2018.

33 See, for example, Islamic Relief's emergency appeal at: https://www.islamic-relief.org.uk/yemen-emergency-appeal/.

34 https://www.aljazeera.com/indepth/opinion/uk-owes-rohingya-protection-170919100556527.html, accessed 1 May 2018.

Law and Domestic Politics

Legal and arbitration processes involving Muslims were also the subject of considerable public attention throughout 2017. In May, a disciplinary case against five Birmingham-based senior teachers accused of professional misconduct in the so-called Trojan Horse inquiry collapsed after the National College for Teaching and Leadership (NCTL) committee, which was considering life bans for the teachers, concluded that the Government's lawyers' repeated failure to share crucial evidence had "brought the integrity of the process into disrepute".[35] The case's collapse brought to a close proceedings stemming from (now discredited) allegations made in 2014 of a plot to "Islamify" several state schools in Birmingham. In a recent scholarly analysis, the proceedings stemming from the "Trojan Horse" case were described as having inflicted a "major injustice" upon the defendants, as well as other individuals accused of being involved in the alleged plot.[36]

Following this case, in October, the Al-Hijrah school, also in Birmingham, was judged in *EWCA Civ 1426* to have contravened the *Equalities Act 2010* by separating pupils by gender in all lessons, at break times and in movement around the school from Year 5 (age 9) onwards. Al-Hijrah has been a voluntary aided faith school since 2001 (that is, it is funded by the State with support from an independent foundation or trust), and is one of 27 such Islamic schools in the UK. The case was brought by the Office for Standards in Education, Children's Services and Skills (Ofsted), which appealed a previous court judgement that allowed a judicial review of a negative evaluation, in its 2016 inspection, of gender segregation. Previously, a judicial review had been allowed on the grounds that Ofsted had failed to show how gender segregation was to the detriment of either boys or girls as groups. In *EWCA Civ 1426*, however, the court sided with Ofsted, which had contended that harm was being done to individual girls and boys at the school as they were deprived of the possibility of interacting with members of the opposite sex.[37]

Both of these cases illustrate how, especially since 2015, counter extremism laws and policies have come to influence the operations of various spheres of local and national governance in the UK. The British government's initial

---

35 http://www.bbc.co.uk/news/uk-england-birmingham-40094333, accessed 23 March 2018. http://www.theguardian.com/world/2017/sep/01/trojan-horse-the-real-story-behind-the-fake-islamic-plot-to-take-over-schools, accessed 23 March 2018.

36 Holmwood, John, and Therese O'Toole, *Countering Extremism in British Schools: the Truth about the Birmingham Trojan Horse Affair* (Bristol: Policy Press, 2018).

37 http://www.bailii.org/cgi-bin/format.cgi?doc=/ew/cases/EWCA/Civ/2017/1426.html &query=(al-hijrah), accessed 23 March 2018.

inquiry into the "Trojan Horse" case was compiled by retired senior police officer Peter Clarke, the former head of the London Metropolitan Police's counter-terrorism unit. Similarly, in the case of Al-Hijrah, Ofsted's negative evaluation, which was ultimately supported by the appeal court, was heavily influenced by the duties outlined in the *Counter Terrorism and Security Act 2015*. In separating children by gender, Al-Hijrah was judged not only to have allowed discriminatory practices but also to have failed to operate in accordance with "fundamental British values", the promotion of which form a central part of the 2015 Act. This penetration of spheres of governance by counter-terror measures remains controversial, in part because it has led to flaws in process: the undisclosed evidence in the NCTL hearing was gathered in the Clarke inquiry. In the view of many critics, the Act has led to regulations being applied inconsistently or even in a vexatious manner. As critics of the Al-Hijrah judgement noted, many élite schools in the UK–both private and public–are single sex, and none of these have been criticised or penalised by the State for failing to prepare their students for life in modern Britain. Indeed, as John Holmwood observed in his comments on the appeal court's judgement, "[T]he Trust responsible for Al-Hijrah school [...] could apply to create two separate schools for boys and girls in two adjacent buildings, or in a single building properly divided and offering similar facilities, as indeed, is the case with other schools in Birmingham [...], and be exempt from criticism under the [Equality] Act".[38]

Elsewhere, family law became a topic of public controversy following a fostering case in the London Borough of Tower Hamlets, which prompted a front page story in *The Times* newspaper in August that read: "Christian girl forced into Muslim care".[39] This headline, like many others repeated in other publications, strongly implied Muslims were unfit to be foster parents to children from another faith, despite this being fairly common in the case of Christian families. It also proved to be factually inaccurate: the five-year-old girl at the centre of this story had dual Christian and Muslim heritage according to court documents, and it was later reported that she had a warm relationship with her Muslim carers and missed them after being removed from their care. Claims that her female carers wore a niqab also proved to be unfounded; in early online versions of the story, some publications doctored a stock image of a Muslim mother, pasting on a niqab.[40] This particular issue further illustrated

---

[38] https://discoversociety.org/2017/12/06/focus-liberal-anxiety-and-the-education-of-muslim-children-a-tale-of-two-schools/, accessed 22 March 2018.

[39] https://www.thetimes.co.uk/article/christian-child-forced-into-muslim-foster-care-by-tower-hamlets-council-3gcp6l8cs, accessed 22 March 2018.

[40] http://www.theguardian.com/commentisfree/2017/oct/04/newspapers-trade-muslim-baiting-christian-girl-muslim-foster-care, accessed 22 March 2018.

the deeply embedded Islamophobia in sections of the British press, and raised questions about safeguarding and the extent to which cultural and religious matching were considered when young children are placed in short term care.

Finally, in November 2017 the Director and Chief Inspector of Ofsted, Amanda Spielman, recommended inspectors question Muslim primary school girls if they wore a head scarf in order to ascertain whether they have been forced to do so.[41] Spielman claimed that parents of these children were "creating an environment where primary school children are expected to wear the hijab [which] could be interpreted as sexualisation of young girls".[42] Her views seemed not to be shared by the wider UK public, however. In a YouGov app-based poll, whose results were posted on 21 November 2017, 40% agreed head scarf-wearing Muslim primary school girls should be interviewed by government inspectors, whereas 47% of Britons responded that they should not (14% of respondents were uncertain).[43]

Alongside the negotiations relating to the UK's withdrawal from the EU, the major event in domestic politics was a snap general election, which was announced by Theresa May in May and took place on 8 June. In the national elections, many Muslim organisations actively encouraged people to register to vote. Some advocacy groups such as MEND even produced a "manifesto" of concerns and issues to consider when choosing who to vote for.[44] About 85% of Muslims voted for the Labour party and around 11% supported the Conservatives.[45] The number of Muslims elected to Parliament rose to 15, with twelve of 13 previous incumbents retaining their seats. According to analysis from the Muslim Council of Britain, 39 constituencies with dense Muslim populations may have caused a high to medium swing away from the Conservatives to the Labour Party.[46]

---

41 https://www.thetimes.co.uk/article/school-inspectors-to-quiz-girls-in-hijabs-3fl2hlkjv, accessed 23 March 2018.

42 http://www.theguardian.com/education/2017/nov/19/school-inspectors-to-question-primary-school-girls-who-wear-hijab, accessed 19 March 2018.

43 https: //yougov.co.uk/news/2017/11/21/hijabs-schools-counter-terrorism-classes-poetry/, accessed 26 March 2018.

44 https://mend.org.uk/wp-content/uploads/2017/05/MEND-Muslim-Manifesto-2017-SUMMARY.pdf, accessed 26 March 2018.

45 http://www.brin.ac.uk/2017/religious-affiliation-and-party-choice-at-the-2017-general-election/, accessed 26 March 2018.

46 http://muslimnews.co.uk/newspaper/home-news/record-number-muslim-mps-elected/, accessed 26 March 2018.

Activities and Initiatives of Main Muslim Organisations

Alongside traditional Muslim institutions such as mosques, there are a growing number of faith-based campaigning and advocacy platforms, civil society groups, charities, professional and artistic networks and social media-based initiatives active in the UK.[47] Largest among these is the Muslim Council of Britain (MCB) which, despite being shunned by the Government since 2006, has expanded its work under its present General Secretary, Harun Khan. Most notable of its initiatives is an annual "Visit My Mosque Day", which in 2017 grew to include 150 mosques opening their doors to the public, up from 80 in 2016 and 20 in 2015.[48] Like a number of Muslim organisations, the MCB was also active in countering negative portrayals of Muslims, especially through its Assistant Secretary General, Miqdaad Versi, who secured over 40 corrections to stories about Muslims between November 2016 and April 2018.[49] Most prominent among organisations countering anti-Muslim prejudice is Tell MAMA, which in 2017 drew particular attention to online harassment of Muslims.[50]

There is also an increasing number of women's and women-led organisations that are raising gender issues, challenging Islamophobia and developing inter-faith activism and supporting the needs of Muslim women, such as the Muslim Women's Council (MWC) and the Bradford based "Muslim Women in Prison Project", which serves the needs of Muslim women offenders in UK prisons.[51] In 2017 the MWC continued its campaign for a women-led mosque in Bradford,[52] while the Women's Muslim College, which operates seven centres across the UK, was launched in September.[53]

More informally, local Muslims were among the first people to respond to the tragic fire that engulfed Grenfell Tower, a 24-storey block of public housing flats in London in mid-June. The Grenfell Tower fire, which was started by a domestic appliance, left 71 dead and over 70 injured in large part due to the blaze

---

47 Lewis, Philip, and Sadek Hamid (eds.), *British Muslims: New Directions in Islamic Thought, Creativity and Activism* (Edinburgh: Edinburgh University Press, 2018).
48 http://www.visitmymosque.org/about/, accessed 25 April 2018.
49 https://www.theguardian.com/commentisfree/2018/apr/27/islamophobia-not-british-press-issue-got-to-be-kidding, accessed 25 April 2018.
50 https://tellmamauk.org/fear-lives-offline-online-experiences-anti-muslim-hostility/, accessed 26 April 2018.
51 https://muslimhands.org.uk/_ui/uploads/87djpw/MWIP_Report.pdf, accessed 21 March 2018.
52 http://sister-hood.com/bana-gora/want-build-first-women-led-mosque-uk/, accessed 25 April 2018.
53 http://alimahsonline.com/index.php/2017/09/21/launch-of-womens-muslim-college/, accessed 25 April 2018.

being accelerated by the building's exterior cladding.[54] Residents had previously expressed concerns about the building's safety and the fire accordingly prompted significant, and sustained, public protest. The Manchester-based Islamic charity Human Appeal raised nearly £170,000 for the survivors of the Grenfell Tower fire, as well as the homeless, during the month of Ramadan.[55]

According to the Ipsos MORI/Social Research Institute review *Survey of Research on Muslims in Britain*, nearly 20% of Muslims said that they had given unpaid help or worked as volunteers for local, national or international organisation or charities in the last twelve months, and three quarters donated to charity in the last year.[56] These efforts are generally not well-recognised. Many British Muslims have expressed frustrations that their achievements are not appreciated and left unacknowledged by politicians. This was a point stressed in Citizens UK's important study *The Missing Muslims*, published in 2017, which provided a detailed set of recommendations for Government, the media, business leaders, civil society and Muslim communities to achieve greater social equality.[57]

Muslim Population: History and Demographics

The 2011 Census remains the most comprehensive source of population data on British Muslims, although 2017 saw the publications of helpful new data and forecasts that shed light on the growth of the country's Muslim population. While a Muslim presence in the British Isles can be found as far back as the seventh century,[58] the Muslim population remained very small until the 1950s. In 1951, England and Wales was host to 21,000 Muslims (or 0.05% of the population);[59] in 2011, the same figure was 2.7 million (or 5%). This figure is

---

54 https://www.independent.co.uk/news/uk/home-news/london-fire-help-mosques-churches-temples-grenfell-tower-injured-safe-how-to-a7789281.html, accessed 21 March 2018.
55 https://humanappeal.org.uk/news/press-releases/2017/muslim-charity-raises-170-000-for-british-people-in-need-across-manchester-and-london-during-ramadan/, accessed 21 March 2018.
56 https://www.ipsos.com/sites/default/files/ct/publication/documents/2018-03/a-review-of-survey-research-on-muslims-in-great-britain-ipsos-mori_0.pdf, accessed 21 March 2018.
57 Citizens UK, *The Missing Muslims: Unlocking British Muslim Potential for the Benefit of All*, (London: Citizens UK, 2017).
58 Gilliat-Ray, Sophie, *Muslims in Britain: an Introduction* (Cambridge: Cambridge University Press, 2010), pp. 6–7.
59 Lewis, Philip, *Young, British and Muslim* (London: Continuum, 2007), p. 19.

certain to have increased markedly in the last few years due to natural growth, immigration and the arrival of refugees and asylum seekers. According to the Pew Research Center's 2017 report, *Europe's Growing Muslim Population*, the number of Muslims in the UK was an estimated 4.13 million in 2016, and this will have increased further since.[60]

The British Muslim population has been shaped by Britain's colonial past, with a majority of British Muslims originating from India, Pakistan and Bangladesh. This has influenced the Islamic traditions that are found in the country, although over time many British Islamic institutions have diverged from their South Asian and Middle Eastern contexts of origin. The South Asian Barelwi and Deobandi traditions are the most influential–with an estimated 65% of mosques belonging to one of those two traditions[61]–while Salafi, modernist, Jamaat-i-Islami-inspired and Shi'i groups, among others, all have a presence. Since the 1970s, and especially since the turn of the millennium, migration to the UK has diversified away from Commonwealth countries.[62] While the number of South Asian Muslims has continued to expand, proportionately this population has declined as Somalis, Afghans, Iraqis and Syrians, among others, have migrated to the UK.[63] While these populations are less established in terms of religious infrastructure, they have made it harder to generalise about the varieties of Islam that predominate in the British context.

The UK is the second most popular destination in Europe for Muslim migrants, after Germany, and the leading destination for Muslim migrants coming to Europe for economic reasons.[64] Relatively few recent immigrants to the UK have been refugees–which reflects the country's increasingly hostile attitude toward those seeking political asylum–but more than 1.5 million "regular" migrants arrived between mid-2010 and mid-2016. Overall, an estimated 43% of all migrants to the UK in that time were Muslims.[65] The Muslim population

---

60 Pew Research Center, *Europe's Growing Muslim Population* (Washington DC: Pew Research Center, 2017), p. 29, http://assets.pewresearch.org/wp-content/uploads/sites/11/2017/11/29103550/FULL-REPORT-FOR-WEB-POSTING.pdf, accessed 21 March 2018.
61 http://www.muslimsinbritain.org/resources/masjid_report.pdf, accessed 21 March 2018.
62 Vertovec, Steven. "Super-diversity and its implications", *Ethnic and Racial Studies*, vol. 30, no. 6 (November 2007), pp. 1024–1054.
63 Jones, Stephen H., "The 'metropolis of dissent': Muslim participation in Leicester and the 'failure' of multiculturalism in Britain", *Ethnic and Racial Studies*, vol. 38, no. 11 (September 2, 2015), pp. 1969–1985; CoDE, *How Has Ethnic Diversity Grown 1991–2001–2011?* (Manchester: CoDE, 2012); http://www.ethnicity.ac.uk/medialibrary/briefings/dynamicsofdiversity/how-has-ethnic-diversity-grown-1991-2001-2011.pdf.
64 Pew Research Center, *Europe's Growing Muslim Population*.
65 Pew Research Center, *Europe's Growing Muslim Population*.

is also comparatively young: 48.4% of Muslims in the 2011 census for England and Wales are under 25, compared with 25.5% of Christians and 30.7% per cent of the general population.[66] The age momentum of the Muslim population means that, even without any further migration, the proportion of British Muslims is all but guaranteed to grow.

Muslim Population	2011: 2,786,635 (4.4%, census records)[67]
	2016: 4,130,000 (6.3%, estimated).[68]
Ethnic/National Backgrounds	England and Wales (as of 2011): 2,706,000
	Scotland: 76,000
	Northern Ireland: 3,800.
	White total (all figures for England and Wales only): 210,620 (8%)
	Mixed ethnic group: 102,582 (4%)
	Asian/Asian British: 1,830,560 (68%), this includes Pakistani 1,028,459 (38%), Bangladeshi 402,428 (15%) and Indian 197,161 (7%)
	Black/African/Caribbean/Black British: 272,015 (10%)
	Other Muslims: 290,289 (11%), this includes a new category for Arabs at 178,195 (7%).
Inner-Islamic Groups	No official data is available, but according to unofficial sources in 2017, 41.2% of mosques in the United Kingdom were Deobandi, 23.7% were Barelwi,[69] 9.4% were Salafi, and just under 6% belonged to some form of Shi'i Islam.[70] This is in addition to a variety of different theological groups and political tendencies.[71]

---

66 https://www.nomisweb.co.uk/census/2011/DC2107EW/view/2092957703?rows=c_relpuk11&cols=c_age, accessed 18 January 2018.
67 All census data extracted from NOMIS, see https://www.nomisweb.co.uk/census/2011, accessed 21 March 2018.
68 Pew Research Center, *Europe's Growing Muslim Population*.
69 The Barelwi Muslim population is actually thought to be larger than the Deobandi, but the latter has greater institutional infrastructures.
70 http://www.muslimsinbritain.org/resources/masjid_report.pdf, accessed 21 March 2018.
71 See Hamid, *Sufis, Salafis and Islamists*.

UNITED KINGDOM 717

Geographical Spread	Greater London Authority (GLA) data, drawing on the ONS Annual Population Survey, puts the Muslim population in London at 15% of the total population of the GLA area in 2015.[72] Muslims are the third largest religious group in the capital after Christians (49%) and "No Religion" (25%). Elsewhere in the country, Blackburn has a Muslim population of 27% of the total, and Bradford, Luton, Slough, and Birmingham each have Muslim populations of over 20%.
Number of Mosques	An unofficial record of mosques suggests there were 2,006 mosques across the UK as of 2017, and 1,836 in England.[73]
Muslim Burial Sites	– Garden of Peace, Elmbridge Road, Hainault, Ilford IG6 3SW – City of London, City of London Cemetery, Aldersbrook Road, London, E12 5DQ – Bury Cemetery, St Peter's Road, Bury–Brookwood Cemetery, Glades House, Cemetery Pales, Brookwood, Woking, Surrey GU24 0BL – North Watford Cemetery, North Western Avenue, Watford, WD25 0AW. – Southern Cemetery, Manchester, M21 7GL.
"Chaplaincy" in State Institutions	Muslim chaplaincy is increasingly well-established in the UK, with Muslims chaplains being found in prisons, hospitals and higher education and represented through the Muslim Chaplains Association (MCA). Most higher education institutions have a chaplaincy or faith advisor who represents the Islamic tradition. Funding models vary, although many work in a voluntary capacity, with some being

---

72 https://data.london.gov.uk/dataset/percentage-population-religion-borough/resource/abfb6175-f489-4c6e-add2-f4d323183224#, accessed 21 March 2018.
73 http://www.muslimsinbritain.org/resources/masjid_report.pdf, accessed 21 March 2018.

linked to local mosques or are academic staff who happen to be Muslim. Universities with religiously diverse student bodies tend to have the most well-developed chaplaincy support for religious minorities, including Muslims. Muslim chaplaincy is also well-established in prisons, in part due to the high proportion of Muslim offenders, with the MCA offering a prisoner resettlement programme.[74] In this setting, however, the situation has been complicated by questions over the chaplains' role in the implementation of Prevent, and unsubstantiated allegations about chaplains' allegedly "anti-British" attitudes.

Halal Products

Halal slaughter is permitted in the UK, and halal products are relatively easy to obtain, although there have been occasional moral panics about halal slaughter in the British press.[75] Products are becoming more easily available in supermarkets, with some operating a halal meat counter (e.g. the Asda store in Barking and Morrisons in Preston). Shazan and Haloodies are two halal brands readily available in supermarkets.

Dress Code

The UK has few restrictions on religious dress, and wearing religious dress has a relatively strong legal protection. Under the *Equality Act 2010* and its predecessors, employers and public bodies are prohibited from discriminating on grounds of faith, and are required to make "reasonable accommodation" for religious beliefs. Employers have been required to pay damages for rejecting job applicants because they wear a head scarf (see *Noah vs Sarah Desrosiers t/a Wedge, 2008*). Despite this, regular

---

74 See http://mca-hmps.co.uk/services/, accessed 21 March 2018.
75 For example, http://www.thetimes.co.uk/article/more-animals-die-in-pain-because-scholars-are-ignorant-of-stunning-fsz83krtn, accessed 30 November 2016.

calls have been made in the media to prohibit the niqab in teaching, courts and in general. There have also been calls to more strictly regulate the wearing of a head scarf in primary schools.

Places of Islamic Learning and Education

For full details of Muslim schools and seminaries in the UK, see the Association of Muslim Schools website: http://ams-uk.org/. Details can also be found in the UK government Department of Communities and Local Government report *The Training and Development of Muslim Faith Leaders*.[76] Notable institutions include:

- Cambridge Muslim College (14 St. Paul's Road, Cambridge, CB1 2EZ, tel.: ++44 1223355235, www.cambridgemuslimcollege.org).
- Oxford Centre for Islamic Studies (Marston Road, Oxford OX3 0EE, www.oxcis.ac.uk/).
- The Islamic College, London (133 High Road, Willesden, London, NW10 2SW, tel.: ++44 2084519993, www.islamic-college.ac.uk/).
- The Markfield Institute of Higher Education (MIHE, The Islamic Foundation, Markfield Conference Centre, Ratby Lane, Markfield, Leicestershire, LE67 9SY, www.islamicfoundation.org.uk/User/Home.aspx).
- Cambridge Islamic College (58 Sturton Street, Cambridge CB1 2QA, tel.: ++44 1223 655223, www.cambridgeislamiccollege.org).
- Al-Mahdi Institute, Birmingham (60 Weoley Park Road, Birmingham, B29 6RB, tel.: +44 1214465047, https://www.almahdi.edu/).
- Ebrahim College, London (80–82 Greenfield Rd, Whitechapel, London E1 1EJ, tel.: ++44 2073776677, https://ebrahimcollege.org.uk/).

---

76 https://www.gov.uk/government/uploads/system/uploads/attachment_data/file/6155/1734121.pdf, accessed 27 March 2018.

Muslim Media and Publications

- *The Muslim News* (PO Box 380, Harrow, Middlesex, HA2 6LL, www.muslimnews.co.uk/).
- British Muslim TV (www.britishmuslim.tv/).
- Islam Channel (428–432 Ley Street, Ilford, Essex, IG2 7BS, www.islamchannel.tv/).
- *The Muslim Weekly* (Suite 8, Montefiore Centre, Hanbury Street, London E1 5HZ, www.themuslimweekly.com/).
- *emel* Magazine (1 Canfield Place, London, NW6 3BT, +44 2073287300 http://emel.com/).

Main Muslim Organisations

- Muslim Council of Britain (PO Box 57330, London, E1 2WJ, tel.: ++44 8452626786, www.mcb.org.uk/). The MCB is a national Muslim umbrella body with over 500 affiliated national, regional, and local organisations, mosques, charities, and schools. It was established in 1997 and remains the most prominent British Muslim organisation.
- Muslim Youth Helpline (MYH FREEPOST RTRZ-RXTY-AUZR, tel.: ++44 2074358171, www.myh.org.uk/). A service set up to cater for the distinctive problems faced by Muslim youth.
- Muslim Engagement and Development (MEND, email: info@mend.org.uk, http://mend.org.uk/advocacy/). MEND is an organisation that seeks to empower and encourage British Muslims to be more actively involved in British media and politics.
- The New Muslims Project, The Islamic Foundation (Ratby Lane, Markfield, Leicestershire, LE67 9SY, tel.: ++44 1530243937, www.newmuslimsproject.net). A network for new Muslims.
- Ahmadiyya Muslim Community UK (http://www.loveforallhatredfornone.org). The umbrella body for the UK's Ahmadi institutions.
- Al-Khoei Foundation (Stone Hall, Chevening Road, London, NW6 6TN, tel.: ++44 2073724049, ++44 2073720694). The Al-Khoei Foundation is one of the largest international Shi'i Muslim organisations. It operates numerous Islamic schools, colleges, universities, and community centres around the world.
- Faith Matters (Fourth Floor, Hamilton House, Mabledon Place, Bloomsbury, London, WC1H 9BB, tel.: ++44 8000280826, www.faith-matters.org). Faith Matters is a group that focuses on inter-faith and community work, including countering extremism. Its leadership also directs Tell MAMA (see below).

- Muslim Council of Wales (Broadway House, Broadway, Cardiff, CF24 1PU, tel.: ++44 2920487667, www.muslimcouncilwales.org.uk/muslimcouncil/). A broad-based umbrella organisation for Islamic organisations in Wales.
- Muslim Women's Council (Carlisle Business Centre, Carlisle Road, Bradford, BD8 8BD, ++44 1274223230, http://www.muslimwomenscouncil.org.uk/). The MWC is a relatively recently established organisation that seeks to empower Muslim women, most notably through its women-led mosque project.
- Islamic Relief UK (16 Lower Marsh, London SE1 7RJ, tel.: ++44 2075933232, www.islamic-relief.org.uk/). Charity organisation.
- Human Appeal (1 Cheadle Point, Carrs Road, Cheadle, SK8 2BL, https://humanappeal.org.uk). Charity organisation.
- Inspire (https://wewillinspire.com/). Inspire is a non-governmental counter-extremism and women's rights organisation. Its founder, Sara Khan, was appointed Lead Commissioner for the Home Office's Commission for Countering Extremism in December 2018.
- Quilliam (Office 109, 4 Little Portland Street, London, W1W 7JB, tel.: ++44 2071827273, https://www.quilliaminternational.com/). Quilliam is a "counter-extremism think tank" that has played a significant role in shaping Prevent and other counter-extremism measures in the UK.
- CAGE (Premier Business Centre, 47–49 Park Royal Road, London, NW10 7LQ, tel.: ++44 2073776700, www.cageuk.org). An independent advocacy organisation working to empower communities impacted by the so-called War on Terror.
- Tell MAMA (http://tellmamauk.org/). Tell MAMA supports victims of anti-Muslim hate, and measures and monitors anti-Muslim incidents.
- Federation of Student Islamic Societies (FOSIS, 38 Mapesbury Road, London, NW2 4JD, tel.: ++44 2084524493, www.fosis.org.uk). Established in 1963, FOSIS is a body that caters to the needs of Muslim students in further and higher education across the UK and Ireland.
- Muslim Association of Britain (MAB, 124 Harrowdene Road, Wembley, Middlesex HA0 2JF, tel.: +44 2089089109, www.mabonline.net/). Initially an offshoot of the Arab Muslim Brotherhood, the MAB is an umbrella organisation that has been active in the Stop the War coalition, an initiative established after 9/11.

Printed in the United States
By Bookmasters